The *Vault/MCCA Guide to Law Firm Diversity Programs* is underwritten by the following law firms:

AKIN GUMP STRAUSS HAUER & FELD LLP
Attorneys at Law

Arent Fox
ATTORNEYS AT LAW

BAKER
&
HOSTETLER LLP
COUNSELLORS AT LAW

BOIES, SCHILLER & FLEXNER, LLP

BROWN RAYSMAN
BROWN RAYSMAN MILLSTEIN FELDER & STEINER LLP

CLEARY
GOTTLIEB

CLIFFORD
CHANCE

COVINGTON & BURLING

CRAVATH, SWAINE & MOORE LLP

Day, Berry & Howard LLP
COUNSELLORS AT LAW

FINNEGAN
HENDERSON
FARABOW
GARRETT &
DUNNER LLP

FOLEY
HOAG LLP
ATTORNEYS AT LAW

FRIED FRANK

Greenberg
Traurig

HellerEhrman
ATTORNEYS

Challenging the laws of convention.™

The *Vault/MCCA Guide to Law Firm Diversity Programs* is
underwritten by the following law firms:

JENNER&BLOCK
WHEN IT'S A MATTER OF IMPORTANCE

KELLEY
DRYE

KILPATRICK
STOCKTON LLP

KRAMER LEVIN
Kramer Levin Naftalis & Frankel LLP

LATHAM&WATKINS LLP

LITTLER MENDELSON®
THE NATIONAL EMPLOYMENT & LABOR LAW FIRM®

LOWENSTEIN SANDLER PC
Attorneys at Law

The *Vault/MCCA Guide to Law Firm Diversity Programs* is
underwritten by the following law firms:

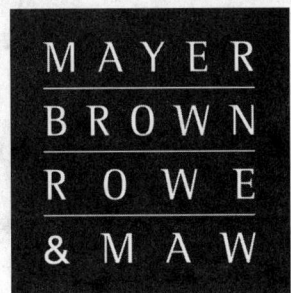

ATTORNEYS AT LAW

McDermott
Will & Emery

McKenna Long
& Aldridge LLP
Attorneys at Law

MINTZ LEVIN
MINTZ LEVIN COHN FERRIS GLOVSKY AND POPEO PC

Morgan Lewis
COUNSELORS AT LAW

MORRISON & FOERSTER LLP

Munger, Tolles & Olson LLP

NEAL, GERBER & EISENBERG LLP

Paul *Hastings*
ATTORNEYS

Pepper Hamilton LLP
Attorneys at Law

Philadelphia
Diversity
Law Group

PILLSBURY WINTHROP LLP

The *Vault/MCCA Guide to Law Firm Diversity Programs* is underwritten by the following law firms:

It's not just business. *It's personal.*

SEDGWICK
DETERT, MORAN & ARNOLD LLP

SHEARMAN & STERLING LLP

Skadden
Skadden, Arps, Slate, Meagher & Flom LLP & Affiliates

SONNENSCHEIN NATH & ROSENTHAL LLP

SULLIVAN & CROMWELL LLP

Sutherland
Asbill & Brennan LLP
ATTORNEYS AT LAW

Thompson & Knight Impact

TOWNSEND
and
TOWNSEND
and
CREW
LLP

WILMER CUTLER PICKERING
HALE AND DORR LLP

WINSTON & STRAWN LLP

The *Vault/MCCA Guide to Law Firm Diversity Programs* is
underwritten by the following corporate counsel:

ABBOTT LABORATORIES

Allstate
You're in good hands.

AstraZeneca
life inspiring ideas

Bayer

BOEING®

bp

The Coca-Cola Company

CORNING
Discovering Beyond Imagination

Countrywide Financial SM

JOHN DEERE

DEL MONTE FOODS

D≪LL™

Deloitte.

DUPONT®

The *Vault/MCCA Guide to Law Firm Diversity Programs* is
underwritten by the following corporate counsel:

HALLIBURTON

HCA

Honeywell

intel®

JPMorganChase

Johnson&Johnson

Marriott.

The *Vault/MCCA Guide to Law Firm Diversity Programs* is
underwritten by the following corporate counsel:

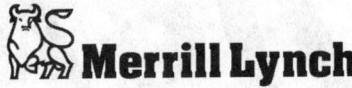

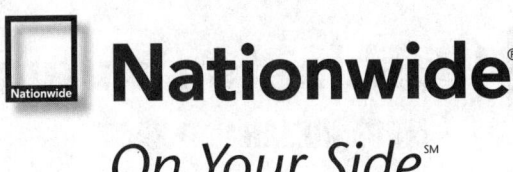

Morgan Stanley

The *Vault/MCCA Guide to Law Firm Diversity Programs* is underwritten by the following corporate counsel:

VAULT/MCCA GUIDE TO
LAW FIRM DIVERSITY PROGRAMS

For information about permission to reproduce selections from this book, contact Vault Inc., 150 West 22nd Street, New York, New York 10011, (212) 366-4212.

Library of Congress CIP Data is available.

ISBN 1-58131-299-7

Printed in the United States of America

ACKNOWLEDGMENTS

Vault could not have put this guide together without the generous help of the following people: Veta Richardson, James C. Diggs, Tom Gottschalk, Rick Palmore, and Gloria Santona. A special thanks to writer extraordinaire Vera Djordjevich and the Vault sales, graphics, editorial, and IT staffs for selling, designing, editing, and programming the guide. Lastly, and especially for making the guide financially possible, a very special thanks to all of the diversity chairs, managers, and coordinators; recruiting staff; and marketing people at the 113 law firms and corporate counsel offices.

Table of Contents

APPENDIX   1313

Preface by Thomas L. Sager

I want to congratulate Vault and MCCA® upon completion of the inaugural *Vault/MCCA Guide to Law Firm Diversity Programs*. It is a valuable source of information that I anticipate will be widely read by lawyers from many sectors of the profession. On behalf of the many grateful readers who, like me, view the guide as an important tool for furthering diversity, I thank the members of the general counsel advisory group – Jim Diggs, Rick Palmore, Tom Gottschalk, and Gloria Santona – for their leadership and support of this worthwhile publication.

For most of my professional life, I have spent time thinking about and trying new approaches to improve diversity in my own company and the primary law firms that are a part of the DuPont Legal network. Admittedly, some of our approaches have worked better than others and being an agent for change can sometimes be very frustrating. It is a continual learning process to which I feel fortunate to be able to contribute. If you are seeking to advance diversity in your organization, my advice to you is to remember that it is a marathon, not a sprint in a race that has no clear finishing line. Building strong diversity programs will continue to demand introspection and action on the part of the legal community. Regardless of age, race, gender, sexual orientation, or physical challenges, we each have a role to play and the opportunity to positively contribute toward greater inclusion.

MCCA is an organization that I am very proud to have helped launch. In fact, one of the most humbling experiences in my professional life was when MCCA chose to name its law firm diversity leadership award the Thomas L. Sager Award, in my honor. Since the first award was given in 1998, 21 law firm programs have been recognized. Their efforts, and those of many other diversity-focused firms, are summarized on the pages that follow. Whether the program is new or has been around a while, steps are being taken in the right direction and I commend every law firm that participated.

For those of us dedicated to building and strengthening diversity programs, this guide should prove to be an instrumental new resource to help further that goal.

Thomas L. Sager
Vice President & Assistant General Counsel
DuPont Company

Acknowledgments from Veta T. Richardson

The Minority Corporate Counsel Association (MCCA®) is proud to have been invited to partner with Vault Inc., the leading media company for career information, to produce this inaugural edition of *The Vault/MCCA Guide to Law Firm Diversity Programs*. We extend our sincere thanks to Vault's CEO, Samer Hamadeh, who had the foresight to suggest that we work together. Since Samer and I first started running with this idea, it has been a whirlwind of positive give and take between our respective organizations!

Founded in 1997, MCCA's mission is to advocate for the expanded hiring, retention, and promotion of minority attorneys in corporate law departments and the law firms that serve them. MCCA accomplishes its mission through the collection and dissemination of information about diversity in the legal profession. We have been proactively and aggressively helping diverse groups of attorneys to succeed and flourish in their workplaces. By leveraging our national focus and network of leaders in the legal profession, MCCA has sought to spotlight the importance of diversity and to keep the issue at the forefront in leading corporations and law firms.

MCCA was pleased to apply what we've learned from our multi-year research initiative, *Creating Pathways to Diversity*®, whose findings provide the foundation upon which MCCA drafted the survey questions. Combined with Vault's top-rate editorial staff and experience at producing informative, user-friendly career resources, the result is the most extensive and informative publication to date on diversity efforts at the nation's top 150 law firms. It has now become a significant addition to Vault's timely and topical set of career development resources addressing the legal profession. We couldn't be more excited about the contribution this guide will make to the legal community and ultimately, advancing our shared goal of a more diverse profession.

Vault and MCCA are deeply indebted to our General Counsel Advisory Board, which was ably led by James Diggs, chief legal officer of PPG Industries, Inc. Jim provided the vision, articulating the need for the general counsel community to receive complete, consistent information in order to make meaningful comparisons among outside counsel diversity efforts. Jim also tapped an influential network of colleagues to ensure that the survey would produce relevant data and receive priority attention from the law firms invited to participate. To our leading general counsel: Jim Diggs, Tom Gottschalk of General Motors, Rick Palmore of Sara Lee, and Gloria Santona of McDonald's, we extend our appreciation on behalf of the many lawyers in corporations, law firms, academia, the public sector, and other workplaces – all of whom will be the beneficiaries of the information contained in the guide.

In closing, it is important to recognize that although this guide is a step forward, it is hardly complete in that it does not cover other diverse populations as break-out categories, such as gay and lesbian attorneys and the physically challenged. The emphasis was intentionally placed on attorneys of color because such a significant number of general counsel and law firm partners have shared a frustration that progress has been much slower within this group as compared to whites of either gender. Rest assured that plans are already underway to address this void by incorporating appropriate feedback to revise the form to cover additional diverse groups in future surveys.

Veta T. Richardson
Executive Director
Minority Corporate Counsel Association

Letter from James C. Diggs

As General Counsel, it's our job to ensure that our legal departments and the outside counsel that we retain deliver high-quality legal services. However, as leading corporations, we've remained mindful that quality legal services can and should be provided by a diverse and inclusive legal team.

Many of us have signed various diversity statements of principle and have made strides within our own organizations. In seeking to develop relationships with various customers, suppliers, and other business associates, we know that building diverse and inclusive workforces enables us to achieve greater levels of success in the global and highly competitive marketplace where we do business each day. The business case is clear and, thus, diversity is more than simply the right thing to do – it's the right thing for our businesses.

However, the relative lack of progress within the law firm community suggests that many firms do not fully appreciate the business case for diversity and may not be doing all that they could to achieve a diverse workforce. In fact, recent data published by the National Association of Law Placement revealed that 43 percent of all U.S. law firms have not one minority partner. In the 21st century, in a nation that takes prides in the diversity of its people, one cannot help but feel startled by such a powerful statistic. But beyond being troubled, we must question how is it that 43 percent of U.S. law firms have not encountered one person of color that is sufficiently qualified to be a partner in their firms? We are compelled to ask what is being done to turn the tide?

As corporate leaders, we believe it is time to put our good principles into practice with a renewed call to action led by the in-house legal community. One factor that has frustrated me and several of my general counsel colleagues has been the lack of a resource that summarizes what larger law firms throughout the country are doing to advance diversity. Also, there has been such inconsistency among the surveys produced to date that we were not in a position to make meaningful comparisons among those law firms that strive for our business.

To address this void, I assembled a General Counsel Advisory Group to work with the Minority Corporate Counsel Association (MCCA®) and Vault. The members of the group were selected for their diverse industry perspectives, recognized leadership on this issue, and personal commitment. With our guidance, MCCA and Vault have published a guide that summarizes the diversity programs currently in place at the nation's largest and most profitable law firms.

Included in this guide is a copy of the letter that members of the advisory group and I sent to the managing partners of approximately 200 law firms listed on page 13. We are pleased to learn that so many law firms accepted our request to participate and, for those that did not, we encourage you to take part in future years.

In closing, I want to again thank my colleagues – Gloria Santona, Rick Palmore and Tom Gottschalk – for their support and many contributions toward the success of this project. It has been my pleasure to work with you to produce this important resource.

James C. Diggs
Senior Vice President, General Counsel & Secretary
PPG Industries, Inc.

How to Use This Guide

Over the past few years, most large U.S. law firms have devoted increasing resources to diversity initiatives as well as to the management and administration of these efforts. Nearly all have developed their own unique cultural approach and methods of administration. This book was developed to provide law students and practicing lawyers with the essential, objective information necessary to meaningfully evaluate these firms' diversity initiatives and programs. We hope that the information contained within this guide will enable law students and mid-career lawyers to match their interests and career objectives with an appropriate firm, as well as, enable corporate in-house counsel, as buyers of legal services, to shed light upon and make meaningful comparisons among the diversity efforts underway at the law firms with which they do business or are considering doing business.

When examining law firm diversity initiatives and comparing firms, we encourage you to look beyond raw numerical data. We encourage you to assess the benchmarks of a supportive, diversity-focused environment:

(1) understands the business case for diversity
(2) receives the commitment of top-management with established systems for measuring progress and accountability
(3) has an internal diversity council, which receives the administrative and financial support needed to spearhead sustainable progress
(4) its diversity efforts enjoy firm-wide ownership and participation
(5) offers superior career developmental programs.

The guide format presents the same information for all firms in a user-friendly way, addressing the degree to which several widely-recognized "best practices" are being incorporated into the firm's diversity program.

The complete survey sent to the law firm is printed in this Guide. In cases where a firm did not respond to a question, the unanswered question is not reprinted in its profile; the question is simply left out. For questions where firms had the option of choosing one or more answers to a question, we listed the answers the firm chose; to see which answers the firm did not choose, please refer to the full text of the survey (starting on p. 13). In addition, many of these questions offered firms the opportunity of providing an additional "Other" response; this additional voluntary information appears in italics at the beginning of the firm's answer. Finally, firms are structured differently when it comes to partnership levels (some firms have equity and non-equity partners, while others have only equity partners; some firms have "of counsel" positions, etc.). We have noted any such idiosyncrasies in notes accompanying the firms' demographic charts. Also note that the row titled "Total" in the demographic charts includes all attorneys of the given category, including white men (therefore, the "Total" is greater than the sum of the previous three rows).

As with many things, however, diversity programs in firms may not be as they appear in a written directory or survey form.

We therefore encourage you to use the information in the Guide as a springboard to ask constructive questions and open a dialogue that will empower you to define your relationship with the law firm. In the case of law students evaluating potential employers, it may be whether the firm's efforts measure up to your personal goals and developmental needs. When making a move laterally, mid-career attorneys will want to carefully evaluate their options and perform due diligence to decide whether a firm is the right fit. Similarly, corporate counsel committed to advancing diversity goals can evaluate whether their outside counsel's efforts are in step with their

corporation's core values around diversity and compare the firm's progress relative to its peers. In addition, law firms will want to use the Guide to do a little benchmarking – are you doing as well as your peers? Are there new approaches you should consider?

MCCA research indicates that most organizations' diversity efforts can be placed on a spectrum that ranges from those who merely seek to comply with federal regulations to those who undertake progressive initiatives to create workplaces of inclusion. We have found that top-down leadership commitment is critical to encouraging the transition and progress through these stages. The more successful, diversity-leading organizations remain focused upon development of a unique set of integrated initiatives that align diversity goals with strategic, business goals. In all cases, the leaders realize that creating a diverse, inclusive workplace is not accomplished easily and at no point is the work complete. Being a diversity-focused leader requires a sustained commitment over time and a willingness to continue to look critically at the organization's successes and failures to chart the next path to progress.

The Numbers

While it is important to underscore that a firm's reported diversity numbers cannot tell the whole story, numbers are a pretty reliable barometer of whether progress is being made. For attorneys considering the firm as an employer or for in-house counsel considering purchasing the firm's legal services, the numbers are important because the closer they are to zero, the less likely you are to encounter a truly diverse and inclusive team.

In addition, the demographic figures reported in this survey are "total numbers" for the entire firm – that is, all U.S. based offices. We have found that within one firm, there may be significant regional disparities so you will want to inquire further into how the particular office with which you are interviewing or in the case of in-house counsel to which you are assigning work, is doing. As you inquire, recognize that recruiting talent to certain locations may be more difficult than other locations. Consider how the office where you would work or place business stacks up against competitors within the same region, as well as nationally.

In-house counsel will need to be proactive. If your company values diversity of representation and you find that, on your matters, the relative percentages of hours billed to your account by minorities or women are disproportionate to the overall diversity percentages within the firm, speak up! Ask why, whenever it appears that the overall diversity within the firm is higher than that reflected on your matters. Take the time to personally get to know more minority and women lawyers at the firm, ask to work with them, and call them directly to place new matters and open engagements.

So that we may all work from the same baseline data, one of the most reliable sources of law firm demographic data is the National Association of Law Placement (NALP). NALP reports that for the similar time period covered by this survey, the percentages of minority and women attorneys in law firms were as follows:

Minority Partners – 4.04

Minority Associates – 14.63

Minority Summer Associates – 18.67

Women Partners – 16.81

Women Associates – 43.02

Women Summer Associates – 49.2

Source: National Association of Law Placement, 2003-2004

Strategic Plan and Diversity Leadership

Once a firm has committed to becoming more diverse, there are various ways in which the firm can advance that commitment. However, it is universally accepted that without the unwavering support of the firm's top management, even the most well-intentioned diversity program will fail. Pay attention to what steps the firm's management has taken to communicate its diversity commitment widely and to develop a clear action plan for progress. Is diversity progress a goal that has been set with firm-wide responsibility and accountability? Do diversity leaders have a voice on management issues? When considering how often the firm's management may review or discuss diversity progress/results, be aware that more often does not necessarily mean better or more committed.

Through working with diversity-leading corporations we have learned that what is valued is measured, and tying compensation to results is a highly effective method for underscoring a priority. Several firms are now starting to adopt this practice and the survey asked whether partner compensation is impacted by diversity results.

Recruitment

This section will prove helpful for law students or attorneys looking to make a lateral move. Law students who are interested in interviewing at a particular law firm will want to check out whether their law school is on the firm's interview schedule. If not, do they recruit at law schools of similar rank and reputation as yours? If so, you'll have a better chance of being considered. Do they plan to interview in your geographic area? There may be an opportunity for you to meet with a representative of the firm when they are in your city.

For laterals, you will need to make the right connections with people already at the firm. Look at their outreach efforts and position yourself to network effectively. In addition, you'll want to invest your time at a place where your career development goals are advanced. The guide will hopefully give you valuable information to start to ask the right questions and evaluate whether a particular firm is a good fit for where you are and what you want to achieve.

Retention and Professional Development

Research indicates that most people care more about the intangibles of their job – such as whether they like what they are doing, whether they see room for growth, and whether they feel they are being fairly treated – than they do the tangibles such as how much they are paid or how big their office is. Very few people move solely for monetary reasons, but they will often jump ship for a better opportunity and will actively seek out that opportunity when they feel they are not valued by their current employer.

Let's face it – at most law firms the turnover rates are high in every category, minorities and women especially. But this section's set of questions was designed to offer information about what the firm may be doing to stem the tide.

The answers to the questions about working less than a full-time schedule and the influence on partnership opportunities are worth reading carefully. Just because a firm has elected to partnership someone who at one time worked less than a full-time schedule does not necessarily mean that the partnership will elect attorneys currently working a part-time schedule. In some firms, working less than a full-time schedule will mean that you must either return full-time to make partner or if already a partner, relinquish being a partner while you are working part-time. In other firms, the partnership simply proportionately adjusts compensation and benefits to reflect a part-time schedule. It's your choice as to which environment better serves your needs. Just recognize that there is a big difference.

Note, too, that in-house counsel can play an important role in influencing the work assignments of minority and women lawyers and thereby further your corporation's diversity goals involving outside counsel.

Management Profile

In every organization, the perspectives and priorities of the management have far-reaching impact. Who is leading the organization? Are diverse opinions included? Have people other than white males been elevated into key management positions; do they lead practice groups? For law students in the enviable position of evaluating several offers and attempting to match their interests to practice areas, perhaps the diversity of the practice group may be an important consideration.

For in-house counsel, look at the information in the guide as an opportunity to assist your diversity goals for outside counsel. If a woman or a minority has worked her way up the ladder to head the practice group of a major law firm, you really don't need to question whether he or she is a good lawyer. Take that as a given. When you find yourself in need of legal help in those areas of law, pick up the phone and place your business through one of these outstanding lawyers. And if the law firm is one that you already work with, have you met the women and minority practice leaders yet? If not, perhaps you should.

What "The Firm Says"

This section of the firm's diversity profile consists of a narrative composed by the firm. There were no requirements regarding what had to be addressed (although we admit to having made a few suggestions). This section offers a great place for the firm to elaborate on some of its answers to the survey question and discuss things they are doing that we may have failed to cover.

In conclusion, we hope that this book assists you in identifying law firms that are a good match to your diversity values and needs. Remember: although you can get a quick impression by flipping through these pages and looking at diversity program overviews and yes/no responses, the most important factor is the commitment of the partnership to meet defined diversity goals and to support programs that enable diverse attorneys to succeed and flourish. This guide is intended to be your first step in learning how to assess a firm's diversity commitment within the context of the firm's unique culture and measured against your personal developmental goals. We hope you find it of value!

Letter from General Counsel Advisory Group to Managing Partners

May 25, 2004
Re: Important General Counsel-Led Diversity Initiative – Response Required

Dear Managing Partner:

We are writing to alert you to a very exciting project and to ask for your involvement in what promises to be an effective means to track law firm performance in the critical area of diversity.

The undersigned chief legal officers have formed the General Counsel Advisory Group and have joined with the Minority Corporate Counsel Association, one of the nation's leading advocates for a more diverse legal profession, and with Vault Inc., a premier source of employment information that enjoys a high degree of visibility among law students and lawyers, to develop the attached Law Firm Diversity Survey. We also solicited the feedback of managing partners at several law firms before finalizing the document. We are asking that all firms listed below complete the survey, as we think it is the best way to stimulate diversity progress and achieve a measure of consistency in how diversity information is reported.

Vault will compile all of the completed surveys into a directory called the Vault/MCCA Guide to Law Firm Diversity Programs. The guide's purpose is to educate the legal community on the commitment and types of diversity programs in place at over 200 large and prestigious law firms (see list on page 13). The objectives of publishing the guide are:

- To provide a consistent profile of current law firm diversity planning, implementation and representation;

- To identify the best practices for the design and implementation of diversity initiatives in law firms; and

- To outline the strategies, programs, and metrics that law firms use to increase the recruitment, retention and promotion of minority and women attorneys.

This guide differs from some of Vault's other publications, such as the Vault Guide to the Top 100 Law Firms, in two significant ways:

- There are no rankings. Rather, Vault is simply gathering and presenting information about each firm's diversity efforts. Law firm profiles will appear in alphabetical order, in a format similar to that of the recently released Vault Guide to Law Firm Pro Bono Programs.

- All information is self-reported by each firm. Each firm's data will be published virtually as submitted, with only minor editing from Vault for clarity and length, and all edits will be reviewed and approved by the firm prior to publication.

The Vault/MCCA Guide to Law Firm Diversity Programs will be distributed free of charge to every law firm that submits a completed survey, to the career offices of every accredited law school in the United States and to the 200+ MCCA member general counsel.

We hope that you will join us in this effort by completing and returning the attached survey in a timely manner.

If you have any questions, please direct them to MCCA's executive director, Veta Richardson, at (202) 371-5910 or Vault's CEO, Samer Hamadeh, at (212) 366-5513.

Sincerely,

James C. Diggs
General Counsel
PPG Industries, Inc.

Tom Gottschalk
General Counsel
General Motors Corporation

Roderick A. Palmore
General Counsel
Sara Lee Corporation

Gloria Santona
General Counsel
McDonald's Corporation

Firms Invited to Participate in Law Firm Diversity Survey

Akerman Senterfitt

Akin Gump Strauss Hauer & Feld LLP

Allen & Overy LLP

Allen Matkins Leck Gamble & Mallory LLP

Alston & Bird LLP

Andrews Kurth LLP

Arent Fox PLLC

Arnold & Porter LLP

Baker & Daniels

Baker & Hostetler LLP

Baker & McKenzie LLP

Baker Botts L.L.P.

Baker, Donelson, Bearman, Caldwell & Berkowitz, PC

Ballard Spahr Andrews & Ingersoll, LLP

Barnes & Thornburg LLP

Bell, Boyd & Lloyd LLC

Bingham McCutchen LLP

Blackwell Sanders Peper Martin LLP

Blank Rome LLP

Boies, Schiller & Flexner LLP

Bracewell & Patterson, L.L.P.

Brown Raysman Millstein Felder & Steiner, LLP

Brown Rudnick Berlack Israels LLP

Bryan Cave LLP

Buchanan Ingersoll PC

Cadwalader, Wickersham & Taft LLP

Cahill Gordon & Reindel LLP

Carlton Fields, P.A.

Chadbourne & Parke LLP

Chapman and Cutler LLP

Choate, Hall & Stewart

Cleary, Gottlieb, Steen & Hamilton

Clifford Chance LLP

Cooley Godward LLP

Coudert Brothers LLP

Covington & Burling

Cozen O'Connor

Cravath, Swaine & Moore LLP

Crowell & Moring LLP

Davis Polk & Wardwell

Davis Wright Tremaine LLP

Day, Berry & Howard, LLP

Debevoise & Plimpton LLP

Dechert LLP

Dewey Ballantine LLP

Dickstein Shapiro Morin & Oshinsky, LLP

Dorsey & Whitney LLP

Dow, Lohnes & Albertson, PLLC

Drinker Biddle & Reath LLP

Duane Morris LLP

Dykema Gossett PLLC

Edwards & Angell LLP

Epstein Becker & Green, P.C.

Faegre & Benson LLP

Fenwick & West LLP

Finnegan, Henderson, Farabow, Garrett & Dunner, L.L.P.

Fish & Neave

Fish & Richardson P.C.

Fitzpatrick, Cella, Harper & Scinto

Foley & Lardner LLP

Foley Hoag LLP

Fox Rothschild LLP

Fried, Frank, Harris, Shriver & Jacobson LLP

Frost Brown Todd LLC

Fulbright & Jaworski L.L.P.

Gardere Wynne Sewell LLP

Gardner Carton & Douglas LLP

Gibson, Dunn & Crutcher LLP

Godwin Gruber LLP

Goodwin Procter LLP

Gray Cary Ware & Freidenrich, LLP

Greenberg Traurig, LLP

Gunderson Dettmer Stough Villeneuve Franklin & Hachigian, LLP

Hale and Dorr LLP

Haynes and Boone, LLP

Heller Ehrman White & McAuliffe LLP

Hinshaw & Culbertson LLP

Hogan & Hartson LLP.

Holland & Hart LLP

Holland & Knight LLP

Honigman Miller Schwartz and Cohn LLP

Howard, Rice, Nemerovski, Canady, Falk & Rabkin, P.C.

Howrey Simon Arnold & White, LLP

Hughes Hubbard & Reed LLP

Hunton & Williams LLP

Husch & Eppenberger, LLC

Ice Miller

Irell & Manella LLP

Jackson Lewis LLP

Jackson Walker LLP

Jeffer, Mangels, Butler & Marmaro LLP

Jenkens & Gilchrist

Jenner & Block LLP

Jones Day

Katten Muchin Zavis Rosenman

Kaye Scholer LLP

Kelley Drye & Warren LLP

Kenyon & Kenyon

Kilpatrick Stockton LLP

King & Spalding LLP

Kirkland & Ellis LLP

Kirkpatrick & Lockhart LLP

Knobbe Martens Olson & Bear LLP

Kramer Levin Naftalis & Frankel LLP

Kutak Rock LLP

Latham & Watkins LLP

LeBoeuf, Lamb, Greene & MacRae, L.L.P.

Littler Mendelson, P.C.

Locke Liddell & Sapp LLP

Loeb & Loeb LLP

Lord, Bissell & Brook LLP

Lowenstein Sandler

Luce, Forward, Hamilton & Scripps LLP

Manatt, Phelps & Phillips, LLP

Mayer, Brown, Rowe & Maw LLP

McCarter & English, LLP

McDermott, Will & Emery LLP

McGuireWoods LLP

McKenna, Long & Aldridge LLP

Michael Best & Friedrich LLP

Milbank, Tweed, Hadley & McCloy, LLP

Miller, Canfield, Paddock and Stone, P.L.C.

Mintz Levin Cohn Ferris Glovsky and Popeo PC

Moore & Van Allen PLLC

Morgan, Lewis & Bockius LLP

Morrison & Foerster LLP

Munger, Tolles & Olson LLP

Neal, Gerber & Eisenberg LLP

Nelson Mullins Riley & Scarborough, L.L.P.

Nixon Peabody LLP

O'Melveny & Myers LLP

Oppenheimer Wolff & Donnelly LLP

Orrick, Herrington & Sutcliffe LLP

Palmer & Dodge LLP

Patterson, Belknap, Webb & Tyler LLP

Patton Boggs LLP

Paul, Hastings, Janofsky & Walker LLP

Paul, Weiss, Rifkind, Wharton & Garrison LLP

Pepper Hamilton LLP

Perkins Coie LLP

Pillsbury Winthrop LLP

Piper Rudnick, LLP

Porter Wright Morris & Arthur LLP

Powell, Goldstein, Frazer & Murphy LLP

Preston Gates & Ellis LLP

Proskauer Rose LLP

Quarles & Brady LLP

Quinn Emanuel Urquhart Oliver & Hedges, LLP

Reed Smith LLP

Robbins, Kaplan, Miller & Ciresi L.L.P.

Ropes & Gray LLP

Sanchez & Daniels

Saul Ewing LLP

Schiff Hardin LLP

Schnader Harrison Segal & Lewis LLP

Schulte Roth & Zabel LLP

Sedgwick, Detert, Moran & Arnold LLP

Seyfarth Shaw LLP

Shaw Pittman LLP

Shearman & Sterling LLP

Sheppard, Mullin, Richter & Hampton LLP

Shook, Hardy & Bacon LLP

Sidley Austin Brown & Wood LLP

Simpson Thacher & Bartlett LLP

Skadden, Arps, Slate, Meagher & Flom LLP

Snell & Wilmer L.L.P.

Sonnenschein Nath & Rosenthal LLP

Squire, Sanders & Dempsey L.L.P.

Steel Hector & Davis

Steptoe & Johnson LLP

Stinson Morrison Hecker LLP

Stoel Rives LLP

Strasburger & Price, LLP

Stroock & Stroock & Lavan

Sullivan & Cromwell

Sutherland Asbill & Brennan LLP

Swidler Berlin Shereff Friedman, LLP

Testa, Hurwitz & Thibeault, LLP

Thacher Proffitt & Wood LLP

Thelen Reid & Priest LLP

Thompson & Knight LLP

Thompson Coburn LLP

Thompson Hine LLP

Townsend and Townsend and Crew LLP

Troutman Sanders LLP

Vedder, Price, Kaufman & Kammholz, P.C.

Venable LLP

Vinson & Elkins L.L.P.

Vorys, Sater, Seymour and Pease LLP

Wachtell, Lipton, Rosen & Katz

Weil, Gotshal & Manges LLP

White & Case LLP

Wildman, Harrold, Allen & Dixon LLP

Wiley Rein & Fielding LLP

Williams & Connolly LLP

Willkie Farr & Gallagher LLP

Wilmer, Cutler & Pickering LLP

Wilson Sonsini Goodrich & Rosati P.C.

Wilson, Elser, Moskowitz, Edelman & Dicker LLP

Winstead Sechrest & Minick P.C.

Winston & Strawn LLP

Wolf, Block, Schorr and Solis-Cohen LLP

Womble Carlyle Sandridge & Rice, PLLC

Vault/MCCA Law Firm Diversity Survey

Introduction

Welcome to the inaugural effort of the Vault/MCCA Guide to Law Firm Diversity Programs (2005 Edition). In anticipation of questions and comments regarding this survey, we have prepared the following instruction sheet to guide you. Of course, if you still have questions, please do not hesitate to contact us at the phone numbers and e-mail addresses below.

This year, we decided to collect data on minorities in total and not to split up the different categories of minorities by race; for the second edition, we will likely ask you to break out your minority attorney data by race. This year, we elected to focus on diversity within the U.S. attorney population only; for the second edition, we may ask you about diversity within your administrative ranks. This year, we are defining diversity simply as minorities and women; for the second edition, we will include questions on the gay and lesbian populations as well.

We thank you for your understanding and welcome comments and feedback as we seek to improve the survey for future editions.

The Process

Participation is straightforward and entirely free of charge. We ask that a representative or group of representatives from your firm complete the attached questionnaire (in MS Word format) within the next four weeks. You are free to skip any question that you do not wish to answer, but we encourage you to be as thorough as possible. Please note that each firm should complete and return only ONE questionnaire. Please e-mail the completed questionnaire to editor Vera Djordjevich at vera@staff.vault.com.

The Timeframe

The book will be officially unveiled at MCCA's Creating Pathways to Diversity conference on November 3rd in New York City, which means that we face an especially compressed publication schedule. We therefore ask that you please return the completed questionnaire no later than Wednesday, JUNE 23, 2004. We appreciate your cooperation and regret that Vault will not be able to include any firms whose responses we do not receive in time.

Distribution

The Vault/MCCA Guide to Law Firm Diversity Programs will be distributed free of charge to every law firm that submits a completed survey, to the career offices of every accredited law school in the United States and to the 200+ MCCA member general counsel. The guide will also be sold through college and university bookstores and on the Internet. Excerpts from the Guide will also be available free at www.vault.com. At no additional charge, moreover, the entire Guide will be available to Vault Gold subscribers and to law schools that have subscribed to the Vault Online Law Career Library.

Instructions

Global Definitions

Also use the following definitions to answer Section II, Question 10, and Section VI.

1. All answers should reflect permanent attorney staff in the United States. Do not include any non-attorney staff, except for summer associates.

2. Do not include contract attorneys or office locations outside of the U.S.

3. For this survey, diversity is defined as male and female minorities and white women but does not include gay and lesbian attorneys.

4. For this survey, minorities are defined as those whose race is other than White/Caucasian (e.g., African-American/Black, Latino/Hispanic, Asian, Native American, Middle Eastern, and Asian Indian).

Section II.

The terms are defined as follows:

Associate: A non-partner lawyer who has no ownership rights or responsibilities but who has an opportunity to become an owner; associates are employees of the firm and are considered on partnership track, even if they ultimately leave the firm or are not chosen for partnership.

Summer Associate: A law student, usually between second and third year (called a 3L, in that case), who serves as a law associate for the summer and is supervised by a lawyer or lawyers.

Equity partner: A part owner who has the right to share in the profits of the firm and may be individually liable for the obligations of the partnership.

Non-equity partner: A law firm employee who has been promoted from an associate position and who does not have interests in the profits or capital of the firm.

New hire: An attorney who has joined the firm sometime during the year indicated on the table (i.e., in 2002 or in 2003); include all first-year associates, laterals, and partners (both equity and non-equity).

Section III.

Question 3. Count only attorneys, not administrative staff, who serve on the diversity committee.

Question 7. When checking the boxes, refer only to your minority attorneys.

Section IV.

Question 10. Count only 3Ls, because 2Ls do not generally receive or accept offers of full-time employment at the end of the summer.

Question 11. Please use definitions from Section II.

Section VII.

In the narrative, some points you may address or provide include:

• The firm's diversity mission statement

• Diversity scholarships for summer associates or first-years or other attorneys

• More detail on part-time/flex-time programs

• More detail on the workings of your diversity committee

• The names of the minority bar associations with which you have relationships and the nature of those relationships

• List and description of diversity awards and honors

• How the firm has communicated to partners the link between diversity and business success

• If the firm provides financial support or pro bono services to minority public interest organizations and if so, name those organizations

• If the firm provides billable credit for work related to diversity initiatives

• The nature and scope of the firm's Equal Employment Opportunity and Prevention of Harassment policy

• If the firm ties progress on diversity initiatives to compensation in any way

Best regards,

Samer Hamadeh

Samer Hamadeh
Co-founder & CEO, Vault
(212) 366-5513
samer@vault.com

Veta Richardson

Veta Richardson, Esq.
Executive Director, MCCA
(202) 371-5910
vetarichardson@mcca.com

I. Firm Contact Info

Contact Person: _____ Title: _____

Managing Partner: _____ (name & title)

Diversity Team Leader: _____ (name & title)

Firm Name: _____

Address: _____

City: _____ State: _____ Zip: _____

Phone: _____ Fax: _____ Email: _____

Office Locations (worldwide): _____

(note that this survey addresses diversity efforts in the U.S. offices only)

II. Law Firm Demographic Profile

(Numbers requested are firm totals for all U.S. offices on 12/31/03 and on 12/31/02. See instructions for definitions.)

	TOTAL (ALL ATTYS) 2003/2002		MINORITY MEN 2003/2002		MINORITY WOMEN 2003/2002		WHITE WOMEN 2003/2002	
1. Number of associates								
2. Number of summer associates								
3. Number of equity partners								
4. Number of non-equity partners								
5. Number of new hires								

MINORITY CORPORATE COUNSEL ASSOCIATION

III. Strategic Plan and Diversity Leadership

1. How does the firm's leadership communicate the importance of diversity to everyone at the firm? (e.g., e-mails, web site, newsletters, meetings, etc.) _____
_____

2. Who has primary responsibility for leading diversity initiatives at your firm? Name of person and his/her title: _____

3. (a) Does your law firm currently have a diversity committee?   Yes ☐   No ☐

   (b) If yes, does the committee's representation include one or more members of the firm's management/executive committee (or the equivalent)?   Yes ☐   No ☐

   (c) If yes, how many attorneys are on the committee, and in 2003, what was the total number of hours collectively spent by the committee in furtherance of the firm's diversity initiatives?

   Total Attorneys on Committee: _____   *Total Hours Spent on Diversity:* _____

4. Does the committee and/or diversity leader establish and set goals or objectives consistent with management's priorities?   Yes ☐   No ☐   Partially ☐

   (explain): _____

5. Has the firm undertaken a formal or informal diversity program or set of initiatives aimed at increasing the diversity of the firm?   Yes, formal ☐   Yes, informal ☐   No ☐

6. (a) How often does the firm's management review the firm's diversity progress/results?
   - ☐ Monthly
   - ☐ Quarterly
   - ☐ Twice a year
   - ☐ Annually
   - ☐ Does not review/measure progress/results
   - ☐ Other, please specify _____

   (b) How is the firm's diversity committee and/or firm management held accountable for achieving results? _____
   _____

7. The inclusion and advancement of minority lawyers in large law firms continues to lag behind the progress made in the case of white women and white men. What are your firm's diversity priorities aimed at improving the representation of minority lawyers at your firm? Please check all that have been completed or that you are currently addressing, or indicate if not a current priority. You may elaborate on any point in the final question, which is a narrative.

LAW FIRM DIVERSITY INITIATIVES	ALREADY COMPLETED	CURRENTLY ADDRESSING	NOT A CURRENT PRIORITY
Undertake communication from firm management that diversity is a top priority of the firm.			
Formalize diversity plan and committee with action steps and accountability to management.			
Conduct firm-wide diversity training for all attorneys and staff.			
Increase the number of minority attorneys at the associate level.			
Increase the number of minority attorneys at the partnership level.			
Develop/expand relationships with minority bar associations to offer firm's support of these networks.			
Focus on strengthening firm's mentoring program, including for benefit of minority attorneys.			
Conduct internal diversity needs assessment and/or retain diversity consultant to examine how firm culture might be more welcoming of minorities.			
Support law firm's internal affinity networks (e.g., women, minority attorney networks).			
Manage/monitor allocation of work assignments and/or hours billed to ensure women and minority attorneys have equal access/inclusion on top client matters.			

IV. Recruitment

A. New Associates

8. Does your firm annually recruit at any of the following types of institutions? (Check all that apply and list the schools).

☐ Ivy League schools: _____

☐ Public state schools: _____

☐ Private schools: _____

☐ Historically Black Colleges and Universities (HBCUs): _____

☐ Native American Tribal Universities: _____

☐ Other predominantly minority and/or women's colleges: _____

9. Of the law schools that you listed above, do you have any special outreach efforts directed to encourage minority law students to consider your firm?

☐ Hold a reception for minority law students

☐ Advertise in minority law student association publication(s)

☐ Participate in/host minority law student job fair(s)

☐ Sponsor minority law student association events

☐ Firm's lawyers participate on career panels at school

☐ Outreach to leadership of minority student organizations

☐ Scholarships or intern/fellowships for minority students

☐ Other: _____

10. What were your summer/new associate demographics for the most recently completed summer class?

SUMMER ASSOCIATE STATISTICS: SUMMER 2003 (INCLUDE ONLY 3LS)	MINORITY MEN	MINORITY WOMEN	WHITE WOMEN	TOTAL
Summer associates				
Summer associates who received an offer of full-time employment				
Summer associates who accepted an offer of full-time employment*				

B. Lateral Associates and Partners

11. What were your demographics for lateral hires and new partners in the past year?

LATERAL ASSOCIATES AND PARTNERS: 1/1/03-12/31/03	MINORITY MEN	MINORITY WOMEN	WHITE WOMEN	TOTAL
Number of lateral associate hires				
Number of lateral partner hires (equity and non-equity)				
Number of new partners (equity and non-equity) promoted from associate rank				
Number of new equity partners				

12. (a) What activities does the firm undertake to attract minority and women attorneys?

☐ Partner programs with women and minority bar associations

☐ Participate at minority job fairs

☐ Seek referrals from other attorneys

☐ Utilize online job services (e.g., MCCA/DuPont Primary Law Firm Job Bank)

☐ Other, please specify: _____

(b) Do you use executive recruiting/search firms to seek to identify new diversity hires (partners or associates)?   Yes ☐   No ☐

(c) If yes, list all women- and/or minority-owned executive search/recruiting firms to which the firm paid a fee for placement services in the past 12 months: _____

V. Retention & Professional Development

13. What is the total number of attorneys who voluntarily or involuntarily left your firm's employ in 2003?

_____

a. Of this total, how many were white women? _____

b. How many were minority women? _____

c. How many were minority men? _____

14. How do 2003 attrition rates generally compare to those experienced in the prior year period?

☐ Higher than in prior years

☐ Lower than in prior years

☐ About the same as in prior years

15. Please identify the specific steps you are taking to reduce the attrition rate of minority and women attorneys. (It is suggested that you elaborate on this issue in the final question of this survey.)

☐ Develop and/or support internal employee affinity groups (e.g., minority or women networks within the firm

☐ Increase/review compensation relative to competition

☐ Increase/improve current work/life programs

☐ Adopt dispute resolution process

☐ Succession plan includes emphasis on diversity

☐ Work with minority and women attorneys to develop career advancement plans

☐ Introduce minority and women attorneys to key clients, including to lead engagements

☐ Review work assignments and hours billed to key client matters to make sure minority and women attorneys are not being excluded

☐ Strengthen mentoring program for all attorneys, including minorities and women

☐ Professional skills development program, including minority and women attorneys

☐ Other, please specify _____

16. Does your firm have part-time/flex-time policies that permit attorneys (male or female) to work alternative schedules?　　Yes ☐　　No ☐　　Comments: _____

17. What impact, if any, will the decision to work part-time have on an attorney's ability to make partner or, if already a partner, to remain a partner at your firm? _____

_____

18. Have any attorneys who chose to work a part-time schedule made partner at your firm?

Yes ☐　　　No ☐　　How many? _____

Comments: _____

VI. Management Demographic Profile (as of 12/31/03)

	MINORITY MEN	MINORITY WOMEN	WHITE WOMEN	TOTAL
Number of attorneys on the Executive/Management Committee or equivalent				
Number of attorneys on the Hiring Committee or equivalent				
Number of attorneys on the Partner/Associate Review Committee or equivalent				

Please provide information regarding all minority and women attorneys who head offices or practice groups of your law firm:

Minorities heading offices (list names and locations): _____

Women heading offices (list names and locations): _____

Minorities heading practice groups (list names and departments): _____

Women heading practice groups (list names and departments): _____

VII. Additional Information

In a narrative of two pages or less, please provide any additional information regarding your firm's diversity initiatives that you wish to share. See instructions for details and suggestions.

LAW FIRM
UNDERWRITERS

**FROM
DIVERSE
PARTS—**

**BUILDING
A GREATER
WHOLE**

Baltimore
Berlin
Boston
Brussels
London
Munich
New York
Northern Virginia
Oxford
Princeton
Waltham
Washington

A vibrant community of ideas can only grow from a rich variety
of perspectives, skills and experiences.

When we begin with diversity, there is no end to what we can create.

wilmerhale.com

**WILMER CUTLER PICKERING
HALE AND DORR LLP**

Commitment to Diversity is always

WorthWeil

At Weil, Gotshal & Manges, we are proud of our long tradition of public commitment to diversity and equal opportunity. We work actively to foster an inclusive work environment, support minority-owned vendors and enrich our firm's culture through our diversity and inclusion initiatives for our lawyers and staff.

Our goal is clear – to create a workplace that enables everyone to succeed.
To learn more about Weil Gotshal, please visit us at *www.weil.com*

WEIL, GOTSHAL & MANGES LLP

AUSTIN   BOSTON   BRUSSELS   BUDAPEST   DALLAS   FRANKFURT   HOUSTON   LONDON   MIAMI

MUNICH   NEW YORK   PARIS   PRAGUE   SILICON VALLEY   SINGAPORE   WARSAW   WASHINGTON, D.C.

WHEN YOUR CITY'S FINANCES ARE
DISTRESSED, AND ITS FUTURE IS UNCERTAIN,
YOU TAKE IT PERSONALLY.
GLENN R. MAHONE
CORPORATE & SECURITIES GROUP

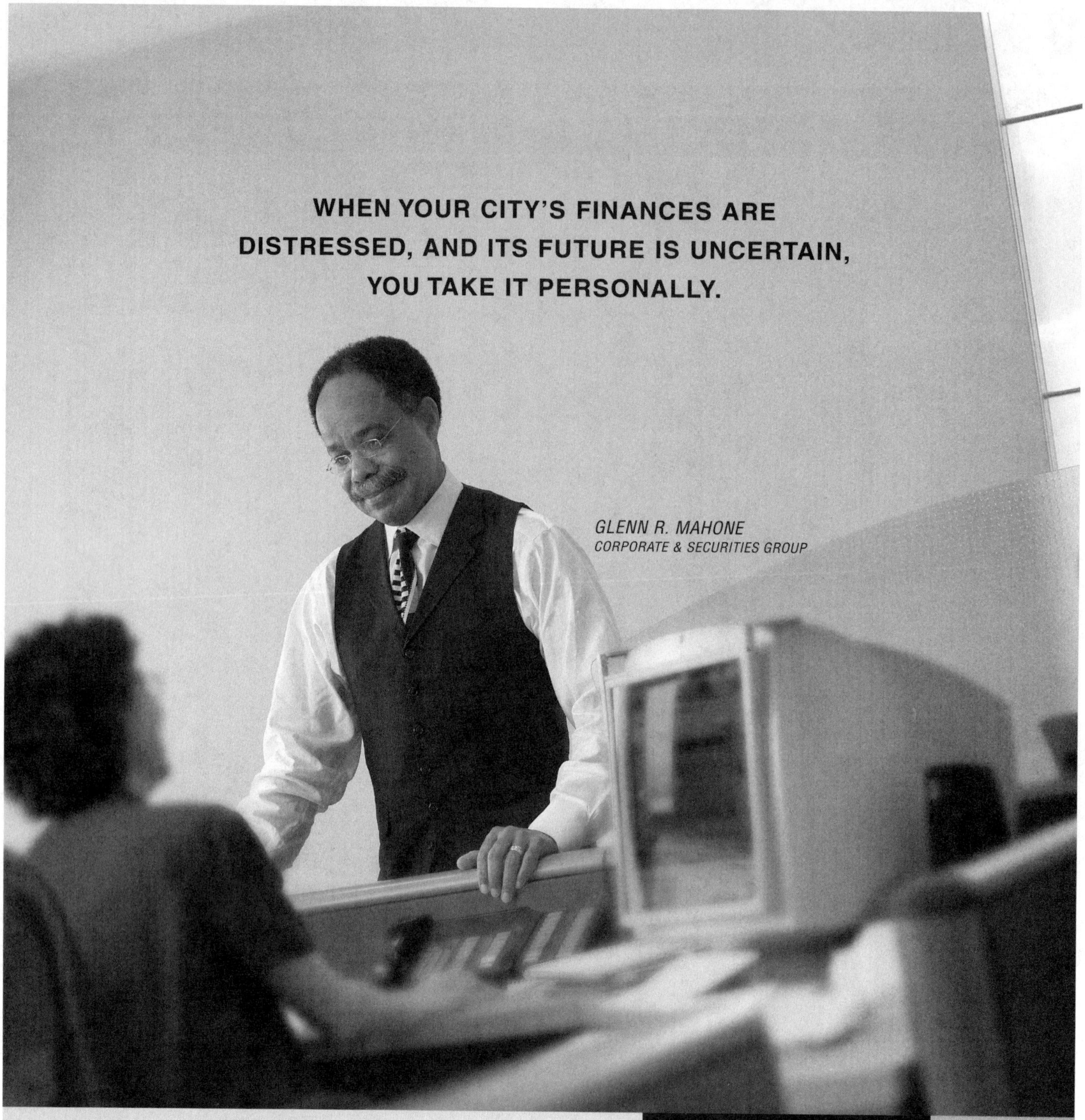

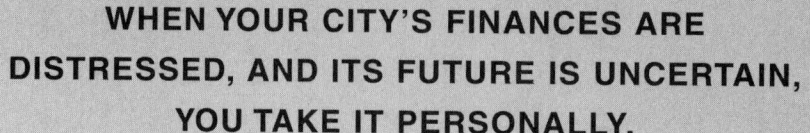

Beyond Words and Numbers

Diversity

MCAA's Thomas L. Sager Award

The Sager Award is given annually to law firms that have demonstrated a sustained commitment to improve the hiring, promotion and retention of minority groups.

Some firms speak of "achieving diversity." At Akin Gump, diversity is more than what you achieve – it's what you believe. After all, diversity speaks not just to numbers but to ideas, innovation and a dynamic culture.

As a three-time recipient of the Minority Corporate Counsel Association's Thomas L. Sager Award, Akin Gump remains committed to the firmwide advancement of minority attorneys. At Akin Gump, it's our culture.

1.866.AKIN LAW

akingump.com

AKIN GUMP
STRAUSS HAUER & FELD LLP
Attorneys at Law

© 2004 Akin Gump Strauss Hauer & Feld LLP

Think we're all the same?

Think again.

Challenging legal problems.
Demanding clients.
Supportive colleagues.

We are commited to making these a reality for all of our lawyers—
regardless of gender, ethnicity, sexual orientation or physical capabilities.

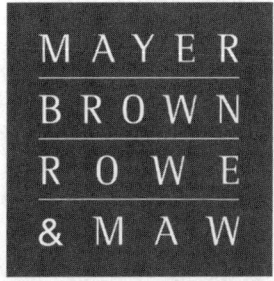

MAYER BROWN ROWE & MAW

www.mayerbrownrowe.com

Brussels • Charlotte • Chicago • Cologne • Frankfurt • Houston • London
Los Angeles • Manchester • New York • Palo Alto • Paris • Washington, D.C.

At KIRKLAND & ELLIS LLP,

Diversity is a priority.
Inclusion is a necessity.

At Kirkland & Ellis LLP, we realize that improving diversity within our Firm requires a fresh approach to recruit outstanding diverse attorneys of all backgrounds and new initiatives to encourage their success at the Firm. It's one of the reasons we have awarded minority students scholarships totaling over a quarter of a million dollars. It's one of the reasons we established the firmwide Diversity Committee and the Women's Leadership Initiative. It's one of the reasons the Firm sponsors a quarterly lunch for our diverse attorneys. It's one of the reasons we created the Diversity Digest – an internal firmwide publication to improve communication and awareness of the Firm's diversity initiatives. We are working hard at Kirkland & Ellis to create an atmosphere of inclusion so that all our employees feel welcome and have an equal opportunity to succeed.

KIRKLAND & ELLIS LLP

www.kirkland.com

Chicago   London   Los Angeles   New York   San Francisco   Washington, D.C.

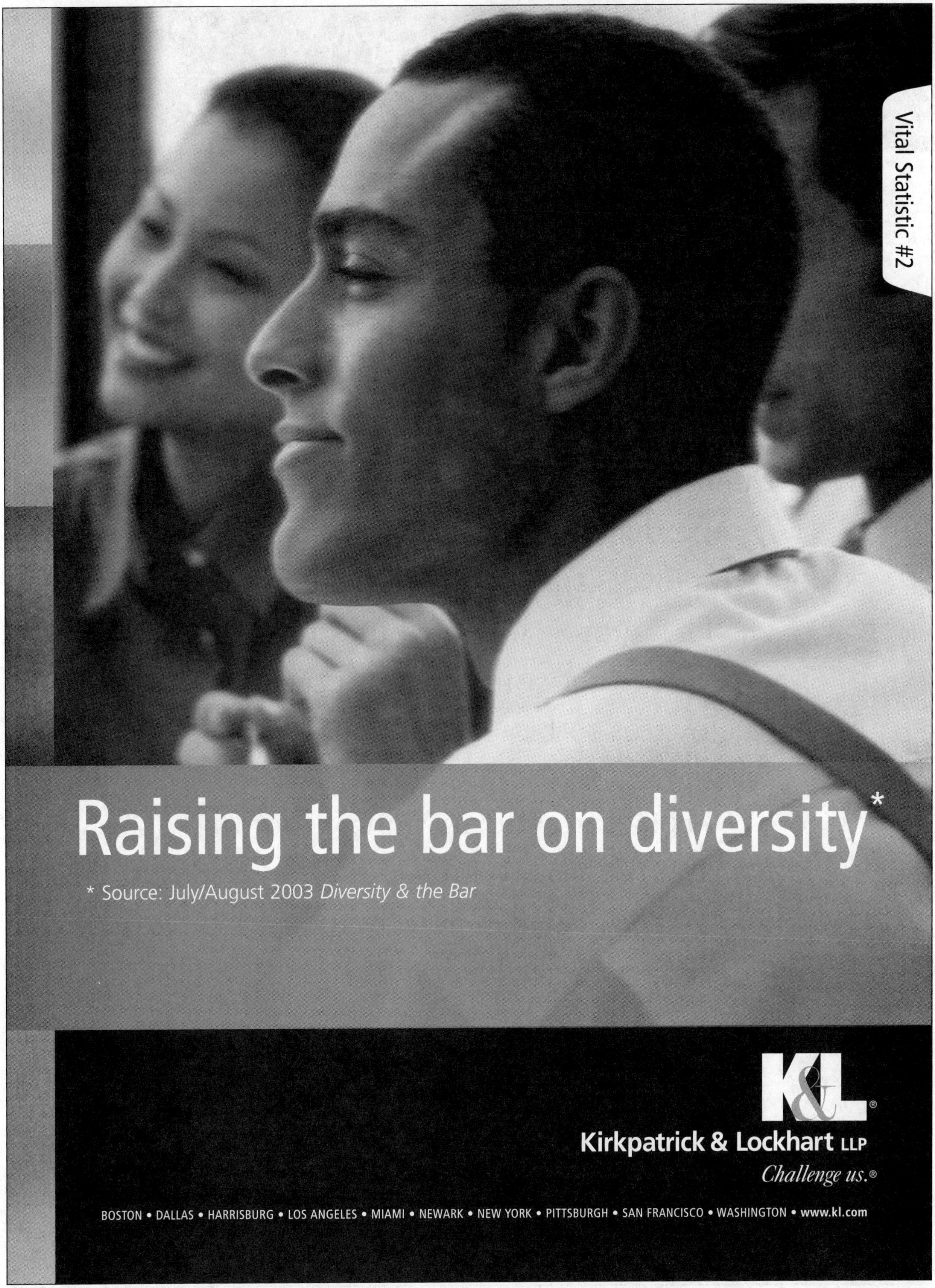
Vital Statistic #2
Raising the bar on diversity*
* Source: July/August 2003 Diversity & the Bar
K&L
Kirkpatrick & Lockhart LLP
Challenge us.®
BOSTON • DALLAS • HARRISBURG • LOS ANGELES • MIAMI • NEWARK • NEW YORK • PITTSBURGH • SAN FRANCISCO • WASHINGTON • www.kl.com

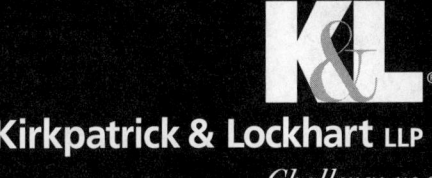

Personal Respect and Individual Worth.

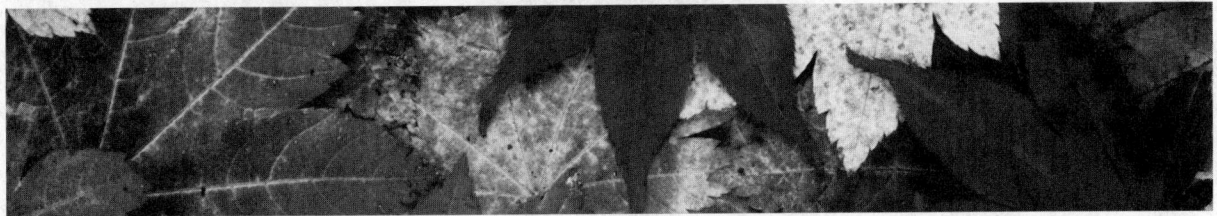

Broad Range

Brown Raysman Millstein Felder & Steiner LLP has long recognized that having attorneys from a cross-section of cultures is essential to a successful practice.

Cultural change is constant and we are constantly changing with it. To help our clients best manage their interests, we must understand change and its impact. Our diversity of attorneys keeps us well connected and provides important perspective in developing successful client strategies.

We've built our business on helping clients manage change, and we will continue to do so by attracting the best legal minds to keep us a step ahead.

For additional information, visit the firm's website: www.brownraysman.com or contact Wanda Woods, Legal Recruitment Manager, at 212-895-2000.

BROWNRAYSMAN

BROWN RAYSMAN MILLSTEIN FELDER & STEINER LLP

Munger, Tolles & Olson LLP
Los Angeles • San Francisco
www.mto.com
(213) 683-9100

At Munger, Tolles & Olson LLP, we value diversity. We believe that a diverse work force improves our ability to serve the needs of our clients and creates a more dynamic workplace for our attorneys. We have a long tradition of supporting diversity. Munger, Tolles & Olson LLP had one of the first women partners in the city, and we believe we had the first openly gay person to serve as Managing Partner at a major law firm.

We have placed a particular emphasis on minority recruitment of attorneys for many years, and we believe that our firm can be a platform for success for every lawyer we hire. We are dedicated to addressing the tough issues, in our firm and society, that impair success for women and minority lawyers. Our Diversity Committee is led by senior partners and has the support of the entire partnership.

We actively encourage employment applications from women and members of minority and other underrepresented groups. In our 2004 Summer Associate Program, which is the firm's main vehicle for the hiring of new attorneys, women and minority law students represent 65% of the group. Additionally, as part of our on-going effort to recruit, retain and promote exceptional attorneys who also contribute to the diversity of our firm and our profession, we have established a 1L Summer Program to specifically target exceptional first year law students of diverse backgrounds. These 1L Summer Program positions will be offered to students who are members of racial or ethnic minority groups, are gay, lesbian, bisexual or transgender, are physically challenged, or are from disadvantaged socioeconomic backgrounds.

For more information, please visit our website at mto.com or contact Kevinn Villard, Director of Legal Recruiting at (213) 683-9242.

DIVERSITY NEEDS CHAMPIONS

We've seen the results

Our focus on diversity is helping us attract the best legal talent and deliver the highest quality services to clients. Our recent successes are gratifying, but our work is far from over—because the more diverse we become, the better we are as a law firm.

www.lordbissell.com

LORD BISSELL ▽ BROOK LLP

BUSINESS NEEDS CHAMPIONS

BOIES, SCHILLER & FLEXNER, LLP

NEW YORK

WASHINGTON DC

FLORIDA

CALIFORNIA

NEW HAMPSHIRE

NEW JERSEY

5301 Wisconsin Avenue N.W.
Washington, D.C. 20015
Tel.: 202 237 2727

333 Main Street
Armonk, NY 10504
Tel.: 914 749 8200

1999 Harrison Street
Oakland, CA 94612
Tel.: 510 874 1000

Bank of America Tower
100 Southeast 2nd Street
Miami, FL 33131-2144
Tel.: 305 539 8400

570 Lexington Avenue
New York, NY 10022
Tel.: 212 446 2300

10 North Pearl Street
Albany, NY 12207
Tel.: 518 434 0600

300 S.E. 2nd Street
Fort Lauderdale, FL 33301
Tel.: 954 356 9911

150 JFK Parkway
Short Hills, NJ 07078
Tel.: 973 218 1111

255 South Orange Avenue
Orlando, FL 32801
Tel.: 407 425 7118

CRAVATH, SWAINE & MOORE LLP

Consistent with our long-held view that excellence is found in many places, diversity is a bedrock principle at Cravath. We embrace the importance of recruiting and retaining outstanding lawyers from different backgrounds and we are committed to promoting diversity at all levels.

We support Vault and MCCA in their efforts to produce the Guide to Law Firm Diversity Programs.

NEW YORK · LONDON

Clifford Chance is proud to join Vault and the Minority Corporate Counsel Association in underwriting the first-ever Guide to Law Firm Diversity Programs. As the leading global provider of legal services, recognition of, and respect for, diversity are at the core of who we are and what we do.

At Clifford Chance, having a diverse workforce isn't just a good idea - it's the only way we do business.

CLIFFORD CHANCE

DOES DIVERSITY MATTER TO YOU?

At Kilpatrick Stockton, we believe it does. That's why we're proud to work with clients who, like us, are actively advancing diversity within their own corporate environments. Together, it's how we're making a difference—to our companies, to our communities, and beyond. To learn more, visit www.KilpatrickStockton.com.

KILPATRICK
STOCKTON LLP
Attorneys at Law

INGENIOUS FOCUS

RAYMOND LOEWY was the father of industrial design. With an eye for function and styling, he created unforgettable international icons. Coca-Cola® dispensers, the Greyhound® bus, and logos for Exxon® and Shell®. Loewy changed the shape of our world. And then he set his sights even higher. For seven years, he concentrated his imaginative talents on the Saturn-Apollo and Skylab projects. He designed living quarters, the simulation of zero gravity, and NASA's first porthole. Without his contributions, mission crews would have faced immense difficulties. Without his focus, we might never have ventured so far.

Focus is the catalyst for exceptional problem solving. At Howrey, focus provides clients with legal and business solutions to their most high-stakes challenges. Focus is a powerful approach and an even more powerful advantage.

HOWREY
HOWREY SIMON ARNOLD & WHITE
ATTORNEYS AT LAW

THE ADVANTAGE OF FOCUS™

AMSTERDAM BRUSSELS CHICAGO HOUSTON
IRVINE LONDON LOS ANGELES MENLO PARK
SAN FRANCISCO WASHINGTON, DC

HOWREY FOCUSES ON LITIGATION, IP AND ANTITRUST

KRAMER LEVIN

Kramer Levin Naftalis & Frankel LLP

COMMITTED TO DIVERSITY

Kramer Levin Naftalis & Frankel LLP

is committed to diversity and to the

programs that are geared to supporting

the associated issues.

AT MANATT, WE PRACTICE DIVERSITY

At Manatt, we strive to be the best kind of meritocracy. Our professionals thrive in an atmosphere that encourages and supports responsibility and aspirations. We believe lateral partner and associate candidates of color will choose to develop their careers at a firm that offers true opportunity equal to their commitment to success and advancement. That's the history of opportunity we have at Manatt, where all professionals with talent and drive are rewarded with a nurturing, dynamic and energizing climate for long-term diversity and commitment.

www.manatt.com

DIVERSITY COMMITTED HERE.

Exhibit A	**Rankings:** • First among New Jersey's largest law firms with the greatest number of minority partners. • Second among New Jersey's largest law firms with the greatest number of women and minority associates.
Exhibit B	**Leadership:** • First major law firm in New Jersey to appoint an African American to Chair its 110 attorney Litigation Department. • Women and minorities appointed to key leadership positions in firm management and are members of various committees such as the executive, strategic planning, diversity, recruiting and ethics.
Exhibit C	**Recruiting:** • Regular participation in minority job fairs across the country. • Partnership with legal recruiters who specialize in placing diverse candidates. • Sponsorship and participation in the Rutgers Minority Summer Program where each year the Firm hires at least one first year minority student as a summer law clerk.
Closing Argument	**Visit our Diversity Mission Statement at:** http://www.lowenstein.com/recruiting/diversitystatement.html

Lowenstein Sandler is Committed to Promoting Diversity in the Workplace.

Contact:
Lynda A. Bennett,
Chair of the Diversity Initiatives Committee
973.597.2386
lbennett@lowenstein.com

LOWENSTEIN SANDLER PC
Attorneys at Law

65 Livingston Avenue
Roseland, New Jersey 07068
Telephone 973.597.2500
Fax 973.597.2400

1251 Avenue of the Americas
New York, New York 10020
Telephone 212.262.6700
Fax 212.262.7402

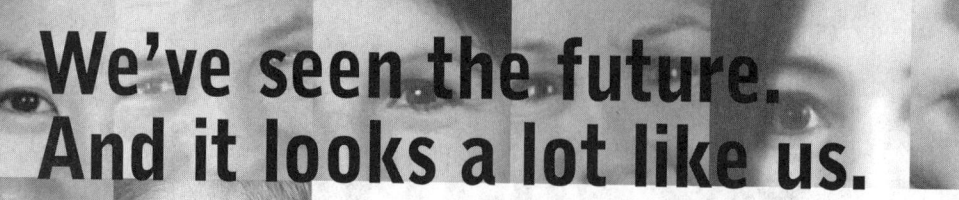

We've seen the future.
And it looks a lot like us.

For well over 200 years, people from all over the world have come to America in search of freedom and a better way of life. The result is a nation that is as diverse as it is vast. While some view America's cultural diversity as an obstacle, we see it as an opportunity for businesses to embrace the future.

We're Littler Mendelson, the nation's largest employment and labor law firm, and we understand the challenges posed by the multicultural workplace. Today, nearly every employer risks miscommunication as it struggles to diversify. At Littler, we've assembled a team of attorneys whose backgrounds and experience are as diverse as the businesses we serve. That's why when the nation's employers need someone to steer them clear of the social and cultural pitfalls that can taint the workplace, they come to us. Every day, we work with employers of all nationalities, sizes and industries, and advise and defend them in every matter of employment and labor law.

To learn more about how we can help ease the future a little closer to you today, visit www.littler.com or call us directly at 1.888.LITTLER.

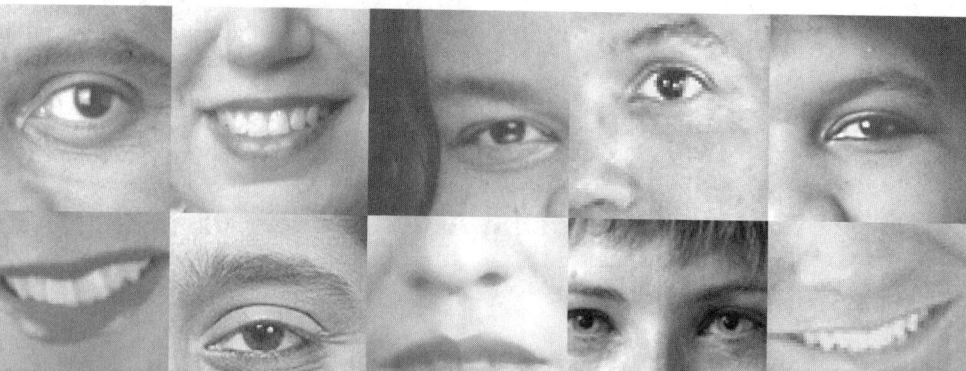

LITTLER MENDELSON®

THE NATIONAL EMPLOYMENT & LABOR LAW FIRM®
400 ATTORNEYS   28 OFFICES   NATIONWIDE

Diversity Matters

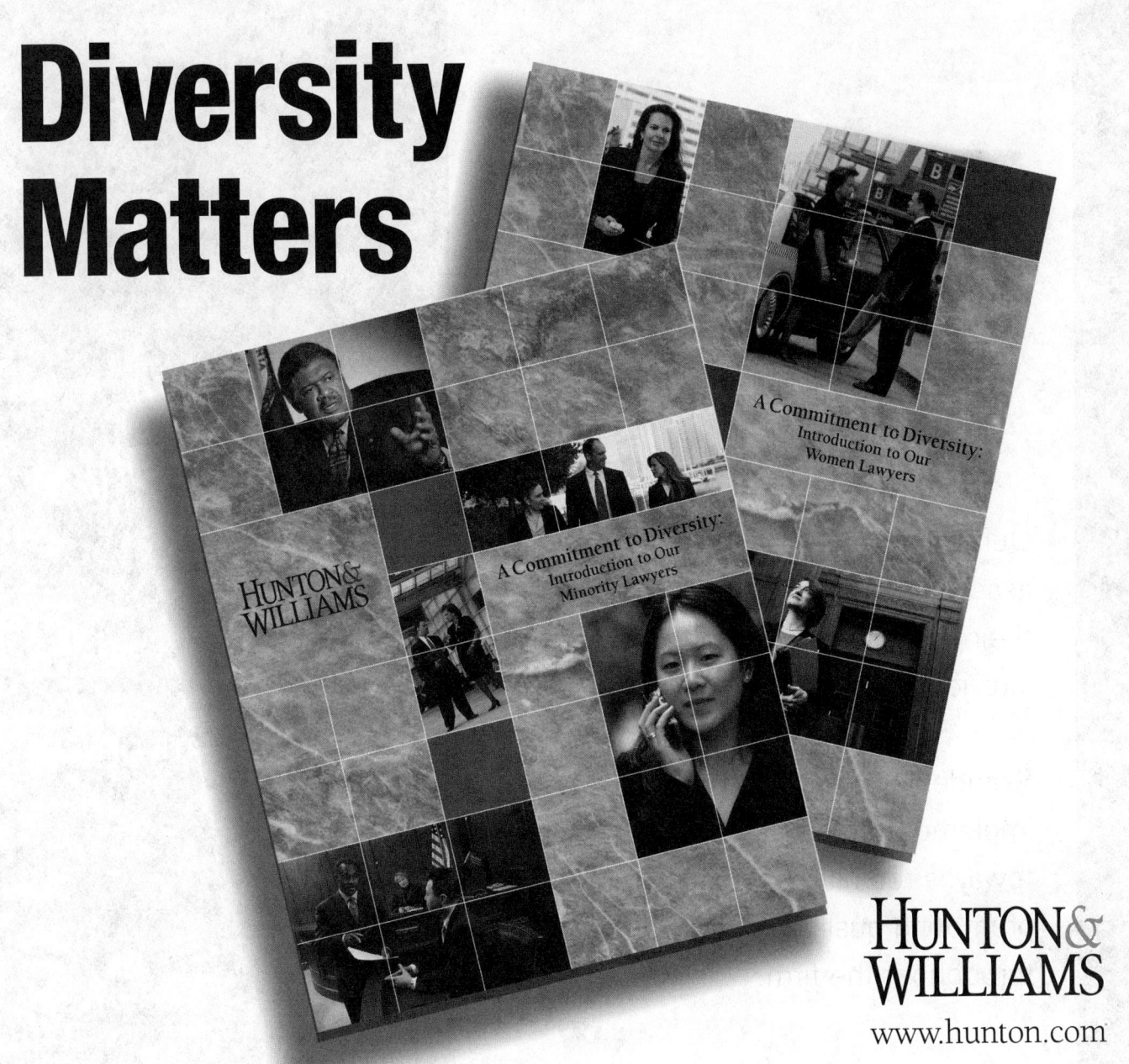

HUNTON&
WILLIAMS

www.hunton.com

We live in a diverse world in which the challenges of meeting the current and future needs of our clients are ever increasing. To meet those challenges, a law firm needs a diverse corps of legal talent. Our brochures, **Introduction to Our Minority Lawyers** and **Introduction to Our Women Lawyers**, illustrate Hunton & Williams' commitment to fostering diversity for ourselves and our clients.

For a copy of our brochures or to learn more about diversity at Hunton & Williams, please contact A. Todd Brown at (704) 378-4727 or tbrown@hunton.com.

ATLANTA AUSTIN BANGKOK BRUSSELS CHARLOTTE DALLAS HONG KONG KNOXVILLE LONDON McLEAN MIAMI NEW YORK NORFOLK RALEIGH RICHMOND SINGAPORE WASHINGTON

What's a lawyer?

Heller Ehrman **V.** Conformity   At Heller Ehrman, diversity isn't merely an asset, it's a necessity. As a global network of attorneys with unique experience and varied backgrounds, we are all working toward one goal. To achieve great things for our clients. Each point of view translates to another option with a potential upside. For our clients. And for ourselves.

W W W . H E W M . C O M

HellerEhrman
ATTORNEYS

Challenging the laws of convention.™

Diversity at McDermott Will & Emery.

Is a part of our attitude, culture of collaboration and a long-term commitment that we take seriously. An atmosphere of inclusion benefits all McDermott lawyers and staff and provides our clients with varied perspectives and backgrounds to their legal issues. Join us in valuing diversity.

Michael Boykins
Co-Chair, Racial and Ethnic Diversity Committee
312.984.7599
mboykins@mwe.com

Andrea Kramer
Co-Chair, Gender Diversity Committee
312.984.6480
akramer@mwe.com

McDermott Will & Emery

227 West Monroe Street
Chicago, Illinois 60606-5096

www.mwe.com

Boston   Brussels   Chicago   Düsseldorf   London   Los Angeles   Miami   Milan   Munich   New York   Orange County   Rome
San Diego   Silicon Valley   Washington, D.C.

Thompson & Knight. Making a difference.

TOP FROM LEFT: PARTNERS Victor Alcorta III - Austin, Kennedy Barnes - Dallas, Timothy R. Brown - Houston, Roxella T. Cavazos - Houston, E.F. Mano DeAyala - Houston, Cheryl E. Diaz - Dallas, Marcie Y. Flores - Dallas Boris A. Hidalgo - Houston, Ricky A. Raven - Houston ROW TWO: David M. Abner - Dallas, Isabel Amadeo - Dallas, Melanie S. Bruce - Dallas, Adrienne E. Dominguez - Dallas, Nichole Dotson-Olajuwon - Houston, Pablo C. Ferrante - Houston, Kristen Roberts Gibson - Houston, Tracy L. Hamilton - Dallas, David W. Henderson - Houston, Lily Nguyen Hoang-Dao - Houston ROW THREE: Isaac Johnson, IV - Houston, Jai-Prakash Phillip Kumar - Houston Michelle M. Kwon - Dallas, Jennine R. Lunceford-Ebron - Dallas, Kim McCrea - Dallas, Sarah E. McLean - Houston, Monica M. Smith - Dallas, Luke A. Walker - Dallas, Cara Clophus Wright - Houston, Thomas Yoo - Dallas

Thompson & Knight's impact on our clients' success is energized
by the diversity of our lawyers.

CORPORATE AND SECURITIES   CORPORATE REORGANIZATION AND CREDITORS' RIGHTS   ENERGY   ENVIRONMENTAL   FINANCE   GOVERNMENT RELATIONS AND PUBLIC POLICY   INTELLECTUAL PROPERTY   INTERNATIONAL   LABOR AND EMPLOYMENT   OIL AND GAS   REAL ESTATE AND BANKING   TAX, BENEFITS, AND ESTATE PLANNING   TECHNOLOGY   TRIAL AND APPELLATE

ALGIERS   AUSTIN   DALLAS   FORT WORTH   HOUSTON   MONTERREY   PARIS   RIO DE JANEIRO   WWW.TKLAW.COM

Thinking about your future?
We are.

Paul, Hastings, Janofsky & Walker LLP, founded in 1951, is an international law firm representing Fortune 500 companies with nearly 950 attorneys located in 15 offices: Atlanta, Beijing, Brussels, Hong Kong, London, Los Angeles, New York, Orange County, Paris, San Diego, San Francisco, Shanghai, Stamford, Tokyo and Washington, DC.

Paul Hastings is committed to providing a work environment that offers equal opportunity to all and reflects the diverse communities in which we operate.

Paul Hastings
ATTORNEYS

www.paulhastings.com
Paul, Hastings, Janofsky & Walker LLP

Atlanta	Los Angeles	San Francisco
Beijing	New York	Shanghai
Brussels	Orange County	Stamford
Hong Kong	Paris	Tokyo
London	San Diego	Washington, DC

LOEB&LOEB LLP

We're serious about

DIVERSITY

HAPPY THEN, HAPPY NOW

Ranked in the Top 3 in "**Best Firms to Work For**" for five consecutive years.

THIS YEAR, ALSO RANKED TOP 5 IN...

Satisfaction, Offices, Compensation, Mentoring, Diversity for Minorities,
Associate/Partner Relations, Pro Bono, and Overall Diversity.

Vault Guide to the Top 100 Law Firms, 7th Ed.

WINSTON & STRAWN LLP

CHICAGO   GENEVA   LONDON   LOS ANGELES   NEW YORK   PARIS   SAN FRANCISCO   WASHINGTON, D.C.

NEAL, GERBER & EISENBERG LLP

NETWORK

GROW

EXPERIENCE

A full service law firm located in the heart of the Loop, NGE is committed to excellence both in the workplace and in the practice of law. We take pride in our client service and our creative, innovative approach to meeting client needs and furthering client goals and objectives. The hallmark of our client service is our people. We have a diverse group of talented individuals, each of whom brings a unique background and perspective to the legal matters they handle. We value that diversity and the way it enhances our environment and our practice.

"We are proud to have a broad array of different personalities, backgrounds and experiences represented at our Firm. This diversity makes NGE a comfortable place for our attorneys to practice, and helps us to best represent our clients' interests and further their goals and objectives."

Victoria Donati, Chair, Diversity Committee

NGE

MAKE YOUR MOVE

NEAL, GERBER & EISENBERG LLP

Two North LaSalle Street • Suite 2200 • Chicago, IL 60602-3801

312-269-8000 • www.ngelaw.com

Day, Berry & Howard LLP . . .

Where the people make a world of difference

Day, Berry & Howard LLP
COUNSELLORS AT LAW

Philadelphia Diversity Law Group

Growing Opportunities Through a Diverse Legal Community

Philadelphia Diversity Law Group

(PDLG) is a Pennsylvania non-profit, equal opportunity corporation formed in 2001. Composed of large law firms and the legal departments of regional corporations and working collaboratively; its goal is to develop programs that will enhance recruitment and retention of diverse attorneys working in the Greater Philadelphia Region.

In collaboration with area educational institutions, businesses and others, the PDLG develops initiatives and programs to increase diversity within our profession.

One such initiative is the PDLG Summer 1L Program, a competitive program which enables first year law students at regional law schools who have overcome obstacles in pursuing a legal career, or who come from disadvantaged backgrounds or backgrounds underrepresented in the Philadelphia legal community to obtain summer clerkships with our member firms and organizations.

Philadelphia Diversity Law Group, Inc.
150 Market Street
Philadelphia, PA 19103
215-979-1179

www.philadiversitylaw.org

Philadelphia Diversity Law Group, Inc. is a Pennsylvania non-profit corporation.

Two cities. One firm. Smart move.
A **go-to firm** for some of America's largest companies —*Corporate Counsel*
Ranked 13th nationally for **attorney satisfaction** and 8th for associate-partner relations —*Vault*
Ranked 7th nationally for **commitment to *pro bono* work** —*Vault*
Nationally ranked 3rd in **overall diversity**, 2nd in diversity for gay and lesbian lawyers, 5th in diversity for women, and 7th in minority divers1ity. —*Vault*
Ranked the **best place to work** out of all Washington, D.C.-based law firms —*The American Lawyer*
To get a smart start on your career in either New York or Washington, D.C., visit **www.arentfox.com.**
Smart in Your World.℠
Arent Fox
ATTORNEYS AT LAW

CORPORATE
COUNSEL
UNDERWRITERS

one **reason** *barbara whittaker*

GM has purchased more than $44.3 billion in goods and services from minority suppliers over the last 36 years. One reason? Barbara Whittaker. As Executive Director of Machinery & Equipment and Indirect Purchasing, Barbara works directly with GM suppliers from all over the globe, including more than 600 certified minority suppliers like The Bartech Group. Formed under the sponsorship of GM in 1976, The Bartech Group is now a $200 million company, and one of the largest staffing companies in the nation. Which means that they not only help Barbara diversify GM's supplier base, they help to diversify GM's workforce as well.

GM awards more than $7 billion in purchasing and contracts annually to minority firms. Barbara Whittaker is just one reason GM is committed to increasing that number each and every year. For information about GM's Supplier Diversity Program visit www.gmsupplypower.com.

CHEVROLET   SAAB   PONTIAC   GMAC   OLDSMOBILE   SATURN   BUICK   CADILLAC   HUMMER   GMC

gm.com

McDonald's Corporation is
dedicated to Diversity.

i'm lovin' it

inspiring
PEOPLE

Sara Lee Corporation's mission is to feed, clothe and care for consumers
and their families the world over. Providing for the everyday needs
of people is not only our business mandate, but also it is the commitment
we make to the communities in which we conduct business.

It is with this spirit that Sara Lee supports the
Minority Corporate Counsel Association.

Del Monte makes

it easy to create

great tasting and

nutritious meals for

your whole family,

including your pets.

DEL MONTE FOODS

www.delmonte.com

Diversity

Support it...
celebrate it.

As the world's premier payments organization,
Visa is proud to be a sponsor of **Vault and MCCA**
in celebrating the individual differences, experiences,
and strengths of Corporate Counsel.

I want to make a difference.

AstraZeneca is one of the world's leading pharmaceutical companies. As a member of our global workforce of over 60,000, you'll be contributing to our efforts in helping people all over the world lead healthier lives.

At AstraZeneca, our employees are valued for their individuality and diversity; for the passion they bring to their work; and the commitment they bring to our business. We sponsor several networking groups within our organization, which offer mentoring, career guidance and networking opportunities. Along with our innovative Work/Life programs which offer flexibility and support, it is easy to see why AstraZeneca has been named *DiversityInc's* **Number 1 Company for Executive Women** and one of *FORTUNE* magazine's **100 Best Companies to Work For**.

AstraZeneca Legal is a dynamic team working closely with all parts of the company to address a range of complex, cutting edge legal issues. AstraZeneca offers career opportunities with growth, development and advancement throughout our organization.

Visit www.AstraZenecaCareers.com for a complete list of all our U.S. job opportunities and to apply online. Please reference Source Code 08676505 in your application. Diversity is the source of our science, our careers and our lives. We are an equal opportunity employer.

FORTUNE
100 BEST
COMPANIES
TO WORK FOR 2004

www.AstraZenecaCareers.com

AstraZeneca
life inspiring ideas

Just Do It.

nike.com

*We believe that diversity makes a
difference. Diverse ideas, experiences,
and talents, challenge us and make us grow.*

*We are on a journey to understand and leverage
the differences among us so that we can better serve
our clients, our profession, and our community.*

We plan to make **A Difference**

The Legal Department of Shell Oil Company

WE ENCOURAGE ALL DREAMERS.

A diverse workplace is

critical to our success. It lets

us approach challenges from

different viewpoints, bridge

differences between people

and cultures, and meet the

needs of our customers, our

communities, and the world.

www.boeing.com

Forever New Frontiers

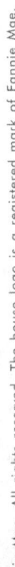

At Fannie Mae, we believe the **American Dream** should be open to everyone.
So we started with our own doors.

Long ago, Fannie Mae realized that diversity was a driving force for both innovation and change. We saw that the more our work force reflected the shifting demographics of our nation, the more competitive we would be. So to help us realize the potential of such visionary thinking, we created the Office of Diversity.

By providing pathways for all employees to grow, we have increased minority representation in our legal department to 36 percent. And nearly 60 percent of attorneys are women.

The energy of our diverse work force has been instrumental in helping Fannie Mae successfully meet the diverse housing needs of American families. And in 2003, we did just that by helping over 10 million families into homes of their own. At Fannie Mae, we are committed to breaking down the barriers to homeownership while opening the doors of opportunity.

Visit www.fanniemae.com/careers to learn about career opportunities in Fannie Mae's Legal Department.

Pictured above (l to r): Fannie Mae employees Donald Remy, Senior Vice President and Deputy General Counsel; Ann Kappler, Senior Vice President and General Counsel; Renie Grohl, Senior Vice President and Deputy General Counsel; and Anthony Marra, Senior Vice President and Deputy General Counsel.

www.fanniemae.com

Be yourself. Race. Ethnicity. Religion. Nationality. Gender. Sexual orientation. In the end, there's just one variety of human being. The individual. All six billion of us. Be bullish.

ml.com

Merrill Lynch

What's inside Dell?

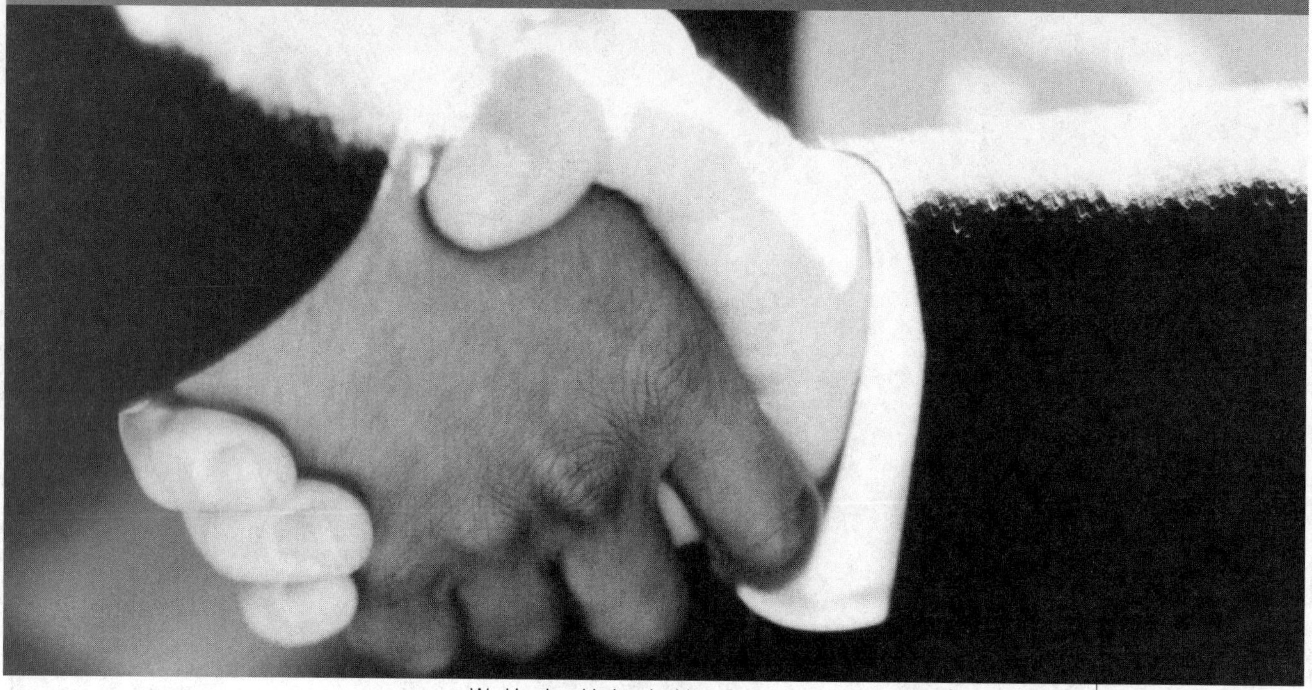

Working hand in hand with our partners to open the doors of opportunity for the people
in the communities we serve is just a part of our commitment at Dell.

Dell | Talent Acquisition

A commitment to building a diverse workforce. In fact, it's an important part of our winning culture. Let Dell open up a world of professional possibilities for you.

Easy as

To submit your resume online, visit **www.discoverdell.com**.

Brighter
futures

Working here takes you places.

Exceptional performance is driven by exceptional people—working at a place where they can leverage their experiences, strengths and perspectives. At JPMorgan Chase, we've created an environment where everyone can reach their fullest potential. Our people build strong networks, meet new challenges head-on, grow their careers and take themselves—and our firm—to new heights.

jpmorganchase.com

Working for diversity because diversity works.

VIACOM

Viacom is an equal opportunity/affirmative action employer supporting workforce diversity.

Alex, Mecole,
Stephanie & Sam,
Wal-Mart In-House Counsel

"At Wal-Mart, we think it is important that
our outside counsel embrace and reflect our
company culture and *commitment to diversity*."

-Sam Reeves,
Sr. Assistant General Counsel
Outside Counsel Management

↘ The face of Countrywide.

From the beginning, Countrywide's goal has been to make it easier to buy a home for all Americans through our flexible and affordable loan programs. Equally as important, as a Fortune 500 company, we are committed to building a diverse workforce and management team. So if you're looking for a home loan, a business partner, or a career opportunity, click on Countrywide.com today—and discover how the new face at Countrywide could be you.

Countrywide is committed to leveraging the talent of a diverse workforce to create great opportunities for our business and our people. EOE. M/F/D/V.

Please visit our website at: **www.countrywidecareers.com**

Home Loans
Loan Closing
Insurance
Banking
Capital Markets
Global Operations

Countrywide Financial SM

Realize your dreams. SM

A more human way of working.

At HP, diversity is more than a catchphrase. It's at the heart of what we do. Having a workforce that reflects the world we serve provides us with a never-ending source of ideas - each one as dynamic and original as the people who have them. HP—where the best ideas go to work.

Please visit **www.jobs.hp.com**

OUR STAND

EMBRACING DIVERSITY
PUTS US ALL IN GOOD HANDS.®

ALLSTATE IS PROUD TO SUPPORT
THE MINORITY CORPORATE COUNSEL ASSOCIATION.

Allstate.
You're in good hands.

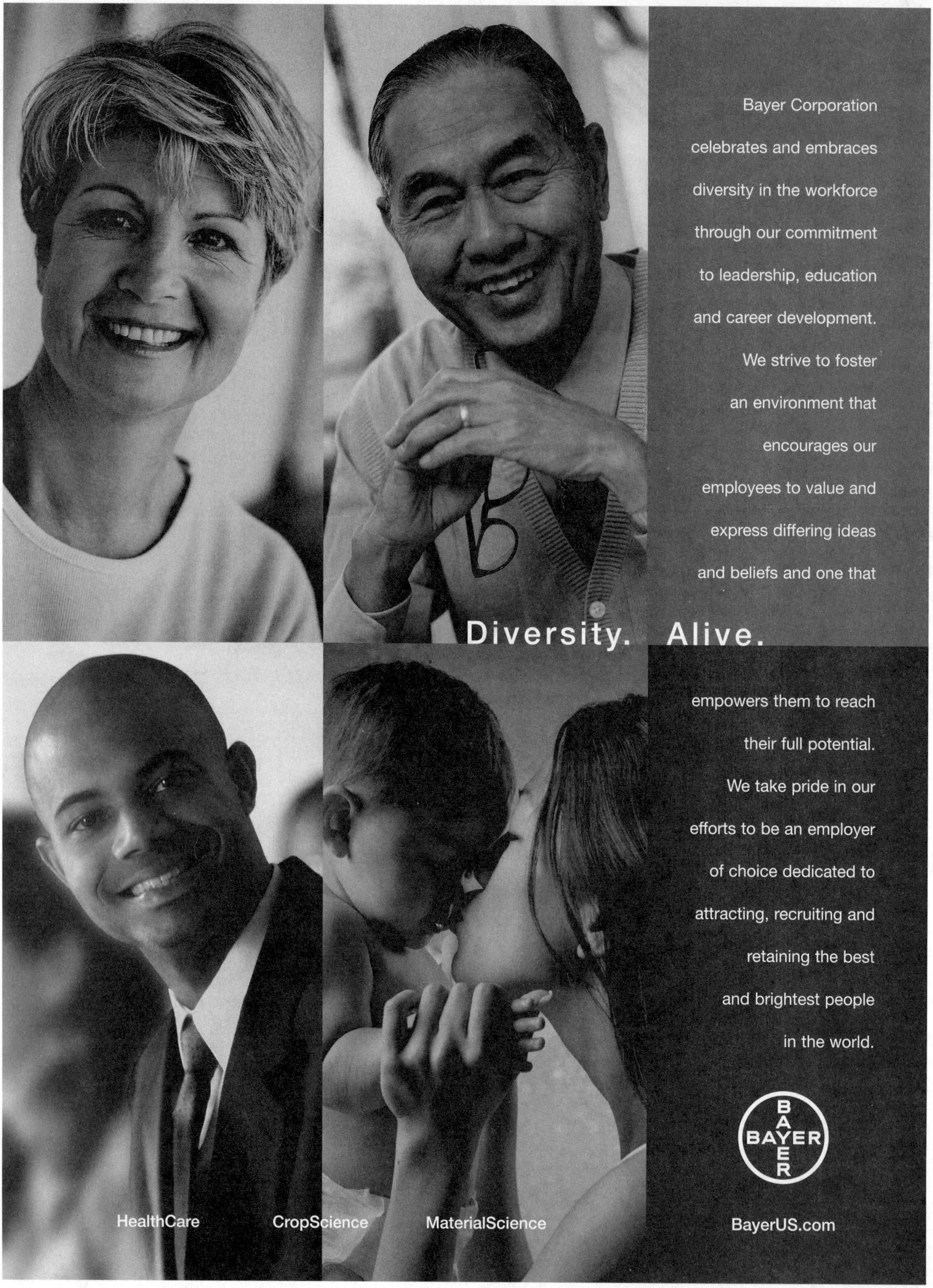
Bayer Corporation celebrates and embraces diversity in the workforce through our commitment to leadership, education and career development. We strive to foster an environment that encourages our employees to value and express differing ideas and beliefs and one that
Diversity. Alive.
empowers them to reach their full potential. We take pride in our efforts to be an employer of choice dedicated to attracting, recruiting and retaining the best and brightest people in the world.
BAYER
HealthCare
CropScience
MaterialScience
BayerUS.com

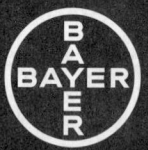

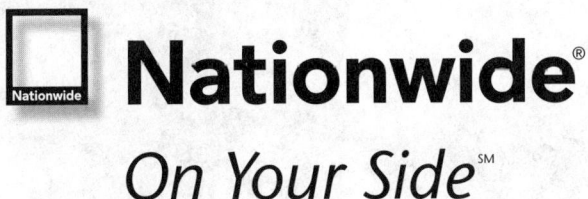

Different perspectives.

Diverse minds create solutions.

At Deloitte & Touche USA LLP, diversity isn't a policy. It's how we do things. It helps us present ideas from people with many backgrounds and a range of experiences, giving clients a 360° perspective on complex issues they face, from assurance and tax to financial advisory and consulting. That's why we're able to build such strong, enduring relationships with clients— who appreciate our multi-dimensional approach, our respect for their business and their culture, and our conviction that teamwork invariably produces the best results.

To learn more about our people and how they think, visit us at www.deloitte.com/us.

Deloitte.

Audit . Tax . Consulting . Financial Advisory.

www.deloitte.com/us

GE Company Picnic Photo 2004

At GE, imagination comes from all over the world. Our 300,000 employees span over 35 countries and represent countless different backgrounds. Put all that together and you have one of the most diverse companies making 25,000 products around the world. Not to mention, a pretty big group photo.

To learn more, visit www.ge.com.

 imagination at work

Seize the moment...

"100 Best Companies to Work For"
— *Fortune,*® *2002, 2003*

"One of the Most Admired Pharmaceutical Companies in America"
— *Fortune,*® *2002, 2003*

"100 Best Places for Latinos to Work"
— *Hispanic Magazine, 2000, 2001, 2002*

At Pfizer, it's our passion for what we do that makes us the world's leading pharmaceutical company. It's also why we believe in recruiting and working with exceptional people with diverse backgrounds and experiences. We know the only way to attract the best people is to offer them a fulfilling working experience with boundless opportunities. Whether it's in Marketing, Finance, Information Technology, Research & Development, or Legal, if you're committed to excellence, your skills will be recognized at Pfizer.

Visit us at **www.pfizer.com** to submit your resume or send it to us at Pfizer Inc., 235 E. 42nd St., 235/13, New York, NY 10017. Pfizer is an Equal Opportunity Employer.

OPPORTUNITY

Life is our life's work.®

www.pfizer.com

Pitney Bowes Community Investments

Engaging our employees.

Partnering effectively.

Delivering solutions that improve
literacy and communication.

Making our communities better places
to live and work.

Engineering the flow of communication™

www.pitneybowes.com

Developing breakthrough medical technologies that advance patient care

www.abbott.com

It's amazing what you can do here.

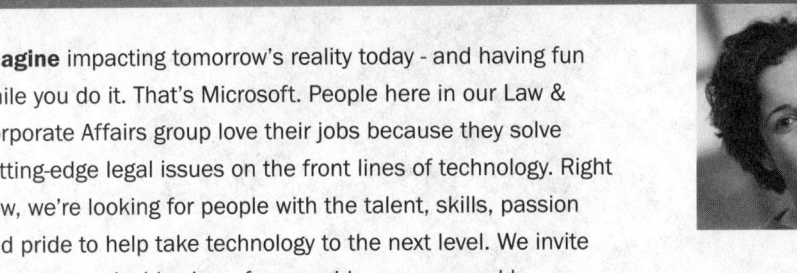

Microsoft

Imagine impacting tomorrow's reality today - and having fun while you do it. That's Microsoft. People here in our Law & Corporate Affairs group love their jobs because they solve cutting-edge legal issues on the front lines of technology. Right now, we're looking for people with the talent, skills, passion and pride to help take technology to the next level. We invite you to get an inside view of our world - one powered by creative people a lot like you.

At Microsoft we are looking for talented professionals for our growing Law & Corporate Affairs department at Microsoft corporate headquarters in the beautiful Pacific Northwest in Redmond, Washington.

Join us to put your passions for law and technology to work in a dynamic, collegial environment. Visit our website to learn more about current opportunities.

microsoft.com/**careers**

Careers

Why should you work
in pharmaceuticals?

Why you should
work for Merck.

Talented professionals have an increasing range of options when it comes to pursuit of a career. At Merck, we like to think that delivering novel medicines to the people who need them most is a calling worthy of your consideration. And that following such a call by joining Merck offers unique challenges and rewards.

After all, what could be more vital than improving the quality of life for people around the world? By joining Merck, you not only engage in that endeavor, but also do it with one of the "100 Best Companies to Work For" according to *FORTUNE* Magazine.

Indeed, Merck & Co., Inc. is a global leader in the research, development, manufacturing and delivery of world-class pharmaceutical products and services. Add to thatbenefits such as programs for job-sharing, mentoring, onsite day care at some facilities, education assistance, and more and you have compelling reasons why you should look into opportunities at Merck. If you would like to explore opportunities with Merck and to learn more about us, please visit: www.merck.com/careers.

Janine C.
Business Manager, two-time VP Club winner,
Merck Masters Club member

MERCK

Committed to bringing
out the best in medicine.
And in people.

www.merck.com/careers

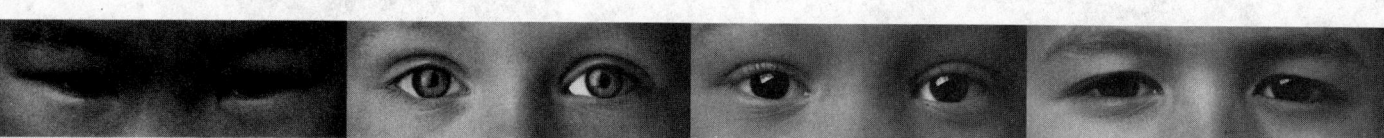

Diversity

It's not an obligation—it's an opportunity.

To make a difference, a company must keep its eyes
open to different ways of thinking.

That's why we take diversity seriously in all aspects
of our business—from our employees, to our
customers, to the companies that supply us with the
goods and services that enable us to do business.

At Morgan Stanley, we understand that diversity
is not an obligation—it's an opportunity.

www.morganstanley.com/about/diversity/

MorganStanley

Just a few steps can change everything.

The world around her is changing as much as she is. Our nation is continually becoming more diverse. That's why Johnson & Johnson is committed to supporting diversity programs within our company as well as within the community. So while she's learning to walk, we'll be taking steps to continue building a more diverse work force that reflects the changing world around us.

Johnson & Johnson

www.baby.com

WELCOME TO FREE ENTERPRISE.

The new advantage of enterprise mobility.

Today, the most productive and profitable enterprise is the free enterprise. Free to capture, move and manage information in real time. Free to adapt more readily. To grow more quickly. To get the most from its people and processes. The foundation for this newfound freedom: rich and robust solutions from Symbol. The Enterprise Mobility Company.™ In markets ranging from retail to manufacturing, transportation and logistics to wholesale distribution, healthcare to government, Symbol provides mobility solutions that meet business' most essential needs. Whether reducing inventory levels to increase working capital... driving retail customer satisfaction without driving up operating costs... or speeding supply chain velocity at every critical link... mobility solutions from Symbol are creating powerful new advantages. So welcome to free enterprise, and the new advantage it enables. Welcome to Symbol. The Enterprise Mobility Company.

Call +1.800.722.6234 or visit www.symbol.com

symbol®
The Enterprise Mobility Company™

ADVANCED DATA CAPTURE | MOBILE COMPUTING | WIRELESS INFRASTRUCTURE | MOBILITY MANAGEMENT SOFTWARE | SYMBOL ENTERPRISE MOBILITY SERVICES | GLOBAL BUSINESS PARTNERS

At Office Depot, we are committed to creating an inclusive environment where all people are valued and respected. **Diversity** is an important dimension of respect for the individual — one of our core values — and to our success in a global marketplace.

Office Depot is proud to support Vault and the Minority Corporate Counsel Association in underwriting research on law firm diversity programs.

WITHOUT the imagination of our talented people, we'd have no words, no pictures, no entertainment to give the world. At Time Warner, we wouldn't be half as successful without the many employees whose creativity and determination help make us a world leader in media and entertainment.

To explore opportunities, visit our career site at www.timewarner.com/careers

    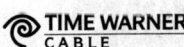

**At BP America Inc.,
Diversity and Inclusion are
deeply embedded within our
organizational values.**

Our vision is to be known internally and externally as an employer and partner of choice for all, as a company with an inclusive culture in which a diverse global workforce contributes and realizes its individual and collective potential.

THE MORE PERSPECTIVES THE CLEARER THE VISION

WE'RE IN THE PEOPLE BUSINESS. THAT'S WHY WE INVEST IN OUR COMMUNITY.

At Washington Mutual, we believe that a diverse environment is invaluable. We know that when every voice is accounted for, we are better able to follow through on our longstanding commitment to making customer service and the community our top priority. So, when Fortune® magazine rated us 19th on the list of the "50 Best Companies for Minorities," we were proud to have our efforts towards diversity noticed. Here at Washington Mutual, we know diversity is a key to unlocking the door to our success. To learn more, visit wamu.com and click on "Job opportunities."

Washington Mutual

MORE **HUMAN** INTEREST™

At Corning Incorporated, the boundless imagination of our people has guided our path for more than 153 years. Our global team has helped make possible some of the world's most life-changing innovations. And we continue that rich legacy today, with products that help make the air cleaner ... help people communicate more quickly and clearly ... and help provide a rich visual experience on televisions, computer screens and more.

With more than 20,000 employees around the world, we represent a richly diverse set of skills, backgrounds, and creative approaches to solving some of the world's toughest scientific problems. Yet there are many things we share ... including an unwavering devotion to our core Values, which continue to guide all our actions. At the heart of our Values is our commitment to The Individual and the our fundamental belief that the contributions of each employee will determine our success.

Our diversity — and within that diversity, our common commitment to our Values — help us to adapt to change. And that's exactly what we'll keep doing ... for the next 153 years, and beyond.

CORNING
Discovering Beyond Imagination

Corning Incorporated   One Riverfront Plaza
Corning, NY 14831
607.974.9000
www.corning.com

LOOK BEYOND THE OBVIOUS.

You're an ideas person. You're open to new approaches. And you look beyond the obvious. At Goldman Sachs, we value people just like you. People who are ready to express their personality, share their ideas, and put their creativity to work. So if you're looking for a place where individuality is welcomed, look no further.

Goldman, Sachs & Co. is proud to support the Minority Corporate Counsel Association.

PLEASE VISIT GS.COM/CAREERS TO COMPLETE AN ONLINE APPLICATION.

GS.COM/CAREERS

Tenet
Working for Our Communities

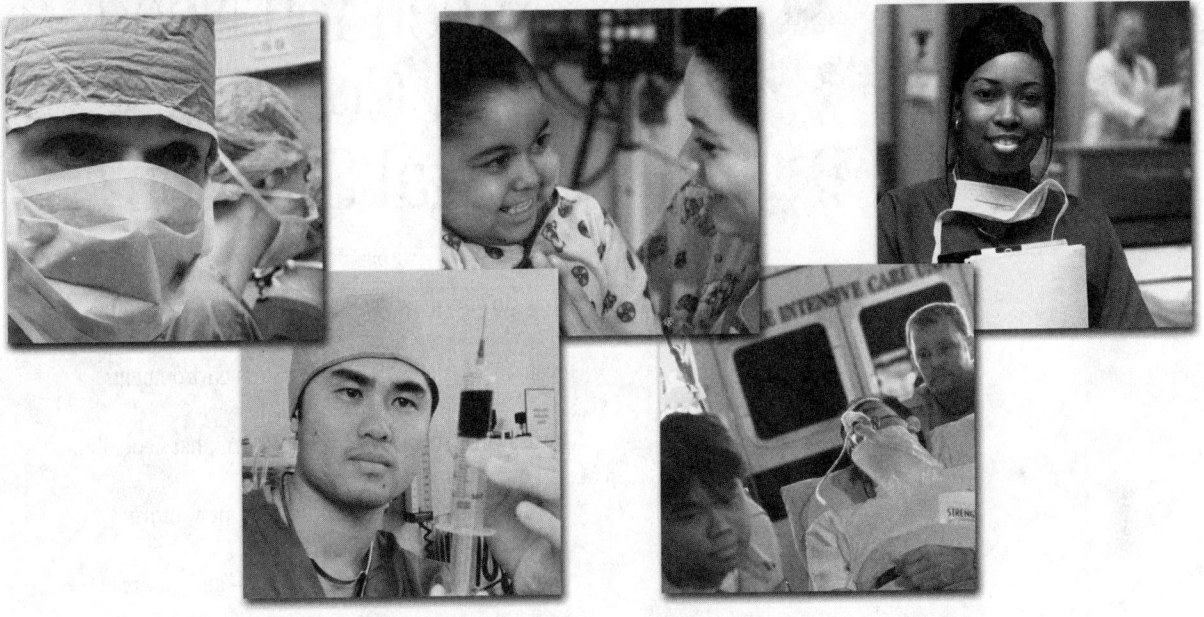

At Tenet, we believe in serving our communities in many ways –
and not just with our hospital services.

We cherish diversity, and we show it through our corporate giving
and support of community programs.

At Tenet, we're working for positive change
in our industry and in our world.

For information on career opportunities with Tenet, visit us at www.tenethealth.com.

So What Happens When You Need A Creative Legal Solution?

How do you meet the legal challenges presented

by an increasingly diverse business environment?

By drawing from a spectrum of talent that's equally

as diverse. When you can do that, new, more

colorful perspectives are shared – and an array

of creative ideas springs forth. That's why

DuPont and the law firms that represent us are

so committed to making the case for diversity.

We know that the more diverse our legal teams

are, the more diverse our thinking, the more

insightful our questions, the more valuable

the answers.

Vision.

A single view of the enterprise supports the CEO's strategic vision.

To realize its vision, a company must synchronize the efforts of all its moving parts. Only then can it execute its strategy with consistent success. Creating a process that works is the most important act of the CEO.

The answer is a single view of the business. Discover how some of the world's top companies achieve it. Read an excerpt from the book, **The Value Factor** *(Bloomberg Press),* by Mark Hurd, President and CEO, and Lars Nyberg, Chairman of NCR Corporation, available online at: **Teradata.com/thevaluefactor**

You've never seen your business like this before.

Diversity Fuels Our Success

Ryder delivers customized transportation, distribution and supply chain solutions for *Fortune* 1000 customers on four continents. Over the past 70 years we've learned that our most effective solutions come from the unique experiences, talents, cultures and ideas of our diverse workforce. To fuel Ryder's industry leadership far into the future, we place a high value on diversity in the people we hire and in the outside resources we use to support our business.

Ryder®
Logistics & Transportation
Solutions Worldwide

If you'd like to learn more about opportunities with Ryder visit us today at

www.ryder.com

Difference does make a difference.

Diversity.
In our eyes, it's an essential ingredient for success.
Because without the talents and insights of many
different people, we would never be able to grow
and adapt to the ever-changing challenges of
the world around us.

To learn more about how Intel supports diversity, visit intel.com/diversity.

At Gap Inc., diversity is who we are...

Our dedication to diversity is reinforced by workplace policies that are not just well-intentioned — they're essential to how we do business. We're committed to supporting and furthering the diversity — in experience, culture, opinion, style and viewpoint — of our valued employees, customers, and the communities we serve.

Gap Inc. is a proud supporter of the Minority Corporate Counsel Association's ongoing commitment to diversity.

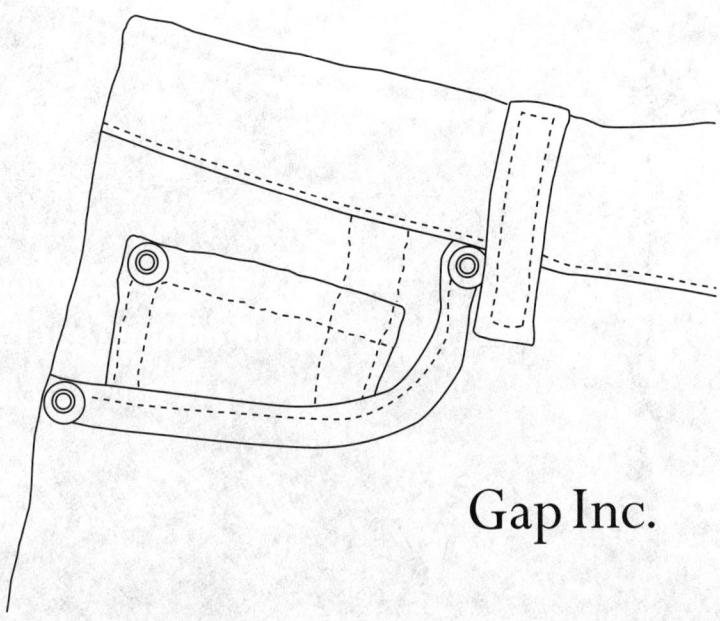

Gap Inc.

The Secret Formula...
Our People.

We understand that it's not our Company that holds the secret ingredient to our success — it's something that emerges from each and every one of our employees.

The Coca-Cola Company

"LegalWATCH is helping Halliburton manage legal risk. And Halliburton is helping me roll out my training program to other companies. We've been working together 3 years, and I'm more impressed every day. Halliburton is always there with scholarships, mentoring and creating solid business opportunities."

Jean Johnson, LegalWATCH

"Halliburton is a great partner"

If you have a minority or woman-owned business,

Halliburton and our subsidiary, KBR, want to talk to you.

HALLIBURTON

Helping to build success through supplier diversity.

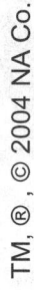

DIVERSITY

OUR MISSION

OUR PRACTICE

OUR SUCCESS

LAW FIRM DIVERSITY PROGRAMS

Akerman Senterfitt

255 South Orange Avenue, 17th Floor
Citrus Center Building
Orlando, FL 32801
Phone: (407) 843-7860
Fax: (407) 843-6610

FIRM LEADERSHIP

Managing Partner: J. Thomas Cardwell, CEO
Diversity Team Leader: Joseph W. Hatchett, Diversity Committee Chair

LOCATIONS

Orlando, FL (HQ)
Fort Lauderdale, FL
Jacksonville, FL
Miami, FL
Tallahassee, FL
Tampa, FL
Washington, DC
West Palm Beach, FL

LAW FIRM DEMOGRAPHIC PROFILES

FULL-TIME ASSOCIATES	2003	2002
Minority men	16	18
Minority women	18	19
White women	51	53
Total*	164	117

SUMMER ASSOCIATES	2003	2002
Minority men	0	0
Minority women	1	0
White women	1	0
Total*	2	0

EQUITY PARTNERS	2003	2002
Minority men	17	21
Minority women	1	0
White women	35	32
Total*	190	195

NON-EQUITY PARTNERS	2003	2002
Minority men	0	0
Minority women	0	0
White women	0	0
Total*	0	0

Note: The firm does not have any non-equity partners.

NEW HIRES	2003	2002
Minority men	1	0
Minority women	4	1
White women	17	12
Total*	37	0

* Includes "of counsel" attorneys

Strategic Plan and Diversity Leadership

How does the firm's leadership communicate the importance of diversity to everyone at the firm? (e.g., e-mails, web site, newsletters, meetings, etc.)

Through firm-wide diversity training, e-mails, and shareholder and board meetings.

Who has primary responsibility for leading diversity initiatives at your firm? Name of person and his/her title:

The diversity committee has the primary responsibility. The committee is chaired by Joseph W. Hatchett, formerly a chief judge of the U.S. Court of Appeals for the 11th Circuit and a justice of the Supreme Court of Florida.

Does your law firm currently have a diversity committee?

Yes

Does the committee's representation include one or more members of the firm's management/executive committee (or the equivalent)?

Yes

How many attorneys are on the committee, and in 2003, what was the total number of hours collectively spent by the committee in furtherance of the firm's diversity initiatives?

Total attorneys on committee: 7

Total hours spent on diversity: N/A

Does the committee and/or diversity leader establish and set goals or objectives consistent with management's priorities?

Yes

Has the firm undertaken a formal or informal diversity program or set of initiatives aimed at increasing the diversity of the firm?

Yes, formal

How often does the firm's management review the firm's diversity progress/results?

Periodically, at least several times per year.

How is the firm's diversity committee and/or firm management held accountable for achieving results?

The committee drafts diversity initiatives each year and its results are measured against these goals.

LAW FIRM DIVERSITY INITIATIVES	ALREADY COMPLETED	CURRENTLY ADDRESSING	NOT A CURRENT PRIORITY
Undertake communication from firm management that diversity is a top priority of the firm.		✓	
Formalize diversity plan and committee with action steps and accountability to management.	✓		
Conduct firm-wide diversity training for all attorneys and staff.	✓		
Increase the number of minority attorneys at the associate level.		✓	
Increase the number of minority attorneys at the partnership level.		✓	
Develop/expand relationships with minority bar associations to offer firm's support of these networks.		✓	
Focus on strengthening firm's mentoring program, including for benefit of minority attorneys.		✓	
Conduct internal diversity needs assessment and/or retain diversity consultant to examine how firm culture might be more welcoming of minorities.			✓
Support law firm's internal affinity networks (e.g., women, minority attorney networks).		✓	
Manage/monitor allocation of work assignments and/or hours billed to ensure women and minority attorneys have equal access/inclusion on top client matters.	✓		

Recruitment – New Associates

Does your firm annually recruit at any of the following types of institutions? (Check all that apply and list the schools).

Ivy League schools: Harvard University

Public state schools: Florida State University, University of Florida

Private schools: University of Miami

Historically Black Colleges and Universities (HBCUs): Howard University

Do you have any special outreach efforts directed to encourage minority law students to consider your firm?

• *Support the University of Miami and St. Thomas University Professional Opportunities Programs.*

• Advertise in minority law student association publication(s)
• Participate in/host minority law student job fair(s)
• Sponsor minority law student association events
• Firm's lawyers participate on career panels at school
• Outreach to leadership of minority student organizations

SUMMER ASSOCIATE STATISTICS: SUMMER 2003	MINORITY MEN	MINORITY WOMEN	WHITE WOMEN	TOTAL
Summer associates	0	1	1	2
Summer associates who received an offer of full-time employment	0	1	0	1
Summer associates who accepted an offer of full-time employment	0	1	0	1

Recruitment – Lateral Associates and Partners

What activities does the firm undertake to attract minority and women attorneys?

• Participate at minority job fairs
• Seek referrals from other attorneys

Do you use executive recruiting/search firms to seek to identify new diversity hires (partners or associates)?

Yes

LATERAL ASSOCIATES AND PARTNERS: 1/1/03 – 12/31/03	MINORITY MEN	MINORITY WOMEN	WHITE WOMEN	TOTAL
Number of lateral associate hires	3	2	13	34
Number of lateral partner hires (equity and non-equity)	0	0	1	3
Number of new partners (equity and non-equity) promoted from associate rank	1	1	3	11
Number of new equity partners	1	0	3	7

Retention & Professional Development

Please identify the specific steps you are taking to reduce the attrition rate of minority and women attorneys.

• Develop and/or support internal employee affinity groups (e.g., minority or women networks within the firm)
• Increase/review compensation relative to competition
• Increase/improve current work/life programs
• Review work assignments and hours billed to key client matters to make sure minority and women attorneys are not being excluded
• Strengthen mentoring program for all attorneys, including minorities and women
• Professional skills development program, including minority and women attorneys

Does your firm have part-time/flex-time policies that permit attorneys (male or female) to work alternative schedules?

Yes, the firm has an alternative work arrangement policy which provides for flex-time, compressed time, flexi-place and reduced work schedule options.

What impact, if any, will the decision to work part-time have on an attorney's ability to make partner or, if already a partner, to remain a partner at your firm?

The attorney will be evaluated, and will progress toward shareholder status, based on the same standards as full-time lawyers.

Have any attorneys who chose to work a part-time schedule made partner at your firm?

Too early to comment; our alternative work policy was instituted in late 2003.

Management Demographic Profile (as of 12/31/03)

	MINORITY MEN	MINORITY WOMEN	WHITE WOMEN	TOTAL
Number of attorneys on the Executive/Management Committee or equivalent	0	0	1	9
Number of attorneys on the Hiring Committee or equivalent	N/A	N/A	N/A	N/A
Number of attorneys on the Partner/Associate Review Committee or equivalent	0	0	1	8

Please provide information regarding all minority and women attorneys who head offices or practice groups of your law firm:

Minorities heading practice groups: Joseph Hatchett is the head of the firm's appellate practice.

The Firm Says

The firm's diversity mission is to develop professional opportunities and to foster an environment in which minorities and women may perform proudly and give the firm's clients the benefits of a law firm balanced fully in terms of race, ethnicity and gender.

Akerman Senterfitt is consistently ranked as a leader in law firm diversity. The firm was ranked No. 3 for the highest percentage of minority attorneys in the 2002 Minority Law Journal's Diversity Scorecard. In 2003, the Diversity Scorecard ranked Akerman Senterfitt second with regard to the highest percentage of Hispanic-American attorneys.

To advance the firm's efforts in relation to diversity issues, Akerman Senterfitt appointed shareholder Joseph W. Hatchett to chair the firm's Committee on Diversity. Mr. Hatchett's distinguished jurist career includes serving as chief judge of the U.S. Court of Appeals for the Eleventh Circuit and as a justice on the Supreme Court of Florida. Mr. Hatchett was the first African-American to serve on the Florida Supreme Court and the first African-American to serve as a chief judge of a federal appellate court in the southern United States.

The Diversity Committee drafts annual diversity initiatives which are translated into specific goals for the coming year. Overall, the firm's diversity efforts have resulted in establishing some programs that other law firms are yet to envision. The firm has established an Alternative Work Plan, allowing lawyers to accommodate family responsibilities, and a Maternity Leave Policy, allowing for childbirth and child nurturing responsibilities for male and female lawyers without loss of partnership possibilities.

One of the goals for 2004 is a Sensitivity Training Program for everyone in the firm, including staff. The firm retained an outside expert in diversity to travel to each of the firm's offices in July 2004 to offer multiple sessions on diversity. The goals for our firm-wide diversity training are to build awareness and competency in the areas of diversity knowledge, self-awareness, productive interpersonal relationships and diversity communication skills. The sessions for the firm's attorneys and management include training on their leadership roles in the area of diversity and the importance of our diversity success to our clients.

Recruitment of minority lawyers is a day-to-day, ongoing process supervised by the firm's recruiting director and the Diversity Committee. The recruiting director contacts prospects by mailing letters to placement officers at major law schools and by having Recruiting Committee members visit law school campuses to interview prospective graduates. These on-campus visits include Howard University Law School, the greatest provider of African-American lawyers in the United States. Contacts are also made with minority organizations at the law schools, such as the Asian/Pacific American Law Student Association and the Hispanic Law Student Association. The firm maintains an especially close relationship with the Black Law Students Association at all of the law schools in Florida. The firm provides financial support to the University of Miami's Professional Opportunities Program for Black Law Students.

The firm's ability to retain minority lawyers is greater than that of the national average. Success in retention has resulted from the firm's practice of providing associates with appraisals of their performance and realistic evaluations regarding their potential for promotion. In addition, the Diversity Committee stays in continuous

contact with the firm's minority lawyers, seeking their perceptions and suggestions, then immediately reacting to correct problems, if any exist.

In the area of mentoring, the firm has been sensitive to the importance of providing full opportunities for associates to form mentoring relationships with more senior lawyers. This practice, however, is not devoted merely to minority lawyers, but is part of an overall program of mentoring for all associates. It is stressed continuously to the firm's minority lawyers that they are expected to develop their practice skills to a level that will allow them the opportunity to be invited to become full ownership partners in the firm. Minority lawyers soon learn that promotion is possible simply by observing the participation of other minority partners who are members of the board of directors, office managers and leaders of practice groups.

The firm collaborates with the Florida Bar, the National Bar Association and the American Bar Association in seeking to increase the number of minority lawyers in all law firms. Several of the firm's lawyers play active roles in the collaboration process. Partner Joseph Hatchett, who is a member of the National Bar Association, the Florida Bar Association and the board of directors of the Lawyers' Committee for Civil Rights Under Law, constantly engages in bar activities and speaking engagements involving the recruitment, training and retention of minority lawyers.

Another partner is the past president of the Hispanic Bar Association of Florida and now serves as its general counsel. Yet another partner chaired the city of Orlando's efforts to have the Florida A&M University Law School locate its new campus in Orlando. Now that the law school has been established in Orlando, firm partners serve as adjunct professors and advisors. In addition, the firm sends delegates to most of the major diversity networking conferences.

The firm has an Anti-Discrimination and Harassment Committee, which is chaired by a woman. Of the committee's other four members, one is a minority male and two are female. The firm has a clear anti-harassment policy with specific reporting, investigation and resolutions methods. The firm is an equal employment opportunity employer and is committed to the principles of equal employment opportunity without regard to such factors as race, color, sex, religion, national origin, age, disability, sexual orientation or any other protected status.

Beyond Words and Numbers

Diversity

MCAA's Thomas L. Sager Award

The Sager Award is given annually to law firms that have demonstrated a sustained commitment to improve the hiring, promotion and retention of minority groups.

Some firms speak of "achieving diversity." At Akin Gump, diversity is more than what you achieve – it's what you believe. After all, diversity speaks not just to numbers but to ideas, innovation and a dynamic culture.

As a three-time recipient of the Minority Corporate Counsel Association's Thomas L. Sager Award, Akin Gump remains committed to the firmwide advancement of minority attorneys. At Akin Gump, it's our culture.

1.866.AKIN LAW
akingump.com

AKIN GUMP
STRAUSS HAUER & FELD LLP
Attorneys at Law

Akin Gump Strauss Hauer & Feld, LLP

1333 New Hampshire Ave., N.W.
Washington, DC 20036
Phone: (202) 887-4000
Fax: (202) 887-4288

FIRM LEADERSHIP

Managing Partner: R. Bruce McLean, Chairman
Diversity Team Leader: Peter Haviland, Chair,
Firm-wide Diversity Committee

LOCATIONS

Washington, DC (HQ)
Austin, TX
Dallas, TX
Houston, TX
Los Angeles, CA
New York, NY
Philadelphia, PA
Riverside, CA
San Antonio, TX
San Francisco, CA
Brussels
London
Moscow
Riyadh (affiliate)

LAW FIRM DEMOGRAPHIC PROFILES

FULL-TIME ASSOCIATES	2003	2002
Minority men	35	34
Minority women	27	37
White women	160	162
Total	483	538

SUMMER ASSOCIATES	2003	2002
Minority men	13	7
Minority women	15	11
White women	29	32
Total	84	83

EQUITY PARTNERS*	2003	2002
Minority men	22	18
Minority women	8	7
White women	37	38
Total	315	328

* Equity and non-equity partner totals are combined
pursuant to firm policy.

Strategic Plan and Diversity Leadership

How does the firm's leadership communicate the importance of diversity to everyone at the firm? (e.g., e-mails, web site, newsletters, meetings, etc.)

The firm's leadership communicates the importance of diversity through firm-wide distribution of our Statement on Diversity. Weekly newsletters also highlight attorneys' achievements, speaking engagements, pro bono activities and published articles. In addition, the chairman periodically distributes firm-wide e-mails discussing the firm's priorities.

Who has primary responsibility for leading diversity initiatives at your firm? Name of person and his/her title:

Peter Haviland, chair of the firm-wide Diversity Committee, in conjunction with R. Bruce McLean, chairman.

Does your law firm currently have a diversity committee?

Yes

Does the committee's representation include one or more members of the firm's management/executive committee (or the equivalent)?

Yes

How many attorneys are on the committee, and in 2003, what was the total number of hours collectively spent by the committee in furtherance of the firm's diversity initiatives?

Total attorneys on committee: 7

Total hours spent on diversity: The firm does not currently separately track hours spent on diversity. Our diversity efforts are integrally linked to our recruitment, attorney professional development and client service activities.

Does the committee and/or diversity leader establish and set goals or objectives consistent with management's priorities?

Yes

Has the firm undertaken a formal or informal diversity program or set of initiatives aimed at increasing the diversity of the firm?

Yes, formal

How often does the firm's management review the firm's diversity progress/results?

Annually

How is the firm's diversity committee and/or firm management held accountable for achieving results?

The Diversity Committee reports regularly to the chairman and the firm's management.

LAW FIRM DIVERSITY INITIATIVES	ALREADY COMPLETED	CURRENTLY ADDRESSING	NOT A CURRENT PRIORITY
Undertake communication from firm management that diversity is a top priority of the firm.	✓		
Formalize diversity plan and committee with action steps and accountability to management.		✓	
Conduct firm-wide diversity training for all attorneys and staff.		✓	
Increase the number of minority attorneys at the associate level.		✓	
Increase the number of minority attorneys at the partnership level.		✓	
Develop/expand relationships with minority bar associations to offer firm's support of these networks.		✓	
Focus on strengthening firm's mentoring program, including for benefit of minority attorneys.		✓	
Conduct internal diversity needs assessment and/or retain diversity consultant to examine how firm culture might be more welcoming of minorities.	✓		
Support law firm's internal affinity networks (e.g., women, minority attorney networks).	✓		
Manage/monitor allocation of work assignments and/or hours billed to ensure women and minority attorneys have equal access/inclusion on top client matters.	✓		
Include minority and female partners in the firm's management structure; ensure that minority and female partners have leadership roles and participate in client service teams.	✓		

Recruitment - New Associates

Does your firm annually recruit at any of the following types of institutions? (Check all that apply and list the schools).

Ivy League schools: Columbia University, Cornell University, Harvard University, University of Pennsylvania, Yale University

Public state schools: University of California-Berkeley (Boalt Hall), University of California-Hastings, UCLA, George Mason University, University of Michigan, University of Minnesota, University of Virginia, University of Texas

Private schools: American University, Baylor University, Boston College, Boston University, Catholic University of America, Duke University, Emory University, Fordham University, George Washington University, Georgetown University, University of Houston, Loyola Law School in Los Angeles, NYU, Pepperdine University, Rutgers University, SMU, St. Mary's University, Stanford University, Temple University, Tulane University, University of Chicago, USC, Vanderbilt University, Washington University in St. Louis

153

Historically Black Colleges and Universities (HBCUs): Howard University through participation in the Mid-Atlantic NBLSA Annual Job Fair

Native American Tribal Universities: Through participation in the American Indian Law Conference

Of the law schools that you listed above, do you have any special outreach efforts directed to encourage minority law students to consider your firm?

• *Offices hold recruiting dinners for minority law students who have received offers for summer associate positions*

• *Lawyers participate in panel discussions with minority law students to discuss practicing law in a large firm environment*

• *Firm participates in the Federal Bar Association's annual American Indian Law Conference and holds recruiting reception for Native American students.*

• Hold a reception for minority law students

• Advertise in minority law student association publication(s)

• Participate in/host minority law student job fair(s)

• Sponsor minority law student association events

• Firm's lawyers participate on career panels at school

• Outreach to leadership of minority student organizations

• Scholarships or intern/fellowships for minority students

SUMMER ASSOCIATE STATISTICS: SUMMER 2003	MINORITY MEN	MINORITY WOMEN	WHITE WOMEN	TOTAL
Summer associates	13	15	29	84
Summer associates who received an offer of full-time employment	12	13	29	76
Summer associates who accepted an offer of full-time employment	9	8	22	57

Recruiting – Lateral Associates and Partners

What activities does the firm undertake to attract minority and women attorneys?

• Partner programs with women and minority bar associations

• Participate at minority job fairs

• Seek referrals from other attorneys

Do you use executive recruiting/search firms to seek to identify new diversity hires (partners or associates)?

Yes

If yes, list all women- and/or minority-owned executive search/recruiting firms to which the firm paid a fee for placement services in the past 12 months:

Unknown

LATERAL ASSOCIATES AND PARTNERS: 1/1/03 – 12/31/03	MINORITY MEN	MINORITY WOMEN	WHITE WOMEN	TOTAL
Number of lateral associate hires	3	6	23	56
Number of lateral partner hires (equity and non-equity)	2	0	1	13
Number of new partners (equity and non-equity) promoted from associate rank	2	1	4	15
Number of new equity partners	0	0	0	0

Retention & Professional Development

Please identify the specific steps you are taking to reduce the attrition rate of minority and women attorneys.

• *The firm has retained a consultant to help develop effective measures that will lead to long-term results.* • *Develop and/or support internal employee affinity groups (e.g., minority or women networks within the firm)*
• Increase/improve current work/life programs
• Succession plan includes emphasis on diversity
• Work with minority and women attorneys to develop career advancement plans
• Introduce minority and women attorneys to key clients, including to lead engagements
• Strengthen mentoring program for all attorneys, including minorities and women
• Professional skills development program, including minority and women attorneys

Does your firm have part-time/flex-time policies that permit attorneys (male or female) to work alternative schedules?

Yes. Akin Gump's reduced work schedule policy allows attorneys to arrange a reduced workload in connection with parenting and family care responsibilities as well as to pursue activities designed to enhance the attorney's professional development or stature in the legal community.

What impact, if any, will the decision to work part-time have on an attorney's ability to make partner or, if already a partner, to remain a partner at your firm?

An attorney's decision to seek a reduced work schedule does not negatively impact that attorney's promotion to counsel or to the partnership or maintaining his/her status in the firm. However, it is anticipated that a lawyer who has worked a reduced work schedule or is working a reduced work schedule may require a longer tenure to meet the criteria for counsel or partner.

Have any attorneys who chose to work a part-time schedule made partner at your firm?

Yes

Management Demographic Profile (as of 12/31/03)

Please provide information regarding all minority and women attorneys who head offices or practice groups of your law firm:

Minorities heading practice groups: Smith W. Davis, Domestic Policy (DC); Edward Fernandes, Litigation (Austin); Hushmand Sohaili, Real Estate (LA)

Women heading practice groups: Valerie A. Slater, International Trade (DC); Karol A. Kepchar, Copyright and Internet (DC); Diana Dutton, Energy (Dallas); Marilyn Doria, Energy (DC)

The Firm Says

In a narrative of two pages or less, please provide any additional information regarding your firm's diversity initiatives that you wish to share. See instructions for details and suggestions.

Akin Gump Strauss Hauer & Feld LLP ranks as one of the largest law firms in the nation. Founded in 1945, Akin Gump today has offices in 14 cities worldwide and employs more than 900 attorneys from diverse backgrounds. Of these attorneys, 34 are African American, 30 are Hispanic, 42 are Asian/Pacific Islander and three are Native American. In total, attorneys of color comprise over 11 percent of our firm-wide legal team. In addition, there are 267 women and 13 self-identified GLBT attorneys firm-wide.

Akin Gump was founded with the ideals of building and maintaining an inclusive working environment. The following excerpt from our current Partnership Admissions Policy summarizes Akin Gump's commitment to diversity:

As historical barriers to achievement in the legal profession have continued to fall, the best and brightest lawyers in their fields, and the best and brightest young lawyers emerging from law schools, come from ever more diverse backgrounds. Our success in the global market, and our success in meeting internal objectives of excellence in mentoring, supervision and professional development, depends on ensuring that we achieve and maintain a critical mass of diversity in our partnership and in our associate population.

Firm leadership

This commitment to diversity is implemented through active participation by our minority and female partners in the firm's leadership. An African American partner, a Hispanic partner, a Native American partner and an Asian partner serve on the Management Committee, and four of the partners on the committee are women. An African American partner also sits on the Compensation Committee. In addition, a female partner heads our Partnership Acceptance Committee. She is joined by an African American, a Hispanic and two other women partners. In addition to these firm-wide management roles, four female partners and two African Americans serve as section managers for various practice areas within the firm. Our firm-wide Diversity Committee reflects the diversity of Akin Gump, consisting of minority, women, openly gay and non-minority attorneys from our offices.

Attorney retention

Retention of our attorneys is another critical component of our efforts to maintain an inclusive environment. A diverse partnership leads to long-term success because it sends an unequivocal signal to our associates and counsel that they can advance professionally at Akin Gump. Minority attorneys currently comprise 10.6 percent

of our partnership, and women make up 16.3 percent of our partnership. These partners actively mentor our associates and counsel and are instrumental in guiding the professional development of our junior lawyers. The diversity of practice areas represented by our minority and female partners guarantee that a minority associate has access to a partner mentor in his/her specific field of interest. Although the firm also encourages mentoring between associates of color and non-minority partners, we are extremely proud of the partners of color who support our mentorship programs.

Our women partners have helped strengthen our retention efforts by leading the Women's Professional Development Forum. This initiative, established in 2001, is a quarterly educational and networking program for all our women attorneys. In each office, the Forum includes a mentoring component as well as a speaker series. This past year, the Forum sponsored several events, including a panel discussion by several female general counsel regarding the achievement of work-life balance in the legal field. The Forum also provides a venue for our female attorneys to develop marketing initiatives and discuss retention issues.

Active promotion of women and minority attorneys sustains our inclusive environment. In 2003, 26 percent of attorneys promoted to partner were minorities and 20 percent were women. In our counsel program, an interim promotion for our associates who are on partnership track, 28 percent of the associates promoted to counsel were minorities and women. As a result of these promotions, women and minorities comprise 33 percent of our current counsel program – a significantly diverse population eligible for partnership.

Recruiting initiatives

Although we believe that a diverse management structure, effective mentoring by our diverse partnership and active promotion of our attorneys are the most effective ways to attract young lawyers of diverse backgrounds, we complement these efforts with innovative recruiting initiatives sponsored by our Diversity Committee. We sponsor fellowship programs with Georgetown University Law Center, the University of Texas and New York University. Through these programs, first-year minority students are assigned mentors from the firm, actively participate in a variety of firm activities throughout the year and are guaranteed a summer associate position after their first year of law school. We are currently expanding our fellowship programs to include other law schools in our major markets.

In addition, this year we will be the first private law firm to host an intern from American University's Washington Semester American Indian Program. By working closely with attorneys and advisors in our American Indian Law and Policy Practice, this internship will provide a law student with firsthand experience in this practice area. This past year the firm also hosted a recruiting reception for Native American law students during the Federal Bar Association's Annual Indian Law Conference, where members of our Hiring Committee met with over 50 Native American law students.

The bottom line

While we are proud of these results, we are dedicated to building upon our record of success. We are a three-time recipient of MCCA's Sager Award and will continue to uphold the diversity principles recognized by this achievement. The firm was founded on principles of diversity, and our tradition challenges us to remain resolute in our commitment to an inclusive environment. At Akin Gump, diversity is not about numbers, it is how we define excellence.

Allen & Overy LLP

1221 Avenue of the Americas
New York, NY 10020
Phone: (212) 610-6300
Fax: (212) 610-6399

FIRM LEADERSHIP

Managing Partner: Mark Welling
Diversity Team Leader: Mark Welling,
Managing Partner

LOCATIONS

London
New York
Amsterdam
Antwerp
Bangkok
Beijing
Bratislava
Brussels
Budapest
Dubai
Frankfurt
Hamburg
Hong Kong
Luxembourg
Madrid
Milan
Moscow
Paris
Prague
Rome
Shanghai
Singapore
Tokyo
Turin
Warsaw

LAW FIRM DEMOGRAPHIC PROFILES

FULL-TIME ASSOCIATES	2003	2002
Minority men	13	19
Minority women	7	7
White women	29	26
Total	116	99

SUMMER ASSOCIATES	2003	2002
Minority men	5	2
Minority women	4	0
White women	4	10
Total	19	18

EQUITY PARTNERS	2003	2002
Minority men	0	0
Minority women	0	0
White women	2	2
Total	23	18

NON-EQUITY PARTNERS	2003	2002
Minority men	0	0
Minority women	0	0
White women	0	0
Total	1	1

NEW HIRES	2003	2002
Minority men	6	2
Minority women	1	1
White women	9	4
Total	33	14

MINORITY CORPORATE COUNSEL ASSOCIATION

Strategic Plan and Diversity Leadership

How does the firm's leadership communicate the importance of diversity to everyone at the firm? (e.g., e-mails, web site, newsletters, meetings, etc.)

Allen & Overy LLP's leadership communicates the importance of diversity to everyone at the firm through a formalized set of internal values, which range from "respecting and including every individual" to "working together as one firm." In addition, Allen & Overy informally fosters diversity by a strong and inclusive global network of communication and respect driven by all members of the firm who share, believe in and practice these values. Monitoring of and compliance with the Allen & Overy's detailed values program is embedded also into its staff (legal and non-legal) and partner appraisal processes. Structurally, Allen & Overy New York has instituted a diversity and inclusion training program, which it will introduce to all members of its legal and non-legal staff. Finally, from a recruitment perspective, the New York office participates in diversity recruitment fairs and continues to seek applicants from a diverse candidate pool.

Who has primary responsibility for leading diversity initiatives at your firm?

Mark Welling, Managing Partner

Does your law firm currently have a diversity committee?

No, but Allen & Overy is currently developing a range of programs and initiatives to further reinforce its internal values program and commitment to diversity which may include the establishment of a diversity committee.

Does the committee and/or diversity leader establish and set goals or objectives consistent with management's priorities?

Yes

Has the firm undertaken a formal or informal diversity program or set of initiatives aimed at increasing the diversity of the firm?

Yes, formal

How often does the firm's management review the firm's diversity progress/results?

Monthly. Allen & Overy's local and global management review on a monthly basis a range of personnel-related data which periodically includes detailed diversity and recruitment data to measure progress on a range of criteria including diversity.

How is the firm's diversity committee and/or firm management held accountable for achieving results?

Due to the firm's commitment to growth in this area, the New York office has appointed several members of the management team to assist the partnership in accomplishing its goals. Since the Allen & Overy global network is fully committed to enhancing its formal and informal diversity policies and initiatives, all offices and departments participate in global initiatives (which are outside the scope of this survey which has been limited to the U.S.).

LAW FIRM DIVERSITY INITIATIVES	ALREADY COMPLETED	CURRENTLY ADDRESSING	NOT A CURRENT PRIORITY
Undertake communication from firm management that diversity is a top priority of the firm.	✔		
Formalize diversity plan and committee with action steps and accountability to management.		✔	
Conduct firm-wide diversity training for all attorneys and staff.	✔ *		
Increase the number of minority attorneys at the associate level.		✔	
Increase the number of minority attorneys at the partnership level.		✔	
Develop/expand relationships with minority bar associations to offer firm's support of these networks.		✔	
Focus on strengthening firm's mentoring program, including for benefit of minority attorneys.		✔	
Conduct internal diversity needs assessment and/or retain diversity consultant to examine how firm culture might be more welcoming of minorities.	✔ *		
Support law firm's internal affinity networks (e.g., women, minority attorney networks).		✔	
Manage/monitor allocation of work assignments and/or hours billed to ensure women and minority attorneys have equal access/inclusion on top client matters.			✔

In progress

Recruitment – New Associates

Does your firm annually recruit at any of the following types of institutions? (Check all that apply and list the schools).

Ivy League schools: Harvard University, Yale University, Columbia University, University of Pennsylvania

Public state schools: University of Texas, UVA, University of Michigan, BLSA Job Fairs (which includes public schools)

Private schools: NYU, Duke University, Georgetown University, Stanford University, University of Chicago

Do you have any special outreach efforts directed to encourage minority law students to consider your firm?

• Advertise in minority law student association publication(s)

• Participate in/host minority law student job fair(s)

• Firm's lawyers participate on career panels at school

SUMMER ASSOCIATE STATISTICS: SUMMER 2003	MINORITY MEN	MINORITY WOMEN	WHITE WOMEN	TOTAL
Summer associates	5	4	4	19
Summer associates who received an offer of full-time employment	4	4	4	17
Summer associates who accepted an offer of full-time employment	4	3**	3**	11*

Three offers are outstanding
*** One offer is outstanding*

Recruitment – Lateral Associates and Partners

What activities does the firm undertake to attract minority and women attorneys?

• Participate at minority job fairs
• Seek referrals from other attorneys

Do you use executive recruiting/search firms to seek to identify new diversity hires (partners or associates)?

No

LATERAL ASSOCIATES AND PARTNERS: 1/1/03 – 12/31/03	MINORITY MEN	MINORITY WOMEN	WHITE WOMEN	TOTAL
Number of lateral associate hires	2	1	3	15
Number of lateral partner hires (equity and non-equity)	0	0	0	2
Number of new partners (equity and non-equity) promoted from associate rank	0	0	0	2
Number of new equity partners	1	0	0	4

Retention & Professional Development

ATTORNEYS WHO LEFT THE FIRM: 2003	MINORITY MEN	MINORITY WOMEN	WHITE WOMEN	TOTAL
Number of attorneys who voluntarily or involuntarily left your firm's employ in 2003	0	1	2	5

How do 2003 attrition rates generally compare to those experienced in the prior year period?

About the same as in prior years

Please identify the specific steps you are taking to reduce the attrition rate of minority and women attorneys.

• Increase/review compensation relative to competition
• Increase/improve current work/life programs
• Succession plan includes emphasis on diversity
• Work with minority and women attorneys to develop career advancement plans
• Introduce minority and women attorneys to key clients, including to lead engagements
• Strengthen mentoring program for all attorneys, including minorities and women
• Professional skills development program, including minority and women attorneys

Does your firm have part-time/flex-time policies that permit attorneys (male or female) to work alternative schedules?

Yes. Allen & Overy has a part-time and flex-time program in which several associates participate.

What impact, if any, will the decision to work part-time have on an attorney's ability to make partner or, if already a partner, to remain a partner at your firm?

None whatsoever.

Have any attorneys who chose to work a part-time schedule made partner at your firm?

No, not in the U.S. This is due to the fact that the associates who currently have part-time schedules are too junior to be considered for partnership. In the U.S. we have one senior counsel member who joined the firm with a part-time arrangement but has not been with Allen & Overy long enough to be considered for partnership.

Management Demographic Profile (as of 12/31/03)

Please provide information regarding all minority and women attorneys who head offices or practice groups of your law firm:

Minorities or women heading offices: N/A (Our only U.S. domestic office is in New York, and it is currently headed by Mark Welling.)

Women heading practice groups: Cathleen McLaughlin, Head of Latin America Group; Helena Sprenger, Head of Dutch Desk

The Firm Says

Diversity and inclusion are key issues for Allen & Overy LLP because we aim to recruit the best people for an international business. We need to harness the talents of a diverse professional body which has to be instinctively international in outlook. We need to be effective individually and collectively in every jurisdiction (we operate in 20 countries), particularly as we come together to work on cross-border transactions. This requires a real appreciation of other cultures. The power of our legal practice and the advice we give comes from effective cooperation across borders, working in teams which are multi-disciplinary and made up of different nationalities. Amongst our lawyers globally, no nationality represents an absolute majority. Cultural diversity is therefore central to the firm.

We have a declared set of values which help us to achieve a diverse and inclusive legal practice. In particular, our values of '"helping people achieve their 'potential" and '"respecting and including every 'individual" incorporate our commitment to diversity. In setting these as clear standards we aim to create a challenging environment in which our people can excel. We try to value different opinions, give people scope to be themselves and demonstrate respect for life outside work. Our performance management process is aligned with our values so that when we review an individual's performance we consider their contribution in this context.

Our induction courses for new joiners to the firm include reference to our values and our stance on equal opportunities and diversity. We also provide in-house and external training for our recruiters. Our development courses for lawyers and support managers focus on effective team work, including the leadership of culturally diverse teams. Cultural awareness training is seen as essential for individuals being considered for overseas secondments.

In summary, we dedicate time, energy and resources to diversity and inclusion in many different ways and do so with the full support of partners and our board.

Allen & Overy LLP's Diversity and Inclusion Statement

With offices in 20 countries, Allen & Overy LLP takes great pride in its international and diverse work force. Our employees mirror the diversity of the societies in which we operate and with which we interact. Our worldwide "Values into Action" program is an example of Allen & Overy's fundamental commitment to promoting respect and inclusion by striving to fulfill the promise of a collegial working environment where every employee is valued for his or her contribution. We aim to continue Allen & Overy's commitment to diversity and inclusion with the following principles in mind:

• Promote inclusiveness in our policies, practices and business relationships;

• Proactively recruit candidates from a diverse and talented applicant pool;

• Reinforce the value of diversity through education and training; and

• Evaluate our effectiveness in creating and sustaining a diverse and inclusive working environment.

Allen & Overy LLP's values

• Excellence in everyone and everything

• Dedication to our clients

• Helping our people to achieve their potential

• Respecting and including every individual

• Working together as one firm

• Entrepreneurial spirit and energy

Alston & Bird LLP

One Atlantic Center
1201 West Peachtree Street
Atlanta, GA 30309
Phone: (404) 881-7000
Fax: (404) 881-7777

FIRM LEADERSHIP

Managing Partner: Ben Johnson
Diversity Team Leader: John Latham, Diversity
Partner

LOCATIONS

Atlanta, GA (HQ)
Charlotte, NC
New York, NY
Raleigh, NC
Washington, DC

LAW FIRM DEMOGRAPHIC PROFILES

FULL-TIME ASSOCIATES	2003	2002
Minority men	19	15
Minority women	30	26
White women	126	123
Total	365	352

SUMMER ASSOCIATES	2003	2002
Minority men	10	11
Minority women	15	8
White women	29	31
Total	86	91

EQUITY PARTNERS	2003	2002
Minority men	5	4
Minority women	2	1
White women	17	17
Total	143	144

NON-EQUITY PARTNERS	2003	2002
Minority men	2	1
Minority women	4	4
White women	22	19
Total	117	102

NEW HIRES	2003	2002
Minority men	8	4
Minority women	5	10
White women	31	38
Total	91	108

Strategic Plan and Diversity Leadership

How does the firm's leadership communicate the importance of diversity to everyone at the firm? (e.g., e-mails, web site, newsletters, meetings, etc.)

In 2001, the managing partner announced at a firm meeting the appointment of John Latham as diversity partner and the creation of a Diversity Committee comprised of lawyers and staff members from our various offices. In 2003, Alston & Bird engaged Roosevelt Thomas Consulting and Training, Inc. to conduct a series of focus groups and to conduct a mandatory firm-wide diversity training seminar for our lawyers and staff.

The importance of diversity is regularly communicated in numerous meetings, including firm meetings, practice group leader training sessions, summer associate orientation, new Associate orientation, staff meetings and partners' breakfast (at which the Diversity Leadership Award is announced). The firm has also prepared a Diversity Brochure which is made available to all attorneys and staff in the firm. The Alston & Bird web site reflects our commitment to diversity (www.alston.com/index.cfm?fuseaction=diversity). And the firm sends e-mail communications to lawyers and staff on various diversity-related matters.

Who has primary responsibility for leading diversity initiatives at your firm?

John L. Latham, diversity partner and chairman of Diversity Committee

Does your law firm currently have a diversity committee?

Yes

Does the committee's representation include one or more members of the firm's management/executive committee (or the equivalent)?

Yes

How many attorneys are on the committee, and in 2003, what was the total number of hours collectively spent by the committee in furtherance of the firm's diversity initiatives?

Total attorneys on committee: 17

Total hours spent on diversity: Data not available

Does the committee and/or diversity leader establish and set goals or objectives consistent with management's priorities?

Yes

Has the firm undertaken a formal or informal diversity program or set of initiatives aimed at increasing the diversity of the firm?

Yes, formal

How often does the firm's management review the firm's diversity progress/results?

Monthly. The diversity partner is a member of the Administrative Committee which meets every two weeks. In addition, the diversity partner meets regularly with the managing partner to update him on diversity initiatives and issues.

How is the firm's diversity committee and/or firm management held accountable for achieving results?

Mr. Latham's role as the diversity partner is dependent upon the firm achieving results consistent with management's expectations. In addition, partners are advised that their compensation is affected by their commitment to the firm's diversity initiatives.

LAW FIRM DIVERSITY INITIATIVES	ALREADY COMPLETED	CURRENTLY ADDRESSING	NOT A CURRENT PRIORITY
Undertake communication from firm management that diversity is a top priority of the firm.	✓		
Formalize diversity plan and committee with action steps and accountability to management.	✓		
Conduct firm-wide diversity training for all attorneys and staff.	✓		
Increase the number of minority attorneys at the associate level.		✓	
Increase the number of minority attorneys at the partnership level.		✓	
Develop/expand relationships with minority bar associations to offer firm's support of these networks.		✓	
Focus on strengthening firm's mentoring program, including for benefit of minority attorneys.		✓	
Conduct internal diversity needs assessment and/or retain diversity consultant to examine how firm culture might be more welcoming of minorities.	✓		
Support law firm's internal affinity networks (e.g., women, minority attorney networks).		✓	
Manage/monitor allocation of work assignments and/or hours billed to ensure women and minority attorneys have equal access/inclusion on top client matters.		✓	
Increase the business development opportunities available to minority lawyers		✓	

Recruitment – New Associates

Does your firm annually recruit at any of the following types of institutions? (Check all that apply and list the schools).

Ivy League schools: Harvard University, Yale University, Columbia University, University of Pennsylvania

Public state schools: University of Georgia, University of Texas, University of Tennessee, University of South Carolina, University of North Carolina, University of Virginia, University of Michigan, University of California-Berkeley, Georgia State University

Private schools: Duke University, Vanderbilt University, Stanford University, Emory University, Wake Forest University, University of Chicago, NYU

Historically Black Colleges and Universities (HBCUs): Howard University

Do you have any special outreach efforts directed to encourage minority law students to consider your firm?

• *Distribute a Diversity Brochure which documents the firm's commitment to diversity.*

• Advertise in minority law student association publication(s)

• Participate in/host minority law student job fair(s)

• Sponsor minority law student association events

• Firm's lawyers participate on career panels at school

• Outreach to leadership of minority student organizations

• Scholarships or intern/fellowships for minority students

SUMMER ASSOCIATE STATISTICS: SUMMER 2003	MINORITY MEN	MINORITY WOMEN	WHITE WOMEN	TOTAL
Summer associates	11	14	32	91
Summer associates who received an offer of full-time employment	6	12	29	72
Summer associates who accepted an offer of full-time employment*	5	11	15	52

* Declines include summer associates who accepted judicial clerkships and were unable to accept offers of full-time employment with Alston & Bird by reason of judge's requirements.

Recruitment – Lateral Associates and Partners

What activities does the firm undertake to attract minority and women attorneys?

• Partner programs with women and minority bar associations

• Participate at minority job fairs

• Seek referrals from other attorneys

Do you use executive recruiting/search firms to seek to identify new diversity hires (partners or associates)?

Yes

If yes, list all women- and/or minority-owned executive search/recruiting firms to which the firm paid a fee for placement services in the past 12 months:

Our records do not include information about the ownership of search firms engaged by this firm.

LATERAL ASSOCIATES AND PARTNERS: 1/1/03 – 12/31/03	MINORITY MEN	MINORITY WOMEN	WHITE WOMEN	TOTAL
Number of lateral associate hires	1	2	5	10
Number of lateral partner hires (equity and non-equity)	2	0	0	7
Number of new partners (equity and non-equity) promoted from associate rank	1	2	4	21
Number of new equity partners	1	1	3	13

Retention & Professional Development

ATTORNEYS WHO LEFT THE FIRM: 2003	MINORITY MEN	MINORITY WOMEN	WHITE WOMEN	TOTAL
Number of attorneys who voluntarily or involuntarily left your firm's employ in 2003	2	1	27	54

How do 2003 attrition rates generally compare to those experienced in the prior year period?

About the same as in prior years

Please identify the specific steps you are taking to reduce the attrition rate of minority and women attorneys.

• Develop and/or support internal employee affinity groups (e.g., minority or women networks within the firm)
• Increase/review compensation relative to competition
• Increase/improve current work/life programs
• Work with minority and women attorneys to develop career advancement plans
• Introduce minority and women attorneys to key clients, including to lead engagements
• Review work assignments and hours billed to key client matters to make sure minority and women attorneys are not being excluded
• Strengthen mentoring program for all attorneys, including minorities and women

Does your firm have part-time/flex-time policies that permit attorneys (male or female) to work alternative schedules?

Yes

What impact, if any, will the decision to work part-time have on an attorney's ability to make partner or, if already a partner, to remain a partner at your firm?

Associates are permitted to work reduced hours for up to two years and remain eligible for partnership consideration upon their return to full-time practice.

Have any attorneys who chose to work a part-time schedule made partner at your firm?

Yes. Our records do not enable us to quantify the number with confidence.

Management Demographic Profile (as of 12/31/03)

	MINORITY MEN	MINORITY WOMEN	WHITE WOMEN	TOTAL
Number of attorneys on the Executive/Management Committee or equivalent	0	1	1	11
Number of attorneys on the Hiring Committee or equivalent	4	6	25	77
Number of attorneys on the Partner/Associate Review Committee or equivalent	1	2	11	33

Please provide information regarding all minority and women attorneys who head offices or practice groups of your law firm:

Minorities heading practice groups: Karol Mason, Public Finance

Women heading practice groups: Karol Mason, Public Finance; Janine Brown, Technology; Donna Bergeson, Regulatory Healthcare; Martha Barber, Trademark; Laura Owens, Products Liability; Pinney Allen, Tax

The Firm Says

Establishing accountability

We have designated a senior partner, John Latham, with responsibility for supporting and enhancing (not just monitoring) diversity. John reports directly to the firm's managing partner and chairs a 23-member Diversity Committee, comprising attorneys and staff from all five offices, responsible for implementing an established firm policy for diversity enhancement. The Diversity Committee meets monthly and its efforts are funded through a pre-approved budgeting process.

In 2003 every partner, associate and staff member attended an educational session on diversity management conducted by Roosevelt Thomas Consulting & Training (RTCT), experts in the diversity and diversity management field. We continue to work with RTCT in the development of more comprehensive and focused diversity educational programs that will be offered to our attorneys and staff in the future.

The firm's professional personnel partner, Jon Lowe, is a key member of the Diversity Committee. Jon is the partner at the firm primarily responsible for attorney recruitment and attorney professional development.

Each of our practice group leaders is held accountable by the firm's management for the diversity enhancement efforts of her or his practice group, and the success or failure of these efforts directly impacts the evaluation and compensation decisions for our practice group leaders.

Achieving results in every area

• Alston & Bird's workplace environment has been praised as one of the most open and receptive in the United States, not only among law firms, but also among all businesses. In each of the last four years, Fortune magazine has recognized Alston & Bird as one of the "100 Best Companies to Work For" in the United States. This year we are ranked second, and we are the only law firm ever to make the top 10 for three consecutive years.

• Of our 21 partners elected for 2004, six are women. Two of these women are minorities.

• The firm received the 2004 Ally Award from the Georgia Commission on Women (a state agency) recognizing the firm's "support of women, their issues and their work environment."

• Women and minorities lead six of our practice areas: health care-regulatory, IP-trademarks and copyrights, products liability, public finance, tax and technology.

• Minority and women partners continue to serve in leadership roles within Alston & Bird:

• In 2001, Pinney Allen, tax group coordinator, was elected to chair the firm's governing body, the Partners' Committee.

• In 2003, Bernard Taylor, an African-American partner and a highly regarded litigator, was elected chair of the firm's Partners' Committee.

Selected external initiatives

• This year, our diversity partner was a featured panelist at the ABA Commission on Racial and Ethnic Diversity in the Profession's meeting in Philadelphia and will serve as a panelist at the commission meeting in Atlanta this August, where he will speak on "15 Tips for Retaining Minority Lawyers."

• Alston & Bird is a founding member of the Atlanta Large Law Firm Diversity Alliance and our diversity partner and firm will be active in the Alliance during 2004-2005.

• Alston & Bird is a sponsor of the Minority Corporate Counsel Association.

• Alston & Bird is a sponsor of the National Bar Association and the Hispanic and Asian Bar Associations. One of our partners, Luis Aguilar, is on the Executive Committee of the Hispanic Bar Association and has been nominated to serve as president-elect.

• Alston & Bird sponsors "Charting Your Own Course," a program which provides a unique opportunity to bring minority in-house counsel and outside lawyers together.

Andrews Kurth LLP

600 Travis, Suite 4200
Houston, TX 77002
Phone: (713) 220-4200
Fax: (713) 220-4285

FIRM LEADERSHIP

Managing Partner: Howard T. Ayers, Co-Chair
Diversity Team Leader: Jonathan S. Day, Co-Chair

LOCATIONS

Houston, TX (HQ)
Austin, TX
Dallas, TX
The Woodlands, TX
Los Angeles, CA
New York, NY
Washington, DC
London

LAW FIRM DEMOGRAPHIC PROFILES

FULL-TIME ASSOCIATES	2003	2002
Minority men	10	6
Minority women	10	11
White women	55	51
Total	164	155

SUMMER ASSOCIATES	2003	2002
Minority men	3	3
Minority women	1	2
White women	17	28
Total	34	53

EQUITY PARTNERS	2003	2002
Minority men	4	7
Minority women	3	3
White women	20	19
Total	135	132

NON-EQUITY PARTNERS	2003	2002
Minority men	4	0
Minority women	0	0
White women	8	4
Total	45	12

NEW HIRES	2003	2002
Minority men	6	1
Minority women	2	3
White women	20	22
Total	77	57

Strategic Plan and Diversity Leadership

How does the firm's leadership communicate the importance of diversity to everyone at the firm? (e.g., e-mails, web site, newsletters, meetings, etc.)

Through e-mails, web site postings, and written and oral communications from our managing partner, we announce and celebrate our diversity initiatives.

Who has primary responsibility for leading diversity initiatives at your firm?

Howard T. Ayers, managing partner

**Does your law firm currently have a diversity committee? **

Yes

Does the committee's representation include one or more members of the firm's management/executive committee (or the equivalent)?

Yes

How many attorneys are on the committee, and in 2003, what was the total number of hours collectively spent by the committee in furtherance of the firm's diversity initiatives?

Total attorneys on committee: 13

Total hours spent on diversity: 500+

Does the committee and/or diversity leader establish and set goals or objectives consistent with management's priorities?

Yes

Has the firm undertaken a formal or informal diversity program or set of initiatives aimed at increasing the diversity of the firm?

Yes, formal

How often does the firm's management review the firm's diversity progress/results?

Annually

How is the firm's diversity committee and/or firm management held accountable for achieving results?

As part of the annual evaluation of the performance of the firm's leaders.

LAW FIRM DIVERSITY INITIATIVES	ALREADY COMPLETED	CURRENTLY ADDRESSING	NOT A CURRENT PRIORITY
Undertake communication from firm management that diversity is a top priority of the firm.		✓	
Formalize diversity plan and committee with action steps and accountability to management.		✓	
Conduct firm-wide diversity training for all attorneys and staff.		✓	
Increase the number of minority attorneys at the associate level.		✓	
Increase the number of minority attorneys at the partnership level.		✓	
Develop/expand relationships with minority bar associations to offer firm's support of these networks.		✓	
Focus on strengthening firm's mentoring program, including for benefit of minority attorneys.		✓	
Conduct internal diversity needs assessment and/or retain diversity consultant to examine how firm culture might be more welcoming of minorities.			
Support law firm's internal affinity networks (e.g., women, minority attorney networks).		✓	
Manage/monitor allocation of work assignments and/or hours billed to ensure women and minority attorneys have equal access/inclusion on top client matters.		✓	

Recruitment - New Associates

Does your firm annually recruit at any of the following types of institutions? (Check all that apply and list the schools).

Ivy League schools: Columbia University, Cornell University, Harvard University, Yale University

Public state schools: George Washington University, New York University, University of Texas at Austin, University of Chicago, University of Houston, University of Virginia, College of William & Mary

Private schools: Baylor University, Brooklyn Law School, Duke University, Emory University, Fordham University, Georgetown University, Pace University, Southern Methodist University, South Texas College of Law, Stanford University, Tulane University, Vanderbilt University, Wake Forest University, Washington & Lee University

Historically Black Colleges and Universities (HBCUs): Texas Southern University

Do you have any special outreach efforts directed to encourage minority law students to consider your firm?

• Participate in/host minority law student job fair(s)
• Sponsor minority law student association events
• Scholarships or intern/fellowships for minority students

MINORITY CORPORATE COUNSEL ASSOCIATION

SUMMER ASSOCIATE STATISTICS: SUMMER 2003	MINORITY MEN	MINORITY WOMEN	WHITE WOMEN	TOTAL
Summer associates	1	1	13	24
Summer associates who received an offer of full-time employment	1	1	10	19
Summer associates who accepted an offer of full-time employment	0	1	6	9

Recruitment – Lateral Associates and Partners

What activities does the firm undertake to attract minority and women attorneys?

• *We encourage minority and women candidates for lateral attorney positions as part of our regular lateral recruiting process.*

• Seek referrals from other attorneys

Do you use executive recruiting/search firms to seek to identify new diversity hires (partners or associates)?

No

LATERAL ASSOCIATES AND PARTNERS: 1/1/03 – 12/31/03	MINORITY MEN	MINORITY WOMEN	WHITE WOMEN	TOTAL
Number of lateral associate hires	1	2	5	19
Number of lateral partner hires (equity and non-equity)	0	0	2	20
Number of new partners (equity and non-equity) promoted from associate rank	2	0	2	17
Number of new equity partners	0	0	0	0

Retention & Professional Development

ATTORNEYS WHO LEFT THE FIRM: 2003	MINORITY MEN	MINORITY WOMEN	WHITE WOMEN	TOTAL
Number of attorneys who voluntarily or involuntarily left your firm's employ in 2003	2	3	12	33

How do 2003 attrition rates generally compare to those experienced in the prior year period?

Lower than in prior years

Please identify the specific steps you are taking to reduce the attrition rate of minority and women attorneys.

• Develop and/or support internal employee affinity groups (e.g., minority or women networks within the firm)

• Increase/review compensation relative to competition

• Increase/improve current work/life programs

• Succession plan includes emphasis on diversity

• Work with minority and women attorneys to develop career advancement plans

• Introduce minority and women attorneys to key clients, including to lead engagements

• Strengthen mentoring program for all attorneys, including minorities and women

• Professional skills development program, including minority and women attorneys

Does your firm have part-time/flex-time policies that permit attorneys (male or female) to work alternative schedules?

Yes

What impact, if any, will the decision to work part-time have on an attorney's ability to make partner or, if already a partner, to remain a partner at your firm?

For associates, the individual remains on track for partnership, but partnership consideration likely will be deferred to account for slower accumulation of experience. For partners, there is no impact on partnership status.

Have any attorneys who chose to work a part-time schedule made partner at your firm?

No. Our Flex-path program is too new. Candidates are progressing through the program now and we expect that most will become partners.

Management Demographic Profile (as of 12/31/03)

	MINORITY MEN	MINORITY WOMEN	WHITE WOMEN	TOTAL
Number of attorneys on the Executive/Management Committee or equivalent	2	1	2	18
Number of attorneys on the Hiring Committee or equivalent	2	2	3	14
Number of attorneys on the Partner/Associate Review Committee or equivalent	0/0*	1/1*	2/6*	16/22*

Partner Review Committee/Associate Review Committee

Please provide information regarding all minority and women attorneys who head offices or practice groups of your law firm:

Women heading offices: Lynne Uniman, New York Office Managing Partner

Minorities heading practice groups: Gene Locke, Public Law

Women heading practice groups: Rosemarie Donnelly, Litigation; Mary Bearden, Health Law; Bennee Jones, Employment Law; Melinda Brunger, Corporate Compliance (Sarbanes Oxley)

Arent Fox PLLC

1050 Connecticut Avenue, N.W.
Washington, DC 20036-5339
Phone: (202) 857-6000
Fax: (202) 857-6395

FIRM LEADERSHIP

Managing Partner: William R. Charyk
Diversity Team Leader: Henry Morris, Partner

LOCATIONS

Washington, DC (HQ)
New York, NY

LAW FIRM DEMOGRAPHIC PROFILES

FULL-TIME ASSOCIATES	2003	2002
Minority men	9	11
Minority women	19	14
White women	47	43
Total	144	130

SUMMER ASSOCIATES	2003	2002
Minority men	1	2
Minority women	4	5
White women	7	8
Total	19	19

EQUITY PARTNERS	2003	2002
Minority men	1	2
Minority women	1	1
White women	13	11
Total	92	91

NON-EQUITY PARTNERS	2003	2002
Minority men	1	1
Minority women	1	1
White women	8	6
Total	32	31

NEW HIRES	2003	2002
Minority men	2	5
Minority women	10	5
White women	17	6
Total	52	38

MINORITY CORPORATE COUNSEL ASSOCIATION

Strategic Plan and Diversity Leadership

How does the firm's leadership communicate the importance of diversity to everyone at the firm? (e.g., e-mails, web site, newsletters, meetings, etc.)

All attorney e-mails; web site; policy statements

Who has primary responsibility for leading diversity initiatives at your firm?

Henry Morris, partner

Does your law firm currently have a diversity committee?

Yes

Does the committee's representation include one or more members of the firm's management/executive committee (or the equivalent)?

Yes

Does the committee and/or diversity leader establish and set goals or objectives consistent with management's priorities?

Yes

Has the firm undertaken a formal or informal diversity program or set of initiatives aimed at increasing the diversity of the firm?

Yes, informal

How often does the firm's management review the firm's diversity progress/results?

Annually

LAW FIRM DIVERSITY INITIATIVES	ALREADY COMPLETED	CURRENTLY ADDRESSING	NOT A CURRENT PRIORITY
Undertake communication from firm management that diversity is a top priority of the firm.		✓	
Formalize diversity plan and committee with action steps and accountability to management.		✓	
Conduct firm-wide diversity training for all attorneys and staff.		✓	
Increase the number of minority attorneys at the associate level.		✓	
Increase the number of minority attorneys at the partnership level.		✓	
Develop/expand relationships with minority bar associations to offer firm's support of these networks.		✓	
Focus on strengthening firm's mentoring program, including for benefit of minority attorneys.		✓	
Conduct internal diversity needs assessment and/or retain diversity consultant to examine how firm culture might be more welcoming of minorities.		✓	
Support law firm's internal affinity networks (e.g., women, minority attorney networks).		✓	
Manage/monitor allocation of work assignments and/or hours billed to ensure women and minority attorneys have equal access/inclusion on top client matters.		✓	

Recruitment – New Associates

Does your firm annually recruit at any of the following types of institutions? (Check all that apply and list the schools).

Ivy League schools: Harvard University, Columbia University, Cornell University, University of Pennsylvania

Public state schools: University of Virginia, University of Maryland, College of William & Mary, George Mason University, University of North Carolina, University of Michigan

Private schools: American University, Emory University, Fordham University, Georgetown University, George Washington University, Duke University, Vanderbilt University, Boston University, Boston College, Northwestern University, New York University

Historically Black Colleges and Universities (HBCUs): Howard University

Do you have any special outreach efforts directed to encourage minority law students to consider your firm?

• Hold a reception for minority law students
• Participate in/host minority law student job fair(s)
• Sponsor minority law student association events
• Firm's lawyers participate on career panels at school
• Outreach to leadership of minority student organizations
• Scholarships or intern/fellowships for minority students

SUMMER ASSOCIATE STATISTICS: SUMMER 2003	MINORITY MEN	MINORITY WOMEN	WHITE WOMEN	TOTAL
Summer associates	1	4	7	19
Summer associates who received an offer of full-time employment	0	2	7	15
Summer associates who accepted an offer of full-time employment	0	1	7	13

Recruitment – Lateral Associates and Partners

What activities does the firm undertake to attract minority and women attorneys?

• Partner programs with women and minority bar associations
• Participate at minority job fairs
• Seek referrals from other attorneys
• Utilize online job services (e.g., MCCA/DuPont Primary Law Firm Job Bank)

Do you use executive recruiting/search firms to seek to identify new diversity hires (partners or associates)?

Yes

If yes, list all women- and/or minority-owned executive search/recruiting firms to which the firm paid a fee for placement services in the past 12 months:

Carter White & Shaw, LLC

LATERAL ASSOCIATES AND PARTNERS: 1/1/03 – 12/31/03	MINORITY MEN	MINORITY WOMEN	WHITE WOMEN	TOTAL
Number of lateral associate hires	2	10	15	35
Number of lateral partner hires (equity and non-equity)	0	0	2	13
Number of new partners (equity and non-equity) promoted from associate rank	0	0	2	2
Number of new equity partners	0	0	1	2

Retention & Professional Development

ATTORNEYS WHO LEFT THE FIRM: 2003	MINORITY MEN	MINORITY WOMEN	WHITE WOMEN	TOTAL
Number of attorneys who voluntarily or involuntarily left your firm's employ in 2003	3	4	7	32

How do 2003 attrition rates generally compare to those experienced in the prior year period?

Lower than in prior years

Please identify the specific steps you are taking to reduce the attrition rate of minority and women attorneys.

• Develop and/or support internal employee affinity groups (e.g., minority or women networks within the firm)
• Increase/review compensation relative to competition
• Introduce minority and women attorneys to key clients, including to lead engagements
• Review work assignments and hours billed to key client matters to make sure minority and women attorneys are not being excluded
• Strengthen mentoring program for all attorneys, including minorities and women
• Professional skills development program, including minority and women attorneys

Does your firm have part-time/flex-time policies that permit attorneys (male or female) to work alternative schedules?

Yes

Have any attorneys who chose to work a part-time schedule made partner at your firm?

Yes, two attorneys.

Management Demographic Profile (as of 12/31/03)

	MINORITY MEN	MINORITY WOMEN	WHITE WOMEN	TOTAL
Number of attorneys on the Executive/Management Committee or equivalent	0	0	1	9
Number of attorneys on the Hiring Committee or equivalent	1	2	5	13
Number of attorneys on the Partner/Associate Review Committee or equivalent	0	0	1	6

Women heading practice groups: Elizabeth Cohen, Trademark; Barbara Wahl, Commercial Litigation; Mary Jo Dowd, Bankruptcy and Financial Restructuring; Larri Short, Life Sciences; Suzy Hung, Immigration; Quana Jew, Chair, Employment Committee; Joanne Schehl, Chair, Professional Development; Deanne Ottaviano, Chair, Pro Bono Committee

The Firm Says

Arent Fox is proud that its commitment to diversity has been recognized in recent Vault rankings. We have achieved an exciting atmosphere in which teamwork and strategic initiatives are encouraged and rewarded. A high priority for the next 12 months will be working with the very impressive talent we have attracted among our minority attorneys so as to actualize their entrepreneurial potential and enable them to envision and achieve satisfying career goals.

We continue to sponsor a number of receptions, bar association events and diversity clerkship opportunities, all of which are designed to increase our profile in the area of diversity and promote the message that we want to attract minority candidates who will share our vision of strategic growth.

Arnold & Porter LLP

555 12th Street, NW
Washington, DC 20004
Phone: (202) 942-5000
Fax: (202) 942-5999

FIRM LEADERSHIP

Managing Partner: James Sandman, Managing
Partner
Diversity Team Leader: William Cook, Partner

LOCATIONS

Washington, DC (HQ)
Denver, CO
Los Angeles, CA
McLean, VA
New York, NY
Brussels
London.

LAW FIRM DEMOGRAPHIC PROFILES

FULL-TIME ASSOCIATES	2003	2002
Minority men	43	39
Minority women	44	45
White women	131	124
Total	393	388

SUMMER ASSOCIATES	2003	2002
Minority men	11	14
Minority women	9	17
White women	20	20
Total	62*	75*

We had five pre-clerk summer associates in 2002 and 2003

EQUITY PARTNERS	2003	2002
Minority men	8	8
Minority women	4	4
White women	36	35
Total	237	231

NEW HIRES	2003	2002
Minority men	10	10
Minority women	15	7
White women	22	32
Total	81	94

Strategic Plan and Diversity Leadership

How does the firm's leadership communicate the importance of diversity to everyone at the firm? (e.g., e-mails, web site, newsletters, meetings, etc.)

E-mails, speeches, training, web site and brochures.

Who has primary responsibility for leading diversity initiatives at your firm?

James Sandman, managing partner

Does your law firm currently have a diversity committee?

Yes

Does the committee and/or diversity leader establish and set goals or objectives consistent with management's priorities?

Yes

Has the firm undertaken a formal or informal diversity program or set of initiatives aimed at increasing the diversity of the firm?

Yes, formal

How often does the firm's management review the firm's diversity progress/results?

Monthly

How is the firm's diversity committee and/or firm management held accountable for achieving results?

Results are reported regularly to the partners of the firm.

LAW FIRM DIVERSITY INITIATIVES	ALREADY COMPLETED	CURRENTLY ADDRESSING	NOT A CURRENT PRIORITY
Undertake communication from firm management that diversity is a top priority of the firm.	✓		
Formalize diversity plan and committee with action steps and accountability to management.		✓	
Conduct firm-wide diversity training for all attorneys and staff.	✓	✓	
Increase the number of minority attorneys at the associate level.	✓	✓	
Increase the number of minority attorneys at the partnership level.	✓	✓	
Develop/expand relationships with minority bar associations to offer firm's support of these networks.	✓	✓	
Focus on strengthening firm's mentoring program, including for benefit of minority attorneys.	✓	✓	
Conduct internal diversity needs assessment and/or retain diversity consultant to examine how firm culture might be more welcoming of minorities.	✓		
Support law firm's internal affinity networks (e.g., women, minority attorney networks).	✓	✓	
Manage/monitor allocation of work assignments and/or hours billed to ensure women and minority attorneys have equal access/inclusion on top client matters.	✓	✓	
Solicit feedback from the firm's internal affinity networks		✓	

Recruitment – New Associates

Does your firm annually recruit at any of the following types of institutions? (Check all that apply and list the schools).

Ivy League schools: Columbia University, Cornell University, Harvard University, University of Pennsylvania, Yale University

Public state schools: University of California-Boalt Hall, University of California-Davis, University of California-Hastings, UCLA, Indiana University, University of Michigan, University of Virginia, University of Minnesota, University of North Carolina, University of Iowa, University of Maryland, University of Texas, College of William & Mary, George Mason University, University of Colorado

Private schools: Boston University, Brooklyn Law School, Northwestern University, Brigham Young University, Wake Forest University, University of Denver, Georgetown University, New York University, Stanford University, Fordham University, Benjamin Cardozo School of Law, American University, Emory University, George Washington University, Duke University, University of Chicago, Vanderbilt University, Washington and Lee University, Washington University in St. Louis, Catholic University of America, Franklin Pierce Law Center, Syracuse University, Thomas Jefferson School of Law, Tulane University, University of Notre Dame, University of Southern California

Historically Black Colleges and Universities (HBCUs): Howard University

Do you have any special outreach efforts directed to encourage minority law students to consider your firm?

• Hold a reception for minority law students
• Advertise in minority law student association publication(s)
• Participate in/host minority law student job fair(s)
• Sponsor minority law student association events
• Firm's lawyers participate on career panels at school
• Outreach to leadership of minority student organizations
• Scholarships for minority students

SUMMER ASSOCIATE STATISTICS: SUMMER 2003	MINORITY MEN	MINORITY WOMEN	WHITE WOMEN	TOTAL
Summer associates	10	7	19	55
Summer associates who received an offer of full-time employment	8	7	19	52
Summer associates who accepted an offer of full-time employment	5	5	14	34

Recruitment – Lateral Associates and Partners

What activities does the firm undertake to attract minority and women attorneys?

• Participate in minority job fairs
• Seek referrals from attorneys in the firm

Do you use executive recruiting/search firms to seek to identify new diversity hires (partners or associates)?

Yes

LATERAL ASSOCIATES AND PARTNERS: 1/1/03 – 12/31/03	MINORITY MEN	MINORITY WOMEN	WHITE WOMEN	TOTAL
Number of lateral associate hires	2	2	0	7
Number of lateral partner hires (equity and non-equity)	0	0	0	2
Number of new partners (equity and non-equity) promoted from associate rank	0	0	0	5
Number of new equity partners	0	0	0	5

Retention & Professional Development

ATTORNEYS WHO LEFT THE FIRM: 2003	MINORITY MEN	MINORITY WOMEN	WHITE WOMEN	TOTAL
Number of attorneys who voluntarily or involuntarily left your firm's employ in 2003	6	15	20	79

How do 2003 attrition rates generally compare to those experienced in the prior year period?

About the same as in prior years

Please identify the specific steps you are taking to reduce the attrition rate of minority and women attorneys.

• *Provide access ato and pay for networking activities outside the firm.*
• Develop and/or support internal employee affinity groups (e.g., minority or women networks within the firm)
• Increase/improve current work/life programs
• Work with minority and women attorneys to develop career advancement plans
• Introduce minority and women attorneys to key clients, including to lead engagements
• Review work assignments and hours billed to key client matters to make sure minority and women attorneys are not being excluded
• Strengthen mentoring program for all attorneys, including minorities and women
• Professional skills development program, including minority and women attorneys

Does your firm have part-time/flex-time policies that permit attorneys (male or female) to work alternative schedules?

Yes

What impact, if any, will the decision to work part-time have on an attorney's ability to make partner or, if already a partner, to remain a partner at your firm?

Part-time associates are eligible for election to the partnership. Working part-time may extend the period before an associate is elected partner. We have a number of part-time partners.

Have any attorneys who chose to work a part-time schedule made partner at your firm?

Yes, at least 3 attorneys.

Management Demographic Profile (as of 12/31/03)

	MINORITY MEN	MINORITY WOMEN	WHITE WOMEN	TOTAL
Number of attorneys on the Executive/Management Committee or equivalent	0	0	1	3
Number of attorneys on the Hiring Committee or equivalent	6	4	15	52
Number of attorneys on the Partner/Associate Review Committee or equivalent	1	2	5	23
Number of attorneys on the Policy Committee	0	0	3	15

Please provide information regarding all minority and women attorneys who head offices or practice groups of your law firm:

Minorities heading offices: Michael Oshima, Administrative Partner, New York

Women heading offices: Marleen VanKerckhove, Brussels

Women heading practice groups: Ellen Reisman, Products Liability

The Firm Says

Arnold & Porter LLP has been honored by the Minority Corporate Counsel Association seven times for our commitment to diversity – more than any other firm in the U.S. We are the only law firm ever to be designated an "Employer of Choice" by the MCCA and have received MCCA's Thomas L. Sager Award six times. We were recognized once again as one of the top firms for diversity in the United States in the 2005 Vault Guide to the Top 100 Law Firms. We ranked No. 4 nationwide for overall diversity, No. 4 for minority diversity, No. 12 for gender diversity and No. 8 in diversity, for gays/lesbians.

The firm actively supports our self-formed affinity group of lawyers of color, called "Minorities at Arnold & Porter," or MAP. MAP members assist the Hiring Committee in working with minority law student associations and placement offices and participate in a number of career development programs and job fairs. We have a minority recruitment brochure, which is distributed on-campus to encourage minority law students to apply to our firm, and we devote 25 percent of our general recruitment brochure to diversity. We have a "Diversity" section on our website.

We have distributed brochures to clients with practice profiles of our women and minority partners and counsel. This information is also available on the "Diversity" section of our website. We recognize that diversity is important to our clients, and we work to have diverse teams of attorneys work on our clients' matters.

During the fall recruitment season, we hold a panel discussion, reception and dinner in Washington for all minority law students to whom we have offered associate or summer associate positions. We pay the expenses of everyone who comes and invite minority law students with offers from all of our domestic offices, not just Washington, to underscore our firm-wide interest in promoting diversity. Arnold & Porter provides two scholarships for minority law students at each of 12 law schools nationwide. The firm holds a luncheon reception in each of our offices for local recipients of the scholarship awards.

Our director of professional development is working with MAP to enhance training, mentoring and career. Earlier this year, we hired a career development specialist to assist all lawyers in all of our offices on career development and advancement matters. Arnold & Porter is partnering with another law firm to develop and coordinate for all Washington minority lawyers a quarterly "Minority Networking Series" to commence in 2005. This year we gave all our African American attorneys the opportunity to attend a professional development conference entitled "Charting Your Own Course." We also sponsored the conference.

We also have a group, "Women at Arnold & Porter," or WAP, for women to discuss issues common to them. Both MAP and WAP work to help the firm identify ways in which we can increase the recruitment and retention of minorities and women. The firm supports their efforts and funds periodic lunches to promote collegiality. These groups have helped to foster informal mentoring relationships. WAP holds breakfasts during the summer for women attorneys and summer associates. MAP hosts a reception each year at the home of one of our minority partners for our minority attorneys and summer associates.

We actively recruit gay and lesbian lawyers. We reach out to gay and lesbian law student associations to inform them of our commitment to inclusion and diversity. We have a number of openly gay and lesbian partners and associates and support their networking and social events.

We consider facilitating work/life balance an important part of promoting diversity, and we try to be a leader in this area. We have appeared five times on Working Mother magazine's list of the "100 Best Companies for Working Mothers." The firm has an on-site Children's Center in our Washington office that offers full- or part-time child care for employees' children on a space-available basis, as well as free back-up emergency child care. We also have arrangements with child care facilities in New York, Los Angeles, and Northern Virginia to assist with emergency back-up child care needs for employees in those offices. The firm offers women 12 weeks of paid maternity leave and additional leave under FMLA. We also have six weeks of paid parental leave and offer adoption assistance for all employees.

We have a part-time work policy that our lawyers really use. More than 8 percent of the attorneys in all of our offices work part time. We have designated a partner to serve as an advisor and facilitator for lawyers who are considering working or are currently working part-time. This partner works part time herself and uses the Children's Center for her two children.

Women and/or minority attorneys serve on many of the firm's committees. Women serve as chair and vice-chair of our Hiring Committee. The executive director and chief financial officer of the firm is a woman, as are a majority of the directors for the various administrative departments in all our offices.

The firm has an extensive diversity training program in which participation is mandatory for all lawyers and staff.

Our work environment was recognized this year by our inclusion as one of only three law firms on Fortune's 2004 list of the "100 Best Companies to Work For." We also appeared on Fortune's 2003 list. We are on The American Lawyer's "A-List" of law firms, which takes account of a firm's diversity, pro bono commitment and associate development, in addition to financial success.

We try to manage our firm in a way that promotes the treatment of every person with dignity and respect, values the contribution that each person makes as an individual, eschews all stereotypes, enables our colleagues to be comfortable being themselves and permits every person to realize his or her potential. Our diversity has made Arnold & Porter a stronger and a better law firm.

Baker & Daniels

300 North Meridian Street, Suite 2700
Indianapolis, IN 46204
Phone: (317) 237-0300
Fax: (317) 237-1000

FIRM LEADERSHIP

Managing Partner: Brian K. Burke, Firm
Managing Partner
Diversity Team Leader: Brian K. Burke, Firm
Managing Partner

LOCATIONS

Elkhart, IN
Fort Wayne, IN
Indianapolis, IN
South Bend, IN
Washington, DC
Beijing, China
Qingdao, China

LAW FIRM DEMOGRAPHIC PROFILES

FULL-TIME ASSOCIATES	2003	2002
Minority men	8	10
Minority women	5	5
White women	63	63
Total	136	137

SUMMER ASSOCIATES	2003	2002
Minority men	2	1
Minority women	1	3
White women	7	8
Total	25	23

EQUITY PARTNERS	2003	2002
Minority men	4	5
Minority women	0	0
White women	16	16
Total	137	138

NEW HIRES	2003	2002
Minority men	1	5
Minority women	1	5
White women	9	7
Total	30	25

Strategic Plan and Diversity Leadership

How does the firm's leadership communicate the importance of diversity to everyone at the firm? (e.g., e-mails, web site, newsletters, meetings, etc.)

Meetings

Who has primary responsibility for leading diversity initiatives at your firm?

Brian K. Burke, firm managing partner

Does your law firm currently have a diversity committee?

Yes

Does the committee's representation include one or more members of the firm's management/executive committee (or the equivalent)?

Yes

How many attorneys are on the committee, and in 2003, what was the total number of hours collectively spent by the committee in furtherance of the firm's diversity initiatives?

Total attorneys on committee: 6

Total hours spent on diversity: N/A. The Diversity Committee is a 2004 Initiative.

Does the committee and/or diversity leader establish and set goals or objectives consistent with management's priorities?

Yes

Has the firm undertaken a formal or informal diversity program or set of initiatives aimed at increasing the diversity of the firm?

Yes, informal, prior to 2004.

How often does the firm's management review the firm's diversity progress/results?

Quarterly

LAW FIRM DIVERSITY INITIATIVES	ALREADY COMPLETED	CURRENTLY ADDRESSING	NOT A CURRENT PRIORITY
Undertake communication from firm management that diversity is a top priority of the firm.		✓	
Formalize diversity plan and committee with action steps and accountability to management.		✓	
Conduct firm-wide diversity training for all attorneys and staff.		✓	
Increase the number of minority attorneys at the associate level.		✓	
Increase the number of minority attorneys at the partnership level.		✓	
Develop/expand relationships with minority bar associations to offer firm's support of these networks.		✓	
Focus on strengthening firm's mentoring program, including for benefit of minority attorneys.		✓	
Conduct internal diversity needs assessment and/or retain diversity consultant to examine how firm culture might be more welcoming of minorities.		✓	
Support law firm's internal affinity networks (e.g., women, minority attorney networks).		✓	
Manage/monitor allocation of work assignments and/or hours billed to ensure women and minority attorneys have equal access/inclusion on top client matters.		✓	

Recruitment - New Associates

Does your firm annually recruit at any of the following types of institutions? (Check all that apply and list the schools).*

Public state schools: Indiana University, University of Illinois, University of Michigan, Michigan State University

Private schools: Duke University, University of Notre Dame, Valparaiso University, Vanderbilt University

Historically Black Colleges and Universities (HBCUs): Howard University

*Note: Answer assumes "annually recruit" refers to participation in on-campus interview programs. Baker & Daniels does solicit resumes from law schools not identified above.

Of the law schools that you listed above, do you have any special outreach efforts directed to encourage minority law students to consider your firm?

• Participate in/host minority law student job fair(s)

• Firm's lawyers participate on career panels at school

• Outreach to leadership of minority student organizations

SUMMER ASSOCIATE STATISTICS: SUMMER 2003	MINORITY MEN	MINORITY WOMEN	WHITE WOMEN	TOTAL
Summer associates	1	1	6	14
Summer associates who received an offer of full-time employment	0	0	6	12
Summer associates who accepted an offer of full-time employment	0	0	5	10

Recruitment – Lateral Associates and Partners

What activities does the firm undertake to attract minority and women attorneys?

• Participate at minority job fairs

• Seek referrals from other attorneys

Do you use executive recruiting/search firms to seek to identify new diversity hires (partners or associates)?

No

LATERAL ASSOCIATES AND PARTNERS: 1/1/03 – 12/31/03	MINORITY MEN	MINORITY WOMEN	WHITE WOMEN	TOTAL
Number of lateral associate hires	1	0	3	12
Number of lateral partner hires (equity and non-equity)	0	0	1	4
Number of new partners (equity and non-equity) promoted from associate rank	0	0	1	4
Number of new equity partners	0	0	0	0

Retention & Professional Development

ATTORNEYS WHO LEFT THE FIRM: 2003	MINORITY MEN	MINORITY WOMEN	WHITE WOMEN	TOTAL
Number of attorneys who voluntarily or involuntarily left your firm's employ in 2003	3	1	13	26

How do 2003 attrition rates generally compare to those experienced in the prior year period?

Higher than in prior years

Please identify the specific steps you are taking to reduce the attrition rate of minority and women attorneys.

See narrative response.

Does your firm have part-time/flex-time policies that permit attorneys (male or female) to work alternative schedules?

Yes. See narrative response.

What impact, if any, will the decision to work part-time have on an attorney's ability to make partner or, if already a partner, to remain a partner at your firm?

Though attorneys with a reduced hours partner-track arrangement have a longer track (depending on the amount of the reduction from the standard goal), there is no other consequence of a reduced hours arrangement.

Have any attorneys who chose to work a part-time schedule made partner at your firm?

Yes, five attorneys.

Management Demographic Profile (as of 12/31/03)

	MINORITY MEN	MINORITY WOMEN	WHITE WOMEN	TOTAL
Number of attorneys on the Executive/Management Committee or equivalent	0	0	1	11
Number of attorneys on the Hiring Committee or equivalent	0	1	2	10
Number of attorneys on the Partner/Associate Review Committee or equivalent	N/A	N/A	N/A	N/A

The Firm Says

Baker & Daniels encourages, supports and values diversity and equal employment opportunities for minorities and women. We believe our philosophy and actions demonstrate our commitment to workplace equality. Over the years, the firm has provided opportunities for women and minorities to further their professional development and assume leadership roles in the profession, in the community and within the firm. Baker & Daniels has implemented several programs designed to promote diversity initiatives with the goal of attracting and retaining a diverse attorney base:

• The firm has established, by partnership action, a standing committee called "Women in the Profession." The broad goals of this committee are to advance the interests of the firm's women attorneys in the business community and to further improve the retention of our women attorneys.

• In addition to traditional on-campus recruiting programs, we participate in Gateway to Diversity: A Summer Employment Program in the Indiana Legal Community, which is sponsored by the Indiana Conference for Legal Education Opportunity (Indiana CLEO) and the Indiana State Bar Association's Committee for Racial Diversity in the Legal Profession.

• Our summer clerkship programs for law students have successfully recruited minorities and female law students. This year's program, totaling 18, includes nine women, two African-American law students and one Asian/Pacific Islander.

• Baker & Daniels has been an active participant and sponsor of "Charting Your Own Course," an organization of minority in-house and outside counsel committed to the development of career opportunities for minority lawyers. A number of our minority attorneys have participated in programs offered by Charting Your Own Course, and one of our partners has been a member of the core group that created and continues to lead the organization.

• In an effort to attract and retain a diverse group of talented lawyers, we have taken a very open and creative approach to accommodating the need for flexible or reduced hours schedules. The firm has adopted a formal policy that permits any and all attorneys qualified by experience and demonstrated aptitude, irrespective of gender, to remain at the firm but to work reduced hours established on an individual basis, while continuing to advance toward partnership. We believe our approach and this policy is highly unusual, at least in the legal profession. However, it is working to allow us to retain some of our most promising attorneys, and we presently have 11 attorneys (10 female and one male) on reduced-hour, partnership-track arrangements, and many others with individualized flexible schedule arrangements.

Baker & Daniels also encourages women and minority professionals at the firm to assume leadership roles within the firm and values the diversity that their involvement in the business and the management of the firm brings. Women and minority attorneys hold key positions in the firm's planning, marketing, recruiting and compensation-setting efforts.

Baker & Daniels does not tolerate discrimination. Baker & Daniels is proud of its tradition of providing a collegial work environment in which all individuals are treated with respect and dignity. Baker & Daniels intends to continue to be a leader in eliminating barriers and in encouraging diversity in the legal profession, as well as our community.

Baker & Daniels is in full compliance with all federal, state and local laws regarding equal employment opportunity and affirmative action that are applicable to our firm. Our Equal Employment Opportunity Policy states as follows:

Baker & Daniels is an Equal Opportunity Employer. It is the policy of the firm to provide equal employment opportunity to all qualified persons, consistent with federal, state and local laws. This policy shall apply to all phases of the employment relationship, including the hiring, interviewing, promoting, compensating and terminating of personnel. Any complaint of discrimination should be reported to the Executive Director or the Director of Personnel and Benefits.

201

Baker & Hostetler LLP

3200 National City Center
1900 East 9th Street
Cleveland, OH 44114
Phone: (216) 621-0200
Fax: (216) 696-0740

FIRM LEADERSHIP

Managing Partner: Alec Wightman and R. Steven Kestner, Executive Partners
Diversity Team Leader: Alec Wightman, Executive Partner

LOCATIONS:

Cleveland, OH (HQ)
Cincinnati, OH
Columbus, OH
Costa Mesa, CA
Denver, CO
Houston, TX
Los Angeles, CA
New York, NY
Orlando, FL
Washington DC
Juarez, Mexico*
Sao Paulo, Brazil*
*Affiliates

LAW FIRM DEMOGRAPHIC PROFILES

FULL-TIME ASSOCIATES	2003	2002
Minority men	21	25
Minority women	19	18
White women	80	72
Total	226	208

SUMMER ASSOCIATES	2003	2002
Minority men	10	6
Minority women	14	17
White women	12	15
Total	59	54

EQUITY PARTNERS	2003	2002
Minority men	3	3
Minority women	0	0
White women	19	16
Total	140	133

NON-EQUITY PARTNERS	2003	2002
Minority men	8	6
Minority women	7	6
White women	29	35
Total	142	138

NEW HIRES	2003	2002
Minority men	3	14
Minority women	6	8
White women	26	24
Total	72	82

Strategic Plan and Diversity Leadership

How does the firm's leadership communicate the importance of diversity to everyone at the firm? (e.g., e-mails, web site, newsletters, meetings, etc.)

Baker & Hostetler communicates the importance of diversity to everyone in the firm through prominent and ongoing articles, statements and updates on the firm's web site; through firm internal and external newsletters; through executive partner updates to everyone in the firm; and by including diversity updates at all significant management meetings, retreats and other programs throughout the year.

Who has primary responsibility for leading diversity initiatives at your firm?

Baker & Hostetler is led by Executive Partners Alec Wightman and R. Steven Kestner. Mr. Wightman also serves as chair of the Diversity Committee and Mr. Kestner is one of several management members on the committee.

Does your law firm currently have a diversity committee?

Yes

Does the committee's representation include one or more members of the firm's management/executive committee (or the equivalent)?

Yes

If yes, how many attorneys are on the committee, and in 2003, what was the total number of hours collectively spent by the committee in furtherance of the firm's diversity initiatives?

Total attorneys on committee: 16

Total hours spent on diversity: Although the specific hours they spend working on the firm's diversity initiatives are not tracked, they meet on a regular basis.

Does the committee and/or diversity leader establish and set goals or objectives consistent with management's priorities?

Yes. Because Baker & Hostetler management is actively involved in the firm's Diversity Committee, the committee's goals and objectives are consistent with those of management. For example, management's goals include accelerated growth of the firm, improved communication and migration of the firm's client base to more sophisticated work. The goals of the Diversity Committee coincide with these firm goals in several ways. The firm's accelerated growth plans include the addition of strong lateral partners. The Diversity Committee has a goal of ensuring that minority candidates are strongly considered. The firm's goal of improved communication includes reporting information to everyone in the firm on all significant firm initiatives, including diversity – a goal shared by the Diversity Committee. The firm's goal of migrating the client base to increase the amount of sophisticated legal work for large clients includes the use of diverse teams of attorneys for significant clients – also a goal shared by the Diversity Committee.

Has the firm undertaken a formal or informal diversity program or set of initiatives aimed at increasing the diversity of the firm?

Yes, formal. These and other initiatives are described in the firm's narrative response below.

How often does the firm's management review the firm's diversity progress/results?

Quarterly. Diversity demographics are tracked, reviewed and reported on a quarterly basis. Also, there is ongoing analysis of diversity staffing reports for major clients, to ensure that minority attorneys receive an opportunity to provide meaningful work and decision making for the firm's high-profile clients. Baker & Hostetler has found the collection, analysis and reporting of this data to be extremely valuable in assessing diversity progress and maintaining accountability.

How is the firm's diversity committee and/or firm management held accountable for achieving results?

The firm's executive partners, Management Committees, the Diversity Committee and key clients receive these reports. This open disclosure is an essential aspect of establishing accountability for achieving results.

LAW FIRM DIVERSITY INITIATIVES	ALREADY COMPLETED	CURRENTLY ADDRESSING	NOT A CURRENT PRIORITY
Undertake communication from firm management that diversity is a top priority of the firm.	✔	✔	
Formalize diversity plan and committee with action steps and accountability to management.	✔	✔	
Conduct firm-wide diversity training for all attorneys and staff.			
Increase the number of minority attorneys at the associate level.	✔	✔	
Increase the number of minority attorneys at the partnership level.	✔	✔	
Develop/expand relationships with minority bar associations to offer firm's support of these networks.	✔	✔	
Focus on strengthening firm's mentoring program, including for benefit of minority attorneys.	✔	✔	
Conduct internal diversity needs assessment and/or retain diversity consultant to examine how firm culture might be more welcoming of minorities.			
Support law firm's internal affinity networks (e.g., women, minority attorney networks).	✔	✔	
Manage/monitor allocation of work assignments and/or hours billed to ensure women and minority attorneys have equal access/inclusion on top client matters.	✔	✔	
Conduct annual minority conferences.	✔	✔	

* The above items, while "already completed," will continue to be addressed.

Recruitment – New Associates

Does your firm annually recruit at any of the following types of institutions? (Check all that apply and list the schools).

Ivy League schools: Columbia University, Cornell University, Harvard University, University of Pennsylvania, Yale University

Public state schools: Cleveland State University, Florida State University, Indiana University-Bloomington, Ohio State University, University of California-Berkeley, University of California-Hastings, University of California-Los Angeles, University of Cincinnati, University of Colorado, University of Florida, University of Houston, University of Michigan, University of North Carolina, University of Texas, University of Virginia

Private schools: Capital University, Case Western Reserve University, Duke University, Georgetown University, Loyola Law School, New York University, Northwestern University, Stanford University, Stetson University, University of Chicago, University of Denver, University of Miami, University of Notre Dame, University of Southern California, Vanderbilt University

Historically Black Colleges and Universities (HBCUs): Howard University

Do you have any special outreach efforts directed to encourage minority law students to consider your firm?

• *We prominently feature our Annual Minority Business Development Conference, its attendees and speakers in LEAP, our law school recruiting publication. This demonstrates to students that if they join Baker & Hostetler, there will be opportunities for professional and personal development to help them succeed.*

• Hold a reception for minority law students

• Advertise in minority law student association publication(s)

• Participate in/host minority law student job fair(s)

• Sponsor minority law student association events

• Firm's lawyers participate on career panels at school

• Outreach to leadership of minority student organizations

• Scholarships or intern/fellowships for minority students

SUMMER ASSOCIATE STATISTICS: SUMMER 2003	MINORITY MEN	MINORITY WOMEN	WHITE WOMEN	TOTAL
Summer associates	7	8	8	43
Summer associates who received an offer of full-time employment	4	6	6	33
Summer associates who accepted an offer of full-time employment	2	5	6	26

Recruitment – Lateral Associates and Partners

What activities does the firm undertake to attract minority and women   attorneys?

• Partner programs with women and minority bar associations

• Participate at minority job fairs

• Seek referrals from other attorneys

Do you use executive recruiting/search firms to seek to identify new diversity hires (partners or associates)?

Yes

LATERAL ASSOCIATES AND PARTNERS: 1/1/03 – 12/31/03	MINORITY MEN	MINORITY WOMEN	WHITE WOMEN	TOTAL
Number of lateral associate hires	1	2	11	29
Number of lateral partner hires (equity and non-equity)	0	0	0	9
Number of new partners (equity and non-equity) promoted from associate rank	2	1	1	10
Number of new equity partners	0	0	4	10

Recruitment – Retention & Professional Development

ATTORNEYS WHO LEFT THE FIRM: 2003	MINORITY MEN	MINORITY WOMEN	WHITE WOMEN	TOTAL
Number of attorneys who voluntarily or involuntarily left your firm's employ in 2003	5	5	20	44

How do 2003 attrition rates generally compare to those experienced in the prior year period?

Lower than in prior years

Please identify the specific steps you are taking to reduce the attrition rate of minority and women attorneys.

• Develop and/or support internal employee affinity groups (e.g., minority or women networks within the firm)

• Increase/review compensation relative to competition

• Increase/improve current work/life programs

• Work with minority and women attorneys to develop career advancement plans

• Introduce minority and women attorneys to key clients, including to lead engagements (Staffing approach includes diversity consideration; proposal, presentation process includes diversity consideration)

• Review work assignments and hours billed to key client matters to make sure minority and women attorneys are not being excluded (quarterly review)

• Strengthen mentoring program for all attorneys, including minorities and women

Does your firm have part-time/flex-time policies that permit attorneys (male or female) to work alternative schedules?

Yes. Baker & Hostetler is sensitive to the importance of a balanced life for female and male attorneys and offers part-time/flex-time policies that permit attorneys to work alternative schedules.

What impact, if any, will the decision to work part-time have on an attorney's ability to make partner or, if already a partner, to remain a partner at your firm?

A part-time attorney may be delayed in achieving partner status due to a delay in sufficient experiences but can achieve partner status once they have sufficient experiences. The firm does not discriminate against attorneys on the basis of work schedule.

Have any attorneys who chose to work a part-time schedule made partner at your firm?

Yes. Part-time attorneys have become partners and other partners have reduced their hours to become part-time.

Management Demographic Profile (as of 12/31/03)

	MINORITY MEN	MINORITY WOMEN	WHITE WOMEN	TOTAL
Number of attorneys on the Executive/Management Committee or equivalent	1	0	2	14
Number of attorneys on the Hiring Committee or equivalent	1	0	3	11
Number of attorneys on the Partner/Associate Review Committee or equivalent	1	0	2	14

Women heading offices Lisa Pennington, Houston Office Managing Partner

Minorities heading practice groups Mike Asensio, Employment and Labor, Columbus Office Practice Group Coordinator; Ron Okada, Litigation, Cleveland Office Practice Group Coordinator; Cranston Williams, Litigation, Los Angeles Office Unassigned Practice Group Coordinator; Naomi Young, Employment and Labor, Los Angeles Office Practice Group Co-coordinator.

Women heading practice groups Angela Agrusa, Litigation, Los Angeles Office Practice Group Coordinator; Mary Bittence, Litigation, Cleveland Office Unassigned Practice Group Co-coordinator; Robin Harvey, Litigation, Cincinnati Office Practice Group Coordinator; Rosemary O'Shea, Employment and Labor, Orlando Office Practice Group Coordinator; Georgeann Peters, Tax, Personal Planning and Employee Benefits, Columbus Office Practice Group Coordinator; Teresa Tracy, Employment and Labor, Los Angeles Office Practice Group Co-coordinator; Naomi Young, Employment and Labor, Los Angeles Office Practice Group Co-coordinator.

The Firm Says

Baker and Hostetler LLP has made a long-term commitment to incorporate diversity within our work force and business strategies by recruiting, retaining and promoting minority and female attorneys at all levels. Through clearly focused and sustained efforts, we have increased the number of minority partners and associates, reached a milestone in minority scholarships, monitored diversity staffing of major projects, conducted annual Minority Conferences and built a more inclusive environment by participating in numerous collaborative efforts with our community, law schools and bar associations.

Firm-wide, over half of our new associates have been women and minorities for the last five years, and we significantly exceed the national average of minority attorney representation among large law firms as reported by NALP. As of January 1, 2004, Baker & Hostetler had 20 minority partners, or 6.71 percent. This progress in the diversity of our work force is the result of many factors, including targeted recruiting of minorities at the law school and lateral level.

In honor of the firm's first African-American partner who joined the firm in 1968, we established the Paul White Scholarship (PWS) in 1997. The scholarship provides financial assistance and practical experience to minority law students by furnishing a paid summer clerkship and a $5,000 net cash award. As of 2003, the PWS is offered in eight offices and reached the milestone of granting more than $1 million in related summer associate and scholarship monies.

One of our most successful strategies in retaining minority attorneys has been our commitment to listen, learn and act upon suggestions. Our Diversity Task Force, established in 1995, has now become a permanent standing committee in the firm. Alec Wightman, who serves as executive partner of the firm with R. Steven Kestner, chairs the Diversity Committee, which includes Mr. Kestner. Other members include members of the Policy Committee, office managing partners, partners and associates. Exemplifying the goal of true diversity, the committee includes minorities, non-minorities, men and women.

A diversity initiative directed by the Diversity Committee has been the development and ongoing analysis of diversity staffing reports for major clients. By tracking the staffing of minority attorneys for these clients, the firm ensures that minority attorneys receive an opportunity to provide meaningful work and decision making for the firm's high-profile clients. Another successful initiative was the establishment of a supplemental mentoring program for associates in their fourth year – a crucial year for the success and development of attorneys.

In October 2003, the firm held its Fourth Annual Minority Business Development and Minority Retention Conference. This conference was inclusive of all firm minority attorneys nationwide. In addition to firm management's active involvement, successful minority partners from within and outside the firm shared experiences and advice. The conference also focused on practical "real world" tools for networking and establishing and maintaining client relationships.

Everyone at all levels of the firm understands that diversity is not a project or program, but a commitment to continued progress. To reinforce this principle, firm management includes diversity as an important agenda topic at all the significant management meetings, retreats and other programs throughout the year. These diversity updates ensure that the firm is driving real change that everyone understands and can embrace.

The firm has cultivated a community of minority attorneys from sundry backgrounds by sponsoring and actively participating in numerous conferences sponsored by minority bar associations and organizations. For the last four years, the firm has sponsored the Charting Your Own Course Conference. The firm was both a sponsor and

presenter at the Third Annual MCCA CLE Expo. There are numerous other diversity sponsorships with organizations, companies, bar associations, governmental agencies and nonprofit organizations

Realizing the importance of diversity within the community, our minority and female attorneys are involved in the leadership of local organizations and bar associations. In 2004 alone, 15 women partners were designated by the press as "Super Lawyers" in Ohio, California and Texas. In April 2004, the firm participated in a "matchmaker" program for law firms which provided minority vendors an opportunity to present their products and services to major law firms. Our Columbus, Los Angeles and New York offices have been key signatories for diversity efforts by their respective bar associations. All of these initiatives work toward increasing the number of minorities and female partners, increasing representation within management, and providing networking opportunities, client development activities and mentoring programs.

In addition to the Diversity Committee, Baker & Hostetler has formed a Women's Committee to provide recommendations to management with respect to issues facing women in the legal profession. Both committees include a cross-section of lawyers by geography, practice group and position. Our Houston office was a key signatory for the Women's Initiative by the Houston Bar Association, and our Houston office managing partner was the first woman to manage a major law firm in Texas. A female minority partner in our firm was recently named one of America's Leading Lawyers by Black Enterprise magazine (April 2004). Our Columbus office managing partner was a recipient of a Commitment to Diversity Award presented by the Ohio State University Moritz College of Law Chapter of the National Black Law Students Association.

Diversity continues to be a core value for Baker & Hostetler. Through strategic recruitment, strong community and professional involvement, and a dedicated commitment to diversity, there has been significant progress. While we are proud of these results, we recognize that all of us need to continue to work to make diversity a reality of an inclusive environment where individual differences are appreciated and valued.

Baker & McKenzie LLP

One Prudential Plaza
130 E. Randolph Drive
Chicago, IL 60601
Phone: (312) 861-8000
Fax: (312) 861-2898
E-mail: info@bakernet.com

FIRM LEADERSHIP

Managing Partner: John Conroy, North
American Managing Partner
Diversity Team Leader: Nam H. Paik, Chair of
the Diversity Oversight Committee and Equal
Employment Opportunity Program Partner

LOCATIONS

Chicago, IL
Dallas, TX
Houston, TX
Miami, FL
New York, NY
Palo Alto, CA
San Diego, CA
San Francisco, CA
Washington DC
60 other locations worldwide

*"Baker & McKenzie International is a Swiss
Verein domiciled in Zurich, Switzerland. The
global Firm's principal executive offices are in
Chicago. The principal executive offices of
Baker & McKenzie LLP, which is a member firm
of Baker & McKenzie International, also are
located in Chicago."*

LAW FIRM DEMOGRAPHIC PROFILES

FULL-TIME ASSOCIATES	2003	2002
Minority men	25	30
Minority women	28	33
White women	101	122
Total	280	302

SUMMER ASSOCIATES	2003	2002
Minority men	3	1
Minority women	3	3
White women	8	8
Total	30	21

EQUITY PARTNERS	2003	2002
Minority men	9	11
Minority women	2	2
White women	16	14
Total	152	150

NON-EQUITY PARTNERS	2003	2002
Minority men	7	4
Minority women	3	2
White women	16	15
Total	72	73

NEW HIRES	2003	2002
Minority men	6	1
Minority women	5	4
White women	16	17
Total	58	49

MCCA
MINORITY CORPORATE COUNSEL ASSOCIATION

Strategic Plan and Diversity Leadership

How does the firm's leadership communicate the importance of diversity to everyone at the firm? (e.g., e-mails, web site, newsletters, meetings, etc.)

E-mails, meetings and diversity workshops.

Who has primary responsibility for leading diversity initiatives at your firm?

Nam H. Paik, EEOP partner (Equal Employment Opportunity Program partner) and chair of the Diversity Oversight Committee.

Does your law firm currently have a diversity committee?

Yes

Does the committee's representation include one or more members of the firm's management/executive committee (or the equivalent)?

Yes

How many attorneys are on the committee, and in 2003, what was the total number of hours collectively spent by the committee in furtherance of the firm's diversity initiatives?

Total attorneys on committee: 9

Total hours spent on diversity: N/A

Does the committee and/or diversity leader establish and set goals or objectives consistent with management's priorities?

Yes

Has the firm undertaken a formal or informal diversity program or set of initiatives aimed at increasing the diversity of the firm?

Yes, formal

How often does the firm's management review the firm's diversity progress/results?

Twice a year

How is the firm's diversity committee and/or firm management held accountable for achieving results?

The firm's Diversity Oversight Committee budget is partially tied to the objectives and goals accomplished by the committee.

LAW FIRM DIVERSITY INITIATIVES	ALREADY COMPLETED	CURRENTLY ADDRESSING	NOT A CURRENT PRIORITY
Undertake communication from firm management that diversity is a top priority of the firm.	✔		
Formalize diversity plan and committee with action steps and accountability to management.	✔		
Conduct firm-wide diversity training for all attorneys and staff.		✔	
Increase the number of minority attorneys at the associate level.		✔	
Increase the number of minority attorneys at the partnership level.		✔	
Develop/expand relationships with minority bar associations to offer firm's support of these networks.		✔	
Focus on strengthening firm's mentoring program, including for benefit of minority attorneys.		✔	
Conduct internal diversity needs assessment and/or retain diversity consultant to examine how firm culture might be more welcoming of minorities.		✔	
Support law firm's internal affinity networks (e.g., women, minority attorney networks).		✔	
Manage/monitor allocation of work assignments and/or hours billed to ensure women and minority attorneys have equal access/inclusion on top client matters.		✔	

Recruitment – New Associates

Does your firm annually recruit at any of the following types of institutions? (Check all that apply and list the schools).

Ivy League schools: Columbia University, Harvard Law School, University of Pennsylvania

Public state schools: University of Illinois, University of Michigan, University of Texas, University of Florida, University of Houston, University of Virginia, William & Mary School of Law, University of California at Berkeley (Boalt Hall)

Private schools: University of Chicago, Northwestern University, Georgetown University, Southern Methodist University, University of Miami, New York University, University of San Diego, George Washington University, Washington and Lee University, Stanford Law School

Historically Black Colleges and Universities (HBCUs): Howard University

Do you have any special outreach efforts directed to encourage minority law students to consider your firm?

• Hold a reception for minority law students

• Participate in/host minority law student job fair(s)

• Sponsor minority law student association events

• Firm's lawyers participate on career panels at school

• Outreach to leadership of minority student organizations

• Scholarships or intern/fellowships for minority students

SUMMER ASSOCIATE STATISTICS: SUMMER 2003	MINORITY MEN	MINORITY WOMEN	WHITE WOMEN	TOTAL
Summer associates	3	4	8	23
Summer associates who received an offer of full-time employment	2	3	4	17
Summer associates who accepted an offer of full-time employment	1	3	3	15

Recruitment – Lateral Associates and Partners

What activities does the firm undertake to attract minority and women attorneys?

• *Work with recruiting firms that specialize in minority recruiting.*

• Partner programs with women and minority bar associations

• Participate at minority job fairs

• Seek referrals from other attorneys

Do you use executive recruiting/search firms to seek to identify new diversity hires (partners or associates)?

Yes

LATERAL ASSOCIATES AND PARTNERS: 1/1/03 – 12/31/03	MINORITY MEN	MINORITY WOMEN	WHITE WOMEN	TOTAL
Number of lateral associate hires	5	5	12	38
Number of lateral partner hires (equity and non-equity)	0	0	2	15
Number of new partners (equity and non-equity) promoted from associate rank	1	0	3	12
Number of new equity partners	0	0	0	0

Retention & Professional Development

ATTORNEYS WHO LEFT THE FIRM: 2003	MINORITY MEN	MINORITY WOMEN	WHITE WOMEN	TOTAL
Number of attorneys who voluntarily or involuntarily left your firm's employ in 2003	7	10	25	98

How do 2003 attrition rates generally compare to those experienced in the prior year period?

Somewhat higher than in prior years

Please identify the specific steps you are taking to reduce the attrition rate of minority and women attorneys. (It is suggested that you elaborate on this issue in the final question of this survey.)

• Develop and/or support internal employee affinity groups (e.g., minority or women networks within the firm)

• Work with minority and women attorneys to develop career advancement plans

• Strengthen mentoring program for all attorneys, including minorities and women

• Professional skills development program, including minority and women attorneys

Does your firm have part-time/flex-time policies that permit attorneys (male or female) to work alternative schedules?

Yes

What impact, if any, will the decision to work part-time have on an attorney's ability to make partner or, if already a partner, to remain a partner at your firm?

We have several partners working on a part-time basis. While an associate who works on a part-time basis may be delayed in becoming a partner, we have elevated associates working on a part-time basis to partnership.

Have any attorneys who chose to work a part-time schedule made partner at your firm?

Yes, seven attorneys.

Management Demographic Profile (as of 12/31/03)

	MINORITY MEN	MINORITY WOMEN	WHITE WOMEN	TOTAL
Number of attorneys on the Executive/Management Committee or equivalent	0	0	3	26
Number of attorneys on the Hiring Committee or equivalent	1	3	4	26
Number of attorneys on the Partner/Associate Review Committee or equivalent	1	0	2	10

Please provide information regarding all minority and women attorneys who head offices or practice groups of your law firm:

Minorities heading practice groups: None

Women heading practice groups: Susan Stone, Tax; Teresa Gleason, International Commercial; Elise Healy, Executive Transfers; Cynthia Jackson, Employment; Paula Krasny, Intellectual Property; Abby Silverman, Litigation/Employment.

The Firm Says

Baker & McKenzie promotes and actively encourages an extremely diverse global workplace, with offices in 38 countries around the world, and men and women from a variety of nationalities, cultures, religions and races. Our high regard for diversity is the very foundation of our firm. It is inherent in our capacity as a truly global law firm and it makes our workplace a myriad of talent and culture – a healthy place for our employees and clients to conduct business. Indeed, over 25 languages are spoken by our lawyers and staff in our U.S. offices alone. We also are proud to be the largest legal service provider headed by a woman. As the French poet Paul Valery wrote, "Enrichessez-vous de vos differences," or, "Enrich yourselves through your differences." We stand by this philosophy. As an equal opportunity employer, we celebrate and encourage people of any race, color, religion, gender, sexual orientation, national origin, disability or age to fulfill their professional aspirations at Baker & McKenzie – one of the most exciting, and diverse, legal environments within which to work.

The firm's Diversity Oversight Committee for North America oversees diversity issues on a region-wide basis. The Diversity Oversight Committee focuses not only on increasing minority representation within North America, but also on educating and training internally to encourage an atmosphere that appreciates and supports diversity and inclusion. The goals of this committee are to enhance our minority scholarship program, create a strategic plan on diversity for North America, collaborate more closely with clients on diversity initiatives, increase the firm's communication efforts in relation to diversity and promote a general environment supportive of all our differences – differences that weave a strong fabric that is the essence of Baker & McKenzie. We are proud to have distributed over $1.3 million to U.S. law schools for scholarships to minority students, including $90,000 in 2003-2004.

Our recent internal diversity initiatives include the creation of a multi-year strategic plan for diversity within our North American region. Additionally, we have implemented in one of our offices a monthly professional development program designed to enhance the skills of all of our attorneys, including women and minority attorneys.

The firm financially supports a number of minority bar associations and minority outreach efforts, including the Chicago Committee on Minorities in Large Law Firms (focused on increasing racial and ethnic diversity within the large firms). The chair of the Diversity Oversight Committee serves on the board of that organization. Additionally, the firm provided in-kind support to the Chicago Committee by providing office space and office services to its executive director for two years.

Baker & McKenzie Chair Christine Lagarde has invested considerable amounts of time to the advancement of women through her participation in various leadership forums addressing issues commonly faced by women in business and legal careers. Most recently she spoke at the American Bar Association's Women in Leadership event in Chicago. She also spoke at the Forum for Women Entrepreneurs in Paris, The Wall Street Journal's

Women in Business Summit in London and the Women in Leadership Conference organized by the Conference Board in Barcelona.

In addition, Abby Silverman, a partner in our San Diego office, recently received the Pinnacle Award for her leadership in the advancement of women.

The firm has received numerous awards for its pro bono efforts in providing direct legal services to disadvantaged and underserved communities. For instance, in December 2003, the Public Interest Law Initiative, located in Chicago, presented its first-ever pro bono achievement award to Baker & McKenzie for outstanding dedication to increasing service to the public through direct legal services. Furthermore, CorporateProBono.org, a project of the American Corporate Counsel Association and the Pro Bono Institute at Georgetown University Law Center, recognized Baker & McKenzie, Abbott Laboratories and the Midwest Immigrant & Human Rights Center for helping Chicago area immigrants to become naturalized U.S. citizens. Nam H. Paik, one of the partners in our Chicago office, received an award from the Korean American Bar Association for creating a pro bono legal clinic which serves the Chicago Korean-American community.

Baker Botts L.L.P.

One Shell Plaza
910 Louisiana Street
Houston, TX 77002
Phone: (713) 229-1234
Fax: (713) 229-1522

FIRM LEADERSHIP

Managing Partner: Walter J. Smith
Diversity Team Leader: Joe Caldwell, Diversity
Committee Chair
Contact Person: Melissa Moss, Manager of
Attorney Employment

LOCATIONS

Houston, TX (HQ)
Austin, TX
Dallas, TX
New York, NY
Washington, DC

LAW FIRM DEMOGRAPHIC PROFILES

FULL-TIME ASSOCIATES	2003	2002
Minority men	24	22
Minority women	27	21
White women	127	123
Total	430	419

SUMMER ASSOCIATES	2003	2002
Minority men	5	9
Minority women	9	11
White women	36	24
Total	99	114

EQUITY PARTNERS	2003	2002
Minority men	8	9
Minority women	3	4
White women	37	31
Total	247	253

NEW HIRES	2003	2002
Minority men	6	4
Minority women	10	4
White women	30	22
Total	85	97

Strategic Plan and Diversity Leadership

How does the firm's leadership communicate the importance of diversity to everyone at the firm? (e.g., e-mails, web site, newsletters, meetings, etc.)

Intranet site within the firm; e-mails; web site recruiting and marketing materials

Who has primary responsibility for leading diversity initiatives at your firm? Name of person and his/her title:

Joe Caldwell, Diversity Committee chair

Does your law firm currently have a diversity committee?

Yes

Does the committee's representation include one or more members of the firm's management/executive committee (or the equivalent)?

Yes

How many attorneys are on the committee, and in 2003, what was the total number of hours collectively spent by the committee in furtherance of the firm's diversity initiatives?

Total attorneys on committee: 7

Does the committee and/or diversity leader establish and set goals or objectives consistent with management's priorities?

Yes

Has the firm undertaken a formal or informal diversity program or set of initiatives aimed at increasing the diversity of the firm?

Yes, formal

How often does the firm's management review the firm's diversity progress/results?

Monthly

LAW FIRM DIVERSITY INITIATIVES	ALREADY COMPLETED	CURRENTLY ADDRESSING	NOT A CURRENT PRIORITY
Undertake communication from firm management that diversity is a top priority of the firm.	✓		
Formalize diversity plan and committee with action steps and accountability to management.		✓	
Conduct firm-wide diversity training for all attorneys and staff.		✓	
Increase the number of minority attorneys at the associate level.		✓	
Increase the number of minority attorneys at the partnership level.		✓	
Develop/expand relationships with minority bar associations to offer firm's support of these networks.		✓	
Focus on strengthening firm's mentoring program, including for benefit of minority attorneys.		✓	
Conduct internal diversity needs assessment and/or retain diversity consultant to examine how firm culture might be more welcoming of minorities.		✓	
Support law firm's internal affinity networks (e.g., women, minority attorney networks).	✓		
Manage/monitor allocation of work assignments and/or hours billed to ensure women and minority attorneys have equal access/inclusion on top client matters.		✓	

Recruitment – New Associates

Does your firm annually recruit at any of the following types of institutions? (Check all that apply and list the schools).

Ivy League schools: Columbia University, Harvard University, University of Pennsylvania and Yale University

Public state schools: University of Houston, Louisiana State University, University of Texas, Texas Tech, University of Michigan, University of Virginia

Private schools: Baylor University, Boston College, Brooklyn Law School, Cardozo Law School, Emory University, Fordham University, George Washington University, University of Notre Dame, Southern Methodist University, South Texas University, Tulane University, Vanderbilt University, University of Chicago, Duke University, Georgetown University, Northwestern University, New York University, Stanford University

Historically Black Colleges and Universities (HBCUs): Howard University and Texas Southern University

Of the law schools that you listed above, do you have any special outreach efforts directed to encourage minority law students to consider your firm?

• Participate in/host minority law student job fair(s)
• Sponsor minority law student association events
• Firm's lawyers participate on career panels at school
• Outreach to leadership of minority student organizations

SUMMER ASSOCIATE STATISTICS: SUMMER 2003	MINORITY MEN	MINORITY WOMEN	WHITE WOMEN	TOTAL
Summer associates	5	9	36	99
Summer associates who received an offer of full-time employment	5	7	28	89
Summer associates who accepted an offer of full-time employment	4	6	20	53

Recruitiment – Lateral Associates and Partners

What activities does the firm undertake to attract minority and women attorneys?

• Partner programs with women and minority bar associations
• Participate at minority job fairs
• Seek referrals from other attorneys

Do you use executive recruiting/search firms to seek to identify new diversity hires (partners or associates)?

Yes

If yes, list all women- and/or minority-owned executive search/recruiting firms to which the firm paid a fee for placement services in the past 12 months:

MS Legal Search, L.L.C.; MBD Search, DBA Michaels Barrett Doblo, L.L.C.

LATERAL ASSOCIATES AND PARTNERS: 1/1/03 – 12/31/03	MINORITY MEN	MINORITY WOMEN	WHITE WOMEN	TOTAL
Number of lateral associate hires	2	0	6	16
Number of lateral partner hires (equity and non-equity)	0	0	0	1
Number of new partners (equity and non-equity) promoted from associate rank	0	1	3	12
Number of new equity partners	N/A	N/A	N/A	N/A

Retention & Professional Development

ATTORNEYS WHO LEFT THE FIRM: 2003	MINORITY MEN	MINORITY WOMEN	WHITE WOMEN	TOTAL
Number of attorneys who voluntarily or involuntarily left your firm's employ in 2003	6	4	27	88

How do 2003 attrition rates generally compare to those experienced in the prior year period?

About the same as in prior years

Please identify the specific steps you are taking to reduce the attrition rate of minority and women attorneys.

• Develop and/or support internal employee affinity groups (e.g., minority or women networks within the firm)
• Increase/improve current work/life programs
• Introduce minority and women attorneys to key clients, including to lead engagements
• Strengthen mentoring program for all attorneys, including minorities and women
• Professional skills development program, including minority and women attorneys

Does your firm have part-time/flex-time policies that permit attorneys (male or female) to work alternative schedules?

Yes

What impact, if any, will the decision to work part-time have on an attorney's ability to make partner or, if already a partner, to remain a partner at your firm?

No impact

Have any attorneys who chose to work a part-time schedule made partner at your firm?

Yes, four attorneys.

Management Demographic Profile (as of 12/31/03)

	MINORITY MEN	MINORITY WOMEN	WHITE WOMEN	TOTAL
Number of attorneys on the Executive/Management Committee or equivalent	0	0	2	11
Number of attorneys on the Hiring Committee or equivalent	4	3	11	49
Number of attorneys on the Partner/Associate Review Committee or equivalent	N/A	N/A	N/A	N/A

Please provide information regarding all minority and women attorneys who head offices or practice groups of your law firm:

Minorities heading practice groups: Pam Giblin, Environmental (firm-wide); and Joe Caldwell, Litigation (Washington, DC)

Women heading practice groups: Pam Giblin, Environmental (firm-wide); Kathryn Vaughn, General Assignment (Houston); Pat Stanton, Global Projects (Dallas); Marley Lott, Real Estate (firm-wide); Maria Boyce, Litigation (Houston); Samara Kline, Appellate (Dallas); and Tamar Stanley, Tax (Washington, DC)

The Firm Says

Baker Botts is steadily committed to recruiting and retaining a diverse work force. The firm is comprised of women and men from a broad variety of racial, religious and ethnic backgrounds. Baker Botts is an equal opportunity employer and abides by its policy prohibiting discrimination on the basis of race, color, creed, national origin, age, gender, sexual orientation, religion, marital and/or parental status, disability, military status, or status as Vietnam-era or disabled veteran.

The firm has participated in many efforts to address diversity issues and continues to challenge itself to better manage these issues internally and externally. Representative activities include:

• Establishing a Diversity Committee and goals for increasing the hiring, retention and promotion of women and minorities

• Formation of a Professional Development Women's Council dedicated to offering professional development opportunities to women clients and lawyers

• Support of associate mentoring programs

• Creation of flexible and part-time work schedules

• Recruitment and retention of a diverse and dynamic work force

• Launching a vendor supplier diversity program to ensure that women and minority-owned businesses are supported as current and potential suppliers of services to Baker Botts

These efforts have a common goal of providing firm clients the premier legal service they expect of Baker Botts, its lawyers and employees. Baker Botts is committed to continuing its active approach to addressing diversity matters and ensuring its clients are satisfied with the resources the firm provides.

Baker Botts' Diversity Committee

The firm created a Diversity Committee to examine the firm's recruiting, retention and promotion efforts. Membership in the committee consists of lawyers and staff from various offices. The firm's managing partner is also a member of the committee.

Mission Statement

Baker Botts is strongly committed to diversity in the workplace and seeks to become the employer of choice for a diverse pool of lawyers and staff. Through the firm's recruitment, retention and advancement efforts of women and minorities, Baker Botts strives to create a climate of inclusion, grow our talent pool and foster innovation. We believe a diverse organization is essential to support the clients and communities which the firm serves.

Goals

• Increase representation and advancement of women and minorities in the firm

• Develop policies and practices that define and communicate the firm's commitment to diversity

• Establish goals for recruitment, retention and advancement of women and minorities and measure progress

Retention

Baker Botts understands that retention of a diverse work force is a very important part of its commitment to diversity. Therefore, the firm seeks to provide meaningful work assignments and opportunities to women and minorities, encourages participation and feedback, and supports a variety of activities for our women lawyers.

Promotion

The third key component of Baker Botts' diversity initiative is promotion. For example, in 2004, 15 percent of women eligible to make partner did so. That same year, 16 percent of men eligible to make partner did so. Baker Botts strives to continue this trend.

Vendor supplier diversity programs

Firm staff have attended several workshops and training seminars on how to implement a successful vendor supplier diversity program. While the firm is in the early stages of its research, plans call for such a program to be instituted in all U.S. offices this year. This aspect of the diversity initiative is important to the firm and to our clients. Baker Botts knows that the firm can impact diversity across many areas – not just the recruiting, retention and promotion of its lawyers and staff, but also that of the many suppliers the firm employs to provide services to its clients.

Baker, Donelson, Bearman, Caldwell & Berkowitz

Commerce Center Suite 1000
211 Commerce Street
Nashville, TN 37201
Phone: (615) 726-5600
Fax: (615) 744-0464

FIRM LEADERSHIP

Managing Partner: Ben Adams, Chairman and
Chief Executive Officer
Diversity Team Leader: Clarence Risin,
Diversity Committee Chair

LOCATIONS

Nashville, TN (HQ)
Atlanta, GA
Birmingham, AL
Chattanooga, TN
Jackson, MS
Johnson City, TN
Knoxville, TN
Memphis, TN
New Orleans, LA
Washington, DC
Beijing, China

LAW FIRM DEMOGRAPHIC PROFILES

FULL-TIME ASSOCIATES	2003	2002
Minority men	8	5
Minority women	5	5
White women	61	47
Total	166	137

SUMMER ASSOCIATES	2003	2002
Minority men	4	5
Minority women	4	5
White women	16	15
Total	46	33

EQUITY PARTNERS	2003	2002
Minority men	4	3
Minority women	0	0
White women	18	13
Total	93	104

NON-EQUITY PARTNERS	2003	2002
Minority men	1	1
Minority women	1	0
White women	13	5
Total	45	32

NEW HIRES	2003	2002
Minority men	4	2
Minority women	4	1
White women	30	9
Total	95	31

Strategic Plan and Diversity Leadership

How does the firm's leadership communicate the importance of diversity to everyone at the firm? (e.g., e-mails, web site, newsletters, meetings, etc.)

Firm retreats; web site

Who has primary responsibility for leading diversity initiatives at your firm? Name of person and his/her title:

Clarence Risin, Diversity Committee chair

Does your law firm currently have a diversity committee?

Yes

Does the committee's representation include one or more members of the firm's management/executive committee (or the equivalent)?

Yes

How many attorneys are on the committee, and in 2003, what was the total number of hours collectively spent by the committee in furtherance of the firm's diversity initiatives?

Total attorneys on committee: 12

Total hours spent on diversity: Not tracked

Does the committee and/or diversity leader establish and set goals or objectives consistent with management's priorities?

Yes

Has the firm undertaken a formal or informal diversity program or set of initiatives aimed at increasing the diversity of the firm?

Yes, formal

How often does the firm's management review the firm's diversity progress/results?

As needed

How is the firm's diversity committee and/or firm management held accountable for achieving results?

Each year, the Diversity Committee and firm management compare the diversity goals set with the results achieved.

LAW FIRM DIVERSITY INITIATIVES	ALREADY COMPLETED	CURRENTLY ADDRESSING	NOT A CURRENT PRIORITY
Undertake communication from firm management that diversity is a top priority of the firm.		✓	
Formalize diversity plan and committee with action steps and accountability to management.		✓	
Conduct firm-wide diversity training for all attorneys and staff.			✓
Increase the number of minority attorneys at the associate level.	✓		
Increase the number of minority attorneys at the partnership level.	✓		
Develop/expand relationships with minority bar associations to offer firm's support of these networks.	✓		
Focus on strengthening firm's mentoring program, including for benefit of minority attorneys.		✓	
Conduct internal diversity needs assessment and/or retain diversity consultant to examine how firm culture might be more welcoming of minorities.			✓
Support law firm's internal affinity networks (e.g., women, minority attorney networks).			✓
Manage/monitor allocation of work assignments and/or hours billed to ensure women and minority attorneys have equal access/inclusion on top client matters.	✓		

Recruitment – New Associates

Does your firm annually recruit at any of the following types of institutions? (Check all that apply and list the schools).

Public state schools: University of Arkansas, University of Alabama, University of Florida, University of Georgia, University of Kentucky, LSU, University of Memphis, University of Mississippi, University of Tennessee, University of Texas, UNC, University of Virginia, College of William & Mary

Private schools: Cumberland School of Law (Samford University), Duke University, Emory University, Georgetown University, Loyola University, Mississippi College, Tulane University, Vanderbilt University, Wake Forest University, Washington & Lee University

Historically Black Colleges and Universities (HBCUs): North Carolina Central University and Southern University

Do you have any special outreach efforts directed to encourage minority law students to consider your firm?

• Advertise in minority law student association publication(s)

• Participate in/host minority law student job fair(s)

• Sponsor minority law student association events

- Firm's lawyers participate on career panels at school
- Outreach to leadership of minority student organizations
- Scholarships or intern/fellowships for minority students

SUMMER ASSOCIATE STATISTICS: SUMMER 2003	MINORITY MEN	MINORITY WOMEN	WHITE WOMEN	TOTAL
Summer associates	1	3	14	40
Summer associates who received an offer of full-time employment	0	2	9	25
Summer associates who accepted an offer of full-time employment	0	1	6	14

Recruitment – Lateral Associates and Partners

What activities does the firm undertake to attract minority and women attorneys?

- Partner programs with women and minority bar associations
- Participate at minority job fairs
- Seek referrals from other attorneys

Do you use executive recruiting/search firms to seek to identify new diversity hires (partners or associates)?

No

LATERAL ASSOCIATES AND PARTNERS: 1/1/03 – 12/31/03	MINORITY MEN	MINORITY WOMEN	WHITE WOMEN	TOTAL
Number of lateral associate hires	2	1	13	41
Number of lateral partner hires (equity and non-equity)	0	1	13	38
Number of new partners (equity and non-equity) promoted from associate rank	0	0	1	4
Number of new equity partners	1	0	6	25

Retention & Professional Development

ATTORNEYS WHO LEFT THE FIRM: 2003	MINORITY MEN	MINORITY WOMEN	WHITE WOMEN	TOTAL
Number of attorneys who voluntarily or involuntarily left your firm's employ in 2003	1	0	10	29

How do 2003 attrition rates generally compare to those experienced in the prior year period?

About the same as in prior years

Please identify the specific steps you are taking to reduce the attrition rate of minority and women attorneys.

• Increase/improve current work/life programs

• Succession plan includes emphasis on diversity

• Strengthen mentoring program for all attorneys, including minorities and women

• Professional skills development program, including minority and women attorneys

Does your firm have part-time/flex-time policies that permit attorneys (male or female) to work alternative schedules?

No, we do have attorneys who work part-time, but no formal policy.

What impact, if any, will the decision to work part-time have on an attorney's ability to make partner or, if already a partner, to remain a partner at your firm?

It would increase the difficulty of making partner. Once partnership is reached, it would have no impact.

Have any attorneys who chose to work a part-time schedule made partner at your firm?

No

Management Demographic Profile (as of 12/31/03)

	MINORITY MEN	MINORITY WOMEN	WHITE WOMEN	TOTAL
Number of attorneys on the Executive/Management Committee or equivalent	0	0	1	9
Number of attorneys on the Hiring Committee or equivalent	5	3	19	61
Number of attorneys on the Partner/Associate Review Committee or equivalent	1	0	6	38

Please provide information regarding all minority and women attorneys who head offices or practice groups of your law firm:

Women heading offices: Denise Killebrew, Birmingham; Susan Rich, Chattanooga; Kelli Thompson, Knoxville

Minorities heading practice groups: Clarence Risin, Tort Litigation

Women heading practice groups: Fern Singer, Labor & Employment; Danielle Trostorff, Health Law Department; Joan McEntee, International Department; Linda Hall Daschle, Public Policy Department; Betty Anderson, Public Strategies

The Firm Says

Baker, Donelson, Bearman, Caldwell & Berkowitz is committed to minority hiring, an important part of the firm's strategic plan and lateral partner and new associate recruiting efforts. We recognize that individuals with varying cultures and backgrounds provide unique perspectives and approaches to solving our clients' legal problems.

Firm-wide there are 110 female attorneys, of whom 38 are shareholders, 13 are of counsel and 54 are associates. Five of our public policy advisors are female. Baker Donelson has 22 minority attorneys, six of whom are shareholders and 16 of whom are associates.

Baker Donelson's Strategic Plan contains the stated goal of increasing its minority population by 100 percent by August 2004. Since the Strategic Plan's adoption in August 2002, the firm has grown from 11 minority attorneys to 22. The firm plans to hire several more minority attorneys in the fall of 2004. Following are some of the efforts undertaken by the firm in pursuit of its commitment to diversity:

- Several years ago, the firm increased its efforts to attract minority lawyers by recruiting established and successful attorneys who could serve as role models and assist in the recruiting and mentoring of young minority lawyers. In January 2000, Barry Ford, a veteran African-American trial judge in Mississippi, was approached about joining the firm. Judge Ford subsequently became a shareholder in the firm's Jackson office and is actively involved in recruiting and mentoring our younger minority attorneys in Jackson and throughout the firm.

- Following Judge Ford's successful transition into the firm, Baker Donelson has continued to seek out other established minority lawyers, and in 2002 we recruited Cyrus Booker, a noted African-American lawyer, to our Nashville office.

- In April 2004, the firm was pleased to announce the hiring of Herman Morris as a shareholder in the Memphis office. Mr. Morris is the former general counsel and CEO of Memphis Light, Gas & Water, one of America's largest electric, gas, and water municipal utilities. Mr. Morris is one of only a few African-Americans to lead, as CEO, a $1.5 billion enterprise.

- With the firm's encouragement and financial support, Clarence Risin, a shareholder in the Knoxville office, is an active participant in the American Bar Association's Minority Counsel Program.

- Baker Donelson's director of attorney recruitment & development, Sue Hunter, is a member of the Nashville Bar Association's Minority Opportunities Committee, and for the past seven years has served as chairperson for the Second-Year Clerkship Committee, which promotes the hiring of minority clerks by Nashville legal employers.

- As part of our ongoing effort to attract minority counsel to the firm, Baker Donelson annually participates in two minority job fairs: the Southeastern Minority Job Fair in Atlanta, Ga.; and the First-Year Minority Job Fair in Nashville, Tenn.

- Baker Donelson also actively recruits at historically African-American law schools such as North Carolina Central, Howard University and Southern University in order to raise its visibility with minority law students.

- Each year, Baker Donelson serves as a sponsor for the National Black Law Students Association's annual meeting.

- For seven consecutive years, Baker Donelson has received the Leadership Award, given by the Nashville Bar Association's Minority Opportunities Program. Leadership Award recipients are judged on four criteria: minority lawyer recruitment and hiring; minority lawyer retention; minority summer associate programs; and business referrals to minority lawyers. Firm contributions to the Minority Opportunities Program are also considered.

- Baker Donelson contributed 20 percent of the endowment for the Julian Blackshear Scholarship at the University of Tennessee College of Law, which specifically provides financial support for minority law students.

- For the past six years, Baker Donelson has hosted the Nashville 1L Minority Job Fair in its Nashville office.

- Both the Nashville and Memphis offices' first-year summer associate programs are exclusively reserved for minority law students.

- Baker Donelson provides financial support to the Napier-Looby Bar Association, an affiliate of the National Bar Association comprised of judges and lawyers of different races and nationalities, and also pays the dues of all the firm's attorneys who wish to be members of the organization.

Ballard Spahr Andrews & Ingersoll, LLP

1735 Market Street, 51st Floor
Philadelphia, PA 19103-7599
Phone: (215) 665-8500
Fax: (215) 864-8999

FIRM LEADERSHIP

Management Partner: Robert C. Gerlach,
Management Partner
Diversity Team Leader: Maureen M. Rayborn,
Chair, Diversity Committee

LOCATIONS

Philadelphia, PA (HQ)
Baltimore, MD
Denver, CO
Salt Lake City, UT
Voorhees, NJ
Washington, DC
Wilmington, DE

LAW FIRM DEMOGRAPHIC PROFILES

FULL-TIME ASSOCIATES	2003	2002
Minority men	6	8
Minority women	18	10
White women	103	109
Total	242	243

SUMMER ASSOCIATES	2003	2002
Minority men	3	3
Minority women	6	9
White women	14	11
Total	35	42

EQUITY PARTNERS	2003	2002
Minority men	1	1
Minority women	3	3
White women	36	34
Total	200	197

NEW HIRES	2003	2002
Minority men	1	4
Minority women	10	6
White women	18	32
Total	58	90

Strategic Plan and Diversity Leadership

How does the firm's leadership communicate the importance of diversity to everyone at the firm? (e.g., e-mails, web site, newsletters, meetings, etc.)

Providing attorney and staff diversity training; posting of firm's Statement of Commitment to Diversity on firm's external web site and on in-house web site.

Who has primary responsibility for leading diversity initiatives at your firm? Name of person and his/her title:

The Chair of the Diversity Committee.

Does your law firm currently have a diversity committee?

Yes

How many attorneys are on the committee, and in 2003, what was the total number of hours collectively spent by the committee in furtherance of the firm's diversity initiatives?

Total attorneys on committee: 11

Total hours spent on diversity: Not recorded

How often does the firm's management review the firm's diversity progress/results?

Quarterly

LAW FIRM DIVERSITY INITIATIVES	ALREADY COMPLETED	CURRENTLY ADDRESSING	NOT A CURRENT PRIORITY
Undertake communication from firm management that diversity is a top priority of the firm.	✔		
Formalize diversity plan and committee with action steps and accountability to management.		✔	
Conduct firm-wide diversity training for all attorneys and staff.	✔		
Increase the number of minority attorneys at the associate level.		✔	
Increase the number of minority attorneys at the partnership level.		✔	
Develop/expand relationships with minority bar associations to offer firm's support of these networks.		✔	
Focus on strengthening firm's mentoring program, including for benefit of minority attorneys.		✔	
Conduct internal diversity needs assessment and/or retain diversity consultant to examine how firm culture might be more welcoming of minorities.	✔		
Support law firm's internal affinity networks (e.g., women, minority attorney networks).	✔		
Manage/monitor allocation of work assignments and/or hours billed to ensure women and minority attorneys have equal access/inclusion on top client matters.	✔		

Recruitment – New Associates

Does your firm annually recruit at any of the following types of institutions? (Check all that apply and list the schools).

Ivy League schools: Columbia University, Harvard University, University of Pennsylvania, Yale University

Public state schools: University of Michigan, University of Pittsburgh, Rutgers University, Temple University, University of Virginia

Private schools: Duke University, George Washington University, Georgetown University, NYU, Villanova University, Widener University

Historically Black Colleges and Universities (HBCUs): Howard University

Do you have any special outreach efforts directed to encourage minority law students to consider your firm?

• *Legal Recruiting Administrators of Philadelphia reception for 1L minority students*

• Hold a reception for minority law students (see narrative section below)

• Participate in/host minority law student job fair(s)

• Sponsor minority law student association events

SUMMER ASSOCIATE STATISTICS: SUMMER 2003	MINORITY MEN	MINORITY WOMEN	WHITE WOMEN	TOTAL
Summer associates	3	2	13	25
Summer associates who received an offer of full-time employment	3	2	10	22
Summer associates who accepted an offer of full-time employment	2	1	8	18

Recruitment – Lateral Associates and Partners

What activities does the firm undertake to attract minority and women attorneys?

• Partner programs with women and minority bar associations

• Participate at minority job fairs

• Seek referrals from other attorneys

• Utilize online job services (e.g., MCCA/DuPont Primary Law Firm Job Bank)

Do you use executive recruiting/search firms to seek to identify new diversity hires (partners or associates)?

Yes

List all women- and/or minority-owned executive search/recruiting firms to which the firm paid a fee for placement services in the past 12 months:

None

LATERAL ASSOCIATES AND PARTNERS: 1/1/03 – 12/31/03	MINORITY MEN	MINORITY WOMEN	WHITE WOMEN	TOTAL
Number of lateral associate hires	1	2	5	22
Number of lateral partner hires (equity and non-equity)	0	0	0	0
Number of new partners (equity and non-equity) promoted from associate rank	0	0	3	7
Number of new equity partners	0	0	3	7

Retention & Professional Development

ATTORNEYS WHO LEFT THE FIRM: 2003	MINORITY MEN	MINORITY WOMEN	WHITE WOMEN	TOTAL
Number of attorneys who voluntarily or involuntarily left your firm's employ in 2003	3	2	23	53

How do 2003 attrition rates generally compare to those experienced in the prior year period?
About the same as in prior years

Please identify the specific steps you are taking to reduce the attrition rate of minority and women attorneys.
• Develop and/or support internal employee affinity groups (e.g., minority or women networks within the firm)
• Increase/review compensation relative to competition
• Work with minority and women attorneys to develop career advancement plans
• Introduce minority and women attorneys to key clients, including to lead engagements
• Review work assignments and hours billed to key client matters to make sure minority and women attorneys are not being excluded
• Strengthen mentoring program for all attorneys, including minorities and women
• Professional skills development program, including minority and women attorneys

Does your firm have part-time/flex-time policies that permit attorneys (male or female) to work alternative schedules?
Yes

What impact, if any, will the decision to work part-time have on an attorney's ability to make partner or, if already a partner, to remain a partner at your firm?
None, other than timing for entering partnership (for associates).

Have any attorneys who chose to work a part-time schedule made partner at your firm?
Yes, one attorney.

Management Demographic Profile (as of 12/31/03)

	MINORITY MEN	MINORITY WOMEN	WHITE WOMEN	TOTAL
Number of attorneys on the Executive/Management Committee or equivalent	0	1	1	10
Number of attorneys on the Hiring Committee or equivalent	0	3	10	32
Number of attorneys on the Partner/Associate Review Committee or equivalent	0/0	0/1	1/3	6/12

Professional Personnel Committee/Evaluation & Compensation Committee

Please provide information regarding all minority and women attorneys who head offices or practice groups of your law firm:

Minorities heading offices: Tobey Daluz, Wilmington, DE

Women heading offices: Lynn Axelroth, Philadelphia, PA; Tobey Daluz, Wilmington, DE

Minorities heading practice groups: Charisse R. Lillie, Litigation Department

Women heading practice groups: Regina O. Thomas, Family Wealth Management; Lynn Axelroth, Construction; Jean Hemphill, Health Care; Jean Hemphill, HIPAA; Jamie Bischoff, Intellectual Property; Beverly Quail, Real Estate Finance; Lisa Sloan, Securitization

The Firm Says

Ballard Spahr Andrews & Ingersoll, LLP, is an equal opportunity employer committed to achieving the goal of full participation of minorities and women in the work of the firm. It seeks to reflect, in both its professional and its support staffs, the racial, gender and ethnic diversity of the urban areas in which it has offices, and to comply fully with all applicable federal, state and local laws, ordinances and regulations implementing EEO objectives. It seeks to accomplish this by meeting the letter of the law and contractual requirements, and by carrying out the spirit of the concept. It strives to maintain and grow diversity in the firm, not just because it is the right thing to do, but because it makes the firm a better firm.

To assist in accomplishing these goals, the firm has a Diversity Committee, comprised of partners, associates and staff, which is responsible for implementing the firm's diversity policy. A professional outside consultant has conducted extensive interviews with partners, associates and staff, and conducted diversity training sessions for all attorneys, summer associates, key committees and administrative department heads in several of the firm's offices. The diversity initiative and training are being expanded to all offices. The action plan adopted by the executive board of the firm following the first phase of diversity training commits the firm to:

- offer regular, systematic and in-depth diversity education courses for all firm management and lawyers;

- create a welcoming environment for all new associates to reaffirm the firm's commitment to their professional development;

- re-invigorate the mentor program, including providing minority associates with the choice of an additional minority mentor; and

• partner with clients who are committed to diversity to help develop business opportunities for the firm's minority lawyers.

As part of its commitment to equal employment opportunity, the firm is developing a voluntary affirmative action plan for each of its offices.

The firm focuses on recruiting minority candidates for its legal professional positions. It pays particular attention to its associate hiring efforts and participates in a variety of recruitment endeavors, including job fairs that promote a diverse candidate base. Since 1997, Ballard Spahr has coordinated the annual Legal Minority Job Fair sponsored by DuPont and coordinates an annual minority job fair for law firms in Philadelphia. The firm recruits from the fairs' participating candidates. It also uses its annual summer associate program as a primary tool for hiring new associates, and makes a special effort to attract a diverse class of participants. In addition, the firm recruits from several other minority job fairs, including Harvard and BALSA, and from Howard Law School.

Diversity of gender in the firm's lawyer and staff ranks is also an important goal. The firm promotes the hiring and promotion of women to management and other leadership positions in the firm. Thirty-six percent of the firm's lawyers are women. Seven of the partners-in-charge of the firm's 31 specialty practice groups are women. The chair of the firm's litigation department is an African-American woman. Two of the firm's seven office managing partners are women (one of whom is African-American). Four of the five office administrators are women and five of the nine staff department directors are women (two of whom are African-American).

In 2003, the firm received the Pennsylvania Bar Association Award for the Promotion of Women to Leadership Positions, and Charisse Lillie, its litigation department chair, received the Association's prestigious Anne X. Alpern Award, for supporting women in the legal profession.

The firm is an original signatory of the Philadelphia Bar Association Statement of Goals of the Philadelphia Law Firms and Legal Departments for Increasing Minority Representation and Retention, through which the firm has committed to greater participation of gender and racial minorities among its attorneys. The firm is also an active member and financial supporter of the Minority Counsel Program of the ABA's Commission on Racial and Ethnic Diversity. Charisse Lillie has served as chair of the Commission and Stephanie Franklin-Suber, an African-American partner in the firm's business and finance department, has served as co-chair of the annual Minority Counsel Program. Ms. Lillie also serves on the Pennsylvania Supreme Court Committee on Racial and Gender Bias in the Justice System.

The firm works closely with its clients in their efforts to promote diversity. A prominent example is the firm's partnering with DuPont. DuPont has selected its primary law firms based upon their excellence and their commitment to the DuPont Legal Model, which applies "business discipline" to the practice of law, making strategic partnering, information technology, metrics, diversity and other initiatives the cornerstones of DuPont's business approach. Because DuPont encourages its primary law firms to use women and minorities for its work, the firm has aggressively taken up this challenge and has been recognized by DuPont for excelling in benchmark DuPont surveys, for making direct financial contributions supporting DuPont diversity initiatives and for participating in DuPont's Minority Job Fairs. The firm also offers its minority and female summer associates mentoring opportunities through the DuPont Program. The firm has been a six-time recipient of DuPont's Challenge Award.

The firm's labor and employment group offers its clients corporate diversity legal services, including strategic planning, employee training, audits, investigations and development of affirmative action plans.

The firm also regularly supports civic and charitable events that promote diversity in the cities in which it has offices.

Barnes & Thornburg LLP

11 South Meridian Street
Indianapolis, IN 46204
Phone: (317) 236-1313
Fax: (317) 231-7433

FIRM LEADERSHIP

Managing Partner: Alan A. Levin, Firm
Managing Partner
Diversity Team Leader: R. Anthony Prather,
Chairman of Diversity Committee

LOCATIONS

Indianapolis, IN (HQ)
Chicago, IL
Elkhart, IN
Fort Wayne, IN
Grand Rapids, MI
South Bend, IN
Washington, DC

LAW FIRM DEMOGRAPHIC PROFILES

FULL-TIME ASSOCIATES	2003	2002
Minority men	2	2
Minority women	5	4
White women	47	50
Total	130	134

SUMMER ASSOCIATES	2003	2002
Minority men	3	3
Minority women	4	3
White women	12	8
Total	27	23

EQUITY PARTNERS	2003	2002
Minority men	4	4
Minority women	1	0
White women	20	19
Total	164	141

NEW HIRES	2003	2002
Minority men	1	0
Minority women	4	1
White women	17	12
Total	69	32

Strategic Plan and Diversity Leadership

How does the firm's leadership communicate the importance of diversity to everyone at the firm? (e.g., e-mails, web site, newsletters, meetings, etc.)

The firm leadership has communicated the importance of diversity in several fashions. First, diversity was a significant agenda item for the partners' retreats in 2001, 2003 and 2004. At the 2003 meeting, the Diversity Action Plan was introduced to the partners. In 2004, there was an outside speaker at the meeting, interacting with the partners on the importance of diversity. Furthermore, diversity has been emphasized with regard to various orientation programs for the associate classes as well as the summer associates.

Who has primary responsibility for leading diversity initiatives at your firm?

Alan A. Levin, firm managing partner

Does your law firm currently have a diversity committee?

Yes

Does the committee's representation include one or more members of the firm's management/executive committee (or the equivalent)?

Yes

How many attorneys are on the committee, and in 2003, what was the total number of hours collectively spent by the committee in furtherance of the firm's diversity initiatives?

Total attorneys on committee: 13

Total hours spent on diversity by lawyer: 50

Does the committee and/or diversity leader establish and set goals or objectives consistent with management's priorities?

Yes

Has the firm undertaken a formal or informal diversity program or set of initiatives aimed at increasing the diversity of the firm?

Yes, formal

How often does the firm's management review the firm's diversity progress/results?

The firm has implemented a semiannual review process. For specific initiatives, an informal review may be more frequent.

How is the firm's diversity committee and/or firm management held accountable for achieving results?

The committee is held accountable in two ways. First, the committee members' continued participation is based on performance, contributions and results. Also, these type of administrative contributions are factors in determining a partner's compensation.

LAW FIRM DIVERSITY INITIATIVES	ALREADY COMPLETED	CURRENTLY ADDRESSING	NOT A CURRENT PRIORITY
Undertake communication from firm management that diversity is a top priority of the firm.	✓		
Formalize diversity plan and committee with action steps and accountability to management.	✓		
Conduct firm-wide diversity training for all attorneys and staff.		✓	
Increase the number of minority attorneys at the associate level.		✓	
Increase the number of minority attorneys at the partnership level.		✓	
Develop/expand relationships with minority bar associations to offer firm's support of these networks.	✓		
Focus on strengthening firm's mentoring program, including for benefit of minority attorneys.		✓	
Conduct internal diversity needs assessment and/or retain diversity consultant to examine how firm culture might be more welcoming of minorities.	✓		
Support law firm's internal affinity networks (e.g., women, minority attorney networks).	✓		
Manage/monitor allocation of work assignments and/or hours billed to ensure women and minority attorneys have equal access/inclusion on top client matters.		✓	

Recruitment – New Associates

Does your firm annually recruit at any of the following types of institutions? (Check all that apply and list the schools).

Ivy League schools: The firm does not interview at these schools, but does hire write-in candidates

Public state schools: Indiana University, University of Michigan, University of Illinois and Ohio State University

Private schools: Northwestern University, University of Notre Dame, Washington University in St. Louis, Duke University, Georgetown University, University of Chicago, Vanderbilt University and Valparaiso University

Historically Black Colleges and Universities (HBCUs): Howard University

Do you have any special outreach efforts directed to encourage minority law students to consider your firm?

• *Gateway to Diversity Program sponsored by the Indiana CLEO program and the ISBA Opportunities for Minorities Committee*

• Hold a reception for minority law students

• Participate in/host minority law student job fair(s)

• Firm's lawyers participate on career panels at school

 VAULT

243

 M|C|C|A
MINORITY CORPORATE COUNSEL ASSOCIATION

SUMMER ASSOCIATE STATISTICS: SUMMER 2003	MINORITY MEN	MINORITY WOMEN	WHITE WOMEN	TOTAL
Summer associates	2	3	4	16
Summer associates who received an offer of full-time employment	2	3	3	15
Summer associates who accepted an offer of full-time employment	2	3	3	14

Recruitment – Lateral Associates and Partners

What activities does the firm undertake to attract minority and women attorneys?

• Participate at minority job fairs

• Seek referrals from other attorneys

Do you use executive recruiting/search firms to seek to identify new diversity hires (partners or associates)?

No

LATERAL ASSOCIATES AND PARTNERS: 1/1/03 – 12/31/03	MINORITY MEN	MINORITY WOMEN	WHITE WOMEN	TOTAL
Number of lateral associate hires	0	1	5	18
Number of lateral partner hires (equity and non-equity)	0	1	1	23
Number of new partners (equity and non-equity) promoted from associate rank	0	0	0	5
Number of new equity partners	N/A	N/A	N/A	N/A

Retention & Professional Development

ATTORNEYS WHO LEFT THE FIRM: 2003	MINORITY MEN	MINORITY WOMEN	WHITE WOMEN	TOTAL
Number of attorneys who voluntarily or involuntarily left your firm's employ in 2003	1	2	19	37

How do 2003 attrition rates generally compare to those experienced in the prior year period?

Higher than in prior years

Please identify the specific steps you are taking to reduce the attrition rate of minority and women attorneys.

The following initiatives are being taken by firm management and the Diversity Committee

• Develop and/or support internal employee affinity groups (e.g., minority or women networks within the firm)

• Work with minority and women attorneys to develop career advancement plans

• Strengthen mentoring program for all attorneys, including minorities and women

• Professional skills development program, including minority and women attorneys

Does your firm have part-time/flex-time policies that permit attorneys (male or female) to work alternative schedules?

Yes

What impact, if any, will the decision to work part-time have on an attorney's ability to make partner or, if already a partner, to remain a partner at your firm?

The firm has adopted a part-time lawyer policy. Part-time lawyers have the opportunity to continue their legal practice with the firm as partners.

Have any attorneys who chose to work a part-time schedule made partner at your firm?

Yes, seven attorneys.

Management Demographic Profile (as of 12/31/03)

	MINORITY MEN	MINORITY WOMEN	WHITE WOMEN	TOTAL
Number of attorneys on the Executive/Management Committee or equivalent	0	0	1	15
Number of attorneys on the Hiring Committee or equivalent	1	1	6	20
Number of attorneys on the Partner/Associate Review Committee or equivalent	0	0	3	19

Please provide information regarding all minority and women attorneys who head offices or practice groups of your law firm:

Women heading offices: None. However, as indicated below, the chair of the firm's largest department, Business, Tax & Real Estate, is a woman (Catherine L. Bridge), and the chair of the firm-wide Marketing Committee is also a woman (Teresa E. Morton).

Minorities heading practice groups: Alan K. Mills, Creditors' Rights; Mari Y. Regnier, Japanese Practice Group

Women heading practice groups: Catherine L. Bridge, Business, Tax & Real Estate; Deborah L. Thorne, Creditors' Rights; Jan M. Carroll, Media; Carolyn D. Gray, ADA; Mariana Richmond, Immigration; Teresa E. Morton, Telecommunications; Mari Y. Regnier, Japanese Practice Group; Alice O. Martin, Bio-Tech Practice Group

The Firm Says

Barnes & Thornburg LLP is committed to diversity in the workplace. In 1971, the firm became the first major Indiana firm to name a woman partner, Shirley A. Shideler. As a firm that conducts business throughout the world, we value the richness of differences in individuals and cultures. Diverse thinking improves our ability to communicate with increasingly diverse constituencies, such as clients, colleagues, judges and juries, regulators and corporate decision-makers.

To cultivate a diverse workplace, we recruit and develop highly skilled minority and women practitioners to assume leadership roles within the firm. Minority and women attorneys participate in firm management, regularly taking first-chair trial responsibility and managing some of our largest legal practices. Six of the firm's women partners are listed in Best Lawyers in America and 49 of our female attorneys are listed in Martindale-Hubbell's Bar Register of Preeminent Lawyers. Barnes & Thornburg is the only Indiana law firm member in the ABA's Conference of Minority Partners in Majority Corporate Law Firms. Four minority partners are registered in the Conference's national directory. Four attorneys are featured in the 2003-2004 edition of Who's Who in Black Indianapolis. Additional statistical information regarding our diversity efforts is as follows:

New associate classes (firm-wide):

> 2002 – 50% women; 7% minority
>
> 2003 – 53% women; 20% minority
>
> 2004 – 31% women; 31% minority

New associates (Indianapolis):

> 2003 – 70% women; 30% minority
>
> 2004 – 40% women; 40% minority

Attorneys as of September 2004:

> 25% women; 5% minority

The numbers of women and minorities in the firm reflect not only the changing populations of law schools, but also the firm's commitment to hire excellent lawyers regardless of race, color, religion, national origin, gender, age, disability, veteran's status, marital status or sexual orientation. The firm provides same-sex domestic partnership benefits. Barnes & Thornburg strives to provide an environment to attract, nurture and retain these valuable minority employees.

Barnes & Thornburg is committed to being all-inclusive in hiring decisions for both lawyers and staff. In 2003, B&T's Management Committee adopted an action plan for increasing diversity. The committee formed to implement the plan includes the managing partner and chairs of the Diversity and Legal Personnel-Recruiting Committees. Women partners include a Management Committee member and chairs of the business, tax & real estate department; the media, immigration, Japanese, telecommunications and financial institutions practice areas; and the Client and Community Relations Committee. An African-American partner chairs the Diversity Committee. Specific action points in the plan cover recruiting and retention efforts, a formal mentoring process, sponsorship of events attended by minority lawyers and an enhanced orientation program reviewing differences in cultures. The plan requires semiannual progress reports presented to firm leadership and an annual report by the firm's managing partner to all partners.

Minority recruiting efforts include encouraging minority candidates at all campus interviews, as well as write-ins; participating in the Gateway to Diversity program sponsored by the Indiana Conference for Legal Education Opportunity and the Indiana State Bar Association Opportunities for Minorities Committee; and recruiting at the Black Law Students Association Midwest Minority Recruitment Conference, Howard University and the Cook County Bar Association Minority Law Student Job Fair. The firm hired at least one summer associate each year for the last nine years from the Gateway to Diversity program or its predecessor program. We have also worked with Eli Lilly & Co. to recruit and attract minority candidates from the Southern University School of Law.

To improve the rate of retention of minorities, the firm offers career development beginning with summer associates. Each summer associate has two advisors who strive to ensure that the experience is rewarding. When a new attorney joins the firm, partner and associate advisors and mentoring programs assist in easing the transition from student to attorney. The firm has held several diversity special events on networking and the alternative work plan policy and regularly scheduled lunches with new minority attorneys and firm leadership. New minority attorneys also have been introduced to prominent community leaders and others in the legal profession.

This year, Barnes & Thornburg was nominated for the Indianapolis Mayor's Celebration of Diversity Award, the only law firm to be nominated. Barnes & Thornburg has received a Madame C.J. Walker Award for its continuous dedication and contributions to the Central Indiana African-American community. The firm also received the Rabb Emison Award, which was created by the Indiana State Bar Association Opportunities for Minorities Committee to honor organizations that demonstrate a commitment to promote diversity and equality in the legal profession and in the membership of the Indiana State Bar Association.

The Diversity Committee has participated in and supported a number of Indianapolis area events over the last several years such as the annual Women and the Law Conference. The firm participated in Indiana Black Expo's Corporate Luncheon in 2003 and was a major sponsor of the Minority Corporate Counsel Association's CLE Expo in 2004. Since the first dinner four years ago, the firm has been a sponsor each year of the Lambda Legal Defense Dinner in Indianapolis. The firm is also a regular sponsor of the Central Indiana Women's Fund.

The firm has been a leader in a formal pro bono program in which all of the firm lawyers are strongly encouraged to give of their time. This, in turn, helps foster a giving and inclusive culture.

In conclusion, the firm is strongly committed to diversity. To us, diversity means more than filling out the roster. The firm strives to incorporate minorities and women at all levels of the organization. The firm is extremely proud that minorities and women lead key practice areas, departments and internal committees within the firm as well as play active roles in the communities in which we practice.

Bingham McCutchen LLP

150 Federal Street
Boston, MA 02110
Phone: (617) 951-8000
Fax: (617) 951-8736

FIRM LEADERSHIP

Managing Partner: Jay S. Zimmerman,
Chairman
Diversity Team Leader: Ralph C. Martin II,
Chair of Diversity Task Force

LOCATIONS

Boston, MA
Hartford, CT
Los Angeles, CA
New York, NY
Orange County, CA
San Francisco, CA
Silicon Valley, CA
Walnut Creek, CA
Washington, DC
London
Tokyo

LAW FIRM DEMOGRAPHIC PROFILES

FULL-TIME ASSOCIATES	2003	2002
Minority men	39	41
Minority women	63	48
White women	197	175
Total	488	450

SUMMER ASSOCIATES	2003	2002
Minority men	8	12
Minority women	10	13
White women	31	34
Total	76	87

EQUITY PARTNERS	2003	2002
Minority men	19	15
Minority women	2	2
White women	53	47
Total	304	277

NON-EQUITY PARTNERS	2003	2002
Minority men	0	0
Minority women	0	0
White women	3	1
Total	9	2

NEW HIRES	2003	2002
Minority men	16	13
Minority women	26	9
White women	72	39
Total	194	111

Strategic Plan and Diversity Leadership

How does the firm's leadership communicate the importance of diversity to everyone at the firm? (e.g., e-mails, web site, newsletters, meetings, etc.)

The leadership of our firm regularly affirms our commitment to diversity and its importance to our firm in numerous ways. Our chair, Jay Zimmerman, focuses on diversity in meetings with partners and associates by, for example, highlighting in firm-wide e-mails the work of the Diversity Task Force and the appointment of Ralph Martin to lead the task force and noting recent developments at the firm through meetings, e-mail announcements, letters and communications on our web site. Furthermore, Ralph Martin communicates the firm's commitment to diversity through in-person meetings (including recently conducted meetings with groups of partners and associates in our domestic offices), reports to the Diversity Task Force, and liaisons with the Committee on Associates (COA) and the recruiting department. In addition, the heads of the COA and our national hiring partner regularly focus and report on diversity and recent diversity efforts in meetings, e-mails, training sessions and videoconferences with attorneys throughout our offices.

Who has primary responsibility for leading diversity initiatives at your firm?

Ralph C. Martin II, Bingham McCutchen partner, managing director of Bingham Consulting (Bingham Consulting is a subsidiary business of Bingham McCutchen) and chair of Diversity Task Force.

Does your law firm currently have a diversity committee?

Yes

Does the committee's representation include one or more members of the firm's management/executive committee (or the equivalent)?

Yes

How many attorneys are on the committee, and in 2003, what was the total number of hours collectively spent by the committee in furtherance of the firm's diversity initiatives?

Total attorneys on committee: 23

Total hours spent on diversity: 1,200

Does the committee and/or diversity leader establish and set goals or objectives consistent with management's priorities?

Yes. Bingham McCutchen has recently augmented its historic approach to goal and objective setting in this area (including its commitment to the diversity principles referenced below) with the commitment to conduct an internal diversity audit (beginning in third quarter 2004), aimed at identifying our current strengths and capacities, and targeting areas for improvement. Once this is completed, the firm, possibly in concert with an external consultant, will develop a new formal diversity plan, which will include developing timetables for achieving the goals set forth therein.

Has the firm undertaken a formal or informal diversity program or set of initiatives aimed at increasing the diversity of the firm?

Yes, formal and informal

How often does the firm's management review the firm's diversity progress/results?

Quarterly

How is the firm's diversity committee and/or firm management held accountable for achieving results?

Bingham McCutchen has signed onto a number of bar association objectives that are designed to promote the more meaningful participation of minority groups in majority law firms. Additionally, upon completion of the diversity benchmarking audit, the firm will be devising a formal diversity plan that will be monitored by Bingham's chairman and the firm's Management Committee.

LAW FIRM DIVERSITY INITIATIVES	ALREADY COMPLETED	CURRENTLY ADDRESSING	NOT A CURRENT PRIORITY
Undertake communication from firm management that diversity is a top priority of the firm.	✔	✔	
Formalize diversity plan and committee with action steps and accountability to management.		✔	
Conduct firm-wide diversity training for all attorneys and staff.			✔
Increase the number of minority attorneys at the associate level.		✔	
Increase the number of minority attorneys at the partnership level.		✔	
Develop/expand relationships with minority bar associations to offer firm's support of these networks.		✔	
Focus on strengthening firm's mentoring program, including for benefit of minority attorneys.		✔	
Conduct internal diversity needs assessment and/or retain diversity consultant to examine how firm culture might be more welcoming of minorities.		✔	
Support law firm's internal affinity networks (e.g., women, minority attorney networks).		✔	
Manage/monitor allocation of work assignments and/or hours billed to ensure women and minority attorneys have equal access/inclusion on top client matters.		✔	

Bingham McCutchen has committed to certain bar association goals in the area of diversity:·

• The firm's New York office has signed onto the Statement of Diversity Principles for the Association of the Bar of the City of New York. As a signatory member, we have committed to achieving several goals that are set out by the Association for member firms, within specific time frames relating to hiring, retention, promotion, leadership and other strategies that will enhance diversity in New York law firms.

• Bingham McCutchen adopted the Bar Association of San Francisco's (BASF) Year 2000 Proposal, co-written by partner Ray Marshall, establishing hiring goals and timetables for minority lawyers, which calls for 25 percent associates/counsel (which the firm exceeded) and 10 percent partners. Bingham McCutchen has pledged to meet the BASF Year 2005 Proposal (35 percent associates; 12 percent partners) firm-wide.

• Bingham McCutchen is one of the participants of the BASF "No Glass Ceiling" Initiative signed in May 2002, where more than 50 public and private law firms agreed to seek to have at least one quarter of their partnership slots filled by women within the next two years. A Bingham McCutchen partner, Charlene (Chuck) Shimada, was on the task force which designed the initiative, and the firm was an early signatory.

Recruitment - New Associates

Does your firm annually recruit at any of the following types of institutions? (Check all that apply and list the schools).

Ivy League schools: Columbia University, Cornell University, Harvard University, University of Pennsylvania, Yale University

Public state schools: University of California-Los Angeles, University of California-Berkeley (Boalt Hall), University of California-Hastings, University of Connecticut, University of Michigan, University of Toronto, University of Virginia

Private schools: Boston College, Boston University, Duke University, Fordham University, Georgetown University, Loyola Law School, McGill University, New England School of Law, New York University, Northeastern University, Northwestern University, Stanford University, Suffolk University, University of Chicago, University of Notre Dame, University of San Francisco, Western New England College

Historically Black Colleges and Universities (HBCUs): Howard University

Do you have any special outreach efforts directed to encourage minority law students to consider your firm?

• *Initiation of and continued participation in The Boston Lawyers Group (BLG) pipeline program designed to encourage minority college students to attend law school. Also, miscellaneous programs geared toward minority law students, including mock interview programs, the Howard University School of Law internship program, mentoring of minority law students and substantive programs around the practice of law.*

• Hold a reception for minority law students

• Advertise in minority law student association publication(s)

• Participate in/host minority law student job fair(s)

• Sponsor minority law student association events

• Firm's lawyers participate on career panels at school

• Outreach to leadership of minority student organizations

• Scholarships or intern/fellowships for minority students

SUMMER ASSOCIATE STATISTICS: SUMMER 2003	MINORITY MEN	MINORITY WOMEN	WHITE WOMEN	TOTAL
Summer associates	7	9	31	68
Summer associates who received an offer of full-time employment	7	9	29	62
Summer associates who accepted an offer of full-time employment	6*	7*	26*	52*

* In any given year, a number of offers remain outstanding on account of post-graduate clerkships.

Recruitment – Lateral Associates and Partners

What activities does the firm undertake to attract minority and women attorneys?

• *Requesting that search firms identify diversity candidates*

• Partner programs with women and minority bar associations

• Participate at minority job fairs

• Seek referrals from other attorneys

• Utilize online job services (e.g., MCCA/DuPont Primary Law Firm Job Bank)

Do you use executive recruiting/search firms to seek to identify new diversity hires (partners or associates)?

Yes

List all women- and/or minority-owned executive search/recruiting firms to which the firm paid a fee for placement services in the past 12 months:

Mestel and Company; CMRW Legal Search; New England Legal Search; Jane Sender Legal Search; McMorrow Savarese.

LATERAL ASSOCIATES AND PARTNERS: 1/1/03 – 12/31/03	MINORITY MEN	MINORITY WOMEN	WHITE WOMEN	TOTAL
Number of lateral associate hires	8	10	44	188
Number of lateral partner hires (equity and non-equity)	4	0	6	40
Number of new partners (equity and non-equity) promoted from associate rank	1	0	0	6
Number of new equity partners	5	0	6	46

* Bingham McCutchen has a one-tier partnership system without distinction between equity and non-equity. In 2003, five contract partners joined the firm, and they are included in our numbers for lateral partner hires and number of new partners.

Retention & Professional Development

ATTORNEYS WHO LEFT THE FIRM: 2003	MINORITY MEN	MINORITY WOMEN	WHITE WOMEN	TOTAL
Number of attorneys who voluntarily or involuntarily left your firm's employ in 2003	N/A	N/A	N/A	N/A

*Firm policy does not permit the external release of departure information.

How do 2003 attrition rates generally compare to those experienced in the prior year period?**

**Given the merger-related expansion of our firm in mid-2002 and again in 2003, we are not able to provide an accurate comparison of attrition rates across the firm.

Please identify the specific steps you are taking to reduce the attrition rate of minority and women attorneys.

• *Market-leading parental leave policy and part-time policy; New Mom's Group*

• Develop and/or support internal employee affinity groups (e.g., minority or women networks within the firm)

• Increase/review compensation relative to competition

• Increase/improve current work/life programs

• Work with minority and women attorneys to develop career advancement plans

• Introduce minority and women attorneys to key clients, including to lead engagements

• Review work assignments and hours billed to key client matters to make sure minority and women attorneys are not being excluded

• Strengthen mentoring program for all attorneys, including minorities and women

• Professional skills development program, including minority and women attorneys

Does your firm have part-time/flex-time policies that permit attorneys (male or female) to work alternative schedules?

Yes. Bingham McCutchen has a progressive part-time policy. Currently 69 attorneys are working a part-time schedule.

What impact, if any, will the decision to work part-time have on an attorney's ability to make partner or, if already a partner, to remain a partner at your firm?

Ordinarily, an associate's decision to work part-time will only affect the length of time prior to consideration for partnership, depending on factors such as the length of time of the part-time arrangement. Our policy does not limit the amount of time our lawyers may maintain a part-time schedule and many of our lawyers remain part-time for a period of years. A partner's decision to work part-time will ordinarily not affect partnership status.

Have any attorneys who chose to work a part-time schedule made partner at your firm?

Yes, three attorneys.

Management Demographic Profile (as of 12/31/03)

	MINORITY MEN	MINORITY WOMEN	WHITE WOMEN	TOTAL
Number of attorneys on the Executive/Management Committee or equivalent	1	0	2	17
Number of attorneys on the Hiring Committee or equivalent	6	5	25	66
Number of attorneys on the Partner/Associate Review Committee or equivalent	N/A	N/A	N/A	N/A

*Bingham McCutchen does not have a Partner/Associate Review Committee.

Please provide information regarding all minority and women attorneys who head offices or practice groups of your law firm:

Women heading offices: Tina Brozman, New York; Mary Huser, Silicon Valley

Minorities heading practice groups (list names and departments): Jiro Murase, Japanese Practice; Saturo Murase, Japanese Practice; Ray Marshall, White Collar Crime and Business Regulation; Ralph C. Martin II, Managing Director of the Bingham Consulting Group (a subsidiary business of Bingham McCutchen).

Women heading practice groups (list names and departments): Amy Kyle, Finance Area Deputy Chair; Tina Brozman, Financial Restructuring; Tara Higgins, Project Finance; Carol Dillon, Real Estate; Randy Michelson, Insolvency and Financial Services Litigation; Mary Huser, Intellectual Property Litigation; Debra Fischer, Labor and Employment Litigation; Debbie Freeman, Labor and Employment Litigation; Janice Howe, Products Liability Litigation; Julia Frost Davies (with Randy Michelson for Insolvency and Financial Restructuring Litigation); Elaine McChesney, Appellate Group; Gerry Alexis, Antitrust and Trade Regulation Group; Sarah Gagan, Commercial Technology and Trademark Group.

The Firm Says

Bingham McCutchen has undertaken a variety of initiatives that support the success of women and minority attorneys. Our initiatives reflect both the firm-wide commitment to diversity and the importance of forging relationships with local community organizations to achieve this important goal.

Bingham McCutchen ranked among the top 10 law firms with the most minority partners, according to The American Lawyer's June 2004 annual survey. The firm was named one of the "25 Most Diverse Law Firms in America" in 2003 by the Minority Law Journal; Bingham McCutchen was the highest-ranking national firm. Bingham McCutchen was the inaugural winner of the Drucilla Stender Ramey Award for diversity in a law firm, sponsored by the California Minority Counsel Program (November 2002). The firm is a founding member and active supporter of the California Minority Counsel Program.

Leadership

San Francisco

Partner Raymond Marshall, an African-American, recently served as president of the State Bar of California and president of the Bar Association of San Francisco (BASF). Partner Charlene Sachi Shimada was the first woman to be named office managing partner. She also served on the task force of BASF's "No Glass Ceiling" Initiative. Partner Angel Garganta currently serves as a director of BASF and the ACLU of Northern California, and has served as director of La Raza Centro Legal and the Lawyers' Committee for Civil Rights of the San Francisco Bay Area. Partner Michael Isaku Begert serves as a director of both the Lawyers' Committee for Civil Rights of the San Francisco Bay Area and the National Asian Pacific American Legal Consortium and is former president of the Asian Law Caucus.

Boston

Partner Ralph C. Martin II serves as vice-chair of the Greater Boston Chamber of Commerce and chair of the Massachusetts Judicial Nominating Committee. Partner Janice Howe serves on the Eastern Regional Committee of the Judicial Nominating Council as well as the Judicial Nominating Council for the Juvenile Court. Partner Julia Frost-Davies is the president of the board of trustees of the Women's Bar Foundation and has served as secretary of the Women's Bar Association of Massachusetts and clerk of the ACLU of Massachusetts. Partner Meerie Joung and associate Nga Nguyen serve as board members of the Asian American Lawyers Association of Massachusetts.

Of counsel Sabita Singh is the advisor to the Asian American Support and Research Agency, the founding member and president of the South Asian Bar Association of Greater Boston, and the president-elect of the National South Asian Bar Association. Partner Beth I. Z. Boland is former president of the Women's Bar Association of Massachusetts. During her tenure she and Elaine McChesney co-authored a WBA report on part-time work in the profession which received national attention. She is also a member of the Boston Bar Association's Committee on Work/Life Issues in the Profession.

Recruitment and retention

Bingham McCutchen is a founding member of both the Boston Lawyers Group (BLG) and the newly reconstituted Connecticut Lawyers Group, which are consortia of law firms and legal employers supporting the recruitment, retention and advancement of attorneys of color in their respective states. We vigorously recruit at job fairs directed at students of color, including the BLSA Job Fair and the BLG Job Fairs (Boston and Washington). In 2003, Bingham McCutchen initiated a formal recruiting relationship with Howard University School of Law, which includes on-campus interviews for all our domestic offices, an internship program in our Washington, D.C., office and sponsorship of Howard's mock interview program.

The San Francisco office sponsors a 3 year, $10,000 per year scholarship for Bay Area minority students, participates in the BASF Minority Clerkship Program each summer and contributes annually to minority student organizations at law schools. Our attorneys also serve as mentors to students of color at local law schools, engage in targeted programs at the firm for students of color, regularly speak at local law schools and participate in efforts to support students at these schools, including judging moot court competitions. Additionally, the firm sponsors student affinity group conferences and activities. The firm will conduct a firm-wide retreat for attorneys of color during the fourth quarter of 2004.

Community service

The Boston office, in collaboration with the BLG and the Posse Foundation (with which the Boston and New York offices are active), founded an annual summer internship program for urban college students from diverse backgrounds who may be interested in going to law school. The program includes attorney mentoring for students, opportunities to interact with summer associates, a series of seminars and events that teach the students about how a law firm works and what it is like to be a lawyer, in addition to the actual work performed. This summer, the program, now a signature program of the BLG, increased in size by 20 percent and resulted in a diverse group of college students now actively considering law school.

For several years, attorneys in Boston and San Francisco have assisted inner-city middle school and high school students with local mock trial programs, designed to expose young people to the legal profession with the hope that some of them will pursue law as a career. Bingham McCutchen recently instituted a reading program in several of its offices in which attorneys and staff travel to an inner-city elementary school on a weekly or biweekly basis, to read to and with children.

For more than 20 years, Bingham McCutchen has handled major impact pro bono litigation involving civil rights, including matters involving racial discrimination, desegregation of schools, voting rights and the use of excessive force by police. Many of our offices are involved in a variety of additional minority mentoring and outreach initiatives, such as the Charting Your Legal Future programs with the BLG in Boston, New York and Washington, D.C. Attorneys in our LA office have handled over 250 adoptions of special needs children through the LA Public Counsel's Adoption Project.

BOIES, SCHILLER & FLEXNER, LLP

NEW YORK

WASHINGTON DC

FLORIDA

CALIFORNIA

NEW HAMPSHIRE

NEW JERSEY

5301 Wisconsin Avenue N.W.
Washington, D.C. 20015
Tel.: 202 237 2727

333 Main Street
Armonk, NY 10504
Tel.: 914 749 8200

1999 Harrison Street
Oakland, CA 94612
Tel.: 510 874 1000

Bank of America Tower
100 Southeast 2nd Street
Miami, FL 33131-2144
Tel.: 305 539 8400

570 Lexington Avenue
New York, NY 10022
Tel.: 212 446 2300

10 North Pearl Street
Albany, NY 12207
Tel.: 518 434 0600

300 S.E. 2nd Street
Fort Lauderdale, FL 33301
Tel.: 954 356 9911

150 JFK Parkway
Short Hills, NJ 07078
Tel.: 973 218 1111

255 South Orange Avenue
Orlando, FL 32801
Tel.: 407 425 7118

Boies, Schiller & Flexner LLP

333 Main Street
Armonk, NY 10504-1710
Phone: (914) 749-8200
Fax: (914) 749-8300
www.bsfllp.com

FIRM LEADERSHIP

Managing Partners: David Boies; Jonathan Schiller; Donald Flexner

LOCATIONS

Armonk, NY (HQ)
Albany, NY
Fort Lauderdale, FL
Hanover, NH
Miami, FL
New York, NY
Oakland, CA
Orlando, FL
Short Hills, NJ
Washington, DC

The Firm Says

Boies, Schiller & Flexner is committed to diversity as an integral part of its professional hiring and development program. We believe that many of our best lawyers contribute to that objective. The goal of diversity is not only important to the firm, it is also important to many of the firm's clients.

Broad Range

Brown Raysman Millstein Felder & Steiner, LLP

900 Third Avenue
New York, NY 10022
Phone: (212) 895-2000
Fax: (212) 895-2900

FIRM LEADERSHIP

Managing Partner: Peter Brown, Richard Raysman and Julian S. Millstein, Co-Managing Partners
Diversity Team Leader: Barry G. Felder and Sarah Hewitt, Co-Chairs Diversity Committee

LOCATIONS

New York, NY (HQ)
Hartford, CT
Los Angeles, CA
Morristown, NJ

LAW FIRM DEMOGRAPHIC PROFILES

FULL-TIME ASSOCIATES	2003	2002
Minority men	5	4
Minority women	10	7
White women	38	41
Total	113	107

SUMMER ASSOCIATES	2003	2002
Minority men	0	1
Minority women	1	0
White women	3	5
Total	8	7

EQUITY PARTNERS	2003	2002
Minority men	0	0
Minority women	0	0
White women	5	5
Total	40	38

NON-EQUITY PARTNERS	2003	2002
Minority men	0	0
Minority women	0	0
White women	8	6
Total	40	34

NEW HIRES	2003	2002
Minority men	3	0
Minority women	2	1
White women	6	9
Total	27	25

Strategic Plan and Diversity Leadership

How does the firm's leadership communicate the importance of diversity to everyone at the firm? (e.g., e-mails, web site, newsletters, meetings, etc.)

The firm's Diversity Mission Statement and the activities of the Diversity Committee are discussed periodically at partner meetings, orientations for new attorneys and associate meetings. The firm has developed a diversity page on the firm's web site that outlines our goals, accomplishments and the Diversity Mission Statement. This information is also available in the firm's recruitment brochure and on our intranet system for reference by all employees.

Who has primary responsibility for leading diversity initiatives at your firm? Name of person and his/her title:

Barry G. Felder and Sarah Hewitt, co-chairs of Diversity Committee

Does your law firm currently have a diversity committee?

Yes

Does the committee's representation include one or more members of the firm's management/executive committee (or the equivalent)?

Yes

How many attorneys are on the committee, and in 2003, what was the total number of hours collectively spent by the committee in furtherance of the firm's diversity initiatives?

Total attorneys on committee: 3

Total hours spent on diversity: 150 or more per year

Does the committee and/or diversity leader establish and set goals or objectives consistent with management's priorities?

Yes

Has the firm undertaken a formal or informal diversity program or set of initiatives aimed at increasing the diversity of the firm?

Yes, formal

How often does the firm's management review the firm's diversity progress/results?

Twice a year

How is the firm's diversity committee and/or firm management held accountable for achieving results?

The Diversity Committee is required to set annual goals and periodically report on action steps and achievements of those goals to the Executive Committee.

LAW FIRM DIVERSITY INITIATIVES	ALREADY COMPLETED	CURRENTLY ADDRESSING	NOT A CURRENT PRIORITY
Undertake communication from firm management that diversity is a top priority of the firm.	✓		
Formalize diversity plan and committee with action steps and accountability to management.	✓		
Conduct firm-wide diversity training for all attorneys and staff.		✓	
Increase the number of minority attorneys at the associate level.	✓	✓	
Increase the number of minority attorneys at the partnership level.		✓	
Develop/expand relationships with minority bar associations to offer firm's support of these networks.	✓		
Focus on strengthening firm's mentoring program, including for benefit of minority attorneys.		✓	
Conduct internal diversity needs assessment and/or retain diversity consultant to examine how firm culture might be more welcoming of minorities.		✓	
Support law firm's internal affinity networks (e.g., women, minority attorney networks).	✓		
Manage/monitor allocation of work assignments and/or hours billed to ensure women and minority attorneys have equal access/inclusion on top client matters.		✓	

Recruitment - New Associates

Does your firm annually recruit at any of the following types of institutions? (Check all that apply and list the schools).

Ivy League schools: Columbia University, Harvard University, University of Pennsylvania

Private schools: New York University, Fordham University, Cardozo School of Law, Brooklyn Law School, Georgetown University, St. John's University, Boston University, Boston College

Historically Black Colleges and Universities (HBCUs): Howard University

Do you have any special outreach efforts directed to encourage minority law students to consider your firm?

• Hold a reception for minority law students

• Advertise in minority law student association publication(s)

• Participate in/host minority law student job fair(s)

• Sponsor minority law student association events

• Firm's lawyers participate on career panels at school

• Outreach to leadership of minority student organizations

SUMMER ASSOCIATE STATISTICS: SUMMER 2003	MINORITY MEN	MINORITY WOMEN	WHITE WOMEN	TOTAL
Summer associates	0	1*	3	8
Summer associates who received an offer of full-time employment	0	1*	3	8
Summer associates who accepted an offer of full-time employment	0	0	3	7

*NOTE: This student did not accept the firm's offer of full-time employment because she and her family decided not to settle in New York.

Recruitment – Lateral Associates and Partners

What activities does the firm undertake to attract minority and women attorneys?

• *The firm has established successful relationships with search firms that specialize in lateral minority attorney candidates.*

• Partner programs with women and minority bar associations

• Participate at minority job fairs

• Seek referrals from other attorneys

Do you use executive recruiting/search firms to seek to identify new diversity hires (partners or associates)?

Yes

List all women- and/or minority-owned executive search/recruiting firms to which the firm paid a fee for placement services in the past 12 months:

Elaine P. Dine, Inc.

LATERAL ASSOCIATES AND PARTNERS: 1/1/03 – 12/31/03	MINORITY MEN	MINORITY WOMEN	WHITE WOMEN	TOTAL
Number of lateral associate hires	2	1	3	21
Number of lateral partner hires (equity and non-equity)	1	0	2	9
Number of new partners (equity and non-equity) promoted from associate rank	0	0	0	0
Number of new equity partners	0	0	0	0

Retention & Professional Development

ATTORNEYS WHO LEFT THE FIRM: 2003	MINORITY MEN	MINORITY WOMEN	WHITE WOMEN	TOTAL
Number of attorneys who voluntarily or involuntarily left your firm's employ in 2003	0	2	14	43

How do 2003 attrition rates generally compare to those experienced in the prior year period?

About the same as in prior years

Please identify the specific steps you are taking to reduce the attrition rate of minority and women attorneys.

• Develop and/or support internal employee affinity groups (e.g., minority or women networks within the firm)

• Increase/review compensation relative to competition

• Increase/improve current work/life programs

• Succession plan includes emphasis on diversity

• Introduce minority and women attorneys to key clients, including to lead engagements

• Professional skills development program, including minority and women attorneys

Does your firm have part-time/flex-time policies that permit attorneys (male or female) to work alternative schedules?

Yes

What impact, if any, will the decision to work part-time have on an attorney's ability to make partner or, if already a partner, to remain a partner at your firm?

The firm currently has one woman equity partner who works on a part-time schedule and has remained a partner. The associates who are currently taking advantage of a part-time schedule are junior associates or are associates that are "off track" by choice. Therefore, they will not be eligible for partnership for a number of years.

Have any attorneys who chose to work a part-time schedule made partner at your firm?

No. The associates who are currently taking advantage of a part-time schedule are junior associates or are associates that are "off track" by choice. Therefore, they will not be eligible for partnership for a number of years.

Management Demographic Profile (as of 12/31/03)

	MINORITY MEN	MINORITY WOMEN	WHITE WOMEN	TOTAL
Number of attorneys on the Executive/Management Committee or equivalent	0	0	0	9
Number of attorneys on the Hiring Committee or equivalent	0	2	2	9
Number of attorneys on the Partner/Associate Review Committee or equivalent	0	0	2	11

Please provide information regarding all minority and women attorneys who head offices or practice groups of your law firm:

Women heading practice groups: Beverly Garofalo, Labor & Employment Group, Harford, CT; JoAnne C. Adlerstein, Immigration Group, New York, NY

The Firm Says

Brown Raysman Millstein Felder & Steiner LLP has long recognized that diversity is an important element in ensuring that we serve our clients with the best legal talent possible. Diversity has aided us to be recognized as a renowned general practice law firm in the new millennium. We know that it is important to take our diversity initiatives even further by ensuring that the women and minority attorneys that work in the firm are provided with essential tools to satisfy their career development goals. With the full support of the firm's Executive Committee, the Diversity Committee has put forth a solid firm-wide diversity plan that focuses on recruitment, retention and career development.

Recruitment

Enlisting the assistance of search firms that specialize in minority partner and lateral attorney hiring has been an important element in increasing the number of minority attorneys in all of our offices and departments. The Diversity Committee also has initiated an aggressive campaign to hire more women and minority law school students. We routinely contact women and minority organizations at law schools and encourage students to come to our offices and meet with partners and associates at the firm. We also fund various cultural and pro bono events that support women and minority causes at law schools.

Retention

The firm's commitment to diversity is prevalent in our everyday work environment. We strive to make sure that all women and minority attorneys feel included, respected and valued in every aspect of their career at the firm. As a result, department heads strive to have women and minority attorneys staffed on high-level and challenging work in order to gain exposure to important clients. The Diversity Committee also has supported women and minority associates to participate in programs that facilitate career development, networking opportunities and pairing with mentors. The firm supports attorneys that participate in diversity-oriented bar associations and women and minority affinity groups. We currently have several attorneys taking advantage of the telecommuting and part-time options offered by the firm. Our part-time attorneys are important role models who provide encouragement for those who may be concerned that the price of a successful career is the sacrifice of family commitments.

Career development

Each department has adopted a "Career Development Goals" assessment plan, which guides associates through the skills that they should be able to perform by the end of each year with the firm. Regular and frequent feedback is provided to associates on a formal and informal basis. We also provide in-house training for all attorneys on topical industry issues that are relevant to our legal practice and overall client development.

In addition to the foregoing, the firm also supports the Minority Corporate Counsel Association's Northeast Regional Diversity Dinner and Pathways to Diversity Conference. The firm is also a signatory to the Association of the Bar of the City of New York's Statement of Diversity Principles. Finally, the firm has adopted the following mission statement that we believe captures our true dedication to diversity in the legal community:

> Brown Raysman Millstein Felder & Steiner, LLP recognizes that we live in a diverse world in which the challenges of meeting the current and future needs of our clients are ever increasing. In order to participate in a global marketplace that will allow us to continue to serve our clients with the best legal talent they have come to expect from our firm, we openly embrace the fact that we need to reflect the fact of the multicultural society in which we live and practice. We believe that diversity encourages a drive of innovative ideas and changes through the exchange of a wide range of perspectives from people with differing backgrounds. We have high admiration and respect for the range of vision that the diversity of our attorneys brings to our clients and the firm.

> We recognize that the firm's continued success is attributable to the many talented people we employ. Therefore, the firm is deliberate in maintaining a culture that supports and promotes diversity so that all attorneys feel included, respected and valued. We make every effort to recruit talented attorneys of all minority backgrounds and work harder to retain them by providing the opportunities and resources needed to advance their careers. The firm vigorously supports the career development of all attorneys of the firm and actively strives to meet this goal day after day, understanding that our strong commitment to diversity in all of our offices will contribute to our continued success now and in the future.

Brown Rudnick Berlack Israels LLP

One Financial Center
Boston, MA 02111
Phone: (617) 856-8200
Fax: (617) 856-8201

FIRM LEADERSHIP

Managing Partner: Joseph F. Ryan, Chief
Executive Officer
Diversity Team Leader: Joseph F. Ryan, Chief
Executive Officer

LOCATIONS

Boston, MA (HQ)
Hartford, CT
New York, NY
Providence, RI
Washington, DC
Dublin
London

LAW FIRM DEMOGRAPHIC PROFILES

FULL-TIME ASSOCIATES	2003	2002
Minority men	3	3
Minority women	4	6
White women	31	28
Total	75	79

SUMMER ASSOCIATES	2003	2002
Minority men	1	0
Minority women	2	2
White women	4	10
Total	13	16

EQUITY PARTNERS	2003	2002
Minority men	1	1
Minority women	0	0
White women	5	5
Total	57	59

CONTRACT PARTNERS	2003	2002
Minority men	1	2
Minority women	0	0
White women	2	3
Total	24	26

NON-EQUITY PARTNERS	2003	2002
Minority men	0	0
Minority women	0	0
White women	4	5
Total	17	17

NEW HIRES	2003	2002
Minority men	0	0
Minority women	0	0
White women	7	7
Total	9	21*

* Includes 8 contract partners

MINORITY CORPORATE COUNSEL ASSOCIATION

Strategic Plan and Diversity Leadership

How does the firm's leadership communicate the importance of diversity to everyone at the firm? (e.g., e-mails, web site, newsletters, meetings, etc.)

Through circulation of policies; workshops; firm-wide diversity initiatives; report on diversity statistics at monthly Management Committee meetings.

Who has primary responsibility for leading diversity initiatives at your firm? Name of person and his/her title:

Joseph F. Ryan, chief executive officer

Does your law firm currently have a diversity committee?

Yes

Does the committee's representation include one or more members of the firm's management/executive committee (or the equivalent)?

Yes

How many attorneys are on the committee, and in 2003, what was the total number of hours collectively spent by the committee in furtherance of the firm's diversity initiatives?

Total attorneys on committee: 6

Total hours spent on diversity: Difficult to determine

Does the committee and/or diversity leader establish and set goals or objectives consistent with management's priorities?

Yes

Has the firm undertaken a formal or informal diversity program or set of initiatives aimed at increasing the diversity of the firm?

Yes, formal

How often does the firm's management review the firm's diversity progress/results?

Monthly

How is the firm's diversity committee and/or firm management held accountable for achieving results?

Managing directors are held accountable to Management Committee for diversity objectives.

LAW FIRM DIVERSITY INITIATIVES	ALREADY COMPLETED	CURRENTLY ADDRESSING	NOT A CURRENT PRIORITY
Undertake communication from firm management that diversity is a top priority of the firm.		✓	
Formalize diversity plan and committee with action steps and accountability to management.		✓	
Conduct firm-wide diversity training for all attorneys and staff.		✓	
Increase the number of minority attorneys at the associate level.		✓	
Increase the number of minority attorneys at the partnership level.		✓	
Develop/expand relationships with minority bar associations to offer firm's support of these networks.		✓	
Focus on strengthening firm's mentoring program, including for benefit of minority attorneys.		✓	
Conduct internal diversity needs assessment and/or retain diversity consultant to examine how firm culture might be more welcoming of minorities.		✓	
Support law firm's internal affinity networks (e.g., women, minority attorney networks).		✓	
Manage/monitor allocation of work assignments and/or hours billed to ensure women and minority attorneys have equal access/inclusion on top client matters.		✓	

Recruitment – New Associates

Does your firm annually recruit at any of the following types of institutions? (Check all that apply and list the schools).

Ivy League schools: Harvard University, Cornell University, Columbia University, University of Pennsylvania

Public state schools: University of Connecticut, University of Michigan, University of Virginia

Private schools: Boston College, Boston University, Franklin Pierce Law Center, Georgetown University, Northeastern University, Northwestern University, New York University, Roger Williams School of Law, Suffolk University

Do you have any special outreach efforts directed to encourage minority law students to consider your firm?

• *Boston Lawyers Group Job Fairs*

• Participate in/host minority law student job fair(s)

• Firm's lawyers participate on career panels at school

SUMMER ASSOCIATE STATISTICS: SUMMER 2003	MINORITY MEN	MINORITY WOMEN	WHITE WOMEN	TOTAL
Summer associates	1	2	4	13
Summer associates who received an offer of full-time employment	1	2	3	11
Summer associates who accepted an offer of full-time employment	1	2	3	11

Recruitment – Lateral Associates and Partners

What activities does the firm undertake to attract minority and women attorneys?

• *1L job opportunities*

• Participate at minority job fairs

• Seek referrals from other attorneys

Do you use executive recruiting/search firms to seek to identify new diversity hires (partners or associates)?

Yes

LATERAL ASSOCIATES AND PARTNERS: 1/1/03 – 12/31/03	MINORITY MEN	MINORITY WOMEN	WHITE WOMEN	TOTAL
Number of lateral associate hires	0	0	0	0
Number of lateral partner hires (equity and non-equity)	0	0	0	0
Number of new partners (equity and non-equity) promoted from associate rank	0	0	0	4
Number of new equity partners	0	0	0	2

Retention & Professional Development

ATTORNEYS WHO LEFT THE FIRM: 2003	MINORITY MEN	MINORITY WOMEN	WHITE WOMEN	TOTAL
Number of attorneys who voluntarily or involuntarily left your firm's employ in 2003	1	2	3	13

How do 2003 attrition rates generally compare to those experienced in the prior year period?

Lower than in prior years

Please identify the specific steps you are taking to reduce the attrition rate of minority and women attorneys.

• Develop and/or support internal employee affinity groups (e.g., minority or women networks within the firm)

• Increase/review compensation relative to competition

• Increase/improve current work/life programs

• Adopt dispute resolution process

• Succession plan includes emphasis on diversity

• Work with minority and women attorneys to develop career advancement plans

• Introduce minority and women attorneys to key clients, including to lead engagements

• Review work assignments and hours billed to key client matters to make sure minority and women attorneys are not being excluded

• Strengthen mentoring program for all attorneys, including minorities and women

• Professional skills development program, including minority and women attorneys

Does your firm have part-time/flex-time policies that permit attorneys (male or female) to work alternative schedules?

Yes

What impact, if any, will the decision to work part-time have on an attorney's ability to make partner or, if already a partner, to remain a partner at your firm?

Reduced-hour lawyers will be considered on the equivalent time standard of full-time lawyers but on a pro-rated basis. For example, an associate working 60 percent time will be advanced one class for each 20 months worked. Other than this elongated schedule, it will have no other impact on an attorney's career.

Have any attorneys who chose to work a part-time schedule made partner at your firm?

Yes

Management Demographic Profile (as of 12/31/03)

	MINORITY MEN	MINORITY WOMEN	WHITE WOMEN	TOTAL
Number of attorneys on the Executive/Management Committee or equivalent	0	0	0	6
Number of attorneys on the Hiring Committee or equivalent	3	1	6	15
Number of attorneys on the Partner/Associate Review Committee or equivalent	0	0	0	7

Please provide information regarding all minority and women attorneys who head offices or practice groups of your law firm:

Women heading practice groups: Franca DeRosa, Energy; Cheryl Cronin, Government Law & Strategies

Buchanan Ingersoll PC

One Oxford Centre
301 Grant Street, 20th Floor
Pittsburgh, PA 15219
Phone: (412) 562-8800
Fax: (412) 562-1041

FIRM LEADERSHIP

Managing Partner: Thomas L. VanKirk, CEO
Diversity Team Leader: Homer L. Harris,
Shareholder

LOCATIONS

Pittsburgh, PA (HQ)
Aventura, FL
Buffalo, NY
Harrisburg, PA
Miami, FL
New York, NY
Philadelphia, PA
Princeton, NJ
San Diego, CA
Tampa, FL
Washington, DC
Wilmington, DE

LAW FIRM DEMOGRAPHIC PROFILES

FULL-TIME ASSOCIATES	2003	2002
Minority men	9	7
Minority women	11	12
White women	59	54
Total	163	176

SUMMER ASSOCIATES	2003	2002
Minority men	1	4
Minority women	5	4
White women	7	15
Total	23	40

EQUITY PARTNERS	2003	2002
Minority men	1	1
Minority women	0	0
White women	11	10
Total	87	81

NON-EQUITY PARTNERS	2003	2002
Minority men	3	3
Minority women	1	1
White women	25	30
Total	100	112

NEW HIRES	2003	2002
Minority men	3	2
Minority women	3	3
White women	18	20
Total	48	58

Strategic Plan and Diversity Leadership

How does the firm's leadership communicate the importance of diversity to everyone at the firm? (e.g., e-mails, web site, newsletters, meetings, etc.)

Firm leadership communicates the importance of diversity through our intranet, e-mail, meetings, newsletters, annual reports, and hosting receptions and events.

Who has primary responsibility for leading diversity initiatives at your firm?

Homer L. Harris, shareholder

Does your law firm currently have a diversity committee?

Yes

Does the committee's representation include one or more members of the firm's management/executive committee (or the equivalent)?

Yes

How many attorneys are on the committee, and in 2003, what was the total number of hours collectively spent by the committee in furtherance of the firm's diversity initiatives?

Total attorneys on committee: 10

Total hours spent on diversity: The firm does not formally track the many, many hours the Diversity Committee spends on diversity matters. Nonetheless, it is a very substantial number.

Does the committee and/or diversity leader establish and set goals or objectives consistent with management's priorities?

Yes

Has the firm undertaken a formal or informal diversity program or set of initiatives aimed at increasing the diversity of the firm?

Yes, formal

How often does the firm's management review the firm's diversity progress/results?

Monthly

How is the firm's diversity committee and/or firm management held accountable for achieving results?

Our CEO requests regular updates on the progress concerning diversity.

LAW FIRM DIVERSITY INITIATIVES	ALREADY COMPLETED	CURRENTLY ADDRESSING	NOT A CURRENT PRIORITY
Undertake communication from firm management that diversity is a top priority of the firm.	✓		
Formalize diversity plan and committee with action steps and accountability to management.		✓	
Conduct firm-wide diversity training for all attorneys and staff.			✓
Increase the number of minority attorneys at the associate level.		✓	
Increase the number of minority attorneys at the partnership level.		✓	
Develop/expand relationships with minority bar associations to offer firm's support of these networks.	✓		
Focus on strengthening firm's mentoring program, including for benefit of minority attorneys.		✓	
Conduct internal diversity needs assessment and/or retain diversity consultant to examine how firm culture might be more welcoming of minorities.			✓
Support law firm's internal affinity networks (e.g., women, minority attorney networks).		✓	
Manage/monitor allocation of work assignments and/or hours billed to ensure women and minority attorneys have equal access/inclusion on top client matters.			✓

Recruitment – New Associates

Does your firm annually recruit at any of the following types of institutions?*

Ivy League schools: Columbia University, Harvard University, University of Pennsylvania

Public state schools: Rutgers University-Camden, Temple University, University of Florida, University of North Carolina, University of Pittsburgh, Penn State-Dickinson School of Law, University of California-Berkeley, UCLA, University of Virginia

Private schools: Boston College, Boston University, Duquesne University, Fordham University, Villanova University, University of Miami, Duke University, Georgetown University, George Washington University, New York University, Northwestern University, University of Notre Dame, Stanford University, University of Chicago, Vanderbilt University

Historically Black Colleges and Universities (HBCUs): Howard University

*Buchanan Ingersoll also recruits through participation in the Northeast BLSA Job Fair and the Philadelphia Minority Job Fair.

Of the law schools that you listed above, do you have any special outreach efforts directed to encourage minority law students to consider your firm?

- Hold a reception for minority law students
- Advertise in minority law student association publication(s)
- Participate in/host minority law student job fair(s)
- Sponsor minority law student association events
- Firm's lawyers participate on career panels at school
- Outreach to leadership of minority student organizations
- Scholarships or intern/fellowships for minority students

SUMMER ASSOCIATE STATISTICS: SUMMER 2003	MINORITY MEN	MINORITY WOMEN	WHITE WOMEN	TOTAL
Summer associates	1	4	7	20
Summer associates who received an offer of full-time employment	0	2	5	12
Summer associates who accepted an offer of full-time employment	0	2	4	10

Recruitment – Lateral Associates and Partners

What activities does the firm undertake to attract minority and women attorneys?

- Partner programs with women and minority bar associations
- Participate at minority job fairs
- Seek referrals from other attorneys

Do you use executive recruiting/search firms to seek to identify new diversity hires (partners or associates)?

Yes

If yes, list all women- and/or minority-owned executive search/recruiting firms to which the firm paid a fee for placement services in the past 12 months:

Melba N.G. Hughes, Hughes Consultants, LLC

LATERAL ASSOCIATES AND PARTNERS: 1/1/03 – 12/31/03	MINORITY MEN	MINORITY WOMEN	WHITE WOMEN	TOTAL
Number of lateral associate hires	2	0	10	21
Number of lateral partner hires (equity and non-equity)	0	0	1	10
Number of new partners (equity and non-equity) promoted from associate rank	0	0	1	10
Number of new equity partners	0	0	1	8

Retention & Professional Development

ATTORNEYS WHO LEFT THE FIRM: 2003	MINORITY MEN	MINORITY WOMEN	WHITE WOMEN	TOTAL
Number of attorneys who voluntarily or involuntarily left your firm's employ in 2003	1	4	14	69

Please identify the specific steps you are taking to reduce the attrition rate of minority and women attorneys.

• Develop and/or support internal employee affinity groups (e.g., minority or women networks within the firm)

• Strengthen mentoring program for all attorneys, including minorities and women

• Professional skills development program, including minority and women attorneys

Does your firm have part-time/flex-time policies that permit attorneys (male or female) to work alternative schedules?

Yes

What impact, if any, will the decision to work part-time have on an attorney's ability to make partner or, if already a partner, to remain a partner at your firm?

It has no impact. The firm has had a number of attorneys participate in part-time or alternative work schedules.

Have any attorneys who chose to work a part-time schedule made partner at your firm?

Yes, one attorney.

Management Demographic Profile (as of 12/31/03)

	MINORITY MEN	MINORITY WOMEN	WHITE WOMEN	TOTAL
Number of attorneys on the Executive/Management Committee or equivalent	1	0	1	20
Number of attorneys on the Hiring Committee or equivalent	4	0	15	39
Number of attorneys on the Partner/Associate Review Committee or equivalent	1	0	1	15

Please provide information regarding all minority and women attorneys who head offices or practice groups of your law firm:

Women heading offices: Karen Crawford, San Diego

The Firm Says

Buchanan Ingersoll recognizes the value and importance of a diverse community and workplace. To this end, it has included diversity as an integral prong of Buchanan Ingersoll's Strategic Plan to ensure the firm actively promotes and maintains a firm culture that supports and promotes diversity among lawyers, legal assistants and staff. Buchanan Ingersoll believes that diversity should be reflected in recruiting, retention and promotion of lawyers and non-lawyers, as well as in administration, operations and programs. We diligently work with clients, bar associations and others to support and promote diversity in the legal community and profession and the community at large.

Buchanan Ingersoll has shown its commitment to diversity through a number of initiatives, including:

• Appointing a board of directors member to focus strictly on diversity

• Assigning representatives in each office to be responsible for furthering our diversity objectives

• Signing and fully supporting bar association Diversity Statements in Harrisburg, Philadelphia and Pittsburgh

• Sponsoring academic scholarships for minority law students

• Supporting minority and women law student organizations financially and otherwise

• Partnering with clients and others to hold diversity focused seminars

• Supporting minority professional organizations in law-related fields, such as the African American Real Estate Professionals of New York

• Donating nearly 18,000 hours of pro bono service to community and charitable organizations

• Supporting diversity-related bar associations and law-related organizations, including the American Bar Association Commission on Racial and Ethnic Diversity in the Profession, Metropolitan Black Bar Association, NAACP Legal Defense and Education Fund, Minority Corporate Counsel Association, the Philadelphia Diversity Law Group and the Cuban American Bar Association

• Establishing and supporting the Executive Women's Forum which addresses issues affecting the total development of the professional woman in corporate culture

As a firm, Buchanan Ingersoll is committed to providing opportunities and challenges for its women lawyers to succeed. The Women's Business Development Committee is just one example of the support women receive at Buchanan Ingersoll. Under the leadership of Mary Ann Dunham, a shareholder in the firm's corporate finance section, the WBDC:

• Fosters an environment of inclusion and mentoring within the firm

• Provides opportunities for our professionals to network with their colleagues in business, industry, government and the nonprofit sector

• Raises the profile of Buchanan Ingersoll women attorneys in the business and legal communities

• Encourages the development of leadership skills, service excellence and entrepreneurial creativity

• Celebrates a common mission of achievement while fostering individual growth and responsibility

Our women lawyers hold many important roles in our firm and serve as shareholders, corporate managers and members of the firm's board of directors. Two of Buchanan Ingersoll's former female attorneys are now serving on the bench, one as a U.S. District Court judge and the other as a Pennsylvania Commonwealth Court judge.

Cadwalader, Wickersham & Taft LLP

100 Maiden Lane
New York, NY 10038
Phone: (212) 504-6000
Fax: (212) 504-6666

FIRM LEADERSHIP

Managing Partner: Robert O. Link, Managing
Partner
Diversity Team Leader: Adam Rogoff, Partner
and Chair of the Diversity Task Force

LOCATIONS

New York, NY (HQ)
Charlotte, NC
Washington, DC
London

LAW FIRM DEMOGRAPHIC PROFILES

FULL-TIME ASSOCIATES	2003	2002
Minority men	33	21
Minority women	31	26
White women	90	83
Total	342	285

SPECIAL COUNSEL	2003	2002
Minority men	2	3
Minority women	2	2
White women	14	14
Total	42	42

SUMMER ASSOCIATES	2003	2002
Minority men	3	12
Minority women	4	10
White women	19	19
Total	49	81

EQUITY PARTNERS	2003	2002
Minority men	4	4
Minority women	1	1
White women	8	10
Total	85	88

NON-EQUITY PARTNERS*	2003	2002
Minority men	0	0
Minority women	0	0
White women	3	3
Total	18	17

Figures represent counsel

NEW HIRES	2003	2002
Minority men	18	9
Minority women	10	7
White women	30	31
Total	110	98

Strategic Plan and Diversity Leadership

How does the firm's leadership communicate the importance of diversity to everyone at the firm? (e.g., e-mails, web site, newsletters, meetings, etc.)

Diversity has been stressed as a priority by the managing partner in his State of the Firm Address. Diversity initiatives and proposed programs have been discussed at partner meetings and announced through firm-wide e-mail messages from the managing partner. In addition, information about diversity programs and events is included in monthly e-bulletins and quarterly newsletters. There is also a page dedicated to diversity on the firm's web site.

Who has primary responsibility for leading diversity initiatives at your firm? Name of person and his/her title:

Adam Rogoff, partner and chair of the Diversity Task Force

Does your law firm currently have a diversity committee?

Yes

Does the committee's representation include one or more members of the firm's management/executive committee (or the equivalent)?

Yes

How many attorneys are on the committee, and in 2003, what was the total number of hours collectively spent by the committee in furtherance of the firm's diversity initiatives?

Total attorneys on committee: 18

Total hours spent on diversity: N/A Diversity Task Force was created in 2004

Does the committee and/or diversity leader establish and set goals or objectives consistent with management's priorities?

Yes

Has the firm undertaken a formal or informal diversity program or set of initiatives aimed at increasing the diversity of the firm? *

*The firm is in the process of creating a formal program. We retained a leading consultant to conduct a comprehensive assessment of each of our U.S. offices. The consultant reported their findings to firm management and is working with the Diversity Task Force to develop our programs.

How often does the firm's management review the firm's diversity progress/results?

During this development phase of the diversity action plan, the chair of the Diversity Task Force is in regular communication with management.

How is the firm's diversity committee and/or firm management held accountable for achieving results?

To be determined. The Diversity Task Force is in the process of developing an action plan, which will be implemented in the coming months. Accountability for achieving results will be addressed, and metrics and measures for each point of the action plan will be presented at that time.

LAW FIRM DIVERSITY INITIATIVES	ALREADY COMPLETED	CURRENTLY ADDRESSING	NOT A CURRENT PRIORITY
Undertake communication from firm management that diversity is a top priority of the firm.	✓		
Formalize diversity plan and committee with action steps and accountability to management.		✓	
Conduct firm-wide diversity training for all attorneys and staff.		✓	
Increase the number of minority attorneys at the associate level.		✓	
Increase the number of minority attorneys at the partnership level.		✓	
Develop/expand relationships with minority bar associations to offer firm's support of these networks.		✓	
Focus on strengthening firm's mentoring program, including for benefit of minority attorneys.		✓	
Conduct internal diversity needs assessment and/or retain diversity consultant to examine how firm culture might be more welcoming of minorities.	✓		
Support law firm's internal affinity networks (e.g., women, minority attorney networks).	✓	✓	
Manage/monitor allocation of work assignments and/or hours billed to ensure women and minority attorneys have equal access/inclusion on top client matters.		✓	

Recruitment – New Associates

Does your firm annually recruit at any of the following types of institutions? (Check all that apply and list the schools).*

Ivy League schools: Columbia University, Cornell University, Harvard University, University of Pennsylvania and Yale University

Public state schools: University of California at Berkeley (Boalt Hall), University of Michigan, University of North Carolina at Chapel Hill, University of Texas, University of Virginia, College of William & Mary

Private schools: Boston College, Boston University, Brooklyn Law School, Benjamin N. Cardozo Law School, University of Chicago, Duke University, Emory University, Fordham University, George Washington University, Georgetown University, Northwestern University, New York University, St. John's University, Stanford University, Temple University, Vanderbilt University, Villanova University, Wake Forest University, Washington and Lee University

Historically Black Colleges and Universities (HBCUs): Howard University, BLSA Northeast Job Fair

Other predominantly minority and/or women's colleges: Southeastern Minority Job Fair

*The firm also recruits at the Midwestern Law Consortium and the Southeastern Law Placement Consortium.

Do you have any special outreach efforts directed to encourage minority law students to consider your firm?

• Advertise in minority law student association publication(s)

• Participate in/host minority law student job fair(s)

• Sponsor minority law student association events

• Outreach to leadership of minority student organizations

SUMMER ASSOCIATE STATISTICS: SUMMER 2003	MINORITY MEN	MINORITY WOMEN	WHITE WOMEN	TOTAL
Summer associates	3	4	19	49
Summer associates who received an offer of full-time employment	3	3	19	48
Summer associates who accepted an offer of full-time employment	3	2	19	41

Recruitment – Lateral Associates and Partners

What activities does the firm undertake to attract minority and women attorneys?

• *Other activities will be undertaken as the firm's Diversity Action Plan is rolled out, including using minority-owned executive search firms.*

• Partner programs with women and minority bar associations

• Seek referrals from other attorneys

Do you use executive recruiting/search firms to seek to identify new diversity hires (partners or associates)?

Yes

LATERAL ASSOCIATES AND PARTNERS: 1/1/03 – 12/31/03	MINORITY MEN	MINORITY WOMEN	WHITE WOMEN	TOTAL
Number of lateral associate hires	17	9	30	103
Number of lateral partner hires (equity and non-equity)	1	0	0	5
Number of new partners (equity and non-equity) promoted from associate rank	0	0	1	7
Number of new equity partners	0	0	0	1

Retention & Professional Development

ATTORNEYS WHO LEFT THE FIRM: 2003	MINORITY MEN	MINORITY WOMEN	WHITE WOMEN	TOTAL
Number of attorneys who voluntarily or involuntarily left your firm's employ in 2003	6	2	30	68

How do 2003 attrition rates generally compare to those experienced in the prior year period?

About the same as in prior years

Please identify the specific steps you are taking to reduce the attrition rate of minority and women attorneys.

• *When the diversity action plan is completed (the third quarter of 2004), a variety of additional steps will be announced to address attrition of minorities and women.*

• Develop and/or support internal employee affinity groups (e.g., minority or women networks within the firm)

• Adopt dispute resolution process

• Strengthen mentoring program for all attorneys, including minorities and women

Does your firm have part-time/flex-time policies that permit attorneys (male or female) to work alternative schedules?

Yes

What impact, if any, will the decision to work part-time have on an attorney's ability to make partner or, if already a partner, to remain a partner at your firm?

To be determined.

Have any attorneys who chose to work a part-time schedule made partner at your firm?

No

Management Demographic Profile (as of 12/31/03)

	MINORITY MEN	MINORITY WOMEN	WHITE WOMEN	TOTAL
Number of attorneys on the Executive/Management Committee or equivalent	1	0	1	7
Number of attorneys on the Hiring Committee or equivalent	0	0	0	6*
Number of attorneys on the Partner/Associate Review Committee or equivalent**	N/A	N/A	N/A	N/A

*These partners are responsible for summer and entry-level hiring in each of their offices. Laterals are handled strictly on a department basis.
**Reviews are handled on a department basis. All partners in a department participate.

Please provide information regarding all minority and women attorneys who head offices or practice groups of your law firm:

Minorities heading practice groups: Andrew Perel, Environmental; Ray Shirazi, Derivatives and Swaps

Women heading practice groups: Linda Swartz, Tax; Karen Gelernt, Mortgage Banking/Whole Loan Trading; Maurine Bartlett, Broker/Dealer

The Firm Says

Cadwalader is committed to developing a comprehensive program that educates attorneys and staff about diversity, promotes awareness of cultural backgrounds and stresses the benefits of embracing diversity. The Management Committee communicated to the partnership the high priority Cadwalader needs to place on diversity. The managing partner has stressed that diversity is critical to maintaining a competitive advantage in attracting and retaining the best talent and clients. A more diverse work force enriches the firm's environment and enhances our ability to deliver the best work product and client service.

Cadwalader's appreciation for diversity, exemplified in such programs as the Cadwalader Women's Initiative, was greatly expanded upon during the second half of 2003, when the firm retained a diversity consultant specializing in assisting law firms develop inclusive work environments. The consultant had led workshops for Cadwalader's summer associates in previous years. The consultant conducted a diversity study of Cadwalader's practices and procedures, using one-on-one interviews and focus groups to gather information on issues of diversity and inclusion. Interviews were conducted with members of the Management Committee, the Firm Committee and the Hiring Committee; department chairs; assigning partners; and focus groups made up of Asian, African-American, Hispanic, openly gay, white and women attorneys.

Following the assessment, a Diversity Task Force was created for the purpose of addressing the issues raised in the assessment and working with the consultant to draft a Diversity Action Plan for Cadwalader. The membership of the Diversity Task Force includes partners, counsel, associates, women, men, openly gay, Hispanic, Asian and African-American attorneys. The mission of the Cadwalader Diversity Task Force is to promote awareness of and respect for diversity, encourage a fulfilling work environment to enhance inclusion and retention of highly talented individuals, and foster a sense of commitment to community and teamwork. The task force intends to achieve these goals by assessing current systems, identifying the specific issues facing Cadwalader and developing a strategic plan. The task force will also propose mechanisms to ensure that the firm remains vigilant to ever changing diversity issues.

The task force kicked off its work in 2004 by participating in a two-day retreat with the consultant that included diversity awareness training. It is anticipated that the Diversity Task Force will have an action plan presented to the Management Committee for approval in the third quarter of 2004. The task force will be succeeded by a diversity committee, charged with the long-term goal of implementing the Diversity Action Plan and continuing Cadwalader's diversity initiatives.

In the meantime, Cadwalader's support for diversity in the community continues to grow. In the past year, Cadwalader has supported a variety of minority organizations including: Asian American Arts Alliance; Asian American Bar Association of New York; Asian American Legal Defense and Education Fund; Asian Pacific American Law Students Association; Association of Black Women Attorneys; Association of the Bar of the City of New York, Office of Diversity; Association of the Bar of the City of New York, Committee on LGBT Rights; Black Law Students Association; Hispanic Bar Association of DC; Korean American League for Civil Action;

Korean American Mentorship; Lambda Legal; Latin American Law Students Association; Lesbian and Gay Law Association Foundation of Greater New York (LeGal); Metropolitan Black Bar Association; Minority Corporate Counsel Association; National Association of Women Judges; New York County Lawyers Association, Committee on LGBT Issues; New York Women's Foundation; Northeast Black Law Students Association; National Lesbian and Gay Law Association; OUTLaw; South Asian Law Students Association; and Washington Lawyers Committee for Civil Rights and Urban Affairs.

Over the past year, Cadwalader representatives have participated in diversity conferences hosted by MCCA, ABCNY and NALP. Cadwalader is a signatory to the Association of the Bar of the City of New York's Statement of Diversity Principles and a sponsor of the MCCA Creating Pathways to Diversity Conference. In December 2003 Cadwalader was the recipient of the Saludos Hispanos 2003 Leaders of Distinction Gold Metal Achievement Award for the firm's leadership role in providing attainment and success among the Hispanic community.

In addition to the foregoing, efforts with respect to diversity include:

Anti-Harassment Policy:

Cadwalader is committed to a work environment free from unlawful discrimination or harassment, including unlawful discrimination or harassment based on race, color, religion, sex, sexual orientation, gender identity and expression, national origin, age, disability, marital status, status as a veteran, or status in any group protected by federal, state or local law. This policy applies to everyone working at the Firm, whether as partners, counsel, associates, legal assistants, or support staff and to all terms and conditions of employment, including but not limited to, hiring, placement, promotion, termination, layoff, recall, transfer, leaves of absence, compensation and training. The Firm will not tolerate any form of unlawful discrimination or harassment, whether in the office, at work assignments outside the office, at office-sponsored social functions, or at other work-related settings.

Non-Discrimination Policy:

Cadwalader is impartial in all its relations with its employees and applicants, and does not discriminate because of age, color, creed, citizenship, disability, veteran or marital status, national origin, race, religion, sex, sexual orientation, or any other legally protected status.

Carlton Fields, P.A.

P.O. Box 3239
Tampa, FL 33601-3239
Phone: (813) 223-7000
Fax: (813) 229-4133

FIRM LEADERSHIP

Managing Partner: Thomas A. Snow, President and CEO
Diversity Team Leader: Jason M. Murray, Chair, Diversity Recruiting & Retention Committee

LOCATIONS

Tampa, FL (HQ)
Atlanta, GA
Miami, FL
Orlando, FL
St. Petersburg, FL
Tallahassee, FL
West Palm Beach, FL

LAW FIRM DEMOGRAPHIC PROFILES

FULL-TIME ASSOCIATES	2003	2002
Minority men	8	7
Minority women	13	10
White women	31	33
Total	75	82

SUMMER ASSOCIATES	2003	2002
Minority men	3	4
Minority women	1	0
White women	4	4
Total	12	13

EQUITY PARTNERS	2003	2002
Minority men	3	3
Minority women	0	0
White women	16	16
Total	87	87

NON-EQUITY PARTNERS	2003	2002
Minority men	3	3
Minority women	2	1
White women	6	8
Total	41	36

NEW HIRES	2003	2002
Minority men	2	4
Minority women	5	4
White women	9	8
Total	32	30

Strategic Plan and Diversity Leadership

How does the firm's leadership communicate the importance of diversity to everyone at the firm? (e.g., e-mails, web site, newsletters, meetings, etc.)

A firm-wide survey on diversity was conducted to analyze the firm's attitudes and current condition with respect to the issue of diversity, including awareness about diversity issues and the attitudes of lawyers within the firm; diversity issues are discussed at shareholder meetings and firm retreats; our diversity initiative is prominently placed on the firm's web site.

Who has primary responsibility for leading diversity initiatives at your firm?

Jason M. Murray, chair, Diversity Recruiting & Retention Committee

Does your law firm currently have a diversity committee?

Yes

Does the committee's representation include one or more members of the firm's management/executive committee (or the equivalent)?

Yes

How many attorneys are on the committee, and in 2003, what was the total number of hours collectively spent by the committee in furtherance of the firm's diversity initiatives?

Total attorneys on committee: 17

Total hours spent on diversity: Not tracked

Does the committee and/or diversity leader establish and set goals or objectives consistent with management's priorities?

Yes

Has the firm undertaken a formal or informal diversity program or set of initiatives aimed at increasing the diversity of the firm?

Yes, formal

How often does the firm's management review the firm's diversity progress/results?

Monthly

LAW FIRM DIVERSITY INITIATIVES	ALREADY COMPLETED	CURRENTLY ADDRESSING	NOT A CURRENT PRIORITY
Undertake communication from firm management that diversity is a top priority of the firm.	✔		
Formalize diversity plan and committee with action steps and accountability to management.	✔		
Conduct firm-wide diversity training for all attorneys and staff.		✔	
Increase the number of minority attorneys at the associate level.		✔	
Increase the number of minority attorneys at the partnership level.		✔	
Develop/expand relationships with minority bar associations to offer firm's support of these networks.	✔		
Focus on strengthening firm's mentoring program, including for benefit of minority attorneys.		✔	
Conduct internal diversity needs assessment and/or retain diversity consultant to examine how firm culture might be more welcoming of minorities.		✔	
Support law firm's internal affinity networks (e.g., women, minority attorney networks).		✔	
Manage/monitor allocation of work assignments and/or hours billed to ensure women and minority attorneys have equal access/inclusion on top client matters.		✔	

Recruitment – New Associates

Does your firm annually recruit at any of the following types of institutions? (Check all that apply and list the schools).

Public state schools: University of Florida, Florida State University, University of Virginia, College of William & Mary

Private schools: Duke University, Georgetown University, Nova Southeastern University, St. Thomas University, Stetson University, University of Miami, Vanderbilt University

Historically Black Colleges and Universities (HBCUs): Howard University, North Carolina Central University

Do you have any special outreach efforts directed to encourage minority law students to consider your firm?

• Participate in/host minority law student job fair(s)

• Sponsor minority law student association events

• Firm's lawyers participate on career panels at school

• Outreach to leadership of minority student organizations

• Scholarships or intern/fellowships for minority students

SUMMER ASSOCIATE STATISTICS: SUMMER 2003	MINORITY MEN	MINORITY WOMEN	WHITE WOMEN	TOTAL
Summer associates	3	1	4	12
Summer associates who received an offer of full-time employment	2	1	3	7
Summer associates who accepted an offer of full-time employment	2	1	2	5

Recruitment – Lateral Associates and Partners

What activities does the firm undertake to attract minority and women attorneys?

• Partner programs with women and minority bar associations

• Participate at minority job fairs

• Seek referrals from other attorneys

Do you use executive recruiting/search firms to seek to identify new diversity hires (partners or associates)?

Yes

If yes, list all women- and/or minority-owned executive search/recruiting firms to which the firm paid a fee for placement services in the past 12 months:

Ankus & Bunt, Inc. (principal: Abbe Bunt)

LATERAL ASSOCIATES AND PARTNERS: 1/1/03 – 12/31/03	MINORITY MEN	MINORITY WOMEN	WHITE WOMEN	TOTAL
Number of lateral associate hires	0	2	6	13
Number of lateral partner hires (equity and non-equity)	0	1	0	6
Number of new partners (equity and non-equity) promoted from associate rank	0	0	2	9
Number of new equity partners	0	0	1	6

Retention & Professional Development

ATTORNEYS WHO LEFT THE FIRM: 2003	MINORITY MEN	MINORITY WOMEN	WHITE WOMEN	TOTAL
Number of attorneys who voluntarily or involuntarily left your firm's employ in 2003	2	1	12	31

How do 2003 attrition rates generally compare to those experienced in the prior year period?

Higher than in prior years

Please identify the specific steps you are taking to reduce the attrition rate of minority and women attorneys.

• *The firm has established a retention program, a minority lawyer network and a Diversity Strategic Plan. The action plan developed to achieve the goals of the Diversity Strategic Plan includes recruiting lateral minority shareholders and senior attorneys to serve as role models for junior associates, communicating to all attorneys and staff the importance of diversity to the firm's success, cultivating and promoting qualified senior minority associates to shareholders, creating networks of minority lawyers within the firm that can support minority lawyers and provide them with an outlet to express their concerns and receive feedback from practice group leaders and senior management, and many other actions.*

• Develop and/or support internal employee affinity groups (e.g., minority or women networks within the firm)

• Increase/review compensation relative to competition

• Increase/improve current work/life programs

• Work with minority and women attorneys to develop career advancement plans

• Introduce minority and women attorneys to key clients, including to lead engagements

• Review work assignments and hours billed to key client matters to make sure minority and women attorneys are not being excluded

• Strengthen mentoring program for all attorneys, including minorities and women

• Professional skills development program, including minority and women attorneys

Does your firm have part-time/flex-time policies that permit attorneys (male or female) to work alternative schedules?

Yes. Carlton Fields has a strong history of attempting to provide creative and flexible alternative work schedule opportunities for lawyers with child care, elder care and other family responsibilities, for lawyers who require a less demanding practice, and in other appropriate circumstances.

What impact, if any, will the decision to work part-time have on an attorney's ability to make partner or, if already a partner, to remain a partner at your firm?

Associates who work on alternative work schedules gain pro-rated credit toward shareholder consideration. Working on an alternative work schedule does not adversely impact a shareholder's ability to remain a shareholder.

Have any attorneys who chose to work a part-time schedule made partner at your firm?

Yes, seven attorneys.

Management Demographic Profile (as of 12/31/03)

	MINORITY MEN	MINORITY WOMEN	WHITE WOMEN	TOTAL
Number of attorneys on the Executive/Management Committee or equivalent	1	0	0	3
Number of attorneys on the Hiring Committee or equivalent	4	2	4	23
Number of attorneys on the Partner/Associate Review Committee or equivalent	0	2	2	18

Please provide information regarding all minority and women attorneys who head offices or practice groups of your law firm:

Minorities heading offices: Luis Prats, Tampa

Women heading offices: Nancy Linnan, Tallahassee

Minorities heading practice groups: Gary Sasso, Litigation and Dispute Resolution

Women heading practice groups: Sylvia Walbolt, Appellate Practice and Trial Support; Nancy Linnan, Government Law & Consulting; Edith Osman, Family Law

The Firm Says

Diversity Mission Statement

Carlton Fields' goal is to recruit, retain and promote attorneys who are racially and ethnically diverse. We strive to create a climate of inclusion, to grow our talent pool, to foster innovation and creativity to compete in the global market, and to become the employer of choice for racially and ethnically diverse attorneys and staff.

Diversity program

The Diversity Recruiting & Retention Committee is chaired by Miami shareholder Jason Murray, past president of the Black Lawyers Association of Miami-Dade County and past appointed member of the county's Black Affairs Advisory Board. The program was created in 2001 to further the firm's efforts to:

• Increase representation of minority lawyers in the firm;

• Develop policies and practices that define and transmit the firm's commitment to diversity; and

• Establish accountability standards and measure progress.

The committee is composed of shareholders and associates from all offices, the firm's president, the director of attorney recruitment and training/client services, and the director of human resources.

Carlton Fields is committed to recruiting and hiring minorities at every opportunity. As demonstrated by recent statistical information, Carlton Fields compares favorably in this regard with peer institutions:

	CARLTON FIELDS FIRM-WIDE	NATIONAL LAW FIRMS(101-250)	FLORIDA LAW FIRMS
Shareholders of Color	6.71%	3.25%	7.05%
Associates of Color	26.47%	11.73%	14.42%

Source: NALP 2003-2004 Directory of Legal Employers

Carlton Fields believes that persons with diverse backgrounds enhance and enrich the firm's work environment and add immeasurable value to the legal services that we provide and the overall culture of the firm. We continue to undertake proactive efforts to increase the employment and advancement of minorities throughout the firm.

Carlton Fields has been the recipient of numerous awards in recognition of the firm's support and promotion of diversity. Representative examples include:

• Carlton Fields ranked No. 3 for the highest percentage of Hispanic American attorneys and No. 47 overall among the 250 largest firms in the country on the Diversity Scorecard published in the Spring 2004 Minority Law Journal.

• The Florida Bar selected Carlton Fields shareholder Jason M. Murray, chair of the firm's Diversity Recruiting & Retention Committee, as the recipient of the 2003 Young Lawyers Division Diversity Award. The award recognizes a person and/or entity that demonstrates the highest morality and respect for all persons and diversity, for efforts and allegiance to creating diversity, and for promoting a more diverse workplace.

• Carlton Fields ranked in the top 10 for the third consecutive year in The American Lawyer's 2003 Midlevel Associate Satisfaction Survey. The firm ranked No. 1 nationally in the 2002 Summer Associate Survey.

• Carlton Fields ranked among the top 200 U.S. law firms for the second consecutive year in the August 2003 edition of The American Lawyer magazine, and is among the "honored top quarter" based on revenue per lawyer, pro bono hours, diversity and associate satisfaction. Carlton Fields is the only Florida law firm named in the top 50 and is one of few law firms its size on the top quarter list.

• Carlton Fields is featured in America's Greatest Places to Work with a Law Degree.

The firm proactively recruits minority students at law school job fairs. We co-sponsor events and provide scholarship funds for students selected by the George Edgecomb Bar Association, the Tampa chapter of the National Bar Association, and the Wilkie D. Ferguson, Jr. Bar Association in Miami-Dade county. In 2004, we established the Carlton Fields Diversity Fellowship Program at Stetson University College of Law. We participate in and donate scholarship funds to the Professional Opportunities Program (POP), developed to provide black law students with summer internship and associate program opportunities in Florida. Members of our firm participate in Young Lawyers Division and Florida Bar mentoring programs.

Women's Initiative Statement

Carlton Fields is committed to promoting a supportive, gender-friendly work environment for all employees. Recognizing the value of women in the work force, Carlton Fields strives to recruit, train, advance and retain our women attorneys. We promote a workplace that supports one's ability to balance one's professional and personal life through formal written programs and policies that are applied consistently to all attorneys. In 1966, at a time when such policies were unheard of, the firm created an alternative work schedule allowing a woman to work part-time after the birth of her first child. That woman is now serving her sixth term as Chair of our

Board of Directors. Our women attorneys have achieved positions of power in the bar, in civic organizations and in their respective communities.

• The firm received The Florida Bar Young Lawyers Division 2004 Michael K. Reese Quality of Life Award.

• The Palm Beach County Bar Association honored Carlton Fields with its 2004 Professionalism Award. The firm was chosen for its nationally recognized Mentor Program.

• The firm was the recipient of the Athena Society's 2002 Level Playing Fields Award presented for the promotion of women in the workplace.

• Carlton Fields was awarded the Women's Chamber of Commerce of Miami-Dade County's 2002 Thelma Gibson Excellence Award in recognition of our professional advancement of women, business excellence and community involvement.

• Carlton Fields was the recipient of the 2000 Family Friendly Business Award from the Greater Tampa Chamber of Commerce.

• The Florida Commission on the Status of Women recognized Carlton Fields as one of the "Best Florida Employers for Working Women" in 2000.

• The firm was the recipient of The Florida Bar Gender Friendly Award in 1998.

	CARLTON FIELDS	NATIONAL LAW FIRMS(101-250)	FLORIDA LAW FIRMS
Women Shareholders	21.64%.	16.4%	17.31%
Women Associates	60.29%	43.11%	46.98%

Source: NALP 2003-2004 Directory of Legal Employers

Chadbourne & Parke LLP

30 Rockefeller Plaza
New York, NY 10112
Phone: (212) 408-5100
Fax: (212) 541-5369

FIRM LEADERSHIP

Managing Partner: Charles K. O'Neill,
Managing Partner
Diversity Team Leader: Vincent Dunn, Partner

LOCATIONS

New York, NY (HQ)
Houston, TX
Los Angeles, CA
Washington, DC
Beijing
Kyiv
London
Moscow
Warsaw

LAW FIRM DEMOGRAPHIC PROFILES

FULL-TIME ASSOCIATES	2003	2002
Minority men	19	17
Minority women	22	19
White women	80	74
Total	226	210

SUMMER ASSOCIATES	2003	2002
Minority men	2	4
Minority women	2	4
White women	6	11
Total	17	28

EQUITY PARTNERS	2003	2002
Minority men	4	2
Minority women	0	0
White women	8	7
Total	80	74

NON-EQUITY PARTNERS	2003	2002
Minority men	2	3
Minority women	0	0
White women	6	5
Total	28	24

NEW HIRES	2003	2002
Minority men	6	10
Minority women	7	8
White women	18	19
Total	52	75

MCCA
MINORITY CORPORATE COUNSEL ASSOCIATION

Strategic Plan and Diversity Leadership

How does the firm's leadership communicate the importance of diversity to everyone at the firm? (e.g., e-mails, web site, newsletters, meetings, etc.)

The firm has communicated the importance of diversity via numerous avenues, including meetings and in written form.

Who has primary responsibility for leading diversity initiatives at your firm?

Vincent Dunn, partner

Does your law firm currently have a diversity committee?

Yes. See "The Firm Says" on page 303.

Does the committee's representation include one or more members of the firm's management/executive committee (or the equivalent)?

No. See "The Firm Says" on page 303.

How many attorneys are on the committee, and in 2003, what was the total number of hours collectively spent by the committee in furtherance of the firm's diversity initiatives?

See "The Firm Says" on page 303.

Does the committee and/or diversity leader establish and set goals or objectives consistent with management's priorities?

See "The Firm Says" on page 303.

Has the firm undertaken a formal or informal diversity program or set of initiatives aimed at increasing the diversity of the firm?

Yes, informal

How often does the firm's management review the firm's diversity progress/results?

Annually

How is the firm's diversity committee and/or firm management held accountable for achieving results?

As more fully described in the narrative below, the firm is in the process of establishing a diversity committee and more formal diversity programs and objectives. At this point, the firm has not addressed accountability, but it is an issue which the firm will be addressing in the near future.

LAW FIRM DIVERSITY INITIATIVES	ALREADY COMPLETED	CURRENTLY ADDRESSING	NOT A CURRENT PRIORITY
Undertake communication from firm management that diversity is a top priority of the firm.	✓		
Formalize diversity plan and committee with action steps and accountability to management.		✓	
Conduct firm-wide diversity training for all attorneys and staff.		✓	
Increase the number of minority attorneys at the associate level.		✓	
Increase the number of minority attorneys at the partnership level.		✓	
Develop/expand relationships with minority bar associations to offer firm's support of these networks.		✓	
Focus on strengthening firm's mentoring program, including for benefit of minority attorneys.		✓	
Conduct internal diversity needs assessment and/or retain diversity consultant to examine how firm culture might be more welcoming of minorities.		✓	
Support law firm's internal affinity networks (e.g., women, minority attorney networks).		✓	
Manage/monitor allocation of work assignments and/or hours billed to ensure women and minority attorneys have equal access/inclusion on top client matters.		✓	

Recruitment – New Associates

Does your firm annually recruit at any of the following types of institutions? (Check all that apply and list the schools).

Ivy League schools: Cornell University, Columbia University, Harvard University, University of Pennsylvania

Public state schools: University of California-Boalt Hall, University of Michigan, UCLA, University of Virginia

Private schools: Emory University, Fordham University, Georgetown University, NYU, Northwestern University, Pace University, Stanford University

Do you have any special outreach efforts directed to encourage minority law students to consider your firm?

• *Home office to the Northeast BLSA Job Fair*

• Participate in/host minority law student job fair(s)

• Firm's lawyers participate on career panels at school

• Outreach to leadership of minority student organizations

SUMMER ASSOCIATE STATISTICS: SUMMER 2003	MINORITY MEN	MINORITY WOMEN	WHITE WOMEN	TOTAL
Summer associates	2	2	6	17
Summer associates who received an offer of full-time employment	2	2	6	16
Summer associates who accepted an offer of full-time employment	2	1	6	14

Recruitment – Lateral Associates and Partners

What activities does the firm undertake to attract minority and women attorneys?

Participate at minority job fairs

Do you use executive recruiting/search firms to seek to identify new diversity hires (partners or associates)?

No

LATERAL ASSOCIATES AND PARTNERS: 1/1/03 – 12/31/03	MINORITY MEN	MINORITY WOMEN	WHITE WOMEN	TOTAL
Number of lateral associate hires	6	7	18	52
Number of lateral partner hires (equity and non-equity)	0	0	0	2
Number of new partners (equity and non-equity) promoted from associate rank	0	0	2	4
Number of new equity partners	2	0	3	8

Retention & Professional Development

ATTORNEYS WHO LEFT THE FIRM: 2003	MINORITY MEN	MINORITY WOMEN	WHITE WOMEN	TOTAL
Number of attorneys who voluntarily or involuntarily left your firm's employ in 2003	5	2	9	29

How do 2003 attrition rates generally compare to those experienced in the prior year period?

About the same as in prior years

Please identify the specific steps you are taking to reduce the attrition rate of minority and women attorneys.

• Develop and/or support internal employee affinity groups (e.g., minority or women networks within the firm)

• Increase/review compensation relative to competition

• Increase/improve current work/life programs

• Adopt dispute resolution process

• Succession plan includes emphasis on diversity

• Introduce minority and women attorneys to key clients, including to lead engagements

• Review work assignments and hours billed to key client matters to make sure minority and women attorneys are not being excluded

• Strengthen mentoring program for all attorneys, including minorities and women

• Professional skills development program, including minority and women attorneys

Does your firm have part-time/flex-time policies that permit attorneys (male or female) to work alternative schedules?

Yes

What impact, if any, will the decision to work part-time have on an attorney's ability to make partner or, if already a partner, to remain a partner at your firm?

None

Have any attorneys who chose to work a part-time schedule made partner at your firm?

Yes, one attorney.

Management Demographic Profile (as of 12/31/03)

	MINORITY MEN	MINORITY WOMEN	WHITE WOMEN	TOTAL
Number of attorneys on the Executive/Management Committee or equivalent	0	0	0	5
Number of attorneys on the Hiring Committee or equivalent	1	0	2	8
Number of attorneys on the Partner/Associate Review Committee or equivalent	2	0	11	25

Please provide information regarding all minority and women attorneys who head offices or practice groups of your law firm:

Women heading offices: Laura Brank, Moscow; Jaroslawa Johnson, Kyiv

Women heading practice groups: Cindy Wenig, Real Estate

The Firm Says

Chadbourne & Parke LLP is in the process of establishing a Diversity Committee. Vincent Dunn, a corporate partner of the firm, will chair the committee. The firm has retained a consultant to advise on the firm's diversity goals and objectives and on the best methods for achieving them. The managing partner of the firm as well as other partners have attended seminars and other meetings regarding diversity issues in the workplace in conjunction with the firm's effort to structure a more comprehensive diversity program.

The following information includes certain of the firm's policies, outlines of some of the initiatives the firm has undertaken to recruit, hire and retain minorities and women, and demonstrates the firm's commitment to equal opportunity employment and diversity.

• Chadbourne is a signatory to the Association of the Bar of the City of New York's Committee on Recruitment and Retention of Lawyers' 1991 Statement of Goals of New York Law Firms and Corporate Legal Departments for Increasing Minority Hiring, Retention and Promotion; to the Association's revised goals and mission statement of 1998; to the Statement of Goals of New York Law Firms and Legal Departments for the Retention and Promotion of Women; and to the Association's 2003 Statement of Diversity Principles.

• Chadbourne has participated in the Association of the Bar of the City of New York's Committee on the Recruitment and Retention of Lawyers' Fellowship Program since its inception in 1991. The Fellowship Program places minority law school students in paid clerkships at participating firms. Each summer Chadbourne has a law student from the program in our summer associate program.

• Chadbourne is among the first 16 law firms to sign the New York County Lawyers' Association's Diversity Statement, supporting both its reporting and implementation plans.

• Chadbourne is a participant in the activities of the Association of the Bar of the City of New York's Committee to Enhance Diversity in the Legal Profession.

• In recent years, Chadbourne has participated in a number of job fairs (for example, the Northeast Black Law Students' Association Job Fair, the job fair formerly known as the Crimson & Brown Associates' Job Fair and the Association of the Bar of the City of New York's Minority Lateral Job Fair) geared toward increasing the hiring of minority law school students and lawyers.

• Chadbourne, for several years running, has hosted a series of promotional receptions at several national law schools to which we have invited, among others, the members of minority and women's organizations, clubs and journals at those law schools. In addition, the firm was a "Platinum Sponsor" of the inaugural Paul Robeson Conference, organized by the Columbia [Law School] Black Law Students' Association. The conference included presentations and discussions focusing on such important topics as affirmative action and business and economic development.

• Chadbourne has joined the American Bar Association's Legal Opportunities Scholarship Fund for Justice and Education and pledged a substantial contribution for the years 2001 through 2003.

• Since 2001, Chadbourne has provided the Northeast BLSA Job Fair with their home office and operational support, and works with its director and staff on new initiatives.

• Chadbourne was one of the first law firms to establish, and is one of the few firms with, an ombuds program to advise attorneys on various career development and workplace issues.

• Women partners at the firm hold regular meetings with women associates to discuss issues of common concern and the firm sponsors seminars on professional issues in conjunction with the Professional Women's Alliance of New York City.

• Chadbourne requires all partners and employees to attend a sensitivity training program which covers policies relating to discrimination, harassment and diversity.

Chapman and Cutler LLP

111 W. Monroe Street
Chicago, IL 60603
Phone: (312) 845-3000
Fax: (312) 701-2361

FIRM LEADERSHIP

Managing Partner: Richard Cosgrove, Chief
Executive Partner
Diversity Team Leader: David McMullen, Chair
of the Diversity Committee

LOCATIONS

Chicago, IL (HQ)
Salt Lake City, UT
San Francisco, CA

FULL-TIME ASSOCIATES	2003	2002
Minority men	4	5
Minority women	4	4
White women	18	19
Total	70	69

SUMMER ASSOCIATES	2003	2002
Minority men	1	0
Minority women	2	1
White women	0	1
Total	9	8

EQUITY PARTNERS	2003	2002
Minority men	2	2
Minority women	0	0
White women	8	6
Total	75	71

NON-EQUITY PARTNERS	2003	2002
Minority men	3	2
Minority women	0	0
White women	12	11
Total	39	37

NEW HIRES	2003	2002
Minority men	1	1
Minority women	2	1
White women	4	7
Total	13	26

Strategic Plan and Diversity Leadership

How does the firm's leadership communicate the importance of diversity to everyone at the firm? (e.g., e-mails, web site, newsletters, meetings, etc.)

Our chief executive partner (CEP) and chief operating partner (COP) have communicated the importance of diversity at our annual attorney dinner, at associate meetings and through various written memoranda. In addition, diversity topics are addressed in our all-firm marketing newsletter, Marketing Matters, and our all-firm weekly newsletter, the C&C Bulletin. Finally, the firm is currently working on an expansion of the diversity section of our web page.

Who has primary responsibility for leading diversity initiatives at your firm?

David B. McMullen, chair of the Diversity Committee

Does your law firm currently have a diversity committee?

Yes

Does the committee's representation include one or more members of the firm's management/executive committee (or the equivalent)?

Yes

How many attorneys are on the committee, and in 2003, what was the total number of hours collectively spent by the committee in furtherance of the firm's diversity initiatives?

Total attorneys on committee: 8 (two members are also members of the firm's management/executive committee)

Total hours spent on diversity: Previously, diversity at our firm was a mandate of several different committees at the firm, including the Employment Committee and our Policy Committee (the management committee of the firm). This year, our diversity initiatives were consolidated into one committee, the Diversity Committee. Hours previously spent on specific diversity initiatives were not tracked separately and the committee responsible for the initiative included these hours in its annual total. Going forward, the hours will be tracked through the Diversity Committee.

Does the committee and/or diversity leader establish and set goals or objectives consistent with management's priorities?

Yes

Has the firm undertaken a formal or informal diversity program or set of initiatives aimed at increasing the diversity of the firm?

Yes, formal

How often does the firm's management review the firm's diversity progress/results?

Quarterly

How is the firm's diversity committee and/or firm management held accountable for achieving results?

The Diversity Committee is responsible for reporting its progress to the firm's Policy Committee and the performance of the members of the committee is one factor taken into account when the firm evaluates partner performance.

LAW FIRM DIVERSITY INITIATIVES	ALREADY COMPLETED	CURRENTLY ADDRESSING	NOT A CURRENT PRIORITY
Undertake communication from firm management that diversity is a top priority of the firm.	✔		
Formalize diversity plan and committee with action steps and accountability to management.	✔		
Conduct firm-wide diversity training for all attorneys and staff.		✔	
Increase the number of minority attorneys at the associate level.		✔	
Increase the number of minority attorneys at the partnership level.		✔	
Develop/expand relationships with minority bar associations to offer firm's support of these networks.		✔	
Focus on strengthening firm's mentoring program, including for benefit of minority attorneys.		✔	
Conduct internal diversity needs assessment and/or retain diversity consultant to examine how firm culture might be more welcoming of minorities.		✔	
Support law firm's internal affinity networks (e.g., women, minority attorney networks).			✔
Manage/monitor allocation of work assignments and/or hours billed to ensure women and minority attorneys have equal access/inclusion on top client matters.			✔

Recruitment – New Associates

Does your firm annually recruit at any of the following types of institutions? (Check all that apply and list the schools).

Ivy League schools: Cornell University

Public state schools: University of Illinois, University of Iowa, University of Virginia, University of Minnesota, University of Michigan, University of California at Berkeley, University of California at Davis, University of California at Hastings

Private schools: University of Notre Dame, Northwestern University, Loyola University-Chicago, DePaul University, Chicago-Kent College of Law, University of Chicago, Washington University in St. Louis, Georgetown University

Do you have any special outreach efforts directed to encourage minority law students to consider your firm?

• Participate in/host minority law student job fair(s)

• Sponsor minority law student association events

• Firm's lawyers participate on career panels at school

• Scholarships or intern/fellowships for minority students

SUMMER ASSOCIATE STATISTICS: SUMMER 2003	MINORITY MEN	MINORITY WOMEN	WHITE WOMEN	TOTAL
Summer associates	1	2	0	9
Summer associates who received an offer of full-time employment	1	2	0	9
Summer associates who accepted an offer of full-time employment	1	2	0	9

Recruitment – Lateral Associates and Partners

What activities does the firm undertake to attract minority and women attorneys?

• *Partner programs with women and minority professional associations such as Women in Public Finance.*

• Participate at minority job fairs

Do you use executive recruiting/search firms to seek to identify new diversity hires (partners or associates)?

Yes

List all women- and/or minority-owned executive search/recruiting firms to which the firm paid a fee for placement services in the past 12 months:

Nichols & Sciabica Attorney Search

LATERAL ASSOCIATES AND PARTNERS: 1/1/03 – 12/31/03	MINORITY MEN	MINORITY WOMEN	WHITE WOMEN	TOTAL
Number of lateral associate hires	0	0	4	10
Number of lateral partner hires (equity and non-equity)	1	0	2	8
Number of new partners (equity and non-equity) promoted from associate rank	0	0	0	3
Number of new equity partners	0	0	1	4

Retention & Professional Development

ATTORNEYS WHO LEFT THE FIRM: 2003	MINORITY MEN	MINORITY WOMEN	WHITE WOMEN	TOTAL
Number of attorneys who voluntarily or involuntarily left your firm's employ in 2003	1	1	5	15

How do 2003 attrition rates generally compare to those experienced in the prior year period?

About the same as in prior years

Please identify the specific steps you are taking to reduce the attrition rate of minority and women attorneys.

• Increase/review compensation relative to competition

• Increase/improve current work/life programs

• Work with minority and women attorneys to develop career advancement plans

• Introduce minority and women attorneys to key clients, including to lead engagements

• Strengthen mentoring program for all attorneys, including minorities and women

• Professional skills development program, including minority and women attorneys

Does your firm have part-time/flex-time policies that permit attorneys (male or female) to work alternative schedules?

Yes. Currently, we have 12 attorneys who are working alternative schedules, seven of whom are associates, which represents 10 percent of our current associates.

What impact, if any, will the decision to work part-time have on an attorney's ability to make partner or, if already a partner, to remain a partner at your firm?

Attorneys on alternate schedules will still be required to meet minimum levels of experience to achieve partnership. Alternate schedules have no effect on an attorney's ability to remain a partner.

Have any attorneys who chose to work a part-time schedule made partner at your firm?

Yes, two attorneys.

Management Demographic Profile (as of 12/31/03)

	MINORITY MEN	MINORITY WOMEN	WHITE WOMEN	TOTAL
Number of attorneys on the Executive/Management Committee or equivalent	1	0	1	12
Number of attorneys on the Hiring Committee or equivalent	1	0	2	7
Number of attorneys on the Partner/Associate Review Committee or equivalent	1	0	1	14

Please provide information regarding all minority and women attorneys who head offices or practice groups of your law firm:*

Women heading offices: Melanie J. Gnazzo, Co-Head of San Francisco Office

*Several of the firm's major committees are chaired by women or minorities: the Professional Personnel Committee, which is responsible for associate compensation and advancement, is chaired by an African-American partner; the hiring partner of the firm, who also serves as chair of the Employment Committee, is a woman partner; and the firm's Marketing Committee is chaired by a woman partner.

Three of the firm's managing partners are openly gay. Additionally, an openly gay man is a member of the executive/management committee, co-head of the firm's San Francisco office and chair of the firm's Diversity Committee.

The Firm Says

Chapman and Cutler LLP has embraced the diversity of its attorneys and staff and is proud of our collegial work environment. We value attorneys and staff who are not only experts in their chosen fields, but who also enhance our workplace environment with their individual experiences. Because of this, we have encouraged our attorneys to devote their time and experience to improve our firm's diversity and to help the community through our pro bono and service opportunities.

In the past, the firm leadership has looked to a variety of committees, including the Employment and Professional Personnel Committees to achieve our diversity initiatives. These groups have participated and have encouraged our attorneys to participate in programs such as minority job fairs (including the Cook County Minority Job Fair) and the Chicago Committee of Minorities in Large Law Firms; to engage in pro bono opportunities serving women, gay and lesbians and other minority groups; to serve on the boards of charitable and nonprofit organizations (such as the Lambda Legal Defense and Education Fund and Gads Hill Center, which provides services to the Latino community); to speak at law schools to diverse student groups; and to be active in minority professional associations.

In addition to the firm's diversity initiatives, the firm has demonstrated its commitment to a diverse workplace through its formal policies. For example, the firm has had an extensive Harassment Policy in place for over 10 years which covers sexual harassment as well as harassment based on sex, age, race, national origin, religion, sexual orientation, marital status, disability and membership in other protected groups. Our policy requires that all firm personnel take responsibility for a harassment-free workplace, and asks that any employee who witnesses harassment report the incident to the appropriate manager.

Another example of the firm's commitment to diversity through formal policies is the firm's equal employment opportunity policy which covers recruitment, hiring, placement, promotion, training and compensation for all jobs without regard to marital or parental status, national origin, ancestry, pregnancy, sexual orientation, source of income or housing status, in addition to the traditional classes covered by such policies. Our EEO policy has been in place for over 10 years.

Recently, the firm's leadership has formalized the firm's various diversity initiatives by forming a Diversity Committee comprised of managing partners who report directly to the firm's chief operating partner and the firm's Policy Committee, which is the executive committee/management committee of the firm. The Diversity Committee is charged with developing and implementing formal policies designed to improve the diversity of

the firm and to foster a workplace that not only embraces diversity, but also anticipates (and not just responds to) the needs of firm personnel. The performance of the members of this committee, and the performance of other partners in achieving these objectives, is a factor in evaluating partner performance and compensation. The firm also provides hours credit to associates working to foster its diversity initiatives, which count toward the firm's hours requirement.

The Diversity Committee's mission statement is as follows: Chapman and Cutler LLP is committed to and has placed the highest priority on achieving workplace diversity; a workplace where individuals of different race, ethnicity, religion, age, sex, sexual orientation, family status or disability have equal opportunity to participate in the firm at all levels to the greatest extent of their ability. Areas of focus for the Diversity Committee include: recruitment, retention, promotion, community and pro bono partnerships and service and education and communication.

Choate, Hall & Stewart

53 State Street, Exchange Place
Boston, MA 02109
Phone: (617) 248-5000
Fax: (617) 248-4000

FIRM LEADERSHIP

Managing Partner: John Nadas and William Gelnaw
Diversity Team Leader: John Nadas, Managing Partner and Co-Chair; Macey Russell, Litigation Partner

LOCATIONS

Boston, MA

LAW FIRM DEMOGRAPHIC PROFILES

FULL-TIME ASSOCIATES	2003	2002
Minority men	1	2
Minority women	7	5
White women	31	33
Total	77	79

SUMMER ASSOCIATES	2003	2002
Minority men	1	0
Minority women	3	2
White women	5	5
Total	14	14

EQUITY PARTNERS	2003	2002
Minority men	1	1
Minority women	0	0
White women	7	6
Total	54	52

NON-EQUITY PARTNERS	2003	2002
Minority men	1	0
Minority women	0	0
White women	11	10
Total	37	35

NEW HIRES	2003	2002
Minority men	0	2
Minority women	3	0
White women	6	12
Total	16	24

Strategic Plan and Diversity Leadership

How does the firm's leadership communicate the importance of diversity to everyone at the firm? (e.g., e-mails, web site, newsletters, meetings, etc.)

Meetings, e-mails, firm intranet site, interoffice mailings, speaker's series and Diversity Action Plan.

Who has primary responsibility for leading diversity initiatives at your firm?

John Nadas, managing partner, and Macey Russell, litigation partner

Does your law firm currently have a diversity committee?

Yes

Does the committee's representation include one or more members of the firm's management/executive committee (or the equivalent)?

Yes

How many attorneys are on the committee, and in 2003, what was the total number of hours collectively spent by the committee in furtherance of the firm's diversity initiatives?

Total attorneys on committee: 10

Total hours spent on diversity: More than 500

Does the committee and/or diversity leader establish and set goals or objectives consistent with management's priorities?

Yes

Has the firm undertaken a formal or informal diversity program or set of initiatives aimed at increasing the diversity of the firm?

Yes, formal

How often does the firm's management review the firm's diversity progress/results?

Quarterly, depending on the year

How is the firm's diversity committee and/or firm management held accountable for achieving results?

Periodically reviewed by the firm's Management Committee and directly tied to review of partner compensation.

LAW FIRM DIVERSITY INITIATIVES	ALREADY COMPLETED	CURRENTLY ADDRESSING	NOT A CURRENT PRIORITY
Undertake communication from firm management that diversity is a top priority of the firm.	✓		
Formalize diversity plan and committee with action steps and accountability to management.	✓		
Conduct firm-wide diversity training for all attorneys and staff.		✓	
Increase the number of minority attorneys at the associate level.		✓	
Increase the number of minority attorneys at the partnership level.		✓	
Develop/expand relationships with minority bar associations to offer firm's support of these networks.		✓	
Focus on strengthening firm's mentoring program, including for benefit of minority attorneys.		✓	
Conduct internal diversity needs assessment and/or retain diversity consultant to examine how firm culture might be more welcoming of minorities.	✓		
Support law firm's internal affinity networks (e.g., women, minority attorney networks).	✓		
Manage/monitor allocation of work assignments and/or hours billed to ensure women and minority attorneys have equal access/inclusion on top client matters.		✓	

Recruitment – New Associates

Does your firm annually recruit at any of the following types of institutions? (Check all that apply and list the schools).

Ivy League schools: Harvard University, Yale University, Columbia University, University of Pennsylvania, Cornell University

Public state schools: University of Connecticut, University of Virginia

Private schools: NYU, Georgetown University, George Washington University, Boston University, Boston College, University of Chicago, Suffolk University, Northeastern University, University of Notre Dame, Duke University

Historically Black Colleges and Universities (HBCUs): Howard University

Do you have any special outreach efforts directed to encourage minority law students to consider your firm?

• Hold a reception for minority law students

• Advertise in minority law student association publication(s)

• Participate in/host minority law student job fair(s)

• Sponsor minority law student association events

• Firm's lawyers participate on career panels at school

• Outreach to leadership of minority student organizations

SUMMER ASSOCIATE STATISTICS: SUMMER 2003	MINORITY MEN	MINORITY WOMEN	WHITE WOMEN	TOTAL
Summer associates	1	3	5	14
Summer associates who received an offer of full-time employment	0	3	5	13
Summer associates who accepted an offer of full-time employment	0	2	5	11

Recruitment – Lateral Associates and Partners

What activities does the firm undertake to attract minority and women attorneys?

• *Boston Lawyer's Group Mentor Program*

• Partner programs with women and minority bar associations

• Participate at minority job fairs

• Seek referrals from other attorneys

Do you use executive recruiting/search firms to seek to identify new diversity hires (partners or associates)?

No

LATERAL ASSOCIATES AND PARTNERS: 1/1/03 – 12/31/03	MINORITY MEN	MINORITY WOMEN	WHITE WOMEN	TOTAL
Number of lateral associate hires	0	1	2	4
Number of lateral partner hires (equity and non-equity)	0	0	0	3
Number of new partners (equity and non-equity) promoted from associate rank	0	0	2	4
Number of new equity partners	0	0	0	2

Retention & Professional Development

ATTORNEYS WHO LEFT THE FIRM: 2003	MINORITY MEN	MINORITY WOMEN	WHITE WOMEN	TOTAL
Number of attorneys who voluntarily or involuntarily left your firm's employ in 2003	1	1	8	21

How do 2003 attrition rates generally compare to those experienced in the prior year period?

About the same as in prior years

Please identify the specific steps you are taking to reduce the attrition rate of minority and women attorneys.

- Develop and/or support internal employee affinity groups (e.g., minority or women networks within the firm)
- Increase/review compensation relative to competition
- Increase/improve current work/life programs
- Work with minority and women attorneys to develop career advancement plans
- Introduce minority and women attorneys to key clients, including to lead engagements
- Review work assignments and hours billed to key client matters to make sure minority and women attorneys are not being excluded
- Strengthen mentoring program for all attorneys, including minorities and women
- Professional skills development program, including minority and women attorneys

Does your firm have part-time/flex-time policies that permit attorneys (male or female) to work alternative schedules?

Yes

What impact, if any, will the decision to work part-time have on an attorney's ability to make partner or, if already a partner, to remain a partner at your firm?

Although part-time status may affect the timing for partnership consideration, it has no effect on an associate's ability to make partner (and we routinely elevate part-time associates to partner status). Likewise, part-time status has no adverse impact on a partner's ability to remain a partner at the firm.

Have any attorneys who chose to work a part-time schedule made partner at your firm?

Yes, four attorneys.

Management Demographic Profile (as of 12/31/03)

	MINORITY MEN	MINORITY WOMEN	WHITE WOMEN	TOTAL
Number of attorneys on the Executive/Management Committee or equivalent	0	0	2	8
Number of attorneys on the Hiring Committee or equivalent	1	1	5	16
Number of attorneys on the Partner/Associate Review Committee or equivalent	0	0	3	7

Please provide information regarding all minority and women attorneys who head offices or practice groups of your law firm:

Women or minorities heading offices: None (we have no branch offices)

Women heading practice groups: Sarah Columbia, Intellectual Property Litigation Practice Group

The Firm Says

Diversity hiring and retention programs

Choate, Hall & Stewart's commitment to hiring, retaining and encouraging people from diverse backgrounds extends to every level and department of the firm. We are a founding member of and very active in the Boston Lawyers Group, a consortium dedicated to enhancing recruitment and retention of attorneys of color. We are also active in the Massachusetts Association of Hispanic Attorneys, the Hispanic National Bar Association, the Asian American Lawyers Association and the South Asian American Law Students Association. We routinely work with faculty members and administrators from law schools around the country, sponsoring activities to help students capitalize on opportunities available in Boston.

A commitment to diversity

Choate, Hall & Stewart is committed to fostering a diverse and inclusive work environment that understands, welcomes, values and supports individuals of all backgrounds. To achieve these goals, the firm has established a Diversity Committee comprised of lawyers and non-lawyers which is co-chaired by one of the managing partners. As an initial step, we retained a Boston-based consulting firm, which conducted a workplace diversity assessment. The goal of the assessment was to gain a better understanding of the perspectives and experiences of individuals within Choate's work force with regard to diversity issues and to identify steps that ensure the firm offers a work environment in which we can all thrive. Having completed the assessment, the firm's Diversity Committee then generated an Action Plan to implement the following steps which include but are not limited to:

1. The institutionalization of a standing Diversity Committee, and the creation of three new standing Subcommittees; one Subcommittee on the Recruitment and Retention of Attorneys and Staff of Color; one Subcommittee on the Retention and Promotion of Women Attorneys; and one Subcommittee on Increasing Diversity Awareness and Improving Diversity Communication Across the Firm.

2. Continuation of "Diversity Dine Around Dinners" for the lawyers and diversity workshops for the staff and others.

3. The establishment of a speaker series to address diversity issues with the involvement of clients and experts.

4. Continual review of our part-time work policy.

5. Systematic coordination of efforts among the Diversity Committee, human resources, professional development, marketing and legal recruitment departments to enhance the firm's ability to attract, retain and promote a diverse work force and to advance specific recommendations set forth in each subcommittee's plan.

Cleary, Gottlieb, Steen & Hamilton

One Liberty Plaza
New York, NY 10006
Phone: (212) 225-2000
Fax: (212) 225-3999

FIRM LEADERSHIP

Managing Partner: Peter Karasz, Managing Partner
Diversity Team Leader: Seth Grosshandler, Chair, Committee on Diversity Issues

LOCATIONS

New York, NY (HQ)
Washington, DC
Brussels
Cologne
Frankfurt
Hong Kong
London
Milan
Moscow
Paris
Rome
Tokyo

LAW FIRM DEMOGRAPHIC PROFILES

FULL-TIME ASSOCIATES	2003	2002
Minority men	45	41
Minority women	68	59
White women	169	123
Total	407	378

SUMMER ASSOCIATES	2003	2002
Minority men	13	4
Minority women	14	16
White women	33	32
Total	80	101

EQUITY PARTNERS	2003	2002
Minority men	7	6
Minority women	2	1
White women	14	12
Total	98	91

COUNSEL & SENIOR ATTORNEYS	2003	2002
Minority men	1	1
Minority women	2	0
White women	11	11
Total	27	25

NEW HIRES	2003	2002
Minority men	6	8
Minority women	13	20
White women	32	33
Total	98	97

MINORITY CORPORATE COUNSEL ASSOCIATION

Strategic Plan and Diversity Leadership

How does the firm's leadership communicate the importance of diversity to everyone at the firm? (e.g., e-mails, web site, newsletters, meetings, etc.)

The Committee on Diversity Issues (which, as described below, includes the managing partner and several senior partners) is charged with communicating the importance of diversity. These communications can take several forms. For example, e-mails are sent from the chair of the Diversity Committee to all attorneys (and summer associates) and administrative staff in the New York office for certain New York office events, such as the recent event we hosted in celebration of the 50th Anniversary of Brown v. Board of Education where we honored Judge Constance Baker Motley and the event we hosted in February in celebration of the 10th anniversary of the end of apartheid in South Africa where we honored Justice Richard Goldstone. (We also invited Cleary Gottlieb alumni to the Brown celebration.) For other events, e-mails might be sent by one or more members of the Diversity Committee announcing various "affinity" events. So, for example, the chair of the Diversity Committee (an openly gay partner) will, together with other gay or lesbian partners, send e-mails to all attorneys (and summer associates) inviting them to the regular lunches for gay and lesbian attorneys. Similarly, the vice-chair of the Diversity Committee (a Latino) sends e-mails to all attorneys (and summer associates) of color inviting them to the semi-annual dinner for attorneys (and summer associates) of color. Women's Working Group lunches and other events are also announced through e-mails to all women attorneys (and summer associates). News of these events is also generally available through the firm's daily information bulletin.

Certain events, such as meetings of the associates of color, are held under the auspices of the Diversity Committee, but do not typically involve partner participation. These events are typically announced by e-mail by associates on the Diversity Committee.

The chair of the Diversity Committee speaks at the new associate orientation for New York and Washington associates regarding the firm's commitment to diversity and the activities of the Diversity Committee. The firm's anti-discrimination and sexual harassment policy is included in the materials given to new associates and is periodically re-circulated to all attorneys and staff.

The chair of the Diversity Committee also speaks at a summer associate event devoted to that purpose each summer. While in prior years this event was held over lunch, this year it will take place in the early evening to promote even greater participation by senior lawyers at the event and a greater dialogue with all in attendance.

Each summer associate is invited to a lunch with several associate and partner members of the Diversity Committee to discuss the role of the Diversity Committee and diversity issues at the firm. There are approximately 10 of these lunches each summer, with groups of 5 to 15 attorneys and summer associates in attendance at each lunch.

Who has primary responsibility for leading diversity initiatives at your firm?

Seth Grosshandler, chair of the Diversity Committee. His term will end on December 31, 2004, and Ricardo Anzaldua, the vice-chair of the Diversity Committee, will become chair for a two-year term.

Does your law firm currently have a diversity committee?

Yes

Does the committee's representation include one or more members of the firm's management/executive committee (or the equivalent)?

Yes

How many attorneys are on the committee, and in 2003, what was the total number of hours collectively spent by the committee in furtherance of the firm's diversity initiatives?

Total attorneys on committee: 19

Total hours spent on diversity: 495. We are in the process of implementing procedures to more methodically track time spent on Diversity Committee matters. For the first six months of 2004, we've recorded 379 hours on Diversity Committee matters.

Does the committee and/or diversity leader establish and set goals or objectives consistent with management's priorities?

Yes. The firm is managed by committees, of which the Diversity Committee is one. The Diversity Committee discusses and reports on its initiatives and progress periodically at meetings of all New York and Washington office partners.

Has the firm undertaken a formal or informal diversity program or set of initiatives aimed at increasing the diversity of the firm?

Yes, formal

How often does the firm's management review the firm's diversity progress/results?

The Diversity Committee discusses and reports on its initiatives and progress periodically at meetings of all New York and Washington partners.

How is the firm's diversity committee and/or firm management held accountable for achieving results?

The Diversity Committee discusses and reports on its initiatives and progress periodically at meetings of all New York and Washington partners.

LAW FIRM DIVERSITY INITIATIVES*	ALREADY COMPLETED	CURRENTLY ADDRESSING	NOT A CURRENT PRIORITY
Undertake communication from firm management that diversity is a top priority of the firm.	✓	✓	
Formalize diversity plan and committee with action steps and accountability to management.	✓	✓	
Conduct firm-wide diversity training for all attorneys and staff.	✓	✓	
Increase the number of minority attorneys at the associate level.	✓	✓	
Increase the number of minority attorneys at the partnership level.	✓	✓	
Develop/expand relationships with minority bar associations to offer firm's support of these networks.		✓	
Focus on strengthening firm's mentoring program, including for benefit of minority attorneys.	✓	✓	
Conduct internal diversity needs assessment and/or retain diversity consultant to examine how firm culture might be more welcoming of minorities.	✓	✓	
Support law firm's internal affinity networks (e.g., women, minority attorney networks).	✓	✓	
Manage/monitor allocation of work assignments and/or hours billed to ensure women and minority attorneys have equal access/inclusion on top client matters.	✓	✓	

*Note: We do not believe that any of the items above is ever truly "completed." Instead, even in those areas where the firm has made great progress (and which we have thus marked as "already completed") there is still more progress to be made (and we have therefore also marked them as "currently addressing").

Recruitment – New Associates

Does your firm annually recruit at any of the following types of institutions? (Check all that apply and list the schools).*

Ivy League schools: Columbia University, Harvard University, University of Pennsylvania, Yale University

Public state schools: University of California-Boalt Hall, University of Michigan, Ohio State University, Rutgers University-Newark, University of Virginia

Private schools: Brooklyn Law School, Benjamin Cardozo School of Law, University of Chicago, Duke University, Fordham University, Georgetown University, New York University, New York Law School, Northwestern University, St. John's University, Stanford University, Tulane University

Historically Black Colleges and Universities (HBCUs): Howard University

*The schools listed above are those at which the firm recruits on campus. The firm also recruits at the BC/BU-NYC Job Fair, Cornell NYC Job Fair and the Northeast BLSA Job Fair.

Do you have any special outreach efforts directed to encourage minority law students to consider your firm?

• *Attorneys of color in the New York office host dinners in the fall for law students of color who have offers outstanding.*

• Hold a reception for minority law students

• Participate in/host minority law student job fair(s)

• Sponsor minority law student association events

• Firm's lawyers participate on career panels at school

• Outreach to leadership of minority student organizations

• Scholarships or intern/fellowships for minority students

SUMMER ASSOCIATE STATISTICS: SUMMER 2003	MINORITY MEN	MINORITY WOMEN	WHITE WOMEN	TOTAL
Summer associates	13	14	33	80
Summer associates who received an offer of full-time employment	13	14	33	80
Summer associates who accepted an offer of full-time employment*	6	11	17	46

These numbers do not include those summer associates who are clerking in 2004-2005 and therefore unable to accept their offers of full-time employment.

Lateral Associates and Partners

What activities does the firm undertake to attract minority and women attorneys?

• Partner programs with women and minority bar associations

• Participate at minority job fairs

Do you use executive recruiting/search firms to seek to identify new diversity hires (partners or associates)?

No. We have not used search firms specifically for the purpose of identifying "diversity hires."

LATERAL ASSOCIATES AND PARTNERS: 1/1/03 – 12/31/03	MINORITY MEN	MINORITY WOMEN	WHITE WOMEN	TOTAL
Number of lateral associate hires	2	1	4	11
Number of lateral partner hires	0	0	0	1
Number of New Partners, Counsel & Senior Attorneys Promoted from Associate Rank	1	3	2	13
Number of new equity partners	1	1	2	11

Retention & Professional Development

ATTORNEYS WHO LEFT THE FIRM: 2003	MINORITY MEN	MINORITY WOMEN	WHITE WOMEN	TOTAL
Number of attorneys who voluntarily or involuntarily left your firm's employ in 2003	7	6	15	45

How do 2003 attrition rates generally compare to those experienced in the prior year period?

Lower than in prior years

Please identify the specific steps you are taking to reduce the attrition rate of minority and women attorneys.

• *All of the steps below are taken for all attorneys, not just minority and woman attorneys, and are part of the training and acculturation of associates designed, in part, to reduce attrition.*

• Develop and/or support internal employee affinity groups (e.g., minority or women networks within the firm)

• Increase/review compensation relative to competition

• Increase/improve current work/life programs

• Work with minority and women attorneys to develop career advancement plans

• Introduce minority and women attorneys to key clients, including to lead engagements

• Review work assignments and hours billed to key client matters to make sure minority and women attorneys are not being excluded

• Strengthen mentoring program for all attorneys, including minorities and women

• Professional skills development program, including minority and women attorneys

Does your firm have part-time/flex-time policies that permit attorneys (male or female) to work alternative schedules?

Yes

What impact, if any, will the decision to work part-time have on an attorney's ability to make partner or, if already a partner, to remain a partner at your firm?

There is no fixed relationship between the duration of reduced schedule status and the timing of one's consideration for partnership. The most important factor in the timing of partnership is experience. For many years, there have been partners who have worked on a reduced schedule in both the New York and Washington offices.

Have any attorneys who chose to work a part-time schedule made partner at your firm?

Yes, three attorneys.

Management Demographic Profile (as of 12/31/03)

	MINORITY MEN	MINORITY WOMEN	WHITE WOMEN	TOTAL
Number of attorneys on the Executive/Management Committee or equivalent	0	0	1	8
Number of attorneys on the Hiring Committee or equivalent	0	1	2	11
Number of attorneys on the Partner/Associate Review Committee or equivalent	2	0	2	11

Please provide information regarding all minority and women attorneys who head offices or practice groups of your law firm:

Minorities heading practice groups: Although the firm does not have formal departments with formal heads of practice groups, following is a list of minority partners, counsel and senior attorneys and their practice areas.

Ricardo A. Anzaldua-Montoya – Corporate; Kimberly B. Blacklow – Corporate; Francisco L. Cestero – Corporate; Laura G. Ciabarra – Real Estate; Carmen A. Corrales – Corporate; Jaime A. El Koury – Corporate; Sandra Galvis – Corporate; Jorge U. Juantorena – Corporate; Sung K. Kang – Corporate; Gabriel J. Mesa – Corporate; Paul J. Shim – Corporate

Women heading practice groups: Although the firm does not have formal departments, a number of women and minority attorneys have been and continue to be leaders in various practice areas and firm committees.

Mary E. Alcock – Corporate; Robin M. Bergen – Corporate; Kimberly B. Blacklow – Corporate; Deborah M. Buell – Litigation / Bankruptcy; Penelope L. Christophorou – Corporate; Laura G. Ciabarra – Real Estate; Carmen Corrales – Corporate; Ellen M. Creede – Corporate; Ana Demel – Corporate; Janet L. Fisher – Corporate; Dana G. Fleischman – Corporate; Sandra L. Flow – Corporate; Sandra Galvis – Corporate; Lindsee P. Granfield – Bankruptcy; Dawn Jasiak – Corporate; Judith Kassel – Trusts and Estate; Karen A. Kerr – Corporate; Jennifer L. Kroman – Litigation; Deborah E. Kurtzberg – ERISA; Joyce E. McCarty – Structured Finance / Environmental; Erika W. Nijenhuis – Tax; Wanda J. Olson – Corporate; Andrea G. Podolsky – Corporate; Sandra M. Rocks – Corporate; Nancy Ruskin – Litigation; Sara Schotland – Litigation and Energy Regulatory; Linda J. Soldo – Corporate; Yvette P. Teofan – Corporate; Mary Watson – Litigation; Janet Weller – Environmental

The Firm Says

The Diversity Committee, which includes partners, associates and administrative staff, is charged in the New York office with promoting diversity and communicating the importance of diversity. A partner from the Washington office and the firm's diversity consultant also attend the twice-monthly meetings.

As set forth in the first question, the Diversity Committee sponsors or is involved with a number of regular and special events, including summer associate lunches and presentations, to which all attorneys are invited. The Diversity Committee also sponsors or is involved with meetings of "affinity" groups, including attorneys of color dinners, associates of color dinners, gay/lesbian lunches and other events, and Women's Working Group lunches and other events. While most of the regular events do not involve members of the administrative staff or alumni, some of the special events (such as the recent celebrations of the 50th Anniversary of Brown v. Board of Education and the 10th anniversary of the end of apartheid in South Africa) do.

Many of the firm's pro bono and public service efforts are also diversity-related and involve administrative as well as legal staff. In 1991, Gottlieb initiated a partnership with a New York City public school located near the firm's offices, in order to help at-risk students at a predominantly minority high school improve their academic performance and preparedness for college. The partnership's programs include one-on-one mentoring, college advising, SAT preparation courses and sponsoring annual events that promote the various academic and cultural talents of the students. The firm also hosts the NYC Legal Outreach Program, a one-week program designed to give a select group of minority students an experience that gives them a taste of life as a lawyer, including negotiating mock contracts and litigating a case before a group of volunteer "judges." We have a pro-bono "partnership" with Acción NY, a micro lender that provides credit to small business owners who do not have access to traditional forms of credit. The majority of Acción's clients are Hispanic, and over half are women. We currently represent over 50 asylum seekers from all over the world in various stages and types of immigration proceedings, including individuals persecuted on the grounds of their race, religion, gender, nationality and/or sexual orientation. In Virginia, we work with the Lawyers' Committee on Civil Rights Under the Law to challenge congressional redistricting plans that discriminate against minority voters. The Vault Guide to Law Firm Pro Bono Programs provides more details about our pro bono practice, which are also available on our web site at www.cgsh.com.

The firm is an original signatory to the Association of the Bar of the City of New York's Diversity Principles and the vice-chair of our Diversity Committee has been an active participant in the City Bar's Statistics Subcommittee, which is responsible for setting the parameters of firms' reporting of diversity information to the City Bar's Office of Diversity. Cleary Gottlieb is pleased to be a part of this process and to work to achieve the goals in the Diversity Principles. There are two items in particular in the Diversity Principles that are the subject of current Diversity Committee focus: first, the Diversity Committee is in the process of developing a Mission Statement; and second, the Diversity Committee is in the initial stages of planning a formal diversity training program for all attorneys (the last formal training took place a number of years ago). Formal diversity training for administrative staff is currently under way.

The Diversity Committee has been working recently on helping to build and establish communities among attorneys of difference – principally attorneys of color and openly gay/lesbian attorneys. The Diversity Committee believes that fostering such communities will make the firm an even more welcoming and supportive institution for attorneys of difference, creating an environment where attorneys of difference can thrive in the

context of the larger community of Cleary Gottlieb lawyers. The events described above are one means to create this sense of community.

Another means to create this community is through our recruiting efforts. Of course, successfully recruiting applicants of difference is a necessary step to creating communities of attorneys of difference. In this regard, the Diversity Committee focuses a good deal of attention on recruiting issues – the chair of the Diversity Committee sits on the Recruiting Committee and the chair of the Recruiting Committee sits on the Diversity Committee – and the partner and associate members of the Diversity Committee have worked on (and will continue to work on) initiatives to recruit successfully applicants of difference. That process itself can help build communities, not only for the applicants, but for the attorneys. For example, the attorneys of color who have attended the dinner held in the fall for applicants of color with outstanding offers believe that the event itself is community-building for them and the applicants.

Cleary Gottlieb is committed to continuing to be a diverse, welcoming and supporting environment for all attorneys, no matter their background.

Clifford Chance is proud to join Vault and the Minority Corporate Counsel Association in underwriting the first-ever Guide to Law Firm Diversity Programs. As the leading global provider of legal services, recognition of, and respect for, diversity are at the core of who we are and what we do.

At Clifford Chance, having a diverse workforce isn't just a good idea - it's the only way we do business.

C L I F F O R D
C H A N C E

CLIFFORD CHANCE US LLP
PROVIDING SEAMLESS LEGAL ADVICE ACROSS 29 MARKETS WORLDWIDE

AMSTERDAM · BANGKOK · BARCELONA · BEIJING · BERLIN · BRUSSELS · BUDAPEST · DUBAI · DÜSSELDORF
FRANKFURT · HONG KONG · LONDON · LUXEMBOURG · MADRID · MILAN · MOSCOW · MUNICH · NEW YORK · PADUA
PALO ALTO · PARIS · PRAGUE · ROME · SÃO PAULO · SHANGHAI · SINGAPORE · TOKYO · WARSAW · WASHINGTON, DC

→ www.cliffordchance.com

Clifford Chance US LLP

31 West 52nd Street
New York, NY 10019
Phone: (212) 878-8000
Fax: (212) 878-8375

FIRM LEADERSHIP

Managing Partner: John Carroll, Regional
Managing Partner
Diversity Team Leader: Keila Ravelo, Partner &
Chair of Diversity Committee

LOCATIONS

New York, NY (HQ)
Los Angeles, CA
Palo Alto, CA
San Diego, CA
San Francisco, CA
Washington, DC
Amsterdam
Bangkok
Barcelona
Beijing
Berlin
Brussels
Budapest
Dubai
Dusseldorf
Frankfurt
Hong Kong
London
Luxembourg
Madrid
Milan
Moscow
Munich
Padua
Paris
Prague
Rome
São Paulo
Shanghai
Singapore
Tokyo
Warsaw

LAW FIRM DEMOGRAPHIC PROFILES

FULL-TIME ASSOCIATES	2003	2002
Minority men	20	24
Minority women	25	35
White women	88	116
Total	318	381

SUMMER ASSOCIATES	2003	2002
Minority men	4	4
Minority women	6	7
White women	10	18
Total	33	39

EQUITY PARTNERS	2003	2002
Minority men	1	1
Minority women	2	2
White women	10	13
Total	82	94

NON-EQUITY PARTNERS	2003	2002
Minority men	0	0
Minority women	0	1
White women	4	5
Total	32	38

NEW HIRES	2003	2002
Minority men	4	11
Minority women	8	14
White women	31	49
Total	67	145

Strategic Plan and Diversity Leadership

How does the firm's leadership communicate the importance of diversity to everyone at the firm? (e.g., e-mails, web site, newsletters, meetings, etc.)

The firm is a signatory of the Association of the Bar of the City of New York's (ABCNY) Statement of Goals for Increasing Minority Retention and Promotion, and we currently have two representatives on the ABCNY Committee to Enhance Diversity in the Legal Profession. The firm's leadership communicates the importance of diversity to everyone at the firm through, among other things, mandatory diversity awareness workshops for all lawyers and director-level staff, regularly communicating updates regarding the initiative, publishing materials on the firm's internal and external web sites, holding regular meetings of the firm's Diversity Committee, as well as through an ongoing, firm-wide guest speaker series on important topics in this area. The firm also emphasizes the importance of fostering diversity at the firm by including "commitment to diversity" as one of several key criteria by which attorneys are evaluated.

Who has primary responsibility for leading diversity initiatives at your firm?

Keila Ravelo, partner and chair of the Diversity Committee; George Schieren, partner and senior advisor to the Diversity Committee

Does your law firm currently have a diversity committee?

Yes

Does the committee's representation include one or more members of the firm's management/executive committee (or the equivalent)?

Yes

How many attorneys are on the committee, and in 2003, what was the total number of hours collectively spent by the committee in furtherance of the firm's diversity initiatives?

Total attorneys on committee: 16

Total hours spent on diversity: 500

Does the committee and/or diversity leader establish and set goals or objectives consistent with management's priorities?

Yes

Has the firm undertaken a formal or informal diversity program or set of initiatives aimed at increasing the diversity of the firm?

Yes, formal

How often does the firm's management review the firm's diversity progress/results?

Annually

How is the firm's diversity committee and/or firm management held accountable for achieving results?

As one of the signatories to the ABCNY's Statement of Goals for Increasing Minority Retention and Promotion and Statement of Diversity Principles, the firm has committed itself to achieving certain measurable results in the area of diversity within a specific timeframe, including (I) hiring entry-level classes that substantially reflect the diversity of graduating law students (within the next two years); (II) achieving a level of diversity throughout an incoming associate's class's progression that is at least as great as when the class was first hired (within the next four years); (III) to reflect diversity not just in the first-year class but through the point when associates are promoted to senior positions, including counsel and partner; and (IV) to achieve leadership positions throughout the firm that reflect the diversity among our senior legal professionals.

LAW FIRM DIVERSITY INITIATIVES	ALREADY COMPLETED	CURRENTLY ADDRESSING	NOT A CURRENT PRIORITY
Undertake communication from firm management that diversity is a top priority of the firm.	✓		
Formalize diversity plan and committee with action steps and accountability to management.	✓		
Conduct firm-wide diversity training for all attorneys and staff.	✓		
Increase the number of minority attorneys at the associate level.		✓	
Increase the number of minority attorneys at the partnership level.		✓	
Develop/expand relationships with minority bar associations to offer firm's support of these networks.	✓		
Focus on strengthening firm's mentoring program, including for benefit of minority attorneys.		✓	
Conduct internal diversity needs assessment and/or retain diversity consultant to examine how firm culture might be more welcoming of minorities.	✓		
Support law firm's internal affinity networks (e.g., women, minority attorney networks).	✓		
Manage/monitor allocation of work assignments and/or hours billed to ensure women and minority attorneys have equal access/inclusion on top client matters.		✓	

Recruitment – New Associates

Does your firm annually recruit at any of the following types of institutions?

Ivy League schools: Columbia University, Cornell University, Harvard University, University of Pennsylvania, Yale University

Public state schools: University of California-Boalt Hall, University of Virginia, University of Michigan, University of Texas

Private schools: Albany Law School (Union University), Brooklyn Law School, Boston College, Boston University, Benjamin Cardozo School of Law, University of Chicago, Duke University, Fordham University, Georgetown University, Hofstra University, University of Notre Dame, Northwestern University, New York University, St. John's University, Villanova University

Historically Black Colleges and Universities (HBCUs): Howard University

Do you have any special outreach efforts directed to encourage minority law students to consider your firm?

• Hold a reception for minority law students

• Advertise in minority law student association publication(s)

• Participate in/host minority law student job fair(s)

• Sponsor minority law student association events

• Firm's lawyers participate on career panels at school

• Outreach to leadership of minority student organizations

• Scholarships or intern/fellowships for minority students

SUMMER ASSOCIATE STATISTICS: SUMMER 2003	MINORITY MEN	MINORITY WOMEN	WHITE WOMEN	TOTAL
Summer associates	3	4	7	21
Summer associates who received an offer of full-time employment	3	4	7	21
Summer associates who accepted an offer of full-time employment	2	4	5	18

Lateral Associates and Partners

What activities does the firm undertake to attract minority and women attorneys?

• *Hire search consultants specializing in minority candidates*

• Partner programs with women and minority bar associations

• Participate at minority job fairs

• Seek referrals from other attorneys

• Utilize online job services (e.g., MCCA/DuPont Primary Law Firm Job Bank)

Do you use executive recruiting/search firms to seek to identify new diversity hires (partners or associates)?

Yes

MCCA
MINORITY CORPORATE COUNSEL ASSOCIATION

VAULT

LATERAL ASSOCIATES AND PARTNERS: 1/1/03 – 12/31/03	MINORITY MEN	MINORITY WOMEN	WHITE WOMEN	TOTAL
Number of lateral associate hires	0	1	9	10
Number of lateral partner hires (equity and non-equity)	0	0	1	2
Number of new partners (equity and non-equity) promoted from associate rank	0	0	1	5
Number of new equity partners	0	0	1	2

Retention & Professional Development

ATTORNEYS WHO LEFT THE FIRM: 2003	MINORITY MEN	MINORITY WOMEN	WHITE WOMEN	TOTAL
Number of attorneys who voluntarily or involuntarily left your firm's employ in 2003	6	10	40	141

How do 2003 attrition rates generally compare to those experienced in the prior year period?

Higher than in prior years

Please identify the specific steps you are taking to reduce the attrition rate of minority and women attorneys.

• *Among other things, the Diversity Committee collaborates with the managing partner for the Americas region on a management-sponsored lecture series featuring speakers of different professional and ethnic backgrounds and interests. The Diversity Committee also sponsors a buddy program for all incoming attorneys of color. In addition to a first-year mentor, each attorney of color is assigned an associate "buddy" whose role is to facilitate the new associate's transition into the firm.*

• Develop and/or support internal employee affinity groups (e.g., minority or women networks within the firm)

• Increase/improve current work/life programs

• Adopt dispute resolution process

• Succession plan includes emphasis on diversity

• Work with minority and women attorneys to develop career advancement plans

• Introduce minority and women attorneys to key clients, including to lead engagements

• Review work assignments and hours billed to key client matters to make sure minority and women attorneys are not being excluded

• Strengthen mentoring program for all attorneys, including minorities and women

• Professional skills development program, including minority and women attorneys

Does your firm have part-time/flex-time policies that permit attorneys (male or female) to work alternative schedules?

Yes. Flex-time policy: Associates who have practiced full time at the firm for a minimum of three years are eligible to be considered for a flexible work arrangement with the firm. The flexible work arrangement may consist of either (I) working a reduced schedule of no less than 60 percent of the full-time annual billable target

and being paid a pro-rated portion of the associate's annual class compensation, or (II) moving to hourly status and being paid for actual hours worked. Part-time policy: Under the firm's child care leave policy, the firm permits attorneys returning to the firm after a parental leave to choose to work a reduced schedule for a period of up to six months following the leave period.

What impact, if any, will the decision to work part-time have on an attorney's ability to make partner or, if already a partner, to remain a partner at your firm?

None

Have any attorneys who chose to work a part-time schedule made partner at your firm?

Yes, one attorney. One associate worked as a part-time associate for several years and was ultimately promoted to partner. Several other associates who have worked part-time/flex-time schedules have been promoted to counsel.

Management Demographic Profile (as of 12/31/03)

	MINORITY MEN	MINORITY WOMEN	WHITE WOMEN	TOTAL
Number of attorneys on the Executive/Management Committee or equivalent	0	0	1	14
Number of attorneys on the Hiring Committee or equivalent	2	1	15	39
Number of attorneys on the Partner/Associate Review Committee or equivalent	1	2	4	20

Please provide information regarding all minority and women attorneys who head offices or practice groups of your law firm:

Women heading practice groups: Margot Schonholtz, Banking and Financial Restructuring; Blair Soyster, Employment Law

The Firm Says

As a global law firm, Clifford Chance is comprised of individuals representing a significant portion of the world's cultures, races, religions and nationalities. Recognition of, and respect for, diversity are at the core of the firm's identity. We believe that diversity is the foundation for producing an environment that maximizes each person's development into a productive and fulfilled professional and each person's ability to work harmoniously with colleagues. In the Americas, the goal of excelling as a diverse society also serves to guide the firm's efforts to recruit and retain the best lawyers from across the country to enrich the Clifford Chance culture and deepen its perspectives.

Commitment to diversity is also an important element of our business strategy. Just as Clifford Chance is diverse, so are its clients. They expect and demand that we be diverse so that we can serve them well and be attentive to the needs of their own customers. We believe that diversity produces a much-needed variety of experiences and perspectives, which creates a competition of ideas out of which the very best work product emerges.

Thus, our firm has included "commitment to diversity" as one of the seven key criteria by which our lawyers are evaluated. Every lawyer must be committed to supporting the firm's diversity efforts and fostering a supportive work environment in which all employees can develop to their fullest potential. More specifically, Clifford Chance believes that a lawyer's commitment to diversity should be shown in five areas:

Recruiting

Our lawyers should take reasonable steps to assist the firm in its effort to recruit and retain attorneys of all backgrounds, without regard to race, religion, color, national origin, age, gender, sexual orientation or disability.

Staffing

Our lawyers should be inclusive when making assignments and staffing projects, and should take reasonable steps to ensure that all attorneys have an opportunity to work on interesting, challenging and substantial assignments.

Mentoring

Our lawyers should take reasonable steps to ensure that all attorneys are given appropriate guidance, support, advice and counsel. Our lawyers should include among their mentoring responsibility efforts to communicate and reflect the firm's commitment to diversity.

Setting an example

Our lawyers should serve as role models to other attorneys by being inclusive in their personal and professional behavior and by fostering a supportive work environment for all employees.

Participation

Our lawyers should participate in the firm's efforts to foster diversity, including firm-sponsored diversity programs and workshops, and should make individual efforts to become aware of and increasingly sensitive to issues affecting individuals of diverse backgrounds.

Among other efforts we have made to address the challenges facing our firm with respect to the recruitment, retention and advancement of attorneys of diverse backgrounds, we have articulated the following Mission Statement for the firm's overall Diversity Initiative:

Clifford Chance is committed to enhancing diversity at the Firm and to fostering a supportive work environment in which all employees, regardless of racial or ethnic background, gender, or sexual orientation, can develop to their fullest potential and contribute their best work to the success of the Firm and its clients.

In 2001, we established a Diversity Committee, which comprises an ethnically diverse group of partners and associates representing our New York, Washington and California offices. A senior partner and member of management sits on the Diversity Committee as senior advisor.

All lawyers are required to participate in diversity awareness workshops, and such workshops have been part of the summer associate curriculum for the past four years. We host lecture series, including panels on steps to success, minority guest speakers from important firm clients, renowned authors and reporters on topics such as race and class in America, and leading human rights activists.

We actively participate in numerous minority job fairs and use search firms specializing in the recruitment of minority lawyers. Firm social events include an Annual Diversity Reception, among other activities.

The Diversity Committee sponsors a buddy program for all attorneys of color, as well as affinity groups for associates of color and gay and lesbian attorneys. An associate relations manager has responsibility for monitoring the specific needs of minority associates and assisting with the implementation of the Diversity Initiative. We encourage all of our lawyers, and specifically our attorneys of color, to get involved in minority bar associations, pro bono and community affairs work.

Clifford Chance demonstrates a strong commitment to women's issues through assisting its women lawyers in professional development and advancement, the development of part-time and flex-time policies and support for a working mothers' affinity group. The Diversity Committee develops these programs to improve the firm's success in the recruitment, retention and advancement of women. The Women's Initiative Group is developing networking opportunities for women both internally and externally. Over the past two years, the firm has, among other things, sponsored more than 80 women partners and associates to join the New York Women's Bar Association. Many are active in this organization on the officer, director and committee-chair levels. Clifford Chance women have designed and co-hosted three successful city-wide seminars, participated in city-wide mentoring groups and served on judicial screening committees to vet New York State judges. Clifford Chance women also lead committees on business law, legislation, international women's rights and pro bono service. A group of our women lawyers currently edits the Women's Bar Association's monthly newsletter. One of our attorneys recently received the 2004 Galaxy Award for "extraordinary" leadership from the New York Women's Agenda. The Women's Bar has also recognized the firm on many occasions for its leadership and service.

Cooley Godward LLP

3000 El Camino Real, 5 Palo Alto Square
Palo Alto, CA 94306
Phone: (650) 843-5000
Fax: (650) 857-0663

FIRM LEADERSHIP

Managing Partner: Stephen C. Neal, Chief
Executive Officer
Diversity Team Leader: James Donato, Partner

LOCATIONS

Palo Alto, CA (HQ)
Broomfield, CO
Reston, VA
San Diego, CA
San Francisco, CA

LAW FIRM DEMOGRAPHIC PROFILES

FULL-TIME ASSOCIATES	2003	2002
Minority men	40	39
Minority women	32	31
White women	89	113
Total	328	366

SUMMER ASSOCIATES	2003	2002
Minority men	5	3
Minority women	6	11
White women	17	15
Total	44	53

EQUITY PARTNERS	2003	2002
Minority men	2	3
Minority women	2	2
White women	25	29
Total	143	148

NEW HIRES	2003	2002
Minority men	8	6
Minority women	11	6
White women	19	15
Total	74	59

Strategic Plan and Diversity Leadership

How does the firm's leadership communicate the importance of diversity to everyone at the firm? (e.g., e-mails, web site, newsletters, meetings, etc.)

Vision & Values Statement; formation of Diversity Committee; minority recruiting initiatives; web site

Who has primary responsibility for leading diversity initiatives at your firm?

James Donato, partner

Does your law firm currently have a diversity committee?

Yes

Does the committee's representation include one or more members of the firm's management/executive committee (or the equivalent)?

No

How many attorneys are on the committee, and in 2003, what was the total number of hours collectively spent by the committee in furtherance of the firm's diversity initiatives?

Total attorneys on committee: 6

Total hours spent on diversity: Approximately 75

Does the committee and/or diversity leader establish and set goals or objectives consistent with management's priorities?

Yes

Has the firm undertaken a formal or informal diversity program or set of initiatives aimed at increasing the diversity of the firm?

Yes, formal

How often does the firm's management review the firm's diversity progress/results?

Twice a year

LAW FIRM DIVERSITY INITIATIVES	ALREADY COMPLETED	CURRENTLY ADDRESSING	NOT A CURRENT PRIORITY
Undertake communication from firm management that diversity is a top priority of the firm.	✓		
Formalize diversity plan and committee with action steps and accountability to management.		✓	
Conduct firm-wide diversity training for all attorneys and staff.		✓	
Increase the number of minority attorneys at the associate level.		✓	
Increase the number of minority attorneys at the partnership level.		✓	
Develop/expand relationships with minority bar associations to offer firm's support of these networks.		✓	
Focus on strengthening firm's mentoring program, including for benefit of minority attorneys.		✓	
Conduct internal diversity needs assessment and/or retain diversity consultant to examine how firm culture might be more welcoming of minorities.	✓		
Support law firm's internal affinity networks (e.g., women, minority attorney networks).		✓	
Manage/monitor allocation of work assignments and/or hours billed to ensure women and minority attorneys have equal access/inclusion on top client matters.	✓		

Recruitment – New Associates

Does your firm annually recruit at any of the following types of institutions? (Check all that apply and list the schools).

Ivy League schools: Cornell University, Columbia University, Harvard University, University of Pennsylvania, Yale University

Public state schools: University of Virginia, University of Texas, George Mason University, University of Michigan, University of California-Hastings, University of California-Boalt, UCLA, UC Davis, University of Colorado

Private schools: University of Chicago, Georgetown University, George Washington University, Northwestern University, Duke University, New York University, Richmond University, University of San Diego, University of Denver, Santa Clara University

Historically Black Colleges and Universities (HBCUs): Howard University

MINORITY CORPORATE COUNSEL ASSOCIATION

Do you have any special outreach efforts directed to encourage minority law students to consider your firm?

• Hold a reception for minority law students

• Participate in/host minority law student job fair(s)

• Sponsor minority law student association events

• Firm's lawyers participate on career panels at school

• Outreach to leadership of minority student organizations

SUMMER ASSOCIATE STATISTICS: SUMMER 2003	MINORITY MEN	MINORITY WOMEN	WHITE WOMEN	TOTAL
Summer associates	5	6	17	44
Summer associates who received an offer of full-time employment	5	6	17	43
Summer associates who accepted an offer of full-time employment	4	4	12	32

Recruitment – Lateral Associates and Partners

What activities does the firm undertake to attract minority and women attorneys?

• Participate at minority job fairs

• Seek referrals from other attorneys

Do you use executive recruiting/search firms to seek to identify new diversity hires (partners or associates)?

No

LATERAL ASSOCIATES AND PARTNERS: 1/1/03 – 12/31/03	MINORITY MEN	MINORITY WOMEN	WHITE WOMEN	TOTAL
Number of lateral associate hires	4	3	7	31
Number of lateral partner hires (equity and non-equity)	0	0	3	5
Number of new partners (equity and non-equity) promoted from associate rank	0	0	2	10
Number of new equity partners	0	0	5	15

Retention & Professional Development

ATTORNEYS WHO LEFT THE FIRM: 2003	MINORITY MEN	MINORITY WOMEN	WHITE WOMEN	TOTAL
Number of attorneys who voluntarily or involuntarily left your firm's employ in 2003	7	8	44	105

How do 2003 attrition rates generally compare to those experienced in the prior year period?

Lower than in prior years

Please identify the specific steps you are taking to reduce the attrition rate of minority and women attorneys.

• Develop and/or support internal employee affinity groups (e.g., minority or women networks within the firm)

• Increase/improve current work/life programs

• Work with minority and women attorneys to develop career advancement plans

• Introduce minority and women attorneys to key clients, including to lead engagements

• Review work assignments and hours billed to key client matters to make sure minority and women attorneys are not being excluded

• Strengthen mentoring program for all attorneys, including minorities and women

• Professional skills development program, including minority and women attorneys

Does your firm have part-time/flex-time policies that permit attorneys (male or female) to work alternative schedules?

Yes

What impact, if any, will the decision to work part-time have on an attorney's ability to make partner or, if already a partner, to remain a partner at your firm?

Determined on a case-by-case basis

Have any attorneys who chose to work a part-time schedule made partner at your firm?

Yes

Management Demographic Profile (as of 12/31/03)

	MINORITY MEN	MINORITY WOMEN	WHITE WOMEN	TOTAL
Number of attorneys on the Executive/Management Committee or equivalent	0	0	2	10
Number of attorneys on the Hiring Committee or equivalent	2	2	3	19
Number of attorneys on the Partner/Associate Review Committee or equivalent*	0	0	7	28

Multiple committees

Please provide information regarding all minority and women attorneys who head offices or practice groups of your law firm:

Women heading practice groups: Janet Cullum, Litigation; Barbara Kosacz, Life Sciences Transactions; Laura Berezin, Investment Banking; Nancy Wojtas, Public Securities; Kathleen Goodhart, Environmental; Ann Mooney, Insureds' Rights; Anne Peck, Trademark, Copyright & Advertising; Barbara Borden, Business Group, San Diego; Suzanne Hooper, Partner Nominating Committee; Susan Philpot, Business Opinion Committee; Susan Philpot, Audit Letter Committee; Kay Chandler, Hiring Committee; Maureen Alger, Pro Bono Counsel; Ann Mooney, Risk Management Committee; Jodie Bourdet, Business Associate Review Committee; Jodie Bourdet, Business Associate Compensation Committee; Andrea Bitar, Associate Committee; Amy Hartman, Litigation Associate Review Committee

The Firm Says

We want to ensure that everyone who works at Cooley Godward feels like they belong. To that end, we strive to recruit and retain a work force that not only welcomes but supports and promotes the interests of women, families and people of any ethnicity or sexual orientation.

The firm's Diversity Committee was created to help us reflect the diversity of our communities and to promote communication and understanding among all of those who comprise the firm. The Committee addresses issues faced by people of color and involving women attorneys and sexual orientation. The Diversity Committee has been a springboard for a number of programs and groups within the firm focused on diversity concerns. The firm has a group devoted to gay, lesbian and bisexual issues, and women associates hold monthly meetings in the Palo Alto Square office that have been expanded to other offices as well.

Cooley was one of the first law firms to commit to the Bar Association of San Francisco's 1988 goals and timetables for minority attorney hiring and advancement. In May 2002, Cooley joined other firms in the San Francisco Bay Area as a signatory to the San Francisco Bar Association's "No Glass Ceiling" commitments which are intended to promote women in leadership roles within the legal profession. That same year, firm management took further steps to demonstrate its commitment to diversity by creating a Diversity Task Force to identify specific steps the firm should take at all levels, including recruitment of entry-level attorneys, lateral hiring and retention of minority attorneys. Among the initiatives already implemented is outreach to law schools to ensure we recruit a diverse range of new attorneys. These and other initiatives within the firm underscore Cooley's commitment to an inclusive workplace.

In addition to its internal commitment, Cooley regularly sponsors events and organizations supporting diversity in the legal profession. Among other activities, Cooley has sponsored:

• The Tom Steel Fellowship Award, San Francisco, Calif.
• Annual AIDS Walk, San Francisco and San Diego, Calif.
• Asian American Bar Association
• Asian Law Alliance Santa Clara County
• Asian Pacific American Law Students Association of the Bay Area
• BASF Drucilla Ramey Fund for Diversity
• Chinese for Affirmative Action
• Harvard Black Law Students Association

- Japan Society
- La Raza Centro Legal
- La Raza Lawyers Association
- Stanford Black Law Students Association

Coudert Brothers LLP

1114 Avenue of the Americas
New York, NY 10036
Phone: (212) 626-4400
Fax: (212) 626-4120

FIRM LEADERSHIP

Chair, Diversity Committee: Stephen M. Hudspeth

LOCATIONS

New York, NY (HQ)
Los Angeles, CA
Palo Alto, CA
San Francisco, CA
Washington, DC
Almaty
Antwerp
Bangkok
Beijing
Berlin
Brussels
Frankfurt
Ghent
Hong Kong
Jakarta
London
Moscow
Paris
Stockholm
Shanghai
Singapore
St. Petersburg
Sydney
Tokyo

LAW FIRM DEMOGRAPHIC PROFILES

FULL-TIME ASSOCIATES	2003	2002
Minority men	8	6
Minority women	23	19
White women	42	42
Total	131	130

SUMMER ASSOCIATES	2003	2002
Minority men	0	1
Minority women	7	8
White women	8	10
Total	26	25

EQUITY PARTNERS	2003	2002
Minority men	1	1
Minority women	2	2
White women	11	11
Total	66	75

NON-EQUITY PARTNERS	2003	2002
Minority men	2	1
Minority women	2	2
White women	0	0
Total	15	20

NEW HIRES	2003	2002
Minority men	3	3
Minority women	9	2
White women	7	8
Total	31	17

MCCA
MINORITY CORPORATE COUNSEL ASSOCIATION

Strategic Plan and Diversity Leadership

How does the firm's leadership communicate the importance of diversity to everyone at the firm? (e.g., e-mails, web site, newsletters, meetings, etc.)

E-mails and meetings

Who has primary responsibility for leading diversity initiatives at your firm?

Stephen M. Hudspeth, partner and Diversity Committee chair

Does your law firm currently have a diversity committee?

Yes

Does the committee's representation include one or more members of the firm's management/executive committee (or the equivalent)?

Yes

How many attorneys are on the committee, and in 2003, what was the total number of hours collectively spent by the committee in furtherance of the firm's diversity initiatives?

Total attorneys on committee: 16

Total hours spent on diversity: 0 (Committee was formed in 2004.)

Does the committee and/or diversity leader establish and set goals or objectives consistent with management's priorities?

Yes

Has the firm undertaken a formal or informal diversity program or set of initiatives aimed at increasing the diversity of the firm?

Yes, formal

How often does the firm's management review the firm's diversity progress/results?

Annually

How is the firm's diversity committee and/or firm management held accountable for achieving results?

Our hope and expectation is that our diversity statistics will improve and we will be judged, as will our general managers, principally on those statistics.

LAW FIRM DIVERSITY INITIATIVES	ALREADY COMPLETED	CURRENTLY ADDRESSING	NOT A CURRENT PRIORITY
Undertake communication from firm management that diversity is a top priority of the firm.		✓	
Formalize diversity plan and committee with action steps and accountability to management.		✓	
Conduct firm-wide diversity training for all attorneys and staff.		✓	
Increase the number of minority attorneys at the associate level.		✓	
Increase the number of minority attorneys at the partnership level.		✓	
Develop/expand relationships with minority bar associations to offer firm's support of these networks.		✓	
Focus on strengthening firm's mentoring program, including for benefit of minority attorneys.		✓	
Conduct internal diversity needs assessment and/or retain diversity consultant to examine how firm culture might be more welcoming of minorities.		✓	
Support law firm's internal affinity networks (e.g., women, minority attorney networks).		✓	
Manage/monitor allocation of work assignments and/or hours billed to ensure women and minority attorneys have equal access/inclusion on top client matters.		✓	

Recruitment - New Associates

Does your firm annually recruit at any of the following types of institutions? (Check all that apply and list the schools).

Ivy League schools: Columbia University, Cornell University, Harvard University, University of Pennsylvania

Public state schools: University of Virginia

Private schools: Boston College, Boston University, Brooklyn Law School, Duke University, Emory University, Fordham University, Georgetown University, NYU, Northwestern University, Pace University, Vanderbilt University

Historically Black Colleges and Universities (HBCUs): Howard University

Do you have any special outreach efforts directed to encourage minority law students to consider your firm?

• Advertise in minority law student association publication(s)

• Participate in/host minority law student job fair(s)

• Sponsor minority law student association events

• Firm's lawyers participate on career panels at school

SUMMER ASSOCIATE STATISTICS: SUMMER 2003	MINORITY MEN	MINORITY WOMEN	WHITE WOMEN	TOTAL
Summer associates	0	7	8	26
Summer associates who received an offer of full-time employment	0	4	5	15
Summer associates who accepted an offer of full-time employment	0	4	5	14

Recruitment – Lateral Associates and Partners

What activities does the firm undertake to attract minority and women attorneys?
- Partner programs with women and minority bar associations
- Participate at minority job fairs

Do you use executive recruiting/search firms to seek to identify new diversity hires (partners or associates)?
No

LATERAL ASSOCIATES AND PARTNERS: 1/1/03 – 12/31/03	MINORITY MEN	MINORITY WOMEN	WHITE WOMEN	TOTAL
Number of lateral associate hires	2	3	1	11
Number of lateral partner hires (equity and non-equity)	1	0	0	3
Number of new partners (equity and non-equity) promoted from associate rank	0	0	0	0
Number of new equity partners	0	0	0	3

Retention & Professional Development

ATTORNEYS WHO LEFT THE FIRM: 2003	MINORITY MEN	MINORITY WOMEN	WHITE WOMEN	TOTAL
Number of attorneys who voluntarily or involuntarily left your firm's employ in 2003	1	5	8	25

How do 2003 attrition rates generally compare to those experienced in the prior year period?
Lower than in prior years

Excellence in Our Practice Knows No Boundaries

COVINGTON & BURLING

WASHINGTON
NEW YORK
SAN FRANCISCO
LONDON
BRUSSELS

COV.COM

Covington & Burling

1201 Pennsylvania Avenue, NW
Washington, DC 20004
Phone: (202) 662-6000
Fax: (202) 662-6291

FIRM LEADERSHIP

Managing Partner: Stuart C. Stock, Chairman
of the Management Committee
Diversity Team Leader: Thomas S. Williamson
Jr., and Linda C. Goldstein, Co-Chairs,
Diversity Committee

LOCATIONS

Washington, DC (HQ)
New York, NY
San Francisco, CA
Brussels
London

LAW FIRM DEMOGRAPHIC PROFILES

FULL-TIME ASSOCIATES	2003	2002
Minority men	23	21
Minority women	16	18
White women	70	72
Total	247	250

SUMMER ASSOCIATES	2003	2002
Minority men	5	10
Minority women	7	5
White women	22	16
Total	61	61

EQUITY PARTNERS	2003	2002
Minority men	5	5
Minority women	3	3
White women	23	21
Total	153	148

NEW HIRES	2003	2002
Minority men	6	4
Minority women	5	9
White women	21	20
Total	63	69

SENIOR COUNSEL, OF COUNSEL & SPECIAL COUNSEL	2003	2002
Minority men	1	1
Minority women	1	1
White women	17	11
Total	68	61

Strategic Plan and Diversity Leadership

How does the firm's leadership communicate the importance of diversity to everyone at the firm? (e.g., e-mails, web site, newsletters, meetings, etc.)

The firm's leadership views communicating the importance of diversity as an ongoing, multifaceted process. The firm's recruiting resume includes a section entitled "Diversity" and refers to diversity as a "core value" of the firm:

We welcome diversity and steadfastly believe that excellence in the practice of law knows no racial, ethnic, gender, religious, sexual orientation or other boundaries.

This message is delivered annually during the course of orientation presentations for new associates. Earlier this year at the firm's retreat for partners and of counsel the program included a formal report and discussion on the firm's diversity goals and challenges. It was the consensus of the firm's senior lawyers that improving the level of diversity of our attorneys is one of the firm's current top priorities. The Management Committee has also established a standing Diversity Committee which, among other duties, is responsible for communicating the importance of diversity as a firm priority and fostering dialogue within the firm regarding diversity issues.

Who has primary responsibility for leading diversity initiatives at your firm?

Thomas S. Williamson Jr. and Linda C. Goldstein, partners and co-chairs, Diversity Committee

Does your law firm currently have a diversity committee?

Yes

Does the committee's representation include one or more members of the firm's management/executive committee (or the equivalent)?

No, but there is a member of the Management Committee who is the designated liaison for the Diversity Committee.

How many attorneys are on the committee, and in 2003, what was the total number of hours collectively spent by the committee in furtherance of the firm's diversity initiatives?

Total attorneys on committee: 23

Does the committee and/or diversity leader establish and set goals or objectives consistent with management's priorities?

Yes

Has the firm undertaken a formal or informal diversity program or set of initiatives aimed at increasing the diversity of the firm?

Yes, informal

How often does the firm's management review the firm's diversity progress/results?

Annually, the issue is frequently discussed throughout year, with one formal evaluation annually.

How is the firm's diversity committee and/or firm management held accountable for achieving results?

The principal accountability mechanism is the reporting relationship to the Management Committee. In addition, there is regular communication regarding diversity between the leadership of the Diversity Committee, the leadership of the Hiring Committee for regular associates, as well as the subcommittee for recruiting and hiring summer associates and the Management Committee. There is a woman partner on the Management Committee and another woman partner who is co-chair of the Diversity Committee. Also, the firm has seven African American partners, all of whom play active roles in monitoring and facilitating the firm's performance in promoting diversity.

LAW FIRM DIVERSITY INITIATIVES	ALREADY COMPLETED	CURRENTLY ADDRESSING	NOT A CURRENT PRIORITY
Undertake communication from firm management that diversity is a top priority of the firm.	✓	✓	
Formalize diversity plan and committee with action steps and accountability to management.		✓	
Conduct firm-wide diversity training for all attorneys and staff.			✓
Increase the number of minority attorneys at the associate level.		✓	
Increase the number of minority attorneys at the partnership level.		✓	
Develop/expand relationships with minority bar associations to offer firm's support of these networks.		✓	
Focus on strengthening firm's mentoring program, including for benefit of minority attorneys.		✓	
Conduct internal diversity needs assessment and/or retain diversity consultant to examine how firm culture might be more welcoming of minorities.		✓	
Support law firm's internal affinity networks (e.g., women, minority attorney networks).		✓	
Manage/monitor allocation of work assignments and/or hours billed to ensure women and minority attorneys have equal access/inclusion on top client matters.		✓	
Summer associate reception sponsored by the firm's Diversity Committee; panel participants in "road show" presentations to assist minority students in how to interview with large law firms.	✓	✓	

Recruitment – New Associates

Does your firm annually recruit at any of the following types of institutions? (Check all that apply and list the schools).

Ivy League schools: Harvard University, Yale University, Columbia University, Cornell University, University of Pennsylvania

Public state schools: UC Berkeley, George Mason University, University of Maryland, University of Michigan, University of North Carolina, University of Texas, University of Virginia, College of William & Mary

Private schools: Boston College, Boston University, Brigham Young University, University of Chicago, Duke University, George Washington University, Georgetown University, NYU, Northwestern University, Stanford University, Vanderbilt University, Washington & Lee University

Historically Black Colleges and Universities (HBCUs): Howard University

Do you have any special outreach efforts directed to encourage minority law students to consider your firm?

• *Lead or participate on panels to give minority students guidance on how to interview with large law firms.*

• Participate in/host minority law student job fair(s)

• Sponsor minority law student association events

• Firm's lawyers participate on career panels at school

SUMMER ASSOCIATE STATISTICS: SUMMER 2003	MINORITY MEN	MINORITY WOMEN	WHITE WOMEN	TOTAL
Summer associates	5	7	22	61
Summer associates who received an offer of full-time employment	5	7	20	57
Summer associates who accepted an offer of full-time employment*	0	2	10	23

* *To date*

Recruitment – Lateral Associates and Partners

What activities does the firm undertake to attract minority and women attorneys?

• Participate at minority job fairs

• Seek referrals from other attorneys

Do you use executive recruiting/search firms to seek to identify new diversity hires (partners or associates)?

Yes

If yes, list all women- and/or minority-owned executive search/recruiting firms to which the firm paid a fee for placement services in the past 12 months:

None.

LATERAL ASSOCIATES AND PARTNERS:* 1/1/03 – 12/31/03	MINORITY MEN	MINORITY WOMEN	WHITE WOMEN	TOTAL
Number of lateral associate hires	0	1	3	7
Number of lateral partner hires (equity and non-equity)	0	0	2	4
Number of new partners (equity and non-equity) promoted from associate rank	0	0	1	2
Number of new equity partners	0	0	3	8

U.S .offices only

Retention & Professional Development

ATTORNEYS WHO LEFT THE FIRM: 2003	MINORITY MEN	MINORITY WOMEN	WHITE WOMEN	TOTAL
Number of attorneys who voluntarily or involuntarily left your firm's employ in 2003	4	7	17	55

How do 2003 attrition rates generally compare to those experienced in the prior year period?

About the same as in prior years

Please identify the specific steps you are taking to reduce the attrition rate of minority and women attorneys.

• *Reviewing benefit programs*

• Develop and/or support internal employee affinity groups (e.g., minority or women networks within the firm)

• Increase/review compensation relative to competition

• Increase/improve current work/life programs

• Introduce minority and women attorneys to key clients, including to lead engagements

• Review work assignments and hours billed to key client matters to make sure minority and women attorneys are not being excluded (selected clients)

• Strengthen mentoring program for all attorneys, including minorities and women

• Professional skills development program, including minority and women attorneys

Does your firm have part-time/flex-time policies that permit attorneys (male or female) to work alternative schedules?

Yes. As a general matter, requests to work part-time are normally accommodated.

What impact, if any, will the decision to work part-time have on an attorney's ability to make partner or, if already a partner, to remain a partner at your firm?

Attorneys who work part-time remain eligible for consideration for partnership. If the cumulative effect of the attorney's individual, part-time arrangement is to omit more than the equivalent of a full year during the associate years, consideration for partnership will ordinarily be deferred accordingly. We currently have eight partners working on a part-time basis in the U.S., two of whom are women.

Have any attorneys who chose to work a part-time schedule made partner at your firm?

Yes, four attorneys. Eight partners currently work part-time.

Management Demographic Profile (as of 12/31/03)

	MINORITY MEN	MINORITY WOMEN	WHITE WOMEN	TOTAL
Number of attorneys on the Executive/Management Committee or equivalent	0	0	1	7
Number of attorneys on the Hiring Committee or equivalent	0	1	1	8
Number of attorneys on the Partner/Associate Review Committee or equivalent	0	2	3	18

Please provide information regarding all minority and women attorneys who head offices or practice groups of your law firm:

Minorities heading practice groups: Phyllis Thompson, States; Tom Williamson, Employment; Jennifer Johnson, Communications & Media

Women heading practice groups: Ellen Corenswet, Private Equity; Amy Moore, Employee Benefits; Doris Blazek-White, Trusts and Estates; Carolyn Corwin, Industries Regulatory Legislative; Ellen Flannerym Food and Drug; Phyllis Thompson, States; Linda Morgan, Transportation; Sonya Winner, Litigation and Intellectual Property; Erin Egan and Jetty Tielemans, Privacy and Data Security; Laurie Self, Trademark & Copyright

The Firm Says

Covington's success has been founded on the firm's ability to attract and retain exceptionally talented and resourceful lawyers. We understand that sustaining this success depends critically on recruiting and developing a diverse community of lawyers. Accordingly, we recognize the differences among us as a genuine asset and source of strength. We welcome diversity and steadfastly believe that excellence in the practice of law knows no racial, ethnic, gender, religious, sexual orientation or other boundaries.

The firm prides itself on several decades of inclusiveness in the partnership and the associate ranks. There have been women partners at Covington since 1974, and we now have a total of 27 women partners in the United States (with more in our international offices), including one who serves on the Management Committee, the firm's senior governing body. The great majority of our women partners have families, and those partners have combined a successful legal career with their family responsibilities. The firm is continually striving to ensure that we improve ourselves as a family-friendly environment.

The firm made its first African-American partner in 1975, and today there are seven African American partners – four men and three women. These individuals are leading practitioners in a variety of different fields that range from white-collar crime to corporate, to communications, to employment law, to bankruptcy, to health law. Our African-American partners are also well integrated into the leadership of the firm's practice groups and key functional committees such as the firm's hiring committee and the evaluation committee that recommends candidates for partnership.

An African-American male partner and a woman partner currently co-chair the firm's Diversity Committee. Both partners and associates are members of the Diversity Committee, and there is a Management Committee liaison partner. The mandate of the Diversity Committee is to promote and enhance diversity at the firm. In furtherance of this mandate the Diversity Committee has chosen to focus its attention primarily on three aspects of the operation of the firm: (1) recruitment and hiring, (2) career development and opportunities for associates, and (3) the process for evaluating and selecting associates to become partners. Although the firm subscribes to the view that diversity within our ranks extends well beyond gender and race, the primary constituency groups addressed by the Diversity Committee are women, African-Americans, Hispanics, Asians, and gay and lesbian lawyers.

The Diversity Committee's current focus on career development is designed to address the key issue of retention of minority and women lawyers. In part, we are addressing the issue of retention by actively encouraging use of the firm's successful and longstanding policy permitting part-time work.

We believe that the measure of opportunity and support at Covington & Burling is demonstrated by the advancement of associates of all backgrounds and the growth of diversity within our own partnership. Thus, since electing our first African-American and women partners more than a generation ago, the overwhelming majority of our women and minority partners have come from within our own ranks. Today, for example, all but one of our African-American partners started their legal careers at Covington & Burling. Likewise the two openly gay lawyers who have become partners began their legal work as associates. The same is true for almost all of our U.S.-based women partners.

We work continuously to enhance our recruitment of a diverse group of individuals. For example, we attend minority job fairs and conferences, participate in minority recruitment programs and interview at law schools with substantial minority enrollment. We work with law school faculty, firm alumni and minority law student organizations to identify talented individuals of all backgrounds, and we also make many other efforts to hire a diverse group of law students and lawyers. In Washington, New York and San Francisco our firm has joined with other major firms in making public commitments to increase diversity within our ranks.

We also find that many of our clients share our commitment to diversity. Increasingly, women and minorities are achieving senior positions as in-house counsel, and they expect their outside law firms to be similarly diverse at all levels of the career ladder. We welcome this challenge and fully endorse the idea that we can provide the best service by drawing from the broadest talent pool and ensuring that equal opportunity is a day-to-day reality in every aspect of our firm.

Cozen O'Connor

1900 Market Street
Philadelphia, PA 19103
Phone: (215) 665-2000
Fax: (215) 665-2013

FIRM LEADERSHIP

Managing Partner: Thomas A.
Decker,Managing Partner
Diversity Team Leader: Sarah E. Davies,
Member of the Firm

LOCATIONS

Philadelphia, PA (HQ)
Atlanta, GA
Charlotte, NC
Cherry Hill, NJ
Chicago, IL
Dallas, TX
Denver, CO
Houston, TX
Las Vegas, NV
Los Angeles, CA
Newark, NJ
New York, NY
San Diego, CA
San Francisco, CA
Seattle, WA
Trenton, NJ
Washington, DC
West Conshohocken, PA
Wichita, KS
Wilmington, DE
London

LAW FIRM DEMOGRAPHIC PROFILES

FULL-TIME ASSOCIATES	2003	2002
Minority men	10	5
Minority women	6	9
White women	109	95
Total	291	257

SUMMER ASSOCIATES	2003	2002
Minority men	2	2
Minority women	4	2
White women	11	14
Total	27	29

EQUITY PARTNERS	2003	2002
Minority men	2	0
Minority women	0	0
White women	11	11
Total	122	115

NON-EQUITY PARTNERS	2003	2002
Minority men	3	5
Minority women	0	0
White women	10	14
Total	75	79

NEW HIRES	2003	2002
Minority men	5	2
Minority women	0	1
White women	22	20
Total	65	64

Strategic Plan and Diversity Leadership

How does the firm's leadership communicate the importance of diversity to everyone at the firm? (e.g., e-mails, web site, newsletters, meetings, etc.)

The firm's Diversity Statement is included on the firm's web site, which is widely viewed by firm clients, prospects, lateral recruits, and law students and staff.

Who has primary responsibility for leading diversity initiatives at your firm?

Sarah E. Davies, member of the firm

Does your law firm currently have a diversity committee?

Yes

Does the committee's representation include one or more members of the firm's management/executive committee (or the equivalent)?

No

How many attorneys are on the committee, and in 2003, what was the total number of hours collectively spent by the committee in furtherance of the firm's diversity initiatives?

Total attorneys on committee: 22

Does the committee and/or diversity leader establish and set goals or objectives consistent with management's priorities?

Yes

Has the firm undertaken a formal or informal diversity program or set of initiatives aimed at increasing the diversity of the firm?

Yes, informal

How often does the firm's management review the firm's diversity progress/results?

Other: No set frequency

How is the firm's diversity committee and/or firm management held accountable for achieving results?

Currently under discussion

LAW FIRM DIVERSITY INITIATIVES	ALREADY COMPLETED	CURRENTLY ADDRESSING	NOT A CURRENT PRIORITY
Undertake communication from firm management that diversity is a top priority of the firm.	✓		
Formalize diversity plan and committee with action steps and accountability to management.		✓	
Conduct firm-wide diversity training for all attorneys and staff.			✓
Increase the number of minority attorneys at the associate level.		✓	
Increase the number of minority attorneys at the partnership level.		✓	
Develop/expand relationships with minority bar associations to offer firm's support of these networks.		✓	
Focus on strengthening firm's mentoring program, including for benefit of minority attorneys.		✓	
Conduct internal diversity needs assessment and/or retain diversity consultant to examine how firm culture might be more welcoming of minorities.			✓
Support law firm's internal affinity networks (e.g., women, minority attorney networks).		✓	
Manage/monitor allocation of work assignments and/or hours billed to ensure women and minority attorneys have equal access/inclusion on top client matters.			✓

Recruitment – New Associates

Does your firm annually recruit at any of the following types of institutions? (Check all that apply and list the schools).

Ivy League schools: University of Pennsylvania

Public state schools: Temple University, Rutgers University, University of Pittsburgh, Dickinson School of Law (Penn State), University of Washington, University of California-Los Angeles, University of Texas, University of Virginia

Private schools: George Washington University, Villanova University, Northwestern University, American University, Catholic University of America, Seattle University, University of San Diego, South Texas College, Georgetown University, Syracuse University

Historically Black Colleges and Universities (HBCUs): Howard University

Other predominantly minority and/or women's colleges: We participate in minority job fairs.

367

Do you have any special outreach efforts directed to encourage minority law students to consider your firm?

• Hold a reception for minority law students
• Advertise in minority law student association publication(s)
• Participate in/host minority law student job fair(s)
• Sponsor minority law student association events
• Firm's lawyers participate on career panels at school
• Outreach to leadership of minority student organizations

SUMMER ASSOCIATE STATISTICS: SUMMER 2003	MINORITY MEN	MINORITY WOMEN	WHITE WOMEN	TOTAL
Summer associates	1	3	8	22
Summer associates who received an offer of full-time employment	1	2	7	18
Summer associates who accepted an offer of full-time employment	1	2	6	17

Lateral Associates and Partners

What activities does the firm undertake to attract minority and women attorneys?

• Partner programs with women and minority bar associations
• Participate at minority job fairs
• Seek referrals from other attorneys

Do you use executive recruiting/search firms to seek to identify new diversity hires (partners or associates)?

Yes

If yes, list all women- and/or minority-owned executive search/recruiting firms to which the firm paid a fee for placement services in the past 12 months:

Cathy Abelson Legal Search, Hayden Legal Search, Inc.

LATERAL ASSOCIATES AND PARTNERS: 1/1/03 – 12/31/03	MINORITY MEN	MINORITY WOMEN	WHITE WOMEN	TOTAL
Number of lateral associate hires	3	0	19	44
Number of lateral partner hires (equity and non-equity)	1	0	3	15
Number of new partners (equity and non-equity) promoted from associate rank	0	0	15	49
Number of new equity partners	0	0	2	8

Retention & Professional Development

ATTORNEYS WHO LEFT THE FIRM: 2003	MINORITY MEN	MINORITY WOMEN	WHITE WOMEN	TOTAL
Number of attorneys who voluntarily or involuntarily left your firm's employ in 2003	0	3	15	40

How do 2003 attrition rates generally compare to those experienced in the prior year period?

About the same as in prior years

Please identify the specific steps you are taking to reduce the attrition rate of minority and women attorneys.

• *Representation of minority and female interests on firm senior management*

• Develop and/or support internal employee affinity groups (e.g., minority or women networks within the firm)

• Increase/review compensation relative to competition

• Increase/improve current work/life programs

• Succession plan includes emphasis on diversity

• Work with minority and women attorneys to develop career advancement plans

• Introduce minority and women attorneys to key clients, including to lead engagements

• Review work assignments and hours billed to key client matters to make sure minority and women attorneys are not being excluded

• Strengthen mentoring program for all attorneys, including minorities and women

• Professional skills development program, including minority and women attorneys

Does your firm have part-time/flex-time policies that permit attorneys (male or female) to work alternative schedules?

Yes

What impact, if any, will the decision to work part-time have on an attorney's ability to make partner or, if already a partner, to remain a partner at your firm?

The firm will consider the amount, duration and quality of work experience of the part-time employee in the same way it considers the amount, duration and quality of work experience of a full-time employee in making promotion decisions. Part-time employment in itself will not preclude employment advancement or eligibility for promotion.

Have any attorneys who chose to work a part-time schedule made partner at your firm?

Yes, seven attorneys.

Management Demographic Profile (as of 12/31/03)

	MINORITY MEN	MINORITY WOMEN	WHITE WOMEN	TOTAL
Number of attorneys on the Executive/Management Committee or equivalent	0	0	1	11
Number of attorneys on the Hiring Committee or equivalent	3	2	14	52
Number of attorneys on the Partner/Associate Review Committee or equivalent	0	0	1	6

Please provide information regarding all minority and women attorneys who head offices or practice groups of your law firm:

Women heading offices: Joann Selleck (San Diego, San Francisco, Los Angeles, Las Vegas) Women heading practice groups: Ann T. Field, Chair National Insurance Litigation Department; Camille Miller, Co-Chair IP Practice Group; Francine L. Semaya, Chair Insurance Corp. and Regulatory Practice Group; Margaret Gallagher Thompson, Estates and Trust Practice Group

The Firm Says

Cozen O'Connor takes its responsibility to foster diversity in the bar seriously. Recognizing the organizational effectiveness that can come from valuing differences, Cozen O'Connor prides itself on its commitment to diversity and its tradition of employing people with diverse backgrounds and experiences. The firm values the breadth of perspectives and the richness of experience made possible by having a diverse complement of lawyers and staff.

In order to promote the goal of a diverse workplace and a diverse bar, the firm has established a Diversity Committee that works closely with the Hiring Committee to increase diversity in the firm and in the bar in general. Cozen O'Connor's commitment to diversity is also demonstrated through the efforts of its attorneys who participate in charitable and community activities whose goals are diversity in our community.

Cozen O'Connor is a leader among law firms committed to the recruitment and retention of lawyers with a wide range of backgrounds and experiences. As a founding member of the Philadelphia Diversity Law Group, the firm partners with other major law firms and corporations to develop programs designed to enhance the recruitment and retention of diverse lawyers. Cozen O'Connor lawyers actively participate in the interview and selection process, and has hired successful candidates from the program as summer associates.

Cozen O'Connor is a signatory to the Philadelphia Bar Association's Statement of Goals of Philadelphia Law Firms to Increase the Advancement of Women in the Profession. Women at Cozen O'Connor serve on the firm's Executive Committee, Management Committee, Hiring Committee, Diversity Committee and various other committees. Women also serve as chairs of practice departments in the firm. Cozen O'Connor is in the forefront of the legal community in providing flexible work arrangements for its attorneys and regularly promotes such attorneys. Both male and female attorneys may work a flexible or reduced schedule, thereby providing them with an opportunity to achieve balance in their personal and professional lives.

The firm recruits at a wide variety of law schools with diverse student populations and participates in minority job fairs throughout the country in an effort to attract and hire lawyers with diverse backgrounds. Cozen

O'Connor is an equal opportunity employer and does not discriminate based upon race, color, gender, national origin or ancestry, religion, age, disability, citizenship, marital status, military or veteran status, sexual preference or orientation, cultural behavior, or any other prohibited bases. The firm's nondiscrimination policy applies to all aspects of the employment relationship including hiring and advancement. As part of Cozen O'Connor's commitment to the hiring and advancement of diverse attorneys in the profession, the firm is a signatory to the Philadelphia Bar Association's Statement of Goals of Philadelphia Law Firms to Increase Minority Hiring.

CRAVATH, SWAINE & MOORE LLP

Consistent with our long-held view that excellence

is found in many places, diversity is a bedrock principle at

Cravath. We embrace the importance of recruiting and

retaining outstanding lawyers from different backgrounds

and we are committed to promoting diversity at all levels.

We support Vault and MCCA in their efforts to

produce the Guide to Law Firm Diversity Programs.

NEW YORK · LONDON

Cravath, Swaine & Moore LLP

Worldwide Plaza, 825 Eighth Avenue
New York, NY 10019
Phone: (212) 474-1000
Fax: (212) 474-3700

FIRM LEADERSHIP

Managing Partner: Robert D. Joffe, Presiding
Partner
Diversity Team Leader: Robert D. Joffe,
Presiding Partner

LOCATIONS

New York, NY (HQ)
London

LAW FIRM DEMOGRAPHIC PROFILES

FULL-TIME ASSOCIATES	2003	2002
Minority men*	49	54
Minority women*	43	50
White women	93	104
Total	379	415

SUMMER ASSOCIATES	2003	2002
Minority men*	10	5
Minority women*	15	7
White women	24	13
Total	85	68

EQUITY PARTNERS	2003	2002
Minority men*	1	1
Minority women*	0	0
White women	9	9
Total	78	74

NEW HIRES	2003	2002
Minority men*	8	16
Minority women*	8	15
White women	13	24
Total	69	95

* Used same guidelines as NALP Survey

Strategic Plan and Diversity Leadership

How does the firm's leadership communicate the importance of diversity to everyone at the firm? (e.g., e-mails, web site, newsletters, meetings, etc.)

Informal meetings with associates and summer associates, memoranda, invitations to diversity-related events.

Who has primary responsibility for leading diversity initiatives at your firm? Name of person and his/her title:

Robert D. Joffe, Presiding Partner

Does your law firm currently have a diversity committee?

Yes

Does the committee's representation include one or more members of the firm's management/executive committee (or the equivalent)?

Yes

How many attorneys are on the committee, and in 2003, what was the total number of hours collectively spent by the committee in furtherance of the firm's diversity initiatives?

Total attorneys on committee: 13

Total hours spent on diversity: Not tracked.

Does the committee and/or diversity leader establish and set goals or objectives consistent with management's priorities?

Yes

Has the firm undertaken a formal or informal diversity program or set of initiatives aimed at increasing the diversity of the firm?

Yes, informal

How often does the firm's management review the firm's diversity progress/results?

Continuously

How is the firm's diversity committee and/or firm management held accountable for achieving results?

The diversity committee includes the presiding partner and the managing and hiring partners for the litigation and corporate groups, so that all partners with administrative responsibilities affecting diversity are on the diversity committee.

LAW FIRM DIVERSITY INITIATIVES	ALREADY COMPLETED	CURRENTLY ADDRESSING	NOT A CURRENT PRIORITY
Undertake communication from firm management that diversity is a top priority of the firm.	✓		
Formalize diversity plan and committee with action steps and accountability to management.		✓	
Conduct firm-wide diversity training for all attorneys and staff.	✓		
Increase the number of minority attorneys at the associate level.		✓	
Increase the number of minority attorneys at the partnership level.		✓	
Develop/expand relationships with minority bar associations to offer firm's support of these networks.		✓	
Focus on strengthening firm's mentoring program, including for benefit of minority attorneys.		✓	
Conduct internal diversity needs assessment and/or retain diversity consultant to examine how firm culture might be more welcoming of minorities.		✓	
Support law firm's internal affinity networks (e.g., women, minority attorney networks).		✓	
Manage/monitor allocation of work assignments and/or hours billed to ensure women and minority attorneys have equal access/inclusion on top client matters.		✓	

Recruitment – New Associates

Does your firm annually recruit at any institutions?

Boalt Hall; Cardozo; Chicago; Columbia; Duke; Fordham; Georgetown; Harvard; Howard; McGill University; Michigan; NYU; North Carolina; Northwestern; Pennsylvania; Rutgers – Newark; Stanford; Texas; Virginia; Yale; Boston College/Boston University Job Fair; Cornell Job Fair; William & Mary/Washington & Lee Job Fair; California/Midwestern Job Fair

Time constraints prevent us from visiting as many schools as we would like. Therefore, we strongly encourage mail-in applications from qualified candidates whose schools we do not visit or who missed us when we interviewed on campus.

Do you have any special outreach efforts directed to encourage minority law students to consider your firm?

• *SEO Program, 1L hiring*

• Hold receptions for minority law students

• Advertise in minority law student association publication(s)

• Participate in/host minority law student job fair(s)

• Sponsor minority law student association events

• Firm's lawyers participate on career panels at school

• Outreach to leadership of minority student organizations

SUMMER ASSOCIATE STATISTICS: SUMMER 2003	MINORITY MEN*	MINORITY WOMEN*	WHITE WOMEN	TOTAL
Summer associates	10	15	24	85
Summer associates who received an offer of full-time employment	10	15	24	84
Summer associates who accepted an offer of full-time employment**	8	8	19	52

Used same guidelines as NALP Survey

*** Response excludes 2003 summer associates who are pursuing clerkships or joint degrees during the 2004-2005 year.*

Recruitment – Lateral Associates and Partners

What activities does the firm undertake to attract minority and women attorneys?

Not applicable. The firm does not hire lateral partners or associates.

Do you use executive recruiting/search firms to seek to identify new diversity hires (partners or associates)?

Not applicable. The firm does not hire lateral partners or associates.

LATERAL ASSOCIATES AND PARTNERS: 1/1/03 – 12/31/03	MINORITY MEN	MINORITY WOMEN	WHITE WOMEN	TOTAL
Number of lateral associate hires	N/A	N/A	N/A	N/A
Number of lateral partner hires (equity and non-equity)	N/A	N/A	N/A	N/A
Number of new partners (equity and non-equity) promoted from associate rank	N/A	N/A	N/A	N/A
Number of new equity partners*	0	0	0	6

Parnters effective 1/1/03

Retention & Professional Development

ATTORNEYS WHO LEFT THE FIRM: 2003	MINORITY MEN	MINORITY WOMEN	WHITE WOMEN	TOTAL
Number of attorneys who voluntarily or involuntarily left your firm's employ in 2003	13	14	23	95

How do 2003 attrition rates generally compare to those experienced in the prior year period?

Higher than in prior year

Please identify the specific steps you are taking to reduce the attrition rate of minority and women attorneys.

• Develop and/or support internal employee affinity groups (e.g., minority or women networks within the firm)

• Increase/improve current work/life programs

• Introduce minority and women attorneys to key clients, including to lead engagements

• Review work assignments and hours billed to key client matters to make sure minority and women attorneys are being given equal opportunities

• Strengthen mentoring program for all attorneys, including minorities and women

• Professional skills development program, including minority and women attorneys

Does your firm have part-time/flex-time policies that permit attorneys (male or female) to work alternative schedules?

Yes. See narrative section.

What impact, if any, will the decision to work part-time have on an attorney's ability to make partner or, if already a partner, to remain a partner at your firm?

None

Have any attorneys who chose to work a part-time schedule made partner at your firm?

No

Management Demographic Profile (as of 12/31/03)

	MINORITY MEN*	MINORITY WOMEN*	WHITE WOMEN	TOTAL
Number of attorneys on the Executive/Management Committee or equivalent	0	0	0	3
Number of attorneys on the Hiring Committee or equivalent	0	0	1	2
Number of attorneys on the Partner/Associate Review Committee or equivalent	0	0	0	2

* Used same guidelines as NALP Survey

Please provide information regarding all minority and women attorneys who head offices or practice groups of your law firm:

Minorities heading offices: Not applicable

Women heading offices: Not applicable

Minorities heading practice groups: Not applicable

Women heading practice groups: Not applicable

The Firm Says

Mission statement

Cravath, Swaine & Moore LLP's overarching goal is to provide the best possible representation to our clients. We have long held the conviction that excellence and diversity go hand in hand, and that we cannot provide our clients with the highest level of representation unless we recruit and retain outstanding lawyers from diverse backgrounds, with different perspectives, experiences and insights. Just as we pride ourselves on the diversity of our practice, we are proud of our committment to promoting the diversity of our people at all levels. As part of this commitment, we established a Diversity Committee to formulate and propose diversity goals for the Firm, develop and implement practices that promote diversity, and analyze and track the Firm's progress in achieving those goals.

We sponsor, host or attend many diversity-related events, including:

- ACLU Lesbian & Gay Rights
- Asian American Legal Defense and Education Fund
- Association of the Bar of the City of New York
- Black Law Student Association (BLSA) at Columbia, Fordham, Harvard, University of Pennsylvania and University of Texas
- Harvard Latino Student Organization
- Hispanic National Bar Association
- LAMBDA GLBT Community Services
- LeGal
- Legal Momentum
- Metropolitan Black Bar Association
- Minority Corporate Counsel Association
- New York Women's Foundation
- Northeast BLSA
- University of Pennsylvania's Latin American Law Students' Association

Policies on equal employment opportunity, anti-discrimination and harassment

Freedom from harassment – Cravath, Swaine & Moore LLP is committed to maintaining a work environment in which all individuals are treated with respect and dignity. Each individual has the right to work in a professional atmosphere that promotes equal employment opportunities and prohibits discriminatory practices, including sexual harassment. To that end, Cravath expects that all relationships among persons in the workplace will be businesslike and free of bias, prejudice and harassment.

Equal employment opportunity and anti-discrimination – Cravath is an equal opportunity employer. It is the policy of the Firm to ensure equal employment opportunity without discrimination or harassment on the basis of race, color, national origin, religion, sex, age, disability, citizenship, marital status, sexual orientation, pregnancy or any other classification protected by law. This Policy applies to recruiting, hiring, placement, promotions, training, discipline, terminations, layoffs, transfers, leaves of absence, compensation and all other terms and conditions of employment.

Part-time work policy

Availability – Cravath supports associates who need or wish to work part-time.

• The Firm will attempt to make part-time work arrangements available to allow associates to fulfill family responsibilities or other obligations on a case-by-case basis.

• The availability of part-time arrangements may vary among the Firm's departments and will depend upon the needs of each practice group, client needs, the level of the associate's experience and the degree of flexibility in the desired arrangements.

• Part-time arrangements will generally not be available to newly hired associates. Working part-time at the beginning of an associate's legal career makes it difficult for the associate to receive the training, experience and exposure necessary for his or her professional development and delays the time when the associate is able to work independently.

Part-time work schedules – Part-time associates are expected to develop a flexible schedule that allows them to handle "mainstream" assignments within his or her practice area. Although part-time associates may establish a "target" schedule that generally allows them to be away from the office on certain days of the week, they must be sufficiently flexible to be available, as needed, to respond to client needs. In most cases, part-time associates are expected to work at least 60% of the average number of hours worked by full-time associates. Each part-time associate's schedule will be worked out on an individual basis.

Process for requesting part-time work – One partner from each department has been designated as the partner responsible for supervising the part-time program in that department. In addition, the Legal Personnel Director is available to answer questions and help associates structure a workable part-time plan. Each associate requesting a part-time arrangement is expected to prepare a written plan outlining his or her proposed arrangement as a basis for discussion with the appropriate partner(s).

Duration of part-time schedule: effect on review process and partnership opportunities – Each part-time associate's work arrangements, as well as his or her performance, generally will be reviewed at least once per year. The Firm believes that part-time arrangements work best when they are used as a step toward a return to full-time status. A part-time associate may be asked to return to full-time status if the Firm considers the change to be in the best interest of the associate or necessary to the Firm and its clients.

The Firm does not believe that there is any fixed minimum or maximum period of time that every associate must work before being considered, or after which he or she will no longer be considered, for partnership. Consequently, there is no fixed rule as to how part-time work will be counted for purposes of determining when an associate will be considered for partnership. However, in general, part-time associates should expect to return to full-time status for at least one year before being considered for admission to the Firm.

Compensation, bacation and benefits – Part-time associates are paid on an hourly basis, receiving one hour's pay for each hour worked. In addition, vacation time, benefits and bonuses are prorated to reflect the part-time associate's individual arrangements. Any associate may obtain a description of the precise method for computing part-time hourly rates, bonuses, vacation pay and benefits by contacting the Director of Legal Personnel.

To assist part-time associates' ability to work from home, the Firm will provide all part-time associates with a home computer, a combination printer/fax machine and a second phone line.

380

Crowell & Moring LLP

1001 Pennsylvania Avenue, NW
Washington, DC 20004
Phone: (202) 624-2500
Fax: (202) 628-5116

FIRM LEADERSHIP

Managing Partner: John Macleod, Chair
Diversity Team Leader: Wilma Lewis and
Luther Zeigler, Diversity Task Force Co-Chairs

LOCATIONS

Washington, DC (HQ)
Irvine, CA
Brussels
London

LAW FIRM DEMOGRAPHIC PROFILES

FULL-TIME ASSOCIATES	2003	2002
Minority men	12	7
Minority women	14	14
White women	60	52
Total	161	140

SUMMER ASSOCIATES	2003	2002
Minority men	1	3
Minority women	4	5
White women	6	13
Total	13	36

EQUITY PARTNERS	2003	2002
Minority men	2	2
Minority women	2	2
White women	9	9
Total	82	80

NON-EQUITY PARTNERS	2003	2002
Minority men	0	0
Minority women	0	0
White women	8	5
Total	30	27

NEW HIRES	2003	2002
Minority men	4	1
Minority women	1	2
White women	11	9
Total	33	23

MCCA
MINORITY CORPORATE COUNSEL ASSOCIATION

Strategic Plan and Diversity Leadership

How does the firm's leadership communicate the importance of diversity to everyone at the firm? (e.g., e-mails, web site, newsletters, meetings, etc.)

Firm leaders communicate their commitment to diversity through e-mails and the firm intranet and in periodic meetings with different groups of lawyers and staff.

Who has primary responsibility for leading diversity initiatives at your firm?

The eight partners on the Diversity Task Force are Wilma Lewis (co-chair), Luther Zeigler (co-chair), Ellen Dwyer, Cliff Hendler, Mike Martinez, Kris Meade, Beth Nolan and Jennifer Waters.

Does your law firm currently have a diversity committee?

Yes. As explained in the narrative statement below, the firm also has a Diversity Task Force.

Does the committee's representation include one or more members of the firm's management/executive committee (or the equivalent)?

Yes. One of the co-chairs of the Diversity Task Force was a member of the firm's management board at the time of the task force's creation.

How many attorneys are on the committee, and in 2003, what was the total number of hours collectively spent by the committee in furtherance of the firm's diversity initiatives?

Total attorneys on committee: 15

Total attorneys on task force: 8

Total hours spent on diversity: Approximately 500

Does the committee and/or diversity leader establish and set goals or objectives consistent with management's priorities?

Yes. See "The Firm Says."

Has the firm undertaken a formal or informal diversity program or set of initiatives aimed at increasing the diversity of the firm?

Yes, formal

How often does the firm's management review the firm's diversity progress/results?

See "The Firm Says."

How is the firm's diversity committee and/or firm management held accountable for achieving results?

See "The Firm Says."

LAW FIRM DIVERSITY INITIATIVES	ALREADY COMPLETED	CURRENTLY ADDRESSING	NOT A CURRENT PRIORITY
Undertake communication from firm management that diversity is a top priority of the firm.	✓		
Formalize diversity plan and committee with action steps and accountability to management.		✓	
Conduct firm-wide diversity training for all attorneys and staff.		✓	
Increase the number of minority attorneys at the associate level.		✓	
Increase the number of minority attorneys at the partnership level.		✓	
Develop/expand relationships with minority bar associations to offer firm's support of these networks.		✓	
Focus on strengthening firm's mentoring program, including for benefit of minority attorneys.		✓	
Conduct internal diversity needs assessment and/or retain diversity consultant to examine how firm culture might be more welcoming of minorities.	✓		
Support law firm's internal affinity networks (e.g., women, minority attorney networks).	✓		
Manage/monitor allocation of work assignments and/or hours billed to ensure women and minority attorneys have equal access/inclusion on top client matters.		✓	

Recruitment – New Associates

Does your firm annually recruit at any of the following types of institutions? (Check all that apply and list the schools).

Ivy League schools: Columbia University, Cornell University, Harvard University, University of Pennsylvania, Yale University

Public state schools: George Mason University, University of Maryland, University of Michigan, UC Berkeley (Boalt), UC Davis, UC Hastings, UCLA, University of Virginia, College of William & Mary

Private schools: University of Chicago, Duke University, Emory University, George Washington University, Georgetown University, Northwestern University, University of Notre Dame, NYU, Stanford University, USC, Washington & Lee University

Historically Black Colleges and Universities (HBCUs): Howard University

Do you have any special outreach efforts directed to encourage minority law students to consider your firm?
• *Sponsor WALRAA's Minority Reception and sponsor the D.C. Road Show*
• Participate in/host minority law student job fair(s)
• Scholarships or intern/fellowships for minority students

SUMMER ASSOCIATE STATISTICS: SUMMER 2003	MINORITY MEN	MINORITY WOMEN	WHITE WOMEN	TOTAL
Summer associates	0	4	6	12
Summer associates who received an offer of full-time employment	0	4	5	11
Summer associates who accepted an offer of full-time employment	0	2	2	6

Recruitment – Lateral Associates and Partners

What activities does the firm undertake to attract minority and women attorneys?

• Participate at minority job fairs

• Seek referrals from other attorneys

Do you use executive recruiting/search firms to seek to identify new diversity hires (partners or associates)?

Yes

If yes, list all women- and/or minority-owned executive search/recruiting firms to which the firm paid a fee for placement services in the past 12 months:

Lerner & Associates; Coonan Attorney Search

LATERAL ASSOCIATES AND PARTNERS: 1/1/03 – 12/31/03	MINORITY MEN	MINORITY WOMEN	WHITE WOMEN	TOTAL
Number of lateral associate hires	3	1	9	27
Number of lateral partner hires (equity and non-equity)	0	0	2	6
Number of new partners (equity and non-equity) promoted from associate rank	0	0	0	3
Number of new equity partners	0	0	0	1

Retention & Professional Development

ATTORNEYS WHO LEFT THE FIRM: 2003	MINORITY MEN	MINORITY WOMEN	WHITE WOMEN	TOTAL
Number of attorneys who voluntarily or involuntarily left your firm's employ in 2003	1	2	9	25

How do 2003 attrition rates generally compare to those experienced in the prior year period?

About the same as in prior years

Please identify the specific steps you are taking to reduce the attrition rate of minority and women attorneys.

• Develop and/or support internal employee affinity groups (e.g., minority or women networks within the firm)

• Increase/review compensation relative to competition

• Work with minority and women attorneys to develop career advancement plans

• Review work assignments and hours billed to key client matters to make sure minority and women attorneys are not being excluded

• Strengthen mentoring program for all attorneys, including minorities and women

• Professional skills development program, including minority and women attorneys

Does your firm have part-time/flex-time policies that permit attorneys (male or female) to work alternative schedules?

Yes. Crowell & Moring has a lawyer-friendly policy that allows flexibility. All full-time attorneys work flexible hours, taking into account the needs of the firm and its clients. Part-time schedules are considered and arranged on a case-by-case basis.

What impact, if any, will the decision to work part-time have on an attorney's ability to make partner or, if already a partner, to remain a partner at your firm?

Part-time issues are evaluated on a case-by-case basis, but as a general rule the decision to work part-time will neither disqualify a lawyer from making partner nor preclude someone who is already a partner from remaining one.

Have any attorneys who chose to work a part-time schedule made partner at your firm?

Yes, one attorney. Part-time status is not a barrier to promotion to partner.

Management Demographic Profile (as of 12/31/03)

	MINORITY MEN	MINORITY WOMEN	WHITE WOMEN	TOTAL
Number of attorneys on the Executive/Management Committee or equivalent	0	0	0	7
Number of attorneys on the Hiring Committee or equivalent	3	3	11	29
Number of attorneys on the Partner/Associate Review Committee or equivalent	1	1	8	29

Please provide information regarding all minority and women attorneys who head offices or practice groups of your law firm:

Women heading practice groups: Cathy Gebhard, Chair of Life Sciences Group

The Firm Says

Crowell & Moring appreciates that its success as a law firm and its well-being as a community depend upon creating and maintaining a diverse team of talented professionals. We value individual differences and recognize that the vitality of our culture is in large measure a function of the very different perspectives, histories and experiences that our individual lawyers and staff bring to the firm. For these reasons, we seek to recruit, retain and encourage people of diverse backgrounds.

C&M is fortunate already to have in its partnership a number of nationally recognized diverse lawyers, including the former United States Attorney for the District of Columbia who was also named by the Harvard Law Bulletin alumni magazine as one of the school's 50 most distinguished women graduates (Wilma Lewis); a former clerk to Justice Thurgood Marshall and a current member of the board of trustees of the NAACP Legal Defense and Education Fund (Karen Hastie Williams); an alumna of the Justice Department's Office of Legal Counsel and the current chair of the Committee on Grievances for the U.S. District Court for the District of Columbia (Laurel Pyke Malson); a patent litigator recently named as an intellectual property law "Superlawyer" for 2004 by Los Angeles Magazine (Kim Nobles); a former assistant U.S. Attorney and recipient of the Gallinghouse Award for Excellence in Financial Litigation from former Attorney General Janet Reno (Mike Martinez); and a former articles editor of the Columbia Law Review who is now a prominent Washington tax practitioner (Charles Hwang).

To give focus and renewed energy to the firm's commitment to diversity, its management board in March 2004 appointed eight partners to a newly constituted Diversity Task Force. Although the firm has long had an active Diversity Committee, this new task force was given the special responsibility of preparing a strategic plan for the firm on diversity issues affecting our lawyers. To assist it in this effort, the task force retained one of the nation's leading consultants on law firm diversity – an expert highly recommended by the Minority Corporate Counsel Association. Our consultant has completed a wide-ranging assessment of diversity needs within the firm, including a survey of all lawyers and extensive individual interviews. We are happy to report that the participation rate in the survey and interviews was enthusiastic, reflecting broad-based support throughout the firm for this initiative.

Over the coming weeks, the task force and its consultant will work together to develop a comprehensive strategy for addressing diversity at the firm, with an initial emphasis on issues of race and ethnicity. A primary goal of that plan will be to integrate diversity into all aspects of firm life. Although the strategic planning process is still underway, among the important issues that the task force and its consultant are working on:

• improving recruitment strategies and methods, both in the law school and lateral markets, to increase the diversity of our lawyers;

• strengthening mentoring and professional development programs and other support mechanisms for minority lawyers;

• assessing the firm's evaluation and promotion processes;

• providing increased education concerning diversity issues so as to promote a firm culture that will support long-term diversity;

• developing mechanisms (including metrics, where appropriate) to hold partners and practice groups accountable for addressing diversity objectives;

• examining the firm's existing structures (committees and otherwise) to ensure that institutional mechanisms are in place to meaningfully address diversity issues; and

• formulating communications strategies that provide for regular and clear communications about the firm's commitment to diversity.

The firm expects to have a strategic plan for diversity in place by the fall of 2004.

In connection with the firm's 25th anniversary in June 2004, C&M also announced a number of exciting, new initiatives that reflect the seriousness of this renewed commitment to the values of diversity. These include:

• the establishment of a $25,000 scholarship program to be awarded annually to a minority law student in the District of Columbia to help defray the costs of his or her legal education;

• the creation and funding of two public service summer internships for Howard University law students;

• a commitment by C&M lawyers to participate regularly in Howard Law School's annual moot court competitions;

• the establishment of an educational outreach program in the community adjacent to the firm's Irvine, Calif., office to serve the predominantly Hispanic students who attend the poorest middle school in Orange County; and

• the initiation of a "Celebrating Diversity" speaker series that will bring to the firm an array of diverse speakers from different walks of life to speak on issues of interest to our lawyers and staff.

We are enthusiastic about all of these new diversity initiatives and look forward to their further development and implementation over the coming weeks and months.

Davis Polk & Wardwell

450 Lexington Avenue
New York, NY 10017
Phone: (212) 450-4000
Fax: (212) 450-3800

FIRM LEADERSHIP

Managing Partner: John R. Ettinger
Diversity Team Leader: Yukako Kawata, Chair
of Personnel Committee

LOCATIONS

New York, NY (HQ)
Menlo Park, CA
Washington, DC
Frankfurt
Hong Kong
London
Madrid
Paris
Tokyo

LAW FIRM DEMOGRAPHIC PROFILES

FULL-TIME ASSOCIATES	2003	2002
Minority men	64	56
Minority women	83	86
White women	155	153
Total Associates	522	521

SUMMER ASSOCIATES	2003	2002
Minority men	4	10
Minority women	21	11
White women	23	36
Total Summer Associates	83	100

EQUITY PARTNERS	2003	2002
Minority men	7	7
Minority women	1	1
White women	29	28
Total Equity Partners	145	140

NEW HIRES	2003	2002
Minority men	11	11
Minority women	12	16
White women	30	25
Total New Hires	92	102

Includes "of counsel" attorneys

Strategic Plan and Diversity Leadership

How does the firm's leadership communicate the importance of diversity to everyone at the firm? (e.g., e-mails, web site, newsletters, meetings, etc.)

Firm web site, firm resume, orientation sessions for new lawyers

Who has primary responsibility for leading diversity initiatives at your firm?

Yukako Kawata, chair of Personnel Committee

Does your law firm currently have a diversity committee?

Yes. Our Personnel Committee oversees personnel matters, including diversity issues.

Does the committee's representation include one or more members of the firm's management/executive committee (or the equivalent)?

No

How many attorneys are on the committee, and in 2003, what was the total number of hours collectively spent by the committee in furtherance of the firm's diversity initiatives?

Total attorneys on committee: 13

Does the committee and/or diversity leader establish and set goals or objectives consistent with management's priorities?

Yes

Has the firm undertaken a formal or informal diversity program or set of initiatives aimed at increasing the diversity of the firm?

Yes, informal

How often does the firm's management review the firm's diversity progress/results?

Ongoing

LAW FIRM DIVERSITY INITIATIVES	ALREADY COMPLETED	CURRENTLY ADDRESSING	NOT A CURRENT PRIORITY
Undertake communication from firm management that diversity is a top priority of the firm.	✓	✓	
Formalize diversity plan and committee with action steps and accountability to management.	✓	✓	
Conduct firm-wide diversity training for all attorneys and staff.		✓	
Increase the number of minority attorneys at the associate level.	✓	✓	
Increase the number of minority attorneys at the partnership level.	✓	✓	
Develop/expand relationships with minority bar associations to offer firm's support of these networks.	✓	✓	
Focus on strengthening firm's mentoring program, including for benefit of minority attorneys.	✓	✓	
Conduct internal diversity needs assessment and/or retain diversity consultant to examine how firm culture might be more welcoming of minorities.		✓	
Support law firm's internal affinity networks (e.g., women, minority attorney networks).	N/A		
Manage/monitor allocation of work assignments and/or hours billed to ensure women and minority attorneys have equal access/inclusion on top client matters.	✓	✓	

Recruitment – New Associates

Does your firm annually recruit at any of the following types of institutions? (Check all that apply and list the schools).

Ivy League schools: Please see firm web site.

Public state schools: Please see firm web site.

Private schools: Please see firm web site.

Historically Black Colleges and Universities (HBCUs): Please see firm web site.

Do you have any special outreach efforts directed to encourage minority law students to consider your firm?

• *Minority and women lawyers are actively made available on an individual basis for interviewing and post-offer discussions.*

• Hold a reception for minority law students

• Advertise in minority law student association publication(s)

• Participate in/host minority law student job fair(s)

• Sponsor minority law student association events

• Firm's lawyers participate on career panels at school

• Scholarships or intern/fellowships for minority students

SUMMER ASSOCIATE STATISTICS: SUMMER 2003	MINORITY MEN	MINORITY WOMEN	WHITE WOMEN	TOTAL
Summer associates	4	19	25	81
Summer associates who received an offer of full-time employment	4	19	25	81
Summer associates who accepted an offer of full-time employment*	N/A	N/A	N/A	N/A

* We do not provide information on acceptance data.

Recruitment – Lateral Associates and Partners

What activities does the firm undertake to attract minority and women attorneys?

• *Minority and women lawyers are actively made available on an individual basis for interviewing and post-offer discussions.*

• Participate at minority job fairs

• Seek referrals from other attorneys

Do you use executive recruiting/search firms to seek to identify new diversity hires (partners or associates)?

Yes

List all women- and/or minority-owned executive search/recruiting firms to which the firm paid a fee for placement services in the past 12 months:

Greene Levin Snyder

LATERAL ASSOCIATES AND PARTNERS: 1/1/03 – 12/31/03	MINORITY MEN	MINORITY WOMEN	WHITE WOMEN	TOTAL
Number of lateral associate hires	0	1	2	5
Number of lateral partner hires (equity and non-equity)	0	0	0	0
Number of new partners (equity and non-equity) promoted from associate rank	0	0	1	6
Number of new equity partners	0	0	1	6

Retention & Professional Development

ATTORNEYS WHO LEFT THE FIRM: 2003	MINORITY MEN	MINORITY WOMEN	WHITE WOMEN	TOTAL
Number of attorneys who voluntarily or involuntarily left your firm's employ in 2003*	N/A	N/A	N/A	N/A

We do not provide this information for any purposes.

How do 2003 attrition rates generally compare to those experienced in the prior year period?

We do not provide this information for any purposes.

Please identify the specific steps you are taking to reduce the attrition rate of minority and women attorneys.

• *We work with all of our attorneys to focus on development through mentoring, training and other professional endeavors.*

• Increase/review compensation relative to competition

• Increase/improve current work/life programs

• Introduce minority and women attorneys to key clients, including to lead engagements

• Review work assignments and hours billed to key client matters to make sure minority and women attorneys are not being excluded

• Strengthen mentoring program for all attorneys, including minorities and women

• Professional skills development program, including minority and women attorneys

Does your firm have part-time/flex-time policies that permit attorneys (male or female) to work alternative schedules?

Yes. We've had an active part-time/flex-time program since the 1980s.

What impact, if any, will the decision to work part-time have on an attorney's ability to make partner or, if already a partner, to remain a partner at your firm?

All part-time decisions are made on a case-by-case basis. We currently have 22 non-partner lawyers and one partner working part-time.

Have any attorneys who chose to work a part-time schedule made partner at your firm?

Yes.

Management Demographic Profile (as of 12/31/03)

Please provide information regarding all minority and women attorneys who head offices or practice groups of your law firm:

Minorities heading offices: Andres Gil, Madrid; Eugene Gregor, Tokyo

Women heading offices: Meg Tahyar, Paris (co-head)

Minorities heading practice groups: Yukako Kawata, IMG (co-head); Andres Gil, Spain and Latin American Practice Group

Women heading practice groups: Nora Jordan, IMG (co-head); Yukako Kawata, IMG (co-head); Beverly Chase, T&E; Gail Flesher, Environmental; Barbara Nims, Employee Benefits Group

The Firm Says

At Davis Polk, we are strongly committed to cultivating a diverse and supportive workplace. We believe that diversity in backgrounds, experiences and ideas enriches our lives and enhances the quality of the work we do for our clients. Our differences enable us to look at problems from a fresh perspective and to be creative, thus strengthening the firm's collaborative approach.

Fifteen or more years ago, Davis Polk & Wardwell initiated programs and embarked on a committed effort to hire and retain minority lawyers. A group of partners met with minority lawyers to discuss how to create and maintain a comfortable and attractive environment for lawyers of diverse backgrounds, particularly those of color. We are proud of our efforts and successes in this area, and continue to work toward further diversity on a daily basis.

• In 1999, the Minority Corporate Counsel Association (MCCA) awarded Davis Polk the first New York City-based Thomas L. Sager Award in recognition of the firm's success in and commitment to the hiring, retention and promotion of minority lawyers.

• In 2002, International Paper awarded the Lighthouse Award to Davis Polk in recognition of the firm's diversity goals.

• Davis Polk routinely ranks among the top firms in *The American Lawyer*'s A-List ranking of elite U.S. law firms (including first place for three consecutive years from 2001-2003), which measures the firm's financial performance, pro bono activity, associate satisfaction and lawyer diversity.

• In June 2003, The American Lawyer ranked Davis Polk first among the country's largest law firms based on the percentage of women partners at the firm.

• According to the Minority Law Journal's Diversity Scorecard 2004, Davis Polk ranked in the top 15 among New York general practice firms as measured by the percentage of United States citizen minority lawyers at the firm.

Our diversity hiring programs start before law school begins. Each summer we hire three or four future law students through the Sponsors for Educational Opportunity (SEO) program, which provides law firm jobs to minority law students the summer prior to starting law school. We also host an informational session and cocktail party of all SEOs throughout the city.

We visit over 30 law schools and job fairs, including Howard University, the Northeast Minority Job Fair, the Hispanic National Bar Association Job Fiar, and the Lavendar Law Career Fair. Throughout our recruiting programs and interviews, we consider the needs of each applicant, particularly minority candidates. For example, in interviewing students, we attempt to match minority students with minority lawyers as well as with other lawyers who share a similar educational background or other interests. This allows us to fully and fairly evaluate the applicant and provides the student with an opportunity to ask any questions he or she might have.

Each year we host, through the assistance of career services offices, two or more informational programs for law students who are interested in learning more about practicing law at a large New York City law firm. In the past, we have contacted specific minority student groups and sponsored various career-related events. We have also sponsored programs organized by minority student organizations, including BLSA conferences, the National Asian Pacific American Conference and Latino Law Student Association symposiums and dinners.

Our assignment system reflects an attempt to ensure that all lawyers are provided with equal access to work opportunities. All new associates may choose the department in which they wish to work, and all corporate associates rotate through a variety of groups and are eligible for overseas assignments. Two or more partners and administrators in each practice area are responsible for managing the allocation of assignments and tracking the workload of our associates. We also regularly monitor hours of our newest associates to ensure the even distribution of work assignments within the class. In 1990, we introduced a partner mentor program, whereby each new associate is assigned a partner mentor for his/her first year at the firm. We encourage the development of these and other mentoring relationships throughout one's career at Davis Polk and believe that this also contributes to our development of minority lawyers.

We believe that our success in hiring and promoting female lawyers is also indicative of our overall approach to providing a diverse workplace. Davis Polk has long offered a part-time program for lawyers. As of April 2004, 23 lawyers participate in the program. Of the 23 lawyers who participate, 21 are women. Many of our part-time lawyers have elected to work on a reduced schedule for child care or family reasons.

We believe that our deep commitment to community and pro bono activities, while clearly providing benefits to our community and to all of our lawyers, also permits us to attract and retain more minority lawyers by providing them with significant opportunities to be involved in programs outside of the firm itself, but which have the full support of the firm. By way of example, in one program our lawyers and legal assistants have mentored more than 250 students from Bushwick High School over the past 11 years and have also provided SAT tutoring and other services to Bushwick students.

While we are proud of our programs and initiatives, we are by no means satisfied. We continue to evaluate and improve our recruiting, retention and promotion efforts and to consider new ways to increase the diversity of our work force in years to come.

Davis Wright Tremaine LLP

2600 Century Square, 1501 Fourth Avenue
Seattle, WA 98101-1688
Phone: (206) 622-3150
Fax: (206) 628-7699

FIRM LEADERSHIP

Managing Partner: Richard D. Ellingsen
Diversity Team Leader: Richard W. Elliott,
Chairman, DWT PRISM Group

LOCATIONS

Seattle, WA (HQ)
Anchorage, AK
Bellevue, WA
Los Angeles, CA
New York, NY
Portland, OR
San Francisco, CA
Washington, DC
Shanghai

LAW FIRM DEMOGRAPHIC PROFILES

FULL-TIME ASSOCIATES	2003	2002
Minority men	14	11
Minority women	13	12
White women	60	61
Total	142	143

SUMMER ASSOCIATES	2003	2002
Minority men	3	3
Minority women	7	4
White women	6	9
Total	21	23

EQUITY PARTNERS	2003	2002
Minority men	10	10
Minority women	3	3
White women	32	31
Total	186	185

NON-EQUITY PARTNERS	2003	2002
Minority men	2	2
Minority women	0	0
White women	10	11
Total	51	43

NEW HIRES	2003	2002
Minority men	5	5
Minority women	4	2
White women	23	15
Total	61	48

Strategic Plan and Diversity Leadership

How does the firm's leadership communicate the importance of diversity to everyone at the firm? (e.g., e-mails, web site, newsletters, meetings, etc.)

Firm leadership communicates the importance of diversity to attorneys and staff through multiple means, including: broad distribution of the Managing Partner's Annual Report on Diversity to attorneys and through the firm's web site; articles on diversity and diverse firm attorneys in the firm's electronic newsletter ("eSource"); attorney retreat functions, such as having an all-attorney luncheon presentation by a diverse general counsel at our 2003 retreat; and presentations by members of the firm's diversity committee, the PRISM Group, and our diversity consultant, Peggy Nagae, to groups of attorneys and different offices within the firm, as well as to management groups such as partners-in-charge of offices, office administrators and practice group chairs.

Who has primary responsibility for leading diversity initiatives at your firm?

Richard D. Ellingsen, managing partner, as assisted by Richard W. Elliott, chair of the PRISM Group.

Does your law firm currently have a diversity committee?

Yes

Does the committee's representation include one or more members of the firm's management/executive committee (or the equivalent)?

Yes

How many attorneys are on the committee, and in 2003, what was the total number of hours collectively spent by the committee in furtherance of the firm's diversity initiatives?

Total attorneys on committee: 13

Total hours spent on diversity: 1,500 estimated

Does the committee and/or diversity leader establish and set goals or objectives consistent with management's priorities?

Yes

Has the firm undertaken a formal or informal diversity program or set of initiatives aimed at increasing the diversity of the firm?

Yes, formal

How often does the firm's management review the firm's diversity progress/results?

Monthly

How is the firm's diversity committee and/or firm management held accountable for achieving results?

DWT is governed by an Executive Committee made up of lawyers from our various offices who are elected by the partnership. The Executive Committee has adopted the following Diversity Strategic Objectives for 2004: recruitment; retention; cultural competency; buying power (vendor diversity); and communication. The managing partner makes an annual report to the Executive Committee on progress achieved during the preceding year toward achieving the Strategic Objectives. The chair of DWT's PRISM Group is responsible to the managing partner for working with the PRISM Group and firm management in implementing specific actions to achieve the Strategic Goals. The managing partner and PRISM Group chair work closely together and communicate frequently through e-mail, telephone conversations and personal meetings regarding progress on diversity initiatives.

LAW FIRM DIVERSITY INITIATIVES	ALREADY COMPLETED	CURRENTLY ADDRESSING	NOT A CURRENT PRIORITY
Undertake communication from firm management that diversity is a top priority of the firm.	✓		
Formalize diversity plan and committee with action steps and accountability to management.	✓		
Conduct firm-wide diversity training for all attorneys and staff.		✓	
Increase the number of minority attorneys at the associate level.		✓	
Increase the number of minority attorneys at the partnership level.		✓	
Develop/expand relationships with minority bar associations to offer firm's support of these networks.	✓	✓	
Focus on strengthening firm's mentoring program, including for benefit of minority attorneys.		✓	
Conduct internal diversity needs assessment and/or retain diversity consultant to examine how firm culture might be more welcoming of minorities.	✓		
Support law firm's internal affinity networks (e.g., women, minority attorney networks).	✓		
Manage/monitor allocation of work assignments and/or hours billed to ensure women and minority attorneys have equal access/inclusion on top client matters.		✓	

Recruitment – New Associates

Does your firm annually recruit at any of the following types of institutions? (Check all that apply and list the schools).

Ivy League schools: Columbia University and Harvard University

Public state schools: University of Alaska, University of Michigan, University of Oregon, University of California-Boalt Hall, University of California-Hastings, University of Virginia, University of Washington

Private schools: Georgetown University, University of Chicago, Duke University, Lewis & Clark University, New York University, Northwestern University, Willamette University, Seattle University, Stanford University

Historically Black Colleges and Universities (HBCUs): Howard University

Other predominantly minority and/or women's colleges: Northwest Minority Job Fair and the Oregon Minority Job Fair

Do you have any special outreach efforts directed to encourage minority law students to consider your firm?

• *DWT's Seattle and Portland offices do the most recruiting of new associates and they do all of the outreach efforts outlined above. Other DWT offices also participate in minority job fairs and sponsor minority law student association events.*

• Hold a reception for minority law students

• Advertise in minority law student association publication(s)

• Participate in/host minority law student job fair(s)

• Sponsor minority law student association events

• Firm's lawyers participate on career panels at school

• Outreach to leadership of minority student organizations

• Scholarships or intern/fellowships for minority students

SUMMER ASSOCIATE STATISTICS: SUMMER 2003	MINORITY MEN	MINORITY WOMEN	WHITE WOMEN	TOTAL
Summer associates	2	4	5	13
Summer associates who received an offer of full-time employment	2	2	4	10
Summer associates who accepted an offer of full-time employment	2	0	4	9

Recruitment – Lateral Associates and Partners

What activities does the firm undertake to attract minority and women attorneys?

• Partner programs with women and minority bar associations

• Participate at minority job fairs

• Seek referrals from other attorneys

Do you use executive recruiting/search firms to seek to identify new diversity hires (partners or associates)?

Yes

If yes, list all women- and/or minority-owned executive search/recruiting firms to which the firm paid a fee for placement services in the past 12 months:

NW Legal Search, Inc. (women-owned)

LATERAL ASSOCIATES AND PARTNERS: 1/1/03 – 12/31/03	MINORITY MEN	MINORITY WOMEN	WHITE WOMEN	TOTAL
Number of lateral associate hires	2	2	9	18
Number of lateral partner hires (equity and non-equity)	1	0	5	17
Number of new partners (equity and non-equity) promoted from associate rank	0	0	1	6
Number of new equity partners	0	0	3	10

Retention & Professional Development

ATTORNEYS WHO LEFT THE FIRM: 2003	MINORITY MEN	MINORITY WOMEN	WHITE WOMEN	TOTAL
Number of attorneys who voluntarily or involuntarily left your firm's employ in 2003	3	1	24	44

How do 2003 attrition rates generally compare to those experienced in the prior year period?

About the same as in prior years

Please identify the specific steps you are taking to reduce the attrition rate of minority and women attorneys.

• Develop and/or support internal employee affinity groups (e.g., minority or women networks within the firm)

• Increase/improve current work/life programs

• Work with minority and women attorneys to develop career advancement plans

• Introduce minority and women attorneys to key clients, including to lead engagements

• Strengthen mentoring program for all attorneys, including minorities and women

• Professional skills development program, including minority and women attorneys

Does your firm have part-time/flex-time policies that permit attorneys (male or female) to work alternative schedules?

Yes. DWT has a longstanding policy of granting part-time status to partners, of-counsel and associate attorneys who either cannot or do not want to work full-time. The arrangement depends on the individual's needs, and there is no general rule that attorneys must work full-time to succeed at DWT.

What impact, if any, will the decision to work part-time have on an attorney's ability to make partner or, if already a partner, to remain a partner at your firm?

As shown by our past performance, our associate lawyers have made partner while on part-time status. It may be more difficult for certain individuals to make partner on the same timeframe as their full-time colleagues because they will not have had nor dedicated the time to demonstrating the propensity to build a practice.

Have any attorneys who chose to work a part-time schedule made partner at your firm?

Yes, 17 attorneys.

Management Demographic Profile (as of 12/31/03)

Please provide information regarding all minority and women attorneys who head offices or practice groups of your law firm:

Women heading offices: Susan G. Duffy, Partner-in-Charge, Seattle Office; Sharon L. Schneier, Partner-in-Charge, New York Office

Women heading practice groups: Mary E. Drobka, Employment/Labor Law; Cassi Kinkead, Litigation (Deputy Chair); Lynn T. Manolopolous, Environmental Law; Alexandra Nicholson, Intellectual Property; Anne L. Northrup, Employee Benefits; Jane Potter, Life Sciences; Kelli L. Sager, Media Law (Deputy Chair); LaVerne Woods, Tax-Exempt Organizations

The Firm Says

Increasing diversity of our attorneys and staff is central to DWT's ability to fulfill its commitments to clients and the community. A core value of the firm, we believe diversity is critical to DWT's long-term success. Formed in 2000, our diversity committee, the PRISM Group, has since grown in size and stature and is now a significant part of firm management. PRISM works closely with a professional diversity consultant, Peggy Nagae, on fostering diversity and implementing specific diversity goals for DWT. PRISM Chair Richard W. Elliott reports directly to Managing Partner Richard D. Ellingsen, who is committed to advancing diversity at DWT.

Our diversity initiatives are guided by the following Diversity Mission Statement, adopted by the firm's executive governing body:

• Hire and retain the best people we can find, all the time helping them achieve their highest and best purpose;

• Maintain a work environment that respects its constituent parts – each of us – and helps us respect and support each other as we work, communicate and resolve conflict together; and

• Define leadership to include only those who recognize, seek out and honor the valued contributions the firm can and should expect when diverse individuals band together to pursue a set of common goals.

Furthermore, a set of five Strategic Objectives guide firm management in taking diversity to the next level at DWT:

• Recruitment – DWT's focus is to recruit more broadly – increasing opportunities to hire outstanding diverse attorneys that reflect the diversity of the communities in which we live and the clients we serve. Successful at recruiting minority associates, our current emphasis is on recruitment of minority lateral attorneys who can bring strong practices and serve as role models to younger minority attorneys within the firm. We are actively seeking such opportunities through a legal recruiter. And our managing partner is working with practice group chairs to further address increasing diversity of lateral hires.

• Retention – We believe there is a strong link between retention of diverse attorneys (and non-diverse attorneys as well) on the one hand, and effective mentoring and professional development programs on the other hand. Consequently, the PRISM Group and our diversity consultant have always strongly supported creation and enhancement of mentoring and professional development programs within DWT offices. This has been especially evident in our larger offices (Seattle and Portland) and now we are expanding this effort to other DWT offices. In addition, we are implementing steps to ensure our diverse associates have opportunities to interact with top work generators to discuss marketing, team building and client relations skills.

• Cultural competency – Cultural competency relates to the ability and confidence of our attorneys and staff, firm-wide, in talking about issues of diversity. In the past, diversity presentations and training have been presented to specific DWT offices on an ad-hoc basis. Efforts are underway to expand that effort through design of a more interactive training program on diversity that fosters discussion and a comfort level when addressing diversity subjects and issues. Our diversity communications efforts, described above, are integral to our cultural competency initiatives.

• Buying power – DWT will use its buying power to further our diversity mission. We are establishing a policy to track and grow vendor diversity with respect to services and goods purchased by the firm. We are actively reviewing existing vendor relationships and identifying the extent of our engagement with minority- and women-owned business enterprises. DWT recently became a member of the Northwest Minority Business Council, a clearinghouse for minority vendors. Through this membership, we will gain valuable information on minority vendors and be able to create a realistic vendor diversity policy.

• Communication – DWT's goal is to communicate to our colleagues, clients and communities our commitment to diversity, the progress we are making and the work yet to be done. Two members of the firm's marketing department, including Marketing Director Michael Breda, are members of the PRISM Group. A Diversity Strategic Communications Plan is in the works. We have made a special effort to keep clients informed by sending them copies of our Managing Partner's Report on Diversity. Our lawyers meet with key clients to update them on our progress, and we respond regularly to client requests for demographic information. DWT also makes a special effort to support our diverse attorneys' activities involving minority bar associations and diversity/civil rights groups. Examples include: Supporting the 2004 Loren Miller Bar Association and Brown v. Board of Education Celebration; hosting a luncheon in 2004 for the National Asian Pacific American Legal Consortium; supporting a minority partner in her appointment to the American Bar Association's Commission on Racial and Ethnic Diversity in the Profession and another minority attorney in his board membership with the Understanding Racism Foundation. (For more examples, please see page 8 of the 2003 Managing Partner's Report on Diversity.)

Our commitment to diversity is further evidenced by the recent establishment of a diversity scholarship honoring our founder: the John M. Davis Diversity Scholarship at the University of Washington School of Law.

Established at $150,000, this scholarship will be awarded by the dean of the School of Law based on academic merit, and given to first-year students who are members of minority groups, including gay/lesbian, disabled or other students who are underrepresented in law school enrollments and/or in the legal profession. Also, contribution to diversity activities and goals has been recently made a specific factor in determining the compensation of partners in the share determination process.

DWT has made substantial progress in the four years since diversity became a firm priority, yet we realize much work remains to be done. Management remains committed to achieving the Strategic Objectives outlined above and has allocated the resources for success.

Day, Berry & Howard LLP...

Where the people make a world of difference

Day, Berry & Howard LLP

COUNSELLORS AT LAW

BOSTON	GREENWICH	HARTFORD	NEW HAVEN	NEW YORK	STAMFORD
260 Franklin Street	One East Putnam Avenue	CityPlace I	700 State Street	126 East 56th Street	One Canterbury Green
Boston, MA 02110	Greenwich, CT 06830	Hartford, CT 06103	New Haven, CT 06511	New York, NY 10022	Stamford, CT 06901
(617) 345-4600	(203) 862-7800	(860) 275-0100	(203) 752-5000	(212) 446-6800	(203) 977-7300

www.dbh.com

Day, Berry & Howard, LLP

CityPlace, 185 Asylum Street
Hartford, CT 06103
Phone: (860) 275-0100
Fax: (860) 275-0343

FIRM LEADERSHIP

Managing Partner: James Sicilian, Chair of
Executive Committee
Diversity Team Leader: Elizabeth A. Alquist,
Chair of Diversity & Sensitivity Committee

LOCATIONS

Hartford, CT (HQ)
Boston, MA
Greenwich, CT
New Haven, CT
New York, NY
Stamford, CT
West Hartford, CT

LAW FIRM DEMOGRAPHIC PROFILES

FULL-TIME ASSOCIATES	2003	2002
Minority men	8	7
Minority women	8	4
White women	49	46
Total	121	106

SUMMER ASSOCIATES	2003	2002
Minority men	0	2
Minority women	2	2
White women	10	5
Total	13	14

PARTNERS*	2003	2002
Minority men	2	2
Minority women	1	1
White women	14	12
Total	99	87

* The firm has equity and non-equity partners, but does not,
as a matter of policy, provide data that would differentiate
equity partners from non-equity partners.

NEW HIRES	2003	2002
Minority men	2	4
Minority women	4	2
White women	11	12
Total	32	35

Strategic Plan and Diversity Leadership

How does the firm's leadership communicate the importance of diversity to everyone at the firm? (e.g., e-mails, web site, newsletters, meetings, etc.)

The firm's leadership communicates the importance of diversity in many ways. For example, our Executive Committee has adopted and embraced diversity as a formal firm-wide strategic goal. Individual partner contributions to diversity factor into partner compensation determination and non-partner bonus awards. Our marketing department publishes a brochure highlighting the DBH Statement of Commitment to Diversity, featuring photographs of DBH minority attorneys, describing their practice areas and providing their contact information. The Diversity & Sensitivity Committee publishes a periodic newsletter to provide updates on our diversity initiatives. We post ongoing diversity-related activities and relevant articles of interest on the DBH Intranet. Our DBH web site features a page describing the firm's diversity efforts. Each quarter, the firm's Executive Committee, together with the chairs of the Hiring Committee and the Diversity & Sensitivity Committee, meet with all attorneys of color to discuss diversity issues based on agendas set by the attorneys of color. We also demonstrate our commitment by providing a home to the executive director of the Connecticut Lawyers Group, lending support, office space and resources.

Who has primary responsibility for leading diversity initiatives at your firm?

Stanley A. Twardy, Jr., partner and Executive Committee liaison to Diversity & Sensitivity Committee; Elizabeth A. Alquist, partner and chair of Diversity & Sensitivity Committee and Women Working Together® (WWT); Lynn Anne Baronas, director of professional development

Does your law firm currently have a diversity committee?

Yes

Does the committee's representation include one or more members of the firm's management/executive committee (or the equivalent)?

Yes

How many attorneys are on the committee, and in 2003, what was the total number of hours collectively spent by the committee in furtherance of the firm's diversity initiatives?

Total attorneys on committee: 12

Total hours spent on diversity: 531

Does the committee and/or diversity leader establish and set goals or objectives consistent with management's priorities?

Yes

Has the firm undertaken a formal or informal diversity program or set of initiatives aimed at increasing the diversity of the firm?

Yes, formal

How often does the firm's management review the firm's diversity progress/results?

Quarterly

How is the firm's diversity committee and/or firm management held accountable for achieving results?

The Diversity & Sensitivity Committee submits an annual report to the Executive Committee describing the committee's accomplishments throughout the year. At quarterly dinner meetings with DBH minority attorneys, the Executive Committee, Hiring Committee, and Diversity & Sensitivity Committee respond to specific inquiries posed by the minority attorneys about benchmarking, minority hiring, workload distribution, the status of various initiatives designed to support diversity and other issues of import to the group

LAW FIRM DIVERSITY INITIATIVES	ALREADY COMPLETED	CURRENTLY ADDRESSING	NOT A CURRENT PRIORITY
Undertake communication from firm management that diversity is a top priority of the firm.	✓		
Formalize diversity plan and committee with action steps and accountability to management.	✓		
Conduct firm-wide diversity training for all attorneys and staff.		✓	
Increase the number of minority attorneys at the associate level.		✓	
Increase the number of minority attorneys at the partnership level.		✓	
Develop/expand relationships with minority bar associations to offer firm's support of these networks.	✓		
Focus on strengthening firm's mentoring program, including for benefit of minority attorneys.	✓		
Conduct internal diversity needs assessment and/or retain diversity consultant to examine how firm culture might be more welcoming of minorities.		✓	
Support law firm's internal affinity networks (e.g., women, minority attorney networks).	✓		
Manage/monitor allocation of work assignments and/or hours billed to ensure women and minority attorneys have equal access/inclusion on top client matters.	✓		
Encourage the education of all attorneys by supporting their attendance at conferences and seminars designed to increase knowledge of and awareness about minority and women's issues		✓	

Recruitment - New Associates

Does your firm annually recruit at any of the following types of institutions? (Check all that apply and list the schools).

Ivy League schools: Harvard University, Yale University, University of Pennsylvania, Columbia University and Cornell University

Public state schools: University of Connecticut, University of Virginia

Private schools: Boston College, Boston University, Duke University, Fordham University, Georgetown University, George Washington University, New York University and Quinnipiac University

Historically Black Colleges and Universities (HBCUs): Howard University

Do you have any special outreach efforts directed to encourage minority law students to consider your firm?

• *WWT holds receptions for women law students*

• Participate in/host minority law student job fair(s)

• Sponsor minority law student association events

• Firm's lawyers participate on career panels at school

• Outreach to leadership of minority student organizations

• Scholarships or intern/fellowships for minority students

SUMMER ASSOCIATE STATISTICS: SUMMER 2003	MINORITY MEN	MINORITY WOMEN	WHITE WOMEN	TOTAL
Summer associates	0	1	8	10
Summer associates who received an offer of full-time employment	0	1	8	9
Summer associates who accepted an offer of full-time employment	0	1	7	8

Recruitment - Lateral Associates and Partners

What activities does the firm undertake to attract minority and women attorneys?

• Partner programs with women and minority bar associations

• Participate at minority job fairs

• Seek referrals from other attorneys

Do you use executive recruiting/search firms to seek to identify new diversity hires (partners or associates)?

Yes

List all women- and/or minority-owned executive search/recruiting firms to which the firm paid a fee for placement services in the past 12 months:

We have partnered with Erica M. Menard, Esq., of Strategic Workforce Solutions in New York, and Julia Sweeney, Special Counsel, in Washington, D.C., but have not yet been asked to pay a fee for services provided.

LATERAL ASSOCIATES AND PARTNERS: 1/1/03 – 12/31/03	MINORITY MEN	MINORITY WOMEN	WHITE WOMEN	TOTAL
Number of lateral associate hires	0	1	4	10
Number of lateral partner hires (equity and non-equity)	0	0	1	5
Number of new partners (equity and non-equity) promoted from associate rank	0	0	1	4
Number of new equity partners	0	0	1	4

Retention & Professional Development

ATTORNEYS WHO LEFT THE FIRM: 2003	MINORITY MEN	MINORITY WOMEN	WHITE WOMEN	TOTAL
Number of attorneys who voluntarily or involuntarily left your firm's employ in 2003	2	0	9	18

How do 2003 attrition rates generally compare to those experienced in the prior year period?

Lower than in prior years

Please identify the specific steps you are taking to reduce the attrition rate of minority and women attorneys.

• *Encourage attendance at seminars and other programs designed to increase awareness of diversity issues*

• Develop and/or support internal employee affinity groups (e.g., minority or women networks within the firm)

• Increase/review compensation relative to competition

• Increase/improve current work/life programs

• Succession plan includes emphasis on diversity

• Work with minority and women attorneys to develop career advancement plans

• Introduce minority and women attorneys to key clients, including to lead engagements

• Review work assignments and hours billed to key client matters to make sure minority and women attorneys are not being excluded

• Strengthen mentoring program for all attorneys, including minorities and women

• Professional skills development program, including minority and women attorneys

Does your firm have part-time/flex-time policies that permit attorneys (male or female) to work alternative schedules?

Yes. Please see "The Firm Says" on page 410.

What impact, if any, will the decision to work part-time have on an attorney's ability to make partner or, if already a partner, to remain a partner at your firm?

None.

Have any attorneys who chose to work a part-time schedule made partner at your firm?

Yes, seven attorneys.

Management Demographic Profile (as of 12/31/03)

Please provide information regarding all minority and women attorneys who head offices or practice groups of your law firm:

Minorities or women heading offices: We do not have any attorneys who head our offices. All are overseen by the Executive Committee, which is chaired by one attorney.

Women heading practice groups: Elizabeth C. Barton, Environmental and Land Use Department

The Firm Says

Day, Berry & Howard LLP is committed to developing a work force that reflects our community and our clients. We have established programs and policies to recruit and retain minority and women attorneys and staff, and to encourage community involvement.

We provide equal employment opportunity at all times without regard to race, color, religion, gender, citizenship status, age, national origin, disability, veteran status, sexual orientation, or any other state or federal law protected status. This applies to recruiting, hiring, training, promoting, evaluating, terminating, compensating, benefits eligibility, working conditions and other employment issues. We actively recruit and retain a diverse workforce which both supports our Equal Employment Opportunity Policy and furthers our ability to provide our clients excellent legal service.

This statement, which the partners have adopted, embodies our commitment to diversity:

Each of us at Day, Berry and Howard, working individually and together, is committed to the principle that every person at the Firm deserves to be treated with dignity and respect. We are proud of our tradition of fostering and maintaining a work environment in which the diversity of each individual is valued and celebrated. We aspire to develop and manage a strong and inclusive Day, Berry and Howard, firm-wide.

We believe that the contributions of each individual are essential to our continued growth and to our ultimate goal of providing to our clients the highest quality legal services in a timely manner at a reasonable cost. We believe that our diversity contributes to our ability to serve our clients more effectively.

We are committed to, and each of us is expected to support, our efforts to foster an inclusive atmosphere that seeks actively to employ people of diverse backgrounds at all levels of the Firm, and to provide, wherever possible, challenging opportunities, meaningful guidance and positive incentives to assist each person to achieve his or her greatest potential.

We are committed to taking full advantage of the rich backgrounds and abilities of our colleagues and to promoting greater diversity and inclusiveness whenever and wherever possible. We are committed to encouraging individual initiatives and contributions as well as teamwork and collaboration.

We believe that we can create advantage from our differences to build richer, broader common values and goals.

Recruiting

We constantly strive to increase the numbers of our minority and women attorney colleagues. We recruit through law school placement offices, participate in non-traditional recruiting venues, including the University of Connecticut Law School's Cultural Diversity Initiative, the Boston Lawyers Group annual job fair and the Hispanic National Bar Association's annual convention.

Retention

We understand that we must do more than simply bring minority and women attorneys through the door; we strive to offer an environment that will enable our attorneys to thrive. These initiatives help ensure that the voices of minority and women attorneys are heard:

Our Diversity & Sensitivity Committee, comprised of attorneys and staff from every firm office, provides a forum to address women and minority issues. The committee sponsors the firm's participation in the Boston Lawyers Group, the Connecticut Lawyers Group, the Connecticut Hispanic Bar Association and the George W. Crawford Law Association.

The Minority Attorney Mentoring Program pairs each member of the firm's Executive Committee with one or more minority associate to ensure that minority associates have a direct communication line to the firm's leadership. These partners and associates attend quarterly dinner meetings to discuss firm diversity initiatives.

- Women Working Together (WWT)® is charged with promoting women's issues inside and outside the firm. WWT's mission includes:
  - Enhancing opportunities for DBH women to succeed and become leaders in the profession;
  - Establishing a forum for DBH women lawyers and women in the legal and business communities meet and develop professional opportunities;
  - Maintaining a supportive environment for DBH women; and
  - Supporting women's initiatives in the greater community.

- Available to all firm attorneys, our Part-time/Flex-time Program, enables attorneys to make reduced, but proportionate, commitments to billable client work and professional and client development. Part-time attorneys are compensated proportionally to full-time attorneys and are eligible for partnership consideration when they accumulate the requisite seniority.

- We participate in the Boston and Connecticut Lawyers Groups, which focus on the hiring, retaining and promoting minority talent. We have taken a leadership role in these organizations, which are comprised of leading firms and in-house law departments and work to educate the profession about diversity. We provide the CLG executive director, who resides in our Hartford office, with support staff and resources.

• We sponsor diversity activities dedicated to the minority community concerns. Each year the firm celebrates Black History Month with a firm-wide trivia contest. We publicize book, movie and recipe recommendations reflecting African-American history and culture. Each office celebrates African-American fare, art and music. We invite speakers from cultural institutions such as the Amistad Foundation, to speak. We sponsor the ASPIRA of New York, Inc. Annual Circle of Latino Achievers luncheon and our local Juneteenth celebration. Our attorneys have opportunities to mentor minority law students from the University of Connecticut School of Law.

Business case for diversity

The firm communicates the link between diversity and business success in many ways, including a presentation at a partners' meeting by the senior vice president and general counsel of the American Corporate Counsel Association, Susan Hackett, on the business case for diversity. After this event, firm leadership included diversity as a stated factor in partner compensation.

Debevoise & Plimpton LLP

919 Third Avenue
New York, NY 10022
Phone: (212) 909-6000
Fax: (212) 909-6836

FIRM LEADERSHIP

Managing Partner: Martin Frederick Evans,
Presiding Partner
Diversity Team Leader: Richard D. Bohm,
Partner and Diversity Committee Chair

LOCATIONS

New York, NY (HQ)
Washington, DC
Frankfurt
Hong Kong
London
Moscow
Paris
Shanghai

LAW FIRM DEMOGRAPHIC PROFILES

FULL-TIME ASSOCIATES	2003	2002
Minority men	28	22
Minority women	66	53
White women	140	122
Total	374	352

SUMMER ASSOCIATES	2003	2002
Minority men	7	3
Minority women	8	14
White women	37	31
Total	95	76

EQUITY PARTNERS	2003	2002
Minority men	2	2
Minority women	1	1
White women	16	15
Total	105	106

COUNSEL	2003	2002
Minority men	1	1
Minority women	1	0
White women	8	8
Total	29	22

NEW HIRES	2003	2002
Minority men	6	5
Minority women	14	18
White women	34	35
Total	87	100

Strategic Plan and Diversity Leadership

How does the firm's leadership communicate the importance of diversity to everyone at the firm? (e.g., e-mails, web site, newsletters, meetings, etc.)

The firm's web site includes a section on diversity at Debevoise, and the firm's intranet includes a diversity page, including information on the committee's activities and the firm's Diversity Policy. In addition, the presiding partner publishes quarterly reports to the entire firm that have included Diversity Committee news. On a periodic basis, the chair of the Diversity Committee reports to the firm's partners on diversity initiatives.

Who has primary responsibility for leading diversity initiatives at your firm?

The Diversity Committee, currently chaired by partner Richard Bohm

Does your law firm currently have a diversity committee?

Yes

Does the committee's representation include one or more members of the firm's management/executive committee (or the equivalent)?

No. The eight partners on the Diversity Committee make regular reports to the Management Committee and report frequently to the presiding partner of the firm.

How many attorneys are on the committee, and in 2003, what was the total number of hours collectively spent by the committee in furtherance of the firm's diversity initiatives?

Total attorneys on committee: 27

Total hours spent on diversity: 800 hours for the one-year period from June 1, 2003 to May 31, 2004.

Does the committee and/or diversity leader establish and set goals or objectives consistent with management's priorities?

Yes

Has the firm undertaken a formal or informal diversity program or set of initiatives aimed at increasing the diversity of the firm?

Yes, formal

How often does the firm's management review the firm's diversity progress/results?

Quarterly

How is the firm's diversity committee and/or firm management held accountable for achieving results?

The Diversity Committee is formulating a diversity action plan, and the committee meets on a monthly or more frequent basis to review progress on initiatives and programs being implemented by the committee. In addition, the committee regularly reviews hiring and attrition statistics to monitor trends in hiring and retention for race and gender.

LAW FIRM DIVERSITY INITIATIVES	ALREADY COMPLETED	CURRENTLY ADDRESSING	NOT A CURRENT PRIORITY
Undertake communication from firm management that diversity is a top priority of the firm.	✓		
Formalize diversity plan and committee with action steps and accountability to management.		✓	
Conduct firm-wide diversity training for all attorneys and staff.			✓
Increase the number of minority attorneys at the associate level.		✓	
Increase the number of minority attorneys at the partnership level.		✓	
Develop/expand relationships with minority bar associations to offer firm's support of these networks.		✓	
Focus on strengthening firm's mentoring program, including for benefit of minority attorneys.		✓	
Conduct internal diversity needs assessment and/or retain diversity consultant to examine how firm culture might be more welcoming of minorities.	✓		
Support law firm's internal affinity networks (e.g., women, minority attorney networks).	✓		
Manage/monitor allocation of work assignments and/or hours billed to ensure women and minority attorneys have equal access/inclusion on top client matters.		✓	
One strategy of Debevoise's Diversity Committee is that diversity training should be a regular, ongoing component of existing lawyer orientation and skills/substantive training programs where appropriate.		✓	

Recruitment – New Associates

Does your firm annually recruit at any of the following types of institutions? (Check all that apply and list the schools).

Ivy League schools: Columbia University, Cornell University, Harvard University, University of Pennsylvania, Yale University

Public state schools: University of California-Boalt, University of Texas, Rutgers University, University of Michigan, University of Virginia, College of William & Mary

Private schools: Albany University, Boston College, Boston University, Brigham Young University, Brooklyn Law School, Cardozo Law School, University of Chicago, Duke University, Emory University, Fordham University, Georgetown University, New York Law School, NYU, Northwestern University, St. John's University, Stanford University, Tulane University, Washington & Lee University

Historically Black Colleges and Universities (HBCUs): Howard University

Do you have any special outreach efforts directed to encourage minority law students to consider your firm?

- Hold a reception for minority law students
- Participate in/host minority law student job fair(s)
- Sponsor minority law student association events
- Firm's lawyers participate on career panels at school
- Outreach to leadership of minority student organizations

SUMMER ASSOCIATE STATISTICS: SUMMER 2003	MINORITY MEN	MINORITY WOMEN	WHITE WOMEN	TOTAL
Summer associates	7	8	37	95
Summer associates who received an offer of full-time employment	7	8	37	95
Summer associates who accepted an offer of full-time employment	7	7	20	60

Recruitment – Lateral Associates and Partners

LATERAL ASSOCIATES AND PARTNERS: 1/1/03 – 12/31/03	MINORITY MEN	MINORITY WOMEN	WHITE WOMEN	TOTAL
Number of lateral associate hires	1	0	2	5
Number of lateral partner hires (equity and non-equity)	0	0	0	1
Number of new partners (equity and non-equity) promoted from associate rank	0	0	1	2
Number of new equity partners	0	0	1	2

Retention & Professional Development

ATTORNEYS WHO LEFT THE FIRM: 2003	MINORITY MEN	MINORITY WOMEN	WHITE WOMEN	TOTAL
Number of attorneys who voluntarily or involuntarily left your firm's employ in 2003	3	3	13	39

How do 2003 attrition rates generally compare to those experienced in the prior year period?

Lower than in prior years

Please identify the specific steps you are taking to reduce the attrition rate of minority and women attorneys.

• *Part-time program*

• Develop and/or support internal employee affinity groups (e.g., minority or women networks within the firm)

• Increase/improve current work/life programs

• Strengthen mentoring program for all attorneys, including minorities and women

• Professional skills development program, including minority and women attorneys

Does your firm have part-time/flex-time policies that permit attorneys (male or female) to work alternative schedules?

Yes

What impact, if any, will the decision to work part-time have on an attorney's ability to make partner or, if already a partner, to remain a partner at your firm?

The firm has a written part-time work policy that includes a statement that part-time lawyers are eligible for partnership consideration.

Have any attorneys who chose to work a part-time schedule made partner at your firm?

Yes, seven attorneys.

Management Demographic Profile (as of 12/31/03)

	MINORITY MEN	MINORITY WOMEN	WHITE WOMEN	TOTAL
Number of attorneys on the Executive/Management Committee or equivalent	0	0	1	8
Number of attorneys on the Hiring Committee or equivalent	0	0	2	5
Number of attorneys on the Partner/Associate Review Committee or equivalent	0	0	5	22

Please provide information regarding all minority and women attorneys who head offices or practice groups of your law firm:

Minorities heading practice groups: Byungkwon Lim, Chair of the Derivatives and Structured Finance Group; Ivan Mattei, Chair of the Project Finance Group

Women heading practice groups: Mary Jo White, Chair of the Litigation Department; Franci Blassberg and Margaret Davenport, Co-Chairs of the Private Equity Group

The Firm Says

Diversity Mission Statement

Debevoise & Plimpton LLP has long been committed to attracting, retaining and promoting a diverse population of lawyers and administrative staff as part of building the strongest possible firm. To ensure continuing focus on that commitment, the firm has an active Diversity Committee that manages diversity issues at the firm in three general areas: recruiting, retention and professional development, and education and communications. The committee is organized in three subcommittees that have responsibility for defining and implementing strategies and programs to realize diversity objectives in these three areas. The committee coordinates with the Hiring Committee to enhance the firm's ability to recruit talented lawyers and staff of diverse backgrounds. The committee reviews and develops activities and programs to promote professional development and training opportunities that enhance the retention and advancement of our diverse community. The committee also works to promote awareness, provide education and encourage open and ongoing discussions about diversity issues throughout the firm.

The Diversity Committee created a policy statement both to help focus the committee's efforts and to convey to our community the firm's policy on diversity.

Diversity Policy

Scope: This policy applies to all members of the Debevoise community.

Statement: One of the greatest strengths of Debevoise & Plimpton LLP is its community. The fundamental values of the firm articulate the importance of "cohesiveness and collegiality within the firm, founded in the character of those we select as partners, counsel, associates and staff and in fundamental principles of fairness and cooperation" with "an emphasis on the success of the firm as a whole."

Debevoise is committed to creating a work environment that values each individual's contributions to our community. We recognize that we must work together every day to respect the different backgrounds, perspectives and experiences of people at the firm and to support our colleagues so they have the ability to develop to their full potential. These values are a foundation of our firm and strengthen our ability to work together as a team so that we can provide our clients with the best legal services available.

Debevoise is committed to promoting the diversity of our community. This commitment stems naturally from the values that shape our firm. To continue to flourish, our firm will strive to recruit and develop the finest talent of all backgrounds and beliefs. Our ability to respond to the needs of our clients, in an increasingly open and global environment, requires that the members of our community have a broad range of skills and experiences. The firm's commitment to diversity furthers these goals.

Part-time program

Debevoise & Plimpton LLP has an established part-time work program. The firm recognizes the difficulties of balancing our professional and family lives and assigns a high priority to helping lawyers in the firm find and maintain the right balance for them. In some cases, lawyers wish to work on a part-time basis following the birth or adoption of a child, or for other family reasons. The firm is as supportive and flexible as possible in assisting lawyers who wish to consider this option. Currently, seven U.S.-based partners, three counsel and 27 associates are working a part-time schedule.

Diversity pro bono services

Debevoise lawyers support diversity in their pro bono commitments, including the following recent or current representations:

• Venture Capital Association of Nigeria (VCAN) in conjunction with the Community Development Venture Capital Alliance. This project relates to possible amendments to recent regulations that require Nigerian banks to set aside 10 percent of their pre-tax profits to make equity investments within Nigeria.

• Harlem Textile Works, an organization that provides Black and Latino young adults with design training and job readiness skills.

• The African American Music Hall of Fame and Museum (TAAMHOF), an organization established to chronicle, celebrate and preserve the legacy of African American performing artists.

• Girls Action Network, Inc. (GAN), an organization established to empower girls through vocational awareness and to increase the likelihood of their success in terms of skill sets, salary, self-esteem, community, civic and corporate participation. GAN serves girls in grades 7 to 12 with a particular focus on girls from under-served communities. A Debevoise lawyer founded and sits on the board of directors of GAN.

• Lawyers Committee for Human Rights asylum cases for clients from all over the world, including Columbia, the Democratic Republic of Congo, Zimbabwe and the People's Republic of China, among many other countries.

Diversity financial support

Debevoise & Plimpton has provided financial contributions to various minority public interest organizations, including the Africa-America Institute, the Asian American Legal Defense & Education Fund, the Minority Corporate Counsel Association, the Japanese Chamber of Commerce, the Lambda Legal Gala Defense Fund, NOW Legal Defense and Education Fund, and the Office of Diversity of the Association of the Bar of the City of New York.

2004 diversity developments

In 2004, Debevoise & Plimpton added a lateral minority male partner and promoted to partner a minority male from its associate ranks.

Dewey Ballantine LLP

1301 Avenue of the Americas
New York, NY 10019
Phone: (212) 259-8000
Fax: (212) 259-6333

FIRM LEADERSHIP

Managing Partner: Sanford W. Morhouse and
Morton A. Pierce, Chairpersons of the
Management Committee
Diversity Team Leader: Janis M. Meyer,
Chairperson, Diversity Committee

LOCATIONS

New York, NY (HQ)
Austin, TX
East Palo Alto, CA
Houston, TX
Los Angeles, CA
Washington, DC
Budapest
Frankfurt
London
Milan
Prague
Rome
Warsaw

LAW FIRM DEMOGRAPHIC PROFILES

FULL-TIME ASSOCIATES	2003	2002
Minority men	29	32
Minority women	36	34
White women	101	110
Total	315	310

SUMMER ASSOCIATES	2003	2002
Minority men	8	7
Minority women	11	13
White women	33	22
Total	80	70

EQUITY PARTNERS	2003	2002
Minority men	3	3
Minority women	2	2
White women	18	15
Total	106	105

NON-EQUITY PARTNERS	2003	2002
Minority men	1	0
Minority women	1	1
White women	3	5
Total	32	32

NEW HIRES	2003	2002
Minority men	5	6
Minority women	13	16
White women	28	45
Total	85	137

Strategic Plan and Diversity Leadership

How does the firm's leadership communicate the importance of diversity to everyone at the firm? (e.g., e-mails, web site, newsletters, meetings, etc.)

E-mails, web site, meetings, newsletters, sponsorship of diversity functions

Who has primary responsibility for leading diversity initiatives at your firm?

Janis M. Meyer, Chairperson, Diversity Committee

Does your law firm currently have a diversity committee?

Yes

Does the committee's representation include one or more members of the firm's management/executive committee (or the equivalent)?

Yes

How many attorneys are on the committee, and in 2003, what was the total number of hours collectively spent by the committee in furtherance of the firm's diversity initiatives?

Total attorneys on committee: 17

Total hours spent on diversity: N/A (Committee was formed in first quarter of 2004.)

Does the committee and/or diversity leader establish and set goals or objectives consistent with management's priorities?

Yes

Has the firm undertaken a formal or informal diversity program or set of initiatives aimed at increasing the diversity of the firm?

Yes, formal

How often does the firm's management review the firm's diversity progress/results?

Twice a year

How is the firm's diversity committee and/or firm management held accountable for achieving results?

The firm strives to reach the goals set by the Statement of Diversity Principles of the Association of the Bar of the City of New York. Time spent on diversity initiatives is one factor in partner performance measurements.

LAW FIRM DIVERSITY INITIATIVES	ALREADY COMPLETED	CURRENTLY ADDRESSING	NOT A CURRENT PRIORITY
Undertake communication from firm management that diversity is a top priority of the firm.	✓		
Formalize diversity plan and committee with action steps and accountability to management.		✓	
Conduct firm-wide diversity training for all attorneys and staff.	✓		
Increase the number of minority attorneys at the associate level.		✓	
Increase the number of minority attorneys at the partnership level.		✓	
Develop/expand relationships with minority bar associations to offer firm's support of these networks.		✓	
Focus on strengthening firm's mentoring program, including for benefit of minority attorneys.		✓	
Conduct internal diversity needs assessment and/or retain diversity consultant to examine how firm culture might be more welcoming of minorities.		✓	
Support law firm's internal affinity networks (e.g., women, minority attorney networks).		✓	
Manage/monitor allocation of work assignments and/or hours billed to ensure women and minority attorneys have equal access/inclusion on top client matters.		✓	

Recruitment – New Associates

Does your firm annually recruit at any of the following types of institutions? (Check all that apply and list the schools).

Ivy League schools: Columbia University, Cornell University, Harvard University, University of Pennsylvania, Yale University

Public state schools: SUNY-Buffalo, University of Michigan, University of Minnesota, University of Virginia, College of William & Mary

Private schools: Albany Law School, Boston College, Boston University, Brookyn Law School, Cardozo Law School, University of Chicago, Duke University, Emory University, Fordham University, Georgetown University, Hofstra University, Northwestern University, University of Notre Dame, NYU, Stanford University, St. John's University, Syracuse University, Washington and Lee University, Washington University

Historically Black Colleges and Universities (HBCUs): Howard University

Do you have any special outreach efforts directed to encourage minority law students to consider your firm?

• *Hiring 1L minority students for summer program*

• Hold receptions for minority law students

• Advertise in minority law student association publication(s)

• Participate in/host minority law student job fair(s)

• Sponsor minority law student association events

• Firm's lawyers participate on career panels at school

• Outreach to leadership of minority student organizations

• Scholarships or intern/fellowships for minority students

SUMMER ASSOCIATE STATISTICS: SUMMER 2003	MINORITY MEN	MINORITY WOMEN	WHITE WOMEN	TOTAL
Summer associates	8	11	33	80
Summer associates who received an offer of full-time employment	8	11	33	78
Summer associates who accepted an offer of full-time employment	6	10	27	65

Recruitment – Lateral Associates and Partners

What activities does the firm undertake to attract minority and women attorneys?

• Partner programs with women and minority bar associations

• Participate at minority job fairs

• Seek referrals from other attorneys

Do you use executive recruiting/search firms to seek to identify new diversity hires (partners or associates)?

No

LATERAL ASSOCIATES AND PARTNERS: 1/1/03 – 12/31/03	MINORITY MEN	MINORITY WOMEN	WHITE WOMEN	TOTAL
Number of lateral associate hires	2	0	4	15
Number of lateral partner hires (equity and non-equity)	0	0	1	7
Number of new partners (equity and non-equity) promoted from associate rank	1	0	1	6
Number of new equity partners	0	0	1	7

Retention & Professional Development

ATTORNEYS WHO LEFT THE FIRM: 2003	MINORITY MEN	MINORITY WOMEN	WHITE WOMEN	TOTAL
Number of attorneys who voluntarily or involuntarily left your firm's employ in 2003	8	12	37	105

How do 2003 attrition rates generally compare to those experienced in the prior year period?

Higher than in prior years

Please identify the specific steps you are taking to reduce the attrition rate of minority and women attorneys.

• Increase/review compensation relative to competition

• Increase/improve current work/life programs

• Succession plan includes emphasis on diversity

• Work with minority and women attorneys to develop career advancement plans

• Introduce minority and women attorneys to key clients, including to lead engagements

• Review work assignments and hours billed to key client matters to make sure minority and women attorneys are not being excluded

• Strengthen mentoring program for all attorneys, including minorities and women

• Professional skills development program, including minority and women attorneys

Does your firm have part-time/flex-time policies that permit attorneys (male or female) to work alternative schedules?

Yes

What impact, if any, will the decision to work part-time have on an attorney's ability to make partner or, if already a partner, to remain a partner at your firm?

Participation in a flexible work arrangement does not change an associate's eligibility for promotion, including eligibility for partnership. However, participation in certain flexible work arrangements may impact the timing of an associate's career progression. Partial workload associates are mindful that attaining the required proficiency for promotion may take more time, simply because less time is spent on professional pursuits. Accordingly, it may take longer to meet the criteria for promotion. The ability to work a flexible arrangement as a partner would be considered based on the respective practice area needs. Seven partners currently work flexible schedules.

Have any attorneys who chose to work a part-time schedule made partner at your firm?

Yes, two attorneys.

Management Demographic Profile (as of 12/31/03)

	MINORITY MEN	MINORITY WOMEN	WHITE WOMEN	TOTAL
Number of attorneys on the Executive/Management Committee or equivalent	0	0	0	5/15*
Number of attorneys on the Hiring Committee or equivalent	3	1	6	28
Number of attorneys on the Partner/Associate Review Committee or equivalent	3	2	5	26

* Numbers listed as: Executive Committee/Management Committee

Please provide information regarding all minority and women attorneys who head offices or practice groups of your law firm:

Minorities heading offices: James D. Smith, Austin; Jeannine Sano, East Palo Alto

Women heading offices: Jeannine Sano, East Palo Alto

Minorities heading practice groups: Junaid Chida, Leasing

The Firm Says

Dewey Ballantine LLP is an initial signatory to the Statement of Diversity Principles of the Association of the Bar of the City of New York and a founding contributor to the newly established Office of Diversity of the City Bar. A firm partner serves on the City Bar's Committee to Enhance Diversity in the Profession and Committee on Recruitment and Retention. The firm has participated for a number of years in the Minority Fellowship Program sponsored by the City Bar and the Equal Justice America Fellowship Program.

The firm has established a Diversity Committee whose members include partners from our U.S. and European offices. The Diversity Committee is currently working on initiatives to increase hiring, retention and promotion of minorities and to ensure that Dewey Ballantine continues to maintain a working environment that is respectful and welcoming to all.

Members of the firm's Executive and Diversity Committees meet periodically with representatives of bar associations and minority organizations to discuss ways to develop procedures and programs to make the firm a welcoming place for all who work here. We also give financial support to bar and student groups that represent minorities. We encourage our lawyers to be active in such groups to ensure the continued flow of ideas. Some of the groups we support include the Asian American Bar Association of New York, Asian American Legal Defense and Education Fund, Asian Americans for Equality, Asian Professional Extension, Asian Pacific American Law Students Association, Black Law Students Association, Latin American Law Students Association, Metropolitan Black Bar Association, National Asian Pacific American Bar Association, the Thurgood Marshall Scholarship Fund, and the Lesbian and Gay Law Association Foundation of Greater New York.

The firm does a significant amount of pro bono work on behalf of organizations that serve minority communities. We support, among others, the Martin Luther King High School Mock Trial Program in New York State, the New York State Defenders Association Immigration Defense Project, the Auschwitz Jewish Center Foundation and

the New York Women's Foundation, Sakhi for South Asian Women, New York Asian Women's Center, Korean American Family Service Center and the Coalition for Asian American Children and Families. We are currently working with community leaders to develop pro bono relationships with additional not-for-profit organizations supporting minority issues.

We also meet with law student organizations to maintain an open dialogue between these groups and the firm and to increase awareness of the firm among students of color. We host a number of events focused specifically on the needs and interests of minority students. The firm has provided grants to several law schools to provide scholarships for students of underrepresented populations and to fund diversity-related projects.

Members of the firm's Executive Committee and Diversity Committee meet with associates to discuss diversity-related issues and consider the associates' perspectives. We have developed a new mentoring program firm-wide with the goal of assisting in ensuring that all of our associates are given the opportunity to develop their careers in an environment where they can seek the advice and counsel of a more senior lawyer. As part of this program, our lawyers will recieve mentoring training. All new employees receive training on diversity and prevention of harassment training. In addition, a comprehensive training program is conducted every two years for all employees.

Dickstein Shapiro Morin & Oshinsky, LLP

2101 L. Street NW
Washington, DC 20037-1526
Phone: (202) 785-9700
Fax: (202) 887-0689

FIRM LEADERSHIP

Managing Partner: Michael E. Nannes
Diversity Team Leader: Peter Kadzik and
Emanuel Faust, Diversity Committee Co-Chairs
Diversity Counsel: C. Elaine Arabatzis

LOCATIONS

Washington, DC (HQ)
New York, NY

LAW FIRM DEMOGRAPHIC PROFILES

FULL-TIME ASSOCIATES	2003	2002
Minority men	13	16
Minority women	16	13
White women	66	72
Total	196	217

SUMMER ASSOCIATES	2003	2002
Minority men	6	2
Minority women	3	4
White women	11	10
Total	30	28

EQUITY PARTNERS	2003	2002
Minority men	2	2
Minority women	0	0
White women	16	17
Total	105	101

NON-EQUITY PARTNERS	2003	2002
Minority men	1	1
Minority women	0	0
White women	2	1
Total	14	7

NEW HIRES	2003	2002
Minority men	3	6
Minority women	5	2
White women	9	13
Total	39	38

Strategic Plan and Diversity Leadership

Who has primary responsibility for leading diversity initiatives at your firm?

Diversity Committee Co-Chairs Peter Kadzik and Emanuel Faust and Diversity Counsel Elaine Arabatzis

Does your law firm currently have a diversity committee?

Yes

Does the committee's representation include one or more members of the firm's management/executive committee (or the equivalent)?

No

How many attorneys are on the committee, and in 2003, what was the total number of hours collectively spent by the committee in furtherance of the firm's diversity initiatives?

Total attorneys on committee: 5

Total hours spent on diversity: 1,450

Does the committee and/or diversity leader establish and set goals or objectives consistent with management's priorities?

Yes

Has the firm undertaken a formal or informal diversity program or set of initiatives aimed at increasing the diversity of the firm?

Yes, formal

How often does the firm's management review the firm's diversity progress/results?

Monthly. The managing partner is actively involved in the firm's diversity program and reviews diversity activities and progress on at least a monthly basis.

How is the firm's diversity committee and/or firm management held accountable for achieving results?

There is no formal accountability process for diversity, but the efforts and results of the process are factored into individual evaluations for partners, associates and staff participating in those activities.

LAW FIRM DIVERSITY INITIATIVES	ALREADY COMPLETED	CURRENTLY ADDRESSING	NOT A CURRENT PRIORITY
Undertake communication from firm management that diversity is a top priority of the firm.	✓		
Formalize diversity plan and committee with action steps and accountability to management.	✓		
Conduct firm-wide diversity training for all attorneys and staff.	✓		
Increase the number of minority attorneys at the associate level.	✓		
Increase the number of minority attorneys at the partnership level.	✓		
Develop/expand relationships with minority bar associations to offer firm's support of these networks.		✓	
Focus on strengthening firm's mentoring program, including for benefit of minority attorneys.		✓	
Conduct internal diversity needs assessment and/or retain diversity consultant to examine how firm culture might be more welcoming of minorities.	✓		
Support law firm's internal affinity networks (e.g., women, minority attorney networks).		✓	
Manage/monitor allocation of work assignments and/or hours billed to ensure women and minority attorneys have equal access/inclusion on top client matters.		✓	

Recruitment - New Associates

Does your firm annually recruit at any of the following types of institutions? (Check all that apply and list the schools).

Ivy League schools: Columbia University, Cornell University, University of Pennsylvania, Harvard University

Public state schools: University of Illinois, University of Maryland, Rutgers University, University of Virginia, University of Michigan, University of North Carolina

Private schools: American University, Catholic University of America, Duke University, Fordham University, George Washington University, Georgetown University, NYU, McGill University, Cardozo Law School, University of Chicago.

Historically Black Colleges and Universities (HBCUs): Howard University

Do you have any special outreach efforts directed to encourage minority law students to consider your firm?

• Hold a reception for minority law students

• Advertise in minority law student association publication(s)

• Participate in/host minority law student job fair(s)

• Sponsor minority law student association events

• Firm's lawyers participate on career panels at school

• Outreach to leadership of minority student organizations

SUMMER ASSOCIATE STATISTICS: SUMMER 2003	MINORITY MEN	MINORITY WOMEN	WHITE WOMEN	TOTAL
Summer associates	5	3	9	24
Summer associates who received an offer of full-time employment	3	3	8	21
Summer associates who accepted an offer of full-time employment	3	3	6	17

Recruitment – Lateral Associates and Partners

What activities does the firm undertake to attract minority and women attorneys?

• Participate at minority job fairs

• Seek referrals from other attorneys

Do you use executive recruiting/search firms to seek to identify new diversity hires (partners or associates)?

Yes

If yes, list all women- and/or minority-owned executive search/recruiting firms to which the firm paid a fee for placement services in the past 12 months:

None.

LATERAL ASSOCIATES AND PARTNERS: 1/1/03 – 12/31/03	MINORITY MEN	MINORITY WOMEN	WHITE WOMEN	TOTAL
Number of lateral associate hires	0	3	3	14
Number of lateral partner hires (equity and non-equity)	0	0	0	8
Number of new partners (equity and non-equity) promoted from associate rank	0	0	1	5
Number of new equity partners	0	0	0	0

Retention & Professional Development

ATTORNEYS WHO LEFT THE FIRM: 2003	MINORITY MEN	MINORITY WOMEN	WHITE WOMEN	TOTAL
Number of attorneys who voluntarily or involuntarily left your firm's employ in 2003	3	1	13	43

How do 2003 attrition rates generally compare to those experienced in the prior year period?

About the same as in prior years

Please identify the specific steps you are taking to reduce the attrition rate of minority and women attorneys.

• Develop and/or support internal employee affinity groups (e.g., minority or women networks within the firm)

• Increase/review compensation relative to competition

• Increase/improve current work/life programs

• Work with minority and women attorneys to develop career advancement plans

• Introduce minority and women attorneys to key clients, including to lead engagements

• Strengthen mentoring program for all attorneys, including minorities and women

• Professional skills development program, including minority and women attorneys

Does your firm have part-time/flex-time policies that permit attorneys (male or female) to work alternative schedules?

Yes

What impact, if any, will the decision to work part-time have on an attorney's ability to make partner or, if already a partner, to remain a partner at your firm?

The firm has a formal flexible work schedule policy that provides that attorneys maintaining a 50 percent or greater work schedule are eligible for partnership. The decision to work part-time has no impact on an attorney's ability to make partner or, if already a partner, to remain a partner, although an attorney who works a substantially reduced schedule as a junior associate may take more time to acquire the skills and experience necessary to make partner.

Have any attorneys who chose to work a part-time schedule made partner at your firm?

Yes, five part-time attorneys have been made partner at the firm.

Management Demographic Profile (as of 12/31/03)

	MINORITY MEN	MINORITY WOMEN	WHITE WOMEN	TOTAL
Number of attorneys on the Executive/Management Committee or equivalent	0	0	1	10
Number of attorneys on the Hiring Committee or equivalent	0	1	3	11
Number of attorneys on the Partner/Associate Review Committee or equivalent	0	0	3	7

Please provide information regarding all minority and women attorneys who head offices or practice groups of your law firm:

Women heading offices: Robin Cohen, New York

Women heading practice groups: Elaine Metlin, D.C. Litigation; Karen Bush, Insurance Coverage

The Firm Says

At Dickstein Shapiro Morin & Oshinsky LLP, diversity is a top priority. Our Diversity Committee's Mission Statement speaks to the firm's level of commitment:

The Diversity Committee, whose members include staff, managers, associates and partners of diverse backgrounds, is charged with the responsibility of developing, implementing and overseeing the progress of the Firm's diversity initiatives, to increase diversity throughout the Firm. The Committee's objective is to improve the recruitment, retention and advancement of diverse employees and attorneys.

The Diversity Committee is comprised of partners, associates and staff members from our D.C. and New York offices. The committee, which meets on a biweekly basis, works closely with the firm's diversity consultant and has developed and implemented a three-year Strategic Plan that includes goals, objectives and action items regarding recruitment, retention and the ongoing role of the Diversity Committee. The firm's diversity consultant, Dr. Arin N. Reeves of The Athens Group, conducted an in-depth assessment of the firm and then presented the results and made recommendations to the full partnership for future diversity initiatives that were incorporated into the diversity Strategic Plan. Dr. Reeves then facilitated the ensuing diversity dialogues among the partners and trained over 30 in-house dialogue facilitators. She also oversees ongoing diversity dialogues for all attorneys and staff.

In 2004, Dickstein Shapiro created the full-time position of diversity and pro bono counsel to focus on the firm's expanding diversity and pro bono initiatives. Our diversity counsel and diversity consultant are presently working together to develop the next phase of the firm's diversity programs. The firm has also assembled a library of materials relating to diversity issues.

The firm has also made great progress toward its strategic goal of increasing the number of diverse partners. We recently brought on three new diverse partners along with a number of diverse counsel and associates. Our 2004 summer associate program similarly reflects our commitment to diversity, with 10 diverse summer associates in this year's summer program.

The firm has also been added to DuPont's Primary Law Firm (PLF) and Service Provider Network. In the DuPont Legal Model, PLFs and service providers are carefully selected to serve as "strategic partners" with DuPont on the basis of competence, technology, contribution to women and minorities, creativity, financial costs and rewards, innovation and more.

Dickstein Shapiro's internal Policy Manual, which is provided to all employees, states that the firm is committed "to creating a work environment in which all employees, regardless of race, color, national origin, sex, age, physical handicap, matriculation, family responsibilities, personal appearance, political affiliation, credit status, marital status, religious affiliation or sexual orientation, enjoy equal opportunities in their employment relationship with the firm." Additionally, the firm, through its Executive Committee, has established and published to all employees its "Core Values of excellence, loyalty, respect (amplified to emphasize the

importance of respect for 'our clients, our attorneys, and our staff, and belief in an environment that offers equal opportunity for all'), initiative and integrity."

Enhancing diversity at all levels is part of the firm's current Strategic Plan. To achieve this goal the firm strives to promote diversity through example and education. Since 2003, the firm has implemented an ongoing series of diversity speaker presentations which have involved high-profile leaders in the community coming to the firm to speak to all partners, attorneys and staff, about diversity-related issues. Speakers have included Elizabeth Birch, former executive director of the Human Rights Campaign, the nation's largest gay, lesbian, bisexual and transgender advocacy organization; Hilary Rosen, an on-air business and political commentator for CNBC and the former chairman and chief executive officer of the Recording Industry Association of America (RIAA); Debra Lee, president and chief operating officer of Black Entertainment Television (BET); Kurt L. Schmoke, dean of Howard University School of Law and former mayor of Baltimore; Dr. Benjamin Hooks, former executive director of the NAACP and U.S. Rep. Barney Frank, the first openly gay member of Congress.

The firm recruits minority candidates aggressively and participates in a number of minority recruiting activities and conferences, including participation in the BLSA Mid-Atlantic Job Fair and the Minority Corporate Counsel Association's (MCCA) Diversity 2000 Club. The firm also sponsored the 2003 and 2004 MCCA annual conferences and several of the related diversity dinners. The firm recently ranked sixth in diversity initiatives in The American Lawyer's Summer Associate Survey.

438

Dorsey & Whitney LLP

50 South Sixth Street, Suite 1500
Minneapolis, MN 55402
Phone: (612) 340-2600
Fax: (612) 340-2868

FIRM LEADERSHIP

Managing Partner: Peter Hendrixson, Managing
Partner
Diversity Team Leader: Sandy Edelman,
Diversity Partner

LOCATIONS

Anchorage, AK
Denver, CO
Des Moines, IA
Fargo, ND
Great Falls, MT
Irvine, CA
Minneapolis, MN
Missoula, MT
New York, NY
Palo Alto, CA
Salt Lake City, UT
Seattle, WA
Washington, DC
Hong Kong
London
Shanghai
Toronto
Vancouver

LAW FIRM DEMOGRAPHIC PROFILES

FULL-TIME ASSOCIATES	2003	2002
Minority men	25	26
Minority women	28	20
White women	124	101
Total	363	305

SUMMER ASSOCIATES	2003	2002
Minority men	2	3
Minority women	4	4
White women	8	16
Total	28	58

EQUITY PARTNERS	2003	2002
Minority men	13	12
Minority women	1	1
White women	38	34
Total	244	229

NON-EQUITY PARTNERS	2003	2002
Minority men	2	1
Minority women	1	0
White women	2	3
Total	24	20

NEW HIRES	2003	2002
Minority men	2	6
Minority women	9	4
White women	27	34
Total	77	94

MINORITY CORPORATE COUNSEL ASSOCIATION

Strategic Plan and Diversity Leadership

How does the firm's leadership communicate the importance of diversity to everyone at the firm? (e.g., e-mails, web site, newsletters, meetings, etc.):

Web site and meetings

Who has primary responsibility for leading diversity initiatives at your firm?

Name of person and his/her title: Sandy Edelman, diversity partner

Does your law firm currently have a diversity committee?

Yes

Does the committee's representation include one or more members of the firm's management/executive committee (or the equivalent)?

Yes

How many attorneys are on the committee, and in 2003, what was the total number of hours collectively spent by the committee in furtherance of the firm's diversity initiatives?

Total attorneys on committee: 25

Does the committee and/or diversity leader establish and set goals or objectives consistent with management's priorities?

Yes

Has the firm undertaken a formal or informal diversity program or set of initiatives aimed at increasing the diversity of the firm?

Yes, formal

How often does the firm's management review the firm's diversity progress/results?

Quarterly

How is the firm's diversity committee and/or firm management held accountable for achieving results?

The diversity partners give a quarterly report to the managing partner. Each group head is held accountable for diversity in his or her group, which is reviewed each year.

LAW FIRM DIVERSITY INITIATIVES	ALREADY COMPLETED	CURRENTLY ADDRESSING	NOT A CURRENT PRIORITY
Undertake communication from firm management that diversity is a top priority of the firm.	✓	✓	
Formalize diversity plan and committee with action steps and accountability to management.	✓		
Conduct firm-wide diversity training for all attorneys and staff.		✓	
Increase the number of minority attorneys at the associate level.		✓	
Increase the number of minority attorneys at the partnership level.		✓	
Develop/expand relationships with minority bar associations to offer firm's support of these networks.		✓	
Focus on strengthening firm's mentoring program, including for benefit of minority attorneys.		✓	
Conduct internal diversity needs assessment and/or retain diversity consultant to examine how firm culture might be more welcoming of minorities.			✓
Support law firm's internal affinity networks (e.g., women, minority attorney networks).	✓	✓	
Manage/monitor allocation of work assignments and/or hours billed to ensure women and minority attorneys have equal access/inclusion on top client matters.		✓	

Recruitment – New Associates

Does your firm annually recruit at any of the following types of institutions? (Check all that apply and list the schools).

Ivy League schools: Columbia University, Cornell University, Harvard University, Yale University

Public state schools: University of Iowa, University of Michigan, University of Minnesota, University of Virginia, University of Washington, University of Wisconsin, University of California-Berkeley (Boalt Hall), University of California-Hastings, University of Colorado

Private schools: George Washington University, Georgetown University, Hamline University, NYU, Northwestern University, Santa Clara University, Seattle University, University of Chicago, St. Thomas University, University of Denver, William Mitchell College of Law

Historically Black Colleges and Universities (HBCUs): Howard University

Do you have any special outreach efforts directed to encourage minority law students to consider your firm?

• Participate in/host minority law student job fair(s)

SUMMER ASSOCIATE STATISTICS: SUMMER 2003	MINORITY MEN	MINORITY WOMEN	WHITE WOMEN	TOTAL
Summer associates	2	4	8	28
Summer associates who received an offer of full-time employment	1	3	7	22
Summer associates who accepted an offer of full-time employment	1	2	2	11*

Six summer associates, including three white women, have not accepted or declined offers due to clerkships.

Recruitment - Lateral Associates and Partners

What activities does the firm undertake to attract minority and women attorneys?

• Participate at minority job fairs

• Sponsorship and participation in minority bar events

Do you use executive recruiting/search firms to seek to identify new diversity hires (partners or associates)?

No

Recruitment - Lateral Associates and Partners

LATERAL ASSOCIATES AND PARTNERS: 1/1/03 – 12/31/03	MINORITY MEN	MINORITY WOMEN	WHITE WOMEN	TOTAL
Number of lateral associate hires	3	2	11	20
Number of lateral partner hires (equity and non-equity)	0	1	2	12
Number of new partners (equity and non-equity) promoted from associate rank	1	0	1	7
Number of new equity partners	0	0	1	2

Retention & Professional Development

ATTORNEYS WHO LEFT THE FIRM: 2003	MINORITY MEN	MINORITY WOMEN	WHITE WOMEN	TOTAL
Number of attorneys who voluntarily or involuntarily left your firm's employ in 2003	5	7	36	120

How do 2003 attrition rates generally compare to those experienced in the prior year period?

About the same as in prior years

Please identify the specific steps you are taking to reduce the attrition rate of minority and women attorneys.

• Develop and/or support internal employee affinity groups (e.g., minority or women networks within the firm)

• Increase/review compensation relative to competition

• Increase/improve current work/life programs

• Work with minority and women attorneys to develop career advancement plans

• Strengthen mentoring program for all attorneys, including minorities and women

• Professional skills development program, including minority and women attorneys

Does your firm have part-time/flex-time policies that permit attorneys (male or female) to work alternative schedules?

Yes

What impact, if any, will the decision to work part-time have on an attorney's ability to make partner or, if already a partner, to remain a partner at your firm?

None

Have any attorneys who chose to work a part-time schedule made partner at your firm?

Yes

Management Demographic Profile (as of 12/31/03)

Please provide information regarding all minority and women attorneys who head offices or practice groups of your law firm:

Minorities heading offices: John Manning, Great Falls and Missoula

Women heading offices: Sarah Herman, Fargo; Kathy Lowe, Irvine

Women heading practice groups: Claire Topp, Health Care; Leslie Anderson, Co-Chair, Employee Benefits; Liz Buckingham, Trademark

	MINORITY MEN	MINORITY WOMEN	WHITE WOMEN	TOTAL
Number of attorneys on the Executive/Management Committee or equivalent	0	0	1	9
Number of attorneys on the Hiring Committee or equivalent	6	2	10	38
Number of attorneys on the Partner/Associate Review Committee or equivalent	1/0	0/0	1/2	13/25

* Numbers listed as Partner Review Committee/Associate Review Committee

The Firm Says

Dorsey & Whitney is highly committed to diversity. The firm understands the value of a diverse work environment and believes that this environment adds to the success of our attorneys and staff. Dorsey is resolved

to recruiting, retaining and promoting attorneys and staff from various diverse backgrounds and strives to be a continued leader on diversity issues.

Dorsey has made a long-term commitment to fostering a diverse workplace. In Dorsey's Statement of Core Values, the firm resolves that it will "develop and nurture a diverse and cooperative workplace that values balance between personal and professional life and promotes community service and leadership." Dorsey established a Diversity Taskforce in 1990. Eventually, a firm-wide Diversity Forum was created, involving partners, associates and staff, that examined and made recommendations about firm recruiting, professional development, community building and the promotion of a "one firm" culture and environment throughout Dorsey's many offices.

More recently, responsibility for achieving the firm's diversity goals has been assigned to the office heads with assistance from designated diversity partners in Dorsey's many locations. The purpose of this new initiative is to move beyond dialogue to "managing for diversity" in order to respond to issues that have been raised. These individuals are dedicated to the mission of assuring that each employee has an equal opportunity to succeed and feels at home and part of the firm community. As we continue to encourage diversity and remove barriers, we know that Dorsey is a better, more inclusive, place to work – and our clients benefit from productive teams, increased efficiency and higher morale.

The top priorities of the office heads and diversity partners include improving attorney skills and career development opportunities, examining further alternative work arrangements, redoubling our efforts to recruit minority law students and lateral candidates, educating ourselves about diversity issues, and nurturing a sense of community within the firm.

The firm is a continued sponsor of many diversity events and conferences including, among others, the Human Rights Campaign Dinner, the Rainbow Families Conference, the Minnesota Women Lawyers Holiday Benefit and Rosalie Wahl Lecture, the National Black Bar Association Conference and the Ann Bancroft Awards Dinner. The firm sponsors and encourages membership for our attorneys in various diversity bar associations including Minnesota Women Lawyers, National Asian Pacific American Bar Association, National Bar Association, Hispanic Bar Association, Lavender Bar Association, National Native American Bar Association, Asian Bar Association of Washington and Minnesota Bar Association.

Dorsey will be hosting the 2004 Northwest Minority Job Fair in our Seattle office and the 2004 Midwest Minority Recruitment Conference in our Minneapolis office. In addition, Dorsey is a platinum plus sponsor of Lavender Law 2004, which will be held in Minneapolis in the fall. The firm actively recruits from various minority job fairs including the Southeastern Minority Job Fair, Cook County Minority Job Fair and BLSA Midwest Recruitment Conference.

The firm provides both financial support through the Dorsey Foundation and legal support from our attorneys who contribute pro bono services to several public interest organizations. Some of the organizations that Dorsey supports include Volunteer Lawyers Network, Minnesota Advocates for Human Rights, Minnesota Civil Liberties Union, American Immigration Lawyer's Association, Children's Law Center, Legal Aid Society of Minneapolis, Innocence Project, Alaska Lawyer for the Day, Legal Aid of Polk County Iowa, Legal Rights Center, United Families of East Harlem, Project for Pride in Living, Human Rights Watch, Lawyers Committee for Human Rights Under Law, African American Men's Project and Central District Legal Clinic in Seattle.

Dorsey was recently ranked 78 out of the 236 firms that reported ethnic data on the Minority Law Journal's 2004 Diversity Scorecard. The Diversity Scorecard ranked firms based on the number of minority U.S. citizen

attorneys out of the total U.S. citizen attorney population at each firm. Dorsey placed well above other law firms whose largest offices are in Minneapolis.

Dorsey & Whitney is committed to attracting and retaining talented lawyers who, along with a strong commitment to the practice, have family concerns necessitating a work arrangement that balances their family needs with the needs of the firm and its clients. The firm has a strong policy of attempting to provide alternative work schedule opportunities for associates with children or dependent family members who cannot care for themselves. The firm believes that associates can and will remain committed professionals while working a reduced schedule, and that the reduced work schedule will not suspend associates' opportunities for professional growth, experience and career advancement. All part-time associates go through the normal evaluation process, which includes an evaluation of the associate's part-time arrangement as well as his or her professional development in accordance with the firm's partnership criteria.

Pursuant to Dorsey's Equal Employment Opportunity Policy, :Dorsey & Whitney will not discriminate against any employee or applicant for employment because of race, color, creed, religion, ancestry, national origin, sex, sexual orientation, disability, age, marital status or status with regard to public assistance. The firm will not make lawyer assignments on the basis of protected class status, including race and sex, nor will it cooperate with clients who may wish to make assignments for stereotypical reasons.

Dorsey's Sexual Harassment Policy provides, in part: Dorsey & Whitney LLP is committed to fostering a work atmosphere that is respectful and cooperative, and which promotes equal opportunity. The firm will not tolerate discrimination or harassment in our workplace. Anyone who engages in discriminatory behavior, including sexual harassment, may be subject to disciplinary action up to and including termination. Retaliation against any person who complains of discrimination or harassment, or who participates in the investigation of a complaint of discrimination or harassment, is prohibited.

Dow, Lohnes & Albertson, PLLC

1200 New Hampshire Avenue, NW
Washington, DC 20036-6802
Phone: (202) 776-2000
Fax: (202) 776-2222

FIRM LEADERSHIP

Managing Partner: John T. Byrnes, Chair,
Management Committee
Diversity Team Leader: David J. Wittenstein,
Member, Management Committee

LOCATIONS (WORLDWIDE):

Washington, DC (HQ)
Atlanta, GA

LAW FIRM DEMOGRAPHIC PROFILES

FULL-TIME ASSOCIATES	2003	2002
Minority men	2	2
Minority women	4	4
White women	22	26
Total	65	70

SUMMER ASSOCIATES	2003	2002
Minority men	1	0
Minority women	5	1
White women	2	7
Total	14	16

EQUITY PARTNERS	2003	2002
Minority men	0	0
Minority women	0	0
White women	5	3
Total	46	40

NON-EQUITY PARTNERS	2003	2002
Minority men	0	0
Minority women	1	0
White women	7	10
Total	20	27

NEW HIRES	2003	2002
Minority men	0	0
Minority women	0	1
White women	2	7
Total	12	11

Strategic Plan and Diversity Leadership

How does the firm's leadership communicate the importance of diversity to everyone at the firm? (e.g., e-mails, web site, newsletters, meetings, etc.)

Currently, e-mails and meetings.

Who has primary responsibility for leading diversity initiatives at your firm?

David J. Wittenstein, member, Management Committee

Does your law firm currently have a diversity committee?

Yes

Does the committee's representation include one or more members of the firm's management/executive committee (or the equivalent)?

Yes

How many attorneys are on the committee, and in 2003, what was the total number of hours collectively spent by the committee in furtherance of the firm's diversity initiatives?

Total attorneys on committee: 7

Total hours spent on diversity: Approximately 400 hours per year

Does the committee and/or diversity leader establish and set goals or objectives consistent with management's priorities?

Yes

Has the firm undertaken a formal or informal diversity program or set of initiatives aimed at increasing the diversity of the firm?

Yes, formal

How often does the firm's management review the firm's diversity progress/results?

Twice a year

How is the firm's diversity committee and/or firm management held accountable for achieving results?

Periodic review of efforts by Management Committee

LAW FIRM DIVERSITY INITIATIVES	ALREADY COMPLETED	CURRENTLY ADDRESSING	NOT A CURRENT PRIORITY
Undertake communication from firm management that diversity is a top priority of the firm.	✓		
Formalize diversity plan and committee with action steps and accountability to management.		✓	
Conduct firm-wide diversity training for all attorneys and staff.		✓	
Increase the number of minority attorneys at the associate level.		✓	
Increase the number of minority attorneys at the partnership level.		✓	
Develop/expand relationships with minority bar associations to offer firm's support of these networks.		✓	
Focus on strengthening firm's mentoring program, including for benefit of minority attorneys.		✓	
Conduct internal diversity needs assessment and/or retain diversity consultant to examine how firm culture might be more welcoming of minorities.		✓	
Support law firm's internal affinity networks (e.g., women, minority attorney networks).	✓		
Manage/monitor allocation of work assignments and/or hours billed to ensure women and minority attorneys have equal access/inclusion on top client matters.		✓	

Recruitment – New Associates

Does your firm annually recruit at any of the following types of institutions? (Check all that apply and list the schools).

Ivy League schools: Yale University, Harvard University, Cornell University, University of Pennsylvania

Public state schools: University of California-Berkeley, University of Michigan, University of Wisconsin, University of Virginia

Private schools: Stanford University, George Washington University, Georgetown University, University of Chicago, Duke University, Vanderbilt University

Historically Black Colleges and Universities (HBCUs): Howard University

Of the law schools that you listed above, do you have any special outreach efforts directed to encourage minority law students to consider your firm?

• Participate in/host minority law student job fair(s)

• Outreach to leadership of minority student organizations

SUMMER ASSOCIATE STATISTICS: SUMMER 2003	MINORITY MEN	MINORITY WOMEN	WHITE WOMEN	TOTAL
Summer associates	1	5	1	8
Summer associates who received an offer of full-time employment	1	4	1	7
Summer associates who accepted an offer of full-time employment	1	3	0	4*

*One withdrew before consideration

Recruitment – Lateral Associates and Partners

What activities does the firm undertake to attract minority and women attorneys?

• Participate at minority job fairs

• Seek referrals from other attorneys

• Utilize online job services (e.g., MCCA/DuPont Primary Law Firm Job Bank)

Do you use executive recruiting/search firms to seek to identify new diversity hires (partners or associates)?

Yes

List all women- and/or minority-owned executive search/recruiting firms to which the firm paid a fee for placement services in the past 12 months:

The Kemp Group

LATERAL ASSOCIATES AND PARTNERS: 1/1/03 – 12/31/03	MINORITY MEN	MINORITY WOMEN	WHITE WOMEN	TOTAL
Number of lateral associate hires	0	0	2	12
Number of lateral partner hires (equity and non-equity)	0	0	0	0
Number of new partners (equity and non-equity) promoted from associate rank	0	1	0	5
Number of new equity partners	0	1	0	1

Retention & Professional Development

ATTORNEYS WHO LEFT THE FIRM: 2003	MINORITY MEN	MINORITY WOMEN	WHITE WOMEN	TOTAL
Number of attorneys who voluntarily or involuntarily left your firm's employ in 2003	0	2	8	21

How do 2003 attrition rates generally compare to those experienced in the prior year period?

About the same as in prior years

Please identify the specific steps you are taking to reduce the attrition rate of minority and women attorneys.*

• Develop and/or support internal employee affinity groups (e.g., minority or women networks within the firm)

• Increase/review compensation relative to competition

• Increase/improve current work/life programs

• Work with minority and women attorneys to develop career advancement plans

• Introduce minority and women attorneys to key clients, including to lead engagements*

• Strengthen mentoring program for all attorneys, including minorities and women

• Professional skills development program, including minority and women attorneys

* Note: We do this for all lawyers, including minority and women lawyers.

Does your firm have part-time/flex-time policies that permit attorneys (male or female) to work alternative schedules?

Yes

What impact, if any, will the decision to work part-time have on an attorney's ability to make partner or, if already a partner, to remain a partner at your firm?

Part-time associates do not become ineligible for partnership. Part-time partners can remain partners in the firm indefinitely.

Have any attorneys who chose to work a part-time schedule made partner at your firm?

Yes, one attorney.

Management Demographic Profile (as of 12/31/03)

Please provide information regarding all minority and women attorneys who head offices or practice groups of your law firm:

Minorities heading practice groups: Quyen Truong, Telecommunications

Women heading practice groups: Quyen Truong, Telecommunications

	MINORITY MEN	MINORITY WOMEN	WHITE WOMEN	TOTAL
Number of attorneys on the Executive/Management Committee or equivalent	0	0	1	4
Number of attorneys on the Hiring Committee or equivalent	1	0	5	16
Number of attorneys on the Partner/Associate Review Committee or equivalent*	N/A	N/A	N/A	N/A

* Associate reviews are done by the individual's practice group. Partner's performance is not formally reviewed; however, the COMPART Committee does review partner's compensation annually. This committee has five members.

The Firm Says

Dow, Lohnes & Albertson, PLLC is committed to recruiting employees of diverse backgrounds and supporting all of our employees in their professional development. We seek to foster an environment that welcomes and offers great opportunities to individuals of talent, energy and character, regardless of their race, gender, ethnicity, national origin, sexual orientation, religion, color, disability or age. We recognize that creating a diverse organization is an evolving process that requires a long-term commitment of organizational resources and leadership.

At the deadline for responding to the survey, we are in the process of developing a number of diversity initiatives with the assistance of an outside consulting firm that specializes in diversity and related issues. We expect to implement these initiatives in the coming months.

Drinker Biddle & Reath LLP

One Logan Square
18th & Cherry Streets
Philadelphia, PA 19103
Phone: (215) 988-2700
Fax: (215) 988-2757

FIRM LEADERSHIP

Managing Partner and Diversity Team Leader:
James Sweet, Chairman

LOCATIONS

Philadelphia, PA (HQ)
Berwyn, PA
Florham Park, NJ
Los Angeles, CA
San Francisco, CA
New York, NY
Princeton, NJ
Washington, DC
Wilmington, DE

LAW FIRM DEMOGRAPHIC PROFILES

FULL-TIME ASSOCIATES	2003	2002
Minority men	11	4
Minority women	13	13
White women	100	69
Total	253	250

SUMMER ASSOCIATES	2003	2002
Minority men	1	6
Minority women	5	3
White women	15	14
Total	36	31

EQUITY PARTNERS	2003	2002
Minority men	2	3
Minority women	1	1
White women	24	21
Total	150	149

NON-EQUITY PARTNERS	2003	2002
Minority men	0	0
Minority women	0	0
White women	4	4
Total	23	21

NEW HIRES	2003	2002
Minority men	6	2
Minority women	6	7
White women	22	41
Total	72	106

MINORITY CORPORATE COUNSEL ASSOCIATION

Strategic Plan and Diversity Leadership

How does the firm's leadership communicate the importance of diversity to everyone at the firm? (e.g., e-mails, web site, newsletters, meetings, etc.)

We have just initiated a diversity program firm-wide to increase the representation of minority lawyers in the firm. We are currently using e-mail and physical meetings to communicate the importance to the firm.

Who has primary responsibility for leading diversity initiatives at your firm?

James Sweet, chairman of the firm

Does your law firm currently have a diversity committee?

Yes

Does the committee's representation include one or more members of the firm's management/executive committee (or the equivalent)?

Yes

How many attorneys are on the committee, and in 2003, what was the total number of hours collectively spent by the committee in furtherance of the firm's diversity initiatives?

Total attorneys on committee: 5

Total hours spent on diversity: Committee has just been formed in 2004.

Does the committee and/or diversity leader establish and set goals or objectives consistent with management's priorities?

Yes

Has the firm undertaken a formal or informal diversity program or set of initiatives aimed at increasing the diversity of the firm?

Yes, formal

How is the firm's diversity committee and/or firm management held accountable for achieving results?

We are in the process of establishing this process and measurement of results.

LAW FIRM DIVERSITY INITIATIVES	ALREADY COMPLETED	CURRENTLY ADDRESSING	NOT A CURRENT PRIORITY
Undertake communication from firm management that diversity is a top priority of the firm.	✔		
Formalize diversity plan and committee with action steps and accountability to management.		✔	
Conduct firm-wide diversity training for all attorneys and staff.			
Increase the number of minority attorneys at the associate level.			
Increase the number of minority attorneys at the partnership level.			
Develop/expand relationships with minority bar associations to offer firm's support of these networks.			
Focus on strengthening firm's mentoring program, including for benefit of minority attorneys.			
Conduct internal diversity needs assessment and/or retain diversity consultant to examine how firm culture might be more welcoming of minorities.		✔	
Support law firm's internal affinity networks (e.g., women, minority attorney networks).			
Manage/monitor allocation of work assignments and/or hours billed to ensure women and minority attorneys have equal access/inclusion on top client matters.			

Recruitment – New Associates

Does your firm annually recruit at any of the following types of institutions? (Check all that apply and list the schools).

Ivy League schools: Columbia University, Cornell University, Harvard University, University of Pennsylvania

Public state schools: University of California-Boalt Hall, University of California-Hastings, University of Michigan, Rutgers University-Camden, Rutgers University-Newark, Temple University, University of Virginia, College of William & Mary

Private schools: Boston College, Boston University, University of Chicago, Duke University, Emory University, Fordham University, Georgetown University, George Washington University, New York University, Northwestern University, University of Notre Dame, Seton Hall University, Stanford University, Villanova University

Do you have any special outreach efforts directed to encourage minority law students to consider your firm?

• Hold a reception for minority law students

• Advertise in minority law student association publication(s)

• Participate in/host minority law student job fair(s)

SUMMER ASSOCIATE STATISTICS: SUMMER 2003	MINORITY MEN	MINORITY WOMEN	WHITE WOMEN	TOTAL
Summer associates	1	3	14	33
Summer associates who received an offer of full-time employment	0	9	0	25
Summer associates who accepted an offer of full-time employment	0	2	8	22

Recruitment – Lateral Associates and Partners

What activities does the firm undertake to attract minority and women attorneys?
Participate at minority job fairs

Do you use executive recruiting/search firms to seek to identify new diversity hires (partners or associates)?
No

LATERAL ASSOCIATES AND PARTNERS: 1/1/03 – 12/31/03	MINORITY MEN	MINORITY WOMEN	WHITE WOMEN	TOTAL
Number of lateral associate hires	1	3	7	25
Number of lateral partner hires (equity and non-equity)	0	0	0	1
Number of new partners (equity and non-equity) promoted from associate rank	0	0	2	8
Number of new equity partners	0	0	0	0

Retention & Professional Development

ATTORNEYS WHO LEFT THE FIRM: 2003	MINORITY MEN	MINORITY WOMEN	WHITE WOMEN	TOTAL
Number of attorneys who voluntarily or involuntarily left your firm's employ in 2003	3	5	23	68

How do 2003 attrition rates generally compare to those experienced in the prior year period?
About the same as in prior years

Please identify the specific steps you are taking to reduce the attrition rate of minority and women attorneys.

The firm is undertaking a firm-wide diversity initiative to identify specific diversity issues and assists in the development of appropriate programs to enhance minority representation among our lawyer base. We expect these programs will focus on hiring, retention and development of minority lawyers as a firm-wide program.

Does your firm have part-time/flex-time policies that permit attorneys (male or female) to work alternative schedules?

Yes

What impact, if any, will the decision to work part-time have on an attorney's ability to make partner or, if already a partner, to remain a partner at your firm?

In general, the partnership operates with shared mutual objectives among partners. Although these objectives include a full commitment to the firm, part-time partners are allowed and are equally expected to be fully committed to the firm's success and ideas even though he or she may devote fewer hours to the firm.

Have any attorneys who chose to work a part-time schedule made partner at your firm?

Yes, one attorney.

Management Demographic Profile (as of 12/31/03)

	MINORITY MEN	MINORITY WOMEN	WHITE WOMEN	TOTAL
Number of attorneys on the Executive/Management Committee or equivalent	0	0	1	15
Number of attorneys on the Hiring Committee or equivalent	0	2	4	16
Number of attorneys on the Partner/Associate Review Committee or equivalent	0	0	1	15

Please provide information regarding all minority and women attorneys who head offices or practice groups of your law firm:

Women heading practice groups: Kate Levering, Chair, Litigation Department; Bonnie Barnett, Chair, Environmental Group; Susan Sharko, Co Chair, Products Liability Group; Nora Pomerantz, Vice Chair, Personal Law Department

The Firm Says

To position Drinker Biddle & Reath as a competitive force in the legal market, we know that real diversity within our attorney base is an important component of our overall mission. Unlike our efforts to diversify our administrative staff, the firm's efforts over the past several years to diversify our lawyer base have had mixed results. When we did have success hiring minority lawyers, we often struggled to retain those minority lawyers going forward. This firm is committed to creating and sustaining diversity throughout the firm, including a team of talented attorneys who represent the various communities in which we work, live and play.

To focus our efforts for achieving diversity within the firm, DB&R created a Diversity Task Force, which is chaired by James Sweet, chairman of the firm. This task force is charged with beginning the process of thinking through the steps necessary to build diversity within our attorney ranks. The task force has embarked on an ambitious course of action to help the firm achieve its objectives. The timeline envisioned by the task force

anticipates that a full "Diversity Committee" – which will be comprised of representation from all parts of the firm – will be created after we complete some important initial tasks.

As a first step, the task force has retained the assistance of a progressive Diversity Consultant to create a "Needs Assessment on Diversity" for our firm. The results of this Needs Assessment will form the foundation for our program and as a result we will assemble a diversity committee and develop targeted programs to address our firm's diversity issues so that we will know where we stand and what we need to do in order to accomplish our objectives. This Needs Assessment involves both a firm-wide survey and a random interview component. Although we do not expect immediate success, we have already raised diversity to a new level of awareness in the firm and we have committed to have a successful program.

Duane Morris LLP

One Liberty Place
Philadelphia, PA 19103-7396
Phone: (215) 979-1000
Fax: (215) 979-1020

FIRM LEADERSHIP

Managing Partner: Sheldon M. Bonovitz,
Chairman
Diversity Team Leader: Nolan N. Atkinson Jr.,
Chair of Diversity Committee

LOCATIONS

Philadelphia, PA (HQ)
Allentown, PA
Atlanta, GA
Bangor, ME
Boston, MA
Chicago, IL
Detroit, MI
Harrisburg, PA
Houston, TX
Miami, FL
Newark, NJ
New York, NY
Pittsburgh, PA
Princeton, NJ
San Diego, CA
San Francisco, CA
Washington, DC
Westchester, NY
Wilmington, DE
London

LAW FIRM DEMOGRAPHIC PROFILES

FULL-TIME ASSOCIATES	2003	2002
Minority men	15	11
Minority women	17	11
White women	75	77
Total	227	203

SUMMER ASSOCIATES	2003	2002
Minority men	0	0
Minority women	2	1
White women	5	3
Total	13	14

EQUITY PARTNERS	2003	2002
Minority men	4	4
Minority women	1	1
White women	19	18
Total	162	162

NON-EQUITY PARTNERS	2003	2002
Minority men	4	2
Minority women	3	3
White women	24	21
Total	91	77

NEW HIRES	2003	2002
Minority men	10	4
Minority women	9	2
White women	28	30
Total	137	102

Strategic Plan and Diversity Leadership

How does the firm's leadership communicate the importance of diversity to everyone at the firm? (e.g., e-mails, web site, newsletters, meetings, etc.)

Firm-wide meetings of partners; annual meeting of partners and associates

Who has primary responsibility for leading diversity initiatives at your firm?

Nolan N. Atkinson Jr., chair of Diversity Committee

Does your law firm currently have a diversity committee?

Yes

Does the committee's representation include one or more members of the firm's management/executive committee (or the equivalent)?

Yes

How many attorneys are on the committee, and in 2003, what was the total number of hours collectively spent by the committee in furtherance of the firm's diversity initiatives?

Total attorneys on committee: 9

Total hours spent on diversity: Cannot be quantified (large number of hours are spent by the Diversity Committee because individual members have specific assignments).

Does the committee and/or diversity leader establish and set goals or objectives consistent with management's priorities?

Yes

Has the firm undertaken a formal or informal diversity program or set of initiatives aimed at increasing the diversity of the firm?

Yes, formal

How often does the firm's management review the firm's diversity progress/results?

Quarterly

How is the firm's diversity committee and/or firm management held accountable for achieving results?

The Executive Committee grades the performance of the chair of the Diversity Committee on an annual basis.

LAW FIRM DIVERSITY INITIATIVES	ALREADY COMPLETED	CURRENTLY ADDRESSING	NOT A CURRENT PRIORITY
Undertake communication from firm management that diversity is a top priority of the firm.	✓		
Formalize diversity plan and committee with action steps and accountability to management.	✓		
Conduct firm-wide diversity training for all attorneys and staff.		✓	
Increase the number of minority attorneys at the associate level.		✓	
Increase the number of minority attorneys at the partnership level.		✓	
Develop/expand relationships with minority bar associations to offer firm's support of these networks.	✓		
Focus on strengthening firm's mentoring program, including for benefit of minority attorneys.		✓	
Conduct internal diversity needs assessment and/or retain diversity consultant to examine how firm culture might be more welcoming of minorities.		✓	
Support law firm's internal affinity networks (e.g., women, minority attorney networks).		✓	
Manage/monitor allocation of work assignments and/or hours billed to ensure women and minority attorneys have equal access/inclusion on top client matters.	✓		

Recruitment – New Associates

Does your firm annually recruit at any of the following types of institutions? (Check all that apply and list the schools).*

Ivy League schools: Columbia University, Cornell University, Harvard University, University of Pennsylvania

Public state schools: University of Georgia, University of Michigan, College of William and Mary

Private schools: University of Chicago, Duke University, Emory University, George Washington University, Georgetown University, New York University, Northwestern University, University of Notre Dame, University of Pittsburgh, Temple University, Vanderbilt University, Villanova University, Washington University School of Law in St. Louis

Other predominantly minority and/or women's colleges: Southeastern Minority Job Fair, Marietta, GA

* Note : We participate in the on-campus interview program at these schools. We receive and consider resumes from many other schools as well.

Do you have any special outreach efforts directed to encourage minority law students to consider your firm?

• Hold a reception for minority law students

• Advertise in minority law student association publication(s)

• Participate in/host minority law student job fair(s)

• Sponsor minority law student association events

• Outreach to leadership of minority student organizations

SUMMER ASSOCIATE STATISTICS: SUMMER 2003	MINORITY MEN	MINORITY WOMEN	WHITE WOMEN	TOTAL
Summer associates	0	2	5	13
Summer associates who received an offer of full-time employment	0	1	5	11
Summer associates who accepted an offer of full-time employment	0	1	5	10

Recruitment – Lateral Associates and Partners

What activities does the firm undertake to attract minority and women attorneys?

• *Search firms specializing in minority candidates*

• Partner programs with women and minority bar associations

• Participate at minority job fairs

• Seek referrals from other attorneys

Do you use executive recruiting/search firms to seek to identify new diversity hires (partners or associates)?

Yes

If yes, list all women- and/or minority-owned executive search/recruiting firms to which the firm paid a fee for placement services in the past 12 months:

ADHOC Law Associates, Inc.; Audrey Golden Associates, Ltd.; AV Search Consultants; Corrao, Miller, Rush & Wiesenthal; DiCicco & Associates; Grimes Legal, Inc.; Hughes & Sloan; Palmer Kent Associates, Inc.; and Pappas & Associates

LATERAL ASSOCIATES AND PARTNERS: 1/1/03 – 12/31/03	MINORITY MEN	MINORITY WOMEN	WHITE WOMEN	TOTAL
Number of lateral associate hires	6	6	12	79
Number of lateral partner hires (equity and non-equity)	2	1	6	53
Number of new partners (equity and non-equity) promoted from associate rank	3	0	3	13
Number of new equity partners	0	0	0	7

Retention & Professional Development

ATTORNEYS WHO LEFT THE FIRM: 2003	MINORITY MEN	MINORITY WOMEN	WHITE WOMEN	TOTAL
Number of attorneys who voluntarily or involuntarily left your firm's employ in 2003	1	4	17	46

How do 2003 attrition rates generally compare to those experienced in the prior year period?

About the same as in prior years

Please identify the specific steps you are taking to reduce the attrition rate of minority and women attorneys.

• Review work assignments and hours billed to key client matters to make sure minority and women attorneys are not being excluded

• Strengthen mentoring program for all attorneys, including minorities and women

Does your firm have part-time/flex-time policies that permit attorneys (male or female) to work alternative schedules?

Yes

What impact, if any, will the decision to work part-time have on an attorney's ability to make partner or, if already a partner, to remain a partner at your firm?

None

Have any attorneys who chose to work a part-time schedule made partner at your firm?

Yes, two attorneys.

Management Demographic Profile (as of 12/31/03)

	MINORITY MEN	MINORITY WOMEN	WHITE WOMEN	TOTAL
Number of attorneys on the Executive/Management Committee or equivalent	0	0	1	5
Number of attorneys on the Hiring Committee or equivalent	0	1	12	32
Number of attorneys on the Partner/Associate Review Committee or equivalent	0	0	1	11

Please provide information regarding all minority and women attorneys who head offices or practice groups of your law firm:

Minorities heading offices: Joseph Burton, San Francisco

Women heading practice groups: Kathleen Shay, Corporate; Barbara Adams, Capital Markets & Investment Banking

The Firm Says

Duane Morris LLP, which numbers in excess of 500 lawyers, is committed to developing and implementing practices and procedures that will grow the racial, cultural and gender diversity of lawyers working in the firm. Our philosophy is that a diverse group of lawyers will better enable the firm to service the clients it represents throughout the world. Diversity therefore is a core value of the firm.

The firm consists of 20 offices with practice groups that have a national and international platform. We dedicate our best and most efficient lawyers to provide professional services to clients regardless of location. Thus, while we have submitted regional diversity statistics, these numbers do not accurately reflect the participation of diverse lawyers for clients in the Mid-Atlantic region.

Regarding gender diversity, the firm's progress has been profound – women hold positions of leadership at all levels of management and in all practice areas at the firm. Kathleen Shay is chair of the corporate department. Sheila Hollis, of our Washington office, is a member of the firm's five-member Executive Management Committee. Sixteen percent of our partners are females. More profoundly, 43 percent of our associate population are women. This concentration reflects the recognition among women associates of the leadership roles held by the firm's women partners and assures that female partnership percentages will grow in the years to come.

Because substantial progress in achieving racial and cultural diversity has been more difficult, Sheldon Bonovitz in his first year as chairman of the firm in the late '90s decided to take aggressive action in an area where laissez faire practices simply do not work. Firm management committed itself to investing the time and resources necessary to hire and retain lawyers who are diverse, always with the goal of making Duane Morris better and stronger by their presence.

Recognizing that there will be statistical fluctuations in the attorney population from year to year, and that the economy will impact hiring practices, the firm's focus is on the quality of its diversity program, its leadership role and the evaluation of its success in five-year intervals rather than with sometimes volatile/misleading year-to-year numbers. Therefore, the most material statistic on the Law Firm Demographic Profile above is category 5 – the percentage of new hires that are minority. Twelve percent of new hires at our firm are minority. Women lawyers account for 26 percent of new hires. These figures forecast that Duane Morris is building a foundation to be a leader in diversity statistics among the largest firms in the country.

As with gender, diverse attorneys have taken leadership positions in the firm. One example is Joe Burton, an African American who heads our San Francisco office and is a member of the firm's prestigious Partners' Board. Other diverse lawyers have served two-year terms on that board as well.

The Diversity Mission Statement continues to be our compass; and the work of the firm's Diversity Committee the means for achieving our goals. The committee, chaired by Nolan N. Atkinson Jr., has recommended, and the firm's Executive Committee has approved, the following initiatives:

• Requiring all outside recruiters to review the firm's Diversity Mission Statement and adhere to its principles.

• Requiring all practice group leaders and office heads to include in their year-end reports a section summarizing what their group has done to promote diversity.

• Reports to the partnership at all firm-wide meetings to include a census of diverse lawyers and the firm's new diversity initiatives.

• Review of the time records of all diverse associates by the chair of the Diversity Committee, thereby assuring that sufficient work is being assigned to each associate and, if not, to determine why and address the issue.

• Requiring all practice group leaders and office heads to notify the chair of the Diversity Committee if a diverse associate is about to go on probationary status in order to explore every opportunity for retaining the associate.

• Fostering a strong link between the firm's marketing plan for retaining and developing new clients and the firm's commitment to a growing an ever increasing diverse population of lawyers.

In addition, Duane Morris is a founding member of the Philadelphia Diversity Law Group, Inc., a consortium of large law firms and corporations working to increase ethnic and racial diversity in the Greater Philadelphia area. Duane Morris partner Nolan N. Atkinson Jr. is the president. The PDLG is sponsoring a summer program founded in 2003 where member firms have agreed to hire first-year (1L) law students who have "overcome obstacles in pursuing a legal career, come from a disadvantaged background or from backgrounds that are underrepresented in the Philadelphia legal community, and who have the ability to succeed in the program run by member organizations."

In the first year, 2003, 12 students participated. Of that number, eight diverse students were invited to return as second-year (2L) summer associates at participating firms. Duane Morris' summer program this year is made up of diverse students that have been or will be exposed to the workings of large firms and corporation through this program. The 1L student at Duane last year was a 2L summer associate this year and was recently offered an associate position upon graduation. One student from Howard Law School worked for another member firm last year and was a 2L at Duane Morris this summer. She, too, received an offer to join the firm as an associate. And the firm is including a new 1L law clerk for the summer associate program just as it did in the program's founding year.

Duane Morris has been a trailblazer in supporting gender diversity throughout the ranks of the firm beginning a generation ago. Duane Morris diversity programs, addressing racial and national origin, will lead to similar success.

Dykema Gossett PLLC

400 Renaissance Center
Detroit, MI 48243
Phone: (313) 568-6800
Fax: (313) 568-6893

FIRM LEADERSHIP

Managing Partner: Rex E. Schlaybaugh,
Chairman
Diversity Team Leader: Seth M. Lloyd,
Professional Personnel Member

LOCATIONS

Detroit, MI (HQ)
Ann Arbor, MI
Bloomfield Hills, MI
Chicago, IL
Grand Rapids, MI
Lansing, MI
Pasadena, CA
Washington, DC

LAW FIRM DEMOGRAPHIC PROFILES

FULL-TIME ASSOCIATES	2003	2002
Minority men	6	8
Minority women	9	10
White women	62	55
Total	118	113

SUMMER ASSOCIATES	2003	2002
Minority men	0	1
Minority women	6	3
White women	8	8
Total	24	21

EQUITY PARTNERS	2003	2002
Minority men	1	2
Minority women	3	3
White women	20	18
Total	99	96

NON-EQUITY PARTNERS	2003	2002
Minority men	2	2
Minority women	1	1
White women	9	7
Total	45	39

NEW HIRES	2003	2002
Minority men	2	4
Minority women	1	4
White women	17	12
Total	53	30

MINORITY CORPORATE COUNSEL ASSOCIATION

Strategic Plan and Diversity Leadership

How does the firm's leadership communicate the importance of diversity to everyone at the firm? (e.g., e-mails, web site, newsletters, meetings, etc.)

Topic at regular meetings of members; management informed of minority retention program and related monitoring; monthly statistics on minority performance provided to department directors; diversity consultant provided training to all attorneys.

Who has primary responsibility for leading diversity initiatives at your firm?

Seth M. Lloyd, professional personnel member

Does your law firm currently have a diversity committee?

Yes

Does the committee's representation include one or more members of the firm's management/executive committee (or the equivalent)?

Yes

How many attorneys are on the committee, and in 2003, what was the total number of hours collectively spent by the committee in furtherance of the firm's diversity initiatives?

Total attorneys on committee: 3

Total hours spent on diversity: 100+

Does the committee and/or diversity leader establish and set goals or objectives consistent with management's priorities?

Yes

Has the firm undertaken a formal or informal diversity program or set of initiatives aimed at increasing the diversity of the firm?

Yes, formal

How often does the firm's management review the firm's diversity progress/results?

Quarterly

How is the firm's diversity committee and/or firm management held accountable for achieving results?

Results in retaining minority lawyers play an important role in the performance evaluation of department directors.

LAW FIRM DIVERSITY INITIATIVES	ALREADY COMPLETED	CURRENTLY ADDRESSING	NOT A CURRENT PRIORITY
Undertake communication from firm management that diversity is a top priority of the firm.		✔	
Formalize diversity plan and committee with action steps and accountability to management.	✔		
Conduct firm-wide diversity training for all attorneys and staff.	✔		
Increase the number of minority attorneys at the associate level.		✔	
Increase the number of minority attorneys at the partnership level.		✔	
Develop/expand relationships with minority bar associations to offer firm's support of these networks.		✔	
Focus on strengthening firm's mentoring program, including for benefit of minority attorneys.		✔	
Conduct internal diversity needs assessment and/or retain diversity consultant to examine how firm culture might be more welcoming of minorities.	✔		
Support law firm's internal affinity networks (e.g., women, minority attorney networks).	✔		
Manage/monitor allocation of work assignments and/or hours billed to ensure women and minority attorneys have equal access/inclusion on top client matters.		✔	

Recruitment – New Associates

Does your firm annually recruit at any of the following types of institutions? (Check all that apply and list the schools).

Ivy League schools: Harvard University

Public state schools: University of Michigan, University of Illinois, Ohio State University, Wayne State University

Private schools: Case Western Reserve University, Northwestern University, Loyola University (Chicago); Georgetown University

Historically Black Colleges and Universities (HBCUs): Howard University

Do you have any special outreach efforts directed to encourage minority law students to consider your firm?

• *Charter member of Wolverine Bar Association 1L Summer Clerkship Program*

• Participate in/host minority law student job fair(s)

• Sponsor minority law student association events

• Firm's lawyers participate on career panels at school

• Scholarships or intern/fellowships for minority students

MINORITY CORPORATE COUNSEL ASSOCIATION

SUMMER ASSOCIATE STATISTICS: SUMMER 2003	MINORITY MEN	MINORITY WOMEN	WHITE WOMEN	TOTAL
Summer associates	0	3	8	21
Summer associates who received an offer of full-time employment	0	2	7	15
Summer associates who accepted an offer of full-time employment	0	1	6	12

Recruitment – Lateral Associates and Partners

What activities does the firm undertake to attract minority and women attorneys?

• Participate at minority job fairs

• Seek referrals from other attorneys

Do you use executive recruiting/search firms to seek to identify new diversity hires (partners or associates)?

Yes

If yes, list all women- and/or minority-owned executive search/recruiting firms to which the firm paid a fee for placement services in the past 12 months:

Newman Hawkins Legal Search

LATERAL ASSOCIATES AND PARTNERS: 1/1/03 – 12/31/03	MINORITY MEN	MINORITY WOMEN	WHITE WOMEN	TOTAL
Number of lateral associate hires	1	1	9	21
Number of lateral partner hires (equity and non-equity)	0	0	3	13
Number of new partners (equity and non-equity) promoted from associate rank	0	1	1	7
Number of new equity partners	0	0	0	6

Retention & Professional Development

ATTORNEYS WHO LEFT THE FIRM: 2003	MINORITY MEN	MINORITY WOMEN	WHITE WOMEN	TOTAL
Number of attorneys who voluntarily or involuntarily left your firm's employ in 2003	2	1	9	24

How do 2003 attrition rates generally compare to those experienced in the prior year period?

About the same as in prior years

Please identify the specific steps you are taking to reduce the attrition rate of minority and women attorneys.

• Develop and/or support internal employee affinity groups (e.g., minority or women networks within the firm)

• Increase/review compensation relative to competition

• Increase/improve current work/life programs

• Work with minority and women attorneys to develop career advancement plans

• Introduce minority and women attorneys to key clients, including to lead engagements

• Review work assignments and hours billed to key client matters to make sure minority and women attorneys are not being excluded

• Strengthen mentoring program for all attorneys, including minorities and women

• Professional skills development program, including minority and women attorneys

Does your firm have part-time/flex-time policies that permit attorneys (male or female) to work alternative schedules?

Yes

What impact, if any, will the decision to work part-time have on an attorney's ability to make partner or, if already a partner, to remain a partner at your firm?

The decision may delay making partner, depending on the duration and degree of part-time status. There is no impact on remaining partner.

Have any attorneys who chose to work a part-time schedule made partner at your firm?

Yes, three attorneys.

Management Demographic Profile (as of 12/31/03)

	MINORITY MEN	MINORITY WOMEN	WHITE WOMEN	TOTAL
Number of attorneys on the Executive/Management Committee or equivalent	0	0	2	7
Number of attorneys on the Hiring Committee or equivalent	0	1	5	14
Number of attorneys on the Partner/Associate Review Committee or equivalent	0	0	2	9

Please provide information regarding all minority and women attorneys who head offices or practice groups of your law firm:

Women heading offices: Marilyn Peters, Bloomfield Hills, MI

Women heading practice groups: Sandra Cotter, Government Policy; Maria Abrahamsen, Health Care; Kathryn Humphrey, Litigation; Margaret Hunter, Employee Benefits

The Firm Says

Guided by the writings of David Wilkins of Harvard Law School on law firm diversity, Dykema Gossett maintains a program under the direction of the member in charge of professional personnel which monitors on a monthly basis the workload of minority lawyers, both in terms of the quantity of work assigned and the quality of work (as measured by the clients for whom they work and the type of assignments). Department directors are provided such information each month and are required to report at quarterly meetings of the firm's chairman and all directors on steps they have taken to ensure that minority associates are receiving their fair share of the top assignments available.

This retention program furthers Dykema's goal to be in the upper quartile of firms in terms of the number of minority associates and members.

The firm has long been recognized as a leader in terms of employing and advancing women, and women are well represented at all levels of the firm, including two who serve on the firm's executive board, one who serves as a co-leader of the firm's government policy and practice department, and three who serve as leaders of practice groups within the firm's departments. One of the ingredients which has contributed to this success is the firm's policy regarding part-time arrangements for lawyers with the firm for more than one year who, for whatever reason, are not able to maintain a full schedule. Currently, 13 associates work on a reduced-time basis. Three associates, including one African-American woman, have been elected to the firm's membership while on part-time status.

As a law firm whose largest office is located in a city whose population is predominantly African-American, Dykema Gossett is committed to leadership in hiring, retaining and advancing qualified men and women lawyers of color. We will continue to monitor our policies and practices to make sure that the firm accomplishes this goal.

Epstein Becker & Green, P.C.

250 Park Avenue
New York, NY 10177
Phone: (212) 351-4500
Fax: (212) 661-0989

FIRM LEADERSHIP

Managing Partner: George P. Sape, Managing
Partner

LOCATIONS

New York, NY (HQ)
Altanta, GA
Boston, MA
Chicago, IL
Dallas, TX
Houston, TX
Los Angeles, CA
Miami, FL
Newark, NJ
San Francisco, CA
Stamford, CT
Washington, DC

LAW FIRM DEMOGRAPHIC PROFILES

FULL-TIME ASSOCIATES	2003	2002
Minority men	13	8
Minority women	21	13
White women	69	58
Total	156	141

SUMMER ASSOCIATES	2003	2002
Minority men	3	0
Minority women	1	0
White women	7	4
Total	13	6

EQUITY PARTNERS	2003	2002
Minority men	6	5
Minority women	0	0
White women	15	13
Total	91	85

NON-EQUITY PARTNERS	2003	2002
Minority men	5	4
Minority women	2	1
White women	21	13
Total	60	41

NEW HIRES	2003	2002
Minority men	5	5
Minority women	4	6
White women	27	13
Total	66	38

Strategic Plan and Diversity Leadership

How does the firm's leadership communicate the importance of diversity to everyone at the firm? (e.g., e-mails, web site, newsletters, meetings, etc.)

Meetings

Who has primary responsibility for leading diversity initiatives at your firm?

George Sape, Managing Partner

Does your law firm currently have a diversity committee?

Yes

Does the committee's representation include one or more members of the firm's management/executive committee (or the equivalent)?

No

How many attorneys are on the committee, and in 2003, what was the total number of hours collectively spent by the committee in furtherance of the firm's diversity initiatives?

Total attorneys on committee: 6

Total hours spent on diversity: Not tracked

Does the committee and/or diversity leader establish and set goals or objectives consistent with management's priorities?

Yes

Has the firm undertaken a formal or informal diversity program or set of initiatives aimed at increasing the diversity of the firm?

Yes, informal

How often does the firm's management review the firm's diversity progress/results?

Reviews occur on an ongoing basis.

How is the firm's diversity committee and/or firm management held accountable for achieving results?

Committee is newly created in 2004.

LAW FIRM DIVERSITY INITIATIVES	ALREADY COMPLETED	CURRENTLY ADDRESSING	NOT A CURRENT PRIORITY
Undertake communication from firm management that diversity is a top priority of the firm.		✓	
Formalize diversity plan and committee with action steps and accountability to management.		✓	
Conduct firm-wide diversity training for all attorneys and staff.	✓	✓	
Increase the number of minority attorneys at the associate level.		✓	
Increase the number of minority attorneys at the partnership level.		✓	
Develop/expand relationships with minority bar associations to offer firm's support of these networks.		✓	
Focus on strengthening firm's mentoring program, including for benefit of minority attorneys.		✓	
Conduct internal diversity needs assessment and/or retain diversity consultant to examine how firm culture might be more welcoming of minorities.		✓	
Support law firm's internal affinity networks (e.g., women, minority attorney networks).		✓	
Manage/monitor allocation of work assignments and/or hours billed to ensure women and minority attorneys have equal access/inclusion on top client matters.		✓	

Recruitment – New Associates

Does your firm annually recruit at any of the following types of institutions? (Check all that apply and list the schools).

Historically Black Colleges and Universities (HBCUs): Howard University

SUMMER ASSOCIATE STATISTICS: SUMMER 2003	MINORITY MEN	MINORITY WOMEN	WHITE WOMEN	TOTAL
Summer associates	3	1	7	13
Summer associates who received an offer of full-time employment	1	1	4	7
Summer associates who accepted an offer of full-time employment	1	1	4	6

Recruitment – Lateral Associates and Partners

What activities does the firm undertake to attract minority and women attorneys?

• Participate at minority job fairs

• Seek referrals from other attorneys

Do you use executive recruiting/search firms to seek to identify new diversity hires (partners or associates)?

Yes

LATERAL ASSOCIATES AND PARTNERS: 1/1/03 – 12/31/03	MINORITY MEN	MINORITY WOMEN	WHITE WOMEN	TOTAL
Number of lateral associate hires	4	4	17	43
Number of lateral partner hires (equity and non-equity)	0	0	1	19
Number of new partners (equity and non-equity) promoted from associate rank	0	0	3	7
Number of new equity partners	1	0	1	6

Retention & Professional Development

ATTORNEYS WHO LEFT THE FIRM: 2003	MINORITY MEN	MINORITY WOMEN	WHITE WOMEN	TOTAL
Number of attorneys who voluntarily or involuntarily left your firm's employ in 2003	3	10	17	42

How do 2003 attrition rates generally compare to those experienced in the prior year period?

About the same as in prior years

Please identify the specific steps you are taking to reduce the attrition rate of minority and women attorneys.

• Increase/review compensation relative to competition

• Increase/improve current work/life programs

• Strengthen mentoring program for all attorneys, including minorities and women

• Professional skills development program, including minority and women attorneys

Does your firm have part-time/flex-time policies that permit attorneys (male or female) to work alternative schedules?

Yes

What impact, if any, will the decision to work part-time have on an attorney's ability to make partner or, if already a partner, to remain a partner at your firm?

No impact

Have any attorneys who chose to work a part-time schedule made partner at your firm?

Yes, two attorneys.

Management Demographic Profile (as of 12/31/03)

	MINORITY MEN	MINORITY WOMEN	WHITE WOMEN	TOTAL
Number of attorneys on the Executive/Management Committee or equivalent	1	0	2	16
Number of attorneys on the Hiring Committee or equivalent*	N/A	N/A	N/A	N/A
Number of attorneys on the Partner/Associate Review Committee or equivalent*	N/A	N/A	N/A	N/A

*This is an office-by-office, department-by-department type of committee.

Please provide information regarding all minority and women attorneys who head offices or practice groups of your law firm:

Minorities heading offices: A. Martin Wickliff Jr. Houston

Women heading offices: Susan Pravda, Boston; Gayla Crain, Dallas; Maxine Hicks, Atlanta

Minorities heading practice groups: Alton Hall, Co-Chair, Litigation

Women heading practice groups: Maxine Hicks, Real Estate

Faegre & Benson LLP

2200 Wells Fargo Center
90 South Seventh Street
Minneapolis, MN 55402
Phone: (612) 766-7000
Fax: (612) 766-1600

FIRM LEADERSHIP

Managing Partner: Thomas G. Morgan
Diversity Team Leader: Charles S. Ferrell
Dana Gray, Manager of Recruiting and
Diversity Coordinator; Michael Ponto, Chair,
Diversity Committee

LOCATIONS

Minneapolis, MN (HQ)
Boulder, CO
Denver, CO
Des Moines, IA
Frankfurt
London
Shanghai

LAW FIRM DEMOGRAPHIC PROFILES

FULL-TIME ASSOCIATES	2003	2002
Minority men	9	11
Minority women	12	10
White women	67	76
Total	168	186

SUMMER ASSOCIATES	2003	2002
Minority men	3	2
Minority women	5	4
White women	15	10
Total	35	29

EQUITY PARTNERS	2003	2002
Minority men	2	1
Minority women	3	2
White women	50	46
Total	216	206

NEW HIRES	2003	2002
Minority men	4	4
Minority women	4	4
White women	11	31
Total	36	80

Strategic Plan and Diversity Leadership

How does the firm's leadership communicate the importance of diversity to everyone at the firm? (e.g., e-mails, web site, newsletters, meetings, etc.)

The firm adopted a formal and strategic diversity plan in early 2003. There is frequent discussion of diversity topics at firm meetings including at the firm-wide annual meetings. A section of our firm newsletter "Hearsay" is for diversity-related firm announcements and activities. We hold annual programming to highlight diversity issues. We have conducted targeted diversity training.

Who has primary responsibility for leading diversity initiatives at your firm?

Charlie Ferrell, diversity partner and Management Committee member; Michael Ponto, chair of Diversity Committee

Does your law firm currently have a diversity committee?

Yes

Does the committee's representation include one or more members of the firm's management/executive committee (or the equivalent)?

Yes

How many attorneys are on the committee, and in 2003, what was the total number of hours collectively spent by the committee in furtherance of the firm's diversity initiatives?

Total attorneys on committee: 11

Total hours spent on diversity: More than 950

Does the committee and/or diversity leader establish and set goals or objectives consistent with management's priorities?

Yes

Has the firm undertaken a formal or informal diversity program or set of initiatives aimed at increasing the diversity of the firm?

Yes, formal

How often does the firm's management review the firm's diversity progress/results?

Monthly

How is the firm's diversity committee and/or firm management held accountable for achieving results?

Annually, the Diversity Committee reports goals and progress toward such goals. Diversity is also a factor in compensation.

Faegre & Benson LLP

LAW FIRM DIVERSITY INITIATIVES	ALREADY COMPLETED	CURRENTLY ADDRESSING	NOT A CURRENT PRIORITY
Undertake communication from firm management that diversity is a top priority of the firm.	✔		
Formalize diversity plan and committee with action steps and accountability to management.	✔		
Conduct firm-wide diversity training for all attorneys and staff.		✔	
Increase the number of minority attorneys at the associate level.		✔	
Increase the number of minority attorneys at the partnership level.		✔	
Develop/expand relationships with minority bar associations to offer firm's support of these networks.	✔		
Focus on strengthening firm's mentoring program, including for benefit of minority attorneys.	✔		
Conduct internal diversity needs assessment and/or retain diversity consultant to examine how firm culture might be more welcoming of minorities.		✔	
Support law firm's internal affinity networks (e.g., women, minority attorney networks).	✔		
Manage/monitor allocation of work assignments and/or hours billed to ensure women and minority attorneys have equal access/inclusion on top client matters.		✔	

Recruitment – New Associates

Does your firm annually recruit at any of the following types of institutions? (Check all that apply and list the schools).

Ivy League schools: Columbia University, Harvard University, Yale University

Public state schools: University of California (Berkeley), University of Chicago, University of Colorado, University of Illinois, University of Iowa, University of Michigan, University of Minnesota, University of Virginia, University of Wisconsin

Private schools: University of Denver, Drake University, George Washington University, Georgetown University, Hamline University, New York University, Northwestern University, St. Thomas University, Stanford University, Washington University (St. Louis), William Mitchell College of Law

Do you have any special outreach efforts directed to encourage minority law students to consider your firm?

• *Informative meetings with minority organizations*

• Hold a reception for minority law students

• Participate in/host minority law student job fair(s)

• Firm's lawyers participate on career panels at school

• Outreach to leadership of minority student organizations

• Scholarships or intern/fellowships for minority students

481

SUMMER ASSOCIATE STATISTICS: SUMMER 2003	MINORITY MEN	MINORITY WOMEN	WHITE WOMEN	TOTAL
Summer associates	1	2	10	21
Summer associates who received an offer of full-time employment	1	2	10	20
Summer associates who accepted an offer of full-time employment	1	2	8	18

Recruitment – Lateral Associates and Partners

What activities does the firm undertake to attract minority and women attorneys?

• Partner programs with women and minority bar associations

• Participate at minority job fairs

• Seek referrals from other attorneys

• Utilize online job services (e.g., MCCA/DuPont Primary Law Firm Job Bank)

Do you use executive recruiting/search firms to seek to identify new diversity hires (partners or associates)?

Yes

LATERAL ASSOCIATES AND PARTNERS: 1/1/03 – 12/31/03	MINORITY MEN	MINORITY WOMEN	WHITE WOMEN	TOTAL
Number of lateral associate hires	1	0	2	7
Number of lateral partner hires (equity and non-equity)	0	0	2	5
Number of new partners (equity and non-equity) promoted from associate rank	1	1	4	13
Number of new equity partners	1	1	6	18

Retention & Professional Development

ATTORNEYS WHO LEFT THE FIRM: 2003	MINORITY MEN	MINORITY WOMEN	WHITE WOMEN	TOTAL
Number of attorneys who voluntarily or involuntarily left your firm's employ in 2003	3	1	8	50

How do 2003 attrition rates generally compare to those experienced in the prior year period?

About the same as in prior years

Please identify the specific steps you are taking to reduce the attrition rate of minority and women attorneys.

• Develop and/or support internal employee affinity groups (e.g., minority or women networks within the firm)

• Work with minority and women attorneys to develop career advancement plans

• Introduce minority and women attorneys to key clients, including to lead engagements

• Professional skills development program, including minority and women attorneys

Does your firm have part-time/flex-time policies that permit attorneys (male or female) to work alternative schedules?

Yes

What impact, if any, will the decision to work part-time have on an attorney's ability to make partner or, if already a partner, to remain a partner at your firm?

Years of service are pro-rated; otherwise there is no consequence for part-time work.

Have any attorneys who chose to work a part-time schedule made partner at your firm?

Yes

Management Demographic Profile (as of 12/31/03)

	MINORITY MEN	MINORITY WOMEN	WHITE WOMEN	TOTAL
Number of attorneys on the Executive/Management Committee or equivalent	0	0	1	9
Number of attorneys on the Hiring Committee or equivalent	0	1	5	18
Number of attorneys on the Partner/Associate Review Committee or equivalent	N/A	N/A	N/A	N/A

Please provide information regarding all minority and women attorneys who head offices or practice groups of your law firm:

Women heading offices: Linda Rockwood, Denver

Women heading practice groups: Kathlyn Noecker, Labor & Employment Law

The Firm Says

We are proud to be the recipient of the 2004 Thomas L. Sager Award for the Midwest Region. To ensure strong and consistent leadership from the highest level, the firm has designated one of its managing partners as its "diversity partner." The diversity partner is accountable for our diversity efforts and success. Charlie Ferrell, the firm's first diversity partner, completed his first full year in that position in 2004. We also have a diversity coordinator, Dana Gray, whose administrative responsibilities help to ensure follow-through and support for our numerous ongoing initiatives. Charlie and Dana are both members of our active Diversity Committee.

Within the structure of our Strategic Plan, and under this leadership, some of the highlights of our diversity efforts are as follows:

Recruiting

We have adopted multiple initiatives aimed at recruiting a diverse pool of candidates, including:

• Hosting of the Minnesota Minority Recruitment Conference in both 2001 and 2003. We sponsor and interview at this Twin Cities job fair every year.

• Interviewing and hiring from law schools with high minority enrollment and recruitment at minority job fairs, including Southeastern Minority Job Fair, DuPont Legal Minority Job Fairs (Wilmington, Houston and Chicago), Harvard BLSA Job Fairs, Rocky Mountain Career Fair, National Lavender GLBT Job Fair and the Hispanic National Bar Association Job Fair.

• Initiating on-campus informational and networking meetings to introduce minority and GLBT law students to the firm.

• Use of first-year positions in our summer program as opportunities to recruit law students of color who may otherwise overlook our firm.

Retention, mentoring and promotion

Our mentoring has evolved through experience and feedback (including "Mentoring Across Differences") to a multi-dimensional program. Every associate is assigned an associate mentor when they join the firm to assist their integration and acclimation to the firm. Following completion of the first full year, associates are assigned a partner mentor. Partner mentoring is focused on a written practice development plan, prepared jointly by the associate and the mentor. Simultaneously, through a group mentoring program, teams of partners facilitate discussion with small groups of associates on specific development objectives. All attorneys are accountable for their performance as mentors.

We also encourage, facilitate and reward less formal mentoring. Through a series of lunches and informal activities, our lawyers of color help orient the summer associates of color to the firm and the Twin Cities legal community. In 2003, we also promoted internal networking lunches and groups among our women attorneys, attorneys of color and GLBT attorneys and staff.

We credit good mentoring for our relatively modest attrition and increasing promotion. In 2003, the rates of attrition for lawyers of color, women lawyers and GLBT lawyers were in each case less than the rate of attrition for all lawyers. All of our partners of color have been promoted from our associate ranks. In the past two years, four associates of color were promoted to partner. Firm-wide, nine women were promoted to partner in 2004, and 49 women have become partners since 1990.

Internal programming to build awareness and enhance values

Internal programming has been an important aspect of our diversity initiatives. In 2001, "Women, Diversity and the Law: Initiatives and Perspective" was our focus. In 2002, we presented "Making the Business Case for Diversity," which aggressively focused on accountability for diversity as a business imperative. That event included a panel of corporate counsel representing six major clients of the firm. Most recently, in 2003, we focused on "The Community Case for Diversity." Two distinguished panels of community leaders addressed topics such as the challenges and opportunities facing our communities, and the ways in which Faegre & Benson can help to meet those challenges and realize those opportunities. Panelists represented prominent community

organizations, including nonprofits which serve our communities of color, women, economically disadvantaged individuals and the GLBT community.

Collaborative efforts with community and bar associations

A highlight of our external outreach in 2003 was our hosting of a reception and day-long test-taking seminar for minority law students in the Twin Cities' area. We also sponsor, and our lawyers will be participating in, several forthcoming minority bar events important to the advancement of diversity in the profession. In Minnesota, these include the Midwest Regional Conference for Women in the Law, NLGLA Lavender Law Conference and a CLE program to celebrate the 50th anniversary of Brown v. Bd. of Education.

Our Minnesota lawyers have been active in the Twin Cities Committee on Minority Lawyers in Large Law Firms, the Minnesota Chapter of the National Asian Pacific American Bar Association, the University of Minnesota Law School Minority Mentor Program, the Minnesota Minority Lawyers Association, the Minnesota Minority Corporate Counsel Program, the Minnesota American Indian Bar Association, the Lavender Bar Association and the Minnesota Association of Black Lawyers (MABL). One of our Minneapolis associates, Harvey Rupert, is currently serving as the president of MABL.

Peer and client networking

We give high priority to networking with our peers and clients on best diversity practices. For the past two years we have attended MCCA's "Creating Pathways to Diversity" Conference in New York. Attendees this year included our diversity coordinator, two members of our Management Committee (including our diversity partner), and the chair of our Diversity Committee. Many of our attorneys attend the MCCA's annual CLE Expo. This year one of our partners, Felicia Boyd, will be presenting at that seminar.

A highlight of our client diversity networking is our relationship with DuPont. Our lawyers have been leaders in diversity initiatives sponsored by DuPont, including the DuPont Minority Counsel Conference and the Conference on Women and the Practice of Law. We are proud that one of our partners, Dara Mann, won the DuPont Themis Award for women's leadership in 2003.

Fenwick & West LLP

801 California Street
Mountain View, CA 94041
Phone: (650) 988-8500
Fax: (650) 938-5200

Embarcadero Center West
275 Battery Street
San Francisco, CA 94111
Phone: (415) 875-2300
Fax: (415) 281-1350

FIRM LEADERSHIP

Chair: Gordon K. Davidson
Managing Partner: Laird Simons and Ralph Pais, Partners
Diversity Team Leader: Laurence Pulgram, Partner
Hiring Partners: Shawna M. Swanson, Jeffery R. Vetter

LOCATIONS

Mountain View, CA
San Francisco, CA
Strategic Plan and Diversity Leadership

LAW FIRM DEMOGRAPHIC PROFILES

FULL-TIME ASSOCIATES	2003	2002
Minority men	15	18
Minority women	17	18
White women	64	60
Total	151	169

SUMMER ASSOCIATES	2003	2002
Minority men	4	0
Minority women	4	7
White women	2	7
Total	17	30

EQUITY PARTNERS	2003	2002
Minority men	4	3
Minority women	0	1
White women	15	17
Total	76	80

NEW HIRES	2003	2002
Minority men	5	1
Minority women	9	3
White women	6	6
Total	30	22

Strategic Plan and Diversity Leadership

How does the firm's leadership communicate the importance of diversity to everyone at the firm? (e.g., e-mails, web site, newsletters, meetings, etc.)

The chair of the firm, managing partners, Diversity Committee and Recruiting Committee have communicated about diversity within the firm by e-mail, intranet postings, newsletter articles, partnership meetings, full-firm meetings, interviews of associates, focus groups and innumerable other means to engage in a discourse about diversity, its value, benefits and challenges to the firm.

Who has primary responsibility for leading diversity initiatives at your firm?

Name of person and his/her title: Gordon Davidson, chairman of the firm. In addition, Laurence Pulgram, managing partner of the San Francisco office, serves as chair of the Diversity Committee.

Does your law firm currently have a diversity committee?

Yes.

Does the committee's representation include one or more members of the firm's management/executive committee (or the equivalent)?

Yes. The chair of the firm, two of the three managing partners of the firm and an additional Executive Committee member are on the committee.

How many attorneys are on the committee, and in 2003, what was the total number of hours collectively spent by the committee in furtherance of the firm's diversity initiatives?

Total attorneys on committee: 10

Total hours spent on diversity: Several hundred hours – not tracked separately.

Does the committee and/or diversity leader establish and set goals or objectives consistent with management's priorities?

Yes.

Has the firm undertaken a formal or informal diversity program or set of initiatives aimed at increasing the diversity of the firm?

Yes, formal.

How often does the firm's management review the firm's diversity progress/results?

As needed – monthly in some instances, to annually in others.

How is the firm's diversity committee and/or firm management held accountable for achieving results?

The Diversity Committee has matrices to measure the success of its initiative. In addition, the firm subscribes to various objectives, goals and timetables for firms in the Bay Area to which its performance is compared.

LAW FIRM DIVERSITY INITIATIVES	ALREADY COMPLETED	CURRENTLY ADDRESSING	NOT A CURRENT PRIORITY
Undertake communication from firm management that diversity is a top priority of the firm.	✔		
Formalize diversity plan and committee with action steps and accountability to management.	✔		
Conduct firm-wide diversity training for all attorneys and staff.		✔	
Increase the number of minority attorneys at the associate level.	✔		
Increase the number of minority attorneys at the partnership level.		✔	
Develop/expand relationships with minority bar associations to offer firm's support of these networks.	✔		
Focus on strengthening firm's mentoring program, including for benefit of minority attorneys.	✔		
Conduct internal diversity needs assessment and/or retain diversity consultant to examine how firm culture might be more welcoming of minorities.	✔		
Support law firm's internal affinity networks (e.g., women, minority attorney networks).		✔	
Manage/monitor allocation of work assignments and/or hours billed to ensure women and minority attorneys have equal access/inclusion on top client matters.		✔	
Attempt to include diverse attorneys in balanced way in all firm activities, committees, initiatives, functions.	✔		

Recruitment – New Associates

Does your firm annually recruit at any of the following types of institutions? (Check all that apply and list the schools).

Ivy League schools: Harvard University, Columbia University, Cornell University, University of Pennsylvania

Public state schools: University of Michigan, University of California (L.A., Berkeley, Davis and Hastings)

Private schools: Northwestern University, Santa Clara University, NYU, Georgetown University, Duke University, Vanderbilt University

Do you have any special outreach efforts directed to encourage minority law students to consider your firm?

• Hold a reception for minority law students

• Advertise in minority law student association publication(s)

• Participate in/host minority law student job fair(s)

• Sponsor minority law student association events

• Firm's lawyers participate on career panels at school

• Outreach to leadership of minority student organizations

SUMMER ASSOCIATE STATISTICS: SUMMER 2003	MINORITY MEN	MINORITY WOMEN	WHITE WOMEN	TOTAL
Summer associates	4	4	2	17
Summer associates who received an offer of full-time employment	4	4	2	16
Summer associates who accepted an offer of full-time employment	4	3	2	14

Recruitment – Lateral Associates and Partners

What activities does the firm undertake to attract minority and women attorneys?

• Partner programs with women and minority bar associations

• Participate at minority job fairs

• Seek referrals from other attorneys

Do you use executive recruiting/search firms to seek to identify new diversity hires (partners or associates)?

No

LATERAL ASSOCIATES AND PARTNERS: 1/1/03 – 12/31/03	MINORITY MEN	MINORITY WOMEN	WHITE WOMEN	TOTAL
Number of lateral associate hires	5	8	8	30
Number of lateral partner hires (equity and non-equity)	0	0	0	2
Number of new partners (equity and non-equity) promoted from associate rank	1	0	1	5
Number of new equity partners	1	0	1	7

Retention & Professional Development

ATTORNEYS WHO LEFT THE FIRM: 2003	MINORITY MEN	MINORITY WOMEN	WHITE WOMEN	TOTAL
Number of attorneys who voluntarily or involuntarily left your firm's employ in 2003	6	4	10	53

How do 2003 attrition rates generally compare to those experienced in the prior year period?

Lower than in prior years

Please identify the specific steps you are taking to reduce the attrition rate of minority and women attorneys.

• *Focused attention to minorities/women and others who are not getting "traction" at the firm to connect them to the firm through better work experiences.*

• Develop and/or support internal employee affinity groups (e.g., minority or women networks within the firm)

• Increase/improve current work/life programs

• Succession plan includes emphasis on diversity

• Introduce minority and women attorneys to key clients, including to lead engagements

• Review work assignments and hours billed to key client matters to make sure minority and women attorneys are not being excluded

• Strengthen mentoring program for all attorneys, including minorities and women

• Professional skills development program, including minority and women attorneys

Does your firm have part-time/flex-time policies that permit attorneys (male or female) to work alternative schedules?

Yes. The firm has a policy of paying proportionate salary for proportionate work hours, without a "haircut" for part-time attorneys. The firm has approximately 17 attorneys, including five partners – men and women – who are working reduced-time schedules.

What impact, if any, will the decision to work part-time have on an attorney's ability to make partner or, if already a partner, to remain a partner at your firm?

Part-time attorneys remain on ordinary partnership track, although reduced experience due to reduced hours in practice may result in proportionate extension of time to partnership consideration. Numerous partners work part-time.

Have any attorneys who chose to work a part-time schedule made partner at your firm?

Yes

Management Demographic Profile (as of 12/31/03)

	MINORITY MEN	MINORITY WOMEN	WHITE WOMEN	TOTAL
Number of attorneys on the Executive/Management Committee or equivalent*	0	0	1	7
Number of attorneys on the Hiring Committee or equivalent	3	0	5	14
Number of attorneys on the Partner/Associate Review Committee or equivalent	0	0	2	6

*Note: one woman attorney joined the Executive Committee in 2004.

Please provide information regarding all minority and women attorneys who head offices or practice groups of your law firm:

Women heading offices: Kate Fritz, former managing partner, San Francisco

Minorities heading practice groups: Greg Sueoka, Patent

Women heading practice groups: Sally Abel, Trademark; Lisa Kenkel, Licensing

The Firm Says

Fenwick & West LLP recognizes the importance of promoting an environment rich in cultural diversity. We recognize the strength of having a wide range of viewpoints and life experiences. We are dedicated to recruiting and hiring people representative of the multitude of backgrounds and perspectives available in the work force. We recognize that by capitalizing on the unique skills that each individual has to offer we will be most successful in all endeavors. We also recognize that attracting and retaining a diverse work force is essential to our long-term success in meeting client needs and accessing the best talent.

In order to insure our commitment to creating a diverse work environment, we have created a Diversity Committee dedicated to developing strategies to increase diversity within the firm. Our Diversity Committee has worked closely with the attorney recruiting department to increase outreach at law schools targeted particularly to diverse student communities. In addition, numerous members of our firm have been actively involved in various groups and activities that work to promote diversity in the profession and in the community, including, for example, the Asian American Bar Association, Bay Area Lawyers for Individual Freedom (BALIF), and the Section of Litigation Committee for the Minority Trial Lawyer. As indicated in response to this survey, the firm has implemented diversity training, mentoring, assignment tracking, as well as recruiting initiatives in its effort to strengthen diversity within the firm. As part of our effort to embrace diverse heritages, the firm hosts celebrations across cultural lines, including Cinco De Mayo, Chinese New Year and Juneteenth. The firm chair, Gordon Davidson, has consistently articulated diversity as a top priority and fundamental objective for the business success of the firm.

Fenwick & West LLP is an equal opportunity employer. The firm is active in recruiting the best employees of every race, color, religion, national origin, gender, age, disability, marital status, parental status and sexual orientation. The firm will continue to encourage and support its employees' participation in organizations focused on diversity. We will continue to develop and maintain an environment that will provide opportunities for the growth and recognition of minorities. Fenwick & West seeks to hire and promote people of various backgrounds and perspectives to strengthen our work force and increase opportunities for the advancement of minorities.

Finnegan, Henderson Farabow, Garrett & Dunner, L.L.P.

1300 I Street, NW
Washington, DC 20005
Phone: (202) 408-4000
Fax: (202) 408-4400

FIRM LEADERSHIP

Managing Partner: Christopher Foley,
Managing Partner
Diversity Team Leader: Christopher Foley,
Managing Partner

LOCATIONS

Washington, DC (HQ)
Atlanta, GA
Cambridge, MA
Palo Alto, CA
Reston, VA
Brussels
Taipei
Tokyo

Note: The Law Firm Demographic Profile does not accurately reflect our firm's attorney population. We have three groups who do not fit into any of the defined categories: senior counsel, of counsel and contract partners. To include these numbers into any of the already defined categories would not accurately represent them in the survey. Therefore, the senior counsel, of counsel and contract partners are not included in our headcount.

LAW FIRM DEMOGRAPHIC PROFILES

FULL-TIME ASSOCIATES	2003	2002
Minority men	29	33
Minority women	7	10
White women	42	46
Total	171	190

SUMMER ASSOCIATES	2003	2002
Minority men	1	3
Minority women	3	2
White women	7	9
Total	20	30

EQUITY PARTNERS	2003	2002
Minority men	2	1
Minority women	1	1
White women	13	11
Total	86	80

NON-EQUITY PARTNERS	2003	2002
Minority men	0	0
Minority women	0	0
White women	4	4
Total	6	6

NEW HIRES	2003	2002
Minority men	3	15
Minority women	0	3
White women	6	11
Total	22	52

Strategic Plan and Diversity Leadership

How does the firm's leadership communicate the importance of diversity to everyone at the firm? (e.g., e-mails, web site, newsletters, meetings, etc.)

During orientation for new employees and on an ongoing basis via e-mails, newsletters, intranet and regularly scheduled firm events (e.g., attorney lunches).

Who has primary responsibility for leading diversity initiatives at your firm?

Christopher Foley, managing partner

Does your law firm currently have a diversity committee?

Yes

Does the committee's representation include one or more members of the firm's management/executive committee (or the equivalent)?

Yes

How many attorneys are on the committee, and in 2003, what was the total number of hours collectively spent by the committee in furtherance of the firm's diversity initiatives?

Total attorneys on committee: One

Does the committee and/or diversity leader establish and set goals or objectives consistent with management's priorities?

Yes

Has the firm undertaken a formal or informal diversity program or set of initiatives aimed at increasing the diversity of the firm?

Yes, formal

How often does the firm's management review the firm's diversity progress/results?

Monthly

LAW FIRM DIVERSITY INITIATIVES	ALREADY COMPLETED	CURRENTLY ADDRESSING	NOT A CURRENT PRIORITY
Undertake communication from firm management that diversity is a top priority of the firm.	✓		
Formalize diversity plan and committee with action steps and accountability to management.		✓	
Conduct firm-wide diversity training for all attorneys and staff.		✓	
Increase the number of minority attorneys at the associate level.		✓	
Increase the number of minority attorneys at the partnership level.		✓	
Develop/expand relationships with minority bar associations to offer firm's support of these networks.		✓	
Focus on strengthening firm's mentoring program, including for benefit of minority attorneys.		✓	
Conduct internal diversity needs assessment and/or retain diversity consultant to examine how firm culture might be more welcoming of minorities.			✓
Support law firm's internal affinity networks (e.g., women, minority attorney networks).			✓
Manage/monitor allocation of work assignments and/or hours billed to ensure women and minority attorneys have equal access/inclusion on top client matters.			✓

Recruitment- New Associates

Does your firm annually recruit at any of the following types of institutions? (Check all that apply and list the schools).

Ivy League schools: Columbia University, Harvard University, University of Pennsylvania

Public state schools: University of Georgia, University of Washington, University of North Carolina-Chapel Hill, George Mason University, University of Michigan, University of California-Los Angeles, University of California at Berkeley-Boalt Hall, University of California-Hastings, University of California-Davis, University of Virginia

Private schools: Emory University, American University, New York University, Duke University, Georgetown University, George Washington University, Vanderbilt University, Boston University, University of Southern California, Boston College, Stanford University, Santa Clara University

Historically Black Colleges and Universities (HBCUs): Howard University

We also recruit at the following job fairs: Chicago Patent Law Interview Program, San Francisco Intellectual Property Law Association (SFIPLA), Mid-Atlantic Black Law Students Association, American Intellectual Property Law Association (AIPLA) Job Fair.

Do you have any special outreach efforts directed to encourage minority law students to consider your firm?

• *Minority attorneys act as mentors to local minority law students*

• Hold a reception for minority law students

• Participate in/host minority law student job fair(s)

• Sponsor minority law student association events

• Firm's lawyers participate on career panels at school

• Outreach to leadership of minority student organizations

• Scholarships or intern/fellowships for minority students

SUMMER ASSOCIATE STATISTICS: SUMMER 2003	MINORITY MEN	MINORITY WOMEN	WHITE WOMEN	TOTAL
Summer associates	1	2	6	16
Summer associates who received an offer of full-time employment	1	2	5	15
Summer associates who accepted an offer of full-time employment	1	2	5	15

Recruitment – Lateral Associates and Partners

What activities does the firm undertake to attract minority and women attorneys?

Partner programs with women and minority bar associations

Participate at minority job fairs

Seek referrals from other attorneys

Do you use executive recruiting/search firms to seek to identify new diversity hires (partners or associates)?

No

LATERAL ASSOCIATES AND PARTNERS*: 1/1/03 – 12/31/03	MINORITY MEN	MINORITY WOMEN	WHITE WOMEN	TOTAL
Number of lateral associate hires	0	0	0	0
Number of lateral partner hires (equity and non-equity)**	N/A	N/A	N/A	N/A
Number of new partners (equity and non-equity) promoted from associate rank	0	0	3	5
Number of new equity partners	0	0	3	5

*This chart does not include our firm's senior counsel, of counsel and contract partners.

**Our firm does not hire lateral equity or non-equity partners.

Retention & Professional Development

ATTORNEYS WHO LEFT THE FIRM: 2003	MINORITY MEN	MINORITY WOMEN	WHITE WOMEN	TOTAL
Number of attorneys who voluntarily or involuntarily left your firm's employ in 2003	6	3	8	49

How do 2003 attrition rates generally compare to those experienced in the prior year period?

Higher than in prior years

Please identify the specific steps you are taking to reduce the attrition rate of minority and women attorneys.

• Increase/improve current work/life programs

• Strengthen mentoring program for all attorneys, including minorities and women

Does your firm have part-time/flex-time policies that permit attorneys (male or female) to work alternative schedules?

Yes. Both men and women attorneys currently work an alternative schedule.

What impact, if any, will the decision to work part-time have on an attorney's ability to make partner or, if already a partner, to remain a partner at your firm?

If an attorney chooses an alternative work schedule, his or her track to partnership will be adjusted in proportion to that schedule. Attorneys who are already partners are also eligible to work an alternative work schedule.

Have any attorneys who chose to work a part-time schedule made partner at your firm?

No. Our alternative work schedule policy has not been in effect long enough for associates to be eligible yet for partnership consideration.

Management Demographic Profile (as of 12/31/03)

	MINORITY MEN	MINORITY WOMEN	WHITE WOMEN	TOTAL
Number of attorneys on the Executive/Management Committee or equivalent	0	0	1	7
Number of attorneys on the Hiring Committee or equivalent	0	0	2	4
Number of attorneys on the Partner/Associate Review Committee or equivalent	0	0	1	11

Please provide information regarding all minority and women attorneys who head offices or practice groups of your law firm:

Minorities heading practice groups: Jean B. Fordis, Bio/Pharm practice group

Women heading practice groups (list names and departments): Jean B. Fordis, Bio/Pharm practice group

The Firm Says

Finnegan Henderson has a strong commitment to developing diversity in our workplace, and in the field of intellectual property law in general. Over the past year and on a continuing basis, Finnegan Henderson works to ensure a diverse workplace and advance diversity in the legal profession in many ways:

- In 2003, we established the Finnegan Henderson Diversity Scholarship, which is open to application by persons of a minority heritage attending top law schools around the nation. Our first Finnegan Scholar is currently working in the Washington, D.C., office.

- Finnegan Henderson also contributes toward the American Intellectual Property Law Education Minority Scholarship endowment.

- Howard University Law School recently honored Finnegan Henderson for our contributions to the University's Institute of Intellectual Property and Social Justice. We have been pleased to support the Institute since its beginning and began teaching an advanced patent law and social engineering course last year. In 2003, the firm collaborated with Howard University Law School to present a one-day Intellectual Property law Seminar, a two-track program offering both introductory and advanced courses on patent, trademark, copyright and other IP issues. The firm has also created a summer intern program for a student from Howard University Law School. Two of our associates are serving as mentors to the 2005 Howard Law School class and we look forward to continuing our efforts to contribute to the Howard IP community.

- Finnegan Henderson has been a perennial sponsor of the National Asian Pacific American Bar Association (NAPABA) Annual Convention. One of our partners currently serves on the board of NAPABA as the southeast regional governor.

- The firm has been a regular sponsor of the Asian Pacific American Bar Association of the Greater Washington, D.C., Area's Annual Installation Dinners and annually hosts a number of programs and meetings.

- Finnegan Henderson sponsors the APABA Education Fund (AEF) Annual Scholarship Dinner. One of our associates is a former board member of AEF, and another associate is a current board member of AEF.

- Finnegan Henderson also sponsors annual fundraising events for National Asian Pacific American Legal Consortium (NAPALC) and Asian Pacific American Legal Resource Center (APALRC).

- Finnegan Henderson actively supports the Women's Bar Association of D.C. We frequently host WBA events, and one of our associates is co-chair of the Intellectual Property Law Forum.

- Each year, as part of our fall on-campus interview schedule, Finnegan Henderson participates in several minority recruiting job fairs. Our 2004 summer program is comprised of 50 percent women and 14 percent minority students.

- Finnegan Henderson's directors and managers attended a full-day diversity awareness seminar in 2003. The firm has established a Diversity/Leadership Group, including the managing partner, executive director, human resources director, and director of professional recruitment and development, to coordinate ongoing firm-wide diversity awareness initiatives.

- Finnegan Henderson offers an alternative work schedule for attorneys. Associate attorneys may work either an 80 percent or a 60 percent schedule, and are paid a proportionate amount of their salary. Currently, we have

male and female attorneys with part-time schedules. This allows individual attorneys to balance their work and personal lives, while it also benefits the firm by retaining a more diverse population of attorneys.

• Lastly, Finnegan Henderson has a second attorney review policy, mandating that all work, before being sent to a client, must be reviewed by another attorney. This policy ensures that all attorneys receive substantive feedback on their work product and professional mentoring, often from many senior attorneys. We feel that this policy helps develop all of our attorneys' legal skills and ensures that each attorney receives one-on-one professional development and mentoring.

Our firm philosophy encourages attorneys from all offices and practice groups to work together on cases where their backgrounds and abilities may contribute. As a result, the potential for any attorney or a diverse group of attorneys to work on a particular matter is large.

Fish & Neave

1251 Avenue of the Americas
New York, NY 10020
Phone: (212) 596-9000
Fax: (212) 596-9090

FIRM LEADERSHIP

Managing Partner: William J. McCabe

LOCATIONS

New York, NY (HQ)
Palo Alto, CA
Washington, DC

LAW FIRM DEMOGRAPHIC PROFILES

FULL-TIME ASSOCIATES	2003	2002
Minority men	21	22
Minority women	21	19
White women	29	27
Total	125	127

SUMMER ASSOCIATES	2003	2002
Minority men	4	6
Minority women	1	3
White women	5	3
Total	16	25

EQUITY PARTNERS	2003	2002
Minority men	1	1
Minority women	1	1
White women	8	9
Total	50	52

NEW HIRES	2003	2002
Minority men	5	3
Minority women	1	5
White women	3	8
Total	21	30

MINORITY CORPORATE COUNSEL ASSOCIATION

Strategic Plan and Diversity Leadership

How does the firm's leadership communicate the importance of diversity to everyone at the firm? (e.g., e-mails, web site, newsletters, meetings, etc.)

All of the above, including our lawyers manual.

Who has primary responsibility for leading diversity initiatives at your firm?

Denise Loring, partner

Does your law firm currently have a diversity committee?

Yes

Does the committee's representation include one or more members of the firm's management/executive committee (or the equivalent)?

No

How many attorneys are on the committee, and in 2003, what was the total number of hours collectively spent by the committee in furtherance of the firm's diversity initiatives?

Total attorneys on committee: 5

Has the firm undertaken a formal or informal diversity program or set of initiatives aimed at increasing the diversity of the firm?

Yes, informal

LAW FIRM DIVERSITY INITIATIVES	ALREADY COMPLETED	CURRENTLY ADDRESSING	NOT A CURRENT PRIORITY
Undertake communication from firm management that diversity is a top priority of the firm.		✔	
Formalize diversity plan and committee with action steps and accountability to management.		✔	
Conduct firm-wide diversity training for all attorneys and staff.			✔
Increase the number of minority attorneys at the associate level.		✔	
Increase the number of minority attorneys at the partnership level.		✔	
Develop/expand relationships with minority bar associations to offer firm's support of these networks.			✔
Focus on strengthening firm's mentoring program, including for benefit of minority attorneys.		✔	
Conduct internal diversity needs assessment and/or retain diversity consultant to examine how firm culture might be more welcoming of minorities.			✔

LAW FIRM DIVERSITY INITIATIVES (CONTINUED)	ALREADY COMPLETED	CURRENTLY ADDRESSING	NOT A CURRENT PRIORITY
Support law firm's internal affinity networks (e.g., women, minority attorney networks).	✓		
Manage/monitor allocation of work assignments and/or hours billed to ensure women and minority attorneys have equal access/inclusion on top client matters.			✓

Recruitment – New Associates

Does your firm annually recruit at any of the following types of institutions? (Check all that apply and list the schools).

Ivy League schools: Cornell University, Columbia University, University of Pennsylvania, Harvard University, Yale University

Public state schools: UCLA, University of Virginia, University of California-Berkeley, University of Texas

Private schools: Fordham University, NYU, Boston University, Boston College, Vanderbilt University, Santa Clara University, Stanford University, George Washington University, Georgetown University, Northwestern University, Duke University, University of Michigan, University of Chicago, University of Southern California

SUMMER ASSOCIATE STATISTICS: SUMMER 2003	MINORITY MEN	MINORITY WOMEN	WHITE WOMEN	TOTAL
Summer associates	4	1	5	16
Summer associates who received an offer of full-time employment	4	1	5	16
Summer associates who accepted an offer of full-time employment	4	1	5	12

Recruitment – Lateral Associates and Partners

What activities does the firm undertake to attract minority and women attorneys?
Participate at minority job fairs

Do you use executive recruiting/search firms to seek to identify new diversity hires (partners or associates)?
No

LATERAL ASSOCIATES AND PARTNERS: 1/1/03 – 12/31/03	MINORITY MEN	MINORITY WOMEN	WHITE WOMEN	TOTAL
Number of lateral associate hires	0	0	1	2
Number of lateral partner hires (equity and non-equity)	0	0	0	0
Number of new partners (equity and non-equity) promoted from associate rank	1	0	0	3
Number of new equity partners	1	0	0	3

Retention & Professional Development

ATTORNEYS WHO LEFT THE FIRM: 2003	MINORITY MEN	MINORITY WOMEN	WHITE WOMEN	TOTAL
Number of attorneys who voluntarily or involuntarily left your firm's employ in 2003	5	1	8	25

How do 2003 attrition rates generally compare to those experienced in the prior year period?

About the same as in prior years

Please identify the specific steps you are taking to reduce the attrition rate of minority and women attorneys.

• Develop and/or support internal employee affinity groups (e.g., minority or women networks within the firm)

• Strengthen mentoring program for all attorneys, including minorities and women

Does your firm have part-time/flex-time policies that permit attorneys (male or female) to work alternative schedules?

Yes

What impact, if any, will the decision to work part-time have on an attorney's ability to make partner or, if already a partner, to remain a partner at your firm?

It's a case-by-case situation.

Have any attorneys who chose to work a part-time schedule made partner at your firm?

No

Management Demographic Profile (as of 12/31/03)

	MINORITY MEN	MINORITY WOMEN	WHITE WOMEN	TOTAL
Number of attorneys on the Executive/Management Committee or equivalent	0	0	0	6
Number of attorneys on the Hiring Committee or equivalent	1	0	1	3
Number of attorneys on the Partner/Associate Review Committee or equivalent	1	0	1	3

The Firm Says

Our longstanding diversity policy (which is also provided on our web site) is set forth below.

We have a Diversity Committee comprising both partners and associates which is constantly looking for new ways to help recruit and retain minority attorneys. We interview at BLSA Job Fair and the Lavender Job Fair, and we are also a signatory to the Association of the Bar of the City of New York's Statement of Diversity Principles.

Fish & Neave Diversity Policy

We believe in recruiting and retaining a diverse group of people from all walks of life. To fulfill this goal, the firm is dedicated to hiring minority attorneys and to creating an environment in which individuals with diverse backgrounds are able to thrive.

In the Minority Law Journal Summer 2003 Diversity Scorecard, Fish & Neave ranked 8th (out of 215 of the nation's largest law firms): 19.1 percent of the firm's attorneys are minorities. According to the most recent NALP form, 16 percent of the firm's attorneys are black, Hispanic or Asian Americans. Eighteen percent of our partners are women.

Some of the minority organizations the firm supports include Asian American Bar Association, African Heritage Twining, Lambda Legal and Minority Corporate Counsel Association.

In order to achieve our diversity objectives, we created a Diversity Subcommittee of the Associates' Committee. The Diversity Subcommittee is dedicated to addressing the concerns of associates at the firm about minority issues. The Subcommittee, composed of associates, works with members of the partnership to ensure that the firm achieves the diverse environment for which it strives.

We try to provide the best possible experience for our attorneys as they grow at the firm. The strength of our firm culture is reflected by the fact that 80 percent of our partners have spent their entire legal career with us.

The excellence of our people is Fish & Neave's greatest asset. Whether it's a person in the mailroom, a legal assistant, a junior associate or a senior partner, we take great pride in the caliber of our people and the quality of their work. We are committed to providing a high quality work environment with lawyers and staff from diverse social, cultural and personal backgrounds.

508

Fitzpatrick, Cella, Harper & Scinto

30 Rockefeller Plaza
New York, NY 10112
Phone: (212) 218-2100
Fax: (212) 218-2200

FIRM LEADERSHIP

Managing Partner: Dominick Conde, Managing Partner
Diversity Team Leader: Leisa Smith, Partner

LOCATIONS

New York, NY (HQ)
Costa Mesa, CA
Washington, DC

LAW FIRM DEMOGRAPHIC PROFILES

FULL-TIME ASSOCIATES	2003	2002
Minority men	11	11
Minority women	11	9
White women	20	17
Total	93	106

SUMMER ASSOCIATES	2003	2002
Minority men	0	2
Minority women	1	6
White women	4	5
Total	18	24

EQUITY PARTNERS	2003	2002
Minority men	0	1
Minority women	1	1
White women	5	5
Total	59	58

NEW HIRES	2003	2002
Minority men	2	5
Minority women	3	7
White women	6	6
Total	18	27

Strategic Plan and Diversity Leadership

How does the firm's leadership communicate the importance of diversity to everyone at the firm? (e.g., e-mails, web site, newsletters, meetings, etc.)

Internal memoranda, web site, associate handbooks, new client presentation on diversity

Who has primary responsibility for leading diversity initiatives at your firm?

Leisa Smith, Diversity Team Leader; Scott Reed, Chair of Professional Development Committee (retention, advancement and mentoring); Michael Sandonato, Chair of Recruiting Committee (recruiting)

Does your law firm currently have a diversity committee?

Yes, see above.

Does the committee's representation include one or more members of the firm's management/executive committee (or the equivalent)?

Yes

How many attorneys are on the committee, and in 2003, what was the total number of hours collectively spent by the committee in furtherance of the firm's diversity initiatives?

Total attorneys on committee: 23

Total hours spent on diversity: 400

Does the committee and/or diversity leader establish and set goals or objectives consistent with management's priorities?

Yes

Has the firm undertaken a formal or informal diversity program or set of initiatives aimed at increasing the diversity of the firm?

Yes, informal

How often does the firm's management review the firm's diversity progress/results?

Quarterly

How is the firm's diversity committee and/or firm management held accountable for achieving results?

The Professional Development Committee and Recruiting Committees report to the Management Committee.

LAW FIRM DIVERSITY INITIATIVES	ALREADY COMPLETED	CURRENTLY ADDRESSING	NOT A CURRENT PRIORITY
Undertake communication from firm management that diversity is a top priority of the firm.	✔		
Formalize diversity plan and committee with action steps and accountability to management.	✔		
Conduct firm-wide diversity training for all attorneys and staff.		✔	
Increase the number of minority attorneys at the associate level.	✔		
Increase the number of minority attorneys at the partnership level.		✔	
Develop/expand relationships with minority bar associations to offer firm's support of these networks.	✔		
Focus on strengthening firm's mentoring program, including for benefit of minority attorneys.	✔		
Conduct internal diversity needs assessment and/or retain diversity consultant to examine how firm culture might be more welcoming of minorities.		✔	
Support law firm's internal affinity networks (e.g., women, minority attorney networks).	✔		
Manage/monitor allocation of work assignments and/or hours billed to ensure women and minority attorneys have equal access/inclusion on top client matters.	✔		

Recruitment – New Associates

Does your firm annually recruit at any of the following types of institutions?

Ivy League schools: Harvard, Columbia, Cornell, UPenn

Public state schools: William & Mary, George Mason, Rutgers University–Newark, University of California–Berkeley, University of California-Los Angeles, University of Houston, University of Michigan

Private schools: American, BC, BU, Brooklyn, Catholic, Fordham, Franklin Pierce, GWU, Georgetown, Loyola–LA, NYLS, NYU, Northwestern, Pace, Seton Hall, St. John's, Stanford, University of Chicago, University of Notre Dame, University of Southern California, Vanderbilt

Do you have any special outreach efforts directed to encourage minority law students to consider your firm?

• Participate in/host minority law student job fair(s)

• Firm's lawyers participate on career panels at school

SUMMER ASSOCIATE STATISTICS: SUMMER 2003	MINORITY MEN	MINORITY WOMEN	WHITE WOMEN	TOTAL
Summer associates	0	1	4	18
Summer associates who received an offer of full-time employment	0	1	4	18
Summer associates who accepted an offer of full-time employment	8	0	0	14

Recruitment – Lateral Associates and Partners

What activities does the firm undertake to attract minority and women attorneys?

• *Support and encourage participation in minority bar association events. (We support monetarily and by representation on the board of trustees the American Intellectual Property Law Education Foundation. The mission of the organization is to significantly increase the number of underrepresented minorities working as intellectual property lawyers.)*

• Partner programs with women and minority bar associations

• Participate at minority job fairs

• Seek referrals from other attorneys

Do you use executive recruiting/search firms to seek to identify new diversity hires partners or associates)?

No

LATERAL ASSOCIATES AND PARTNERS: 1/1/03 – 12/31/03	MINORITY MEN	MINORITY WOMEN	WHITE WOMEN	TOTAL
Number of lateral associate hires	0	0	1	2
Number of lateral partner hires (equity and non-equity)	0	0	0	1
Number of new partners (equity and non-equity) promoted from associate rank	0	0	0	2
Number of new equity partners	0	0	0	2

Retention & Professional Development

ATTORNEYS WHO LEFT THE FIRM: 2003	MINORITY MEN	MINORITY WOMEN	WHITE WOMEN	TOTAL
Number of attorneys who voluntarily or involuntarily left your firm's employ in 2003	3	4	4	18

How do 2003 attrition rates generally compare to those experienced in the prior year period?

About the same as in prior years

Please identify the specific steps you are taking to reduce the attrition rate of minority and women attorneys.

• Develop and/or support internal employee affinity groups (e.g., minority or women networks within the firm)

• Increase/review compensation relative to competition

• Increase/improve current work/life programs

• Work with minority and women attorneys to develop career advancement plans

• Introduce minority and women attorneys to key clients, including to lead engagements

• Review work assignments and hours billed to key client matters to make sure minority and women attorneys are not being excluded

• Strengthen mentoring program for all attorneys, including minorities and women

• Professional skills development program, including minority and women attorneys

Does your firm have part-time/flex-time policies that permit attorneys (male or female) to work alternative schedules?

Yes

What impact, if any, will the decision to work part-time have on an attorney's ability to make partner or, if already a partner, to remain a partner at your firm?

None

Have any attorneys who chose to work a part-time schedule made partner at your firm?

Yes, one attorney.

Management Demographic Profile (as of 12/31/03)

	MINORITY MEN	MINORITY WOMEN	WHITE WOMEN	TOTAL
Number of attorneys on the Executive/Management Committee or equivalent	0	0	0	7
Number of attorneys on the Hiring Committee or equivalent	1	0	2	10
Number of attorneys on the Partner/Associate Review Committee or equivalent	0	1	2	11

The Firm Says

Diversity in our workplace has long been important to us at Fitzpatrick and has been a particular focus of our firm for at least the last five years.

We believe that a diverse workplace enhances the quality of the legal services that we provide. At its core, a law firm is composed of its people. We have found that when those people are of diverse backgrounds, different perspectives and experiences are brought together, with the resultant synergy stimulating creativity and innovation. A diverse pool of attorneys also provides us with a platform from which we can continue to attract

the best and brightest new candidates to our organization. And having a workplace that mirrors those of our clients allows us to partner more effectively with them. It all just makes good business sense.

We believe that the quality and depth of minority and women attorneys at our firm are the best evidence of our commitment to diversity:

• Nearly 20 percent of our attorneys are minorities, and over 25 percent are women.

• In the last three years, Fitzpatrick has made eight new partners. Three of those partners are women, and one of those women is an African-American.

• Over the past three years, over 30 percent of our newly hired attorneys were minorities, and over 40 percent of our newly hired attorneys were women.

• We have responded positively to every request we have received for more flexible hours and working arrangements, and currently over 5 percent of our attorneys work part-time, telecommute or have schedules that are some combination of the two.

First and foremost, our success in recruiting and retaining minority attorneys is an outgrowth of the energy and resources we devote to recruiting and retaining top-quality legal talent.

Simply put, we have found that if the tasks of legal recruiting and associate development are given the high level of importance that they deserve, then a substantial percentage of minority and women attorneys is a natural result. We take a broad-based approach toward recruiting and look well beyond the traditional factors of law school name and class rank in assessing a candidate's potential abilities. While academic accomplishments are of course a consideration, we also put great emphasis on other, less tangible factors, such as the level of the candidate's motivation and drive, the candidate's judgment and the candidate's ability to function in a team environment.

We pride ourselves in our ability to identify these attributes not only in the nation's "top-10" law schools, but in many law schools often overlooked by other large firms, many of which have significant numbers of minority and women students.

We recruit from these schools routinely and have found some of our best people at them. We also regularly recruit at events specifically targeted toward minorities, such as the Black Law Students Association annual job fair in New York. This approach, we believe, has contributed significantly to the impressive statistics given above.

The success of minority and women attorneys already within our organization is also an important factor in the equation and gives us an advantage in attracting new minority talent.

We are delighted that our minority and women partners, as well as the increasing number of more senior minority and women associates at the firm, have served as role models for their more junior counterparts and aid in their professional growth.

Historically, our firm has enjoyed a very high retention rate, not only with respect to our minority and women associates, but with our associate corps in general. We credit this success largely to the high emphasis we put on mentoring and professional development.

We have an active Professional development Committee, comprised of partners and associates, which oversees formal training, mentoring and associate reviews. Under the guidance of the Professional Development

Committee, our litigation, patent and trademark practice groups each administer a year-long course in their respective areas. Every new associate also completes an in-house writing workshop, given annually. Each associate is assigned to a partner mentor of the associate's choosing, who becomes responsible for keeping track of the progress and needs of the mentee's career at the firm. Our mentors are expected to have frequent meetings or lunches with their mentees, keep track of the evaluations that each mentee receives from other attorneys at the firm, and render advice and suggestions as to how the mentees can improve and grow as lawyers.

By allowing the associate to select his or her mentor, we help ensure that the match will be a successful one, and we optimize the quality of the mentoring that the associate receives. At a broader level, all partners and senior associates at the firm are encouraged to act as informal mentors to the younger lawyers with whom they work, teaching as they go, and making sure that each young lawyer's experience on a project is a developmental one.

In 2002, we were the proud recipients of the Minority Corporate Counsel Association's Thomas L. Sager Diversity Award – and we are the first intellectual property law firm to receive it. In the summer issue of the Minority Law Journal we ranked No. 10 in their 2002 Diversity Scorecard. We believe our efforts to create a diverse workplace over the last several years are best evidenced by our success at doing so.

Foley & Lardner LLP

777 East Wisconsin Avenue
Milwaukee, WI 53202-5367
Phone: (414) 271-2400
Fax: (414) 297-4900

FIRM LEADERSHIP

Managing Partner: Stanley S. Jaspan,
Managing Partner
Diversity Team Leader: Marc McSweeney,
Diversity Partner

LOCATIONS

Milwaukee, WI (HQ)
Chicago, IL
Detroit, MI
Jacksonville, FL
Los Angeles, CA
Madison, WI
New York, NY
Orlando, FL
Palo Alto, CA
Sacramento, CA
San Diego, CA
San Diego/Del Mar, CA
San Francisco, CA
Tallahassee, FL
Tampa, FL
Washington, DC
West Palm Beach, FL
Brussels
Tokyo

LAW FIRM DEMOGRAPHIC PROFILES

FULL-TIME ASSOCIATES	2003	2002
Minority men	29	29
Minority women	26	29
White women	162	163
Total	492	516

SUMMER ASSOCIATES	2003	2002
Minority men	13	8
Minority women	7	9
White women	16	35
Total	70	92

EQUITY PARTNERS	2003	2002
Minority men	5	4
Minority women	8	8
White women	51	48
Total	406	393

NON-EQUITY PARTNERS	2003	2002
Minority men	1	0
Minority women	4	3
White women	1	2
Total	35	52

NEW HIRES	2003	2002
Minority men	6	5
Minority women	8	6
White women	35	37
Total	99	101

Strategic Plan and Diversity Leadership

How does the firm's leadership communicate the importance of diversity to everyone at the firm? (e.g., e-mails, web site, newsletters, meetings, etc.)

Addressed at all firm-wide meetings, firm management committee meetings as well as meetings attended by department chairs, practice group leaders and office managing partners. And we will soon launch an internal diversity extranet, as well as a diversity newsletter.

Who has primary responsibility for leading diversity initiatives at your firm?

Maurice (Marc) McSweeney, diversity partner

Does your law firm currently have a diversity committee?

No, but one is in the process of formation.

Does the committee and/or diversity leader establish and set goals or objectives consistent with management's priorities?

Yes

Has the firm undertaken a formal or informal diversity program or set of initiatives aimed at increasing the diversity of the firm?

Yes, formal

How often does the firm's management review the firm's diversity progress/results?

Quarterly

How is the firm's diversity committee and/or firm management held accountable for achieving results?

The firm has created a diversity plan which includes incremental goals and objectives. Each quarter the diversity partner updates firm management on the status of each initiative, including specifics on the measurable results themselves. Our diversity partner dedicates 1,000 billable hours a year to the firm's diversity initiatives. All of the firm's leadership is held accountable through the diversity partner's reports to the firm's management committee on each partner's contributions.

LAW FIRM DIVERSITY INITIATIVES	ALREADY COMPLETED	CURRENTLY ADDRESSING	NOT A CURRENT PRIORITY
Undertake communication from firm management that diversity is a top priority of the firm.	✓		
Formalize diversity plan and committee with action steps and accountability to management.	✓		
Conduct firm-wide diversity training for all attorneys and staff.		✓	
Increase the number of minority attorneys at the associate level.		✓	
Increase the number of minority attorneys at the partnership level.		✓	
Develop/expand relationships with minority bar associations to offer firm's support of these networks.		✓	
Focus on strengthening firm's mentoring program, including for benefit of minority attorneys.		✓	
Conduct internal diversity needs assessment and/or retain diversity consultant to examine how firm culture might be more welcoming of minorities.	✓		
Support law firm's internal affinity networks (e.g., women, minority attorney networks).	✓		
Manage/monitor allocation of work assignments and/or hours billed to ensure women and minority attorneys have equal access/inclusion on top client matters.		✓	

Recruitment – New Associates

Does your firm annually recruit at any of the following types of institutions? (Check all that apply and list the schools).

Ivy League schools: Columbia University; Cornell University; Harvard University; University of Pennsylvania; Yale University

Public state schools: University of California-Berkley, University of California-Davis, University of California-Hastings, UCLA, University of Florida, Florida State University, University of Georgia, George Mason University, University of Illinois, Indiana University-Bloomington, University of Iowa, University of Michigan, University of Minnesota, ,University of Texas, University of Utah, University of Virginia, University of Wisconsin

Private schools: American University, Brigham Young University, Catholic University of America, University of Chicago, DePaul University, Duke University, Emory University, George Washington University, Georgetown University, IIT (Chicago-Kent), Loyola University-Chicago, Loyola Law School-Los Angeles, Marquette University, New York University, Northwestern University, University of Notre Dame, Stanford University, Stetson University, University of Southern California, University of San Diego, Vanderbilt University, Washington University, St. Louis

Historically Black Colleges and Universities (HBCUs): Howard University

Do you have any special outreach efforts directed to encourage minority law students to consider your firm?

• Participate in/host minority law student job fair(s)

• Sponsor minority law student association events

• Firm's lawyers participate on career panels at school

• Scholarships or intern/fellowships for minority students

SUMMER ASSOCIATE STATISTICS: SUMMER 2003	MINORITY MEN	MINORITY WOMEN	WHITE WOMEN	TOTAL
Summer associates	13	7	16	70
Summer associates who received an offer of full-time employment	11	5	11	54
Summer associates who accepted an offer of full-time employment	8	4	9	40

Recruitment – Lateral Associates and Partners

What activities does the firm undertake to attract minority and women attorneys?

• Participate at minority job fairs

• Seek referrals from other attorneys

Do you use executive recruiting/search firms to seek to identify new diversity hires (partners or associates)?

Yes

LATERAL ASSOCIATES AND PARTNERS: 1/1/03 – 12/31/03	MINORITY MEN	MINORITY WOMEN	WHITE WOMEN	TOTAL
Number of lateral associate hires	5	4	12	45
Number of lateral partner hires (equity and non-equity)	1	1	2	10
Number of new partners (equity and non-equity) promoted from associate rank	2	2	3	15
Number of new equity partners	1	0	3	21

Retention & Professional Development

ATTORNEYS WHO LEFT THE FIRM: 2003	MINORITY MEN	MINORITY WOMEN	WHITE WOMEN	TOTAL
Number of attorneys who voluntarily or involuntarily left your firm's employ in 2003	4	7	36	125

How do 2003 attrition rates generally compare to those experienced in the prior year period?

About the same as in prior years

Please identify the specific steps you are taking to reduce the attrition rate of minority and women attorneys.

• Develop and/or support internal employee affinity groups (e.g., minority or women networks within the firm)

• Increase/improve current work/life programs

• Succession plan includes emphasis on diversity

• Work with minority and women attorneys to develop career advancement plans

• Introduce minority and women attorneys to key clients, including to lead engagements

• Review work assignments and hours billed to key client matters to make sure minority and women attorneys are not being excluded

• Strengthen mentoring program for all attorneys, including minorities and women

Does your firm have part-time/flex-time policies that permit attorneys (male or female) to work alternative schedules?

Yes. The firm recognizes that flexibility in scheduling is necessary and desirable to permit attorneys to respond to certain demands in their personal lives. It is the policy of Foley & Lardner to make alternative work schedule arrangements reasonably available to attorneys, as requested, for the purpose of meeting their needs for child or elder care. Although it is the general policy of the firm to recruit and hire attorneys who practice law on a full-time basis, the firm believes that the availability of such flexible arrangements will benefit both the firm and its clients by facilitating the recruitment of new attorneys and the retention of experienced attorneys. The object of this policy is to strike a fair balance between the business and economic needs of the firm, the demands and expectations of our clients, the impact on other attorneys in the organization, and the needs and goals of the attorney requesting the flexible arrangement.

What impact, if any, will the decision to work part-time have on an attorney's ability to make partner or, if already a partner, to remain a partner at your firm?

If the attorney works part-time for a significant period of time it may extend the time to partnership. It does not impact on the ability to remain a partner.

Have any attorneys who chose to work a part-time schedule made partner at your firm?

Yes, four attorneys.

Management Demographic Profile (as of 12/31/03)

	MINORITY MEN	MINORITY WOMEN	WHITE WOMEN	TOTAL
Number of attorneys on the Executive/Management Committee or equivalent	0	1	1	13
Number of attorneys on the Hiring Committee or equivalent	0	4	9	32
Number of attorneys on the Partner/Associate Review Committee or equivalent	0	1	2	9

Please provide information regarding all minority and women attorneys who head offices or practice groups of your law firm:

Women heading offices: Nancy Sennett,-Milwaukee office; Nancy Geenan, San Francisco & Silicon Valley offices

Minorities heading practice groups: Pavan K. Agarwal, Electronics; Richard T. Choi, Financial Services/Products; Sharon R. Barner, IP Litigation; Denise Rios Rodriguez, Payments/Compliance; Miriam C. Beezy, Trademark & Copyright

Women heading practice groups: Sharon R. Barner, IP Litigation; Denise Rios Rodriguez, Payments/Compliance; Miriam C. Beezy, Trademark & Copyright; Beth A. Burrous, Biotechnology & Pharmaceutical; Janet E. Zeigler, Health Care Finance & Restructuring; Linda E. Benfield, Environmental Regulation; Lisa S. Neubauer, Insurance Dispute Resolution; Maureen A. McGinnity, Tax, Valuation & Fiduciary LIT; Judith A. Waltz, Payments/Compliance

The Firm Says

As one of the highest priorities of our firm, Foley & Lardner is fully invested in establishing an environment that attracts and sustains diversity of gender, ethnicity, religion and sexual preferences. Our diversity partner, in conjunction with our firm's management, has defined our diversity mission as follows:

To be the law firm that is open and inclusive to, provides mentoring and training opportunities for, and maintains a barrier-free workplace that supports the bias-free promotion of all individuals.

Through our Diversity Initiative, and the direct support of the highest levels of our firm, we have established policies and procedures to help us realize our mission. For example, contributing to a diverse work force in a meaningful way is an important element of our partner compensation program. It also is the explicit objective of Foley & Lardner to promote and to invite to partnership women and minority attorneys who meet the firm's criteria for partnership such that, over time, the number of women and minority partners will correspond more closely to the percentage of women and minority attorneys hired by the firm. Our diversity partner, Marc McSweeney, personifies the importance we place on our Diversity Initiative. Marc is a former member of the firm's Management Committee and former national chair of the firm's litigation department.

To increase our ethnic diversity, Foley & Lardner has set a goal of at least 20 percent minority hiring in each associate and summer associate class. To achieve this goal, our firm identifies and actively recruits minority students through placement administrators, faculty members, former summer associates and minority law

student organizations; attends minority job fairs, receptions and forums; establishes and cultivates ties with the minority professional communities in the cities in which our offices are located; participates in minority law student hiring programs sponsored by state bars; and works to include minority students in the firm's summer associate program.

We also are firmly committed to ensuring that assignments are fair and appropriate for women and minority attorneys based upon current roles and responsibilities, and that these assignments provide attorneys with opportunities for success and advancement. To this end, we strive to create a work environment that is open and supportive and we provide formalized training, mentoring, guidance and feedback. The firm's Diversity partner also reviews staffing of all the firm's clients to further improve the diversity of our teams and, ultimately, the service to our clients.

Foley & Lardner's efforts to ensure diversity within our firm, as well as in our profession, continue to be recognized – as exemplified by our Chicago office's receipt of the Sager Award in 2000. This award, bestowed by the Minority Corporate Counsel Association, recognizes law firms that have demonstrated sustained commitment to improving the hiring, retention and promotion of minority attorneys. We also continue to participate in and form strategic alliances with organizations dedicated to the advancement of diversity in the legal profession. We are extremely proud of the recent recognition received by partners Sharon Barner and Alicia Batts in the November 2003 issue of Black Enterprise magazine, in which they were named two of "America's Top Black Lawyers."

In 1998, Foley & Lardner created the Minority Scholarship Program – believed to be the first of its kind among law firms. Through the program, Foley & Lardner awards $5,000 to a minority law student at each of the following schools: Duke, University of Florida, Georgetown, University of Michigan, Northwestern, Stanford, UCLA and University of Wisconsin. The winners are selected based upon their undergraduate records, involvement in community activities and minority student associations, outstanding work and personal achievements.

Foley & Lardner's Women's Network Steering Committee was organized in January 2001 to identify, review and resolve issues relating to the recruiting and retention of women associates and partners at the firm. The committee's mission is to work with firm management, department chairs and practice group leaders to support, educate and promote women associates and partners within the firm. Over time, the Women's Network Steering Committee has furthered its role in the firm with additional subcommittees, including the National Liaison Committee, which coordinates issues raised and programs developed at the local office level; the Compensation Committee, which reviews compensation issues for women; the Mentoring and Practice Development Committee, which supports senior counsel and young partners during their years of developing a partner-level practice; and the Leadership Committee, which identifies leadership opportunities and supports leadership aspirations for women in the firm.

Our firm is a sponsor of both the Athena Foundation and its ATHENA PowerLink mentoring program. Our firm not only provides financial support to the program, but also has a number of attorneys participating as mentors/advisors to women business owners. Foley & Lardner is also a supporter of the Minority Corporate Counsel Association. Foley & Lardner co-sponsored the MCCA's Mentoring Across Differences Research Report, which explores the trends surrounding mentoring relationships in law firms and corporations.

Other local-office sponsorship and membership activities include the following:

• Founding member, the Milwaukee Center for Workplace Diversity

- Corporate sponsor, Black Law Student Association, Midwest Region
- Corporate sponsor, Northwestern Latino Law Students Association
- Participant, Bar Association of San Francisco "No Glass Ceiling" Initiative
- Sponsor, California Minority Corporate Counsel Program
- Corporate sponsor, National Association of Women Business 0wners, Chicago Chapter
- Sponsor, Women's Economic Development Outreach, Chicago
- Sponsor, Springboard Enterprises, Chicago
- Title sponsor, Women Who Mean Business Awards, San Diego
- Member, Wolverine Bar Association, Detroit
- Sponsor, Healthcare Businesswomen's Association, San Francisco Chapter
- Sponsor, Asian Pacific American Bar Association
- Corporate sponsor, The Enterprise Institute, Detroit
- Sponsor, Women Inc.
- Sponsor, Thurgood Marshall Scholarship Fund Luncheon

525

Foley Hoag LLP

Seaport World Trade Center West
155 Seaport Boulevard
Boston, MA 02210-2600
Phone: (617) 832-1000
Fax: (617) 832-7000

FIRM LEADERSHIP

Managing Partner: Peter Rosenblum and
Michele Whitham, Co-Managing Partners

LOCATIONS

Boston, MA (HQ)
Washington, DC

LAW FIRM DEMOGRAPHIC PROFILES

FULL-TIME ASSOCIATES	2003	2002
Minority men	6	5
Minority women	11	10
White women	54	57
Total	145	143

SUMMER ASSOCIATES	2003	2002
Minority men	0	5
Minority women	2	2
White women	10	14
Total	27	38

EQUITY PARTNERS	2003	2002
Minority men	3	3
Minority women	0	0
White women	11	12
Total	73	72

NON-EQUITY PARTNERS	2003	2002
Minority men	0	0
Minority women	0	0
White women	6	5
Total	25	24

NEW HIRES	2003	2002
Minority men	4	2
Minority women	1	3
White women	13	16
Total	39	38

MINORITY CORPORATE COUNSEL ASSOCIATION

Strategic Plan and Diversity Leadership

How does the firm's leadership communicate the importance of diversity to everyone at the firm? (e.g., e-mails, web site, newsletters, meetings, etc.)

Foley Hoag's leadership has outlined their commitment to diversity on the firm's web site. The firm has also made a public statement of its support of diversity in our community by dedicating resources and legal talent to promote the goals of diversity and tolerance through the pro bono work of our lawyers and the contributions of the Foley Hoag Foundation.

Who has primary responsibility for leading diversity initiatives at your firm?

Peter Rosenblum, Co-Managing Partner

Does your law firm currently have a diversity committee?

No

Does the committee and/or diversity leader establish and set goals or objectives consistent with management's priorities?

Yes

Has the firm undertaken a formal or informal diversity program or set of initiatives aimed at increasing the diversity of the firm?

Yes, informal

How often does the firm's management review the firm's diversity progress/results?

Quarterly

LAW FIRM DIVERSITY INITIATIVES	ALREADY COMPLETED	CURRENTLY ADDRESSING	NOT A CURRENT PRIORITY
Undertake communication from firm management that diversity is a top priority of the firm.	✔		
Formalize diversity plan and committee with action steps and accountability to management.		✔	
Conduct firm-wide diversity training for all attorneys and staff.	✔		
Increase the number of minority attorneys at the associate level.		✔	
Increase the number of minority attorneys at the partnership level.		✔	
Develop/expand relationships with minority bar associations to offer firm's support of these networks.		✔	
Focus on strengthening firm's mentoring program, including for benefit of minority attorneys.		✔	
Conduct internal diversity needs assessment and/or retain diversity consultant to examine how firm culture might be more welcoming of minorities.		✔	
Support law firm's internal affinity networks (e.g., women, minority attorney networks).	✔		
Manage/monitor allocation of work assignments and/or hours billed to ensure women and minority attorneys have equal access/inclusion on top client matters.	✔		

Recruitment – New Associates

Does your firm annually recruit at any of the following types of institutions? (Check all that apply and list the schools).

Ivy League schools: Columbia University, Harvard University, University of Pennsylvania, Yale University

Public state schools: University of California-Berkeley, University of Michigan, University of North Carolina, University of Virginia, College of William & Mary

Private schools: Boston College, Boston University, University of Chicago, Duke University, Fordham University, George Washington University, Georgetown University, New York University, Northeastern University, Northwestern University, Stanford University, Suffolk University

Historically Black Colleges and Universities (HBCUs): Howard University

Do you have any special outreach efforts directed to encourage minority law students to consider your firm?

• Hold a reception for minority law students
• Advertise in minority law student association publication(s)
• Participate in/host minority law student job fair(s)
• Sponsor minority law student association events
• Firm's lawyers participate on career panels at school
• Outreach to leadership of minority student organizations

SUMMER ASSOCIATE STATISTICS: SUMMER 2003	MINORITY MEN	MINORITY WOMEN	WHITE WOMEN	TOTAL
Summer associates	0	1	10	24
Summer associates who received an offer of full-time employment	0	1	10	23
Summer associates who accepted an offer of full-time employment	0	0	8	17

Recruitment – Lateral Associates and Partners

What activities does the firm undertake to attract minority and women attorneys?

• *Foley Hoag is a founding member of The Boston Lawyers Group, a consortium of Boston law firms and government and corporate legal offices dedicated to increasing the number of lawyers of color practicing in Boston.*

• Partner programs with women and minority bar associations

• Participate at minority job fairs

• Seek referrals from other attorneys

Do you use executive recruiting/search firms to seek to identify new diversity hires (partners or associates)?

Yes

If yes, list all women- and/or minority-owned executive search/recruiting firms to which the firm paid a fee for placement services in the past 12 months:

Jane Sender and Associates; New England Legal Search

LATERAL ASSOCIATES AND PARTNERS: 1/1/03 – 12/31/03	MINORITY MEN	MINORITY WOMEN	WHITE WOMEN	TOTAL
Number of lateral associate hires	1	0	2	7
Number of lateral partner hires (equity and non-equity)	0	0	0	2
Number of new partners (equity and non-equity) promoted from associate rank	0	0	1	5
Number of new equity partners	0	0	0	3

Retention & Professional Development

ATTORNEYS WHO LEFT THE FIRM: 2003	MINORITY MEN	MINORITY WOMEN	WHITE WOMEN	TOTAL
Number of attorneys who voluntarily or involuntarily left your firm's employ in 2003	3	1	11	29

How do 2003 attrition rates generally compare to those experienced in the prior year period?

About the same as in prior years

Please identify the specific steps you are taking to reduce the attrition rate of minority and women attorneys.

• Develop and/or support internal employee affinity groups (e.g., minority or women networks within the firm)

• Increase/improve current work/life programs

• Work with minority and women attorneys to develop career advancement plans

• Introduce minority and women attorneys to key clients, including to lead engagements

• Review work assignments and hours billed to key client matters to make sure minority and women attorneys are not being excluded

• Strengthen mentoring program for all attorneys, including minorities and women

• Professional skills development program, including minority and women attorneys

Does your firm have part-time/flex-time policies that permit attorneys (male or female) to work alternative schedules?

Yes

What impact, if any, will the decision to work part-time have on an attorney's ability to make partner or, if already a partner, to remain a partner at your firm?

At least for the first year of such work, an attorney working at 80 percent of full-time most likely will gain seniority as if working full-time. In other circumstances, an attorney working a reduced schedule most likely will gain seniority at a pace proportional to the percentage of full-time at which the attorney is working. However, to the extent that an associate demonstrates that despite working a reduced schedule, she or he remains at, or attains over time, the same level of skill and experience as others in her or his law school class, the reduced schedule may not have such an effect.

Have any attorneys who chose to work a part-time schedule made partner at your firm?

Yes, four in recent years. A number of women associates have been promoted to partnership on time with their law school classmates while working part-time schedules.

Management Demographic Profile (as of 12/31/03)

	MINORITY MEN	MINORITY WOMEN	WHITE WOMEN	TOTAL
Number of attorneys on the Executive/Management Committee or equivalent	1	0	1	6
Number of attorneys on the Hiring Committee or equivalent	1	0	3	10
Number of attorneys on the Partner/Associate Review Committee or equivalent	0	0	1	8

Please provide information regarding all minority and women attorneys who head offices or practice groups of your law firm:

Women heading offices: Michele Whitham, Co-Managing Partner of the firm; Janis Brennan, Administrative Partner of the Washington, DC office

Women heading practice groups: Beth Arnold, Patent; Arlene Bender, Business; Stefanie Cantor, Trusts & Estates; Mary Beth Gentleman, Energy; Gloria Larson, Government Strategies; and Susan Montgomery, Trademark

The Firm Says

Foley Hoag's commitment to diversity traces its roots to the founding of the firm in 1943. Henry Foley and Garrett Hoag were determined to hire the very best lawyers, based entirely on individual merit and without exclusion – an attitude that set them very much apart from others in the Boston legal community of that era. Those twin traditions of excellence and inclusiveness have remained guiding forces in the firm's culture. We have brought together at the firm lawyers of different backgrounds, skills and experiences, because we recognize that those individuals bring with them a diversity of thought and perspective that enriches the firm's culture and enhances the quality of our work. We are committed to fostering an environment in which diversity of every type can flourish and in which every lawyer is positioned to thrive.

Recruitment and advancement

Our founders' values drove us to hire a diverse work force – because it was the right thing to do – long before some other firms awoke to the "business case" for diversity. Foley Hoag, for example, was the first large Boston law firm to promote an African-American attorney to the partnership ranks.

Foley Hoag is a founding member of The Boston Lawyers Group (BLG), a consortium of large Boston law firms, minority-owned firms, and government and corporate legal offices dedicated to increasing the number of lawyers of color practicing in Boston. Our co-managing partner and our administrative partner serve on the BLG's Executive Committee, and the BLG's executive offices are currently hosted at our firm.

The firm's lawyers are very active in the BLG's recruitment efforts, interviewing law students at BLG job fairs, mentoring first-year law students of color and participating in career panels and mock interviews held for students at Boston area schools. This year we hosted a dinner, as well as career development panels, for all first-year students of color at Boston law schools. We also hosted a lunchtime seminar for all summer associates of color at BLG member firms. Since its inception, we have participated in the BLG's summer internship program for undergraduates of color who may be interested in legal careers. Foley Hoag is also a regular sponsor and

participant at conferences and job fairs organized by minority law student groups and other affinity organizations dedicated to issues of recruitment, retention and promotion of lawyers of color.

Foley Hoag is a strong supporter of the efforts of The Partnership, Inc., an organization working to make a lasting change in the Boston community by fostering key relationships among existing and emerging leaders and developing programs to strengthen the retention of minority executives and professionals. We have sponsored a number of our associates of color as "Fellows" in The Partnership's Boston Fellows Program, a nine-month program bringing together professionals and executives of color, providing opportunities to meet and develop relationships with Boston's most influential people of color and key non-minority decision-makers as well.

We also support our associates in seeking leadership roles outside the firm to enhance their professional development. For example, associate Maria Lam has been elected to the Boston Bar Association Council, and she also is currently serving as secretary of The Partnership, Inc.

Dedicating our resources

As a leader in the legal and business community, we are dedicated to supporting and expanding diversity throughout the community in which we live and work. We take great pride in the fact that we have been able to employ our own resources and our legal talent to promote the goals of diversity and tolerance. Foley Hoag served as counsel to a group of plaintiffs in the litigation achieving the desegregation of the Boston city school system, and for two decades, we defended on behalf of our client, the NAACP, consent decrees implemented in actions to remove barriers to the integration of the Boston police and fire departments. In 2004, we served as lead trial counsel in a landmark case successfully challenging the Massachusetts legislature's redistricting plan under the Voting Rights Act on the grounds that it discriminated against minority voters.

The Foley Hoag Foundation, established in 1980 by the partners of the firm, seeks to combat racism, especially among youth, in the city of Boston. The Foundation awards grants to organizations that work to improve Boston's racial climate by addressing issues of diversity and race through art and cultural activities, youth leadership, recreational programs or advocacy assistance. The Foley Hoag Foundation was the first and remains the only foundation to focus exclusively on the improvement of race relations in Boston.

Foley Hoag lawyers participate in a number of initiatives to promote the educational development of inner-city students. We are a host firm for the Boston Citizen Schools 8th Grade Academy, an initiative that helps young people to develop their writing and communication skills with the help of volunteer lawyer coaches. We work with high school students in mock-trial programs. Also, a number of Foley Hoag lawyers and staff travel weekly to a Boston public elementary school to read with students as part of Boston Partners in Education's Power Lunch Program, a one-on-one literacy and mentoring program.

The firm's pro bono work and community activities have earned Foley Hoag numerous awards. They include the inaugural Adams Pro Bono Publico Award from the Standing Committee on Pro Bono Legal Services of the Massachusetts Supreme Judicial Court, the Racial Justice Award from the YWCA of Greater Boston, and awards from the Gay and Lesbian Advocates and Defenders, the Political Asylum and Immigrant Representation Project, the Boston Indian Council and the Women's Bar Association of Massachusetts.

Fried, Frank, Harris, Shriver & Jacobson LLP

One New York Plaza
New York, NY 10004
Phone: (212) 859-8000
Fax: (212) 859-4000

1001 Pennsylvania Avenue, N.W.
Washington, DC 20004

350 South Grand Avenue
Los Angeles, CA 90071

FIRM LEADERSHIP

Managing Partner: Paul Reinstein and Valerie
Jacob, Managing Partners
Diversity Team Leader: Peter Cobb, Chair of
New York Diversity Committee; Matt Morley,
Chair of D.C. Diversity Committee

LOCATIONS

Los Angeles, CA
New York, NY
Washington, DC
London
Paris

LAW FIRM DEMOGRAPHIC PROFILES*

FULL-TIME ASSOCIATES	2003	2002
Minority men	35	41
Minority women	46	57
White women	85	93
Total	339	377

SUMMER ASSOCIATES	2003	2002
Minority men	6	9
Minority women	5	10
White women	27	18
Total	66	64

EQUITY PARTNERS	2003	2002
Minority men	2	3
Minority women	5	5
White women	18	17
Total	124	133

NON-EQUITY PARTNERS	2003	2002
Minority men	0	0
Minority women	1	0
White women	10	10
Total	20	22

NEW HIRES	2003	2002
Minority men	9	9
Minority women	9	13
White women	20	26
Total	66	91

*These figures are for senior attorneys (the firm does not have non-equity partners).

MINORITY CORPORATE COUNSEL ASSOCIATION

Strategic Plan and Diversity Leadership

How does the firm's leadership communicate the importance of diversity to everyone at the firm? (e.g., e-mails, web site, newsletters, meetings, etc.)

Generally, the firm uses e-mail and internal memoranda to communicate important matters to its attorneys and staff. Diversity matters are also communicated in periodic newsletters and in formal and informal meetings with attorneys and staff, such as the firm's annual "State of the Firm" meeting where significant current matters relating to the firm and its business are discussed with all of our attorneys. Our web site contains a section devoted to diversity, both in connection with our recruiting efforts and with the concerns of our current legal and non-legal staff. This section of our web site is in the process of being substantially upgraded.

Who has primary responsibility for leading diversity initiatives at your firm?

In the New York office: Paul Reinstein, managing partner; Peter Cobb, chair of the NY Diversity Committee; and Paul Steinberg, executive director for attorney affairs. In the DC office: Matt Morley, chair of the DC Diversity Committee; Terry Miller, director of associate development. In the Los Angeles office, Stephen Alexander, partner.

Does your law firm currently have a diversity committee?

Yes

Does the committee's representation include one or more members of the firm's management/executive committee (or the equivalent)?

Yes

How many attorneys are on the committee, and in 2003, what was the total number of hours collectively spent by the committee in furtherance of the firm's diversity initiatives?

Total attorneys on committee: 11 (NY); 11 (DC)

Total hours spent on diversity: No meaningful records are kept, but in the past year, the partners on the firm's Diversity Committees have devoted many hundreds of hours to diversity-related matters.

Does the committee and/or diversity leader establish and set goals or objectives consistent with management's priorities?

Yes

Has the firm undertaken a formal or informal diversity program or set of initiatives aimed at increasing the diversity of the firm?

Yes, formal

How often does the firm's management review the firm's diversity progress/results?

Because diversity is currently a major focus of the firm, firm management is continually involved in and reviewing our efforts.

How is the firm's diversity committee and/or firm management held accountable for achieving results?

Internally, the Diversity Committees of the New York and Washington, D.C., offices report periodically to the firm's Governance Committee on their plans and programs. In New York, the firm has joined other firms in setting a goal of having an attorney work force that, at all levels of seniority, substantially reflects in its diversity the law student population from which that work force is drawn. On an annual basis, the firm provides data to the Association of the Bar of the City of New York's Committee to Enhance Diversity in the Profession with respect to its efforts and progress in achieving that goal in its New York office.

LAW FIRM DIVERSITY INITIATIVES*	ALREADY COMPLETED	CURRENTLY ADDRESSING	NOT A CURRENT PRIORITY
Undertake communication from firm management that diversity is a top priority of the firm.	✓		
Formalize diversity plan and committee with action steps and accountability to management.	✓	✓	
Conduct firm-wide diversity training for all attorneys and staff.**	✓	✓	
Increase the number of minority attorneys at the associate level.	✓	✓	
Increase the number of minority attorneys at the partnership level.		✓	
Develop/expand relationships with minority bar associations to offer firm's support of these networks.	✓	✓	
Focus on strengthening firm's mentoring program, including for benefit of minority attorneys.		✓	
Conduct internal diversity needs assessment and/or retain diversity consultant to examine how firm culture might be more welcoming of minorities.	✓		
Support law firm's internal affinity networks (e.g., women, minority attorney networks).	✓	✓	
Manage/monitor allocation of work assignments and/or hours billed to ensure women and minority attorneys have equal access/inclusion on top client matters.		✓	

* Note: Many of the potential priorities listed here are ongoing processes that will never be "completed" if we in fact take them seriously. Thus, where we believe we have made significant progress but are continuing our efforts, we have indicated that by checking both the "completed" and the "currently addressing" boxes.

**Completed in the D.C. office

Recruitment – New Associates

Does your firm annually recruit at any of the following types of institutions? (Check all that apply and list the schools).

Ivy League schools: Columbia University, Cornell University, Harvard University, University of Pennsylvania, Yale University

Public state schools: University of Iowa, University of Michigan, University of Minnesota, University of North Carolina, Rutgers University-Newark, University of California-Berkeley, UCLA, University of Virginia, University of Wisconsin

Private schools: American University, Boston University, Brooklyn Law School, Cardozo School of Law, Catholic University of America, University of Chicago, Duke University, Fordham University, Hofstra University, Georgetown University, George Washington University, New York Law School, Northwestern University, NYU, St. Johns University, Stanford University

Historically Black Colleges and Universities (HBCUs): Howard University

Do you have any special outreach efforts directed to encourage minority law students to consider your firm?

- *Maintain close relationships, through our fellowship programs and otherwise, with leading civil rights advocacy organizations like NAACP-LDF and MALDEF, the Lawyers' Committee for Civil Rights under Law and the Washington Lawyer's Committee for Civil Rights and Urban Affairs.•* Hold a reception for minority law students

- Advertise in minority law student association publication(s)

- Participate in/host minority law student job fair(s)

- Sponsor minority law student association events

- Firm's lawyers participate on career panels at school

- Outreach to leadership of minority student organizations

- Scholarships or intern/fellowships for minority students

SUMMER ASSOCIATE STATISTICS: SUMMER 2003	MINORITY MEN	MINORITY WOMEN	WHITE WOMEN	TOTAL
Summer associates	3	5	27	62
Summer associates who received an offer of full-time employment	3	5	25	58
Summer associates who accepted an offer of full-time employment	1	3	20	41

Recruitment – Lateral Associates and Partners

What activities does the firm undertake to attract minority and women attorneys?

• *Speaking at on-campus pro bono and diversity-related events.*

• Participate at minority job fairs

• Seek referrals from other attorneys

Do you use executive recruiting/search firms to seek to identify new diversity hires (partners or associates)?

Yes

If yes, list all women- and/or minority-owned executive search/recruiting firms to which the firm paid a fee for placement services in the past 12 months:

We do not have the data to answer this.

LATERAL ASSOCIATES AND PARTNERS: 1/1/03 – 12/31/03	MINORITY MEN	MINORITY WOMEN	WHITE WOMEN	TOTAL
Number of lateral associate hires	0	0	1	6
Number of lateral partner hires (equity and non-equity)*	0	0	1	2
Number of new partners (equity and non-equity*) promoted from associate rank	1	0	0	3
Number of new equity partners	1	0	0	5

* The firm does not have non-equity partners. We do have several senior attorneys who are of counsel or special counsel and who are not included in the above numbers. In the period 1/1/03 through 12/31/03, we promoted one associate (a minority woman) to the position of special counsel and we laterally hired one attorney (a white woman) as a special counsel.

Retention & Professional Development

ATTORNEYS WHO LEFT THE FIRM: 2003	MINORITY MEN	MINORITY WOMEN	WHITE WOMEN	TOTAL
Number of attorneys who voluntarily or involuntarily left your firm's employ in 2003	14	16	28	107

How do 2003 attrition rates generally compare to those experienced in the prior year period?

About the same as in prior years

Please identify the specific steps you are taking to reduce the attrition rate of minority and women attorneys.

• Develop and/or support internal employee affinity groups (e.g., minority or women networks within the firm)

• Increase/improve current work/life programs

• Work with minority and women attorneys to develop career advancement plans (as part of mentoring)

• Introduce minority and women attorneys to key clients, including to lead engagements (as part of mentoring)

- Review work assignments and hours billed to key client matters to make sure minority and women attorneys are not being excluded (as part of mentoring)
- Strengthen mentoring program for all attorneys, including minorities and women
- Professional skills development program, including minority and women attorneys

Does your firm have part-time/flex-time policies that permit attorneys (male or female) to work alternative schedules?

Yes

What impact, if any, will the decision to work part-time have on an attorney's ability to make partner or, if already a partner, to remain a partner at your firm?

Not an obstacle.

Have any attorneys who chose to work a part-time schedule made partner at your firm?

Yes, at least three attorneys. A number of other partners have chosen to work part-time after becoming partners.

Management Demographic Profile (as of 12/31/03)

Please provide information regarding all minority and women attorneys who head offices or practice groups of your law firm:

Women heading offices: Valerie Jacob is one of the two managing partners of the firm as a whole

Minorities heading practice groups: Carmen Lawrence, co-chair of Securities Enforcement Group

Women heading practice groups: Carmen Lawrence and Dixie Johnson, co-chairs of Securities Enforcement Group; Audrey Strauss, head of White Collar Litigation Practice Group; Valerie Jacob, head of Capital Markets Group; Lois Herzeca, co-head of Private Equity Practice Group and of Corporate Governance Practice group; Ann Lesk, head of Estates and Trusts Group; Laraine Rothenberg, head of Employee Benefits, Executive Compensation and Exempt Organizations Group; Jessica Forbes, head of Investment Company Practice Group; Jennifer Colyer, Pro Bono Counsel (NY office); Karen Grisez, Public Service Counsel (DC office)

	MINORITY MEN	MINORITY WOMEN	WHITE WOMEN	TOTAL
Number of attorneys on the Executive/Management Committee or equivalent*	0	1	3	20
Number of attorneys on the Hiring Committee or equivalent – NY	0	2	1	6
Number of attorneys on the Hiring Committee or equivalent – DC	1	2	5	18
Number of attorneys on the Partner/Associate Review Committee or equivalent**	0	1	3	10

*Governance and Partner Review & Development Committees

**Partnership Candidate Review Committee

The Firm Says

Over the past year, the Diversity Committees in the firm's two major offices – New York and Washington, D.C. – have been extremely active in assessing how well we are pursuing and achieving our goal of creating and sustaining a truly diverse and inclusive law firm. With the help of outside consultants we have obtained the views of a large number of the firm's lawyers through focus groups and individual interviews. As a result of this work, the firm has strengthened the focus of its recruitment processes on diversity, established more extensive mentoring programs and introduced diversity-related segments into its internal professional development and management training programs. During the coming year, we will be focusing our efforts on all of the above programs as well as working to clarify and improve our existing part-time and flex-time programs for attorneys.

Diversity Committee Mission Statement:

Fried Frank supports a policy of equal opportunity for all. The Diversity Committee's mandate is to provide leadership to the firm as we strive to:

• recruit a highly qualified, diverse group of attorneys;

• improve the professional development and advancement of all of our lawyers; and

• enhance the firm's working atmosphere so as to foster respect for diversity and a sense of inclusion and fairness throughout the firm.

The committee provides a forum for the identification, prioritization and discussion of diversity issues, including the development and support of related proposals, initiatives and programs.

For the past 14 years, the firm's New York office has been an active participant in the Sponsors for Educational Opportunity (SEO) program, where each summer we hire two young people of color as interns in the summer between their college graduation and their entry into law school. Many of these SEO interns return to the firm as summer associates and associates. We currently have five associates in the New York office who participated in the SEO program.

The firm has highly successful collaborative fellowship programs with the NAACP Legal Defense and Educational Fund (LDF) and the Mexican-American Legal Defense and Educational Fund (MALDEF). Each year, Fried Frank hires two entry-level attorneys who spend two years in our New York litigation department and then two years as staff attorneys at LDF and MALDEF respectively, the costs of which are borne by Fried Frank. Once a fellow has successfully completed the four-year program, he or she can return to Fried Frank or, in many cases, stay on as a staff member at LDF and MALDEF. Although participation in the program is not restricted to minority attorneys, it has helped us attract many highly talented attorneys, many of whom are minorities, to the firm.

Fried Frank engages in pro bono work for minority public interest organizations. The firm assisted LDF in drafting and filing a response to a motion to dismiss LDF's challenge to the New York felon disfranchisement laws. These laws, argued LDF, which were originally enacted with racial animus, have continued to preclude a number of minority communities from realizing full participation in the democratic system and they violate, among other laws, the federal Voting Rights Act.

Fried Frank is assisting MALDEF in a high-profile Texas case involving the constitutionality of the Texas public school finance system. MALDEF is challenging the current school finance system under the Texas constitution due to the state's inability to provide for equal access to resources for all school districts in the state, including MALDEF's clients, the poorest and most racially diverse school districts in Texas. Trial is set for August 9, 2004, and the issue is expected to reach the Supreme Court of Texas by early next year. A Fried Frank partner is currently serving as chair of the board of trustees of MALDEF.

In 2000, Fried Frank established the Michael R. Diehl Civil Rights Forum, in memory of Michael R. Diehl, a corporate associate who was killed in a tragic swimming accident in 1999. Throughout his life, Michael was committed to the struggle for civil rights for gays and lesbians, as well as for all people who have been denied equal rights in our society. This forum provides the Fried Frank community with an opportunity to engage a prominent person (or persons) with a demonstrable commitment to civil rights in a discussion of social justice issues. Past speakers have included Deborah A. Batts of the U.S. District Court for the Southern District of New York; Elise Boddie, assistant counsel for the NAACP Legal Defense and Educational Fund, Inc; Matthew Coles, director of the ACLU's Gay and Lesbian Project; Leticia Saucedo, MALDEF staff attorney; Kerry Kennedy Cuomo, author; Professor Charles Ogletree Jr. of Harvard Law School; and Anthony D. Romero, executive director of the American Civil Liberties Union.

Although the survey explicitly excludes gay and lesbian issues from the concept of diversity, we believe that it should be explicitly included in the future. Each year we do an outreach letter to gay and lesbian student groups at various law schools introducing them to Fried Frank and our practice areas. Each summer we host a reception for our gay and lesbian attorneys and summer associates. We have sponsored tables at events for a variety of gay and lesbian organizations including Lambda Legal and LeGal Foundation. Fried Frank offers medical and dental insurance for domestic partners of the same sex. The firm represents Hetrick-Martin Institute, a public charity that provides educational and outreach services to gay and lesbian youth in New York City. The firm also represented a number of participants in the vigil to mourn the death of Matthew Shepard, a gay college student who was murdered because of his sexual orientation, who were subjected to police brutality or misconduct during the vigil.

Frost Brown Todd LLC

2200 PNC Center, 201 E. Fifth Street
Cincinnati, OH 45202
Phone: (513) 651-6800
Fax: (513) 651-6981

400 W. Market Street, 32nd Floor
Louisville, KY 40202
Phone: (859) 231-0000
Fax: (859) 231-0011

FIRM LEADERSHIP

Managing Partners: Richard J. Erickson &
Edward C. Glasscock, Members
Diversity Team Leaders: Deborah S. Adams
and Bonita K. Black, Members

LOCATIONS

Cincinnati, OH
Columbus, OH
Lexington, KY
Louisville, KY
Middletown, OH
Nashville, TN
New Albany, IN

LAW FIRM DEMOGRAPHIC PROFILES*

FULL-TIME ASSOCIATES	2003	2002
Minority men	5	2
Minority women	4	5
White women	53	55
Total	122	139

SUMMER ASSOCIATES	2003	2002
Minority men	1	1
Minority women	4	1
White women	8	6
Total	22	13

EQUITY PARTNERS	2003	2002
Minority men	0	0
Minority women	1	0
White women	20	17
Total	134	134

NON-EQUITY PARTNERS	2003	2002
Minority men	0	0
Minority women	0	1
White women	3	6
Total	11	14

NEW HIRES	2003	2002
Minority men	3	1
Minority women	0	0
White women	17	14
Total	47	35

Note: Not all past information available in computer.

Strategic Plan and Diversity Leadership

How does the firm's leadership communicate the importance of diversity to everyone at the firm? (e.g., e-mails, web site, newsletters, meetings, etc.)

All of the above.

Who has primary responsibility for leading diversity initiatives at your firm?

Deborah S. Adams and Bonita K. Black, members and co-chairs of Diversity Committee

Does your law firm currently have a diversity committee?

Yes

How many attorneys are on the committee, and in 2003, what was the total number of hours collectively spent by the committee in furtherance of the firm's diversity initiatives?

Total attorneys on committee: 19

Total hours spent on diversity: 500

Does the committee and/or diversity leader establish and set goals or objectives consistent with management's priorities?

Diversity consultant conducted assessment of focus groups and collected additional data in training sessions. Goals/objectives are being formulated on that basis.

- The Training and Development Committee of the firm has worked with the department chairs and practice group leaders to successfully implement departmental and general training programs for our lawyers. The Training and Development Committee has also updated the firm's formal mentoring program and instituted an informal mentoring program. The firm now gives budgeted time credit for those involved in training and mentoring efforts.

- The firm is conducting a technology assessment to determine new and different ways to help attorneys connect to the office from remote locations. A Communications Committee has been formed to address any perceived communications issues.

- The Diversity Committee is holding a retreat in July where it expects to further advance committee work.

Has the firm undertaken a formal or informal diversity program or set of initiatives aimed at increasing the diversity of the firm?

Yes, formal

How often does the firm's management review the firm's diversity progress/results?

Quarterly

How is the firm's diversity committee and/or firm management held accountable for achieving results?

Compensation Committee review

LAW FIRM DIVERSITY INITIATIVES	ALREADY COMPLETED	CURRENTLY ADDRESSING	NOT A CURRENT PRIORITY
Undertake communication from firm management that diversity is a top priority of the firm.	✓		
Formalize diversity plan and committee with action steps and accountability to management.	✓		
Conduct firm-wide diversity training for all attorneys and staff.	✓		
Increase the number of minority attorneys at the associate level.	✓		
Increase the number of minority attorneys at the partnership level.		✓	
Develop/expand relationships with minority bar associations to offer firm's support of these networks.	✓		
Focus on strengthening firm's mentoring program, including for benefit of minority attorneys.	✓		
Conduct internal diversity needs assessment and/or retain diversity consultant to examine how firm culture might be more welcoming of minorities.	✓		
Support law firm's internal affinity networks (e.g., women, minority attorney networks).	✓		
Manage/monitor allocation of work assignments and/or hours billed to ensure women and minority attorneys have equal access/inclusion on top client matters.	✓		

Recruitment – New Associates

Does your firm annually recruit at any of the following types of institutions?

Ivy League schools; Public state schools; Private Schools

Do you have any special outreach efforts directed to encourage minority law students to consider your firm?
- Minority law reception in partnership with local bar
- Participate in/host minority law student job fairs
- Firm's lawyers participate on career panels at school

SUMMER ASSOCIATE STATISTICS: SUMMER 2003	MINORITY MEN	MINORITY WOMEN	WHITE WOMEN	TOTAL
Summer associates	1	4	8	22
Summer associates who received an offer of full-time employment	0	4	7	20
Summer associates who accepted an offer of full-time employment	0	4	6	17

Recruitment – Lateral Associates and Partners

What activities does the firm undertake to attract minority and women attorneys?

• Partner programs with women and minority bar associations

• Participate at minority job fairs

• Seek referrals from other attorneys

LATERAL ASSOCIATES AND PARTNERS: 1/1/03 – 12/31/03	MINORITY MEN	MINORITY WOMEN	WHITE WOMEN	TOTAL
Number of lateral associate hires	1	0	5	16
Number of lateral partner hires (equity and non-equity)	0	0	0	0
Number of new partners (equity and non-equity) promoted from associate rank	0	0	4	27
Number of new equity partners	0	1	2	16

Retention & Professional Development

ATTORNEYS WHO LEFT THE FIRM: 2003	MINORITY MEN	MINORITY WOMEN	WHITE WOMEN	TOTAL
Number of attorneys who voluntarily or involuntarily left your firm's employ in 2003	0	1	15	29

How do 2003 attrition rates generally compare to those experienced in the prior years period?

Lower than in prior years

Please identify the specific steps you are taking to reduce the attrition rate of minority and women attorneys.

• Develop and/or support internal employee affinity groups (e.g., minority or women networks within the firm)

• Increase/review compensation relative to competition

• Increase/improve current work/life programs

• Adopt dispute resolution process

• Work with minority and women attorneys to develop career advancement plans

• Strengthen mentoring program for all attorneys, including minorities and women

• Professional skills development program, including

Does your firm have part-time/flex-time policies that permit attorneys (male or female) to work alternative schedules?

Yes

What impact, if any, will the decision to work part-time have on an attorney's ability to make partner or, if already a partner, to remain a partner at your firm?

Part-time associates are eligible for partnership on a pro-rated schedule. Reduced schedules for partners are handled through compensation system.

Have any attorneys who chose to work a part-time schedule made partner at your firm?

Yes, two attorneys.

Management Demographic Profile (as of 12/31/03)

	MINORITY MEN	MINORITY WOMEN	WHITE WOMEN	TOTAL
Number of attorneys on the Executive/Management Committee or equivalent	0	0	1	8
Number of attorneys on the Hiring Committee or equivalent	0	1	5	11
Number of attorneys on the Partner/Associate Review Committee or equivalent	0	0	4	24

Please provide information regarding all minority and women attorneys who head offices or practice groups of your law firm:

Women heading offices: Susan L. Williams, New Albany, IN

The Firm Says

Diversity training

The Executive Committee is pleased to announce that Diversity Training for all offices will be June 2, 3, 4, 7, 8 and 9. All firm members and employees are REQUIRED to attend a training session in 2004. Sessions will last approximately two hours each. People unable to attend training in June will be trained by FBT attorneys in the fall.

In addition, the Executive Committee encourages all attorneys to attend the FBT Women's Project/Diversity Committee Sponsored Professional Development Program entitled "The Business Case for Diversity: Why Diversity Should Matter to You" in Cincinnati on June 10, from 9:30 a.m.-1:30 p.m. This program features six of our clients that participated in our diversity assessment process and our diversity consultant. This program promises to be an excellent opportunity to interact with clients and learn how diversity touches our bottom line.

All administrative staff should coordinate with their team and/or cube-mate for coverage in their absence.

Louisville/New Albany

Wednesday, June 2, 9 a.m.-11a.m. (6/2 am), 2 p.m.-4p.m. (6/2 pm)

Thursday, June 3, 9 a.m.-11a.m. (6/3 am), 2 p.m.-4p.m. (6/3 pm)

Thursday, June 3, 5 p.m.-7p.m. (6/3 late)

Friday, June 4, 9 a.m.-11a.m. (6/4 am)

Cincinnati

Monday, June 7, 9 a.m.-11a.m. (6/7 am), 2 p.m.-4p.m. (6/7 pm)

Tuesday, June 8, 8 a.m.-10a.m. (6/8 am)

Wednesday, June 9, 9 a.m.-11a.m. (6/9 am), 2 p.m.-4p.m. (6/9 pm), 5 p.m.-7p.m. (6/9 late)

Lexington

Friday, June 4, 3 p.m.-5p.m. (6/4 Lex)

Middletown

Tuesday, June 8, 12 p.m. (6/8 Mid)

Columbus

Tuesday, June 8, 4 p.m. (6/8 Col)

Nashville

To be determined.

Please note that any members or employees from any office may attend training in any location. If you know you're going to be in another office, and need to participate while in that office, please let us know and we will include you in one of these sessions.

Fulbright & Jaworski L.L.P.

1301 McKinney, Suite 5100
Houston, TX 77010
Phone: (713) 651-5151
Fax: (713) 651-5246

FIRM LEADERSHIP

Managing Partner: Steven B. Pfeiffer
Diversity Team Leader: Cyndi M. Benedict,
Ralph C. Dawson and Tom C. Godbold

LOCATIONS

Houston, TX (HQ)
Austin, TX
Dallas, TX
Los Angeles, CA
Minneapolis, MN
New York, NY
San Antonio, TX
Washington, DC
Hong Kong
London
Munich

LAW FIRM DEMOGRAPHIC PROFILES

FULL-TIME ASSOCIATES	2003	2002
Minority men	30	24
Minority women	27	31
White women	138	121
Total	382	350

SUMMER ASSOCIATES	2003	2002
Minority men	7	9
Minority women	11	9
White women	28	29
Total	74	72

EQUITY PARTNERS	2003	2002
Minority men	8	7
Minority women	3	1
White women	42	38
Total	316	314

NEW HIRES	2003	2002
Minority men	9	7
Minority women	9	9
White women	38	29
Total	91	91

VAULT

MCCA
MINORITY CORPORATE COUNSEL ASSOCIATION

Strategic Plan and Diversity Leadership

How does the firm's leadership communicate the importance of diversity to everyone at the firm? (e.g., e-mails, web site, newsletters, meetings, etc.)

The importance of diversity is communicated in a variety of ways – most importantly, by the firm's actions. Communication is also accomplished via intranet, Internet, policy statements, e-mails, firm-wide diversity training, and support for and participation in numerous diversity related programs sponsored by bar associations, MCCA and a multitude of other organizations.

Who has primary responsibility for leading diversity initiatives at your firm?

Steven B. Pfeiffer, managing partner, through the Committee on Recruitment and Retention of Women and Minorities; Tri-chairs Cyndi M. Benedict, Ralph C. Dawson and Tom C. Godbold.

Does your law firm currently have a diversity committee?

Yes

Does the committee's representation include one or more members of the firm's management/executive committee (or the equivalent)?

Yes. Liaison to Executive Committee

How many attorneys are on the committee, and in 2003, what was the total number of hours collectively spent by the committee in furtherance of the firm's diversity initiatives?

Total attorneys on committee: 9

Total hours spent on diversity: In excess of 250 hours

Does the committee and/or diversity leader establish and set goals or objectives consistent with management's priorities?

Yes

Has the firm undertaken a formal or informal diversity program or set of initiatives aimed at increasing the diversity of the firm?

Yes, formal

How often does the firm's management review the firm's diversity progress/results?

Review is an ongoing matter. In addition, more formal review of achievements and progress is examined at least annually in some form.

How is the firm's diversity committee and/or firm management held accountable for achieving results?

Various review and analyses of progress and achievements and involvement in diversity efforts both firm-wide and office-specific are examined.

LAW FIRM DIVERSITY INITIATIVES	ALREADY COMPLETED	CURRENTLY ADDRESSING	NOT A CURRENT PRIORITY
Undertake communication from firm management that diversity is a top priority of the firm.	✓		
Formalize diversity plan and committee with action steps and accountability to management.	✓	✓	
Conduct firm-wide diversity training for all attorneys and staff.	✓		
Increase the number of minority attorneys at the associate level.	✓	✓	
Increase the number of minority attorneys at the partnership level.	✓	✓	
Develop/expand relationships with minority bar associations to offer firm's support of these networks.	✓	✓	
Focus on strengthening firm's mentoring program, including for benefit of minority attorneys.	✓	✓	
Conduct internal diversity needs assessment and/or retain diversity consultant to examine how firm culture might be more welcoming of minorities.			
Support law firm's internal affinity networks (e.g., women, minority attorney networks).	✓		
Manage/monitor allocation of work assignments and/or hours billed to ensure women and minority attorneys have equal access/inclusion on top client matters.			

Recruitment - New Associates

Does your firm annually recruit at any of the following types of institutions? (Check all that apply and list the schools).

Ivy League schools: Columbia University, Harvard University, University of Pennsylvania, Yale University

Public state schools: University of California-Boalt, University of California-Hastings, George Mason University, University of Houston, University of Iowa, University of Michigan, University of Minnesota, University of Texas, University of Virginia, UCLA

Private schools: Baylor University, Brooklyn Law School, Cardozo, University of Chicago, Duke University, Emory University, Fordham University, Georgetown University, George Washington University, Hamline University, Hofstra University, Loyola Law School (L.A.), Northwestern University, NYU, St. John's University, St. Mary's University, SMU, South Texas College of Law, Stanford University, Tulane University, USC, Vanderbilt University

Historically Black Colleges and Universities (HBCUs): Howard University, Texas Southern University

Do you have any special outreach efforts directed to encourage minority law students to consider your firm?

• Participate in/host minority law student job fair(s)

• Sponsor minority law student association events

• Firm's lawyers participate on career panels at school

• Outreach to leadership of minority student organizations

• Scholarships or intern/fellowships for minority students

SUMMER ASSOCIATE STATISTICS: SUMMER 2003	MINORITY MEN	MINORITY WOMEN	WHITE WOMEN	TOTAL
Summer associates	5	8	22	54
Summer associates who received an offer of full-time employment	3	6	18	42
Summer associates who accepted an offer of full-time employment	1	3	5	17

Recruitment – Lateral Associates and Partners

What activities does the firm undertake to attract minority and women attorneys?

• *Various efforts both at the local office level, community level and firm-wide at the regional and national level through participation in minority and diversity programs and events.*

• Participate at minority job fairs

• Seek referrals from other attorneys

Do you use executive recruiting/search firms to seek to identify new diversity hires (partners or associates)?

No

LATERAL ASSOCIATES AND PARTNERS: 1/1/03 – 12/31/03	MINORITY MEN	MINORITY WOMEN	WHITE WOMEN	TOTAL
Number of lateral associate hires	1	1	5	11
Number of lateral partner hires (equity and non-equity)	0	0	1	6
Number of new partners (equity and non-equity) promoted from associate rank	1	1	1	7
Number of new equity partners	1	1	2	13

Retention & Professional Development

ATTORNEYS WHO LEFT THE FIRM: 2003	MINORITY MEN	MINORITY WOMEN	WHITE WOMEN	TOTAL
Number of attorneys who voluntarily or involuntarily left your firm's employ in 2003	4	5	16	51

How do 2003 attrition rates generally compare to those experienced in the prior year period?

About the same as in prior years.

Please identify the specific steps you are taking to reduce the attrition rate of minority and women attorneys.

• *All of the following represent actions underway at the firm to improve the retention and recruitment of women and minority attorneys, which is a key directive and top priority of firm management. We expect that in focusing on improving our efforts relative to women and minority attorneys we will improve our methods of providing greater opportunity to all of our attorneys.*

• Develop and/or support internal employee affinity groups (e.g., minority or women networks within the firm)

• Increase/review compensation relative to competition

• Increase/improve current work/life programs

• Adopt dispute resolution process

• Succession plan includes emphasis on diversity

• Work with minority and women attorneys to develop career advancement plans

• Introduce minority and women attorneys to key clients, including to lead engagements

• Review work assignments and hours billed to key client matters to make sure minority and women attorneys are not being excluded

• Strengthen mentoring program for all attorneys, including minorities and women

• Professional skills development program, including minority and women attorneys

Does your firm have part-time/flex-time policies that permit attorneys (male or female) to work alternative schedules?

Yes

What impact, if any, will the decision to work part-time have on an attorney's ability to make partner or, if already a partner, to remain a partner at your firm?

As every part-time situation at our firm differs from person to person, each situation and partnership consideration is evaluated according to its own unique facts. In addition, the firm recognizes that greater flexibility with respect to part-time employment may increase our ability to retain talented women attorneys, an important firm goal. To this end the firm has and continues to evaluate and implement opportunities in this area.

Have any attorneys who chose to work a part-time schedule made partner at your firm?

Yes

Management Demographic Profile (as of 12/31/03)

Please provide information regarding all minority and women attorneys who head offices or practice groups of your law firm:

Women heading offices: Joy R. Bode, Austin; Julie A. Tassi, Washington, DC

Minorities heading practice groups: Evelyn H. Biery, Bankruptcy

Women heading practice groups: Evelyn H. Biery, Bankruptcy; Eva Fromm-O'Brien, Environmental

	MINORITY MEN	MINORITY WOMEN	WHITE WOMEN	TOTAL
Number of attorneys on the Executive/Management Committee or equivalent	0	0	2	6
Number of attorneys on the Hiring Committee or equivalent	0	0	3	10*
Number of attorneys on the Partner/Associate Review Committee or equivalent	0	0	1	12

Chairs of individual offices

The Firm Says

Our firm is committed to the goal of strengthening our diversity through recruiting and retaining minority and women attorneys and staff personnel from all backgrounds. Our commitment is consistent with our recognition that it is the outstanding people within Fulbright & Jaworski who have always been the source of our strength. Our colleagues (attorneys and staff) are the firm's greatest assets. We have long embraced the principles of equal employment opportunity. We further recognize that promoting diversity is an integral component of our continuing quest for excellence as individual attorneys and as a firm.

As part of the effort to advance our commitment to diversity throughout the firm, the following initiatives, among others, are being pursued:

• Improvement of the level of diversity within the firm's leadership positions, firm committees and practice development efforts.

• Development of an attorney and senior administrative manager evaluation process to review and recognize the contributions made by our attorneys and managers to advance the firm's efforts to fulfill our commitment to diversity as set forth in this message.

• Emphasis of the firm's longstanding policy that encourages reporting of any discrimination or harassment based on sex, race, national origin or other protected status.

• Participation in opportunities outside the firm to explore diversity initiatives underway with clients, bar associations and minority organizations who share this common objective.

Regarding the firm's current diversity efforts, the firm has recently implemented the "Dignity, Courtesy & Respect" program. This program covers all of the firm's employment related policies, including the Equal Employment Opportunity policy. It involves a formal training program which touches on diversity in the

workplace among many other related topics. Training has been completed in several of our offices. The firm hired an outside consultant to develop and conduct the program and will complete it nationwide in the upcoming year.

The firm also makes affirmative efforts to recruit lawyers who are members of racial or ethnic minority groups. The firm interviews with several programs, including the Sunbelt Minority Conference and the Texas-Tulane Minority Program, specifically designed to introduce minority students to law firms. The firm also interviews at historically black Texas Southern University and Howard University Schools of Law.

Diversity initiatives

- Workplace – creating an inclusive environment

- Diversity training for all firm management

- Diversity training for all lawyers worldwide

- Diversity training for all staff worldwide

- Promoting diversity was key message at fall 2003 worldwide partners meeting

- Mentoring training for partners participating in the mentorship program

- Information sessions for all lawyers where input on diversity issues was solicited

- Commitment to improve diversity among Fulbright's leadership (already have women and minorities on firm's Executive and Policy Committees and serving as department heads, practice group leaders, team leaders, committee chairs)

- Commitment to improve access to promotions and high-caliber work for women and minority attorneys

- Committee recommending next steps in diversity initiatives

- Work force – recruiting and retaining a diverse group of attorneys and staff

- Received 2004 President's Award from the Southern California Chinese Lawyers Association, the oldest Asian American bar association in California, for Fulbright's commitment to advance the professional growth of Chinese and Asian American lawyers, stating that our firm has demonstrated a "genuine commitment to diversity" and that Fulbright's "attorneys' steadfast support in recent years is commendable."

- Recruiting at historically African-American law schools

- Recruiting at Latino Law Student Job Fair

- Sponsorship and participation in numerous job fairs for African-Americans

- Mentorship program for all non-partner attorneys, with emphasis on issues affecting women and minorities

- Mid-year attorney reviews outside of the official attorney evaluation process to identify areas of concern

- Recognition given to attorneys' involvement in promoting diversity

- Creating flexible environment in which many opt to work on reduced hours basis

- Added Martin Luther King Jr. holiday to the list of firm-wide holidays

- Local offices use a "floating holiday" to celebrate community and cultural events

- Marketplace – making a difference with our clients and in our community

- Significant financial participation in the Brown v. Board at 50 celebration in Washington, D.C., in May 2004

- Encourage attorneys to participate in organizations that share our firm's commitment to promoting diversity

- Sole law firm sponsor of Prairie View A&M's 125th anniversary documentary

- Sponsor and participate in Minority Corporate Counsel Association

- Participate in diversity task forces in legal organizations like the Association of Legal Administrators

- Sponsor and active in leadership of Texas Minority Council of the State Bar of Texas, designed to increase business development opportunities for women and minorities

- Sponsored and participated in Dallas Hispanic Bar Association's mock trial competitions

- Sponsor Just the Beginning Foundation, a national organization for African-American judges

- Received the NAACP's "Foot Soldiers in the Sands" award for active sponsorship and participation

- Sponsoring minority scholarship at a Texas law school

- Undergraduate college scholarship to the UNCF/The College Fund

- Sponsored the Women in Leadership Symposium hosted by the Texas Diversity Council

- Will be looking at Fulbright's vendors to promote diversity

- Will be seeking partnership sponsorships with firm clients who focus on diversity

Results

- Number of minority lawyers up 38 percent in five years

- Number of women lawyers up 30 percent in five years

- Fifteen percent of our current partners are women and minorities

- Fifty-two percent of our current associates are women and minorities

Gardere Wynne Sewell LLP

1601 Elm Street, Suite 3000
Dallas, TX 75201
Phone: (214) 999-3000
Fax: (214) 999-4667

FIRM LEADERSHIP

Managing Partner: Stephen D. Good, Managing Partner
Diversity Team Leader: Dwight Francis, Partner

LOCATIONS

Dallas, TX (HQ)
Austin, TX
Houston, TX
Washington, DC
Mexico City

LAW FIRM DEMOGRAPHIC PROFILES

FULL-TIME ASSOCIATES	2003	2002
Minority men	4	3
Minority women	8	7
White women	38	39
Total	112	112

SUMMER ASSOCIATES	2003	2002
Minority men	3	3
Minority women	5	4
White women	8	13
Total	28	35

EQUITY PARTNERS	2003	2002
Minority men	2	1
Minority women	0	0
White women	15	15
Total	103	107

NON-EQUITY PARTNERS	2003	2002
Minority men	5	5
Minority women	1	1
White women	15	13
Total	61	52

NEW HIRES	2003	2002
Minority men	1	1
Minority women	2	2
White women	3	3
Total	12	13

MCCA
MINORITY CORPORATE COUNSEL ASSOCIATION

Strategic Plan and Diversity Leadership

How does the firm's leadership communicate the importance of diversity to everyone at the firm? (e.g., e-mails, web site, newsletters, meetings, etc.)

Every person is required to attend our one-day "Workplace of Difference" workshop within the first year of employment.

Who has primary responsibility for leading diversity initiatives at your firm?

Dwight Francis, partner

Does your law firm currently have a diversity committee?

Yes

Does the committee's representation include one or more members of the firm's management/executive committee (or the equivalent)?

Yes

How many attorneys are on the committee, and in 2003, what was the total number of hours collectively spent by the committee in furtherance of the firm's diversity initiatives?

Total attorneys on committee: 10

Total hours spent on diversity: Historically, we have not tracked these hours.

Does the committee and/or diversity leader establish and set goals or objectives consistent with management's priorities?

Yes

How often does the firm's management review the firm's diversity progress/results?

Annually. Some portions of the initiatives are reviewed more frequently than annually.

LAW FIRM DIVERSITY INITIATIVES	ALREADY COMPLETED	CURRENTLY ADDRESSING	NOT A CURRENT PRIORITY
Undertake communication from firm management that diversity is a top priority of the firm.		✔	
Formalize diversity plan and committee with action steps and accountability to management.		✔	
Conduct firm-wide diversity training for all attorneys and staff.*	✔		
Increase the number of minority attorneys at the associate level.*	✔	✔	
Increase the number of minority attorneys at the partnership level.*	✔	✔	
Develop/expand relationships with minority bar associations to offer firm's support of these networks.*	✔	✔	
Focus on strengthening firm's mentoring program, including for benefit of minority attorneys.*	✔	✔	
Conduct internal diversity needs assessment and/or retain diversity consultant to examine how firm culture might be more welcoming of minorities.		✔	
Support law firm's internal affinity networks (e.g., women, minority attorney networks).		✔	
Manage/monitor allocation of work assignments and/or hours billed to ensure women and minority attorneys have equal access/inclusion on top client matters.			✔
Identify and address any institutional or systematic roadblocks to the continued promotion of minority lawyers.		✔	

* Iniatives are ongoing

Recruitment- New Associates

Does your firm annually recruit at any of the following types of institutions? (Check all that apply and list the schools).

Ivy League schools: Harvard University*

Public state schools: University of Houston, University of Kansas, Texas Tech University, University of Texas, University of Virginia*

Private schools: Baylor University, Duke University, George Washington University, Georgetown University, SMU Dedman School of Law, St. Mary's University, Vanderbilt University*

Historically Black Colleges and Universities (HBCUs): Texas Southern University (Thurgood Marshall School of Law)

We interview on-campus at the schools listed above. However, we invite students from all accredited law schools to apply. We always interview, and often hire, students who attend schools not included in the list above.

Do you have any special outreach efforts directed to encourage minority law students to consider your firm?

• Hold a reception for minority law students

• Participate in/host minority law student job fair(s)

• Sponsor minority law student association events

• Firm's lawyers participate on career panels at school

SUMMER ASSOCIATE STATISTICS: SUMMER 2003	MINORITY MEN	MINORITY WOMEN	WHITE WOMEN	TOTAL
Summer associates	1	3	7	20
Summer associates who received an offer of full-time employment	0	3	6	15
Summer associates who accepted an offer of full-time employment	0	2	4	10

Recruitment – Lateral Associates and Partners

What activities does the firm undertake to attract minority and women attorneys?

• Partner programs with women and minority bar associations

• Participate at minority job fairs

• Seek referrals from other attorneys

Do you use executive recruiting/search firms to seek to identify new diversity hires (partners or associates)?

Yes

If yes, list all women- and/or minority-owned executive search/recruiting firms to which the firm paid a fee for placement services in the past 12 months:

Counsel Source (Dallas)

Select Legal Search (Dallas)

LATERAL ASSOCIATES AND PARTNERS: 1/1/03 – 12/31/03	MINORITY MEN	MINORITY WOMEN	WHITE WOMEN	TOTAL
Number of lateral associate hires	1	0	4	15
Number of lateral partner hires (equity and non-equity)	0	0	1	4
Number of new partners (equity and non-equity) promoted from associate rank	0	0	2	8
Number of new equity partners	1	0	0	5

Retention & Professional Development

ATTORNEYS WHO LEFT THE FIRM: 2003	MINORITY MEN	MINORITY WOMEN	WHITE WOMEN	TOTAL
Number of attorneys who voluntarily or involuntarily left your firm's employ in 2003	1	0	8	23

How do 2003 attrition rates generally compare to those experienced in the prior year period?

Lower than in prior years

Please identify the specific steps you are taking to reduce the attrition rate of minority and women attorneys.

• Develop and/or support internal employee affinity groups (e.g., minority or women   networks within the firm)

• Work with minority and women attorneys to develop career advancement plans

• Introduce minority and women attorneys to key clients, including to lead   engagements

• Review work assignments and hours billed to key client matters to make sure minority and women attorneys are not being excluded

• Strengthen mentoring program for all attorneys, including minorities and women

• Professional skills development program, including minority and women attorneys

Does your firm have part-time/flex-time policies that permit attorneys (male or female) to work alternative schedules?

Yes

What impact, if any, will the decision to work part-time have on an attorney's ability to make partner or, if already a partner, to remain a partner at your firm?

The flex-time policy has a provision for delaying partnership by a year or two, if appropriate to the circumstances. There is no impact on the existing partner remaining a partner, other than a possible reclassification from equity to non-equity status if appropriate to the circumstances.

Have any attorneys who chose to work a part-time schedule made partner at your firm?

Yes, two attorneys

Management Demographic Profile (as of 12/31/03)

	MINORITY MEN	MINORITY WOMEN	WHITE WOMEN	TOTAL
Number of attorneys on the Executive/Management Committee or equivalent	1	0	3	13
Number of attorneys on the Hiring Committee or equivalent	2	2	12	40
Number of attorneys on the Partner/Associate Review Committee or equivalent	0	2	3	16

Please provide information regarding all minority and women attorneys who head offices or practice groups of your law firm:

Women heading offices: Kim Yelkin, Austin

Women heading practice groups: Suzan Fenner, Tax; Elizabeth Howard, Banking; Deirdre Ruckman, Bankruptcy; Kim Yelkin, Legislative & Regulatory Affairs

The Firm Says

Gardere Wynne Sewell LLP has a long history of commitment to the advancement of minorities and women. The firm has made great efforts to communicate and facilitate its dedication to create a diverse and dynamic workplace and has created policies and programs to support this goal.

The firm has had a diversity committee for over a decade. The committee's role over the years has evolved. The current committee has adopted the following Mission Statement:

1. Improve upon the recruitment of minority law students and lawyers, and accelerate the growth in hiring of minority lawyers, both laterally and from law school;

2. Substantially improve upon the firm's retention of minority lawyers by, for example, instituting structured mentoring programs to insure that minority lawyers develop relationships inside and outside the firm and develop appropriate legal skills;

3. Identify and address any institutional or systematic roadblocks to the continued promotion of minority lawyers through the associate ranks, to income partner, and then to equity partner;

4. Enhance the business development opportunities available to minority lawyers;

5. Increase awareness among all firm lawyers of the benefits (financial, cultural, creative and otherwise) to be derived from increased ethnic diversity, and the necessity of having our ethnic composition reflect the increasingly diverse nature of our clients, prospective clients and the larger community;

6. Increase the level of ethnic and racial diversity throughout all of the firm's offices; and

7. Promote Gardere's image as a firm committed to diversity within the business and legal communities both locally and nationally.

Minority recruiting

We aggressively compete for top minority lawyers and have expanded our on-campus interviews at certain schools to attract more minorities. We participate in the Southeastern Minority Job Fair in Atlanta and the Sunbelt Minority Recruitment Program in Dallas on an annual basis. The firm has also established flexible hiring guidelines which enable us to consider a greater number of minority students for permanent employment.

"Workplace of Difference"

The firm was the first for-profit enterprise to sponsor the "Workplace of Difference" program conducted by the Anti-Defamation League for all lawyers and staff. The seminars are directed toward creating a heightened awareness of issues affecting minorities and provide an appreciation for comments and actions that might be unintentionally discriminatory. Each member of the firm, attorneys and staff alike, participate in this important program during their first year with the firm.

One of the activities that exhibits Gardere's commitment to diversity is the annual Martin Luther King Jr. Speech Competition held in Dallas and Houston. For the past 11 years, the annual program recognizes and encourages the oratorical skills of Dallas and Houston area elementary school children. The students' speeches not only address how Dr. King impacted today's world and the students' vision for the future, but the students' insights into today's society. The annual event has become a well-publicized program in each city and is held during the week of Dr. King's birthday events.

Distinction in pro bono work and other honors

Gardere's attorneys recognize that their skills and time are needed by less fortunate individuals in our communities. Our firm has received many honors and awards for the pro bono efforts of our attorneys on behalf of deserving clients. For five straight years, Gardere was recognized by the Dallas Bar Association as the best in Dallas for pro bono service and was elevated to the Dallas "Pro Bono Hall of Fame."

Gardere has participated, since inception, in the City of Dallas Chamber's programs created to establish goals, measure and annually report the results regarding the dollar amount of purchases from ethnic-minority firms and women-owned firms, the ethnic-minority and female percentage of new hires, and the ethnic-minority and female percentage of promotions and professional/management/board positions held by these two minority groups.

In 1998, the Greater Dallas Chamber presented Gardere with a Dallas Women's Covenant Diamond Cutter Award in recognition of our firm's commitment to the hire, promotion and support of women in business. In 2003, Gardere was once again recognized by the Greater Dallas Chamber when presented with a Dallas Women's Covenant Leadership Award in recognition of our firm's commitment to the promotion of women into management and executive management positions.

Gardere supports a diverse community through participation or leadership positions in the following organizations: Asian American Bar Association; Austin Black Lawyers' Association; Dallas Bar Association's J. L. Turner Society (African American Bar); Dallas Bar Association's Minority Clerkship Program; Dallas Bar Association's Minority Attorney Business Development Initiative; Dallas Bar Association's Asian American Law Section Sponsor; Dallas Black Chamber of Commerce; Dallas Chamber of Commerce Women's Covenant; Dallas Hispanic Chamber of Commerce; Dallas Together Forum; Dallas Women's Foundation; Women's International Network; Houston Bar Association; Mexican American Section; Houston Bar Association Minority Opportunities in the Legal Profession Project; Houston Bar Association's Asian American Section; Mexican-American Bar Association; National Bar Association; Texas Bar Association Minority Counsel Program.

Gardner Carton & Douglas LLP

191 North Wacker Drive, Suite 3700
Chicago, IL 60606-1698
Phone: (312) 569-1000
Fax: (312) 569-3000

FIRM LEADERSHIP

Managing Partner: Harold Kaplan, Chairman
Diversity Team Leader: Liisa Thomas, Partner

LOCATIONS

Chicago, IL (HQ)
Albany, NY
Milwaukee, WI
Washington, DC

LAW FIRM DEMOGRAPHIC PROFILES

FULL-TIME ASSOCIATES	2003	2002
Minority men	12	13
Minority women	10	12
White women	38	37
Total	102	102

SUMMER ASSOCIATES	2003	2002
Minority men	0	1
Minority women	1	2
White women	5	2
Total	8	8

PARTNERS*	2003	2002
Minority men	7	6
Minority women	0	0
White women	32	27
Total	129	115

* We do not classify partners as equity and non-equity. GCD
has only one tier of partnership.

NEW HIRES	2003	2002
Minority men	3	4
Minority women	4	2
White women	14	11
Total	41	37

MINORITY CORPORATE COUNSEL ASSOCIATION

Strategic Plan and Diversity Leadership

How does the firm's leadership communicate the importance of diversity to everyone at the firm? (e.g., e-mails, web site, newsletters, meetings, etc.)

The firm's leadership stresses the importance of diversity at partnership and associate meetings, firm retreats, on the firm web site, in firm marketing materials and through its public support of targeted diversity initiatives. For example, the firm is sponsoring a Minority Business Initiative, led by the minority partners of the firm, whose goal is to provide the highest quality sophisticated legal services to the minority business community and to people and organizations that embrace and value diversity. The firm also demonstrates the importance of diversity through its support of minority bar associations – for example, the Cook County Bar Association and the Hispanic Lawyers Association of Illinois – and minority-focused legal organizations, including the Chicago Committee on Minorities in Large Law Firms and MALDEF.

Who has primary responsibility for leading diversity initiatives at your firm?

Harold Kaplan, chairman of the firm

Does your law firm currently have a diversity committee?

Yes

Does the committee's representation include one or more members of the firm's management/executive committee (or the equivalent)?

Yes

How many attorneys are on the committee, and in 2003, what was the total number of hours collectively spent by the committee in furtherance of the firm's diversity initiatives?

Total attorneys on committee: 10

Total hours spent on diversity: 630

Does the committee and/or diversity leader establish and set goals or objectives consistent with management's priorities?

Yes

Has the firm undertaken a formal or informal diversity program or set of initiatives aimed at increasing the diversity of the firm?

Yes, formal

How often does the firm's management review the firm's diversity progress/results?

Annually

How is the firm's diversity committee and/or firm management held accountable for achieving results?

Department chairs are charged with and held responsible for meeting specific goals to ensure the recruitment, retention and development of minority and female attorneys. Departments that fail to meet these measurable

goals are negatively impacted through our compensation process, and departments that achieve these goals are rewarded during the year-end compensation review process.

LAW FIRM DIVERSITY INITIATIVES	ALREADY COMPLETED	CURRENTLY ADDRESSING	NOT A CURRENT PRIORITY
Undertake communication from firm management that diversity is a top priority of the firm.		✓	
Formalize diversity plan and committee with action steps and accountability to management.	✓		
Conduct firm-wide diversity training for all attorneys and staff.	✓		
Increase the number of minority attorneys at the associate level.		✓	
Increase the number of minority attorneys at the partnership level.		✓	
Develop/expand relationships with minority bar associations to offer firm's support of these networks.		✓	
Focus on strengthening firm's mentoring program, including for benefit of minority attorneys.	✓		
Conduct internal diversity needs assessment and/or retain diversity consultant to examine how firm culture might be more welcoming of minorities.			✓
Support law firm's internal affinity networks (e.g., women, minority attorney networks).	✓		
Manage/monitor allocation of work assignments and/or hours billed to ensure women and minority attorneys have equal access/inclusion on top client matters.		✓	

Recruitment- New Associates

Does your firm annually recruit at any of the following types of institutions?

Public state schools: University of Michigan; University of Illinois; University of Chicago; New York University

Private schools: Washington University at St. Louis; Northwestern University; Georgetown University; Cornell; University of Notre Dame; Loyola Universtiy Chicago; Chicago-Kent

Do you have any special outreach efforts directed to encourage minority law students to consider your firm?

• Hold a reception for minority law students

• Participate in/host minority law student job fair(s)

• Sponsor minority law student association events

• Firm's lawyers participate on career panels at school

• Outreach to leadership of minority student organizations

We have worked with some Chicago-area law schools to provide minority students at these schools the opportunity to have their initial "on-campus" interview at GCD. This will allow these students an additional opportunity to meet us outside of the more formal on-campus recruiting process.

SUMMER ASSOCIATE STATISTICS: SUMMER 2003	MINORITY MEN	MINORITY WOMEN	WHITE WOMEN	TOTAL
Summer associates	0	1	5	8
Summer associates who received an offer of full-time employment	0	0	5	5
Summer associates who accepted an offer of full-time employment	0	0	4	4*

* One offer is outstanding; summer associate has until May 2005 to accept offer (extra time given while summer associate completes clerkship)

Recruitment- Lateral Associates and Partners

What activities does the firm undertake to attract minority and women attorneys?
• Participate at minority job fairs
• Seek referrals from other attorneys
• Utilize online job services (e.g., MCCA/DuPont Primary Law Firm Job Bank)

Do you use executive recruiting/search firms to seek to identify new diversity hires (partners or associates)?
Yes   We indicate to our search firms that we want, and expect, to see minority candidates.

LATERAL ASSOCIATES AND PARTNERS: 1/1/03 – 12/31/03	MINORITY MEN	MINORITY WOMEN	WHITE WOMEN	TOTAL
Number of lateral associate hires	3	4	9	27
Number of lateral partner hires	0	0	4	10
Number of new partners promoted from associate rank	0	1	1	5

Retention & Professional Development

ATTORNEYS WHO LEFT THE FIRM: 2003	MINORITY MEN	MINORITY WOMEN	WHITE WOMEN	TOTAL
Number of attorneys who voluntarily or involuntarily left your firm's employ in 2003	3	6	7	25

How do 2003 attrition rates generally compare to those experienced in the prior year period?
About the same as in prior years

Please identify the specific steps you are taking to reduce the attrition rate of minority and women attorneys.

• Work with minority and women attorneys to develop career advancement plans

• Review work assignments and hours billed to key client matters to make sure minority and women attorneys are not being excluded

• Strengthen mentoring program for all attorneys, including minorities and women

Does your firm have part-time/flex-time policies that permit attorneys (male or female) to work alternative schedules?

Yes

What impact, if any, will the decision to work part-time have on an attorney's ability to make partner or, if already a partner, to remain a partner at your firm?

No impact

Have any attorneys who chose to work a part-time schedule made partner at your firm?

Yes, one attorney:

Management Demographic Profile (as of 12/31/03)

	MINORITY MEN	MINORITY WOMEN	WHITE WOMEN	TOTAL
Number of attorneys on the Executive/Management Committee or equivalent	0	0	0	8
Number of attorneys on the Hiring Committee or equivalent	0	0	1	1
Number of attorneys on the Partner/Associate Review Committee or equivalent	1	0	8	15

Please provide information regarding all minority and women attorneys who head offices or practice groups of your law firm:

Minorities heading offices: None

Women heading offices: None

Minorities heading practice groups: Mark Latham, Environmental; Liisa Thomas, Privacy; Alan King, Labor & Employment

Women heading practice groups: Annette Ahlers, Tax (Co-Chair); Virginia Boylan, Tribal Governments; Kimberly Rubel, Securities; Stephanie Wickouski, Corporate Restructuring and Financial Institutions; Susan Macaulay, Banking Practice; Mary Lee Turk, Wealth Planning (Vice Chair); Tina Kourasis, Retail and Apparel; Cathy Austin, Information Technology; Liisa Thomas, Privacy

The Firm Says

In a narrative of two pages or less, please provide any additional information regarding your firm's diversity initiatives that you wish to share. See instructions for details and suggestions.

Throughout the history of the firm, Gardner Carton & Douglas LLP has been a leader in its commitment to the diversity of its partners, associates and staff. More than a principle, a policy or a well-crafted statement, this commitment is an attitude in practice, reflected in the work of our Diversity Committee – and the firm as a whole – to foster the professional growth of our talented minority attorneys.

Why this commitment to diversity? By more accurately reflecting our clients and our communities, we are more effectively positioned to understand their needs and objectives, in all their many facets. Creativity, innovation, cooperation and mutual respect are the natural result of an environment in which individual contributions are valued, where biases based on gender, race and other factors are absent, and legal knowledge combines with unique worldviews.

More than a decade ago, the firm established our Diversity Committee. Comprised of minority and majority representative partners and associates of the firm, the committee's primary objective is to proactively recruit, retain and foster the professional development of talented minority attorneys. The firm also has a Women's Committee with an objective similar to the Diversity Committee with regard to supporting our women attorneys. Throughout all of our practice groups and as a whole, the firm is as committed as ever to fostering the diversity of our people and to providing our clients with innovative, effective and solution-oriented legal services.

Recruitment

The firm's commitment to diversity is demonstrated in its many efforts to recruit women and minority law school graduates and experienced attorneys. We regularly help coordinate and participate in a number of minority attorney recruitment programs, such as the Cook County Bar Association Minority Law Student Fair. Members of our hiring committee and recruitment staff travel to law schools around the country, meeting with first-year women and minority students to increase interest in the firm's summer associate program and conducting interviews with graduating students for our new-associate positions.

Further, the firm regularly offers time, money and other resources to help support and encourage women and minority students as they pursue their educational and professional goals. We work with student groups at various law schools to provide mentoring and financial assistance; for example, we sponsor scholarships given annually to deserving minority law students by the Hispanic Lawyers Scholarship Fund of Illinois and the Cook County Bar Association.

Retention and professional development

Once an attorney has joined our firm, our work is far from complete. A stable, supportive environment is key to encouraging the exploration of professional interests and the ongoing development of legal skills.

The firm has established a mentoring program that pairs new associates with senior associates and partners. The committee is currently focused on the development of additional ways to target and address issues specific to our women and minority associates and partners.

As a firm, we understand the value of relationships – with clients and peers – to a successful career in the law. Therefore, we assist our women and minority attorneys in building a sustained client base and important

networks with other legal professionals. Working with the Chicago Committee on Minorities in Large Law Firms, an organization chaired by Jesse Ruiz, one of our partners, we hosted a series of 12 roundtable discussions focused on strengthening the ties between established corporations and minority lawyers. We have also supported the development of a special program designed to foster a dialogue that will raise mutual awareness between minority business owners and our attorneys.

The firm has long hosted an annual women's networking event so that our women attorneys have the opportunity to build relationships and enhance their client development opportunities.

On June 30, 2004, the firm launched its Minority Business Initiative. The MBI Group is comprised of all the minority partners in the firm – we are very proud that we have minority partners and associates in every department of the firm. The MBI Group's mission is to provide the highest quality sophisticated legal services to the minority business community and to people and organizations that embrace and value diversity. This effort is led by GCD minority attorneys and is supported by the entire firm. The firm has initiated this effort to provide greater practice development support to minority attorneys and to increase the number of minority partners and associates at the firm.

We are also very proud that most of our women and minority partners have important leadership roles in the firm. For example, our securities law practice is chaired by Kimberly Rubel, our environmental practice is chaired by Mark Latham, our labor and employment practice is chaired by Alan King, the firm's Business Development Committee is co-chaired by Jesse Ruiz and the firm's Pro Bono Committee is chaired by Kevin Freeman.

Professional and civic participation

Our attorneys regularly take a leadership role in professional and civic organizations dedicated to advancing the interests of minorities in the community. They have held positions as presidents, board members or committee chairs of:

• the Chicago Committee on Minorities in Large Law Firms, a not-for-profit organization supporting the education and professional growth of minority attorneys;

• the Cook County Bar Association Minority Job Fair Committee;

• the Scholarship Committee of the American Intellectual Property Law Foundation, which awards annual scholarships to minority law students who have a demonstrated interest in practicing intellectual property law;

• the Hispanic Lawyers Scholarship Fund of Illinois; and

• the Hispanic Lawyers Association of Illinois.

Gibson, Dunn & Crutcher LLP

333 South Grand Avenue
Los Angeles, CA 90071
Phone: (213) 229-7000
Fax: (213) 229-7520

FIRM LEADERSHIP

Managing Partner: Kenneth M. Doran,
Managing Partner
Diversity Team Leader: Barbara L. Becker,
Partner

LOCATIONS

Los Angeles, CA (HQ)
Century City, CA
Dallas, TX
Denver, CO
Irvine, CA
New York, NY
Palo Alto, CA
San Francisco, CA
Washington, DC
Brussels
London
Munich
Paris

Note: Law Firm demographic figures are for U.S. offices only and do not include European offices.

LAW FIRM DEMOGRAPHIC PROFILES

FULL-TIME ASSOCIATES	2003	2002
Minority men	33	29
Minority women	44	45
White women	178	172
Total	503	490

SUMMER ASSOCIATES	2003	2002
Minority men	6	8
Minority women	9	9
White women	34	46
Total	98	114

EQUITY PARTNERS	2003	2002
Minority men	6	6
Minority women	1	1
White women	31	29
Total	235	231

NEW HIRES	2003	2002
Minority men	8	4
Minority women	10	15
White women	46	53
Total	125	122

Strategic Plan and Diversity Leadership

How does the firm's leadership communicate the importance of diversity to everyone at the firm? (e.g., e-mails, web site, newsletters, meetings, etc.)

Gibson Dunn is deeply committed to improve diversity at all levels of the firm. This strategic priority was recently underscored in a speech given by our managing partner to all lawyers of the firm. The Management Committee regularly discusses our progress on diversity initiatives with the chairs of our Diversity Committee, the Associates Committee and the Hiring Committee, as well as the partners in charge of our offices.

Who has primary responsibility for leading diversity initiatives at your firm?:

Barbara Becker, partner and chair of Diversity Committee and Leslie Ripleg, Director of Legal Recruiting & Diversity

Does your law firm currently have a diversity committee?

Yes

Does the committee's representation include one or more members of the firm's management/executive committee (or the equivalent)?

Yes

How many attorneys are on the committee, and in 2003, what was the total number of hours collectively spent by the committee in furtherance of the firm's diversity initiatives?

Total attorneys on committee: over 100

Total hours spent on diversity: Estimated to be in excess of 1,000 hours in 2003

Does the committee and/or diversity leader establish and set goals or objectives consistent with management's priorities?

Yes

Has the firm undertaken a formal or informal diversity program or set of initiatives aimed at increasing the diversity of the firm?

Yes, formal

How often does the firm's management review the firm's diversity progress/results?

The firm's management reviews the firm's diversity progress/results on an ongoing basis.

How is the firm's diversity committee and/or firm management held accountable for achieving results?

Diversity in our workplace is a top priority of our firm's management. The chair of the firm's Diversity Committee is directly accountable to the firm's managing partner and regularly reports to the managing partner concerning the Diversity Committee and the progress of our diversity efforts. Our managing partner reports on the progress of our diversity efforts to the firm's senior management on a quarterly basis. We believe that the marketplace will be the ultimate arbiter of our firm's success with diversity, both in terms of our successful

recruitment and retention of attorneys of diverse backgrounds and of our being hired by clients who value diversity in their outside counsel.

LAW FIRM DIVERSITY INITIATIVES	ALREADY COMPLETED	CURRENTLY ADDRESSING	NOT A CURRENT PRIORITY
Undertake communication from firm management that diversity is a top priority of the firm.	✓		
Formalize diversity plan and committee with action steps and accountability to management.	✓		
Conduct firm-wide diversity training for all attorneys and staff.		✓	
Increase the number of minority attorneys at the associate level.		✓	
Increase the number of minority attorneys at the partnership level.		✓	
Develop/expand relationships with minority bar associations to offer firm's support of these networks.		✓	
Focus on strengthening firm's mentoring program, including for benefit of minority attorneys.		✓	
Conduct internal diversity needs assessment and/or retain diversity consultant to examine how firm culture might be more welcoming of minorities.	✓		
Support law firm's internal affinity networks (e.g., women, minority attorney networks).	✓		
Manage/monitor allocation of work assignments and/or hours billed to ensure women and minority attorneys have equal access/inclusion on top client matters.	✓		

Recruitment- New Associates

Does your firm annually recruit at any of the following types of institutions? (Check all that apply and list the schools).

Ivy League schools: Columbia University, Cornell University, Harvard University, University of Pennsylvania, Yale University

Public state schools: University of California-Boalt Hall, UCLA, University of Colorado, University of Michigan, University of Minnesota, University of Texas, University of Virginia, University of California-Davis

Private schools: University of Chicago, Duke University, Fordham University, George Washington University, Georgetown University, Loyola University, NYU, University of San Diego, Stanford University, Southern Methodist University, USC, Vanderbilt University, William & Mary

Do you have any special outreach efforts directed to encourage minority law students to consider your firm?

• *Host mock interview programs*

• *Ongoing dialogue with Career Services Diversity Administrators*

• *Targeted 1L Program*

• Hold a reception for minority law students

• Advertise in minority law student association publication(s)

• Participate in/host minority law student job fair(s)

• Sponsor minority law student association events

• Firm's lawyers participate on career panels at school

• Outreach to leadership of minority student organizations

• Scholarships or intern/fellowships for minority students

SUMMER ASSOCIATE STATISTICS: SUMMER 2003	MINORITY MEN	MINORITY WOMEN	WHITE WOMEN	TOTAL
Summer associates	7	9	34	98
Summer associates who received an offer of full-time employment	5	8	29	90
Summer associates who accepted an offer of full-time employment	3	8	25	70

Recruitment- Lateral Associates and Partners

What activities does the firm undertake to attract minority and women attorneys?

• *In the hiring process at law schools around the country each "team leader" is specifically tasked with responsibility for identifying the most effective methods for recruiting minority candidates for associate positions at the firm. In addition, members of the Diversity Committee are active participants in our recruiting efforts by hosting hospitality suites and other outreach efforts at the law schools.*

• Partner programs with women and minority bar associations

• Participate at minority job fairs

• Seek referrals from other attorneys

Do you use executive recruiting/search firms to seek to identify new diversity hires (partners or associates)?

Yes

LATERAL ASSOCIATES AND PARTNERS: 1/1/03 – 12/31/03	MINORITY MEN	MINORITY WOMEN	WHITE WOMEN	TOTAL
Number of lateral associate hires	1	3	8	23
Number of lateral partner hires (equity and non-equity)	0	0	0	7
Number of new partners (equity and non-equity) promoted from associate rank	0	0	4	7
Number of new equity partners	0	0	4	14

Retention & Professional Development

ATTORNEYS WHO LEFT THE FIRM: 2003	MINORITY MEN	MINORITY WOMEN	WHITE WOMEN	TOTAL
Number of attorneys who voluntarily or involuntarily left your firm's employ in 2003	3	11	39	100

How do 2003 attrition rates generally compare to those experienced in the prior year period?

About the same as in prior years

Please identify the specific steps you are taking to reduce the attrition rate of minority and women attorneys.

• Develop and/or support internal employee affinity groups (e.g., minority or women networks within the firm)

• Increase/review compensation relative to competition

• Increase/improve current work/life programs

• Work with minority and women attorneys to develop career advancement plans

• Introduce minority and women attorneys to key clients, including to lead engagements

• Review work assignments and hours billed to key client matters to make sure minority and women attorneys are not being excluded

• Strengthen mentoring program for all attorneys, including minorities and women

• Professional skills development program, including minority and women attorneys

Does your firm have part-time/flex-time policies that permit attorneys (male or female) to work alternative schedules?

Yes, Gibson Dunn & Crutcher's part-time policies for associates and partners permit part-time schedules for periods of time during an attorney's career.

What impact, if any, will the decision to work part-time have on an attorney's ability to make partner or, if already a partner, to remain a partner at your firm?

The fact that an attorney works on a part-time basis for a period of time will not affect the attorney's ability to become a partner or to remain a partner.

Have any attorneys who chose to work a part-time schedule made partner at your firm?

Yes

Management Demographic Profile (as of 12/31/03)

	MINORITY MEN	MINORITY WOMEN	WHITE WOMEN	TOTAL
Number of attorneys on the Executive/Management Committee or equivalent	0	0	1	18
Number of attorneys on the Hiring Committee or equivalent	1	2	11	35
Number of attorneys on the Partner/Associate Review Committee or equivalent	0	0	5	38

Please provide information regarding all minority and women attorneys who head offices or practice groups of your law firm:

Women heading offices: Marjorie E. Lewis, Los Angeles; Kathryn A. Coleman, Bay Area; Stephanie R. Bess, London; Stephanie Tsacoumis, Washington, DC

Minorities heading practice groups: Miguel Estrada, Appellate & Constitutional Law; Marcellus McRae, Business Crimes & Investigations

Women heading practice groups: Gail Lees, Consumer Class Actions; Amy Rudnick, Financial Institutions; Judith Lee, International Trade & Customs; Deborah Clarke, Labor & Employment

The Firm Says

Gibson Dunn believes that diversity among our attorneys is essential to our continued success as one of the leading law firms in the world. Diversity among our attorneys creates a more vibrant and stimulating workplace. By creating an environment that is comfortable for each attorney at our firm, we believe our attorneys will thrive and the firm and our clients will benefit from each attorney's unique perspective. The recruitment, retention and promotion of attorneys of diverse backgrounds are top goals of our firm's management. Consistent with these goals, Gibson Dunn proudly supports a Diversity Committee comprised of associates and partners throughout the firm.

The Diversity Committee focuses on recruiting, retaining and promoting a diverse group of law students and attorneys. The committee also facilitates a continuing and evolving dialogue within the firm on a wide range of issues. The activities of our Diversity Committee include:

• Coordinating the firm's recruitment efforts for diverse candidates through active participation in the hiring process, as well as consulting on recruitment policies and practices;

• Hosting receptions across the country for members of law school organizations that are focused on diversity;

• Mentoring associates from diverse backgrounds;

• Working with outside consultants to assist in developing more effective mentoring programs;

• Sponsoring the activities of various local and national special interest organizations focused on diversity issues, including: the American Bar Association (ABA) Minority Demonstration Program, the American Civil Liberties Union's (ACLU) Lesbian & Gay Rights and AIDS Projects Summer Attorney Reception, the American Indian Law Student Association, the Asian American Legal Defense and Education Fund (AALDEF)

Summer Reception, various Asian Pacific American Law Students Association (APALSA) conferences, the annual Harvard Law School Black Law Students' Association (BLSA) Spring Conference, the Law Students of African Descent Placement Night and the Minority Corporate Counsel Association;

• Participating as speakers to address diversity issues in various forums ranging from law schools to professional conferences and community organizations; and

• Hosting prominent educational and professional leaders to speak on issues of diversity at firm events.

By further increasing the diversity of our attorneys, we will enhance the environment that has allowed us to attract and retain top quality attorneys. We believe that this will further increase our ability to provide the highest level of service to our clients.

Gray Cary Ware & Freidenrich

2000 University Avenue
East Palo Alto, CA 94303
Phone: (650) 833-2253
Fax:(650) 833-2001

LOCATIONS

East Palo Alto, CA (HQ)
Austin, TX
Sacramento, CA
San Diego, CA San Francisco, CA
Seattle, WA
Washington, DC

LAW FIRM DEMOGRAPHIC PROFILES

FULL-TIME ASSOCIATES	2003	2002
Minority men	16	19
Minority women	14	16
White women	63	82
Total	234	271

SUMMER ASSOCIATES	2003	2002
Minority men	1	11
Minority women	2	3
White women	11	18
Total	26	46

EQUITY PARTNERS	2003	2002
Minority men	5	3
Minority women	1	1
White women	24	27
Total	108	114

NON-EQUITY PARTNERS	2003	2002
Minority men	6	7
Minority women	2	3
White women	21	21
Total	49	47

NEW HIRES	2003	2002
Minority men	3	0
Minority women	3	1
White women	2	6
Total	18	24

MCCA
MINORITY CORPORATE COUNSEL ASSOCIATION

Strategic Plan and Diversity Leadership

Does your law firm currently have a diversity committee?

No

Does the committee and/or diversity leader establish and set goals or objectives consistent with management's priorities?

N/A

Has the firm undertaken a formal or informal diversity program or set of initiatives aimed at increasing the diversity of the firm?

Yes, informal

How often does the firm's management review the firm's diversity progress/results?

Annually

LAW FIRM DIVERSITY INITIATIVES	ALREADY COMPLETED	CURRENTLY ADDRESSING	NOT A CURRENT PRIORITY
Undertake communication from firm management that diversity is a top priority of the firm.		✓	
Formalize diversity plan and committee with action steps and accountability to management.			
Conduct firm-wide diversity training for all attorneys and staff.	✓*	✓*	
Increase the number of minority attorneys at the associate level.		✓	
Increase the number of minority attorneys at the partnership level.		✓	
Develop/expand relationships with minority bar associations to offer firm's support of these networks.		✓	
Focus on strengthening firm's mentoring program, including for benefit of minority attorneys.		✓	
Conduct internal diversity needs assessment and/or retain diversity consultant to examine how firm culture might be more welcoming of minorities.			
Support law firm's internal affinity networks (e.g., women, minority attorney networks).		✓	
Manage/monitor allocation of work assignments and/or hours billed to ensure women and minority attorneys have equal access/inclusion on top client matters.			

* Have done in the past and will do in the future.

Recruitment- New Associates

Do you have any special outreach efforts directed to encourage minority law students to consider your firm?

• Participate in/host minority law student job fair(s)

• Sponsor minority law student association events

• Firm's lawyers participate on career panels at law schools

SUMMER ASSOCIATE STATISTICS: SUMMER 2003	MINORITY MEN	MINORITY WOMEN	WHITE WOMEN	TOTAL
Summer associates	1	2	11	26
Summer associates who received an offer of full-time employment	0	2	10	23*
Summer associates who accepted an offer of full-time employment	0	2	8	19

* Five of these were offers to return summer 2004; these were 1L/joint degree students.

Recruitment- Lateral Associates and Partners

What activities does the firm undertake to attract minority and women attorneys?

• Partner programs with women and minority bar associations

• Participate at minority job fairs

• Seek referrals from other attorneys

Do you use executive recruiting/search firms to seek to identify new diversity hires (partners or associates)?

No

LATERAL ASSOCIATES AND PARTNERS: 1/1/03 – 12/31/03	MINORITY MEN	MINORITY WOMEN	WHITE WOMEN	TOTAL
Number of lateral associate hires	0	3	2	11
Number of lateral partner hires (equity and non-equity)	3	0	0	7
Number of new partners (equity and non-equity) promoted from associate rank	0	0	3	10
Number of new equity partners	0	0	0	2

Retention & Professional Development

ATTORNEYS WHO LEFT THE FIRM: 2003	MINORITY MEN	MINORITY WOMEN	WHITE WOMEN	TOTAL
Number of attorneys who voluntarily or involuntarily left your firm's employ in 2003	3	4	15	45

How do 2003 attrition rates generally compare to those experienced in the prior year period?

Higher than in prior years

Please identify the specific steps you are taking to reduce the attrition rate of minority and women attorneys.

• Develop and/or support internal employee affinity groups (e.g., minority or women networks within the firm)

• Increase/review compensation relative to competition

• Increase/improve current work/life programs

• Work with minority and women attorneys to develop career advancement plans

• Introduce minority and women attorneys to key clients, including to lead engagements

• Strengthen mentoring program for all attorneys, including minorities and women

• Professional skills development program, including minority and women attorneys

Does your firm have part-time/flex-time policies that permit attorneys (male or female) to work alternative schedules?

Yes

Have any attorneys who chose to work a part-time schedule made partner at your firm?

Yes

Management Demographic Profile (as of 12/31/03)

	MINORITY MEN	MINORITY WOMEN	WHITE WOMEN	TOTAL
Number of attorneys on the Executive/Management Committee or equivalent	0	0	2	9
Number of attorneys on the Hiring Committee or equivalent	2	2	5	17
Number of attorneys on the Partner/Associate Review Committee or equivalent	N/A	N/A	N/A	N/A

Please provide information regarding all minority and women attorneys who head offices or practice groups of your law firm:

Women heading offices: Margaret Kavalaris, Washington, D.C.

Minorities heading practice groups: Robert Brownlie, Corporate & Commercial Disputes

Women heading practice groups: Marcie Mihaila, Litigation Department; Luanne Sacks, Trade Regulation and Consumer Liability Division

The Firm Says

Gray Cary offers free legal services to minorities through its work with the Palo Alto Volunteer Attorney Program, Stanford Community Law Clinic, San Diego Volunteer Program, Silicon Valley Campaign for Legal Services, Legal Aid Societies of San Mateo and San Diego, Santa Clara Community Law Center, Planned Partenhood, and Families and Children's' Counseling Services, among others. Gray Cary also owrks with minority communities as a partner with the City of East Palo Alto battling nuisance/drug houses.

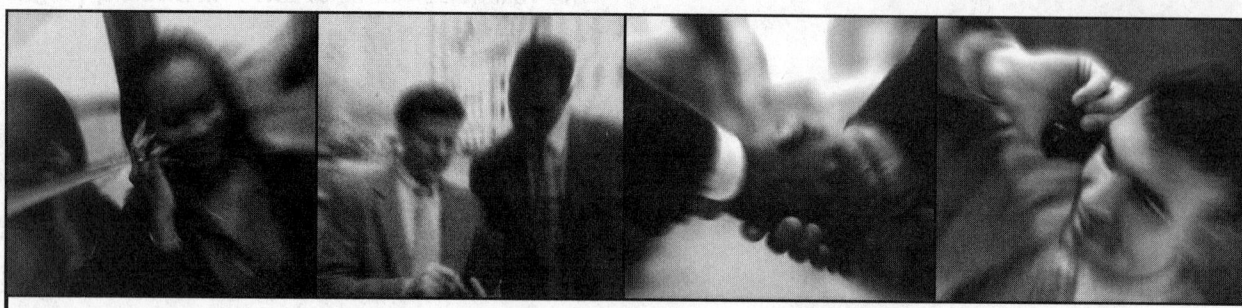

Most Law Firms Have Diversity Committees.
We Have Diversity.

Greenberg Traurig, LLP

1221 Brickell Avenue
Miami, FL 33131
Phone: (305) 579-0500
Fax: (305) 579-0717

FIRM LEADERSHIP

Managing Partner: Cesar L. Alvarez, President
and CEO
Diversity Team Leader: Cesar L. Alvarez,
President and CEO

LOCATIONS

Miami, FL (HQ)*
Albany, NY
Atlanta, GA
Boca Raton, FL
Boston, MA
Chicago, IL
Dallas, TX
Denver, CO
East Palo Alto, CA
Florham Park, NJ
Fort Lauderdale, FL
Irvine, CA
Los Angeles, CA
New York, NY
Orlando, FL
Philadelphia, PA
Phoenix, AZ
Tallahassee, FL
Tysons Corner, VA
Washington, DC
West Palm Beach, FL
Wilmington, DE
Amsterdam
Zurich

*Greenberg Traurig is a national firm and does
not have a "principal" or "headquarter"
office. Miami is the firm's founding office.*

LAW FIRM DEMOGRAPHIC PROFILES

FULL-TIME ASSOCIATES	2003	2002
Minority men	56	37
Minority women	55	30
White women	123	111
Total	433	357

SUMMER ASSOCIATES	2003	2002
Minority men	8	2
Minority women	3	7
White women	9	8
Total	28*	22

EQUITY PARTNERS	2003	2002
Minority men	20	11
Minority women	1	2
White women	32	23
Total	280	205

NON-EQUITY PARTNERS	2003	2002
Minority men	44	31
Minority women	15	6
White women	75	67
Total	372	341

NEW HIRES	2003	2002
Minority men	23	11
Minority women	23	15
White women	45	42
Total	184	173

Strategic Plan and Diversity Leadership

How does the firm's leadership communicate the importance of diversity to everyone at the firm? (e.g., e-mails, web site, newsletters, meetings, etc.)

At Greenberg Traurig, diversity is addressed from the top down. We lead by example, starting with our president and CEO, Cesar L. Alvarez. Greenberg Traurig supports and promotes diversity in a variety of ways, such as firm retreats, minority job fairs, university support, career development opportunities, minority business support, employer counseling, training and policy development, and philanthropic endeavors. The firm posts its EEO policies on its Intranet, accessible to all employees and attorneys.

Who has primary responsibility for leading diversity initiatives at your firm?

Cesar L. Alvarez, president and CEO.

Does your law firm currently have a diversity committee?

No In general, Greenberg Traurig does not operate by committee for its business functions. The CEO views as an important part of his job, fostering minority involvement within the firm.

Does the committee's representation include one or more members of the firm's management/executive committee (or the equivalent)?

Yes. Our CEO is the person in charge.

How many attorneys are on the committee, and in 2003, what was the total number of hours collectively spent by the committee in furtherance of the firm's diversity initiatives?

We do not operate by committee.

Does the committee and/or diversity leader establish and set goals or objectives consistent with management's priorities?

No. Our CEO does this.

Has the firm undertaken a formal or informal diversity program or set of initiatives aimed at increasing the diversity of the firm?

Yes, formal and informal

How often does the firm's management review the firm's diversity progress/results?

Promoting diversity enters into decision-making on a daily basis.

How is the firm's diversity committee and/or firm management held accountable for achieving results?

This is an important part of the CEO's job.

LAW FIRM DIVERSITY INITIATIVES	ALREADY COMPLETED	CURRENTLY ADDRESSING	NOT A CURRENT PRIORITY
Undertake communication from firm management that diversity is a top priority of the firm.		✓	
Formalize diversity plan and committee with action steps and accountability to management.			
Conduct firm-wide diversity training for all attorneys and staff.		✓	
Increase the number of minority attorneys at the associate level.		✓	
Increase the number of minority attorneys at the partnership level.		✓	
Develop/expand relationships with minority bar associations to offer firm's support of these networks.		✓	
Focus on strengthening firm's mentoring program, including for benefit of minority attorneys.		✓	
Conduct internal diversity needs assessment and/or retain diversity consultant to examine how firm culture might be more welcoming of minorities.		✓ *	
Support law firm's internal affinity networks (e.g., women, minority attorney networks).		✓	
Manage/monitor allocation of work assignments and/or hours billed to ensure women and minority attorneys have equal access/inclusion on top client matters.		✓	

*Informal

Note: Greenberg Traurig is one of the fastest growing law firms in the U.S. (The National Law Journal Millennium 250 Survey). Its commitment to diversity hiring and promotion is, therefore, constant. A time when it is already completed is not conceivable.

Recruitment – New Associates

Does your firm annually recruit at any of the following types of institutions?

Ivy League schools: Harvard University, Columbia University, University of Pennsylvania

Public state schools: Arizona State University, University of California at Los Angeles , University of Illinois, University of Florida, University of Michigan, University of North Carolina, University of Texas

Private schools: Duke University, New York University, University of Chicago, Northwestern University, Georgetown University, Emory University, Stanford University

Historically Black Colleges and Universities (HBCUs): Florida International University

Do you have any special outreach efforts directed to encourage minority law students to consider your firm?

• Participate in/host minority law student job fair(s) (Greenberg Traurig participates in the Delaware Minority Job Fair, the Southeastern Minority Job Fair and the Northeastern Black Law Students Association Job Fair.)

• Scholarships or intern/fellowships for minority students (As the largest funder in the country of fellowships for Equal Justice Works, GT makes it possible for students and lawyers to work for the public interest for such organizations as the Florida Immigrant Advocacy Center, the Center for Battered Women Legal Services in New York and the Legal Aid Society of Chicago.)

• Our CEO speaks at law schools regularly. For example, in October, he will speak at the eighth annual National Latino Law Student Association Conference at the University of Denver College of Law.

SUMMER ASSOCIATE STATISTICS: SUMMER 2003	MINORITY MEN & WOMEN	WOMEN	TOTAL*
Summer associates	11	9	28
Summer associates who received an offer of full-time employment	9	7	23
Summer associates who accepted an offer of full-time employment	8	7	22

* Figure represents all women summer associates (both minority and white).

Recruitment – Lateral Associates and Partners

What activities does the firm undertake to attract minority and women attorneys?

• Partner programs with women and minority bar associations
• Participate at minority job fairs
• Seek referrals from other attorneys (e.g. MCCA/DuPont Primary Law Firm Job Bank)

Do you use executive recruiting/search firms to seek to identify new diversity hires (partners or associates)?

Yes

List all women- and/or minority-owned executive search/recruiting firms to which the firm paid a fee for placement services in the past 12 months:

Confidential

LATERAL ASSOCIATES AND PARTNERS: 1/1/03 – 12/31/03	MINORITY MEN	MINORITY WOMEN	WHITE WOMEN	TOTAL
Number of lateral associate hires	14	21	40	124
Number of lateral partner hires (equity and non-equity)	9	2	5	60
Number of new partners (equity and non-equity) promoted from associate rank	0	1	5	22
Number of new equity partners	5	2	7	53

Retention & Professional Development

ATTORNEYS WHO LEFT THE FIRM: 2003	MINORITY MEN	MINORITY WOMEN	WHITE WOMEN	TOTAL
Number of attorneys who voluntarily or involuntarily left your firm's employ in 2003	7	10	27	92

How do 2003 attrition rates generally compare to those experienced in the prior year period?

Lower than in prior years

Please identify the specific steps you are taking to reduce the attrition rate of minority and women attorneys.

• Develop and/or support internal employee affinity groups (e.g., minority or women networks within the firm)

• Increase/review compensation relative to competition

• Increase/improve current work/life programs

• Work with minority and women attorneys to develop career advancement plans

• Introduce minority and women attorneys to key clients, including to lead engagements

• Strengthen mentoring program for all attorneys, including minorities and women

• Professional skills development program, including minority and women attorneys

Does your firm have part-time/flex-time policies that permit attorneys (male or female) to work alternative schedules?

Yes. The firm recognizes that despite a strong commitment to the practice of law, an individual lawyer may find that personal and/or family concerns necessitate requesting a work arrangement which reduces the amount of time devoted to practicing law. The firm has a strong policy of providing interesting and productive alternative work schedule opportunities for lawyers with small children or in other circumstances.

What impact, if any, will the decision to work part-time have on an attorney's ability to make partner or, if already a partner, to remain a partner at your firm?

An alternative work schedule for a period not to exceed six months will not in and of itself hold back an associate's progression toward becoming a shareholder. The impact on shareholder eligibility, salary and

benefits for individuals working an alternative work schedule longer than six months will be determined at the discretion of the lawyer's department head and the CEO.

Have any attorneys who chose to work a part-time schedule made partner at your firm?
Yes, two attorneys in the recent past.

Management Demographic Profile (as of 12/31/03)

	MINORITY MEN	MINORITY WOMEN	WHITE WOMEN	TOTAL
Number of attorneys on the Executive/Management Committee or equivalent	1	0	1	12

Please provide information regarding all minority and women attorneys who head offices or practice groups of your law firm:

Minorities heading offices: Cesar L. Alvarez, President/CEO; Orlando L. Evora, Co-Managing Shareholder, Orlando

Women heading offices: N/A

Minorities heading practice groups: Carl A. Fornaris, Co-Chair, Financial Institutions; Oscar Levin, Co-Chair, Business Immigration; Patricia Menendez Cambo, Chair, Global

Women heading practice groups: Hilarie Bass, Chair, Litigation; Patricia Menendez Cambo, Chair, Global Business Practice; Shirley Z. Johnson, Chair, Antitrust & Trade Regulation; Diana P. Scott, Co-Chair, Labor & Employment; Nancy Taylor, Co-Chair, Health Business; Laura Foote Reiff, Co-Chair, Business Immigration

The Firm Says

In a narrative of two pages or less, please provide any additional information regarding your firm's diversity initiatives that you wish to share. See instructions for details and suggestions.

Most law firms have diversity committees. Greenberg Traurig has diversity.

Diversity starts from within
Greenberg Traurig is committed to diversity in the workplace. It has been and continues to be the goal of Greenberg Traurig to foster a well-balanced work force which contains a significant presence of minority group members and women. That commitment is reflected in significant increases year-to-year in the number of minorities and women. Firm-wide, as of July 31, 2004, we had a total of 2,600 U.S. employees, of which 867 met the definition of minority persons, reflecting a total of 33 percent of the firm's employment base. Of these employees, 1,478, or 57 percent, are women.

Diversity in firm recognition
It's no coincidence that Greenberg Traurig strongly supports diversity initiatives and has received firm and individual recognition for our efforts. Not only are we the only AmLaw 100 law firm with an Hispanic or

African-American president or CEO, but one-third of our more than 2,600 employees in 24 offices throughout the United States and Europe are minorities.

As compared to other law firms, we take pride in the following recent recognition:

Minority Law Journal, 2004

• First place, most Hispanic Americans/highest number category
• Second place, most minority partners/highest number category
• Top 10 ranking, most minority partners/highest percentage category

Vault Guide to the Top 100 Law Firms, 2004

• Top 10 ranking, best in diversity for minorities
• Top 15 ranking, best in diversity for women

Diversity in individual recognition

Our attorneys have received worldwide recognition for their efforts to promote diversity and aid minorities. Honors include:

• Attorney of the Year Award, Hispanic National Bar Association
• Pioneer Award, African-American Judges of Florida
• Silver Medallion Award, National Conference for Community and Justice
• Put Something Back Award, 11th Judicial Court
• Young Hispanic Leadership Award, Hispanic Heritage Festival
• Torch of Liberty Award, Anti-Defamation League

Diversity through action

• Charitable community projects nationwide benefit from millions of dollars in funding available through the Greenberg Traurig Foundation.
• Greenberg Traurig Fellowship Foundation provides funding for attorneys to work with public interest groups.
• We are the largest sponsor of Equal Justice Works fellowships in the country.
• Our nation's officer corps chose Greenberg Traurig as party and co-counsel to an amicus brief filed with the Supreme Court supporting affirmative action.
• We provide and participate in minority business support, university support and minority job fairs.

Creating access for minority law students

Greenberg Traurig lawyers have made an on-going commitment to fostering diversity inside and outside the firm. The firm's internal efforts are best evidenced by its growing numbers of minorities. Outside the firm, for example, our CEO, concerned with the small numbers of minorities enrolled in law schools, successfully lobbied with other community leaders to establish two diversity-focused law schools. These schools, Florida International University School of Law and Florida A&M College of Law, offer a diverse student population many advantages, including location in urban areas and the convenience of night and weekend curriculum options. The success of both programs has led to the American Bar Association (ABA) recommending accreditation to the ABA House of Delegates.

Hale and Dorr LLP*

60 State Street
Boston, MA 02109
Phone: (617) 526-6000
Fax: (617) 526-5000

FIRM LEADERSHIP

Managing Partner: William F. Lee, Managing Partner
Diversity Team Leader: John G. Fabiano and Wendell C. Taylor, Co-Chairs of the Diversity Committee

LOCATIONS

Boston, MA (HQ)
New York, NY
Reston, VA
Princeton, NJ
Waltham, MA
Washington, DC
London
Munich
Oxford

NOTE: On June 1, 2004, Hale and Dorr LLP merged with Wilmer Cutler Pickering LLP to form Wilmer Cutler Pickering Hale and Dorr LLP. The information below reflects Hale and Dorr's diversity programs in 2002 and 2003. The combined firm will report its 2004 diversity initiatives in next year's edition of the Vault/MCCA Law Firm Diversity Guide (2006).

LAW FIRM DEMOGRAPHIC PROFILES

FULL-TIME ASSOCIATES*	2003	2002
Minority men	15	17
Minority women	19	20
White women	114	122
Total	285	310

* Includes counsel and staff attorneys.

SUMMER ASSOCIATES	2003	2002
Minority men	3	3
Minority women	3	2
White women	17	20
Total	37	40

EQUITY PARTNERS	2003	2002
Minority men	5	5
Minority women	0	0
White women	25	25
Total	157	154

NON-EQUITY PARTNERS	2003	2002
Minority men	0	0
Minority women	0	0
White women	4	3
Total	11	14

NEW HIRES	2003	2002
Minority men	1	2
Minority women	7	3
White women	12	33
Total	43	51

Strategic Plan and Diversity Leadership

How does the firm's leadership communicate the importance of diversity to everyone at the firm? (e.g., e-mails, web site, newsletters, meetings, etc.)

The firm's leadership communicates the importance of the diversity initiative through discussions at meetings of the firm's executive and hiring committees, firm-wide meetings of the partners and various meetings with associates and staff. In these discussions, the firm's management stresses the moral and business imperatives that underlie the firm's diversity initiative.

Who has primary responsibility for leading diversity initiatives at your firm?

Two partners of the firm: John G. Fabiano and Wendell C. Taylor, co-chairs of the Diversity Committee

Does your law firm currently have a diversity committee?

Yes

If yes, does the committee's representation include one or more members of the firm's management/executive committee (or the equivalent)?

Yes

If yes, how many attorneys are on the committee, and in 2003, what was the total number of hours collectively spent by the committee in furtherance of the firm's diversity initiatives?

Total attorneys on committee: 11

Total hours spent on diversity: 400

Does the committee and/or diversity leader establish and set goals or objectives consistent with management's priorities?

Yes

Has the firm undertaken a formal or informal diversity program or set of initiatives aimed at increasing the diversity of the firm?

Yes, formal

How often does the firm's management review the firm's diversity progress/results?

Quarterly

How is the firm's diversity committee and/or firm management held accountable for achieving results?

The success of the firm's diversity initiative is one of the factors considered by the firm's compensation committee in setting partner compensation.

LAW FIRM DIVERSITY INITIATIVES	ALREADY COMPLETED	CURRENTLY ADDRESSING	NOT A CURRENT PRIORITY
Undertake communication from firm management that diversity is a top priority of the firm.	✔		
Formalize diversity plan and committee with action steps and accountability to management.	✔		
Conduct firm-wide diversity training for all attorneys and staff.			✔
Increase the number of minority attorneys at the associate level.		✔	
Increase the number of minority attorneys at the partnership level.		✔	
Develop/expand relationships with minority bar associations to offer firm's support of these networks.		✔	
Focus on strengthening firm's mentoring program, including for benefit of minority attorneys.		✔	
Conduct internal diversity needs assessment and/or retain diversity consultant to examine how firm culture might be more welcoming of minorities.		✔	
Support law firm's internal affinity networks (e.g., women, minority attorney networks).		✔	
Manage/monitor allocation of work assignments and/or hours billed to ensure women and minority attorneys have equal access/inclusion on top client matters.		✔	

Recruitment - New Associates

Does your firm annually recruit at any of the following types of institutions? (Check all that apply and list the schools).

Ivy League schools: Columbia University, Cornell University, Harvard University, University of Pennsylvania, Yale University

Public state schools: University of Michigan, University of Virginia

Private schools: Boston College, Boston University, University of Chicago, Duke University, Georgetown University, Northeastern University, Northwestern University, New York University, Suffolk University

Do you have any special outreach efforts directed to encourage minority law students to consider your firm?

• Hold a reception for minority law students

• Participate in/host minority law student job fair(s)

• Sponsor minority law student association events

• Firm's lawyers participate on career panels at school

• Outreach to leadership of minority student organizations

• Scholarships or intern/fellowships for minority students

MINORITY CORPORATE COUNSEL ASSOCIATION

SUMMER ASSOCIATE STATISTICS: SUMMER 2003	MINORITY MEN	MINORITY WOMEN	WHITE WOMEN	TOTAL
Summer associates	0	2	17	30
Summer associates who received an offer of full-time employment	0	1	16	28
Summer associates who accepted an offer of full-time employment	0	0	15	25

Recruitment – Lateral Associates and Partners

What activities does the firm undertake to attract minority and women attorneys?

• Participate at minority job fairs

• Seek referrals from other attorneys

• Partner programs with women and minority bar associations

Do you use executive recruiting/search firms to seek to identify new diversity hires (partners or associates)?

No

LATERAL ASSOCIATES AND PARTNERS: 1/1/03 – 12/31/03	MINORITY MEN	MINORITY WOMEN	WHITE WOMEN	TOTAL
Number of lateral associate hires	2	3	2	15
Number of lateral partner hires (equity and non-equity)	0	0	1	2
Number of new partners (equity and non-equity) promoted from associate rank	0	0	0	4
Number of new equity partners	0	0	0	5

Retention & Professional Development

Please identify the specific steps you are taking to reduce the attrition rate of minority and women attorneys.

• *Encourage the development of internal affinity groups.*

• Develop and/or support internal employee affinity groups (e.g., minority or women networks within the firm)

• Increase/review compensation relative to competition

• Increase/improve current work/life programs

• Succession plan includes emphasis on diversity

• Work with minority and women attorneys to develop career advancement plans

• Introduce minority and women attorneys to key clients, including to lead engagements

• Review work assignments and hours billed to key client matters to make sure minority and women attorneys are not being excluded

• Strengthen mentoring program for all attorneys, including minorities and women

• Professional skills development program, including minority and women attorneys

Does your firm have part-time/flex-time policies that permit attorneys (male or female) to work alternative schedules?

Yes. The firm offers both part-time and flex-time to attorneys.

What impact, if any, will the decision to work part-time have on an attorney's ability to make partner or, if already a partner, to remain a partner at your firm?

None.

Have any attorneys who chose to work a part-time schedule made partner at your firm?

Yes, three attorneys in 2002

Management Demographic Profile (as of 12/31/03)

	MINORITY MEN	MINORITY WOMEN	WHITE WOMEN	TOTAL
Number of attorneys on the Executive/Management Committee or equivalent	1	0	3	11
Number of attorneys on the Hiring Committee or equivalent	2	0	3	17
Number of attorneys on the Partner/Associate Review Committee or equivalent	0	0	7	35

Please provide information regarding all minority and women attorneys who head offices or practice groups of your law firm:

Minorities heading offices: William F. Lee, Managing Partner of Hale and Dorr; David Sylvester, Reston, VA.

Women heading practice groups: Susan W. Murley, Vice Chair, Corporate Department; Meghan H. Magruder, Vice Chair, Environmental Department; Hollie L. Baker, Vice Chair, Intellectual Property Department; Karen F. Green, Chair, Litigation Department; Michelle D. Miller, Vice Chair, Litigation Department; Jennifer C. Snyder, Chair, Private Client Department; A. Silvana Giner, Vice Chair, Private Client Department; Katharine E. Bachman, Vice Chair, Real Estate Department.

Haynes and Boone, LLP

901 Main Street, Suite 3100
Dallas, TX 75202
Phone: (214) 651-5000
Fax: (214) 651-5940

FIRM LEADERSHIP

Kathleen M. Beasley, Hiring Partner
Managing Partner: Robert E. Wilson
Diversity Team Leaders: Kathleen M. Beasley
and Lamont Jefferson, Esqs.

LOCATIONS

Dallas, TX (HQ)
Austin, TX
Fort Worth, TX
Houston, TX
New York, NY
Richardson, TX
San Antonio, TX
Washington, DC
Mexico City

LAW FIRM DEMOGRAPHIC PROFILES

FULL-TIME ASSOCIATES	2003	2002
Minority men	19	16
Minority women	15	12
White women	71	70
Total	234	222

SUMMER ASSOCIATES	2003	2002
Minority men	6	8
Minority women	9	7
White women	31	38
Total	78	100

EQUITY PARTNERS	2003	2002
Minority men	8	9
Minority women	1	1
White women	26	26
Total	158	158

NON-EQUITY PARTNERS	2003	2002
Minority men	0	0
Minority women	0	0
White women	1	2
Total	3	5

NEW HIRES	2003	2002
Minority men	8	5
Minority women	4	4
White women	24	22
Total	70	57

MINORITY CORPORATE COUNSEL ASSOCIATION

Strategic Plan and Diversity Leadership

How does the firm's leadership communicate the importance of diversity to everyone at the firm? (e.g., e-mails, web site, newsletters, meetings, etc.)

Meetings and attorney retreats

Who has primary responsibility for leading diversity initiatives at your firm?

Kathy Beasley and Lamont Jefferson, Esqs.

Does your law firm currently have a diversity committee?

Yes

Does the committee's representation include one or more members of the firm's management/executive committee (or the equivalent)?

Yes

How many attorneys are on the committee, and in 2003, what was the total number of hours collectively spent by the committee in furtherance of the firm's diversity initiatives?

Total attorneys on committee: 10

Total hours spent on diversity: Not tracked

Does the committee and/or diversity leader establish and set goals or objectives consistent with management's priorities?

Yes

Has the firm undertaken a formal or informal diversity program or set of initiatives aimed at increasing the diversity of the firm?

Yes, informal

How often does the firm's management review the firm's diversity progress/results?

Annually. The board of directors reviews annually, but certain board members review our progress/results on a quarterly basis.

How is the firm's diversity committee and/or firm management held accountable for achieving results?

Through results of surveys and how we do on these surveys, the board of directors is updated annually on how well we are doing.

LAW FIRM DIVERSITY INITIATIVES	ALREADY COMPLETED	CURRENTLY ADDRESSING	NOT A CURRENT PRIORITY
Undertake communication from firm management that diversity is a top priority of the firm.	✓		
Formalize diversity plan and committee with action steps and accountability to management.		✓	
Conduct firm-wide diversity training for all attorneys and staff.	✓		
Increase the number of minority attorneys at the associate level.		✓	
Increase the number of minority attorneys at the partnership level.		✓	
Develop/expand relationships with minority bar associations to offer firm's support of these networks.		✓	
Focus on strengthening firm's mentoring program, including for benefit of minority attorneys.		✓	
Conduct internal diversity needs assessment and/or retain diversity consultant to examine how firm culture might be more welcoming of minorities.		✓	
Support law firm's internal affinity networks (e.g., women, minority attorney networks).		✓	
Manage/monitor allocation of work assignments and/or hours billed to ensure women and minority attorneys have equal access/inclusion on top client matters.		✓	
We are currently addressing relationships with minority bar associations, in light of the roles of our attorneys in those organizations, and our sponsorship of programs.		✓	

Recruitment – New Associates

Does your firm annually recruit at any of the following types of institutions? (Check all that apply and list the schools).

Ivy League schools: Columbia University, Cornell University, Harvard University, University of Pennsylvania and Yale University

Public state schools: On-campus: Texas Tech University, University of Texas, University of Houston, University of Michigan, University of Oklahoma, University of Virginia

Solicit Resumes: George Mason University, University of California, UCLA, University of Colorado, University of Florida, University of Iowa, University of Indiana, University of Kansas, University of Nebraska, University of Notre Dame

Private schools: On-campus: Baylor University, Duke University, Georgetown University, George Washington University, NYU, Northwestern University, Southern Methodist University, Stanford University, St. Mary's University, Tulane University, University of Chicago, Vanderbilt University

Solicit Resumes: Boston College, Boston University, Brigham Young University, Case Western Reserve University, Creighton University, Emory University, Franklin Pierce Law Center, Pepperdine University, Texas

Wesleyan University, Washington University in St. Louis, Washington and Lee University, Loyola Patent Interview Program in Chicago (patent job fair open to all schools)

Historically Black Colleges and Universities: Texas Southern University-Thurgood Marshall School of Law

Do you have any special outreach efforts directed to encourage minority law students to consider your firm?

• Hold a reception for minority law students

• Advertise in minority law student association publications

• Participate in/host minority law student job fair(s)

• Sponsor minority law student association events

• Firm's lawyers participate on career panels at school

• Outreach to leadership of minority student organizations

• Scholarships or intern/fellowships for minority students

SUMMER ASSOCIATE STATISTICS: SUMMER 2003	MINORITY MEN	MINORITY WOMEN	WHITE WOMEN	TOTAL
Summer associates	3	5	29	68
Summer associates who received an offer of full-time employment	1	3	12	33
Summer associates who accepted an offer of full-time employment	1	1	8	26

Recruitment – Lateral Associates and Partners

What activities does the firm undertake to attract minority and women attorneys?

• Partner programs with women and minority bar associations

• Participate at minority job fairs

• Seek referrals from other attorneys

Do you use executive recruiting/search firms to seek to identify new diversity hires (partners or associates)?

Yes

LATERAL ASSOCIATES AND PARTNERS: 1/1/03 – 12/31/03	MINORITY MEN	MINORITY WOMEN	WHITE WOMEN	TOTAL
Number of lateral associate hires	1	2	3	21
Number of lateral partner hires (equity and non-equity)	0	0	0	1
Number of new partners (equity and non-equity) promoted from associate rank	0	0	2	7
Number of new equity partners	0	0	0	1

Retention & Professional Development

ATTORNEYS WHO LEFT THE FIRM: 2003	MINORITY MEN	MINORITY WOMEN	WHITE WOMEN	TOTAL
Number of attorneys who voluntarily or involuntarily left your firm's employ in 2003	6	0	18	53

How do 2003 attrition rates generally compare to those experienced in the prior year period?

About the same as in prior years

Please identify the specific steps you are taking to reduce the attrition rate of minority and women attorneys.

• Develop and/or support internal employee affinity groups (e.g., minority or women networks within the firm)

• Increase/improve current work/life programs

• Strengthen mentoring program for all attorneys, including minorities and women

• Professional skills development program, including minority and women attorneys

Does your firm have part-time/flex-time policies that permit attorneys (male or female) to work alternative schedules?

Yes. We are currently reviewing policy.

What impact, if any, will the decision to work part-time have on an attorney's ability to make partner or, if already a partner, to remain a partner at your firm?

Case-by-case basis.

Management Demographic Profile (as of 12/31/03)

	MINORITY MEN	MINORITY WOMEN	WHITE WOMEN	TOTAL
Number of attorneys on the Executive/Management Committee or equivalent	0	0	3	13
Number of attorneys on the Hiring Committee or equivalent	8	3	18	84
Number of attorneys on the Partner/Associate Review Committee or equivalent	1	0	6	16

Please provide information regarding all minority and women attorneys who head offices or practice groups of your law firm:

Minorities heading offices: Lamont Jefferson, San Antonio

Women heading offices: Ellen McGinnis, Washington, DC

Minorities heading practice groups: Ernest Martin, Insurance Litigation

Women heading practice groups: Stacey Jernigan, Bankruptcy; Sue Murphy/Ellen McGinnis, Financial Transactions; Ann Saegert, Real Estate; Sharon Freytag, Appellate; Noel Hensley, Securities Litigation

MINORITY CORPORATE COUNSEL ASSOCIATION

The Firm Says

Haynes and Boone is committed to the principle of equal opportunity for all individuals commensurate with their abilities, and not limited by discrimination based on race, color, religion, age, disability, national origin, gender or sexual orientation.

We are proud of the ethnic and cultural diversity of our people and the pivotal role women and minorities have played in our firm's development. Haynes and Boone's growth in terms of diversity, number of lawyers and experience has been noteworthy. We have aggressively recruited outstanding students from the best law schools in the country. While in our early years we interviewed only at law schools in Texas, today approximately 36 percent of our lawyers are graduates of law schools located outside of Texas. Furthermore, our lawyers come from more than 40 states and 15 foreign countries.

Our firm is committed to recruiting, retaining and promoting women and minority lawyers. As evidence of this commitment, Haynes and Boone received the Minority Corporate Counsel Association's prestigious 2002 Thomas L. Sager Award. We also have established the Haynes and Boone Minority Scholars Program available to first-year students at SMU Dedman School of Law and the University of Texas School of Law. Haynes and Boone scholars receive a monthly stipend, a summer clerkship at Haynes and Boone and a mentor to provide guidance during the student's first year in law school.

We recognize that to be responsive to the changing business environment and our evolving client base, our lawyers must reflect the diversity of our clients and the communities in which we live. According to a recent national survey of the 250 largest U.S. law firms, we ranked 40th in percentage of minority lawyers. As of December 31, 2003, 13 (8 percent) of our partners and 42 (15 percent) of our associates and of counsel are minorities.

Our firm also ranks in the top 50 among the nation's 200 largest U.S. law firms in percentage of women lawyers. As of December 31, 2003, 28 (17 percent) of our partners and 104 (37 percent) of our associates and of counsel are women. We strongly believe that cultural and ethnic diversity enhances innovation and the delivery of quality legal services to a diverse marketplace.

We have two partners who co-chair the firm's Development and Diversity Program, which is devoted to ensuring the advancement and retention of all attorneys, including our women and minority attorneys. Special attention is paid to mentoring and training, to assist each attorney in excelling in all aspects of the practice of law, including the development of legal and business development skills and community involvement. The Development and Diversity co-chairs solicit input and assistance from a cross-section of the firm, including a large number of the firm's women and minority attorneys.

Haynes and Boone actively recruits minority candidates as part of our recruiting program. As part of this effort, we engage in the following activities:

• We attend the Southeastern Minority Job Fair and Sunbelt Minority Job Fair.

• We recruit on campus at schools with significant minority representation (Columbia, Harvard, NYU, St. Mary's, Tulane, Texas Southern University, University of Texas and South Texas).

• We include minority attorneys in all facets of our recruiting program from on-campus and in-office interviewing to decision making on the extension of offers.

- We seek recommendations from professors at various schools regarding minority students.

- We sponsor minority student career development events, including our annual sponsorship of "Career Night" held by the Dallas Asian American Bar Association for North Texas law students and participation in the Dallas Asian American Leadership Educational Conference.

- We sponsor dinners and other social events for our female and minority attorneys.

- We support our Asian American attorneys' sponsorship of an annual dinner for incoming first-year Asian American associates.

- We encourage our minority attorneys to participate and take significant leadership roles in local, state and national minority bar associations and events, including attendance at the events sponsored by the Minority Corporate Counsel Association, Texas Minority Counsel Program, the National Asian Pacific American Bar Association, Hispanic National Bar Association, National Bar Association and Asia-Pacific Interest Section of the State Bar of Texas.

- We solicit resumes from minority organizations at various law schools.

- We sponsor a party for our female summer associates and attorneys as a part of our summer associate program.

- We sponsor a table at the Houston Bar Association's Minority Summer Associate Luncheon as a part of our summer associate program.

- We participate in the Greater Houston Diversity Coalition and the Houston CEO Diversity Roundtable.

- We target prospective hires among minority students.

- The firm is a party to the Houston Bar Association's 2003 Gender Initiative Commitment Statement; the State Bar of Texas's 1997 Statement of Goals of San Antonio Law Firms and Corporate Legal Departments for Increasing Minority Hiring, Retention and Promotion; and Statements of Goals for Austin, Dallas, Fort Worth and Houston.

- We participate in the Houston Bar Association's program for Minority Opportunities in the Legal Profession. Through that program, the firm commits to hire, as a summer associate, a minority first-year law student from one of the Houston law schools.

- We regularly hire minority attorneys laterally.

- We use executive search firms to help identify minority attorneys and post attorney positions on minority web sites.

- We sponsor minority and diversity programs offered by bar associations and other attorney organizations.

- We offer scholarships to minority students at Southern Methodist University and the University of Texas.

- We offer diversity training for all attorneys in the firm.

- We sponsor and attend the Dallas Bar Association Minority Clerkship Luncheon.

- We support our attorneys' participation in programs and forums sponsored by minority law student organizations.

What's a lawyer?

Heller Ehrman v. Conformity At Heller Ehrman, diversity isn't merely an asset, it's a necessity. As a global network of attorneys with unique experience and varied backgrounds, we are all working toward one goal. To achieve great things for our clients. Each point of view translates to another option with a potential upside. For our clients. And for ourselves.

WWW.HEWM.COM

HellerEhrman
ATTORNEYS

Challenging the laws of convention.™

Heller Ehrman White & McAuliffe LLP

333 Bush Street
San Francisco, CA 94104
Phone: (415) 772-6000
Fax: (415) 772-6268

FIRM LEADERSHIP

Managing Partner: Barry S. Levin, Chairman
Diversity Team Leader: Warrington S. Parker III
(Co-Chair, Ethnic Diversity Task Force and
Michael L. Rugen (Co-Chair, Ethnic Diversity
Task Force)

LOCATIONS

San Francisco, CA (HQ)
Anchorage, AK
Los Angeles, CA
Madison, WI
Menlo Park, CA
New York, NY
Portland, OR
San Diego, CA
Seattle, WA
Washington, DC
Beijing
Hong Kong
Singapore

LAW FIRM DEMOGRAPHIC PROFILES

FULL-TIME ASSOCIATES	2003	2002
Minority men	44	41
Minority women	44	35
White women	138	117
Total	457	411

SUMMER ASSOCIATES	2003	2002
Minority men	2	2
Minority women	7	3
White women	14	7
Total	66	62

EQUITY PARTNERS	2003	2002
Minority men	11	9
Minority women	1	2
White women	41	35
Total	216	170

NON-EQUITY PARTNERS	2003	2002
Minority men	0	0
Minority women	0	0
White women	2	2
Total	32	35

NEW HIRES	2003	2002
Minority men	13	11
Minority women	10	5
White women	43	29
Total	171	78

Strategic Plan and Diversity Leadership

How does the firm's leadership communicate the importance of diversity to everyone at the firm? (e.g., e-mails, web site, newsletters, meetings, etc.)

The firm uses a variety of methods to communicate the importance of diversity, including e-mails, web site pages, company intranet ("splash screen" and "announcements"), regular community celebrations (such recent events include the Philippine Independence Day Lunch, Gay Pride Breakfast, Black History Celebration and others), and Dignity and Respect Training (a class designed to explore the importance of respect in the workplace is provided to all attorneys, managers and supervisors).

Who has primary responsibility for leading diversity initiatives at your firm?

Warrington S. Parker III (co-chair, Ethnic Diversity Task Force) and Michael L. Rugen (co-chair, Ethnic Diversity Task Force)

Does your law firm currently have a diversity committee?

Yes

Does the committee's representation include one or more members of the firm's management/executive committee (or the equivalent)?

Yes

How many attorneys are on the committee, and in 2003, what was the total number of hours collectively spent by the committee in furtherance of the firm's diversity initiatives?

Total attorneys on committee: 13

Total hours spent on diversity: Approximately 800

Does the committee and/or diversity leader establish and set goals or objectives consistent with management's priorities?

Yes

Has the firm undertaken a formal or informal diversity program or set of initiatives aimed at increasing the diversity of the firm?

Yes, formal

How often does the firm's management review the firm's diversity progress/results?

Quarterly

How is the firm's diversity committee and/or firm management held accountable for achieving results?

Chairs of the Ethnic Diversity Task Force report to the firm's Executive and Policy Committees on diversity efforts and successes of individual offices, as well as the successes of the entire firm.

LAW FIRM DIVERSITY INITIATIVES	ALREADY COMPLETED	CURRENTLY ADDRESSING	NOT A CURRENT PRIORITY
Undertake communication from firm management that diversity is a top priority of the firm.	✓		
Formalize diversity plan and committee with action steps and accountability to management.	✓	✓	
Conduct firm-wide diversity training for all attorneys and staff.	✓	✓	
Increase the number of minority attorneys at the associate level.	✓	✓	
Increase the number of minority attorneys at the partnership level.		✓	
Develop/expand relationships with minority bar associations to offer firm's support of these networks.		✓	
Focus on strengthening firm's mentoring program, including for benefit of minority attorneys.		✓	
Conduct internal diversity needs assessment and/or retain diversity consultant to examine how firm culture might be more welcoming of minorities.	✓	✓	
Support law firm's internal affinity networks (e.g., women, minority attorney networks).	✓	✓	
Manage/monitor allocation of work assignments and/or hours billed to ensure women and minority attorneys have equal access/inclusion on top client matters.		✓	

Recruitment – New Associates

Does your firm annually recruit at any of the following types of institutions? (Check all that apply and list the schools).

Ivy League schools: Columbia University, Cornell University, Harvard University, University of Pennsylvania, Yale University

Public state schools: University of Arizona, University of California-Berkeley, University of California-Davis, University of California-Hastings, University of California-Los Angeles, George Mason University, University of Michigan, University of Texas, University of Virginia, University of Washington, University of Wisconsin

Private schools: New York University, Santa Clara University, Benjamin N. Cardozo School of Law at Yeshiva University, Brooklyn Law School, University of Chicago, Fordham University, George Washington University, Georgetown University, Loyola Law School-Los Angeles, University of San Diego, Stanford University, University of Southern California

Do you have any special outreach efforts directed to encourage minority law students to consider your firm?

• Hold a reception for minority law students

• Participate in/host minority law student job fair(s)

• Sponsor minority law student association events

• Firm's lawyers participate on career panels at school

• Outreach to leadership of minority student organizations

• Scholarships or intern/fellowships for minority students

SUMMER ASSOCIATE STATISTICS: SUMMER 2003	MINORITY MEN	MINORITY WOMEN	WHITE WOMEN	TOTAL
Summer associates	4	7	11	34
Summer associates who received an offer of full-time employment	4	5	8	28
Summer associates who accepted an offer of full-time employment	0	3	4	14

Recruitment – Lateral Associates and Partners

What activities does the firm undertake to attract minority and women attorneys?

• Partner programs with women and minority bar associations

• Participate at minority job fairs

• Seek referrals from other attorneys

• Utilize online job services (e.g., MCCA/DuPont Primary Law Firm Job Bank)

Do you use executive recruiting/search firms to seek to identify new diversity hires (partners or associates)?

Yes

List all women- and/or minority-owned executive search/recruiting firms to which the firm paid a fee for placement services in the past 12 months:

Audrey Golden and Associates (women-owned); McClure & Feuer (women-owned); North, Berman, and Beebe (women-owned); Patricia Wilson and Associates (women-owned)

Heller Ehrman also works to build relationships with executive search firms that focus on diverse clientele.

LATERAL ASSOCIATES AND PARTNERS: 1/1/03 – 12/31/03	MINORITY MEN	MINORITY WOMEN	WHITE WOMEN	TOTAL
Number of lateral associate hires	5	7	17	80
Number of lateral partner hires (equity and non-equity)	3	0	6	44
Number of new partners (equity and non-equity) promoted from associate rank	0	0	4	8
Number of new equity partners	3	0	10	50

Retention & Professional Development

ATTORNEYS WHO LEFT THE FIRM: 2003	MINORITY MEN	MINORITY WOMEN	WHITE WOMEN	TOTAL
Number of attorneys who voluntarily or involuntarily left your firm's employ in 2003	15	8	16	63

How do 2003 attrition rates generally compare to those experienced in the prior year period?

Lower than in prior years

Please identify the specific steps you are taking to reduce the attrition rate of minority and women attorneys.

• Develop and/or support internal employee affinity groups (e.g., minority or women networks within the firm)

• Increase/review compensation relative to competition

• Strengthen mentoring program for all attorneys, including minorities and women

• Professional skills development program, including minority and women attorneys

Does your firm have part-time/flex-time policies that permit attorneys (male or female) to work alternative schedules?

Yes

What impact, if any, will the decision to work part-time have on an attorney's ability to make partner or, if already a partner, to remain a partner at your firm?

None.

Have any attorneys who chose to work a part-time schedule made partner at your firm?

Yes. During the firm's history, some part-time attorneys have made partner, but we do not keep these records so we cannot provide an accurate count regarding the number.

Management Demographic Profile (as of 12/31/03)

	MINORITY MEN	MINORITY WOMEN	WHITE WOMEN	TOTAL
Number of attorneys on the Executive/Management Committee or equivalent	0	0	1	5
Number of attorneys on the Hiring Committee or equivalent	2	1	5	16
Number of attorneys on the Partner/Associate Review Committee or equivalent	0	0	1	8

Please provide information regarding all minority and women attorneys who head offices or practice groups of your law firm:

Minorities heading practice groups: Warrington S. Parker III (Appeals and Strategy)

Women heading practice groups: Mary L. Azcuenaga (Antitrust & Trade Regulation); Nancy Sher Cohen (Insurance Coverage); Patricia K. Gillette (Labor and Employment); Lynn J. Loacker (Corporate Finance); Judith C. Miles (Real Estate); M. Patricia Thayer (Intellectual Property Litigation)

The Firm Says

Since 1890, Heller Ehrman has embraced and celebrated diversity in our work force. While the firm's founders demonstrated their commitment to diversity by assembling (uncharacteristically for the time) a group of lawyers from disparate religious backgrounds, today that commitment is manifested on many more levels. We believe that diversity enhances the quality of service we provide to clients and makes Heller Ehrman a rich and rewarding place to work, for both attorneys and professional staff.

We have set aggressive hiring and advancement goals for minority attorneys, defined as African-Americans, Asians/Pacific Islanders, Hispanics/Latinos, Native Americans, and self-identified gays and lesbians. In addition, the firm supports the Heller Ehrman Lesbian/Gay/Bisexual/Transgender Alliance (HELGA) as well as a variety of ethnic and cultural activities, including participation in World AIDS Day, celebration of Black History Month and various multicultural events within the firm and in the communities in which we live and work.

Initiatives

Although we have made great strides toward creating a diverse attorney population, we believe that we must continue to improve. The firm's Ethnic Diversity Task Force is re-examining all aspects of hiring, retention and promotion practices. For example:

• We are implementing a program to identify and recruit minority lateral shareholders in all offices. Having a critical mass of senior attorneys of color at the firm will be our single best asset in recruiting and retaining additional minority attorneys.

• In 2003, we established a Diversity Fellowship Program that provides four fellowships (based on geographic areas Northwest, Bay Area, Southern California and East Coast) to minority students who have completed their first year of law school. Each fellowship winner will receive summer employment at the office of their choice, plus a $7,500 scholarship for the following academic year.

• All firm-wide and office-wide committees are being studied to ensure that minorities are appropriately represented, and our associate mentoring and assignment programs are being reviewed especially as they affect attorneys of color.

• We recently instituted a program of internal and external events designed to increase awareness of diversity issues. Our first event was a firm-wide videoconference discussion by the team of Heller Ehrman attorneys who represent the Lawyers' Committee for Civil Rights Under Law, the NAACP, the National Women's Law Center and other civil rights groups before the Supreme Court in the University of Michigan case which addresses the constitutionality of race-conscious admissions policies.

• We held our first firm-wide Ethnic Diversity Summit in June 2004. This summit provides opportunities for all minority attorneys at Heller Ehrman to network, discuss issues that face attorneys of color and get involved in various diversity initiatives.

• Our Recruiting, Retention, Development and Diversity Committee (R2D2), which includes shareholders, associates and human resources professionals, addresses minority hiring, retention and advancement issues.

• Awareness of diversity enables us to understand the value of differences. Our Managing With Respect Training, a class designed to explore the importance of respect in the workplace, is provided to all attorneys, managers and supervisors.

Results

We are proud of our diversity and are pleased recently to have been acknowledged for our efforts and our success to date:

• Diversity & The Bar has recognized our firm as one of four law firms with exceptional diversity initiatives.

• Currently, members of minority groups, including self-identified gay men and lesbians, make up 7 percent of our shareholders and 22 percent of our associates.

In addition to ethnic diversity, the firm also focuses on participation of women in the attorney and senior staff management work force. Women at Heller Ehrman comprise 19 percent of shareholders, 45 percent of associates, 43 percent of summer associates and 44 percent of senior staff management.

Heller Ehrman Equal Opportunity Employer Statement

Heller Ehrman is an equal opportunity employer and partnership; the firm actively seeks diversity among its attorneys. The firm does not discriminate on the basis of race, religion, color, gender, age, medical condition, physical or sensorial disability, marital status, national origin, sexual orientation or veteran's status. The firm seeks to hire, develop and advance, on the basis of professional ability, attorneys of varying backgrounds in sufficient numbers to ensure that the composition of the firm at all levels – shareholders and associates alike – reflects the diversity of the communities where the firm practices.

Hinshaw & Culbertson LLP

222 N. LaSalle St. #300
Chicago, IL 60601
Phone: (312) 704-3000
Fax: (312) 704-3001

FIRM LEADERSHIP

Managing Partner: Donald L. Mrozek, Chairman of the Firm
Diversity Team Leader: Jeffrey R. Glass, Chairman of the Diversity Committee

LOCATIONS

Chicago, IL (HQ)
Appleton, WI
Belleville, IL
Champaign, IL
Crystal Lake, IL
Ft. Lauderdale, FL
Jacksonville, FL
Joliet, IL
Lisle, IL
Los Angeles, CA
Miami, FL
Milwaukee, WI
Minneapolis, MN
New York, NY
Peoria, IL
Phoenix, AZ
Portland, OR
Rockford, IL
San Francisco, CA
Schererville, IN
Springfield, IL
St. Louis, MO
Tampa, FL
Waukegan, IL

LAW FIRM DEMOGRAPHIC PROFILES

FULL-TIME ASSOCIATES	2003	2002
Minority men	14	11
Minority women	10	12
White women	66	63
Total	162	155

SUMMER ASSOCIATES	2003	2002
Minority men	1	4
Minority women	4	3
White women	5	3
Total	12	13

EQUITY PARTNERS	2003	2002
Minority men	3	2
Minority women	0	0
White women	10	9
Total	85	83

NON-EQUITY PARTNERS	2003	2002
Minority men	3	4
Minority women	2	2
White women	25	21
Total	132	119

NEW HIRES	2003	2002
Minority men	4	6
Minority women	2	9
White women	13	26
Total	49	73

Strategic Plan and Diversity Leadership

How does the firm's leadership communicate the importance of diversity to everyone at the firm? (e.g., e-mails, web site, newsletters, meetings, etc.)

Through e-mails, web site, intranet, Diversity Committee meetings, attorney orientation and the all-attorney firm meeting

Who has primary responsibility for leading diversity initiatives at your firm?

Jeffrey R. Glass, chairman of the Diversity Committee, partner and member of the Executive Committee

Does your law firm currently have a diversity committee?

Yes

Does the committee's representation include one or more members of the firm's management/executive committee (or the equivalent)?

Yes

How many attorneys are on the committee, and in 2003, what was the total number of hours collectively spent by the committee in furtherance of the firm's diversity initiatives?

Total attorneys on committee: 7 The committee includes the director of human resources and administration, legal recruitment manager and the marketing director.

Total hours spent on diversity: 1,000

Does the committee and/or diversity leader establish and set goals or objectives consistent with management's priorities?

Yes

Has the firm undertaken a formal or informal diversity program or set of initiatives aimed at increasing the diversity of the firm?

Yes, formal

How often does the firm's management review the firm's diversity progress/results?

Monthly – Reports are distributed
Quarterly – Diversity Committee meets

How is the firm's diversity committee and/or firm management held accountable for achieving results?

The firm has developed reports which track minority hiring and retention as well as promotions to partners and positions of prominence such as office heads. At the annual compensation review by the Management Committee, the Diversity Committee chairman and members of the Diversity Committee are specifically reviewed for their activities during the year and progress toward the firm's diversity goals. That review is a component taken into account by the Management Committee in recommending new annual compensation.

LAW FIRM DIVERSITY INITIATIVES	ALREADY COMPLETED	CURRENTLY ADDRESSING	NOT A CURRENT PRIORITY
Undertake communication from firm management that diversity is a top priority of the firm.	✓		
Formalize diversity plan and committee with action steps and accountability to management.	✓		
Conduct firm-wide diversity training for all attorneys and staff.		✓	
Increase the number of minority attorneys at the associate level.		✓	
Increase the number of minority attorneys at the partnership level.		✓	
Develop/expand relationships with minority bar associations to offer firm's support of these networks.	✓		
Focus on strengthening firm's mentoring program, including for benefit of minority attorneys.	✓		
Conduct internal diversity needs assessment and/or retain diversity consultant to examine how firm culture might be more welcoming of minorities.		✓	
Support law firm's internal affinity networks (e.g., women, minority attorney networks).	✓		
Manage/monitor allocation of work assignments and/or hours billed to ensure women and minority attorneys have equal access/inclusion on top client matters.	✓		

Recruitment – New Associates

Does your firm annually recruit at any of the following types of institutions? (Check all that apply and list the schools).

No

SUMMER ASSOCIATE STATISTICS: SUMMER 2003	MINORITY MEN	MINORITY WOMEN	WHITE WOMEN	TOTAL
Summer associates	1	3	6	12
Summer associates who received an offer of full-time employment	1	2	3	8
Summer associates who accepted an offer of full-time employment	1	2	3	7

Recruitment – Lateral Associates and Partners

What activities does the firm undertake to attract minority and women attorneys?

• Partner programs with women and minority bar associations

• Participate at minority job fairs

• Seek referrals from other attorneys

Do you use executive recruiting/search firms to seek to identify new diversity hires (partners or associates)?

Yes

List all women- and/or minority-owned executive search/recruiting firms to which the firm paid a fee for placement services in the past 12 months:

Seltzer, Fontaine, Beckwith – Los Angeles (women-owned)

LATERAL ASSOCIATES AND PARTNERS: 1/1/03 – 12/31/03	MINORITY MEN	MINORITY WOMEN	WHITE WOMEN	TOTAL
Number of lateral associate hires	4	3	11	38
Number of lateral partner hires (equity and non-equity)	0	0	1	12
Number of new partners (equity and non-equity) promoted from associate rank	0	1	4	13
Number of new equity partners	1	0	1	3

Retention & Professional Development

ATTORNEYS WHO LEFT THE FIRM: 2003	MINORITY MEN	MINORITY WOMEN	WHITE WOMEN	TOTAL
Number of attorneys who voluntarily or involuntarily left your firm's employ in 2003	5	6	11	44

How do 2003 attrition rates generally compare to those experienced in the prior year period?

About the same as in prior years

Please identify the specific steps you are taking to reduce the attrition rate of minority and women attorneys.

• Develop and/or support internal employee affinity groups (e.g., minority or women networks within the firm)

• Introduce minority and women attorneys to key clients, including to lead engagements

• Review work assignments and hours billed to key client matters to make sure minority and women attorneys are not being excluded

• Strengthen mentoring program for all attorneys, including minorities and women

• Professional skills development program, including minority and women attorneys

Does your firm have part-time/flex-time policies that permit attorneys (male or female) to work alternative schedules?

Yes

What impact, if any, will the decision to work part-time have on an attorney's ability to make partner or, if already a partner, to remain a partner at your firm?

There is no impact if the attorney is already a partner. Other part-time lawyers are considered individually.

Have any attorneys who chose to work a part-time schedule made partner at your firm?

No

Management Demographic Profile (as of 12/31/03)

	MINORITY MEN	MINORITY WOMEN	WHITE WOMEN	TOTAL
Number of attorneys on the Executive/Management Committee or equivalent	1	0	3	26
Number of attorneys on the Hiring Committee or equivalent	1	1	3	15
Number of attorneys on the Partner/Associate Review Committee or equivalent	0	0	0	1

Please provide information regarding all minority and women attorneys who head offices or practice groups of your law firm:

Minorities heading offices: Robert Romero, San Francisco, CA

Women heading offices: Cheryl Wilke, Ft. Lauderdale, FL; Renee Mortimer, Schererville, IN; Teri Drew, St. Louis, MO

Women heading practice groups: Specialty Practice Group Leaders: Beth Culp – Insurance Coverage; Teri Drew – General Liability; Laurie Randolph – Construction; Cheryl Wilke – Workers Compensation

The Firm Says

In 2001, Hinshaw began planning a formal firm-wide Diversity Initiative which relates to its nine regions and 24 offices. During the first year of the Diversity Initiative, the number of minority attorneys in the firm doubled from an average of 17 to 35. The contents of the Initiative include, among other attributes:

• Financial incentives are in place to encourage regional directors and office in-charge partners to hire minority attorneys. Regional directors and office heads are evaluated and compensated in large part upon the profitability of their respective region/office. Hinshaw's Diversity Initiative provides that when a minority attorney is hired, the expense of that individual's compensation is not allocated to the specific office, but is instead pro rated on a per attorney basis across the firm. The income attributable to the minority attorney is allocated to the specific office, however. Thus, there is a built-in incentive for those with hiring authority to search for and hire well-qualified minorities since success in this regard will have a positive impact on the profitability of the office for which the office head is responsible. Additionally, reports are circulated quarterly

by the Diversity Committee to regional directors and office heads reflecting the individual office expense savings by virtue of the hired minority attorneys as a means of constantly reminding the in-charge attorneys of the benefits of this management tool.

• The Initiative requires each of the firm's nine regions to develop and update a specific diversity plan for each region. The plans include specific goals as to hiring of minority attorneys and also include specific mentor program guidelines for minorities. These plans are in turn regularly reviewed by the Diversity Committee for progress on meeting goals and with recommendations for updates.

• The Initiative provides referral bonuses for attorneys who refer minorities to the firm. The bonus is paid half at time of hire and half at the first-year anniversary of the minority attorney with the firm.

• The Initiative provides an annual award known as the Chairman's Diversity Award which is awarded by the chairman of the firm to the region, with a separate award given to the office, which have most advanced the firm's diversity goals. The award includes a substantial cash contribution by the firm to a charity of the recipient's choosing whose mission is, in part, the advancement of diversity within the legal profession.

The firm has established a Diversity Committee headed by a longstanding member of the firm's Executive Committee who is also a regional director. The Diversity Committee is composed of seven partners, including three Executive Committee members and three minority partners, one of whom also sits on the Executive Committee. Committee members also include the head of human resources, the firm's recruiting executive, and the firm's marketing department executive. The Diversity Committee meets quarterly. Meetings are held on a rotating basis at different offices of the firm. The meeting agenda typically lasts between six and seven hours as the committee reviews all aspects of the functioning of the firm's Diversity Initiative, the metrics of accomplishment of goals and plans for participation in upcoming diversity events across the country. The committee is given a sizable budget by the firm each year and has independent discretion on committing funds toward diversity efforts on behalf of the firm. Progress on the firm's diversity goals is a specific element of the evaluation of members of the Diversity Committee at compensation time.

Hinshaw has developed metrics for measuring progress on numerous diversity goals. Separate reports have been developed and are routinely reviewed by the Diversity Committee. These include, among others:

• Minority hire and separation reports published each month.

• Evaluative reports as to separation and retention of minorities and women. These analyze the reasons why minorities and women may have left the firm over the preceding quarter and provide information from exit interviews and the like.

• Report of minority attorneys' utilization. This report tracks the number of hours each minority attorney has posted from various billing attorney sources. The report also tracks the hours and percentage of billable time the minority attorney has spent on specific firm clients. This report is used by the Diversity Committee to monitor and evaluate the quality and type of work being provided to minority attorneys to insure that they are receiving work from prime partners. The committee also uses this report to insure that minorities are provided matters for key clients of the firm.

Hinshaw has established a formal mentoring program applicable to all offices of the firm. The program emphasizes mutual responsibility between the mentor and associate for regular meetings and participation in activities for professional growth. Each associate is assigned a prime mentor and, in addition, the firm has a pool of over 30 partner affinity mentors across the firm who are available to any associate in the firm. The affinity

mentors are partners who have been identified as natural teachers and counselors who have credibility with the firm and among associates. Associates are encouraged to develop relationships with affinity mentors in addition to the formal relationship with the prime mentor.

The firm has created a diversity channel e-mail group which is designed for easy sharing of comments and thoughts regarding diversity issues among not only minority attorneys, but also all attorneys who are specifically interested in diversity issues.

Hinshaw actively encourages and financially supports minority attorney participation in minority bar associations across the country. Hinshaw also regularly provides contributions and supports participation in activities of prominent organizations whose mission includes diversity in the legal field.

Hogan & Hartson LLP

555 13th Street, NW
Washington, DC 20004
Phone: (202) 637-5600
Fax: (202) 637-5910

FIRM LEADERSHIP

Managing Partner: J. Warren Gorrell Jr.
Diversity Team Leader: Claudette M. Christian
(Partner) and Robert H. Kapp (Of Counsel)

LOCATIONS

Washington, DC (HQ)
Baltimore, MD
Boulder, CO
Colorado Springs, CO
Denver, CO
Los Angeles, CA
McLean, VA
Miami, FL
New York, NY
Beijing; Berlin
Brussels
Budapest
London
Moscow
Munich
Paris
Prague
Tokyo
Warsaw

LAW FIRM DEMOGRAPHIC PROFILES

FULL-TIME ASSOCIATES	2003	2002
Minority men	23	30
Minority women	46	46
White women	187	177
Total	440	462

SUMMER ASSOCIATES	2003	2002
Minority men	3	3
Minority women	8	8
White women	18	37
Total	45	67

EQUITY PARTNERS	2003	2002
Minority men	8	8
Minority women	3	3
White women	44	46
Total	279	260

NON-EQUITY PARTNERS	2003	2002
Minority men	2	2
Minority women	6	2
White women	36	32
Total	97	104

NEW HIRES	2003	2002
Minority men	6	13
Minority women	13	18
White women	42	50
Total	113	125

Strategic Plan and Diversity Leadership

How does the firm's leadership communicate the importance of diversity to everyone at the firm? (e.g., e-mails, web site, newsletters, meetings, etc.)

The chairman of the firm emphasizes the high priority placed on diversity in his annual State of the Firm message; the Executive Committee of the firm has appointed a standing committee on diversity; the managing partner-practice administration is a member of the Diversity Committee; the firm's web site includes a section on diversity; and the firm distributes a diversity brochure in connection with its recruitment program.

Who has primary responsibility for leading diversity initiatives at your firm?

Name of person and his/her title: Claudette M. Christian, partner, and Robert H. Kapp, of counsel, co-chairs of the Diversity Committee.

Does your law firm currently have a diversity committee?

Yes

Does the committee's representation include one or more members of the firm's management/executive committee (or the equivalent)?

Yes

How many attorneys are on the committee, and in 2003, what was the total number of hours collectively spent by the committee in furtherance of the firm's diversity initiatives?

Total attorneys on Committee: 29

Total hours spent on diversity: The firm does not maintain a record of hours spent on diversity. The hours are substantial and include the time of management personnel, recruitment committee personnel, mentors, practice area administrators, associate review committee personnel, those working on professional development and others. The Diversity Committee meets on average once each month.

Does the committee and/or diversity leader establish and set goals or objectives consistent with management's priorities?

Yes

Has the firm undertaken a formal or informal diversity program or set of initiatives aimed at increasing the diversity of the firm?

Yes, formal

How often does the firm's management review the firm's diversity progress/results?

Periodically during the year.

How is the firm's diversity committee and/or firm management held accountable for achieving results?

Through meetings with, and reports furnished to, the chairman, the managing partner-practice administration and the Executive Committee.

LAW FIRM DIVERSITY INITIATIVES	ALREADY COMPLETED	CURRENTLY ADDRESSING	NOT A CURRENT PRIORITY
Undertake communication from firm management that diversity is a top priority of the firm.	✓		
Formalize diversity plan and committee with action steps and accountability to management.	✓		
Conduct firm-wide diversity training for all attorneys and staff.		✓	
Increase the number of minority attorneys at the associate level.		✓	
Increase the number of minority attorneys at the partnership level.		✓	
Develop/expand relationships with minority bar associations to offer firm's support of these networks.		✓	
Focus on strengthening firm's mentoring program, including for benefit of minority attorneys.		✓	
Conduct internal diversity needs assessment and/or retain diversity consultant to examine how firm culture might be more welcoming of minorities.		✓	
Support law firm's internal affinity networks (e.g., women, minority attorney networks).		✓	
Manage/monitor allocation of work assignments and/or hours billed to ensure women and minority attorneys have equal access/inclusion on top client matters.		✓	

Recruitment – New Associates

Does your firm annually recruit at any of the following types of institutions? (Check all that apply and list the schools).

Ivy League schools: Columbia University; Cornell Job Fair; Harvard University; Harvard BLSA; University of Pennsylvania; Yale University

Public state schools: University of Baltimore; University of California-Boalt Hall ; UC Hastings; UC Davis; UCLA; University of Colorado; University of Florida; George Mason University; University of Maryland; University of Michigan; University of Texas; University of Virginia; College of William & Mary

Private schools: American University; Boston College/Boston University NY Job Fair; Boston College/Boston University DC Job Fair; Cardozo Law School; Catholic University of America; University of Chicago; University of Denver; Duke University; Fordham University; George Washington University; Georgetown University; Loyola University; University of Miami; Northwestern University; NYU; University of Richmond; Stanford University; USC; Vanderbilt University; Washington and Lee University; Washington University, Tulane University, University of Miami Job Fair

Historically Black Colleges and Universities (HBCUs): Howard University

Other predominantly minority and/or women's colleges: Lavender Law; Latina-o Law Conference; Northeast BLSA Job Fair; NLGLA; MABLSA; Rocky Mountain Minority Legal Career Fair; West Coast Interview Program (Vanderbilt, American, Tulane, Miami, Washington Universities)

Do you have any special outreach efforts directed to encourage minority law students to consider your firm?

• *Invite minority students to meet with partners after offers have been extended. Extensive follow-up by associates and partners after offers have been conveyed.*

• Hold a reception for minority law students

• Advertise in minority law student association publication(s)

• Participate in/host minority law student job fair(s)

• Sponsor minority law student association events

• Firm's lawyers participate on career panels at school

• Outreach to leadership of minority student organizations

SUMMER ASSOCIATE STATISTICS: SUMMER 2003	MINORITY MEN	MINORITY WOMEN	WHITE WOMEN	TOTAL
Summer associates	1	8	18	42
Summer associates who received an offer of full-time employment	1	8	18	41
Summer associates who accepted an offer of full-time employment	1	4	12	28

Recruitment – Lateral Associates and Partners

What activities does the firm undertake to attract minority and women attorneys?

• Participate at minority job fairs

• Seek referrals from other attorneys

Do you use executive recruiting/search firms to seek to identify new diversity hires (partners or associates)

Yes

List all women- and/or minority-owned executive search/recruiting firms to which the firm paid a fee for placement services in the past 12 months:

Of the fees that were paid to search firms last year, over 50 percent of the fees were paid to women- and/or minority-owned organizations.

LATERAL ASSOCIATES AND PARTNERS: 1/1/03 – 12/31/03	MINORITY MEN	MINORITY WOMEN	WHITE WOMEN	TOTAL
Number of lateral associate hires	1	4	13	37
Number of lateral partner hires (equity and non-equity)	0	1	2	15
Number of new partners (equity and non-equity) promoted from associate rank	0	2	5	16
Number of new equity partners	0	0	2	33

Retention & Professional Development

ATTORNEYS WHO LEFT THE FIRM: 2003	MINORITY MEN	MINORITY WOMEN	WHITE WOMEN	TOTAL
Number of attorneys who voluntarily or involuntarily left your firm's employ in 2003	14	9	40	127

How do 2003 attrition rates generally compare to those experienced in the prior year period?

About the same as in prior years

Please identify the specific steps you are taking to reduce the attrition rate of minority and women attorneys.

• Develop and/or support internal employee affinity groups (e.g., minority or women networks within the firm)

• Increase/review compensation relative to competition

• Increase/improve current work/life programs

• Work with minority and women attorneys to develop career advancement plans

• Introduce minority and women attorneys to key clients, including to lead engagements

• Review work assignments and hours billed to key client matters to make sure minority and women attorneys are not being excluded

• Strengthen mentoring program for all attorneys, including minorities and women

• Professional skills development program, including minority and women attorneys

Does your firm have part-time/flex-time policies that permit attorneys (male or female) to work alternative schedules?

Yes

What impact, if any, will the decision to work part-time have on an attorney's ability to make partner or, if already a partner, to remain a partner at your firm?

Part-time associates on two-thirds time or more remain on the partnership track. Currently, the firm has 27 part-time partners.

Have any attorneys who chose to work a part-time schedule made partner at your firm?

Yes, nine attorneys.

Management Demographic Profile (as of 12/31/03)

	MINORITY MEN	MINORITY WOMEN	WHITE WOMEN	TOTAL
Number of attorneys on the Executive/Management Committee or equivalent	0	0	2	12
Number of attorneys on the Hiring Committee or equivalent	3	6	15	52
Number of attorneys on the Partner/Associate Review Committee or equivalent	5	2	15	55

Please provide information regarding all minority and women attorneys who head offices or practice groups of your law firm:

Women heading offices: Office Managing Partner: Ann Morgan Vickery, DC; Office Administrative Partner: Niki Tuttle, Denver

Minorities heading practice groups: Practice Group Director: Daniel Gonzalez, Litigation

Women heading practice groups: Practice Group Directors: Patricia Brannan, CSD; Michelle Farquhar, Communications; Ann Vickery, Health; Emily Yinger, Litigation; Jeanne Archibald, International Trade. Executive Committee: Christine Varney. Practice Area Administrators: Donna Boswell and Lori Sostowski. Managing Partner-Practice Administration: Jeanne Archibald

The Firm Says

The following statement is set forth in the firm's recruitment brochure:

Diversity at Hogan & Hartson is a Firm Priority

Hogan & Hartson has long been committed to recruiting, retaining and promoting lawyers with diverse backgrounds and experience. The firm was one of the first major law firms in the country to achieve a critical mass of women and people of color, and we strive to build upon that tradition. Women and attorneys of color represent many of the firm's largest and most high-profile clients, and hold key positions in the firm and in numerous bar and other professional organizations. We take pride in the firm's diversity and are dedicated to recruiting and retaining attorneys who reflect the diversity of our clients and communities.

Of the major law firms based in Washington, D.C., Hogan & Hartson L.L.P. (H&H) was among the first to have minority equity partners and a critical mass of women attorneys and equity partners. Women and minority partners represent many of the firm's largest and most high-profile clients. One of the minority partners has served on the firm's Executive Committee, one presently serves as co-chair of both the Recruitment Committee and the Diversity Committee, and several have been among the firm's most highly compensated partners. Female partners are presently serving on the firm's Executive Committee, as managing partners and as practice group directors.

H&H has a vigorous program to promote diversity in its professional ranks. The program includes the following components:

1. The establishment of a Diversity Committee as a standing committee of the firm, composed of a racially diverse group of partners and associates, dedicated to the task of recruiting and retaining a diverse group of attorneys.

2. Recent initiatives to recruit a diverse group of attorneys include the following:

   (a) The preparation and distribution to applicants of a diversity brochure to emphasize the firm's commitment to diversity and the priority that it places on diversity in its recruitment efforts.

   (b) The creation of a separate diversity section of the firm's web site to convey a warm, encouraging and welcoming message to minority, female and other applicants.

   (c) Sending a personalized letter to the minority student organizations at each of the law schools at which the firm interviews student applicants, encouraging their membership to consider employment opportunities at H&H. The letter profiles a number of our minority partners and includes descriptions of their practices and professional accomplishments. It is designed to convey the message that minorities are welcome and can succeed at H&H.

   (d) Sending firm representatives, and in some cases delegations of minority lawyers, to various collaborative events – receptions for minority summer associates, "road shows" at law school campuses, and so on – designed to introduce minority candidates to the major law firms. H&H is also participating in various job fairs – for example, Lavender Law, Mid-Atlantic BLSA – which extend the firm's recruitment outreach to a diverse constituency.

   (e) An improved process of reviewing minority student applications which is designed to ensure careful consideration and to demonstrate the firm's commitment to diversity. This process includes a review by a member of the Diversity Committee prior to making "fly-back'" decisions and, insofar as possible, participation by top management personnel in minority student "fly-back" interviews.

   (f) Following extension of summer employment offers, all minority offerees are invited back to the firm for a "second look" at the firm and encouragement to accept the offer of employment.

3. Initiatives to foster the career development, retention and promotion of a diverse group of associates include the following:

   (a) The firm has established a small working group consisting of the co-chairs of the Diversity Committee, the managing partner for practice administration and representatives of other committees to assess the progress of minority associates and to foster their career development. In consultation with the firm practice area administrators, the working group assigns partners from pertinent practice areas to provide guidance, oversee professional development and ensure appropriate work assignments for many minority associates.

   (b) The firm's African American partners and associates meet for lunch on a regular basis to discuss matters of common interest and concern.

   (c) The H&H Academy, an institutionalized educational program within the firm, provides widespread training on substantive areas of law, as well as on legal skills of general applicability, such as drafting, public speaking, negotiations and ethics, and on subjects such as business development and client service. The H&H Academy is piloting an individualized professional development

program for associates with an enhanced mentoring component. All associates receive regularly scheduled evaluations of performance, and more senior associates also receive assessments of their advancement prospects.

The firm provides financial support and pro bono services to the NAACP Legal Defense and Education Fund, Inc., the National Association for the Advancement of Colored People (NAACP), Mexican American Legal Defense and Education Fund (MALDEF) and the Lawyers' Committee for Civil Rights Under Law, among others.

Holland & Hart LLP

555 Seventeenth Street, Suite 3200
Denver, CO 80202
Phone: (303) 295-8000
Fax: (303) 295-8261

FIRM LEADERSHIP

Managing Partner: Edward H. Flitton III,
Partner
Diversity Team Leader: Peter C. Houtsma,
Partner

LOCATIONS

Denver CO (HQ)
Aspen, CO
Billings, MT
Boise, ID
Boulder, CO
Cheyenne, WY
Colorado Springs, CO
Denver Tech Center, CO
Jackson, WY
Salt Lake City, UT
Santa Fe, NM
Washington, DC

LAW FIRM DEMOGRAPHIC PROFILES

FULL-TIME ASSOCIATES	2003	2002
Minority men	5	3
Minority women	4	7
White women	41	40
Total	96	92

SUMMER ASSOCIATES	2003	2002
Minority men	1	0
Minority women	1	2
White women	6	3
Total	8	10

EQUITY PARTNERS	2003	2002
Minority men	1	1
Minority women	1	1
White women	33	30
Total	143	136

NEW HIRES	2003	2002
Minority men	2	2
Minority women	0	2
White women	13	15
Total	46	39

Strategic Plan and Diversity Leadership

How does the firm's leadership communicate the importance of diversity to everyone at the firm? (e.g., e-mails, web site, newsletters, meetings, etc.)

Statement of commitment to diversity supplied to every new hire. Framed statements supplied and hung in every attorney office. Firm maintains a diversity section on its web sites and management sends e-mails to entire firm regarding diversity achievements and events.

Who has primary responsibility for leading diversity initiatives at your firm?

Peter C. Houtsma, partner and chair of Diversity Committee

Does your law firm currently have a diversity committee?

Yes

Does the committee's representation include one or more members of the firm's management/executive committee (or the equivalent)?

No

How many attorneys are on the committee, and in 2003, what was the total number of hours collectively spent by the committee in furtherance of the firm's diversity initiatives?

Total attorneys on committee: 9

Total hours spent on diversity: Numerous

Does the committee and/or diversity leader establish and set goals or objectives consistent with management's priorities?

Yes

Has the firm undertaken a formal or informal diversity program or set of initiatives aimed at increasing the diversity of the firm?

Yes, formal

How often does the firm's management review the firm's diversity progress/results?

Quarterly

How is the firm's diversity committee and/or firm management held accountable for achieving results?

The Diversity Committee reports to the Management Committee quarterly.

LAW FIRM DIVERSITY INITIATIVES	ALREADY COMPLETED	CURRENTLY ADDRESSING	NOT A CURRENT PRIORITY
Undertake communication from firm management that diversity is a top priority of the firm.	✔	✔	
Formalize diversity plan and committee with action steps and accountability to management.	✔	✔	
Conduct firm-wide diversity training for all attorneys and staff.	✔	✔	
Increase the number of minority attorneys at the associate level.	✔	✔	
Increase the number of minority attorneys at the partnership level.		✔	
Develop/expand relationships with minority bar associations to offer firm's support of these networks.	✔	✔	
Focus on strengthening firm's mentoring program, including for benefit of minority attorneys.	✔	✔	
Conduct internal diversity needs assessment and/or retain diversity consultant to examine how firm culture might be more welcoming of minorities.	✔	✔	
Support law firm's internal affinity networks (e.g., women, minority attorney networks).	✔	✔	
Manage/monitor allocation of work assignments and/or hours billed to ensure women and minority attorneys have equal access/inclusion on top client matters.	✔	✔	

Recruitment – New Associates

Does your firm annually recruit at any of the following types of institutions? (Check all that apply and list the schools).

Public state schools: University of Colorado-Boulder, University of Virginia, University of Michigan, University of Utah, University of Wyoming, University of New Mexico, University of Idaho, University of Montana

Private schools: University of Denver, Brigham Young University

Do you have any special outreach efforts directed to encourage minority law students to consider your firm?

• *Mailings to diverse law students*

• Hold a reception for minority law students

• Participate in/host minority law student job fair(s)

• Sponsor minority law student association events

• Firm's lawyers participate on career panels at school

• Outreach to leadership of minority student organizations

• Scholarships or intern/fellowships for minority students

SUMMER ASSOCIATE STATISTICS: SUMMER 2003	MINORITY MEN	MINORITY WOMEN	WHITE WOMEN	TOTAL
Summer associates	0	1	6	7
Summer associates who received an offer of full-time employment	0	1	6	7
Summer associates who accepted an offer of full-time employment	0	1	4	5

Recruitment – Lateral Associates and Partners

What activities does the firm undertake to attract minority and women attorneys?

• *See other activities with law schools listed above.*

• Partner programs with women and minority bar associations

• Participate at minority job fairs

• Seek referrals from other attorneys

Do you use executive recruiting/search firms to seek to identify new diversity hires (partners or associates)?

No

LATERAL ASSOCIATES AND PARTNERS: 1/1/03 – 12/31/03	MINORITY MEN	MINORITY WOMEN	WHITE WOMEN	TOTAL
Number of lateral associate hires	1	0	7	20
Number of lateral partner hires (equity and non-equity)	0	0	0	7
Number of new partners (equity and non-equity) promoted from associate rank	0	0	3	5
Number of new equity partners	0	0	3	12

Retention & Professional Development

ATTORNEYS WHO LEFT THE FIRM: 2003	MINORITY MEN	MINORITY WOMEN	WHITE WOMEN	TOTAL
Number of attorneys who voluntarily or involuntarily left your firm's employ in 2003	1	4	10	23

How do 2003 attrition rates generally compare to those experienced in the prior year period?

About the same as in prior years

Please identify the specific steps you are taking to reduce the attrition rate of minority and women attorneys.

• Develop and/or support internal employee affinity groups (e.g., minority or women networks within the firm)

• Increase/review compensation relative to competition

• Succession plan includes emphasis on diversity

• Work with minority and women attorneys to develop career advancement plans

• Introduce minority and women attorneys to key clients, including to lead engagements

• Review work assignments and hours billed to key client matters to make sure minority and women attorneys are not being excluded

• Strengthen mentoring program for all attorneys, including minorities and women

• Professional skills development program, including minority and women attorneys

Does your firm have part-time/flex-time policies that permit attorneys (male or female) to work alternative schedules?

Yes. Holland & Hart is known as a leader in the industry for its part-time/flex-time policies.

What impact, if any, will the decision to work part-time have on an attorney's ability to make partner or, if already a partner, to remain a partner at your firm?

No impact on partnership but partnership consideration may be delayed in proportion to the amount an attorney's schedule is reduced.

Have any attorneys who chose to work a part-time schedule made partner at your firm?

Yes

Management Demographic Profile (as of 12/31/03)

	MINORITY MEN	MINORITY WOMEN	WHITE WOMEN	TOTAL
Number of attorneys on the Executive/Management Committee or equivalent	0	0	1	6
Number of attorneys on the Hiring Committee or equivalent	0	1	4	9
Number of attorneys on the Partner/Associate Review Committee or equivalent	1	0	2	9

Please provide information regarding all minority and women attorneys who head offices or practice groups of your law firm:

Women heading offices: Wendy J. Pifher, Colorado Springs; Teresa A. Buffington, Cheyenne; Rachel A. Yates, Denver Tech

Women heading practice groups: Risa L. Wolf-Smith, Bankruptcy, Business Department; Betty C. Arkell, Corporate Finance, Business Department; Jane O. Francis, Employee Benefits, Business Department; Elizabeth A. Sharrer, Real Estate, Business Department; Elizabeth R. Carney, Financial, Business Department; Marcy G. Glenn, Appellate, Litigation Department

The Firm Says

In addition to the continuing efforts by our hiring committees to attract and retain female/minority attorneys (see answers to questions above), early in 2004, our firm's Associate Committee, with the assistance of the Diversity Committee, undertook an extensive and comprehensive survey of our non-partner attorneys. The results of this survey were used to evaluate and measure the firm's commitment to diversity, the firm culture, firm leadership, how to better serve associate needs and to address attorneys' concerns with regard to communication, technology, mentoring/supervision, and so on.

The results of the survey were very positive and several recommendations were made, with many initiatives instituted or continued. These include:

1. Continued emphasis on the importance of business development training for associates in all departments and heightened emphasis on business development training and opportunities geared specifically toward minorities/women in the firm.

2. Clarify standards regarding what is expected of associates in connection with business development in particular and other matters deemed important for satisfactory progress toward partnership.

3. Continued emphasis on mentoring/supervision programs and training.

4. Establish a forum for female attorneys in the firm to communicate with respect to issues of greatest concern to them.

5. Continue periodic meetings between firm management and associates to discuss matters of current interest.

6. Publish results of pro bono investigation indicating that all parts of the firm are making fair contributions on the pro bono front.

7. Incorporate diversity/gender matters into programs and discussions for partnership.

Holland & Knight LLP

195 Broadway, 24th Floor
New York, NY 10007
Phone: (212) 513-3200
Fax: (212) 385-9010

FIRM LEADERSHIP

Managing Partner: Howell W. Melton Jr.,
Managing Partner
Diversity Team Leader: Raymond P. Carpenter,
Partner

LOCATIONS

Annapolis, MD
Atlanta, GA
Bethesda, MD
Boston, MA
Bradenton, FL
Chicago, IL
Fort Lauderdale, FL
Jacksonville, FL
Lakeland, FL
Los Angeles, CA
McLean, VA
Miami, FL
New York, NY
Orlando, FL
Portland, OR
Providence, RI
Rancho Santa Fe, CA
San Antonio, TX
San Francisco, CA
St. Petersburg, FL
Seattle, WA
Tallahassee, FL
Tampa, FL
Washington, DC
West Palm Beach, FL
Beijing; Caracas*
Helsinki*
Jyväskylä, Finland*
Mexico City
Rio de Janeiro
São Paulo
Tampere, Finland*
Tel Aviv*
Tokyo
*Representative office

LAW FIRM DEMOGRAPHIC PROFILES

FULL-TIME ASSOCIATES	2003	2002
Minority men	49	50
Minority women	53	49
White women	213	204
Total	527	530

SUMMER ASSOCIATES	2003	2002
Minority men	10	17
Minority women	11	11
White women	19	26
Total	58	66

EQUITY PARTNERS	2003	2002
Minority men	21	20
Minority women	4	6
White women	46	48
Total	457	449

NON-EQUITY PARTNERS	2003	2002
Minority men	16	24
Minority women	7	7
White women	61	42
Total	288	296

NEW HIRES	2003	2002
Minority men	17	11
Minority women	13	7
White women	56	36
Total	141	112

Strategic Plan and Diversity Leadership

How does the firm's leadership communicate the importance of diversity to everyone at the firm? (e.g., e-mails, web site, newsletters, meetings, etc.)

The firm's web site contains information on our Women's and Minority Initiatives. It also is updated for achievements and accomplishments in this area such as awards from community or bar association groups, and such achievements also are included in the weekly internal marketing newsletter. In addition, the firm leadership addresses diversity at every opportunity in its communication with the firm on goals and objectives for firm operations. This is done in speeches by the managing partner and in written communications distributed firm-wide.

Who has primary responsibility for leading diversity initiatives at your firm?

Raymond P. Carpenter, partner

Does your law firm currently have a diversity committee?

No. It is anticipated that a formal diversity committee will be established in the near future. The firm conducts its diversity efforts through the Minority and Women's Initiatives. Each of these groups has its own operational budget, internal structure, and goals and objectives established on a firm-wide basis. Each initiative has a local office structure and a national structure for accomplishing firm-wide objectives and plans. The chairs of each of these initiatives report directly to the managing partner.

Does the committee and/or diversity leader establish and set goals or objectives consistent with management's priorities?

No. The firm has established very broad goals for the development of a culture in which lawyers of all racial, gender, ethnic, religious, sexual and national backgrounds can work together and realize their own personal and professional goals. We will know that this program is working as the firm grows and prospers through the efforts of this diverse group of lawyers.

Has the firm undertaken a formal or informal diversity program or set of initiatives aimed at increasing the diversity of the firm?

Yes, formal

How often does the firm's management review the firm's diversity progress/results?

Annually

How is the firm's diversity committee and/or firm management held accountable for achieving results?

The managing partner and the section chairs include in their analysis of a partner's performance an element which recognizes support for and advancement of the firm's core values. The extent to which the firm management and each partner participate in achieving a more diverse working environment is a part of the consideration of compensation that is not tied to economic performance. The determination for each lawyer is made by the managing partner and the section chairs, with input from around the firm.

LAW FIRM DIVERSITY INITIATIVES	ALREADY COMPLETED	CURRENTLY ADDRESSING	NOT A CURRENT PRIORITY
Undertake communication from firm management that diversity is a top priority of the firm.	✓		
Formalize diversity plan and committee with action steps and accountability to management.		✓	
Conduct firm-wide diversity training for all attorneys and staff.			✓
Increase the number of minority attorneys at the associate level.		✓	
Increase the number of minority attorneys at the partnership level.		✓	
Develop/expand relationships with minority bar associations to offer firm's support of these networks.		✓	
Focus on strengthening firm's mentoring program, including for benefit of minority attorneys.		✓	
Conduct internal diversity needs assessment and/or retain diversity consultant to examine how firm culture might be more welcoming of minorities.	✓		
Support law firm's internal affinity networks (e.g., women, minority attorney networks).	✓		
Manage/monitor allocation of work assignments and/or hours billed to ensure women and minority attorneys have equal access/inclusion on top client matters.		✓	

Recruitment – New Associates

Does your firm annually recruit at any of the following types of institutions? (Check all that apply and list the schools).

Ivy League schools: Columbia University, Cornell University, Harvard University, University of Pennsylvania, Yale University

Public state schools: Florida State University, Georgia State University, University of California-Berkeley (Boalt Hall), University of California-Los Angeles, University of California-Hastings College of Law, University of Connecticut, University of Florida, University of Georgia, University of Illinois, University of Michigan, University of North Carolina, University of Texas-Austin, University of Virginia, University of Washington

Private schools: Baylor University, Boston College, Boston University, Duke University, Emory University, Fordham University, George Washington University, Georgetown University, Lewis & Clark College, Loyola Law School, Mercer University, New York University, Northwestern University, St. Mary's Law School, Stanford University, Stetson University, Suffolk University, University of Chicago, University of Miami, University of Southern California, Vanderbilt University, Washington & Lee University

Historically Black Colleges and Universities (HBCUs): Howard University

Do you have any special outreach efforts directed to encourage minority law students to consider your firm?

- *Women and Minorities in the Profession Committee of the Georgia State Bar – Holland & Knight partner served as a featured speaker at this bar exam preparation workshop for minority and women law students.*

- *Emory University School of Law Symposium on Diversity in the Legal Profession – firm lawyers attend this annual conference sponsored by the Atlanta Diversity Consortium, Inc.*

- *Black History Month Events – invited all Black Law Student Association (BLSA) members from the Georgia law schools at which we recruit to attend these events in our Atlanta office.*

- *University of Georgia School of Law 1L Reception – Holland & Knight lawyers and recruiting staff attended this event to improve our recruiting efforts at the University of Georgia and target 1L minority students for our summer associate program.*

- *"Demystifying the Large Firm Practice" Seminar – an annual event held in our Atlanta office to target top 1Ls at law schools in Georgia, including minority students.*

- *Law School Admission Council (LSAC) Minority Recruitment Forum – Holland & Knight hosted a reception in conjunction with Northwestern University School of Law for minority undergraduate students interested in attending law school.*

- *Georgia Association of Women Lawyers (GAWL) – firm lawyers participated in a recent art auction fundraiser presented by GAWL for law school scholarships, as well as a recent reception in honor of GAWL's recently released in-depth study titled "It's About Time: Part-Time Policies and Practices."*

- *Southeastern Minority Job Fair (SEMJF)*

- *Hispanic National Bar Association (HNBA) Job Fair*

- *Harvard Black Law Students Job Fair*

- *Hispanic West Coast Job Fair*

- *Black Law Student Association Northeast Job Fair*

- *National Black Law Student Association (NBLSA) Reception – a Holland & Knight lawyer spoke at the reception, and the firm purchased a table at the event.*

- *"Leaping Into the Great Beyond: How to Make a Right Career Decision for You" – Presentation sponsored by our Boston office's Diversity Committee.*

- *Boston Lawyers Group – members of this group, including Holland & Knight, mentor minority 1L students.*

- *Professional Opportunities Program – Holland & Knight sponsors this program, which targets minority students from South Florida schools.*

- *Firm Night Reception – the firm hosts this event for University of Miami 1L students.*

- *Third Annual Career Fair at the University of Miami Law School.*

- *University of Maryland Diversity Conference – a firm representative attended this conference.*

- *University of Miami Hispanic Law Student Association (HLSA) Banquet – the firm purchased a table at this event.*

- *Florida Bar Journal Diversity Symposium – a Holland & Knight representative attended this event.*

- *University of Miami Law School Reception – the firm hosts a reception for University of Miami 2L students who will be interviewed on campus.*

- *Metropolitan Black Bar Association Dinner.*

- *University of Washington Diversity Dinner – the firm purchased a table at this event.*

- *Los Angeles-area Asian Lawyers Happy Hour – the firm sponsored one of these for law students.*

• Hold a reception for minority law students

• Advertise in minority law student association publication(s)

• Participate in/host minority law student job fair(s)

• Sponsor minority law student association events

• Firm's lawyers participate on career panels at school

• Outreach to leadership of minority student organizations

• Scholarships or intern/fellowships for minority students

SUMMER ASSOCIATE STATISTICS: SUMMER 2003	MINORITY MEN	MINORITY WOMEN	WHITE WOMEN	TOTAL
Summer associates	10	11	20	59
Summer associates who received an offer of full-time employment	7	10	10	39
Summer associates who accepted an offer of full-time employment	4	9	9	34

Recruitment – Lateral Associates and Partners

What activities does the firm undertake to attract minority and women attorneys?

• *D.C. Road Show (program in which majority Washington, D.C., firms visit national law schools, including University of Virginia, Duke University, Columbia and New York University, to inform African American students about practicing in D.C.), interview at schools such as Howard University and Georgia State with high minority enrollments.*

• Partner programs with women and minority bar associations

• Participate at minority job fairs

• Seek referrals from other attorneys

Do you use executive recruiting/search firms to seek to identify new diversity hires (partners or associates)?

Yes

List all women- and/or minority-owned executive search/recruiting firms to which the firm paid a fee for placement services in the past 12 months:

E M Messick Consulting, Inc.

LATERAL ASSOCIATES AND PARTNERS: 1/1/03 – 12/31/03	MINORITY MEN	MINORITY WOMEN	WHITE WOMEN	TOTAL
Number of lateral associate hires	14	12	53	122
Number of lateral partner hires (equity and non-equity)	3	1	3	24
Number of new partners (equity and non-equity) promoted from associate rank	2	0	6	20
Number of new equity partners	3	0	4	40

Retention & Professional Development

ATTORNEYS WHO LEFT THE FIRM: 2003	MINORITY MEN	MINORITY WOMEN	WHITE WOMEN	TOTAL
Number of attorneys who voluntarily or involuntarily left your firm's employ in 2003	19	12	52	160

How do 2003 attrition rates generally compare to those experienced in the prior year period?

Lower than in prior years

Please identify the specific steps you are taking to reduce the attrition rate of minority and women attorneys.

• Develop and/or support internal employee affinity groups (e.g., minority or women networks within the firm)

• Increase/improve current work/life programs

• Adopt dispute resolution process

• Succession plan includes emphasis on diversity

• Work with minority and women attorneys to develop career advancement plans

• Introduce minority and women attorneys to key clients, including to lead engagements

• Review work assignments and hours billed to key client matters to make sure minority and women attorneys are not being excluded

• Strengthen mentoring program for all attorneys, including minorities and women

Does your firm have part-time/flex-time policies that permit attorneys (male or female) to work alternative schedules?

Yes

What impact, if any, will the decision to work part-time have on an attorney's ability to make partner or, if already a partner, to remain a partner at your firm?

Per policy, this should have no impact on partnership consideration.

Have any attorneys who chose to work a part-time schedule made partner at your firm?

Yes, at least one. We have not tracked this until recently.

Management Demographic Profile (as of 5/31/04)

	MINORITY MEN	MINORITY WOMEN	WHITE WOMEN	TOTAL
Number of attorneys on the Executive/Management Committee or equivalent	5	0	5	22
Number of attorneys on the Hiring Committee or equivalent	3	1	6	35
Number of attorneys on the Partner/Associate Review Committee or equivalent	1	1	4	24

Please provide information regarding all minority and women attorneys who head offices or practice groups of your law firm: (as of 6/21/04)

Minorities heading offices: La Fonte Nesbitt, Annapolis, Bethesda, McLean and Washington, DC; Peter Prieto, Miami

Women heading offices: Deborah Barnard, Deputy Executive Partner, Boston; Marie Lefere, Fort Lauderdale

Minorities heading practice groups: Alcides Avila, Banking and Finance; Jorge Hernandez-Toraño, Business-South Florida practice group, Entertainment and Sports Law team; Brett Hayes, Real Estate (Los Angeles); Raymond Carpenter, Tax and Employee Benefits; Roderic Woodson, District of Columbia Team; South Florida-International*; International Litigation*

Women heading practice groups: Ruth Lansner, Business Section Deputy Section Leader for Professional Development and Recruiting; Martha Barnett, Government Section deputy section leader for Marketing and Practice Development; Deborah Barnard, Litigation Section deputy section leader for Professional Development and Recruiting; Janis Schiff, Real Estate Section deputy section leader for Marketing and Practice Development; Melissa Turra, Real Estate-Jacksonville; Lola Hale; Public Companies – Securities & Corporate Governance; Amy Edwards, Environment; Laurie Webb Daniel, Appellate; Tracy Nichols, Securities Litigation; Shari Levitan, Private Wealth Services-New England; Tara Scanlon, Retail Development & Leasing; Karen Walker and woman Co-Chair*, National Defense & Government Procurement; Restructuring, Creditors' Rights and Insolvency*; Alternative Dispute Resolution*; Land Use & Government*

*Leaders could not be reached prior to deadline to approve the release of their names.

The Firm Says

Holland & Knight is committed to the development of a diverse work force of lawyers, professionals and staff from across racial, gender, age, ethnic, national origin, sexual orientation and religious lines. In this way, we can provide our clients the benefit of an experienced pool of professionals that reflects the national and international marketplace in which we do business.

The mission of our diversity program is to promote an internal, community and global standard of economic development and opportunity for all people, regardless of nationality, race, gender and/or sexual orientation. To support this mission and our diversity goals, the firm adopted a diversity plan that addresses recruitment and hiring, mentoring, grievance procedures and cultural recognition, with a periodic internal diversity report to track our progress in reaching our goals.

Diversity commitment

Holland & Knight's diversity commitment is defined and implemented through the Minority and Women's Initiatives. The goals of our Minority Initiative are to create a positive and supportive environment for the professional and personal development of minority attorneys, to foster the firm's recruitment and retention of minority attorneys, and to encourage professional and civic contributions by minority attorneys. The cornerstone of our diversity commitment is to hire men and women with diverse backgrounds and superior academic and professional credentials who will excel as lawyers and become partners and leaders at Holland & Knight.

The Women's Initiative serves as a forum for the women of Holland & Knight and promotes a culture that is sensitive to a wide range of women's issues. Regular Women's Initiative luncheons and meetings provide the firm's women the opportunity to address issues ranging from economic and professional development to flex-time.

The Women's Initiative launched its Rising Stars program in early 2003 for women attorneys in their seventh year of practice and beyond. Each year, five of our talented and dedicated women partners and senior associates are selected to participate in this year-long program in leadership, marketing, management, professional mentoring and experiential learning. The goal is to enhance these lawyers' leadership positions in the firm, elevate their profiles within the legal profession and the community, and increase their success in business development.

Recruiting, retention and promotion

The firm has recognized that in order to increase the number and retention of minority associates, the firm had to increase the number of minorities in the partnership. This would give associates confidence that remaining with the firm and staying the course to partnership would result in promotion and not disappointment. Holland & Knight is committed to identifying and recruiting successful minority partners in practices that do well in this law firm economic environment to promote a critical mass of minorities. The internal initiatives provide support for career development and professional development by encouraging lawyers to actively participate in their local bars and communities to build relationships that promote their professional economic development. The firm also encourages non-minority attorneys to partner with minority attorneys in the marketing of their practices and in the performance of client work to field a diverse team at every opportunity.

The firm has established a comprehensive mentoring program for all associates, with special provisions to address the needs and concerns of minority and women associates. The program is designed to ensure that the business, professional and social development of those being mentored meets firm and personal expectations, and that they receive the support they need to operate effectively within the firm's culture. A firm-wide committee that tracks the progress of this program pays special attention to meeting these needs for minority associates, lateral partners and senior counsel. Our partner mentors are trained in their responsibilities, reviewed in regard to their performance and rewarded based upon their results. Holland & Knight also offers a Balanced Work/Life Program to those lawyers who are balancing family and work priorities.

Equal employment opportunity and grievance procedures

Holland & Knight is committed to providing a work environment that is free from unlawful discrimination and harassment in any form. In accordance with the provisions of federal and local laws, the firm's policy is not to discriminate by reason of race, color, religion, sex, pregnancy, national origin, age, disability, veteran status or any other factor prohibited by law.

Sexual harassment is unacceptable at Holland & Knight, and it is not tolerated. We have established and trained a Fair Employment Practices Committee, which receives and investigates reports of alleged sexual harassment and facilitates appropriate action in response to those reports. The committee does not currently address equal employment or discrimination issues, but it is anticipated that its scope will expand when the group has received appropriate training.

Awards and recognition

• Spring 2004 – for the fourth year in a row, the Minority Law Journal's Diversity Scorecard of the nation's 250 largest law firms ranked Holland & Knight No. 1 in the number of minority partners and in the top five in the number of African American and Hispanic American attorneys.

• November 2003 – Miami partner Marilyn Holifield was named one of America's Top Lawyers by Black Enterprise Magazine.

• September 2003 – the Defense Research Institute presented Holland & Knight with its Law Firm Diversity Award for demonstrating a significant commitment to diversity. Criteria for selection include a formal diversity plan set forth by law firm management and the promotion of minority and women attorneys.

Other diversity recognition awards we have received include the Athena Society's 2001 Level Playing Field Award, the Minority Corporate Counsel Association's 1999 Thomas L. Sager Award (Atlanta), the 2000 Arnold Z. Rosoff Award for Achievement in Workforce Diversity, the 2000 Employer of the Year Award from the Marriott Foundation for People with Disabilities and the Association of Black Women Attorneys' Award for Excellence in Corporate Diversity, as well as various awards and honors given to individual attorneys.

Honigman Miller Schwartz and Cohn LLP

2290 First National Building
660 Woodward Ave.
Detroit, MI 48226
Phone: (313) 465-7000
Fax: (313) 465-8000

FIRM LEADERSHIP

Managing Partner: Alan S. Schwartz, CEO and Chairman
Diversity Team Leader: Alex L. Parrish, Partner

LOCATIONS

Detroit, MI (HQ)
Bingham Farms, MI
Lansing, MI

LAW FIRM DEMOGRAPHIC PROFILES

FULL-TIME ASSOCIATES	2003	2002
Minority men	1	1
Minority women	1	4
White women	18	18
Total	50	54

SUMMER ASSOCIATES	2003	2002
Minority men	1	0
Minority women	0	1
White women	1	4
Total	6	13

EQUITY PARTNERS	2003	2002
Minority men	1	1
Minority women	1	1
White women	18	17
Total	102	99

NON-EQUITY PARTNERS	2003	2002
Minority men	0	0
Minority women	1	1
White women	12	12
Total	28	28

NEW HIRES	2003	2002
Minority men	0	1
Minority women	0	2
White women	6	4
Total	14	14

Strategic Plan and Diversity Leadership

How does the firm's leadership communicate the importance of diversity to everyone at the firm? (e.g., e-mails, web site, newsletters, meetings, etc.)

Vision statement; web site; e-mails; meetings/discussions.

Who has primary responsibility for leading diversity initiatives at your firm?

Alex L. Parrish, partner and chair of Task Force on Issues Affecting Minority Attorneys

Does your law firm currently have a diversity committee?

Yes

Does the committee's representation include one or more members of the firm's management/executive committee (or the equivalent)?

Yes

How many attorneys are on the committee, and in 2003, what was the total number of hours collectively spent by the committee in furtherance of the firm's diversity initiatives?

Total attorneys on committee: 7

Total hours spent on diversity: Varies

Does the committee and/or diversity leader establish and set goals or objectives consistent with management's priorities?

Yes

Has the firm undertaken a formal or informal diversity program or set of initiatives aimed at increasing the diversity of the firm?

Yes, informal

How often does the firm's management review the firm's diversity progress/results?

Periodically at management meetings

How is the firm's diversity committee and/or firm management held accountable for achieving results?

No formal review process at this time.

LAW FIRM DIVERSITY INITIATIVES	ALREADY COMPLETED	CURRENTLY ADDRESSING	NOT A CURRENT PRIORITY
Undertake communication from firm management that diversity is a top priority of the firm.		✓	
Formalize diversity plan and committee with action steps and accountability to management.		✓	
Conduct firm-wide diversity training for all attorneys and staff.			✓
Increase the number of minority attorneys at the associate level.		✓	
Increase the number of minority attorneys at the partnership level.		✓	
Develop/expand relationships with minority bar associations to offer firm's support of these networks.		✓	
Focus on strengthening firm's mentoring program, including for benefit of minority attorneys.		✓	
Conduct internal diversity needs assessment and/or retain diversity consultant to examine how firm culture might be more welcoming of minorities.			✓
Support law firm's internal affinity networks (e.g., women, minority attorney networks).	✓		
Manage/monitor allocation of work assignments and/or hours billed to ensure women and minority attorneys have equal access/inclusion on top client matters.	✓		

Recruitment – New Associates

Does your firm annually recruit at any of the following types of institutions? (Check all that apply and list the schools).

Ivy League schools: Harvard University

Historically Black Colleges and Universities (HBCUs): Howard University

Do you have any special outreach efforts directed to encourage minority law students to consider your firm?

• Participate in/host minority law student job fair(s)

• Sponsor minority law student association events

• Firm's lawyers participate on career panels at school

SUMMER ASSOCIATE STATISTICS: SUMMER 2003	MINORITY MEN	MINORITY WOMEN	WHITE WOMEN	TOTAL
Summer associates	1	0	1	6
Summer associates who received an offer of full-time employment	1	0	1	5
Summer associates who accepted an offer of full-time employment	1	0	1	5

Recruitment – Lateral Associates and Partners

What activities does the firm undertake to attract minority and women attorneys?

• Participate at minority job fairs

• Seek referrals from other attorneys

Do you use executive recruiting/search firms to seek to identify new diversity hires (partners or associates)?

Yes

List all women- and/or minority-owned executive search/recruiting firms to which the firm paid a fee for placement services in the past 12 months:

Newman-Hawkins

LATERAL ASSOCIATES AND PARTNERS: 1/1/03 – 12/31/03	MINORITY MEN	MINORITY WOMEN	WHITE WOMEN	TOTAL
Number of lateral associate hires	0	0	2	7
Number of lateral partner hires (equity and non-equity)	0	0	0	2
Number of new partners (equity and non-equity) promoted from associate rank	0	1	3	8
Number of new equity partners	0	0	2	5

Retention & Professional Development

ATTORNEYS WHO LEFT THE FIRM: 2003	MINORITY MEN	MINORITY WOMEN	WHITE WOMEN	TOTAL
Number of attorneys who voluntarily or involuntarily left your firm's employ in 2003	1	4	5	22

How do 2003 attrition rates generally compare to those experienced in the prior year period?

Higher than in prior years

Please identify the specific steps you are taking to reduce the attrition rate of minority and women attorneys.

• Develop and/or support internal employee affinity groups (e.g., minority or women networks within the firm)

• Increase/review compensation relative to competition

• Increase/improve current work/life programs

• Work with minority and women attorneys to develop career advancement plans

• Introduce minority and women attorneys to key clients, including to lead engagements

• Review work assignments and hours billed to key client matters to make sure minority and women attorneys are not being excluded

• Strengthen mentoring program for all attorneys, including minorities and women

• Professional skills development program, including minority and women attorneys

Does your firm have part-time/flex-time policies that permit attorneys (male or female) to work alternative schedules?

Yes. Firm is willing to work with any reasonable schedule that works for the lawyer and the firm.

What impact, if any, will the decision to work part-time have on an attorney's ability to make partner or, if already a partner, to remain a partner at your firm?

Depending on the selected schedule, may delay partnership decision for one year; if already a partner, then no impact.

Have any attorneys who chose to work a part-time schedule made partner at your firm?

Yes, four attorneys (all women).

Management Demographic Profile (as of 12/31/03)

	MINORITY MEN	MINORITY WOMEN	WHITE WOMEN	TOTAL
Number of attorneys on the Executive/Management Committee or equivalent	1	0	1	15
Number of attorneys on the Hiring Committee or equivalent	1	0	5	24
Number of attorneys on the Partner/Associate Review Committee or equivalent	0	0	0	5

Please provide information regarding all minority and women attorneys who head offices or practice groups of your law firm:

Women heading practice groups: Sherill Siebert, Employee Benefits Department

The Firm Says

Our firm's Guiding Principles provide:

We will commit ourselves, individually and collectively, to the principle that each and every person at the firm deserves to be treated with dignity and respect. We will encourage a work environment in which an individual's diversity is valued. We will strive to promote diversity by creating an environment that attracts and retains the best persons for all positions in the firm regardless of gender, racial, ethnic or other diverse characteristics, and by providing challenging opportunities, sufficient guidance, and positive incentives to assist each person to achieve his/her greatest potential.

Approximately one-half of law school students are women. The current proportion of women associates (18 of 50) and non-equity partners (12 of 28) at our firm is approaching that level which reflects the firm's commitment to recruiting women attorneys. The firm also involves female attorneys in its recruiting activities on campus at law schools and on its recruiting activities and personnel committee. A woman partner, Linda Ross, chairs the firm's recruiting and personnel committee.

The firm participates in the Midwest Black Law Students Recruiting Association Conference and the Wolverine Bar Association summer associate program, both of which focus on the recruitment of minorities. In fact, our summer associate program for 2004 includes a 1L minority Wolverine Bar student and a 2L minority student who was our 1L Wolverine Bar student last summer. We also focus on-campus recruiting at law schools with a large percentage of minority law students.

As noted on our web site, the firm is amenable to alternative work arrangements. Accordingly, the firm has several female attorneys who work on a part-time basis. A number of part-time women attorneys also have become partners. The firm also sponsors a women's executive breakfast at least once each year. The breakfast features women clients as speakers and promotes our women lawyers to clients and prospective clients who are invited as guests to the breakfast. The firm also sponsors regular in-house luncheons for its women lawyers at which various career development topics are discussed.

In addition to the initiatives noted above, the firm has a committee on Issues Affecting Minority Attorneys chaired by two minority attorneys and staffed by several other attorneys. That committee has a subcommittee on partner development and retention and another subcommittee on associate development and recruitment. Each of those subcommittees is chaired by a minority attorney. Additionally, the firm has an associate development committee that focuses on various issues of interest to associates in the firm and on establishing productive mentor/mentee relationships. Both women and minority attorneys have served on that committee as well.

The firm participates in the Federal Judicial Externship program which involves including minority attorneys in various summer associate activities at the firm. The firm supports law school and community programs focused on women and minorities, such as the Butch Carpenter Dinner at University of Michigan Law School and the Barrister's Ball.

655

Howrey Simon Arnold & White, LLP

1299 Pennsylvania Avenue, NW
Washington, DC 20004
Phone: (202) 783-0800
Fax: (202) 383-6610

FIRM LEADERSHIP

Managing Partner: Robert F. Ruyak, Managing
Partner and CEO
Diversity Team Leader: Patricia G. Butler,
Partner and Chair of Diversity Committee

LOCATIONS

Washington, DC (HQ)
Chicago, IL
Houston, TX
Irvine, CA
Los Angeles, CA
Menlo Park, CA
San Francisco, CA
Amsterdam
Brussels
London

LAW FIRM DEMOGRAPHIC PROFILES

FULL-TIME ASSOCIATES	2003	2002
Minority men	25	29
Minority women	35	36
White women	80	84
Total	298	294

SUMMER ASSOCIATES	2003	2002
Minority men	5	1
Minority women	7	8
White women	11	11
Total	40	36

EQUITY PARTNERS	2003	2002
Minority men	2	1
Minority women	2	2
White women	17	16
Total	120	120

NON-EQUITY PARTNERS	2003	2002
Minority men	11	7
Minority women	5	2
White women	18	16
Total	113	98

NEW HIRES	2003	2002
Minority men	10	2
Minority women	7	9
White women	14	15
Total	66	68

Strategic Plan and Diversity Leadership

How does the firm's leadership communicate the importance of diversity to everyone at the firm? (e.g., e-mails, web site, newsletters, meetings, etc.)

Presentation at annual partnership meeting, posting of firm Diversity Statement on firm web site, inclusion of Diversity Statement in firm literature and client/potential client presentations. See narrative for additional information.

Who has primary responsibility for leading diversity initiatives at your firm?

Patricia G. Butler, chair of Diversity Committee

Does your law firm currently have a diversity committee?

Yes

Does the committee's representation include one or more members of the firm's management/executive committee (or the equivalent)?

No

How many attorneys are on the committee, and in 2003, what was the total number of hours collectively spent by the committee in furtherance of the firm's diversity initiatives?

Total attorneys on committee: 12

Total hours spent on diversity: 200+

Does the committee and/or diversity leader establish and set goals or objectives consistent with management's priorities?

Yes

Has the firm undertaken a formal or informal diversity program or set of initiatives aimed at increasing the diversity of the firm?

Yes, formal

How often does the firm's management review the firm's diversity progress/results?

Annually

How is the firm's diversity committee and/or firm management held accountable for achieving results?

No direct accountability measures.

LAW FIRM DIVERSITY INITIATIVES	ALREADY COMPLETED	CURRENTLY ADDRESSING	NOT A CURRENT PRIORITY
Undertake communication from firm management that diversity is a top priority of the firm.	✓		
Formalize diversity plan and committee with action steps and accountability to management.	✓		
Conduct firm-wide diversity training for all attorneys and staff.			✓
Increase the number of minority attorneys at the associate level.	✓	✓	
Increase the number of minority attorneys at the partnership level.	✓	✓	
Develop/expand relationships with minority bar associations to offer firm's support of these networks.	✓	✓	
Focus on strengthening firm's mentoring program, including for benefit of minority attorneys.			
Conduct internal diversity needs assessment and/or retain diversity consultant to examine how firm culture might be more welcoming of minorities.			✓
Support law firm's internal affinity networks (e.g., women, minority attorney networks).	✓	✓	
Manage/monitor allocation of work assignments and/or hours billed to ensure women and minority attorneys have equal access/inclusion on top client matters.		✓	

Recruitment – New Associates

Does your firm annually recruit at any of the following types of institutions? (Check all that apply and list the schools).

Ivy League schools: Harvard University, University of Pennsylvania, Columbia University, Cornell University

Public state schools: University of Virginia, College of William and Mary, University of Texas, University of California

Private schools: Stanford University, Vanderbilt University, NYU, Washington and Lee University

Historically Black Colleges and Universities (HBCUs): Howard University

Do you have any special outreach efforts directed to encourage minority law students to consider your firm?

• Hold receptions for minority law students

• Advertise in minority law student association publication(s)

• Participate in/host minority law student job fair(s)

• Sponsor minority law student association events

• Firm's lawyers participate on career panels at school

• Outreach to leadership of minority student organizations

• Scholarships or intern/fellowships for minority students

MINORITY CORPORATE COUNSEL ASSOCIATION

SUMMER ASSOCIATE STATISTICS: SUMMER 2003	MINORITY MEN	MINORITY WOMEN	WHITE WOMEN	TOTAL
Summer associates	5	8	10	38
Summer associates who received an offer of full-time employment	4	7	9	30
Summer associates who accepted an offer of full-time employment	3	6	7	26

Recruitment – Lateral Associates and Partners

What activities does the firm undertake to attract minority and women attorneys?

• *Howrey has several partners that participate and hold positions in minority bars, including Karen Lockwood, president-elect of the Women's Bar Association of the District of Columbia; Christina Sarchio, vice president and member of the Hispanic Bar Association; and Mark Whitaker, chair of the Diversity Committee of the AIPLA (American Intellectual Property Law Association).*

• Partner programs with women and minority bar associations

Do you use executive recruiting/search firms to seek to identify new diversity hires (partners or associates)?

No

LATERAL ASSOCIATES AND PARTNERS: 1/1/03 – 12/31/03	MINORITY MEN	MINORITY WOMEN	WHITE WOMEN	TOTAL
Number of lateral associate hires	7	7	14	54
Number of lateral partner hires (equity and non-equity)	3	0	3	12
Number of new partners (equity and non-equity) promoted from associate rank	1	3	1	15
Number of new equity partners	0	0	1	7

Retention & Professional Development

ATTORNEYS WHO LEFT THE FIRM: 2003	MINORITY MEN	MINORITY WOMEN	WHITE WOMEN	TOTAL
Number of attorneys who voluntarily or involuntarily left your firm's employ in 2003	7	5	19	68

How do 2003 attrition rates generally compare to those experienced in the prior year period?

About the same as in prior years*

*Note: 2003 attrition was about the same as in 2002, but lower than 2001 and 2000.

Please identify the specific steps you are taking to reduce the attrition rate of minority and women attorneys.

See "The Firm Says" below.

Does your firm have part-time/flex-time policies that permit attorneys (male or female) to work alternative schedules?

Yes

What impact, if any, will the decision to work part-time have on an attorney's ability to make partner or, if already a partner, to remain a partner at your firm?

Pro rata reduction in hours/years accrued toward partnership. The partnership track is 7.5 years.

Have any attorneys who chose to work a part-time schedule made partner at your firm?

Yes, three attorneys.

Management Demographic Profile (as of 12/31/03)

	MINORITY MEN	MINORITY WOMEN	WHITE WOMEN	TOTAL
Number of attorneys on the Executive/Management Committee or equivalent	0	1	1	7
Number of attorneys on the Hiring Committee or equivalent	1	2	7	20
Number of attorneys on the Partner/Associate Review Committee or equivalent	0	1	9	36

Please provide information regarding all minority and women attorneys who head offices or practice groups of your law firm:

Minorities heading practice groups: Cecilia Gonzalez, Partner, Intellectual Property – Executive Management Team

Women heading practice groups: Cecilia Gonzalez, Partner, Intellectual Property – Executive Management Team

The Firm Says

Howrey's diversity efforts focus on three main areas: (1) hiring, (2) retention and (3) promotion of minority and women attorneys. Our promotion statistics best show the success of our efforts to fulfill those mandates. Howrey is proud that 44 percent of the associates that Howrey elected to partnership last year in the D.C. office were minority attorneys and 30 percent were women attorneys.

Our hiring and retention efforts are equally indicative of our focus. In 2003 minority associates were 21 percent of all associates. Forty-four percent of associates were women. Twelve percent of the non-equity partners were minority and 26 percent were women. Five percent of the equity partners were minorities and 12 percent were women. New attorney hires were 26 percent minority and 31 percent women. Our 2003 summer associate class was 30 percent minority and 50 percent women. Howrey continued these recruiting efforts during the 2003

recruiting season and recruited a 2004 summer class that is 34 percent minority and 43 percent women. Under our Howrey Externs for Legal Pro Bono Service (HELPS) program, we also have hired two first-year law students for summer externships with the Archdiocesan Legal Network and the Legal Aid Society. Both are minorities.

We believe this strong and consistent progress results from dedicated investment, persistent effort and innovative thinking. For example, a primary focus of Howrey's recruiting efforts is to attract, aggressively recruit and hire minority and women candidates. Howrey continued its tradition of holding receptions for local minority law students to recruit them for Howrey's summer program. Howrey's unique summer program has an online application process and we encourage all interested candidates nationwide to apply. To evaluate our efforts to attract minority students, we gave the online applicants the option of indicating ethnicity. This helps us determine if we are successful in our efforts. Of the applicants who self-selected for our 2004 Bootcamp program, 31 percent were minority. We also bolstered our efforts by inviting all of our minority candidates to attend a dinner in Washington. One hundred percent of the attendees who received offers accepted and another recruiting tradition was born.

Howrey also undertook the following diversity recruiting efforts:

• Identified students from law school minority resume books and personally invited those students to on-campus receptions or encouraged them to apply.

• For each law school where Howrey held recruiting receptions, we identified and sent personalized invitations to minority student law groups (including Black Law Student Associations, Latino/Hispanic American Law Students Associations, Asian Pacific American Law Students Associations, South Asian Law Students Associations and Native American Law Students Associations).

• Howrey participated in job fairs hosted by Harvard BLSA, the Northeast BLSA and the MABLSA.

We have raised awareness within our firm of our diversity efforts. Howrey incorporated a presentation on diversity at its annual partner retreat to emphasize the importance and success of the firm's diversity initiatives as well as the importance of diversity to the firm's clients. An important part of the presentation is Howrey's statistical success at all levels – summer associate, associate and partnership. The presentation also includes information about the firm's clients that have their own diversity initiatives and requirements. This presentation, along with our Diversity Statement, is a staple of our client pitches.

Howrey is proud that minorities and women participate in at all levels of firm management and professional and business development activities. Minorities and women serve on all of the firm's six operating committees – Recruiting, Assignment, Evaluation, Diversity, Pro Bono and Associate Affairs – and on the umbrella managing Attorney Development Committee. Minorities and women also serve on the Executive Committee, Partnership Committee, as co-chair of the Business Affairs Committee and on the management team of the firm's intellectual property practice group.

Howrey's Diversity Committee is a budgeted operating committee of the firm. In 2003, to better inform its retention and mentoring efforts, Howrey's Diversity Committee circulated a survey to minority attorneys and solicited information on experiences and suggestions on future activities to assist its retention efforts. No surprise – what the Diversity Committee learned is that Howrey's minority attorneys are interested in the tools and information to enable them to take charge of their careers and success at the firm. To that end, the Diversity Committee instituted a series of business development training seminars for minority and women attorneys.

Howrey's longstanding Women's Leadership Initiative is an integral part of Howrey's efforts to retain and promote its women attorneys.

Howrey has continued to support minority and women bar associations and diversity-supporting aspects of majority bar associations. Howrey attorneys hold positions in the Women's Bar Association, the Hispanic Bar Association and the American Intellectual Property Law Association Diversity Committee. Howrey's sponsorships have included the National Bar Association, the Minority Corporate Counsel Association, the National Association of Women Judges, the Women's Bar Association and the Women's Corporate Counsel Conference.

Diversity Matters

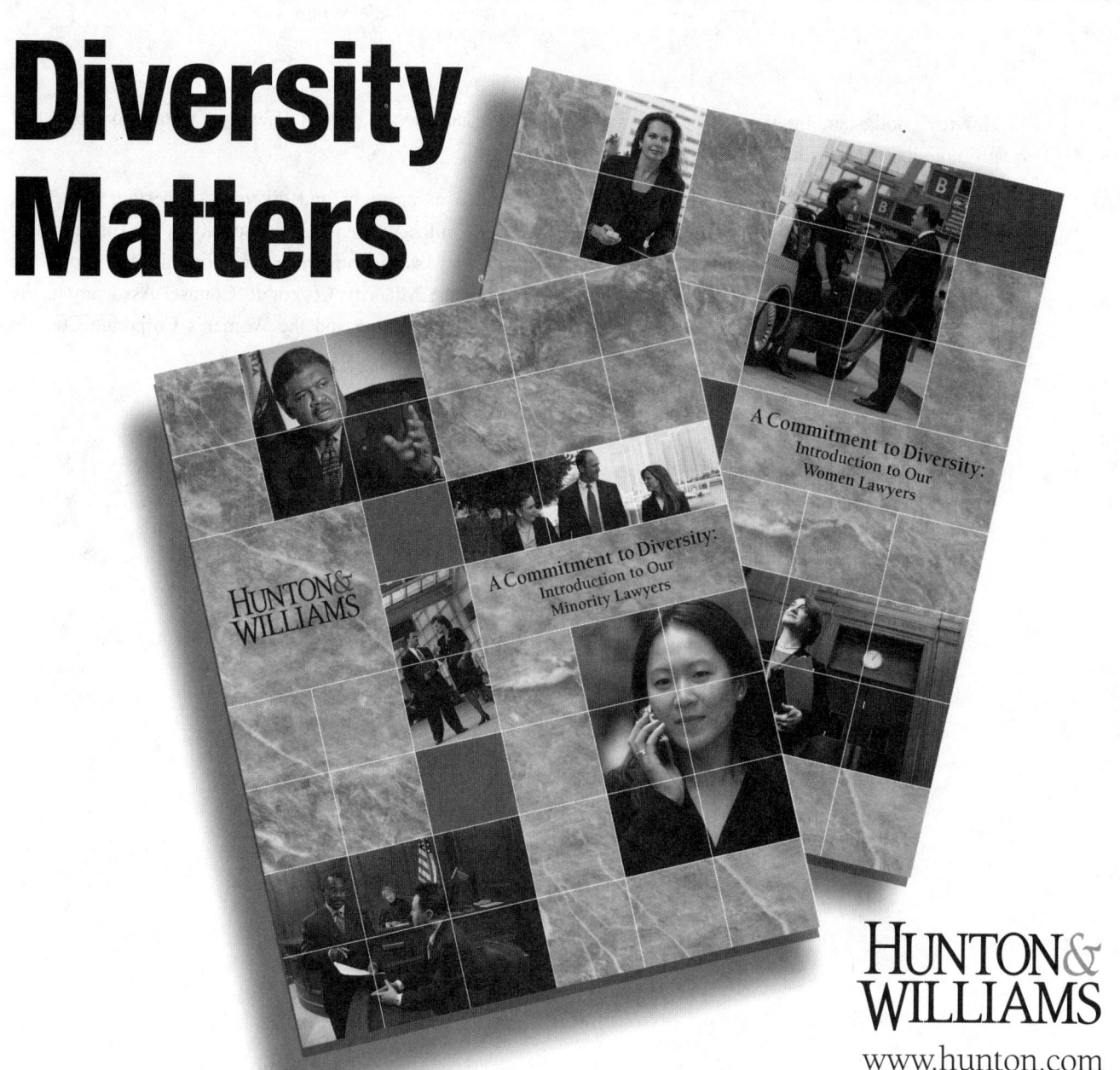

A Commitment to Diversity: Introduction to Our Women Lawyers

A Commitment to Diversity: Introduction to Our Minority Lawyers

HUNTON & WILLIAMS

HUNTON& WILLIAMS
www.hunton.com

We live in a diverse world in which the challenges of meeting the current and future needs of our clients are ever increasing. To meet those challenges, a law firm needs a diverse corps of legal talent. Our brochures, **Introduction to Our Minority Lawyers** and **Introduction to Our Women Lawyers**, illustrate Hunton & Williams' commitment to fostering diversity for ourselves and our clients.

For a copy of our brochures or to learn more about diversity at Hunton & Williams, please contact A. Todd Brown at (704) 378-4727 or tbrown@hunton.com.

ATLANTA   AUSTIN   BANGKOK   BRUSSELS   CHARLOTTE   DALLAS   HONG KONG   KNOXVILLE   LONDON   McLEAN   MIAMI   NEW YORK   NORFOLK   RALEIGH   RICHMOND   SINGAPORE   WASHINGTON

Hunton & Williams LLP

Riverfront Plaza, East Tower
951 East Byrd Street
Richmond, VA 23219-4074
Phone: (804) 788-8200
Fax: (804) 788-8218

FIRM LEADERSHIP

Managing Partner: Thurston R. Moore,
Managing Partner
Diversity Team Leader: A. Todd Brown,
Chairman, Diversity Activities Committee

LOCATIONS

Richmond, VA (HQ)
Atlanta, GA
Austin, TX
Charlotte, NC
Dallas, TX
Knoxville, TN
McLean, VA
Miami, FL
New York, NY
Norfolk, VA
Raleigh, NC
Washington, DC
Bangkok
Brussels
Hong Kong
London
Singapore

LAW FIRM DEMOGRAPHIC PROFILES

FULL-TIME ASSOCIATES	2003	2002
Minority men	32	29
Minority women	36	41
White women	155	169
Total	464	492

SUMMER ASSOCIATES	2003	2002
Minority men	6	9
Minority women	8	7
White women	15	38
Total	73	106

EQUITY PARTNERS	2003	2002
Minority men	17	17
Minority women	5	6
White women	33	32
Total	283	269

NON-EQUITY PARTNERS	2003	2002
Minority men	2	2
Minority women	0	0
White women	7	5
Total	42	40

NEW HIRES	2003	2002
Minority men	13	10
Minority women	4	13
White women	28	41
Total	103	123

MINORITY CORPORATE COUNSEL ASSOCIATION

Strategic Plan and Diversity Leadership

How does the firm's leadership communicate the importance of diversity to everyone at the firm? (e.g., e-mails, web site, newsletters, meetings, etc.)

At quarterly partners' meetings, the firm's managing partner and the Chairman of the Executive Committee stress the importance of diversity. Likewise, at quarterly associate meetings, the firm's managing partner discusses various aspects of diversity. Additionally, the firm's diversity policy and initiatives are communicated through memoranda, e-mails, brochures and a web site.

Who has primary responsibility for leading diversity initiatives at your firm?

Thurston R. Moore, managing partner; A. Todd Brown, partner and chair of Diversity Activities Committee; Andrea Bear Field and Frank E. Emory Jr., partners and co-chairs of the Diversity Strategies Committee; and Susan H. Gunn, human resources director.

Does your law firm currently have a diversity committee?

Yes

Does the committee's representation include one or more members of the firm's management/executive committee (or the equivalent)?

Yes

How many attorneys are on the committee, and in 2003, what was the total number of hours collectively spent by the committee in furtherance of the firm's diversity initiatives?

Total attorneys on committee: Diversity Activities – 24; Diversity Strategies – 19

Total hours spent on diversity: 1,922

Does the committee and/or diversity leader establish and set goals or objectives consistent with management's priorities?

Yes

Has the firm undertaken a formal or informal diversity program or set of initiatives aimed at increasing the diversity of the firm?

Yes, formal

How often does the firm's management review the firm's diversity progress/results?

Monthly

How is the firm's diversity committee and/or firm management held accountable for achieving results?

The firm's managing partner has responsibility for leading the planning, implementation, and achievement of the firm's diversity initiatives. The managing partner monitors the progress of these efforts and reports regularly to the firm's Executive Committee and its partners. Senior management and practice group leaders are directed to

incorporate the firm's diversity goals and objectives into their overall planning process and are held accountable for diversity results through informal monitoring as well as a formal annual evaluation process.

LAW FIRM DIVERSITY INITIATIVES*	ALREADY COMPLETED	CURRENTLY ADDRESSING	NOT A CURRENT PRIORITY
Undertake communication from firm management that diversity is a top priority of the firm.	✓		
Formalize diversity plan and committee with action steps and accountability to management.	✓		
Conduct firm-wide diversity training for all attorneys and staff.		✓	
Increase the number of minority attorneys at the associate level.	✓		
Increase the number of minority attorneys at the partnership level.	✓		
Develop/expand relationships with minority bar associations to offer firm's support of these networks.		✓	
Focus on strengthening firm's mentoring program, including for benefit of minority attorneys.	✓		
Conduct internal diversity needs assessment and/or retain diversity consultant to examine how firm culture might be more welcoming of minorities.	✓		
Support law firm's internal affinity networks (e.g., women, minority attorney networks).	✓		
Manage/monitor allocation of work assignments and/or hours billed to ensure women and minority attorneys have equal access/inclusion on top client matters.	✓		

* Firm management at Hunton & Williams has previously addressed, and continues to address, diversity goals and initiatives as an on-going practice.

Recruitment – New Associates

Does your firm annually recruit at any of the following types of institutions? (Check all that apply and list the schools).

Ivy League schools: Columbia University, Cornell University (job fair), Harvard University, University of Pennsylvania, Yale University

Public state schools: University of North Carolina, McGill University, University of Virginia, University of California-Boalt, College of William & Mary, University of Texas, Georgia State, University of Georgia, Florida State University, University of Michigan, University of South Carolina, University of Tennessee, University of Florida

Private schools: Emory University, Mercer University, Vanderbilt University, Wake Forest University, Stanford University, University of Chicago, University of Notre Dame, Washington and Lee University, University of Richmond, SMU, Baylor University, Tulane University, NYU, Fordham University, BU/BC (job fair), Duke University, George Washington University, Georgetown University, University of Miami

Historically Black Colleges and Universities (HBCUs): Howard University

Do you have any special outreach efforts directed to encourage minority law students to consider your firm?

• *Outreach to law school professors*

• Hold a reception for minority law students

• Participate in/host minority law student job fair(s): BLSA (Harvard, Mideast, Northeast), SEMJF

• Sponsor minority law student association events: University of Texas

• Firm's lawyers participate on career panels at school: Georgetown, UVA, W&M, Richmond, Univ. of Texas, Emory, Georgia State, Univ. of Georgia.

• Outreach to leadership of minority student organizations

• Scholarships or intern/fellowships for minority students

SUMMER ASSOCIATE STATISTICS: SUMMER 2003	MINORITY MEN	MINORITY WOMEN	WHITE WOMEN	TOTAL
Summer associates	6	5	23	77
Summer associates who received an offer of full-time employment	4	2	18	55
Summer associates who accepted an offer of full-time employment	4	2	9	29

Recruitment – Lateral Associates and Partners

What activities does the firm undertake to attract minority and women attorneys?

• Partner programs with women and minority bar associations

• Participate at minority job fairs

• Seek referrals from other attorneys

Do you use executive recruiting/search firms to seek to identify new diversity hires (partners or associates)?

Yes

List all women- and/or minority-owned executive search/recruiting firms to which the firm paid a fee for placement services in the past 12 months:

One of the firm's former minority associates left the firm to start his own search firm. We have not hired anyone through the agency to date, but Hunton & Williams has an ongoing working relationship with them and we hope to place candidates presented by the search firm in the future. Additionally, the firm has made it known to all search firms with whom we deal that we would like a diverse pool of candidates presented for each and every position they are attempting to fill on our behalf.

LATERAL ASSOCIATES AND PARTNERS: 1/1/03 – 12/31/03	MINORITY MEN	MINORITY WOMEN	WHITE WOMEN	TOTAL
Number of lateral associate hires	9	3	16	58
Number of lateral partner hires (equity and non-equity)	0	0	2	10
Number of new partners (equity and non-equity) promoted from associate rank	1	0	4	25
Number of new equity partners	1	0	4	25

Retention & Professional Development

ATTORNEYS WHO LEFT THE FIRM: 2003	MINORITY MEN	MINORITY WOMEN	WHITE WOMEN	TOTAL
Number of attorneys who voluntarily or involuntarily left your firm's employ in 2003	9	11	39	122

How do 2003 attrition rates generally compare to those experienced in the prior year period?

Higher than in prior years

Please identify the specific steps you are taking to reduce the attrition rate of minority and women attorneys.

• Develop and/or support internal employee affinity groups (e.g., minority or women networks within the firm)

• Increase/improve current work/life programs

• Adopt dispute resolution process

• Succession plan includes emphasis on diversity

• Work with minority and women attorneys to develop career advancement plans

• Introduce minority and women attorneys to key clients, including to lead engagements

• Review work assignments and hours billed to key client matters to make sure minority and women attorneys are not being excluded

• Strengthen mentoring program for all attorneys, including minorities and women

• Professional skills development program, including minority and women attorneys

Does your firm have part-time/flex-time policies that permit attorneys (male or female) to work alternative schedules?

Yes

What impact, if any, will the decision to work part-time have on an attorney's ability to make partner or, if already a partner, to remain a partner at your firm?

Lawyers who are working under an approved reduced hour arrangement (or who have done so at some point during their employment with the firm) may be considered for partnership provided that they otherwise meet the firm's standards for partnership admission.

Have any attorneys who chose to work a part-time schedule made partner at your firm?

No. We have not had part-time associates make partner from the associate ranks; however we have partners who work part-time.

Management Demographic Profile (as of 12/31/03)

	MINORITY MEN	MINORITY WOMEN	WHITE WOMEN	TOTAL
Number of attorneys on the Executive/Management Committee or equivalent	1	0	2	15
Number of attorneys on the Hiring Committee or equivalent	13	5	24	98
Number of attorneys on the Partner/Associate Review Committee or equivalent	1/2*	0/0*	2/4*	15/13*

* *Partner review committee/Associate review committee. At Hunton & Williams, our equivalents to the Partner Review Committee (PRC) and the Associate Review Committee (ARC) are separate committees, thus separate numbers above.*

Please provide information regarding all minority and women attorneys who head offices or practice groups of your law firm:

Women heading offices: Andrea Bear Field, Washington

Minorities heading practice groups: Pauline A. Schneider, head of the Public Finance and Real Estate practice in Washington; John Charles Thomas, head of Appellate Practice Group; Frank E. Emory Jr., head of the Litigation practice in Charlotte; A. Todd Brown, head of the Labor practice in Charlotte; and Fernando C. Alonso and Carlos E. Loumiet, co-heads of our Latin American Practice Group.

Women heading practice groups: Kathy Robb, head of our Resources, Regulatory & Environmental Law Team; Margaret P. Eisenhauer (Peggy), head of our Privacy Practice Group; Pauline A. Schneider, head of the Public Finance and Real Estate practice in Washington; and Caryl Greenberg Smith, head of the Public Finance practice in Atlanta and co-head of the firm's Public Finance Practice Group.

The Firm Says

Hunton & Williams (H&W) maintains a vigorous and expanding Diversity Program designed to attract and develop a work force representative of the firm's global law practice. The firm believes that a diverse group of lawyers and staff members allows us to better serve our clients in an international forum. In the 2004 Diversity Scorecard of the Minority Law Journal, H&W ranked in the top 10 percent of national law firms for the largest number of minority partners. In addition to 68 minority and women partners, the firm currently employs 300 minority and women associates and is the top-fifth law firm employer of Hispanic American attorneys.

The components of our Diversity Program include a diversity policy which enthusiastically supports the strong commitment to diversity issued by a large group of chief legal officers of U.S. and international corporations entitled Diversity in the Workplace: A Statement of Principle. The firm also has (1) a policy on equal employment; (2) an Affirmative Action Plan that provides a comprehensive blueprint for implementing diversity and equal employment opportunity; and (3) a strong Policy against Harassment, which applies to sexual harassment as well as harassment based on race, national origin, disability religion, sexual orientation and any

other protected categories. Our legal recruiting program, which seeks to attract exceptionally able lawyers, incorporates a focused minority recruiting effort, including regular participation in regional minority law student job fairs.

Additional components of our Diversity Program are:

• Work-life programs: The firm strives to provide a family-friendly working environment that recognizes the importance of our commitments to our loved ones as well as to our clients. Several committees and task forces within the firm, including the Women Partners Group, the Committee on Diversity, the Associates Committee and the firm-sponsored Women's Networking Forum, regularly address such issues as reduced hour arrangements, leave policies, child care, mentoring and other methods of assisting lawyers and staff in the challenge of balancing work and family life.

• Community outreach: Hunton & Williams' community service and outreach initiatives reflect the broad interests of our lawyers and staff in providing legal services and other types of assistance to a wide variety of pro bono clients and charitable groups. Projects supported by the firm include maintaining a neighborhood pro bono office in the oldest and poorest community in Richmond, Va.; staffing an elder law clinic; assisting an AIDS service organization; participating in domestic violence programs; supporting battered women's shelters; and representing refugees from Haiti, Turkey, Tibet, Sierra Leone, Senegal and Indonesia in proceedings for political asylum in conjunction with the Lawyers Committee for Human Rights.

• Corporate partnership: H&W is a regular patron and sponsor of the Minority Corporate Counsel Association's events and programs. The firm seeks to partner with our clients in the area of diversity. For example, we recently have partnered with Sodexho, Inc. and Duke Energy to sponsor summer internships for minority law school students. We also work with our clients to ensure that the team of lawyers we provide for their matters also reflects the importance of diversity to their organizations.

• Firm, bar and community leadership: H&W is proud of the leadership contributions our lawyers provide to the firm, the local and national bar and the communities in which we live and practice. The firm is proactive in ensuring that women and minority lawyers play prominent roles not only in their practice areas, but also in firm administration and bar and civic organizations. Such bar and civic involvement includes participation in the National Hispanic Bar Association's National Moot Court Competition; the ABA Commission on Racial and Ethnic Diversity in the Profession; the Atlanta Legal Diversity Consortium; and the New York Bar Symposium on Diversity.

The firm also appreciates that the breadth of gender, race, ethnicity, and all the other rich, growing and ever-changing differences among us are assets only if they are effectively incorporated in the client, professional and cultural growth and success of the firm. Diversity is a strategic and cultural asset and integral part of the core values of Hunton & Williams. The firm has established the following committees to promote diversity within the firm:

Diversity Strategies Committee: The mission of this committee is to focus on how the firm's growing diversity can best be used to serve existing clients, develop new clients or further distinguish our law firm. The committee focuses on the most effective and efficient use of diversity in our client relations and business development, including liaising with our firm-wide Business Development Committee for appropriate consideration of diversity; participating in ongoing team and individual attorney planning processes to ensure diversity is well considered; responding appropriately to clients who have stated diversity expectations; and analyzing new and

strategic business development opportunities where diversity may be a value differentiator or may provide entree.

Diversity Activities Committee: The mission of this committee is to provide a forum for Hunton & Williams' lawyers, staff and recruits to enjoy and appreciate the breadth and richness of cultural, ethnic, gender and other differences among us through an agenda of initiatives and programs. The committee reviews the firm's communications, recruiting, professional development and social activities to determine how we can best reflect the richness of our diversity and to provide our teams and practice groups with the support and tools they need to ensure the cultural leadership and versatility of our firm.

Jackson Lewis LLP

One North Broadway (Administrative Offices)
White Plains, NY 10601
Phone: (914) 328-0404
Fax: (914) 328-1882

FIRM LEADERSHIP

Managing Partner: William A. Krupman
Diversity Team Leader: William J. Anthony,
Partner (Hartford, CT)

LOCATIONS

White Plains, NY (HQ)
Atlanta, GA
Boston, MA
Chicago, IL
Dallas, TX
Greenville, SC
Hartford, CT
Melville, NY
Los Angeles, CA
Miami, FL
Minneapolis, MN
Morristown, NJ
New York, NY
Orlando, FL
Pittsburgh, PA
Sacramento, CA
San Francisco, CA
Seattle, WA
Stamford, CT
Vienna, VA

LAW FIRM DEMOGRAPHIC PROFILES

FULL-TIME ASSOCIATES	2003	2002
Minority men	7	17
Minority women	18	19
White women	70	73
Total	173	188

PARTNERS	2003	2002
Minority men	5	4
Minority women	1	1
White women	30	27
Total	153	141

NEW HIRES	2003	2002
Minority men	3	3
Minority women	3	8
White women	16	17
Total	33	48

Strategic Plan and Diversity Leadership

How does the firm's leadership communicate the importance of diversity to everyone at the firm? (e.g., e-mails, web site, newsletters, meetings, etc.)

Jackson Lewis communicates diversity initiatives through face-to-face meetings, teleconferences, e-mail updates and memoranda.

Who has primary responsibility for leading diversity initiatives at your firm?

William J. Anthony and Kathleen G. Maylin are co-chairs of the firm's Diversity Committee. Both are partners.

Does your law firm currently have a diversity committee?

Yes

Does the committee's representation include one or more members of the firm's management/executive committee (or the equivalent)?

Yes

How many attorneys are on the committee, and in 2003, what was the total number of hours collectively spent by the committee in furtherance of the firm's diversity initiatives?

Total attorneys on committee: 25

Total hours spent on diversity: N/A

Does the committee and/or diversity leader establish and set goals or objectives consistent with management's priorities?

Yes

Has the firm undertaken a formal or informal diversity program or set of initiatives aimed at increasing the diversity of the firm?

Yes, formal

How often does the firm's management review the firm's diversity progress/results?

Quarterly

LAW FIRM DIVERSITY INITIATIVES	ALREADY COMPLETED	CURRENTLY ADDRESSING	NOT A CURRENT PRIORITY
Undertake communication from firm management that diversity is a top priority of the firm.	✓		
Formalize diversity plan and committee with action steps and accountability to management.	✓		
Conduct firm-wide diversity training for all attorneys and staff.			✓
Increase the number of minority attorneys at the associate level.		✓	
Increase the number of minority attorneys at the partnership level.		✓	
Develop/expand relationships with minority bar associations to offer firm's support of these networks.	✓		
Focus on strengthening firm's mentoring program, including for benefit of minority attorneys.	✓		
Conduct internal diversity needs assessment and/or retain diversity consultant to examine how firm culture might be more welcoming of minorities.	✓		
Support law firm's internal affinity networks (e.g., women, minority attorney networks).	✓		
Manage/monitor allocation of work assignments and/or hours billed to ensure women and minority attorneys have equal access/inclusion on top client matters.	✓		

Recruitment – New Associates

Do you have any special outreach efforts directed to encourage minority law students to consider your firm?

• Participate in/host minority law student job fair(s)

• Scholarships or intern/fellowships for minority students (See narrative section below)

Recruitment – Lateral Associates and Partners

What activities does the firm undertake to attract minority and women attorneys?

• *Advertise with specialty bar associations*

• Partner programs with women and minority bar associations

• Participate at minority job fairs

• Seek referrals from other attorneys

• Utilize online job services (e.g., MCCA/DuPont Primary Law Firm Job Bank)

Do you use executive recruiting/search firms to seek to identify new diversity hires (partners or associates)?

Yes

Retention & Professional Development

Please identify the specific steps you are taking to reduce the attrition rate of minority and women attorneys.

• Develop and/or support internal employee affinity groups (e.g., minority or women networks within the firm)

• Increase/review compensation relative to competition

• Increase/improve current work/life programs

• Introduce minority and women attorneys to key clients, including to lead engagements

• Review work assignments and hours billed to key client matters to make sure minority and women attorneys are not being excluded

• Strengthen mentoring program for all attorneys, including minorities and women

• Professional skills development program, including minority and women attorneys

Does your firm have part-time/flex-time policies that permit attorneys (male or female) to work alternative schedules?

Yes

What impact, if any, will the decision to work part-time have on an attorney's ability to make partner or, if already a partner, to remain a partner at your firm?

Part-time attorneys are not eligible for partnership.

Management Demographic Profile (as of 12/31/03)

	MINORITY MEN	MINORITY WOMEN	WHITE WOMEN	TOTAL
Number of attorneys on the Executive/Management Committee or equivalent	0	0	0	8
Number of attorneys on the Partner/Associate Review Committee or equivalent	0	0	3	5

Please provide information regarding all minority and women attorneys who head offices or practice groups of your law firm:

Women heading offices: Lynn C. Outwater (Pittsburgh); Diane E. Stanton (Orlando)

Women heading practice groups: Felice B. Ekelman (co-chair, Traditional Labor); Lynn C. Outwater (co-chair, Management Training); Susan B. McKenna (co-chair, Employment Litigation)

The Firm Says

Centered on a workplace philosophy of preventive strategies and positive solutions, Jackson Lewis draws strength and energy from the diversity of our attorneys, our staff and the employer community we serve. Since 1958, our core legal business has involved working with management to respect, honor and value the differences and the similarities among their employees, address discrimination issues and counsel on diversity and affirmative action initiatives. These same issues and opportunities challenge Jackson Lewis as an employer of 800 individuals of different sex, race, age, physical and mental ability, ethnicity, religion, national origin, sexual orientation and family status in 20 offices coast to coast. Our diversity assists us in meeting the needs of our clients for broad-based policies, programs, strategies and solutions.

To achieve our goal of being the best possible workplace law firm in the country, Jackson Lewis strives to attract and retain the most qualified legal talent and support staff. In each of our 20 offices we reach out to a wide applicant pool and create incentives to enhance everyone's work experience. Our credibility as leading employment lawyers and our viability as an employer of choice depend on our ability to provide a variety of options and opportunities for those committed to delivering exemplary services to a diverse client community. One of the rewards of our commitment to diversity comes from the recognition of clients that demand nothing less from their legal service providers.

Directing the diversity initiative firm-wide is the Jackson Lewis Diversity Committee made of partners, associates and representatives of our human resources department. Under the Diversity "umbrella," formalized affinity groups, such as the African American, Hispanic, Asian American, Women's, and Gay & Lesbian groups, provide Jackson Lewis attorneys with specialized professional and business development support to grow and be competitive in a vigorous global marketplace. Through relationships with organizations such as the Minority Corporate Counsel Association and Hispanic and Asian bar associations, Jackson Lewis participates in the exchange of information and ideas that vitalize our role as legal counselors and as an employer committed to nurturing, sustaining and expanding the diverse talents and resources of our work force.

We sponsor a scholarship at the University of Michigan School of Law for minority students whose application and course work reveal an interest in employment law. The scholarship provides assistance to students who demonstrate financial need and who come from a disadvantaged background or a historically underrepresented minority group.

The firm conducts annual Women's Employment Law Conferences and is a sponsor of the annual Out & Equal Workplace Summit, the preeminent organization devoted to the gay, lesbian, bisexual and transgender community in workplace settings.

Jenkens & Gilchrist

1445 Ross Avenue, Suite 3200
Dallas, TX 75202
Phone: (214) 855-4500
Fax: (214) 855-4300

FIRM LEADERSHIP

Managing Partner: Thomas H. Cantrill,
Chairman
Diversity Team Leader: Chris Auguste, Chair of
Diversity Committee

LOCATIONS

Dallas, TX (HQ)
Austin, TX
Chicago, IL
Houston, TX
Los Angeles, CA
New York, NY
Pasadena, CA
San Antonio, TX
Washington, DC

LAW FIRM DEMOGRAPHIC PROFILES

FULL-TIME ASSOCIATES	2003	2002
Minority men	14	13
Minority women	14	11
White women	81	81
Total	240	262

SUMMER ASSOCIATES	2003	2002
Minority men	4	3
Minority women	6	14
White women	13	18
Total	52	66

EQUITY PARTNERS	2003	2002
Minority men	5	4
Minority women	0	0
White women	14	15
Total	131	153

NON-EQUITY PARTNERS	2003	2002
Minority men	3	5
Minority women	0	0
White women	12	14
Total	69	78

NEW HIRES	2003	2002
Minority men	3	3
Minority women	7	3
White women	21	17
Total	60	57

Strategic Plan and Diversity Leadership

How does the firm's leadership communicate the importance of diversity to everyone at the firm? (e.g., e-mails, web site, newsletters, meetings, etc.)

The firm's leadership has a serious commitment to becoming more diverse and has communicated the importance of diversity to everyone at the firm by directing all of the firm's management and operating committees to create policies and implement changes to enhance and increase diversity at the firm.

Who has primary responsibility for leading diversity initiatives at your firm?

Christopher Auguste, shareholder and chair of Diversity Committee

Does your law firm currently have a diversity committee?

Yes

If yes, does the committee's representation include one or more members of the firm's management/executive committee (or the equivalent)?

Yes

If yes, how many attorneys are on the committee, and in 2003, what was the total number of hours collectively spent by the committee in furtherance of the firm's diversity initiatives?

Total attorneys on committee: 15

Total hours spent on diversity: 200

Does the committee and/or diversity leader establish and set goals or objectives consistent with management's priorities?

Yes

Has the firm undertaken a formal or informal diversity program or set of initiatives aimed at increasing the diversity of the firm?

Yes, informal

How often does the firm's management review the firm's diversity progress/results?

The Diversity Committee is presently and actively developing diversity initiatives. A member of the firm's Operating Committee serves on the Diversity Committee. The committee has monthly meetings and regularly meets with members of management and the various management committees to discuss and effectuate its diversity initiatives.

How is the firm's diversity committee and/or firm management held accountable for achieving results?

When the firm management analyzes each attorney's contribution to the firm during the prior year, the firm's management takes into account each attorney's contribution to diversity.

LAW FIRM DIVERSITY INITIATIVES	ALREADY COMPLETED	CURRENTLY ADDRESSING	NOT A CURRENT PRIORITY
Undertake communication from firm management that diversity is a top priority of the firm.	✔		
Formalize diversity plan and committee with action steps and accountability to management.		✔	
Conduct firm-wide diversity training for all attorneys and staff.		✔	
Increase the number of minority attorneys at the associate level.		✔	
Increase the number of minority attorneys at the partnership level.		✔	
Develop/expand relationships with minority bar associations to offer firm's support of these networks.		✔	
Focus on strengthening firm's mentoring program, including for benefit of minority attorneys.	✔		
Conduct internal diversity needs assessment and/or retain diversity consultant to examine how firm culture might be more welcoming of minorities.		✔	
Support law firm's internal affinity networks (e.g., women, minority attorney networks).		✔	
Manage/monitor allocation of work assignments and/or hours billed to ensure women and minority attorneys have equal access/inclusion on top client matters.		✔	
Increase minority recruiting by adding predominantly minority law schools to our annual recruitment program.		✔	
Coordinate recruiting and diversity efforts.		✔	
Partner with key client to reach out to minority law students.		✔	

Recruitment – New Associates

Does your firm annually recruit at any of the following types of institutions? (Check all that apply and list the schools).

Predominantly minority and/or women's colleges: We attend job fairs that include those schools.

Do you have any special outreach efforts directed to encourage minority law students to consider your firm?

• Hold a reception for minority law students

• Advertise in minority law student association publication(s)

• Participate in/host minority law student job fair(s)

• Sponsor minority law student association events

• Firm's lawyers participate on career panels at school

• Outreach to leadership of minority student organizations

SUMMER ASSOCIATE STATISTICS: SUMMER 2003	MINORITY MEN	MINORITY WOMEN	WHITE WOMEN	TOTAL
Summer associates	4	5	10	43
Summer associates who received an offer of full-time employment	4	5	10	41
Summer associates who accepted an offer of full-time employment	4	4	9	29

Recruitment – Lateral Associates and Partners

What activities does the firm undertake to attract minority and women attorneys?

• Participate at minority job fairs

• Seek referrals from other attorneys

Do you use executive recruiting/search firms to seek to identify new diversity hires (partners or associates)?

No

LATERAL ASSOCIATES AND PARTNERS: 1/1/03 – 12/31/03	MINORITY MEN	MINORITY WOMEN	WHITE WOMEN	TOTAL
Number of lateral associate hires	3	1	10	33
Number of lateral partner hires (equity and non-equity)	0	0	0	4
Number of new partners (equity and non-equity) promoted from associate rank	3	0	4	17
Number of new equity partners	2	0	1	8

Retention & Professional Development

ATTORNEYS WHO LEFT THE FIRM: 2003	MINORITY MEN	MINORITY WOMEN	WHITE WOMEN	TOTAL
Number of attorneys who voluntarily or involuntarily left your firm's employ in 2003	4	6	26	101

How do 2003 attrition rates generally compare to those experienced in the prior year period?

Comparable

Please identify the specific steps you are taking to reduce the attrition rate of minority and women attorneys.

• Develop and/or support internal employee affinity groups (e.g., minority or women networks within the firm)

• Increase/improve current work/life programs

• Work with minority and women attorneys to develop career advancement plans

• Introduce minority and women attorneys to key clients, including to lead engagements

• Review work assignments and hours billed to key client matters to make sure minority and women attorneys are not being excluded

• Strengthen mentoring program for all attorneys, including minorities and women

• Professional skills development program, including minority and women attorneys

Does your firm have part-time/flex-time policies that permit attorneys (male or female) to work alternative schedules?

Yes

What impact, if any, will the decision to work part-time have on an attorney's ability to make partner or, if already a partner, to remain a partner at your firm?

None. Jenkens promotes part-time associates to partner.

Have any attorneys who chose to work a part-time schedule made partner at your firm?

Yes, two attorneys.

Management Demographic Profile (as of 12/31/03)

	MINORITY MEN	MINORITY WOMEN	WHITE WOMEN	TOTAL
Number of attorneys on the Executive/Management Committee or equivalent	0	0	0	5
Number of attorneys on the Hiring Committee or equivalent	2	2	6	19
Number of attorneys on the Partner/Associate Review Committee or equivalent	N/A	N/A	N/A	N/A

Please provide information regarding all minority and women attorneys who head offices or practice groups of your law firm:

Minorities heading offices: Washington, DC

Women heading offices: New York and Washington, DC

Women heading practice groups: Estate Planning and Intellectual Property

The Firm Says

Diversity statement

Jenkens & Gilchrist has an unyielding commitment to diversity. We are proud of our attorneys' diverse backgrounds and appreciate the many unique qualities that each of them brings to the firm. Our diversity efforts remain true to our core values of integrity, excellence, service, hard work and collegiality, particularly when it comes to the talented individuals who make Jenkens & Gilchrist such an exciting place to work. To provide leadership for our diversity initiatives, a Diversity Committee was formed to guide, research, identify and propose recommendations to recruit, retain and advance minority and women lawyers. Today, the Diversity Committee is completing an assessment of our current programs and reviewing proposed initiatives.

Jenkens & Gilchrist actively recruits minority and female law students and laterals. We strive to create well-balanced interview teams of women and men from different backgrounds and practices who are knowledgeable about issues affecting minorities and women. The firm also hosts and sponsors on-campus initiatives of such organizations as Black Law Students Association, Hispanic Law Students Association and other organizations with diverse membership, and is developing a 1L program designed to increase our diversity.

Jenkens & Gilchrist has created attorney development and mentoring programs to ensure that all of our associates are integrated into the firm, their sections and the practice of law. At their core, these programs are designed to ensure that all of our associates have equal access to formal and informal training in the skills and abilities our firm expects all of our lawyers to develop as they build their careers. The overriding purpose of these programs is to promote the development and retention of lawyers who reflect the firm's commitment to excellence, professionalism and diversity; who meet and exceed the needs of our clients; who sustain the firm's culture; and who will enhance its future performance.

Jenkens & Gilchrist provides its women and minority associates the essential skills, training, community exposure and opportunities to succeed throughout every step of their careers. The firm targets high-value cases in which they can become involved and collaborates with associates to get them involved in various aspects of business development.

We are pleased with our progress in establishing and improving our procedures in order to achieve our long-range goals to date, but recognize we must continue to seek opportunities to expand our efforts. As we continue to strive to increase the diversity of our firm, Jenkens & Gilchrist will provide our lawyers and staff with an experience rich in perspectives, culture and opportunities.

685

You must be *the* change you wish to see *in the* world.

—*Mahatma Gandhi*

Diversity is a top-of-mind issue at K&L. Because diversity of opinions, ideas, attitudes, experiences and perspectives makes for a stronger work environment. And better client solutions. With the appointment of Carl Cooper, the first management committee-level Chief Diversity Officer in a national law firm, we continue to answer the challenge of diversity. More is on the way. We know we can't change the world, but we are changing K&L. You have our word.

Kirkpatrick & Lockhart LLP

Challenge us.®

www.kl.com

Diversity as a Journey

By
Peter J. Kalis

As my friend and colleague, Carl Cooper, is fond of saying, diversity is less a destination than a journey. By our lights at K&L, it is a journey through the American experience, one that welcomes aboard the rich blend of perspectives, experiences and contributions that give content and meaning to our lives as Americans. It is this very journey that makes us a better, more resilient, and embracing organization, and one best suited to serve our clients.

As we enter this dawning century, our challenge is not what it was 50 years ago when *Brown v. Board of Education* was handed down. Now, we're confronted by myriad legacy issues whose subtlety and virulence require nuanced and determined responses. At K&L, we've concluded that diversity simply cannot be "in the mix" with other laudable institutional goals. Rather, our leadership is convinced that

it must get out front on this issue, and we have attempted to do so in a variety of ways.

First, we recognized our own limitations and sought the very best leadership in the country on diversity questions. We found that leadership in Carl Cooper, a leading attorney with both private sector and public sector experience, a successful law professor, a graduate of the Howard University School of Law, and a former Teaching Fellow at Harvard Law School. And, by the way, beyond those formal credentials, Carl is a unique combination of idealism, empathy, vision, creativity, and pragmatism.

Second, we concluded that it simply wasn't enough to invite Carl to K&L. We had to empower him. And, thus, Carl, in his role as Chief Diversity Officer, participates in every meeting of our Management Committee on the

same level, for example, as does our Chief Financial Officer. Carl is always at the table, and he always has one mission: diversity. We believe that he is the first officeholder at any major law firm to fill such a role.

Third, we specifically defined Carl's role as one of a "change agent." Carl is expected to drive change not only within K&L but also within the profession at large. We invite you to learn from Carl about how he has changed us. As for the profession at large, perhaps the greatest testimonial is the number of law firms that followed in our wake to appoint people to positions not unlike Carl's.

Fourth, we understood that, while Carl drives this bus, we all had to be passengers. We have embarked upon firmwide mentoring training that has included well over 500 of our attorneys. This is just one example of how diversity has made us a better organization for all personnel.

Fifth, we are taking diversity into places where few law firms tread. Our Work/Life Task Force, which is attacking the vexing issues associated with a proper balance between paid work and personal life, is one example. And the K&L Health Challenge — an extraordinary initiative aimed at the wellness of all of our personnel — is another example. Both of these pro-grams have their roots, in various ways, in our diversity initiative.

So, at K&L, our journey continues. We're excited by what we've learned and what we've accomplished, and we're equally excited about meeting tomorrow's challenges.

You are the rising generation within our profession. You have many decisions ahead of you, and one important one concerns where you will begin your career. If the issue of diversity is on your mind, know that earlier generations have diversity on their minds as well. At K&L, we're trying to translate this concern into tangible progress, and we're convinced that we're succeeding.

I hope that you have an opportunity to learn more about K&L, and that we have an opportunity to learn more about you.

Diversity

"A difference; variety; unlikeness" (Webster's Dictionary)

By
Carl G. Cooper

As the first, and at one time, the only Chief Diversity Officer of a major law firm, you can imagine how often I'm asked, "Why does a law firm need a Chief Diversity Officer?" Of course the short answer is, because our law firm wants to be more diverse, firm wide and firm deep. As the Chief Diversity Officer ("CDO"), my job is to "promote, achieve and then maintain" diversity within the law firm and simultaneously act as an agent for change in the profession at large. Diversity, consequently, is my full-time job.

The longer answer to the "Why diversity" question is more complex and confusing.

Diversity programs have been around for over twenty-five years and the legal industry has been estimated to be about eight (8) billion dollars!

Recently validated in the Supreme Court case of *Grutter*, the court held that diversity was a compelling interest and, consequently, public institutions could factor race into their decisions about admissions to their schools of higher education. By implication, it is assumed that the drive for diversity in the private sector will continue and, indeed, increase substantially.

In the year 2004, with America celebrating *Brown vs. Board of Education*'s fiftieth anniversary, diversity is being promoted more now than at any previous time in its history.

The confusion is that, the celebration over the *Brown* decision notwithstanding, less has changed in fact than all the fanfare would suggest. *Brown* aspired to integrate public education, which is more segregated today than it was 50 years ago. And while we applaud and celebrate diversity, in law as elsewhere, there is more talk on the subject than actually reflected in a multi-cultural workforce.

Indeed on June 2, 2004, K&L released its Second Annual Survey of In-House Counsel, which concluded that "when counsel is actually being chosen today, there is very little relationship between a law firm's diversity and its likelihood of being selected to provide legal services." Moreover, the survey revealed that, "in fact, racial diversity ranked below effective communications, working as a team, hourly rates, and working with enjoyable attorneys." Given our mission at K&L, diversity ranks much higher.

Diversity at K&L is part of our organizational DNA! As Chief Diversity Officer, I participate at every Management Committee meeting, and the first order of business at each of these meetings is a report by each of our offices on its effort in the area of diversity.

At K&L, this year's summer associate class reflects our collective efforts in this regard. Fifty percent of our summer class of 2004 is composed of women and thirty percent of the class are minority members. All summer associates have a recently trained mentor who will guide them through their summer experience and make certain that they are assimilated into the organizational fabric here at K&L. From summer associate to partnership is an extremely long period and, consequently, our goal is not merely to recruit; our broader mission is to retain and promote our new associates as they grow into the culture at K&L and become the future leaders of our firm.

We understand that our commitment is to a marathon and not a sprint. We believe in diversity because it produces better results for our clients and greater intellectual benefit for our colleagues, and it is good for our profession and the broader community. Retention will be the key going forward, as diversity is not a commodity, but rather a value that adds to the quality of the environment of a law firm or any other organization. Diversity permeates a firm's culture, creating a dynamic and enriched organization. This will be reflected not only in how many different people come, but also in how many different people stay and become partners and members of the firm's committees and management team.

By having a full-time diversity officer, K&L has developed the prototype of an officer devoted solely to the promotion and fulfillment of making true diversity, in all aspects of the word, a living reality. The responsibility for the diversity agenda cannot be placed on a partner or associate who toils in the diversity field while also attempting to meet other enterprising goals.

At K&L, we realize that diversity is a process as well as a result. It cannot happen solely by mandate from the top down, nor by virtue of discontent from the bottom up. In short, it is expansive, encompassing and enriching in its aspiration and application. This is truly a humbling yet remarkable undertaking for our firm, as our character will be measured not by what we do for the majority among us, but by how we consider those least able to voice their concerns. The choice is ours and at K&L we're committed, no matter how long or difficult the path may be. Period!

Kirkpatrick & Lockhart LLP

Challenge us.®

www.kl.com

BOSTON • DALLAS • HARRISBURG • LOS ANGELES • MIAMI • NEWARK • NEW YORK • PITTSBURGH • SAN FRANCISCO • WASHINGTON

Jenner & Block LLP

One IBM Plaza
Chicago, IL 60611-7603
Phone: (312) 222-9350
Fax: (312) 527-0484

FIRM LEADERSHIP

Managing Partner: Robert L. Graham, Managing Partner
Diversity Team Leader: Jeffrey D. Colman, E. Lynn Grayson, Reginald J. Hill and William M. Hohengarten, Co-Chairs

LOCATIONS

Chicago, IL (HQ)
Dallas, TX
Washington, DC

LAW FIRM DEMOGRAPHIC PROFILES

FULL-TIME ASSOCIATES	2003	2002
Minority men	22	20
Minority women	13	6
White women	70	79
Total	232	222

SUMMER ASSOCIATES	2003	2002
Minority men	6	15
Minority women	7	13
White women	32	28
Total	88	115

EQUITY PARTNERS	2003	2002
Minority men	4	2
Minority women	0	0
White women	27	26
Total	159	141

NON-EQUITY PARTNERS	2003	2002
Minority men	1	1
Minority women	0	0
White women	4	4
Total	15	22

NEW HIRES*	2003	2002
Minority men	10	7
Minority women	9	3
White women	20	23
Total	80	82

Excludes summer associates

Strategic Plan and Diversity Leadership

How does the firm's leadership communicate the importance of diversity to everyone at the firm? (e.g., e-mails, web site, newsletters, meetings, etc.)

As part of the "Core Values" section of the firm's mission statement, featured in Annual Reports, Diversity Newsletter published three times per year, the diversity web site section, Women's Forum meetings, sponsorship of minority causes, employee handbook and training materials and hiring practice.

Who has primary responsibility for leading diversity initiatives at your firm?

The four co-chairs of our Diversity Committee: Jeffrey D. Colman, E. Lynn Grayson, Reginald J. Hill and William M. Hohengarten.

Does your law firm currently have a diversity committee?

Yes

Does the committee's representation include one or more members of the firm's management/executive committee (or the equivalent)?

Yes

How many attorneys are on the committee, and in 2003, what was the total number of hours collectively spent by the committee in furtherance of the firm's diversity initiatives?

Total attorneys on committee: 25

Total hours spent on diversity: N/A

Does the committee and/or diversity leader establish and set goals or objectives consistent with management's priorities?

Yes

Has the firm undertaken a formal or informal diversity program or set of initiatives aimed at increasing the diversity of the firm?

Yes, formal

How often does the firm's management review the firm's diversity progress/results?

Monthly

How is the firm's diversity committee and/or firm management held accountable for achieving results?

Everyone in the firm is subject to strict accountability under its Strategic Business Plan, which identifies "Diversity" as one of five "Core Values."

LAW FIRM DIVERSITY INITIATIVES	ALREADY COMPLETED	CURRENTLY ADDRESSING	NOT A CURRENT PRIORITY
Undertake communication from firm management that diversity is a top priority of the firm.	✓		
Formalize diversity plan and committee with action steps and accountability to management.	✓		
Conduct firm-wide diversity training for all attorneys and staff.		✓	
Increase the number of minority attorneys at the associate level.	✓		
Increase the number of minority attorneys at the partnership level.		✓	
Develop/expand relationships with minority bar associations to offer firm's support of these networks.	✓		
Focus on strengthening firm's mentoring program, including for benefit of minority attorneys.	✓		
Conduct internal diversity needs assessment and/or retain diversity consultant to examine how firm culture might be more welcoming of minorities.		✓	
Support law firm's internal affinity networks (e.g., women, minority attorney networks).		✓	
Manage/monitor allocation of work assignments and/or hours billed to ensure women and minority attorneys have equal access/inclusion on top client matters.		✓	

Recruitment – New Associates

Do you have any special outreach efforts directed to encourage minority law students to consider your firm?

- Hold a reception for minority law students
- Participate in/host minority law student job fair(s)
- Sponsor minority law student association events
- Firm's lawyers participate on career panels at school
- Outreach to leadership of minority student organizations

SUMMER ASSOCIATE STATISTICS: SUMMER 2003	MINORITY MEN	MINORITY WOMEN	WHITE WOMEN	TOTAL
Summer associates	1	5	24	62
Summer associates who received an offer of full-time employment	1	5	19	51
Summer associates who accepted an offer of full-time employment	1	2	14	38

Recruitment – Lateral Associates and Partners

What activities does the firm undertake to attract minority and women attorneys?

• Partner programs with women and minority bar associations

• Participate at minority job fairs

• Seek referrals from other attorneys

Do you use executive recruiting/search firms to seek to identify new diversity hires (partners or associates)?

Yes

If yes, list all women- and/or minority-owned executive search/recruiting firms to which the firm paid a fee for placement services in the past 12 months:

None, to which the firm paid a fee for placement services.

LATERAL ASSOCIATES AND PARTNERS: 1/1/03 – 12/31/03	MINORITY MEN	MINORITY WOMEN	WHITE WOMEN	TOTAL
Number of lateral associate hires	3	4	11	33
Number of lateral partner hires (equity and non-equity)	1	0	3	11
Number of new partners (equity and non-equity) promoted from associate rank	2	0	2	12
Number of new equity partners	2	0	2	12

Retention & Professional Development

ATTORNEYS WHO LEFT THE FIRM: 2003	MINORITY MEN	MINORITY WOMEN	WHITE WOMEN	TOTAL
Number of attorneys who voluntarily or involuntarily left your firm's employ in 2003	6	2	26	59

How do 2003 attrition rates generally compare to those experienced in the prior year period?

About the same as in prior years

Please identify the specific steps you are taking to reduce the attrition rate of minority and women attorneys.

• Develop and/or support internal employee affinity groups (e.g., minority or women networks within the firm)

• Introduce minority and women attorneys to key clients, including to lead engagements

• Strengthen mentoring program for all attorneys, including minorities and women

• Professional skills development program, including minority and women attorneys

Does your firm have part-time/flex-time policies that permit attorneys (male or female) to work alternative schedules?

Yes

What impact, if any, will the decision to work part-time have on an attorney's ability to make partner or, if already a partner, to remain a partner at your firm?

None. Many female attorneys have made partner under this scenario.

Have any attorneys who chose to work a part-time schedule made partner at your firm?

Yes. Definitive historical information is not readily available.

Management Demographic Profile (as of 12/31/03)

	MINORITY MEN	MINORITY WOMEN	WHITE WOMEN	TOTAL
Number of attorneys on the Executive/Management Committee or equivalent	0	0	2	14
Number of attorneys on the Hiring Committee or equivalent	3	2	7	27
Number of attorneys on the Partner/Associate Review Committee or equivalent	N/A	N/A	N/A	N/A

Please provide information regarding all minority and women attorneys who head offices or practice groups of your law firm:

Minorities heading practice groups: Many minorities serve on our Diversity, Pro Bono Committee and Hiring Committees. In addition, Jenner & Block has four senior partners who are 65 years old or older who continue to make outstanding contributions to their firm, the bench, the bar and the profession.

Women heading practice groups: Debbie L. Berman, Co-Chair, Trade Secrets and Unfair Competition Practice; Paula C. Goedert, Chair, Association Practice; Teri A. Lindquist, Co-Chair, Corporate Finance Practice; Linda L. Listrom, Co-Chair, Defense and Aerospace Practice; Gail H. Morse, Chair, State and Local Tax Practice, and Co-Chair, Tax and Tax Controversy Practices; Stephanie A. Scharf, Co-Chair, Products Liability and Mass Tort Defense Practice; Lise T. Spacapan, Co-Chair, Products Liability and Mass Tort Defense Practice; Barbara S. Steiner, Co-Chair, Antitrust and Trade Regulation Practice.

In addition, many women serve on our Policy, Management, Diversity, Pro Bono and Hiring Committees.

The Firm Says

In support of Jenner & Block's core value of "Respect and Reward Our People," the firm states the following: "Diversity is important to the Firm. We are committed to maintaining and promoting diversity in hiring, development, promotion and success of all legal and non-legal personnel. People within our Firm will always treat each other with respect."

Jenner & Block is not a newcomer to the diversity issue. Over the years the firm has won numerous awards for its longtime commitment to diversity. Recently our leadership on diversity initiatives has been recognized by

the following organizations and awards: Minority Corporate Counsel Association Rainbowmaker Award, 2003; the Chicago Bar Association Alliance for Women Alta May Hulett Award, 2002; the Mexican American Legal Defense and Education Fund Legal Service Award, 2002; the National Association of Women Lawyers President's Award, 2002; the Women's Bar Association of Illinois Women With Vision Award, 2002.

The American Lawyer's "A-List" recognizes the top 20 law firms in the nation by evaluating their business performance as well as their record of pro bono service, associate satisfaction and commitment to diversity. Our continued commitment to diversity was recognized when Jenner & Block was named one of the 20 law firms that "lead the pack" and the only Chicago-headquartered law firm to make the prestigious *American Lawyer* A-List for the second year in a row.

Recruitment

Minority and women attorneys of the firm share their diverse perspectives while serving as members of the firm's Hiring Committee. They also recruit on campus and host minority job fairs, including spring and fall Black Law Student Association (BLSA) events at various law schools. Minority attorneys also host an annual reception at the firm for Latino/Latina Law Student Association (LLSA) members from local law schools.

Mentoring, personal development and training

Jenner & Block develops minority and women attorneys through a mentoring program for associates in the first through the fourth years, with senior partners focusing on minority and women associates.

To foster opportunities for professional, social and personal growth for its women attorneys, Jenner & Block instituted the Women's Forum. The Women's Forum convenes on a quarterly basis, with guest speakers from various industries addressing issues that are of concern to female attorneys. Women partners serve as mentors and advisors to women associates on both professional and personal development.

Client relationships and firm management

At Jenner & Block, diverse partners manage some of the firm's largest client relationships and serve in leadership positions on the firm's Policy Committee, Management Committee and in practice group management.

Alliance partnerships

Jenner & Block has established several alliance partnerships with organizations committed to improving diversity in the legal profession.

In May 2003 Jenner & Block was the First Patron Sponsor of Harvard Law School's "Celebration 50," a three-day CLE event in honor of the 50th anniversary of the law school's first woman graduate. The salute to the storied school's female alums who have worked for Jenner & Block as well as to its female alums everywhere was one of the largest gatherings of women lawyers and of Harvard Law School alumni ever.

For the third year in a row, Jenner & Block was the Premier Sponsor of the Minority Corporate Counsel Association's CLE Expo. Jenner & Block co-sponsored the National Association of Women Lawyers' "Taking Charge of Your Career: Best Practices for Women Lawyers & Their Firms" conference on March 12, 2004 in Washington, D.C.

Service to the bar

Our firm's commitment in supporting diversity and equal rights is also demonstrated by our senior partners' leadership roles in bar-related women and minority activities. For instance, Richard J. Gray serves as co-chair of the Diversity Plan Implementation Committee of the ABA Section of Litigation, is a member of the ABA President's Advisory Committee on Diversity in the Profession, and is a member of the ABA committee charged with raising funds to support ABA-granted Legal Opportunity Scholarships to law students. Stephanie A. Scharf is president of the National Association of Women Lawyers. Daniel J. Hurtado is a board member of the Chicago Committee on Minorities in Large Law firms. E. Lynn Grayson is co-chair of the Chicago Bar Association Alliance for Women and a member of the Illinois State Bar Association Standing Committee on Women in the Law.

Over the years, the firm has worked on important cases involving diversity issues such as fighting for the voting rights of African-Americans and combating race discrimination in housing. In a recent U.S. Supreme Court term, the firm played a key role in getting 65 major corporations to join in the firm's amicus brief to the U.S. Supreme Court in support of the University of Michigan's affirmative action policies.

Retired Jenner & Block Partner Joan M. Hall is a co-founder of the Young Women's Leadership Charter School of Chicago, which provides inner-city young women of color a challenging curriculum in a small school environment, nurturing the girls' self-confidence and optimism, and inspiring them to achieve in math, science and technology.

Diversity communications

Jenner & Block is one of the few law firms in the country that communicates about its diverse work force and diversity issues through firm-sponsored publications. Equal Time, the firm's diversity newsletter, is distributed to clients, alumni, law school students and faculty, and the media. In closing, we at Jenner & Block will continue to live our values and reflect our commitment to diversity in our operations, in our service to clients, and in our work in the profession and community.

Jones Day

51 Louisiana Avenue, N.W.
Washington, DC 20001-2113
Phone: (202) 879-3939
Fax: (202) 626-1700

FIRM LEADERSHIP

Managing Partner: Stephen J. Brogan
Diversity Team Leader: Alison B. Marshall,
Chair, Diversity Task Force

LOCATIONS

Atlanta, GA
Chicago, IL
Cleveland, OH
Columbus, OH
Dallas, OH
Houston, TX
Irvine, CA
Los Angeles, CA
Menlo Park, CA
New York, NY
Pittsburgh, PA
San Diego, CA
San Francisco, CA
Washington, DC
Beijing
Brussels
Frankfurt
Hong Kong
London
Madrid
Milan
Munich
New Delhi
Paris
Shanghai
Singapore
Sydney
Taipei
Tokyo

LAW FIRM DEMOGRAPHIC PROFILES

FULL-TIME ASSOCIATES	2003	2002
Minority men	53	47
Minority women	61	48
White women	396	360
Total	999	924

SUMMER ASSOCIATES	2003	2002
Minority men	11	13
Minority women	20	14
White women	80	68
Total	206	183

PARTNERS	2003	2002
Minority men	13	9
Minority women	4	2
White women	74	66
Total	474	445

NEW HIRES	2003	2002
Minority men	13	23
Minority women	21	13
White women	95	94
Total	261	277

Strategic Plan and Diversity Leadership

How does the firm's leadership communicate the importance of diversity to everyone at the firm? (e.g., e-mails, web site, newsletters, meetings, etc.)

The importance of diversity is discussed at a variety of different meetings including Advisory Committee meetings, recruitment meetings and practice group meetings. Diversity is also addressed on the firm's web site.

Who has primary responsibility for leading diversity initiatives at your firm?

Alison B. Marshall, chair, Diversity Task Force

Does your law firm currently have a diversity committee?

Yes

Does the committee's representation include one or more members of the firm's management/executive committee (or the equivalent)?

Yes

How many attorneys are on the committee, and in 2003, what was the total number of hours collectively spent by the committee in furtherance of the firm's diversity initiatives?

Total attorneys on committee: 10

Total hours spent on diversity: Not available

Does the committee and/or diversity leader establish and set goals or objectives consistent with management's priorities?

Partially. A collaborative effort with the offices.

Has the firm undertaken a formal or informal diversity program or set of initiatives aimed at increasing the diversity of the firm?

Yes, informal

How often does the firm's management review the firm's diversity progress/results?

Monthly

LAW FIRM DIVERSITY INITIATIVES	ALREADY COMPLETED	CURRENTLY ADDRESSING	NOT A CURRENT PRIORITY
Undertake communication from firm management that diversity is a top priority of the firm.		✓	
Formalize diversity plan and committee with action steps and accountability to management.		✓	
Conduct firm-wide diversity training for all attorneys and staff.		✓	
Increase the number of minority attorneys at the associate level.		✓	
Increase the number of minority attorneys at the partnership level.		✓	
Develop/expand relationships with minority bar associations to offer firm's support of these networks.		✓	
Focus on strengthening firm's mentoring program, including for benefit of minority attorneys.		✓	
Conduct internal diversity needs assessment and/or retain diversity consultant to examine how firm culture might be more welcoming of minorities.		✓	
Support law firm's internal affinity networks (e.g., women, minority attorney networks).		✓	
Manage/monitor allocation of work assignments and/or hours billed to ensure women and minority attorneys have equal access/inclusion on top client matters.		✓	

Note: Each of the items listed above, as do all diversity initiatives, require ongoing attention; therefore, we cannot properly respond to any category as "already completed."

Recruitment – New Associates

List of Law Schools Jones Day Annually Recruits At (as of 9/16/04)

American University, Washington College of Law; Benjamin Cardozo School of Law; Boston University; Case Western Reserve University; Catholic University of America; Chicago-Kent College of Law; Cleveland State University; Columbia University; Duke University; Emory University; Fordham University; George Mason University; George Washington University; Georgetown University; Georgia State University; Harvard University; Indiana University – Bloomington; Loyola University, Chicago; Loyola Law School, Los Angeles; New York University; Northwestern University; Ohio State University; Pepperdine University; South Texas College of Law; Southern Methodist University; Stanford University; Texas Tech University; Tulane University; Vanderbilt University; University of Akron; University of California – Berkeley (Boalt Hall); University of California – Davis; University of California – Hastings; University of California – Los Angeles; University of Chicago; University of Cincinnati; University of Georgia; University of Houston; University of Illinois; University of Iowa; University of Michigan; University of Minnesota; University of North Carolina; University of Notre Dame; University of Pennsylvania; University of Pittsburgh; University of San Diego; University of Southern California; University of Texas; University of Virginia; University of Wisconsin; Washington and Lee University; Washington University; Yale Law School

Do you have any special outreach efforts directed to encourage minority law students to consider your firm?

• Hold a reception for minority law students

• Participate in/host minority law student job fair(s)

• Sponsor minority law student association events

• Firm's lawyers participate on career panels at school

• Outreach to leadership of minority student organizations

SUMMER ASSOCIATE STATISTICS: SUMMER 2003	MINORITY MEN	MINORITY WOMEN	WHITE WOMEN	TOTAL
Summer associates	11	20	80	206
Summer associates who received an offer of full-time employment	9	17	67	164
Summer associates who accepted an offer of full-time employment	9	13	58	134

Recruitment – Lateral Associates and Partners

What activities does the firm undertake to attract minority and women attorneys?

• Partner programs with women and minority bar associations

• Participate at minority job fair

• Seek referrals from other attorneys

Do you use executive recruiting/search firms to seek to identify new diversity hires (partners or associates)?

Yes

If yes, list all women- and/or minority-owned executive search/recruiting firms to which the firm paid a fee for placement services in the past 12 months:

Jones Day has had a relationship with women- and/or minority-owned search firms; however, it is our practice not to share such information.

LATERAL ASSOCIATES AND PARTNERS: 1/1/03 – 12/31/03	MINORITY MEN	MINORITY WOMEN	WHITE WOMEN	TOTAL
Number of lateral associate hires	2	9	27	70
Number of lateral partner hires	2	1	2	16
Number of new partners promoted from associate rank	2	1	7	25

Retention & Professional Development

How do 2003 attrition rates generally compare to those experienced in the prior year period?

About the same as in prior years

Please identify the specific steps you are taking to reduce the attrition rate of minority and women attorneys.

• *Jones Day gives particular emphasis to training for its associates.*

• Introduce minority and women attorneys to key clients, including to lead engagements

• Review work assignments and hours billed to key client matters to make sure minority and women attorneys are not being excluded

• Professional skills development program, including minority and women attorneys

Does your firm have part-time/flex-time policies that permit attorneys (male or female) to work alternative schedules?

Yes

What impact, if any, will the decision to work part-time have on an attorney's ability to make partner or, if already a partner, to remain a partner at your firm?

A part-time schedule may have an impact on professional development and, consequently, on advancement toward or within the partnership. The extent of the impact will depend on the duration of the part-time arrangement, the quality and quantity of work performed and whether the lawyer effectively assumed increasing levels of responsibility while maintaining a reduced schedule.

Have any attorneys who chose to work a part-time schedule made partner at your firm?

Yes, data is not available on how many.

Management Demographic Profile (as of 12/31/03)

	MINORITY MEN	MINORITY WOMEN	WHITE WOMEN	TOTAL
Number of attorneys on the Executive/Management Committee or equivalent	2	1	6	41
Number of attorneys on the Hiring Committee or equivalent	0	1	6	18
Number of attorneys on the Partner/Associate Review Committee or equivalent*	1	0	3	23

* Non-Partner Review Committee

Please provide information regarding all minority and women attorneys who head offices or practice groups of your law firm:

Minorities heading offices: Elwood Lui, San Francisco (Asian male)

Women heading offices: Laura E. Ellsworth, Pittsburgh (white female); Mary Ellen Powers, Washington, DC (white female)

Minorities heading practice groups: Jayant W. Tambe, New Associates Group Office Coordinator (Asian male)

Women heading practice groups: Sydney McDole, Group Coordinator, New Associates Group (white female); Lizanne Thomas, Business Practice Group Office Group Coordinator (white female); Janine Metcalf, New Associates Group Office Coordinator (white female); Maria K. Nelson, New Associates Group Office Coordinator (white female); S. Louise Rankin, New Associates Group Office Coordinator (white female)

The Firm Says

Jones Day's culture is one of teamwork, and the firm prides itself on being "One Firm Worldwide." As the firm's web site describes, our lawyers are "hands-on" and believe that dedication to and effort for common goals are the keys to success. Our lawyers, at all levels, expect to be involved meaningfully as members of the team on client projects. Our culture is for everyone to pitch in to support client service. Jones Day lawyers routinely work together not only as professionals but also as enthusiastic colleagues and friends with the advancement of the client's interest as the paramount goal. This core culture of teamwork is one that supports and nurtures diversity and inclusion and permits attorneys from all backgrounds to flourish.

Jones Day's Diversity Task Force supports the domestic office and practice group leaders in four primary areas: (1) entry-level recruitment, (2) lateral recruitment, (3) development and retention of attorneys, and (4) diversity awareness. The firm maintains a formal Nondiscrimination Program related to both lawyer and staff employment. The firm also participates in a wide variety of activities connected with increasing diversity within the legal profession, and is continually looking for new opportunities.

For example, Jones Day participates in the Columbus Bar Association Minority Clerkship Program and the Georgetown Minority Law Clerk program and has hired part-time law clerks through this program to work at the firm during the school year. In addition, Jones Day sponsors and participates in minority recruiting events at Harvard Law School, specifically, the Harvard Black Law Students Association (BLSA) Annual Spring Conference and Job Fair, the BLSA 1L Job Fair and the BLSA 2L/3L Job Fair. We also participate each year in the National Asian Pacific American Conference on Law and Public Policy, put on by the Conference of the Asian Pacific American Law Students Association at Harvard Law School. The firm participates in the annual Cook County Bar Association Minority Lawyer Conference, and has sponsored BLSA conferences at Case Western Reserve University and USC law schools. Firm offices have conducted mock interviews, receptions and other events in an attempt to assist minority applicants in finding positions within the legal community. The Atlanta office sponsors interns from Morehouse College. In addition, the firm contributes support to minority law student associations, nationally and at individual law schools, including but not limited to APALSA, the Latino Law Student Association and NBLSA.

The firm also sponsors and sends minority lawyers to participate in minority recruiting road shows. The road shows are designed to provide opportunities for practicing minority lawyers to share their career development path and job search tips with minority law students. This year, Jones Day lawyers will attend road shows at U.C. Berkeley, New York University, Georgetown, University of Illinois, Stanford and the University of Michigan.

Jones Day has also participated in and sponsored the NALP Foundation Pathways Partnership Summit, in which minority recruiting and retention issues were addressed. The firm also actively participated in the American Bar Association National Conference for Minority Lawyers, which brought together in-house counsel and lawyers from private practice to discuss methods of increasing diversity and awareness of minority recruiting issues. In addition, the firm is a member of the ABA Conference of Minority Partners in Majority Corporate Law Firms.

The firm is a signatory to various minority hiring goals and initiatives established by local bar associations in Chicago, Columbus, Dallas, Los Angeles, New York City, Pittsburgh and Washington, D.C. , and a number of offices have been actively involved in local initiatives to increase diversity within the bar. For example, the Jones Day Columbus office participates, along with other area law firms, in the Managing Partners' Diversity Initiative. Columbus firms are making progress in a collaborative effort to significantly increase the number of minority attorneys recruited, hired and promoted. Similarly, the Jones Day Los Angeles office joined several L.A.-area law firms in forming a Managing Partners' Roundtable. The roundtable's goal is to determine initiatives for improving hiring and retention for minority and female lawyers in the Los Angeles region. Discussions at recent meetings have centered on planning two conferences to be held in Los Angeles. The conferences will provide corporate law firms and their clients an opportunity to share perspectives on diversity lawyer hiring and retention issues. One conference will address minority lawyer hiring and retention; another will focus primarily on female lawyer hiring and retention issues. The Atlanta, Cleveland and Dallas offices are also each currently involved in similar initiatives.

Jones Day's pro bono activities also reflect its commitment to diversity and issues of concern to communities of color. For example, in 2003, Jones Day submitted an amicus brief to the United States Supreme Court in support of the University of Michigan's position in the Bollinger affirmative action cases. Filed on behalf of MIT, Stanford University, IBM, DuPont, National Academy of Sciences, National Academy of Engineering and the National Action Council for Minorities in Engineering, Jones Day argued in support of affirmative action particularly in the context of science and technology education. In 2004, Jones Day attorneys are devoting considerable time to handling a major housing discrimination action, Dalle et al. v. Winarsky, pending in the U.S. District Court for the District of Maryland, on behalf of a number of tenants in a housing complex who allege that the owner engaged in racial discrimination by evicting them from their apartments so that the apartments could be renovated and then occupied by non-minority tenants.

Katten Muchin Zavis Rosenman

525 West Monroe Street, Suite 1600
Chicago, IL 60661-3693
Phone: (312) 902-5200
Fax: (312) 902-1061
Web site: www.kmzr.com

FIRM LEADERSHIP

National Managing Partner: Vincent A.F. Sergi

LOCATIONS

Chicago, IL (HQ)
Charlotte, NC
Inving, TX
Los Angeles, CA
New York, NY
Palo Alto, CA
Washington, DC

The Firm Says

Katten Muchin Zavis Rosenman is currently in the process of evaluating and restructuring its diversity policies and initiatives. Toward that end, the firm has recently hired a new diversity consultant. More information shall be made available for the next edition of the Vault/MCCA Guide to Law Firm Diversity Programs. If you need additional information, please contact Leslie D. Dent, chair of the Katten Muchin Zavis Rosenman Diversity Committee.

Kaye Scholer LLP

425 Park Avenue
New York, NY 10022-3598
Phone: (212) 836-8000
Fax: (212) 836-8689

FIRM LEADERSHIP

Managing Partner: Barry Willner, Managing Partner
Diversity Team Leader: Sheila Boston, Partner and Chair of Diversity Committee

LOCATIONS

New York, NY (HQ)
Chicago, IL
Los Angeles, CA
Washington DC
West Palm Beach, FL
Frankfurt
Hong Kong
London
Shanghai

LAW FIRM DEMOGRAPHIC PROFILES

FULL-TIME ASSOCIATES	2003	2002
Minority men	25	23
Minority women	24	24
White women	81	80
Total	270	271

SUMMER ASSOCIATES	2003	2002
Minority men	2	4
Minority women	5	8
White women	12	18
Total	31	52

EQUITY PARTNERS	2003	2002
Minority men	2	2
Minority women	2	2
White women	17	14
Total	136	130

NEW HIRES	2003	2002
Minority men	6	7
Minority women	6	6
White women	21	14
Total	56	50

Strategic Plan and Diversity Leadership

How does the firm's leadership communicate the importance of diversity to everyone at the firm? (e.g., e-mails, web site, newsletters, meetings, etc.)

E-mail, web sites, meetings

Who has primary responsibility for leading diversity initiatives at your firm?

Sheila Boston, chair Diversity Committee; James Herschlein, co-chair Recruiting Committee, Executive Committee; Bea Drechsler, co-chair Recruiting Committee

Does your law firm currently have a diversity committee?

Yes

Does the committee's representation include one or more members of the firm's management/executive committee (or the equivalent)?

Yes

How many attorneys are on the committee, and in 2003, what was the total number of hours collectively spent by the committee in furtherance of the firm's diversity initiatives?

Total attorneys on committee: 21

Total hours spent on diversity: In excess of 800 hours

Does the committee and/or diversity leader establish and set goals or objectives consistent with management's priorities?

Yes

Has the firm undertaken a formal or informal diversity program or set of initiatives aimed at increasing the diversity of the firm?

Yes, formal

How often does the firm's management review the firm's diversity progress/results?

Quarterly

LAW FIRM DIVERSITY INITIATIVES	ALREADY COMPLETED	CURRENTLY ADDRESSING	NOT A CURRENT PRIORITY
Undertake communication from firm management that diversity is a top priority of the firm.	✔		
Formalize diversity plan and committee with action steps and accountability to management.		✔	
Conduct firm-wide diversity training for all attorneys and staff.	✔		
Increase the number of minority attorneys at the associate level.		✔	
Increase the number of minority attorneys at the partnership level.		✔	
Develop/expand relationships with minority bar associations to offer firm's support of these networks.		✔	
Focus on strengthening firm's mentoring program, including for benefit of minority attorneys.		✔	
Conduct internal diversity needs assessment and/or retain diversity consultant to examine how firm culture might be more welcoming of minorities.	✔		
Support law firm's internal affinity networks (e.g., women, minority attorney networks).	✔		
Manage/monitor allocation of work assignments and/or hours billed to ensure women and minority attorneys have equal access/inclusion on top client matters.		✔	

Recruitment - New Associates

Does your firm annually recruit at any of the following types of institutions?

Ivy League schools: Harvard, Yale, Columbia, Cornell, Penn

Public state schools: Michigan UCLA

Private schools: BC, BLSA, Brooklyn, BU, Cardozo, Duke, Fordham, GW, Georgetown, Hofstra, Northwestern, NYU, NY Law, PLIP, Rutgers, St. John's, Stanford

Historically Black Colleges and Universities (HBCUs): Howard University

Do you have any special outreach efforts directed to encourage minority law students to consider your firm?

• Participate in/host minority law student job fair(s)

• Firm's lawyers participate on carrer panels at school

• Outreach to leadership of minority student organizations

• Scholarships or intern/fellowships for minority students

SUMMER ASSOCIATE STATISTICS: SUMMER 2003	MINORITY MEN	MINORITY WOMEN	WHITE WOMEN	TOTAL
Summer associates	0	4	9	31
Summer associates who received an offer of full-time employment	0	4	9	31
Summer associates who accepted an offer of full-time employment	0	4	8	29

Recruitment – Lateral Associates and Partners

What activities does the firm undertake to attract minority and women attorneys?

• Partner programs with women and minority bar associations

• Participate at minority job fairs

• Seek referrals from other attorneys

Do you use executive recruiting/search firms to seek to identify new diversity hires (partners or associates)?

Yes

LATERAL ASSOCIATES AND PARTNERS: 1/1/03 – 12/31/03	MINORITY MEN	MINORITY WOMEN	WHITE WOMEN	TOTAL
Number of lateral associate hires	2	0	2	20
Number of lateral partner hires (equity and non-equity)	0	0	2	3
Number of new partners (equity and non-equity) promoted from associate rank	0	1	1	7
Number of new equity partners	0	1	3	10

Retention & Professional Development

ATTORNEYS WHO LEFT THE FIRM: 2003	MINORITY MEN	MINORITY WOMEN	WHITE WOMEN	TOTAL
Number of attorneys who voluntarily or involuntarily left your firm's employ in 2003	0	0	7	32

How do 2003 attrition rates generally compare to those experienced in the prior year period?

About the same as in prior years

Please identify the specific steps you are taking to reduce the attrition rate of minority and women attorneys.

• Develop and/or support internal employee affinity groups (e.g., minority or women networks within the firm)

• Increase/review compensation relative to competition

- Increase/improve current work/life programs
- Succession plan includes emphasis on diversity
- Work with minority and women attorneys to develop career advancement plans
- Introduce minority and women attorneys to key clients, including to lead engagements
- Review work assignments and hours billed to key client matters to make sure minority and women attorneys are not being excluded
- Strengthen mentoring program for all attorneys, including minorities and women
- Professional skills development program, including minority and women attorneys

Does your firm have part-time/flex-time policies that permit attorneys (male or female) to work alternative schedules?

Yes

What impact, if any, will the decision to work part-time have on an attorney's ability to make partner or, if already a partner, to remain a partner at your firm?

None

Management Demographic Profile (as of 12/31/03)

	MINORITY MEN	MINORITY WOMEN	WHITE WOMEN	TOTAL
Number of attorneys on the Executive/Management Committee or equivalent	0	0	1	11
Number of attorneys on the Hiring Committee or equivalent	2	2	10	27
Number of attorneys on the Partner/Associate Review Committee or equivalent	1	0	2	13

Please provide information regarding all minority and women attorneys who head offices or practice groups of your law firm:

Women/Minority Heads of Practice Groups: Alice Young, Chair, Asia Pacific Group, America (Minority); Sheri Jeffery, Chair Entertainment

The Firm Says

At Kaye Scholer we have a commitment to fostering and supporting diversity. We believe that the richer the mix of people, the stronger and more vital the firm.

The Diversity and Recruiting Committees work together to ensure a diverse workplace. We recruit at job fairs such as the BLSA Northeast Job Fair and the DuPont Minority Job Fair. We conduct on-campus interviews and actively recruit diverse candidates at all of the law schools at which we interview.

The firm is one of the original signatories of the New York City Bar's Statement of Diversity Principles, and has participated in the City Bar Fellowship Program since its inception.

Last year Kaye Scholer entered into a partnership with the Bronx School for Law, Government and Justice. Kaye Scholer attorneys have coached the school's mock trial team in a state competition, conducted a mock labor negotiation with the students and judged several moot court competitions at the school. Next year we will initiate a mentor program.

Our partners' commitment to diversity extends well beyond the firm. This fall one of our partners will become chair of the Committee on Recruitment and Retention of Lawyers of the Association of the Bar of the City of New York. Among other organizations in which our partners are involved are the Asian American Bar Association of New York, Legal Momentum (formerly NOW), Inwood House and Just One Break.

We actively seek out applications from candidates with a wide variety of backgrounds, interests and life experience. Please join us as we build a more diverse legal community.

Kilpatrick Stockton LLP

Suite 2800
1100 Peachtree Street
Atlanta, GA 30309
Phone: (404) 815-6500
Fax: (404) 815-6555

FIRM LEADERSHIP

Monica D. Jones, Diversity Program Manager
Managing Partner: William H. Brewster,
Managing Partner
Diversity Team Leader: W. Randy Eaddy,
Partner who serves as Diversity Council Chair

LOCATIONS

Atlanta, GA (HQ)
Augusta, GA
Charlotte, NC
New York, NY
Raleigh, NC
Winston-Salem, NC
Washington, DC
London
Stockholm

LAW FIRM DEMOGRAPHIC PROFILES

FULL-TIME ASSOCIATES	2003	2002
Minority men	16	18
Minority women	20	21
White women	54	73
Total	204	233

SUMMER ASSOCIATES	2003	2002
Minority men	6	5
Minority women	7	7
White women	18	16
Total	54	57

EQUITY PARTNERS	2003	2002
Minority men	3	3
Minority women	0	1
White women	11	12
Total	117	119

NON-EQUITY PARTNERS	2003	2002
Minority men	1	1
Minority women	1	2
White women	19	19
Total	83	81

NEW HIRES	2003	2002
Minority men	3	0
Minority women	4	12
White women	14	15
Total	54	57

MINORITY CORPORATE COUNSEL ASSOCIATION

Strategic Plan and Diversity Leadership

How does the firm's leadership communicate the importance of diversity to everyone at the firm? (e.g., e-mails, web site, newsletters, meetings, etc.)

The firm's communications about the importance of diversity in our workplace and our efforts to improve the firm's diversity come directly from firm's Executive Committee, in the form of statements and proclamations sent firm wide via e-mail. Our Diversity Council and its chair are also responsible for carrying the messages to all at the firm via group presentations at partners' meetings, e-mail announcements and newsletter articles. Our diversity program manager regularly updates the firm on diversity matters via the diversity intranet site, newsletter submissions.

Who has primary responsibility for leading diversity initiatives at your firm?

W. Randy Eaddy, partner who serves as Diversity Council chair.

Does your law firm currently have a diversity committee?

Yes

Does the committee's representation include one or more members of the firm's management/executive committee (or the equivalent)?

Yes

How many attorneys are on the committee, and in 2003, what was the total number of hours collectively spent by the committee in furtherance of the firm's diversity initiatives?

Total attorneys on committee: 8

Total hours spent on diversity: 1,000.30

Does the committee and/or diversity leader establish and set goals or objectives consistent with management's priorities?

Yes

Has the firm undertaken a formal or informal diversity program or set of initiatives aimed at increasing the diversity of the firm?

Yes, formal

How often does the firm's management review the firm's diversity progress/results?

Twice a year. The managing partner receives a monthly report from the Diversity Council, and diversity matters is a standing agenda item for the monthly meetings of the Executive Committee. The Diversity Council chair reports semi-annually to the Executive Committee.

LAW FIRM DIVERSITY INITIATIVES	ALREADY COMPLETED	CURRENTLY ADDRESSING	NOT A CURRENT PRIORITY
Undertake communication from firm management that diversity is a top priority of the firm.	✔		
Formalize diversity plan and committee with action steps and accountability to management.	✔		
Conduct firm-wide diversity training for all attorneys and staff.		✔	
Increase the number of minority attorneys at the associate level.		✔	
Increase the number of minority attorneys at the partnership level.		✔	
Develop/expand relationships with minority bar associations to offer firm's support of these networks.		✔	
Focus on strengthening firm's mentoring program, including for benefit of minority attorneys.		✔	
Conduct internal diversity needs assessment and/or retain diversity consultant to examine how firm culture might be more welcoming of minorities.		✔	
Support law firm's internal affinity networks (e.g., women, minority attorney networks).	✔		
Manage/monitor allocation of work assignments and/or hours billed to ensure women and minority attorneys have equal access/inclusion on top client matters.		✔	

Other Diversity Initiatives at Kilpatrick

The firm officially adopted a Statement of Commitment to Diversity in July 2002. Since that statement, the firm has put into place a Diversity Action Program and established a Diversity Council and two teams, an attorney team and a staff team, to work together to address the diversity concerns of Kilpatrick Stockton. The teams, under the direction of the Council, developed the firm's Strategic Action Plan for Implementing Diversity Commitment (SAP). The SAP has separate components for attorney and staff roles, but has a common commitment and overarching goals to enhance diversity throughout the firm. Action steps that address each of the above priorities and many others are included in the SAP. Additionally, the firm has a full-time diversity program manager and has established a separate budget to help drive the strategic initiatives of the SAP. We believe that these aspects of the SAP will help ensure the long-term successes of our program.

Recruitment - New Associates

Does your firm annually recruit at any of the following types of institutions? (Check all that apply and list the schools).

Ivy League schools: Harvard University, Columbia University

Public state schools: University of Alabama, University of Georgia, University of Florida, University of Tennessee, University of Virginia, University of North Carolina, University of South Carolina, College of William & Mary

Private schools: Emory University, Washington & Lee University, Duke University, Wake Forest University, Georgetown University

Historically Black Colleges and Universities (HBCUs): Howard University, North Carolina Central University

Do you have any special outreach efforts directed to encourage minority law students to consider your firm?

• Hold a reception for minority law students

• Advertise in minority law student association publication(s)

• Participate in/host minority law student job fair(s)

• Sponsor minority law student association events

• Outreach to leadership of minority student organizations

• Scholarships or intern/fellowships for minority students

SUMMER ASSOCIATE STATISTICS: SUMMER 2003	MINORITY MEN	MINORITY WOMEN	WHITE WOMEN	TOTAL
Summer associates	4	5	12	37
Summer associates who received an offer of full-time employment	3	3	9	28
Summer associates who accepted an offer of full-time employment	2	3	8	21

Recruitment – Lateral Associates and Partners

What activities does the firm undertake to attract minority and women attorneys?

• Participate at minority job fairs

• Seek referrals from other attorneys

Do you use executive recruiting/search firms to seek to identify new diversity hires (partners or associates)?

Yes

LATERAL ASSOCIATES AND PARTNERS: 1/1/03 – 12/31/03	MINORITY MEN	MINORITY WOMEN	WHITE WOMEN	TOTAL
Number of lateral associate hires	2	3	4	24
Number of lateral partner hires (equity and non-equity)	0	0	3	11
Number of new partners (equity and non-equity) promoted from associate rank	0	0	2	8
Number of new equity partners	0	0	3	6

Retention & Professional Development

ATTORNEYS WHO LEFT THE FIRM: 2003	MINORITY MEN	MINORITY WOMEN	WHITE WOMEN	TOTAL
Number of attorneys who voluntarily or involuntarily left your firm's employ in 2003	4	7	33	85

How do 2003 attrition rates generally compare to those experienced in the prior year period?

Lower than in prior years

Please identify the specific steps you are taking to reduce the attrition rate of minority and women attorneys.

• Develop and/or support internal employee affinity groups (e.g., minority or women networks within the firm)

• Introduce minority and women attorneys to key clients, including to lead engagements

• Strengthen mentoring program for all attorneys, including minorities and women

• Professional skills development program, including minority and women attorneys

Does your firm have part-time/flex-time policies that permit attorneys (male or female) to work alternative schedules?

Yes

What impact, if any, will the decision to work part-time have on an attorney's ability to make partner or, if already a partner, to remain a partner at your firm?

None with respect to eligibility or the applicable criteria. As a practical matter, however, it may take more time (years) for an attorney who works part-time to acquire requisite practice experience to become a partner.

Have any attorneys who chose to work a part-time schedule made partner at your firm?

Yes , two attorneys.

Management Demographic Profile (as of 12/31/03)

	MINORITY MEN	MINORITY WOMEN	WHITE WOMEN	TOTAL
Number of attorneys on the Executive/Management Committee or equivalent	0	0	2	13
Number of attorneys on the Hiring Committee or equivalent	3	1	4	19
Number of attorneys on the Partner/Associate Review Committee or equivalent	0	0	5	18

Please provide information regarding all minority and women attorneys who head offices or practice groups of your law firm:

Minorities heading practice groups: W. Randy Eaddy, Securities practice leader

Women heading practice groups: Diane Prucino, Labor & Employment group leader

The Firm Says

At Kilpatrick Stockton, promoting diversity and its social imperative for fair treatment in our workplace without regard to racial, ethnic, religious, gender, sexual orientation and other self-defining factors is a core value – a part of the fabric for our institutional life. We recognize both the social responsibility and the business opportunity of promoting diversity. It is the right thing to do, and it is good for business.

Kilpatrick Stockton's commitment to diversity as a core value leads us to pursue initiatives that seek to make every aspect of our work environment more open and fulfilling for all our personnel. We have adopted as our guiding principle the following statement about what diversity means to us, which we refer to as the Kilpatrick Stockton diversity principle:

At Kilpatrick Stockton, all persons, without regard to differences among them that do not matter in the workplace, shall be respected and valued fully, so that each person may maximize his or her potential to contribute to the common good of our firm and to benefit fairly from doing so.

For us, diversity in our workplace is about action, continually seeking better ways to empower and energize our varied personnel for success. Their individual successes enhance both our ability to provide world-class services to clients and our collective and individual contributions to the strength and vitality of the communities in which we work and live.

The centerpiece of our overall Diversity Action Program is our recently adopted Strategic Action Plan for Implementing Diversity Commitment (the "Plan" or "SAP"), which we are already implementing to guide, monitor and measure ourselves and our actions. A summary of the Initiatives and select action steps under the Plan are set forth at the end of this section.

Kilpatrick Stockton's 125-year history includes a legacy of inclusiveness that precedes the emergence of diversity as a contemporary concept. We are proud that our firm practiced diversity before most institutions had any conception of it, and we are inspired by our early recognitions and accomplishments, such as:

• The first large firm in the Southeast to have a female partner.

• Establishing the James S. Dockery Jr. Scholarship at Wake Forest Law School to support outstanding minority students.

• Being awarded (in 1999) Georgia's first Thomas L. Sager Award by the Minority Corporate Counsel Association.

We recognize that creating and sustaining a diverse environment is not a matter of happenstance, but requires strategic, purposeful initiatives. Through the SAP, we will ensure that diversity flourishes as a core value throughout our firm – today and in the future.

Kilpatrick Stockton Diversity Strategic Action Plan

Attorney initiatives

I – To develop and implement institutional structures and standard operating procedures that solidify and facilitate our commitment to diversity as a "core value" of the Firm.

II – To engage in proactive and innovative hiring practices, at all levels ... to exceed relevant NALP averages and reflect ... the diversity profile of ... [our] communities .

III – To improve significantly our retention and advancement of diversity attorneys ... by developing and implementing programs and support systems that train, mentor and empower our attorneys ....

IV – To increase the participation of women and minority attorneys in management and other leadership roles within the Firm, and to ensure the proper sharing by all attorneys in the financial benefits provided by the Firm.

V – To facilitate the refinement, implementation and coordination of policies and related models for successful advancement ... by attorneys who desire a reduced or other alternative time commitment for their practice of law.

VI – To communicate ... our diversity commitment, our diversity attorneys and our diversity successes to persons and organizations who ... can benefit from awareness of our diversity activities and results.

Select action steps

• Conduct a firm-wide Diversity Audit, and raise overall awareness about diversity among all personnel through professionally facilitated education and training programs.

• Refine and formalize institutional procedures that help ensure the proactive consideration and assessment of diversity issues in all key management functions of the Firm.

• Establish training program to prepare firm leaders and partners to better manage diversity attorneys.

• Institutionalize mentoring/coaching program, with coaches who are specifically trained and held accountable for effectiveness, and develop award system to promote same.

• Monitor each Practice Group's commitment to ensuring quality work assignments to and proactive integration of diversity associates into the success matrix of the Group.

• Ensure that the composition of client services committees, the leadership of Practice Groups, the delegation of client relationship responsibilities, etc. reflect commitment to diversity.

• Encourage and support participation by women and minority attorneys in high-profile positions within applicable bar association of their respective affinity.

• Foster and support the establishment of voluntary affinity groups to increase communication, relationship building, and collaborative support systems among diversity attorneys.

• Monitor and confirm compliance with the Firm's reduced hours policy.

• Explore an alternative "success model" built on a reduced hours or flex-time commitment.

• Develop appropriate "business case" criteria for assessing potential lateral candidates in light of long-term diversity objectives.

• Increase the pool of candidates for summer program recruitment, and institutionalize coaching program to enhance yield from summer associates.

King & Spalding LLP

191 Peachtree Street
Atlanta, GA 30303-1763
Phone: (404) 572-4600
Fax: (404) 572-5100

FIRM LEADERSHIP

Managing Partner: Walter W. Driver Jr.,
Chairman
Diversity Team Leader: Ralph B. Levy,
Chairman, Diversity Committee

LOCATIONS

Atlanta, GA (HQ)
Houston, TX
New York, NY
Washington, DC
London

LAW FIRM DEMOGRAPHIC PROFILES

FULL-TIME ASSOCIATES*	2003	2002
Minority men	22	27
Minority women	43	38
White women	192	176
Total	514	481

*Includes, where applicable, staff attorneys, associates, counsel and of counsel.

SUMMER ASSOCIATES	2003	2002
Minority men	2	8
Minority women	18	12
White women	43	46
Total	115	122

EQUITY PARTNERS	2003	2002
Minority men	6	6
Minority women	1	1
White women	17	17
Total	149	160

NON-EQUITY PARTNERS	2003	2002
Minority men	3	3
Minority women	1	0
White women	20	18
Total	62	58

NEW HIRES*	2003	2002
Minority men	7	9
Minority women	13	13
White women	62	42
Total	146	121

**Includes, where applicable, individuals who were promoted from temporary attorney to staff attorney, associate, counsel or of counsel in the year in question.

Strategic Plan and Diversity Leadership

How does the firm's leadership communicate the importance of diversity to everyone at the firm? (e.g., e-mails, web site, newsletters, meetings, etc.)

The firm's Diversity Committee is a standing committee, currently led by our former firm-wide managing partner. The chairman of our Diversity Committee reports directly to the chairman of the firm and the Policy Committee. The chairman of our Diversity Committee briefs our Operating Committee twice each year and our Policy Committee at least once each year on the firm's diversity initiatives and progress. At the most recent Partners' Retreat, Dr. Roosevelt Thomas, the CEO of the American Institute for Managing Diversity, was a featured speaker. A section of the firm's web site is dedicated to diversity. Among other things, this web site highlights recent efforts by the firm to promote diversity. Recently, the firm launched a resume-sharing program to encourage our clients to share the resumes of qualified women and minority lawyers who apply for positions with their company, in cases where their company does not have an open position. To launch this program, the chairman of our Diversity Committee sent an e-mail to all of our lawyers asking them whether their clients should be sent a letter introducing the resume-sharing program to them.

Who has primary responsibility for leading diversity initiatives at your firm?

Ralph B. Levy, chairman of the Diversity Committee

Does your law firm currently have a diversity committee?

Yes

Does the committee's representation include one or more members of the firm's management/executive committee (or the equivalent)?

Two members of the Policy Committee are ad hoc members of the Diversity Committee and attend Dviersity Committee meetings to provide input and ensure appropriate support.

How many attorneys are on the committee, and in 2003, what was the total number of hours collectively spent by the committee in furtherance of the firm's diversity initiatives?

Total attorneys on committee: 13

Total hours spent on diversity: Approximately 850

Does the committee and/or diversity leader establish and set goals or objectives consistent with management's priorities?

Yes

Has the firm undertaken a formal or informal diversity program or set of initiatives aimed at increasing the diversity of the firm?

Yes, formal

How often does the firm's management review the firm's diversity progress/results?

Twice a year by the Operating Committee. Annually – minimum review by Policy Committee.

How is the firm's diversity committee and/or firm management held accountable for achieving results?

The chairman of our Diversity Committee briefs our Operating Committee twice each year and our Policy Committee at least once annually on the firm's diversity initiatives and progress.

LAW FIRM DIVERSITY INITIATIVES	ALREADY COMPLETED	CURRENTLY ADDRESSING	NOT A CURRENT PRIORITY
Undertake communication from firm management that diversity is a top priority of the firm.	✔		
Formalize diversity plan and committee with action steps and accountability to management.	✔		
Conduct firm-wide diversity training for all attorneys and staff.		✔	
Increase the number of minority attorneys at the associate level.		✔	
Increase the number of minority attorneys at the partnership level.		✔	
Develop/expand relationships with minority bar associations to offer firm's support of these networks.		✔	
Focus on strengthening firm's mentoring program, including for benefit of minority attorneys.		✔	
Conduct internal diversity needs assessment and/or retain diversity consultant to examine how firm culture might be more welcoming of minorities.		✔	
Support law firm's internal affinity networks (e.g., women, minority attorney networks).	✔		
Manage/monitor allocation of work assignments and/or hours billed to ensure women and minority attorneys have equal access/inclusion on top client matters.			✔
Help design diversity training for law firm leaders		✔	
Cooperate with clients who request us to manage/monitor allocation of work assignments and/or hours billed to ensure women and minority attorneys have meaningful access/inclusion to their work.		✔	

Recruitment – New Associates

Does your firm annually recruit at any of the following types of institutions? (Check all that apply and list the schools).

Ivy League schools: Harvard University, Yale University, University of Pennsylvania, Cornell University, Columbia University

Public state schools: Florida State University, Georgia State University, University of Florida, University of Georgia, University of Houston, University of Kentucky, University of Maryland, University of Michigan, UNC, University of South Carolina, University of Texas, University of Virgina, University of California (Boalt Hall)

Private schools: Boston University, Duke University, Emory University, Fordham University, George Washington University, Georgetown University, Hofstra University, Mercer University, Northwestern University, New York University, University of Chicago, University of Notre Dame, Southeasrt Methodist University, St. John's University, St. Louis University, Stanford University, Tulane University, Vanderbilt University

Historically Black Colleges and Universities (HBCUs): Howard University

Do you have any special outreach efforts directed to encourage minority law students to consider your firm?

• Hold a reception for minority law students

• Advertise in minority law student association publication(s)

• Participate in/host minority law student job fair(s)

• Sponsor minority law student association events

• Firm's lawyers participate on career panels at school

• Outreach to leadership of minority student organizations

• Scholarships or intern/fellowships for minority students

SUMMER ASSOCIATE STATISTICS: SUMMER 2003*	MINORITY MEN	MINORITY WOMEN	WHITE WOMEN	TOTAL
Summer associates	1	16	43	112
Summer associates who received an offer of full-time employment	1	13	40	103
Summer associates who accepted an offer of full-time employment**	1	10	27	67

* *Includes 3Ls only; does not include individuals in JD/MBA program. Individuals who spent time in two firm offices counted only once.*

***Eleven offers (four to white women) could not be accepted due to intervening judicial clerkship.*

Recruitment – Lateral Associates and Partners

What activities does the firm undertake to attract minority and women attorneys?

• Partner programs with women and minority bar associations

• Participate at minority job fairs

• Seek referrals from other attorneys

Do you use executive recruiting/search firms to seek to identify new diversity hires (Partners or associates)?

Yes

List all women- and/or minority-owned executive search/recruiting firms to which the firm paid a fee for placement services in the past 12 months:

We have paid a fee to the following firms that are either owned by women and/or minorities, founded by women and/or minorities, or that have senior management that is diverse:

Counsel on Call; Hughes & Sloan; Corrao Miller Rush & Wiesenthal; The PeterSan Group (one male owner & one female owner); Wooldridge & associates; and Greenburg & Associates.

LATERAL ASSOCIATES AND PARTNERS: 1/1/03 – 12/31/03	MINORITY MEN	MINORITY WOMEN	WHITE WOMEN	TOTAL
Number of lateral associate hires*	2	7	32	72
Number of lateral partner hires (equity and non-equity)	0	0	3	5
Number of new partners (equity and non-equity) promoted from associate rank**	1	0	3	11
Number of new equity partners***	0/1	0/0	1/0	3/3

* *Includes, where applicable, staff attorneys, associates, counsel and of counsel. Includes, where applicable, individuals who were promoted from temporary attorney to staff attorney, associate, counsel or of counsel in 2003.*

** *Includes one lawyer who moved to London from New York.*

*** *Data for "new equity partners" is divided into lateral hires and those promoted from partner to equity partner. (Laterals/Partner to Equity Partner)*

Retention & Professional Development

ATTORNEYS WHO LEFT THE FIRM: 2003	MINORITY MEN	MINORITY WOMEN	WHITE WOMEN	TOTAL
Number of attorneys who voluntarily or involuntarily left your firm's employ in 2003	11	11	42	118

How do 2003 attrition rates generally compare to those experienced in the prior year period?

About the same as in prior years

Please identify the specific steps you are taking to reduce the attrition rate of minority and women attorneys. (It is suggested that you elaborate on this issue in the final question of this survey.)

• *See ombudsmen description in narrative Section VII.*

• Develop and/or support internal employee affinity groups (e.g., minority or women networks within the firm)

• Increase/improve current work/life programs

• Strengthen mentoring program for all attorneys, including minorities and women

• Professional skills development program, including minority and women attorneys

Does your firm have part-time/flex-time policies that permit attorneys (male or female) to work alternative schedules?

Yes

What impact, if any, will the decision to work part-time have on an attorney's ability to make partner or, if already a partner, to remain a partner at your firm?

Part-time attorneys are eligible to be elected partner while they are on a part-time basis. However, any part-time partner who wishes to be considered for election to equity partner must return to full-time status for at least two full calendar years before his/her election as an equity partner becomes effective.

Have any attorneys who chose to work a part-time schedule made Partner at your firm?

Yes, one attorney.

Management Demographic Profile (as of 12/31/03)

	MINORITY MEN	MINORITY WOMEN	WHITE WOMEN	TOTAL
Number of attorneys on the Executive/Management Committee or equivalent	0	0	0	10
Number of attorneys on the Hiring Committee or equivalent*	3	2	24	65
Number of attorneys on the Partner/Associate Review Committee or equivalent	2	0	2	11

King & Spalding has separate Hiring Committees in each U.S. office; numbers are for all four offices combined.

Please provide information regarding all minority and women attorneys who head offices or practice groups of your law firm:

Minorities heading practice groups: Grace Rodriguez, Special Matters/Government Investigations; Carlos Treistman – Deputy, Global Projects

Women heading practice groups: Sarah Borders, Co-Leader, Financial Restructuring; Suzanne Feese, Tax; Caryn Hemsworth, Deputy, Financial Transactions; Peggy O'Neil, Financial Transactions; Grace Rodriguez, Special Matters/Government Investigations; Carol Wood, Deputy, Houston Litigation

The Firm Says

We believe that our firm and our clients benefit from our diversity. However, we are hardly satisfied that we have attained our goal and we know we can do much more. We are committed to increasing the diversity in our firm and actively seek out and welcome people of varying backgrounds, cultural influences and experience, who have the ability and desire to assist us in rendering excellent client service.

Recent activities which King & Spalding has undertaken to promote diversity include:

• Diversity training for law firm leaders. King & Spalding helped to create the Large Law Firm Alliance, a group of 11 law firms in Atlanta that have agreed to partner with the American Institute for Managing Diversity to create a training program for individuals who hold leadership positions within large law firms.

• Part-time coordinator. Recently, in an effort to insure that our part-time policy is benefiting those who wish to take advantage of it, our chairman has decided that he will appoint a coordinator for part-time work.

- Women's initiatives. The firm sponsors a number of activities designed to advance women's issues within the firm, including informal lunches with associates and partners to discuss career development, a book club focusing on women's issues in the professional world, training sessions to discuss marketing tips and a woman's intranet page.

- Resume-sharing program. Recently, we launched a resume-sharing program to encourage our clients to share the resumes of qualified women and minority lawyers who apply for positions with their company, in cases where their company does not have an open position. The goal of this program is to help us identify additional minority applicants.

- Houston Bar Association Gender Initiative. In September, we signed the Houston Bar Association's 2003 Gender Initiative Commitment Statement. As part of this Commitment, we have committed to take concrete actions to materially increase the number of women at the partnership level by year-end 2007; achieve approximately equal retention rates for both men and women attorneys for 2007 and beyond; obtain feedback from employees on their assessment of gender issues in the workplace and address unconscious stereotypes and perceptions of gender bias; offer formal or informal networking opportunities, client development activities and mentoring programs to women attorneys at all levels to help women establish their professional profiles and develop client bases; identify and promote opportunities for women at all levels to participate in challenging projects and firm opportunities; and embrace the concept of part-time partners and flexible work schedules.

- The Association of the Bar of the City of New York Statement of Diversity Principles. As a signatory to the Statement of Principles, the firm has adopted goals relating to hiring, retaining and promoting a diverse work force. We have also committed to achieve leadership positions throughout the firm that reflect the diversity among the senior legal professionals at the firm, to conduct diversity training, to implement and maintain diversity-enhancing programs, and to measure the success of our diversity initiatives.

- Lloyd M. Johnson Scholarship Program. The firm has pledged $32,500 over the next three years to the scholarship program and, as one of the first 10 firms to agree to sponsor the program, King & Spalding has been asked to sit on the Scholarship Selection Committee.

- Ombudsmen. The firm recently created an ombudsman position within each of its domestic offices. This position is held by one or more partners and is designed to allow our lawyers to have confidential conversations about issues of importance to them. The goal is for the individual and the ombudsman to create a plan of action to address the issues or concerns.

- Women's client retreat. Each year, King & Spalding sponsors a retreat for our women partners and clients. In addition to allowing for social exchange, these retreats provide an opportunity for CLE and/or other learning opportunities.

- Partner retreat. At our Spring 2004 Partners' Retreat, one of the featured speakers was Dr. Roosevelt Thomas, CEO of the American Institute for Managing Diversity. As part of his discussion, Dr. Thomas explored the differences between preferences and requirements and laid out a framework to help the firm continue to think about the issue of diversity.

- Executive dinner. Lynn Martin, former Secretary of Labor under President George H.W. Bush, was the featured speaker at our Fall Executive Dinner in 2003. The Honorable Ms. Martin is a frequent speaker on the subject of diversity.

- 2L clerkship. Although we do not normally hire first-year law students for our summer associate program, we hire a bar-sponsored, first-year minority law student in our Atlanta, New York and Houston offices.

- Atlanta Legal Diversity Consortium, Inc. King & Spalding is a member of the Atlanta Legal Diversity Consortium, Inc. and the chairman of our Diversity Committee is currently a member of its board.

- Campus and community efforts. King & Spalding participates and supports a number of campus and community efforts designed to improve diversity within the legal profession and our firm. Among the community sponsorships and activities that King & Spalding has participated in are the following: National Association of Women Lawyers; The King Center; United Negro College Fund; Anti-Defamation League; Women International; Hispanic Bar Association; the NBLSA; State Bar of Georgia, Women and Minorities in the Profession Committee; League of Women Voters of Atlanta, Fulton County; YMCA Salute to Women of Achievement Luncheon; National Coalition of One Hundred Black Women Chapter-Stone Mountain/Lithonia Chapter; Lawyers Committee for Civil Rights Under Law; ABA Commission on the 50th Anniversary of Brown vs. Board of Education; NOW Legal Defense and Education Fund; InMotion; Medical Education of South African Blacks; Mexican-American Bar Association of Houston; and Sheltering Arms.

At KIRKLAND & ELLIS LLP,

Diversity is a priority.
Inclusion is a necessity.

At Kirkland & Ellis LLP, we realize that improving diversity within our Firm requires a fresh approach to recruit outstanding diverse attorneys of all backgrounds and new initiatives to encourage their success at the Firm. It's one of the reasons we have awarded minority students scholarships totaling over a quarter of a million dollars. It's one of the reasons we established the firmwide Diversity Committee and the Women's Leadership Initiative. It's one of the reasons the Firm sponsors a quarterly lunch for our diverse attorneys. It's one of the reasons we created the Diversity Digest – an internal firmwide publication to improve communication and awareness of the Firm's diversity initiatives. We are working hard at Kirkland & Ellis to create an atmosphere of inclusion so that all our employees feel welcome and have an equal opportunity to succeed.

KIRKLAND & ELLIS LLP

www.kirkland.com

Chicago   London   Los Angeles   New York   San Francisco   Washington, D.C.

Kirkland & Ellis LLP

Aon Center
200 East Randolph Drive
Chicago, IL 60601
Phone: (312) 861-2000
Fax: (312) 861-2200

FIRM LEADERSHIP

Diversity Team Leaders: Paul R. Garcia, Co-Chair, Firm-wide Diversity Committee
Michael D. Jones, Co-Chair, Firm-wide Diversity Committee
Managing Partner: Thomas D. Yannucci, Chairman, Management Committee

LOCATIONS

Chicago, IL
Los Angeles, CA
New York, NY
San Francisco, CA
Washington, DC

LAW FIRM DEMOGRAPHIC PROFILES

FULL-TIME ASSOCIATES	2003	2002
Minority men	45	43
Minority women	52	44
White women	144	130
Total	538	500

SUMMER ASSOCIATES	2003	2002
Minority men	10	7
Minority women	11	13
White women	49	27
Total	129	99

PARTNERS*	2003	2002
Minority men	12	11
Minority women	6	1
White women	65	60
Total	388	346

Kirkland & Ellis does not distinguish between equity and non-equity partners.

NEW HIRES	2003	2002
Minority men	14	17
Minority women	22	14
White women	41	41
Total	184	151

Strategic Plan and Diversity Leadership

How does the firm's leadership communicate the importance of diversity to everyone at the firm? (e.g., e-mails, web site, newsletters, meetings, etc.)

The importance of diversity at Kirkland & Ellis LLP is regularly communicated through a number of different means, including e-mail notice to attorneys of diversity-related events, initiatives and commitments; through our web site (www.kirkland.com) and, specifically, our diversity web page; during our Diversity Lunch wherein diverse attorneys meet with Diversity Committee members as well as other committee members and partners to discuss professional development issues, hiring and recruiting efforts, as well as diversity initiatives and commitments; in firm-wide Diversity Committee meetings; at our share partner and all partner meetings; in our Diversity Digest, a newsletter published periodically and provided to all attorneys within the firm; through Kirkland-funded sponsorships of various diverse organizations and to minority law school organizations and events; through the funding of our eleven $15,000 law school minority fellowships at The University of Chicago Law School, Columbia University Law School, Georgetown University Law Center, Harvard Law School, Howard University School of Law, University of Michigan Law School, New York University School of Law, Northwestern School of Law, University of Notre Dame Law School, Stanford Law School and Yale Law School; by approving attorneys' requests to attend diversity-related conferences and events and funding the costs for such attendance; through communications from our firm's Management Committee; at Kirkland's annual Summer Associate Diversity Dinner and Summer Associate Women's Dinner hosted in our various offices, and at Diversity Committee-sponsored receptions; at Recruiting Committee meetings; via Kirkland-created advertisements in legal publications; through our recruiting at minority job fairs and the sponsoring of various minority law student receptions; by the firm's membership in the Chicago Committee on Minorities in Large Law Firms of which one of our partners is a board member; and through the firm's participation and sponsorship at the Minority Corporate Counsel Association's CLE Expo March 31-April 2, 2004.

Who has primary responsibility for leading diversity initiatives at your firm?

Paul R. Garcia, co-chair, firm-wide Diversity Committee (Chicago), and Michael D. Jones, co-chair, firm-wide Diversity Committee (Washington, D.C.)

Does your law firm currently have a diversity committee?

Yes

Does the committee's representation include one or more members of the firm's management/executive committee (or the equivalent)?

Yes

How many attorneys are on the committee, and in 2003, what was the total number of hours collectively spent by the committee in furtherance of the firm's diversity initiatives?

Total attorneys on committee: 31

Total hours spent on diversity: 800

Does the committee and/or diversity leader establish and set goals or objectives consistent with management's priorities?

Yes

Has the firm undertaken a formal or informal diversity program or set of initiatives aimed at increasing the diversity of the firm?

Yes, formal.

How often does the firm's management review the firm's diversity progress/results?

Routinely. Our diversity progress and results are regularly in the forefront of the minds of our firm's management, and discussed and reviewed in a variety of contexts.

How is the firm's diversity committee and/or firm management held accountable for achieving results?

The Diversity Committee and our law firm's Management Committee are principally held accountable by our clients, who have increasingly clear diversity guidelines. We produce diversity-related reports on behalf of a number of key clients and monitor results on a regular basis. We are also a signatory to the 2003 Statement of Diversity Principles promulgated by the Association of the Bar of the City of New York (ABCNY) and crafted by the ABCNY's Committee to Enhance Diversity in the Profession. The 2003 Statement requires that we commit to and achieve a number of diversity goals.

LAW FIRM DIVERSITY INITIATIVES	ALREADY COMPLETED	CURRENTLY ADDRESSING	NOT A CURRENT PRIORITY
Undertake communication from firm management that diversity is a top priority of the firm.	✔		
Formalize diversity plan and committee with action steps and accountability to management.	✔		
Conduct firm-wide diversity training for all attorneys and staff.		✔	
Increase the number of minority attorneys at the associate level.	✔	✔	
Increase the number of minority attorneys at the partnership level.		✔	
Develop/expand relationships with minority bar associations to offer firm's support of these networks.	✔		
Focus on strengthening firm's mentoring program, including for benefit of minority attorneys.	✔	✔	
Conduct internal diversity needs assessment and/or retain diversity consultant to examine how firm culture might be more welcoming of minorities.		✔	
Support law firm's internal affinity networks (e.g., women, minority attorney networks).	✔		

LAW FIRM DIVERSITY INITIATIVES (CONTINUED)	ALREADY COMPLETED	CURRENTLY ADDRESSING	NOT A CURRENT PRIORITY
Manage/monitor allocation of work assignments and/or hours billed to ensure women and minority attorneys have equal access/inclusion on top client matters.	✓		
Establishment, growth and continued support of the firm-wide Diversity Committee.	✓	✓	
Creation and approval of our annual diversity budget.	✓		
Role of Attorney Development Department in the spearheading and support of diversity initiatives.	✓		

Recruitment – New Associates

Does your firm annually recruit at any of the following types of institutions? (Check all that apply and list the schools).

Ivy League schools: Columbia University Law School, Cornell Law School, Harvard Law School, University of Pennsylvania Law School, Yale Law School

Public state schools: Arizona State University College of Law, University of California at Berkeley, Boalt Hall School Law, University of California, Hastings College of Law, University of Illinois College of Law, Indiana University School of Law – Bloomington, University of Michigan Law School, Ohio State University College of Law, University of Texas School of Law, UCLA School of Law, University of Utah College of Law, University of Virginia School of Law

Private schools: Boston College Law School, Boston University School of Law, Brigham Young University Law School, Brooklyn Law School, University of Chicago Law School, Chicago-Kent College of Law, Benjamin N. Cardozo School of Law, DePaul University College of Law, Duke University School of Law, Emory University School of Law, Fordham University School of Law, Georgetown University Law Center, George Washington University Law School, Howard University School of Law, Loyola University Chicago School of Law, Loyola Law School – Los Angeles, Northwestern University School of Law, University of Notre Dame Law School, New York University School of Law, Pepperdine University School of Law, Santa Clara University School of Law, Stanford Law School, University of Southern California Law Center, Washington University School of Law

Historically Black Colleges and Universities (HBCUs): Howard University School of Law

Do you have any special outreach efforts directed to encourage minority law students to consider your firm?

• *Host reception for minority summer associates. Additional outreach efforts on the part of Kirkland include pursuing the establishment of a one-on-one relationship and, thereafter, regular contact between minority summer associate candidates who have received offers and attorney members of our offices' recruiting committees. In addition, Diversity Committee members meet with minority law school professors and administrators, law school directors of minority affairs and law school deans in an attempt to better understand the minority law student population and their interests.*

• Hold a reception for minority law students

- Advertise in minority law student association publication(s)
- Participate in/host minority law student job fair(s)
- Sponsor minority law student association events
- Firm's lawyers participate on career panels at school
- Outreach to leadership of minority student organizations
- Fellowships for minority students at certain law schools

SUMMER ASSOCIATE STATISTICS: SUMMER 2003	MINORITY MEN	MINORITY WOMEN	WHITE WOMEN	TOTAL
Summer associates	10	8	43	117
Summer associates who received an offer of full-time employment	10	7	42	115
Summer associates who accepted an offer of full-time employment	6	5	34	88

Lateral Associates and Partners

What activities does the firm undertake to attract minority and women attorneys?

- *In January 2004, Kirkland created the Kirkland & Ellis LLP Women's Leadership Initiative (WLI). The goal of the WLI is to provide a forum for discussion of issues that are relevant to women in the firm and legal community, foster opportunities and provide a supportive network for our female attorneys. Each Kirkland office hosts WLI events throughout the year.*
- Partner programs with women and minority bar associations
- Participate at minority job fairs
- Seek referrals from other attorneys

Do you use executive recruiting/search firms to seek to identify new diversity hires (partners or associates)?

Yes

If yes, list all women- and/or minority-owned executive search/recruiting firms to which the firm paid a fee for placement services in the past 12 months:

Audrey Golden Associates, Ltd.; McCormack Schreiber Legal Search, Inc.; Nichols & Sciabica Attorney Search; Russo & Fondell, Inc.; Smallwood Keller & Lewis, P.C.; and Zenner Consulting Group, LLC.

LATERAL ASSOCIATES AND PARTNERS: 1/1/03 – 12/31/03	MINORITY MEN	MINORITY WOMEN	WHITE WOMEN	TOTAL
Number of lateral associate hires	9	9	13	77
Number of lateral partner hires*	0	0	2	13
Number of new partners promoted from associate rank*	3	5	6	53

* Kirkland & Ellis does not distinguish between equity and non-equity partners.

Retention & Professional Development

ATTORNEYS WHO LEFT THE FIRM: 2003	MINORITY MEN	MINORITY WOMEN	WHITE WOMEN	TOTAL
Number of attorneys who voluntarily or involuntarily left your firm's employ in 2003	11	8	23	99

How do 2003 attrition rates generally compare to those experienced in the prior year period?

Lower than in prior years

Please identify the specific steps you are taking to reduce the attrition rate of minority and women attorneys.

• Develop and/or support internal employee affinity groups (e.g., minority or women networks within the firm)

• Increase/review compensation relative to competition

• Increase/improve current work/life programs

• Succession plan includes emphasis on diversity

• Introduce minority and women attorneys to key clients, including to lead engagements

• Review work assignments and hours billed to key client matters to make sure minority and women attorneys are not being excluded

• Strengthen mentoring program for all attorneys, including minorities and women

• Professional skills development program, including minority and women attorneys

Does your firm have part-time/flex-time policies that permit attorneys (male or female) to work alternative schedules?

Yes. Kirkland recognizes that an individual lawyer may determine that personal concerns make it desirable to request an alternative work schedule arrangement. Kirkland expects that lawyers can and will remain committed professionals while working a reduced schedule and believes that such a schedule should not suspend opportunities for professional growth, experience and career advancement. Kirkland makes reasonable efforts to accommodate such requests as appropriate to the particular circumstances of the individual situations. To work effectively, the alternative work schedule must be fair to both the lawyer working a reduced schedule and the other lawyers in the office and consistent with the best interests of the firm and the needs of its clients. Non-share partners and associates are eligible to request an alternative work schedule. Kirkland appoints a partner in each office as an advisor to work with lawyers seeking approval of an alternative work schedule. Such partner or advisor will assist in preparation of alternative schedule requests and may ask other lawyers to cooperate and participate in making the alternative work schedule program successful. Upon approval of a lawyer's reduced-hours plan, the advisor shall be responsible for working with and obtaining the cooperation of others in carrying out the plan.

What impact, if any, will the decision to work part-time have on an attorney's ability to make partner or, if already a partner, to remain a partner at your firm?

As referenced above, Kirkland & Ellis has a longstanding and flexible policy on alternative work schedules, which recognizes individual needs. We have a two-tier partnership and part-time attorneys may be and have been elected to the first tier of partnership, non-share partner. However, non-share partners on alternative work schedule status will not typically be eligible for election to the share partnership.

Have any attorneys who chose to work a part-time schedule made partner at your firm?

Yes, 15 attorneys.

Management Demographic Profile (as of 12/31/03)

	MINORITY MEN	MINORITY WOMEN	WHITE WOMEN	TOTAL
Number of attorneys on the Executive/Management Committee or equivalent	0	0	1	15
Number of attorneys on the Hiring Committee or equivalent	14	12	46	118
Number of attorneys on the Partner/Associate Review Committee or equivalent	4	0	10	93

The Firm Says

Diversity is an increasing focus of all areas of the firm. The formalization of diversity as an issue of prime import to Kirkland is reflected in terms of the firm's commitment of time, budget and resources. Kirkland's commitment to diversity is reinforced by the work performed by Kirkland's firm-wide Diversity Committee. The Diversity Committee's focus is the recruitment, retention and advancement of attorneys in a manner that promotes diversity at all levels within the firm. The 31-member committee is co-chaired by Paul Garcia, an intellectual property partner in our Chicago office, and Michael D. Jones, a litigation partner in our Washington, D.C., office. The Diversity Committee also includes four members of Kirkland's Management Committee, each of our office's recruiting chair partners, as well as associates and partners from every office of the firm.

The Diversity Committee budget supports the diverse initiatives Kirkland has created and continues to develop, permitting sponsorship of a broad range of diverse organizations, events and activities. In 2003, the Kirkland & Ellis Foundation contributed in excess of $550,000 to the sponsorship of nonprofit organizations, foundations and initiatives that directly or indirectly benefit diversity-related initiatives. Kirkland's Attorney Development Department works with the Diversity Committee to coordinate its initiatives and to ensure that minority and women lawyers receive training, professional development and challenging opportunities.

At Kirkland's most recent annual partners' meeting, the single longest presentation specifically addressed the hiring, retention and promotion of women and minority attorneys. Two partners in our Chicago office made presentations with respect to these two issues at the behest of Kirkland's Management Committee chairman, Thomas D. Yannucci. Our Diversity Lunch, wherein diverse attorneys meet with Diversity Committee members as well as other committee members and partners, provides an opportunity for Kirkland to solicit and draw upon the inspiration, thoughts and varied experiences of our diverse lawyers in our attempt to enhance diversity in the workplace.

From 1997 – 2004, Kirkland sponsored 16 minority scholarships at Northwestern University School of Law and the University of Chicago Law School. Through these scholarships the firm provided $304,000 in minority awards. This Fall 2004, Kirkland created the Kirkland & Ellis LLP Minority Fellowship at eleven law schools across the country. This program will award a $15,000 stipend and a summer associate position in one of our law firm's domestic offices after the student has completed his/her second year of law school. Finalists who do

not receive a Fellowship may receive an offer to join our summer associate program. The underlying goal of this Fellowship is to facilitate an increase of minority lawyers within the Firm, and more broadly, the practice of law.

The Chicago Lawyer 2004 and 2003 Diversity Survey ranked Kirkland & Ellis first in number of minority lawyers. In 2001, the firm received the prestigious Thomas L. Sager Award from the Minority Corporate Counsel Association. The Sager Award is presented to law firms that have demonstrated a sustained commitment to improve the hiring, retention and promotion of minority attorneys.

Kirkland has provided financial support to the following organizations: Mexican American Legal Defense & Educational Fund, Puerto Rican Legal Defense & Education Fund, Asian Pacific American Legal Center and the Asian Pacific American Bar Association Education Fund.

Kirkland lawyers are members of minority bar associations across the country, including, but not limited to the Armenian Bar Association, Asian American Bar Association, Black Women Lawyers' Association of Greater Chicago, Black Women Lawyers' Association of Los Angeles, California Minority Law Association, Hispanic Lawyers' Association of Illinois, Hispanic National Bar Association, Indian American Bar Association, John M. Langston Bar Association of Los Angeles, Korean American Bar Association, National Bar Association, National Lesbian and Gay Law Association, Puerto Rican Bar Association, Southern California Chinese Law Association and Women Lawyers' Association of Los Angeles.

Kirkland & Ellis complies with all applicable local, state and federal civil rights laws prohibiting discrimination in employment. All employment decisions, including the recruiting, hiring, placement, training, promotion, compensation, evaluation, discipline and termination of employees (if necessary) are made without regard to the employee's race, color, creed, religion, sex, pregnancy or childbirth, personal appearance, family responsibilities, sexual orientation or preference, political affiliation, source of income, place of residence, national or ethnic origin, ancestry, age, marital status, veteran status, unfavorable discharge from military service, or on the basis of physical or mental disability which is unrelated to the individual's ability to perform essential functions of a particular job or position, or is unrelated to the individual's qualifications for employment, or on any other basis prohibited by applicable law.

Kirkland's policy prohibiting sexual harassment applies to every employee and partner of Kirkland & Ellis LLP. Excerpts of our policy are provided here. The firm prohibits verbal or physical conduct of a sexual nature where such conduct has the purpose or effect of unreasonably (1) interfering with an individual's work performance or (2) creating an intimidating, hostile or offensive work environment. The firm also prohibits harassment not overtly sexual in nature but improperly directed at, or commenting on attributes or characteristics of, a person solely because of, or on the basis of, his or her sex. The firm prohibits retaliation against a person who refuses or objects to unwelcome verbal or physical conduct of a sexual nature, who reports any of the above conduct or who cooperates in the firm's investigation of a complaint of sexual harassment. Repeated comments or conduct of a sexual nature, or repeated instances of harassment not sexual in nature but directed at a person solely because of, or on the basis of, his or her sex, made after a request to stop such behavior and which have the purpose or effect of interfering unreasonably with an employee's work or work environment generally will be found to be in violation of the firm's policy. Finally, Kirkland will not countenance sexual harassment of Kirkland & Ellis employees and partners by third parties and will deal with sexual harassment by third parties in accordance with our policy and guidelines.

Kirkpatrick & Lockhart LLP

Henry W. Oliver Building
535 Smithfield Street
Pittsburgh, PA 15222
Phone: (412) 355-6500
Fax: (412) 355-6501

FIRM LEADERSHIP

Managing Partner: Peter J. Kalis, Chair,
Management Committee
Diversity Team Leader: Carl G. Cooper, Chief
Diversity Officer

LOCATIONS

Boston, MA
Dallas, TX
Harrisburg, PA
Los Angeles, CA
Miami, FL
Newark, NJ
New York, NY
Pittsburgh, PA
San Francisco, CA
Washington, DC

Note: Kirkpatrick & Lockhart LLP does not include Middle Eastern individuals as minorities, as defined by this survey. The EEOC defines Middle Eastern individuals within the "White" race/ethnic category, and K&L adheres to the EEOC's definitions for purposes of race/ethnic self-identification and record keeping.

LAW FIRM DEMOGRAPHIC PROFILES

FULL-TIME ASSOCIATES*	2003	2002
Minority men	22	21
Minority women	43	44
White women	141	134
Total	395	390

* Includes Counsel

SUMMER ASSOCIATES	2003	2002
Minority men	7	3
Minority women	15	3
White women	23	21
Total	71	53

EQUITY PARTNERS	2003	2002
Minority men	3	2
Minority women	0	1
White women	19	16
Total	200	203

NON-EQUITY PARTNERS*	2003	2002
Minority men	3	3
Minority women	2	0
White women	17	17
Total	128	88

* Includes Of Counsel

NEW HIRES	2003	2002
Minority men	6	6
Minority women	9	8
White women	37	30
Total	111	94

Note: In the charts above, the numbers exclude Retired Partners

Strategic Plan and Diversity Leadership

How does the firm's leadership communicate the importance of diversity to everyone at the firm? (e.g., e-mails, web site, newsletters, meetings, etc.)

K&L uses the following methods to communicate the importance of diversity: e-mail communications from our Management Committee and Chief Diversity Officer (CDO), quarterly Diversity Committee newsletters, weekly firm bulletins, internal and external web site postings, firmwide videoconferences with our CDO and Diversity Committee, local office visits from our CDO with all levels of firm employees, and first year and summer associate orientation programming.

Who has primary responsibility for leading diversity initiatives at your firm?

Carl G. Cooper, Chief Diversity Officer

Does your law firm currently have a diversity committee?

Yes

Does the committee's representation include one or more members of the firm's management/executive committee (or the equivalent)?

Yes

How many attorneys are on the committee, and in 2003, what was the total number of hours collectively spent by the committee in furtherance of the firm's diversity initiatives?

Total attorneys on committee: 11

Total hours spent on diversity: 3,856.15 This number does not include hours spent by certain non-attorney members of the Diversity Committee and administrative, recruitment and marketing staff who support the needs and initiatives of the Diversity Committee.

Does the committee and/or diversity leader establish and set goals or objectives consistent with management's priorities?

Yes

Has the firm undertaken a formal or informal diversity program or set of initiatives aimed at increasing the diversity of the firm?

Yes, formal

How often does the firm's management review the firm's diversity progress/results?

Monthly

How is the firm's diversity committee and/or firm management held accountable for achieving results?

The firm's CDO must report monthly to the firm's Management Committee on all diversity initiatives, development and progress. In addition, each office's Administrative Partner reports monthly to the Management Committee on the office's diversity statistics.

LAW FIRM DIVERSITY INITIATIVES	ALREADY COMPLETED	CURRENTLY ADDRESSING	NOT A CURRENT PRIORITY
Undertake communication from firm management that diversity is a top priority of the firm.	✔ *		
Formalize diversity plan and committee with action steps and accountability to management.	✔ *		
Conduct firm-wide diversity training for all attorneys and staff.	✔ *		
Increase the number of minority attorneys at the associate level.		✔	
Increase the number of minority attorneys at the partnership level.		✔	
Develop/expand relationships with minority bar associations to offer firm's support of these networks.		✔	
Focus on strengthening firm's mentoring program, including for benefit of minority attorneys.	✔ *		
Conduct internal diversity needs assessment and/or retain diversity consultant to examine how firm culture might be more welcoming of minorities.		✔	
Support law firm's internal affinity networks (e.g., women, minority attorney networks).	✔ *		
Manage/monitor allocation of work assignments and/or hours billed to ensure women and minority attorneys have equal access/inclusion on top client matters.		✔	
Establish regular firm-wide meetings with all minority attorneys to raise issues and highlight developments.	✔ *		

* K&L provides continued commitment, analysis and development to these priorities.

Recruitment – New Associates

Does your firm annually recruit at any of the following types of institutions? (Check all that apply and list the schools).

Ivy League schools: Columbia University, Cornell University, Harvard University, University of Pennsylvania, Yale University

Public state schools: Dickinson School of Law (Pennsylvania State University), Ohio State University, Rutgers University, State University of New York (SUNY) at Buffalo, University of California-Berkeley (Boalt Hall), University of California-Davis, University of California-Hastings, University of California-Los Angeles (UCLA), University of Florida, University of Iowa, University of Michigan, University of Minnesota, University of Pittsburgh, University of Texas, University of Virginia, West Virginia University, College of William & Mary (Marshall-Wythe School of Law)

Private schools: American University, Boston College, Boston University, Case School of Law, Catholic University of America, Duke University, Duquesne University, Fordham University, George Washington University, Georgetown University, Loyola Law School, New York University, Northeastern University, Northwestern University, Pace University, Seton Hall University, Stanford University, Suffolk University,

Syracuse University, Tulane University, University of Chicago, University of Miami, University of Notre Dame, University of San Francisco, University of Southern California, University of Tulsa, Vanderbilt University, Wake Forest University, Washington & Lee University, Widener University

Historically Black Colleges and Universities (HBCUs): Howard University, Texas Southern University (Thurgood Marshall School of Law)

Do you have any special outreach efforts directed to encourage minority law students to consider your firm?

• *The firm's CDO meets with law school deans to discuss expressly the firm's recruitment of minority law students. The firm sponsors the James M. Nabrit Lecture Series at Howard University School of Law, which this year was in commemoration of the 50th Anniversary of the Supreme Court decision* Brown v. Board of Education.

• Hold a reception for minority law students

• Advertise in minority law student association publication(s)

• Participate in/host minority law student job fair(s)

• Sponsor minority law student association events

• Firm's lawyers participate on career panels at school

• Outreach to leadership of minority student organizations

• Scholarships or intern/fellowships for minority students

SUMMER ASSOCIATE STATISTICS: SUMMER 2003	MINORITY MEN	MINORITY WOMEN	WHITE WOMEN	TOTAL
Summer associates	4	11	21	58
Summer associates who received an offer of full-time employment	2	10	17	50
Summer associates who accepted an offer of full-time employment	2	10	16	46

Recruitment – Lateral Associates and Partners

What activities does the firm undertake to attract minority and women attorneys?

• *The firm partners with corporate clients on diversity issues, including hosting and moderating the first General Counsel Roundtable Discussion on Diversity for* Corporate Legal Times. *Our CDO has written and is currently writing articles on issues of diversity for publication in legal journals in order to resonate the firm's commitment to diversity in all arenas.*

• Partner programs with women and minority bar associations

• Participate at minority job fairs

• Seek referrals from other attorneys

• Utilize online job services (e.g., MCCA/DuPont Primary Law Firm Job Bank)

Do you use executive recruiting/search firms to seek to identify new diversity hires (partners or associates)?

Yes

List all women- and/or minority-owned executive search/recruiting firms to which the firm paid a fee for placement services in the past 12 months:

Berman International, Inc., Ridgefield, CT; Gardiner Simpson, New York, NY; MBD Search LLC, Dallas, TX; North Berman & Beebe Ltd., Washington, DC; Oxford Legal Associates, Inc., Fort Washington, PA; Preferred Placement, New York, NY

LATERAL ASSOCIATES AND PARTNERS: 1/1/03 – 12/31/03	MINORITY MEN	MINORITY WOMEN	WHITE WOMEN	TOTAL
Number of lateral associate hires	3	7	17	38
Number of lateral partner hires (equity and non-equity)*	1	1	3	27
Number of new partners (equity and non-equity) promoted from associate rank	0	0	1	12
Number of new equity partners	1	0	3	17

* Includes only Equity Partners and Income Partners.

Retention & Professional Development

ATTORNEYS WHO LEFT THE FIRM: 2003	MINORITY MEN	MINORITY WOMEN	WHITE WOMEN	TOTAL
Number of attorneys who voluntarily or involuntarily left your firm's employ in 2003	3	9	25	65

How do 2003 attrition rates generally compare to those experienced in the prior year period?

About the same as in prior years

Please identify the specific steps you are taking to reduce the attrition rate of minority and women attorneys.

• *The firm partnered with PPG, Inc. to create the K&L/PPG Diversity Fellowship for a selected minority associate to work closely with PPG's legal team to strengthen the attorney's skills, to promote diversity and to build the relationship between the firm and its client.*

• Develop and/or support internal employee affinity groups (e.g., minority or women networks within the firm)

• Increase/review compensation relative to competition

• Increase/improve current work/life programs

• Succession plan includes emphasis on diversity

• Work with minority and women attorneys to develop career advancement plans

• Introduce minority and women attorneys to key clients, including to lead engagements

• Review work assignments and hours billed to key client matters to make sure minority and women attorneys are not being excluded

• Strengthen mentoring program for all attorneys, including minorities and women

• Professional skills development program, including minority and women attorneys

Does your firm have part-time/flex-time policies that permit attorneys (male or female) to work alternative schedules?

Yes

What impact, if any, will the decision to work part-time have on an attorney's ability to make partner or, if already a partner, to remain a partner at your firm?

No fixed relationship exists between the duration of part-time status and the timing of an associate's consideration for partnership. As with all lawyers, one who has worked or is working on a part-time schedule will be considered for partnership when the firm believes his/her experience and development make consideration appropriate. Likewise, consistent with the interests of the firm and its clients, the firm is flexible in its review of the proposed periods of time for part-time status as a partner.

Have any attorneys who chose to work a part-time schedule made partner at your firm?

Yes, seven attorneys. The firm has not maintained detailed historical records on this issue; this number reflects those individuals we can confirm at this time.

Management Demographic Profile (as of 12/31/03)

	MINORITY MEN	MINORITY WOMEN	WHITE WOMEN	TOTAL
Number of attorneys on the Executive/Management Committee or equivalent	2	0	2	19
Number of attorneys on the Hiring Committee or equivalent	7	7	20	73
Number of attorneys on the Partner/Associate Review Committee or equivalent*	3/2	1/0	20/15	65/66

All attorneys/Partners only

Please provide information regarding all minority and women attorneys who head offices or practice groups of your law firm:

Minorities heading offices: Paul W. Sweeney Jr., Los Angeles

Minorities heading practice groups: Bonnie Berry LaMon, Entertainment – Coordinator; C. Dirk Peterson, Broker-Dealer – Co-Coordinator; Jerome Walker, Bank Regulatory & Compliance – Coordinator

Women heading practice groups: Diane Ambler, Anti-Money Laundering – Coordinator; Bonnie Berry LaMon, Entertainment – Coordinator; Christine Ethridge, Intellectual Property – Co-Coordinator; Eileen Smith Ewing, Life Sciences – Coordinator; Janice Hartman, Corporate – Co-Coordinator; Mergers & Acquisitions – Coordinator; Securities – Co-Coordinator; Rebecca Laird, Financial Institutions – Co-Coordinator; Cary Meer, Derivatives, Structured Products and Futures – Coordinator; Hedge Funds and Venture Funds – Co-Coordinator; Susan Mussman, Nonprofit Organizations – Coordinator; Suzan Onel, Food, Drug, Medical Device and Cosmetic – Co-Coordinator

The Firm Says

In the late 1990s, recognizing the critical importance of promoting, achieving and maintaining a diverse and open workforce, K&L conducted an intensive self-evaluation in all aspects of diversity, including diversity sensitivity training for its employees. As a result, K&L established a firm-wide Diversity Committee, which continues to this day. The committee is comprised of at least one representative from each of K&L's 10 offices and is chaired by a partner who is also a member of the firm's Management Committee.

To further its diversity initiatives, in February 2003 K&L entered into a new era with the appointment of Carl G. Cooper as the firm's, indeed the legal community's, first Chief Diversity Officer (CDO). Importantly, the CDO reports directly to the chair of the Management Committee, and he acts with the assurance and commitment from the entire Management Committee. With the innovation of the CDO, diversity is now "top of mind" on every decision that the Management Committee makes. The CDO has undertaken the diversity initiative with help of a diversity project manager and an administrative assistant.

Both the CDO and the Diversity Committee focus on three major objectives with respect to attorneys: (i) expanding recruiting activities; (ii) enhancing retention of minority and female attorneys; and (iii) building relationships and promoting the law firm's diversity initiatives among minority constituencies as well as in the wider community-at-large.

Recruitment

K&L participates in minority job fairs, including BLSA, Boston Lawyers Group Job Fair/Students of Color, DuPont Minority Job Fair, Lavender Law Career Fair and The Southeastern Minority Job Fair, and intensely recruits highly qualified minority candidates during on-campus interviews at targeted law schools around the country, such as Howard University School of Law and Texas Southern University's Thurgood Marshall School of Law.

In a momentous event, K&L made a substantial commitment to be the sole sponsor of the James M. Nabrit Lecture Series at Howard University School of Law. This year, the series commemorated the Supreme Court's decision in *Brown v. Board of Education*, with the collaboration of Howard Law faculty, the NAACP Legal and Educational Defense Fund, and the NAACP. The program featured Professor Charles Ogletree of Harvard Law School as the inaugural speaker for the series and included an informal "Conversation with the Supreme Court," with Justice Stephen Breyer. It truly was a proud day in the history of the firm.

As a result of these initiatives and commitments, the total number of minority and women lawyers at K&L has been increasing steadily. In addition, during the last round of partner elections, which took effect on March 1, 2004, eight of the sixteen newly elected partners are women, including one minority woman. K&L has made it a strategic priority that these numbers continue to increase at all levels within all offices.

Retention

In the first year, K&L's CDO has endeavored to open and maintain direct lines of communication with all groups within K&L to ensure that the interests and perspectives of all K&L attorneys and employees are considered in firm decisions. In collaboration with other departments at K&L, the diversity team has created a Diversity Newsletter, which is both for internal and external purposes. Monthly Diversity Committee conference calls, diversity e-mail groups and semiannual large-scale meetings keep attorneys informed about the CDO's endeavors and diversity-related items.

As another significant development to increase attorney retention, K&L's CDO and Chief Officer for Recruitment and Development designed and launched together a firmwide mentoring initiative, with an additional focus on diversity issues. All lawyers were invited to half-day mentoring training sessions led by nationally recognized consultants in the field. In order to ensure the effective implementation of the mentoring program, K&L designated attorney mentor coordinators and hired additional administrative staff. Most recently, continuing innovative leadership in law firm management, the firm appointed a Director of Professional and Personal Life Integration to lead the firm in further developing a corporate culture and policies that promote and sustain a healthy integration of professional and personal responsibilities.

Since the CDO has taken office, minority and women attorneys have become increasingly engaged at K&L. They have taken on leadership roles that currently include service on the Management Committee and senior practice leadership positions.

Relationships

Additionally, K&L has partnered with like-minded corporate clients on the diversity front. On July 24, 2003, K&L's New York office hosted and our CDO moderated the first General Counsel Roundtable discussion on Diversity for Corporate Legal Times. The "Dream Team" of general counsel included Jim Diggs of PPG; Stacey Mobley of DuPont; Ken Frazier of Merck; Rick Palmore of Sara Lee; Don Liu of IKON; and Michele Coleman Mayes of Pitney Bowes. From this partnering, the CDO and general counsel of PPG, Inc., Jim Diggs, have instituted a position known as the K&L/PPG Diversity Fellowship. The Fellowship consists of a carefully chosen K&L minority associate working closely with PPG's legal team in the general commercial and corporate area, in order to promote diversity and the relationship between the firm and the corporation.

Moreover, minority and women attorneys at K&L have taken on leadership roles in community organizations whose missions embrace diversity goals; in bar and other professional organizations with diversity and gender agendas; and through participation in recruitment and networking aimed at minorities and women attorneys. The CDO also instituted an initiative for each office to develop or sponsor an outreach program in its respective community.

In the July/August 2003 issue of the Minority Corporate Counsel Association's publication Diversity & The Bar, K&L was featured in an article entitled "Above the Cut: Law Firms Raise the Bar." The article identified four law firms in the United States, including K&L, which "are stepping outside the norm, displaying an

unprecedented level of commitment and new strategies for achieving diversity." K&L was recognized as the first major law firm to appoint a Management Committee-level Chief Diversity Officer – an officer who participates on the same plane in firm management as the Chief Financial Officer and whose sole purpose is to promote, achieve and maintain a diverse work force, firmwide and firm deep. By having a full-time CDO, K&L has developed the prototype of an officer devoted solely to the promotion and fulfillment of making true diversity, in all aspects of the word, a living reality. Needless to say, K&L is very proud to have been recognized for this achievement.

Latham & Watkins

Founding Office:
633 West Fifth Street
Suite 4000
Los Angeles, CA 90071-2007
Phone: (213) 485-1234
Fax: (213) 891-8763
www.lw.com

FIRM LEADERSHIP

Managing Partner: Robert Dell
Diversity Team Leader: Mark Newell, Chair of
the Diversity Committee

OFFICE LOCATIONS

Boston, MA
Chicago, IL
Costa Mesa, CA
Los Angeles, CA
Menlo Park, CA
Newark, NJ
New York, NY
Reston, VA
San Diego, CA
San Francisco, CA
Washington, DC
Brussels
Frankfurt
Hamburg
Hong Kong
London
Milan
Moscow
Paris
Rome
Singapore
Tokyo

LAW FIRM DEMOGRAPHIC PROFILES

FULL-TIME ASSOCIATES	2003	2002
Minority men	71	78
Minority women	93	96
White women	258	264
Total	826	875

SUMMER ASSOCIATES	2003	2002
Minority men	19	11
Minority women	26	24
White women	48	50
Total	144	138

PARTNERS*	2003	2002
Minority men	13	9
Minority women	6	6
White women	58	51
Total	396	377

* For the purposes of this survey, we will not distinguish equity from non-equity.

NEW HIRES	2003	2002
Minority men	12	19
Minority women	23	26
White women	53	59
Total	154	202

MINORITY CORPORATE COUNSEL ASSOCIATION

Strategic Plan and Diversity Leadership

How does the firm's leadership communicate the importance of diversity to everyone at the firm? (e.g., e-mails, web site, newsletters, meetings, etc.):

Latham & Watkins discusses the firm's commitment to diversity in virtually every setting in which the firm operates. This includes discussions within the firm's Executive Committee and with its Chairs Group, which consists of all the principal leaders of the firm, including the office managing partners, global department chairs and major committee heads. We also regularly communicate to the firm our commitment to equal opportunity. In addition, we formed a Diversity Committee comprised of representatives of the firm's principal committees to reinforce our commitment to diversity and monitor our progress toward goals and objectives, which have been communicated in a firm-wide memorandum. In each of our offices, our attorneys, paralegals, managers and staff meet on a regular basis to discuss, among other things, concerns that arise in the workplace. The frequency and types of such meetings vary from office to office. Typically, attorneys meet once a month and office managers meet two to three times a month. In addition, at the firm's annual meeting for new partners, we devote a session to the firm's diversity commitment.

Who has primary responsibility for leading diversity initiatives at your firm?:

Mark Newell, the firm's chief operating partner and a member of the Executive Committee, is also the chair of the firm's Diversity Committee. The members of the Diversity Committee are: Michael Bond (Private Equity Strategy Committee, London), Sharon Bowen (Recruiting Committee, New York), Kim Marie Boylan (Associates Committee, Washington, D.C.), Bruce Howard (Training & Career Enhancement Committee, Orange County), Mimi Krumholz (Director of Global Human Resources, Northern Virginia), Belinda Lee (Los Angeles), Juli Wilson Marshall (Marketing Strategy Committee, Chicago), Thomas Pfister (EEO Review Board, Los Angeles), John Shyer (EEO Review Board and Paralegal Coordinator Committee, New York), Karen Silverman (Income Partner and Counsel Review Committee, San Francisco) and John Tang (Associates Committee, Silicon Valley).

Does your law firm currently have a diversity committee?

Yes

Does the committee's representation include one or more members of the firm's management/executive committee (or the equivalent)?

Yes

How many attorneys are on the committee, and in 2003, what was the total number of hours collectively spent by the committee in furtherance of the firm's diversity initiatives?

Total attorneys on committee: 11

Total hours spent on diversity: We only recently established a separate mechanism for recording the number of hours collectively spent by the committee members; however, since diversity is a focus of all our committees and our diversity efforts are integral to the business of the firm, overall time spent in this area is not recorded separately.

Does the committee and/or diversity leader establish and set goals or objectives consistent with management's priorities?

Yes. The Diversity Committee meets regularly to review the firm's progress on diversity initiatives and to establish goals and objectives.

Has the firm undertaken a formal or informal diversity program or set of initiatives aimed at increasing the diversity of the firm?

Yes, formal

How often does the firm's management review the firm's diversity progress/results?

Monthly

How is the firm's diversity committee and/or firm management held accountable for achieving results?

Latham's Executive Committee, which serves as the firm's top-level management, is actively involved in directing and monitoring diversity activities through its chief operating partner's role as chair of the Diversity Committee. In this capacity, the chair regularly communicates with the various relevant managers to discuss diversity-related issues, initiatives and progress. In addition, the Executive Committee regularly solicits each partner's feedback with respect to such partner's diversity efforts. This feedback is sought in the year-end Partnership Self-Assessment Questionnaire.

LAW FIRM DIVERSITY INITIATIVES*	ALREADY COMPLETED	CURRENTLY ADDRESSING	NOT A CURRENT PRIORITY
Undertake communication from firm management that diversity is a top priority of the firm.	✔		
Formalize diversity plan and committee with action steps and accountability to management.	✔		
Conduct firm-wide diversity training for all attorneys and staff.	✔		
Increase the number of minority attorneys at the associate level.		✔	
Increase the number of minority attorneys at the partnership level.		✔	
Develop/expand relationships with minority bar associations to offer firm's support of these networks.	✔		
Focus on strengthening firm's mentoring program, including for benefit of minority attorneys.		✔	
Conduct internal diversity needs assessment and/or retain diversity consultant to examine how firm culture might be more welcoming of minorities.		✔	
Support law firm's internal affinity networks (e.g., women, minority attorney networks).	✔		
Manage/monitor allocation of work assignments and/or hours billed to ensure women and minority attorneys have equal access/inclusion on top client matters.	✔		

In connection with the above, we note that even those items marked as "completed" are ongoing within the firm, and we regularly focus on how to improve our diversity program, including monitoring our progress with respect to our objectives. Further, in order to promote diversity within the firm, the firm committee chairs seek nominations from a variety of sources and make appointments to include women and minority attorneys. In addition, the firm panels and presentations include women and minority presenters and instructors. In order to avoid ambiguity with respect to the firm's part-time policy, the firm committed the policy to writing and has its implementation overseen by the Associates Committee or Executive Committee, as the case may be.

SUMMER ASSOCIATE STATISTICS: SUMMER 2003	MINORITY MEN	MINORITY WOMEN	WHITE WOMEN	TOTAL
Summer associates	12	22	47	128
Summer associates who received an offer of full-time employment	10	20	47	123
Summer associates who accepted an offer of full-time employment	8	16	44	109

Recruitment- New Associates

Does your firm annually recruit at any of the following types of institutions?

Ivy League schools: Columbia University, Cornell University, Harvard University, University of Pennsylvania, Yale University

Public state schools: University of Alabama, University of Arizona, Arizona State University, University of California-Boalt Hall, University of Colorado, University of California-Davis, University of Florida, George Mason University, University of Georgia, University of California-Hastings, University of Illinois, University of Indiana, University of Iowa, University of Kansas, University of Maryland, University of Miami, University of Michigan, University of Minnesota, University of Missouri-Columbia, University of North Carolina, Ohio State University, University of Oregon, Penn State University, Rutgers University-Camden, Rutgers University-Newark, University of Tennessee, University of Texas, University of Toronto, UCLA, University of Utah, University of Virginia, University of Washington, College of William & Mary, University of Wisconsin

Private schools: American University, Baylor University, Boston College, Boston University, Brooklyn Law School, BYU, Cardozo Law School, Case Western Reserve University, Catholic University of America, University of Chicago, University of Cincinnati, Duke University, Emory University, Fordham University, George Washington University, Georgetown University, Loyola Law School, McGeorge School of Law, New York Law School, Northwestern University, University of Notre Dame, NYU, Pace University, Pepperdine University, Santa Clara University, Seton Hall University, SMU, St. John's University, Stanford University, Syracuse University, Temple University, Tulane University, USC, University of San Diego, University of San Francisco, Vanderbilt University, Villanova University, Wake Forest University, Washington & Lee University, Washington University in St. Louis

Historically Black Colleges and Universities (HBCUs): Howard University

Do you have any special outreach efforts directed to encourage minority law students to consider your firm?

• Hold a reception for minority law students

• Advertise in minority law student association publication(s)

• Participate in/host minority law student job fair(s)

• Sponsor minority law student association events

• Firm's lawyers participate on career panels at school

• Outreach to leadership of minority student organizations

• Scholarships or intern/fellowships for minority students

• Annual Diversity Weekend for minority law student recruits.

LATERAL ASSOCIATES AND PARTNERS: 1/1/03 – 12/31/03	MINORITY MEN	MINORITY WOMEN	WHITE WOMEN	TOTAL
Number of lateral associate hires	1	3	8	34
Number of lateral partner hires (equity and non-equity)	0	0	2	10
Number of new partners (equity and non-equity) promoted from associate rank	4	0	6	21
Number of new equity partners*	N/A	N/A	N/A	N/A

* For the purposes of this survey, we will not distinguish equity from non-equity.

Recruitment- Lateral Associates and Partners

What activities does the firm undertake to attract minority and women attorneys?

• Partner programs with women and minority bar associations

• Participate at minority job fairs

• Seek referrals from other attorneys

• Utilize online job services (e.g., MCCA/DuPont Primary Law Firm Job Bank)

Do you use executive recruiting/search firms to seek to identify new diversity hires (partners or associates)?

Yes

If yes, list all women- and/or minority-owned executive search/recruiting firms to which the firm paid a fee for placement services in the past 12 months:

Greene-Levin-Snyder Legal Search Group, New York, NY; McCormack Schreiber Legal Search Inc., Chicago, IL; Reece Legal Search, Inc., Los Angeles, CA; Russo & Fondell, Beverly Hills, CA; Seltzer Fontaine Beckwith, Los Angeles, CA; Swan Legal Search, Los Angeles, CA.

Retention & Professional Development

Please identify the specific steps you are taking to reduce the attrition rate of minority and women attorneys.

• Develop and/or support internal employee affinity groups (e.g., minority or women networks within the firm)

• Increase/review compensation relative to competition

• Increase/improve current work/life programs

• Adopt dispute resolution process

• Succession plan [process] includes emphasis on diversity

• Work with minority and women attorneys to develop career advancement plans

• Introduce minority and women attorneys to key clients, including to lead engagements

• Review work assignments and hours billed to key client matters to make sure minority and women attorneys are not being excluded

• Strengthen mentoring program for all attorneys, including minorities and women

• Professional skills development program, including minority and women attorneys

The Associates Committee has met with a diversity consultant as part of an ongoing effort to be proactive with respect to diversity at the firm. In addition, the Associates Committee oversees the assigning of work to all junior associates, in order to ensure an equitable distribution of assignments. The firm also holds a diversity weekend for law student recruits and the Diversity Committee meets regularly and advises other committees throughout the firm.

Does your firm have part-time/flex-time policies that permit attorneys (male or female) to work alternative schedules?

Yes. The firm invites all attorneys to participate in the flexible schedule program.

What impact, if any, will the decision to work part-time have on an attorney's ability to make partner or, if already a partner, to remain a partner at your firm?

Depending upon the aggregate amount of time an associate has worked part-time, an associate may fall back one class year or may maintain his or her class rank. Associates have made partner working part-time on an extended part-time basis, including the year in which they became partners. With respect to partners, any part-time arrangement is highly individualized and is worked out between the particular partner and the Executive Committee. However, this does not affect a partner's ability to remain a partner at the firm.

Have any attorneys who chose to work a part-time schedule made partner at your firm?

Yes, eleven attorneys

Management Demographic Profile (as of 12/31/03)

	MINORITY MEN	MINORITY WOMEN	WHITE WOMEN	TOTAL
Number of attorneys on the Executive/Management Committee or equivalent	0	0	1	8
Number of attorneys on the Hiring Committee or equivalent	3	7	10	39
Number of attorneys on the Partner/Associate Review Committee or equivalent	2	1	10	52

Please provide information regarding all minority and women attorneys who head offices or practice groups of your law firm:

Women heading offices: Ora Fisher, Silicon Valley (as of 2004); Anya Goldin, Moscow; Virginia Grogan, Orange County; Martha Jordan, Los Angeles.

Minorities heading practice groups: Marcelo Halpern, Corporate/Technology Transactions; Jiyeon Lee-Lim, Tax/ International Tax

Women heading practice groups: Vicki Marmorstein, Global Department Chair, Finance & Real Estate; Julia Hatcher, Environment, Land & Resources/Air Quality; Maureen Mahoney, Litigation/Appellate; Robin Struve, Tax/Benefits & Compensation; Carolyne Hathaway, Corporate/Chemical & Pesticide Regulation; Katherine Lauer, Litigation/Health Care & Life Sciences; Juli Wilson Marshall, Litigation/Intellectual Property & Technology; Ursula Hyman, Tax/Public & Tax-Exempt Finance; Jiyeon Lee-Lim, Tax/International Tax; Oonagh Whitty, Tax/International Tax; Lucinda Starrett, Environment, Land & Resources/Air Quality; Kimberly Wilkinson, Corporate/Public Company Representation; Laurie Smilan, Litigation/Securities Litigation & Professional Liability; Laura DeFelice, Finance & Real Estate/Structured Finance; Catherine Palmer, Vice Global Department Chair, Litigation Department/White Collar & Corporate Compliance; Beth Wilkinson, Litigation/White Collar & Corporate Compliance.

The Firm Says

Our commitment to diversity is not just a philosophy. It's something we work at and try to achieve at every turn. In the most recent *Vault Guide to the Top 100 Law Firms*, a Latham associate said Latham "welcomes a more diverse population." A female associate at Latham recalled, "One big reason I chose Latham was the number and high profile of women partners." And a gay Latham associate added, "People judge you here by your work and commitment, not by your private life." In addition, Latham ranked fourth for the highest number of Asian American attorneys in the *Minority Law Journal*'s 2004 Diversity Scorecard.

We have continued our efforts by forming a Diversity Committee with representatives from the Recruiting, Associates, Marketing, Executive and Training Committees, among others, and our internal EEO Board, which provides an additional forum for addressing any discrimination or harassment issues.

Management

Attorneys of diverse racial, ethnic backgrounds and sexual orientation have long been represented on the firm's management committees responsible for promotions to partnership, recruiting and training, among other responsibilities. One of our African American partners, who previously served on our Executive Committee, currently chairs our Associates Committee. The managing partners in the Moscow, Orange County and Silicon Valley offices are women, as are the department chair of the firm's global finance and real estate department, the vice chair of the global litigation department, the chair of the Global Recruiting Committee, two local corporate department chairs, one local tax department chair, 12 practice group chairs/co-chairs firm-wide and the firm's top non-lawyer executive.

Recruiting

Our goal is to increase the diversity of our attorneys at all levels through improved recruitment and retention of lawyers of diverse backgrounds. Our efforts at minority recruitment and hiring include sponsorship of and participation in events designed to introduce the firm to minority recruits and vice versa. For example, Latham sponsored the ABA's first National Conference for Minority Lawyers. We also have a Diversity Subcommittee of our Global Recruiting Committee devoted to minority recruiting, as well as a Recruiting Committee member on the Diversity Committee.

Training

Latham continuously reviews its hiring, evaluation and compensation practices to ensure that all of our lawyers and staff have an equal and ample opportunity to achieve excellence in the practice of law. Our Training and Career Enhancement (TACE) Committee develops and implements comprehensive training and education programs in all practice areas at each stage of an associate's career, with a focus on interactive training. Our TACE Committee also regularly includes presentations on the firm's equal opportunity policies and obligations, including an extensive session at the First Year Academy.

Mentoring

Latham has traditionally been a firm of close working relationships among its partners, associates and staff. As our firm has grown, we have been sensitive to the importance of preserving opportunities for our associates to form mentoring relationships with senior lawyers. Mentoring programs in a number of our offices help associates of all backgrounds understand the inner workings of the firm and the resources and opportunities available to them.

Professional and civic participation

We represented the University of Michigan Law School in its closely watched affirmative action case which was argued before the U.S. Supreme Court by one of our women partners who chairs our appellate practice group.

We participate in initiatives of bar associations to promote minority attorney hiring and advancement. We are a charter signatory to the Los Angeles County Bar Association's Statement of Goals and Principles on Minority Hiring, Retention and Promotion; the Bar Association of San Francisco's Glass Ceiling Initiative; and the New York City Bar's Statement of Goals of New York Law Firms and Corporate Legal Departments for Increasing Minority Hiring, Retention and Promotion. We serve on the Executive Committee of the California Minority Counsel Program.

Our minority attorneys work as community leaders. A Latham associate initiated a voting rights program that resulted in her and the firm being honored by the National Coalition on Black Civic Participation. Another Latham associate was awarded the Ally of Justice Award by the National Human Rights Campaign for his work in creating and launching a project on behalf of gay and lesbian Americans to review federal and state law providing benefits and responsibilities for individuals and their domestic partners. In addition, a Latham partner serves as secretary to the Washington, D.C., National Bar Association.

Pro bono/community service

We have committed substantial resources, both through formal pro bono activities and the efforts of our individual attorneys, to assist our local communities and their residents. These efforts have resulted in widespread recognition, including a pro bono award by *The National Law Journal*, a profile on ABC's "World News Tonight" and in *The New York Times*, and a sixth-place spot in *The American Lawyer*'s 2003 pro bono rankings. Most recently, Latham received the American Bar Association's Pro Bono Publico Award, perhaps the most prestigious pro bono award in the United States.

Pro bono matters are treated the same as other work, with the same high standards applied and the same billable hour credit given to attorneys. In 2003, about 78 percent of the firm's U.S. attorneys represented pro bono clients in all areas of the law, from complex litigation on behalf of detained children to sophisticated transactions for legal services agencies. Our international offices are quickly building impressive pro bono programs as well, appropriate to their local legal cultures, from work in legal services clinics in Paris to counseling refugee organizations in Hamburg.

LeBoeuf, Lamb, Greene & MacRae, L.L.P

125 West 55th Street
New York, NY 10019
Phone: (212) 424-8000
Fax: (212) 424-8500

FIRM LEADERSHIP

Managing Partner: Steven Davis, Chairman of
the Firm
Diversity Team Leader: Brian Betancourt,
Director of Diversity

OFFICE LOCATIONS

New York, NY (HQ)
Albany, NY
Boston, MA
Harrisburg, PA
Hartford, CT
Houston, TX
Jacksonville, FL
Los Angeles, CA
Newark, NJ
Pittsburgh, PA
Salt Lake City, UT
San Francisco, CA
Washington, DC
Almaty; Beijing
Brussels
Bishkek
Johannesburg
London
Moscow
Paris
Riyadh

LAW FIRM DEMOGRAPHIC PROFILES

FULL-TIME ASSOCIATES	2003	2002
Minority men	32	29
Minority women	40	34
White women	140	132
Total	332	350

SUMMER ASSOCIATES	2003	2002
Minority men	6	6
Minority women	8	10
White women	22	15
Total	56	51

EQUITY PARTNERS	2003	2002
Minority men	6	6
Minority women	3	3
White women	23	27
Total	167	198

NEW HIRES	2003	2002
Minority men	6	14
Minority women	7	12
White women	17	26
Total	62	76

Strategic Plan and Diversity Leadership

How does the firm's leadership communicate the importance of diversity to everyone at the firm? (e.g., e-mails, web site, newsletters, meetings, etc.)

The firm utilizes a number of ways to communicate the importance of diversity to everyone at the firm including (1) diversity training; (2) e-mails from the managing partners, director of diversity and executive director; (3) diversity survey for all associates; (4) naming the director of diversity to the firm's Practice Leadership Committee. In addition, a panel of in-house counsel relating to the issues of diversity was the main event at the 2003 Partner's Retreat.

Who has primary responsibility for leading diversity initiatives at your firm?

The responsibilities are shared by Steven Davis, chairman, and Brian Betancourt, director of diversity; Donna Gordon, associate director of diversity; Stephen DiCarmine, executive director; and Diane Costigan, director of legal personnel.

Does your law firm currently have a diversity committee?

Yes

Does the committee's representation include one or more members of the firm's management/executive committee (or the equivalent)?

Yes

How many attorneys are on the committee, and in 2003, what was the total number of hours collectively spent by the committee in furtherance of the firm's diversity initiatives?

Total attorneys on committee: 15

Total hours spent on diversity: Over 2,500 hours

Does the committee and/or diversity leader establish and set goals or objectives consistent with management's priorities?

Yes

Has the firm undertaken a formal or informal diversity program or set of initiatives aimed at increasing the diversity of the firm?

Yes, formal

How often does the firm's management review the firm's diversity progress/results?

Monthly

How is the firm's diversity committee and/or firm management held accountable for achieving results?

The director of diversity is required to give monthly updates to firm management regarding the progress of all diverse associates at the firm. Such reports include hours billed, matters worked on, and so on. In addition, the director of diversity meets regularly with all department heads and office heads to review the progress of diverse associates and to implement ways to make sure the diverse associates are fully engaged and are getting the opportunity to work on major matters.

LAW FIRM DIVERSITY INITIATIVES	ALREADY COMPLETED	CURRENTLY ADDRESSING	NOT A CURRENT PRIORITY
Undertake communication from firm management that diversity is a top priority of the firm.	✓		
Formalize diversity plan and committee with action steps and accountability to management.	✓		
Conduct firm-wide diversity training for all attorneys and staff.	✓		
Increase the number of minority attorneys at the associate level.	✓		
Increase the number of minority attorneys at the partnership level.		✓	
Develop/expand relationships with minority bar associations to offer firm's support of these networks.		✓	
Focus on strengthening firm's mentoring program, including for benefit of minority attorneys.	✓		
Conduct internal diversity needs assessment and/or retain diversity consultant to examine how firm culture might be more welcoming of minorities.	✓		
Support law firm's internal affinity networks (e.g., women, minority attorney networks).		✓	
Manage/monitor allocation of work assignments and/or hours billed to ensure women and minority attorneys have equal access/inclusion on top client matters.	✓		

Recruitment - New Associates

Does your firm annually recruit at any of the following types of institutions?

Ivy League schools: Harvard University, Yale University, Columbia University, Cornell University; University of Pennsylvania

Public state schools: University of California-Boalt Hall, University of California-Hastings, UCLA, University of Connecticut, University of Florida, University of Michigan, Rutgers University-Newark, University of Texas, University of Utah, University of Virginia

Private schools: Boston College, Brigham Young University, Brooklyn Law School, Duke University, Fordham University, Georgetown University, Loyola Law School, New York University, New York Law School, Seton Hall University, Stanford University, University of Chicago, University of Southern California

Historically Black Colleges and Universities (HBCUs): Howard University

Do you have any special outreach efforts directed to encourage minority law students to consider your firm?

• Hold a reception for minority law students

• Advertise in minority law student association publication(s)

• Participate in/host minority law student job fair(s)

• Sponsor minority law student association events

- Firm's lawyers participate on career panels at school
- Outreach to leadership of minority student organizations
- Scholarships or intern/fellowships for minority students

SUMMER ASSOCIATE STATISTICS: SUMMER 2003	MINORITY MEN	MINORITY WOMEN	WHITE WOMEN	TOTAL
Summer associates	6	5	21	48
Summer associates who received an offer of full-time employment	6	5	21	48
Summer associates who accepted an offer of full-time employment	5	5	19	44

Recruitment- Lateral Associates and Partners

What activities does the firm undertake to attract minority and women attorneys?

- Partner programs with women and minority bar associations
- Participate at minority job fairs
- Seek referrals from other attorneys
- Utilize online job services (e.g., MCCA/DuPont Primary Law Firm Job Bank)

Do you use executive recruiting/search firms to seek to identify new diversity hires (partners or associates)?

Yes

List all women- and/or minority-owned executive search/recruiting firms to which the firm paid a fee for placement services in the past 12 months:

Mestel & Company; Vintage Legal; Audrey Golden, Inc.; Seder Associates

LATERAL ASSOCIATES AND PARTNERS: 1/1/03 – 12/31/03	MINORITY MEN	MINORITY WOMEN	WHITE WOMEN	TOTAL
Number of lateral associate hires	2	1	8	23
Number of lateral partner hires (equity and non-equity)	0	0	1	5
Number of new partners (equity and non-equity) promoted from associate rank	0	0	0	2
Number of new equity partners	0	0	1	7

Retention & Professional Development

ATTORNEYS WHO LEFT THE FIRM: 2003	MINORITY MEN	MINORITY WOMEN	WHITE WOMEN	TOTAL
Number of attorneys who voluntarily or involuntarily left your firm's employ in 2003	5	7	55	151

How do 2003 attrition rates generally compare to those experienced in the prior year period?

About the same as in prior years

Please identify the specific steps you are taking to reduce the attrition rate of minority and women attorneys.

- Develop and/or support internal employee affinity groups (e.g., minority or women networks within the firm)
- Increase/improve current work/life programs
- Succession plan includes emphasis on diversity
- Introduce minority and women attorneys to key clients, including to lead engagements
- Review work assignments and hours billed to key client matters to make sure minority and women attorneys are not being excluded
- Strengthen mentoring program for all attorneys, including minorities and women

Does your firm have part-time/flex-time policies that permit attorneys (male or female) to work alternative schedules?

Yes

What impact, if any, will the decision to work part-time have on an attorney's ability to make partner or, if already a partner, to remain a partner at your firm?

May serve to lengthen the partnership track.

Have any attorneys who chose to work a part-time schedule made partner at your firm?

No

Management Demographic Profile (as of 12/31/03)

	MINORITY MEN	MINORITY WOMEN	WHITE WOMEN	TOTAL
Number of attorneys on the Executive/Management Committee or equivalent	0	0	2	11
Number of attorneys on the Hiring Committee or equivalent	0	2	2	9
Number of attorneys on the Partner/Associate Review Committee or equivalent	0	0	5	18

Please provide information regarding all minority and women attorneys who head offices or practice groups of your law firm:

Minorities heading offices: Ingrid Zhu-Clark, Beijing; Andrew Fawbush, Jacksonville; Jude Kearney, Johannesburg; Women heading offices:Ingrid Zhu-Clark, Beijing; Margaret Keane, Pittsburgh; Mary Lopatto, Washington, DC

Women heading practice groups: Jane Boisseau, Insurance; Vivian Polak, Litigation/IP

The Firm Says

In September 1991, LeBoeuf, Lamb, Greene & MacRae, L.L.P. was one of the original 35 signatories to the Statement of Goals of New York Law Firms and Corporate Legal Departments for Minority Representation and Retention prepared by The Association of the Bar of the City of New York (ABCNY). The firm also signed the ABCNY 1998 Restatement of Goals for the Hiring, Retention and Promotion of Attorneys of Color and the Retention and Promotion of Women. In August 2003, the firm renewed its compliance with the Statement of Goals by signing ABCNY's 2003 Statement of Diversity Principles, which includes an updated Statement of Diversity Goals and Diversity Practices for New York Law Firms and Law Departments.

LeBoeuf has established a Diversity Initiatives Group, presently comprising the firm's executive director, the director of legal personnel and professional development, four partners and 11 associates from the New York and regional U.S. offices. The Diversity Initiatives Group meets on a regular basis to review and monitor the firm's overall progress and activities in the area of equal opportunity, with special emphasis on the recruitment, retention and advancement of associates who are racial minorities; disabled; gay, lesbian, bisexual or transgender persons. The firm has also appointed a director of diversity and an associate director of diversity to address concerns and policy issues.

As part of LeBoeuf's commitment to the retention and advancement of diverse associates, the firm has adopted the Diversity Plan set forth below. LeBoeuf has also committed to improving the Diversity Plan by instituting programs that address the Minority Corporate Counsel Association's Top Ten Diversity Recommended Practices, which include development and communication of the business case for diversity, involvement of senior partners in diversity efforts, top-down diversity training, accountability, development of effective mentoring programs, lateral hiring, work-life balance, expanded recruiting, incentives for diversity initiatives and equal treatment programs.

The firm feels that the Statement of Diversity Principles serves as an important reminder to the legal community regarding appropriate hiring, retention and promotion practices. LeBoeuf's actual minority hiring percentages have historically exceeded the minimum percentages required by the Statement of Diversity Principles and the firm fully supports its objectives. Our Equal Opportunity Statement and Policy, which has been in place since December 1987, provides in part:

It is the policy of LeBoeuf, Lamb, Greene & MacRae, L.L.P. to recruit, develop, and advance qualified attorneys without discrimination based upon sex, age, color, national origin, disability, race, religion, sexual orientation, or marital, parental or veteran status, and to take affirmative actions, including, but not limited to, those outlined in the Firm's Diversity Plan.

Diversity Plan

I. Attorney Orientation

The Firm's Equal Opportunity Plan will be stated clearly in all procedural manuals, employee handbooks, recruiting material and in other internal publications. All attorneys will also receive a copy of this Diversity Plan.

II. Recruitment/Professional Outreach Program

The Firm will continue its annual participation in BLSA Minority Law Student Recruiting Job Fairs and Conferences.

The Firm will continue to pursue contacts with law school Placement Directors and minority law student organizations to achieve participation of minority interviewees.

The Firm will continue its participation in Legal Outreach, Inc., a program involving inner-city high school students intended to encourage careers in the law.

The Firm will continue to participate in local and regional bar association diversity recruitment and retention programs, including The Association of the Bar of the City of New York.

The Firm will utilize specialized minority recruiters as a referral source for lateral attorneys.

The Firm will continue to be a participant in and supporter of the Sponsors for Educational Opportunity Corporate Law Career Program.

III. Development and Advancement

The partners in the Diversity Initiatives Group will provide introductory profiles of all diverse associates to the Firm's Steering and Administrative Committees on an annual basis.

The Director of Diversity and the partners in the Diversity Initiatives Group will meet regularly with department heads and office heads of the Firm in order to monitor the progress of diverse associates.

The Director of Diversity will review the evaluations and utilization rates of diverse associates on an ongoing basis in order to ascertain the development of diverse associates.

The Director of Diversity and the Associate Director of Diversity will address special concerns of diverse associates and will liaise with the Firm's administration in order to resolve workplace issues related to diversity.

IV. Role of the Diversity Initiatives Group

To foster implementation of the Firm's diversity goals and policies as outlined in this Diversity Plan.

To continuously seek and develop means and opportunities to further the Firm's diversity goals and policies.

To publicize and emphasize throughout all levels of the Firm, the Firm's commitment to its diversity policies and goals.

To confer with and seek counsel from the diverse associates who are not Diversity Initiatives Group members with respect to diversity concerns.

V. Role of the Associates on the Diversity Initiatives Group

To hold and participate in frequent discussion meetings open to diverse associates firm-wide.

To sponsor events which promote diversity for all LeBoeuf attorneys.

To, on behalf of diverse associates firm-wide, advise the Diversity Initiatives Group regarding issues concerning diverse associates.

To liaise with the Firm's Associates and Recruiting Committees with respect to concerns of diverse associates.

We've seen the future.
And it looks a lot like us.

For well over 200 years, people from all over the world have come to America in search of freedom and a better way of life. The result is a nation that is as diverse as it is vast. While some view America's cultural diversity as an obstacle, we see it as an opportunity for businesses to embrace the future.

We're Littler Mendelson, the nation's largest employment and labor law firm, and we understand the challenges posed by the multicultural workplace. Today, nearly every employer risks miscommunication as it struggles to diversify. At Littler, we've assembled a team of attorneys whose backgrounds and experience are as diverse as the businesses we serve. That's why when the nation's employers need someone to steer them clear of the social and cultural pitfalls that can taint the workplace, they come to us. Every day, we work with employers of all nationalities, sizes and industries, and advise and defend them in every matter of employment and labor law.

To learn more about how we can help ease the future a little closer to you today, visit www.littler.com or call us directly at 1.888.LITTLER.

LITTLER MENDELSON®

THE NATIONAL EMPLOYMENT & LABOR LAW FIRM®
400 ATTORNEYS   28 OFFICES   NATIONWIDE

Littler Mendelson, P.C.

650 California Street, 20th Floor
San Francisco, CA 94108
Phone: (415) 433-1940

FIRM LEADERSHIP

Managing Partner: Wendy Tice-Wallner Title:
President/Managing Shareholder
Diversity Team Leader: Jaffe Dickerson and
Dudley Rochelle, Diversity Council Co-Chairs

OFFICE LOCATIONS

San Francisco, CA (HQ)
Atlanta, GA
Bakersfield, CA
Boston, MA
Charlotte, NC
Chicago, IL
Columbus, OH
Dallas, TX
Denver, CO
Fresno, CA
Houston, TX
Las Vegas, NV
Los Angeles, CA
Miami, FL
Minneapolis, MN
Newark, NJ
New York, NY
Philadelphia, PA
Phoenix, CA
Pittsburgh, PA
Reno, NV
Sacramento, CA
San Diego, CA
San Jose, CA
Santa Maria, CA
Seattle, WA
Stockton, CA
Walnut Creek, CA
Washington, DC

LAW FIRM DEMOGRAPHIC PROFILES

FULL-TIME ASSOCIATES	2003	2002
Minority men	15	15
Minority women	21	17
White women	92	89
Total	200	194

SUMMER ASSOCIATES	2003	2002
Minority men	2	1
Minority women	5	4
White women	9	7
Total	20	21

EQUITY PARTNERS	2003	2002
Minority men	6	5
Minority women	3	2
White women	28	29
Total	133	133

NON-EQUITY PARTNERS	2003	2002
Minority men	5	3
Minority women	3	2
White women	19	13
Total	59	49

NEW HIRES	2003	2002
Minority men	9	5
Minority women	9	3
White women	24	17
Total	68	40

Strategic Plan and Diversity Leadership

How does the firm's leadership communicate the importance of diversity to everyone at the firm? (e.g., e-mails, web site, newsletters, meetings, etc.)

Presentations at annual shareholder meeting, office managing shareholder meetings, board of directors updates, presentation of Diversity Roundtable and white paper on "The Changing Workforce" at Littler's National Employer Conference, web site information, web site update to provide intranet site for attorneys.

Who has primary responsibility for leading diversity initiatives at your firm?

Jaffe Dickerson and Dudley Rochelle, shareholders and members of the board of directors, co-chair the Diversity Council.

Does your law firm currently have a diversity committee?

Yes

Does the committee's representation include one or more members of the firm's management/executive committee (or the equivalent)?

Yes

How many attorneys are on the committee, and in 2003, what was the total number of hours collectively spent by the committee in furtherance of the firm's diversity initiatives?

Total attorneys on committee: 26

Total hours spent on diversity: 2000+

Does the committee and/or diversity leader establish and set goals or objectives consistent with management's priorities?

Yes

Has the firm undertaken a formal or informal diversity program or set of initiatives aimed at increasing the diversity of the firm?

Yes, formal

How often does the firm's management review the firm's diversity progress/results?

Quarterly

How is the firm's diversity committee and/or firm management held accountable for achieving results?

The Diversity Council is overseen by the board of directors, including the managing director and senior officers of the firm, and communicates initiatives and expectations to various management personnel throughout the firm.

LAW FIRM DIVERSITY INITIATIVES	ALREADY COMPLETED	CURRENTLY ADDRESSING	NOT A CURRENT PRIORITY
Undertake communication from firm management that diversity is a top priority of the firm.	✓		
Formalize diversity plan and committee with action steps and accountability to management.	✓		
Conduct firm-wide diversity training for all attorneys and staff.		✓	
Increase the number of minority attorneys at the associate level.	✓	✓	
Increase the number of minority attorneys at the partnership level.	✓	✓	
Develop/expand relationships with minority bar associations to offer firm's support of these networks.	✓	✓	
Focus on strengthening firm's mentoring program, including for benefit of minority attorneys.	✓	✓	
Conduct internal diversity needs assessment and/or retain diversity consultant to examine how firm culture might be more welcoming of minorities.	✓		
Support law firm's internal affinity networks (e.g., women, minority attorney networks).		✓	
Manage/monitor allocation of work assignments and/or hours billed to ensure women and minority attorneys have equal access/inclusion on top client matters.		✓	

Recruitment – New Associates

Does your firm annually recruit at any of the following types of institutions?*

Ivy League schools: Columbia University, Cornell University, Harvard University, University of Pennsylvania

Public state schools: University of Colorado, University of Georgia, Georgia State University, University of California-Hastings, UC Berkeley (Boalt), UC Davis, UCLA, University of Houston, University of Illinois, University of Michigan, University of Minnesota, University of North Carolina, Ohio State University, University of Oregon, University of Pittsburgh, University of Tennessee, University of Texas, USF, Vanderbilt University, Villanova University, University of Virginia, University of Washington, College of William & Mary

Private schools: Baylor University, Boston College, Boston University, University of Chicago, Duke University, Duquesne University, Emory University, Fordham University, George Washington University, Georgetown University, Loyola Law School, Northwestern University, University of Notre Dame, NYU, Santa Clara University, SMU, Stanford University, USC, USF, Vanderbilt University, Villanova University

Historically Black Colleges and Universities (HBCUs): Howard University

* Each year, Littler Mendelson visits over 40 law schools and job fairs to interview second-year law students for summer associate positions and third-year law students for entry-level associate positions. We often send an attorney from one of our offices geographically closest to the law school/job fair to interview candidates on

behalf of all of our firm's offices. This year, Littler Mendelson plans to interview at the law schools and job fairs indicated above.

Do you have any special outreach efforts directed to encourage minority law students to consider your firm?

• Advertise in minority law student association publication(s)

• Participate in/host minority law student job fair(s)

• Sponsor minority law student association events

• Firm's lawyers participate on career panels at school

• Outreach to leadership of minority student organizations

SUMMER ASSOCIATE STATISTICS: SUMMER 2003	MINORITY MEN	MINORITY WOMEN	WHITE WOMEN	TOTAL
Summer associates	1	5	5	19
Summer associates who received an offer of full-time employment	0	3	3	14
Summer associates who accepted an offer of full-time employment	0	1	2	10

Recruitment- Lateral Associates and Partners

What activities does the firm undertake to attract minority and women attorneys?

• Partner programs with women and minority bar associations

• Participate at minority job fairs

• Seek referrals from other attorneys

Do you use executive recruiting/search firms to seek to identify new diversity hires (partners or associates)?

Yes

LATERAL ASSOCIATES AND PARTNERS*: 1/1/03 – 12/31/03	MINORITY MEN	MINORITY WOMEN	WHITE WOMEN	TOTAL
Number of lateral associate hires	5	6	16	40
Number of lateral partner hires (equity and non-equity)	2	3	3	17
Number of new partners (equity and non-equity) promoted from associate rank	0	1	2	12
Number of new equity partners	1	1	2	9

All information of ethnicity and gender is based on voluntary self-identification by our associates and partners.

Retention & Professional Development

ATTORNEYS WHO LEFT THE FIRM: 2003	MINORITY MEN	MINORITY WOMEN	WHITE WOMEN	TOTAL
Number of attorneys who voluntarily or involuntarily left your firm's employ in 2003	6	3	23	65

How do 2003 attrition rates generally compare to those experienced in the prior year period?

About the same as in prior years. The overall attrition rate was about the same as in 2002. However, the total number of minority women who left in 2003 was significantly lower than in 2002.

Please identify the specific steps you are taking to reduce the attrition rate of minority and women attorneys.

• Increase/review compensation relative to competition

• Increase/improve current work/life programs

• Adopt dispute resolution process

• Succession plan includes emphasis on diversity

• Work with minority and women attorneys to develop career advancement plans

• Introduce minority and women attorneys to key clients, including to lead engagements

• Review work assignments and hours billed to key client matters to make sure minority and women attorneys are not being excluded (emerging)

• Strengthen mentoring program for all attorneys, including minorities and women (emerging)

• Professional skills development program, including minority and women attorneys

Does your firm have part-time/flex-time policies that permit attorneys (male or female) to work alternative schedules?

Yes

What impact, if any, will the decision to work part-time have on an attorney's ability to make partner or, if already a partner, to remain a partner at your firm?

A decision to work part-time does not preclude the ability of an associate to make partner, or to remain partner.

Have any attorneys who chose to work a part-time schedule made partner at your firm?

Yes. Firm has not kept accurate data.

Management Demographic Profile (as of 12/31/03)

	MINORITY MEN	MINORITY WOMEN	WHITE WOMEN	TOTAL
Number of attorneys on the Executive/Management Committee or equivalent	2	0	3	19
Number of attorneys on the Hiring Committee or equivalent	0	1	2	5
Number of attorneys on the Partner/Associate Review Committee or equivalent	0	2	7	31

Please provide information regarding all minority and women attorneys who head offices or practice groups of your law firm:

Minorities heading offices: Paul Bateman;

Women heading offices: Shelline Bennet, Lori Brown ,Marilyn Culp, Linda Headley, Kate Wilson

Minorities heading practice groups: N/A

Women heading practice groups: N/A

The Firm Says

Diversity statement

At Littler Mendelson, we recognize the importance of diversity on the long-term success of our firm. We are committed to creating an inclusive, open and respectful culture comprised of individuals from diverse backgrounds each of whom are given a platform for success. We recognize that "diversity" encompasses an infinite range of individual characteristics and experiences, including gender, age, race, national origin, religion, political affiliation, marital status, disability, geographic background, sexual orientation and family relationships. The firm's goal is to create a work environment in which the unique attributes, perspectives, backgrounds, skills and abilities of each individual are valued.

We acknowledge that diversity among our attorneys and staff is beneficial to the firm's morale, productivity and success. We believe diversity fosters a positive and creative environment that attracts talented individuals; encourages our attorneys and staff to maximize their potential; and enhances our ability to respond quickly with innovative solutions to the rapidly changing needs of our clients.

Diversity is not new to Littler Mendelson. We are proud to have assembled a staff of lawyers with diverse and accomplished backgrounds. Diversity remains a critical part of Littler Mendelson's short- and long-term strategic goals. We are committed to all issues affecting diversity, including without limitation, recruiting and hiring attorneys from all walks of life, ensuring that all attorneys have an equal opportunity to prosper in the practice of law, creating a work environment that values the perspectives and varied experience, which are found only in a diverse workplace, and capitalizing on that diversity so that we may provide our clients with a broader, richer environment, which produces more creative thinking and solutions. We believe that promoting diversity is essential to the success of our firm.

As part of Littler Mendelson's ongoing commitment to diversity, we will:

• Enhance our recruiting efforts to promote the hiring of qualified individuals from diverse backgrounds, especially women and persons of color;

• Financially and philosophically support the firm's Diversity Council which is committed to promoting diversity within the firm and encouraging those from diverse backgrounds to network with others in our profession to gain knowledge, develop business and encourage one another;

• Include attorneys from diverse backgrounds in our firm's management, leadership, training and client development opportunities;

• Participate in bar association and community activities that advance diversity in our firm, in the legal profession and in the communities in which we live and work; and

• Commit the time and resources necessary to accomplish these objectives.

• Through our collective and individual efforts, we will capitalize on the strengths emanating from our diversity and foster understanding, communication and respect so that we may provide extraordinary service to our clients and set a standard for other law firms to model.

Locke Liddell & Sapp LLP

2200 Ross Ave., Suite 2200
Dallas, TX 75201
Phone: (214) 740-8000
Fax: (214) 740-8800

FIRM LEADERSHIP

Managing Partner: Bryan Goolsby, Managing Partner
Diversity Team Leader: David Cabrales, Diversity Committee Chairman

OFFICE LOCATIONS

Austin, TX
Dallas, TX
Houston, TX
New Orleans, LA

LAW FIRM DEMOGRAPHIC PROFILES

FULL-TIME ASSOCIATES	2003	2002
Minority men	18	23
Minority women	18	20
White women	46	46
Total	175	185

SUMMER ASSOCIATES	2003	2002
Minority men	6	7
Minority women	6	7
White women	22	29
Total	43	57

EQUITY PARTNERS	2003	2002
Minority men	6	5
Minority women	1	1
White women	29	30
Total	168	179

NON-EQUITY PARTNERS	2003	2002
Minority men	1	1
Minority women	0	0
White women	3	3
Total	28	22

NEW HIRES	2003	2002
Minority men	4	2
Minority women	3	1
White women	10	8
Total	23	17

MCCA
MINORITY CORPORATE COUNSEL ASSOCIATION

Strategic Plan and Diversity Leadership

How does the firm's leadership communicate the importance of diversity to everyone at the firm? (e.g., e-mails, web site, newsletters, meetings, etc.)

The firm has an active Diversity Committee that is designed to assure we actively recruit and retain minority students and attorneys. We communicate regularly with our partners to remind them of the importance of mentoring minority attorneys and also including them in their business development plans.

Who has primary responsibility for leading diversity initiatives at your firm?

David Cabrales, chairman of firm-wide Diversity Committee

Does your law firm currently have a diversity committee?

Yes

Does the committee's representation include one or more members of the firm's management/executive committee (or the equivalent)?

Yes. Management Committee members are ex-officio members of every firm committee.

How many attorneys are on the committee, and in 2003, what was the total number of hours collectively spent by the committee in furtherance of the firm's diversity initiatives?

Total attorneys on committee: 10

Total hours spent on diversity: 500+

Does the committee and/or diversity leader establish and set goals or objectives consistent with management's priorities?

Yes

Has the firm undertaken a formal or informal diversity program or set of initiatives aimed at increasing the diversity of the firm?

Yes, informal

How often does the firm's management review the firm's diversity progress/results?

Varies by initiative item.

How is the firm's diversity committee and/or firm management held accountable for achieving results?

All Diversity Committee recommendations are submitted and approved by the Management Committee; the Management Committee is also empowered to appoint and remove members from the committee.

LAW FIRM DIVERSITY INITIATIVES	ALREADY COMPLETED	CURRENTLY ADDRESSING	NOT A CURRENT PRIORITY
Undertake communication from firm management that diversity is a top priority of the firm.	✓		
Formalize diversity plan and committee with action steps and accountability to management.	✓		
Conduct firm-wide diversity training for all attorneys and staff.		✓	
Increase the number of minority attorneys at the associate level.	✓	✓	
Increase the number of minority attorneys at the partnership level.	✓	✓	
Develop/expand relationships with minority bar associations to offer firm's support of these networks.	✓		
Focus on strengthening firm's mentoring program, including for benefit of minority attorneys.		✓	
Conduct internal diversity needs assessment and/or retain diversity consultant to examine how firm culture might be more welcoming of minorities.			✓
Support law firm's internal affinity networks (e.g., women, minority attorney networks).	✓	✓	
Manage/monitor allocation of work assignments and/or hours billed to ensure women and minority attorneys have equal access/inclusion on top client matters.		✓	
Seeking to determine the extent to which diversity is a priority among firm clients..		✓	

Recruitment – New Associates

Does your firm annually recruit at any of the following types of institutions?

Ivy League schools: Cornell University, Columbia University, Harvard University, Yale University

Public state schools: University of Texas, University of Michigan, University of Virginia, University of Houston, University of North Carolina, College of William & Mary

Private schools: Baylor University, SMU, Duke University, Georgetown University, Vanderbilt University, NYU, Emory University, Washington & Lee University, Washington University

Do you have any special outreach efforts directed to encourage minority law students to consider your firm?

• Hold a reception for minority law students

• Participate in/host minority law student job fair(s)

• Sponsor minority law student association events

• Firm's lawyers participate on career panels at school

• Outreach to leadership of minority student organizations

Locke Liddell & Sapp LLP

SUMMER ASSOCIATE STATISTICS: SUMMER 2003	MINORITY MEN	MINORITY WOMEN	WHITE WOMEN	TOTAL
Summer associates	1	3	16	40
Summer associates who received an offer of full-time employment	1	3	12	32
Summer associates who accepted an offer of full-time employment	0	1	3	11

Recruitment – Lateral Associates and Partners

What activities does the firm undertake to attract minority and women attorneys?

• Partner programs with women and minority bar associations

• Participate at minority job fairs

• Utilize online job services (e.g., MCCA/DuPont Primary Law Firm Job Bank)

Do you use executive recruiting/search firms to seek to identify new diversity hires (partners or associates)?

We do not limit our lateral hiring to minority applicants.

LATERAL ASSOCIATES AND PARTNERS: 1/1/03 – 12/31/03	MINORITY MEN	MINORITY WOMEN	WHITE WOMEN	TOTAL
Number of lateral associate hires	N/A	N/A	N/A	N/A
Number of lateral partner hires (equity and non-equity)	N/A	N/A	N/A	N/A
Number of new partners (equity and non-equity) promoted from associate rank	N/A	N/A	N/A	N/A
Number of new equity partners	N/A	N/A	N/A	N/A

Note: Data on Lateral Associates and Partners is "Not Available"

Retention & Professional Development

ATTORNEYS WHO LEFT THE FIRM: 2003	MINORITY MEN	MINORITY WOMEN	WHITE WOMEN	TOTAL
Number of attorneys who voluntarily or involuntarily left your firm's employ in 2003	6	5	15	49

How do 2003 attrition rates generally compare to those experienced in the prior year period?

About the same as in prior years

Please identify the specific steps you are taking to reduce the attrition rate of minority and women attorneys.

• Develop and/or support internal employee affinity groups (e.g., minority or women networks within the firm)

• Increase/review compensation relative to competition

• Work with minority and women attorneys to develop career advancement plans

• Introduce minority and women attorneys to key clients, including to lead engagements

• Strengthen mentoring program for all attorneys, including minorities and women

• Professional skills development program, including minority and women attorneys

Does your firm have part-time/flex-time policies that permit attorneys (male or female) to work alternative schedules?

Yes. On occasion, some attorneys will work part-time or reduced hours. Requests are submitted through the section head and upon their approval then submitted to the Management Committee; each request is considered individually and the decision on how to implement the request is based on individual circumstance.

What impact, if any, will the decision to work part-time have on an attorney's ability to make partner or, if already a partner, to remain a partner at your firm?

The factors considered for making partner are numerous and complex. Thus it is difficult to assess the impact of any one factor.

Have any attorneys who chose to work a part-time schedule made partner at your firm?

Yes, they are eligible.

Management Demographic Profile (as of 12/31/03)

	MINORITY MEN	MINORITY WOMEN	WHITE WOMEN	TOTAL
Number of attorneys on the Executive/Management Committee or equivalent	0	0	1	7
Number of attorneys on the Hiring Committee or equivalent*	3	1	14	45
Number of attorneys on the Partner/Associate Review Committee or equivalent	0	0	4	10

Each office has its own Employment Committee that reports to the Management Committee.

Please provide information regarding all minority and women attorneys who head offices or practice groups of your law firm:

Women heading practice groups: Jerry Clements, Litigation; Stephanie Donaho, Chair, Firm Recruiting Committee; Jennifer Jackson-Spencer, Chair, Firm Paralegal Committee

The Firm Says

Achieving diversity in hiring, retaining and promoting women and minority attorneys at Locke Liddell & Sapp is a key component of our client service, not just a "numbers game." We recruit new lawyers and make lateral hires of women and minority individuals who do outstanding legal work and manage client relationships. We give minority and women associates important tasks and provide them every opportunity to advance to partnership.

Our focus on diversity is working. Our minority hiring percentage for 2003 increased to 27 percent (from approximately 18 percent in 2002). In 2003, minorities accounted for approximately 11 percent, and women accounted for approximately 26 percent, of our attorney population. The December 2003 Texas Lawyer Legal Almanac notes that our firm has the second-highest percentage of minority associates in Texas. And in 2004 the LLS Austin office was named the most diverse office in the city, according to the 2004 Hispanic Bar Association of Austin and Austin Black Lawyers Association's Annual Minority Report.

Some of our historical and current efforts are highlighted below:

- In 1997, we formed a Diversity Committee whose sole focus is the hiring, advancement and retention of minority and women attorneys. Today, the committee is co-chaired by a minority partner and a woman partner.

- In 1998, the firm established the Rod Sands Diversity Scholarship at the University of Texas School of Law to provide financial aid to minority and economically disadvantaged students in honor of our deceased friend and partner, Rod Sands.

- In 1999, Locke Liddell received an award from the Hispanic Bar Association of Houston in connection with the Bar's issuance of its five-year report regarding the Statement of Goals. Locke Liddell exceeded the Statement's goal of obtaining a 10 percent minority hiring level over those five years by achieving a 13 percent hiring level during that period.

- In 2001, our firm was one of the few major Houston firms to participate in the Diversity Focus Groups sponsored by MCCA and used to produce MCCA's report on law firm diversity best practices. In 2002 and 2003, we participated as a Diamond Level sponsor of the MCCA Diversity Dinner.

- In 2003, the Austin Black Lawyers Association and the Hispanic Bar Association of Austin awarded our firm with an "A" or "Excellent" grade for the third consecutive year on its Annual Minority Report Card. Grades are awarded to the 25 largest law firms in Austin based on a variety of factors, including number of minority attorneys in the firm, number of minority summer law clerks hired and additional efforts made to increase/promote diversity within the firm. Our Austin office, with 19.4 percent minority attorneys, is currently the second most diverse legal office in Austin.

- In 2002 and 2003, the firm was a member of the Dallas Consortium for Minority Hiring. Each year Consortium members recruit at minority recruiting events throughout the U.S., including the Southeast Minority Job Fair and the Northeast Minority Job Fair. We also conduct on-campus interviews at the Sunbelt Minority Job Fair. Through the Dallas Consortium for Minority Hiring, we currently co-sponsor a $2,500 scholarship for a minority candidate completing his/her first year of law school.

- Flyers are sent to minority student organizations at law schools across the country, introducing the firm and encouraging students to drop their resumes with us in connection with on-campus interviews.

- In 2003, the firm's Houston office initiated a mentorship program available to all associates to focus on developing business. The mentoring partners are encouraged to ensure that diversity concerns are addressed. The firm's Diversity Committee is using the Houston program as a model in rolling out mentoring programs in the firm's other offices. The Dallas office participates in the Dallas Independent School District's "adopt a school" program and provides tutors/mentors to the primarily Hispanic Medrano Elementary School. In addition, an Hispanic associate in our Austin office chairs the Hispanic Bar Association's Elementary School Minority Outreach Program and personally mentors/tutors Hispanic law students at the University of Texas at Austin.

- The firm has participated in the Houston Bar Association's Subcommittee on Minority Opportunities program for five years. We provide a summer clerkship for a law student who would not otherwise have the opportunity to clerk at our firm. We also participate in the Dallas Bar Association/Dallas Public Summer Law Intern Program and the Belo Corporation's Paul Quinn College legal intern program.

- For the ninth year, our firm hosted an event in Houston for our female clients and attorneys providing a networking opportunity specifically for women.

- Locke Liddell was one of the few AmLaw 100 firms in the nation to have a woman serve as its leader. Harriet Miers led our firm as co-managing partner until 2001; she now serves as deputy chief of staff to President Bush. We are also pleased to have a woman, Jerry Clements, serve on the firm's Management Committee and as head of litigation. Stephanie Donaho is the hiring partner for the firm.

- During 2003, the firm successfully recruited two African American attorneys as partners. Bill Jones, former general counsel for Texas Governor Rick Perry, joined our firm as a partner in the Austin office, and Brian Q. Carmichael joined as a partner in Houston. Raul Gonzalez joined our firm in 1999 after serving as justice of the Texas Supreme Court and Roland Garcia joined our firm as a partner in 1996. Roland has served as president of both the Houston Bar Association and the Association for the Advancement of Mexican Americans.

- Diversity is valued as an important component of Locke Liddell's client service. We promote the use of diverse client service teams, recognizing the importance of respecting and mirroring the diversity of our clients' work forces.

DIVERSITY NEEDS CHAMPIONS

We've seen the results

Our focus on diversity is helping us attract the best legal
talent and deliver the highest quality services to clients.
Our recent successes are gratifying, but our work is
far from over—because the more diverse we
become, the better we are as a law firm.

www.lordbissell.com

LORD BISSELL ⧩ BROOK LLP

BUSINESS NEEDS CHAMPIONS

Lord, Bissell & Brook LLP

115 S. LaSalle Street
Chicago, IL 60603
Phone: (312) 443-0700
Fax: (312) 443-0336

FIRM LEADERSHIP

Managing Partner: Dan Schlessinger, Partner
Diversity Team Leader: Peg Anderson, Partner
and Janet Love, Partner, Co-Chairs

LOCATIONS

Chicago, IL (HQ)
Atlanta, GA
Los Angeles, CA
New York, NY

LAW FIRM DEMOGRAPHIC PROFILES

FULL-TIME ASSOCIATES	2003	2002
Minority men	14	9
Minority women	18	17
White women	37	44
Total	138	139

SUMMER ASSOCIATES	2003	2002
Minority men	1	2
Minority women	3	6
White women	8	2
Total	24	21

EQUITY PARTNERS	2003	2002
Minority men	1	1
Minority women	4	4
White women	12	12
Total	121	127

NON-EQUITY PARTNERS	2003	2002
Minority men	1	1
Minority women	0	0
White women	10	8
Total	33	32

NEW HIRES	2003	2002
Minority men	6	4
Minority women	6	7
White women	4	15
Total	46	42

MINORITY CORPORATE COUNSEL ASSOCIATION

Strategic Plan and Diversity Leadership

How does the firm's leadership communicate the importance of diversity to everyone at the firm? (e.g., e-mails, web site, newsletters, meetings, etc.)

Our web site contains our Diversity Statement, adopted by our Executive Committee:

We believe that diversity is essential to our business as a law firm. A diverse work force strengthens our firm by helping us attract the best legal talent and deliver the highest quality legal services to our clients. We have a strong commitment to attracting, retaining and promoting attorneys of all backgrounds and have made this commitment part of our strategic business plan. We actively promote diversity in our recruiting activities and through our emphasis on the mentoring and training of all of our attorneys.

At our partnership retreat in June of 2002 we conducted a diversity panel consisting of one general counsel and one senior inside counsel from two of our large corporate clients and our diversity consultant. The panel presented the business case for diversity and engaged our partners in active dialogue concerning diversity issues. We also held diversity training for all attorneys in the firm in October of 2002 stressing the business case for diversity, the importance of mentoring and various mentoring techniques.

Our minority associates meet regularly with our diversity consultant to discuss any issues or matters of importance to them, and these issues are brought to the Diversity Committee. This process has resulted in a presentation to our partners of issues that concern our minority attorneys.

We also focus on expanding attendance at various diversity events. For example, we filled three tables with partners, associates and guests at the Minority Corporate Counsel Association's Midwest dinner in Chicago last March.

We celebrate Martin Luther King Day by giving our entire Chicago office the option to give a day of community service rather than a day at the office. In 2003, the first year of our celebration, approximately 80 people participated, and in 2004 over 100 people participated in this event, including partners, associates and staff. The event starts with a breakfast at which we ask speakers to come in to talk to us about King Day. This has been a very effective way to communicate our commitment to diversity as well as to promote closer relationships among our attorneys and staff. On King Day, our partners work side-by-side with associates and staff cleaning, painting, sorting clothes, serving meals in soup kitchens, visiting schools for the underprivileged and any number of other tasks. This event instantly became a widely-anticipated firm tradition and has been a huge success in promoting camaraderie and goodwill within the firm. We look forward to our third annual event in January 2005.

Who has primary responsibility for leading diversity initiatives at your firm?

Janet Love and Peg Anderson, partners and co-chairs of the Diversity Committee; Dan Schlessinger, managing partner

Does your law firm currently have a diversity committee?

Yes

Does the committee's representation include one or more members of the firm's management/executive committee (or the equivalent)?

No. The Diversity Committee includes two members of the Compensation Committee and the chair of the Hiring Committee. The chair of the Legal Personnel Committee and the personnel partner are ex officio members.

How many attorneys are on the committee, and in 2003, what was the total number of hours collectively spent by the committee in furtherance of the firm's diversity initiatives?

Total attorneys on committee: 14

Total hours spent on diversity: 827 (committee only); 1,010 (all attorneys)

Does the committee and/or diversity leader establish and set goals or objectives consistent with management's priorities?

Yes. Our Diversity Committee is in the process of preparing a Strategic Plan for Diversity which we anticipate will be presented to our Executive Committee for formal adoption. The Plan sets general policies and goals that cover diversity events and activities as well as policies for addressing attorney evaluation and long-term advancement, mentoring, recruiting, communicating and other diversity-driven matters, as well as an action list. As we proceed through the drafting stage, we are asking for input from our minority associates and communicating with them so that the Plan will be sure to address their concerns. We have begun to implement many of the processes and procedures from the Plan as we incorporate them into the Plan document.

Has the firm undertaken a formal or informal diversity program or set of initiatives aimed at increasing the diversity of the firm?

Yes, formal and informal

Formal: Our formal diversity program will be reflected in our Strategic Plan for Diversity discussed above. In addition, our Hiring Committee has adopted initiatives aimed at increasing the number of minority candidates considered for summer associate positions with the goal of increasing our diversity hiring. Our general practice is to limit the number of students that we call back for office interviews from each law school campus. We place no limits on the number of minority candidates that can be called back. In addition, we interview at minority job fairs. When making hiring decisions we also consider a candidate's diverse background as being one of many important characteristics to consider.

Informal: We have made changes to the questions that partners must answer when preparing their year-end self-evaluation memos in order to stress the importance of mentoring and reaching out to associates. We have also made changes to our associate year-end evaluation forms in order to highlight the importance of mentoring and to structure the associates' annual reports of their work in a way that is responsive to associates' comments and concerns. We are also sponsoring regular culturally diverse social events for our attorneys and/or staff to stress the importance of diversity in our firm culture. In addition, as we work with our Legal Personnel Committee to overhaul our mentoring program for associates, we are in the process of adopting in the short term a more informal mentoring panel of various partners willing to serve as mentors to minorities.

How often does the firm's management review the firm's diversity progress/results?

Our Diversity Committee and managing partner monitor our minority hiring as a percentage of our summer program and of our incoming first-year associate class, our total number of minorities by office and rank, and

our general progress at promoting diversity in the firm. This is done with regularity, though informally. Our Diversity Committee also monitors the effectiveness of our diversity efforts through the feedback that we receive from our minority associates in connection with their regular minority associate meetings.

How is the firm's diversity committee and/or firm management held accountable for achieving results?

Whether we have achieved our desired results is a factor that our Compensation Committee considers in determining the compensation of the co-chairs of our Diversity Committee and, to a lesser extent, the other partner members of the Diversity Committee.

LAW FIRM DIVERSITY INITIATIVES	ALREADY COMPLETED	CURRENTLY ADDRESSING	NOT A CURRENT PRIORITY
Undertake communication from firm management that diversity is a top priority of the firm.	✔		
Formalize diversity plan and committee with action steps and accountability to management.		✔	
Conduct firm-wide diversity training for all attorneys and staff.	✔		
Increase the number of minority attorneys at the associate level.		✔	
Increase the number of minority attorneys at the partnership level.		✔	
Develop/expand relationships with minority bar associations to offer firm's support of these networks.		✔	
Focus on strengthening firm's mentoring program, including for benefit of minority attorneys.		✔	
Conduct internal diversity needs assessment and/or retain diversity consultant to examine how firm culture might be more welcoming of minorities.	✔		
Support law firm's internal affinity networks (e.g., women, minority attorney networks).		✔	
Manage/monitor allocation of work assignments and/or hours billed to ensure women and minority attorneys have equal access/inclusion on top client matters.		✔	

Recruitment – New Associates

Does your firm annually recruit at any of the following types of institutions?

Ivy League Schools: Cornell University*, Harvard University, University of Pennsylvania*

Public State Schools: Georgia State University, University of California – Los Angeles, University of Florida, University of Georgia, University of Illinois, University of Iowa, University of Michigan, University of Minnesota*, University of North Carolina*, College of William and Mary*, University of Wisconsin

Private Schools: Georgetown University*, DePaul University, Duke University, Emory University, Fordham University, George Washington University, Loyola Law School (Los Angeles), Northwestern University, University of Chicago, University of Notre Dame, University of Southern California, Washington University at St. Louis, New York University*

Minority Job Fairs: Chicago Cook County Minority Job Fair, Southeastern Minority Job Fair

Denotes interviewing at job fairs.

Do you have any special outreach efforts directed to encourage minority law students to consider your firm?

• Hold a reception for minority law students

• Advertise in minority law student association publication(s)

• Participate in/host minority law student job fair(s)

• Sponsor minority law student association events

• Firm's lawyers participate on career panels at school

• Outreach to leadership of minority student organizations

SUMMER ASSOCIATE STATISTICS: SUMMER 2003	MINORITY MEN	MINORITY WOMEN	WHITE WOMEN	TOTAL
Summer associates	1	3	8	24
Summer associates who received an offer of full-time employment	1	3	8	22
Summer associates who accepted an offer of full-time employment	1	2	5	14

Recruitment – Lateral Associates and Partners

What activities does the firm undertake to attract minority and women attorneys?

• Partner programs with women and minority bar associations

• Participate at minority job fairs

• Seek referrals from other attorneys

• Utilize online job services (e.g., MCCA/DuPont Primary Law Firm Job Bank)

Do you use executive recruiting/search firms to seek to identify new diversity hires (partners or associates)?

Yes

List all women- and/or minority-owned executive search/recruiting firms to which the firm paid a fee for placement services in the past 12 months:

We use The Alexander Group to identify diversity hires, but it is not a woman- and/or minority owned firm.

LATERAL ASSOCIATES AND PARTNERS: 1/1/03 – 12/31/03	MINORITY MEN	MINORITY WOMEN	WHITE WOMEN	TOTAL
Number of lateral associate hires	5	1	2	19
Number of lateral partner hires (equity and non-equity)	0	0	0	5
Number of new partners (equity and non-equity) promoted from associate rank	0	0	0	5
Number of new equity partners	0	0	1	3

Retention & Professional Development

ATTORNEYS WHO LEFT THE FIRM: 2003	MINORITY MEN	MINORITY WOMEN	WHITE WOMEN	TOTAL
Number of attorneys who voluntarily or involuntarily left your firm's employ in 2003	2	5	13	49

How do 2003 attrition rates generally compare to those experienced in the prior year period?

About the same as in prior years

Please identify the specific steps you are taking to reduce the attrition rate of minority and women attorneys.

• Develop and/or support internal employee affinity groups (e.g., minority or women networks within the firm)

• Increase/review compensation relative to competition

• Increase/improve current work/life programs

• Work with minority and women attorneys to develop career advancement plans

• Introduce minority and women attorneys to key clients, including to lead engagements

• Review work assignments and hours billed to key client matters to make sure minority and women attorneys are not being excluded

• Strengthen mentoring program for all attorneys, including minorities and women

• Professional skills development program, including minority and women attorneys

Does your firm have part-time/flex-time policies that permit attorneys (male or female) to work alternative schedules?

Yes. Our firm has a Policy on Alternate Work Arrangements that has been cited as a significant benefit and a successful program by attorneys who have used it. Under this policy, numerous associates and income partners have arranged part-time work schedules, lasting for periods from six months to several years. In addition, we believe that our FMLA leave policy for attorneys is more advantageous than at most large law firms, allowing 12 weeks with pay and the ability to add vacation and holidays to the 12-week leave. In addition, our annual performance and compensation review system annualizes maternity and family medical leaves for purposes of calculating annual billable hours.

What impact, if any, will the decision to work part-time have on an attorney's ability to make partner or, if already a partner, to remain a partner at your firm?

Our attorneys are evaluated for purposes of advancement to partnership on the basis of many factors, including the attorney's experience, skills, performance and value to their practice area and the firm. An attorney on an alternate work arrangement need not return to full-time status in order to be considered for partnership. Being on an alternate work arrangement could adversely affect an attorney's readiness for partnership status for several reasons, including decreased profitability and slower professional development. The effect of any alternate work arrangement on progression to partnership will, as with all decisions regarding partnership progression, remain in the discretion of the firm.

Have any attorneys who chose to work a part-time schedule made partner at your firm?

Yes, two attorneys. In addition, two partners went on alternative work schedules after becoming partners.

Management Demographic Profile (as of 12/31/03)

	MINORITY MEN	MINORITY WOMEN	WHITE WOMEN	TOTAL
Number of attorneys on the Executive/Management Committee or equivalent	0	0	0*	7
Number of attorneys on the Hiring Committee or equivalent	0	1	5	17
Number of attorneys on the Partner/Associate Review Committee or equivalent	0	2	5	15

A female equity partner was elected to the Management Committee effective June 1, 2004.

Please provide information regarding all minority and women attorneys who head offices or practice groups of your law firm:

Minorities heading offices: An African American female partner was named partner-in-charge of the Atlanta office effective June 2004.

Women heading offices: An African American female partner was named partner-in-charge of the Atlanta office effective June 2004.

Women heading practice groups: Canella Woyar, Wealth Preservation and Estate Planning

Minorities heading practice groups: An Asian male partner is the head of our Media & Entertainment practice group.

The Firm Says

Our Diversity Committee ("DC") is charged with focusing on the recruiting, retention and promotion of minority attorneys. The chair of our Hiring Committee is on the Diversity Committee, and one of the co-chairs of the Diversity Committee is on the Hiring Committee. The DC is comprised of nine equity partners (two of whom are on the Compensation Committee and one of whom is the partner-in-Charge of our Atlanta office), two income partners, one of counsel and three associates. Our DC meetings are regularly attended by the chair of our Professional Personnel Committee and our personnel partner (who is in charge of all non-equity partner

personnel matters in the firm). The DC meets regularly, usually shortly after the regular quarterly meeting of our minority associates. Our outside diversity consultant attends all DC meetings.

We sponsor regular quarterly meetings for our minority associates as well as regular off-site informal gatherings. The informal gatherings engender camaraderie and provide opportunities to raise issues of common concern. The quarterly meetings are facilitated by our outside diversity consultant and are not attended by partners unless requested by the minority associates. This structure allows our associates to raise concerns and issues anonymously. Any issues are brought by our consultant to the Diversity Committee.

For the last several years, the firm has made a conscious effort to reach out to minorities in its recruiting program for summer associates. We have interviewed students at various minority student venues and actively provide sponsorship of events organized by minority law student organizations and attend minority student job-related events at law schools. The percentage of minority law students in the firm's summer program has been 20 percent, 22 percent, 33 percent, 15 percent and 43 percent in the summers of 2000, 2001, 2002, 2003 and 2004, respectively. The percentage of minorities entering the firm as first-year associates has increased markedly as well, resulting in 18 percent, 23 percent, 35 percent, 37 percent and 18 percent minority first year associates in the fall of the years 2000 through 2004, respectively. We presently have six minority partners, one minority of counsel and 28 minority associates.

We recognize that making the firm environment comfortable and inclusive is essential. In May 2001, we hired diversity consultants, Springborg & Associates, to conduct mentor/diversity training for all attorneys who had a role in either mentoring or being a "sibling" to a summer associate, as well as several senior partners, including our managing partner. That training was uniformly well received. In October of 2002, we engaged The Athens Group, headed by Dr. Arin Reeves, to conduct diversity awareness and mentor training for the entire firm. This training focused on mentoring skills and diversity awareness for partners, and for associates emphasized practical skills aimed at helping associates understand how to get the mentoring they need.

We have also focused on achieving "partner buy-in" to our diversity efforts. At our Partners' Retreat in June 2002, we conducted a diversity panel discussion. The written evaluations from the partners indicated that many partners wanted to know how they could help in the diversity effort and how the firm might go about improving its retention of minority attorneys.

Our diversity efforts reach beyond our office to our community. In January 2003 we held our first annual celebration of King Day as described above. This event became an instant success that the firm wholeheartedly embraced, and has quickly become a widely anticipated firm tradition. In addition to the firm-sponsored community activities, the firm encourages its attorneys to become involved in minority organizations. Lord, Bissell & Brook provides funds for membership fees, seminar attendance and event sponsorships.

We also promote initiatives that focus on opportunities for our women attorneys. We have a Women's Initiative Group that focuses on professional development and advancement of our women attorneys. We also have a Women in Insurance Group, an active group of women attorneys who work together to promote business among women in the insurance industry. In addition, a woman sits on our Executive Committee, the partner-in-charge of our Atlanta office is an African American woman and one of the co-chairs of the Diversity Committee is an Asian woman. There are three women on the Compensation Committee; six women on the Hiring Committee, six women on the Legal Personnel Committee and six women on the Diversity Committee, which is chaired by two women.

Our associates have formed an Associates Committee. Its main focus is to provide a forum for issues of interest and concern to associates and to facilitate communication between and among associates and partners. The committee meets monthly and holds at least one annual meeting for all associates. This committee provides a forum in which associates can raise any topic, including gender- and diversity-related issues or concerns. The Diversity Committee has a representative on the Associates Committee who regularly attends the Associate Committee meetings as the DC liaison.

In September 2002 our Los Angeles office won the Thomas L. Sager Award, presented by the Minority Corporate Counsel Association. We are proud of our diversity progress but we know the importance of continuing our efforts because we already see how diversity efforts impress and attract more and more qualified candidates for attorney positions.

DIVERSITY COMMITTED HERE.

Exhibit A	**Rankings:** • First among New Jersey's largest law firms with the greatest number of minority partners. • Second among New Jersey's largest law firms with the greatest number of women and minority associates.
Exhibit B	**Leadership:** • First major law firm in New Jersey to appoint an African American to Chair its 110 attorney Litigation Department. • Women and minorities appointed to key leadership positions in firm management and are members of various committees such as the executive, strategic planning, diversity, recruiting and ethics.
Exhibit C	**Recruiting:** • Regular participation in minority job fairs across the country. • Partnership with legal recruiters who specialize in placing diverse candidates. • Sponsorship and participation in the Rutgers Minority Summer Program where each year the Firm hires at least one first year minority student as a summer law clerk.
Closing Argument	**Visit our Diversity Mission Statement at:** http://www.lowenstein.com/recruiting/diversitystatement.html

Lowenstein Sandler

65 Livingston Avenue
Roseland, NJ 07068
Phone: (973) 597-2500
Fax: (973) 597-2400

FIRM LEADERSHIP

Managing Partner: Michael L. Rodburg,
Director/Managing Partner
Diversity Team Leader: Lynda A. Bennett,
Director/Chair of Diversity Initiatives
Committee

OFFICE LOCATIONS

Roseland, NJ (HQ)
New York, NY
Somerville, NJ

LAW FIRM DEMOGRAPHIC PROFILES

FULL-TIME ASSOCIATES	2003	2002
Minority men	6	5
Minority women	10	9
White women	52	48
Total	157	123

SUMMER ASSOCIATES	2003	2002
Minority men	1	2
Minority women	2	1
White women	5	4
Total	15	13

EQUITY PARTNERS	2003	2002
Minority men	2	2
Minority women	1	1
White women	5	4
Total	60	58

NON-EQUITY PARTNERS	2003	2002
Minority men	0	0
Minority women	0	0
White women	0	0
Total	6	4

NEW HIRES	2003	2002
Minority men	2	0
Minority women	2	2
White women	13	13
Total	52	28

MINORITY CORPORATE COUNSEL ASSOCIATION

Strategic Plan and Diversity Leadership

How does the firm's leadership communicate the importance of diversity to everyone at the firm? (e.g., e-mails, web site, newsletters, meetings, etc.)

The firm uses a variety of methods, including posting a diversity mission statement on our web site; encouraging participation in minority bar associations, MCCA and other diversity-focused organizations; encouraging participation in law school outreach activities sponsored by minority student organizations; and including the Diversity Initiatives Committee within the firm's management structure.

Who has primary responsibility for leading diversity initiatives at your firm?

Lynda A. Bennett, Director/Chair of Diversity Initiatives Committee

Does your law firm currently have a diversity committee?

Yes

Does the committee's representation include one or more members of the firm's management/executive committee (or the equivalent)?

Yes

How many attorneys are on the committee, and in 2003, what was the total number of hours collectively spent by the committee in furtherance of the firm's diversity initiatives?

Total attorneys on committee: 8

Total hours spent on diversity: 260

Does the committee and/or diversity leader establish and set goals or objectives consistent with management's priorities?

Yes

Has the firm undertaken a formal or informal diversity program or set of initiatives aimed at increasing the diversity of the firm?

Yes, formal

How often does the firm's management review the firm's diversity progress/results?

Annually

How is the firm's diversity committee and/or firm management held accountable for achieving results?

The effectiveness of the Diversity Initiatives Committee is evaluated in connection with each director's annual performance management plan.

LAW FIRM DIVERSITY INITIATIVES	ALREADY COMPLETED	CURRENTLY ADDRESSING	NOT A CURRENT PRIORITY
Undertake communication from firm management that diversity is a top priority of the firm.		✓	
Formalize diversity plan and committee with action steps and accountability to management.	✓		
Conduct firm-wide diversity training for all attorneys and staff.	✓		
Increase the number of minority attorneys at the associate level.		✓	
Increase the number of minority attorneys at the partnership level.		✓	
Develop/expand relationships with minority bar associations to offer firm's support of these networks.		✓	
Focus on strengthening firm's mentoring program, including for benefit of minority attorneys.	✓		
Conduct internal diversity needs assessment and/or retain diversity consultant to examine how firm culture might be more welcoming of minorities.		✓	
Support law firm's internal affinity networks (e.g., women, minority attorney networks).	✓		
Manage/monitor allocation of work assignments and/or hours billed to ensure women and minority attorneys have equal access/inclusion on top client matters.		✓	
Outreach to area law schools to foster relationships with diverse law students and/or specialty student organizations.	✓		

Recruitment – New Associates

Does your firm annually recruit at any of the following types of institutions?

Ivy League schools: Cornell University, Columbia University, Harvard University, University of Pennsylvania

Public state schools: Rutgers University-Newark, Rutgers University-Camden, University of North Carolina, University of Virginia, University of Texas, University of Michigan, College of William and Mary

Private schools: Boston College, Boston University, Case Western Reserve University, Duke University, Emory University, Fordham University, George Washington University, Georgetown University, New York University, Northwestern University, Northeastern University, Seton Hall University, Suffolk University, University of Chicago, University of Notre Dame, University of Southern California, Vanderbilt University, Wake Forest University, Washington and Lee University, Washington University in St. Louis, Yeshiva University

Do you have any special outreach efforts directed to encourage minority law students to consider your firm?

• Hold a reception for minority law students
• Participate in/host minority law student job fair(s)

- Sponsor minority law student association events
- Firm's lawyers participate on career panels at school
- Outreach to leadership of minority student organizations
- Scholarships or intern/fellowships for minority students

SUMMER ASSOCIATE STATISTICS: SUMMER 2003	MINORITY MEN	MINORITY WOMEN	WHITE WOMEN	TOTAL
Summer associates	1	2	5	14
Summer associates who received an offer of full-time employment	1	2	5	11
Summer associates who accepted an offer of full-time employment	1	2	4	10

Recruitment- Lateral Associates and Partners

What activities does the firm undertake to attract minority and women attorneys?
- Partner programs with women and minority bar associations
- Participate at minority job fairs
- Seek referrals from other attorneys

Do you use executive recruiting/search firms to seek to identify new diversity hires (partners or associates)?
Yes

If yes, list all women- and/or minority-owned executive search/recruiting firms to which the firm paid a fee for placement services in the past 12 months:
None

LATERAL ASSOCIATES AND PARTNERS: 1/1/03 – 12/31/03	MINORITY MEN	MINORITY WOMEN	WHITE WOMEN	TOTAL
Number of lateral associate hires	2	3	8	34
Number of lateral partner hires (equity and non-equity)	0	0	0	5
Number of new partners (equity and non-equity) promoted from associate rank	0	0	1	5
Number of new equity partners	0	0	1	6

Retention & Professional Development

ATTORNEYS WHO LEFT THE FIRM: 2003	MINORITY MEN	MINORITY WOMEN	WHITE WOMEN	TOTAL
Number of attorneys who voluntarily or involuntarily left your firm's employ in 2003	1	2	9	17

How do 2003 attrition rates generally compare to those experienced in the prior year period?

Lower than in prior years

Please identify the specific steps you are taking to reduce the attrition rate of minority and women attorneys.

• Develop and/or support internal employee affinity groups (e.g., minority or women networks within the firm)

• Increase/improve current work/life programs

• Succession plan includes emphasis on diversity

• Work with minority and women attorneys to develop career advancement plans

• Strengthen mentoring program for all attorneys, including minorities and women

• Professional skills development program, including minority and women attorneys

Does your firm have part-time/flex-time policies that permit attorneys (male or female) to work alternative schedules?

Yes. About 7 percent of our work force currently utilizes alternative work schedules.

What impact, if any, will the decision to work part-time have on an attorney's ability to make partner or, if already a partner, to remain a partner at your firm?

None

Have any attorneys who chose to work a part-time schedule made partner at your firm?

Yes, one attorney. This past year we elected our first part-time partner, who had maintained part-time status for more than three years prior to being promoted. She was considered in the ordinary course of the firm's partnership track.

Management Demographic Profile (as of 12/31/03)

	MINORITY MEN	MINORITY WOMEN	WHITE WOMEN	TOTAL
Number of attorneys on the Executive/Management Committee or equivalent	0	0	1	7
Number of attorneys on the Hiring Committee or equivalent	1	0	5	9
Number of attorneys on the Partner/Associate Review Committee or equivalent	0	0	1	7

Please provide information regarding all minority and women attorneys who head offices or practice groups of your law firm:

Minorities heading practice groups: David L. Harris, Head of Litigation Department

Women heading practice groups: Martha L. Lester, Employment Practice Group

The Firm Says

Lowenstein Sandler has a strong commitment to a diverse workplace. The firm requires all attorneys and staff to attend diversity training. As reflected in the following Diversity Mission Statement, the firm also has several policies and procedures in place to retain and mentor diverse attorneys. While many of those policies and procedures have yielded positive results, the firm recognizes that enhancing diversity requires an ongoing commitment. Accordingly, the Diversity Initiatives Committee is charged with the task of continually evaluating and, where necessary, improving firm practices.

Lowenstein Sandler Diversity Mission Statement

Lowenstein Sandler PC is committed to promoting diversity in the workplace and to fulfilling the promise of a collegial and respectful working environment in which each person is encouraged and assisted in reaching his or her fullest potential. Lowenstein Sandler has implemented several policies and programs to encourage the recruitment, retention and promotion of lawyers from diverse social, economic, cultural and personal backgrounds. The firm's commitment to diversity is reinforced at all levels of the firm, from senior management, throughout the partnership ranks, within the associate recruiting, training and mentoring programs, and among the staff. As a result of these efforts, Lowenstein Sandler ranks:

• first among New Jersey's largest law firms with the greatest number of minority partners between 1995 and 2003, according to the November 3, 2003 issue of the *New Jersey Law Journal*.

• second among New Jersey's largest law firms with the greatest number of women and minority associates, according to the November 3, 2003 issue of the *New Jersey Law Journal*.

The firm's commitment to diversity is implemented primarily by three separate committees of the firm: the Diversity Initiatives Committee, the Recruiting Committee and the Associate Life & Training Committee.

The Diversity Initiatives Committee, composed of partners and associates, has the specific task of evaluating the effectiveness of the firm's existing policies affecting diversity and developing new ones that will further promote a diverse workplace at Lowenstein Sandler. Among other things, the Diversity Initiatives Committee reviews programs at other firms and recommends to senior management improvements in existing programs, new initiatives for this firm based on other firms' programs and promising new approaches.

The Recruiting Committee and its full-time professional staff is charged with ensuring that new and lateral associates hired by the firm reflect the best possible quality attorneys and law students, with diversity as an important component of the overall hiring evaluation. To fulfill these objectives, the Recruiting Committee participates in the following:

• Partnership with legal recruiters that specialize in placing diverse candidates.

• Sponsorship and participation in the Rutgers Minority Summer Program. Each year, the firm attends a recruitment fair sponsored by Rutgers University School of Law and hires at least one first-year minority student as a summer law clerk.

- Sponsorship of the Rutgers Law School Program, whereby the firm funds a student to work for the summer in the public interest law or government sector.
- Participation in minority job fairs across the country, including the Northeast BLSA Job Fair (30 law schools), the New Jersey Minority Job Fair (three law schools) and the Philadelphia Minority Job Fair (five law schools).
- Sponsorship of and membership in New Jersey Law Firm Group, a nonprofit organization that is designed to assist minority students attending Seton Hall University School of Law and Rutgers University School of Law in obtaining employment with New Jersey's larger law firms.
- Sponsorship of and membership in the Minority Corporate Counsel Association.

The Associate Life & Training Committee is composed of partners and associates with a full-time professional staff responsible for developing and implementing firm wide programs of orientation, training, continuing legal education, mentoring, and performance evaluation and review. As part of its mandate, the Associate Life & Training Committee is sensitive to and strives to promote the goals of a diverse workplace. In addition to the firm's mentoring program, the firm participates in the New Jersey Law Firm Group's mentoring program that pairs first-year students with practicing attorneys and is designed to assist minority students in developing career objectives.

In addition to the work of the committees, the firm sponsors an organization, the Women Lawyers of Lowenstein Sandler (WLLS). WLLS is a proactive group of women partners and associates dedicated to providing a forum for women's issues in the law. During the past year, WLLS has sponsored several events with significant numbers of outside invitees, designed to provide networking opportunities for women, discuss ways to successfully navigate a career path as a professional woman and exchange ideas about how to balance the demands of work and family.

Lowenstein Sandler offers a work environment that is conducive to working parents. For example, the firm's maternity leave policy provides full pay for three months and allows an attorney to take an additional three months at home with her newborn child without penalty to partnership track or case responsibility. The firm also offers part-time and flexible hours for attorneys to accommodate child care responsibilities and quality of life decisions. Moreover, the firm has eliminated the myth of "mommy track" by developing a policy that facilitates the promotion of part-time attorneys to directors of the firm. Currently, more than 7 percent of the firm's attorneys have reduced work schedules.

To solidify senior management's commitment to diversity, the firm has integrated women and minority directors into key leadership positions in firm management such as the Executive Committee, department chairs, practice group leaders, the New Directors Qualifications Committee, the Strategic Growth and Planning Committee and the Recruiting Committee.

Luce, Forward, Hamilton & Scripps LLP

600 West Broadway, Suite 2600
San Diego, CA 92101-3372
Phone: (619) 236-1414
Fax: (619) 232-8311
www.luce.com

FIRM LEADERSHIP

Managing Partner: Robert J. Bell
Diversity Team Leader: Michael J. Pérez,
Partner and Chair of Diversity Committee

LOCATIONS

San Diego, CA (HQ)
Carmel Valley/Del Mar, CA
Los Angeles, CA
San Francisco, CA

The Firm Says

Luce, Forward, Hamilton & Scripps welcomes, supports and promotes the interests of women, families and people of all races, ethnicities and sexual orientations. One of California's premier global law firms, Luce Forward has long recognized the importance and value of diversity since it was founded in 1873. In furtherance of Luce Forward's commitment to diversity, Luce Forward has created a Diversity Committee to help our firm reflect the diversity of our communities and to promote communication and understanding among all of those who comprise the firm. The Diversity Committee addresses issues faced by women and minority attorneys, and involving differences among people including race, religion, age, ethnicity, national origin, sexual orientation, gender, language, medical condition or disability, and culture.

The firm's Diversity Committee is comprised of minority and non-minority partners and associates, as well as members of the Recruiting and Human Resources Departments (http://luceweb/lfhsdirectory/committees.htm). Through its subcommittees, the Diversity Committee addresses issues related to community outreach efforts and the recruitment, retention and evaluation of a diverse group of associates and partners. The Diversity Committee is also helping the firm to shape, expand and restate its policies and programs to support the goals of diversity.

The Diversity Committee has identified specific steps that the firm will take to recruit, retain and promote diversity at all levels, including law students and lateral hires. Among the initiatives already implemented is an expanded outreach to law schools to ensure that we recruit a diverse range of new attorneys. Moreover, the firm is focusing on associate development and mentoring. The firm recognizes that each lawyer develops individually and that our mentoring efforts must be structured accordingly. In addition to its internal commitment, the firm regularly sponsors community events

at organizations supporting diversity in the legal profession. Among other organizations, the firm has sponsored the Tom Homann Law Association, the Earl B. Gilliam Bar Association, Pan Asian Bar Association, La Raza Lawyers Association, the NCCJ Martin Luther King Jr. Breakfast, the San Diego County Bar Association's Ethnic Minority Relations Committee's Unity Breakfast, the Lawyers Club, the National Asian Pacific Bar Association, the Hispanic National Bar Association and the National Bar Association.

The firm is committed to fostering understanding, communication and respect among all people of the firm. The firm believes it can and should capitalize on the strengths emanating from these differences. Luce Forward believes that, by drawing on the talents of all of the firm's personnel, we will create an optimal workplace which will attract and retain the best and the brightest, who will in turn help us to better serve varying markets and approach services to clients more effectively. In short, Luce Forward recognizes the beneficial impact a successful diversity program will have on firm morale, productivity and legal strategies. A diverse legal team will support the success and advancement of the firm's legal efforts and foster an environment that supports innovation and creative problem solving.

807

AT MANATT, WE PRACTICE DIVERSITY

At Manatt, we strive to be the best kind of meritocracy. Our professionals thrive in an atmosphere that encourages and supports responsibility and aspirations. We believe lateral partner and associate candidates of color will choose to develop their careers at a firm that offers true opportunity equal to their commitment to success and advancement. That's the history of opportunity we have at Manatt, where all professionals with talent and drive are rewarded with a nurturing, dynamic and energizing climate for long-term diversity and commitment.

www.manatt.com

Albany

Los Angeles

Mexico City

New York

Orange County

Palo Alto

Sacramento

Washington D.C.

manatt
manatt | phelps | phillips

Manatt, Phelps & Phillips, LLP

11355 W. Olympic Blvd.
Los Angeles, CA 90064
Phone: (310) 312-4000
Fax: (310) 314-4224

FIRM LEADERSHIP

Managing Partner: Paul H. Irving, Chief
Executive and Managing Partner
Diversity Team Leader: Johnnie A. James and
Jack S. Yeh, Partners and Co-Chairs of
Diversity Committee

LOCATIONS

Los Angeles, CA (HQ)
Albany, NY
Costa Mesa, CA
New York, NY
Palo Alto, CA
Sacramento, CA
Washington, DC
Mexico City

LAW FIRM DEMOGRAPHIC PROFILES

FULL-TIME ASSOCIATES*	2003	2002
Minority men	19	18
Minority women	14	12
White women	46	33
Total	141	116

Includes counsels: 42/35

SUMMER ASSOCIATES	2003	2002
Minority men	1	0
Minority women	2	0
White women	0	3
Total	4	7

EQUITY PARTNERS	2003	2002
Minority men	2	2
Minority women	0	0
White women	11	8
Total	51	45

NON-EQUITY PARTNERS	2003	2002
Minority men	3	2
Minority women	4	2
White women	14	11
Total	92	77

NEW HIRES	2003	2002
Minority men	6	8
Minority women	7	6
White women	31	7
Total	86	41

Strategic Plan and Diversity Leadership

How does the firm's leadership communicate the importance of diversity to everyone at the firm? (e.g., e-mails, web site, newsletters, meetings, etc.)

At Manatt our commitment to diversity is an integral business priority and core value. Because diversity is a firm priority, our diversity goals and objectives are summarized in a living document – a plan – that is concrete, easy to understand and public. Firm leadership including the firm's chief executive and managing partner have made a strong commitment to this plan. On a regular basis, the Diversity Committee provides updates regarding the firm's progress and new initiatives. In addition, our commitment to diversity is an integral part of our recruiting and marketing materials and will continue to be featured as a key component of our Web site and firm intranet.

Who has primary responsibility for leading diversity initiatives at your firm?

Johnnie A. James and Jack S. Yeh, partners and co-chairs of the Diversity Committee

Does your law firm currently have a diversity committee?

Yes

Does the committee's representation include one or more members of the firm's management/executive committee (or the equivalent)?

Yes

How many attorneys are on the committee, and in 2003, what was the total number of hours collectively spent by the committee in furtherance of the firm's diversity initiatives?

Total attorneys on committee: 3

Total hours spent on diversity: More than 100

Does the committee and/or diversity leader establish and set goals or objectives consistent with management's priorities?

Yes

Has the firm undertaken a formal or informal diversity program or set of initiatives aimed at increasing the diversity of the firm?

Yes, formal

How often does the firm's management review the firm's diversity progress/results?

Quarterly and annually.

How is the firm's diversity committee and/or firm management held accountable for achieving results?

A minority attorney who joins Manatt as a new or lateral hire immediately becomes the focus of a mentoring program in which senior firm attorneys take an active role to encourage career development. Mentors actively work with their mentees, helping them form business plans and involving them in firm-wide marketing and

cross-selling opportunities. The mentoring program is designed to create accountability for mentors and their mentee's progress.

LAW FIRM DIVERSITY INITIATIVES	ALREADY COMPLETED	CURRENTLY ADDRESSING	NOT A CURRENT PRIORITY
Undertake communication from firm management that diversity is a top priority of the firm.	✓		
Formalize diversity plan and committee with action steps and accountability to management.	✓		
Conduct firm-wide diversity training for all attorneys and staff.	✓		
Increase the number of minority attorneys at the associate level.		✓	
Increase the number of minority attorneys at the partnership level.		✓	
Develop/expand relationships with minority bar associations to offer firm's support of these networks.		✓	
Focus on strengthening firm's mentoring program, including for benefit of minority attorneys.	✓		
Conduct internal diversity needs assessment and/or retain diversity consultant to examine how firm culture might be more welcoming of minorities.		✓	
Support law firm's internal affinity networks (e.g., women, minority attorney networks).		✓	
Manage/monitor allocation of work assignments and/or hours billed to ensure women and minority attorneys have equal access/inclusion on top client matters.		✓	

Recruitment – New Associates

Does your firm annually recruit at any of the following types of institutions?

Ivy League schools: Columbia University, Cornell University, Harvard University and Yale University

Public state schools: University of California-Boalt Hall, University of California-Davis and UCLA

Private schools: NYU, University of San Diego, Georgetown University, Stanford University, USC and Loyola Law School

Do you have any special outreach efforts directed to encourage minority law students to consider your firm?

• *In addition to participating in several minority regional and local job fairs and receptions, Manatt proudly contributes significant financial and other resources to student-run, nonprofit organizations that provide grant awards to underrepresented communities in our local area*

• Participate in/host minority law student job fair(s)

• Sponsor minority law student association events

• Firm's lawyers participate on career panels at school

• Outreach to leadership of minority student organizations

SUMMER ASSOCIATE STATISTICS: SUMMER 2003	MINORITY MEN	MINORITY WOMEN	WHITE WOMEN	TOTAL
Summer associates	1	2	0	4
Summer associates who received an offer of full-time employment	1	2	0	4
Summer associates who accepted an offer of full-time employment	0	2	0	3

Recruitment – Lateral Associates and Partners

What activities does the firm undertake to attract minority and women attorneys?

• *Diversity success at Manatt is accomplished by the people we trust and value most — our own associates, partners, recruiters and clients contribute their experiences and insights in identifying the kind of qualified candidates that we have in mind. Manatt regularly contributes significant financial and other resources, as well the time and dedication of our management and attorneys, to the Minority Corporate Counsel Association, the California Minority Counsel Program and numerous other national and regional minority bar organizations and minority civic organizations.*

• Participate at minority job fairs

• Seek referrals from other attorneys

Do you use executive recruiting/search firms to seek to identify new diversity hires (partners or associates)?

Yes

List all women- and/or minority-owned executive search/recruiting firms to which the firm paid a fee for placement services in the past 12 months:

The Brunswick Group, E.P. Dine Inc., Prestige Nationwide Search Consultants, The Artemis Group, LTD., Garb Jaffe and Associates and The Mestel Group

LATERAL ASSOCIATES AND PARTNERS: 1/1/03 – 12/31/03	MINORITY MEN	MINORITY WOMEN	WHITE WOMEN	TOTAL
Number of lateral associate hires	6	4	16	53
Number of lateral partner hires (equity and non-equity)	1	3	16	35
Number of new partners (equity and non-equity) promoted from associate rank	0	0	0	2
Number of new equity partners	0	0	0	2

Retention & Professional Development

ATTORNEYS WHO LEFT THE FIRM: 2003	MINORITY MEN	MINORITY WOMEN	WHITE WOMEN	TOTAL
Number of attorneys who voluntarily or involuntarily left your firm's employ in 2003	5	3	15	56

How do 2003 attrition rates generally compare to those experienced in the prior year period?

Higher than in prior years

Please identify the specific steps you are taking to reduce the attrition rate of minority and women attorneys.

• *Manatt is committed to becoming actively involved in the personal growth, leadership and career development goals and initiatives for our minority attorneys. To that end, the firm has implemented a mentoring program to help associates and partners build a vision for their short- and long-term career development goals. Each attorney is provided assistance with the development of a personal business plan, a plan for marketing and cross-selling within the firm, guidance and support in building important client relationships, and general assistance in increasing their profile inside and outside of the firm.*

• Succession plan includes emphasis on diversity (in process)

• Work with minority and women attorneys to develop career advancement plans

• Introduce minority and women attorneys to key clients, including to lead engagements

• Strengthen mentoring program for all attorneys, including minorities and women

• Professional skills development program, including minority and women attorneys

Does your firm have part-time/flex-time policies that permit attorneys (male or female) to work alternative schedules?

Yes

What impact, if any, will the decision to work part-time have on an attorney's ability to make partner or, if already a partner, to remain a partner at your firm?

Manatt attorneys who work part-time may have slightly longer paths to partnership but are nevertheless treated like any other partner in terms of respect, support, compensation and level determinations.

Have any attorneys who chose to work a part-time schedule made partner at your firm?

Yes, three attorneys.

Management Demographic Profile (as of 12/31/03)

	MINORITY MEN	MINORITY WOMEN	WHITE WOMEN	TOTAL
Number of attorneys on the Executive/Management Committee or equivalent	1	0	1	11
Number of attorneys on the Hiring Committee or equivalent	5	1	1	13
Number of attorneys on the Partner/Associate Review Committee or equivalent	1	0	3	7

Please provide information regarding all minority and women attorneys who head offices or practice groups of your law firm:

Minorities heading offices: John Ray, Washington, D.C.

Women heading offices: Ellen Marshall, Orange County, California

Minorities heading practice groups: Johnnie James, Employment & Labor; Arman Pahlavan, Venture Capital & Technology

Women heading practice groups: Linda Goldstein, Advertising, Marketing & Media; Laurie Soriano, Entertainment Industry; Deborah Bachrach, Healthcare Industry; Marcia Alazraki and Maggie Levy, Insurance Industry; Jill Pietrini, Intellectual Property/Internet; Lisa Specht, Real Estate & Land Use

The Firm Says

Diversity is a core value at Manatt, Phelps & Phillips, LLP. It's inseparable from our commitment to meritocracy, because the best people reflect the widest possible perspectives, experiences and backgrounds. The basic qualities that we seek in all our professionals — commitment, judgement, creativity, entrepreneurial drive, business skill, civic responsibility and a desire to be the best — are deeply enriched by diverse cultural experiences. These qualities define the way we practice law and offer services to clients, and they are greatly strengthened by our active and effective efforts to recruit and retain minority lawyers.

We understand the practical importance of diversity to our clients and to the communities where we practice. We consider it an imperative business priority to ensure that our firm, from the top down, reflect the diverse communities that we serve. In our major office locations, from New York to Washington, D.C., to Los Angeles, the multiple strengths of African-American, Latino, Asian and many other cultures are inseparable from the rapid development of the global economy. The directors of the largest corporations, like the owners of the newest entrepreneurial businesses, increasingly reflect this kind of multicultural perspective and increasingly require it of the law firms they use. Manatt embraces the challenge as a mission of the firm.

Our efforts to promote diversity have ranked us in the top 15 percent of the nation's 250 largest law firms on the Minority Law Journal's Diversity Scorecard. We realize, however, that means we have much more to do. Our efforts are founded on our understanding that the key to retaining talented minority lawyers — and therefore the key to nurturing a commitment to diversity — is creating a distinctive environment that supports the needs of minority professionals. We focus on the following key areas to accomplish our mission.

Clear diversity statement. Manatt's commitment to diversity begins with and is summarized in a living document — a plan — that is concrete, easy to understand and public. It demonstrates in writing to each and every law school student, lateral candidate, recruiter, existing client and potential client that we are serious about creating a workplace that mirrors the breadth of the communities where we and our clients live and work. Manatt's commitment to diversity is an integral part of our recruiting and marketing materials and will continue to be featured as a key component of our web site.

Targeted recruitment. At Manatt, recruiting minority attorneys doesn't begin and end on law school campuses. Granted, we make special efforts to seek out and interview law students who share our core values in ways shaped and enhanced by their own experience involving race, color, sexual orientation, gender or religion. Beyond this, however, we have a targeted recruitment outreach campaign that calls on the members of the firm and our most trusted outside colleagues to locate talented minority lawyers. Our associates and partners, as well

as select recruiters and clients, are provided with specific information about our diversity commitment, philosophy and recruiting initiatives. We urge our friends, colleagues and clients to identify the kind of qualified candidates we want and spread our message that we want to talk to minority attorneys with drive, energy, intelligence and a history of excellence.

Firsthand experience. Because diversity is a firm priority and business objective, we make a point of demonstrating that firsthand to minority recruits. Our most senior and high-profile lawyers meet with candidates to share Manatt's culture and diversity philosophy and goals as well as the many opportunities that are available to minority attorneys in our firm. We also offer candidates the chance to meet and speak with other minority lawyers in the firm.

Mentoring as a cornerstone. A minority attorney who joins Manatt as a new or lateral hire immediately becomes the focus of a mentoring program in which senior firm attorneys take an active role to encourage career development. We believe professionals who will be key long-term players with existing and prospective clients — clients that are becoming more racially diverse — must have the opportunity to lead, prosper in our system and maximize their skills and experiences. Mentors guide and enhance that career development through their own experience and relationships.

Mentors actively work with their proteges, helping them form business plans and involving them in firm-wide marketing and cross-selling opportunities. Building visibility with firm colleagues, clients and the business community is an important part of the help that mentors provide. Mentors are held accountable for their roles and their proteges' progress at becoming successful and productive members of the firm.

Access to opportunity. At Manatt we believe that the key to retaining talented minority lawyers — and therefore the key to the success of our diversity efforts — is providing a distinctive experience that offers clear and open access to professional accomplishment. We make a concerted effort to provide minority lawyers and minority partners with important responsibilities and leadership opportunities in client development activities, complex litigation, large transactional matters and high-profile community and civic organizations. We also encourage and support minority lawyers who take leadership positions within the firm and outside in the community at large, and help to facilitate the development of their professional profile.

Long-term commitment. Manatt strives to be the best kind of meritocracy. Our professionals thrive in an atmosphere that encourages and supports responsibility and aspirations. We believe lateral partner and associate candidates of color will choose to develop their careers at a firm that offers true opportunity equal to their commitment to success and advancement. That's the history of opportunity we have at Manatt, where all professionals with talent and drive are rewarded with a nurturing, dynamic and energizing climate for long-term diversity and commitment. Diversity at Manatt is more than just a goal. It is who we are and what we demand of ourselves.

Challenging legal problems.
Demanding clients.
Supportive colleagues.

We are commited to making these a reality for all of our lawyers—
regardless of gender, ethnicity, sexual orientation or physical capabilities.

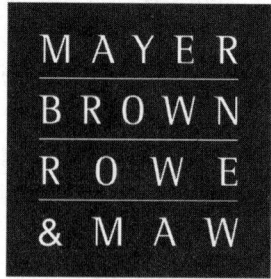

MAYER
BROWN
ROWE
& MAW

www.mayerbrownrowe.com

Brussels • Charlotte • Chicago • Cologne • Frankfurt • Houston • London
Los Angeles • Manchester • New York • Palo Alto • Paris • Washington, D.C.

Mayer, Brown, Rowe & Maw is a combination of two limited liability partnerships,
each named Mayer, Brown, Rowe & Maw LLP, one established in Illinois, USA, and one incorporated in England.

Mayer, Brown, Rowe & Maw LLP

1675 Broadway
New York, NY 10019
Phone: (212) 506-2500
Fax: (212) 262-1910

FIRM LEADERSHIP

Managing Partner: Debora de Hoyos, Managing
Partner
Diversity Team Leader: Committee on Diversity
& Inclusion, c/o Linda Bushlow

LOCATIONS

Charlotte, NC
Chicago, IL
Houston, TX
Los Angeles, CA
New York, NY
Palo Alto, CA
Washington, DC
Brussels
Cologne
Frankfurt
London
Manchester
Paris

LAW FIRM DEMOGRAPHIC PROFILES

FULL-TIME ASSOCIATES	2003	2002
Minority men	48	39
Minority women	47	43
White women	204	206
Total	611	619

SUMMER ASSOCIATES	2003	2002
Minority men	11	6
Minority women	15	8
White women	40	24
Total	113	69

PARTNERS*	2003	2002
Minority men	7	4
Minority women	5	3
White women	50	44
Total	372	344

As a matter of firm policy, we do not distinguish between equity and non-equity partners externally. The chart above includes data for both equity and non-equity partners.

NEW HIRES	2003	2002
Minority men	12	14
Minority women	15	17
White women	34	34
Total	121	128

Strategic Plan and Diversity Leadership

How does the firm's leadership communicate the importance of diversity to everyone at the firm? (e.g., e-mails, web site, newsletters, meetings, etc.)

At our annual partners meeting, members of our Policy & Planning Committee address all partners on the importance of making diversity a priority as a business imperative. Semi-annually our Committee on Diversity & Inclusion leads discussions with the firm's practice leaders to establish diversity priorities and future goals. Our Committee on Diversity & Inclusion holds periodic roundtables with our associates at which they present an overview of our most recent diversity initiatives. This quarter, our firm will release a new expanded diversity web site in order to keep our attorneys updated regarding our progress in the area of diversity; inform law student and lateral candidates of our commitment to diversity in our hiring, development and promotion efforts; and share with our clients news about our diversity initiatives.

Who has primary responsibility for leading diversity initiatives at your firm?

The partner members of the Committee on Diversity & Inclusion which includes among its members Debora de Hoyos, managing partner; Ty Fahner, partner and chair of the Policy & Planning Committee, the firm's senior management committee; the co-chairs of the Committee on Associates; and hiring partners from the various offices.

Does your law firm currently have a diversity committee?

Yes

Does the committee's representation include one or more members of the firm's management/executive committee (or the equivalent)?

Yes

How many attorneys are on the committee, and in 2003, what was the total number of hours collectively spent by the committee in furtherance of the firm's diversity initiatives?

Total attorneys on committee: 23

Total hours spent on diversity: At our firm, hours are not tracked in this manner. However, in addition to monthly committee meetings and an annual full-day meeting, committee members actively participate in a variety of internal and external diversity related initiatives involving mentoring, panel discussions, interviewing, and so on, and the contribution of their hours is considerable.

Does the committee and/or diversity leader establish and set goals or objectives consistent with management's priorities?

Yes

Has the firm undertaken a formal or informal diversity program or set of initiatives aimed at increasing the diversity of the firm?

Yes, formal

How often does the firm's management review the firm's diversity progress/results?

Twice a year

How is the firm's diversity committee and/or firm management held accountable for achieving results?

The Committee on Diversity & Inclusion prepares semi-annual reports to the Policy & Planning Committee which outline accomplishments and an action plan for the next six months. Practice leaders are also expected to report to the Partner Promotion Committee the efforts of their practice to train and develop diverse attorneys. Each year, all partners are expected to summarize their contributions to "firm welfare," which includes their efforts aimed at advancing our diversity objectives in recruiting, development and promotion of diverse attorneys.

LAW FIRM DIVERSITY INITIATIVES	ALREADY COMPLETED	CURRENTLY ADDRESSING	NOT A CURRENT PRIORITY
Undertake communication from firm management that diversity is a top priority of the firm.	✔		
Formalize diversity plan and committee with action steps and accountability to management.	✔		
Conduct firm-wide diversity training for all attorneys and staff.		✔ *	
Increase the number of minority attorneys at the associate level.		✔	
Increase the number of minority attorneys at the partnership level.		✔	
Develop/expand relationships with minority bar associations to offer firm's support of these networks.		✔	
Focus on strengthening firm's mentoring program, including for benefit of minority attorneys.		✔	
Conduct internal diversity needs assessment and/or retain diversity consultant to examine how firm culture might be more welcoming of minorities.		✔	
Support law firm's internal affinity networks (e.g., women, minority attorney networks).		✔	
Manage/monitor allocation of work assignments and/or hours billed to ensure women and minority attorneys have equal access/inclusion on top client matters.		✔	
Partnering with clients and undergraduate and law schools to improve the representation of minorities and women in the profession. Some specific details of our current initiatives are outlined in our narrative response below.		✔	

* Only for new entry-level associates

Recruitment – New Associates

Does your firm annually recruit at any of the following types of institutions?

Ivy League schools: Columbia University, Cornell University, Harvard University, University of Pennsylvania and Yale University

Public state schools: University of California-Boalt, University of Houston, University of Illinois, Indiana University, University of Iowa, University of Michigan, University of Minnesota, University of North Carolina, Ohio State University, University of Texas, UCLA, University of Virginia, College of William & Mary, and University of Wisconsin

Private schools: American University, Boston College, Boston University, Case Western Reserve University, University of Chicago, De Paul University, Duke University, Emory University, Fordham University, Georgetown University, George Washington University, John Marshall Law School, Chicago-Kent College of Law, Loyola University–Chicago, Loyola Law School–Los Angeles, New York University, Northwestern University, University of Notre Dame, St. Johns University, Stanford University, Tulane University, USC, Valparaiso University, Vanderbilt University, Wake Forest University, Washington University in St. Louis, and Washington and Lee University

Historically Black Colleges and Universities (HBCUs): Howard University

Do you have any special outreach efforts directed to encourage minority law students to consider your firm?
• Hold a reception for minority law students
• Advertise in minority law student association publication(s)
• Participate in/host minority law student job fair(s)
• Sponsor minority law student association events
• Firm's lawyers participate on career panels at school
• Outreach to leadership of minority student organizations
• Scholarships or intern/fellowships for minority students
• City-wide panels for minority law students on "How to Succeed in Law School" or mock interview programs

SUMMER ASSOCIATE STATISTICS: SUMMER 2003	MINORITY MEN	MINORITY WOMEN	WHITE WOMEN	TOTAL
Summer associates	11	15	40	113
Summer associates who received an offer of full-time employment	10	13	37	101
Summer associates who accepted an offer of full-time employment	5	11	23	62

Recruitment – Lateral Associates and Partners

What activities does the firm undertake to attract minority and women attorneys?

• *Sponsor a variety of student-focused programs at which we offer resume reviews, panel presentations, networking receptions, and so on.*

• Partner programs with women and minority bar associations

• Participate at minority job fairs

• Seek referrals from other attorneys

Do you use executive recruiting/search firms to seek to identify new diversity hires (partners or associates)?

Yes

If yes, list all women- and/or minority-owned executive search/recruiting firms to which the firm paid a fee for placement services in the past 12 months:

We do not track information about the ownership structure of the search firms who have placed attorneys at our firm.

LATERAL ASSOCIATES AND PARTNERS: 1/1/03 – 12/31/03	MINORITY MEN	MINORITY WOMEN	WHITE WOMEN	TOTAL
Number of lateral associate hires	6	7	17	53
Number of lateral partner hires (equity and non-equity)	1	1	2	22
Number of new partners (equity and non-equity) promoted from associate rank	2	1	4	24
Number of new equity partners*	3	2	6	46

* As a matter of firm policy, we do not distinguish between equity and non-equity partners externally. Our response to "Number of New Equity Partners" above includes both equity and non-equity partners.

Retention & Professional Development

ATTORNEYS WHO LEFT THE FIRM: 2003	MINORITY MEN	MINORITY WOMEN	WHITE WOMEN	TOTAL
Number of attorneys who voluntarily or involuntarily left your firm's employ in 2003	2	7	29	82

How do 2003 attrition rates generally compare to those experienced in the prior year period?

About the same as in prior years

Please identify the specific steps you are taking to reduce the attrition rate of minority and women attorneys.

- *Hold an annual Diversity Retreat for our diverse attorneys and an annual Women's Symposium for our women attorneys*
- Develop and/or support internal employee affinity groups (e.g., minority or women networks within the firm)
- Increase/improve current work/life programs
- Work with minority and women attorneys to develop career advancement plans
- Introduce minority and women attorneys to key clients, including to lead engagements
- Review work assignments and hours billed to key client matters to make sure minority and women attorneys are not being excluded
- Strengthen mentoring program for all attorneys, including minorities and women
- Professional skills development program, including minority and women attorneys

Does your firm have part-time/flex-time policies that permit attorneys (male or female) to work alternative schedules?

Yes

What impact, if any, will the decision to work part-time have on an attorney's ability to make partner or, if already a partner, to remain a partner at your firm?

Attorneys who are working part-time receive full consideration for promotion to partner along with other attorneys. Partner candidates are evaluated based on a number of factors including legal skills, managing major matters, ability to expand business with existing clients or with new clients, and overall contribution to the firm. In some cases, working reduced hours may delay partnership consideration because the part-time attorney's development and readiness for partnership may be slower as compared to full-time attorneys. Each attorney is evaluated individually and advanced based on his or her demonstrated achievements.

Have any attorneys who chose to work a part-time schedule made partner at your firm?

Yes. While we can confirm that attorneys have made partner while working part-time, we do not track information on whether or not our partners were working part-time at the time of their promotion to the position.

Management Demographic Profile (as of 12/31/03)

	MINORITY MEN	MINORITY WOMEN	WHITE WOMEN	TOTAL
Number of attorneys on the Executive/Management Committee or equivalent	0	0	2	14
Number of attorneys on the Hiring Committee or equivalent	4	5	12	51
Number of attorneys on the Partner/Associate Review Committee or equivalent	1	1	3	17

Please provide information regarding all minority and women attorneys who head offices or practice groups of your law firm:

Minorities heading offices: none

Women heading offices: Debora de Hoyos, Managing Partner (firm-wide)

Minorities heading practice groups: Dean Pappas, Real Estate (Los Angeles); Javier Rubinstein, Litigation (Chicago)

Women heading practice groups: Delilah Flaum, Health Care (firm-wide); Donna Morgan, Wealth Management (firm-wide); Kathleen Walsh, Corporate (New York)

The Firm Says

Mayer, Brown, Rowe & Maw LLP has found that diversity strengthens our work force, improves the breadth and quality of our practices, and makes our firm more responsive to the varied needs of our worldwide clientele.

Inclusion begins with opportunity. We ensure that all associates at the firm are provided exciting and challenging work experiences and the guidance necessary for success. We continue to seek innovative and effective ways to increase the number of minority, gay and female students interested in law school and to recruit diverse law students and lateral candidates.

Mayer Brown builds programs for students at all levels of schooling to increase the pool of lawyers of diverse backgrounds. Through conferences, job fairs, panel discussions and workshops, we make the legal profession less abstract and more accessible to students of all backgrounds. In the past year, we have conducted panel discussions for minority students at Chicago, New York and Washington, D.C. area law schools; organized a Constitutional Law Program with Northside Preparatory High School in Chicago; and held panel discussions for affinity groups such as BLSA, LALSA and APALSA at Chicago, New York, Los Angeles, Houston and D.C. area law schools.

A commitment to the professional development and advancement of our diverse attorneys is central to our diversity and inclusion programs. Members of our Committee on Diversity & Inclusion include the chairman, the managing partner, the co-chairs of our Committee on Associates and the chair of the Partner Promotion Committee. A primary component of their mission is to ensure that practice leaders and other partners responsible for the advancement of associates are focused on the successful development of our diverse attorneys. This development is facilitated by effective processes for work assignments, performance feedback and training programs, all of which are monitored by our committee leaders.

Our annual Diversity Retreat is a cornerstone of our internal diversity and inclusion program. One of the main objectives of our retreat is to provide our diverse associates with an additional opportunity to interact with the firm's senior management. In developing the programming for this event, we make it a priority to include topics on business development skills and what it takes to make partner. The firm uses the wealth of knowledge and insight gathered and shared at the retreat to guide our diversity efforts.

The Committee on Diversity & Inclusion members in each office host periodic sessions with all attorneys to share information about the firm's diversity efforts and to solicit ideas and comments regarding events and future initiatives. In addition, minority attorneys meet informally to provide ongoing opportunities for building

relationships within the firm. Our firm also has a dedicated partner for associate development and recruiting. One of his significant responsibilities is to monitor progress of associates, including diverse associates.

The partners on the Committee on Diversity & Inclusion meet regularly with practice leaders to discuss the progress of their diverse associates. Working with the managing partner and chairman, the committee strives to increase awareness of diversity among practice leaders and partners generally, both as a firm value and a component of excellence; to promote best practices with respect to inclusion; to develop strategies for improving the recruitment and retention of diverse attorneys; and to provide a forum for associate concerns.

In addition to a wide array of internal legal education programs, our lawyers also attend numerous external networking and educational conferences designed for diverse lawyers, such as the ABA Commission on Racial and Ethnic Diversity in the Profession Conference; MCCA's Annual Pathways to Diversity Conference and CLE Expo; the Texas Minority Counsel Program, "Diversity: A World of Opportunity"; the National South Asian Bar Association's Conference; and the Minority Outside Counsel Networking Conference. We are a national platinum sponsor of the Minority Corporate Counsel Association. In addition, all of our new entry-level attorneys participate in a workplace diversity training workshop as part of their new associate orientation program.

Driven by the leadership and active participation of managing partner Debora de Hoyos and other female leaders at the firm, Mayer, Brown, Rowe & Maw offers a variety of initiatives and opportunities focused on the interests and talents of our female attorneys. The firm hosts Women's Forums annually for all female attorneys to participate in workshops, panel discussions, networking receptions and presentations led by our female partners and by leaders from the legal and business community. Our quarterly e-letter provides updates on local events for women to learn, share experiences and network, and each office hosts informal lunches for female attorneys. In recognition of the demands of balancing work and family, Mayer Brown has implemented programs for part-time work opportunities, back-up child care service, domestic partner benefits and a six-week paid parental leave for both birth and adoptive parents.

Mayer Brown is committed to providing a thriving workplace for gay, lesbian and bisexual attorneys. The firm has provisions for same-gender relationships in its domestic partner benefits program. We support a number of gay- and lesbian-related organizational events and pro bono matters. We participate annually in the Lavender Law Career Fair, and the Committee on Diversity & Inclusion includes gay partners who monitor and advocate for progress in this important area.

Through event participation and sponsorships of awards dinners and conferences initiated by organizations such as South Asian Bar Association, Puerto Rican Bar Association, Black Women Lawyers Association, BLSA, APALSA, PRLDEF, LAMDA and Catalyst, and through pro bono work for entities like the NAACP and the Mexican Fine Arts Center Museum, we provide vital support to those who seek to advance the goal of diversity at all levels of society.

Diversity at McDermott Will & Emery.

Is a part of our attitude, culture of collaboration and a long-term commitment that we take seriously. An atmosphere of inclusion benefits all McDermott lawyers and staff and provides our clients with varied perspectives and backgrounds to their legal issues. Join us in valuing diversity.

Michael Boykins
Co-Chair, Racial and Ethnic Diversity Committee
312.984.7599
mboykins@mwe.com

Andrea Kramer
Co-Chair, Gender Diversity Committee
312.984.6480
akramer@mwe.com

McDermott Will&Emery

227 West Monroe Street
Chicago, Illinois 60606-5096

www.mwe.com

Boston Brussels Chicago Düsseldorf London Los Angeles Miami Milan Munich New York Orange County Rome San Diego Silicon Valley Washington, D.C.

McDermott Will & Emery LLP

227 West Monroe Street, Suite 4400
Chicago, IL 60606
Phone: (312) 372-2000
Fax: (312) 984-7700

FIRM LEADERSHIP

Managing Partner: Harvey W. Freishtat, Chairman
Diversity Team Leaders: Michael L. Boykins, Racial & Ethnic Diversity Committee Co-Chair, and Andrea S. Kramer, Gender Diversity Committee Co-Chair

OFFICE LOCATIONS

Chicago, IL
Boston, MA
Irvine, CA
Los Angeles, CA
Miami, FL
New York, NY
Palo Alto, CA
San Diego, CA
Washington, DC
Brussels
Düsseldorf
London
Milan
Munich
Rome

LAW FIRM DEMOGRAPHIC PROFILES

FULL-TIME ASSOCIATES	2003	2002
Minority men	25	20
Minority women	21	28
White women	108	130
Total	369	411

SUMMER ASSOCIATES	2003	2002
Minority men	10	4
Minority women	10	2
White women	18	13
Total	54	45

EQUITY PARTNERS	2003	2002
Minority men	7	7
Minority women	3	3
White women	38	39
Total	275	271

NON-EQUITY PARTNERS	2003	2002
Minority men	11	10
Minority women	9	11
White women	74	81
Total	227	231

NEW HIRES	2003	2002
Minority men	21	11
Minority women	12	10
White women	30	22
Total	114	111

MINORITY CORPORATE COUNSEL ASSOCIATION

Strategic Plan and Diversity Leadership

How does the firm's leadership communicate the importance of diversity to everyone at the firm? (e.g., e-mails, web site, newsletters, meetings, etc.)

McDermott communicates the importance of diversity though firm-wide e-mails, the firm web site, newsletters and monthly diversity committee meetings.

Who has primary responsibility for leading diversity initiatives at your firm?

Michael L. Boykins, Racial and Ethnic Diversity Committee co-chair, and Andrea S. Kramer, Gender Diversity Committee co-chair

Does your law firm currently have a diversity committee?

Yes

Does the committee's representation include one or more members of the firm's management/executive committee (or the equivalent)?

Yes

How many attorneys are on the committee, and in 2003, what was the total number of hours collectively spent by the committee in furtherance of the firm's diversity initiatives?

Total attorneys on Racial and Ethnic Diversity Committee: 10

Total hours spent on diversity: 250 hours

Total attorneys on Gender Diversity Committee: 12

Total hours spent on diversity: 1,000 hours (Racial & Ethnic Committee); 1,000 hours (Gender Diversity Committee)

Does the committee and/or diversity leader establish and set goals or objectives consistent with management's priorities?

Yes

Has the firm undertaken a formal or informal diversity program or set of initiatives aimed at increasing the diversity of the firm?

Yes, formal

How often does the firm's management review the firm's diversity progress/results?

Monthly

How is the firm's diversity committee and/or firm management held accountable for achieving results?

Progress reports are provided to the Management Committee from the co-chairs of the diversity committees on a regular basis. The co-chairs of both diversity committees are also on the Compensation Committee.

LAW FIRM DIVERSITY INITIATIVES	ALREADY COMPLETED	CURRENTLY ADDRESSING	NOT A CURRENT PRIORITY
Undertake communication from firm management that diversity is a top priority of the firm.	✓		
Formalize diversity plan and committee with action steps and accountability to management.	✓		
Conduct firm-wide diversity training for all attorneys and staff.		✓	
Increase the number of minority attorneys at the associate level.	✓		
Increase the number of minority attorneys at the partnership level.	✓		
Develop/expand relationships with minority bar associations to offer firm's support of these networks.		✓	
Focus on strengthening firm's mentoring program, including for benefit of minority attorneys.	✓		
Conduct internal diversity needs assessment and/or retain diversity consultant to examine how firm culture might be more welcoming of minorities.		✓	
Support law firm's internal affinity networks (e.g., women, minority attorney networks).	✓	✓	
Manage/monitor allocation of work assignments and/or hours billed to ensure women and minority attorneys have equal access/inclusion on top client matters.		✓	

Recruitment – New Associates

Does your firm annually recruit at any of the following types of institutions?

Ivy League schools: Harvard University, Yale University, Columbia University, Cornell University, University of Pennsylvania

Public state schools: University of California at Boalt, Davis, Hastings and Los Angeles; University of Illinois, University of Iowa, University of Michigan, University of North Carolina, University of Virginia, University of Wisconsin

Private schools: Boston College, Duke University, Fordham University, George Washington University, Georgetown University, Loyola Law School (LA), Loyola University (Chicago), Northwestern University, Pepperdine University, Santa Clara University, University of Chicago, Wake Forest University, Stanford University, University of Southern California

Do you have any special outreach efforts directed to encourage minority law students to consider your firm?

• Hold a reception for minority law students

• Participate in/host minority law student job fair(s)

• Sponsor minority law student association events

- Firm's lawyers participate on career panels at school
- Outreach to leadership of minority student organizations

SUMMER ASSOCIATE STATISTICS: SUMMER 2003	MINORITY MEN	MINORITY WOMEN	WHITE WOMEN	TOTAL
Summer associates	12	11	17	54
Summer associates who received an offer of full-time employment	10	9	16	49
Summer associates who accepted an offer of full-time employment	9	7	15	44

Recruitment- Lateral Associates and Partners

What activities does the firm undertake to attract minority and women attorneys?

- Participate at minority job fairs
- Seek referrals from other attorneys

Do you use executive recruiting/search firms to seek to identify new diversity hires (partners or associates)?

Yes

LATERAL ASSOCIATES AND PARTNERS: 1/1/03 – 12/31/03	MINORITY MEN	MINORITY WOMEN	WHITE WOMEN	TOTAL
Number of lateral associate hires	6	7	17	44
Number of lateral partner hires (equity and non-equity)	4	0	3	19
Number of new partners (equity and non-equity) promoted from associate rank	0	2	8	22
Number of new equity partners*	0	0	0	0

* McDermott does not hire equity partners.

Retention & Professional Development

ATTORNEYS WHO LEFT THE FIRM: 2003	MINORITY MEN	MINORITY WOMEN	WHITE WOMEN	TOTAL
Number of attorneys who voluntarily or involuntarily left your firm's employ in 2003	5	15	42	123

How do 2003 attrition rates generally compare to those experienced in the prior year period?

About the same as in prior years

Please identify the specific steps you are taking to reduce the attrition rate of minority and women attorneys.

• Develop and/or support internal employee affinity groups (e.g., minority or women networks within the firm)

• Increase/improve current work/life programs

• Work with minority and women attorneys to develop career advancement plans

• Introduce minority and women attorneys to key clients, including to lead engagements

• Review work assignments and hours billed to key client matters to make sure minority and women attorneys are not being excluded

• Strengthen mentoring program for all attorneys, including minorities and women

• Professional skills development program, including minority and women attorneys

Does your firm have part-time/flex-time policies that permit attorneys (male or female) to work alternative schedules?

Yes

What impact, if any, will the decision to work part-time have on an attorney's ability to make partner or, if already a partner, to remain a partner at your firm?

While working part-time may lengthen the time required to achieve partnership, McDermott promotes part-time lawyers to partner and part-time status does not affect a lawyer's ability to remain partner.

Have any attorneys who chose to work a part-time schedule made partner at your firm?

Yes

Management Demographic Profile (as of 12/31/03)

	MINORITY MEN	MINORITY WOMEN	WHITE WOMEN	TOTAL
Number of attorneys on the Executive/Management Committee or equivalent*	0/1	0/0	1/3	8/21
Number of attorneys on the Hiring Committee or equivalent	1	0	2	11
Number of attorneys on the Associate Review Committee or equivalent	1	1	26	70

* Numbers listed as: Executive Committee/Management Committee

Please provide information regarding all minority and women attorneys who head offices or practice groups of your law firm:

Minorities heading offices: Anthony de Alcuaz, Silicon Valley

Women heading offices: Helen R. Friedli, Chicago

Minorities heading practice groups: Shirley Fujimoto, Telecommunications; Jorge Arciniega, Los Angeles Intellectual Property

Women heading practice groups: Andrea Kramer, Energy; Margaret Duncan, Chicago Intellectual Property; Donna Tanguay, Washington, DC, Intellectual Property; Sandra Murphy, Family Law; Marilyn Lamar, Information Technology; Elizabeth Majers, Corporate Finance; Melise Blakeslee, e-Business; Marsha Croninger, Environmental; Margaret Warner, Insurance; Shirley Fujimoto, Telecommunications; Christine Gill, Telecommunications; Karen Dewis, Washington, DC, Corporate; Cathryn Campbell, San Diego Intellectual Property; Donna Tanguay, Washington, DC, Intellectual Property; Andrea Kramer, Financial Products, Trading and Derivatives; Susan Cooke, Environmental

McGuireWoods LLP

One James Center, 901 E. Cary St
Richmond, VA 23219
Phone: (804) 775-1000
Fax: (804) 775-1061

FIRM LEADERSHIP

Managing Partner: William J. Strickland,
Managing Partner
Diversity Team Leader: Jacquelyn E. Stone,
Firm-wide Hiring Partner & Chair of the
Recruitment Committee

LOCATIONS

Richmond, VA (HQ)
Atlanta, GA
Baltimore, MD
Charlotte, NC
Charlottesville, VA
Chicago, IL
Detroit, MI
Jacksonville, FL
New York, NY
Norfolk, VA
Pittsburgh, PA
Tysons Corner, VA
Washington, DC
Almaty, Kazakstan
Brussels, Belgium

LAW FIRM DEMOGRAPHIC PROFILES

FULL-TIME ASSOCIATES	2003	2002
Minority men	12	9
Minority women	19	15
White women	120	128
Total	326	324

SUMMER ASSOCIATES	2003	2002
Minority men	1	1
Minority women	4	6
White women	20	12
Total	53	32

EQUITY PARTNERS	2003	2002
Minority men	4	5
Minority women	1	2
White women	19	19
Total	184	188

NON-EQUITY PARTNERS	2003	2002
Minority men	5	3
Minority women	2	2
White women	39	39
Total	179	174

NEW HIRES	2003	2002
Minority men	6	3
Minority women	6	3
White women	25	17
Total	85	73

MINORITY CORPORATE COUNSEL ASSOCIATION

Strategic Plan and Diversity Leadership

How does the firm's leadership communicate the importance of diversity to everyone at the firm? (e.g., e-mails, web site, newsletters, meetings, etc.)

The majority of the Firm's strong support for diversity is communicated through meetings, where the Firm's management has articulated its views on the benefits of a diverse group of lawyers within the firm. This viewpoint is supported in many other official communications. It was clearly stated in the Firm's Strategic Plan. The Firm's web site has an extensive section entitled "Commitment to the Minority Community," which outlines many of the Firm's activities to attract minority lawyers and support minority communities. The Firm's Strategic Plan states its goals of continuing to recruit, train and retain minority lawyers. The Firm's newsletter has carried several stories celebrating the successes of the Firm's minority lawyers and alumni, as well as articles on awards that McGuireWoods has received for its commitment to hiring, retaining and promoting ethic minority lawyers.

Who has primary responsibility for leading diversity initiatives at your firm?

Jacquelyn E. Stone, Firm-wide Hiring Partner and Chair of the Recruitment Committee.

Does your law firm currently have a diversity committee?

Yes

Does the committee's representation include one or more members of the firm's management/executive committee (or the equivalent)?

Yes

How many attorneys are on the committee, and in 2003, what was the total number of hours collectively spent by the committee in furtherance of the firm's diversity initiatives?

Total attorneys on committee: 8

Total hours spent on diversity: 100

Does the committee and/or diversity leader establish and set goals or objectives consistent with management's priorities?

Yes

Has the firm undertaken a formal or informal diversity program or set of initiatives aimed at increasing the diversity of the firm?

Yes, – It is part of the Firm's Strategic Plan.

How often does the firm's management review the firm's diversity progress/results?

It is done on an ongoing basis.

How is the firm's diversity committee and/or firm management held accountable for achieving results?

There is a clear process set forth in the Firm's Strategic Plan in what the Firm seeks to achieve with regards to diversity, and we ensure these goals are met as we regularly review progress on the Strategic Plan in meetings of the board of partners, which includes both minority and female partners.

LAW FIRM DIVERSITY INITIATIVES	ALREADY COMPLETED	CURRENTLY ADDRESSING	NOT A CURRENT PRIORITY
Undertake communication from firm management that diversity is a top priority of the firm.	✔		
Formalize diversity plan and committee with action steps and accountability to management.	✔		
Conduct firm-wide diversity training for all attorneys and staff.	✔		
Increase the number of minority attorneys at the associate level.	✔ *		
Increase the number of minority attorneys at the partnership level.	✔ *		
Develop/expand relationships with minority bar associations to offer firm's support of these networks.	✔		
Focus on strengthening firm's mentoring program, including for benefit of minority attorneys.	✔		
Conduct internal diversity needs assessment and/or retain diversity consultant to examine how firm culture might be more welcoming of minorities.		✔	
Support law firm's internal affinity networks (e.g., women, minority attorney networks).	✔		
Manage/monitor allocation of work assignments and/or hours billed to ensure women and minority attorneys have equal access/inclusion on top client matters.	✔		
Ensure minority representation on firm committees and in leadership positions.	✔		

* These activities have programs in place, but are a continual priority for the firm.

Recruitment – New Associates

Does your firm annually recruit at any of the following types of institutions?

Ivy League schools: Harvard University, University of Pennsylvania

Public state schools: University of Michigan, University of Florida, George Mason University, University of North Carolina, University of Illinois, University of Virginia, University of Georgia, University of Maryland, University of Pittsburgh, University of Iowa, University of Baltimore

Private schools: Georgetown University, University of Notre Dame, DePaul University, Chicago-Kent at Illinois Institute of Technology, Duquesne University, Washington and Lee University, Loyola University-Chicago, Vanderbilt University

Do you have any special outreach efforts directed to encourage minority law students to consider your firm?

• *Maintain regular contact with professors and career services representatives to encourage minority law students to interview*

• Participate in/host minority law student job fair(s)

• Firm's lawyers participate on career panels at school

• Outreach to leadership of minority student organizations

• Scholarships or intern/fellowships for minority students

• Sponsor bar association reception for minority summer associates

SUMMER ASSOCIATE STATISTICS: SUMMER 2003	MINORITY MEN	MINORITY WOMEN	WHITE WOMEN	TOTAL
Summer associates	1	3	19	45
Summer associates who received an offer of full-time employment	1	2	18	38
Summer associates who accepted an offer of full-time employment	1	1	16	31

Recruitment – Lateral Associates and Partners

What activities does the firm undertake to attract minority and women attorneys?

• Sponsor programs and partner with women and minority bar associations

• Participate at minority job fairs

• Seek referrals from other attorneys

• Utilize online job services (e.g., MCCA/DuPont Primary Law Firm Job Bank)

Do you use executive recruiting/search firms to seek to identify new diversity hires (partners or associates)?

Yes

List all women- and/or minority-owned executive search/recruiting firms to which the firm paid a fee for placement services in the past 12 months:

We emphasize that we want women and minority candidates with all executive search firms used, but we do not compile information on the ownership of the search firms used.

LATERAL ASSOCIATES AND PARTNERS: 1/1/03 – 12/31/03	MINORITY MEN	MINORITY WOMEN	WHITE WOMEN	TOTAL
Number of lateral associate hires	5	4	28	74
Number of lateral partner hires (equity and non-equity)	1	0	21	105
Number of new partners (equity and non-equity) promoted from associate rank	1	0	3	12
Number of new equity partners	0	0	5	48

Retention & Professional Development

ATTORNEYS WHO LEFT THE FIRM: 2003	MINORITY MEN	MINORITY WOMEN	WHITE WOMEN	TOTAL
Number of attorneys who voluntarily or involuntarily left your firm's employ in 2003	1	4	32	87

How do 2003 attrition rates generally compare to those experienced in the prior year period?

About the same as in prior years

Please identify the specific steps you are taking to reduce the attrition rate of minority and women attorneys.

• *Ensure that women and minority lawyers are in positions of leadership in all levels of the firm, which positively impacts the overall inclusive environment within McGuireWoods.*

• Develop and/or support internal employee affinity groups (e.g., minority or women networks within the firm)

• Increase/review compensation relative to competition

• Increase/improve current work/life programs

• Succession plan includes emphasis on diversity

• Work with minority and women attorneys to develop career advancement plans

• Introduce minority and women attorneys to key clients, including to lead engagements

• Review work assignments and hours billed to key client matters to make sure minority and women attorneys are not being excluded

• Strengthen mentoring program for all attorneys, including minorities and women

• Professional skills development program, including minority and women attorneys

Does your firm have part-time/flex-time policies that permit attorneys (male or female) to work alternative schedules?

Yes

What impact, if any, will the decision to work part-time have on an attorney's ability to make partner or, if already a partner, to remain a partner at your firm?

Partnership tracks are determined on an individual basis. At McGuireWoods, associates do not go off track for being considered for partnership if they are part-time, and the firm does have part-time partners. The Partnership Agreement was amended six years ago to confirm that part-timers were eligible for election to all levels of partnership.

Have any attorneys who chose to work a part-time schedule made partner at your firm?

Yes, three attorneys

Management Demographic Profile (as of 12/31/03)

	MINORITY MEN	MINORITY WOMEN	WHITE WOMEN	TOTAL
Number of attorneys on the Executive/Management Committee or equivalent	0	1	5	27
Number of attorneys on the Hiring Committee or equivalent	1	2	8	23
Number of attorneys on the Partner/Associate Review Committee or equivalent*	N/A	N/A	N/A	N/A

* Associate reviews are done through each department. Our firm does not have a "Partner/Associate Review Committee."

Please provide information regarding all minority and women attorneys who head offices or practice groups of your law firm:

Minorities heading offices: Alan C. Cason, managing partner of the Baltimore office

Women heading offices: M. Melissa Glassman, managing partner of the Tysons Corner office

Women heading practice groups: Until a few months ago, a woman chaired the products liability department, but stepped down due to her client workload. Additionally a woman previously chaired the real estate/environmental department, but stepped down after being appointed to the Firm's Board of Partners.

The Firm Says

McGuireWoods has more minority partners than most firms of our size. Since January 1, 1999, McGuireWoods has hired 276 women and minority lawyers. The firm has 43 minority lawyers (and seven international lawyers on whom we do not track ethnicity) and 194 lawyers who are women. There are 13 minority partners (and two international lawyers on whom we do not track ethnicity) and 58 women partners.

Women and minority lawyers occupy many leadership positions. Anne Marie Whittemore is on the Executive Committee. Five of the 19 members of the Board of Partners are women. Jacquelyn Stone, an African-American female, is on our Board of Partners, is the Firm-Wide Hiring Partner and chairs the Recruitment Committee. Alan Cason, also African-American, is the Managing Partner in Baltimore. Melissa Glassman is the Managing Partner in Tysons Corner, VA. Eva Tashjian-Brown is the Firm's Executive director, as well as an Equity Partner. The Firm's Chief Financial Officer is also a woman. McGuireWoods' Equal Employment Opportunity policy prohibits discrimination on the basis of race, color, sex, sexual orientation, religion, national origin, age or

disability. No act of discrimination is tolerated and is subject to disciplinary action up to and including discharge. McGuireWoods insists that all employees shall be treated with dignity and respect. McGuireWoods is committed to diversity in the workplace and an environment free from harassment and discrimination.

Our commitment to diversity includes merging with a minority-owned law firm, entering into joint ventures with other minority law firms and hiring laterally. We have recruited minority students and associates at numerous minority job fairs: Dupont Job Fairs, Southeast Minority Job Fair, BLSA Mid-Atlantic Job Fair, BLSA Northeast Job Fair and Cook County Job Fair. We participate in seminars on minority hiring sponsored by law school placement offices and student organizations. We have used Wallace Law Registry's minority database as a resource for recruiting minority lawyers and paralegals.

As a result of a recent strategic planning process, McGuireWoods formed a Human Resources Task Force and established a minority recruitment and retention subcommittee. McGuireWoods recognizes that to attract and retain talented lawyers, it should provide flexibility in the work schedule. Partners and associates may choose to work part-time, while maintaining full benefits. Associates who are part-time may continue on the partnership track.

In recognition of McGuireWoods' commitment to diversity, the Firm the inaugural recipient of International Paper's Lighthouse Award — an award presented to International Paper's legal department supplier who, by example and leadership, has distinguished itself in the area of diversity. In 1999, McGuireWoods was awarded the prestigious Minority Corporate Counsel Association's Thomas L. Sager Award for our sucess in hiring, retaining and promoting minority lawyers. The firm has been active with the MCCA as a member of the Outside Counsel Strategic Planning Committee and in raising funds from the DuPont Private Law Firm Network to support the association's Minority Job Bank. McGuireWoods provides significant support to the MCCA's annual CLE Expos. We were selected to participate in the ABA's Minority Counsel Demonstration Program due to our diversity record.

McGuireWoods lawyers are active participants in minority bar associations. Alan Cason has held leadership roles in Baltimore's Monumental City Bar Association. Zola-Mari Williams is involved in the Annual Scholarship Banquet of the D.W. Perkins Bar Association in Jacksonville, Fla. The firm has made financial contributions to the Gate City Bar Association in Atlanta and two of the firm's partners are active in it. Greta Weathersby has been active in the Cook County Bar Association and served on the Chicago Committee on Minorities in Large Law Firms. Several African-American partners of McGuireWoods have been leaders in the Old Dominion Bar Association in Virginia. Jacquelyn Stone served on the Millennium Diversity Initiative Committee of the Virginia State Bar Association. Many of our African-American lawyers, also are active in the National Bar Association.

McGuireWoods' Atlanta office provides employment to pre-qualified Spelman College students interested in law with paid internships or as litigation management assistants. Spelman is historically attended by African-American women. Of the 12 women who went through the Spelman Intern Program, nine have gone onto law school. One is an associate in our Atlanta office.

The firm is active in several programs for underprivileged children, including "Tomorrow's Promise," a college scholarship program established by to assist children of public housing tenants. McGuireWoods helped establish The Carver Promise, a nationally recognized group to help underprivileged, predominately minority children work toward high school graduation and college admission. A McGuireWoods partner is the founder and president of The Chicago Challenge, which provides some of Chicago's most economically disadvantaged inner-city children with quality education, health care, psychological counseling, after-school tutoring and

extracurricular activities. A partner in the firm's Washington, D.C., office is on the board of the DC Urban League.

Alan Cason is the chairman of the Baltimore City Bar Association's Minority Clerkship Program, which identifies exceptional minority students at Maryland law schools for summer employment at large Baltimore law firms. The firm is developing a minority scholarship program.

Over the decades, the firm has provided hundreds of hours in free legal time, handling a wide variety of legal aid matters and court-appointed cases for people of all races who need legal assistance but cannot afford it. The firm's pro bono activities have not only aided individuals, but organizations. In partnership with NAACP Executive Director Kweisi Mfumi, McGuireWoods helped create the African American Festival Foundation, a nonprofit organization dedicated to organizing an annual festival in Baltimore. We also provide pro bono legal services to the foundation. The firm formed the Slave Museum in Fredricksburg, Va., helped it obtain tax-exempt status and provided pro bono legal services to it for eight years. McGuireWoods also provides pro bono legal services to First Tee, a nonprofit group whose mission is to give minority youth access to the game of golf.

McKenna Long & Aldridge LLP

1900 K Street, NW
Washington, DC 20006
Phone: (202) 496-7500
Fax: (202) 496-7756

FIRM LEADERSHIP

Managing Partner: T. Mark Flanagan Jr., Firm-wide Managing Partner
Diversity Team Leader: Tami Lyn Azorsky, Chair, Firm-wide Diversity Committee

LOCATIONS

Atlanta, GA
Denver, CO
Los Angeles, CA
Philadelphia, PA
San Diego, CA
San Francisco, CA
Washington, DC
Brussels

LAW FIRM DEMOGRAPHIC PROFILES

FULL-TIME ASSOCIATES	2003	2002
Minority men	9	11
Minority women	16	17
White women	58	58
Total	175	166

SUMMER ASSOCIATES	2003	2002
Minority men	3	2
Minority women	7	2
White women	9	4
Total	28*	17*

* Summer associate totals include 1L and 2L students.

EQUITY PARTNERS	2003	2002
Minority men	3	3
Minority women	1	1
White women	13	13
Total	103	100

NON-EQUITY PARTNERS	2003	2002
Minority men	2	2
Minority women	3	3
White women	11	14
Total	63	76

NEW HIRES	2003	2002
Minority men	1	1
Minority women	1	4
White women	5	5
Total	24	23

Strategic Plan and Diversity Leadership

How does the firm's leadership communicate the importance of diversity to everyone at the firm? (e.g., e-mails, web site, newsletters, meetings, etc.)

An identified critical task in the firm's recently adopted and published Strategic Plan is to "develop firm-wide approaches to the hiring, training and retention of diverse and high quality professionals." In addition, we use the following MLA resources to communicate diversity: firm-wide Diversity Committee, web site diversity page, intranet diversity page, monthly updates and posted Diversity Committee meeting minutes, Hiring & Professional Development Committee meetings and recent firm-wide partners meeting.

Who has primary responsibility for leading diversity initiatives at your firm?

Tami Lyn Azorsky, chair, firm-wide Diversity Committee

Does your law firm currently have a diversity committee?

Yes

Does the committee's representation include one or more members of the firm's management/executive committee (board of directors)?

Yes

How many attorneys are on the committee, and in 2003, what was the total number of hours collectively spent by the committee in furtherance of the firm's diversity initiatives?

Total attorneys on committee: 4

Total hours spent on diversity: 150

Does the committee and/or diversity leader establish and set goals or objectives consistent with management's priorities?

Yes

Has the firm undertaken a formal or informal diversity program or set of initiatives aimed at increasing the diversity of the firm?

Yes, formal

How often does the firm's management review the firm's diversity progress/results?

Quarterly

How is the firm's diversity committee and/or firm management held accountable for achieving results?

The Diversity Committee reports to the chair of the Hiring & Professional Development Committee, who is also the vice-chair of the firm.

LAW FIRM DIVERSITY INITIATIVES	ALREADY COMPLETED	CURRENTLY ADDRESSING	NOT A CURRENT PRIORITY
Undertake communication from firm management that diversity is a top priority of the firm.	✓		
Formalize diversity plan and committee with action steps and accountability to management.	✓		
Conduct firm-wide diversity training for all attorneys and staff.		✓	
Increase the number of minority attorneys at the associate level.		✓	
Increase the number of minority attorneys at the partnership level.		✓	
Develop/expand relationships with minority bar associations to offer firm's support of these networks.		✓	
Focus on strengthening firm's mentoring program, including for benefit of minority attorneys.	✓		
Conduct internal diversity needs assessment and/or retain diversity consultant to examine how firm culture might be more welcoming of minorities.		✓	
Support law firm's internal affinity networks (e.g., women, minority attorney networks).	✓		
Manage/monitor allocation of work assignments and/or hours billed to ensure women and minority attorneys have equal access/inclusion on top client matters.		✓	
Participation and membership in diversity-focused committees and organizations.	✓		

Recruitment – New Associates

Does your firm annually recruit at any of the following types of institutions?

Ivy League schools: Harvard University, Columbia University

Public state schools: University of Georgia, Georgia State University, University of Michigan, UCLA, University of Virginia

Private schools: Duke University, Emory University, George Washington University, Georgetown University, Loyola Law School of LA, Mercer University, NYU, Pepperdine University, Southwestern University, USC

Historically Black Colleges and Universities (HBCUs): Howard University

Do you have any special outreach efforts directed to encourage minority law students to consider your firm?

• Hold a reception for minority law students

• Advertise in minority law student association publication(s)

• Participate in/host minority law student job fair(s)

- Sponsor minority law student association events
- Firm's lawyers participate on career panels at school
- Outreach to leadership of minority student organizations
- Scholarships or intern/fellowships for minority students
- Mentoring programs for minority law students

SUMMER ASSOCIATE STATISTICS: SUMMER 2003*	MINORITY MEN	MINORITY WOMEN	WHITE WOMEN	TOTAL
Summer associates	2	5	7	22
Summer associates who received an offer of full-time employment	2	4	7	21
Summer associates who accepted an offer of full-time employment	2	4	3**	16**

This chart identifies only 2L students from our 2003 summer program (who were eligible for new associate positions).
** We have three outstanding offers to students who will be completing clerkships in 2004-05. Of those, two are white women.*

Recruitment – Lateral Associates and Partners

What activities does the firm undertake to attract minority and women attorneys?

- Partner programs with women and minority bar associations
- Participate at minority job fairs
- Seek referrals from other attorneys
- Work with diverse student organizations on campuses.

Do you use executive recruiting/search firms to seek to identify new diversity hires (partners or associates)?

Yes

If yes, list all women- and/or minority-owned executive search/recruiting firms to which the firm paid a fee for placement services in the past 12 months:

Two placements with Mestel & Company, one with The Newin Co., and one with Hughes & Sloan

LATERAL ASSOCIATES AND PARTNERS: 1/1/03 – 12/31/03	MINORITY MEN	MINORITY WOMEN	WHITE WOMEN	TOTAL
Number of lateral associate hires	1	1	4	19
Number of lateral partner hires (equity and non-equity)	0	0	1	5
Number of new partners (equity and non-equity) promoted from associate rank	0	0	1	7
Number of new equity partners	0	0	0	3

Retention & Professional Development

ATTORNEYS WHO LEFT THE FIRM: 2003	MINORITY MEN	MINORITY WOMEN	WHITE WOMEN	TOTAL
Number of attorneys who voluntarily or involuntarily left your firm's employ in 2003	4	3	17	55

How do 2003 attrition rates generally compare to those experienced in the prior year period?

Higher than in prior years. 2003 was our post-merger year.

Please identify the specific steps you are taking to reduce the attrition rate of minority and women attorneys.

• Develop and/or support internal employee affinity groups (e.g., minority or women networks within the firm)

• Increase/review compensation relative to competition

• Increase/improve current work/life programs

• Work with minority and women attorneys to develop career advancement plans

• Introduce minority and women attorneys to key clients, including to lead engagements

• Review work assignments and hours billed to key client matters to make sure minority and women attorneys are not being excluded

• Strengthen mentoring program for all attorneys, including minorities and women

• Professional skills development program, including minority and women attorneys

Does your firm have part-time/flex-time policies that permit attorneys (male or female) to work alternative schedules?

Yes

What impact, if any, will the decision to work part-time have on an attorney's ability to make partner or, if already a partner, to remain a partner at your firm?

An attorney working part-time remains eligible for partnership consideration. Primary issues considered in the decision include commitment, experience and contribution. Information regarding our part-time policy is available upon request.

Have any attorneys who chose to work a part-time schedule made partner at your firm?

Yes. Six attorneys.

Management Demographic Profile (as of 12/31/03)

	MINORITY MEN	MINORITY WOMEN	WHITE WOMEN	TOTAL
Number of attorneys on the Executive/Management Committee or equivalent	0	0	1	19*
Number of attorneys on the Hiring Committee or equivalent	2	3	9	31**
Number of attorneys on the Partner/Associate Review Committee or equivalent	1	0	1	10***

* Includes two firm-wide co chairs, two co-vice-chairs, two co-managing partners and 13 attorneys on the board of directors (we don't double-count co-chairs or vice-chair).
** Count includes hiring committees in Atlanta (12), D.C. (9), L.A. (5) and HPD Committee (5).
*** Count includes eight firm-wide department heads and two co-managing partners (Comp).

Please provide information regarding all minority and women attorneys who head offices or practice groups of your law firm:

Minorities heading practice groups: Song Jung, Intellectual Property Department; Farah Nicol, Toxic Tort Litigation Team Leader

Women heading practice groups: Tami Lyn Azorsky, Co-Chair, Litigation Department; Debby Ebel, Litigation Team Leader; Ann-Marie McGaughey, Corporate Team Leader; Kellie Newton, Corporate Team Leader; Lisa Oberg, Toxic Tort Litigation Team Leader

The Firm Says

Diversity Initiative

McKenna Long & Aldridge LLP is committed to achieve the goals of diversity and inclusiveness. The Diversity Initiative is based on both moral and business imperatives: we believe diversity in law firms reflects the values of the society in which we practice law; we also believe that the firm's present business and its future business opportunities will be enhanced by assuring each of our lawyers an environment which furthers the progress and success of her/his practice. The following principles are the foundation of this commitment:

- To provide full access to career opportunity to everyone throughout the firm;
- To be inclusive of everyone, regardless of differences in race, color, national origin, gender, religion, age, disability, sexual orientation, culture or lifestyle; and
- To recruit, develop, promote and retain a world-class talent base that reflects the diversity of the communities in which we live.

We believe that recruiting, hiring and developing a diverse work force makes MLA a stronger and more competitive law firm. MLA is committed to attracting and retaining the best and brightest employees who reflect the diversity of our society. To that end, MLA has established relationships with key universities and student and professional organizations, and has established an internal Diversity Committee.

Our commitment to diversity will be fulfilled through the adoption and implementation of an annual Diversity Action Plan. Highlights of past and ongoing projects are listed below.

Program sponsorship

D.C. Law Students in Court Program: MLA's D.C. office offers financial and volunteer support for this nonprofit legal clinic that provides legal services to the poor. The clinic is supported by five area law schools and is staffed largely by minority students.

Racial & Ethnic Minority Diversity in Law Firms Seminar, Southern California Managing Partners Roundtable: The Managing Partners Roundtable, of which MLA is a charter member, hosted this seminar (its first) to create a forum for a confidential, candid and constructive dialogue on race an ethnicity at L.A. firms. MLA sent seven representatives to the all-day program.

Minority Student Scholarship Fund, Georgia State University College of Law: The firm was one of three founding sponsors to establish the endowment of this minority student scholarship fund.

Atlanta Bar Minority Clerkship Program: MLA has participated in this program since its inception by hiring a 1L law clerk each year.

Women of Color Collective Spring Symposium, Georgetown University Law Center: MLA co-sponsored and provided an attorney panelist for this year's symposium, "Lives in the Balance: Meeting the Needs of Career and Family in the 21st Century."

Youth Internship Program, Constitutional Rights Foundation: This program provides under-served high school students from the Greater Los Angeles Area the opportunity to participate in an innovative eight-week program. MLA has sponsored a student each summer in 2003 and 2004.

Annual Business Development Conference, California Minority Counsel Program: As a co-sponsor, MLA attorneys of color representing the San Francisco, San Diego and Los Angeles offices attended the 14th annual conference in November 2003.

Prejudice Awareness Summit, Georgia Tech University: For the fourth year, MLA is a co-sponsor of the Atlanta Summit, part of a nationwide program that works with middle school students to examine the roots of prejudice and develop ongoing programs in schools to educate children to value the differences among people.

Professional Women's Roundtable: This fall marks the sixth roundtable the firm has sponsored for its women clients and prospective clients. This year's all-day program will include presentations by two nationally known speakers who will lead discussions on hiring and retaining women and people of color and communication and negotiating skills.

Law school programs

- Writing seminars for diverse law student organizations at selected Atlanta schools
- Interviewing workshop panel presentations and mock interview programs at selected schools in Atlanta, Washington, D.C., and Los Angeles
- First-Year Minority Law Student Open House for students at D.C. law schools
- Speaker's program on Marcus Dixon case and reception, Georgetown University Law Center
- Co-creator, Women of Color Collective Mentor Program, Georgetown University Law Center

Organization memberships

- California Minority Counsel Program (CMCP)
- Founding member, The Atlanta Legal Diversity Consortium, Inc.

• Southern California Managing Partners Roundtable Diversity Committee (two members)

• Los Angeles Area Legal Recruitment Association (LAALRA) Diversity Committee

Honors and awards

• Justice Benham "Friend of BLSA Award," Georgia State University School of Law

• Southern Region BLSA Trailblazer Award

• Special Recognition for Commitment to Increasing Diversity in the Legal Profession, BLSA, Emory University School of Law

Milbank, Tweed, Hadley & McCloy, LLP

1 Chase Manhattan Plaza
New York, NY 10005
Phone: (212) 530-5000
Fax: (212) 530-5219

FIRM LEADERSHIP

Managing Partner: Mel Immergut, Chairman
Diversity Team Leader: Errol Taylor and Elihu
Robertson, Chairmen of the Diversity
Committee

LOCATIONS

New York, NY (HQ)
Los Angeles, CA
Palo Alto, CA
Washington, DC
Frankfurt
London
Munich
Hong Kong
Singapore
Tokyo

LAW FIRM DEMOGRAPHIC PROFILES

FULL-TIME ASSOCIATES	2003	2002
Minority men	30	36
Minority women	39	35
White women	82	89
Total	318	325

SUMMER ASSOCIATES	2003	2002
Minority men	5	8
Minority women	14	15
White women	22	30
Total	56	91

EQUITY PARTNERS	2003	2002
Minority men	7	5
Minority women	3	3
White women	4	4
Total	105	104

NEW HIRES	2003	2002
Minority men	9	9
Minority women	9	12
White women	22	26
Total	85	105

Strategic Plan and Diversity Leadership

How does the firm's leadership communicate the importance of diversity to everyone at the firm? (e.g., e-mails, web site, newsletters, meetings, etc.)

E-mail, regular meetings and web site; diversity training for all lawyers.

Who has primary responsibility for leading diversity initiatives at your firm?

Errol Taylor and Elihu Robertson, chairmen of the Diversity Committee

Does your law firm currently have a diversity committee?

Yes

Does the committee's representation include one or more members of the firm's management/executive committee (or the equivalent)?

Yes

How many attorneys are on the committee, and in 2003, what was the total number of hours collectively spent by the committee in furtherance of the firm's diversity initiatives?

Total attorneys on committee: 10

Total hours spent on diversity: Weekly meetings

Does the committee and/or diversity leader establish and set goals or objectives consistent with management's priorities?

Yes

Has the firm undertaken a formal or informal diversity program or set of initiatives aimed at increasing the diversity of the firm?

Yes, formal

How often does the firm's management review the firm's diversity progress/results?

Quarterly

How is the firm's diversity committee and/or firm management held accountable for achieving results?

The Diversity Committee reports to the Executive Committee and periodically to the firm. Practice group quarterly meeting agenda includes review of efforts regarding diversity. Partners are encouraged to address efforts in diversity in annual self-appraisal.

LAW FIRM DIVERSITY INITIATIVES	ALREADY COMPLETED	CURRENTLY ADDRESSING	NOT A CURRENT PRIORITY
Undertake communication from firm management that diversity is a top priority of the firm.	✔		
Formalize diversity plan and committee with action steps and accountability to management.	✔		
Conduct firm-wide diversity training for all attorneys and staff.	✔		
Increase the number of minority attorneys at the associate level.		✔	
Increase the number of minority attorneys at the partnership level.		✔	
Develop/expand relationships with minority bar associations to offer firm's support of these networks.		✔	
Focus on strengthening firm's mentoring program, including for benefit of minority attorneys.	✔		
Conduct internal diversity needs assessment and/or retain diversity consultant to examine how firm culture might be more welcoming of minorities.	✔		
Support law firm's internal affinity networks (e.g., women, minority attorney networks).	✔		
Manage/monitor allocation of work assignments and/or hours billed to ensure women and minority attorneys have equal access/inclusion on top client matters.		✔	

Recruitment – New Associates

Does your firm annually recruit at any of the following types of institutions?

Ivy League schools: Harvard University, Columbia University, Yale University, University of Pennsylvania

Public state schools: SUNY, Rutgers University, University of Michigan, UCLA, University of Virginia

Historically Black Colleges and Universities (HBCUs): Howard University

Do you have any special outreach efforts directed to encourage minority law students to consider your firm?

• Advertise in minority law student association publication(s)

• Participate in/host minority law student job fair(s)

• Sponsor minority law student association events

• Firm's lawyers participate on career panels at school

• Outreach to leadership of minority student organizations

• Scholarships or intern/fellowships for minority students

SUMMER ASSOCIATE STATISTICS: SUMMER 2003	MINORITY MEN	MINORITY WOMEN	WHITE WOMEN	TOTAL
Summer associates	2	13	18	46
Summer associates who received an offer of full-time employment	2	13	18	43
Summer associates who accepted an offer of full-time employment	1	9	12	29

Recruitment – Lateral Associates and Partners

What activities does the firm undertake to attract minority and women attorneys?

• Partner programs with women and minority bar associations

• Participate at minority job fairs

• Seek referrals from other attorneys

Do you use executive recruiting/search firms to seek to identify new diversity hires (partners or associates)?

Yes

LATERAL ASSOCIATES AND PARTNERS: 1/1/03 – 12/31/03	MINORITY MEN	MINORITY WOMEN	WHITE WOMEN	TOTAL
Number of lateral associate hires	3	0	3	12
Number of lateral partner hires (equity and non-equity)	1	0	0	7
Number of new partners (equity and non-equity) promoted from associate rank	1	0	0	2

Retention & Professional Development

Please identify the specific steps you are taking to reduce the attrition rate of minority and women attorneys.

• Develop and/or support internal employee affinity groups (e.g., minority or women networks within the firm)

• Increase/improve current work/life programs

• Work with minority and women attorneys to develop career advancement plans

• Introduce minority and women attorneys to key clients, including to lead engagements

• Review work assignments and hours billed to key client matters to make sure minority and women attorneys are not being excluded

• Strengthen mentoring program for all attorneys, including minorities and women

• Professional skills development program, including minority and women attorneys

Does your firm have part-time/flex-time policies that permit attorneys (male or female) to work alternative schedules?

Yes

What impact, if any, will the decision to work part-time have on an attorney's ability to make partner or, if already a partner, to remain a partner at your firm?

Partnership track may be extended for part-time associates – otherwise, no impact.

Have any attorneys who chose to work a part-time schedule made partner at your firm?

No

Management Demographic Profile (as of 12/31/03)

	MINORITY MEN	MINORITY WOMEN	WHITE WOMEN	TOTAL
Number of attorneys on the Executive/Management Committee or equivalent	0	0	0	3
Number of attorneys on the Hiring Committee or equivalent	7	3	7	24

Please provide information regarding all minority and women attorneys who head offices or practice groups of your law firm:

Women heading practice groups: Georgiana Slade, Trusts & Estates Department

Mintz, Levin, Cohn, Ferris, Glovsky and Popeo PC

One Financial Center
Boston, MA 02111
Phone: (617) 542-6000
Fax: (617) 542-2241

FIRM LEADERSHIP

Cherie Kiser, Managing Partner-Integration &
Chair of the Diversity Committee

LOCATIONS

Boston, MA (HQ)
Los Angeles, CA
New Haven, CT
New York, NY
Reston, VA
Washington, DC
London

LAW FIRM DEMOGRAPHIC PROFILES

FULL-TIME ASSOCIATES	2003	2002
Minority men	9	10
Minority women	16	17
White women	104	108
Total	255	273

SUMMER ASSOCIATES*	2003	2002
Minority men	2	2
Minority women	1	1
White women	12	6
Total	27	20

Summer associates from 6/1/02-9/1/02 and 6/1/03 – 9/1/03

EQUITY PARTNERS	2003	2002
Minority men	0	0
Minority women	0	0
White women	8	7
Total	68	60

NON-EQUITY PARTNERS	2003	2002
Minority men	5	6
Minority women	0	0
White women	25	27
Total	96	109

NEW HIRES	2003	2002
Minority men	2	2
Minority women	3	2
White women	14	22
Total	43	42

Strategic Plan and Diversity Leadership

How does the firm's leadership communicate the importance of diversity to everyone at the firm? (e.g., e-mails, web site, newsletters, meetings, etc.)

Firm leadership communicates the significance of diversity at firm functions such as the firm's annual meeting and various partnership retreats. Additionally, the firm's Diversity Committee uses the firm's web site and intranet site as a means of communicating important issues respecting diversity to the firm.

Who has primary responsibility for leading diversity initiatives at your firm?

Cherie Kiser, managing partner-integration

Does your law firm currently have a diversity committee?

Yes

Does the committee's representation include one or more members of the firm's management/executive committee (or the equivalent)?

Yes

How many attorneys are on the committee, and in 2003, what was the total number of hours collectively spent by the committee in furtherance of the firm's diversity initiatives?

Total attorneys on committee: 13

Total hours spent on diversity: 5-10 hours/month

Does the committee and/or diversity leader establish and set goals or objectives consistent with management's priorities?

Yes

Has the firm undertaken a formal or informal diversity program or set of initiatives aimed at increasing the diversity of the firm?

Yes, formal

How often does the firm's management review the firm's diversity progress/results?

Twice a year

How is the firm's diversity committee and/or firm management held accountable for achieving results?

Mintz Levin's Diversity Committee reports directly to the firm's policy and management committees, both of which are responsible for the firm's strategic direction and day-to-day operation.

LAW FIRM DIVERSITY INITIATIVES	ALREADY COMPLETED	CURRENTLY ADDRESSING	NOT A CURRENT PRIORITY
Undertake communication from firm management that diversity is a top priority of the firm.	✓		
Formalize diversity plan and committee with action steps and accountability to management.		✓	
Conduct firm-wide diversity training for all attorneys and staff.		✓	
Increase the number of minority attorneys at the associate level.		✓	
Increase the number of minority attorneys at the partnership level.		✓	
Develop/expand relationships with minority bar associations to offer firm's support of these networks.	✓		
Focus on strengthening firm's mentoring program, including for benefit of minority attorneys.	✓		
Conduct internal diversity needs assessment and/or retain diversity consultant to examine how firm culture might be more welcoming of minorities.	✓		
Support law firm's internal affinity networks (e.g., women, minority attorney networks).	✓		
Manage/monitor allocation of work assignments and/or hours billed to ensure women and minority attorneys have equal access/inclusion on top client matters.		✓	

Recruitment – New Associates

Does your firm annually recruit at any of the following types of institutions?

Ivy League schools: Harvard University, Cornell University, University of Pennsylvania, Columbia University

Public state schools: University of Virginia, College of William & Mary, University of Michigan

Private schools: Boston College, Boston University, Northeastern University, George Washington University, Georgetown University, American University, Suffolk University, NYU, Duke University, New England School of Law, Catholic University of America, Franklin Pierce Law Center

Historically Black Colleges and Universities (HBCUs): Howard University

Do you have any special outreach efforts directed to encourage minority law students to consider your firm?

• *Host mock interview workshop for local law students of color (generally occurs every February in Boston)*

• Hold a reception for minority law students

• Participate in/host minority law student job fair(s)

• Sponsor minority law student association events

- Firm's lawyers participate on career panels at school
- Outreach to leadership of minority student organizations
- Scholarships or intern/fellowships for minority students

SUMMER ASSOCIATE STATISTICS: SUMMER 2003	MINORITY MEN	MINORITY WOMEN	WHITE WOMEN	TOTAL
Summer associates	2	0	10	20
Summer associates who received an offer of full-time employment	2	0	10	18
Summer associates who accepted an offer of full-time employment	2	0	7	12*

* Three offers are outstanding

Recruitment – Lateral Associates and Partners

What activities does the firm undertake to attract minority and women attorneys?

• Direct outreach to student bar associations; host mock interview workshop for local law students of color.
- Partner programs with women and minority bar associations
- Participate at minority job fairs (BLG DC/Boston Fall Job Fairs, Harvard BLSA Job Fair)
- Seek referrals from other attorneys
- Utilize online job services (e.g., MCCA/DuPont Primary Law Firm Job Bank)

Do you use executive recruiting/search firms to seek to identify new diversity hires (partners or associates)?

Yes

List all women- and/or minority-owned executive search/recruiting firms to which the firm paid a fee for placement services in the past 12 months

None.

LATERAL ASSOCIATES AND PARTNERS: 1/1/03 – 12/31/03	MINORITY MEN	MINORITY WOMEN	WHITE WOMEN	TOTAL
Number of lateral associate hires	0	1	5	15
Number of lateral partner hires (equity and non-equity)	0	0	0	3
Number of new partners (equity and non-equity) promoted from associate rank	0	0	4	10
Number of new equity partners	0	0	1	14

Retention & Professional Development

ATTORNEYS WHO LEFT THE FIRM: 2003	MINORITY MEN	MINORITY WOMEN	WHITE WOMEN	TOTAL
Number of attorneys who voluntarily or involuntarily left your firm's employ in 2003	5	4	27	69

How do 2003 attrition rates generally compare to those experienced in the prior year period?

Lower than in prior years

Please identify the specific steps you are taking to reduce the attrition rate of minority and women attorneys.

• Develop and/or support internal employee affinity groups (e.g., minority or women networks within the firm)

• Work with minority and women attorneys to develop career advancement plans

• Introduce minority and women attorneys to key clients, including to lead engagements

• Review work assignments and hours billed to key client matters to make sure minority and women attorneys are not being excluded

• Strengthen mentoring program for all attorneys, including minorities and women

• Professional skills development program, including minority and women Attorneys

Does your firm have part-time/flex-time policies that permit attorneys (male or female) to work alternative schedules?

Yes

What impact, if any, will the decision to work part-time have on an attorney's ability to make partner, or if already a partner to remain a partner at your firm?

None. Attorneys on part-time schedules are fully eligible for partnership opportunities.

Have any attorneys who chose to work a part-time schedule made partner at your firm?

Yes, one attorney.

Management Demographic Profile (as of 12/31/03)

	MINORITY MEN	MINORITY WOMEN	WHITE WOMEN	TOTAL
Number of attorneys on the Executive/Management Committee or equivalent	0	0	1	17
Number of attorneys on the Hiring Committee or equivalent	2	1	3	16
Number of attorneys on the Partner/Associate Review Committee or equivalent	0	0	2	10

Please provide information regarding all minority and women attorneys who head offices or practice groups of your law firm:

Women heading offices: Cherie Kiser, Washington; Jennifer Rubin, New Haven

Minorities heading practice groups: Anthony Hubbard, Business & Finance

Women heading practice groups: Linda Bentley, Healthcare; Betsy Burnett, Litigation; Rosemary Allen, IP; Kim Marrkand, Litigation; Susan Cohen, Immigration; Cherie Kiser, Communications/IT

The Firm Says

Mintz Levin Cohn Ferris Glovsky and Popeo, PC has a genuine commitment to diversity and is involved in encouraging diversity both at the firm and in the legal profession. We adhere to a strict policy of equal opportunity, both in letter and spirit, and value diversity among our employees, which we consistently work to foster. The firm is a diverse workplace defined by an open, supportive, collegial environment.

Mintz Levin's commitment to diversity is driven by its diversity mission: "To fully understand and value diversity in its employees, clients and other constituencies, and to integrate this appreciation into the Firm's values, vision, mission, culture, policies and practices." The firm has a 14-member Diversity Committee to weave this mission into the firm's strategic direction. The committee consists of 10 partners, three associates and a non-attorney professional, each representing a different constituency group. Our Diversity Committee reflects our firm's diversity and is chaired by one of the four managing partners. The committee meets every month and is charged with formulating and adopting policies that impact recruiting, retention, mentoring and promoting a diverse work force, including attorneys, other legal professionals and support staff.

In addition to the Diversity Committee, the firm actively encourages the establishment of so-called affinity groups within the firm. In late 2003, a GLBT (gay, lesbian, bisexual, transgender) Group was established, consisting of approximately 17 partners, associates and senior professionals that meet quarterly. The Minority Attorneys Group has been meeting for over a decade on a quarterly basis. These forums provide an opportunity for mutual support, sharing concerns and establishing informal mentoring.

Mintz Levin has been on the forefront of issues respecting lawyers of color and women. In 1986, two Mintz Levin partners were instrumental in creating the Boston Lawyers Group (BLG), a nonprofit organization founded by a consortium of major Boston firms committed to improving the hiring and retention of lawyers of color. Today, the BLG has over 30 prominent legal organizations, including two minority law firms and a number of public sector entities ranging from the city of Boston corporation counsel to the offices of the Massachusetts attorney general and the U.S. attorney. Mintz Levin partners are active members of the BLG's executive committee and a Mintz Levin associate serves on the associate advisory board. The BLG is credited with raising awareness of the diversity issue at the senior levels of all major Boston law firms, enhancing the image of Boston as a place to live and work for attorneys of color, and dramatically increasing the numbers of attorneys of color practicing in the firms.

In 2002, the firm made Boston history by electing four lawyers of color to its partnership ranks in a single year. One of these partners is now the firm's hiring partner. Mintz Levin is proud to have elected Boston's first female partner in 1966. Today, Mintz Levin's women partners lead numerous practice groups within the firm and nearly half of all attorneys at the firm are women. In June 2003, Mintz Levin was recognized by The American Lawyer as exceeding the national average for woman partners. Additionally, the firm was among the first firms

nationwide to employ part-time and other flexible work arrangements to meet the needs of its women attorneys. Since 1993, the firm has offered employee benefits to same-sex partners of employees.

Our commitment to diversity is exemplified by the service of Mintz Levin partners and associates in leadership positions both inside and outside the firm, including offices and board appointments at the Metropolitan Black Bar Association, the Massachusetts Black Lawyers Association, the South Asian Bar Association, the Massachusetts Association of Hispanic Attorneys, the Hispanic-American Chamber of Commerce, the Women's Bar Association of Massachusetts and the National Lesbian and Gay Bar Association.

The firm participates in and supports numerous diversity-related efforts sponsored by organizations including MCCA, the Boston Women's Fund, Women in Cable and Communications, GLAD, ABA Commission on Racial and Ethnic Diversity in the Profession, the Charting Your Own Course Foundation, Massachusetts Lesbian and Gay Bar Association, the Jewish Federation of the North Shore, Citizen Schools, The Commonwealth Institute's Top 100 Women-Led Businesses Project, Springboard Enterprises, the Northeastern Black Law Students Association and the National Black Law Students Association.

On the recruiting front, Mintz Levin hosts an annual mock interview workshop for Boston area law students of color and participates in job fairs for law students of color in Washington, D.C., and New York. Mintz Levin lawyers mentor women law students and law students of color, support on-campus student organizations and speak at diversity and recruiting symposiums. The firm also supports the AIPLA minority student scholarship fund.

The firm's pro bono activities also reflect its commitment to diversity. For over a decade, Mintz Levin has committed itself to a program of community service, focusing on domestic violence prevention. The decision to focus on domestic violence was built upon the experience and resources the firm had already developed in this area through its pro bono Domestic Violence Project. Through the Domestic Violence Project's pro bono client representation and legislative activity, Mintz Levin has demonstrated a strong commitment to issues surrounding domestic violence and the rights of abused women and children. Our domestic violence initiatives enable us to utilize our skills as legal advocates and to identify opportunities for legislative initiatives at both the state and federal levels. Since 1989, attorneys have represented over 185 victims of domestic violence.

In addition, the firm is one of four firms nationwide that has represented the Human Rights Campaign (the largest national GLBT advocacy organization) over the last several years, providing assistance with federal legislative and constitutional issues, including hate crime measures and anti-discrimination legislation. In recognition of this service, HRC presented Mintz Levin with its Corporate Community Service Awards in 1995 and 1996. In 2002, a Mintz Levin attorney received the National Ally of Justice Award for the significant pro bono efforts she had undertaken on behalf of the HRC.

Moore & Van Allen PLLC

100 N. Tryon Street, Suite 4700
Charlotte, NC 28202-4003
Phone: (704) 331-1000
Fax: (704) 331-1159

FIRM LEADERSHIP

Managing Partner: Ernest W. Reigel, Member
Diversity Team Leaders: John S. Chinuntdet,
Member, and Valecia M. McDowell, Associate

LOCATIONS

Charlotte, NC (HQ)
Charleston, SC
Durham, NC

LAW FIRM DEMOGRAPHIC PROFILES

FULL-TIME ASSOCIATES	2003	2002
Minority men	7	6
Minority women	2	3
White women	33	30
Total	98	99

SUMMER ASSOCIATES	2003	2002
Minority men	3	2
Minority women	0	1
White women	8	12
Total	24	30

EQUITY PARTNERS	2003	2002
Minority men	1	0
Minority women	0	0
White women	2	5
Total	56	63

NON-EQUITY PARTNERS	2003	2002
Minority men	0	1
Minority women	1	1
White women	10	11
Total	50	60

NEW HIRES	2003	2002
Minority men	0	2
Minority women	0	0
White women	8	16
Total	24	31

Strategic Plan and Diversity Leadership

How does the firm's leadership communicate the importance of diversity to everyone at the firm? (e.g., e-mails, web site, newsletters, meetings, etc.)

Matters of diversity are communicated by way of the firm's external web site, internal intranet site, e-mail and Daily Bulletin postings, as well as through quarterly diversity meetings and presentations on various diversity issues.

Who has primary responsibility for leading diversity initiatives at your firm?

John S. Chinuntdet, member (Financial Services) and Valecia M. McDowell, associate (Litigation), co-chairs of Diversity Committee.

Does your law firm currently have a diversity committee?

Yes

Does the committee's representation include one or more members of the firm's management/executive committee (or the equivalent)?

No

How many attorneys are on the committee, and in 2003, what was the total number of hours collectively spent by the committee in furtherance of the firm's diversity initiatives?

Total attorneys on committee: 17

Total hours spent on diversity: 256.58

Does the committee and/or diversity leader establish and set goals or objectives consistent with management's priorities?

Yes

Has the firm undertaken a formal or informal diversity program or set of initiatives aimed at increasing the diversity of the firm?

Yes, informal

How often does the firm's management review the firm's diversity progress/results?

Quarterly

LAW FIRM DIVERSITY INITIATIVES	ALREADY COMPLETED	CURRENTLY ADDRESSING	NOT A CURRENT PRIORITY
Undertake communication from firm management that diversity is a top priority of the firm.		✓	
Formalize diversity plan and committee with action steps and accountability to management.		✓	
Conduct firm-wide diversity training for all attorneys and staff.			✓
Increase the number of minority attorneys at the associate level.		✓	
Increase the number of minority attorneys at the partnership level.		✓	
Develop/expand relationships with minority bar associations to offer firm's support of these networks.	✓		
Focus on strengthening firm's mentoring program, including for benefit of minority attorneys.		✓	
Conduct internal diversity needs assessment and/or retain diversity consultant to examine how firm culture might be more welcoming of minorities.			✓
Support law firm's internal affinity networks (e.g., women, minority attorney networks).		✓	
Manage/monitor allocation of work assignments and/or hours billed to ensure women and minority attorneys have equal access/inclusion on top client matters.		✓	

Recruitment - New Associates

Does your firm annually recruit at any of the following types of institutions? (Check all that apply and list the schools).

Ivy League schools: Harvard University, Yale University

Public state schools: University of North Carolina, University of Virginia, University of Texas, University of Georgia, University of Michigan, College of William and Mary

Private schools: Duke University, Wake Forest University, Emory University, NYU, Vanderbilt University, USC

Historically Black Colleges and Universities (HBCUs): Howard University, North Carolina Central University

Other predominantly minority and/or women's colleges: National Black Law Students Association Northeastern Job Fair, Southeastern Minority Job Fair

 VAULT

867

MINORITY CORPORATE COUNSEL ASSOCIATION

Do you have any special outreach efforts directed to encourage minority law students to consider your firm?

• Hold a reception for minority law students

• Participate in/host minority law student job fair(s)

• Sponsor minority law student association events

• Firm's lawyers participate on career panels at school

• Outreach to leadership of minority student organizations

SUMMER ASSOCIATE STATISTICS: SUMMER 2003	MINORITY MEN	MINORITY WOMEN	WHITE WOMEN	TOTAL
Summer associates	3	0	8	24
Summer associates who received an offer of full-time employment	1	0	4	13
Summer associates who accepted an offer of full-time employment	1	0	4	8

Recruitment – Lateral Associates and Partners

What activities does the firm undertake to attract minority and women attorneys?

• *Utilize services of search firms specializing in the placement of minority and female candidates.*

• Partner programs with women and minority bar associations

• Participate at minority job fairs

• Seek referrals from other attorneys

• Utilize online job services (e.g., MCCA/DuPont Primary Law Firm Job Bank)

Do you use executive recruiting/search firms to seek to identify new diversity hires (partners or associates)?

Yes

If yes, list all women- and/or minority-owned executive search/recruiting firms to which the firm paid a fee for placement services in the past 12 months:

None.

LATERAL ASSOCIATES AND PARTNERS: 1/1/03 – 12/31/03	MINORITY MEN	MINORITY WOMEN	WHITE WOMEN	TOTAL
Number of lateral associate hires	0	0	1	5
Number of lateral partner hires (equity and non-equity)	0	0	1	6
Number of new partners (equity and non-equity) promoted from associate rank	0	0	0	7
Number of new equity partners	0	0	0	4

Moore & Van Allen PLLC

Retention & Professional Development

ATTORNEYS WHO LEFT THE FIRM: 2003	MINORITY MEN	MINORITY WOMEN	WHITE WOMEN	TOTAL
Number of attorneys who voluntarily or involuntarily left your firm's employ in 2003	1	0	9	39*

* Office consolidation in Raleigh/Durham, N.C., resulted in an unusually high number of lawyer departures (voluntary) in 2003.

How do 2003 attrition rates generally compare to those experienced in the prior year period?

Higher than in prior years (see note* above)

Please identify the specific steps you are taking to reduce the attrition rate of minority and women attorneys

• *Limited use of employer-sponsored child care center based on tenancy of building owned by child care center sponsor. Additional employer-sponsored backup child care program available to attorneys and staff.*

• Develop and/or support internal employee affinity groups (e.g., minority or women networks within the firm)

• Increase/improve current work/life programs

• Professional skills development program, including minority and women attorneys

Does your firm have part-time/flex-time policies that permit attorneys (male or female) to work alternative schedules?

Yes. We presently have the following attorneys on alternative schedules: six members, two associates and nine counsels. In addition, the following attorneys telecommute: one member and one associate.

What impact, if any, will the decision to work part-time have on an attorney's ability to make partner or, if already a partner, to remain a partner at your firm?

In order to retain benefits and the option of remaining on a modified membership track, hours pro-rated by 75 percent of the average, full-time attorney are necessary. Lawyers may work part-time schedules consisting of fewer than 75 percent hours, with no benefits or membership track options.

Have any attorneys who chose to work a part-time schedule made partner at your firm?

Yes, one attorney.

Management Demographic Profile (as of 12/31/03)

	MINORITY MEN	MINORITY WOMEN	WHITE WOMEN	TOTAL
Number of attorneys on the Executive/Management Committee or equivalent	0	0	0	8
Number of attorneys on the Hiring Committee or equivalent	2	1	9	33
Number of attorneys on the Partner/Associate Review Committee or equivalent	0	0	2	5

MINORITY CORPORATE COUNSEL ASSOCIATION

Please provide information regarding all minority and women attorneys who head offices or practice groups of your law firm:

Minorities heading practice groups: John S. Chinuntdet, Co-Head of Investment Team/Financial Services

Women heading practice groups: Arlene Hanks, Intellectual Property

The Firm Says

Moore & Van Allen is committed to minority recruitment and fostering diversity within the firm. Our firm actively recruits qualified women and minority candidates. To this end, the firm established an active Diversity Committee in 2000 to evaluate and make recommendations regarding the recruitment and retention of traditionally underrepresented groups, and to lead the firm in shaping a culture which values differences and encourages all employees to reach their fullest potential.

Since the inception of Moore & Van Allen's Diversity Committee in 2000, the firm has seen a 175 percent increase in its number of minority attorneys. That number is based on the following:

- 2000 minority attorneys: one member, three associates
- 2004 minority attorneys: two members, nine associates

Under the leadership of the Diversity Committee, Moore & Van Allen and the Charlotte Chamber of Commerce spearheaded two city-wide minority events featuring noted speakers addressing issues facing minority professionals in the community. Beginning in 2002, the firm has partnered with the Afro-American Cultural Center, a cultural, educational and community-based organization. The Diversity Committee is also actively involved in partnering with law schools and other employers to identify and develop relationships with minority candidates.

Associates may earn up to 50 hours of total billable credit during each calendar year toward their billable hour goal for bonus eligibility by participating in approved recruiting, diversity, pro bono and/or public service activities.

Morgan, Lewis & Bockius LLP

1701 Market Street
Philadelphia, PA 19103-2921
Phone: (215) 963-5000
Fax: (215) 963-5001
Diversity Contact: Francis M. Milone, Chair

FIRM LEADERSHIP

Managing Partners:
- Robert A. Dufek, Managing Partner for Practice (Litigation and Regulatory)
- Thomas J. Sharbaugh, Managing Partner for Operations
- Philip H. Werner, Managing Partner for Practice (Transactional, International and Interdisciplinary)

Diversity Team Leader:
- Christopher P. Reynolds, Partner and Chair of Firm-wide Diversity Committee

LOCATIONS

Philadelphia, PA (HQ)
Boston, MA
Chicago, IL
Dallas, TX
Harrisburg, PA
Irvine, CA
Los Angeles, CA
Miami, FL
New York, NY
Palo Alto, CA
Pittsburgh, PA
Princeton, NJ
San Francisco, CA
Washington, DC
Brussels; Frankfurt
London
Paris
Tokyo

LAW FIRM DEMOGRAPHIC PROFILES

FULL-TIME ASSOCIATES	2003	2002
Minority men	43	43
Minority women	56	50
White women	227	224
Total	620	607

SUMMER ASSOCIATES	2003	2002
Minority men	8	7
Minority women	13	9
White women	35	34
Total	83	63

PARTNERS*	2003	2002
Minority men	14	7
Minority women	5	4
White women	58	43
Total	391	331

* We do not distinguish between equity and non-equity partners

NEW HIRES	2003	2002
Minority men	21	17
Minority women	27	13
White women	96	48
Total	306	169

Strategic Plan and Diversity Leadership

How does the firm's leadership communicate the importance of diversity to everyone at the firm? (e.g., e-mails, web site, newsletters, meetings, etc.)

Morgan Lewis communicates the importance of diversity to everyone at the firm in a number of ways. First, and foremost, our chair, Francis M. Milone, communicates directly with all personnel to convey the importance of diversity in our workplace. In April 2003, he approved the following diversity mission statement to summarize and communicate our commitment to all firm personnel:

Morgan Lewis serves a global array of clients throughout the United States and the world. The clients we serve and the communities in which we operate are diverse. We value the breadth of perspectives and the richness of experience made possible by having a diverse complement of lawyers and staff. We are committed to achieving greater diversity within the firm as an important element of maintaining our excellence.

This statement of diversity is both complete and emphatic. It recognizes that we are not just waking up to diversity, and our chair has challenged us to move forward in this area.

Second, we communicate our efforts externally. The firm's diversity efforts have a prominent place on our web site, our recruiting materials and our client proposals. We are, in fact, one of the few firms of our size and caliber to have placed diversity as a top-line item on the home page of our web page. When you "click" on www.morganlewis.com, the diversity heading appears on the home page, and links to internal, as well as external, resources relating to our diversity efforts.

Finally, we communicate our efforts through a series of internal mechanisms. In November 2003, we established a diversity committee, consisting of a chair and five partner members, with support from human resources and marketing. The committee meets quarterly and focuses on five areas of accountability: recruiting, retention, policies and procedures, external affairs and client development. Each of the partners has underlying accountability for a particular area. These partners are in constant communication with each other and members of the firm to ensure that our diversity efforts are a top-line item for the firm. A discussion of our diversity efforts was presented to our summer associates during our firm-wide kickoff orientation program and we plan on having a session on this subject at our fall All Partner meeting.

Who has primary responsibility for leading diversity initiatives at your firm?

Christopher P. Reynolds, partner (labor & employment law practice group) and chair of Firm-wide Diversity Committee

Does your law firm currently have a diversity committee?

Yes

Does the committee's representation include one or more members of the firm's management/executive committee (or the equivalent)?

Yes. Steven R. Wall, a member of the firm's Advisory Board, monitors on behalf of firm management the Diversity Committee's activities. The committee is directly responsible to the chair of the firm.

How many attorneys are on the committee, and in 2003, what was the total number of hours collectively spent by the committee in furtherance of the firm's diversity initiatives?

Total attorneys on committee: 5

Total hours spent on diversity: Not tracked

Does the committee and/or diversity leader establish and set goals or objectives consistent with management's priorities?

Yes

Has the firm undertaken a formal or informal diversity program or set of initiatives aimed at increasing the diversity of the firm?

Yes, formal

How often does the firm's management review the firm's diversity progress/results?

Annually

How is the firm's diversity committee and/or firm management held accountable for achieving results?

The Diversity Committee sets general objectives (not numerical) and identifies areas where we can make increasing our recruitment and retention of minority attorneys a priority. Examples include further development of our relationship with law schools with larger numbers of minority law students, identifying client service teams that can be enhanced by including minority attorneys.

The chair and members of the Diversity Committee must demonstrate quarterly to the Management Committee our progress on the five broad areas of focus: recruiting, retention, policies and procedures, external affairs and client development.

LAW FIRM DIVERSITY INITIATIVES	ALREADY COMPLETED	CURRENTLY ADDRESSING	NOT A CURRENT PRIORITY
Undertake communication from firm management that diversity is a top priority of the firm.	✓		
Formalize diversity plan and committee with action steps and accountability to management.	✓		
Conduct firm-wide diversity training for all attorneys and staff.	✓		
Increase the number of minority attorneys at the associate level.		✓	
Increase the number of minority attorneys at the partnership level.		✓	
Develop/expand relationships with minority bar associations to offer firm's support of these networks.	✓		
Focus on strengthening firm's mentoring program, including for benefit of minority attorneys.		✓	

MINORITY CORPORATE COUNSEL ASSOCIATION

LAW FIRM DIVERSITY INITIATIVES (CONTINUED)	ALREADY COMPLETED	CURRENTLY ADDRESSING	NOT A CURRENT PRIORITY
Conduct internal diversity needs assessment and/or retain diversity consultant to examine how firm culture might be more welcoming of minorities.		✔	
Support law firm's internal affinity networks (e.g., women, minority attorney networks).		✔	
Manage/monitor allocation of work assignments and/or hours billed to ensure women and minority attorneys have equal access/inclusion on top client matters.	✔		

Recruitment - New Associates

Does your firm annually recruit at any of the following types of institutions?

Ivy League schools: Columbia University, Cornell University, Harvard University, University of Pennsylvania and Yale University

Public state schools: Rutgers University, Temple University, University of Virginia, University of Michigan, University of California-Hastings, UCLA

Private schools: University of Chicago, Duke University, Georgetown University, Stanford University, University of San Francisco, USC

Historically Black Colleges and Universities (HBCUs): Howard University

Do you have any special outreach efforts directed to encourage minority law students to consider your firm?

• *Please see our narrative response below describing the Morgan Lewis Book Scholarship Program.*

• Hold a reception for minority law students

• Advertise in minority law student association publication(s)

• Participate in/host minority law student job fair(s)

• Sponsor minority law student association events

• Firm's lawyers participate on career panels at school

• Outreach to leadership of minority student organizations

• Scholarships or intern/fellowships for minority students

SUMMER ASSOCIATE STATISTICS: SUMMER 2003	MINORITY MEN	MINORITY WOMEN	WHITE WOMEN	TOTAL
Summer associates	3	11	31	70
Summer associates who received an offer of full-time employment	2	10	25	61
Summer associates who accepted an offer of full-time employment	2	7	18	45

Recruitment – Lateral Associates and Partners

What activities does the firm undertake to attract minority and women attorneys?

• Partner programs with women and minority bar associations

• Participate at minority job fairs

• Seek referrals from other attorneys

• Utilize online job services (e.g., MCCA/DuPont Primary Law Firm Job Bank)

Do you use executive recruiting/search firms to seek to identify new diversity hires (partners or associates)?

Yes

List all women- and/or minority-owned executive search/ recruiting firms to which the firm paid a fee for placement services in the past 12 months:

Sandra Green Legal Placement, Inc.; Marilyn Wolk & Associates; Garb & Associates; Settzer, Fontaine & Beckwith; Abelson Legal Search; Liz Shapiro Legal Search; Leace Kapress, LLC

LATERAL ASSOCIATES AND PARTNERS: 1/1/03 – 12/31/03	MINORITY MEN	MINORITY WOMEN	WHITE WOMEN	TOTAL
Number of lateral associate hires	13	16	47	145
Number of lateral partner hires (equity and non-equity)	5	2	12	71
Number of new partners (equity and non-equity) promoted from associate rank	1	1	7	17
Number of new equity partners*	N/A	N/A	N/A	N/A

* We do not distinguish between equity and non-equity partners

Retention & Professional Development

ATTORNEYS WHO LEFT THE FIRM: 2003	MINORITY MEN	MINORITY WOMEN	WHITE WOMEN	TOTAL
Number of attorneys who voluntarily or involuntarily left your firm's employ in 2003	20	22	65	232

How do 2003 attrition rates generally compare to those experienced in the prior year period?

Higher than in prior years

Please identify the specific steps you are taking to reduce the attrition rate of minority and women attorneys.

• *We are working to further improve many of our work and family human resources policies and procedures including our policy on part-time employment and flex-time work schedules to make them more attractive to women. We are studying ways to offer better mentoring opportunities for our minority lawyers. We are*

strengthening our relationships with certain law schools where we recruit and who have larger numbers of minority students.

- Develop and/or support internal employee affinity groups (e.g., minority or women networks within the firm)
- Increase/review compensation relative to competition
- Increase/improve current work/life programs
- Work with minority and women attorneys to develop career advancement plans
- Introduce minority and women attorneys to key clients, including to lead engagements
- Review work assignments and hours billed to key client matters to make sure minority and women attorneys are not being excluded
- Strengthen mentoring program for all attorneys, including minorities and women
- Professional skills development program, including minority and women attorneys

Does your firm have part-time/flex-time policies that permit attorneys (male or female) to work alternative schedules?

Yes. Morgan Lewis fully supports attorneys who choose to work alternative schedules. A significant number of attorneys have flexible work schedules that allow them to maintain a balance between their careers and their families. Approximately 87 of our senior lawyers (including partners, of counsel, senior counsel and special counsel) work flexible schedules. We work with these individuals to tailor their schedules to meet the demands of their personal commitments, their practices and our clients.

What impact, if any, will the decision to work part-time have on an attorney's ability to make partner or, if already a partner, to remain a partner at your firm?

At Morgan Lewis, the decision to adopt a flexible part-time schedule does not impact an attorney's ability to make or remain a partner. Women who work part-time are regularly elevated to partner and remain partner once elected.

Have any attorneys who chose to work a part-time schedule made partner at your firm?

Yes, eighteen partners are part-time. Thirteen were part-time when they became partners.

Management Demographic Profile (as of 12/31/03)

	MINORITY MEN	MINORITY WOMEN	WHITE WOMEN	TOTAL
Number of attorneys on the Executive/Management Committee or equivalent	0	1	3	22
Number of attorneys on the Hiring Committee or equivalent	2	3	35	82
Number of attorneys on the Partner/Associate Review Committee or equivalent	1	1	7	36

Please provide information regarding all minority and women attorneys who head offices or practice groups of your law firm:

Minorities heading offices: Rollin B. Chippy, Deputy Office Managing Partner, San Francisco

Women heading offices: Marlee Myers, Office Managing Partner, Pittsburgh

Minorities heading practice groups: Grace E. Speights, Partner, Co-Head Complex Employment Litigation Team, Labor & Employment Law Practice Group

Women heading practice groups: Marlee S. Myers, Co-Chair, Technology Practice; Kathryn L. Gleason, Leader, FDA/Healthcare Regulatory Practice; Carol M. Merchasin, Executive Director, Morgan Lewis Resources; Eleanor Pelta, Managing Director, Morgan Lewis Resources; Grace E. Speights, Co-Head, Complex Employment Litigation Team; Doreen S. Davis, Co-Head, Traditional Labor Team; Kathryn Doyle, Assistant Practice Group Leader, Patent Practice Group; Karen A. Butcher, Assistant Leader, Trademark/Copyright Practice Group; Jami Wintz McKeon, Office Leader, Business & Corporate Area, Litigation Practice Group Christina Fournaris, Assistant Leader, Personal Law Practice Group

The Firm Says

Morgan Lewis Book Scholarship Program at Penn Law School

Morgan Lewis is sponsoring the Morgan Lewis Book Scholarship Program at the University of Pennsylvania Law School. Under this program, 20 book scholarships will be awarded to students selected this spring by student organizations under the umbrella of the United Law Students of Color Council. This new program is part of Morgan Lewis's ongoing efforts to strengthen its bonds with students of color.

Our commitment to diversity

At Morgan Lewis, achieving greater diversity within the firm is essential to delivering excellent service to our clients. As a global firm that serves a wide array of national and international companies and institutions, we understand that having a diverse complement of attorneys and staff gives our clients a greater breadth of perspective, thereby contributing to the success of our firm and our clients. When we provide our clients with teams of lawyers to support their legal needs, diversity is just as essential a consideration as industry expertise, relevant experience, cost-effective staffing and personal chemistry.

The following summarizes Morgan Lewis's specific efforts to achieve greater diversity at our firm, for our clients and within the legal marketplace.

Building a diverse core: Internally, our commitment to diversity permeates all levels of our firm's governance-and it shows. Female and minority partners and executives hold many prominent positions within Morgan Lewis. Senior female lawyers and lawyers of color serve on our advisory board, as office managing partners and on management committees. Within practices, female partners hold a number of leadership positions. In the labor and employment law practice, for example, women constitute a quarter of the senior lawyers, and lead three of the five practice areas. Three out of four firm-wide administrative departments, including information systems, human resources and marketing, are headed by women. In addition, women hold eight of the 16 director of administration positions throughout the firm's offices.

Encouraging diversity in the legal marketplace: The firm also encourages diversity in the legal marketplace. For example, Morgan Lewis is a premier sponsor of the Minority Corporate Counsel Association (MCCA). We

participate in that organization's events nationwide, including its annual CLE Expo, regional diversity dinners and the Creating Pathways to Diversity Conference. Our partners often serve as guest speakers at many of these events.

In addition, Morgan Lewis attorneys participate actively in Charting Your Own Course, an organization that develops networking and mentoring opportunities for minority lawyers across the country. We also support various publications that have special editions devoted to diversity, such as L Magazine, the Vault Guides, Minority Law Journal and the Mid-Atlantic Black Law Students Association newsletter.

Diversity and recruiting

Diversity at Morgan Lewis permeates every facet of the firm – from recruiting to mentoring and career development to the firm's management. We know that achieving greater diversity within the firm is essential to delivering exceptional service to our clients.

But diversity is not just a smart business decision. Ensuring the inclusion of diverse cultural, economic, social and personal backgrounds makes working at Morgan Lewis a more enriching experience and makes for a stronger firm. Below are some highlights of our diversity initiatives.

Recruiting and diversity: We work hard to develop relationships with law schools, governmental organizations and undergraduate schools to increase the diversity in our recruitment pool. Morgan Lewis lawyers and staff also participate in and/or sponsor recruitment events for organizations such as the Asian American Legal Defense and Education Fund, the Black Law Students Association and the National Latina/o Student Conference. In addition, the firm actively recruits at minority job fairs at top law schools all over the country.

Working together to achieve results: Improving diversity at Morgan Lewis is everyone's job. To quote our EEO policy, we must all "accept a full share of responsibility in making Morgan, Lewis & Bockius LLP an equal opportunity employer in every sense of the term." To that end, Morgan Lewis:

• Annually participates in and recruits from job fairs for minority law students.
• Maintains a network of minority partners who assist in recruiting interested and qualified minority candidates.
• Actively participates in local bar association summer associate diversity initiatives.
• Funds law school programs designed to expand opportunities for minority law students.
• Hosts receptions for law school affinity groups to introduce students to Morgan Lewis.
• Actively recruits established and high-quality minority and female lawyers from other firms.

Law firms are dynamic organizations, and building and maintaining diversity to create positive change and build successful careers requires constant and focused effort and attention. At Morgan Lewis, diversity is one of our top priorities.

Morrison & Foerster LLP

425 Market Street
San Francisco, CA 94105-2482
Phone: (415) 268-7000
Fax: (415) 268-7522

FIRM LEADERSHIP

Managing Partner: Keith C. Wetmore, Chair of
the Firm
Diversity Team Leader: Keith C. Wetmore,
Chair of the Firm

LOCATIONS

San Francisco, CA (HQ)
Century City, CA
Denver, CO
Irvine, CA
Los Angeles, CA
McLean, VA
New York, NY
Palo Alto, CA
Sacramento, CA
San Diego, CA
Walnut Creek, CA
Washington, DC
Beijing
Brussels
Hong Kong
London
Shanghai
Singapore
Tokyo

LAW FIRM DEMOGRAPHIC PROFILES

FULL-TIME ASSOCIATES*	2003	2002
Minority men	62	71
Minority women	77	74
White women	141	138
Total	477	484

SUMMER ASSOCIATES*	2003	2002
Minority men	8	8
Minority women	30	14
White women	29	23
Total	92	68

EQUITY PARTNERS*	2003	2002
Minority men	14	13
Minority women	7	6
White women	47	54
Total	277	276

NEW HIRES*	2003	2002
Minority men	14	19
Minority women	19	16
White women	29	43
Total	112	124

Includes U.S. offices only

Strategic Plan and Diversity Leadership

How does the firm's leadership communicate the importance of diversity to everyone at the firm? (e.g., e-mails, web site, newsletters, meetings, etc.)

E-mail communications; town hall meetings, partnership, practice and interviewer training; firm-wide and office attorney recruiting committee meetings, whose membership is composed of partners, attorneys and our attorney recruiters; meetings of the firm-wide Diversity Committee that includes attorneys and staff; annual write-ups of office diversity plans; annual write-ups of attorney recruiting diversity plans; discussions and reports at meetings of staff involved in attorney recruiting and of staff involved in staff recruiting; Diversity Strategy Committee recommendations to the Board of Directors.

Who has primary responsibility for leading diversity initiatives at your firm?

Keith C. Wetmore, Chair of the Firm

Does your law firm currently have a diversity committee?

Yes. Morrison & Foerster has three committees responsible for leading diversity initiatives at the firm, as follows:

Firm-wide Diversity Committee (co-chaired by partner Arturo González and Kathleen Dykstra, Managing Director of Human Resources)

The firm created a Diversity Committee in 1992 that includes attorney and staff representatives from our U.S. offices. The committee reports directly to senior management and discusses a wide range of diversity issues, oversees diversity training/awareness programs focused on issues of race and gender that have included, since the early 1990s, the retention of an outside consultant who holds role playing and other training programs in every office of the firm. Members of the Diversity Committee also play important roles in their individual offices planning numerous educational sessions in celebration of many events during the year, including, for example, Black History Month, Latino History Month, Daughters & Sons Day in April, Gay Pride Month and Asian Pacific Heritage Month. The Diversity Committee reports to management of the firm and is assisted by our outside consultant and a firm-wide human resources assistant.

Diversity Strategy Committee (chaired by partner Rachel Krevans)

The Diversity Strategy Committee was formed in 2003 and has as its primary mission recommending to the Board of Directors and management what the firm's major diversity objectives should be and providing strategic direction to the firm to achieve those goals. This committee is composed of senior and mid-level partners, including the Chair of the Firm and the firm's three Managing Partners for Operations. The Diversity Strategy Committee reports to the Board of Directors and is assisted by a member of our Professional Development Group (an attorney) and the firm's Managing Director of Human Resources.

Minority Recruiting Committee (chaired by partner Hector Gallegos)

As a subcommittee of the firm-wide Attorney Recruiting Committee, the MRC is responsible for receptions and outreach to law students of color at law schools at which we recruit. It is composed of partners and associates from six U.S. offices. The MRC is assisted by the Senior Recruiting Manager (firm-wide) and the Attorney Recruiting Managers in the individual offices.

Does the committee's representation include one or more members of the firm's management/executive committee (or the equivalent)?

Diversity Committee – Yes

Diversity Strategy Committee – Yes

Minority Recruiting Committee – No

How many attorneys are on the committee, and in 2003, what was the total number of hours collectively spent by the committee in furtherance of the firm's diversity initiatives?

Total attorneys on Diversity Committee: 35 (13 partners and 22 associates/counsel) plus 54 staff and legal assistants

Total attorneys on Diversity Strategy Committee: 10 (10 partners)

Total attorneys on Minority Recruiting Committee: 7 (2 partners and 5 associates)

Total hours spent on diversity: 1,065 hours for these committee members and others.

Does the committee and/or diversity leader establish and set goals or objectives consistent with management's priorities?

Yes

Has the firm undertaken a formal or informal diversity program or set of initiatives aimed at increasing the diversity of the firm?

Yes, formal

How often does the firm's management review the firm's diversity progress/results?

Frequently – on a periodic basis, no set schedule.

How is the firm's diversity committee and/or firm management held accountable for achieving results?

The above committees are accountable to the firm's board of directors.

LAW FIRM DIVERSITY INITIATIVES	ALREADY COMPLETED	CURRENTLY ADDRESSING	NOT A CURRENT PRIORITY
Undertake communication from firm management that diversity is a top priority of the firm.	✓		
Formalize diversity plan and committee with action steps and accountability to management.	✓		
Conduct firm-wide diversity training for all attorneys and staff.	✓		
Increase the number of minority attorneys at the associate level.	✓		
Increase the number of minority attorneys at the partnership level.	✓		
Develop/expand relationships with minority bar associations to offer firm's support of these networks.	✓		

LAW FIRM DIVERSITY INITIATIVES (CONTINUED)	ALREADY COMPLETED	CURRENTLY ADDRESSING	NOT A CURRENT PRIORITY
Focus on strengthening firm's mentoring program, including for benefit of minority attorneys.	✔		
Conduct internal diversity needs assessment and/or retain diversity consultant to examine how firm culture might be more welcoming of minorities.	✔		
Support law firm's internal affinity networks (e.g., women, minority attorney networks).	✔		
Manage/monitor allocation of work assignments and/or hours billed to ensure women and minority attorneys have equal access/inclusion on top client matters.	✔		

Recruitment – New Associates

Does your firm annually recruit at any of the following types of institutions?

Ivy League schools: Columbia University, Cornell University, Harvard University, Yale University, University of Pennsylvania

Public state schools: University of California-Berkeley (Boalt Hall), University of California-Davis, University of California-Hastings, University of California-Los Angeles, University of Colorado, University of Michigan, University of Virginia

Private schools: University of Denver, Fordham University, Georgetown University, Loyola Law School (L.A.), University of San Diego, Santa Clara University, Stanford University

Historically Black Colleges and Universities (HBCUs): Howard University

Do you have any special outreach efforts directed to encourage minority law students to consider your firm?

• Hold a reception for minority law students

• Advertise in minority law student association publication(s)

• Participate in/host minority law student job fair(s)

• Sponsor minority law student association events

• Firm's lawyers participate on career panels at school

• Outreach to leadership of minority student organizations

• Scholarships or intern/fellowships for minority students

SUMMER ASSOCIATE STATISTICS: SUMMER 2003*	MINORITY MEN	MINORITY WOMEN	WHITE WOMEN	TOTAL
Summer associates	14	19	25	83**
Summer associates who received an offer of full-time employment	13	16	24	73
Summer associates who accepted an offer of full-time employment	10	14	18	55

*Includes U.S. offices only

**In 2003, the firm had 97 summer associates firm-wide. Fourteen of the 97 summer associates either were first-years (entering their second year of law school) and not qualified for consideration of full-time offers or were in our Hong Kong or Tokyo offices during the summer.

Recruitment – Lateral Associates and Partners

What activities does the firm undertake to attract minority and women attorneys?

• Partner programs with women and minority bar associations

• Participate at minority job fairs

• Seek referrals from other attorneys

Do you use executive recruiting/search firms to seek to identify new diversity hires (partners or associates)?

No, not specifically. We do not use search firms specifically to seek to identify new diversity hires, but we do make clear to all of the search firms, in the second paragraph of our agreement letter that we use firm-wide, that we are an Equal Opportunity/Affirmative Action Employer, as follows:

Equal Opportunity/Affirmative Action Employer. Morrison & Foerster is an equal opportunity employer. You agree to present candidates to us regardless of race, color, sex, religion, ethnic or national origin, age, disability (including persons infected with the HIV virus or persons with AIDS), veteran status, marital status, sexual orientation, gender identity, domestic partner status, weight or height.

List all women- and/or minority-owned executive search/recruiting firms to which the firm paid a fee for placement services in the past 12 months:

We do not inquire about women- and/or minority owned status.

LATERAL ASSOCIATES AND PARTNERS*: 1/1/03 – 12/31/03	MINORITY MEN	MINORITY WOMEN	WHITE WOMEN	TOTAL
Number of lateral associate hires	6	10	15	56
Number of lateral partner hires (equity and non-equity)	1	1	1	16
Number of new partners (equity and non-equity) promoted from associate and of counsel rank	1	0	0	9
Number of new equity partners	2	1	1	25

+ Includes U.S. offices only

* Includes partners promoted from associate and of counsel ranks. Note that as of 1/1/04, the firm added as equity partners from within its ranks two minority men, two minority women and two white women.

Retention & Professional Development

Please identify the specific steps you are taking to reduce the attrition rate of minority and women attorneys.

• Develop and/or support internal employee affinity groups (e.g., minority or women networks within the firm)

• Increase/improve current work/life programs

• Work with minority and women attorneys to develop career advancement plans

• Introduce minority and women attorneys to key clients, including to lead engagements

• Review work assignments and hours billed to key client matters to make sure minority and women attorneys are not being excluded

• Strengthen mentoring program for all attorneys, including minorities and women

• Professional skills development program, including minority and women attorneys

Does your firm have part-time/flex-time policies that permit attorneys (male or female) to work alternative schedules?

Yes

What impact, if any, will the decision to work part-time have on an attorney's ability to make partner or, if already a partner, to remain a partner at your firm?

Case-by-case determination – depends on the circumstances.

Have any attorneys who chose to work a part-time schedule made partner at your firm?

Yes, four attorneys. Four individuals since 2002 have been elected to the partnership while working a part-time schedule.

Management Demographic Profile (as of 12/31/03)*

	MINORITY MEN	MINORITY WOMEN	WHITE WOMEN	TOTAL
Number of attorneys on the Executive/Management Committee or equivalent	2	1	7	32
Number of attorneys on the Hiring Committee or equivalent**	3	0	4	16
Number of attorneys on the Partner/Associate Review Committee or equivalent***	1	0	3	10

*Includes all offices *Morrison & Foerster Board of Directors, including the Executive Committee
**Firm-wide Attorney Recruiting Committee – attorney members
***Firm-wide Partnership Review Committee

Please provide information regarding all minority and women attorneys who head offices or practice groups of your law firm:

Minorities heading offices: Joseph Anderson, Singapore

Women heading offices: Rachel Krevans, San Francisco; Karen Hagberg, New York

Minorities heading practice groups: Arturo González, Chair, Trial Practice Group; Angela Padilla and Cedric Chao, Co-Chairs, Consumer Litigation Practice; Gladys Monroy, Co-Chair, Patent

Women heading practice groups: Lori Schechter, Chair, Litigation Department; Angela Padilla, Co-Chair, Consumer Litigation Practice; Gladys Monroy, Co-Chair, Patent; Barbara Mendelson, Chair, Financial Services; Kathy Johnstone, Co-Chair, Financial Transactions Group

The Firm Says

Morrison & Foerster's Diversity Mission Statement was articulated in 1992 and defines our cultural values today:

> *We at Morrison & Foerster will continue our work to break down barriers to equal opportunity, to value fully the differences among people in our organization while recognizing our similarities, and to create an atmosphere in which each individual can develop his or her potential to the fullest extent possible.*

> *We believe that diversity adds value to our organization by attracting the most talented people possible, by making the best use of the talents of those who work here, and finally, by enhancing our ability to attract, retain and, most importantly, to serve our clients. We want our firm to act as a model of diversity which others will follow.*

The firm has a long history of nurturing tolerance, inclusion and mutual respect. The first African American associate joined the firm in 1969 and became a partner in 1976. The first female associate joined the firm in 1967. In 1978, a female associate became a partner. An associate of Chinese American descent became a partner in 1983 and a Latino associate became a partner in 1992. Currently, 11 percent of our partners and 31 percent of our associates are lawyers of color. Women comprise 19 percent of our partnership and 45 percent of our associate ranks. Our summer associate program averages 35 to 40 percent summer associates of color and over 50 percent women. Over 50 of our lawyers are openly gay or lesbian.

One of the hallmarks of Morrison & Foerster's culture is being ahead of the curve in exploring and addressing concepts such as glass ceilings, maternity leave, part-time work, sexual harassment prevention and diversity sensitivity training. In the 1980s, the firm helped found and continues to participate in programs that are important to the acceptance and integration of attorneys of color into the legal community, including the American Bar Association's Minority Demonstration Program. Partners in our firm helped spearhead the creation of the Goals and Timetables for Minority Hiring and Advancement developed by the Bar Association of San Francisco in 1989, as well as similar programs establishing hiring goals sponsored by the Los Angeles County Bar and related activities sponsored by bar associations in other cities, including New York and Denver.

The firm's Diversity Committee oversees a long-term diversity training program that initially started with the management group and one office of the firm in 1992. The program generally rotates to several U.S. offices each year. The firm's diversity efforts have also included town meetings focused on diversity issues, training in related areas such as sexual harassment and workplace violence prevention, celebration of Black History, Asian

American Awareness, Latino/Mexican American and Gay Pride Months, and many other events. For the past decade, the firm has sponsored workshops for attorneys of color to improve their experience at the firm.

The Minority Recruiting Committee, a subcommittee of the firm-wide Attorney Recruiting Committee, focuses on recruiting efforts at law schools. The MRC is composed of partners and associates from our U.S. offices who host receptions for students of color at several law schools each fall. A group of Morrison & Foerster lawyers of color travels to the receptions from various offices in the U.S. to speak to law students of color about "what it is like to be a lawyer of color and to practice at Morrison & Foerster."

The firm's Diversity Strategy Committee, formed in 2003, has as its primary mission recommending to the board of directors and management what the firm's major diversity objectives should be and providing strategic direction to the firm to achieve those goals.

The Morrison & Foerster Foundation has funded many programs designed to assist students in the pursuit of their careers. The firm has sponsored minority law students at UCLA and four three-year Minority Law Student Scholarships awarded through the Bar Association of San Francisco Endowment Fund; funded a Kennedy-King scholarship for minority students transferring from junior college to complete their degrees; and, through the Thurgood Marshall Scholarship Fund Summer Test Program, subsidized the Princeton Review course costs at Howard University for over 20 minority students studying for the LSAT. The firm awards a fellowship each year to a first-year student at Boalt Law School who has obtained employment at an environmentally oriented public interest or public sector organization. The Foundation also has sponsored fellowships for Equal Justice Works fellows for several years.

The firm is proud to have been recognized for its support of attorneys of color and women in the legal profession. The firm was one of three organizations to be honored with the Catalyst Award in 1993 and the only law firm to have ever received the award, which is presented annually to corporations and professional firms that demonstrate a commitment to the leadership development of female employees. The firm received the Thomas L. Sager Award from MCCA in 2001, 2002 and 2003 for its sustained commitment to hiring, retaining and promoting minority attorneys. The firm was recognized by the Minority Law Journal as sixth in diversity among U.S. law firms in 2004, and the latest Vault Guide to the Top 100 Law Firms ranked the firm:

- No. 1 Firm to Work For
- No. 1 Firm for Diversity
- No. 1 Firm in Northern California
- No. 1 Firm in Pro Bono
- No. 2 Firm in Informal Training and Mentoring

The firm's extensive pro bono efforts also have resulted in numerous awards, the most prestigious of which is the 2002 ABA Law Firm of the Year Award. Morrison & Foerster lawyers have served in leadership positions in bar associations nationwide, including the American Bar Association, the State Bar of California, the Bar Associations adn Barr9sters Clubs of Los Angeles and San Francisco, the Northern Virginia chapter of the Federal Bar Association, the Asian American Bar Association of the Greater Bay Area, the Filipino Bar Association of Northern California, the InterPacific Bar Association and the Irish American Bar Association.

Munger, Tolles & Olson LLP
Los Angeles • San Francisco
www.mto.com
(213) 683-9100

*"There never were in the world two opinions alike,
no more than two hairs or two grains;
the most universal quality is diversity."*

Michel de Montaigne

At Munger, Tolles & Olson LLP, we value diversity. We believe that a diverse work force improves our ability to serve the needs of our clients and creates a more dynamic workplace for our attorneys. We have a long tradition of supporting diversity. Munger, Tolles & Olson LLP had one of the first women partners in the city, and we believe we had the first openly gay person to serve as Managing Partner at a major law firm.

We have placed a particular emphasis on minority recruitment of attorneys for many years, and we believe that our firm can be a platform for success for every lawyer we hire. We are dedicated to addressing the tough issues, in our firm and society, that impair success for women and minority lawyers. Our Diversity Committee is led by senior partners and has the support of the entire partnership.

We actively encourage employment applications from women and members of minority and other underrepresented groups. In our 2004 Summer Associate Program, which is the firm's main vehicle for the hiring of new attorneys, women and minority law students represent 65% of the group. Additionally, as part of our on-going effort to recruit, retain and promote exceptional attorneys who also contribute to the diversity of our firm and our profession, we have established a 1L Summer Program to specifically target exceptional first year law students of diverse backgrounds. These 1L Summer Program positions will be offered to students who are members of racial or ethnic minority groups, are gay, lesbian, bisexual or transgender, are physically challenged, or are from disadvantaged socioeconomic backgrounds.

For more information, please visit our website at mto.com or contact Kevinn Villard, Director of Legal Recruiting at (213) 683-9242.

Munger, Tolles & Olson LLP

355 S. Grand Avenue, 35th Floor
Los Angeles, CA 90071-1560
Phone: (213) 683-9100
Fax: (213) 687-3702

FIRM LEADERSHIP

Managing Partner: Robert K. Johnson and R. Gregory Morgan, Co-Managing Partners
Diversity Team Leader: Kristin S. Escalante, R. Gregory Morgan and Bart H. Williams, Chairs of Diversity Committee

LOCATIONS

Los Angeles, CA (HQ)
San Francisco, CA

LAW FIRM DEMOGRAPHIC PROFILES

FULL-TIME ASSOCIATES	2003	2002
Minority men	10	9
Minority women	4	5
White women	32	31
Total	74	79

SUMMER ASSOCIATES	2003	2002
Minority men	6	4
Minority women	2	6
White women	4	3
Total	21	16

EQUITY PARTNERS	2003	2002
Minority men	6	5
Minority women	2	2
White women	8	8
Total	81	76

NON-EQUITY PARTNERS	2003	2002
Minority men	0	0
Minority women	0	0
White women	0	0
Total	0	0

NEW HIRES	2003	2002
Minority men	3	4
Minority women	0	3
White women	8	10
Total	14	21

Strategic Plan and Diversity Leadership

How does the firm's leadership communicate the importance of diversity to everyone at the firm? (e.g., e-mails, web site, newsletters, meetings, etc.)

Web site and firm meetings; discussion at attorney retreats.

Who has primary responsibility for leading diversity initiatives at your firm?

Kristin S. Escalante, R. Gregory Morgan and Bart H. Williams, chairs of the Diversity Committee

Does your law firm currently have a diversity committee?

Yes

Does the committee's representation include one or more members of the firm's management/executive committee (or the equivalent)?

Yes

How many attorneys are on the committee, and in 2003, what was the total number of hours collectively spent by the committee in furtherance of the firm's diversity initiatives?

Total attorneys on committee: 37

Total hours spent on diversity: We do not track non-billable hours (other than discrete pro bono matters). Because we do not track time spent on committees, we cannot accurately report.

Does the committee and/or diversity leader establish and set goals or objectives consistent with management's priorities?

Yes

Has the firm undertaken a formal or informal diversity program or set of initiatives aimed at increasing the diversity of the firm?

Yes, formal

How often does the firm's management review the firm's diversity progress/results?

Quarterly

LAW FIRM DIVERSITY INITIATIVES	ALREADY COMPLETED	CURRENTLY ADDRESSING	NOT A CURRENT PRIORITY
Undertake communication from firm management that diversity is a top priority of the firm.	✔		
Formalize diversity plan and committee with action steps and accountability to management.		✔	
Conduct firm-wide diversity training for all attorneys and staff.		✔	
Increase the number of minority attorneys at the associate level.		✔	
Increase the number of minority attorneys at the partnership level.		✔	
Develop/expand relationships with minority bar associations to offer firm's support of these networks.		✔	
Focus on strengthening firm's mentoring program, including for benefit of minority attorneys.		✔	
Conduct internal diversity needs assessment and/or retain diversity consultant to examine how firm culture might be more welcoming of minorities.	✔		
Support law firm's internal affinity networks (e.g., women, minority attorney networks).	✔		
Manage/monitor allocation of work assignments and/or hours billed to ensure women and minority attorneys have equal access/inclusion on top client matters.		✔	
Women lawyers' monthly networking meeting where topics of interest to the firm's women lawyers are discussed.	✔		

Recruitment - New Associates

Does your firm annually recruit at any of the following types of institutions? (Check all that apply and list the schools).

Ivy League schools: Columbia University, Harvard University, Yale University, University of Pennsylvania

Public state schools: University of California-Boalt Hall, University of Michigan, UCLA

Private schools: University of Chicago, New York University, Stanford University, USC

Historically Black Colleges and Universities (HBCUs): Occasionally at Howard University

Do you have any special outreach efforts directed to encourage minority law students to consider your firm?

• Participate in/host minority law student job fair(s)

• Firm's lawyers participate on career panels at school

• Intern/fellowships for minority students

895

SUMMER ASSOCIATE STATISTICS: SUMMER 2003	MINORITY MEN	MINORITY WOMEN	WHITE WOMEN	TOTAL
Summer associates	6	2	4	21
Summer associates who received an offer of full-time employment	6	2	3	19
Summer associates who accepted an offer of full-time employment	2	0	1	8*

* There is no deadline for offer acceptance at MTO. Offers can be outstanding for several years as attorneys complete clerkship and internship programs.

Lateral Associates and Partners

What activities does the firm undertake to attract minority and women attorneys?

• *MTO 1L Summer Program*

• Participate at minority job fairs

Do you use executive recruiting/search firms to seek to identify new diversity hires (partners or associates)?

Yes

List all women- and/or minority-owned executive search/recruiting firms to which the firm paid a fee for placement services in the past 12 months:

Seltzer Fontaine

LATERAL ASSOCIATES AND PARTNERS: 1/1/03 – 12/31/03	MINORITY MEN	MINORITY WOMEN	WHITE WOMEN	TOTAL
Number of lateral associate hires	0	0	2	2
Number of lateral partner hires (equity and non-equity)	0	0	0	1
Number of new partners (equity and non-equity) promoted from associate rank	1	0	0	4
Number of new equity partners	1	0	0	5

Retention & Professional Development

ATTORNEYS WHO LEFT THE FIRM: 2003	MINORITY MEN	MINORITY WOMEN	WHITE WOMEN	TOTAL
Number of attorneys who voluntarily or involuntarily left your firm's employ in 2003	3	1	8	18

How do 2003 attrition rates generally compare to those experienced in the prior year period?

Higher than in prior years

Please identify the specific steps you are taking to reduce the attrition rate of minority and women attorneys.

- *Attrition rates was a topic for discussion at the firm's 2004 Attorney Retreat; diversity in the firm and the legal community was a topic for discussion at the 2003 Attorney Retreat.*
- Develop and/or support internal employee affinity groups (e.g., minority or women networks within the firm)
- Increase/improve current work/life programs
- Introduce minority and women attorneys to key clients, including to lead engagements
- Strengthen mentoring program for all attorneys, including minorities and women
- Professional skills development program, including minority and women attorneys

Does your firm have part-time/flex-time policies that permit attorneys (male or female) to work alternative schedules?

Yes

What impact, if any, will the decision to work part-time have on an attorney's ability to make partner or, if already a partner, to remain a partner at your firm?

MTO's partnership track is very short but flexible. Because we hire extraordinary new lawyers and give them meaningful opportunities early on, we generally consider our associates for partnership anywhere from four to seven years at the firm. We recognize that each attorney develops at his or her own pace, and that some lawyers may work part-time for some portion of their associate years. Therefore, we do not have a rigid preconception of the minimum or maximum amount of time it can take to attain partnership, and we have no "up-or-out" policy.

Have any attorneys who chose to work a part-time schedule made partner at your firm?

Yes, one attorney.

Management Demographic Profile (as of 12/31/03)

	MINORITY MEN	MINORITY WOMEN	WHITE WOMEN	TOTAL
Number of attorneys on the Executive/Management Committee or equivalent	2	0	2	17
Number of attorneys on the Hiring Committee or equivalent	6	1	10	37
Number of attorneys on the Partner/Associate Review Committee or equivalent	2	0	2	20

Please provide information regarding all minority and women attorneys who head offices or practice groups of your law firm:

MTO does not have office or practice group heads. Our co-managing partner from 1999 to 2002 was Ruth E. Fisher.

The Firm Says

At Munger, Tolles & Olson LLP, we value diversity. We believe that a diverse work force improves our ability to serve the needs of our clients and creates a more dynamic workplace for our attorneys. We have a long tradition of supporting diversity. Munger, Tolles & Olson (MTO) had one of the first women partners in Los Angeles, and we believe we had the first openly gay person to serve as managing partner at a major law firm.

While many of our attorneys have received awards and recognitions, we are especially proud of the accomplishments of our women and minority attorneys. Our partner, Vilma Martinez, the former president and general counsel of the Mexican American Legal Defense Fund and a recipient of the American Bar Association's Margaret Brent Award, was recently listed as one of the 50 Most Powerful Women lawyers in Los Angeles. Charles Siegel has actively championed the rights of the disabled and was recognized for his activities when the Western Law Center for Disability Rights named their prestigious President's Award in his honor. In 2004, Terry Sanchez and Bart Williams were recognized by their colleagues of the bar, who nominated them "Super Lawyers," the top 3 percent of lawyers in Southern California as evaluated by their peers.

Women and minority attorneys participate in all aspects of the firm's governance, which is done through attorney committees. All attorneys are expected to actively participate and are encouraged to focus on the areas of firm governance that interest them most. One of our former partners, Ruth Fisher, was the firm's co-managing partner from 1999 to 2002.

Our Diversity Committee is led by senior partners and has the support of the entire partnership. Women and minority attorneys are active participants on the Diversity Committee, which is chaired by Kristin Escalante (woman partner), Greg Morgan (co-managing partner) and Bart Williams (African-American partner).

We have placed a particular emphasis on recruitment of minority attorneys for many years, and we believe that our firm can be a platform for success for every lawyer we hire. We are dedicated to addressing the tough issues, in our firm and society, that impair success for women and minority lawyers. The retention of women and minority attorneys was a topic of discussion at the firm's 2004 Attorney Retreat; diversity in the firm and the legal community was a topic of discussion at the 2003 Attorney Retreat. Several of our partners were members

of a planning committee which organized and sponsored a Managing Partners Roundtable Diversity Conference in Los Angeles in September 2003. As a result of that conference, a "Diversity Roundtable" group was created, and as many as 18 major Los Angeles law firms now meet bimonthly to discuss diversity issues. The firm is a member of the California Minority Lawyers Association and of the Minority Corporate Counsel Association. In 2001, MTO was a national sponsor of the MCCA's report, "Creating Pathways to Diversity," on recommended practices to make diversity programs at law firms more successful.

We actively encourage employment applications from women and members of minority and other underrepresented groups. Women and minority law students represent 65 percent of our 2004 summer associate program, which is the firm's main vehicle for the hiring of new attorneys. Additionally, as part of our ongoing effort to recruit, retain and promote exceptional attorneys who also contribute to the diversity of our firm and our profession, we have established a 1L summer program to specifically target exceptional first-year law students of diverse backgrounds. These 1L summer positions will be offered to students who are members of racial or ethnic minority groups, are gay, lesbian, bisexual or transgender, are physically challenged, or are from disadvantaged socioeconomic backgrounds.

Mentoring is an important tool used by the firm to encourage new attorneys and familiarize them with MTO's culture and systems. Each new attorney is assigned two mentors for the first year – a senior and a junior attorney who will answer questions, provide advice and guidance, and take an interest in the new attorney's professional development. Also, the firm realizes that attorneys may have other priorities in their lives that sometimes take precedence over work, such as families and personal interests. MTO allows attorneys considerable flexibility in determining their own schedules, subject to client requirements, and part-time work schedules are not unusual.

The firm and its attorneys have sponsored many events for women and minority organizations, and its attorneys are members of various minority and women's bar associations, such as the Japanese American Bar Association, the National Conference of Women's Bar Association and the Women Lawyers Association of Los Angeles which is a member of the Multicultural Bar Alliance, a loose organization of all minority bar associations in the Los Angeles area. Two of our women attorneys are very active in WLALA and serve as the current president and sit on the finance committee.

MTO actively encourages attorney participation in pro bono activities and has recently provided pro bono services to many minority organizations such as:

• Mexican American Legal Defense and Education Fund, Mexican American Bar Association, La Raza, El Proyecto Del Barrio, Plaza de Cultura y Arte Foundation, El Arca

• Minority Business Enterprise Legal Defense and Education Fund

• Thai Community Development Center, LTSC (Asian) Community Development Corporation, Asian Pacific Legal Foundation

• Lake County Indians

• San Francisco Bar Association Minority Scholarship Program; School to College and Law Academy, which provides mentoring, education and summer jobs to minority high school students in San Francisco; San Francisco's "No Glass Ceiling" Commission

For more information on the firm's pro bono program and activities, please refer to our web site at www.mto.com or review the recent Vault Guide to Law Firm Pro Bono Programs.

NEAL, GERBER & EISENBERG LLP

NETWORK

GROW

EXPERIENCE

A full service law firm located in the heart of the Loop, NGE is committed to excellence both in the workplace and in the practice of law. We take pride in our client service and our creative, innovative approach to meeting client needs and furthering client goals and objectives. The hallmark of our client service is our people. We have a diverse group of talented individuals, each of whom brings a unique background and perspective to the legal matters they handle. We value that diversity and the way it enhances our environment and our practice.

"We are proud to have a broad array of different personalities, backgrounds and experiences represented at our Firm. This diversity makes NGE a comfortable place for our attorneys to practice, and helps us to best represent our clients' interests and further their goals and objectives."

Victoria Donati, Chair, Diversity Committee

NGE

MAKE YOUR MOVE

NEAL, GERBER & EISENBERG LLP

Two North LaSalle Street • Suite 2200 • Chicago, IL 60602-3801

312-269-8000 • www.ngelaw.com

Neal, Gerber & Eisenberg LLP

Two North LaSalle Street
Chicago, IL 60602-3801
Phone: (312) 269-8000
Fax: (312) 269-1747

FIRM LEADERSHIP

Managing Partner: Jerry H. Biederman, Partner,
Corporate & Securities
Diversity Team Leader: Victoria L. Donati,
Partner and Chair of Diversity Committee

LOCATIONS

Chicago, IL (HQ)

LAW FIRM DEMOGRAPHIC PROFILES

FULL-TIME ASSOCIATES	2003	2002
Minority men	3	2
Minority women	2	3
White women	21	20
Total	49	40

SUMMER ASSOCIATES	2003	2002
Minority men	1	0
Minority women	3	0
White women	2	2
Total	6	5

EQUITY PARTNERS	2003	2002
Minority men	1	0
Minority women	0	0
White women	11	6
Total	72	61

NON-EQUITY PARTNERS	2003	2002
Minority men	1	0
Minority women	1	1
White women	11	14
Total	21	19

NEW HIRES	2003	2002
Minority men	3	0
Minority women	0	1
White women	13	4
Total	41	16

Strategic Plan and Diversity Leadership

How does the firm's leadership communicate the importance of diversity to everyone at the firm? (e.g., e-mails, web site, newsletters, meetings, etc.)

We publicize our activities with minority groups through e-mails, meetings and personal conversations, and we encourage attorney participation at such events/activities. We publicize our diversity statement on our web site, feature minority and women attorneys in our newsletters and firm brochures, and participate in minority job fairs. We actively participate in events and activities put on by the MCCA and by the Chicago Committee on Minorities in Large Law Firms, and we encourage attorneys to participate in minority bar associations and events. Orientation of new attorneys to the firm includes information about our diversity initiatives.

Who has primary responsibility for leading diversity initiatives at your firm? Name of person and his/her title:

Victoria L. Donati, partner and chair of Diversity Committee

Does your law firm currently have a diversity committee?

Yes

Does the committee's representation include one or more members of the firm's management/executive committee (or the equivalent)?

Yes

How many attorneys are on the committee, and in 2003, what was the total number of hours collectively spent by the committee in furtherance of the firm's diversity initiatives?

Total attorneys on committee: 7

Total hours spent on diversity: 160

Does the committee and/or diversity leader establish and set goals or objectives consistent with management's priorities?

Yes

Has the firm undertaken a formal or informal diversity program or set of initiatives aimed at increasing the diversity of the firm?

Yes, informal

How often does the firm's management review th e firm's diversity progress/results?

Annually

How is the firm's diversity committee and/or firm management held accountable for achieving results?

It hasn't been measurably accountable to date. Our goal for 2004 is to develop appropriate metrics to measure success and to impose greater accountability.

LAW FIRM DIVERSITY INITIATIVES	ALREADY COMPLETED	CURRENTLY ADDRESSING	NOT A CURRENT PRIORITY
Undertake communication from firm management that diversity is a top priority of the firm.	✔		
Formalize diversity plan and committee with action steps and accountability to management.		✔	
Conduct firm-wide diversity training for all attorneys and staff.		✔	
Increase the number of minority attorneys at the associate level.	✔		
Increase the number of minority attorneys at the partnership level.		✔	
Develop/expand relationships with minority bar associations to offer firm's support of these networks.	✔		
Focus on strengthening firm's mentoring program, including for benefit of minority attorneys.	✔		
Conduct internal diversity needs assessment and/or retain diversity consultant to examine how firm culture might be more welcoming of minorities.		✔	
Support law firm's internal affinity networks (e.g., women, minority attorney networks).	✔		
Manage/monitor allocation of work assignments and/or hours billed to ensure women and minority attorneys have equal access/inclusion on top client matters.		✔	

Recruitment - New Associates

Does your firm annually recruit at any of the following types of institutions? (Check all that apply and list the schools).

Public state schools: University of Illinois, University of Iowa, University of Michigan, and others based on write-ins

Private schools: Northwestern University, University of Chicago, Chicago-Kent College of Law, Case Western Reserve University, and others based on write-ins

Do you have any special outreach efforts directed to encourage minority law students to consider your firm?

• Hold a reception for minority law students

• Advertise in minority law student association publication(s)

• Participate in/host minority law student job fair(s)

• Sponsor minority law student association events

• Firm's lawyers participate on career panels at school

• Outreach to leadership of minority student organizations

• Scholarships or intern/fellowships for minority students

SUMMER ASSOCIATE STATISTICS: SUMMER 2003	MINORITY MEN	MINORITY WOMEN	WHITE WOMEN	TOTAL
Summer associates	1	3	2	6
Summer associates who received an offer of full-time employment	1	3	2	6
Summer associates who accepted an offer of full-time employment	1	2	2	5

Recruitment – Lateral Associates and Partners

What activities does the firm undertake to attract minority and women attorneys?

• Participate at minority job fairs

• Seek referrals from other attorneys

Do you use executive recruiting/search firms to seek to identify new diversity hires (partners or associates)?

Yes

List all women- and/or minority-owned executive search/recruiting firms to which the firm paid a fee for placement services in the past 12 months:

Watson & Rosenbaum; Nicolas & Sciabica; Mestel & Company; Zenner Consulting Group

LATERAL ASSOCIATES AND PARTNERS: 1/1/03 – 12/31/03	MINORITY MEN	MINORITY WOMEN	WHITE WOMEN	TOTAL
Number of lateral associate hires	2	0	7	21
Number of lateral partner hires (equity and non-equity)	1	0	3	14
Number of new partners (equity and non-equity) promoted from associate rank	0	0	0	1
Number of new equity partners	0	0	2	3

Retention & Professional Development

ATTORNEYS WHO LEFT THE FIRM: 2003	MINORITY MEN	MINORITY WOMEN	WHITE WOMEN	TOTAL
Number of attorneys who voluntarily or involuntarily left your firm's employ in 2003	1	0	5	10

How do 2003 attrition rates generally compare to those experienced in the prior year period?

About the same as in prior years

Please identify the specific steps you are taking to reduce the attrition rate of minority and women attorneys.

• Develop and/or support internal employee affinity groups (e.g., minority or women networks within the firm)

• Increase/review compensation relative to competition

• Increase/improve current work/life programs

• Work with minority and women attorneys to develop career advancement plans

• Introduce minority and women attorneys to key clients, including to lead engagements

• Strengthen mentoring program for all attorneys, including minorities and women

• Professional skills development program, including minority and women attorneys

Does your firm have part-time/flex-time policies that permit attorneys (male or female) to work alternative schedules?

Yes, the firm has been a leader in permitting attorneys to work on a part-time and/or flex-time basis.

What impact, if any, will the decision to work part-time have on an attorney's ability to make partner or, if already a partner, to remain a partner at your firm?

By allowing us to attract and retain highly talented attorneys, we think that our part-time/flex-time policies have a positive impact on an individual's ability to become and to remain a partner. It certainly has no adverse impac

Have any attorneys who chose to work a part-time schedule made partner at your firm?

Yes, nine attorneys. This includes partners currently at the firm who work a part-time schedule. It does not include the several others who made partner but then left for other positions (e.g., in-house positions) or to exit the work force entirely.

Management Demographic Profile (as of 12/31/03)

	MINORITY MEN	MINORITY WOMEN	WHITE WOMEN	TOTAL
Number of attorneys on the Executive/Management Committee or equivalent	0	0	0	7
Number of attorneys on the Hiring Committee or equivalent	1	0	2	11
Number of attorneys on the Partner/Associate Review Committee or equivalent	1	0	2	12

Please provide information regarding all minority and women attorneys who head offices or practice groups of your law firm:

Women heading practice groups: Jill Coleman, Finance; Ellen Friedler, Commercial Leasing; Patricia Cain, ERISA; Frances Gecker, Bankruptcy; Diana McKenzie, Information Technology; Lisa Zebovitz, Environmental Litigation

The Firm Says

Neal, Gerber & Eisenberg LLP is strongly committed to diversity. We have made great strides in recent years with respect to our diversity efforts and, yet, we recognize that the drive to diversify is a mission that can never be "completed." It is a goal that requires constant vigilance and continuous effort. We are dedicated to nurturing a truly diverse environment.

We value diversity

We recognize that diversity is a vital component of our culture, identity, strategic planning and overall well-being. It fosters equal opportunity; creates an open, positive and satisfying work environment; and promotes the highest standards and ideals of our legal system. By embracing diversity, we reflect that which is great about our community and society at large; we best serve our clients' interests; we fulfill our obligations as members of the bar; and we promote creativity, opportunity and professional development at every level.

We foster diversity

NGE has fostered individual growth and development and the diversity of our firm members in a number of ways:

• Allowing attorneys and staff to balance commitments to work, family, community and personal life by pioneering the development and maintenance of a flexible work environment (including part-time and flexible work schedules and job-sharing);

• Encouraging attorneys and staff to support professional, civic and community organizations that advance the interests of minorities and women in the legal community and the community at large;

• Giving billable credit to partners and associates for work on pro bono matters, including many that support the minority community;

• Conducting an annual and ongoing evaluation of our processes – including policies, procedures and firm communications – to ensure that we affirmatively reach out to minorities and women and that we follow the spirit and objectives of equal employment opportunity;

• Continuing to enhance our mentoring programs to assure that attorneys are included in meaningful work assignments and provided feedback that allows them to develop to the fullest of their abilities;

• Continuously evaluating vendor relationships to assure that we work with minority and women-owned vendors to provide us goods and services;

• Supporting the Chicago Committee on Minorities in Large Law Firms;

• Supporting and working with other organizations, such as the Minority Corporate Counsel Association, to increase opportunity and diversity within the legal profession generally;

• Participating in minority recruitment programs such as the Cook County Bar Association Minority Law Student Job Fair and other minority law student and bar association events, including sponsorship of the Black Law Students Association, Latino Law Student and Asian Pacific American Law Students Association at Northwestern University, the University of Chicago Law School South Asian Law Students Association and the University of Illinois Black Law Students Association;

• Sponsoring and donating time and in-kind benefits to a variety of minority and women student bar associations to help groom leaders within their ranks and prepare their student members for the practice of law; and

• Providing scholarship support to minority students.

We continue to look for ways to demonstrate our commitment and desire to make the legal profession a more diverse, and thereby more dynamic, field, and we welcome the opportunity to affect individuals at all stages of their careers, both within NGE and beyond.

We recognize that there still is much to be done and have taken steps to be active agents of change. NGE formalized its diversity efforts with the formation of a Diversity Committee in 2002, which is comprised of seven attorney members (five equity partners and two associates) and three director-level administrators, including members of representative groups within the firm and a member of the firm's Executive Committee. The committee is accountable directly to the firm's managing partner and Executive Committee. Over the last two years, the Diversity Committee has laid the foundation to launch a full-scale diversity initiative.

We look to the future

In 2004, our primary mission is to further our diversity efforts. Our goal is to get more attorneys involved in our efforts, to share in the benefits of diversity and to clearly communicate the value and rewards that derive from each individual's contribution to the effort. We also are looking for ways to better measure our success – for a system of metrics that will work in a law firm setting. We hope to establish an appropriate system of measurement and reward that will help us to capture and capitalize upon our successes and that will further incentivize positive behaviors.

We will continue to strive to respect, support and reward individuals on the basis of personal achievement and contribution, and to encourage attorneys and staff to recognize the value of diversity in achieving a better work environment and a stronger firm.

Nelson Mullins Riley & Scarborough, L.L.P.

1320 Main Street, 17th Floor
Columbia, SC 29201
Phone: (803) 799-2000
Fax: (803) 256-7500
www.nelsonmullins.com

FIRM LEADERSHIP

Managing Partner: David E. Dukes, Managing
Partner
Diversity Team Leader: Stuart M. Andrews,
Partner and Chair of Diversity Committee

LOCATIONS

Columbia, SC (HQ)
Atlanta, GA
Charleston, SC
Charlotte, NC
Greenville, SC
Myrtle Beach, SC
Raleigh, NC
Washington, DC
Winston-Salem, NC

LAW FIRM DEMOGRAPHIC PROFILES

FULL-TIME ASSOCIATES	2003	2002
Minority men	2	2
Minority women	6	3
White women	42	42
Total	134	121

SUMMER ASSOCIATES	2003	2002
Minority men	3	2
Minority women	4	5
White women	29	21
Total	69	66

EQUITY PARTNERS	2003	2002
Minority men	1	1
Minority women	0	0
White women	15	12
Total	116	99

NON-EQUITY PARTNERS	2003	2002
Minority men	7	7
Minority women	2	1
White women	30	25
Total	73	65

NEW HIRES	2003	2002
Minority men	0	1
Minority women	4	3
White women	15	13
Total	59	37

Strategic Plan and Diversity Leadership

How does the firm's leadership communicate the importance of diversity to everyone at the firm? (e.g., e-mails, web site, newsletters, meetings, etc.)

We have relied principally on the creation of a diversity committee. We also have featured diversity as a panel discussion at the firm's annual meeting, at which several general counsel of major national companies that are firm clients discussed the significance of demonstrated commitment to diversity in the law firms that serve them.

Who has primary responsibility for leading diversity initiatives at your firm? Name of person and his/her title:

Stuart M. Andrews, chair of Diversity Committee

Does your law firm currently have a diversity committee?

Yes

Does the committee's representation include one or more members of the firm's management/executive committee (or the equivalent)?

Yes

How many attorneys are on the committee, and in 2003, what was the total number of hours collectively spent by the committee in furtherance of the firm's diversity initiatives?

Total attorneys on committee: 25

Total hours spent on diversity: 150

Does the committee and/or diversity leader establish and set goals or objectives consistent with management's priorities?

Yes

Has the firm undertaken a formal or informal diversity program or set of initiatives aimed at increasing the diversity of the firm?

Yes, informal

How often does the firm's management review the firm's diversity progress/results?

Annually

How is the firm's diversity committee and/or firm management held accountable for achieving results?

Annual review

LAW FIRM DIVERSITY INITIATIVES	ALREADY COMPLETED	CURRENTLY ADDRESSING	NOT A CURRENT PRIORITY
Undertake communication from firm management that diversity is a top priority of the firm.	✔	✔	
Formalize diversity plan and committee with action steps and accountability to management.		✔	
Conduct firm-wide diversity training for all attorneys and staff.		✔	
Increase the number of minority attorneys at the associate level.		✔	
Increase the number of minority attorneys at the partnership level.		✔	
Develop/expand relationships with minority bar associations to offer firm's support of these networks.		✔	
Focus on strengthening firm's mentoring program, including for benefit of minority attorneys.		✔	
Conduct internal diversity needs assessment and/or retain diversity consultant to examine how firm culture might be more welcoming of minorities.		✔	
Support law firm's internal affinity networks (e.g., women, minority attorney networks).		✔	
Manage/monitor allocation of work assignments and/or hours billed to ensure women and minority attorneys have equal access/inclusion on top client matters.		✔	

Recruitment – New Associates

Does your firm annually recruit at any of the following types of institutions? (Check all that apply and list the schools).

Public state schools: University of South Carolina, University of North Carolina, University of Virginia, University of Georgia, Georgia State University

Private schools: Duke University, Vanderbilt University, Mercer University, Emory University

Do you have any special outreach efforts directed to encourage minority law students to consider your firm?

• *Host meetings of the Georgia Association of Black Women Attorneys, that has members that are African American female law students; Conduct workshops for Resume Drafting and Interview Techniques; Southeastern Law Consortium.*

• Advertise in minority law student association publication(s)

• Participate in/host minority law student job fair(s)

• Firm's lawyers participate on career panels at school

• Outreach to leadership of minority student organizations

• Scholarships or intern/fellowships for minority students

911

SUMMER ASSOCIATE STATISTICS: SUMMER 2003	MINORITY MEN	MINORITY WOMEN	WHITE WOMEN	TOTAL
Summer associates	3	3	17	42
Summer associates who received an offer of full-time employment	3	2	12	27
Summer associates who accepted an offer of full-time employment	2**	2	18*	18

*Two offers pending to judicial clerks   **One offer pending

Recruitment – Lateral Associates and Partners

What activities does the firm undertake to attract minority and women attorneys?

• Partner programs with women and minority bar associations

• Participate at minority job fairs

• Seek referrals from other attorneys

Do you use executive recruiting/search firms to seek to identify new diversity hires (partners or associates)?

No

LATERAL ASSOCIATES AND PARTNERS: 1/1/03 – 12/31/03	MINORITY MEN	MINORITY WOMEN	WHITE WOMEN	TOTAL
Number of lateral associate hires	0	3	12	33
Number of lateral partner hires (equity and non-equity)	0	1	3	26
Number of new partners (equity and non-equity) promoted from associate rank	0	0	2	5
Number of new equity partners	1	0	3	9

Retention & Professional Development

ATTORNEYS WHO LEFT THE FIRM: 2003	MINORITY MEN	MINORITY WOMEN	WHITE WOMEN	TOTAL
Number of attorneys who voluntarily or involuntarily left your firm's employ in 2003	1	0	7	20

How do 2003 attrition rates generally compare to those experienced in the prior year period?

About the same as in prior years

Please identify the specific steps you are taking to reduce the attrition rate of minority and women attorneys.

• Develop and/or support internal employee affinity groups (e.g., minority or women networks within the firm)

• Increase/review compensation relative to competition

MINORITY CORPORATE COUNSEL ASSOCIATION

• Increase/improve current work/life programs

• Work with minority and women attorneys to develop career advancement plans

• Introduce minority and women attorneys to key clients, including to lead engagements

• Strengthen mentoring program for all attorneys, including minorities and women

• Professional skills development program, including minority and women attorneys

Does your firm have part-time/flex-time policies that permit attorneys (male or female) to work alternative schedules?

Yes. We have had this for approximately 10 years.

What impact, if any, will the decision to work part-time have on an attorney's ability to make partner or, if already a partner, to remain a partner at your firm?

We do have attorneys who have worked part-time and gone on to make partner. We also have partners who have gone part-time and remained a partner.

Have any attorneys who chose to work a part-time schedule made partner at your firm?

Yes, five attorneys.

Management Demographic Profile (as of 12/31/03)

	MINORITY MEN	MINORITY WOMEN	WHITE WOMEN	TOTAL
Number of attorneys on the Executive/Management Committee or equivalent	0	0	0	5
Number of attorneys on the Hiring Committee or equivalent	2	2	9	38
Number of attorneys on the Partner/Associate Review Committee or equivalent	0	1	9	26

Please provide information regarding all minority and women attorneys who head offices or practice groups of your law firm:

Women heading offices: Denise Gunter, Winston-Salem, NC

Women heading practice groups: Sue Harper, Employment; Cherie Blackburn, Employment; Elizabeth Moise, Products Liability Litigation; Karen Crawford, Environmental; Sara Turnipseed, Toxic Tort Litigation

Nixon Peabody LLP

100 Summer Street
Boston, MA 02110-2131
Phone: (617) 345-1000
Fax: (617) 345-1300

FIRM LEADERSHIP

Managing Partner: Harry P. Trueheart III and
Nestor M. Nicholas, Co-Managing Partners
Diversity Team Leader: Harry P. Trueheart III,
Chairman and Co-Managing Partner

LOCATIONS

Boston, MA (HQ)
Albany, NY
Buffalo, NY
Garden City, NY
Hartford, CT
Irvine, CA
McLean, VA
Manchester, NH
New York, NY
Philadelphia, PA
Providence, RI
Rochester, NY
San Francisco, CA
Washington, DC

LAW FIRM DEMOGRAPHIC PROFILES

ASSOCIATES, COUNCIL AND LAW CLERKS*	2003	2002
Minority men	23	18
Minority women	22	23
White women	101	103
Total	282	283

* We have included counsel and law clerks together with
associates.

SUMMER ASSOCIATES	2003	2002
Minority men	5	4
Minority women	4	3
White women	12	15
Total	36	37

PARTNERS*	2003	2002
Minority men	4	5
Minority women	2	1
White women	57	57
Total	332	329

* We do not distinguish between equity and non-equity
partners.

NEW HIRES	2003	2002
Minority men	12	2
Minority women	6	6
White women	19	17
Total	74	48

Strategic Plan and Diversity Leadership

How does the firm's leadership communicate the importance of diversity to everyone at the firm? (e.g., e-mails, web site, newsletters, meetings, etc.)

The firm conducts firm-wide training programs for all attorneys and staff; through the firm's mission statement as well as firm's diversity statement; and through recruiting efforts at the attorney and staff levels.

Who has primary responsibility for leading diversity initiatives at your firm? Name of person and his/her title:

Currently, diversity initiatives are led by partners Kendal Tyre and Elizabeth Moore. Harry Trueheart, chairman and co-managing partner, recently established a Diversity Summit which he leads.

Does your law firm currently have a diversity committee?

Yes

Does the committee's representation include one or more members of the firm's management/executive committee (or the equivalent?)

Yes. See information above regarding the Diversity Summit.

How many attorneys are on the committee, and in 2003, what was the total number of hours collectively spent by the committee in furtherance of the firm's diversity initiatives?

Total attorneys on committee: 12

Total hours spent on diversity: 100+

Does the committee and/or diversity leader establish and set goals or objectives consistent with management's priorities?

Yes. A Diversity Committee meeting was held in June 2004 to further define these goals and objectives.

Has the firm undertaken a formal or informal diversity program or set of initiatives aimed at increasing the diversity of the firm?

Yes, formal. The Diversity Summit develops processes to create and implement the firm's diversity initiatives.

How often does the firm's management review the firm's diversity progress/ results?

Annually, as part of involved attorney's annual evaluation.

LAW FIRM DIVERSITY INITIATIVES	ALREADY COMPLETED	CURRENTLY ADDRESSING	NOT A CURRENT PRIORITY
Undertake communication from firm management that diversity is a top priority of the firm.	✔		
Formalize diversity plan and committee with action steps and accountability to management.		✔	
Conduct firm-wide diversity training for all attorneys and staff.		✔	
Increase the number of minority attorneys at the associate level.		✔	
Increase the number of minority attorneys at the partnership level.		✔	
Develop/expand relationships with minority bar associations to offer firm's support of these networks.	✔		
Focus on strengthening firm's mentoring program, including for benefit of minority attorneys.		✔	
Conduct internal diversity needs assessment and/or retain diversity consultant to examine how firm culture might be more welcoming of minorities.		✔	
Support law firm's internal affinity networks (e.g., women, minority attorney networks).	✔		
Manage/monitor allocation of work assignments and/or hours billed to ensure women and minority attorneys have equal access/inclusion on top client matters.		✔	

Recruitment - New Associates

Does your firm annually recruit at any of the following types of institutions? (Check all that apply and list the schools).

Ivy League schools: All that have law schools

Public state schools: SUNY at Buffalo

Private schools: Albany Law School, Brooklyn Law School, Duke University, Fordham University, George Washington University, Georgetown University, Hofstra University, Northeastern University, Santa Clara University, St. John's University, Stanford University, Suffolk University, Syracuse University, University of San Francisco, University of California (Boalt Hall, Davis, Hastings), University of Michigan, University of Virginia

Historically Black Colleges and Universities (HBCUs): Howard University

Do you have any special outreach efforts directed to encourage minority law students to consider your firm?

• *The firm sponsors a moot court competition at Cornell University for black undergraduate students*

• Hold a reception for minority law students

• Advertise in minority law student association publication(s)

• Participate in/host minority law student job fair(s)

917

- Sponsor minority law student association events
- Firm's lawyers participate on career panels at school
- Outreach to leadership of minority student organizations
- Scholarships or intern/fellowships for minority students

SUMMER ASSOCIATE STATISTICS: SUMMER 2003	MINORITY MEN	MINORITY WOMEN	WHITE WOMEN	TOTAL
Summer associates	1	3	10	24
Summer associates who received an offer of full-time employment	1	3	10	23
Summer associates who accepted an offer of full-time employment	0	3	7	18

Recruitment – Lateral Associates and Partners

What activities does the firm undertake to attract minority and women attorneys?

- Partner programs with women and minority bar associations
- Participate at minority job fairs
- Seek referrals from other attorneys
- The firm partners with corporate client in-house counsel in summer associate diversity initiatives.

Do you use executive recruiting/search firms to seek to identify new diversity hires (partners or associates)?

Yes

LATERAL ASSOCIATES AND PARTNERS: 1/1/03 – 12/31/03	MINORITY MEN	MINORITY WOMEN	WHITE WOMEN	TOTAL
Number of lateral associate hires	9	4	25	65
Number of lateral partner hires (equity and non-equity)	0	0	0	33
Number of new partners (equity and non-equity) promoted from associate rank	0	0	0	6
Number of new equity partners	0	0	0	0

Retention & Professional Development

ATTORNEYS WHO LEFT THE FIRM: 2003	MINORITY MEN	MINORITY WOMEN	WHITE WOMEN	TOTAL
Number of attorneys who voluntarily or involuntarily left your firm's employ in 2003	2	5	20	56

How do 2003 attrition rates generally compare to those experienced in the prior year period?

Higher than in prior years

Please identify the specific steps you are taking to reduce the attrition rate of minority and women attorneys.

• Develop and/or support internal employee affinity groups (e.g., minority or women networks within the firm)

• Increase/review compensation relative to competition

• Increase/improve current work/life programs

• Work with minority and women attorneys to develop career advancement plans

• Introduce minority and women attorneys to key clients, including leading engagements

• Strengthen mentoring program for all attorneys, including minorities and women

• Professional skills development program, including minority and women attorneys

Does your firm have part-time/flex-time policies that permit attorneys (male or female) to work alternative schedules?

Yes. The firm currently has 16 women attorneys (non-partners) who are working a modified schedule of hours with a reduction from 10 percent to 40 percent of the billable/non-billable hour requirements and corresponding office hours. In prior years, several male attorneys have requested and been approved for reduced hours to accommodate their families' needs.

What impact, if any, will the decision to work part-time have on an attorney's ability to make partner or, if already a partner, to remain a partner at your firm?

The firm has an Associate and Counsel Policy on Modified Work Arrangements that states the following regarding eligibility for partnership: Alternative work schedule arrangements will not affect the basic eligibility of attorneys to be considered for partnership. However, attorneys who avail themselves of alternative work schedule arrangements may delay career progression and readiness for partnership status, since such arrangements may lengthen the time it takes to develop partner-level lawyering skills, well-rounded legal experience and practice development/client relations ability and business, all of which are important to meeting the firm's criteria for election to partnership. The firm's criteria for partnership will be applied to all attorneys uniformly regardless of any alternative work schedule arrangements.

Have any attorneys who chose to work a part-time schedule made partner at your firm?

Yes, in the past 4 years, 4 women working a part-time schedule were elected to partner.

Management Demographic Profile (as of 12/31/03)

	MINORITY MEN	MINORITY WOMEN	WHITE WOMEN	TOTAL
Number of attorneys on the Executive/Management Committee or equivalent	0	0	1	18
Number of attorneys on the Hiring Committee or equivalent	1	2	10	25
Number of attorneys on the Partner/Associate Review Committee or equivalent	0	0	2	8

Please provide information regarding all minority and women attorneys who head offices or practice groups of your law firm:

Women heading offices: Susan C. Roney, Buffalo, NY, Office Managing Partner; Tina Wilcox, Washington, DC, Office Managing Partner; Pat Igoe, Providence, RI, Office Managing Partner

Women heading practice groups (list names and departments): Laurie Miller (Team Leader), Government Investigation/White Collar Crime; Martha Anderson, (Deputy Practice Group Leader), Business Group (Marketing/Sales); Lori Green (Deputy Practice Group Leader), Business Group (Business Plan Implementation); Ann Miller (Team Leader), International Team; Patti Morrison (Team Leader), Immigration Team; Laura Wheeler (Team Leader), Corporate Trust Team; Jean McCreary (Practice Group Leader), Energy/Project Finance & Environmental Group; Elizabeth Whittle (Team Leader), Hydroelectricity Team; Monica Sussman (Practice Group Leader), Affordable Housing Group

The Firm Says

The firm's Professional Personnel Committee continuously reviews associate compensation relative to the competition. In recent years, the committee made "market adjustments" to the pay scales for our major metro offices to bring our associate salaries up to the market in those cities.

In 2002, a firm-wide mentor program was introduced. New associates are assigned a senior associate in his/her office to act as a "guide" during their first year of practice. The relationship with a more experienced peer provides the new associate with a comfortable place to go with questions and concerns that he/she might be reluctant to bring to a partner. For the senior associate, the relationship aids in the development of leadership skills and the time spent is recognized as an important contribution to the firm. At the end of the associate's first year of practice, they are matched with partners to act in a more formal, practice group-related mentor capacity over the years as the associate develops.

The firm is committed to providing all firm attorneys with opportunities to strengthen their knowledge and skills in areas specific to their practice area as well as areas important to their growth as professionals.

Firm attorneys are involved in leadership roles in several community organizations, including the New York Urban League. The firm is a founding member of the Greater Rochester Diversity Council. In conjunction with our client, John Hancock, firm attorneys volunteer as mentors to girls attending an inner-city high school in Boston. The firm has hosted receptions and meetings for minority and women's groups, including recently at a hotel trade association meeting in Las Vegas, and is one of the founders of the Women's High Tech Coalition.

Nixon Peabody is a signatory to the American Bar Association's Diversity Pledge, the Statement of Diversity Principles of the Association of the Bar of the City of New York and the Diversity Pledge of the Bar Association of San Francisco, and its minority partners are members of the ABA Committee on Minorities in the Profession. A partner is chief of staff to the president of the National Bar Association and has created an international directory of black attorneys. Firm attorneys have chaired the New York State Bar Association Committee on Minorities in the Profession and have held leadership positions in local chapters of the Hispanic and Puerto Rican Bar Associations.

Firm partners have served in leadership positions in local chapters of the Women's Bar Association and the New York Judges and Lawyers Breast Cancer Alert. A woman partner has received recognition by the bar and the state for her work in providing legal representation to battered women.

O'Melveny & Myers LLP

7 Times Square
New York, NY 10036
Phone: (213) 430-6000
Fax: (213) 430-6407

FIRM LEADERSHIP

Managing Partner: Arthur B. Culvahouse Jr.,
Chair
Diversity Team Leader: Kathryn Sanders and
John Beisner, Partners

LOCATIONS

Los Angeles, CA (HQ)
Century City, CA
Irvine, CA
New York, NY
Newport Beach, CA
San Francisco, CA
Silicon Valley, CA
Washington, DC
Beijing
Brussels
Hong Kong
London
Shanghai
Tokyo

FULL-TIME ASSOCIATES	2003	2002
Minority men	50	47
Minority women	50	43
White women	140	133
Total	626	540

SUMMER ASSOCIATES	2003	2002
Minority men	11	13
Minority women	22	11
White women	40	50
Total	125	98

PARTNERS*	2003	2002
Minority men	14	13
Minority women	3	1
White women	27	26
Total	224	199

*O'Melveny & Myers does not provide a breakdown of equity
and non-equity partners.

NEW HIRES*	2003	2002
Minority men	103	160
Minority women	79	97
White women	50	68
Total	182	257

*O'Melveny & Myers and O'Sullivan merged in 2002.

Strategic Plan and Diversity Leadership

How does the firm's leadership communicate the importance of diversity to everyone at the firm?

The firm's commitment to diversity is one of O'Melveny & Myers' five priorities of the firm's FY 2005 Firm-wide Strategy and Goals which was distributed throughout the firm to attorneys and staff. At the firm's partner offsite meeting in February 2004, members of the Diversity Task Force and the firm's diversity consultant made a presentation on the diversity strategic plan and identified the business case for diversity, the results of the firm's diversity assessment and the key components of the strategic plan. The Diversity Task Force subsequently made similar presentations to the attorneys and staff in each of the firm's U.S. offices. Additional communication tools utilized throughout the year to communicate diversity initiatives include the firm's Internet and intranet web sites; electronic newsletters, including messages from the chair and the Diversity Task Force; and town hall meetings. The firm has also established Embracing Diversity 2004, a firm-wide day set aside to recognize the diverse talents of the people of O'Melveny & Myers.

Who has primary responsibility for leading diversity initiatives at your firm?

The Office of the Chair (OTC), comprised of the firm's chair, vice chairs, a senior partner, an associate and COO, have ultimate responsibility for leading the firm's diversity initiatives. The Diversity Task Force, led by Kathryn Sanders and John Beisner, both of whom are partners and members of the firm's Policy Committee, serves as "internal consultant" to the OTC on matters relating to diversity and is responsible for developing certain portions of the firm's Diversity Task Force Strategic Plan.

Does your law firm currently have a diversity committee?

Yes

Does the committee's representation include one or more members of the firm's management/executive committee (or the equivalent)?

Yes

How many attorneys are on the committee, and in 2003, what was the total number of hours collectively spent by the committee in furtherance of the firm's diversity initiatives?

Total attorneys on committee: 10

Total hours spent on diversity: On average, 100+ hours per attorney per year

Does the committee and/or diversity leader establish and set goals or objectives consistent with management's priorities?

Yes

Has the firm undertaken a formal or informal diversity program or set of initiatives aimed at increasing the diversity of the firm?

Yes, formal

How often does the firm's management review the firm's diversity progress/results?

Monthly

How is the firm's diversity committee and/or firm management held accountable for achieving results?

The Office of the Chair is ultimately responsible for the success of the firm's diversity initiatives and prepares a formal annual report on the firm's progress on diversity initiatives that is distributed throughout the firm.

LAW FIRM DIVERSITY INITIATIVES	ALREADY COMPLETED	CURRENTLY ADDRESSING	NOT A CURRENT PRIORITY
Undertake communication from firm management that diversity is a top priority of the firm.	✔		
Formalize diversity plan and committee with action steps and accountability to management.	✔		
Conduct firm-wide diversity training for all attorneys and staff.		✔	
Increase the number of minority attorneys at the associate level.		✔	
Increase the number of minority attorneys at the partnership level.		✔	
Develop/expand relationships with minority bar associations to offer firm's support of these networks.	✔		
Focus on strengthening firm's mentoring program, including for benefit of minority attorneys.		✔	
Conduct internal diversity needs assessment and/or retain diversity consultant to examine how firm culture might be more welcoming of minorities.	✔		
Support law firm's internal affinity networks (e.g., women, minority attorney networks).		✔	
Manage/monitor allocation of work assignments and/or hours billed to ensure women and minority attorneys have equal access/inclusion on top client matters.		✔	

Recruitment – New Associates

Does your firm annually recruit at any of the following types of institutions?

Ivy League schools: Harvard University, University of Pennsylvania, Columbia University, Yale University

Public state schools: UCLA, University of California-Boalt Hall, University of California-Hastings

Private schools: University of Southern California, New York University, Stanford University, Loyola Law School (CA)

Historically Black Colleges and Universities (HBCUs): Howard University

Do you have any special outreach efforts directed to encourage minority law students to consider your firm?

- *Scholarships at the grade school and high school level in predominantly diverse public schools in the U.S. Scholarships for law students in Beijing and Shanghai.*
- Hold a reception for minority law students
- Advertise in minority law student association publication(s)
- Participate in/host minority law student job fair(s)
- Sponsor minority law student association events
- Firm's lawyers participate on career panels at school
- Outreach to leadership of minority student organizations

SUMMER ASSOCIATE STATISTICS: SUMMER 2003	MINORITY MEN	MINORITY WOMEN	WHITE WOMEN	TOTAL
Summer associates	10	20	40	126
Summer associates who received an offer of full-time employment	8	20	39	115
Summer associates who accepted an offer of full-time employment	4	16	29	78

Recruitment – Lateral Associates and Partners

What activities does the firm undertake to attract minority and women attorneys?

- Partner programs with women and minority bar associations
- Participate at minority job fairs
- Seek referrals from other attorneys

Do you use executive recruiting/search firms to seek to identify new diversity hires (partners or associates)?

Yes

If yes, list all women- and/or minority-owned executive search/recruiting firms to which the firm paid a fee for placement services in the past 12 months:

In process.

LATERAL ASSOCIATES AND PARTNERS: 1/1/03 – 12/31/03	MINORITY MEN	MINORITY WOMEN	WHITE WOMEN	TOTAL
Number of lateral associate hires	1	1	5	13
Number of lateral partner hires (equity and non-equity)	1	0	1	3
Number of new partners (equity and non-equity) promoted from associate rank	1	2	4	13
Number of new equity partners*	N/A	N/A	N/A	N/A

*O'Melveny & Myers does not provide a breakdown of equity and non-equity partners.

Retention & Professional Development

ATTORNEYS WHO LEFT THE FIRM: 2003*	MINORITY MEN	MINORITY WOMEN	WHITE WOMEN	TOTAL
Number of attorneys who voluntarily or involuntarily left your firm's employ in 2003	N/A	N/A	N/A	N/A

*O'Melveny & Myers does not release data regarding attorneys who leave the firm.

Please identify the specific steps you are taking to reduce the attrition rate of minority and women attorneys.

• Develop and/or support internal employee affinity groups (e.g., minority or women networks within the firm)

• Increase/review compensation relative to competition

• Increase/improve current work/life programs

• Adopt dispute resolution process

• Work with minority and women attorneys to develop career advancement plans

• Introduce minority and women attorneys to key clients, including to lead engagements

• Review work assignments and hours billed to key client matters to make sure minority and women attorneys are not being excluded

• Strengthen mentoring program for all attorneys, including minorities and women

• Professional skills development program, including minority and women attorneys

Does your firm have part-time/flex-time policies that permit attorneys (male or female) to work alternative schedules?

Yes

What impact, if any, will the decision to work part-time have on an attorney's ability to make partner or, if already a partner, to remain a partner at your firm?

Part-time attorneys are eligible for consideration for election to the partnership.

Have any attorneys who chose to work a part-time schedule made partner at your firm?

Yes, two attorneys.

Management Demographic Profile (as of 12/31/03)

	MINORITY MEN	MINORITY WOMEN	WHITE WOMEN	TOTAL
Number of attorneys on the Executive/Management Committee or equivalent	1	0	2	19
Number of attorneys on the Hiring Committee or equivalent	30	9	4	82
Number of attorneys on the Partner/Associate Review Committee or equivalent	4	1	5	30

Please provide information regarding all minority and women attorneys who head offices or practice groups of your law firm:

Minorities heading practice groups: H. Chao (Asia Practice); J. Fernandez (Latin America Practice); S. Ikuta (Environmental Practice)

Women heading practice groups: D. Belaga (SF Litigation Department) and (Environmental Class Action Defense Practice); D. Cendali (New York IP & Technology Practice) and (Copyright, Trademark and Internet Practice); K. Dreyfus (Silicon Valley Transactions Department); L. Griffey (Executive Compensation Practice); S. Ikuta (Environmental Practice); K. Newman (Telecoms Practice) K. Sanders (Private Investment Fund Practice); and D. Valentine (Antitrust Practice)

The Firm Says

O'Melveny & Myers LLP is proud of its long-standing commitment to diversity and to promoting equal and nondiscriminatory opportunities for all of our attorneys and staff. Our diversity commitment is prominently reflected in the firm's values statement, which pledges the firm's dedication to "uncompromising excellence," achieved through, among other things, "identifying superior and diverse lawyers." That element of our values statement underscores our devotion to developing and maintaining a professional environment that attracts, retains, and promotes attorneys and staff of all backgrounds — regardless of gender, race, ethnicity, national origin, sexual orientation, age, religion, disability, or any other group. This commitment is reflected in our standing "Statement of Commitment to Diversity," which is set forth below.

According to the Minority Law Journal (Summer 2004), O'Melveny & Myers ranks 17th in attorney diversity among the National Law Journal's Top 250 firms. We are committed to doing more to make O'Melveny & Myers a diversity leader. To that end, we established a firm-wide Diversity Task Force comprised of attorneys and staff, to help guide our work in this area. Based on the results of a firm-wide diversity assessment completed with the assistance of an outside diversity expert, that Task Force has developed a five-year Strategic Plan for improving diversity that has been adopted by the firm and incorporated into the firm's FY2005 Strategies and Goals. Because we recognize that diversity is critical to the firm's efforts to attract and retain the best available talent and deliver the highest quality professional services that clients expect and demand, our firm and its leadership have committed to the following goals for the current fiscal year:

• Implementing the recommendations of the Diversity Task Force and executing diversity initiatives as part of our commitment to excellence and leadership.

• Creating opportunities for professional development, high-level responsibility, and leadership for attorneys, managers, paralegals, and staff of all backgrounds.

• Integrating diversity commitment and accountability into Firm management, compensation, and talent development processes and procedures.

• Assembling teams and developing leaders that reflect the diversity of the markets in which we practice.

The firm is currently conducting diversity training for all lawyers and support staff in its U.S. offices and is establishing other programs demonstrating the firm's commitment to diversity. For example, on June 29, 2004, the firm celebrated its first annual Embracing Diversity Day. The firm devoted an entire day to firm-wide activities designed to celebrate our existing diversity, raise awareness in the O'Melveny & Myers community about various diversity issues, and to highlight our plans to make the firm more diverse. We are also reviewing and revising our work assignment and career development processes to ensure that we are providing equal opportunity to all of our lawyers and staff.

O'Melveny & Myers is a signatory and subscribes to the 2003 Statement of Principles on Minority Hiring of the Association of the Bar of the City of New York and the Bar Association of San Francisco's Breaking the Glass Ceiling Commitment. We have also been active within various national bar associations in promoting diversity.

Statement on Commitment to Diversity

O'Melveny & Myers LLP celebrates and values the diversity of all of our attorneys and staff. As a leading international law firm representing clients in virtually every sector of the global economy, we recognize our collective diversity as a strength and an asset that promotes uncompromising excellence in our work, fosters distinctive leadership in the legal profession and in the communities in which we practice, and cultivates superior citizenship in a rich and dynamic environment where individuals are respected for their unique styles, contributions and differences.

At O'Melveny, we continue to commit ourselves to sustaining long-term efforts, ensuring the development and maintenance of a professional environment that attracts, retains and promotes attorneys and staff of all backgrounds—regardless of gender, race, ethnicity, national origin, sexual orientation, age, religion, disability or any other status as defined and protected by applicable law. In short, we embrace our diversity as fundamental to the promotion of our firm's values and recognize that diversity has an invaluable influence on our firm and all that we aspire to be.

Maintaining our commitment to diversity is the responsibility of the Office of the Chair, which is presently collaborating with the Diversity Task Force to promote innovative approaches that will enhance the diversity of our attorneys and staff and that will recognize diversity as essential to fulfilling our long-term business objectives. Although O'Melveny – like the legal profession at large – has not yet achieved its fullest potential with respect to diversity, we recognize that true diversity is a journey, not a destination, and we are committed to continuous and demonstrable efforts to achieve a truly diverse firm.

Orrick, Herrington & Sutcliffe LLP

666 Fifth Avenue
New York, NY 10103
Phone: (212) 506-5000
Fax: (212) 506-5151

FIRM LEADERSHIP

Managing Partner: Ralph Baxter, Chairman &
Chief Executive Officer
Diversity Team Leader: Joseph Evall, Partner &
Chair of Firm-wide Diversity Committee

LOCATIONS

Irvine, CA
Los Angeles, CA
Menlo Park, CA
New York, NY
Pacific Northwest (Seattle, WA & Portland, OR)
Sacramento, CA
San Francisco, CA
Washington, DC
London
Milan
Paris
Rome
Tokyo

LAW FIRM DEMOGRAPHIC PROFILES

FULL-TIME ASSOCIATES	2003	2002
Minority men	27	27
Minority women	48	44
White women	88	88
Total	315	308

SUMMER ASSOCIATES	2003	2002
Minority men	7	4
Minority women	7	3
White women	11	25
Total	51	53

EQUITY PARTNERS	2003	2002
Minority men	8	6
Minority women	2	3
White women	34	30
Total	225	207

NON-EQUITY PARTNERS	2003*	2002*
Minority men	1	1
Minority women	2	1
White women	13	15
Total	39	44

* Only attorneys designated as "of counsel" at Orrick are
included in this column.

NEW HIRES	2003	2002
Minority men	7	11
Minority women	10	9
White women	24	24
Total	88	98

Strategic Plan and Diversity Leadership

How does the firm's leadership communicate the importance of diversity to everyone at the firm? (e.g., e-mails, web site, newsletters, meetings, etc.)

Orrick's leadership communicates the importance of diversity through e-mails highlighting diversity-related accomplishments, updates relating to the Women's Career Initiative, the firm intranet and Orrick web site, firm-wide training sessions held twice a year and by contributing pro bono legal services and other volunteer time, as well as money, to the communities in which Orrick attorneys practice. In addition, members of the Diversity Committee participate in various firm committees and constantly reiterate the importance of diversity to the firm.

Who has primary responsibility for leading diversity initiatives at your firm?

Joseph Evall, Partner and Chair of Firm-wide Diversity Committee

Does your law firm currently have a diversity committee?

Yes

Does the committee's representation include one or more members of the firm's management/executive committee (or the equivalent)?

Yes

How many attorneys are on the committee, and in 2003, what was the total number of hours collectively spent by the committee in furtherance of the firm's diversity initiatives?

Total attorneys on committee: 75. Orrick's Diversity Committee includes a separate committee for each U.S. office; the chairs of each local office serve as a firm-wide committee. Lawyers at all levels of experience are encouraged to join and participate in the office committees. Such participation is expected to involve at least 10 hours per year.

Does the committee and/or diversity leader establish and set goals or objectives consistent with management's priorities?

Yes

Has the firm undertaken a formal or informal diversity program or set of initiatives aimed at increasing the diversity of the firm?

Yes, formal

How often does the firm's management review the firm's diversity progress/results?

Monthly

How is the firm's diversity committee and/or firm management held accountable for achieving results?

If the firm's Diversity Committee and/or firm management do not achieve good results, then members of the Diversity Committee and management will be replaced.

LAW FIRM DIVERSITY INITIATIVES	ALREADY COMPLETED	CURRENTLY ADDRESSING	NOT A CURRENT PRIORITY
Undertake communication from firm management that diversity is a top priority of the firm.	✔		
Formalize diversity plan and committee with action steps and accountability to management.	✔		
Conduct firm-wide diversity training for all attorneys and staff.		✔	
Increase the number of minority attorneys at the associate level.		✔	
Increase the number of minority attorneys at the partnership level.		✔	
Develop/expand relationships with minority bar associations to offer firm's support of these networks.		✔	
Focus on strengthening firm's mentoring program, including for benefit of minority attorneys.	✔		
Conduct internal diversity needs assessment and/or retain diversity consultant to examine how firm culture might be more welcoming of minorities.	✔		
Support law firm's internal affinity networks (e.g., women, minority attorney networks).	✔		
Manage/monitor allocation of work assignments and/or hours billed to ensure women and minority attorneys have equal access/inclusion on top client matters.		✔	
Train minority law students in interviewing skills and in how to succeed at a law firm; reach out to minority school children in our communities to ensure that they succeed.	✔		

Recruitment - New Associates

Does your firm annually recruit at any of the following types of institutions?

Ivy League schools: Harvard University, Columbia University, University of Pennsylvania, Cornell University, Yale University

Public state schools: University of Virginia, University of California-Davis, UCLA, University of California-Boalt Hall, University of California-Hastings, University of Michigan, University of Washington (Seattle)

Private schools: American University, Boston College, Boston University, University of Chicago, Duke University, Emory University, Fordham University, Georgetown University, Hofstra University, McGeorge School of Law (University of the Pacific), New York University, Northwestern University, Santa Clara University, Seattle University, Stanford University

Do you have any special outreach efforts directed to encourage minority law students to consider your firm?

• *Orrick plans to sponsor a Bay Area Minority Job Fair in 2005.*

• Hold a reception for minority law students

• Advertise in minority law student association publication(s)

• Participate in/host minority law student job fair(s)

• Sponsor minority law student association events

• Firm's lawyers participate on career panels at school

• Outreach to leadership of minority student organizations

• Scholarships or intern/fellowships for minority students

SUMMER ASSOCIATE STATISTICS: SUMMER 2003	MINORITY MEN	MINORITY WOMEN	WHITE WOMEN	TOTAL
Summer associates	5	2	9	34
Summer associates who received an offer of full-time employment	5	2	8	31
Summer associates who accepted an offer of full-time employment	3	1	8	23

Recruitment – Lateral Associates and Partners

What activities does the firm undertake to attract minority and women attorneys?

• Partner programs with women and minority bar associations

• Seek referrals from other attorneys

Do you use executive recruiting/search firms to seek to identify new diversity hires (partners or associates)?

No

LATERAL ASSOCIATES AND PARTNERS: 1/1/03 – 12/31/03	MINORITY MEN	MINORITY WOMEN	WHITE WOMEN	TOTAL
Number of lateral associate hires	3	2	15	35
Number of lateral partner hires (equity and non-equity)*	0	1	3	21
Number of new partners (equity and non-equity) promoted from associate rank	1	0	3	12
Number of new equity partners	0	0	3	16

This row includes lateral partner and lateral of counsel hires.

Retention & Professional Development

ATTORNEYS WHO LEFT THE FIRM: 2003	MINORITY MEN	MINORITY WOMEN	WHITE WOMEN	TOTAL
Number of attorneys who voluntarily or involuntarily left your firm's employ in 2003	5	10	21	70

How do 2003 attrition rates generally compare to those experienced in the prior year period?

Lower than in prior years

Please identify the specific steps you are taking to reduce the attrition rate of minority and women attorneys.

• Develop and/or support internal employee affinity groups (e.g., minority or women networks within the firm)

• Increase/improve current work/life programs

• Adopt dispute resolution process

• Work with minority and women attorneys to develop career advancement plans

• Introduce minority and women attorneys to key clients, including to lead engagements

• Strengthen mentoring program for all attorneys, including minorities and women

• Professional skills development program, including minority and women attorneys

Does your firm have part-time/flex-time policies that permit attorneys (male or female) to work alternative schedules?

Yes

What impact, if any, will the decision to work part-time have on an attorney's ability to make partner or, if already a partner, to remain a partner at your firm?

None.

Have any attorneys who chose to work a part-time schedule made partner at your firm?

No

Management Demographic Profile (as of 12/31/03)

	MINORITY MEN	MINORITY WOMEN	WHITE WOMEN	TOTAL
Number of attorneys on the Executive/Management Committee or equivalent	0	0	1	9
Number of attorneys on the Hiring Committee or equivalent	6	9	34	102
Number of attorneys on the Partner/Associate Review Committee or equivalent	0	1	6	32

Please provide information regarding all minority and women attorneys who head offices or practice groups of your law firm:

Minorities heading offices: Steve Graham, Pacific Northwest; Dora Mao, San Francisco

Women heading offices: Dora Mao, San Francisco; Felicia Graham, Washington, DC

Minorities heading practice groups: Lorraine McGowen, Private Finance (Bankruptcy & Debt Restructuring)

Women heading practice groups: Lorraine McGowen, Private Finance (Bankruptcy & Debt Restructuring); Katharine Crost, Structured Finance

The Firm Says

Orrick's core value of cooperation and individual respect is reflected in its longstanding commitment to diversity. Orrick's Diversity Committee advises management, oversees a diversity committee in each domestic office and takes action to ensure that Orrick's attorneys are diverse and to ensure that all Orrick lawyers are positioned to thrive personally and professionally. The firm-wide and office diversity committees assist in Orrick's lawyer recruiting efforts, associate orientation, the summer program, attorney training and development, the attorney mentoring program, pro bono work and community activities, and numerous other aspects of firm life. All attorneys are encouraged to support and participate in community bar associations and other organizations whose goal is to promote diversity in the legal profession.

The Diversity Committee and Orrick recognize that promoting diversity means more than just creating an equal playing field; it also means helping every lawyer thrive. Orrick's Diversity Committee established the firm-wide mentoring program to ensure that each lawyer has meaningful mentoring relationships within the firm. Attorneys who are women, members of minority groups or openly gay or lesbian play an integral role in the mentoring program. In addition, Orrick has organized a Women's Career Initiative to support the retention and advancement of women lawyers. Local diversity committees organize internal diversity events, including affinity dinners for minority and gay and lesbian attorneys and seminars on a variety of topics relevant to diversity issues.

Much of Orrick's pro bono work relates to the diversity of the communities in which our attorneys practice. Legal services organizations that we partner with include:

- Lawyers Committee for Human Rights
- Lawyers Committee for Civil Rights
- Women's Commission for Refugee Women and Children
- inMotion
- Women Escaping a Violent Environment (WEAVE)
- New York City Gay and Lesbian Anti-Violence Project
- National Center for Lesbian Rights
- ACLU Lesbian and Gay Rights and AIDS Project
- AIDS Legal Referral Panel
- Asian Law Caucus
- Disability Rights Education and Defense Fund

Orrick's contribution to its diverse communities goes beyond legal work. For example, Orrick's New York office has partnered with The Children's Storefront, an independent elementary school in Harlem; attorneys provide legal services for parents and students, and non-legal personnel have served as volunteers and tutors for the school.

Orrick encourages its attorneys to participate in third-party diversity organizations. Orrick attorneys actively participate in several legal organizations and currently serve (or have recently served) on the boards and committees of numerous organizations that support diversity issues and causes, including the following:

• California Minority Counsel Program
• Sacramento County Bar Association's Minority Hiring and Retention Committee
• Amber Charter School
• Hispanic Federation of New York
• New York City Gay and Lesbian Anti-Violence Project
• National Center for Lesbian Rights
• Pride Law Fund
• South Asian Bar Association of Northern California
• Sikh Bar Association of North America
• Indo-US Policy Institute
• Foundation Fighting Blindness
• Womenspace
• East Palo Alto Mural Art Project

Orrick regularly reaches out to the community to encourage women, minorities and gay and lesbian people to become lawyers. Orrick attorneys also work with a variety of other community organizations involved with diversity issues, both to support its own diversity initiatives and to take an active role in developing opportunities for minority lawyers outside of the firm. For example, under the auspices of the U.C. Davis King Hall Outreach Program (KHOP), Orrick's Sacramento office and the Minority Hiring and Retention Committee of the Sacramento County Bar Association co-hosted a reception for minority college students interested in law school. In addition, Orrick's San Francisco public finance group has been actively supporting minority-owned law firms that are new entrants to the public finance legal market, by mentoring and utilizing them as co-bond counsel on important engagements for the city of San Francisco.

In recent years, Orrick attorneys have taken advantage of opportunities to meet minority and gay and lesbian law students by sponsoring and attending receptions, lectures, panel discussions and other events hosted by minority lawyer and law student organizations and local bar associations. As a result, Orrick has built strong relationships with a number of minority student groups around the country. Orrick attorneys have given presentations on legal careers, interviewing skills and other subjects to minority students at Stanford Law School, Columbia Law School, Fordham Law School and others. In addition, Orrick has participated in the Sacramento Bar Association's Minority Fellowship Program and hires one summer associate through the program each year. In 2004, the Silicon Valley office sponsored the Herma Hill Kay Summer Fellowship Fund, which funded a Boalt Law School student working at a women's rights organization.

Orrick has been recognized for its commitment to diversity, most recently by the board of directors and staff of the New York City Gay & Lesbian Anti-Violence Project, which selected Orrick as a recipient of its 2004 Courage Award.

Palmer & Dodge LLP

111 Huntington Avenue at Prudential Center
Boston, MA 02199-7613
Phone: (617) 239-0100
Fax: (617) 239-4420

FIRM LEADERSHIP

Managing Partner: Jeffrey F. Jones, Managing
Partner
Diversity Team Leader: Judith A. Malone,
Hiring Partner & Diversity Committee
Chairperson

LOCATIONS

Boston, MA (HQ)
New York, NY
Washington, DC

LAW FIRM DEMOGRAPHIC PROFILES

FULL-TIME ASSOCIATES	2003	2002
Minority men	3	3
Minority women	8	6
White women	46	45
Total	104	99

SUMMER ASSOCIATES	2003	2002
Minority men	0	0
Minority women	2	0
White women	2	4
Total	13	10

EQUITY PARTNERS*	2003	2002
Minority men	1	1
Minority women	0	1
White women	11	12
Total	63	66

*Palmer & Dodge only has equity partners.

NEW HIRES	2003	2002
Minority men	1	0
Minority women	2	1
White women	7	7
Total	18	18

Strategic Plan and Diversity Leadership

How does the firm's leadership communicate the importance of diversity to everyone at the firm? (e.g., e-mails, web site, newsletters, meetings, etc.)

The importance of diversity is addressed periodically in various venues within the firm, including in meetings of firm management (Executive Committee, department administrators, Hiring Committee), in firm meetings and in the firm's clear and unequivocal commitment to hiring, retention and promotion of people of all backgrounds in all of the firm's policies and practices.

Who has primary responsibility for leading diversity initiatives at your firm?

Judith A. Malone, hiring partner and Diversity Committee chairperson

Does your law firm currently have a diversity committee?

Yes

Does the committee's representation include one or more members of the firm's management/executive committee (or the equivalent)?

Yes

How many attorneys are on the committee, and in 2003, what was the total number of hours collectively spent by the committee in furtherance of the firm's diversity initiatives?

Total attorneys on committee: 7

Total hours spent on diversity: This is a newly formed committee. There are no records of time available.

Does the committee and/or diversity leader establish and set goals or objectives consistent with management's priorities?

Partially. The committee will advise management on policies, practices and objectives to assist in achieving management diversity goals.

Has the firm undertaken a formal or informal diversity program or set of initiatives aimed at increasing the diversity of the firm?

Yes, informal

How often does the firm's management review the firm's diversity progress/results?

No set schedule for review

How is the firm's diversity committee and/or firm management held accountable for achieving results?

Through periodic review of diversity statistics and ongoing informal discussion.

LAW FIRM DIVERSITY INITIATIVES	ALREADY COMPLETED	CURRENTLY ADDRESSING	NOT A CURRENT PRIORITY
Undertake communication from firm management that diversity is a top priority of the firm.		✓	
Formalize diversity plan and committee with action steps and accountability to management.		✓	
Conduct firm-wide diversity training for all attorneys and staff.			✓
Increase the number of minority attorneys at the associate level.		✓	
Increase the number of minority attorneys at the partnership level.		✓	
Develop/expand relationships with minority bar associations to offer firm's support of these networks.		✓	
Focus on strengthening firm's mentoring program, including for benefit of minority attorneys.			✓
Conduct internal diversity needs assessment and/or retain diversity consultant to examine how firm culture might be more welcoming of minorities.			✓
Support law firm's internal affinity networks (e.g., women, minority attorney networks).		✓	
Manage/monitor allocation of work assignments and/or hours billed to ensure women and minority attorneys have equal access/inclusion on top client matters.			✓

Recruitment - New Associates

Does your firm annually recruit at any of the following types of institutions?

Ivy League schools: Cornell University, Harvard University, University of Pennsylvania, Yale University

Public state schools: University of Virginia

Private schools: Boston College, Boston University, Duke University, Georgetown University, New England School of Law, Northeastern University, Suffolk University

Other predominantly minority and/or women's colleges: Boston Lawyers Group Job Fair

Do you have any special outreach efforts directed to encourage minority law students to consider your firm?

• Attend receptions for minority law students

• Advertise in minority law student association publication(s)

• Participate in/host minority law student job fair(s)

• Sponsor minority law student association events

• Firm's lawyers participate on career panels at school

SUMMER ASSOCIATE STATISTICS: SUMMER 2003	MINORITY MEN	MINORITY WOMEN	WHITE WOMEN	TOTAL
Summer associates	0	0	4	10
Summer associates who received an offer of full-time employment	0	0	3	7*
Summer associates who accepted an offer of full-time employment	0	0	1**	5

* Of our 10 summer associates only seven were offer-eligible; the others were 1Ls.

** Only one female summer associate declined our offer; the other is clerking.

Recruitment – Lateral Associates and Partners

What activities does the firm undertake to attract minority and women attorneys?

Participate at minority job fairs

Do you use executive recruiting/search firms to seek to identify new diversity hires (partners or associates)?

No

LATERAL ASSOCIATES AND PARTNERS: 1/1/03 – 12/31/03	MINORITY MEN	MINORITY WOMEN	WHITE WOMEN	TOTAL
Number of lateral associate hires	1	1	1	6
Number of lateral partner hires (equity and non-equity)	0	0	0	0
Number of new partners (equity and non-equity) promoted from associate rank	0	0	0	1
Number of new equity partners*	0	0	0	1

*Palmer & Dodge only has equity partners.

Retention & Professional Development

ATTORNEYS WHO LEFT THE FIRM: 2003	MINORITY MEN	MINORITY WOMEN	WHITE WOMEN	TOTAL
Number of attorneys who voluntarily or involuntarily left your firm's employ in 2003	1	1	8	17

How do 2003 attrition rates generally compare to those experienced in the prior year period?

About the same as in prior years

Please identify the specific steps you are taking to reduce the attrition rate of minority and women attorneys.

• Develop and/or support internal employee affinity groups (e.g., minority or women networks within the firm)

• Increase/improve current work/life programs

• Work with minority and women attorneys to develop career advancement plans

• Strengthen mentoring program for all attorneys, including minorities and women

• Professional skills development program, including minority and women attorneys

Does your firm have part-time/flex-time policies that permit attorneys (male or female) to work alternative schedules?

Yes. The firm has regularly had one of the highest rates of participation in parental leave and part-time work programs of all firms in the U.S.

What impact, if any, will the decision to work part-time have on an attorney's ability to make partner or, if already a partner, to remain a partner at your firm?

Part-time lawyers are considered on the equivalent time standard as full-time associates but pro-rated to take into account part-time service. Lawyers working on part-time schedules have been promoted to partner and have continued on a part-time basis as partners.

Have any attorneys who chose to work a part-time schedule made partner at your firm?

Yes, three attorneys.

Management Demographic Profile (as of 12/31/03)

	MINORITY MEN	MINORITY WOMEN	WHITE WOMEN	TOTAL
Number of attorneys on the Executive/Management Committee or equivalent	0	0	1	7
Number of attorneys on the Hiring Committee or equivalent	0	1	2	8
Number of attorneys on the Partner/Associate Review Committee or equivalent	0	0	1	4

Please provide information regarding all minority and women attorneys who head offices or practice groups of your law firm:

Women heading practice groups: Ruth Dowling, Co-Chair of Litigation department; Laurie Hall, Chair of Private Client department; Kathleen Williams, Co-Chair of Intellectual Property and Life Sciences practice groups; Yvonne Schlaeppi, Chair of International practice group

The Firm Says

Palmer & Dodge is proud of our newly organized Diversity Committee. This committee was created in response to internal desires to create a more diverse work force. After much thought we created a formal structure to convey the importance of this issue both internally and externally. The Diversity Committee has been assigned responsibility for advancing the firm's diversity agenda and has strong support from the Executive Committee for its important mission.

Palmer & Dodge is a founding member of The Boston Lawyer's Group (BLG). The mission of the BLG is to support the efforts of its member organizations to identify, recruit, advance and retain attorneys of color. We are

proud to belong to this organization which has, since its inception in 1986, been a model of cooperative effort by large Boston firms which gather together and address a common problem. Through the BLG, Palmer & Dodge participates in mock interview programs, job fairs targeting 2L students and mentoring programs for students of color.

Palmer & Dodge is well known for part-time and parental leave policies. In 2000 the Employment Issues Committee of the Massachusetts Women's Bar Association published a report on the effect of reduced-hours arrangements on the retention, recruitment and success of women attorneys in law firms. That report looked at the percentage of attorneys with reduced-hours arrangements in NALP firms in 1999 and ranked P&D No. 1 in three categories:

Percentage of all attorneys working part-time: 12.2 percent

Percentage of associates working part-time: 14.1 percent

Percentage of partners working part-time: 8.7 percent

In the fall of 2003 Palmer & Dodge was ranked among the nation's top law firms by The American Lawyer for diversity, pro bono work and business excellence, placing 29th out of the country's largest 200 firms. The American Lawyer publishes the rankings as an indicator of which firms lead the legal industry in business and professional standards, and Palmer & Dodge was one of only two Boston-based firms in the top 50 this year.

Palmer & Dodge has for many years supported the work of the Lawyers' Committee for Civil Rights. That support has been both financial and through pro bono prosecution of claims of racial discrimination on behalf of LCCR. A partner of the firm currently serves as chair of the LCCR board.

Patterson, Belknap, Webb & Tyler LLP

1133 Avenue of the Americas
New York, NY 10036
Phone: (212) 336-2000
Fax: (212) 336-2222
Diversity e-mail fbwarder@pbwt.com

FIRM LEADERSHIP

Managing Partner: Rochelle Korman, Managing Partner
Diversity Team Leader: Frederick B. Warder III, Chair, Diversity Committee

LOCATIONS

New York, NY

Strategic Plan and Diversity Leadership

How does the firm's leadership communicate the importance of diversity to everyone at the firm? (e.g., e-mails, web site, newsletters, meetings, etc.)

Orientation programs for new lawyers and new staff include presentations on the importance to the firm of diversity. Annual "state of the firm" presentations to all lawyers, as well as departmental meetings and retreats, also cover the priority placed by the firm on diversity. Diversity is emphasized by firm management to the Hiring Committee in its guidance, and diversity is discussed by departmental heads in connection with monitoring the mentoring received by every associate at the firm. In connection with a series of diversity training discussions and programs held by the firm in 2003, firm management repeatedly reaffirmed the firm's commitment not just to diversity but to the open and frank discussion of how to improve diversity at this firm and other firms in New York.

Who has primary responsibility for leading diversity initiatives at your firm?

Frederick B. Warder III, chair of Diversity Committee

Does your law firm currently have a diversity committee?

Yes

Does the committee's representation include one or more members of the firm's management/executive committee (or the equivalent)?

Yes

How many attorneys are on the committee, and in 2003, what was the total number of hours collectively spent by the committee in furtherance of the firm's diversity initiatives?

Total attorneys on committee: 18

Total hours spent on diversity: 204

Does the committee and/or diversity leader establish and set goals or objectives consistent with management's priorities?

Yes. The management of the firm is committed to diversity in principle and in practice, and has in many cases set goals for the Diversity Committee rather than the other way around. The firm's managing partner is an active member of the Diversity Committee, as are the firm's executive director and professional development director. Many of the firm's practice leaders have joined various diversity initiatives, and the entire firm (attorneys, paraprofessionals and staff) participated in a series of diversity workshops in 2003. Finally, in the fall of 2003, the firm became one of the first signatories of the groundbreaking Statement of Diversity Principles developed by the Association of the Bar of the City of New York.

Has the firm undertaken a formal or informal diversity program or set of initiatives aimed at increasing the diversity of the firm?

Yes, formal

How often does the firm's management review the firm's diversity progress/results?

Quarterly

How is the firm's diversity committee and/or firm management held accountable for achieving results?

The Diversity Committee and its chair report to management as initiatives are undertaken and as committee discussions result in recommendations. Individual attorneys who participate in the mentoring program report to practice leaders on a quarterly basis on mentoring activities and issues. In addition, the committee chair and his counterpart on the Recruiting Committee meet regularly before and during the annual recruiting season.

LAW FIRM DIVERSITY INITIATIVES	ALREADY COMPLETED	CURRENTLY ADDRESSING	NOT A CURRENT PRIORITY
Undertake communication from firm management that diversity is a top priority of the firm.	✓		
Formalize diversity plan and committee with action steps and accountability to management.	✓		
Conduct firm-wide diversity training for all attorneys and staff.	✓		
Increase the number of minority attorneys at the associate level.	✓		
Increase the number of minority attorneys at the partnership level.	✓		
Develop/expand relationships with minority bar associations to offer firm's support of these networks.		✓	
Focus on strengthening firm's mentoring program, including for benefit of minority attorneys.		✓	
Conduct internal diversity needs assessment and/or retain diversity consultant to examine how firm culture might be more welcoming of minorities.	✓		
Support law firm's internal affinity networks (e.g., women, minority attorney networks).	✓		
Manage/monitor allocation of work assignments and/or hours billed to ensure women and minority attorneys have equal access/inclusion on top client matters.	✓		
Participate in local bar association activities aimed at enhancing diversity in local law firms, coporate law departments and public sector legal divisions.	✓		

Recruitment – New Associates

Do you have any special outreach efforts directed to encourage minority law students to consider your firm?

• Hold a reception for minority law students

• Advertise in minority law student association publication(s)

• Participate in/host minority law student job fair(s)

- Sponsor minority law student association events
- Firm's lawyers participate on career panels at school
- Outreach to leadership of minority student organizations
- Scholarships or intern/fellowships for minority students
- Recruitment – Lateral Associates and Partners
- What activities does the firm undertake to attract minority and women attorneys?
- Partner programs with women and minority bar associations
- Participate at minority job fairs
- Seek referrals from other attorneys

Do you use executive recruiting/search firms to seek to identify new diversity hires (partners or associates)?

Yes

SUMMER ASSOCIATE STATISTICS: SUMMER 2003	MINORITY MEN	MINORITY WOMEN	WHITE WOMEN	TOTAL
Summer associates	1	1	6	11
Summer associates who received an offer of full-time employment	1	1	6	11
Summer associates who accepted an offer of full-time employment	1	1	4	9

Recruitment – Lateral Associates and Partners

LATERAL ASSOCIATES AND PARTNERS: 1/1/03 – 12/31/03	MINORITY MEN	MINORITY WOMEN	WHITE WOMEN	TOTAL
Number of lateral associate hires	0	0	1	1
Number of lateral partner hires (equity and non-equity)	0	0	0	2
Number of new partners (equity and non-equity) promoted from associate rank	0	0	0	2
Number of new equity partners	0	0	0	4

Retention & Professional Development

How do 2003 attrition rates generally compare to those experienced in the prior year period?

Higher than in prior years

Please identify the specific steps you are taking to reduce the attrition rate of minority and women attorneys.

• Develop and/or support internal employee affinity groups (e.g., minority or women networks within the firm)

• Increase/review compensation relative to competition

• Work with minority and women attorneys to develop career advancement plans

• Introduce minority and women attorneys to key clients, including to lead engagements

• Review work assignments and hours billed to key client matters to make sure minority and women attorneys are not being excluded

• Strengthen mentoring program for all attorneys, including minorities and women

• Professional skills development program, including minority and women attorneys

Does your firm have part-time/flex-time policies that permit attorneys (male or female) to work alternative schedules?

Yes

What impact, if any, will the decision to work part-time have on an attorney's ability to make partner or, if already a partner, to remain a partner at your firm?

None. The firm's part-time policy explicitly states that a part-time schedule will not affect an attorney's eligibility for partnership consideration. There is also no minimum requirement for "equivalent years" or other adjustment made to the partnership track for part-time associates. The firm has had a number of part-time partners, three of whom were part-time associates prior to being elected to the partnership. In 2003, the firm had 11 part-time associates, three part-time counsel and two part-time partners. In 2004, the firm has 12 part-time associates, three part-time counsel, and two part-time partners.

Have any attorneys who chose to work a part-time schedule made partner at your firm?

Yes, three attorneys. See comments above.

Management Demographic Profile (as of 12/31/03)

	MINORITY MEN	MINORITY WOMEN	WHITE WOMEN	TOTAL
Number of attorneys on the Executive/Management Committee or equivalent	0	0	2	6
Number of attorneys on the Hiring Committee or equivalent	0	1	3	10
Number of attorneys on the Partner/Associate Review Committee or equivalent*	N/A	N/A	N/A	N/A

*Patterson Belknap does not have a Partner/Associate Review Committee or equivalent.

Partner review: Each partner is reviewed annually by all associates via anonymous survey questionnaires that are reviewed and tabulated by an outside consultant. Partners are also reviewed annually by a small committee of partners consisting of three men and one woman.

Associate review: Each associate is reviewed annually, and the most junior associates semi-annually, by all partners in the associate's department. Evaluations are submitted by all partners, counsel and senior associates with whom the associate has worked during the preceding review period, and these evaluations are then reviewed and discussed by all partners in the associate's department before the associate receives his or her review.

Please provide information regarding all minority and women attorneys who head offices or practice groups of your law firm:

Women heading offices: The firm has only one office. The managing partner of the firm, Rochelle Korman, is a woman.

Women heading practice groups: Antonia M. Grumbach, Exempt Organizations Practice Group; Gloria C. Phares, Transactional Intellectual Property Practice Group; Lisa E. Cleary and Ellen M. Martin, co-heads of the Employment Law Practice Group

The Firm Says

Patterson Belknap is dedicated to being the best place in New York City to practice law. In pursuit of that goal, the firm works hard to maintain an atmosphere of dignity, civility and respect in which all of its attorneys and staff, whatever their backgrounds, are comfortable and can flourish. Promoting diversity has long been an important element of the firm's growth and evolution. Over the past several years, the firm has focused additional attention on recruiting and retaining lawyers with diverse backgrounds and perspectives. Improving diversity at Patterson Belknap is the right thing to do, and that is reason enough for our diversity initiatives. But improving diversity is also good business, and the firm believes that it can fully address its clients' needs only with a group of attorneys as diverse as the problems we and our clients confront.

To that end, Patterson Belknap actively pursues minority law students and clerks during recruiting season and minority lateral hires to fill the needs of expanding practice areas. The firm spends equal energy on retaining its minority lawyers through formal firm programs, such as mentoring and diversity training, and through informal firm initiatives, such as fostering affinity groups and holding discussion lunches. The Patterson Attorneys of Color (PAC) affinity group was established three years ago and has become an important part of the firm's fabric. Patterson takes seriously the commitment it made when it became one of the first signatories of the Statement of Diversity Principles promulgated last year by the Association of the Bar of the City of New York. While the firm had also been a signatory of prior versions of these Principles, the new Statement calls for more openness and accountability for diversity efforts citywide, and the firm believes that this openness will help Patterson Belknap and its New York City neighbors improve our diversity records.

Above all, Patterson Belknap is committed to nurturing a community in which our clients are served in the best way possible and in which everyone can realize his or her potential as a professional. Hiring and retaining a diverse group of attorneys has been and continues to be a fundamental part of that commitment.

Patton Boggs LLP

2550 M Street, NW
Washington, DC 20037
Phone: (202) 457-6000
Fax: (202) 457-6315

FIRM LEADERSHIP

Managing Partner: Stuart Pape, Managing
Partner
Diversity Team Leader: Therese R. Gross,
Chief Human Resources Officer

LOCATIONS

Washington, DC (HQ)
Anchorage, AK
Dallas, TX
Denver, CO
McLean, VA
Doha, Qatar

LAW FIRM DEMOGRAPHIC PROFILES

FULL-TIME ASSOCIATES	2003	2002
Minority men	16	17
Minority women	11	8
White women	67	51
Total	180	164

SUMMER ASSOCIATES	2003	2002
Minority men	1	1
Minority women	2	0
White women	7	2
Total	20	5

EQUITY PARTNERS	2003	2002
Minority men	5	5
Minority women	1	1
White women	12	13
Total	115	122

NON-EQUITY PARTNERS	2003	2002
Minority men	1	1
Minority women	3	4
White women	13	11
Total	62	53

NEW HIRES	2003	2002
Minority men	4	8
Minority women	6	1
White women	35	13
Total	76	44

Strategic Plan and Diversity Leadership

How does the firm's leadership communicate the importance of diversity to everyone at the firm? (e.g., e-mails, web site, newsletters, meetings, etc.)

Meetings; web site; newsletters; orientation.

Who has primary responsibility for leading diversity initiatives at your firm?

Therese Gross, chief human resources officer; Stuart Pape, managing partner; Kara Reidy, director of recruitment/retention; and Ira Fishman, COO.

Does your law firm currently have a diversity committee?

No

Does the committee and/or diversity leader establish and set goals or objectives consistent with management's priorities?

Yes

Has the firm undertaken a formal or informal diversity program or set of initiatives aimed at increasing the diversity of the firm?

Yes, formal

How often does the firm's management review the firm's diversity progress/results?

Continuously

LAW FIRM DIVERSITY INITIATIVES	ALREADY COMPLETED	CURRENTLY ADDRESSING	NOT A CURRENT PRIORITY
Undertake communication from firm management that diversity is a top priority of the firm.	✔		
Formalize diversity plan and committee with action steps and accountability to management.		✔	
Conduct firm-wide diversity training for all attorneys and staff.		✔	
Increase the number of minority attorneys at the associate level.		✔	
Increase the number of minority attorneys at the partnership level.		✔	
Develop/expand relationships with minority bar associations to offer firm's support of these networks.		✔	
Focus on strengthening firm's mentoring program, including for benefit of minority attorneys.		✔	
Conduct internal diversity needs assessment and/or retain diversity consultant to examine how firm culture might be more welcoming of minorities.	✔		

LAW FIRM DIVERSITY INITIATIVES (CONTINUED)	ALREADY COMPLETED	CURRENTLY ADDRESSING	NOT A CURRENT PRIORITY
Support law firm's internal affinity networks (e.g., women, minority attorney networks).		✓	
Manage/monitor allocation of work assignments and/or hours billed to ensure women and minority attorneys have equal access/inclusion on top client matters.		✓	

Recruitment – New Associates

Does your firm annually recruit at any of the following types of institutions? (Check all that apply and list the schools).

Ivy League schools: Harvard University

Public state schools: University of Michigan, University of Chicago, University of Denver, University of Colorado, University of Texas, University of Virginia, George Mason University

Private schools: Georgetown University, Vanderbilt University, George Washington University, Catholic University of America

Historically Black Colleges and Universities (HBCUs): Howard University

Do you have any special outreach efforts directed to encourage minority law students to consider your firm?

• Hold a reception for minority law students

• Advertise in minority law student association publication(s)

• Participate in/host minority law student job fair(s)

• Sponsor minority law student association events

• Outreach to leadership of minority student organizations

SUMMER ASSOCIATE STATISTICS: SUMMER 2003	MINORITY MEN	MINORITY WOMEN	WHITE WOMEN	TOTAL
Summer associates	1	1	5	12
Summer associates who received an offer of full-time employment	1	1	5	12
Summer associates who accepted an offer of full-time employment	1	1	4	11

Recruitment – Lateral Associates and Partners

What activities does the firm undertake to attract minority and women attorneys?

Seek referrals from other attorneys

Do you use executive recruiting/search firms to seek to identify new diversity hires (partners or associates)?

Yes

LATERAL ASSOCIATES AND PARTNERS: 1/1/03 – 12/31/03	MINORITY MEN	MINORITY WOMEN	WHITE WOMEN	TOTAL
Number of lateral associate hires	3	4	23	53
Number of lateral partner hires (equity and non-equity)	0	0	0	5
Number of new partners (equity and non-equity) promoted from associate rank	0	0	1	5
Number of new equity partners*	0	0	0	0

Promoted on 1/1/03

Retention & Professional Development

ATTORNEYS WHO LEFT THE FIRM: 2003	MINORITY MEN	MINORITY WOMEN	WHITE WOMEN	TOTAL
Number of attorneys who voluntarily or involuntarily left your firm's employ in 2003	4	2	11	42

How do 2003 attrition rates generally compare to those experienced in the prior year period?

About the same as in prior years

Please identify the specific steps you are taking to reduce the attrition rate of minority and women attorneys.

• Develop and/or support internal employee affinity groups (e.g., minority or women networks within the firm)

• Increase/improve current work/life programs

• Succession plan includes emphasis on diversity

• Work with minority and women attorneys to develop career advancement plans

• Introduce minority and women attorneys to key clients, including to lead engagements

• Review work assignments and hours billed to key client matters to make sure minority and women attorneys are not being excluded

• Strengthen mentoring program for all attorneys, including minorities and women

• Professional skills development program, including minority and women attorneys

Does your firm have part-time/flex-time policies that permit attorneys (male or female) to work alternative schedules?

Yes

What impact, if any, will the decision to work part-time have on an attorney's ability to make partner or, if already a partner, to remain a partner at your firm?

Attorneys on a lower billable hour track are fully eligible for partner. Associates who are on a schedule that does not require them to be in office full-time are not eligible but can move to either full-hour or lower-hour track and be fully eligible.

Have any attorneys who chose to work a part-time schedule made partner at your firm?

Yes, two attorneys.

Management Demographic Profile (as of 12/31/03)

	MINORITY MEN	MINORITY WOMEN	WHITE WOMEN	TOTAL
Number of attorneys on the Executive/Management Committee or equivalent	0	0	2	16
Number of attorneys on the Hiring Committee or equivalent	0	2	4	12
Number of attorneys on the Partner/Associate Review Committee or equivalent	0	0	7	13

Please provide information regarding all minority and women attorneys who head offices or practice groups of your law firm:

Women heading practice groups: Deborah Lodge, Unassigned

Thinking about your future?
We are.

Paul, Hastings, Janofsky & Walker LLP, founded in 1951, is an international law firm representing Fortune 500 companies with nearly 950 attorneys located in 15 offices: Atlanta, Beijing, Brussels, Hong Kong, London, Los Angeles, New York, Orange County, Paris, San Diego, San Francisco, Shanghai, Stamford, Tokyo and Washington, DC.

Paul Hastings is committed to providing a work environment that offers equal opportunity to all and reflects the diverse communities in which we operate.

Paul Hastings
ATTORNEYS

www.paulhastings.com
Paul, Hastings, Janofsky & Walker LLP

Atlanta	Los Angeles	San Francisco
Beijing	New York	Shanghai
Brussels	Orange County	Stamford
Hong Kong	Paris	Tokyo
London	San Diego	Washington, DC

Paul, Hastings, Janofsky & Walker LLP

515 S. Flower Street, 25th Floor
Los Angeles, CA 90071
Phone: (213) 683-6000
Fax: (213) 683-5918

FIRM LEADERSHIP

Managing Partner: Greg Nitzkowski
Diversity Team Leaders: Charles Hamilton, At-Large Diversity Partner & Chair of the Diversity Policy and Program Committee (DPPC); Anton Mack, Managing Director of Attorney Recruiting, Member of the DPPC & Chair of the Diversity Task Force

LOCATIONS

Atlanta, GA
Costa Mesa, CA
Los Angeles, CA
New York, NY
San Diego, CA
San Francisco, CA
Stamford, CT
Washington, DC
Beijing
Brussels
Hong Kong
London
Paris
Shanghai
Tokyo

LAW FIRM DEMOGRAPHIC PROFILES*

FULL-TIME ASSOCIATES	2003	2002
Minority men	31	30
Minority women	44	45
White women	194	173
Total	516	509

SUMMER ASSOCIATES	2003	2002
Minority men	10	9
Minority women	4	16
White women	26	28
Total	71	81

EQUITY PARTNERS	2003	2002
Minority men	12	9
Minority women	3	3
White women	27	29
Total	197	187

NON-EQUITY PARTNERS	2003	2002
Minority men	1	1
Minority women	0	0
White women	3	3
Total	19	20

NEW HIRES	2003	2002
Minority men	29	5
Minority women	17	18
White women	87	40
Total	255	126

Data in chart reflect totals on 2/01/04 and 2/01/03.

Strategic Plan and Diversity Leadership

How does the firm's leadership communicate the importance of diversity to everyone at the firm? (e.g., e-mails, web site, newsletters, meetings, etc.)

At present, the firm leadership shares its message on diversity through a monthly newsletter.

Who has primary responsibility for leading diversity initiatives at your firm?

Charles Hamilton, at-large diversity partner and chair, DPPC

Does your law firm currently have a diversity committee?

Yes

Does the committee's representation include one or more members of the firm's management/executive committee (or the equivalent)?

Yes

How many attorneys are on the committee, and in 2003, what was the total number of hours collectively spent by the committee in furtherance of the firm's diversity initiatives?

Total attorneys on committee: 10

Total hours spent on diversity: N/A. The DPPC will collect this data at the end of 2004.

Does the committee and/or diversity leader establish and set goals or objectives consistent with management's priorities?

Yes

Has the firm undertaken a formal or informal diversity program or set of initiatives aimed at increasing the diversity of the firm?

Yes, formal

How often does the firm's management review the firm's diversity progress/results?

Twice a year

How is the firm's diversity committee and/or firm management held accountable for achieving results?

The annual DPPC goals and objectives are reviewed by the firm's Policy Committee to determine whether additional efforts and resources are required.

LAW FIRM DIVERSITY INITIATIVES	ALREADY COMPLETED	CURRENTLY ADDRESSING	NOT A CURRENT PRIORITY
Undertake communication from firm management that diversity is a top priority of the firm.	✓		
Formalize diversity plan and committee with action steps and accountability to management.		✓	
Conduct firm-wide diversity training for all attorneys and staff.**		✓	
Increase the number of minority attorneys at the associate level.*	✓	✓	
Increase the number of minority attorneys at the partnership level.*	✓	✓	
Develop/expand relationships with minority bar associations to offer firm's support of these networks.*	✓	✓	
Focus on strengthening firm's mentoring program, including for benefit of minority attorneys.		✓	
Conduct internal diversity needs assessment and/or retain diversity consultant to examine how firm culture might be more welcoming of minorities.		✓	
Support law firm's internal affinity networks (e.g., women, minority attorney networks).		✓	
Manage/monitor allocation of work assignments and/or hours billed to ensure women and minority attorneys have equal access/inclusion on top client matters.**		✓	

*We have made measurable strides, and significant efforts are being made in these areas.

**This is currently under construction.

Recruitment - New Associates

Does your firm annually recruit at any of the following types of institutions? (Check all that apply and list the schools).

Ivy League schools: Columbia University, Cornell University, Harvard University, University of Pennsylvania, Yale University

Public state schools: Boalt Hall (UC Berkeley), University of Connecticut, University of Georgia , Georgia State University, University of California-Hastings, UC Davis, UCLA, University of Michigan, University of North Carolina, University of Virginia

Private schools: Boston College, University of Chicago, Duke University, Emory University, Fordham University, George Washington University, Georgetown University, Loyola Law School (L.A.), New York University, Northwestern University, University of Notre Dame, Stanford University, University of San Diego, University of San Francisco, Vanderbilt University, Washington and Lee University

Historically Black Colleges and Universities (HBCUs): Howard University

Other predominantly minority and/or women's colleges: N/A. As a legal employer, we do not recruit at colleges; however, we regularly hire graduates of these institutions as summer associates during law school and as associates after graduation.

Do you have any special outreach efforts directed to encourage minority law students to consider your firm?

• Hold a reception for minority law students

• Advertise in minority law student association publication(s)

• Participate in/host minority law student job fair(s)

• Sponsor minority law student association events

• Firm's lawyers participate on career panels at school

• Outreach to leadership of minority student organizations

• Scholarships or intern/fellowships for minority students

• Recruitment – Lateral Associates and Partners

SUMMER ASSOCIATE STATISTICS: SUMMER 2003	MINORITY MEN	MINORITY WOMEN	WHITE WOMEN	TOTAL
Summer associates	9	4	23	62
Summer associates who received an offer of full-time employment	9	2	22	56
Summer associates who accepted an offer of full-time employment	6	1	17	46

Recruitment – Lateral Associates and Partners

What activities does the firm undertake to attract minority and women attorneys?

• *National Bar Association web site*

• Partner programs with women and minority bar associations

• Participate at minority job fairs

• Seek referrals from other attorneys

Do you use executive recruiting/search firms to seek to identify new diversity hires (partners or associates)?

Yes

List all women- and/or minority-owned executive search/recruiting firms to which the firm paid a fee for placement services in the past 12 months:

Audrey Golden & Associates, Counsel Search, EM Messick, Garrison & Sisson, Hughes & Sloan, Marina Sirras & Associates, Russo & Fondell, Smythe Masterson & Judd, Sokol Associates, Triumph Search Agency.

LATERAL ASSOCIATES AND PARTNERS: 1/1/03 – 12/31/03	MINORITY MEN	MINORITY WOMEN	WHITE WOMEN	TOTAL*
Number of lateral associate hires	12	7	35	114
Number of lateral partner hires (equity and non-equity)	3	0	1	20
Number of new partners (equity and non-equity) promoted from associate rank	0	0	2	10
Number of new equity partners	3	0	3	30

Period reported is 2/2/03 through 2/1/04 and does not include foreign offices.

Retention & Professional Development

ATTORNEYS WHO LEFT THE FIRM: 2003	MINORITY MEN	MINORITY WOMEN	WHITE WOMEN	TOTAL
Number of attorneys who voluntarily or involuntarily left your firm's employ in 2003	12	14	38	139

How do 2003 attrition rates generally compare to those experienced in the prior year period?

Lower than in prior years

Please identify the specific steps you are taking to reduce the attrition rate of minority and women attorneys.

• Develop and/or support internal employee affinity groups (e.g., minority or women networks within the firm)

• Increase/review compensation relative to competition

• Increase/improve current work/life programs

• Adopt dispute resolution process

• Succession plan includes emphasis on diversity

• Strengthen mentoring program for all attorneys, including minorities and women

• Professional skills development program, including minority and women attorneys

Does your firm have part-time/flex-time policies that permit attorneys (male or female) to work alternative schedules?

Yes

What impact, if any, will the decision to work part-time have on an attorney's ability to make partner or, if already a partner, to remain a partner at your firm?

Paul Hastings has a flexible part-time policy, in which attorneys can return from part-time status for partnership consideration. The flexible policy allows for case-by-case recognition for part-time work. This policy applies to current partners as well.

Have any attorneys who chose to work a part-time schedule made partner at your firm?

Yes, three attorneys. This information only reflects statistics maintained over the past several years.

Management Demographic Profile (as of 12/31/03)

	MINORITY MEN	MINORITY WOMEN	WHITE WOMEN	TOTAL
Number of attorneys on the Executive/Management Committee or equivalent*	3	1	3	44
Number of attorneys on the Hiring Committee or equivalent	5	3	14	42
Number of attorneys on the Partner/Associate Review Committee or equivalent**	0	2	10	35

* Includes the Policy Committee, department, office management, general counsel to the firm and the professional personnel partner.

**Includes the Partnership Evaluation Committee and the Unit Committee.

Please provide information regarding all minority and women attorneys who head offices or practice groups of your law firm:

Minorities heading offices: Elena Baca, Los Angeles; Norman Futami, Los Angeles

Women heading offices: Elena Baca, Los Angeles; Barbara Brown, Washington, DC

Minorities heading practice groups: Jorge Alers, Corp-Latin America; John Gibson, Litigation-Real Estate; Ned Isokawa, Litigation-Product Liability/Toxic Tort/Environmental; Carl Sanchez, Corporate-Mergers & Acquisitions

Women heading practice groups: Nancy Abell, Employment Law (Chair); Julie Allecta, Corporate-Investment Management; Jamie Broder, Litigation-Alternative Dispute Resolution; Siobhan Burke, Corporate-Private Equity; Grace Carter, Litigation-Healthcare; Eve Coddon, Litigation-Insurance Coverage; Erika Collins, Employment-International Employment Law; Victoria Cundiff, Litigation-Trade Secrets/Employee Covenants; Deborah Marlowe, Employment-Immigration

The Firm Says

Paul Hastings is committed to providing a work environment that offers equal opportunity to all and reflects the diverse communities in which we operate.

We actively seek to recruit minority candidates for attorney and staff positions. We do so by reaching out to law students, working with networks and organizations, and through our selection and interview process. And it is working. In national surveys, we continue to strengthen our rankings on the number of minority lawyers in our firm. We also seek to assure that all of our people have equal access to the best opportunities for professional development and growth.

The Diversity Policy and Program Committee is comprised of partners and associates across the firm. They have been chartered with bringing tangible focus to the firm's strategic direction for diversity as well as advising firm management with respect to the adoption of policies and programs that support the further development and achievement of the firm's diversity goals.

The Paul Hastings diversity initiatives include:

• Addressing Diversity in a Challenging Legal Market, University of Maryland, 2004

- ABA Commission on Racial and Ethnic Diversity in the Profession, Host, Multicultural Bar Leaders' Breakfast, 2003
- BLSA Mid-Atlantic, Northeast and Western Job Fairs, 2003
- Boalt Hall Coalitions at the Crossroads Conference, 2003
- Harvard BLSA Spring Conference, Platinum Sponsor, 2003
- Hispanic National Bar Association Latino Law School Job Fair, 2003
- Howard University Legal Partner Program, Gold Sponsor, 2003
- Michigan BLSA 25th Annual Alden J. "Butch" Carpenter Memorial Banquet, Gold Sponsor, 2003
- MCCA Dinners, Diamond/Gold Sponsor, Washington, D.C., New York, San Francisco, 2003
- La Raza Law Student Reception, UCLA, USC, Loyola, 2004
- Lawyers' Committee for Civil Rights Under Law 40th Anniversary Dinner, 2003
- Los Angeles Managing Partners Roundtable Diversity Seminar, 2003
- National BLSA Magazine, 2003
- National Center for Lesbian Rights 26th Anniversary Dinner, 2003
- Northwestern BLSA Diamond Sponsor, 2004
- Penn BLSA15th Annual Sadie T. M. Alexander Commemorative Conference, Gold Sponsor, 2003
- Southeastern Minority Job Fair, 2003
- Stanford APALSA Bay Area Fourth Annual Conference, Silver Sponsor, 2003
- USC Annual Alumni Dinner, Gold Sponsor, 2004

Paul, Weiss, Rifkind, Wharton & Garrison LLP

1285 Avenue of the Americas
New York, NY 10019
Phone: (212) 373-3000
Fax: (212) 757-3990

FIRM LEADERSHIP

Patricia J. Morrissy, Legal Recruitment Director
Managing Partner: Alfred D. Youngwood, Chair of the Firm
Diversity Team Leader: Marco V. Masotti, Corporate Partner and Chair of the Diversity Committee

LOCATIONS

New York, NY (HQ)
Washington, DC
Beijing
Hong Kong
London
Tokyo

LAW FIRM DEMOGRAPHIC PROFILES

FULL-TIME ASSOCIATES	2003	2002
Minority men	33	34
Minority women	41	38
White women	116	113
Total	327	332

SUMMER ASSOCIATES	2003	2002
Minority men	7	5
Minority women	14	19
White women	26	29
Total	77	86

EQUITY PARTNERS	2003	2002
Minority men	4	4
Minority women	2	1
White women	10	9
Total	98	94

NEW HIRES	2003	2002
Minority men	6	6
Minority women	16	13
White women	29	26
Total	78	79

Strategic Plan and Diversity Leadership

How does the firm's leadership communicate the importance of diversity to everyone at the firm? (e.g., e-mails, web site, newsletters, meetings, etc.)

Meetings, firm-wide events, web site and alumni newsletter.

Who has primary responsibility for leading diversity initiatives at your firm?

Marco V. Masotti, corporate partner and chair of the Diversity Committee

Does your law firm currently have a diversity committee?

Yes

Does the committee's representation include one or more members of the firm's management/executive committee (or the equivalent)?

Yes

How many attorneys are on the committee, and in 2003, what was the total number of hours collectively spent by the committee in furtherance of the firm's diversity initiatives?

Total attorneys on committee: 9

Does the committee and/or diversity leader establish and set goals or objectives consistent with management's priorities?

Yes

Has the firm undertaken a formal or informal diversity program or set of initiatives aimed at increasing the diversity of the firm?

Yes, formal

How often does the firm's management review the firm's diversity progress/results?

Twice a year

LAW FIRM DIVERSITY INITIATIVES	ALREADY COMPLETED	CURRENTLY ADDRESSING	NOT A CURRENT PRIORITY
Undertake communication from firm management that diversity is a top priority of the firm.	✓		
Formalize diversity plan and committee with action steps and accountability to management.	✓		
Conduct firm-wide diversity training for all attorneys and staff.	✓		
Increase the number of minority attorneys at the associate level.		✓	
Increase the number of minority attorneys at the partnership level.		✓	
Develop/expand relationships with minority bar associations to offer firm's support of these networks.	✓		
Focus on strengthening firm's mentoring program, including for benefit of minority attorneys.	✓		
Conduct internal diversity needs assessment and/or retain diversity consultant to examine how firm culture might be more welcoming of minorities.		✓	
Support law firm's internal affinity networks (e.g., women, minority attorney networks).		✓	
Manage/monitor allocation of work assignments and/or hours billed to ensure women and minority attorneys have equal access/inclusion on top client matters.		✓	

Recruitment- New Associates

Does your firm annually recruit at any of the following types of institutions? (Check all that apply and list the schools).

Ivy League schools: Columbia University, Cornell University, Harvard University, University of Pennsylvania, Yale University

Public state schools: University of California-Boalt, Osgoode Hall Law School (York University), University of Toronto, University of Virginia, College of William & Mary

Private schools: Boston College, Boston University, Brooklyn Law School, Cardozo Law School, University of Chicago, Duke University, Fordham University, Georgetown University, George Washington University, McGill University, University of Michigan, Northwestern University, New York Law School, New York University, Stanford University, Washington University (St. Louis), Washington and Lee University

Historically Black Colleges and Universities (HBCUs): Howard University

Do you have any special outreach efforts directed to encourage minority law students to consider your firm?

• Hold a reception for minority law students

• Advertise in minority law student association publication(s)

MINORITY CORPORATE COUNSEL ASSOCIATION

- Participate in/host minority law student job fair(s)
- Sponsor minority law student association events
- Firm's lawyers participate on career panels at school
- Outreach to leadership of minority student organizations
- Scholarships or intern/fellowships for minority students

SUMMER ASSOCIATE STATISTICS: SUMMER 2003	MINORITY MEN	MINORITY WOMEN	WHITE WOMEN	TOTAL
Summer associates	7	14	26	77
Summer associates who received an offer of full-time employment	7	14	26	77
Summer associates who accepted an offer of full-time employment	5	10	12	50

Recruitment – Lateral Associates and Partners

What activities does the firm undertake to attract minority and women attorneys?

- Partner programs with women and minority bar associations
- Participate at minority job fairs
- Seek referrals from other attorneys
- Utilize online job services (e.g., MCCA/DuPont Primary Law Firm Job Bank)

Do you use executive recruiting/search firms to seek to identify new diversity hires (partners or associates)?

Yes

LATERAL ASSOCIATES AND PARTNERS: 1/1/03 – 12/31/03	MINORITY MEN	MINORITY WOMEN	WHITE WOMEN	TOTAL
Number of lateral associate hires	0	1	6	14
Number of lateral partner hires (equity and non-equity)	0	0	1	4
Number of new partners (equity and non-equity) promoted from associate rank	0	1	0	3
Number of new equity partners	0	1	1	7

Retention & Professional Development

ATTORNEYS WHO LEFT THE FIRM: 2003	MINORITY MEN	MINORITY WOMEN	WHITE WOMEN	TOTAL
Number of attorneys who voluntarily or involuntarily left your firm's employ in 2003	7	10	28	82

How do 2003 attrition rates generally compare to those experienced in the prior year period?

About the same as in prior years

Please identify the specific steps you are taking to reduce the attrition rate of minority and women attorneys.

• *See narrative section below.*

• Develop and/or support internal employee affinity groups (e.g., minority or women networks within the firm)

• Increase/review compensation relative to competition

• Increase/improve current work/life programs

• Work with minority and women attorneys to develop career advancement plans

• Introduce minority and women attorneys to key clients, including to lead engagements

• Strengthen mentoring program for all attorneys, including minorities and women

• Professional skills development program, including minority and women attorneys

Does your firm have part-time/flex-time policies that permit attorneys (male or female) to work alternative schedules?

Yes

What impact, if any, will the decision to work part-time have on an attorney's ability to make partner or, if already a partner, to remain a partner at your firm?

None.

Have any attorneys who chose to work a part-time schedule made partner at your firm?

Yes

Management Demographic Profile (as of 12/31/03)

	MINORITY MEN	MINORITY WOMEN	WHITE WOMEN	TOTAL
Number of attorneys on the Executive/Management Committee or equivalent	0	0	1	10
Number of attorneys on the Hiring Committee or equivalent	2	2	3	17
Number of attorneys on the Partner/Associate Review Committee or equivalent	N/A	N/A	N/A	N/A

Please provide information regarding all minority and women attorneys who head offices or practice groups of your law firm:

Minorities heading offices: Jeanette K. Chan, Beijing; Lisa Yano, Tokyo

Women heading offices: Jeanette K. Chan, Beijing; Lisa Yano, Tokyo

Minorities heading practice groups: Theodore V. Wells Jr., co-chair of the litigation department and member of the Diversity Committee

Women heading practice groups: Terry Schimek, Financing Practice Group; Judith Thoyer, M&A Practice Group; Marilyn Sobel, Private Equity Practice Group; Carey Ramos, Co-Chair of the Litigation IP Practice Group

The Firm Says

Paul Weiss diversity initiatives are led by the firm's Diversity Committee and Women's Initiatives Committee. The Diversity Committee is entrusted with maintaining and expanding diversity among the lawyers at the firm. Our goal has been, and continues to be, to incorporate an actively pro-diversity agenda into the fabric of firm life. To this end, we have worked to motivate the firm's diverse community to collaborate with our committee in order to design and implement programs and initiatives aimed at increasing diversity through more effective recruitment and retention. Similarly, the firm's Women's Initiatives Committee is dedicated to the career development and retention of our women attorneys.

Recruitment

On the recruitment front, we send outreach letters to all minority groups at all schools at which we interview, inviting their members to sign up with us for an on-campus interview. When minority applicants interview at the firm, we make sure that they meet with at least one minority attorney. After minority candidates receive offers, a Recruitment & Diversity Task Force follows up with them and makes a special effort to have the firm's minority attorneys follow up with them as well. Paul Weiss also supports and participates in numerous minority recruitment activities, such as:

• Harvard Asian Law Society's (HALS) Asia Pacific and Business Conference
• Association of the Bar of the City of New York Fellowship Program
• Sponsors for Educational Opportunity (SEO) Career Program
• Northeast Black Law Students' Association (BLSA) Annual Roundtable in honor of summer associates
• Harvard BLSA Career/Alumni Spring Conference
• Columbia BLSA's Paul Robeson Conference and Annual Spring Alumni Dinner

Similarly, Paul Weiss has implemented a number of initiatives relating to the recruitment of women. First, under the auspices of our Women's Initiatives Committee and Recruitment Committee, we send an outreach letter to law school student organizations. Second, when we visit campuses to interview, we make every effort to ensure women and minority attorneys are well represented. Third, during the in-house interview process, women candidates are scheduled to interview with at least one woman attorney. Fourth, during the follow-up process, our recruitment staff facilitates further interactions between women candidates and lawyers when the candidate wants to address gender-specific concerns. Finally, our summer associate program, one of our major recruiting tools, includes events sponsored by our Women's Initiatives Committee. In addition, the firm's Summer Committee sponsors events at outside organizations aimed toward women's concerns.

Retention

The firm's Diversity Committee, which consists of partners, counsel and associates, has designed a formal mentoring program for our minority associates, which seeks to foster productive mentoring relationships and to enhance the professional lives of the participating partners and associates. The Diversity Committee also hosts diversity networking events, which give Paul Weiss minority associates the opportunity to meet other professionals in the legal and business worlds. These annual networking events attract about 400 guests and

guest speakers, such as John Payton, lead counsel in the University of Michigan affirmative action cases, and Cory Booker, lawyer and former Newark mayoral candidate. On June 22, 2004, we hosted our most recent event featuring as guest speaker Harvard Professor Charles Ogletree Jr., who addressed a crowd of well over 450 guests and signed copies of his new book, All Deliberate Speed: Reflections on the First Half-Century of Brown v. Board of Education.

Similarly, the firm's Women's Initiatives Committee, which consists of partners, counsel and associates, develops and supports programs aimed at promoting women attorneys and providing them with a forum to discuss their goals and experiences. The Women's Initiatives Committee holds an annual Women's Networking Event to allow our women attorneys and women from various industries to develop professional relationships. Prior speakers have included Hillary Clinton, author Anna Quindlen and Emily's List president, Ellen Malcolm. Throughout the year, the Women's Initiatives Committee sponsors a lecture series for our women attorneys, which includes topics such as public speaking and effective networking. The Women's Initiatives Committee also oversees the firm's flex-time/part-time program, which was developed to support those attorneys who choose to work a reduced schedule. The Women's Initiatives Committee continually monitors the program to address the needs of its participants. Currently, the firm is in the process of closely examining issues confronting our women attorneys and creating programs that focus on those issues.

Sponsorships

Paul Weiss has a tradition of sponsoring and participating in various minority forums and programs both inside and outside the firm, including, but not limited to:

- NAACP Legal Defense and Education Fund's National Equal Justice Awards Dinner
- Asian American Legal Defense and Education Fund's (AALDEF) Annual Lunar New Year Celebration
- Asian American Bar Association of New York's (AABANY) Annual Meeting and Dinner
- ABA Commission on Racial and Ethnic Diversity in the Profession's Annual National Conference for the Minority Lawyer
- Metropolitan Black Bar Association Annual Awards and Dinner Dance
- ABA Conference of Minority Partners in Majority Law Firms

Paul Weiss also serves as a signatory of the Association of the Bar of the City of New York's (ABCNY) Statement of Goals of New York Law Firms and Corporate Legal Departments for Increasing Minority Representation and Retention and the Restatement and Reaffirmation of Goals adopted by the ABCNY for the hiring, retention and promotion of female attorneys and attorneys of color.

Awards and honors

Paul Weiss was featured in the April 2004 issue of the Minority Law Journal in a cover story entitled "Practicing what they Preach." The article details the firm's efforts toward diversity recruitment and retention and applauds the firm's accomplishments. In an accompanying article detailing law firm rankings across the country for diversity, Paul Weiss is ranked second.

Pepper Hamilton LLP

3000 Two Logan Square
18th and Arch Streets
Philadelphia, PA 19103
Phone: (215) 981-4000
Fax: (215) 981-4750

FIRM LEADERSHIP

Managing Partner: Robert E. Heideck,
Executive Partner
Diversity Team Leader: There is no team leader
but rather an ad hoc committee of partners
and administrators.

LOCATIONS

Philadelphia, PA (HQ)
Berwyn, PA
Detroit, MI
Harrisburg, PA
Pittsburgh, PA
Princeton, NJ
Washington, DC
Wilmington, DE

LAW FIRM DEMOGRAPHIC PROFILES

FULL-TIME ASSOCIATES	2003	2002
Minority men	8	8
Minority women	7	6
White women	89	82
Total	210	205

SUMMER ASSOCIATES	2003	2002
Minority men	2	4
Minority women	3	1
White women	10	11
Total	24	25

EQUITY PARTNERS	2003	2002
Minority men	1	1
Minority women	1	1
White women	15	18
Total	101	112

NON-EQUITY PARTNERS	2003	2002
Minority men	2	0
Minority women	0	0
White women	8	10
Total	60	63

NEW HIRES	2003	2002
Minority men	5	0
Minority women	2	2
White women	21	8
Total	53	36

MINORITY CORPORATE COUNSEL ASSOCIATION

Strategic Plan and Diversity Leadership

How does the firm's leadership communicate the importance of diversity to everyone at the firm? (e.g., e-mails, web site, newsletters, meetings, etc.)

Diversity was a topic at the firm's annual meeting and our diversity initiative is detailed on our web site (see narrative section below). Events are advertised in our daily e-mail newsletter and by e-mails.

Who has primary responsibility for leading diversity initiatives at your firm?

The responsibilities are shared by members of an ad hoc committee consisting of partners and professional development staff at the direction of the executive partner.

Does your law firm currently have a diversity committee?

Yes. It is an ad hoc committee.

Does the committee's representation include one or more members of the firm's management/executive committee (or the equivalent)?

Yes. The executive partner directs the Diversity Initiative.

How many attorneys are on the committee, and in 2003, what was the total number of hours collectively spent by the committee in furtherance of the firm's diversity initiatives?

Total attorneys on committee: 6

Total hours spent on diversity: In excess of 500

Does the committee and/or diversity leader establish and set goals or objectives consistent with management's priorities?

Yes

Has the firm undertaken a formal or informal diversity program or set of initiatives aimed at increasing the diversity of the firm?

Yes, formal

How often does the firm's management review the firm's diversity progress/results?

Quarterly

How is the firm's diversity committee and/or firm management held accountable for achieving results?

The diversity efforts are regularly reported to clients and to all firm citizens.

LAW FIRM DIVERSITY INITIATIVES	ALREADY COMPLETED	CURRENTLY ADDRESSING	NOT A CURRENT PRIORITY
Undertake communication from firm management that diversity is a top priority of the firm.	✓		
Formalize diversity plan and committee with action steps and accountability to management.		✓	
Conduct firm-wide diversity training for all attorneys and staff.		✓	
Increase the number of minority attorneys at the associate level.	✓		
Increase the number of minority attorneys at the partnership level.		✓	
Develop/expand relationships with minority bar associations to offer firm's support of these networks.		✓	
Focus on strengthening firm's mentoring program, including for benefit of minority attorneys.	✓		
Conduct internal diversity needs assessment and/or retain diversity consultant to examine how firm culture might be more welcoming of minorities.	✓		
Support law firm's internal affinity networks (e.g., women, minority attorney networks).	✓		
Manage/monitor allocation of work assignments and/or hours billed to ensure women and minority attorneys have equal access/inclusion on top client matters.		✓	

Recruitment - New Associates

Does your firm annually recruit at any of the following types of institutions?

Ivy League schools: University of Pennsylvania, Columbia, Harvard

Public state schools: Rutgers, Temple, University of Virginia

Private schools: Emory, New York University, Michigan

Historically Black Colleges and Universities (HBCUs): Howard

Do you have any special outreach efforts directed to encourage minority law students to consider your firm?

• Hold a reception for minority law students

• Participate in/host minority law student job fair(s)

• Sponsor minority law student association events

• Firm's lawyers participate on career panels at school

• Outreach to leadership of minority student organizations

• Scholarships or intern/fellowships for minority students

SUMMER ASSOCIATE STATISTICS: SUMMER 2003	MINORITY MEN	MINORITY WOMEN	WHITE WOMEN	TOTAL
Summer associates	1	3	10	23
Summer associates who received an offer of full-time employment	1	3	10	23
Summer associates who accepted an offer of full-time employment	1	3	9	22

*We had one African-American 1L who was not eligible for a permanent offer.

Recruitment – Lateral Associates and Partners

What activities does the firm undertake to attract minority and women attorneys?

• Partner programs with women and minority bar associations

• Participate at minority job fairs

• Seek referrals from other attorneys

Do you use executive recruiting/search firms to seek to identify new diversity hires (partners or associates)?

Yes

List all women- and/or minority-owned executive search/recruiting firms to which the firm paid a fee for placement services in the past 12 months:

Juristaff and Cathy Abelson

LATERAL ASSOCIATES AND PARTNERS: 1/1/03 – 12/31/03	MINORITY MEN	MINORITY WOMEN	WHITE WOMEN	TOTAL
Number of lateral associate hires	4	3	21	52*
Number of lateral partner hires (equity and non-equity)	1	0	0	6
Number of new partners (equity and non-equity) promoted from associate rank	1	0	1	7
Number of new equity partners	0	0	0	3

*Includes first-year associates according to survey's definitions.

Retention & Professional Development

ATTORNEYS WHO LEFT THE FIRM: 2003	MINORITY MEN	MINORITY WOMEN	WHITE WOMEN	TOTAL
Number of attorneys who voluntarily or involuntarily left your firm's employ in 2003	1	1	20	55

How do 2003 attrition rates generally compare to those experienced in the prior year period?

About the same as in prior years

Please identify the specific steps you are taking to reduce the attrition rate of minority and women attorneys.

- Develop and/or support internal employee affinity groups (e.g., minority or women networks within the firm)
- Increase/review compensation relative to competition
- Increase/improve current work/life programs
- Work with minority and women attorneys to develop career advancement plans
- Review work assignments and hours billed to key client matters to make sure minority and women attorneys are not being excluded
- Strengthen mentoring program for all attorneys, including minorities and women
- Professional skills development program, including minority and women attorneys

Does your firm have part-time/flex-time policies that permit attorneys (male or female) to work alternative schedules?

Yes

What impact, if any, will the decision to work part-time have on an attorney's ability to make partner or, if already a partner, to remain a partner at your firm?

Part-time associates are eligible to be considered for nomination and election as a partner in accordance with normal procedures and standards.

Have any attorneys who chose to work a part-time schedule made partner at your firm?

Yes. Two attorneys.

Management Demographic Profile (as of 12/31/03)

	MINORITY MEN	MINORITY WOMEN	WHITE WOMEN	TOTAL
Number of attorneys on the Executive/Management Committee or equivalent	0	0	2	12
Number of attorneys on the Hiring Committee or equivalent	0	0	2	12
Number of attorneys on the Partner/Associate Review Committee or equivalent	1	0	5	14

Please provide information regarding all minority and women attorneys who head offices or practice groups of your law firm:

Women heading practice groups: Barbara W. Mather, Chair, Litigation and Dispute Resolution Department; Nina M. Gussack, Chair, Health Effects Litigation Practice Group; Deborah F. Cohen, Chair, Insurance Practice Group; Dusty Elias Kirk, Co-Chair, Real Estate Practice Group; Joan C. Arnold, Chair, Tax Practice Group; Barbara T. Sicalides, Vice Chair, Commercial Litigation Practice Group.

The Firm Says

"Our most valued resource is our people." – Pepper Hamilton's vision statement

Pepper Hamilton LLP is committed to advancing diversity, and we work continuously to expand and promote opportunities for all Pepper people. In addition to ensuring that the firm is an attractive and fair place to work, we take seriously our clients' commitment to diversity by making every effort to assemble appropriate project teams that accommodate their diversity requests and requirements.

Pepper is a limited liability partnership in which women and minorities hold ownership interests. Applicants are hired without regard to their age, race, gender, sexual orientation, color, religion, national origin, place of birth, non-job-related disability or any other legally protected status, and once employed by the firm, individuals are treated without regard to any of these criteria.

Recognizing that diverse characteristics and talent enhance any organization, and that a national law firm must reflect our many different cultures and ideas, we actively recruit and encourage the hiring, training and promotion of women and minorities. We participate annually in regional and local minority law student job fairs and other minority recruiting events, and we actively recruit at predominantly minority law schools such as Howard University. Pepper regularly participates in and sponsors diversity initiatives such as:

• American Bar Association's Women in the Profession Research Project on the Retention and Advancement of Women Attorneys of Color

• Philadelphia Diversity Law Group, an organization of law firms and corporate counsel promoting minority lawyer hiring and retention (Pepper is a founding member)

• Wolverine Bar Association, a minority organization in Michigan

• Dauphin County (Pa.) Bar Association's Capital Area Managing Partners Diversity Initiative (Pepper is a charter member)

• Philadelphia Bar Association's Statement of Goals of Philadelphia Law Firms and Legal Departments for the Retention and Promotion of Women (Pepper is a signatory)

• Philadelphia Bar Association's Statement of Goals of Philadelphia Law Firms and Legal Departments for Increasing Minority Representation and Retention (Pepper is a signatory)

In 2003, Pepper launched a diversity initiative to enhance the firm's commitment to the hiring and retention of minority lawyers. The firm engaged a nationally prominent diversity consultant to survey the firm's minority lawyers, both current and alumni, to assess our strengths and shortcomings as a firm in which minority lawyers can reach their professional potential and achieve personal and professional satisfaction.

Using what she had learned as a springboard for discussion, the consultant facilitated diversity workshops for members of the firm's Executive, Associates and Hiring Committees, and all department, practice group and

office heads. The workshops heightened the participants' appreciation of the variety of backgrounds, personal characteristics and skills that contribute to a successful business and professional organization and that need to be consciously cultivated for Pepper to flourish. At an annual firm meeting, the consultant spoke about the role of diversity in the workplace to all of Pepper's lawyers, legal assistants and senior managers, and she conducted a diversity workshop for non-lawyer staff.

As part of our diversity initiative, Pepper has established a mentoring program for all minority associates, which includes training for mentors and proteges, and regular get-togethers of the participants for comparing notes on best mentoring practices and monitoring the program's progress. Our directors of professionalism and associate development work to bring in-depth, creative training programs and opportunities to the firm. We also believe that good mentoring and networking occur outside of the law firm, and we pay dues for minority bar association memberships. We also were one of the first firms in the nation to offer benefits to same-gender domestic partners of our employees.

Our attempts to search out, recruit and encourage promotion of women and minorities have rewarded the firm and the individuals involved. The firm elected its first female partner in 1960, well ahead of most major law firms. We were one of the first large firms to elect a woman as executive partner. Women head our litigation and dispute resolution department, as well as the health effects litigation, insurance, real estate and tax practice groups. Women and minorities serve on the firm's managing committees, including the Executive Committee, of which a woman is vice chairwoman. Pepper legal assistants, managers and staff represent a diverse group of dedicated professionals; more than half are women or minorities or both.

Many of Pepper's minority and women lawyers hold leadership positions outside of the firm. One of our Washington partners, an African-American, is a member of the board of governors of the American Bar Association. A Philadelphia partner is president of the Pennsylvania Bar Association and the first person of color to lead the 29,000-member organization. An African-American in our Detroit office is vice chairman of the Executive Committee of the Detroit Economic Growth Corporation. A female partner was president of the board of directors of the Philadelphia Volunteers for the Indigent Program in 2002, and a female partner was president of the Detroit Bar Association in 1995-96. In 1991, one of our associates (now a partner) was the first African-American to chair the 5,000-member Young Lawyers Section of the Philadelphia Bar Association.

In addition, a number of our lawyers are active board members of minority, women, gay and lesbian, and other bar and community organizations. Historically, Pepper has encouraged and strongly supported its lawyers' involvement in minority organizations. For example, in 1999, one of our partners co-chaired the National Bar Association's annual convention in Philadelphia. Pepper provided substantial in-kind support for the convention and sponsored a major reception during the week-long event. We also participate in Lavender Law, the annual conference of the National Lesbian and Gay Law Association and the National Lesbian and Gay Law Foundation.

Pepper is dedicated to offering equal and fair employment opportunities, and we work continuously to ensure the well-being of our most valued resource – our people.

Perkins Coie LLP

1201 Third Avenue
Suite 4800
Seattle, WA 98101
Phone: (206) 359-8000
Fax: (206) 359-9000

FIRM LEADERSHIP

Managing Partner: Bob Giles, Managing Partner
Diversity Team Leader: Allison Kendrick,
Partner, Women and Minority Lawyers
Committee Chairperson

LOCATIONS

Seattle, WA (HQ)
Anchorage, AK
Bellevue, WA
Boise, ID
Chicago, IL
Denver, CO
Los Angeles, CA
Menlo Park, CA
Olympia, WA
Phoenix, AZ
Portland, OR
San Francisco, CA
Washington, DC
Beijing

LAW FIRM DEMOGRAPHIC PROFILES

FULL-TIME ASSOCIATES	2003	2002
Minority men	27	28
Minority women	22	28
White women	77	86
Total	249	279

SUMMER ASSOCIATES	2003	2002
Minority men	2	5
Minority women	7	5
White women	9	12
Total	29	41

EQUITY PARTNERS	2003	2002
Minority men	6	5
Minority women	1	2
White women	20	20
Total	177	168

NON-EQUITY PARTNERS	2003	2002
Minority men	7	4
Minority women	1	1
White women	13	11
Total	66	54

NEW HIRES	2003	2002
Minority men	8	8
Minority women	4	8
White women	21	22
Total	75	80

Strategic Plan and Diversity Leadership

How does the firm's leadership communicate the importance of diversity to everyone at the firm? (e.g., e-mails, web site, newsletters, meetings, etc.)

E-mail, web site, intranet, meetings (monthly Women and Minority Lawyers Committee; all-lawyer conference held periodically).

Who has primary responsibility for leading diversity initiatives at your firm?

Allison Kendrick, partner and chairperson, Women and Minority Lawyers Committee

Does your law firm currently have a diversity committee?

Yes

Does the committee's representation include one or more members of the firm's management/executive committee (or the equivalent)?

Yes

How many attorneys are on the committee, and in 2003, what was the total number of hours collectively spent by the committee in furtherance of the firm's diversity initiatives?

Total attorneys on committee: 20

Total hours spent on diversity: 500

Does the committee and/or diversity leader establish and set goals or objectives consistent with management's priorities?

Yes

Has the firm undertaken a formal or informal diversity program or set of initiatives aimed at increasing the diversity of the firm?

Yes, formal

How often does the firm's management review the firm's diversity progress/results?

Annually

How is the firm's diversity committee and/or firm management held accountable for achieving results?

Management Committee member Roy Tucker provides oversight of the committee. We formally report annually to the Executive Committee.

LAW FIRM DIVERSITY INITIATIVES	ALREADY COMPLETED	CURRENTLY ADDRESSING	NOT A CURRENT PRIORITY
Undertake communication from firm management that diversity is a top priority of the firm.		✓	
Formalize diversity plan and committee with action steps and accountability to management.		✓	
Conduct firm-wide diversity training for all attorneys and staff.	✓		
Increase the number of minority attorneys at the associate level.		✓	
Increase the number of minority attorneys at the partnership level.		✓	
Develop/expand relationships with minority bar associations to offer firm's support of these networks.	✓		
Focus on strengthening firm's mentoring program, including for benefit of minority attorneys.	✓		
Conduct internal diversity needs assessment and/or retain diversity consultant to examine how firm culture might be more welcoming of minorities.	✓		
Support law firm's internal affinity networks (e.g., women, minority attorney networks).	✓		
Manage/monitor allocation of work assignments and/or hours billed to ensure women and minority attorneys have equal access/inclusion on top client matters.			✓

Recruitment – New Associates

Does your firm annually recruit at any of the following types of institutions? (Check all that apply and list the schools).

Ivy League schools: Columbia University, Cornell University, Harvard University, University of Pennsylvania, Yale University

Public state schools: University of California-Boalt, University of California-Hastings, UC Davis, UCLA, University of Colorado, University of Illinois, University of Oregon, University of Michigan, University of Virginia, University of Washington

Private schools: New York University, George Washington University, Duke University, University of Chicago, Georgetown University, Seattle University, Santa Clara University, University of Denver, Northwestern University, Gonzaga University, Willamette University, Lewis & Clark University, Stanford University

Historically Black Colleges and Universities (HBCUs): Howard University

Do you have any special outreach efforts directed to encourage minority law students to consider your firm?

• Participate in/host minority law student job fair(s)

• Sponsor minority law student association events

- Firm's lawyers participate on career panels at school
- Outreach to leadership of minority student organizations
- Scholarships or intern/fellowships for minority students

SUMMER ASSOCIATE STATISTICS: SUMMER 2003	MINORITY MEN	MINORITY WOMEN	WHITE WOMEN	TOTAL
Summer associates	0	0	6	10
Summer associates who received an offer of full-time employment	0	0	6	9
Summer associates who accepted an offer of full-time employment	0	0	5	8

Recruitment – Lateral Associates and Partners

What activities does the firm undertake to attract minority and women attorneys?

- Partner programs with women and minority bar associations
- Participate at minority job fairs
- Seek referrals from other attorneys

Do you use executive recruiting/search firms to seek to identify new diversity hires (partners or associates)?

Yes

List all women- and/or minority-owned executive search/recruiting firms to which the firm paid a fee for placement services in the past 12 months:

Northwest Legal Search, Portland; Nichols & Sciabica, Chicago; Solutus Legal Search, Menlo Park; Zenner Consulting, Chicago.

LATERAL ASSOCIATES AND PARTNERS: 1/1/03 – 12/31/03	MINORITY MEN	MINORITY WOMEN	WHITE WOMEN	TOTAL
Number of lateral associate hires	8	4	14	43
Number of lateral partner hires (equity and non-equity)	2	0	2	22
Number of new partners (equity and non-equity) promoted from associate rank	0	1	2	18
Number of new equity partners	0	0	1	10

Retention & Professional Development

ATTORNEYS WHO LEFT THE FIRM: 2003	MINORITY MEN	MINORITY WOMEN	WHITE WOMEN	TOTAL
Number of attorneys who voluntarily or involuntarily left your firm's employ in 2003	6	10	29	70

How do 2003 attrition rates generally compare to those experienced in the prior year period?

Higher than in prior years

Please identify the specific steps you are taking to reduce the attrition rate of minority and women attorneys.

• Develop and/or support internal employee affinity groups (e.g., minority or women networks within the firm)

• Increase/improve current work/life programs

• Work with minority and women attorneys to develop career advancement plans

• Introduce minority and women attorneys to key clients, including to lead engagements

• Strengthen mentoring program for all attorneys, including minorities and women

Does your firm have part-time/flex-time policies that permit attorneys (male or female) to work alternative schedules?

Yes

What impact, if any, will the decision to work part-time have on an attorney's ability to make partner or, if already a partner, to remain a partner at your firm?

A number of our lawyers have been promoted to partner from part-time status and we have several part-time partners currently at the firm.

Have any attorneys who chose to work a part-time schedule made partner at your firm?

Yes, several (unsure of historical totals).

Management Demographic Profile (as of 12/31/03)

	MINORITY MEN	MINORITY WOMEN	WHITE WOMEN	TOTAL
Number of attorneys on the Executive/Management Committee or equivalent	1	0	2	16
Number of attorneys on the Hiring Committee or equivalent	5	4	14	56
Number of attorneys on the Partner/Associate Review Committee or equivalent*	1/1	0/0	2/6	17/20

Numbers listed as: Partner/Associate

Women heading practice groups: Janis Cunningham, Seattle Personal Planning Group; Heidi Sachs and Lynne Graybeal, Seattle Trademark Group; Nancy Williams, Seattle Labor & Employment Group.

The Firm Says

Perkins Coie is a large international law firm with a presence on the Pacific Rim. The firm values diversity as integral to the firm's culture and practice of law. The firm is committed to the growth and development of a legal community that reflects the rich diversity of our community at large. We are proud of our history and look forward to continuous improvement in the recruitment, development and retention of a diverse work force.

One of the most visible ways in which the firm illustrates its commitment to diversity is through the Perkins Coie 1L Diversity Student Fellowship. Established in the Seattle office in 1991 by an in-house Minority Hiring Task Force, the fellowship began with a summer associate position and a scholarship award for one diverse University of Washington first-year law student. In 1999, the program was expanded to include students at Seattle University to coincide with the relocation of the law school to the Seattle campus. In 2002, we expanded the program once again and now seek applications from diverse first-year law students from around the country. In the Seattle office, the fellowship is awarded to up to three candidates and continues to offer a summer associate job as well as a $7,500 scholarship award. In 2003, the Portland office began offering a fellowship as well. This pioneering program has been so successful that several other law firms in the Pacific Northwest have followed our lead and have established their own programs.

Our recruiting efforts for second- and third-year law students also reflect our commitment to diversity and have included interviewing at the Northwest Minority Job Fair, the Southeastern Minority Job Fair, the Black Law Student Association's Midwest Minority Recruitment Conference and Howard University School of Law in Washington, D.C. In addition, we provide a diversity contact list so that law students with questions can contact lawyers of color or other diverse backgrounds here at the firm.

Lawyers at all levels of practice, representing almost every U.S. office, serve on the Women and Minority Lawyers Committee. The work of this committee began in 1988 and has provided a forum for discussion and implementation of a variety of programs and policies affecting women and diverse lawyers. Most recently three sub-groups (women, minority and GLBT lawyers) of the committee have undertaken an outreach and education focus to provide an in-depth analysis of our diversity statistics and retention trends. The purpose of this research is twofold: to educate personnel at all levels in the firm as to best practices currently in place pertaining to diversity issues, as well as to reach out to women and diverse lawyers to learn what issues are of importance to them and what the firm can do to improve retention.

The Women and Minority Lawyers Committee also sponsors a firm-wide mentor program for incoming diverse and women entry-level associates. We tailor the mentor program for each individual attorney to provide the best possible mentoring relationship based on that attorney's preferences. In 2003, the committee partnered with the firm's client relations department to create a Diversity Resources Photo-directory that we send to clients quarterly. This, paired with occasional social events between our clients and diverse lawyers, provides an excellent opportunity to foster more meaningful relationships between our diverse lawyers and our clients. We offer alternating in-house lunches for women lawyers, women partners, minority lawyers and GLBT lawyers, which provide excellent networking and relationship-building opportunities. The committee also sponsors membership in specialty bar organizations for the firm's women and diverse attorneys.

Perkins Coie's leadership on diversity issues is also reflected in our pro bono work in the community. For example, we represented the University of Washington School of Law in the class action challenging the use of affirmative action in law school admissions. Our lawyers contributed over 2,000 hours to the successful defense of that important case. As another example, Dave Burman, a litigation partner in our Seattle office, has provided the Washington State Bar Association advice on how to best increase diversity within the board of governors.

Our lawyers are also encouraged to engage in community service through activities such as the Perkins Coie Community Service Fellowship, firm-sponsored volunteer projects, board membership, individual volunteer projects, charitable giving and pro bono legal services. We were pleased to be the co-recipient of the Washington State Bar Association's 2003 Excellence in Diversity Award.

Other diverse lawyers are also connected to and provide leadership in the legal community. To name but a few examples of such leadership, Seattle litigation associate Diankha Linear was awarded the Excellence in the Practice of Law Award by the Loren Miller Bar Association at their annual scholarship dinner in May 2004. Diankha will become president of the Seattle LMBA in 2005. Seattle litigation partner James Williams also received special recognition for his work on the events celebrating the 50th anniversary of Brown v. Board of Education. James is the current chair of the local LMBA Evaluation Committee. Seattle corporate associate Kha Dang previously served on the board of the Asian Bar Association of Washington and was the membership chair. Seattle trademark associate Grace Han is a current board member of the Korean Bar Association of Washington. Fred Rivera, Seattle labor and employment partner, is a prior regional president of the Hispanic National Bar Association.

Finally, we are proud that many of our women, minority and disabled attorneys have gone on from Perkins Coie to become leaders in the community. Some examples are Judges M. Margaret McKeown and Ronald M. Gould of the U.S. Court of Appeals for the Ninth Circuit, Heng-Ping Kiang of Internap, Michelle Wilson of Amazon.com and Bruce Brooks of Federal Home Loan Bank in Seattle.

Only 4% of law firm partners are people of color. Why?

Pillsbury Winthrop is dedicated to changing the status quo. In the Minority Law Journal's "Diversity Scorecard" this spring, we had the 6th highest percentage of minority partners in the country. For us, creating a workplace where everyone can realize their potential makes our work better — and makes our lives better.   www.pillsburywinthrop.com

Pillsbury Winthrop LLP

50 Fremont Street
San Francisco, CA 94105
Phone: (415) 983-1000
Fax: (415) 983-1200

FIRM MANAGEMENT

Managing Partner: Marina Park
Diversity Team Leader: Kevin Fong (Partner)
and Dawn Steel (Senior Attorney)

LOCATIONS

San Francisco, CA (HQ)
Century City, CA
Costa Mesa, CA
Houston, TX
Los Angeles, CA
McLean, VA
New York, NY
Palo Alto, CA
Sacramento, CA
San Diego, CA
San Diego-North County, CA
Stamford, CT
Washington, DC
London
Sydney
Tokyo

LAW FIRM DEMOGRAPHIC PROFILES

FULL-TIME ASSOCIATES	2003	2002
Minority men	37	41
Minority women	39	38
White women	139	129
Total	392	385

SUMMER ASSOCIATES	2003	2002
Minority men	3	7
Minority women	8	15
White women	12	19
Total	46	62

PARTNERS*	2003	2002
Minority men	18	18
Minority women	7	5
White women	59	56
Total	290	273

Includes all partners, without distinction between equity and non-equity.

NEW HIRES	2003	2002
Minority men	8	7
Minority women	15	8
White women	34	33
Total	121	84

Strategic Plan and Diversity Leadership

How does the firm's leadership communicate the importance of diversity to everyone at the firm? (e.g., e-mails, web site, newsletters, meetings, etc.)

We use all means of firm communication to convey our commitment to diversity, including e-mails, our web site, newsletters and meetings.

Who has primary responsibility for leading diversity initiatives at your firm?

Kevin Fong and Dawn Steele, co-chairs of the Diversity Committee.

Does your law firm currently have a diversity committee?

Yes

Does the committee's representation include one or more members of the firm's management/executive committee (or the equivalent)?

Yes

Does the committee and/or diversity leader establish and set goals or objectives consistent with management's priorities?

Yes

Has the firm undertaken a formal or informal diversity program or set of initiatives aimed at increasing the diversity of the firm?

Yes, formal

How often does the firm's management review the firm's diversity progress/results?

Monthly

How is the firm's diversity committee and/or firm management held accountable for achieving results?

Diversity initiatives are measured along with Pillsbury Winthrop's other strategic goals. Our partner compensation program clearly states that partners who take on substantial leadership roles on firm committees and produce measurable results will be given extra compensation credit. The associate compensation program is also designed to recognize contributions that further the firm's core goals, including diversity.

LAW FIRM DIVERSITY INITIATIVES	ALREADY COMPLETED	CURRENTLY ADDRESSING	NOT A CURRENT PRIORITY
Undertake communication from firm management that diversity is a top priority of the firm.	✔	✔	
Formalize diversity plan and committee with action steps and accountability to management.	✔		
Conduct firm-wide diversity training for all attorneys and staff.	✔	✔	
Increase the number of minority attorneys at the associate level.	✔	✔	
Increase the number of minority attorneys at the partnership level.	✔	✔	
Develop/expand relationships with minority bar associations to offer firm's support of these networks.	✔	✔	
Focus on strengthening firm's mentoring program, including for benefit of minority attorneys.		✔	
Conduct internal diversity needs assessment and/or retain diversity consultant to examine how firm culture might be more welcoming of minorities.	✔	✔	
Support law firm's internal affinity networks (e.g., women, minority attorney networks).	✔	✔	
Manage/monitor allocation of work assignments and/or hours billed to ensure women and minority attorneys have equal access/inclusion on top client matters.	✔	✔	

Note: Most of our initiatives are ongoing in nature.

Recruitment – New Associates

Do you have any special outreach efforts directed to encourage minority law students to consider your firm?

• Participate in/host minority law student job fair(s)

• Sponsor minority law student association events

• Firm's lawyers participate on career panels at school

• Outreach to leadership of minority student organizations

SUMMER ASSOCIATE STATISTICS: SUMMER 2003	MINORITY MEN	MINORITY WOMEN	WHITE WOMEN	TOTAL
Summer associates	3	5	11	40
Summer associates who received an offer of full-time employment	3	4	10	33
Summer associates who accepted an offer of full-time employment	3	4	9	30

Recruitment – Lateral Associates and Partners

What activities does the firm undertake to attract minority and women attorneys?

• Partner programs with women and minority bar associations

• Participate at minority job fairs

• Seek referrals from other attorneys

Do you use executive recruiting/search firms to seek to identify new diversity hires (partners or associates)?

Yes

List all women- and/or minority-owned executive search/recruiting firms to which the firm paid a fee for placement services in the past 12 months:

Decline to answer

LATERAL ASSOCIATES AND PARTNERS: 1/1/03 – 12/31/03	MINORITY MEN	MINORITY WOMEN	WHITE WOMEN	TOTAL
Number of lateral associate hires	7	13	30	89
Number of lateral partner hires (equity and non-equity)	1	2	6	35
Number of new partners (equity and non-equity) promoted from associate rank	2	0	1	10
Number of new equity partners	0	0	0	0

Retention & Professional Development

ATTORNEYS WHO LEFT THE FIRM: 2003	MINORITY MEN	MINORITY WOMEN	WHITE WOMEN	TOTAL
Number of attorneys who voluntarily or involuntarily left your firm's employ in 2003	13	11	21	98

How do 2003 attrition rates generally compare to those experienced in the prior year period?

About the same as in prior years

Please identify the specific steps you are taking to reduce the attrition rate of minority and women attorneys.

• Develop and/or support internal employee affinity groups (e.g., minority or women networks within the firm)

• Increase/improve current work/life programs

• Introduce minority and women attorneys to key clients, including to lead engagements

• Review work assignments and hours billed to key client matters to make sure minority and women attorneys are not being excluded

• Strengthen mentoring program for all attorneys, including minorities and women

• Professional skills development program, including minority and women attorneys

MINORITY CORPORATE COUNSEL ASSOCIATION

Does your firm have part-time/flex-time policies that permit attorneys (male or female) to work alternative schedules?

Yes. Pillsbury Winthrop supports flexible work arrangements to meet the needs of our attorneys while still meeting the needs of our clients. The fact that an attorney is part-time is generally invisible to clients; part-time attorneys are expected to continue providing the highest quality client service. Our policy states our commitment to offering a part-time program to retain talented and successful attorneys who, for personal reasons, wish to work a reduced schedule for a defined period of time. Part-time arrangements have been approved for attorneys writing books, devoting time to bar activities, as well as those balancing their commitment to work and their families.

What impact, if any, will the decision to work part-time have on an attorney's ability to make partner or, if already a partner, to remain a partner at your firm?

Depending on the experience and skill set of the individual attorney, part-time attorneys may be eligible for partnership consideration with their class. Alternatively, consideration may be deferred if it is determined that the attorney would benefit from additional time to develop important skills or experience prior to consideration.

Have any attorneys who chose to work a part-time schedule made partner at your firm?

Yes. Approximately a dozen. We did not start tracking these statistics until some time after our formal part-time policy had been adopted. We believe close to a dozen part-time associates have made partner since the formal policy was implemented. However, our firm's informal practices have long supported flexible schedules and work/life balance. Our current managing partner, Marina Park, is a good example. Ms. Park made partner in 1992 after several years as a part-time associate.

Management Demographic Profile (as of 12/31/03)

	MINORITY MEN	MINORITY WOMEN	WHITE WOMEN	TOTAL
Number of attorneys on the Executive/Management Committee or equivalent	0	0	3	11
Number of attorneys on the Hiring Committee or equivalent	1	1	4	17
Number of attorneys on the Partner/Associate Review Committee or equivalent	3*	0	16**	36

*One of whom is co-vice chair.   **One of whom is chair.

Please provide information regarding all minority and women attorneys who head offices or practice groups of your law firm:

Minorities heading offices: Patrick Marshall (San Francisco); Davina Kaile (Silicon Valley)

Women heading offices: Susan Kohlmann (New York); Davina Kaile (Silicon Valley); Sheryl Stein (Los Angeles/Century City); Sue Hodges (San Diego/Carmel Valley)

Minorities heading practice groups and departments: Michael Barr (Environmental); Kevin Fong (Appellate); Stanton Wong (Securities Specialty Team); Jing-Kai Syz (China practice); Takeo Akiyama and Yuji Iwanaga (Japan Practice Co Leaders); Doug Tribble (Litigation Dept-San Diego/Carmel Valley)

Women heading practice groups and departments: Marla Hoehn (Commerce & Technology); Paula Weber (Employment & Labor); Susan Serota (Executive Compensation/Benefits); Jennifer Jordan McCall (Individual Client Services); Elizabeth Fry (Individual Client Services); Jan Cate (Bank Finance); Allison Leopold Tilley (Emerging Companies; South Asia; Technology); Jennifer Mattingly (Global Outsourcing); Jane Stein (Project Finance); Caroline Harcourt (Real Estate Capital Markets); Maureen Corcoran (Healthcare); M. Katharine Davidson (Media & Entertainment); Anna Graves (Restaurant Food & Beverage); Deborah Thoren-Peden (Retail); Charlotta Otterbeck (Swedish); Linda Williams (Business/Corporate Securities & Finance-San Francisco); Sheryl Stein (Business-Los Angeles/Century City); Christine Scheuneman (Business-Orange County); Alison Leopold Tilley (Business-Silicon Valley); Susan Kohlmann (Intellectual Property-New York); Cameo Jones (Life Sciences-San Francisco); Michelle Hallsten (Business-Sacramento); Sarah Flanagan (Litigation-San Francisco); Julie Divola (Tax-San Francisco)

The Firm Says

Pillsbury Winthrop has a demonstrated commitment to diversity in the legal profession. We strive to attract and retain the best attorneys and staff. Our leaders are committed to fostering an environment that is rich in opportunity.

Our Record on Advancing Minority Partners

We have one of the largest groups of minority partners in the country. In the Minority Law Journal's 2004 scorecard, Pillsbury Winthrop had the 6th highest percentage of minority partners in the country (9.3%). With 27 minority partners, we also had the 6th highest number of minority partners in the country.

Our Diverse Leadership

Minority partners are an important part of the firm's leadership. The managing partners of two of our California offices are minority lawyers, including the managing partner of our firm's largest office. Minority partners have chaired or co-chair a number of the firm's committees, including the firm's Attorney Recruitment Committee, and serve on the firm's Compensation Committee (which recommends compensation of partners). A minority partner holds the vice-chair position on our Attorney Development Committee (which reviews the performance of all non-partner attorneys and recommends admission of partners). The firm's Diversity Committee co-chair is a minority partner. In 1999, Pillsbury Winthrop became the first major law firm in the country to promote women to two of its top leadership positions: Mary Cranston is the Chair of the firm's Managing Board, and Marina Park is the firm-wide Managing Partner. Women also serve in leadership positions on firm committees, as Practice Section leaders and as Office Managing Partners.

Our Commitment to Creating Opportunities

We are committed to continuing and expanding our firm's long-standing efforts to hire and promote minority lawyers. In two of the last three years, we have been among the top 20 law firms for overall diversity in the Minority Law Journal's Diversity Scorecard. In 2002, the Minority Law Journal's survey ranked us among the top 10 law firms for "Most Minority Associates".

We are always striving for new ways to promote diversity, including:

• Initiating firm-wide diversity workshops (led by outside consultants) in all offices for all attorneys and staff in the firm.

- Actively recruiting and hiring first-year summer associates from diverse backgrounds (two of whom are now minority partners in the firm).

- Developing a law school outreach program to increase the involvement of Pillsbury Winthrop attorneys in activities at key law schools with diverse students.

- Developing marketing and advertising that feature the practices of minority attorneys in the firm.

- Creating a firm-wide attorney career advisory network-a diverse panel of partners and senior attorneys who will be available to advise associates in any office on career development issues.

- Planning regular conference calls to provide an inter-office forum for open dialog and mentoring among attorneys within minority groups (e.g. African-American attorneys' conference call, Latino attorneys' conference call). This effort builds upon prior regular events-such as annual minority partner meetings and local minority attorney lunches.

The firm encourages minority attorneys to take the initiative to develop their own innovative practices. For example, one senior associate initiated an effort to host annual diversity receptions in our Orange County office. The associate brought together African-American business professionals in Orange County to create networking opportunities; we recently held our third annual reception.

Our lawyers have been active leaders in efforts to promote diversity in the legal profession and business world:

- One of our partner, Richard Odgers, is a former chair of the California Minority Counsel Program.

- Kevin Fong, a partner in our San Francisco office, has served on the steering committee of CMCP and also has served on the board of directors of Lawyers for One America, a national collaboration of organizations working on diversity and pro bono issues in the legal profession.

- Two of our partners, Jeffrey Ross and James Seff, are past presidents of the Bar Association of San Francisco, a leader in promoting diversity; Mr. Ross was a founder of the Law Academy high school program started by BASF and the San Francisco Unified School District in 1997. Our Chair, Mary Cranston, chairs BASF's "No Glass Ceiling" taskforce.

- One of our partners, Susan Kohlmann, has served as co-chair of the Committee on Women and the Law of the Associate of the Bar of the City of New York.

- Our partner, Jorge del Calvo is an adviser to HispanicNet, a national and local network of Hispanic entrepreneurs and business executives in technology markets dedicated to accelerating Hispanics' opportunities to start, build, manage and invest in leading technology companies. Mr. del Calvo has been a frequent speaker at conferences sponsored by HispanicNet, the Asian American Manufacturing Association, and other organizations addressing diversity in technology markets.

In summary, we hope to lead the nation in hiring, retaining and promoting lawyers from diverse backgrounds which reflect the best quality in the country.

Piper Rudnick, LLP

203 North LaSalle Street, Suite 1800
Chicago, Il 60601
Phone: (312) 368-4000
Fax: (312) 236-7516

FIRM MANAGEMENT

Theresa D. Cropper, National Director of
Diversity
Managing Partner: Francis B. Burch Jr. and Lee
I. Miller, co-chairs
Diversity Team Leader: Peter C.B. Bynoe,
partner

LOCATIONS

Chicago, IL (HQ)
Baltimore, MD
Boston, MA
Dallas, TX
Eagan, MN
Easton, MD
Edison, NJ
Las Vegas, NV
Los Angeles, CA
New York, NY
Philadelphia, PA
Reston, VA
San Francisco, CA
Tampa, FL
Washington, DC

LAW FIRM DEMOGRAPHIC PROFILES

FULL-TIME ASSOCIATES	2003	2002
Minority men	32	31
Minority women	39	35
White women	193	189
Total	511	503

SUMMER ASSOCIATES	2003	2002
Minority men	4	6
Minority women	10	10
White women	31	16
Total	68	50

EQUITY PARTNERS	2003	2002
Minority men	2	2
Minority women	0	0
White women	28	27
Total	239	226

NON-EQUITY PARTNERS	2003	2002
Minority men	12	10
Minority women	6	4
White women	46	39
Total	204	173

NEW HIRES	2003	2002
Minority men	24	32
Minority women	22	21
White women	80	110
Total	282	355

Strategic Plan and Diversity Leadership

How does the firm's leadership communicate the importance of diversity to everyone at the firm? (e.g., e-mails, web site, newsletters, meetings, etc.)

The firm's leadership communicates through meetings, e-mail, web site, firm brochures and retreats.

Who has primary responsibility for leading diversity initiatives at your firm?

Peter C.B. Bynoe, partner

Does your law firm currently have a diversity committee?

Yes

Does the committee's representation include one or more members of the firm's management/executive committee (or the equivalent)?

Yes

How many attorneys are on the committee, and in 2003, what was the total number of hours collectively spent by the committee in furtherance of the firm's diversity initiatives?

Total attorneys on committee: 15

Total hours spent on diversity: 600

Does the committee and/or diversity leader establish and set goals or objectives consistent with management's priorities?

Yes

Has the firm undertaken a formal or informal diversity program or set of initiatives aimed at increasing the diversity of the firm?

Yes, formal

How often does the firm's management review the firm's diversity progress/results?

The firm is developing a strategic plan for diversity with specific goals and measurement tools. The Diversity Committee meets twice a year to review diversity data and measure the sucess of specific goals.

How is the firm's diversity committee and/or firm management held accountable for achieving results?

Accountability is part of the strategic plan. The national co-chairs of the firm are members of the Diversity Committee. For the year 2005, the Diversity Committee will implement accountability standards for practice group leaders, managing partners, and the committee itself.

LAW FIRM DIVERSITY INITIATIVES	ALREADY COMPLETED	CURRENTLY ADDRESSING	NOT A CURRENT PRIORITY
Undertake communication from firm management that diversity is a top priority of the firm.	✓	✓	
Formalize diversity plan and committee with action steps and accountability to management.	✓	✓	
Conduct firm-wide diversity training for all attorneys and staff.		✓	
Increase the number of minority attorneys at the associate level.	✓	✓	
Increase the number of minority attorneys at the partnership level.	✓	✓	
Develop/expand relationships with minority bar associations to offer firm's support of these networks.	✓	✓	
Focus on strengthening firm's mentoring program, including for benefit of minority attorneys.		✓	
Conduct internal diversity needs assessment and/or retain diversity consultant to examine how firm culture might be more welcoming of minorities.		✓	
Support law firm's internal affinity networks (e.g., women, minority attorney networks).	✓	✓	
Manage/monitor allocation of work assignments and/or hours billed to ensure women and minority attorneys have equal access/inclusion on top client matters.	✓	✓	
Develop strong relationship with minority student organizations.		✓	

Recruitment – New Associates

Does your firm annually recruit at any of the following types of institutions? (Check all that apply and list the schools).

Ivy League schools: Columbia University, Cornell University, Harvard University, University of Pennsylvania and Yale University.

Public state schools: University of Baltimore, University of California-Boalt Hall, University of California-LA, University of Florida, University of Illinois, University of Maryland, University of Michigan, University of Virginia.

Private schools: American University, Benjamin Cardozo Law School, Boston College, Brooklyn Law School, Catholic University of America, Chicago-Kent College, DePaul University, Duke University, Fordham University, George Washington University, Georgetown University, John Marshall University, Loyola Law School (L.A.), New York University, St. John's University, Stanford University, Tulane University, Vanderbilt University and Villanova University

Historically Black Colleges and Universities (HBCUs): Howard University

Do you have any special outreach efforts directed to encourage minority law students to consider your firm?

• Hold a reception for minority law students

• Advertise in minority law student association publication(s)

• Participate in/host minority law student job fair(s)

• Sponsor minority law student association events

• Firm's lawyers participate on career panels at school

• Outreach to leadership of minority student organizations

• Joint pro bono activities

SUMMER ASSOCIATE STATISTICS: SUMMER 2003	MINORITY MEN	MINORITY WOMEN	WHITE WOMEN	TOTAL
Summer associates	4	6	27	56
Summer associates who received an offer of full-time employment	4	4	25	46
Summer associates who accepted an offer of full-time employment	2	2	21	37

Recruitment – Lateral Associates and Partners

What activities does the firm undertake to attract minority and women attorneys?

• Partner programs with women and minority bar associations

• Participate at minority job fairs

• Seek referrals from other attorneys

• Utilize online job services (e.g., MCCA/DuPont Primary Law Firm Job Bank)

• Chicago Cook County Bar Association Minority Student Job Fair; Harvard BSLA; Sunbelt Minority Recruitment Program; Mid-Atlantic BLSA

Do you use executive recruiting/search firms to seek to identify new diversity hires (partners or associates)?

Yes

List all women- and/or minority-owned executive search/recruiting firms to which the firm paid a fee for placement services in the past 12 months:

McCormack & Schreiber; Winston & Green; Carter-White, Shaw & Messick

LATERAL ASSOCIATES AND PARTNERS: 1/1/03 – 12/31/03	MINORITY MEN	MINORITY WOMEN	WHITE WOMEN	TOTAL
Number of lateral associate hires	3	7	10	38
Number of lateral partner hires (equity and non-equity)	0	1	7	45
Number of new partners (equity and non-equity) promoted from associate rank	2	2	5	23
Number of new equity partners	0	0	2	25

Retention & Professional Development

ATTORNEYS WHO LEFT THE FIRM: 2003	MINORITY MEN	MINORITY WOMEN	WHITE WOMEN	TOTAL
Number of attorneys who voluntarily or involuntarily left your firm's employ in 2003	8	7	35	115

How do 2003 attrition rates generally compare to those experienced in the prior year period?

Lower than in prior years

Please identify the specific steps you are taking to reduce the attrition rate of minority and women attorneys.

• Develop and/or support internal employee affinity groups (e.g., minority or women networks within the firm)

• Increase/review compensation relative to competition

• Increase/improve current work/life programs

• Work with minority and women attorneys to develop career advancement plans

• Introduce minority and women attorneys to key clients, including to lead engagements

• Review work assignments and hours billed to key client matters to make sure minority and women attorneys are not being excluded

• Strengthen mentoring program for all attorneys, including minorities and women

• Professional skills development program, including minority and women attorneys

Does your firm have part-time/flex-time policies that permit attorneys (male or female) to work alternative schedules?

Yes. Part-time and flex-time schedules are available to Piper Rudnick attorneys on an ad hoc basis with no firm policy. It is an arrangement between him/her and the practice group leader.

What impact, if any, will the decision to work part-time have on an attorney's ability to make partner or, if already a partner, to remain a partner at your firm?

If a Piper Rudnick attorney is working at least at 70 percent, he/she is presumed to be on partner track.

Have any attorneys who chose to work a part-time schedule made partner at your firm?

Yes, five attorneys.

Management Demographic Profile (as of 12/31/03)

	MINORITY MEN	MINORITY WOMEN	WHITE WOMEN	TOTAL
Number of attorneys on the Executive/Management Committee or equivalent	2	0	5	34
Number of attorneys on the Hiring Committee or equivalent	3	3	11	42
Number of attorneys on the Partner/Associate Review Committee or equivalent	0	0	1	11

Please provide information regarding all minority and women attorneys who head offices or practice groups of your law firm:

Women heading offices: Ann Hurwitz, Dallas, TX; Cynthia Surrisi, Eagan, MN; and Nancy Spangler, Reston, VA.

The Firm Says

Piper Rudnick is committed to improving diversity within the firm. To that end, we have developed a diversity initiative which includes the provision for a diversity committee, a full-time director and firm-wide resources to support the diversity efforts. In addition, the firm's stated policies bar discrimination in hiring, recruiting, compensation or promotion on the grounds of age, ancestry, citizenship, color, marital status, national origin, pregnancy, race, religion, gender, sexual orientation, veteran status, the physical or mental disability or medical condition of an otherwise qualified individual. The firm is committed to maintaining a working environment in which all individuals are treated with respect and dignity. Each of our employees should be able to work in an atmosphere that promotes equal opportunity, without being subject to discriminatory practices such as harassment. In keeping with this commitment, we will not tolerate harassment of our employees at work by anyone, including any partner, attorney, supervisor, employee, contractor, vendor, client or visitor. We encourage all persons to report information relating to workplace harassment or discrimination without regard to the identity of the accused wrongdoer or victim, and we are committed to investigating all complaints promptly and taking immediate and effective remedial action to stop such conduct.

The Diversity Committee is comprised of representatives from all strategic areas of the firm. The firm's top management, including the national co-chairs, practice group leaders and managing partners join a diverse collective. Piper Rudnick recently hired a new full-time national director of diversity, Theresa D. Cropper, to manage the implementation of the firm's five-year Diversity Plan. This position provides full-time attention to developing effective recruitment, retention and promotion strategies. Ms. Cropper manages the Diversity Committee and liaisons with many of the firm's committees including Association Review and Compensation, Hiring Committees, and Associates and Partners Committees.

As the tenure of our national diversity director has just begun in May 2004, we have many plans underway. To launch the Diversity Plan, we are beginning with quantitative and qualitative assessments of the firm's diversity. Needed to establish a diversity baseline, these assessments will take a snapshot of the firm's diversity by practice area, office and each office's practice area. The assessment will also analyze the firm's top clients and their diversity policies and needs by practice area in the context of the current pool of minority attorneys available.

The Diversity Committee will also explore the need for a minority attorney retreat, which would provide opportunities to network, develop skills and explore strategies for success at the firm. The retreat would also allow for direct input on diversity strategies by minority attorneys. Other issues the Diversity Committee will explore is billable credit for diversity work as well as tying diversity efforts into compensation review.

There are some key institutional clients who require diversity reports and diverse teams of attorneys working on their accounts. There are also clients and potential clients who issue Requests for Proposals and Requests for Information who need diversity information in selecting law firms for representation. These requests provide the backdrop for communicating the link between diversity and business success. We are developing firm policies to provide a coordinated response to those requests which serve as a context for future decisions affecting team selection and service for those clients.

Piper Rudnick enjoys a strong history of pro bono work and many of those clients are minority. Among the many cases we handle, the following are some of the highlights of our pro bono efforts. We joined a team of attorneys to support the NAACP in a nationwide discrimination lawsuit against Cracker Barrel restaurants. We are co-counsel on a Title VII class action suit on behalf of African American and Latino New York City public school teachers, challenging the tests required by the New York State Education Department. We filed amicus briefs in the Bollinger cases in the U.S. Court of Appeals and the U.S. Supreme Court. We have a strong relationship with the Asian American Legal Services Clinic in Chicago. We continue to work to save Black Creek, a Native American archaeological and culture site in New Jersey. We have partnered with the Pennsylvania Coalition Against Domestic Violence to form a network which helps women and children seek appellate relief from domestic violence. And we worked eight years on a class action sexual harassment case against the District of Columbia Department of Corrections.

Piper Rudnick attends minority job fairs across the country, ranging from the Black Law Students Association Northeast Regional Job Fair to the Mid-Atlantic Minority Job Fair, Cook County Bar Association Job Fair and the Sunbelt Minority Job Fair. On a national level, the firm serves as a member of the ABA's Minority Counsel Demonstration Program, a network of selected law firms and in-house counsel working to find business opportunities for minority lawyers in law firms and corporations. The firm has supported many of the efforts of the Minority Corporate Counsel Association, and all of our minority partners are members of the ABA Conference of Minority Partners. We are also active in several local organizations working to increase diversity in the profession, such as the Chicago Committee on Minorities in Large Law Firms and the Washington, D.C., Road Show.

It is an exciting time for diversity efforts at Piper Rudnick. Having solidified staff, structure and resources, the firm will embark up developing new and innovative strategies, programs and activities for the success of the diverse attorney at Piper Rudnick. We are committed to increasing our diversity and exploring opportunities that will enable us to retain and promote minority attorneys. We are committed to the success of the program and we are excited about the opportunities ahead.

Porter, Wright, Morris & Arthur LLP

41 South High Street
Columbus, OH 43215
Phone: (614) 227-2000
Fax: (614) 227-2100

FIRM MANAGEMENT

Managing Partner: Robert W. Trafford, Managing Partner
Diversity Team Leader: Mary Beth M. Clary and Fred G. Pressley Jr., Partners and Co-Chairs of Diversity Committee

LOCATIONS

Columbus, OH (HQ)
Cincinnati, OH
Cleveland, OH
Dayton, OH
Naples, FL
Washington, DC

LAW FIRM DEMOGRAPHIC PROFILES

FULL-TIME ASSOCIATES	2003	2002
Minority men	4	5
Minority women	9	5
White women	46	42
Total	123	116

SUMMER ASSOCIATES	2003	2002
Minority men	3	2
Minority women	9	3
White women	11	10
Total	40	35

EQUITY PARTNERS	2003	2002
Minority men	4	4
Minority women	0	0
White women	‧ 15	15
Total	108	108

NON-EQUITY PARTNERS	2003	2002
Minority men	0	0
Minority women	0	0
White women	8	8
Total	43	39

NEW HIRES	2003	2002
Minority men	1	1
Minority women	4	3
White women	12	8
Total	31	34

MINORITY CORPORATE COUNSEL ASSOCIATION

Strategic Plan and Diversity Leadership

How does the firm's leadership communicate the importance of diversity to everyone at the firm? (e.g., e-mails, web site, newsletters, meetings, etc.)

Firm partners approved the firm's Diversity Statement and Plan at a partners meeting, which was preceded by smaller discussion group meetings. Once approved, the Diversity Statement and Plan were communicated to all employees via e-mail along with a message from the managing partner which stressed the importance of the Diversity Statement and Plan to the firm and its future. The firm's Diversity Statement and Plan is posted on the firm's web site. The importance of diversity is also communicated annually to all associates by including a "What have you done for diversity" question on the associate self-evaluation form.

Who has primary responsibility for leading diversity initiatives at your firm?

Mary Beth M. Clary and Fred G. Pressley Jr., partners and co-chairs of the Diversity Committee

Does your law firm currently have a diversity committee?

Yes

Does the committee's representation include one or more members of the firm's management/executive committee (or the equivalent)?

Yes. The managing partner and two of seven members of the firm's Directing Partners Committee are on the Diversity Committee.

How many attorneys are on the committee, and in 2003, what was the total number of hours collectively spent by the committee in furtherance of the firm's diversity initiatives?

Total attorneys on committee: 11

Total hours spent on diversity: More than 500 hours

Does the committee and/or diversity leader establish and set goals or objectives consistent with management's priorities?

Yes

Has the firm undertaken a formal or informal diversity program or set of initiatives aimed at increasing the diversity of the firm?

Yes, formal

How often does the firm's management review the firm's diversity progress/results?

Annually. Although the entire Diversity Plan is reviewed annually, specific features of the plan are reviewed more frequently, as needed.

How is the firm's diversity committee and/or firm management held accountable for achieving results?

The firm's managing partner participates in or keeps abreast of the firm's diversity initiatives and provides relevant information to the firm's Compensation Committee with respect to the diversity activities of the partners.

LAW FIRM DIVERSITY INITIATIVES	ALREADY COMPLETED	CURRENTLY ADDRESSING	NOT A CURRENT PRIORITY
Undertake communication from firm management that diversity is a top priority of the firm.	✓		
Formalize diversity plan and committee with action steps and accountability to management.	✓		
Conduct firm-wide diversity training for all attorneys and staff.	✓		✓
Increase the number of minority attorneys at the associate level.		✓	
Increase the number of minority attorneys at the partnership level.		✓	
Develop/expand relationships with minority bar associations to offer firm's support of these networks.		✓	
Focus on strengthening firm's mentoring program, including for benefit of minority attorneys.	✓		
Conduct internal diversity needs assessment and/or retain diversity consultant to examine how firm culture might be more welcoming of minorities.			✓
Support law firm's internal affinity networks (e.g., women, minority attorney networks).	✓		
Manage/monitor allocation of work assignments and/or hours billed to ensure women and minority attorneys have equal access/inclusion on top client matters.		✓	
See narrative section below.		✓	

Recruitment – New Associates

Does your firm annually recruit at any of the following types of institutions? (Check all that apply and list the schools).

Ivy League schools: Cornell University, Harvard University, Columbia University, University of Pennsylvania

Public state schools: University of Virginia, University of Michigan, Ohio State University, Cleveland State University, University of Texas, University of Wisconsin, Indiana University, University of Cincinnati, University of Illinois, University of Maryland, William and Mary School of Law

Private schools: University of Dayton, American University, University of Notre Dame, Case Western Reserve University, Boston College, Capital University, Catholic University of America, Northwestern University, Georgetown University, George Washington University, University of Chicago, Wake Forest University, Ohio Northern University, Vanderbilt University, New York University

Historically Black Colleges and Universities (HBCUs): Howard University

Do you have any special outreach efforts directed to encourage minority law students to consider your firm?

• Hold a reception for minority law students

• Participate in/host minority law student job fair(s)

• Sponsor minority law student association events

• Firm's lawyers participate on career panels at school

• Scholarships or intern/fellowships for minority students

SUMMER ASSOCIATE STATISTICS: SUMMER 2003	MINORITY MEN	MINORITY WOMEN	WHITE WOMEN	TOTAL
Summer associates	2	7	11	31
Summer associates who received an offer of full-time employment	2	5	10	27
Summer associates who accepted an offer of full-time employment	2	3	7	22

Recruitment – Lateral Associates and Partners

What activities does the firm undertake to attract minority and women attorneys?

• Partner programs with women and minority bar associations

• Participate at minority job fairs

• Seek referrals from other attorneys

• See narrative section below.

Do you use executive recruiting/search firms to seek to identify new diversity hires (partners or associates)?

No. When we retain a search firm, it is not to specifically identify a minority lawyer for a particular position; however, we do remind the search firms of our diversity commitment to assist them in the search.

If yes, list all women- and/or minority-owned executive search/recruiting firms to which the firm paid a fee for placement services in the past 12 months:

We use the services of Snyder & Associates, a woman-owned executive search firm.

LATERAL ASSOCIATES AND PARTNERS: 1/1/03 – 12/31/03	MINORITY MEN	MINORITY WOMEN	WHITE WOMEN	TOTAL
Number of lateral associate hires	0	2	4	10
Number of lateral partner hires (equity and non-equity)	0	0	0	0
Number of new partners (equity and non-equity) promoted from associate rank	0	0	1	5
Number of new equity partners	0	0	0	2

Retention & Professional Development

ATTORNEYS WHO LEFT THE FIRM: 2003	MINORITY MEN	MINORITY WOMEN	WHITE WOMEN	TOTAL
Number of attorneys who voluntarily or involuntarily left your firm's employ in 2003	1	0	8	25

How do 2003 attrition rates generally compare to those experienced in the prior year period?

About the same as in prior years

Please identify the specific steps you are taking to reduce the attrition rate of minority and women attorneys.

• Develop and/or support internal employee affinity groups (e.g., minority or women networks within the firm)

• Increase/review compensation relative to competition

• Work with minority and women attorneys to develop career advancement plans

• Introduce minority and women attorneys to key clients, including to lead engagements

• Review work assignments and hours billed to key client matters to make sure minority and women attorneys are not being excluded

• Strengthen mentoring program for all attorneys, including minorities and women

• Professional skills development program, including minority and women attorneys

• See narrative section below.

Does your firm have part-time/flex-time policies that permit attorneys (male or female) to work alternative schedules?

Yes

What impact, if any, will the decision to work part-time have on an attorney's ability to make partner or, if already a partner, to remain a partner at your firm?

The decision of a partner to work part-time has no impact on the ability of that partner to remain a partner at the firm. The decision to make an associate or lateral attorney a partner in the firm is based on his or her total contribution to the firm and part-time status in most cases will impact that contribution.

Have any attorneys who chose to work a part-time schedule made partner at your firm?

No. However, the firm does have six partners and seven associates who work on a part-time schedule.

Management Demographic Profile (as of 12/31/03)

	MINORITY MEN	MINORITY WOMEN	WHITE WOMEN	TOTAL
Number of attorneys on the Executive/Management Committee or equivalent	2	0	1	7
Number of attorneys on the Hiring Committee or equivalent	1	0	8	20
Number of attorneys on the Partner/Associate Review Committee or equivalent*	0/1	0/0	0/2	6/7

*Numbers listed as: Partner Review (Compensation) Committee/Associate Review Evaluation Committee

Please provide information regarding all minority and women attorneys who head offices or practice groups of your law firm:

Minorities heading practice groups: Fred G. Pressley Jr., Labor Department; David L. Douglass, White Collar Crime Practice Group

Women heading practice groups: Kathleen Trafford, Appeals Practice Group and Chair of Associate Evaluation Committee; Donna Ruscitti, Intellectual Property; Diane Goulder, Employee Benefits; Polly J. Harris, Partner in Charge of Paralegal Administration

The Firm Says

Porter, Wright, Morris & Arthur LLP has long been committed to diversity in the profession, in our community and in our firm. In 2002, the firm formalized this commitment when its partners unanimously adopted a Diversity Statement and Diversity Plan, both of which can be found on our web site at www.porterwright.com. While the Diversity Statement sets forth our beliefs and aspirations for diversity and our commitment to diversity, our Diversity Plan is a practical and goal-oriented list of action steps specifically tailored to achieve our diversity commitments.

As part of our overall commitment, we have identified in our Diversity Statement six specific commitments to diversity. These are to employ effective methods of recruitment of diverse persons; to promote full and inclusive participation by our attorneys and support staff in our service to clients; to support the success and advancement of members of diverse groups within our firm; to include members of diverse groups within our firm in leadership training and opportunities; to participate in bar association and community activities that advance diversity in our firm, in the legal profession, and in the communities in which we live and work; and to commit the time and resources necessary to accomplish these objectives.

Our Diversity Plan includes over 40 action items centered around these commitments. We would like to highlight just a few of these action items here.

Diversity training. Beginning in 2002, the firm's leadership participated in a diversity training program. The program was facilitated by an outside consultant and was so well received that it was arranged for all lawyers in our headquarters office. All paralegals in all of the firm's offices have participated in this diversity training program. In addition, the consultant has been invited back each year to conduct diversity training as part of our associate orientation program. The program consists of a lecture, videotapes and small group interaction sessions.

Minority clerk programs. The firm has participated in the Columbus Bar Association's Minority Clerk Program since its inception nearly 20 years ago and the Cleveland program for eight years. The programs, coordinated through the local bars, are designed to create opportunities for first-year minority law students to experience a large law firm practice. The Columbus Bar assigns minority law students to participating firms annually, while the Cleveland Bar provides minority law students' resumes to the firm and the firm commits to interviewing at least five candidates and hiring at least one annually. These minority law students then join our regular summer law clerk classes. Until three years ago, the Columbus Bar Association's program prohibited participating firms from making an offer to the program's law students to return to the firms after their second year or for permanent employment after graduation. Since that prohibition was removed, we have made offers to students from the program to return as second-year clerks outside of the program and, in the case of the first-year student who participated in the program three years ago, as a full-time associate in 2004. We also have made offers to law students from the Cleveland Bar Association's program to return as second-year clerks outside of the program and, in the case of two students over the last six years, as full-time associates.

Scholarship program. In an effort to diversify and expand its recruiting efforts regarding lawyers of color, the firm is in the process of establishing a scholarship program for law students of color, with the first scholarship award to be made in the 2004-05 academic year. The award will consist of a paid summer clerkship opportunity with the firm and a stipend for law school expenses following the conclusion of the summer clerkship. Award recipients will be selected based on a variety of factors including, but not limited to, academic record, letters of recommendation and writing ability.

Mentoring program. The firm's mentoring program was improved for all associates as a result of the Diversity Plan. The mentors receive training in mentoring to emphasize the importance of the program to facilitate the ability of a diverse group of associates to maximize their potential and advancement within the firm. The goals of the program are to assist newly hired associates to learn the firm's culture, history, practices and procedures; to introduce them to senior partners in relevant practice areas and develop opportunities to form relationships with such senior partners and with clients; to provide programming to enhance associates' understanding of business concepts, business development, client relations and client satisfaction; and to ensure that associates have the opportunities to perform significant work assignments. The firm has included many of these goals in the law clerk mentoring program.

PWMA Minority Lawyers Network. We have established the PWMA Minority Lawyers Network. The mission of the network is to, among other things, improve performance feedback, associate development, mentoring and retention; assist in setting priorities and providing feedback on the firm's diversity initiatives; assist in business development activities; enhance opportunities for minority attorneys to interact and raise issues and concerns before they become problems; and assist in integrating new minority lawyers into the firm and our communities.

The network meets at least three to four times each year and is led by a minority partner. All minority attorneys are invited (but not required) to participate and the firm covers transportation, lodging and related costs. The meetings consist of a substantive component devoted to issues that confront minority attorneys and a social component such as a reception, lunch or dinner. The substantive component has consisted of roundtable discussions and panel presentations by firm lawyers.

The network has been successful in identifying and addressing concerns of minority lawyers, encouraging minority lawyers to remain in private practice by offering role models who have found a satisfying career at the firm, spotting and resolving problem issues that arise for individual minority lawyers, and articulating the concerns and challenges faced by the minority lawyers to firm management.

Powell Goldstein Frazer & Murphy LLP

191 Peachtree Street, NE
Sixteenth Floor
Atlanta, GA 30303
Phone: (404) 572-6600
Fax: (404) 572-6999

FIRM MANAGEMENT

Managing Partner: James J. McAlpin Jr.,
Chair, Executive Committee and Board of
Partners
Diversity Team Leader: Aasia Mustakeem,
Partner

LOCATIONS

Atlanta, GA (HQ)
Washington, DC

LAW FIRM DEMOGRAPHIC PROFILES

FULL-TIME ASSOCIATES	2003	2002
Minority men	7	N/A
Minority women	17	N/A
White women	52	N/A
Total	132	N/A

SUMMER ASSOCIATES	2003	2002
Minority men	4	N/A
Minority women	7	N/A
White women	14	N/A
Total	34	N/A

EQUITY PARTNERS	2003	2002
Minority men	2	N/A
Minority women	1	N/A
White women	13	N/A
Total	81	N/A

NON-EQUITY PARTNERS	2003*	2002*
Minority men	4	N/A
Minority women	2	N/A
White women	25	N/A
Total	67	N/A

NEW HIRES	2003	2002
Minority men	4	N/A
Minority women	10	N/A
White women	16	N/A
Total	46	N/A

* Includes counsel/of counsel
Note: N/A means "not available" in the above charts

MCCA
MINORITY CORPORATE COUNSEL ASSOCIATION

Strategic Plan and Diversity Leadership

How does the firm's leadership communicate the importance of diversity to everyone at the firm? (e.g., e-mails, web site, newsletters, meetings, etc.)

General announcements (such as e-mails, web site, newsletters); firm sponsorship of various organizations and initiatives; meetings with management; and reports to firm personnel about diversity initiatives.

Who has primary responsibility for leading diversity initiatives at your firm?

Aasia Mustakeem, partner

Does your law firm currently have a diversity committee?

Yes

Does the committee's representation include one or more members of the firm's management/executive committee (or the equivalent)?

Yes

How many attorneys are on the committee, and in 2003, what was the total number of hours collectively spent by the committee in furtherance of the firm's diversity initiatives?

Total attorneys on committee: 11

Total hours spent on diversity: Currently not tracked.

Does the committee and/or diversity leader establish and set goals or objectives consistent with management's priorities?

Yes

Has the firm undertaken a formal or informal diversity program or set of initiatives aimed at increasing the diversity of the firm?

Yes, formal

How often does the firm's management review the firm's diversity progress/results?

Professional staff and diversity committee report periodically to the Executive Committee (and/or firm management) on initiatives, hiring results, and mentoring and retention of minorities.

How is the firm's diversity committee and/or firm management held accountable for achieving results?

Through the compensation process.

LAW FIRM DIVERSITY INITIATIVES*	ALREADY COMPLETED*	CURRENTLY ADDRESSING	NOT A CURRENT PRIORITY
Undertake communication from firm management that diversity is a top priority of the firm.	✓		
Formalize diversity plan and committee with action steps and accountability to management.		✓	
Conduct firm-wide diversity training for all attorneys and staff.	✓		
Increase the number of minority attorneys at the associate level.	✓		
Increase the number of minority attorneys at the partnership level.	✓		
Develop/expand relationships with minority bar associations to offer firm's support of these networks.	✓		
Focus on strengthening firm's mentoring program, including for benefit of minority attorneys.	✓		
Conduct internal diversity needs assessment and/or retain diversity consultant to examine how firm culture might be more welcoming of minorities.	✓		
Support law firm's internal affinity networks (e.g., women, minority attorney networks).	✓		
Manage/monitor allocation of work assignments and/or hours billed to ensure women and minority attorneys have equal access/inclusion on top client matters.	✓		

* Ongoing

Recruitment - New Associates

Does your firm annually recruit at any of the following types of institutions?

Ivy League schools: Harvard University, Yale University

Public state schools: University of Virginia, College of William & Mary, University of Georgia, University of North Carolina, University of Florida, Georgia State University

Private schools: Vanderbilt University, Duke University, Emory University, Mercer University, Catholic University of America, Georgetown University, George Washington University

Historically Black Colleges and Universities (HBCUs): Howard University

Do you have any special outreach efforts directed to encourage minority law students to consider your firm?

• Participate in/host minority law student job fair(s)

• Sponsor minority law student association events

• Firm's lawyers participate on career panels at school

• Outreach to leadership of minority student organizations

SUMMER ASSOCIATE STATISTICS: SUMMER 2003	MINORITY MEN	MINORITY WOMEN	WHITE WOMEN	TOTAL
Summer associates	2	8	13	33
Summer associates who received an offer of full-time employment	1	6	10	26
Summer associates who accepted an offer of full-time employment	1	4	8	20

Recruitment – Lateral Associates and Partners

What activities does the firm undertake to attract minority and women attorneys?

• Partner programs with women and minority bar associations

• Participate at minority job fairs

• Seek referrals from other attorneys

Do you use executive recruiting/search firms to seek to identify new diversity hires (partners or associates)?

Yes

List all women- and/or minority-owned executive search/recruiting firms to which the firm paid a fee for placement services in the past 12 months:

Confidential

LATERAL ASSOCIATES AND PARTNERS: 1/1/03 – 12/31/03	MINORITY MEN	MINORITY WOMEN	WHITE WOMEN	TOTAL
Number of lateral associate hires	1	2	6	13
Number of lateral partner hires (equity and non-equity)	0	0	1	3
Number of new partners (equity and non-equity) promoted from associate rank	1	0	1	4
Number of new equity partners	N/A	N/A	N/A	N/A

Retention & Professional Development

How do 2003 attrition rates generally compare to those experienced in the prior year period?

About the same as in prior years

Please identify the specific steps you are taking to reduce the attrition rate of minority and women attorneys.

• Develop and/or support internal employee affinity groups (e.g., minority or women networks within the firm)

• Increase/review compensation relative to competition

• Increase/improve current work/life programs

• Succession plan includes emphasis on diversity

• Work with minority and women attorneys to develop career advancement plans

• Introduce minority and women attorneys to key clients, including to lead engagements

• Review work assignments and hours billed to key client matters to make sure minority and women attorneys are not being excluded

• Strengthen mentoring program for all attorneys, including minorities and women

• Professional skills development program, including minority and women attorneys

Does your firm have part-time/flex-time policies that permit attorneys (male or female) to work alternative schedules?

Yes

What impact, if any, will the decision to work part-time have on an attorney's ability to make partner or, if already a partner, to remain a partner at your firm?

Not an impediment.

Have any attorneys who chose to work a part-time schedule made partner at your firm?

Yes

Management Demographic Profile (as of 12/31/03)

	MINORITY MEN	MINORITY WOMEN	WHITE WOMEN	TOTAL
Number of attorneys on the Executive/Management Committee or equivalent	0	0	1	12
Number of attorneys on the Hiring Committee or equivalent	2	5	5	23
Number of attorneys on the Partner/Associate Review Committee or equivalent	0	1	6	15

Please provide information regarding all minority and women attorneys who head offices or practice groups of your law firm:

Women heading practice groups: Hilary Harp, Kathryn Knudson, Carol Newman, Cynthia Berry.

The Firm Says

Our firm's longstanding commitment to diversity is well known. The firm was founded in 1909 by a core group of committed lawyers of differing faiths who went on in their careers to play leadership roles in the civil rights movement. Over the past 30 years, the firm has aggressively recruited professionals of various faiths, multicultural and ethnic backgrounds. In addition, the firm continues its commitment to hiring an increasing number of women. Our goal is one of promoting and fostering an environment to attract and retain minority and women attorneys through partnership.

The firm's dedication to hiring women and minorities continues to this day. The core mission of the firm's diversity committee is to promote a culture where individuals of diverse backgrounds feel valued at the firm and have opportunities for professional advancement. Aasia Mustakeem, a partner in our Atlanta office, is chair of the U.S. Law Firm Group's Committee on Ethnic and Racial Diversity. The committee's objective is to attract more minority attorneys to law firms. We seek to combine the most experienced legal talent for each representation, as well as select diverse viewpoints, talents and multicultural backgrounds. We have found, quite simply, that our clients receive the best overall legal services through the utilization of a diverse group of lawyers. In addition, upon reaching the firm's billable hour target, associates receive 50 hours of credit for approved pro bono work, which may include diversity initiatives.

In 2004, the firm was ranked second in the nation in overall diversity by the *Vault Guide to the Top 100 Law Firms*. In other ratings, the firm was first in the country for diversity for minorities, second in the country for diversity for women and seventh in the country for diversity for gays and lesbians.

In addition, in 2003, *The American Lawyer* ranked the firm seventh in the nation among law firms with the highest percentage of female partners. In 2003, the national average for percentage of women partners in large law firms was 16 percent. The firm had 32 women partners, 25 percent of the total number of partners in the firm. The firm also received high rankings for overall percentage of female lawyers: 40 percent. In addition, according to the Minority Law Journal Diversity Scorecard, the firm ranked No. 1 in minority group representation among Atlanta-based law firms. Powell Goldstein ranked 35th of 200 firms nationwide.

Our commitment to increasing diversity goes well beyond the firm's doors. We actively work to assist and to promote minority businesses in the Atlanta community. Firm lawyers are active in the Israeli, Indian and Hispanic Chambers of Commerce. Our lawyers who serve on the board of the Special Olympics of Georgia and the firm's financial support of the Paralympics are just some of the ways the firm demonstrates community commitment to diversity. In addition to our attorneys in Atlanta and Washington serving on numerous local and national boards, the firm financially supports organizations such as the Lawyers' Committee for Civil Rights Under Law, the Whitman-Walker Clinic, Atlanta Urban League, Atlanta Union Mission and a host of other Washington and Atlanta charities.

Preston Gates & Ellis LLP

925 4th Avenue, Suite 2900
Seattle, WA 98104
Phone: (206) 623-7580
Fax: (206) 623-7022

FIRM LEADERSHIP

Managing Partner: B. Gerald Johnson
Diversity Team Leader: Liam B. Lavery, partner
and Anthony R. Miles, associate

LOCATIONS

Seattle, WA (HQ)
Anchorage, AK
Irvine, CA
Portland, OR
San Francisco, CA
Spokane, WA
Washington, DC
Beijing
Hong Kong
Taipei

LAW FIRM DEMOGRAPHIC PROFILES

FULL-TIME ASSOCIATES	2003	2002
Minority men	12	9
Minority women	10	11
White women	66	68
Total	200	188

SUMMER ASSOCIATES	2003	2002
Minority men	4	3
Minority women	3	3
White women	9	7
Total	26	25

EQUITY PARTNERS	2003	2002
Minority men	2	3
Minority women	3	4
White women	31	30
Total	142	140

NON-EQUITY PARTNERS	2003	2002
Minority men	2	2
Minority women	3	1
White women	15	12
Total	61	47

NEW HIRES	2003	2002
Minority men	5	2
Minority women	3	4
White women	24	12
Total	77	45

Strategic Plan and Diversity Leadership

How does the firm's leadership communicate the importance of diversity to everyone at the firm? (e.g., e-mails, web site, newsletters, meetings, etc.)

Firm Statement of Shared Values, firm affirmative action plan, hiring committee, e-mails, firm web site and intranet, department meetings, associate and partner briefings.

Who has primary responsibility for leading diversity initiatives at your firm?

Liam B. Lavery, partner, and Anthony R. Miles, associate, are co-chairs of the diversity committee.

Does your law firm currently have a diversity committee?

Yes

Does the committee's representation include one or more members of the firm's management/executive committee (or the equivalent)?

No

How many attorneys are on the committee, and in 2003, what was the total number of hours collectively spent by the committee in furtherance of the firm's diversity initiatives?

Total attorneys on committee: 12

Total hours spent on diversity: Unable to accurately report time recorded in 2003 as diversity committee work and related activities were billed to multiple billing numbers.

Does the committee and/or diversity leader establish and set goals or objectives consistent with management's priorities?

Yes. Firm management regularly reviews the goals and accomplishments of the committee; committee has liaisons to executive and hiring committees.

Has the firm undertaken a formal or informal diversity program or set of initiatives aimed at increasing the diversity of the firm?

Yes, formal

How often does the firm's management review the firm's diversity progress/results?

Annually

How is the firm's diversity committee and/or firm management held accountable for achieving results?

The committee reports to firm management on an annual basis and as needed throughout the year. Attorneys serving on the committee may be recognized for the time and energy devoted to diversity related efforts through partner and associate compensation processes and are eligible for bonus consideration.

LAW FIRM DIVERSITY INITIATIVES	ALREADY COMPLETED	CURRENTLY ADDRESSING	NOT A CURRENT PRIORITY
Undertake communication from firm management that diversity is a top priority of the firm.	✓		
Formalize diversity plan and committee with action steps and accountability to management.	✓		
Conduct firm-wide diversity training for all attorneys and staff.		✓	
Increase the number of minority attorneys at the associate level.		✓	
Increase the number of minority attorneys at the partnership level.		✓	
Develop/expand relationships with minority bar associations to offer firm's support of these networks.	✓		
Focus on strengthening firm's mentoring program, including for benefit of minority attorneys.	✓		
Conduct internal diversity needs assessment and/or retain diversity consultant to examine how firm culture might be more welcoming of minorities.		✓	
Support law firm's internal affinity networks (e.g., women, minority attorney networks).			✓
Manage/monitor allocation of work assignments and/or hours billed to ensure women and minority attorneys have equal access/inclusion on top client matters.		✓	

Recruitment – New Associates

Does your firm annually recruit at any of the following types of institutions? (Check all that apply and list the schools).

Ivy League schools: Columbia University, Harvard University, Yale University

Public state schools: University of Virginia, University of Oregon, University of Michigan, University of California-Boalt Hall, University of Washington

Private schools: Stanford University, NYU, Georgetown University, Seattle University, University of Chicago, Northwestern University, American University, Duke University, Washington and Lee University

Do you have any special outreach efforts directed to encourage minority law students to consider your firm?

• Participate in/host minority law student job fair(s)

• Sponsor minority law student association events

• Outreach to leadership of minority student organizations

• Scholarships or intern/fellowships for minority students

SUMMER ASSOCIATE STATISTICS: SUMMER 2003	MINORITY MEN	MINORITY WOMEN	WHITE WOMEN	TOTAL
Summer associates	1	1	8	19
Summer associates who received an offer of full-time employment	1	1	7	17
Summer associates who accepted an offer of full-time employment	0	1	6	13

Lateral Associates and Partners

What activities does the firm undertake to attract minority and women attorneys?

• Partner programs with women and minority bar associations

• Participate at minority job fairs

• Seek referrals from other attorneys

Do you use executive recruiting/search firms to seek to identify new diversity hires (partners or associates)?

No

LATERAL ASSOCIATES AND PARTNERS: 1/1/03 – 12/31/03	MINORITY MEN	MINORITY WOMEN	WHITE WOMEN	TOTAL
Number of lateral associate hires	2	0	5	20
Number of lateral partner hires (equity and non-equity)		1	2	13
Number of new partners (equity and non-equity) promoted from associate rank	1	1	2	6
Number of new equity partners	0	0	2	3

Retention & Professional Development

ATTORNEYS WHO LEFT THE FIRM: 2003	MINORITY MEN	MINORITY WOMEN	WHITE WOMEN	TOTAL
Number of attorneys who voluntarily or involuntarily left your firm's employ in 2003	1	1	19	39

How do 2003 attrition rates generally compare to those experienced in the prior year period?

Lower than in prior years

Please identify the specific steps you are taking to reduce the attrition rate of minority and women attorneys.

• Develop and/or support internal employee affinity groups (e.g., minority or women networks within the firm)

• Work with minority and women attorneys to develop career advancement plans

• Introduce minority and women attorneys to key clients, including to lead engagements

• Review work assignments and hours billed to key client matters to make sure minority and women attorneys are not being excluded

• Strengthen mentoring program for all attorneys, including minorities and women

• Professional skills development program, including minority and women attorneys

Does your firm have part-time/flex-time policies that permit attorneys (male or female) to work alternative schedules?

Yes

What impact, if any, will the decision to work part-time have on an attorney's ability to make partner or, if already a partner, to remain a partner at your firm?

Length of time to partner is likely to be longer. We have several successful part-time partners at the firm.

Have any attorneys who chose to work a part-time schedule made partner at your firm?

Yes, three attorneys.

Management Demographic Profile (as of 12/31/03)

	MINORITY MEN	MINORITY WOMEN	WHITE WOMEN	TOTAL
Number of attorneys on the Executive/Management Committee or equivalent	0	0	2	9
Number of attorneys on the Hiring Committee or equivalent	2	3	10	28
Number of attorneys on the Partner/Associate Review Committee or equivalent	1	0	4	18

Please provide information regarding all minority and women attorneys who head offices or practice groups of your law firm:

Minorities heading practice groups: Denise Stiffarm, First Year Associate Department

Women heading practice groups: Denise Stiffarm, First-Year Associate Department; Martha Dawson, Document Analysis and Technology Group; Kari Glover, Firm Managing Partner – Elect; Lisa Johnsen, Tax-Exempt Organizations Practice Group; Liz Thomas, Compensation Committee Chair; Grace Yuan, School Districts Practice Group; Jennifer Coughlin, Anchorage Office Managing Partner

The Firm Says

Establishing and maintaining a diverse and fully inclusive work force is essential to a strong law firm. At Preston Gates & Ellis, we are committed to fostering workplace and attorney diversity to enrich the experience of everyone who currently works at Preston and to make the firm an attractive prospect for those looking to further their legal careers. Preston Gates & Ellis is committed to providing every opportunity for equal employment to qualified applicants and employees.

We endeavor to recruit attorneys and law students from all backgrounds who add to our overall diversity, including people of color. We strive for a diverse group of individuals in our summer program and offer up to three minority fellowships each year to first-year law students. Since 2000, on average, 34 percent of students in our summer program have been minority law students and 48 percent have been women.

We believe that numbers are strong indicators of success on diversity and we work for continuous improvement in trends rather than commitments to strict numerical goals. The overall positive trend in our numbers of recognized minorities in our associate and staff ranks has been positive.

Twenty-five percent of Preston Gates partners are women, compared to a national average of less than 14 percent. Forty-eight percent of the firm's associates are women. The National Law Journal ranked Preston Gates first in the country for the highest percentage of equity partners who are women (24.6 percent), and second in the country for total number of women partners (45). Over the past five years, women attorneys have participated in and led a number of Preston Gates' most visible committees, practice groups and departments.

Other outside indicators confirming that our diversity efforts are bearing fruit include:

• The firm was recently ranked among the top 10 firms nationally in two of Vault's Top 100 diversity lists – for diversity generally and for women – in the 2003 survey compiled by Vault Inc. and published in the Vault Guide to the Top 100 Law Firms. Additionally, the firm received a ranking of 12 in the category of diversity for gays and lesbians.

• Preston Gates was awarded the 2003 Association of Legal Administrators' (Puget Sound Chapter) first annual Achievement in Diversity Award. The award recognized the comprehensive scope and far-reaching nature of the firm's support for diversity initiatives.

• In 2003, the Washington Young Lawyer's Division (WYLD) awarded two of four annual awards to minority associates at Preston Gates. Tony Miles received the WYLD Outstanding Young Lawyer in 2003 Award and Mari Horita received the WYLD Professionalism Award for Community Service.

• The firm received a "diversity scorecard result" in 2002 that was in the highest quartile among 200 firms that responded to the Minority Law Journal's annual Diversity Scorecard survey. The firm received the highest diversity scorecard rating of any firm in the Northwest (No. 37).

• Preston Gates attorney Jamie Pedersen serves as co-chair of the National Board of Education Lambda Legal Defense Fund, which won the landmark Lawrence v. Texas case, finding a constitutional right to privacy for same-sex couples. Jamie also serves a cooperating attorney for Lambda in Andersen v. Sims, the case challenging Washington's ban on marriage by same-sex couples.

The statistical data does not reflect the positive feeling engendered in the firm through our efforts to provide education and support for diversity-related initiatives. Nor does it reflect the firm's commitment to accommodating a variety of lifestyle choices by our attorneys and staff. We are particularly proud of having received the United Cerebral Palsy Association of King and Snohomish Counties Partnership Award for providing employment opportunities for people with physical disabilities. We also have invested significantly in technology to facilitate remote access, telecommuting and the lifestyle needs of our attorneys and staff.

Preston Gates's commitment to diversity extends beyond the walls of our offices. Our attorneys participate in and lead both traditional and minority bar organizations and non-legal community organizations focused on serving minority communities or enhancing opportunities of minority youth. For example, four of our attorneys participated in developing and implementing the King County Bar Foundation's Future of the Law Institute (FLI), a program that brings together minority school children, judges and practitioners for a two-day exploration of the law and legal careers. The firm backs up our attorneys' active engagement with financial support for the program and we are proud that the American Bar Association identified FLI as an exemplary effort to increase diversity in the legal profession and will award it the 2004 Partnership Award.

Proskauer Rose LLP

1585 Broadway
New York, NY 10036
Phone: (212) 969-3000
Fax: (212) 969-2900

FIRM MANAGEMENT

Managing Partner: Alan S. Jaffe, Chairman
Diversity Team Leader: Kathy H. Rocklen,
Corporate Partner

LOCATIONS

New York, NY (HQ)
Boca Raton, FL
Boston, MA
Los Angeles, CA
Newark, NJ
Washington, DC
Paris

LAW FIRM DEMOGRAPHIC PROFILES

FULL-TIME ASSOCIATES	2003	2002
Minority men	17	17
Minority women	38	36
White women	131	131
Total	376	361

SUMMER ASSOCIATES	2003	2002
Minority men	6	3
Minority women	5	13
White women	36	35
Total	68	96

EQUITY PARTNERS*	2003	2002
Minority men	2	2
Minority women	1	1
White women	17	15
Total	157	148

We have no non-equity partners.

SENIOR COUNSEL	2003	2002
Minority men	2	0
Minority women	2	1
White women	11	9
Total	60	52

NEW HIRES	2003	2002
Minority men	5	3
Minority women	12	12
White women	39	31
Total	122	98

Strategic Plan and Diversity Leadership

How does the firm's leadership communicate the importance of diversity to everyone at the firm? (e.g., e-mails, web site, newsletters, meetings, etc.)

The firm's policies with respect to diversity are reflected in various firm publications, marketing materials, employee manuals, web pages, and so forth, and are circulated to all attorneys and staff periodically by reminder e-mails.

Who has primary responsibility for leading diversity initiatives at your firm? Name of person and his/her title:

The chair of the Diversity Committee, Kathy Rocklen (a partner in our corporate department), as well as the committee itself.

Does your law firm currently have a diversity committee?

Yes

Does the committee's representation include one or more members of the firm's management/executive committee (or the equivalent)?

Yes

How many attorneys are on the committee, and in 2003, what was the total number of hours collectively spent by the committee in furtherance of the firm's diversity initiatives?

Total attorneys on committee: 10

Total hours spent on diversity: N/A

Does the committee and/or diversity leader establish and set goals or objectives consistent with management's priorities?

Yes

Has the firm undertaken a formal or informal diversity program or set of initiatives aimed at increasing the diversity of the firm?

Yes, formal

How often does the firm's management review the firm's diversity progress/results?

Annually

How is the firm's diversity committee and/or firm management held accountable for achieving results?

The committee makes periodic reports to the Executive Committee.

LAW FIRM DIVERSITY INITIATIVES*	ALREADY COMPLETED	CURRENTLY ADDRESSING	NOT A CURRENT PRIORITY
Undertake communication from firm management that diversity is a top priority of the firm.	✓		
Formalize diversity plan and committee with action steps and accountability to management.	✓		
Conduct firm-wide diversity training for all attorneys and staff.		✓	
Increase the number of minority attorneys at the associate level.		✓	
Increase the number of minority attorneys at the partnership level.		✓	
Develop/expand relationships with minority bar associations to offer firm's support of these networks.		✓	
Focus on strengthening firm's mentoring program, including for benefit of minority attorneys.		✓	
Conduct internal diversity needs assessment and/or retain diversity consultant to examine how firm culture might be more welcoming of minorities.	✓		
Support law firm's internal affinity networks (e.g., women, minority attorney networks).	✓		
Manage/monitor allocation of work assignments and/or hours billed to ensure women and minority attorneys have equal access/inclusion on top client matters.		✓	

* The firm, through its Diversity Committee, is working on various initiatives to maintain its commitment to diversity and pursue strategies of inclusion. Although some of the above initiatives – the establishment and support of affinity groups, for example – have been in place for some time, we consider our work to support diversity to require ongoing focus and effort.

Recruitment – New Associates

Does your firm annually recruit at any of the following types of institutions?

See our web site (www.proskauer.com) for a list of the law schools at which we conduct on-campus recruiting. In addition, we accept resumes from students at a wide range of other schools.

Of the law schools that you listed above, do you have any special outreach efforts directed to encourage minority law students to consider your firm?

• *The above activities are undertaken to varying degrees at the schools at which we recruit.*

• Hold a reception for minority law students

• Advertise in minority law student association publication(s)

• Participate in/host minority law student job fair(s)

• Sponsor minority law student association events

• Firm's lawyers participate on career panels at school

• Outreach to leadership of minority student organizations

• Scholarships or intern/fellowships for minority students

SUMMER ASSOCIATE STATISTICS: SUMMER 2003	MINORITY MEN	MINORITY WOMEN	WHITE WOMEN	TOTAL
Summer associates	3	5	29	55
Summer associates who received an offer of full-time employment	3	5	26	52
Summer associates who accepted an offer of full-time employment	2	4	22	43

Recruitment – Lateral Associates and Partners

What activities does the firm undertake to attract minority and women attorneys?

• *Work with recruiters who have a large number of minority candidates*

• Partner programs with women and minority bar associations

• Participate at minority job fairs

• Seek referrals from other attorneys

Do you use executive recruiting/search firms to seek to identify new diversity hires (partners or associates)?

Yes

List all women- and/or minority-owned executive search/recruiting firms to which the firm paid a fee for placement services in the past 12 months:

The firm has made significant lateral hires through a woman-owned search firm in the past 12 months.

LATERAL ASSOCIATES AND PARTNERS: 1/1/03 – 12/31/03	MINORITY MEN	MINORITY WOMEN	WHITE WOMEN	TOTAL
Number of lateral associate hires	1	2	8	20
Number of lateral partner hires (equity and non-equity)	0	0	2	11
Number of new partners (equity and non-equity) promoted from associate rank	0	0	0	2
Number of new equity partners	0	0	2	13

Retention & Professional Development

ATTORNEYS WHO LEFT THE FIRM: 2003	MINORITY MEN	MINORITY WOMEN	WHITE WOMEN	TOTAL
Number of attorneys who voluntarily or involuntarily left your firm's employ in 2003	4	9	32	78

How do 2003 attrition rates generally compare to those experienced in the prior year period?

About the same as in prior years

Please identify the specific steps you are taking to reduce the attrition rate of minority and women attorneys.

• Develop and/or support internal employee affinity groups (e.g., minority or women networks within the firm)

• Introduce minority and women attorneys to key clients, including to lead engagements

• Strengthen mentoring program for all attorneys, including minorities and women

• Professional skills development program, including minority and women attorneys

Does your firm have part-time/flex-time policies that permit attorneys (male or female) to work alternative schedules?

Yes

What impact, if any, will the decision to work part-time have on an attorney's ability to make partner or, if already a partner, to remain a partner at your firm?

Eligibility for partnership consideration is not affected by the fact that an associate has been or is on a reduced schedule, although the timing of such consideration may be. Partners who choose to work on reduced schedule may remain partners.

Have any attorneys who chose to work a part-time schedule made partner at your firm?

Yes, one attorney.

Management Demographic Profile (as of 12/31/03)

	MINORITY MEN	MINORITY WOMEN	WHITE WOMEN	TOTAL
Number of attorneys on the Executive/Management Committee or equivalent	0	0	0	6
Number of attorneys on the Hiring Committee or equivalent	1	0	5	18
Number of attorneys on the Partner/Associate Review Committee or equivalent	0	0	3	16

The Firm Says

Proskauer's commitment to diversity

It is Proskauer's policy to ensure equal employment opportunity without discrimination or harassment on the basis of race, color, national origin, sex, age, disability, citizenship, marital status, sexual orientation or any other characteristic protected by law. It is also Proskauer's policy to develop and maintain diversity in its legal and supporting staffs and to conduct programs advancing that policy both internally in the firm and externally, by engaging in activities that support diversity in the profession generally. Following are some of the relevant Proskauer programs and policies:

• The firm has a Diversity Committee to assist in developing and maintaining diversity in its legal staff and advise its governing body with respect to policies and programs to promote diversity.

• The firm is a signatory to and participated actively in the drafting of the 2003 Statement of Diversity Principles of the Association of the Bar of the City of New York (ABCNY). It is also a signatory to the Florida Bar Equal Opportunities Law Section Statement of Principles.

• The firm is an original contributor to the Legal Opportunity Scholarship Fund of the American Bar Association to provide resources to increase the flow of racial and ethnic minority students into the legal profession.

• Partners of the firm are members of the ABCNY's Committee to Enhance Diversity in the Profession and the Committee on Recruitment and Retention of Lawyers, though which the firm participates in the annual summer associate fellowship program.

• A senior counsel of the firm has served as the president of the Women's Bar Association of the State of New York.

• A partner has chaired the Committee on Minorities in the Profession of the Association of the Bar of the City of New York and served on its Task Force on Women in the Profession.

• The firm's law school recruitment practices include attendance at BLSA job fairs, sponsorship of the Lavender Law conference, receptions for students of color, involvement of minority and LGBT attorneys in interviewing and follow-up, and targeting law schools with large numbers of minority students.

• A partner serves as a member of the board of directors of the Lawyers' Committee on Civil Rights, a nationwide organization that promotes diversity in the profession.

• The firm, on a pro bono basis, is general counsel to The Bold Initiative, Inc., a not-for-profit organization that strives to make the business case for diversity in the workplace.

• Partners in the firm have spoken at the 1999 Queer Law Conference and the 2002 LGBT Law Conference. A partner was the program chair of the 2002 New York State Bar Association's Civil Rights Committee's program, "Legal Issues Affecting the LGBT Community."

• A partner of the firm authored the ABCNY's 1997 report on same-sex marriage and is a member of the Same Sex Marriage Committee of the New York State Bar Association.

• The firm has taken on pro bono projects on behalf of the Gay Men's Health Crisis and the Gay Officer's Action League. In addition, a partner served as lead counsel for a Navy officer threatened with expulsion from the

service based on private information the Navy obtained illegally from America Online, making new law under the military's "Don't Ask, Don't Tell, Don't Pursue" policy.

• The firm has established affinity groups to give attorneys of color, LGBT attorneys and women attorneys the opportunity to meet and discuss issues of common interest.

• The firm has maternity leave, child care leave and alternative work schedule policies to assist lawyers who have child-raising responsibilities in balancing the demands of personal life with the responsibilities of professional life.

Personal Respect and Individual Worth.

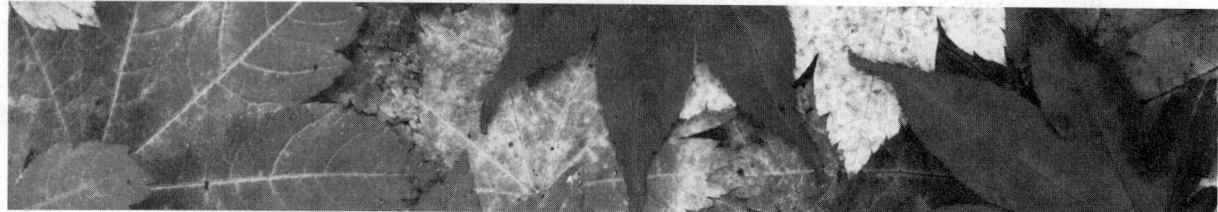

Quarles & Brady LLP

At Quarles & Brady, diversity is more than philosophy, it's an integral part of our practice. As a firm, we are committed to the most fundamental precepts of diversity: personal respect and individual worth. We constantly strive to understand the subtleties of diversity and to capture the benefits for our firm, our clients and our communities. But the true test of our philosophy is how we show it. Here are just a few examples of our commitment: **Minority Clerkships** – For 12 years we have supported internships, mentor programs and law school scholarships. **Leadership** – Women hold nearly 40% of the various leadership roles within the firm. **Involvement** – We enjoy 99% participation by all attorneys and staff in our ongoing diversity awareness program. **Communities** – Through our firmwide diversity initiative, each office provides substantial financial support and talent to organizations and activities that advance diversity. If you would like to learn more about our diversity initiative, please contact our diversity partner Nancy Peterson at 414.277.5515 or our firm managing partner Pat Ryan at 414.277.5181.

Chicago   Madison   Milwaukee   Naples   Phoenix   Tucson

Quarles & Brady LLP

411 E. Wisconsin Avenue, Suite 2040
Milwaukee, WI 53202-4497
Phone: (414) 277-5000
Fax: (414) 271-3552

FIRM MANAGEMENT

Managing Partner: Patrick Ryan, Chair,
Executive Committee
Diversity Team Leader: Nancy Peterson,
Partner and Co-Chair, Diversity Committee

LOCATIONS

Milwaukee, WI (HQ)
Chicago, IL
Madison, WI
Naples, FL
Phoenix, AZ
Tucson, AZ

LAW FIRM DEMOGRAPHIC PROFILES

FULL-TIME ASSOCIATES	2003	2002
Minority men	13	19
Minority women	13	14
White women	45	54
Total	147	170

SUMMER ASSOCIATES	2003	2002
Minority men	1	6
Minority women	9	3
White women	12	2
Total	30	17

EQUITY PARTNERS	2003	2002
Minority men	7	5
Minority women	0	0
White women	33	33
Total	225	227

NON-EQUITY PARTNERS	2003	2002
Minority men	4	0
Minority women	2	1
White women	10	6
Total	36	25

NEW HIRES	2003	2002
Minority men	6	5
Minority women	2	3
White women	10	6
Total	40	32

Strategic Plan and Diversity Leadership

How does the firm's leadership communicate the importance of diversity to everyone at the firm? (e.g., e-mails, web site, newsletters, meetings, etc.)

Quarles & Brady has a firm-wide Diversity Initiative that implements the goals expressed in our Strategic Plan. The Strategic Plan was adopted in 2001 by a vote of all partners. The chair of our Executive Committee and co-chairs of the Diversity Committee report on progress regularly at attorney and staff meetings. At least twice a year we conduct formal diversity events, including training programs and client panels where the business case for diversity is made. Informal events, including celebrations of Black History Month and Cinco de Mayo, are held several times a year. Diversity events, as well as changes in firm policies and procedures resulting from our Diversity Initiative, are typically announced by firm-wide e-mail. We also use our daily firm-wide bulletin for "Diversity Moments," as well as our newsletters and diversity posters to keep the goals of our Diversity Initiative in front of the members of the firm.

Who has primary responsibility for leading diversity initiatives at your firm?

Co-Chairs of the Diversity Committee: Nancy K. Peterson, partner, and Patrick Ryan, chair of Executive Committee.

Does your law firm currently have a diversity committee?

Yes

Does the committee's representation include one or more members of the firm's management/executive committee (or the equivalent)?

Yes

How many attorneys are on the committee, and in 2003, what was the total number of hours collectively spent by the committee in furtherance of the firm's diversity initiatives?

Total attorneys on committee: 16

Total hours spent on diversity: 594.5

Does the committee and/or diversity leader establish and set goals or objectives consistent with management's priorities?

Yes

Has the firm undertaken a formal or informal diversity program or set of initiatives aimed at increasing the diversity of the firm?

Yes, formal

How often does the firm's management review the firm's diversity progress/results?

Quarterly

How is the firm's diversity committee and/or firm management held accountable for achieving results?

The diversity goal is one of 10 goals in our Strategic Plan. The plan is reviewed annually by the Executive Committee. Census statistics are circulated monthly. Performance evaluations are solicited after each diversity program and are reviewed by the members of the Diversity Committee and the Executive Committee.

LAW FIRM DIVERSITY INITIATIVES	ALREADY COMPLETED	CURRENTLY ADDRESSING	NOT A CURRENT PRIORITY
Undertake communication from firm management that diversity is a top priority of the firm.	✔		
Formalize diversity plan and committee with action steps and accountability to management.	✔		
Conduct firm-wide diversity training for all attorneys and staff.	✔		
Increase the number of minority attorneys at the associate level.		✔	
Increase the number of minority attorneys at the partnership level.		✔	
Develop/expand relationships with minority bar associations to offer firm's support of these networks.	✔	✔	
Focus on strengthening firm's mentoring program, including for benefit of minority attorneys.		✔	
Conduct internal diversity needs assessment and/or retain diversity consultant to examine how firm culture might be more welcoming of minorities.	✔		
Support law firm's internal affinity networks (e.g., women, minority attorney networks).		✔	
Manage/monitor allocation of work assignments and/or hours billed to ensure women and minority attorneys have equal access/inclusion on top client matters.		✔	
Minority internships, continuing diversity training		✔	

Recruitment – New Associates

Does your firm annually recruit at any of the following types of institutions? (Check all that apply and list the schools).

Ivy League schools: Harvard University

Public state schools: Arizona State University, University of Arizona, University of Florida, University of Iowa, University of Michigan, University of Minnesota, University of Texas, University of Wisconsin, University of Virginia

Private schools: Georgetown University, Northwestern University, University of Chicago, Chicago-Kent College of Law, Marquette University, Stetson University

Historically Black Colleges and Universities (HBCUs): Howard University

Do you have any special outreach efforts directed to encourage minority law students to consider your firm?

• *We sent our diversity brochure to approximately 200 minority professors.*

• Hold a reception for minority law students

• Participate in/host minority law student job fair(s)

• Sponsor minority law student association events

• Firm's lawyers participate on career panels at school

• Outreach to leadership of minority student organizations

• Scholarships or intern/fellowships for minority students

SUMMER ASSOCIATE STATISTICS: SUMMER 2003	MINORITY MEN	MINORITY WOMEN	WHITE WOMEN	TOTAL
Summer associates	1	9	12	30
Summer associates who received an offer of full-time employment	0	6	7	20
Summer associates who accepted an offer of full-time employment	0	6	6	19

Recruitment – Lateral Associates and Partners

What activities does the firm undertake to attract minority and women attorneys?

• *We participate in the Legal Educational Opportunities Program at the University of Wisconsin Law School through funding and mentoring; participate in the Chicago Committee on Minorities in Large Law Firms; created a summer associate program for first- and second-year Native American students where we partnered with two different Native American communities; sent our diversity brochure to all minority law student groups where we interview on-campus.*

• Partner programs with women and minority bar associations

• Participate at minority job fairs

• Seek referrals from other attorneys

Do you use executive recruiting/search firms to seek to identify new diversity hires (partners or associates)?

Yes

LATERAL ASSOCIATES AND PARTNERS: 1/1/03 – 12/31/03	MINORITY MEN	MINORITY WOMEN	WHITE WOMEN	TOTAL
Number of lateral associate hires	1	1	5	20
Number of lateral partner hires (equity and non-equity)	3	0	3	12
Number of new partners (equity and non-equity) promoted from associate rank	3	1	4	14
Number of new equity partners	2	0	2	8

Retention & Professional Development

ATTORNEYS WHO LEFT THE FIRM: 2003	MINORITY MEN	MINORITY WOMEN	WHITE WOMEN	TOTAL
Number of attorneys who voluntarily or involuntarily left your firm's employ in 2003	7	1	14	54

How do 2003 attrition rates generally compare to those experienced in the prior year period?

Higher than in prior years

Please identify the specific steps you are taking to reduce the attrition rate of minority and women attorneys.

• *We now offer an associate flexible work schedule policy as well as income partner status to help our attorneys balance work and life issues.*

• Develop and/or support internal employee affinity groups (e.g., minority or women networks within the firm)

• Increase/review compensation relative to competition

• Increase/improve current work/life programs

• Work with minority and women attorneys to develop career advancement plans

• Introduce minority and women attorneys to key clients, including to lead engagements

• Strengthen mentoring program for all attorneys, including minorities and women

• Professional skills development program, including minority and women attorneys

Does your firm have part-time/flex-time policies that permit attorneys (male or female) to work alternative schedules?

Yes

What impact, if any, will the decision to work part-time have on an attorney's ability to make partner or, if already a partner, to remain a partner at your firm?

Our income partner status provides the opportunity for associates to remain on track for partnership while working reduced hours and for partners to work reduced hours. A person who becomes an income partner may remain in this position for his or her career, or may be considered for admission as an equity partner with the consent of the Executive Committee.

Have any attorneys who chose to work a part-time schedule made partner at your firm?

Yes, three attorneys.

Management Demographic Profile (as of 12/31/03)

	MINORITY MEN	MINORITY WOMEN	WHITE WOMEN	TOTAL
Number of attorneys on the Executive/Management Committee or equivalent	1	0	1	10
Number of attorneys on the Hiring Committee or equivalent	2	3	6	23
Number of attorneys on the Partner/Associate Review Committee or equivalent	0/1*	0/0*	1/4*	8/16*

* Partner Review Committee/Associate Review Committee

Please provide information regarding all minority and women attorneys who head offices or practice groups of your law firm:

Women heading offices: Ann M. Murphy, Milwaukee, WI; Susan Boswell, Tucson, AZ

Women heading practice groups: Kathyrn M. Buono, Corporate Services; Kathleen A. Gray, Trusts & Estates; and Janice E. Rodgers, Tax Exempt Organizations

The Firm Says

Quarles & Brady's philosophy

Our firm is committed to an aggressive agenda designed to promote and achieve diversity at all levels. The firm's diversity mission statement is found in our comprehensive Strategic Plan, which adopted a diversity goal, together with long-term action items. The stated diversity goal is "to foster an environment of inclusion, understanding, respect and opportunity for employees of different genders, races, ages, cultures, religions, disabilities, sexual orientation, and lifestyles by developing and implementing a long-term diversity program."

The diversity program's foundation is the firm's longstanding policy of fair and equal employment opportunity for every person regardless of age, race, color, creed, religion, disability, marital status, sex, sexual orientation, national origin, ancestry, citizenship or other legally protected status. The firm has long sought to provide a work environment that is free from discrimination, intimidation and harassment based on any of these characteristics. Our written equal opportunity and prohibition of harassment policy, together with formal training on the policy for all personnel, reinforces the Quarles & Brady tradition of developing a diverse work force that treats each other with respect and values the individual.

Diversity committee formed

To advance the firm's diversity goal of greater inclusion, understanding, respect and opportunity, the Executive Committee appointed a Diversity Committee in 2001 to interact with all members of the firm and ensure that diversity is a part of the infrastructure of our organization. The Diversity Committee consists of representatives from each of our offices and includes partners, associates and staff as well as members of the firm's Executive Committee. Quarles & Brady provides billable hours credit to committee members. The importance of the committee's work is further highlighted by the fact that the chair of the firm's Executive Committee is co-chair of the Diversity Committee. The Diversity Committee formulated the diversity initiative that we are now implementing.

Diversity consultant retained – the "business case" presented

Quarles & Brady retained a consultant to assess the diversity climate at our firm. The consultant first spoke to all personnel about the dimensions of diversity and articulated the business case. The consultant next conducted a series of focus group discussions with 500 people, including partners, associates and staff in each of our offices. From information gleaned during these discussions, the consultant developed recommendations to improve our diversity program and created a firm-specific diversity training program. To set the stage for the training program, representatives of seven clients spoke at two events for all attorneys about their diversity initiatives and expectations of outside law firms. Our subsequent firm-wide training program has been attended by 99 percent of all attorneys and staff.

Tangible examples of our diversity commitment:

• Summer associate classes. Individuals of color comprised 33 percent of our summer associate class in 2003, 50 percent in 2002 and 40 percent in 2001.

• Leadership. In two cities (including our largest office), the firm's managing partners are women. Additionally, women hold nearly 40 percent of the firm's various leadership roles.

• Domestic partner benefits. The firm's written policies extend domestic partner benefits to all attorneys and staff.

• Minority clerkships. The firm has joined forces with the Gila River Indian Community of Central Arizona and the Forest County Potawatomi Community of Wisconsin on a joint summer associate program. Native American law students who participate in the program split their time between our Phoenix or Milwaukee office and the legal department of the Gila River or Potawatomi Community. We also participate in the Wisconsin State Bar Minority Clerkship Program as well as the Arizona State University and University of Arizona Minority Intern Programs. The firm is also a member of the Chicago Committee on Minorities in Large Law Firms.

• Mentoring. Quarles & Brady supports a three-year mentor program at the University of Wisconsin Law School. The program connects minority students and "first generation" majority law students with local attorneys who serve as personal and professional mentors. For our own associates, Quarles & Brady provides individual mentoring for new hires for two years and practice group mentoring for all.

• Minority scholarships. Quarles & Brady sponsors four scholarships for minority students at Marquette University, the University of Wisconsin, Arizona State University and the University of Arizona. Each scholarship is for $5,000 for three years. Two of the scholarships have been matched by individual contributions from firm attorneys.

• Maternity/paternity leave. Associate maternity and paternity leave is fully paid, and our partner compensation system explicitly gives compensation credit for maternity and paternity leaves to partners.

• Flexible schedule/part-time. Recognizing that life balance issues can be accommodated in the workplace, the firm offers a flexible, part-time work schedule program for associates and a companion income partner status. The two policies together offer the opportunity for an attorney with a proven record of performance to plan a flexible career with us for the long term.

• Our communities. Our firm and individuals within the firm provide substantial financial support and talent to community organizations, activities and minority bar associations that advance diversity. The firm also offers

extensive pro bono legal services in all offices. The firm and individual lawyers have received awards for outstanding community and pro bono service. Our Tucson office received a Diversity Workforce Inclusion award from SHRM and Jobing.com.

Quarles & Brady values diversity because our people value it. We constantly strive to understand the subtleties of diversity and to capture the benefits for our firm, our clients and our communities.

WHEN YOUR CITY'S FINANCES ARE DISTRESSED, AND ITS FUTURE IS UNCERTAIN, YOU TAKE IT PERSONALLY.

GLENN R. MAHONE
CORPORATE & SECURITIES GROUP

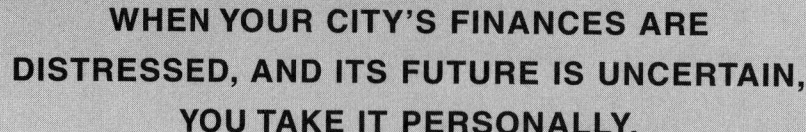

Reed Smith LLP

435 Sixth Avenue
Pittsburgh, PA 15219
Phone: (412) 288-3131
Fax: (412) 288-3063

FIRM LEADERSHIP

Managing Partner: Gregory B. Jordan,
Managing Partner
Diversity Team Leader: Cathy Bissoon, Director
of Diversity

LOCATIONS

Pittsburgh, PA (HQ)
Century City, CA
Falls Church, VA
Harrisburg, VA
Leesburg, VA
Los Angeles, CA
New York, NY
Newark, NJ
Oakland, CA
Philadelphia, PA
Princeton, NJ
Richmond, VA
San Francisco, CA
Washington, DC
Westlake Village, CA
Wilmington, DE
London
Midlands, United Kingdom

LAW FIRM DEMOGRAPHIC PROFILES

FULL-TIME ASSOCIATES	2003	2002
Minority men	21	13
Minority women	34	14
White women	139	104
Total	362	282

SUMMER ASSOCIATES	2003	2002
Minority men	9	9
Minority women	15	16
White women	15	37
Total	61	77

EQUITY PARTNERS	2003	2002
Minority men	4	3
Minority women	2	1
White women	32	24
Total	214	174

NON-EQUITY PARTNERS	2003	2002
Minority men	11	4
Minority women	2	1
White women	41	19
Total	184	104

COUNSEL	2003	2002
Minority men	5	1
Minority women	2	2
White women	34	26
Total	108	96

NEW HIRES	2003	2002
Minority men	27	4
Minority women	32	8
White women	102	55
Total	314	148

Strategic Plan and Diversity Leadership

How does the firm's leadership communicate the importance of diversity to everyone at the firm? (e.g., e-mails, web site, newsletters, meetings, etc.)

Through meetings, electronic mail, the firm web site and in newsletters.

Who has primary responsibility for leading diversity initiatives at your firm?

Cathy Bissoon, Director of Diversity

Does your law firm currently have a diversity committee?

Yes

Does the committee's representation include one or more members of the firm's management/executive committee (or the equivalent)?

Yes. Includes chief human resources officer

How many attorneys are on the committee, and in 2003, what was the total number of hours collectively spent by the committee in furtherance of the firm's diversity initiatives?

Total attorneys on committee: 12

Does the committee and/or diversity leader establish and set goals or objectives consistent with management's priorities?

Yes

Has the firm undertaken a formal or informal diversity program or set of initiatives aimed at increasing the diversity of the firm?

Yes, formal

How often does the firm's management review the firm's diversity progress/results?

Formally quarterly, but updates are continuous.

How is the firm's diversity committee and/or firm management held accountable for achieving results?

All partners, including the Diversity Committee and firm management, are evaluated annually on their contributions to diversity.

LAW FIRM DIVERSITY INITIATIVES	ALREADY COMPLETED	CURRENTLY ADDRESSING	NOT A CURRENT PRIORITY
Undertake communication from firm management that diversity is a top priority of the firm.	✓ *		
Formalize diversity plan and committee with action steps and accountability to management.	✓		
Conduct firm-wide diversity training for all attorneys and staff.	✓ **	✓	
Increase the number of minority attorneys at the associate level.	✓ *		
Increase the number of minority attorneys at the partnership level.	✓ *		
Develop/expand relationships with minority bar associations to offer firm's support of these networks.	✓ *		
Focus on strengthening firm's mentoring program, including for benefit of minority attorneys.	✓ *		
Conduct internal diversity needs assessment and/or retain diversity consultant to examine how firm culture might be more welcoming of minorities.	✓ *		
Support law firm's internal affinity networks (e.g., women, minority attorney networks).	✓ *		
Manage/monitor allocation of work assignments and/or hours billed to ensure women and minority attorneys have equal access/inclusion on top client matters.		✓	

Ongoing   ** *For all managers*

Recruitment – New Associates

Does your firm annually recruit at any of the following types of institutions? (Check all that apply and list the schools).

Ivy League schools: Columbia University, Cornell University, Harvard University, University of Pennsylvania, Yale University

Public state schools: Rutgers University-Camden, Rutgers University-Newark, Temple University, University of North Carolina, UC Berkley, UC Davis, UC Hastings, UCLA, George Mason University, University of Michigan, University of Pittsburgh, Dickinson School of Law (Penn State), University of Virginia, West Virginia University, College of William & Mary

Private schools: American University, Benjamin N. Cardozo School of Law, Boston College, Boston University, Case Western Reserve University, Catholic University of America, Duke University, Duquesne University, Emory University, Fordham University, George Washington University, Georgetown University, Hofstra University, Loyola University, New York University, Northwestern University, Santa Clara University, Seton Hall University, St. John's University, Stanford University, University of Richmond, University of Chicago, University of Notre Dame, University of San Francisco, University of Southern California, Vanderbilt University, Villanova University, Washington and Lee University, Widener University

Historically Black Colleges and Universities (HBCUs): Howard University

Do you have any special outreach efforts directed to encourage minority law students to consider your firm?

• Hold a reception for minority law students

• Advertise in minority law student association publication(s)

• Participate in/host minority law student job fair(s)

• Sponsor minority law student association events

• Firm's lawyers participate on career panels at school

• Outreach to leadership of minority student organizations

• Scholarships or intern/fellowships for minority students

SUMMER ASSOCIATE STATISTICS: SUMMER 2003	MINORITY MEN	MINORITY WOMEN	WHITE WOMEN	TOTAL
Summer associates	7	12	12	52
Summer associates who received an offer of full-time employment	5	10	12	46
Summer associates who accepted an offer of full-time employment	4	8	9	39

Recruitment – Lateral Associates and Partners

What activities does the firm undertake to attract minority and women attorneys?

• Partner programs with women and minority bar associations

• Participate at minority job fairs

• Seek referrals from other attorneys

Do you use executive recruiting/search firms to seek to identify new diversity hires (partners or associates)?

We utilized executive search firms for a variety of hiring needs. We have worked with firms who emphasize minority recruitment.

LATERAL ASSOCIATES AND PARTNERS: 1/1/03 – 12/31/03	MINORITY MEN	MINORITY WOMEN	WHITE WOMEN	TOTAL
Number of lateral associate hires	14	23	43	126
Number of lateral partner hires (equity and non-equity)	7	1	23	102
Number of new partners (equity and non-equity) promoted from associate rank	1	1	12	36
Number of new equity partners	0	0	0	0

Retention & Professional Development

Please identify the specific steps you are taking to reduce the attrition rate of minority and women attorneys.

- Develop and/or support internal employee affinity groups (e.g., minority or women networks within the firm)
- Increase/review compensation relative to competition
- Increase/improve current work/life programs
- Work with minority and women attorneys to develop career advancement plans
- Introduce minority and women attorneys to key clients, including to lead engagements
- Review work assignments and hours billed to key client matters to make sure minority and women attorneys are not being excluded
- Strengthen mentoring program for all attorneys, including minorities and women
- Professional skills development program, including minority and women attorneys

Does your firm have part-time/flex-time policies that permit attorneys (male or female) to work alternative schedules?

Yes

What impact, if any, will the decision to work part-time have on an attorney's ability to make partner or, if already a partner, to remain a partner at your firm?

None. Decisions on whether to promote a part-time attorney to partner, or to retain a part-time attorney as partner, are made without regard to the attorney's part-time status. For part-time attorneys, the firm employs the same criteria as it employs for full-time attorneys and partnership promotion generally. As a practical matter, the firm does recognize that working on a part-time arrangement for an extended period of time may affect an individual's readiness for partnership promotion.

Have any attorneys who chose to work a part-time schedule made partner at your firm?

Yes

Management Demographic Profile (as of 12/31/03)

	MINORITY MEN	MINORITY WOMEN	WHITE WOMEN	TOTAL
Number of attorneys on the Executive/Management Committee or equivalent	1	0	4	17
Number of attorneys on the Hiring Committee or equivalent	5	4	17	60

Please provide information regarding all minority and women attorneys who head offices or practice groups of your law firm:

Women heading offices: Three (Pittsburgh, Oakland and Washington, DC)

Minorities heading practice groups list names and departments: One (Employment)

Women heading practice groups: Seven (Antitrust, Employment, Appellate, Mergers & Acquisitions, Financial Services, Health Care and Life Sciences)

The Firm Says

Reed Smith is a firm that values cultural differences and adheres to policies and practices that are designed to foster an environment in which all attorneys and staff are full participants. Our firm stands side by side with our clients and other businesses and institutions to promote programs that contribute to achieving diversity in the legal profession.

We continuously explore ways to enhance the inclusiveness of our organization and consistently evaluate our own diversity efforts and work-life policies to ensure that they are in keeping with marketplace practices that have proven effective in achieving inclusiveness. We recognize that diversity at all levels of an organization is a true sign of a world-class business and we have made the recruitment, retention and promotion of women and diverse attorneys a top priority.

Consistent with this priority, we have made great efforts to develop work-life programs such as flexible work schedules and supplemental leave for infant child care to better accommodate our firm's working parents. We have instituted domestic partner benefits firm-wide. We have a Diversity Committee, headed by our director of diversity, to address matters related to achieving diversity at all levels of our organization. The Diversity Committee is charged with the tasks, among others, of working with existing internal committees to broaden recruitment efforts – both laterally and at the entry level; of developing new and innovative ways to attract diverse talent; of addressing issues unique to diverse attorneys; and of providing an internal support system for our diverse lawyers. The committee is dedicated to creating a work environment that values our differences.

Over the last three years, Reed Smith has tripled the number of minority lawyers firm-wide and has quadrupled the number of minority partners. Reed Smith continues to be aggressive in its approach to achieving and maintaining a diverse work force and developing an inclusive environment in which all of our attorneys and staff are able to thrive professionally and socially. We look forward to partnering with organizations for whom diversity also is a recognized priority and remain devoted to strengthening our firm through cultural enrichment and a commitment to equality and fairness.

Robins, Kaplan, Miller & Ciresi L.L.P.

2800 LaSalle Plaza, 800 LaSalle Avenue
Minneapolis, MN 55402-2015
Phone: (612) 349-8500
Fax: (612) 339-4181

FIRM MANAGEMENT

Managing Partner: Steven A. Schumeister,
Managing Partner
Diversity Team Leader: B. Todd Jones,
Partner, Diversity Committee Chair

LOCATIONS

Minneapolis, MN (HQ)
Atlanta, GA
Boston, MA
Los Angeles, CA
Naples, FL
St. Paul, MN
Washington, DC

LAW FIRM DEMOGRAPHIC PROFILES

FULL-TIME ASSOCIATES	2003	2002
Minority men	12	9
Minority women	8	6
White women	52	51
Total	145	129

SUMMER ASSOCIATES	2003	2002
Minority men	1	2
Minority women	5	6
White women	3	7
Total	19	21

PARTNERS*	2003	2002
Minority men	3	3
Minority women	1	1
White women	17	15
Total	115	108

* We do not distinguish between equity and non-equity partners

NEW HIRES	2003	2002
Minority men	4	1
Minority women	3	3
White women	7	8
Total	43	29

MINORITY CORPORATE COUNSEL ASSOCIATION

Strategic Plan and Diversity Leadership

How does the firm's leadership communicate the importance of diversity to everyone at the firm?

The importance of issues of diversity, and recent work of the Diversity Committee, is communicated to the firm at quarterly partnership meetings, the annual all-attorney meeting, partnership retreats, department and office manager meetings, and staff communication meetings.

Who has primary responsibility for leading diversity initiatives at your firm?

The Executive Board has primary responsibility for leading diversity initiatives at the law firm. These efforts are lead by Michael V. Ciresi, chairman of the board, and B. Todd Jones, chair of the Diversity Committee, and both are members of the Executive Board.

Does your law firm currently have a diversity committee?

Yes

Does the committee's representation include one or more members of the firm's management/executive committee (or the equivalent)?

Yes

How many attorneys are on the committee, and in 2003, what was the total number of hours collectively spent by the committee in furtherance of the firm's diversity initiatives?

Total Attorneys on committee: 12 (in 2004); 9 (in 2003)

Total hours spent on diversity: 462

Does the committee and/or diversity leader establish and set goals or objectives consistent with management's priorities?

Yes

Has the firm undertaken a formal or informal diversity program or set of initiatives aimed at increasing the diversity of the firm?

Yes, formal

How often does the firm's management review the firm's diversity progress/results?

Quarterly

How is the firm's diversity committee and/or firm management held accountable for achieving results?

Objective benchmarks for success in this area of strategic planning are difficult to quantify beyond demographic statistics. Setting an appropriate tone at the top and establishing an environment of mutual respect and excellent client service based on a diversity of views are the key goals of firm management.

LAW FIRM DIVERSITY INITIATIVES	ALREADY COMPLETED	CURRENTLY ADDRESSING	NOT A CURRENT PRIORITY
Undertake communication from firm management that diversity is a top priority of the firm.	✓		
Formalize diversity plan and committee with action steps and accountability to management.		✓	
Conduct firm-wide diversity training for all attorneys and staff.		✓	
Increase the number of minority attorneys at the associate level.		✓	
Increase the number of minority attorneys at the partnership level.		✓	
Develop/expand relationships with minority bar associations to offer firm's support of these networks.	✓		
Focus on strengthening firm's mentoring program, including for benefit of minority attorneys.		✓	
Conduct internal diversity needs assessment and/or retain diversity consultant to examine how firm culture might be more welcoming of minorities.	✓		
Support law firm's internal affinity networks (e.g., women, minority attorney networks).	✓		
Manage/monitor allocation of work assignments and/or hours billed to ensure women and minority attorneys have equal access/inclusion on top client matters.		✓	

Recruitment - New Associates

Does your firm annually recruit at any of the following types of institutions? (Check all that apply and list the schools).

Ivy League schools: Harvard University, Yale University, Cornell University, Columbia University

Public state schools: University of California-Boalt Hall, George Mason University, University of Wisconsin, University of Minnesota, University of Iowa, University of Georgia, University of Michigan

Private schools: University of Chicago, Emory University, Duke University, Franklin Pierce Law Center, George Washington University, Georgetown University, Northwestern University, Hamline University, University of St. Thomas, William Mitchell College of Law, NYU

Historically Black Colleges and Universities (HBCUs): Howard University

Do you have any special outreach efforts directed to encourage minority law students to consider your firm?

- Hold a reception for minority law students
- Participate in/host minority law student job fair(s)
- Sponsor minority law student association events
- Firm's lawyers participate on career panels at school
- Scholarships or intern/fellowships for minority students

SUMMER ASSOCIATE STATISTICS: SUMMER 2003	MINORITY MEN	MINORITY WOMEN	WHITE WOMEN	TOTAL
Summer associates	0	4	3	14
Summer associates who received an offer of full-time employment	0	3	3	12
Summer associates who accepted an offer of full-time employment	0	3	3	12

Recruitment – Lateral Associates and Partners

What activities does the firm undertake to attract minority and women attorneys?

- Participate at minority job fairs
- Seek referrals from other attorneys

Do you use executive recruiting/search firms to seek to identify new diversity hires (partners or associates)?

Yes

LATERAL ASSOCIATES AND PARTNERS: 1/1/03 – 12/31/03	MINORITY MEN	MINORITY WOMEN	WHITE WOMEN	TOTAL
Number of lateral associate hires	1	0	2	14
Number of lateral partner hires (equity and non-equity)	0	0	1	6
Number of new partners (equity and non-equity) promoted from associate rank	0	0	1	4
Number of new equity partners*	N/A	N/A	N/A	N/A

We do not distinguish between equity and non-equity partners

Retention & Professional Development

Please identify the specific steps you are taking to reduce the attrition rate of minority and women attorneys.

- Develop and/or support internal employee affinity groups (e.g., minority or women networks within the firm)
- Increase/improve current work/life programs
- Succession plan includes emphasis on diversity
- Introduce minority and women attorneys to key clients, including to lead engagements
- Review work assignments and hours billed to key client matters to make sure minority and women attorneys are not being excluded
- Strengthen mentoring program for all attorneys, including minorities and women
- Professional skills development program, including minority and women attorneys

Does your firm have part-time/flex-time policies that permit attorneys (male or female) to work alternative schedules?

Yes

Management Demographic Profile (as of 12/31/03)

	MINORITY MEN	MINORITY WOMEN	WHITE WOMEN	TOTAL
Number of attorneys on the Executive/Management Committee or equivalent	0	0	2	9
Number of attorneys on the Hiring Committee or equivalent	3	0	4	9
Number of attorneys on the Partner/Associate Review Committee or equivalent	2	2	6	24

Please provide information regarding all minority and women attorneys who head offices or practice groups of your law firm:

Women heading practice groups: Kathleen Flynn Peterson, Individual & Mass Tort

Ropes & Gray LLP

One International Place
Boston, MA 02110
Phone: (617) 951-7000
Fax: (617) 951-7050

FIRM LEADERSHIP

Managing Partner: John T. Montgomery,
Managing Partner
Diversity Team Leader: Joan McPhee, Chair of
Diversity Committee

LOCATIONS

Boston, MA (HQ)
New York, NY
San Francisco, CA
Washington, DC

LAW FIRM DEMOGRAPHIC PROFILES

FULL-TIME ASSOCIATES	2003	2002
Minority men	23	20
Minority women	27	21
White women	114	104
Total	337	317

SUMMER ASSOCIATES	2003	2002
Minority men	5	3
Minority women	4	9
White women	26	22
Total	57	56

EQUITY PARTNERS	2003	2002
Minority men	5	4
Minority women	4	3
White women	31	30
Total	201	175

NEW HIRES	2003	2002
Minority men	5	5
Minority women	8	9
White women	30	22
Total	67	85

Strategic Plan and Diversity Leadership

How does the firm's leadership communicate the importance of diversity to everyone at the firm? (e.g., e-mails, web site, newsletters, meetings, etc.)

E-mails, web site, meetings, diversity programs, including workshops and symposia, and diversity awards ceremony.

Who has primary responsibility for leading diversity initiatives at your firm?

Joan McPhee, chair of Diversity Committee

Does your law firm currently have a diversity committee?

Yes

If yes, does the committee's representation include one or more members of the firm's management/executive committee (or the equivalent)?

Yes

If yes, how many attorneys are on the committee, and in 2003, what was the total number of hours collectively spent by the committee in furtherance of the firm's diversity initiatives?

Total attorneys on committee: 6

Total hours spent on diversity: 200

Does the committee and/or diversity leader establish and set goals or objectives consistent with management's priorities?

Yes

Has the firm undertaken a formal or informal diversity program or set of initiatives aimed at increasing the diversity of the firm?

Yes, formal and informal

How often does the firm's management review the firm's diversity progress/results?

Annually

How is the firm's diversity committee and/or firm management held accountable for achieving results?

As a member of the Diversity Committee, the firm's managing partner helps ensure that the committee achieves its objectives. Additionally, contributions made by individual committee members to the firm's diversity goals are considered as a part of the annual attorney review process. The committee itself regularly evaluates all of its programs and other initiatives to ensure their effectiveness.

LAW FIRM DIVERSITY INITIATIVES	ALREADY COMPLETED	CURRENTLY ADDRESSING	NOT A CURRENT PRIORITY
Undertake communication from firm management that diversity is a top priority of the firm.	✔ *		
Formalize diversity plan and committee with action steps and accountability to management.		✔	
Conduct firm-wide diversity training for all attorneys and staff.	✔ *		
Increase the number of minority attorneys at the associate level.	✔ *		
Increase the number of minority attorneys at the partnership level.	✔ *		
Develop/expand relationships with minority bar associations to offer firm's support of these networks.	✔	✔	
Focus on strengthening firm's mentoring program, including for benefit of minority attorneys.	✔	✔	
Conduct internal diversity needs assessment and/or retain diversity consultant to examine how firm culture might be more welcoming of minorities.	✔	✔	
Support law firm's internal affinity networks (e.g., women, minority attorney networks).	✔		
Manage/monitor allocation of work assignments and/or hours billed to ensure women and minority attorneys have equal access/inclusion on top client matters.	✔ *	✔	
Formally recognize diversity contributions at annual Diversity Awards ceremony.	✔ *		

Already completed and ongoing.

Recruitment – New Associates

Does your firm annually recruit at any of the following types of institutions? (Check all that apply and list the schools).

Ivy League schools: Columbia University, Cornell University, Harvard University, University of Pennsylvania, Yale University

Public state schools: Boalt Hall (University of California-Berkeley), UCLA, University of Connecticut, University of Iowa, University of Michigan, University of Minnesota, University of North Carolina, University of Texas, University of Virginia, University of Wisconsin, College of William & Mary

Private schools: American University, Boston College, Boston University, Brigham Young University, Duke University, Fordham University, George Washington University, Georgetown University, NYU, Northeastern University, Northwestern University, Stanford University, Suffolk University, Tulane University, University of Chicago, University of Southern California, Vanderbilt University, Washington & Lee University, Washington University (St. Louis)

Historically Black Colleges and Universities (HBCUs): Howard University

Do you have any special outreach efforts directed to encourage minority law students to consider your firm?

• Hold a reception for minority law students

• Participate in/host minority law student job fair(s)

• Sponsor minority law student association events

• Firm's lawyers participate on career panels at school

SUMMER ASSOCIATE STATISTICS: SUMMER 2003	MINORITY MEN	MINORITY WOMEN	WHITE WOMEN	TOTAL
Summer associates	6	4	25	54
Summer associates who received an offer of full-time employment	6	4	25	54
Summer associates who accepted an offer of full-time employment	4	3	22	45

Recruitment – Lateral Associates and Partners

What activities does the firm undertake to attract minority and women attorneys?

• Partner programs with women and minority bar associations

• Participate at minority job fairs

• Seek referrals from other attorneys

Do you use executive recruiting/search firms to seek to identify new diversity hires (partners or associates)?

Yes

Llist all women- and/or minority-owned executive search/recruiting firms to which the firm paid a fee for placement services in the past 12 months:

None

LATERAL ASSOCIATES AND PARTNERS: 1/1/03 – 12/31/03	MINORITY MEN	MINORITY WOMEN	WHITE WOMEN	TOTAL
Number of lateral associate hires	1	1	1	4
Number of lateral partner hires (equity and non-equity)	1	0	2	6
Number of new partners (equity and non-equity) promoted from associate rank	0	0	3	8
Number of new equity partners	1	0	5	14

Retention & Professional Development

ATTORNEYS WHO LEFT THE FIRM: 2003	MINORITY MEN	MINORITY WOMEN	WHITE WOMEN	TOTAL
Number of attorneys who voluntarily or involuntarily left your firm's employ in 2003	5	4	22	62

How do 2003 attrition rates generally compare to those experienced in the prior year period?

About the same as in prior years

Please identify the specific steps you are taking to reduce the attrition rate of minority and women attorneys.

• Develop and/or support internal employee affinity groups (e.g., minority or women networks within the firm)
• Increase/review compensation relative to competition
• Increase/improve current work/life programs
• Work with minority and women attorneys to develop career advancement plans
• Introduce minority and women attorneys to key clients, including to lead engagements
• Review work assignments and hours billed to key client matters to make sure minority and women attorneys are not being excluded
• Strengthen mentoring program for all attorneys, including minorities and women
• Professional skills development program, including minority and women attorneys

Does your firm have part-time/flex-time policies that permit attorneys (male or female) to work alternative schedules?

Yes

What impact, if any, will the decision to work part-time have on an attorney's ability to make partner or, if already a partner, to remain a partner at your firm?

A lawyer's decision to work part-time has no direct impact on the attorney's ability to make partner.

Have any attorneys who chose to work a part-time schedule made partner at your firm?

Yes, 10 attorneys.

Management Demographic Profile (as of 12/31/03)

	MINORITY MEN	MINORITY WOMEN	WHITE WOMEN	TOTAL
Number of attorneys on the Executive/Management Committee or equivalent	0	0	1	7
Number of attorneys on the Hiring Committee or equivalent	2	1	4	14
Number of attorneys on the Partner/Associate Review Committee or equivalent	0	1	4	23

Minorities heading practice groups: Roscoe Trimmier, Litigation; Dennis Coleman, Sports Law; Adolfo Garcia, International

Women heading practice groups: Lisa Ropple, Litigation; Susan Johnston, Tax & Benefits; Michele Garvin, Health Care; Joan McPhee, Government Enforcement

The Firm Says

Ropes & Gray has long been committed to fostering diversity in the workplace, reflecting the firm's core values of excellence, fairness, collaboration and collegiality. Accordingly, we promote the recruitment, retention and advancement of people of diverse backgrounds at all levels of the firm. At Ropes & Gray, we see our individual differences as an asset which not only enhances the quality of life for each of us, but also strengthens our accomplishments as a firm. We understand that the differences in our backgrounds mean that our lawyers bring a variety of perspectives and ideas to the problems on which we are asked to collaborate, thereby enhancing our ability to serve our clients well and run our firm effectively. As a result of our commitment – and as exemplified by the data reported in our NALP form and by our ranking by Vault as one of the best law firms for diversity among the most prestigious law firms in the country – Ropes & Gray is today a workplace where individuals with diverse backgrounds and life experiences work together in a spirit of openness and collaboration.

We are proud of the diversity we have achieved at Ropes & Gray. We see our work environment as one where all individuals can thrive and are motivated to do their best, strengthened by their different backgrounds, perspectives and life experiences. The firm's continuing effort to that end is led by the Diversity Committee, comprised of both lawyers and staff. With a mandate to provide guidance and recommendations to the firm on policies and programs designed to retain and enhance the firm's diverse work force, the Diversity Committee's primary goals are to attract and retain the most talented and motivated individuals and to maintain a culture of acceptance through education and outreach.

In support of these goals, the Diversity Committee has sponsored various educational and awareness initiatives that address issues relating to community and team building, hiring and retention, marketing and mentoring. One series, "Appreciating Differences," which is designed to promote a healthy dialogue on how to use cultural differences to achieve positive results at work, has been offered to attorneys and staff regularly throughout the year since its introduction in 2001. Other symposiums have featured discussions on the value of diversity by a number of well-known public figures. Another initiative sponsored by the firm's Diversity Committee is the Citizens School's 8th Grade Academy, a mentoring program for Boston middle school students. This program, which pairs students with Ropes & Gray attorneys for after-school tutoring in reading and writing, provides youngsters a valuable opportunity for both academic enrichment and personal growth. In March 2003, the firm established the Trent Hankins Award for Outstanding Contributions to Diversity, which is presented at an annual awards ceremony to recognize achievements that have been made to enhance the firm's diversity efforts.

Ropes & Gray's commitment to diversity has long placed a particular focus on attorneys of color. In 1985, the firm was a founding member of the Boston Lawyers Group (then known as the Boston Law Firm Group). BLG is a consortium of Boston-area law firms, governmental law departments and in-house corporate counsel that collaborates on various programs and initiatives calculated to further BLG's stated mission, which is to support the efforts of its member organizations to identify, recruit, advance and retain attorneys of color. At the time of its founding, BLG was the first citywide collaboration of this sort. Ropes & Gray lawyers have been active not only in founding, but thereafter in carrying out, BLG's vision of a more diverse community. Roscoe Trimmier,

the firm's first African-American partner and head of the litigation department, served as an original member of the BLG's Executive Committee and was instrumental in drafting the charter adopted by the BLG's original member firms. Another partner at Ropes & Gray chaired the inaugural committee of the BLG that addresses issues of retention of minority lawyers. Today, Ropes & Gray lawyers serve as members of BLG's Executive Committee, Hiring & Education Committee, Diversity Best Practices Committee and Associate Advisory Committee. Also, Ropes & Gray regularly participates in the BLG-sponsored job fairs conducted in Boston and Washington, D.C.

The firm has also long been an active participant in programs sponsored by The Partnership, Inc., a nonprofit organization whose mission, in part, has been to attract and retain young professionals of color in the Boston area. We often have sponsored young lawyers in the Partnership's fellowship program, a program designed to introduce Fellows to the corporate, civic, arts and other aspects of Boston city life.

Not only is Ropes & Gray a leader on issues related to attorneys of color, but our attorneys of color hold significant positions within the firm as well. The attorneys of color at Ropes & Gray comprise 10 percent of the lawyers in the firm, are spread across all our major practice areas and occupy a wide range of seniority levels within those departments. Our attorneys of color lead practice groups and serve on a number of the cross-departmental committees and groups that administer the firm on a day-to-day basis, including the Associates Committee, the Hiring Group, the Diversity Committee and the Training Advisory Committee.

The firm also sponsors the Attorneys of Color group for social and professional support of its attorneys of color. The AOC group conducts regular quarterly meetings and leads special events oriented towards the firm's attorneys of color. These meetings and events are intended to provide opportunities for the firm's attorneys of color to share their unique experiences within the firm, to encourage mentoring relationships among the more senior and junior attorneys, and to ensure that attorneys of color feel welcomed and supported.

In addition, Ropes & Gray has implemented a number of programs and policies specifically with the goal of supporting the retention and promotion of women attorneys. In 1996, for example, the firm established the Women's Forum for the purpose of providing a forum for women lawyers to consider matters of common interest, to offer opportunities for mutual support and community, and to generally assist in the development and progress of women lawyers at the firm. The Women's Forum sponsors educational programs designed to help women lawyers manage their careers, augment their skills, and deal with issues faced by women generally. These programs have addressed such topics as mentoring, choosing practice areas, marketing, strategies for career development, and gender-based communications issues. The Women's Forum also organizes social events to enable women from different practice areas to get to know one another better.

The Women's Forum, and other firm programs and policies, also recognize and address the special challenges faced by women lawyers who have children. The Women's Forum hosts informal "brown bag" lunches geared primarily toward matters of interest to women lawyers who have (or are planning or expecting) children. These lunches feature speakers from within and outside the firm on topics such as child care options, estate and financial planning, and the challenges presented in balancing work and family.

Ropes & Gray also has adopted a reduced time policy under which lawyers can work reduced schedules for family, health or other reasons. Currently, a number of women associates and partners are working reduced schedules pursuant to this policy. Four women lawyers have been promoted to partner while working on a reduced time basis, all of whom were working part time to accommodate their child care responsibilities.

Ropes & Gray founded the first emergency child-care facility in the city. At no cost, excellent back-up day care is available to everyone at the firm in the firm's own on-site facility. In addition, the firm has established a private lactation room for nursing mothers. The firm also supplies associates with tools such as remote network access and PDA's to enable lawyers to work from home and remote locations. Together, these policies help support women who are juggling work and family.

Saul Ewing LLP

100 South Charles Street
Baltimore, MD 21201
Phone: (410) 332-8600
Fax: (410) 332-8862

FIRM LEADERSHIP

Leslie T. Long, Diversity Coordinator
Managing Partner: Stephen S. Aichele,
Managing Partner of Saul Ewing LLP
Diversity Team Leader: Ava E. Lias-Booker and
Joseph F. O'Dea Jr., Co-Chairs of the Diversity
Committee

LOCATIONS

Baltimore, MD (HQ)
Chesterbrook, PA
Harrisburg, PA
Philadelphia, PA
Princeton, NJ
Washington, DC
Wilmington, DE

LAW FIRM DEMOGRAPHIC PROFILES

FULL-TIME ASSOCIATES	2003	2002
Minority men	4	3
Minority women	10	9
White women	40	47
Total	115	117

SUMMER ASSOCIATES	2003	2002
Minority men	3	1
Minority women	3	5
White women	6	5
Total	16	15

EQUITY PARTNERS	2003	2002
Minority men	1	1
Minority women	1	1
White women	19	21
Total	93	101

NON-EQUITY PARTNERS	2003	2002
Minority men	1	0
Minority women	0	0
White women	8	3
Total	41	21

NEW HIRES	2003	2002
Minority men	2	1
Minority women	6	3
White women	7	8
Total	38	29

MINORITY CORPORATE COUNSEL ASSOCIATION

Strategic Plan and Diversity Leadership

How does the firm's leadership communicate the importance of diversity to everyone at the firm? (e.g., e-mails, web site, newsletters, meetings, etc.)

Saul Ewing has had regular discussions at firm-wide meetings in regards to diversity, how it is a key component in the growth of the firm, as well as it being each individual's responsibility to uphold the initiative. We have also created a diversity newsletter and are currently in the beginning stages of compiling our diversity information to place on our web site and to be disseminated internally via e-mail.

Who has primary responsibility for leading diversity initiatives at your firm?

Ava E. Lias-Booker, partner, and Joseph F. O'Dea Jr., partner and vice chair of the litigation department. The committee itself is comprised of the heads of most of the firm's standing committees, such as the Executive, Hiring, Career Development and Evaluation Committees, and the head of the summer associates program.

Does your law firm currently have a diversity committee?

Yes

Does the committee's representation include one or more members of the firm's management/executive committee (or the equivalent)?

Yes

How many attorneys are on the committee, and in 2003, what was the total number of hours collectively spent by the committee in furtherance of the firm's diversity initiatives?

Total attorneys on committee: 9

Total hours spent on diversity: 530.5 hours

Does the committee and/or diversity leader establish and set goals or objectives consistent with management's priorities?

Yes

Has the firm undertaken a formal or informal diversity program or set of initiatives aimed at increasing the diversity of the firm?

Yes, formal

How often does the firm's management review the firm's diversity progress/results?

We have implemented a system in which the Diversity Committee provides a formal report regarding the firm's diversity progress/results to the Executive Committee on a quarterly basis. The Executive Committee monitors the achievement of those milestones.

How is the firm's diversity committee and/or firm management held accountable for achieving results?

The Executive Committee also requires the participation of department heads in providing formal reports on the progress in terms of our diversity initiatives in reference to our Diversity Strategic Action Plan.

LAW FIRM DIVERSITY INITIATIVES	ALREADY COMPLETED	CURRENTLY ADDRESSING	NOT A CURRENT PRIORITY
Undertake communication from firm management that diversity is a top priority of the firm.	✔		
Formalize diversity plan and committee with action steps and accountability to management.	✔		
Conduct firm-wide diversity training for all attorneys and staff.	✔		
Increase the number of minority attorneys at the associate level.		✔	
Increase the number of minority attorneys at the partnership level.		✔	
Develop/expand relationships with minority bar associations to offer firm's support of these networks.		✔	
Focus on strengthening firm's mentoring program, including for benefit of minority attorneys.		✔	
Conduct internal diversity needs assessment and/or retain diversity consultant to examine how firm culture might be more welcoming of minorities.	✔		
Support law firm's internal affinity networks (e.g., women, minority attorney networks).		✔	
Manage/monitor allocation of work assignments and/or hours billed to ensure women and minority attorneys have equal access/inclusion on top client matters.		✔	

Recruitment - New Associates

Does your firm annually recruit at any of the following types of institutions? (Check all that apply and list the schools).*

Ivy League schools: Columbia University, University of Pennsylvania

Public state schools: University of Baltimore, Dickinson School of Law (Penn State), University of Maryland, Rutgers University-Camden, Rutgers University-Newark, Temple University, University of Virginia, College of William & Mary

Private schools: American University, Boston College, Boston University, Brooklyn Law School, Catholic University of America, Duke University, Fordham University, George Washington University, Georgetown University, Seton Hall University, Villanova University, Washington and Lee University, Widener University

Historically Black Colleges and Universities (HBCUs): Howard University

* We also collect resumes at many Ivy League, public and private schools.

Do you have any special outreach efforts directed to encourage minority law students to consider your firm?

• *Saul Ewing is a member of the Legal Recruitment Administration and, in conjunction with the top 25 Philadelphia law firms, we take part in hosting the Annual First-Year Minority Reception.*

• Advertise in minority law student association publication(s)
• Participate in/host minority law student job fair(s)
• Sponsor minority law student association events
• Firm's lawyers participate on career panels at school
• Outreach to leadership of minority student organizations

SUMMER ASSOCIATE STATISTICS: SUMMER 2003	MINORITY MEN	MINORITY WOMEN	WHITE WOMEN	TOTAL
Summer associates	3	3	6	16
Summer associates who received an offer of full-time employment	3	3	6	16
Summer associates who accepted an offer of full-time employment	3	3	6	16

Recruitment – Lateral Associates and Partners

What activities does the firm undertake to attract minority and women attorneys?

• Participate at minority job fairs
• Seek referrals from other attorneys

Do you use executive recruiting/search firms to seek to identify new diversity hires (partners or associates)?

Yes

LATERAL ASSOCIATES AND PARTNERS: 1/1/03 – 12/31/03	MINORITY MEN	MINORITY WOMEN	WHITE WOMEN	TOTAL
Number of lateral associate hires	1	2	4	16
Number of lateral partner hires (equity and non-equity)	1	0	1	10
Number of new partners (equity and non-equity) promoted from associate rank	0	0	2	5
Number of new equity partners	0	0	0	1

List all women- and/or minority-owned executive search/recruiting firms to which the firm paid a fee for placement services in the past 12 months:

Mestel & Co., Liz Shapiro Legal Search, Amato Legal Search, Golub Associates, St. Clair Legal, Carter-White & Shaw, Williamson Legal, Marina Sirras & Associates, Major Hagen & Africa.

Retention & Professional Development

ATTORNEYS WHO LEFT THE FIRM: 2003	MINORITY MEN	MINORITY WOMEN	WHITE WOMEN	TOTAL
Number of attorneys who voluntarily or involuntarily left your firm's employ in 2003	1	4	16	34

How do 2003 attrition rates generally compare to those experienced in the prior year period?

Higher than in prior years

Please identify the specific steps you are taking to reduce the attrition rate of minority and women attorneys.

• Develop and/or support internal employee affinity groups (e.g., minority or women networks within the firm)
• Increase/review compensation relative to competition
• Increase/improve current work/life programs
• Succession plan includes emphasis on diversity
• Work with minority and women attorneys to develop career advancement plans
• Introduce minority and women attorneys to key clients, including to lead engagements
• Review work assignments and hours billed to key client matters to make sure minority and women attorneys are not being excluded
• Strengthen mentoring program for all attorneys, including minorities and women
• Professional skills development program, including minority and women attorneys

Does your firm have part-time/flex-time policies that permit attorneys (male or female) to work alternative schedules?

Yes. Currently we have 13 lawyers who work part-time.

What impact, if any, will the decision to work part-time have on an attorney's ability to make partner or, if already a partner, to remain a partner at your firm?

It may elongate the time it takes to become a partner, but has no impact on the attorney's ability to remain a partner.

Have any attorneys who chose to work a part-time schedule made partner at your firm?

Yes, one attorney.

Management Demographic Profile (as of 12/31/03)

	MINORITY MEN	MINORITY WOMEN	WHITE WOMEN	TOTAL
Number of attorneys on the Executive/Management Committee or equivalent	0	0	1	7
Number of attorneys on the Hiring Committee or equivalent	1	0	8	17
Number of attorneys on the Partner/Associate Review Committee or equivalent	0	0	3	7

Please provide information regarding all minority and women attorneys who head offices or practice groups of your law firm:

Women heading offices: Constance B. Foster, Harrisburg; Pamela S. Goodwin, Princeton

Women heading practice groups: Harriet E. Cooperman, Labor and Employment Law; Constance B. Foster, Insurance Group; Sherry H. Flax, Intellectual Property; Nancy S. Cleveland, Telecommunications Group; Wendie C. Stabler, Utility Regulation

The Firm Says

The Executive Committee tasked the Diversity Committee with studying the issue and identifying ways to strengthen and improve the firm. As a result, the Diversity Committee spent the last two years comprehensively studying ways to make Saul Ewing a more diverse and inclusive law firm. The firm engaged in a national search for the leading consultant on the issue of law firm diversity strategies. We retained The Athens Group of Chicago and Dr. Arin Reeves. Dr. Reeves and her staff conducted both a needs assessment (that is, an independent study of how the law firm operates) and diversity dialogues with all attorneys, managers and staff in the spring and fall of 2003. We are proud to be among only a small handful of law firms nationwide that has included not only its attorneys, but also all employees, in the firm's diversity initiatives. This fact alone speaks volumes about our commitment to create an environment in which everyone can succeed.

The wealth of information and thoughtful, energized and firm-minded feedback that poured in through this process was incredible. The needs assessment and diversity dialogues achieved several critical objectives, namely they:

• demonstrated the firm's commitment to diversity
• engaged every person employed by Saul Ewing in the process of improving the diversity of the firm
• made the business case for diversity; and
• prompted critical feedback from all parts of the organization, which the Diversity Committee used to develop the strategies to diversify the firm going forward

While the Diversity Committee is pleased to report this progress, these activities were merely initial steps in a long-range, multi-step process.

The Diversity Committee took the information gained through the diversity dialogues, studied practices at other firms and ultimately crafted a plan. That process culminated earlier this year with the Executive Committee's adoption of the firm's Strategic Plan for Diversity. The Plan outlined a far-reaching list of action items, all intended to strengthen the firm. The Diversity Committee believes that our plan is as comprehensive as any law firm plan in the nation.

Among many new initiatives that the Diversity Committee will be rolling out as we move forward, the Diversity Committee created a newsletter that will serve as a vehicle to keep everyone in the Saul Ewing community abreast of Plan implementation, as well as other diversity related issues in the firm, the profession and the communities in which we practice.

Saul Ewing LLP Vision Statement

At Saul Ewing LLP, we are proudly committed to diversity and to providing equal opportunities for all to succeed. We define diversity broadly as the differences among people, including race, culture, ethnicity, gender,

sexual orientation, religion, language and experiences. We sincerely value the different perspectives that the diversity of our attorneys and staff bring to the firm and our clients. And we not only acknowledge, but enthusiastically embrace, the pivotal role that diversity plays in growing and strengthening us as a firm. To foster that continued growth, Saul Ewing will:

- ensure that firm management is dedicated to taking a leadership role in making diversity a key business priority
- support a standing Diversity Committee, including the leadership of other standing firm committees such as the Hiring Committee, Evaluation Committee, Professional Development Committee and Summer Program
- develop and implement meaningful strategies for the recruitment, hiring, retention and advancement of women and minorities
- promote the active involvement of women and minority attorneys in diversity planning; and
- vigorously encourage a firm culture in which differing points of view are sought out, heard and respected, and in which diversity is truly valued and appreciated as an integral part of the firm

From a business perspective, we recognize that diversity among our professional staff only enriches the quality of the services the firm provides to our clients. We also recognize that our non-professional staff is a vital part of the organization, and that diversity throughout the entire firm is essential to our continued success. And at Saul Ewing, we believe that achieving diversity in the workplace is not only the right thing to do, but is also critical to the health and success of any business, including our own.

Schiff Hardin LLP

6600 Sears Tower
Chicago, IL 60606
Phone: (312) 258-5500
Fax: (312) 258-5600

FIRM MANAGEMENT

Managing Partner: Scott Pickens, Partner
Diversity Team Leader: Marci Eisenstein, Partner

LOCATIONS

Chicago, IL (HQ)
Atlanta, GA
Lake Forest, IL
New York, NY
Washington, DC
Dublin

LAW FIRM DEMOGRAPHIC PROFILES

FULL-TIME ASSOCIATES	2003	2002
Minority men	8	5
Minority women	9	5
White women	44	46
Total	109	99

SUMMER ASSOCIATES	2003	2002
Minority men	0	2
Minority women	0	7
White women	3	6
Total	16	23

EQUITY PARTNERS	2003	2002
Minority men	1	2
Minority women	0	0
White women	15	14
Total	95	92

NON-EQUITY PARTNERS	2003	2002
Minority men	1	0
Minority women	0	0
White women	22	21
Total	70	61

NEW HIRES	2003	2002
Minority men	6	1
Minority women	4	2
White women	12	13
Total	48	31

Strategic Plan and Diversity Leadership

How does the firm's leadership communicate the importance of diversity to everyone at the firm? (e.g., e-mails, web site, newsletters, meetings, etc.)

Partner meetings, attorney meetings, firm-wide announcements, e-mails, web site postings, newsletters.

Who has primary responsibility for leading diversity initiatives at your firm?

Marci Eisenstein, partner and chair of Diversity Committee

Does your law firm currently have a diversity committee?

Yes

Does the committee's representation include one or more members of the firm's management/executive committee (or the equivalent)?

No. However, Marci Eisenstein, the chair of the Diversity Committee, was a member of the Executive Committee until March 2004.

How many attorneys are on the committee, and in 2003, what was the total number of hours collectively spent by the committee in furtherance of the firm's diversity initiatives?

Total attorneys on committee: 5

Total hours spent on diversity: Approximately 200

Does the committee and/or diversity leader establish and set goals or objectives consistent with management's priorities?

Yes

Has the firm undertaken a formal or informal diversity program or set of initiatives aimed at increasing the diversity of the firm?

Yes, formal

How often does the firm's management review the firm's diversity progress/results?

Quarterly

How is the firm's diversity committee and/or firm management held accountable for achieving results?

The Diversity Committee prepares an annual action plan of diversity initiatives. It is accountable to the Executive Committee and the firm's partners for the results.

LAW FIRM DIVERSITY INITIATIVES	ALREADY COMPLETED	CURRENTLY ADDRESSING	NOT A CURRENT PRIORITY
Undertake communication from firm management that diversity is a top priority of the firm.	✓	✓	
Formalize diversity plan and committee with action steps and accountability to management.	✓	✓	
Conduct firm-wide diversity training for all attorneys and staff.		✓	
Increase the number of minority attorneys at the associate level.		✓	
Increase the number of minority attorneys at the partnership level.		✓	
Develop/expand relationships with minority bar associations to offer firm's support of these networks.		✓	
Focus on strengthening firm's mentoring program, including for benefit of minority attorneys.	✓	✓	
Conduct internal diversity needs assessment and/or retain diversity consultant to examine how firm culture might be more welcoming of minorities.	✓	✓	
Support law firm's internal affinity networks (e.g., women, minority attorney networks).	✓	✓	
Manage/monitor allocation of work assignments and/or hours billed to ensure women and minority attorneys have equal access/inclusion on top client matters.	✓	✓	

Recruitment - New Associates

Does your firm annually recruit at any of the following types of institutions? (Check all that apply and list the schools).

Predominantly minority and/or women's colleges

Ivy League schools: Harvard University

Public state schools: University of Michigan, University of Illinois, University of Virginia, University of Wisconsin, University of Iowa, University of Minnesota

Private schools: Northwestern University, Washington University, Georgetown University, George Washington University, Vanderbilt University, Duke University, Chicago-Kent College of Law, DePaul University, Loyola University, University of Chicago

Historically Black Colleges and Universities (HBCUs): Howard University

Do you have any special outreach efforts directed to encourage minority law students to consider your firm?

• *Donated money to minority law student association*
• Hold a reception for minority law students
• Participate in/host minority law student job fair(s)

MINORITY CORPORATE COUNSEL ASSOCIATION

- Sponsor minority law student association events
- Firm's lawyers participate on career panels at school
- Outreach to leadership of minority student organizations
- Scholarships or intern/fellowships for minority students

SUMMER ASSOCIATE STATISTICS: SUMMER 2003	MINORITY MEN	MINORITY WOMEN	WHITE WOMEN	TOTAL
Summer associates	0	0	3	13
Summer associates who received an offer of full-time employment	0	0	3	13
Summer associates who accepted an offer of full-time employment	0	0	0	8

Recruitment – Lateral Associates and Partners

What activities does the firm undertake to attract minority and women attorneys?

- Partner programs with women and minority bar associations
- Participate at minority job fairs
- Seek referrals from other attorneys

Do you use executive recruiting/search firms to seek to identify new diversity hires (partners or associates)?

Yes

LATERAL ASSOCIATES AND PARTNERS: 1/1/03 – 12/31/03	MINORITY MEN	MINORITY WOMEN	WHITE WOMEN	TOTAL
Number of lateral associate hires	5	4	11	33
Number of lateral partner hires (equity and non-equity)	1	0	1	15
Number of new partners (equity and non-equity) promoted from associate rank	0	0	4	9
Number of new equity partners	0	0	1	9

Retention & Professional Development

ATTORNEYS WHO LEFT THE FIRM: 2003	MINORITY MEN	MINORITY WOMEN	WHITE WOMEN	TOTAL
Number of attorneys who voluntarily or involuntarily left your firm's employ in 2003	4	0	8	28

How do 2003 attrition rates generally compare to those experienced in the prior year period?

Higher than in prior years

Please identify the specific steps you are taking to reduce the attrition rate of minority and women attorneys.

• Develop and/or support internal employee affinity groups (e.g., minority or women networks within the firm)
• Increase/review compensation relative to competition
• Increase/improve current work/life programs
• Work with minority and women attorneys to develop career advancement plans
• Introduce minority and women attorneys to key clients, including to lead engagements
• Review work assignments and hours billed to key client matters to make sure minority and women attorneys are not being excluded
• Strengthen mentoring program for all attorneys, including minorities and women
• Professional skills development program, including minority and women attorneys

Does your firm have part-time/flex-time policies that permit attorneys (male or female) to work alternative schedules?

Yes

What impact, if any, will the decision to work part-time have on an attorney's ability to make partner or, if already a partner, to remain a partner at your firm?

Working a part-time or reduced schedule does not preclude advancement to the partnership.

Have any attorneys who chose to work a part-time schedule made partner at your firm?

Yes

Management Demographic Profile (as of 12/31/03)

	MINORITY MEN	MINORITY WOMEN	WHITE WOMEN	TOTAL
Number of attorneys on the Executive/Management Committee or equivalent	0	0	1	5
Number of attorneys on the Hiring Committee or equivalent	3	1	11	35
Number of attorneys on the Partner/Associate Review Committee or equivalent	0	0	2	10

Please provide information regarding all minority and women attorneys who head offices or practice groups of your law firm:

Women heading practice groups: Marci Eisenstein, Class Action Litigation; Barbara Heffernan, Energy, Telecom & Public Utilities; Jill Berkeley, Insurance

The Firm Says

Schiff Hardin has been known for many years for its commitment to diversity in its workplace and in the community. In addition to hiring and mentoring lawyers who are women and members of minority groups, we support our commitment to a diverse work force in other ways as well.

In particular, Schiff Hardin's diversity initiatives span four general areas:

• Communicating and demonstrating a commitment to the value of diversity
• Recruitment strategies and practices
• Retention strategies and practices
• Pro bono services

Due to these efforts, Schiff Hardin has increased its diversity. For example, from 2001 to 2004, the percentage of minority associates has doubled to 16 percent and the percentage of minority summer associates has tripled to 31 percent.

Communicating and demonstrating a commitment to the value of diversity

Schiff Hardin is a signatory to the Policy Statement Regarding the Hiring and Retention of Minority Lawyers. It is also a member of the Chicago Committee on Minorities in Large Law Firms.

In 2003, Schiff Hardin established a Diversity Committee. Marci Eisenstein, a former member of the firm's Executive Committee and a practice group leader, chairs the committee. The mission of the committee is "to enhance the Firm's ability to recruit, hire, develop, retain and promote a diverse professional workforce on the basis of demonstrated merit and performance by continuing the development of an inclusive culture that promotes the likelihood of success for all lawyers at the Firm."

The Diversity Committee regularly reports, and is accountable, to the Executive Committee and the firm's partners on the success of the firm's diversity initiatives. The firm's diversity initiatives are an agenda item for the firm's partners' meetings. In addition, the chair of professional personnel, who also sits on the Diversity Committee, reports on the firm's diversity initiatives in meetings with associate lawyers.

The firm invests in minority-focused organizations. Most recently, it has sponsored events by the Black Women Lawyers' Association (in which a number of our lawyers have leadership roles) and the Chicago Committee on Minorities in Large Law Firms. The firm is continually seeking other partnerships and relationships with minority-focused organizations.

In 1999, the firm established a scholarship for minority students at Loyola University of Chicago in the name of one of its former partners. The firm has contributed $250,000 to endow the scholarship. For the past four years, a second-year minority law student has received a Schiff Hardin/John J. Waldron scholarship.

The firm also has a women attorneys group (known as the Women's Networking Group) that regularly sponsors seminars and other special events designed to serve the needs of women professionals. Our attorneys are active

in organizations that support and promote professional development for women. This group also has a program to mentor and further support the career advancement of female attorneys at Schiff Hardin.

Currently, three of our women lawyers are practice group leaders.

Recruitment strategies and practices

Over the past several years, the firm has modified its recruiting practices to increase the number of minority candidates who are interviewed during the recruiting process. These changes include expanding the number of law schools at which it interviews and taking part in job fairs that focus on minority law students. As noted above, these changes have been successful in increasing the diversity of our lawyers.

Schiff Hardin also has diversity with respect to gender. Fifty percent of our associates are women.

Retention strategies and practices

In 2003, Schiff Hardin hired an outside consultant to help us determine what we could do to improve hiring, retention and advancement of our minority associates. Based upon that study, the firm created a formal coaching program for associates. We experienced a tremendous response from our partners in volunteering to act as coaches. As part of the program, the firm instituted cross-cultural and cross-gender training programs for all coaches and advisees.

Recognizing the need that some of our lawyers have to balance demands outside the workplace, the firm offers flexible, part-time arrangements to lawyers.

In addition to the coaching program, the firm has taken other steps to ensure that all of our lawyers receive full access to professional development opportunities. The firm's chair of professional personnel is charged with the responsibility (along with practice group leaders and the firm's Professional Personnel Committee) to review associates' work and client assignments to make sure that each associate receives appropriate opportunities to develop their skills as lawyers in the firm.

Pro bono services

Schiff Hardin has a historical commitment to advancing diversity in our communities. The firm's lawyers have been legal counsel in several pieces of landmark litigation seeking diversity in residential housing. Its lawyers have represented victims of hate crimes. We were a founding member of the Chicago Lawyers' Committee for Civil Rights Under Law and three of our current partners have served as chairs of that organization. We also founded and continue to staff the first law-firm-based storefront legal aid clinic in the city of Chicago.

Schulte Roth & Zabel LLP

919 Third Avenue
New York, NY 10022
Phone: (212) 756-2000
Fax: (212) 593-5955

FIRM MANAGEMENT

Susan R. Galligan, Special Counsel and
Director of Professional Development
Diversity Team Leader: Mark E. Brossman,
Partner

LOCATIONS

New York, NY (HQ)
London

LAW FIRM DEMOGRAPHIC PROFILES

FULL-TIME ASSOCIATES	2003	2002
Minority men	17	15
Minority women	23	22
White women	84	88
Total	247	236

SUMMER ASSOCIATES	2003	2002
Minority men	0	4
Minority women	1	3
White women	15	12
Total	37	26

EQUITY PARTNERS	2003	2002
Minority men	1	1
Minority women	1	1
White women	8	7
Total	63	61

NON-EQUITY PARTNERS	2003	2002
Minority men	0	0
Minority women	0	0
White women	0	0
Total	1	1

SPECIAL COUNSEL	2003	2002
Minority men	0	0
Minority women	0	0
White women	8	10
Total	15	18

NEW HIRES	2003	2002
Minority men	8	2
Minority women	6	3
White women	20	18
Total	65	57

Strategic Plan and Diversity Leadership

How does the firm's leadership communicate the importance of diversity to everyone at the firm? (e.g., e-mails, web site, newsletters, meetings, etc.)

Policy statements, newsletters, article distribution, meetings, orientation segment, training

Who has primary responsibility for leading diversity initiatives at your firm? Name of person and his/her title:

Mark Brossman, partner and chair of the Diversity Committee

Does your law firm currently have a diversity committee?

Yes

Does the committee's representation include one or more members of the firm's management/executive committee (or the equivalent)?

No

How many attorneys are on the committee, and in 2003, what was the total number of hours collectively spent by the committee in furtherance of the firm's diversity initiatives?

Total attorneys on committee: 8

Does the committee and/or diversity leader establish and set goals or objectives consistent with management's priorities?

Yes

Has the firm undertaken a formal or informal diversity program or set of initiatives aimed at increasing the diversity of the firm?

Yes, informal

How often does the firm's management review the firm's diversity progress/results?

Annually

How is the firm's diversity committee and/or firm management held accountable for achieving results?

Periodic reports to the Executive Committee.

LAW FIRM DIVERSITY INITIATIVES	ALREADY COMPLETED	CURRENTLY ADDRESSING	NOT A CURRENT PRIORITY
Undertake communication from firm management that diversity is a top priority of the firm.		✓	
Formalize diversity plan and committee with action steps and accountability to management.		✓	
Conduct firm-wide diversity training for all attorneys and staff.		✓	
Increase the number of minority attorneys at the associate level.		✓	
Increase the number of minority attorneys at the partnership level.		✓	
Develop/expand relationships with minority bar associations to offer firm's support of these networks.		✓	
Focus on strengthening firm's mentoring program, including for benefit of minority attorneys.		✓	
Conduct internal diversity needs assessment and/or retain diversity consultant to examine how firm culture might be more welcoming of minorities.		✓	
Support law firm's internal affinity networks (e.g., women, minority attorney networks).		✓	
Manage/monitor allocation of work assignments and/or hours billed to ensure women and minority attorneys have equal access/inclusion on top client matters.		✓	

Recruitment - New Associates

Does your firm annually recruit at any of the following types of institutions? (Check all that apply and list the schools).

Ivy League schools: Columbia University, Harvard University, Cornell University, University of Pennsylvania

Public state schools: University of California-Boalt Hall, University of Virginia

Private schools: Tulane University, Northwestern University, New York University, George Washington University, Fordham University, Boston College, Franklin Pierce Law Center, Boston University, Cardozo Law School, Georgetown University

Historically Black Colleges and Universities (HBCUs): Howard University

Do you have any special outreach efforts directed to encourage minority law students to consider your firm?

• Advertise in minority law student association publication(s)
• Participate in/host minority law student job fair(s)
• Sponsor minority law student association events
• Firm's lawyers participate on career panels at school
• Outreach to leadership of minority student organizations

SUMMER ASSOCIATE STATISTICS: SUMMER 2003	MINORITY MEN	MINORITY WOMEN	WHITE WOMEN	TOTAL
Summer associates	0	2	15	37
Summer associates who received an offer of full-time employment	0	1	15	37
Summer associates who accepted an offer of full-time employment	0	1	15	32*

* Plus four clerkships

Recruitment – Lateral Associates and Partners

What activities does the firm undertake to attract minority and women attorneys?

• Partner programs with women and minority bar associations
• Participate at minority job fairs
• Seek referrals from other attorneys

Do you use executive recruiting/search firms to seek to identify new diversity hires (partners or associates)?

Yes

LATERAL ASSOCIATES AND PARTNERS: 1/1/03 – 12/31/03	MINORITY MEN	MINORITY WOMEN	WHITE WOMEN	TOTAL
Number of lateral associate hires	5	2	8	35
Number of lateral partner hires (equity and non-equity)	0	0	0	0
Number of new partners (equity and non-equity) promoted from associate rank	1	0	0	4
Number of new equity partners	1	0	0	4

Retention & Professional Development

ATTORNEYS WHO LEFT THE FIRM: 2003	MINORITY MEN	MINORITY WOMEN	WHITE WOMEN	TOTAL
Number of attorneys who voluntarily or involuntarily left your firm's employ in 2003	4	6	24	55

How do 2003 attrition rates generally compare to those experienced in the prior year period?

About the same as in prior years

Please identify the specific steps you are taking to reduce the attrition rate of minority and women attorneys. (It is suggested that you elaborate on this issue in the final question of this survey.)

• Develop and/or support internal employee affinity groups (e.g., minority or women networks within the firm)
• Increase/improve current work/life programs
• Work with minority and women attorneys to develop career advancement plans
• Introduce minority and women attorneys to key clients, including to lead engagements
• Review work assignments and hours billed to key client matters to make sure minority and women attorneys are not being excluded
• Strengthen mentoring program for all attorneys, including minorities and women
• Professional skills development program, including minority and women attorneys

Does your firm have part-time/flex-time policies that permit attorneys (male or female) to work alternative schedules?

Yes

What impact, if any, will the decision to work part-time have on an attorney's ability to make partner or, if already a partner, to remain a partner at your firm?

For an associate, the track to partnership may be adjusted to take into account the practice time difference due to the reduced work schedule.

Have any attorneys who chose to work a part-time schedule made partner at your firm?

Yes, one attorney.

Management Demographic Profile (as of 12/31/03)

	MINORITY MEN	MINORITY WOMEN	WHITE WOMEN	TOTAL
Number of attorneys on the Executive/Management Committee or equivalent	0	0	0	5
Number of attorneys on the Hiring Committee or equivalent	2	1	7	15
Number of attorneys on the Partner/Associate Review Committee or equivalent	0	0	2	7

The Firm Says

Diversity at SRZ is important to creating an environment that allows our firm to attract and retain a diverse pool of talented attorneys, foster a supportive work environment for all employees and raise awareness within our firm of important diversity issues.

The firm has taken on a number of initiatives to support its commitment to diversity:

- The Diversity Committee at SRZ ensures that the firm's diversity initiatives continue to be successful and that we are proactive with respect to our diversity commitment goals.

- We are a signatory to the Association of the Bar of the City of New York's Statement of Goals for Increasing Minority Representation and Retention. As part of that commitment, we have increased our efforts to hire minority lawyers by interviewing at a broader range of law schools and more regional BLSA job fairs.

- The firm participates in the Association's Summer Bar Fellow Program, a first-year summer associate program for minority students who attend law school in the New York region; the Association of the Bar's Minority Lateral Recruiting Program; and the Lavender Law Career Fair, a National Lesbian and Gay Law Association's Annual Conference.

- Of the 37 summer associates in our 2004 class, five are minorities (including four women) and 11 are white women.

- There are currently 14 attorneys — both men and women — who participate in our alternative work schedule program.

- We also are committed to religious diversity and accommodate dietary needs and religious observances. Our attorneys have a diverse range of beliefs and goals; we recognize that, in order to achieve a balanced life for our lawyers, we must respect and accommodate these differences.

- Schulte Roth & Zabel LLP is an equal opportunity employer. A complete copy of our Non-Discrimination Policy can be viewed on our web site at www.srz.com/recruiting.asp.

Think we're all the same?

Think again.

Sedgwick, Detert, Moran & Arnold LLP

One Embarcadero Center, 16th Floor
San Francisco, CA 94111
Phone: (415) 781-7900
Fax: (415) 781-2635

FIRM LEADERSHIP

Managing Partner: Kevin J. Dunne, Chairman
Diversity Team Leader: Craig S. Barnes,
Partner and Chair of Diversity Committee;
Stephanie A. Sheridan, Partner and Co-Chair of
Diversity Committee

LOCATIONS

San Francisco, CA (HQ)
Chicago, IL
Dallas, TX
Irvine, CA
Los Angeles, CA
New York, NY
Newark, NJ
London
Paris
Zurich

LAW FIRM DEMOGRAPHIC PROFILES

FULL-TIME ASSOCIATES	2003	2002
Minority men	11	4
Minority women	16	10
White women	32	12
Total	131	99

SUMMER ASSOCIATES	2003	2002
Minority men	2	1
Minority women	1	0
White women	8	5
Total	14	9

PARTNERS	2003	2002
Minority men	2	2
Minority women	0	0
White women	15	12
Total	100	89

NEW HIRES	2003	2002
Minority men	5	6
Minority women	7	5
White women	24	17
Total	59	63

Strategic Plan and Diversity Leadership

How does the firm's leadership communicate the importance of diversity to everyone at the firm? (e.g., e-mails, web site, newsletters, meetings, etc.)

E-mails, web site, proposals, meetings, committee, hiring, advertising.

Who has primary responsibility for leading diversity initiatives at your firm? Name of person and his/her title:

We have a full Diversity Committee chaired by Stephanie Sheridan and Craig Barnes.

Does your law firm currently have a diversity committee?

Yes

Does the committee's representation include one or more members of the firm's management/executive committee (or the equivalent)?

No

How many attorneys are on the committee, and in 2003, what was the total number of hours collectively spent by the committee in furtherance of the firm's diversity initiatives?

Total attorneys on committee: 13

Total hours spent on diversity: We have meetings approximately once a month and subcommittees that meet more frequently on given topics and research assignments.

Does the committee and/or diversity leader establish and set goals or objectives consistent with management's priorities?

Yes

Has the firm undertaken a formal or informal diversity program or set of initiatives aimed at increasing the diversity of the firm?

Yes, informal

How often does the firm's management review the firm's diversity progress/results?

Monthly

How is the firm's diversity committee and/or firm management held accountable for achieving results?

The Diversity Committee will report findings back to the firm's Management Committee.

LAW FIRM DIVERSITY INITIATIVES	ALREADY COMPLETED	CURRENTLY ADDRESSING	NOT A CURRENT PRIORITY
Undertake communication from firm management that diversity is a top priority of the firm.		✓	
Formalize diversity plan and committee with action steps and accountability to management.		✓	
Conduct firm-wide diversity training for all attorneys and staff.			✓
Increase the number of minority attorneys at the associate level.		✓	
Increase the number of minority attorneys at the partnership level.		✓	
Develop/expand relationships with minority bar associations to offer firm's support of these networks.		✓	
Focus on strengthening firm's mentoring program, including for benefit of minority attorneys.		✓	
Conduct internal diversity needs assessment and/or retain diversity consultant to examine how firm culture might be more welcoming of minorities.			✓
Support law firm's internal affinity networks (e.g., women, minority attorney networks).		✓	
Manage/monitor allocation of work assignments and/or hours billed to ensure women and minority attorneys have equal access/inclusion on top client matters.			✓
All of the goals outlined above are important to Sedgwick; we have identified those that are the subject of current initiatives.		✓	

Recruitment – New Associates

Does your firm annually recruit at any of the following types of institutions? (Check all that apply and list the schools).

Ivy League schools: Harvard University and Columbia University

Public state schools: University of Virginia, UCLA, UC Berkley, UC Hastings, University of Texas and University of Michigan

Private schools: Stanford University, USC, Southwestern University, Southern Methodist University, University of San Francisco, Pepperdine University, Loyola Law School, Fordham University, Baylor University and New York University

Do you have any special outreach efforts directed to encourage minority law students to consider your firm?

• Participate in/host minority law student job fair(s)
• Firm's lawyers participate on career panels at school

SUMMER ASSOCIATE STATISTICS: SUMMER 2003	MINORITY MEN	MINORITY WOMEN	WHITE WOMEN	TOTAL
Summer associates	3	1	2	14
Summer associates who received an offer of full-time employment	3	0	1	11
Summer associates who accepted an offer of full-time employment	3	0	1	10

Recruitment – Lateral Associates and Partners

What activities does the firm undertake to attract minority and women attorneys?
• Partner programs with women and minority bar associations
• Participate at minority job fairs
• Seek referrals from other attorneys
• Utilize online job services (e.g., MCCA/DuPont Primary Law Firm Job Bank)

Do you use executive recruiting/search firms to seek to identify new diversity hires (partners or associates)?
Yes

List all women- and/or minority-owned executive search/recruiting firms to which the firm paid a fee for placement services in the past 12 months:
Sedgwick has retained a woman-owned search firm to do a state-wide search in California, where we have the most offices. For our other search firms, diversity is a component we ask them to consider in proposing candidates to us.

LATERAL ASSOCIATES AND PARTNERS: 1/1/03 – 12/31/03	MINORITY MEN	MINORITY WOMEN	WHITE WOMEN	TOTAL
Number of lateral associate hires	4	9	17	53
Number of lateral partner hires (equity and non-equity)	0	0	1	3
Number of new partners (equity and non-equity) promoted from associate rank	0	0	3	9

Retention & Professional Development

ATTORNEYS WHO LEFT THE FIRM: 2003	MINORITY MEN	MINORITY WOMEN	WHITE WOMEN	TOTAL
Number of attorneys who voluntarily or involuntarily left your firm's employ in 2003	6	6	27	43

How do 2003 attrition rates generally compare to those experienced in the prior year period?
About the same as in prior years

Please identify the specific steps you are taking to reduce the attrition rate of minority and women attorneys.

• Develop and/or support internal employee affinity groups (e.g., minority or women networks within the firm)

• Increase/improve current work/life programs

• Introduce minority and women attorneys to key clients, including to lead engagements

• Strengthen mentoring program for all attorneys, including minorities and women

• Professional skills development program, including minority and women attorneys

Does your firm have part-time/flex-time policies that permit attorneys (male or female) to work alternative schedules?

Yes

What impact, if any, will the decision to work part-time have on an attorney's ability to make partner or, if already a partner, to remain a partner at your firm?

An associate who is working on a part-time basis may be considered for partnership. It is understood that a part-time associate's progression toward partnership may take longer than it would have if the associate had been working a full-time schedule. The firm has partners on part-time schedules as well.

Have any attorneys who chose to work a part-time schedule made partner at your firm?

Yes. We have two part-time partners.

Management Demographic Profile (as of 12/31/03)

	MINORITY MEN	MINORITY WOMEN	WHITE WOMEN	TOTAL
Number of attorneys on the Executive/Management Committee or equivalent	1	0	1	13
Number of attorneys on the Hiring Committee or equivalent	0	0	2	8
Number of attorneys on the Partner/Associate Review Committee or equivalent	N/A	N/A	N/A	N/A

Please provide information regarding all minority and women attorneys who head offices or practice groups of your law firm:

Women heading practice groups: Cynthia Plevin, Employment & Labor; Marilyn Klinger, Surety

The Firm Says

Sedgwick is proud to have ranked No. 17 for "Overall Diversity" in the 2004 Vault Guide to the Top 100 Law Firms (and No. 10 for diversity with respect to gays and lesbians). We believe these ratings reflect the firm's cultural openness to diversity. Sedgwick is striving to develop a work force that more closely reflects the diverse environment in which we live, and has promulgated policies and practices intended to support those goals, as follows:

Policies

Sedgwick is dedicated to diversity and to the advancement of minorities and women in our firm. The firm is an equal opportunity employer, and employees are selected, hired and promoted on the basis of ability, experience, training, skill and character. To that end, Sedgwick has and enforces an Equal Employment Practices Policy and an Unlawful Harassment Policy. Sedgwick also has a part-time policy in place that may be utilized by female and male associates who wish to be considered for partnership. The firm has a dedicated Diversity Committee, which oversees and coordinates activities designed to recruit and retain talented minority attorneys.

Diversity and promotion of women

Sedgwick believes diverse teams are better positioned to anticipate the needs of our clients and that our employees enjoy working in a diverse environment where all points of view are thoughtfully considered before final decisions are made. Sedgwick is striving to meet the diversity policy articulated by the Association of Corporate Counsel, and has adopted the Bar Association of San Francisco's "No Glass Ceiling" Initiative.

To meet these goals, the firm is bolstering its mentoring efforts for all attorneys and has retained a consultant who has particular experience tailoring mentoring programs for minority and female attorneys.

In 2004, Sedgwick has undertaken particular efforts to support the firm's women. The firm joined Catalyst, a nonprofit research and advisory organization working to advance women in business, which provides strategic consulting services to help firms advance women and build inclusive work environments. The firm kicked off a "Women's Forum," a group designed to provide a platform for Sedgwick's female attorneys to voice their professional development needs, to recommend programs to enhance the role of women in the firm and the profession, and to develop programs related to the advancement of women in the firm.

Pro bono, organizational and charitable support

Many members of the firm participate in organizations dedicated to promoting women and minorities in law and in business, such as the Chicago Committee on Minorities in Large Law Firms, the Women's Bar Association of Illinois, the Minority Corporate Counsel Association, the African American Insurance Professionals Association, CREW (Commercial Real Estate Women), the Women Lawyers Association of Los Angeles, the California Association of Black Lawyers Foundation, the California Minority Counsel Program, the Cuban American Bar Association, the Hispanic National Bar Association and the Asian Law Caucus.

The firm also provides pro bono legal support and financial support to minority and women public interest organizations, including the AIDS Foundation of Chicago, Bay Area Latino Lawyers Fund, Filipino American Council, Now Legal Defense & Education Fund, Inner-City Scholarship Fund, Cabrini Mission Foundation and Project Open Hand. Many of our attorneys serve on the board of directors for local and community nonprofit organizations; and many of our associates participate in public high school mock-trial programs.

Shaw Pittman LLP

2300 N Street, NW
Washington, DC 20037
Phone: (202) 663-8000
Fax: (202) 663-8007

FIRM MANAGEMENT

Managing Partner: Stephen B. Huttler, Partner
Diversity Team Leader: Elizabeth Espin Stern
and Maureen Dwyer, Partners

LOCATIONS

Washington, DC (HQ)
Palo Alto, CA
McLean, VA
New York, NY
London, England
Taipei, Taiwan

LAW FIRM DEMOGRAPHIC PROFILES

FULL-TIME ASSOCIATES	2003	2002
Minority men	13	16
Minority women	10	11
White women	54	67
Total	161	118

SUMMER ASSOCIATES	2003	2002
Minority men	2	5
Minority women	3	6
White women	14	14
Total	29	44

EQUITY PARTNERS	2003	2002
Minority men	2	2
Minority women	2	2
White women	22	26
Total	124	109

NEW HIRES	2003	2002
Minority men	5	3
Minority women	5	4
White women	14	13
Total	61	45

Strategic Plan and Diversity Leadership

How does the firm's leadership communicate the importance of diversity to everyone at the firm? (e.g., e-mails, web site, newsletters, meetings, etc.)

E-mail, meetings with all attorneys and individual practice groups, training sessions, included in statement of firm goals, web site.

Who has primary responsibility for leading diversity initiatives at your firm?

Elizabeth Espin Stern and Maureen Dwyer, partners and co-chairs of Diversity Initiative

Does your law firm currently have a diversity committee?

Yes

Does the committee's representation include one or more members of the firm's management/executive committee (or the equivalent)?

Yes

How many attorneys are on the committee, and in 2003, what was the total number of hours collectively spent by the committee in furtherance of the firm's diversity initiatives?

Total attorneys on committee: 5

Total hours spent on diversity: 50 to 100

Does the committee and/or diversity leader establish and set goals or objectives consistent with management's priorities?

Yes

Has the firm undertaken a formal or informal diversity program or set of initiatives aimed at increasing the diversity of the firm?

Yes, formal

How often does the firm's management review the firm's diversity progress/results?

Quarterly

How is the firm's diversity committee and/or firm management held accountable for achieving results?

The Initiative is taken very seriously and includes both the committee and a Minority Associate Retention Task Force, which augments the associate-wide efforts for career advancement of the Associates' and Professional Development Committees. The managing partner, with the input of the management team, monitors the Diversity Initiative closely. Compensation discussions include a review of the diversity co-chair partners' efforts and progress.

LAW FIRM DIVERSITY INITIATIVES	ALREADY COMPLETED	CURRENTLY ADDRESSING	NOT A CURRENT PRIORITY
Undertake communication from firm management that diversity is a top priority of the firm.	✓		
Formalize diversity plan and committee with action steps and accountability to management.		✓	
Conduct firm-wide diversity training for all attorneys and staff.		✓	
Increase the number of minority attorneys at the associate level.	✓		
Increase the number of minority attorneys at the partnership level.		✓	
Develop/expand relationships with minority bar associations to offer firm's support of these networks.	✓		
Focus on strengthening firm's mentoring program, including for benefit of minority attorneys.	✓		
Conduct internal diversity needs assessment and/or retain diversity consultant to examine how firm culture might be more welcoming of minorities.	✓		
Support law firm's internal affinity networks (e.g., women, minority attorney networks).	✓		
Manage/monitor allocation of work assignments and/or hours billed to ensure women and minority attorneys have equal access/inclusion on top client matters.		✓	

Recruitment – New Associates

Do you have any special outreach efforts directed to encourage minority law students to consider your firm?

• Hold a reception for minority law students
• Advertise in minority law student association publication(s)
• Participate in/host minority law student job fair(s)
• Sponsor minority law student association events
• Firm's lawyers participate on career panels at school
• Outreach to leadership of minority student organizations
• Scholarships or intern/fellowships for minority students

SUMMER ASSOCIATE STATISTICS: SUMMER 2003	MINORITY MEN	MINORITY WOMEN	WHITE WOMEN	TOTAL
Summer associates	1	3	12	26
Summer associates who received an offer of full-time employment	1	2	12	24
Summer associates who accepted an offer of full-time employment	1	2	8	17

Recruitment – Lateral Associates and Partners

What activities does the firm undertake to attract minority and women attorneys?

• Participate at minority job fairs

• Seek referrals from other attorneys

Do you use executive recruiting/search firms to seek to identify new diversity hires (partners or associates)?

Yes

List all women- and/or minority-owned executive search/recruiting firms to which the firm paid a fee for placement services in the past 12 months:

Various D.C.-based legal search firms; decline to provide specific names.

LATERAL ASSOCIATES AND PARTNERS: 1/1/03 – 12/31/03	MINORITY MEN	MINORITY WOMEN	WHITE WOMEN	TOTAL
Number of lateral associate hires	1	3	6	17
Number of lateral partner hires (equity and non-equity)	0	0	1	4
Number of new partners (equity and non-equity) promoted from associate rank*	0	0	0	2
Number of new equity partners	0	0	1	4

* Seven associates were promoted to counsel: five women and two men, including one minority woman and four white women

Retention & Professional Development

ATTORNEYS WHO LEFT THE FIRM: 2003	MINORITY MEN	MINORITY WOMEN	WHITE WOMEN	TOTAL
Number of attorneys who voluntarily or involuntarily left your firm's employ in 2003	3	5	25	75

How do 2003 attrition rates generally compare to those experienced in the prior year period?

About the same as in prior years

Please identify the specific steps you are taking to reduce the attrition rate of minority and women attorneys.

• Develop and/or support internal employee affinity groups (e.g., minority or women networks within the firm)

• Increase/improve current work/life programs

• Work with minority and women attorneys to develop career advancement plans

• Introduce minority and women attorneys to key clients, including to lead engagements

• Strengthen mentoring program for all attorneys, including minorities and women (Includes launch of an "Open

• Door program to include partner mentoring of minority associates in addition to other mentoring programs in place at the firm)

• Professional skills development program, including minority and women attorneys

Does your firm have part-time/flex-time policies that permit attorneys (male or female) to work alternative schedules?

Yes

What impact, if any, will the decision to work part-time have on an attorney's ability to make partner or, if already a partner, to remain a partner at your firm?

No impact on eligibility for promotion or continued success. Compensation is adjusted in accordance with hours worked.

Have any attorneys who chose to work a part-time schedule made partner at your firm?

Yes, four attorneys. This is a proven approach for many years in which part-time attorneys have been promoted both to counsel and to partner.

Management Demographic Profile (as of 12/31/03)

	MINORITY MEN	MINORITY WOMEN	WHITE WOMEN	TOTAL
Number of attorneys on the Executive/Management Committee or equivalent	0	0	0	3
Number of attorneys on the Hiring Committee or equivalent	1	1	5	16
Number of attorneys on the Partner/Associate Review Committee or equivalent	1	1	3	15

Please provide information regarding all minority and women attorneys who head offices or practice groups of your law firm:

Minorities heading practice groups: Elizabeth Espin Stern, Immigration

Women heading practice groups: Elizabeth Espin Stern, Immigration; Sheila Harvey, Environment; Christine Kearns, Commercial Litigation and Employment Advocacy

The Firm Says

Shaw Pittman is fully committed to a diverse work force in all areas and at all levels in the firm. In fact, Shaw Pittman's new managing partner, Stephen Huttler, has identified this commitment to be one of his top priorities. We have two partners, Elizabeth Espin Stern and Maureen Dwyer, designated to co-chair our Diversity Initiative. As part of this initiative, we are reinforcing our commitment to inclusiveness of persons of all backgrounds, because we believe that this type of commitment will enrich our work force and enhance our service to our clients.

Our various recruiting programs throughout the firm are structured to provide identification of minority applicants. One of our most significant recruiting efforts for all candidates, including minority and women candidates, is the personal networking initiatives of our current lawyers. In addition, we make special outreach efforts to increase our pool of minority and women lawyers by participating in events and supporting

organizations whose membership consists primarily of women and minorities. For example, we have been a principal supporter and participant of the Washington Area Legal Recruitment Administrator Association's Diversity Reception, an annual summer event. Our associates are involved with the efforts of the Road Show. The Road Show is a group of African American associates from several large Washington firms who visit law school campuses to talk to African American students about large firm practice. For many years, we have interviewed on campus at Howard University Law School and we frequently attend minority job fairs. At various law schools, we attend and participate in job fairs and career seminars for minority students. We also have launched a minority scholarship program for two law schools per year.

Retention and opportunity for promotion require diligent attention. Our work assignment process and professional development programs for lawyers in the firm are designed to allow all lawyers to work to their full potential, including preparing them for consideration for promotion. Mentor programs can play a significant role in the success of an associate. All new lawyers are assigned associate advisors who have an official, sanctioned role recognized by the firm. Responsibility for associate management is focused in the practice group and many groups also assign partner mentors. The firm's Associates Committee conducts thorough performance reviews and acts as quickly as possible to provide feedback to ensure the professional development and advancement of associates. Our director of professional programs assists the practice groups and the Associates Committee with these programs.

To specifically address minority associate retention and success, we have formed a Minority Associate Retention Task Force that is part of the Diversity Initiative. Led by counsel Kimberly Mann, the task force is involved in obtaining feedback from minority associates and providing open door mentoring for their specific needs. In addition, the task force is developing recommendations for the firm's management team and the leaders of other key committees, including the Associates, Professional Development and Senior Professional Committees, regarding specific programs that would enhance the workplace for minority lawyers. The co-chairs of the Diversity Initiative are working with the task force to launch an "Open Door" program by which a group of partner-mentors would be trained in diversity issues and be available to minority associates for informal discussions and guidance on career issues.

The firm has engaged a diversity consultant to provide quarterly trainings to our lawyers on diversity issues, and to assist in implementing our firm's agenda to attract and retain minority lawyers at all levels in our workplace. Our diversity co-chairs and the diversity consultant are working with practice groups to identify specific needs and enhance lateral recruiting, lawyer retention and overall career opportunities for minority lawyers.

Shearman & Sterling LLP

599 Lexington Avenue
New York, NY 10022
Phone: (212) 848-4000
Fax: (212) 848-7179

FIRM MANAGEMENT

Managing Partner: David W. Heleniak, Senior
Partner
Diversity Team Leader: Denise M. Grant and
William E. Hirschberg, Co-Chairs of Diversity
Committee
Anna L. Brown, Diversity Management
Attorney

LOCATIONS

New York, NY (HQ)
Menlo Park, CA
San Francisco, CA
Washington, DC
Abu Dhabi
Beijing
Brussels
Düsseldorf
Frankfurt
Hong Kong
London
Mannheim
Munich
Paris
Rome
São Paulo
Singapore
Tokyo
Toronto

LAW FIRM DEMOGRAPHIC PROFILES

FULL-TIME ASSOCIATES	2003	2002
Minority men	62	64
Minority women	78	70
White women	138	140
Total	492.5	500

SUMMER ASSOCIATES	2003	2002
Minority men	12	9
Minority women	11	8
White women	17	22
Total	73	74

EQUITY PARTNERS	2003	2002
Minority men	4	4
Minority women	2	1
White women	20.5	21
Total	140.5	142

NEW HIRES	2003	2002
Minority men	10	12
Minority women	20	15
White women	24	36
Total	92	84

Strategic Plan and Diversity Leadership

How does the firm's leadership communicate the importance of diversity to everyone at the firm? (e.g., e-mails, web site, newsletters, meetings, etc.)

The firm's diversity initiative is part of its strategic business plan. The firm utilizes all media of communication, including those listed above, to communicate the importance of this initiative.

Who has primary responsibility for leading diversity initiatives at your firm?

Denise M. Grant and William E. Hirschberg, co-chairs of the Diversity Committee

Does your law firm currently have a diversity committee?

Yes

Does the committee's representation include one or more members of the firm's management/executive committee (or the equivalent)?

Yes

How many attorneys are on the committee, and in 2003, what was the total number of hours collectively spent by the committee in furtherance of the firm's diversity initiatives?

Total attorneys on committee: 23

Total hours spent on diversity: The Diversity Committee meets on a monthly basis. The work of the committee is continuous and ongoing. Partners and associates spend significant time implementing the firm's diversity initiatives. The firm's diversity management attorney devotes her time exclusively to the firm's diversity efforts.

Does the committee and/or diversity leader establish and set goals or objectives consistent with management's priorities?

Yes

Has the firm undertaken a formal or informal diversity program or set of initiatives aimed at increasing the diversity of the firm?

Yes, formal

How often does the firm's management review the firm's diversity progress/results?

Ongoing evaluation of initiatives

Annually

How is the firm's diversity committee and/or firm management held accountable for achieving results?

Partners' contributions to the firm's diversity efforts are considered as part of the annual partner review process.

LAW FIRM DIVERSITY INITIATIVES	ALREADY COMPLETED	CURRENTLY ADDRESSING	NOT A CURRENT PRIORITY
Undertake communication from firm management that diversity is a top priority of the firm.	✔		
Formalize diversity plan and committee with action steps and accountability to management.	✔		
Conduct firm-wide diversity training for all attorneys and staff.		✔	
Increase the number of minority attorneys at the associate level.		✔	
Increase the number of minority attorneys at the partnership level.		✔	
Develop/expand relationships with minority bar associations to offer firm's support of these networks.	✔		
Focus on strengthening firm's mentoring program, including for benefit of minority attorneys.		✔	
Conduct internal diversity needs assessment and/or retain diversity consultant to examine how firm culture might be more welcoming of minorities.	✔		
Support law firm's internal affinity networks (e.g., women, minority attorney networks).	✔		
Manage/monitor allocation of work assignments and/or hours billed to ensure women and minority attorneys have equal access/inclusion on top client matters.		✔	

* See narrative

Recruitment - New Associates

Does your firm annually recruit at any of the following types of institutions? (Check all that apply and list the schools).

Ivy League schools: Harvard University, Columbia University, Yale University, Cornell University, University of Pennsylvania

Public state schools: University of North Carolina, University of Michigan, University of Virginia, University of Cincinnati, UCLA, University of California-Boalt Hall, University of California-Hastings, McGill University, University of Toronto, Osgoode Hall (York University)

Private schools: Brooklyn Law School, Emory University, Tulane University, New York University, Hofstra University, St. John's University, Fordham University, Georgetown University, George Washington University, Cardozo School of Law, Boston College, Boston University, American University, Stanford University, Vanderbilt University, Pace University, Duke University, University of Chicago, Northwestern University, Washington University St. Louis

Historically Black Colleges and Universities (HBCUs): Howard University

Do you have any special outreach efforts directed to encourage minority law students to consider your firm?

• *Annual Open House hosted by the Diversity Committee. The firm presents, hosts and sponsors on-campus workshops, panel discussions and seminars with several minority law student organizations.*

• Hold a reception for minority law students

• Advertise in minority law student association publication(s)

• Participate in/host minority law student job fair(s)

• Sponsor minority law student association events

• Firm's lawyers participate on career panels at school

• Outreach to leadership of minority student organizations

• Scholarships or intern/fellowships for minority students

SUMMER ASSOCIATE STATISTICS: SUMMER 2003	MINORITY MEN	MINORITY WOMEN	WHITE WOMEN	TOTAL
Summer associates	12	11	17	73
Summer associates who received an offer of full-time employment	12	11	17	73
Summer associates who accepted an offer of full-time employment	9	8*	13*	54*

* *Five offers still outstanding, including one minority woman and one white woman*

Recruitment – Lateral Associates and Partners

What activities does the firm undertake to attract minority and women attorneys?

• Partner programs with women and minority bar associations

• Participate at minority job fairs

• Seek referrals from other attorneys

Do you use executive recruiting/search firms to seek to identify new diversity hires (partners or associates)?

Yes

List all women- and/or minority-owned executive search/recruiting firms to which the firm paid a fee for placement services in the past 12 months:

Sandra Green Legal Placement, Hank-Kross, Greene Levin Snyder

LATERAL ASSOCIATES AND PARTNERS: 1/1/03 – 12/31/03	MINORITY MEN	MINORITY WOMEN	WHITE WOMEN	TOTAL
Number of lateral associate hires	2	4	6	20.5
Number of lateral partner hires (equity and non-equity)	0	1	0	2
Number of new partners (equity and non-equity) promoted from associate rank	0	0	2	4
Number of new equity partners	N/A	N/A	N/A	N/A

Retention & Professional Development

Please identify the specific steps you are taking to reduce the attrition rate of minority and women attorneys.

• *The firm works with all attorneys to develop career advancement plans. See "The Firm Says"*
• Develop and/or support internal employee affinity groups (e.g., minority or women networks within the firm)
• Increase/improve current work/life programs
• Strengthen mentoring program for all attorneys, including minorities and women
• Professional skills development program, including minority and women attorneys

Does your firm have part-time/flex-time policies that permit attorneys (male or female) to work alternative schedules?

Yes. The firm is committed to making part-time and flex-time career paths available to associates subject to the needs of the firm and the particular practice area.

What impact, if any, will the decision to work part-time have on an attorney's ability to make partner or, if already a partner, to remain a partner at your firm?

An associate with a part-time or flex-time schedule could be considered to become a counsel or partner and continue to work on a part-time or flex-time basis.

Have any attorneys who chose to work a part-time schedule made partner at your firm?

Yes, four attorneys. This includes both part-time and flex-time arrangements.

Management Demographic Profile (as of 12/31/03)

	MINORITY MEN	MINORITY WOMEN	WHITE WOMEN	TOTAL
Number of attorneys on the Executive/Management Committee or equivalent	1	0	1	11
Number of attorneys on the Hiring Committee or equivalent	N/A	N/A	N/A	N/A
Number of attorneys on the Partner/Associate Review Committee or equivalent	N/A	N/A	N/A	N/A

Please provide information regarding all minority and women attorneys who head offices or practice groups of your law firm:

Minorities heading offices: Lee Edwards, Beijing

Women heading practice groups: Pamela Gibson, Capital Markets/Asia & Europe; Linda Rappaport, Executive Compensation & Employee Benefits; Cynthia Urda Kassis, Project Development and Finance

The Firm Says

Shearman & Sterling LLP's Global Diversity Initiative has four strategic goals; (1) create a firm culture that supports and promotes diversity; (2) facilitate diversity in all aspects of the firm; (3) increase the recruitment, retention, development and advancement of attorneys from diverse backgrounds; and (4) promote diversity through involvement in the global legal community, nonprofit organizations and bar associations and through client relationships.

Diversity committee and innovative practices

Established in 1992, Shearman & Sterling's Diversity Committee includes the firm's senior partners, 11 other partners and 10 associates. The firm also has a full-time diversity management attorney. The committee meets regularly to put into action initiatives that promote diversity within the firm and the legal community. Time spent on such matters is billed to a firm account and included in the annual partner review process.

Shearman & Sterling utilizes formal education programs to promote a clearer understanding of diversity and its value in business and to the firm. Diversity sessions are included in its annual curriculum for new partners, first-year and summer associate orientation programs, annual associate conferences for third- and sixth-year associates and practice group presentations. The firm also continues to strengthen its focus on mentoring, and it encourages attorneys to participate in affinity groups.

The firm has instituted a number of initiatives and benefits designed to increase retention and promotion for all associates. They include sabbaticals, upward review of partners, counsel and senior associates, flexible work options and domestic partner benefits. Many partners and associates have taken advantage of these initiatives and benefits.

The firm is an active member of Catalyst, a nonprofit organization dedicated to the advancement of women in business. Women partners have hosted panel discussions and receptions on issues such as "Women and the Law" and "An Insider's View of Habits of Highly Effective Women Negotiators." The firm and the Association of Black Women Attorneys co-sponsored the panel discussion, "Excelling at Motherhood and the Law." It also teamed with the Metropolitan Black Bar Association as co-sponsors of the program, "Celebrating the Strength and Perseverance of Women."

Scholarships and recruitment initiatives

The Shearman & Sterling LLP/NAACP Legal Defense and Educational Fund, Inc. Scholarship annually awards two outstanding African-American law students with a $15,000 scholarship for the first year of law school. The award is renewable for the second and third years of law school. It also guarantees summer employment at Shearman & Sterling and the NAACP Legal Defense and Educational Fund. The program, now in its 13th year, has benefited more than 25 students.

For the past 11 years, Shearman & Sterling has participated in the Sponsors for Educational Opportunity (SEO) Program, whereby two minority law school students work as summer interns at the firm. Partner and associate mentors are assigned to both students. The firm participates in the Association of the Bar of the City of New York Summer Fellowship Program for Minority Law Students, whereby a first-year minority law student in the New York City area participates in the firm's summer associate program. The firm is also a participant in the Northeast BLSA Job Fair.

Other initiatives include hosting an open house for law students from diverse backgrounds and sponsoring and participating in the Lavender Law Conference. In 2004 the firm hosted its first Pride Luncheon to celebrate Pride Week and the firm's work in the LGBT community.

Shearman & Sterling supports professional events and programs by the Lambda Legal Defense and Education Fund, Asian American Legal Defense and Education Fund, Asian American Bar Association of New York, Hispanic Federation, Metropolitan Black Bar Association and the Minority Corporate Counsel Association, to name a few.

The firm sponsors events like the annual Jazz Foundation of America's "A Great Night in Harlem." The firm also supports many organizations, including Legal Outreach, Harlem Children's Zone, Brotherhood SisterSol, ACORN, Casa Mexico (Project Unity), Bradhurst Harlem Project, Trey Whitfield School, Upper Bronx Neighborhood Association for Puerto Ricans, Louis Carr Internship Foundation, ACLU Gay and Lesbian Rights Project, National Center for Lesbian Rights, Latin America Worker's Project, Haitian Women for Haitian Refugees, Filipino American Human Services, Inc., Black Masa Trust, Alvin Ailey Dance Company, Asian Professional Extension, Inc. (APEX), Museum for African Art, Puerto Rican Bar Association Scholarship Fund and the Smithsonian National Museum of the American Indian.

Shearman & Sterling offers a paid summer internship to minority high school and college students, introducing them to the legal profession and the "world of work." The students are primarily sourced through community outreach organizations, such as the I Have a Dream Foundation, Thurgood Marshall Summer Law Internship Program, Prep for Prep and The Development School for Youth Program.

On a global level, the firm participates in the South African Visiting Lawyers Program, through which a South African attorney of color has the opportunity to work in the firm's New York office for six months to one year. The firm also provides pro bono assistance to the Office of the Prosecution for the International Criminal Tribunal for Rwanda.

Shearman & Sterling is an active member of the Association of the Bar of the City of New York's Committee to Enhance Diversity in the profession. It is also a signatory to the ABCNY's 2003 Statement of Diversity Principles, the Statement of Goals of New York Law Firms and Minority Representation and Retention, and the Restatement and Reaffirmation of Goals adopted by the Association for the hiring, retention and promotion of attorneys of color and women. The Minority Law Journal ranked Shearman & Sterling among the top 10 firms overall in its annual Diversity Scorecard for 2004. Please see the firm's web site and diversity brochure for more information on its diversity initiatives.

Sheppard, Mullin, Richter & Hampton LLP

333 South Hope Street, 48th Floor
Los Angeles, CA 90071
Phone: (213) 620-1780
Fax: (213) 620-1398

FIRM MANAGEMENT

Managing Partner: Guy N. Halgren, Chair, Executive Committee
Diversity Team Leader: Dianne Baquet Smith, Chair, Diversity Committee

LOCATIONS

Los Angeles, CA (HQ)
Century City, CA
Costa Mesa, CA
Del Mar, CA
San Diego, CA
San Francisco, CA
Santa Barbara, CA
Washington, DC

LAW FIRM DEMOGRAPHIC PROFILES

FULL-TIME ASSOCIATES	2003	2002
Minority men	13	13
Minority women	15	13
White women	57	47
Total	172	148

SUMMER ASSOCIATES	2003	2002
Minority men	5	3
Minority women	3	1
White women	5	12
Total	21	21

EQUITY PARTNERS	2003	2002
Minority men	7	6
Minority women	2	2
White women	14	12
Total	133	117

NON-EQUITY PARTNERS	2003	2002
Minority men	0	2
Minority women	0	0
White women	8	7
Total	26	24

NEW HIRES*	2003	2002
Minority men	5	1
Minority women	4	3
White women	9	7
Total	69	22

Includes entry-level and lateral associates and partners, but does not include senior attorneys or special counsel.

MINORITY CORPORATE COUNSEL ASSOCIATION

Strategic Plan and Diversity Leadership

How does the firm's leadership communicate the importance of diversity to everyone at the firm? (e.g., e-mails, web site, newsletters, meetings, etc.)

Through e-mails, meetings, web site, program participation and sponsorships.

Who has primary responsibility for leading diversity initiatives at your firm?

Guy N. Halgren, chair of Executive Committee

Does your law firm currently have a diversity committee?

Yes

Does the committee's representation include one or more members of the firm's management/executive committee (or the equivalent)?

Yes

How many attorneys are on the committee, and in 2003, what was the total number of hours collectively spent by the committee in furtherance of the firm's diversity initiatives?

Total attorneys on committee: 6

Total hours spent on diversity: 500+ hours

Does the committee and/or diversity leader establish and set goals or objectives consistent with management's priorities?

Yes

Has the firm undertaken a formal or informal diversity program or set of initiatives aimed at increasing the diversity of the firm?

Yes, formal

How often does the firm's management review the firm's diversity progress/results?

Monthly

How is the firm's diversity committee and/or firm management held accountable for achieving results?

The Diversity Committee includes members of the firm's Executive Committee who report on monthly meetings. The Diversity Committee prepares a year-end report of the prior calendar year's activities and goals for the future.

LAW FIRM DIVERSITY INITIATIVES	ALREADY COMPLETED	CURRENTLY ADDRESSING	NOT A CURRENT PRIORITY
Undertake communication from firm management that diversity is a top priority of the firm.	✓		
Formalize diversity plan and committee with action steps and accountability to management.	✓		
Conduct firm-wide diversity training for all attorneys and staff.		✓	
Increase the number of minority attorneys at the associate level.		✓	
Increase the number of minority attorneys at the partnership level.	✓		
Develop/expand relationships with minority bar associations to offer firm's support of these networks.	✓		
Focus on strengthening firm's mentoring program, including for benefit of minority attorneys.		✓	
Conduct internal diversity needs assessment and/or retain diversity consultant to examine how firm culture might be more welcoming of minorities.			✓
Support law firm's internal affinity networks (e.g., women, minority attorney networks).		✓	
Manage/monitor allocation of work assignments and/or hours billed to ensure women and minority attorneys have equal access/inclusion on top client matters.	✓		
Joined with other law firms in sponsoring a formal program and in following up regarding diversity efforts.	✓		

Recruitment - New Associates

Does your firm annually recruit at any of the following types of institutions? (Check all that apply and list the schools).

Ivy League schools: Harvard University, Yale University, Columbia University, University of Pennsylvania

Public state schools: University of Michigan, University of Minnesota, UCLA, University of California-Boalt Hall, University of California-Hastings, University of California-Davis, University of Virginia

Private schools: Stanford University, USC, Loyola Law School, Duke University, Northwestern University, University of Chicago, New York University, Georgetown University, University of Notre Dame, Brigham York University, George Washington University

Historically Black Colleges and Universities (HBCUs): Howard University

Do you have any special outreach efforts directed to encourage minority law students to consider your firm?

• Hold a reception for minority law students

• Participate in/host minority law student job fair(s)

• Sponsor minority law student association events

• Firm's lawyers participate on career panels at school

SUMMER ASSOCIATE STATISTICS: SUMMER 2003	MINORITY MEN	MINORITY WOMEN	WHITE WOMEN	TOTAL
Summer associates	4	3	5	18
Summer associates who received an offer of full-time employment	4	3	5	18
Summer associates who accepted an offer of full-time employment	4	3	5	17

Recruitment – Lateral Associates and Partners

What activities does the firm undertake to attract minority and women attorneys?

• Partner programs with women and minority bar associations

• Participate at minority job fairs

• Seek referrals from other attorneys

Do you use executive recruiting/search firms to seek to identify new diversity hires (partners or associates)?

Yes

LATERAL ASSOCIATES AND PARTNERS: 1/1/03 – 12/31/03	MINORITY MEN	MINORITY WOMEN	WHITE WOMEN	TOTAL
Number of lateral associate hires	3	4	9	30
Number of lateral partner hires (equity and non-equity)	1	0	2	19
Number of new partners (equity and non-equity) promoted from associate rank	0	0	0	4
Number of new equity partners	1	0	2	17

Retention & Professional Development

ATTORNEYS WHO LEFT THE FIRM: 2003	MINORITY MEN	MINORITY WOMEN	WHITE WOMEN	TOTAL
Number of attorneys who voluntarily or involuntarily left your firm's employ in 2003	3	1	4	29

How do 2003 attrition rates generally compare to those experienced in the prior year period?

About the same as in prior years

Please identify the specific steps you are taking to reduce the attrition rate of minority and women attorneys.

• Strengthen mentoring program for all attorneys, including minorities and women

• Professional skills development program, including minority and women attorneys

Does your firm have part-time/flex-time policies that permit attorneys (male or female) to work alternative schedules?

Yes

What impact, if any, will the decision to work part-time have on an attorney's ability to make partner or, if already a partner, to remain a partner at your firm?

Case-by-case determination.

Have any attorneys who chose to work a part-time schedule made partner at your firm?

Yes, one attorney.

Management Demographic Profile (as of 12/31/03)

	MINORITY MEN	MINORITY WOMEN	WHITE WOMEN	TOTAL
Number of attorneys on the Executive/Management Committee or equivalent	0	0	1	8
Number of attorneys on the Hiring Committee or equivalent*	2	1	4	12
Number of attorneys on the Partner/Associate Review Committee or equivalent**	1	2	1	15

* L.A. office   ** Two separate committees, combined here.

Please provide information regarding all minority and women attorneys who head offices or practice groups of your law firm:

Women heading offices: M. Elizabeth McDaniel, San Francisco

Shook, Hardy & Bacon LLP

2555 Grand Boulevard
Kansas City, MO 64108
Phone: (816) 474-6550
Fax: (816) 421-5547

FIRM MANAGEMENT

Tina L. Harris, Director of Strategic Diversity Initiatives
Managing Partner: John Murphy, Managing Partner
Diversity Team Leader: Mischa Buford Epps, Partner & Chair, Diversity Committee

LOCATIONS

Kansas City, MO (HQ)
Houston, TX
Irvine, CA
Miami, FL
New Orleans, LA
Overland Park, KS
San Francisco, CA
Tampa, FL
Geneva
London

LAW FIRM DEMOGRAPHIC PROFILES

FULL-TIME ASSOCIATES	2003	2002
Minority men	14	20
Minority women	22	23
White women	88	92
Total	239	252

SUMMER ASSOCIATES	2003	2002
Minority men	3	3
Minority women	4	3
White women	20	22
Total	41	43

EQUITY PARTNERS	2003	2002
Minority men	6	6
Minority women	5	5
White women	35	25
Total	198	190

NON-EQUITY PARTNERS	2003	2002
Minority men	5	5
Minority women	3	1
White women	23	29
Total	66	73

NEW HIRES	2003	2002
Minority men	4	4
Minority women	9	8
White women	23	20
Total	63	74

Strategic Plan and Diversity Leadership

How does the firm's leadership communicate the importance of diversity to everyone at the firm? (e.g., e-mails, web site, newsletters, meetings, etc.)

Diversity is an integral part of the firm's intranet, web site and marketing materials.

Who has primary responsibility for leading diversity initiatives at your firm?

John Murphy, chairman

Does your law firm currently have a diversity committee?

Yes

Does the committee's representation include one or more members of the firm's management/executive committee (or the equivalent)

Yes

How many attorneys are on the committee, and in 2003, what was the total number of hours collectively spent by the committee in furtherance of the firm's diversity initiatives.

Total attorneys on committee: 16

Total hours spent on diversity: 1472.65

Does the committee and/or diversity leader establish and set goals or objectives consistent with management's priorities?

Yes

Has the firm undertaken a formal or informal diversity program or set of initiatives aimed at increasing the diversity of the firm?

Yes, formal

How often does the firm's management review the firm's diversity progress/results?

Annually

How is the firm's diversity committee and/or firm management held accountable for achieving results?

The chair of the Diversity Committee submits an annual report to the firm's Executive Committee. The chair must also obtain budget approval from the Executive Committee.

LAW FIRM DIVERSITY INITIATIVES	ALREADY COMPLETED	CURRENTLY ADDRESSING	NOT A CURRENT PRIORITY
Undertake communication from firm management that diversity is a top priority of the firm.	✓		
Formalize diversity plan and committee with action steps and accountability to management.	✓		
Conduct firm-wide diversity training for all attorneys and staff.		✓	
Increase the number of minority attorneys at the associate level.		✓	
Increase the number of minority attorneys at the partnership level.		✓	
Develop/expand relationships with minority bar associations to offer firm's support of these networks.	✓		
Focus on strengthening firm's mentoring program, including for benefit of minority attorneys.	✓		
Conduct internal diversity needs assessment and/or retain diversity consultant to examine how firm culture might be more welcoming of minorities.		✓	
Support law firm's internal affinity networks (e.g., women, minority attorney networks).			✓
Manage/monitor allocation of work assignments and/or hours billed to ensure women and minority attorneys have equal access/inclusion on top client matters.	✓		

Recruitment – New Associates

Does your firm annually recruit at any of the following types of institutions (Check all that apply and list the schools).

Job fairs: Loyola Patent Law Interview Program, Southeastern Minority Job Fair, DuPont Minority Job Fair, Cook County Minority Job Fair, Louisiana Job Fair, Lavender Law Job Fair

Ivy League schools: Columbia University, Harvard University, University of Pennsylvania, Yale University

Public state schools: University of North Carolina, University of Florida, University of Minnesota, University of Missouri, University of Nebraska, University of Iowa, University of Texas, University of Kansas, Florida State University, Louisiana State University, University of California-Davis, University of California-Berkeley, University of California-Hastings, UCLA, University of Houston, University of Missouri-Kansas City

Private schools: University of Miami, New York University, Duke University, George Washington University, Georgetown University, University of Notre Dame, Tulane University, St. Louis University, Washington University, Emory University, Vanderbilt University, Stetson University, Baylor University, Washburn University, Loyola University-New Orleans, University of San Francisco, South Texas College of Law, University of Southern California

Historically Black Colleges and Universities (HBCUs): Howard University

Do you have any special outreach efforts directed to encourage minority students to consider your firm?

• Participate in/host minority law student job fair(s)
• Sponsor minority law student association events
• Firm's lawyers participate on career panels at school
• Outreach to leadership of minority student organizations
• Scholarships or intern/fellowships for minority students

SUMMER ASSOCIATE STATISTICS: SUMMER 2003	MINORITY MEN	MINORITY WOMEN	WHITE WOMEN	TOTAL
Summer associates	3	4	19	42
Summer associates who received an offer of full-time employment	1	3	13	31*
Summer associates who accepted an offer of full-time employment	1	3	10	25

* Three summer associates deferred offers due to judicial clerkships

Recruitment – Lateral Associates

What activities does the firm undertake to attract minority and women attorneys?

• Participate at minority job fairs
• Seek referrals from other attorneys
• Utilize online job services (e.g., MCCA/DuPont Primary Law Firm Job Bank)

Do you use executive recruiting/search firms to seek to identify new diversity hires (partners or associates)?

No, we have an Executive Recruiter on our staff.

LATERAL ASSOCIATES AND PARTNERS: 1/1/03 – 12/31/03	MINORITY MEN	MINORITY WOMEN	WHITE WOMEN	TOTAL
Number of lateral associate hires	1	4	5	21
Number of lateral partner hires (equity and non-equity)	0	1	0	2
Number of new partners (equity and non-equity) promoted from associate rank	2	1	3	11
Number of new equity partners	1	1	0	8

Retention & Professional Development

ATTORNEYS WHO LEFT THE FIRM: 2003	MINORITY MEN	MINORITY WOMEN	WHITE WOMEN	TOTAL
Number of attorneys who voluntarily or involuntarily left your firm's employ in 2003	9	9	21	76

How do 2003 attrition rates generally compare to those experienced in the prior year period?

Slightly higher than in prior years.

Please identify the specific steps you are taking to reduce the attrition rate of minority and women attorneys.
- Increase/improve current work/life programs
- Introduce minority and women attorneys to key clients, including to lead engagements
- Review work assignments and hours billed to key client matters to make sure minority and women attorneys are not being excluded
- Strengthen mentoring program for all attorneys, including minorities and women
- Professional skills development program, including minorities and women attorneys

Does your firm have part-time/flex-time policies that permit attorneys (male or female) to work alternative schedules?

Yes

Have any attorneys who chose to work a part-time schedule made partner at your firm?

No

Management Demographic Profile (as of 12/31/03)

	MINORITY MEN	MINORITY WOMEN	WHITE WOMEN	TOTAL
Number of attorneys on the Executive/Management Committee or equivalent	0	0	1	9
Number of attorneys on the Hiring Committee or equivalent	1	1	5	16
Number of attorneys on the Partner/Associate Review Committee or equivalent	1	1	8	27

Please provide information regarding all minority and women attorneys who head offices or practice groups of your law firm?

Minorities heading offices: Sandra Phillips, Houston

Women heading offices: Shannon Spangler, San Francisco; Michelle Mangrum, Washington, DC; and Sandra Phillips, Houston

Women heading practice groups: Martha Warren, Product Liability Litigation (Kansas City); Marie Woodbury, Pharmaceutical & Medical Device Litigation Division (Kansas City)

The Firm Says

Shook, Hardy & Bacon LLP (SHB) was honored to receive the Thomas L. Sager Award from the Minority Corporate Counsel Association. We believe that diversity in the workplace is an absolute necessity. SHB recognizes that diversity is not just a committee, program or an annual celebration; SHB's objective is for all of its employees to feel included regardless of gender, race, ethnicity, color, religion, sexual orientation, physical ability, veteran status, marital status, citizenship, national origin, ancestry, life experience, or any protected status under local, state or federal law.

Diversity from a global perspective

SHB embraces diversity as a global issue. To that end, SHB, helped form The London Diversity Working Group at the end of 2001. This group is an initiative of London First, an organization set up to improve and promote London. The Diversity Working Group was established to encourage diversity in the U.K. legal community. The Working Group plans to create a scholarship fund, conduct events for schoolchildren and establish diversity awards for the legal profession.

Innovative diversity initiatives

SHB continues its multifaceted approach to diversity. For example, as part of an SHB year-long Diversity Lecture Series, SHB sponsored a day-long CLE entitled "Women as Advocates." This well-received CLE brought together women from across the nation to discuss the state of women in the legal profession. Other presentations included "Holocaust Remembrance," presented by Holocaust survivors from the Midwest Center for Holocaust Education, "Diversity and the Arts" and "Sexual Orientation in the Workplace." SHB also provided a timely presentation by the Islamic Society shortly after the September 11 attacks. Designed to educate SHB employees on the religion and culture of Islam, the presentation enabled employees to ask questions and deal with feelings and emotions generated after the terrorist attacks.

For the past four years, SHB has incorporated mandatory diversity training as part of a 10-week training program for all new attorneys. Additionally, each summer associate class participates in an interactive presentation with the Diversity Committee and spends one weekend of each summer experiencing Kansas City's rich and diverse heritage. For the past four years, the summer associates have had the honor of hearing a speech from John "Buck" O'Neill, a former Negro Leagues baseball player and legend, at the Negro Leagues Baseball and Kansas City Jazz Museum in the historic 18th and Vine district of Kansas City.

Realizing our potential impact, SHB continues to support diversity in the community at large. The firm supports or partners with Harmony; Project Equality; the local affiliates of the National Bar Association and Hispanic Bar Association; women attorney groups of city, metropolitan and state bar associations; and the Minority Suppliers Council. In addition, SHB Kansas City participates in a metro-wide summer legal intern program (SLIP) that introduces minority high school students to the legal profession. Also, SHB established a charitable foundation which provides scholarships for minority law students.

Recruiting

Every fall, SHB recruits at the following minority job fairs and historically Black colleges and universities: DuPont Minority Job Fair, Southeastern Minority Job Fair, Cook County Minority Job Fair, Sunbelt Minority Job Fair, Midwest Regional BLSA Recruitment Conference, DRI's Minority Job Fair and Howard University.

Moving towards an inclusive work environment

Administratively, SHB has made large strides towards creating an inclusive work environment. For example, it incorporated diversity into its mission statement and strategic plan. With the assistance of the Diversity Committee, the firm audited all of its benefits programs and policies to ensure that we are keeping with our overall diversity goals. For example, domestic partners are now included in policies related to funeral leave, family medical leave and nepotism. Furthermore, the firm instituted a Mentoring Task Force and an Exit Interview Task Force that focuses on attrition and retention rates for women and attorneys of color.

SHB has made a sincere effort to make diversity part of all firm decisions — big and small. For instance, the firm's intranet site includes a Diversity Committee page, a diversity calendar to ensure that programs are not scheduled on any religious holiday, and a reminder of dietary restrictions for religions and cultures. In addition, SHB has taken a great step forward by creating a director of strategic diversity initiatives position. This position allows SHB to provide greater focus on this important area.

SHB and its attorneys have been active in a number of other diversity efforts, including:

• Supporting the efforts of the MCCA and attending each of the Diversity Dinners, including serving as a sponsor of its annual CLE Expo in Chicago;

• Attending national conferences focusing on diversity, including the ABA conference for the Minority Lawyer, National Summit on the Retention of Minority Lawyers in the Private Sector, the National Bar Association Annual Conference, Hispanic National Bar Association Annual Conference and diversity conferences hosted by DuPont;

• Helping found the Emma Bowen Foundation for Minority Interests in Media;

• Acting as a diversity resource to other firms, organizations and clients;

• Spearheading law school and community-wide mentoring programs;

• Diversity training for all on-campus interviewers and members of firm committees; and

• Collaborating with other Kansas City area law firms to develop the Heartland Diversity Legal Job Fair for fall 2005.

• Diversity continues to be a core value of SHB. The firm's commitment to diversity is starting to bear fruit. We continue to take the steps necessary to reach our ultimate goal of creating and maintaining a diverse and inclusive environment that reflects the communities where we work and live.

Sidley Austin Brown & Wood LLP

Bank One Plaza
10 South Dearborn Street
Chicago, IL 60603
Phone: (312) 853-7000
Fax: (312) 853-7036

FIRM LEADERSHIP

Managing Partners: Thomas A. Cole (Chairman of Executive Committee); Charles W. Douglas (Chairman of Management Committee) Theodore N. Miller (Vice Chairman of Management Committee)

Diversity Team Leaders: Stanley B. Stallworth and Carlos A. Rodriguez, Firmwide Co-Chairs, Committee on Racial and Ethnic Diversity; Kathleen Roach and Laurin Blumenthal Kleiman, Firmwide Co-chairs, committee on the Retention and Promotion of Women

LOCATIONS

Chicago, IL
Dallas, TX
Los Angeles, CA
New York, NY
San Francisco, CA
Washington, DC
Beijing
Brussels
Geneva
Hong Kong
London
Shanghai
Singapore
Tokyo

LAW FIRM DEMOGRAPHIC PROFILES

FULL-TIME ASSOCIATES	2003	2002
Minority men	49	50
Minority women	82	67
White women	267	280
Total	766	749

SUMMER ASSOCIATES	2003	2002
Minority men	10	19
Minority women	16	29
White women	39	47
Total	112	168

EQUITY PARTNERS	2003	2002
Minority men	24	20
Minority women	8	7
White women	75	71
Total	513	485

NEW HIRES	2003	2002
Minority men	15	16
Minority women	31	19
White women	49	62
Total	189	208

Strategic Plan and Diversity Leadership

How does the firm's leadership communicate the importance of diversity to everyone at the firm? (e.g., e-mails, web site, newsletters, meetings, etc.)

Targeted presentation at each annual all-partners meeting; periodic presentations at other quarterly partners meetings; periodic reports at associates town hall meetings; targeted presentation at annual new associates orientation; targeted presentation at annual mid-level associates conference; periodic presentations to group heads meetings; inquiry regarding diversity included in annual review of all partners by management; publication of a diversity brochure (every 18 months); inclusion of discussion regarding diversity in most other firm-wide publications (e.g., recruitment brochure).

Who has primary responsibility for leading diversity initiatives at your firm?

Stanley B. Stallworth and Carlos A. Rodriguez, co-chairs of the firmwide Committee on Racial and Ethnic Diversity ("Diversity Committee"); Kathleen Roach and Laurin Blumenthal Kleiman, firm-wide co-chairs of Committee on the Retention and Promotion of Women ("Women's Committee").

Does your law firm currently have a diversity committee?

Yes

Does the committee's representation include one or more members of the firm's management/executive committee (or the equivalent)?

Yes

How many attorneys are on the committee, and in 2003, what was the total number of hours collectively spent by the committee in furtherance of the firm's diversity initiatives?

Total attorneys on committee: 55

Total hours spent on diversity: 7,750

Does the committee and/or diversity leader establish and set goals or objectives consistent with management's priorities?

Yes

Has the firm undertaken a formal or informal diversity program or set of initiatives aimed at increasing the diversity of the firm?

Yes, formal

How often does the firm's management review the firm's diversity progress/results?

Monthly

How is the firm's diversity committee and/or firm management held accountable for achieving results?

Manner of monitoring results: The firm's accounting department generates a diversity report monthly, which contains the raw data about the number of minority attorneys and women and the total number of partners,

associates and counsel in each office. In addition, the Diversity Committee and the Women's Committee regularly request and receive reports about the composition of each class of summer associates and starting associates, by office. The Diversity Committee and the Women's Committee also monitor the performance of associates, by race and by gender, within the classes of associates whose performance has been broken out into group rankings. Much of this information is reported regularly to the Diversity Committee, the Women's Committee and/or to the firm's management.

What metrics are used: We review attrition rates, percentages of minority lawyers and women in each summer class, percentages of minority lawyers and women in each new associates class, qualitative performance data, rates of promotion to partnership, total percentages of minority lawyers and women in the partnership, percentages of committee chair and co-chair positions held by women and minorities, and percentages of the firm's Executive and Management Committees which are women and/or racial minorities.

Manner of holding managers accountable for results: Due to the manner in which we are managed, it is difficult to attribute responsibility or credit for the firm's performance on any one or more of these criteria to any one or more individuals. Our relative success, or lack thereof, is communicated to firm management and is one of the criteria we use to judge our success as a firm from year to year.

LAW FIRM DIVERSITY INITIATIVES	ALREADY COMPLETED	CURRENTLY ADDRESSING	NOT A CURRENT PRIORITY
Undertake communication from firm management that diversity is a top priority of the firm.	✔		
Formalize diversity plan and committee with action steps and accountability to management.	✔		
Conduct firmwide diversity training for all attorneys and staff.		✔*	
Increase the number of minority attorneys at the associate level.	✔		
Increase the number of minority attorneys at the partnership level.		✔	
Develop/expand relationships with minority bar associations to offer firm's support of these networks.	✔		
Focus on strengthening firm's mentoring program, including for benefit of minority attorneys.	✔		
Conduct internal diversity needs assessment and/or retain diversity consultant to examine how firm culture might be more welcoming of minorities.		✔	
Support law firm's internal affinity networks (e.g., women, minority attorney networks).	✔		
Manage/monitor allocation of work assignments and/or hours billed to ensure women and minority attorneys have equal access/inclusion on top client matters.		✔	

* For firm leadership and practice group heads

Recruitment – New Associates

Does your firm annually recruit at any of the following types of institutions? (Check all that apply and list the schools).

Ivy League schools: Columbia University, Cornell University, Harvard University, University of Pennsylvania, Yale University

Public state schools: University of California-Berkeley, University of California-Hastings, University of Illinois, Indiana University, University of Iowa, University of Michigan, University of Minnesota, University of Missouri, UCLA, University of Houston, University of Kentucky, University of Pittsburgh, UNC, University of Texas, University of Washington, University of Virginia, College of William & Mary, University of Wisconsin, University of Toronto (Canada), UBC (Canada)

Private schools: American University, Boston College, Brooklyn Law School, Boston University, Cardozo Law School, University of Chicago, DePaul University, Duke University, Emory University, Fordham University, George Washington University, Georgetown University, John Marshall Law School, Chicago-Kent College of Law, Loyola University-Chicago, Loyola Law School (L.A.), University of Miami, New York Law School, Northwestern University, University of Notre Dame, NYU, Southern Methodist University, Stanford University, St. John's University, St. Louis University, USC, Valparaiso University, Vanderbilt University, Villanova University, Washington University, Washington & Lee University, McGill University (Canada), Osgoode University (Canada)

Historically Black Colleges and Universities (HBCUs): Howard University, Southern University, Texas Southern University

Of the law schools that you listed above, do you have any special outreach efforts directed to encourage minority law students to consider your firm?
• *Make special contacts with law school personnel who have direct contact with minority student groups (e.g., director of minority affairs)*
• Hold a reception for minority law students
• Participate in/host minority law student job fair(s)
• Sponsor minority law student association events
• Firm's lawyers participate on career panels at school
• Outreach to leadership of minority student organizations
• Scholarships or intern/fellowships for minority students

SUMMER ASSOCIATE STATISTICS: SUMMER 2003	MINORITY MEN	MINORITY WOMEN	WHITE WOMEN	TOTAL
Summer associates	10	16	39	112
Summer associates who received an offer of full-time employment	10	15	39	107
Summer associates who accepted an offer of full-time employment	9	8	25	75

Recruitment – Lateral Associates and Partners

What activities does the firm undertake to attract minority and women attorneys?

• *Utilize minority search firms*
• Participate at minority job fairs

Do you use executive recruiting/search firms to seek to identify new diversity hires (partners or associates)?

Yes

If yes, list all women- and/or minority-owned executive search/recruiting firms to which the firm paid a fee for placement services in the past 12 months:

Winston & Green; The Haffner Group, Inc.

LATERAL ASSOCIATES AND PARTNERS: 1/1/03 – 12/31/03	MINORITY MEN	MINORITY WOMEN	WHITE WOMEN	TOTAL
Number of lateral associate hires	3	2	13	38
Number of lateral partner hires (equity and non-equity)	2	1	1	17
Number of new partners (equity and non-equity) promoted from associate rank	4	1	7	26
Number of new equity partners	6	2	8	43

Retention & Professional Development

ATTORNEYS WHO LEFT THE FIRM: 2003	MINORITY MEN	MINORITY WOMEN	WHITE WOMEN	TOTAL
Number of attorneys who voluntarily or involuntarily left your firm's employ in 2003	14	13	74	152

How do 2003 attrition rates generally compare to those experienced in the prior year period?

Higher than in prior years

Please identify the specific steps you are taking to reduce the attrition rate of minority and women attorneys.

• Develop and/or support internal employee affinity groups (e.g., minority or women networks within the firm)
• Increase/improve current work/life programs
• Succession plan includes emphasis on diversity
• Work with minority and women attorneys to develop career advancement plans
• Introduce minority and women attorneys to key clients, including to lead engagements
• Review work assignments and hours billed to key client matters to make sure minority and women attorneys are not being excluded

• Strengthen mentoring program for all attorneys, including minorities and women
• Professional skills development program, including minority and women attorneys

Does your firm have part-time/flex-time policies that permit attorneys (male or female) to work alternative schedules?

Yes. The firm recognizes that one of the biggest challenges for professional women is the challenge of balancing work with the rest of their lives, particularly raising children. Accordingly, the firm has a long history and tradition of supporting part-time work arrangements. A number of our current partners have worked part-time, or reduced hours, for a decade or more. In fact, several of our current partners were promoted to partnership while working reduced hours schedules.

The firm's current reduced hours policy allows attorneys, male and female, partners and associates upon request and on a case by case basis, to work reduced hours. Attorneys working reduced hours are paid proportionately (e.g., 75 percent pay for working 75 percent of the annual billable hours target). Associates who work reduced hours are expected to remain on partnership track and are treated the same as full-time lawyers in terms of evaluations and the types of work assignments available.

The Women's Committee has conducted presentations on part-time or reduced work schedules to demonstrate management support for reduced hours arrangements, explain the reduced hours policy and provide tips for working such a schedule successfully. The Women's Committee has also hosted other presentations relevant to work/life balance issues, including one recently which provided attorneys with information about finding child care (or elder care) and how to pay domestic employment taxes.

What impact, if any, will the decision to work part-time have on an attorney's ability to make partner or, if already a partner, to remain a partner at your firm?

None

Have any attorneys who chose to work a part-time schedule made partner at your firm?

Yes, 12 attorneys. Both male and female associates have made partner while working a percentage of a full-time schedule (part-time).

Management Demographic Profile (as of 12/31/03)

	MINORITY MEN	MINORITY WOMEN	WHITE WOMEN	TOTAL
Number of attorneys on the Executive/Management Committee or equivalent*	1/0	0/0	3/1	41/10
Number of attorneys on the Hiring Committee or equivalent	10	8	41	139
Number of attorneys on the Partner/Associate Review Committee or equivalent	2	0	13	58

Numbers listed as: Management Committee/Executive Committee

Please provide information regarding all minority and women attorneys who head offices or practice groups of your law firm:

Minorities heading practice groups: Deborah Pole, Product Liability; Mass Tort Litigation (Los Angeles) (African American) and Dale Lum, SanFrancisco Securitization (San Francisco)(Asian)

Women heading practice groups: Virginia L. Aronson, Real Estate (National); Maureen Crough, Environmental (New York); Cathy Kaplan, Securitization (New York); Mary Neale, Public Finance (Los Angeles); Deborah Pole, Product Liability and Mass Tort Litigation (Los Angeles) (African American); Judith Praitis, Environmental (Los Angeles) and Eileen Caulfield Schwab, Private Clients Group (New York)

The Firm Says

Firmwide support of diversity

In order to encourage all partners to assist in the creation of a more diverse law firm, each partner is asked during his/her annual partner interview with the Management Committee to report on his/her contributions to the firm's efforts in this area. Diversity receives attention at each annual meeting of partners, ranging from targeted presentations by the firmwide chairs of the Diversity Committee and the Women's Committee to break-out discussion sessions where partners discuss the issues. The firmwide chairs of the Diversity Committee and the Women's Committee make presentations annually at the new associates orientation program and the mid-level associates program. Forty-three percent of the attorneys who were named to the partnership in June 2004 are women and 13.5 percent are racial minorities.

Mentoring

Each domestic office has, or is in process of developing, a mentoring program specifically for its minority associates. Each office has some form of "mentoring circles" where a few minority partners are paired with several minority associates. The circles engage in social activities as well as group discussions about firm matters and practice-related matters.

To assist with monitoring the progress of individual associates, the firmwide co-chairs of the Diversity Committee receive copies of the minority associates' evaluations and discuss the same with the associates to the extent requested or necessary. In addition, to encourage camaraderie among its minority attorneys, the Diversity Committee hosts events specifically for minority attorneys and minority summer associates. Members of the firm's management often attend those events.

Recruitment

Sidley's Recruitment Committee is charged with the mission of aggressively recruiting minority lawyers at law schools where the firm has traditionally recruited. Efforts are made to identify promising law students of color prior to Sidley's on-campus recruiting (such as contacting the director of minority affairs at the law schools). During the call-back interviews, we assure that students are interviewed by a diverse group of lawyers.

Our Outreach Recruitment Program takes us onto law school campuses with high percentages of minority law students. In recent years, we have recruited at Howard University, Southern University, Thurgood Marshall Law School at Texas Southern University, and the University of Miami. With the exception of Howard, all of the foregoing are law schools at which the firm traditionally did not recruit, prior to the inception of the Outreach

Recruitment Program in 2000. Since the program's inception, we have hired eight attorneys from these schools and we currently have eight summer associates from these schools in the 2004 summer program.

Sidley frequently participates in law school minority recruitment conferences, such as the Southeastern Minority Job Fair, the Sunbelt Recruitment Conference, the Cook County Bar Association Recruitment Fair, the Harvard Black Law Students Association's Recruitment Fair and the New York City Minority Recruitment Fair.

When summer associates arrive for their summer internships, the Diversity Committee sponsors an "Off the Record Tips Seminar" that is designed to alert the minority summer associates to common pitfalls that prior summer associates have experienced and offer helpful hints for making the most of the summer experience. Each summer, one or both of the firmwide co-chairs visits each domestic office and hosts both a meeting with all summer associates to discuss the importance of diversity matters to the firm and a social gathering with all minority summer associates and attorneys. This summer, minorities represent approximately 28 percent of the summer associate classes throughout the firm's domestic offices.

Scholarships/intern programs. Each year the firm awards several scholarships to deserving law students. In the name of our deceased partner, Wiley A. Branton, a noted civil rights advocate and former dean at Howard Law School, the firm annually awards a scholarship to the number one ranking law student in the first-year class at Howard. In March 2004, the firm established a chair at Howard to support the law school's lecture series on diversity matters. Sidley also supports programs for undergraduate minority students who are considering careers in law, offering summer interns an opportunity to spend several weeks in Sidley's offices.

Special programs. In recognition of Asian-American Awareness Month (March 2004), the firm sponsored two events in Chicago, a brown-bag luncheon for all firm personnel and a dinner for all minority lawyers at a local Asian restaurant. On May 17, 2004, the firm sponsored a program commemorating the 50th Anniversary of Brown v. Board of Education. The firm's flagship program was held in the Chicago office and each office is hosting an event at some time during this golden anniversary year. The firm awarded eight scholarships to minority law students from Illinois law schools.

Minority and ethnic bar associations and conferences. The firm encourages its minority attorneys to become affiliated with minority and ethnic bar associations. If requested by its minority lawyers, Sidley will pay their dues for membership in one such association. The firm also encourages its lawyers to participate and take leadership roles in national events for minority lawyers. Three of Sidley's minority partners were panelists or featured speakers at each of the MCCA's 2003 and 2004 CLE Conferences in Chicago. Our firmwide Diversity Committee co-chair spoke on two national panels relating to law firm diversity in the last year.

Sidley considers requests, and often funds requests by its minority lawyers, to attend national conferences and seminars, such as the National Conference for the Minority Lawyer, events hosted by the ABA's Commission on Racial and Ethnic Diversity and the national convention of the National Bar Association.

Minority student bar associations. When requested, the firm sponsors events hosted by the minority student bar associations of law schools at which the firm recruits. In addition, the firm's lawyers often participate in such events by speaking at seminars on resume building, interviewing skills and other topics relevant to minority law students.

Simpson Thacher & Bartlett LLP

425 Lexington Avenue
New York, NY 10017
Phone: (212) 455-2000
Fax: (212) 455-2502

FIRM LEADERSHIP

Chairman: Richard I. Beattie, Chairman of the Firm
Chairman: Philip T. Ruegger III, Partner, Chairman of the Executive Committee
Managing Partners: George R. Krouse Jr. and Barry R. Ostrager, Co-Administrative Partners
Diversity Team Leader: David L. Williams, Chairman of the Diversity Committee

LOCATIONS

New York, NY (HQ)
Los Angeles, CA
Palo Alto, CA
Hong Kong
London
Tokyo

LAW FIRM DEMOGRAPHIC PROFILES

FULL-TIME ASSOCIATES	2003	2002
Minority men	48	45
Minority women	71	77
White women	194	197
Total	578	577

SUMMER ASSOCIATES	2003	2002
Minority men	11	11
Minority women	14	12
White women	21	32
Total	65	86

EQUITY PARTNERS	2003	2002
Minority men	2	2
Minority women	1	0
White women	17	16
Total	124	119

NEW HIRES	2003	2002
Minority men	13	8
Minority women	10	21
White women	38	44
Total	106	110

Strategic Plan and Diversity Leadership

How does the firm's leadership communicate the importance of diversity to everyone at the firm? (e.g., e-mails, web site, newsletters, meetings, etc.)

The firm's leadership communicates the importance of diversity through a variety of different means, including updates on activities of the Diversity Committee at monthly partnership meetings, special lunches and other events for interested associates, and a diversity reception for all summer associates and certain associates.

Who has primary responsibility for leading diversity initiatives at your firm?

David L. Williams, partner and chairman of the Diversity Committee

Does your law firm currently have a diversity committee?

Yes

Does the committee's representation include one or more members of the firm's management/executive committee (or the equivalent)?

Yes

How many attorneys are on the committee, and in 2003, what was the total number of hours collectively spent by the committee in furtherance of the firm's diversity initiatives?

Total attorneys on committee: 12

Does the committee and/or diversity leader establish and set goals or objectives consistent with management's priorities?

Yes

Has the firm undertaken a formal or informal diversity program or set of initiatives aimed at increasing the diversity of the firm?

Yes, formal and informal

How often does the firm's management review the firm's diversity progress/results?

Monthly

LAW FIRM DIVERSITY INITIATIVES	ALREADY COMPLETED	CURRENTLY ADDRESSING	NOT A CURRENT PRIORITY
Undertake communication from firm management that diversity is a top priority of the firm.		✓	
Formalize diversity plan and committee with action steps and accountability to management.	✓		
Conduct firmwide diversity training for all attorneys and staff.		✓	
Increase the number of minority attorneys at the associate level.		✓	
Increase the number of minority attorneys at the partnership level.		✓	
Develop/expand relationships with minority bar associations to offer firm's support of these networks.		✓	
Focus on strengthening firm's mentoring program, including for benefit of minority attorneys.		✓	
Conduct internal diversity needs assessment and/or retain diversity consultant to examine how firm culture might be more welcoming of minorities.		✓	
Support law firm's internal affinity networks (e.g., women, minority attorney networks).		✓	
Manage/monitor allocation of work assignments and/or hours billed to ensure women and minority attorneys have equal access/inclusion on top client matters.		✓	

Recruitment – New Associates

Does your firm annually recruit at any of the following types of institutions? (Check all that apply and list the schools).

The student body at some of the law schools where we recruit is over 50 percent women.

Do you have any special outreach efforts directed to encourage minority law students to consider your firm?

- *Participate in SEO Program*
- Hold a reception for minority law students
- Participate in/host minority law student job fair(s)
- Sponsor minority law student association events
- Firm's lawyers participate on career panels at school
- Outreach to leadership of minority student organizations
- Scholarships or intern/fellowships for minority students

SUMMER ASSOCIATE STATISTICS: SUMMER 2003	MINORITY MEN	MINORITY WOMEN	WHITE WOMEN	TOTAL
Summer associates	11	14	21	65
Summer associates who received an offer of full-time employment	11	14	21	65
Summer associates who accepted an offer of full-time employment	6	7	15	43

Recruitment – Lateral Associates and Partners

What activities does the firm undertake to attract minority and women attorneys?
• Partner programs with women and minority bar associations
• Participate at minority job fairs
• Seek referrals from other attorneys

Do you use executive recruiting/search firms to seek to identify new diversity hires (partners or associates)?
No

LATERAL ASSOCIATES AND PARTNERS: 1/1/03 – 12/31/03	MINORITY MEN	MINORITY WOMEN	WHITE WOMEN	TOTAL
Number of lateral associate hires	2	1	6	19
Number of lateral partner hires (equity and non-equity)	0	0	0	0
Number of new partners (equity and non-equity) promoted from associate rank	0	0	2	6
Number of new equity partners	0	0	2	6

Retention & Professional Development

ATTORNEYS WHO LEFT THE FIRM: 2003	MINORITY MEN	MINORITY WOMEN	WHITE WOMEN	TOTAL
Number of attorneys who voluntarily or involuntarily left your firm's employ in 2003	6	16	39	108

How do 2003 attrition rates generally compare to those experienced in the prior year period?
About the same as in prior years   Note that our attrition rates for the past three years were as follows:

2001 — 19 percent
2002 — 17 percent
2003 — 19 percent

Please identify the specific steps you are taking to reduce the attrition rate of minority and women attorneys.

- *The firm's leadership communicates the importance of diversity through a variety of different means including updates on activities of the diversity committee at monthly partnership meetings, special lunches and other events for interested associates, a diversity reception for all summer associates and certain associates, etc.*
- Develop and/or support internal employee affinity groups (e.g., minority or women networks within the firm)
- Increase/improve current work/life programs
- Work with minority and women attorneys to develop career advancement plans
- Review work assignments and hours billed to key client matters to make sure minority and women attorneys are not being excluded
- Strengthen mentoring program for all attorneys, including minorities and women
- Professional skills development program, including minority and women attorneys

Does your firm have part-time/flex-time policies that permit attorneys (male or female) to work alternative schedules?

Yes

What impact, if any, will the decision to work part-time have on an attorney's ability to make partner or, if already a partner, to remain a partner at your firm?

Consideration for partnership for flex-time associates is discussed in the context of annual evaluations just as it is for full-time associates.

Have any attorneys who chose to work a part-time schedule made partner at your firm?

Yes , two attorneys.

Management Demographic Profile (as of 12/31/03)

	MINORITY MEN	MINORITY WOMEN	WHITE WOMEN	TOTAL
Number of attorneys on the Executive/Management Committee or equivalent	0	0	0	9
Number of attorneys on the Hiring Committee or equivalent	1	0	6	24
Number of attorneys on the Partner/Associate Review Committee or equivalent	0	1	5	19

Please provide information regarding all minority and women attorneys who head offices or practice groups of your law firm:

Women heading practice groups: Victoria B. Bjorklund, Exempt Organizations Group; Sarah E. Cogan, Public Registered Funds Practice; Mildred Kalik, Personal Planning Department

The Firm Says

The firm provides billable credit for work related to diversity initiatives. The firm's Diversity Committee meets on a monthly basis and reports periodically to the firm's Executive Committee and to the full partnership.

Skadden, Arps, Slate, Meagher & Flom LLP

4 Times Square
New York, NY 10036
Phone: (212) 735-3000
Fax: (212) 735-2000

FIRM LEADERSHIP

Contact Person: Edwin Bowman, Diversity
Manager
Managing Partner: Robert C. Sheehan,
Executive Partner
Diversity Team Leader: Michael A. Lawson,
Partner

LOCATIONS

New York, NY (HQ)
Boston, MA
Chicago, IL
Houston, TX
Los Angeles, CA
Palo Alto, CA
San Francisco, CA
Washington, DC
Wilmington, DE
Beijing
Brussels
Frankfurt
Hong Kong
London
Moscow
Paris
Singapore
Sydney
Tokyo
Toronto
Vienna

LAW FIRM DEMOGRAPHIC PROFILES

FULL-TIME ASSOCIATES	2003	2002
Minority men	98	104
Minority women	105	112
White women	363	368
Total	1213	1266

SUMMER ASSOCIATES	2003	2002
Minority men	12	19
Minority women	25	19
White women	68	52
Total	187	184

EQUITY PARTNERS	2003	2002
Minority men	10	9
Minority women	5	4
White women	50	48
Total	353	340

NEW HIRES	2003	2002
Minority men	16	24
Minority women	17	14
White women	63	77
Total	186	249

Strategic Plan and Diversity Leadership

How does the firm's leadership communicate the importance of diversity to everyone at the firm? (e.g., e-mails, web site, newsletters, meetings, etc.)

The importance of diversity is communicated through orientation and training of all personnel. A diversity web site is a permanent part of the firm's intranet and is used as a resource for internal and external news about diversity issues, programs and special events.

Who has primary responsibility for leading diversity initiatives at your firm?

Name of person and his/her title: In addition to a diversity committee comprised of partners from each office, the firm has a full-time manager of diversity: Edwin Bowman, diversity manager.

Does your law firm currently have a diversity committee?

Yes

Does the committee's representation include one or more members of the firm's management/executive committee (or the equivalent)?

Yes

How many attorneys are on the committee, and in 2003, what was the total number of hours collectively spent by the committee in furtherance of the firm's diversity initiatives?

Total attorneys on committee: 16

Total hours spent on diversity: Approximately 450 hours on structured events and meetings (Note: does not include full-time diversity manager, recruiting and attorney development administrative time.)

Does the committee and/or diversity leader establish and set goals or objectives consistent with management's priorities?

Yes

Has the firm undertaken a formal or informal diversity program or set of initiatives aimed at increasing the diversity of the firm?

Yes, formal

How often does the firm's management review the firm's diversity progress/results?

Quarterly

How is the firm's diversity committee and/or firm management held accountable for achieving results?

The firm's Diversity Committee periodically reviews progress on achieving its key initiatives by reviewing its overall mission. The diversity manager's goals and objectives, which are linked to the Diversity Committee mission, are evaluated yearly as part of the firm's performance management process.

LAW FIRM DIVERSITY INITIATIVES	ALREADY COMPLETED	CURRENTLY ADDRESSING	NOT A CURRENT PRIORITY
Undertake communication from firm management that diversity is a top priority of the firm.	✔		
Formalize diversity plan and committee with action steps and accountability to management.	✔		
Conduct firmwide diversity training for all attorneys and staff.	✔		
Increase the number of minority attorneys at the associate level.		✔	
Increase the number of minority attorneys at the partnership level.		✔	
Develop/expand relationships with minority bar associations to offer firm's support of these networks.	✔		
Focus on strengthening firm's mentoring program, including for benefit of minority attorneys.	✔		
Conduct internal diversity needs assessment and/or retain diversity consultant to examine how firm culture might be more welcoming of minorities.	✔		
Support law firm's internal affinity networks (e.g., women, minority attorney networks).	✔		
Manage/monitor allocation of work assignments and/or hours billed to ensure women and minority attorneys have equal access/inclusion on top client matters.		✔	

Recruitment – New Associates

Does your firm annually recruit at any of the following types of institutions? (Check all that apply and list the schools).

These are the schools from which we draw the majority of our associates. We recruit at over 70 schools and participate in a multitude of job fairs.

Ivy League schools: Harvard University, Yale University, Columbia University, University of Pennsylvania, Cornell University

Public state schools: Penn State University, Ohio State University, University of Michigan, University of Virginia, University of Texas, UCLA

Private schools: University of Chicago, NYU, Duke University, Georgetown University, Vanderbilt University, Boston College, Fordham University, Stanford University

Historically Black Colleges and Universities (HBCUs): Howard University

Do you have any special outreach efforts directed to encourage minority law students to consider your firm?

• Hold a reception for minority law students
• Participate in/host minority law student job fair(s)

- Sponsor minority law student association events
- Firm's lawyers participate on career panels at school
- Outreach to leadership of minority student organizations
- Scholarships or intern/fellowships for minority students

SUMMER ASSOCIATE STATISTICS: SUMMER 2003	MINORITY MEN	MINORITY WOMEN	WHITE WOMEN	TOTAL
Summer associates	12	25	68	187
Summer associates who received an offer of full-time employment	12	24	66	182
Summer associates who accepted an offer of full-time employment	9	21	54	143

Recruitment – Lateral Associates and Partners

What activities does the firm undertake to attract minority and women attorneys?

- Partner programs with women and minority bar associations
- Participate at minority job fairs
- Seek referrals from other attorneys

Do you use executive recruiting/search firms to seek to identify new diversity hires (partners or associates)?

Yes

If yes, list all women- and/or minority-owned executive search/recruiting firms to which the firm paid a fee for placement services in the past 12 months:

Mestel & Company, Scherzer & Company, Russon & Fondell Search Consultants, Laura Segal & Associates, Elaine P. Dine, Inc., and Levenson Schweitzer, Inc.

LATERAL ASSOCIATES AND PARTNERS: 1/1/03 – 12/31/03	MINORITY MEN	MINORITY WOMEN	WHITE WOMEN	TOTAL
Number of lateral associate hires	2	2	14	29
Number of lateral partner hires (equity and non-equity)	0	0	0	3
Number of new partners (equity and non-equity) promoted from associate rank	1	1	1	14
Number of new equity partners	1	1	1	17

Retention & Professional Development

Please identify the specific steps you are taking to reduce the attrition rate of minority and women attorneys.

• Develop and/or support internal employee affinity groups (e.g., minority or women networks within the firm)
• Increase/improve current work/life programs
• Succession plan includes emphasis on diversity
• Work with minority and women attorneys to develop career advancement plans
• Introduce minority and women attorneys to key clients, including to lead engagements
• Review work assignments and hours billed to key client matters to make sure minority and women attorneys are not being excluded
• Strengthen mentoring program for all attorneys, including minorities and women
• Professional skills development program, including minority and women attorneys

Does your firm have part-time/flex-time policies that permit attorneys (male or female) to work alternative schedules?

Yes

What impact, if any, will the decision to work part-time have on an attorney's ability to make partner or, if already a partner, to remain a partner at your firm?

Part-time associates are eligible for counsel consideration but not partnership. We have accommodated existing partners with part-time schedules.

Have any attorneys who chose to work a part-time schedule made partner at your firm?

Yes, three attorneys.

Management Demographic Profile (as of 12/31/03)

	MINORITY MEN	MINORITY WOMEN	WHITE WOMEN	TOTAL
Number of attorneys on the Executive/Management Committee or equivalent	0	0	3	18
Number of attorneys on the Hiring Committee or equivalent*	2	3	19	72
Number of attorneys on the Partner/Associate Review Committee or equivalent	N/A	N/A	N/A	N/A

Does not include Summer Associate Committee.

Please provide information regarding all minority and women attorneys who head offices or practice groups of your law firm:

Women heading offices: Phyllis G. Korff, Asia Pacific Region

Minorities heading practice groups: Jose R. Allen, San Francisco

Women heading practice groups: Sheila L. Birnbaum, Complex Mass Torts and Insurance Litigation; Dana Freyer, Corporate Compliance; Linda Hayman, UCC; Stacy Kanter, Corporate Finance; Phyllis G. Korff, Asian Practice

The Firm Says

Skadden Arps has a strong commitment to promote diversity at all levels. As a part of this commitment, the firm has established a Diversity Committee. Consistent with Skadden's core value to be an effective and successful meritocracy, the Diversity Committee's mission is to implement proactive policies addressing the issues of recruiting, retaining and promoting qualified attorneys in all practice areas in all offices with the goal to increase the diversity of the firm. In addition, the Diversity Committee monitors existing policies and practices to assure they are consistent with and actively promote the diversity goals of Skadden Arps.

The Diversity Committee is comprised of partners representing all U.S. offices, legal hiring and associate development, and a full-time diversity manager. The Diversity Committee meets regularly to review practices and policies and to monitor progress on strategic initiatives that focus on hiring, promoting, training and retaining women and minority attorneys.

The Diversity Committee, with representation of partners firmwide, has developed strategic plans for implementation of key initiatives in areas of communications, seminars, mentor programs and assignment distribution that support diversity objectives. Each U.S. office has a mentoring program; the assignment process is monitored to assure an equitable distribution of work among all attorneys with a focus on the professional development and the retention of attorneys of color and women. The firm has held seminars on the following topics, among others: Skadden's representation of law students of color in the University of Michigan Law School affirmative action case heard by the U.S. Supreme Court; Project Finance Practice Symposium for South African Visiting Attorneys Program of the Cyrus R. Vance Center for International Initiatives, Association of the Bar of the City of New York; and the Minority Corporate Counsel Association's "Creating Pathways to Diversity" series.

The Diversity Committee has also instituted diversity training to reach all levels of the firm; named a full-time manager of diversity to focus on the development, delivery and implementation of diversity-related procedures, policies and programs consistent with Skadden's mission; and developed a diversity communications link on the firm's intranet to keep employees informed of diversity issues, accomplishments and highlights.

The firm is dedicated to addressing issues of recruitment, promotion and retention as they affect minority and women attorneys as part of the diverse work force. Minority and women attorneys are actively involved with on-campus recruiting, career days and minority law student association activities. Skadden is a supporter of the Sponsors for Employment Opportunities (SEO) Corporate Law Career Program and employs, as summer interns, minority college graduates who will be entering law school. Diversity recruitment teams meet with women and minority law school student association members in organizations such as the Black Law Student Association (BLSA), Latin American Law Student Association (LALSA) and the Asian Pacific American Law

Student Association (APALSA) to share information about the firm and to talk about making the transition from law school to a law firm. Women partners meet with women summer associates to discuss topics such as their experiences developing a successful legal career, balancing work and family, and professional development strategies. Skadden Arps holds receptions, social and cultural events for first-year law students of color to provide networking opportunities for the students with Skadden associates and partners.

Diversity training is an ongoing process at Skadden Arps. We regularly conduct diversity awareness and skills building sessions for summer associates, associates and partners in all offices throughout the firm. Examples of such sessions are as follows:

All summer associates go through a two-hour diversity training session that informs them of the firm's policies and practices, demonstrates through interactive break-out sessions the broad range of diversity, and demonstrates how to manage individual tolerance levels for various diverse characteristics.

New incoming associates attend a 90-minute diversity training session that describes the various dimensions of diversity and assesses the impact of the various dimensions of diversity on the firm.

Skadden hired a top-tier diversity consultant to help develop a training session for partners that focused on giving effective performance feedback and evaluations in a diverse work force. These sessions concentrate on the impact of diversity-related variables on performance appraisals, strategies for performance evaluation success, identification of performance issues and situations, and common performance review pitfalls.

Skadden Arps actively supports the involvement of minority and women attorneys in community-based and bar association activities. As previously mentioned, minority and women attorneys participate in a full range of recruitment activities, lead sessions in mentoring and career education programs, and serve on numerous committees and boards of organizations that focus on minority and women attorneys in the profession. Skadden attorneys have participated in numerous diversity activities in organizations such as:

- Minority Corporate Counsel Association
- Committee to Enhance Diversity in the Profession, Association of the Bar of the City of New York
- Lawyers' Committee for Civil Rights Under the Law
- American Bar Association Council on Racial and Ethnic Justice
- Los Angeles Managing Partners Roundtable
- The Boston Lawyers Group
- Chicago Committee on Minorities in Large Law Firms

Skadden supports the diversity initiatives of various bar associations and takes leadership roles with associations such as the Women's Bar Association, Metropolitan Black Bar Association, National South Asian Bar association, Hispanic National Bar Association, and the Lesbian and Gay Lawyers Association of Los Angeles. Skadden Arps is a signatory to the Statement of Diversity Principles of both the Association of the Bar of the City of New York and the New York County Lawyers Association.

Snell & Wilmer L.L.P.

One Arizona Center
Phoenix, AZ 85004-2202
Phone: (602) 382-6000
Fax: (602) 382-6070

FIRM LEADERSHIP

Managing Partner: John Bouma, Chairman of
the Executive Committee
Diversity Team Leader: Barb Dawson, Partner

LOCATIONS

Phoenix, AZ (HQ)
Tucson, AZ
Irvine, CA
Salt Lake City, UT
Denver, CO
Las Vegas, NV

LAW FIRM DEMOGRAPHIC PROFILES

FULL-TIME ASSOCIATES	2003	2002
Minority men	14	10
Minority women	13	15
White women	68	62
Total	210	198

SUMMER ASSOCIATES	2003	2002
Minority men	1	1
Minority women	1	2
White women	13	13
Total	32	28

PARTNERS*	2003	2002
Minority men	3	3
Minority women	3	2
White women	23	23
Total	151	143

** The firm does not disclose equity vs. non-equity partner
numbers.*

NEW HIRES	2003	2002
Minority men	8	0
Minority women	2	5
White women	15	13
Total	63	52

Strategic Plan and Diversity Leadership

How does the firm's leadership communicate the importance of diversity to everyone at the firm? (e.g., e-mails, web site, newsletters, meetings, etc.)

The firm communicates through its internal newsletter, associate roundtables, attorney retreats (held twice annually) and internal web site.

Who has primary responsibility for leading diversity initiatives at your firm?

Barb Dawson, partner

Does your law firm currently have a diversity committee?

Yes

Does the committee's representation include one or more members of the firm's management/executive committee (or the equivalent)?

No

How many attorneys are on the committee, and in 2003, what was the total number of hours collectively spent by the committee in furtherance of the firm's diversity initiatives?

Total attorneys on committee: 22

Total hours spent on diversity: Unknown. Under the auspices of the firm's Attorney Development Committee (ADC) and as part of our firm culture, thousands of hours have been spent on issues relating to associate welfare, including mentoring and training. The ADC has a specific subgroup focusing solely on diversity outreach. However, as the firm has not established a separate billing number for the Diversity Outreach Group, the specific amount of time spent on diversity issues is not known.

Does the committee and/or diversity leader establish and set goals or objectives consistent with management's priorities?

Partially. The committee and management work together to set priorities and goals.

Has the firm undertaken a formal or informal diversity program or set of initiatives aimed at increasing the diversity of the firm?

Yes, informal

How often does the firm's management review the firm's diversity progress/results?

Quarterly at a minimum

How is the firm's diversity committee and/or firm management held accountable for achieving results?

The firm's Executive Committee receives reports recounting, and evaluates the results of, Hiring Committee and Attorney Development Committee efforts. Typically, those reports are submitted and evaluated on a quarterly basis.

LAW FIRM DIVERSITY INITIATIVES	ALREADY COMPLETED	CURRENTLY ADDRESSING	NOT A CURRENT PRIORITY
Undertake communication from firm management that diversity is a top priority of the firm.		✔	
Formalize diversity plan and committee with action steps and accountability to management.	✔ *		
Conduct firmwide diversity training for all attorneys and staff.			✔ **
Increase the number of minority attorneys at the associate level.		✔	
Increase the number of minority attorneys at the partnership level.		✔	
Develop/expand relationships with minority bar associations to offer firm's support of these networks.		✔	
Focus on strengthening firm's mentoring program, including for benefit of minority attorneys.	✔ *		
Conduct internal diversity needs assessment and/or retain diversity consultant to examine how firm culture might be more welcoming of minorities.		✔	
Support law firm's internal affinity networks (e.g., women, minority attorney networks).		✔	
Manage/monitor allocation of work assignments and/or hours billed to ensure women and minority attorneys have equal access/inclusion on top client matters.		✔	
The firm has a strong culture of community service, including outreach to civic organizations and minority business organizations, pro bono work, and other efforts that benefit diverse groups and enhance relationships between members of the firm and those groups.		✔	

* The firm is reviewing and attempting to improve on an ongoing basis
** The firm is currently addressing as to partners only.

Recruitment – New Associates

Does your firm annually recruit at any of the following types of institutions? (Check all that apply and list the schools).

Job fairs: Loyola IP Job Fair, SFIPLA (San Francisco IP Job Fair), RMDJF (Rocky Mountain Diversity Job Fair)*

Public state schools: University of California-Los Angeles, University of California-Hastings, University of Arizona, Arizona State University, University of Iowa, University of Nevada-Las Vegas, University of Utah, University of Colorado, University of Kansas, University of Virginia

Private schools: University of Notre Dame, Georgetown University, Brigham Young University, University of San Diego, University of Denver, Vanderbilt University, Duke University*

*The firm sends recruiting letters to the vast majority of law schools, but can only conduct on-campus interviews at some of them. The schools listed above are those visited in 2003.

Do you have any special outreach efforts directed to encourage minority law students to consider your firm?

Meeting with administrators and professors at various law schools to discuss additional outreach opportunities

- Participate in/host minority law student job fair(s)
- Firm's lawyers participate on career panels at school
- Outreach to leadership of minority student organizations
- Scholarships or intern/fellowships for minority students

SUMMER ASSOCIATE STATISTICS: SUMMER 2003	MINORITY MEN	MINORITY WOMEN	WHITE WOMEN	TOTAL
Summer associates	1	1	13	32
Summer associates who received an offer of full-time employment	1	1	12	26
Summer associates who accepted an offer of full-time employment	1	1	9	22

Recruitment – Lateral Associates and Partners

What activities does the firm undertake to attract minority and women attorneys?
- Partner programs with women and minority bar associations
- Participate at minority job fairs
- Seek referrals from other attorneys

Do you use executive recruiting/search firms to seek to identify new diversity hires (partners or associates)?

No

If yes, list all women- and/or minority-owned executive search/recruiting firms to which the firm paid a fee for placement services in the past 12 months:
- Hawkins & Associates

Retention & Professional Development

How do 2003 attrition rates generally compare to those experienced in the prior year period?
About the same as in prior years

Please identify the specific steps you are taking to reduce the attrition rate of minority and women attorneys.
- Develop and/or support internal employee affinity groups (e.g., minority or women networks within the firm)
- Increase/review compensation relative to competition*
- Increase/improve current work/life programs*
- Adopt dispute resolution process*
- Work with minority and women attorneys to develop career advancement plans

- Introduce minority and women attorneys to key clients, including to lead engagements
- Review work assignments and hours billed to key client matters to make sure minority and women attorneys are not being excluded
- Strengthen mentoring program for all attorneys, including minorities and women
- Professional skills development program, including minority and women attorneys

The firm takes these steps for all attorneys, not just for minorities and women.

Does your firm have part-time/flex-time policies that permit attorneys (male or female) to work alternative schedules?

Yes

What impact, if any, will the decision to work part-time have on an attorney's ability to make partner or, if already a partner, to remain a partner at your firm?

The decision to work part-time may increase the length of time it takes to make partner.

Have any attorneys who chose to work a part-time schedule made partner at your firm?

Yes, one attorney.

LATERAL ASSOCIATES AND PARTNERS: 1/1/03 – 12/31/03	MINORITY MEN	MINORITY WOMEN	WHITE WOMEN	TOTAL
Number of lateral associate hires	7	3	5	38
Number of lateral partner hires (equity and non-equity)	0	0	1	3
Number of new partners (equity and non-equity) promoted from associate rank	1	1	1	12
Number of new equity partners	N/A*	N/A*	N/A*	N/A*

* The firm does not disclose this information

Retention & Professional Development

ATTORNEYS WHO LEFT THE FIRM: 2003	MINORITY MEN	MINORITY WOMEN	WHITE WOMEN	TOTAL
Number of attorneys who voluntarily or involuntarily left your firm's employ in 2003	3	4	9	40

Management Demographic Profile (as of 12/31/03)

	MINORITY MEN	MINORITY WOMEN	WHITE WOMEN	TOTAL
Number of attorneys on the Executive/Management Committee or equivalent	0	0	0	5
Number of attorneys on the Hiring Committee or equivalent	0	4	12	42
Number of attorneys on the Partner/Associate Review Committee or equivalent*	1	4	9	28

* The firm's equivalent of a "Partner/Associate Review Committe" is its Attorney Development Committe, which is composed of partner and associates from all its offices.

Women heading practice groups: Jody Pokorski, Real Estate; Becky Winterscheidt, Labor & Employment; Nanette Sanders, Bankruptcy

The Firm Says

Snell & Wilmer has a long history of support for minority and women attorneys, as well as a strong culture of commitment to the communities in which its attorneys live and work. The firm was one of the first businesses in Arizona to celebrate Martin Luther King Jr.'s birthday. It also offered strong support for, and helped secure, formal recognition of Dr. King's birthday as a holiday in Arizona when many opposed it. The firm also has been a community leader in hiring minorities and women and electing them into the partnership.

The firm's attorneys have also invested thousands of hours over the years in work with civic organizations devoted to the interests of minorities and women, including minority legal writing programs and minority bar organizations; in pro bono legal work; and in other efforts designed to provide assistance and promote fairness to those in need of such efforts. The firm also has long recognized that its ability to provide superior legal services to its clients arises, in part, from the synergy created by diverse attorneys with diverse backgrounds and outlooks.

In short, the firm has always been committed to diversity. Recently, in efforts to promote diversity, the firm has taken more formal measures. In late 2003, the ABA's Tort Trial and Insurance Practice Section launched its "Ending Lip Service to Diversity" program, a public national forum for law firms to commit to increasing diversity in the profession. Signatories to this program make a commitment to increase the number of women and minorities in the firm to a certain percentage by the year 2008, as well as work to increase diversity awareness. In January, S&W became a signatory to this program. The firm's percentage of women and minorities already exceeds the goal that signatory firms are asked to achieve by 2008.

With substantial input from its Attorney Development Committee, the firm also recently adopted a formal diversity policy (see below). The firm also formed a Diversity Outreach Group of partners and associates interested in and committed to diversity efforts. The firm also plans to focus some of its next partner retreat, to be held in the fall of 2004, on diversity issues. As the firm's attorneys will attest, it is an exciting time to be working on diversity issues at Snell & Wilmer!

Diversity Policy

Snell & Wilmer has a deep and longstanding commitment to developing, maintaining and fostering an inclusive and accepting environment rich in diversity. By hiring and retaining a diverse group of attorneys whose collective talents and creativity are drawn from a broad cross-section of backgrounds and outlooks, we enhance our ability to offer superior legal services to our clients.

To enhance our efforts, Snell & Wilmer's Attorney Development and Hiring Committees and the Diversity Outreach Group will ensure that the firm continues to value and promote diversity through focused hiring, development and community efforts.

Sonnenschein Nath & Rosenthal LLP

8000 Sears Tower
344 South Wacker Drive
Chicago, IL 60606
Phone: (312) 876-8000
Fax: (312) 876-7934

FIRM LEADERSHIP

Helise Harrington, Diversity Manager
Managing Partner: Duane C. Quaini, Chairman
Diversity Team Leader: Kevin P. Chavous,
Partner

LOCATIONS

Chicago, IL (HQ)
Kansas City, MO
Los Angeles, CA
New York, NY
San Francisco, CA
Short Hills, NJ
St. Louis, MO
Washington, DC
West Palm Beach, FL

LAW FIRM DEMOGRAPHIC PROFILES

FULL-TIME ASSOCIATES	2003	2002
Minority men	30	22
Minority women	37	24
White women	124	100
Total*	363	341

SUMMER ASSOCIATES	2003	2002
Minority men	4	2
Minority women	10	4
White women	15	8
Total	37	21

EQUITY PARTNERS	2003	2002
Minority men	4	2
Minority women	2	2
White women	24	22
Total	153	143

NON-EQUITY PARTNERS	2003	2002
Minority men	2	2
Minority women	2	1
White women	44	32
Total	143	128

NEW HIRES	2003	2002
Minority men	14	181*
Minority women	26	10
White women	52	51
Total	169	188

* Includes number of counsel associates

Strategic Plan and Diversity Leadership

How does the firm's leadership communicate the importance of diversity to everyone at the firm? (e.g., e-mails, web site, newsletters, meetings etc.)

Regular meetings of and communications by firm-wide Diversity Committee and local Diversity Committees; the firm web site; e-mails, diversity newsletter. In addition, diversity is included as a central topic in every firm-wide practice retreat and firm-wide partner and associate meeting.

Who has primary responsibility for leading diversity initiatives at your firm?

Helise Harrington, diversity manager and counsel

Does your law firm currently have a diversity committee?

Yes. A firm-wide Diversity Committee (as well as local committees in seven offices).

Does the committee's representation include one or more members of the firm's management/executive committee (or the equivalent)?

Yes

How many attorneys are on the committee, and in 2003, what was the total number of hours collectively spent by the committee in furtherance of the firm's diversity initiatives?

Total attorneys on committee: 13

Total hours spent on diversity: 1,572

Does the committee and/or diversity leader establish and set goals or objectives consistent with management's priorities?

Yes

Has the firm undertaken a formal or informal diversity program or set of initiatives aimed at increasing the diversity of the firm?

Yes, formal

How often does the firm's management review the firm's diversity progress/results?

Annually and ongoing (see answer below)

How is the firm's diversity committee and/or firm management held accountable for achieving results?

Each member of Sonnenschein's management, as well as every other partner in the firm, reports annually to the chairman of the firm and the firm-wide Diversity Committee on what his/her contribution to the Diversity Initiative has been during the previous year and what his/her proposed contribution for the upcoming year will be. In addition, each head of office reports annually to the diversity manager on the measures that have been taken to ensure that each minority associate within that office has received his/her share of "choice" assignments, appropriate training and exposure to skills building and business opportunities. The diversity manager also regularly reviews department assignments and if she determines that a particular associate has not receive an

equitable share of favorable assignments, the diversity manager coordinates with the head of office, the practice group head and the Legal Development Committee to ascertain how the assignments should be reallocated.

LAW FIRM DIVERSITY INITIATIVES	ALREADY COMPLETED	CURRENTLY ADDRESSING	NOT A CURRENT PRIORITY
Undertake communication from firm management that diversity is a top priority of the firm.		✓	
Formalize diversity plan and committee with action steps and accountability to management.	✓		
Conduct firm-wide diversity training for all attorneys and staff.		✓	
Increase the number of minority attorneys at the associate level.		✓	
Increase the number of minority attorneys at the partnership level.		✓	
Develop/expand relationships with minority bar associations to offer firm's support of these networks.		✓	
Focus on strengthening firm's mentoring program, including for benefit of minority attorneys.		✓	
Conduct internal diversity needs assessment and/or retain diversity consultant to examine how firm culture might be more welcoming of minorities.		✓	
Support law firm's internal affinity networks (e.g., women, minority attorney networks).	✓		
Manage/monitor allocation of work assignments and/or hours billed to ensure women and minority attorneys have equal access/inclusion on top client matters.		✓	

Sonnenschein Nath & Rosenthal LLP other goals in the area of diversity

• Each office has evaluated its hiring processes and is currently modifying practices that inhibit diverse recruitment.

• The recruiting committee at each office includes attorneys of diverse backgrounds and at least one member of that office's diversity committee. On-campus recruiters include attorneys of diverse backgrounds.

• Each office actively participates in seminars and related events sponsored by student organizations comprised of minority and women law students, in diversity job fairs and in minority and other diversity-oriented career days at law schools or other organizations within the legal community.

Recruitment – New Associates

Does your firm annually recruit at any of the following types of institutions? (Check all that apply and list the schools).

Ivy League schools: Columbia University, Cornell University, Harvard University, University of Pennsylvania, Yale University

Public state schools: University of Southern Illinois, University of California-Berkeley-Boalt Hall, University of California-Davis, University of California-Hastings, University of Illinois, University of Missouri at Columbia, University of Missouri at Kansas City, University of Kansas, Rutgers University, University of Michigan-Ann Arbor, University of Virginia

Private schools: American University, Boston College, Boston University, Brooklyn Law School, Cardozo School of Law, University of Chicago, DePaul University, Duke University, Fordham University, George Washington University, Georgetown University, John Marshall Law School, Kent School of Law, New York University, Stanford University, Washington University, Northwestern University

Historically Black Colleges and Universities (HBCUs): Howard University

Do you have any special outreach efforts directed to encourage minority law students to consider your firm?

• *Meet with law school deans and admission personnel; mentor first-year law students*
• Hold a reception for minority law students
• Advertise in minority law student association publication(s)
• Participate in/host minority law student job fair(s)
• Sponsor minority law student association events
• Firm's lawyers participate on career panels at school
• Outreach to leadership of minority student organizations
• Scholarships or intern/fellowships for minority students

SUMMER ASSOCIATE STATISTICS: SUMMER 2003	MINORITY MEN	MINORITY WOMEN	WHITE WOMEN	TOTAL
Summer associates	4	10	15	37
Summer associates who received an offer of full-time employment	4	10	14	36
Summer associates who accepted an offer of full-time employment	4	10	13	33

Recruitment – Lateral Associates and Partners

What activities does the firm undertake to attract minority and women attorneys?

• Partner programs with women and minority bar associations
• Participate at minority job fairs
• Seek referrals from other attorneys

Do you use executive recruiting/search firms to seek to identify new diversity hires (partners or associates)?

Yes

List all women- and/or minority-owned executive search/recruiting firms to which the firm paid a fee for placement services in the past 12 months:

- Carter-White & Shaw
- Retention & Professional Development

LATERAL ASSOCIATES AND PARTNERS: 1/1/03 – 12/31/03	MINORITY MEN	MINORITY WOMEN	WHITE WOMEN	TOTAL
Number of lateral associate hires	5	6	19	45
Number of lateral partner hires (equity and non-equity)	2	1	7	31
Number of new partners (equity and non-equity) promoted from associate rank	0	1	6	15
Number of new equity partners	1	0	2	15

Retention & Professional Development

ATTORNEYS WHO LEFT THE FIRM: 2003	MINORITY MEN	MINORITY WOMEN	WHITE WOMEN	TOTAL
Number of attorneys who voluntarily or involuntarily left your firm's employ in 2003	6	5	25	70

How do 2003 attrition rates generally compare to those experienced in the prior year period?

About the same as in prior years

Please identify the specific steps you are taking to reduce the attrition rate of minority and women attorneys.

- *The diversity manager serves as the firm's ombudsman for fielding issues and concerns that minority and women attorneys wish to discuss and have addressed confidentially. In this capacity, the diversity manager has the discretion (with the permission of the reporting attorney) to speak directly with any member of the firm to redress and remedy those concerns as appropriate. Also, at any point at which it is evident that a minority or women attorney is encountering obstacles to his/her attaining an expected level of performance as an attorney with the firm, the diversity manager is consulted on corrective actions or other appropriate measures. The diversity manager also interviews each minority attorney who resigns from the firm to determine the quality of that person's experience in the firm during his or her period of employment. All members of the Policy and Planning Committee and the Legal Development Committee, as well as the national and office practice group heads, have participated in a full day of diversity training. All other attorneys will participate in diversity training workshops prior to the end of 2004.*
- Develop and/or support internal employee affinity groups (e.g., minority or women networks within the firm)
- Adopt dispute resolution process (see narrative section below)
- Succession plan includes emphasis on diversity
- Work with minority and women attorneys to develop career advancement plans
- Introduce minority and women attorneys to key clients, including to lead engagements

- Review work assignments and hours billed to key client matters to make sure minority and women attorneys are not being excluded
- Strengthen mentoring program for all attorneys, including minorities and women
- Professional skills development program, including minority and women attorneys

Does your firm have part-time/flex-time policies that permit attorneys (male or female) to work alternative schedules?

Yes. Going back to at least 1983, lawyers have worked part-time and become partners at Sonnenschein. The firm has also had partners decide to commence part-time schedules.

What impact, if any, will the decision to work part-time have on an attorney's ability to make partner or, if already a partner, to remain a partner at your firm?

In the case of associates, the fact that an associate commences a part-time schedule may, but does not necessarily, lengthen the partnership path. This is handled on a case-by-case basis. The only impact on a partner may be an adjustment of his/her compensation to reflect a reduced workload.

Have any attorneys who chose to work a part-time schedule made partner at your firm?

Yes, at least six attorneys. Since 1994, six associates who worked part-time have become partners at Sonnenschein. Other associates before that time became partners but the exact number before that year is not readily available. In addition, a significant number of attorneys have started working part-time after they become partners.

Management Demographic Profile (as of 12/31/03)

	MINORITY MEN	MINORITY WOMEN	WHITE WOMEN	TOTAL
Number of attorneys on the Executive/Management Committee or equivalent	1	0	1	13
Number of attorneys on the Hiring Committee or equivalent*	8	8	18	63
Number of attorneys on the Partner/Associate Review Committee or equivalent	0	0	3	11

* Seven office Hiring Committes

Please provide information regarding all minority and women attorneys who head offices or practice groups of your law firm:

Minorities heading offices: Robert J. Scoular, Los Angeles

Women heading offices: Pamela Baker, Co-head, Chicago

Minorities heading practice groups (list names and departments): Singleton McAllister, Chair of the Corporate Diversity Counseling Group; Jacqueline Vidmar, Vice Chair of the Environmental Group

Women heading practice groups (list names and departments): Carol Ann Been, Co-Vice Chair, IP&T; Jana Cohen Blackman, Chair, Real Estate; Jacqueline Vidmar, Vice Chair, Environmental; Pamela Baker, Vice Chair, Employee Benefits; Singleton McAllister, Chair, Diversity Corporate Counseling; Linda White, Chair, Telecommunications SBU; Donna Vobornik, Vice Chair, Insurance

The Firm Says

Diversity at Sonnenschein means inclusion, at all levels of seniority, of attorneys of different races, genders, sexual orientations, ethnic backgrounds and abilities/disabilities. The firm's goal is that the demographics of each office reflect the community in which the office is located.

The data provided for this survey shows that 2003 was a successful year firm-wide in recruiting minority and women attorneys. However, the data for 2004 is even more compelling. During the first five months of 2004 Sonnenschein hired four African Americans as partners/of counsel, six Asian-American associates and one Hispanic associate. The firm also promoted three African Americans to partner and promoted one Hispanic attorney to partner. During the same period, the firm hired five women partners/of counsel and 13 women associates and promoted seven women to partner/of counsel.

Sonnenschein's commitment to diversity includes retaining and promoting women and minority attorneys to partnership and leadership positions. An increasing number of women and minority attorneys are being appointed to key management positions within the firm. Nine minority attorneys and 25 women attorneys sit on firm-wide committees, and one minority attorney and one woman attorney chair a firm-wide committee. One of nine heads of office is a minority and one is a woman. Of the firm's nationwide practice groups, one chair and one vice chair are minorities and three chairs and five vice chairs are women.

Perhaps more importantly, we have formalized and rationalized our diversity initiatives, which we believe will result in Sonnenschein's achieving and maintaining a truly meaningful level of diversity. During 2003, the firm-wide Diversity Committee drafted, and in early 2004, the firm adopted, a firm-wide Diversity Plan. The plan advances an aggressive, but realistic, set of initiatives to ensure that meaningful diversity is achieved and maintained throughout the firm. It sets forth time-limited, measurable goals in the areas of recruitment, retention, promotion and leadership and provides for individual partner accountability in achieving these goals. The firm-wide Diversity Committee, a standing committee of which the chairman of the firm is a member, is overseeing the plan's implementation. In addition, the firm has hired a full-time diversity manager, who reports directly to the committee and the chairman, who has the responsibility of monitoring adherence to the plan in all of the firm's offices. Each office also has a local diversity committee, which coordinates local initiatives with those of the firm-wide committee.

To highlight only a few aspects of Sonnenschein's Diversity Plan:

- The firm has adopted targets for each of its offices to attain by the end of 2004, 2005 and 2006, both for an increased percentage of women and minority attorneys and for an increased percentage of women and minority partners.

- All attorneys in positions of leadership have participated in a full day of diversity training in 2004 and all other attorneys will participate in diversity training workshops by the end of the year.

- Each practice group is developing an objective set of skill benchmarks for associates in that group.

- The firm has committed that by no later than December 31, 2005, each firm-wide committee will include at least two diverse members and each of the firm's practice groups will include at least one diverse attorney in a management position.

- In addition to attending minority job fairs and participating in functions of various minority law student organizations, Sonnenschein sponsors programs on law school campuses and in partnership with professional

and civic organizations such as the Minority Corporate Counsel Association. We are a founding member of the Chicago Committee on Minorities in Large Law Firms and signatories of the Diversity Principles of the Association of the Bar of the City of New York and the Kansas City Metropolitan Bar Association. We hold annual receptions in New York, St. Louis, Washington, D.C., and Kansas City for minority 1L students from local law schools and a year-end reception in Chicago sponsored by the Committee for Minority Law Students. The St. Louis and New York offices participate in minority summer clerkship programs. The St Louis office is also participating in an ongoing study sponsored by Washington University Law School on the recruitment and retention of African American attorneys in St. Louis.

• The firm sponsors a Women's Business Development Group, the members of which are the firm's women partners and of counsel. The group's activities further the firm's goal of advancing and enhancing the careers and personal lives of women attorneys within the firm. The group hosts a firm-wide retreat for women partners and of counsel devoted to the topics of career enhancement, business development and networking; sponsors activities of women's groups such as the NOW Legal Defense and Education Fund; and holds social events of interest to Sonnenschein women attorneys and their clients.

• We have also partnered with Pugh, Jones Johnson & Quandi, P.C., a highly respected Chicago-based minority-owned firmThe purpose of the alliance to meet the demands of our multicultural American marketplace; to apply the inherent value and creativity of interpersonal diversity in solving legal problems for our clients; to achieve and sustain an inclusive work force of the best and brightest lawyers and staff; and to exemplify leadership in our community and our profession.

• Sonnenschein is also concerned with being a good corporate citizen and in making positive contributions to underrepresented communities. Among the minority public interest organizations to which Sonnenschein provides pro bono services and/or financial support are Center on Wrongful Conviction; Chicago Coalition for the Homeless; Chicago Lawyers' Committee for Civil Rights Under Law; Chicago Volunteer Legal Services; Heartland Alliance; inMotion; Lambda Legal; Lawyers Alliance for New York; Legal Aid Bureau; Legal Assistance Foundation; Midwest Immigrant and Human Rights Center; National Center on Poverty Law; National Immigration Law Center; Welfare Law Center; Western Center on Law and Poverty; and Women's Law & Public Policy.

Steptoe & Johnson LLP

1330 Connecticut Avenue, NW
Washington, DC 20036
Phone: (202) 429-3000
Fax: (202) 429-3902

FIRM LEADERSHIP

Managing Partner: Roger Warin, Partner
Diversity Team Leader: John Nolan, Partner

LOCATIONS

Washington, DC (HQ)
Los Angeles, CA
Phoenix, AZ
Brussels
London

LAW FIRM DEMOGRAPHIC PROFILES

FULL-TIME ASSOCIATES	2003	2002
Minority men	9	11
Minority women	13	10
White women	51	57
Total	156	164

SUMMER ASSOCIATES	2003	2002
Minority men	2	4
Minority women	5	2
White women	17	15
Total	34	34

EQUITY PARTNERS	2003	2002
Minority men	3	3
Minority women	2	2
White women	22	23
Total	117	117

NEW HIRES	2003	2002
Minority men	1	0
Minority women	4	3
White women	12	16
Total	17	19

Strategic Plan and Diversity Leadership

How does the firm's leadership communicate the importance of diversity to everyone at the firm? (e.g., e-mails, web site, newsletters, meetings, etc.)

Annual addresses from firm management; participation in minority bar events; support of community service programs.

Who has primary responsibility for leading diversity initiatives at your firm?

John Nolan, partner

Does your law firm currently have a diversity committee?

Yes

Does the committee's representation include one or more members of the firm's management/executive committee (or the equivalent)?

Yes

How many attorneys are on the committee, and in 2003, what was the total number of hours collectively spent by the committee in furtherance of the firm's diversity initiatives?

Total attorneys on committee: 8

Total hours spent on diversity: Not tracked

Does the committee and/or diversity leader establish and set goals or objectives consistent with management's priorities?

Yes

Has the firm undertaken a formal or informal diversity program or set of initiatives aimed at increasing the diversity of the firm?

Yes, formal

How often does the firm's management review the firm's diversity progress/results?

Annually

How is the firm's diversity committee and/or firm management held accountable for achieving results?

The Diversity Committee formally reports to firm management annually. Discussion of committee efforts are ongoing throughout the year.

LAW FIRM DIVERSITY INITIATIVES	ALREADY COMPLETED	CURRENTLY ADDRESSING	NOT A CURRENT PRIORITY
Undertake communication from firm management that diversity is a top priority of the firm.	✔		
Formalize diversity plan and committee with action steps and accountability to management.	✔		
Conduct firm-wide diversity training for all attorneys and staff.		✔	
Increase the number of minority attorneys at the associate level.		✔	
Increase the number of minority attorneys at the partnership level.		✔	
Develop/expand relationships with minority bar associations to offer firm's support of these networks.		✔	
Focus on strengthening firm's mentoring program, including for benefit of minority attorneys.	✔		
Conduct internal diversity needs assessment and/or retain diversity consultant to examine how firm culture might be more welcoming of minorities.		✔	
Support law firm's internal affinity networks (e.g., women, minority attorney networks).	✔		
Manage/monitor allocation of work assignments and/or hours billed to ensure women and minority attorneys have equal access/inclusion on top client matters.	✔		

Recruitment – New Associates

Does your firm annually recruit at any of the following types of institutions?

Ivy League schools: Columbia, Harvard, U. Penn, Yale

Public state schools: Boalt, U. Chicago, George Mason, U. Maryland, U. Michigan, NYU, UVA

Private schools: American, Catholic, Duke, GW, Georgetown, Stanford, William & Mary

Historically Black Colleges and Universities (HBCUs): Howard, BLSA Mid-Atlantic Job Fair

Local DC Job Fairs: Boston College, Emory and MidWest Law School Consortium, HNBA Job Fair, Washington University, Tulane and U. Miami job fair.

Do you have any special outreach efforts directed to encourage minority law students to consider your firm?

• *Howard University Law Firm Outreach Program; participate in mock interview programs at law schools.*

• Hold a reception for minority law students

• Advertise in minority law student association publication(s)

• Participate in/host minority law student job fair(s)

• Sponsor minority law student association events

- Firm's lawyers participate on career panels at school
- Outreach to leadership of minority student organizations

SUMMER ASSOCIATE STATISTICS: SUMMER 2003	MINORITY MEN	MINORITY WOMEN	WHITE WOMEN	TOTAL
Summer associates	1	3	10	28*
Summer associates who received an offer of full-time employment	1	1	9	18
Summer associates who accepted an offer of full-time employment	0	1	5	12

* Nine 3Ls were ineligible for associate offers due to pending clerkships. Of those nine, five accepted summer associate offers prior to the clerkships. One of the five was a minority woman.

Recruitment – Lateral Associates and Partners

What activities does the firm undertake to attract minority and women attorneys?

- *Participation in law school events*
- Participate at minority job fairs
- Seek referrals from other attorneys
- Utilize online job services (e.g., MCCA/DuPont Primary Law Firm Job Bank)

Do you use executive recruiting/search firms to seek to identify new diversity hires (partners or associates)?

Yes

LATERAL ASSOCIATES AND PARTNERS: 1/1/03 – 12/31/03	MINORITY MEN	MINORITY WOMEN	WHITE WOMEN	TOTAL
Number of lateral associate hires	0	1	4	13
Number of lateral partner hires (equity and non-equity)	0	0	1	5
Number of new partners (equity and non-equity) promoted from associate rank	0	0	1	2
Number of new equity partners	0	0	1	3

Retention & Professional Development

ATTORNEYS WHO LEFT THE FIRM: 2003	MINORITY MEN	MINORITY WOMEN	WHITE WOMEN	TOTAL
Number of attorneys who voluntarily or involuntarily left your firm's employ in 2003	2	1	12	40

How do 2003 attrition rates generally compare to those experienced in the prior year period?

About the same as in prior years

Please identify the specific steps you are taking to reduce the attrition rate of minority and women attorneys.

• Develop and/or support internal employee affinity groups (e.g., minority or women networks within the firm)

• Increase/review compensation relative to competition

• Increase/improve current work/life programs

• Work with minority and women attorneys to develop career advancement plans

• Introduce minority and women attorneys to key clients, including to lead engagements

• Review work assignments and hours billed to key client matters to make sure minority and women attorneys are not being excluded

• Strengthen mentoring program for all attorneys, including minorities and women

• Professional skills development program, including minority and women attorneys

Does your firm have part-time/flex-time policies that permit attorneys (male or female) to work alternative schedules?

Yes

What impact, if any, will the decision to work part-time have on an attorney's ability to make partner or, if already a partner, to remain a partner at your firm?

Part-time lawyers may continue on partnership track. The length of part-time status may affect the timing of partnership decisions.

Have any attorneys who chose to work a part-time schedule made partner at your firm?

Yes, four attorneys.

Management Demographic Profile (as of 12/31/03)

	MINORITY MEN	MINORITY WOMEN	WHITE WOMEN	TOTAL
Number of attorneys on the Executive/Management Committee or equivalent	0	0	2	13
Number of attorneys on the Hiring Committee or equivalent	5	1	10	28
Number of attorneys on the Partner/Associate Review Committee or equivalent	0	0	3	10

Please provide information regarding all minority and women attorneys who head offices or practice groups of your law firm:

Women heading practice groups: Susan Esserman, International Department

The Firm Says

Steptoe & Johnson LLP has a longstanding commitment to equal opportunity employment. We seek to recruit qualified applicants regardless of race, religion, gender, sexual orientation, disability, national origin and veteran or other protected status. We consider ourselves at the forefront of major D.C. firms in providing opportunities for women and minority lawyers. Steptoe is a Charter Signatory to the Policy Statement Regarding Minority Hiring and Retention of the District of Columbia Conference on Opportunities for Minorities in the Legal Profession.

A new associate's first steps are guided by a more senior associate who serves as an advisor. The advisor monitors work assignments, provides information about the firm's practice and offers insight into the way the firm operates. The advisor ensures that the new associate gets started on the right foot and begins to feel at home as quickly as possible. Associates also select a partner or senior associate to serve as a mentor.

Our firm regularly sponsors and attends minority conferences, receptions and job fairs. In addition, we periodically contact law school placement directors to seek their advice and request their assistance in encouraging minority candidates to consider our firm. Steptoe has sponsored and assisted in the coordination of the Annual D.C. Minority Summer Associate Reception since its inception, and in 1998 Sandy Chamblee, a partner with the firm, served as a keynote speaker.

In 1995, as part of our continuing effort to better recruit and retain minority candidates, we implemented a Standing Committee on Diversity. This committee served as an adjunct to the Hiring Committee. In 2000, the name was changed to the Diversity Committee, but the committee's purpose remains the same. The committee includes the chair of the Hiring Committee and a diverse cross-section of attorneys within the firm who have expressed an interest in assisting us to create strategies for more effective minority recruitment and retention. Attorneys from the Diversity Committee participate in job fairs and conferences aimed at minority recruiting as well as serve as on-campus recruiters.

We are proud of our commitment to equal opportunity and continually strive to do better.

Diversity summary statement

Key elements of our policy include:

• Express commitments to equal opportunity and diversity in recruiting materials and firm policy manuals

• Charter signatory to the Policy Statement Regarding Minority Hiring and Retention of the District of Columbia Conference on Opportunities for Minorities in the Legal Profession

• Diversity Committee helps develop strategies for recruiting minority candidates

• Broad flexibility in alternative career paths for working women, including part-time partnerships, telecommuting, extended leaves and rehires

• Among the many talented and accomplished women and minority attorneys at our firm are the former director of the U.S. Minerals Management Service (Cynthia Quarterman); the former deputy director for science policy and technology transfer at the National Institutes of Health (Sandy Chamblee); and the former deputy U.S. trade representative (Susan Esserman)

Strasburger & Price, LLP

901 Main Street, Suite 4300
Dallas, TX 75202
Phone: (214) 651-4300
Fax: (214) 651-4330

FIRM LEADERSHIP

Managing Partner: Kirk Sniff, Managing Partner
Diversity Team Leader: Arcie Izquierdo Jordan, Chairman of the Diversity and Community Relations Committee

LOCATIONS

Dallas, TX (HQ)
Austin, TX
Collin County, TX
Houston, TX
San Antonio, TX
Washington, DC
Mexico City

LAW FIRM DEMOGRAPHIC PROFILES

FULL-TIME ASSOCIATES	2003	2002
Minority men	3	3
Minority women	5	8
White women	28	24
Total	80	80

SUMMER ASSOCIATES	2003	2002
Minority men	4	0
Minority women	3	1
White women	16	14
Total	34	30

EQUITY PARTNERS	2003	2002
Minority men	1	0
Minority women	1	1
White women	10	11
Total	67	76

NON-EQUITY PARTNERS	2003	2002
Minority men	3	4
Minority women	0	0
White women	13	13
Total	26	32

NEW HIRES	2003	2002
Minority men	1	1
Minority women	1	6
White women	9	6
Total	28	25

MINORITY CORPORATE COUNSEL ASSOCIATION

Strategic Plan and Diversity Leadership

How does the firm's leadership communicate the importance of diversity to everyone at the firm? (e.g., e-mails, web site, newsletters, meetings, etc.)

The firm communicates the importance of diversity to everyone at the firm by way of annual diversity training programs, the firm's Web page, quarterly updates on the firm's diversity initiatives (partner meetings, firm-wide retreats and associate meetings), sponsorships and special events (receptions) with the goal of improving diversity.

Who has primary responsibility for leading diversity initiatives at your firm?

Arcie Izquierdo Jordan, Chairman of Diversity and Community Relations Committee. Local office coordinators: JoAnn Dalrymple, senior counsel (Austin); Monica Alvarez, associate (Collin County); Earsa Jackson, associate (Dallas); Elizabeth Volmert, partner (Houston); Ed Valdespino, partner (San Antonio).

Does your law firm currently have a diversity committee?

Yes

Does the committee's representation include one or more members of the firm's management/executive committee (or the equivalent)?

Yes

How many attorneys are on the committee, and in 2003, what was the total number of hours collectively spent by the committee in furtherance of the firm's diversity initiatives?

Total attorneys on committee: 14

Total hours spent on diversity: Not known

Does the committee and/or diversity leader establish and set goals or objectives consistent with management's priorities?

Yes

Has the firm undertaken a formal or informal diversity program or set of initiatives aimed at increasing the diversity of the firm?

Yes, formal

How often does the firm's management review the firm's diversity progress/results?

Quarterly

How is the firm's diversity committee and/or firm management held accountable for achieving results?

The Chairman of diversity coordinates formal reports to the firm's Policy Committee. These reports include goals of the committee and results for each office. Each office appoints an office coordinator. These coordinators are recognized by the Diversity and Community Relations Committee and the Policy Committee for their individual office participation and overall results.

LAW FIRM DIVERSITY INITIATIVES	ALREADY COMPLETED	CURRENTLY ADDRESSING	NOT A CURRENT PRIORITY
Undertake communication from firm management that diversity is a top priority of the firm.	✔		
Formalize diversity plan and committee with action steps and accountability to management.	✔		
Conduct firm-wide diversity training for all attorneys and staff.	✔		
Increase the number of minority attorneys at the associate level.		✔	
Increase the number of minority attorneys at the partnership level.		✔	
Develop/expand relationships with minority bar associations to offer firm's support of these networks.		✔	
Focus on strengthening firm's mentoring program, including for benefit of minority attorneys.		✔	
Conduct internal diversity needs assessment and/or retain diversity consultant to examine how firm culture might be more welcoming of minorities.	✔		
Support law firm's internal affinity networks (e.g., women, minority attorney networks).	✔		
Manage/monitor allocation of work assignments and/or hours billed to ensure women and minority attorneys have equal access/inclusion on top client matters.	✔		
Increase the number of minority attorneys in management positions. Institutionalize processes designed to heighten sensitivity to diversity priorities in recruitment activities. Develop and implement formal lateral hire integration program so as to improve retention rates of minority attorneys recruited.	✔		

Recruitment – New Associates

Does your firm annually recruit at any of the following types of institutions? (Check all that apply and list the schools).

Sunbelt Minority Recruitment Program: Baylor University, LSU, Texas Tech, SMU, South Texas, Southern University, St. Mary's University, Texas Wesleyan University, Loyola University-New Orleans, Oklahoma City University, Texas Southern, University of Houston, University of Texas, University of New Mexico, Tulane University, University of Tulsa, University of Oklahoma and University of Arizona

Public state schools: University of Texas, Texas Tech University, University of Virginia, University of Houston, University of North Carolina, College of William & Mary

Private schools: Baylor University, Duke University, Georgetown University, Southern Methodist University, St. Mary's University, Vanderbilt University, South Texas College of Law, Washington and Lee University, Wake Forest University

Historically Black Colleges and Universities (HBCUs): Texas Southern University (through participation in the Sunbelt Minority Recruitment Program)

Do you have any special outreach efforts directed to encourage minority law students to consider your firm?

• Hold receptions for minority law students

• Participate in minority law student job fair(s)

• Sponsor minority law student association events

• Firm's lawyers participate on career panels at school

• Scholarships or intern/fellowships for minority students

SUMMER ASSOCIATE STATISTICS: SUMMER 2003	MINORITY MEN	MINORITY WOMEN	WHITE WOMEN	TOTAL
Summer associates	4	4	14	33
Summer associates who received an offer of full-time employment	1	2	6	14
Summer associates who accepted an offer of full-time employment	0	2	6	11

Recruitment – Lateral Associates and Partners

What activities does the firm undertake to attract minority and women attorneys?

• Participate at minority job fairs

• Seek referrals from other attorneys

• Utilize search firms to identify diverse candidates

Do you use executive recruiting/search firms to seek to identify new diversity hires (partners or associates)?

Yes

If yes, list all women- and/or minority-owned executive search/recruiting firms to which the firm paid a fee for placement services in the past 12 months:

Will not disclose.

LATERAL ASSOCIATES AND PARTNERS: 1/1/03 – 12/31/03	MINORITY MEN	MINORITY WOMEN	WHITE WOMEN	TOTAL
Number of lateral associate hires	0	0	3	5
Number of lateral partner hires (equity and non-equity)	0	0	0	1
Number of new partners (equity and non-equity) promoted from associate rank	0	0	0	1
Number of new equity partners	0	1	1	4

Retention & Professional Development

ATTORNEYS WHO LEFT THE FIRM: 2003	MINORITY MEN	MINORITY WOMEN	WHITE WOMEN	TOTAL
Number of attorneys who voluntarily or involuntarily left your firm's employ in 2003	3	3	7	43

How do 2003 attrition rates generally compare to those experienced in the prior year period?

About the same as in prior years

Please identify the specific steps you are taking to reduce the attrition rate of minority and women attorneys.

• *Established minority group within firm. Group meets quarterly.*

• Have developed formal lateral hire integration program so as to improve retention rates of minority attorneys recruited.

• Develop and/or support internal employee affinity groups (e.g., minority and women networks within the firm)

• Increase/review compensation relative to competition

• Work with minority and women attorneys to develop career advancement plans

• Introduce minority and women attorneys to key clients, including to lead engagements

• Review work assignments and hours billed to key client matters to make sure minority and women attorneys are not being excluded

• Strengthen mentoring program for all attorneys, including minorities and women

• Professional skills development program, including minority and women attorneys

Does your firm have part-time/flex-time policies that permit attorneys (male or female) to work alternative schedules?

Yes

What impact, if any, will the decision to work part-time have on an attorney's ability to make partner or, if already a partner, to remain a partner at your firm?

There is no defined response to this situation. The impact, if any, will vary on the basis of specific circumstances.

Have any attorneys who chose to work a part-time schedule made partner at your firm?

Yes, one attorney, although some partners have gone part time upon making partner.

Management Demographic Profile (as of 12/31/03)

	MINORITY MEN	MINORITY WOMEN	WHITE WOMEN	TOTAL
Number of attorneys on the Executive/Management Committee or equivalent	1	0	1	8
Number of attorneys on the Hiring Committee or equivalent	0	0	4	12
Number of attorneys on the Partner/Associate Review Committee or equivalent	0	0	1	4

Please provide information regarding all minority and women attorneys who head offices or practice groups of your law firm:

Minorities heading offices: Ed Valdespino, Partner-in-Charge, San Antonio

Women heading offices: Betsy Kamin, Partner-in-Charge, Houston

Minorities heading practice groups: Arcie Izquierdo Jordan, Head of the International Practice Unit and Chairman of Diversity and Community Relations Committee

Women heading practice groups: Arcie Izquierdo Jordan, Head of the International Practice Unit and Chairman of Diversity and Community Relations Committee; Judith Blakeway, leader of the Antitrust Team; Carol Glendenning, Leader of the Venture Capital Team and Policy Committee member 1998-2002); Marian E. Ladner, Leader of Customs Team; Jane Woods LaFranchi, Leader of Export Compliance & Enforcement Team (Before relocating to Washington, D.C., Jane was the Partner-in-Charge of the firm's Mexico City office); Kimberly S. Moore, Chair of Legal Assistant Committee and Chairman of the firm's web site); Toni Scott Reed, Member of Policy Committee and Hiring Partner; Beth Pace Tiggelaar, Chair of Income Partner Committee; Ashley Kisner, Member of Lawyer Employment Evaluation Team and Chair of Associate Training Committee.

The Firm Says

Strasburger understands that diversity relates to a variety of differences in people. As a firm, we value differences such as life and work experiences; personal values; personality profile; work practice; age; sex; ethnicity; family responsibilities; sexual orientation; education; and cultural, socioeconomic and religious backgrounds. It is through these unique differences that we provide effective, efficient and consistent legal services to our clients. Because Strasburger is committed to providing superb legal services, we strive to recruit attorneys and staff with outstanding legal skills and diverse backgrounds reflective of the communities that we serve. Our diversity efforts have allowed us to represent our clients more effectively.

Formal Diversity Statement

Strasburger embraces diversity and is committed to providing opportunity within all areas of our organization — whether legal, professional or administrative — to all people regardless of race, color, sex, national origin, religion, age, sexual orientation or disability.

Goals

- Execute and support the firm's commitment to diversity;
- Develop diversity training programs and activities for attorneys and non-attorney personnel;
- Integrate formalized diversity objectives into recruiting strategies and continue to enhance minority recruitment efforts;
- Increase participation — both by firm and by individual attorneys — in organizations with a minority, women or community development focus
- Enhance associate mentoring programs and lateral hire integration so as to improve retention rates of minority attorneys recruited; and
- Explore a formal vendor/supplier diversity program.

Spreading the message

Among the events Strasburger sponsors or otherwise participates in is the annual Tom Unis Valuing Diversity Award luncheon sponsored by the Greater Dallas Community Relations Commission. This award recognizes the achievements of individuals who actively work to improve race relations and promote multicultural understanding. The Unis Award selection committee is composed of a cross-section of citizens from the community as a whole. Strasburger is the title sponsor of the awards luncheon. The Unis Award is named for the late Tom Unis, who spent his long career at Strasburger as one of the firm's first partners working with founders Henry Strasburger and Hobert Price. He was founding chairman of the Greater Dallas Community Relations Commission in 1969, at which time he was also a Dallas city councilman.

Other notable recent events in which Strasburger has participated include:

• In conjunction with the Dallas Community of Churches, Strasburger was proud to host a presentation by Dr. James L. Lawson, a hero of the civil rights movement. Dr. Lawson helped to train the "sit-in kids" who advanced the cause of civil rights through their lunchroom sit-ins. The presentation was attended by business, religious and educational leaders.

• Strasburger's Austin office sponsored the 20th Annual Scholarship and Awards Banquet of the Thurgood Marshall Legal Society, a local chapter of the National Black Law Students Association based at the University of Texas at Austin. The office has also participated in and co-hosted a reception at the beginning of the recruiting season for minority law students at the University of Texas Law School to encourage them to consider Strasburger.

• Strasburger is a corporate sponsor for the Annual Dallas Cup/Dallas Is Diversity event that takes place each April. This invitational soccer tournament brings youth soccer teams from all corners of the globe to Dallas for a week of fun and learning. Dallas Is Diversity promotes ethnic and cultural diversity in the Dallas area through various events throughout the year.

• Strasburger has been known for many years for its commitment to diversity in its workplace and in the community. Strasburger is a founding member of the Dallas Bar Association Minority Recruitment effort which visits numerous campuses nationwide. In addition, we actively recruit minority students through the Sunbelt Minority Conference and through various recruiting and outreach programs. In addition to hiring and mentoring lawyers who are women and members of underrepresented groups, we support our goal of a diverse working environment in other ways as well, for example through participating in job fairs.

• Strasburger has established a Diversity and Community Relations Committee composed of attorneys throughout our various offices, as well as human resources and attorney recruiting personnel. The highest echelons of the firm's management are involved, active members of the Diversity and Community Relations Committee. With representation from the firm's Employment Committee, the Diversity and Community Relations Committee's activities are coordinated in a seamless, effective fashion with the firm's recruiting and retention activities and policies.

• To further advance the success of our women attorneys, Strasburger hosts practice development events, training sessions and social activities designed to address issues facing women attorneys, foster relationships among women at the firm and promote business development opportunities.

• In 2002, Strasburger created the "Tom Unis Valuing Diversity Scholarship." This scholarship, in honor of the late Tom Unis, awards a scholarship to a minority student attending classes on a full-time basis who during his or her first year of law school demonstrates exceptional academic performance.

• The firm's diversity goals are not limited to attorneys. Our legal assistants, legal secretaries and other professional and administrative staff reflect the larger community. More than 25 percent of Strasburger's non-attorney staff are from underrepresented ethnic groups and 85 percent are women.

• A number of Strasburger attorneys are active officers and members of legal and business organizations that have an ethnic minority focus. Among these are the Asian American Bar Association, the Dallas Urban League, the J.L. Turner Legal Association, the John C. Ford Program, the Mexican-American Bar Association, the National Bar Association and the San Antonio Hispanic Chamber of Commerce.

Sullivan & Cromwell

125 Broad Street
New York, NY 10004-2498
Phone: (212) 558-4000
Fax: (212) 558-3588

FIRM LEADERSHIP

Kandance Weems Norris, Diversity
Management Attorney
Managing Partner: H. Rodgin Cohen, Chairman
Diversity Team Leader: Gandolfo DiBlasi,
Diversity Committee Chair

LOCATIONS

New York, NY (HQ)
Los Angeles, CA
Palo Alto, CA
Washington, DC
Beijing
Frankfurt
Hong Kong
London
Melbourne
Paris
Sydney
Tokyo

LAW FIRM DEMOGRAPHIC PROFILES

FULL-TIME ASSOCIATES	2003	2002
Minority men	29	34
Minority women	46	51
White women	123	127
Total	459	477

SUMMER ASSOCIATES	2003	2002
Minority men	5	16
Minority women	6	25
White women	18	39
Total	53	130

EQUITY PARTNERS	2003	2002
Minority men	5	4
Minority women	1	0
White women	12	10
Total	122	116

NEW HIRES	2003	2002
Minority men	7	16
Minority women	12	16
White women	25	24
Total	93	113

Strategic Plan and Diversity Leadership

How does the firm's leadership communicate the importance of diversity to everyone at the firm? (e.g., e-mails, web site, newsletters, meetings, etc.)

The firm uses meetings, memos, e-mails and workshops to communicate the importance of diversity.

Who has primary responsibility for leading diversity initiatives at your firm?

Kandance Weems Norris, diversity management attorney

Does your law firm currently have a diversity committee?

Yes

Does the committee's representation include one or more members of the firm's management/executive committee (or the equivalent)?

Yes

How many attorneys are on the committee, and in 2003, what was the total number of hours collectively spent by the committee in furtherance of the firm's diversity initiatives?

Total attorneys on committee: 23

Total hours spent on diversity: The firm does not track hours spent on diversity.

Does the committee and/or diversity leader establish and set goals or objectives consistent with management's priorities?

Yes

Has the firm undertaken a formal or informal diversity program or set of initiatives aimed at increasing the diversity of the firm?

Yes, formal and informal

How often does the firm's management review the firm's diversity progress/results?

Monthly

How is the firm's diversity committee and/or firm management held accountable for achieving results?

The Diversity Committee must prepare a report for the firm's chairman annually, reporting on the previous year's initiatives and results.

LAW FIRM DIVERSITY INITIATIVES	ALREADY COMPLETED	CURRENTLY ADDRESSING	NOT A CURRENT PRIORITY
Undertake communication from firm management that diversity is a top priority of the firm.	✓		
Formalize diversity plan and committee with action steps and accountability to management.		✓	
Conduct firm-wide diversity training for all attorneys and staff.		✓	
Increase the number of minority attorneys at the associate level.		✓	
Increase the number of minority attorneys at the partnership level.		✓	
Develop/expand relationships with minority bar associations to offer firm's support of these networks.		✓	
Focus on strengthening firm's mentoring program, including for benefit of minority attorneys.		✓	
Conduct internal diversity needs assessment and/or retain diversity consultant to examine how firm culture might be more welcoming of minorities.		✓	
Support law firm's internal affinity networks (e.g., women, minority attorney networks).	✓		
Manage/monitor allocation of work assignments and/or hours billed to ensure women and minority attorneys have equal access/inclusion on top client matters.		✓	

Recruitment - New Associates

Does your firm annually recruit at any of the following types of institutions? (Check all that apply and list the schools).

Ivy League schools: Columbia University, Cornell University, Harvard University, University of Pennsylvania, Yale University

Public state schools: University of California-Boalt Hall, University of California-Hastings, UCLA, Rutgers University, University of Michigan, University of Texas, University of Toronto, University of Virginia

Private schools: American University, Boston College, Boston University, Brooklyn Law School, Benjamin Cardozo School of Law, Catholic University of America, Duke University, Fordham University, George Washington University, Georgetown University, McGill University, New York Law School, NYU, Northwestern University, Stanford University, University of Chicago

Historically Black Colleges and Universities (HBCUs): Howard University

Do you have any special outreach efforts directed to encourage minority law students to consider your firm?

• *Meet with professors to ask that they encourage minority law students to apply*

• Hold a reception for minority law students

MINORITY CORPORATE COUNSEL ASSOCIATION

- Participate in/host minority law student job fair(s)
- Sponsor minority law student association events
- Firm's lawyers participate on career panels at school
- Outreach to leadership of minority student organizations
- Scholarships or intern/fellowships for minority students

SUMMER ASSOCIATE STATISTICS: SUMMER 2003	MINORITY MEN	MINORITY WOMEN	WHITE WOMEN	TOTAL
Summer associates	3	5	14	43
Summer associates who received an offer of full-time employment	3	5	14	43
Summer associates who accepted an offer of full-time employment	3	3	11	32

Recruitment – Lateral Associates and Partners

What activities does the firm undertake to attract minority and women attorneys?

S&C typically hires very few lateral attorneys. Lateral hires represented less than 5 percent of all new hires in 2003.

Do you use executive recruiting/search firms to seek to identify new diversity hires (partners or associates)?

No

LATERAL ASSOCIATES AND PARTNERS: 1/1/03 – 12/31/03	MINORITY MEN	MINORITY WOMEN	WHITE WOMEN	TOTAL
Number of lateral associate hires	3	1	2	6
Number of lateral partner hires (equity and non-equity)	0	0	0	0
Number of new partners (equity and non-equity) promoted from associate rank	0	0	2	6
Number of new equity partners	0	0	2	6

Retention & Professional Development

ATTORNEYS WHO LEFT THE FIRM: 2003	MINORITY MEN	MINORITY WOMEN	WHITE WOMEN	TOTAL
Number of attorneys who voluntarily or involuntarily left your firm's employ in 2003	7	3	27	95

How do 2003 attrition rates generally compare to those experienced in the prior year period?

Lower than in prior years

Please identify the specific steps you are taking to reduce the attrition rate of minority and women attorneys.

- *The firm's chairman holds periodic discussions with minority and women associates. The diversity management attorney plans numerous programs for minority and women attorneys and is available to discuss any issues or concerns.*
- Develop and/or support internal employee affinity groups (e.g., minority or women networks within the firm)
- Increase/improve current work/life programs
- Succession plan includes emphasis on diversity
- Strengthen mentoring program for all attorneys, including minorities and women
- Professional skills development program, including minority and women attorneys

Does your firm have part-time/flex-time policies that permit attorneys (male or female) to work alternative schedules?

Yes. S&C's flex-time policy permits attorneys to work on a reduced schedule while remaining on partnership track. Recently, two partners were elected while working on a flex-time schedule.

What impact, if any, will the decision to work part-time have on an attorney's ability to make partner or, if already a partner, to remain a partner at your firm?

None. S&C currently has two part-time partners, one of whom was recently elected while working part-time.

Have any attorneys who chose to work a part-time schedule made partner at your firm?

Yes, two attorneys.

Management Demographic Profile (as of 12/31/03)

	MINORITY MEN	MINORITY WOMEN	WHITE WOMEN	TOTAL
Number of attorneys on the Executive/Management Committee or equivalent	0	0	1	8
Number of attorneys on the Hiring Committee or equivalent	1	0	1	3
Number of attorneys on the Partner/Associate Review Committee or equivalent	N/A	N/A	N/A	N/A

Please provide information regarding all minority and women attorneys who head offices or practice groups of your law firm:

Minorities heading offices: Chun Wei, Beijing and Hong Kong; Izumi Akai, Tokyo

Women heading offices: Chun Wei, Beijing

Minorities heading practice groups: Sergio Galvis, Latin American Practice

Women heading practice groups: Yvonne Quinn, Antitrust; Ann Fisher, Sovereign Issuers; Alison Ressler, Private Equity

The Firm Says

It is the firm's policy to seek out minorities and women in recruiting, to advance them through the associate ranks and to promote them to partnership consistently with the standards applied to all associates. Similarly, it is the firm's policy to advance minority and women partners to positions of responsibility in firm management. In order to implement these policies, the firm must attract and retain qualified minority and women associates in meaningful numbers. The firm's culture and policies are supportive of diversity in its broadest sense, including not only race and gender, but also ethnicity, sexual orientation and religious affiliation. In addition, the firm has recognized the need to take special steps to provide equal professional experiences and opportunities for advancement to all of its associates. The firm maintains a number of diversity initiatives, directed at improving the recruitment, retention and advancement of minorities. Similarly, the firm has implemented a number of programs and policies designed to address work/life issues of concern to women and to ensure that the firm's culture is comfortable for women. The following are some of the most notable programs and initiatives:

• **Minority and women partners.** In 2003, one-third of the lawyers who became partners were minorities and one-third were women. Two women became partners in 2004 who were working on a part-time schedule. Since 2000, eight women have become partners of the firm, almost half of the 17 current women partners.

• **Diversity committee.** The firm has a Diversity Committee that focuses on the hiring, professional development and promotion of minority lawyers and serves as a forum for the firm's ongoing dialogue on diversity issues. The Diversity Committee is comprised of partners and associates at all levels and includes African-American, Asian, Latino, gay, lesbian, Orthodox Jewish and Muslim lawyers. The committee is chaired by a partner who is a member of the firm's management committee.

• **Diversity management attorney.** The firm has a full-time diversity management attorney, whose role is to coordinate recruiting and retention efforts with respect to minorities and women.

• **Flex-time policy.** The firm recently restated its flex-time policy (initially adopted in 1987) to encourage associates with children or other family concerns to remain with the firm while adjusting their working schedules to reflect their individual family needs. The policy restatement was initiated and drafted primarily by women partners, including two women who were working part-time prior to becoming partners.

• **Forums and other gatherings.** The firm sponsors frequent gatherings of women and minority lawyers and holds periodic forums at which women and minority associates are given the opportunity to discuss diversity-related issues with partners. The firm's chairman, H. Rodgin Cohen, takes an active interest in the professional development of women and minority lawyers and has held several breakfast and lunch meetings with minority and women associates to exchange views and proposals on diversity issues.

- **Speakers and diversity workshop.** The firm invites outside speakers to address diversity issues with lawyers and continues to use consultants to develop and conduct seminars and other programs for diversity and other workplace issues. In 2001, the firm devoted significant effort and resources to a diversity workshop designed to help minority associates develop strategies for professional development and to provide feedback to the firm on mentoring, training and assignment issues. The workshop, conducted over two days, was led by David Wilkins, a Harvard Law School professor and leading author on the structure of corporate law firms and the experience of black lawyers, and David Thomas, a Harvard Business School professor and authority on mentoring, executive development and workplace diversity.

- **Recruiting initiatives.** The firm's women and minority lawyers devote significant efforts each year to recruiting; several of them act as recruiting coordinators at individual law schools. Of the firm's three hiring partners, one is a woman and one is a minority. Our diversity management attorney, herself a minority lawyer, heads a Diversity Recruiting Committee, which focuses exclusively on one-on-one recruiting efforts directed at minority candidates. The firm holds special events to attract women and minority lawyers to the firm, including a breakfast discussion series for summer associates and other women and minority lawyers at the firm and diversity and women's receptions at several law schools. The firm also attends receptions hosted by student groups.

- **Professional activities, minority development and scholarship programs.** Beyond our firm, we are committed to improving the diversity of the legal profession. Our lawyers have participated in bar association committees and panels discussing diversity issues, and the firm has hosted countless forums, panel discussions and receptions for minority lawyers and law students. The firm participates in a number of minority development programs, including Sponsors for Educational Opportunity (SEO), Practicing Attorneys for Law Students (PALS), the Thurgood Marshall Legal Internship Program, the Legal Outreach Program and several others that offer internship, mentoring and development opportunities for minority high school, college and law school students. The firm has established a scholarship program at Howard University School of Law to award minority scholarships to two students in each entering class, contributes annually to the ABA minority scholarship program and has formed a partnership with Frederick Douglass Academy in East Harlem, participating in classroom teaching and contributing scholarships and book funds.

We constantly challenge ourselves to be the best. Achievement of that goal requires that we continuously strive to increase the diversity of our lawyers, and we are seriously committed to doing just that.

Sutherland Asbill & Brennan LLP

1275 Pennsylvania Avenue
Washington, DC 20004
Phone: (202) 383-0100
Fax: (202) 637-3593

FIRM LEADERSHIP

Managing Partner: James L. Henderson III,
Managing Partner
Diversity Team Leader: Peter H. Rodgers and
Allegra J. Lawrence, Partners

LOCATIONS

Atlanta, GA
Austin, TX
Houston, TX
New York, NY
Tallahassee, FL
Washington, DC

LAW FIRM DEMOGRAPHIC PROFILES

FULL-TIME ASSOCIATES	2003	2002
Minority men	9	9
Minority women	11	12
White women	61	56
Total	161	157

SUMMER ASSOCIATES	2003	2002
Minority men	3	1
Minority women	4	2
White women	15	22
Total	37	40

EQUITY PARTNERS	2003	2002
Minority men	2	2
Minority women	2	2
White women	24	25
Total	134	141

NON-EQUITY PARTNERS	2003	2002
Minority men	0	0
Minority women	0	0
White women	0	0
Total	4	0

NEW HIRES	2003	2002
Minority men	1	3
Minority women	4	2
White women	16	13
Total	41	39

Strategic Plan and Diversity Leadership

How does the firm's leadership communicate the importance of diversity to everyone at the firm? (e.g., e-mails, web site, newsletters, meetings, etc.)

Diversity is addressed on the firm's web site (www.sablaw.com) and in the firm's five-year strategic plan.

Who has primary responsibility for leading diversity initiatives at your firm?

Partners Peter H. Rodgers, James B. Jordan, Bert Adams and Allegra J. Lawrence

Does your law firm currently have a diversity committee?

No

Does the committee and/or diversity leader establish and set goals or objectives consistent with management's priorities?

Yes

Has the firm undertaken a formal or informal diversity program or set of initiatives aimed at increasing the diversity of the firm?

Yes, informal

How often does the firm's management review the firm's diversity progress/results?

Annually

How is the firm's diversity committee and/or firm management held accountable for achieving results?

Through an annual review of the firm's strategic plan goals.

LAW FIRM DIVERSITY INITIATIVES	ALREADY COMPLETED	CURRENTLY ADDRESSING	NOT A CURRENT PRIORITY
Undertake communication from firm management that diversity is a top priority of the firm.		✓	
Formalize diversity plan and committee with action steps and accountability to management.		✓	
Conduct firm-wide diversity training for all attorneys and staff.		✓	
Increase the number of minority attorneys at the associate level.		✓	
Increase the number of minority attorneys at the partnership level.		✓	
Develop/expand relationships with minority bar associations to offer firm's support of these networks.		✓	
Focus on strengthening firm's mentoring program, including for benefit of minority attorneys.		✓	

LAW FIRM DIVERSITY INITIATIVES (CONTINUED)	ALREADY COMPLETED	CURRENTLY ADDRESSING	NOT A CURRENT PRIORITY
Conduct internal diversity needs assessment and/or retain diversity consultant to examine how firm culture might be more welcoming of minorities.		✔	
Support law firm's internal affinity networks (e.g., women, minority attorney networks).		✔	
Manage/monitor allocation of work assignments and/or hours billed to ensure women and minority attorneys have equal access/inclusion on top client matters.		✔	

Recruitment - New Associates

Does your firm annually recruit at any of the following types of institutions? (Check all that apply and list the schools).

Ivy League schools: Columbia University, Cornell University, Harvard University, University of Pennsylvania, Yale University

Public state schools: University of California-Berkeley, University of Florida, University of Georgia, University of Michigan, University of North Carolina, University of Virginia, College of William & Mary

Private schools: American University, Catholic University, Duke University, Emory University, Georgetown University, George Washington University, University of Notre Dame, Northwestern University, NYU, Tulane University, Vanderbilt University, Wake Forest University, Washington University, Washington & Lee University

Historically Black Colleges and Universities (HBCUs): Howard University, Black Law Student Association job fairs

Do you have any special outreach efforts directed to encourage minority law students to consider your firm?

• Advertise in minority law student association publication(s)

• Participate in/host minority law student job fair(s)

• Sponsor minority law student association events

• Firm's lawyers participate on career panels at school

• Outreach to leadership of minority student organizations

SUMMER ASSOCIATE STATISTICS: SUMMER 2003	MINORITY MEN	MINORITY WOMEN	WHITE WOMEN	TOTAL
Summer associates	3	4	15	37
Summer associates who received an offer of full-time employment	3	2	13	30
Summer associates who accepted an offer of full-time employment	3	2	12	27

Recruitment – Lateral Associates and Partners

What activities does the firm undertake to attract minority and women attorneys?

• Partner programs with women and minority bar associations

• Participate at minority job fairs

• Seek referrals from other attorneys

Do you use executive recruiting/search firms to seek to identify new diversity hires (partners or associates)?

Yes

List all women- and/or minority-owned executive search/recruiting firms to which the firm paid a fee for placement services in the past 12 months:

None

LATERAL ASSOCIATES AND PARTNERS: 1/1/03 – 12/31/03	MINORITY MEN	MINORITY WOMEN	WHITE WOMEN	TOTAL
Number of lateral associate hires	2	3	10	26
Number of lateral partner hires (equity and non-equity)	0	0	0	1
Number of new partners (equity and non-equity) promoted from associate rank	0	1	1	10
Number of new equity partners	0	0	0	0

Retention & Professional Development

ATTORNEYS WHO LEFT THE FIRM: 2003	MINORITY MEN	MINORITY WOMEN	WHITE WOMEN	TOTAL
Number of attorneys who voluntarily or involuntarily left your firm's employ in 2003	3	6	16	44

How do 2003 attrition rates generally compare to those experienced in the prior year period?

Higher than in prior years

Please identify the specific steps you are taking to reduce the attrition rate of minority and women attorneys.

• Increase/improve current work/life programs

• Work with minority and women attorneys to develop career advancement plans

• Introduce minority and women attorneys to key clients, including to lead   engagements

• Strengthen mentoring program for all attorneys, including minorities and women

• Professional skills development program, including minority and women attorneys

Does your firm have part-time/flex-time policies that permit attorneys (male or female) to work alternative schedules?

Yes

What impact, if any, will the decision to work part-time have on an attorney's ability to make partner or, if already a partner, to remain a partner at your firm?

The firm is committed to its part-time program. We work with attorneys on a case-by-case basis to address part-time work schedules. We do not anticipate that part-time schedules will impact individual attorney's ability to provide top-notch client service.

Have any attorneys who chose to work a part-time schedule made partner at your firm?

Yes, two attorneys.

Management Demographic Profile (as of 12/31/03)

	MINORITY MEN	MINORITY WOMEN	WHITE WOMEN	TOTAL
Number of attorneys on the Executive/Management Committee or equivalent	0	0	1	9
Number of attorneys on the Hiring Committee or equivalent	0	1	7	18
Number of attorneys on the Partner/Associate Review Committee or equivalent	1	0	1	6

Please provide information regarding all minority and women attorneys who head offices or practice groups of your law firm:

Minorities heading practice groups: Reginald J. Clark, Atlanta Tax Practice

Women heading practice groups: Elizabeth V. Tanis, Atlanta Deputy Litigation Group Leader; Elisabeth A. Langworthy, Washington IP Group Leader; Patricia B. Cunningham, Atlanta Deputy IP Group Leader

The Firm Says

Sutherland is committed to diversity in our workplace and in our profession because we believe that diverse skills, knowledge, viewpoints, gender, cultural perspectives and national origins make us a stronger, more productive law firm. We are committed to promoting and achieving diversity at all levels and are proud of the pivotal role that women lawyers and lawyers of color have played in our firm's growth and development. Our commitment to diversity is demonstrated by our firm's actions and the leadership roles our attorneys undertake to promote diversity in the legal profession, including the following:

• Past co-chair, American Bar Association Task Force on Women in the Profession
• Founding co-chair, State Bar of Georgia Minority Counsel Program (now called Diversity Program)
• Chair, State Bar of Georgia's Committee on Women and Minorities in the Profession
• Board member, Georgia Asian Pacific American Bar Association
• Past president, Georgia Association for Women Lawyers

• President, Georgia Association of Black Women Attorneys
• Participant, Symposium on Increasing Number of Minority Law Clerks
• Former national co-chairs and current board of directors, Lawyers' Committee for Civil Rights Under the Law
• Participant, Atlanta Large Law Firm Diversity Alliance
• Charter member, Atlanta Legal Diversity Consortium, Inc.
• Board member, Atlanta Legal Diversity Consortium, Inc.

We recruit for diversity by participating in the Southeastern Minority Job Fair, the Mid-Atlantic Black Law Students Association Job Fair and on-campus interviews at Howard University School of Law. We focus on retention and advancement by providing mentoring and training programs to help our attorneys of color excel.

Our broad-based commitment to diversity enables us to provide our clients with a team of professionals possessing a breadth of experiences and perspectives. Sutherland's diverse workplace allows us to staff each matter with the best attorneys possessing a vast array of creativity and problem-solving skills. Our environment of inclusion benefits our clients as well as our firm.

Testa, Hurwitz & Thibeault, LLP

125 High Street
Boston, MA 02110
Phone: (617) 248-7000
Fax: (617) 248-7100

FIRM LEADERSHIP

Managing Partner: William B. Asher, Managing Partner
Diversity Team Leaders: Mark D. Smith and Stephen D. Whetstone, Partners

LOCATIONS

Boston, MA

LAW FIRM DEMOGRAPHIC PROFILES

FULL-TIME ASSOCIATES	2003	2002
Minority men	15	21
Minority women	13	19
White women	88	109
Total	234	306

SUMMER ASSOCIATES	2003	2002
Minority men	2	2
Minority women	1	4
White women	14	15
Total	33	47

EQUITY PARTNERS	2003	2002
Minority men	1	1
Minority women	0	0
White women	11	10
Total	85	84

NEW HIRES	2003	2002
Minority men	3	2
Minority women	7	6
White women	11	19
Total	43	63

Strategic Plan and Diversity Leadership

How does the firm's leadership communicate the importance of diversity to everyone at the firm? (e.g., e-mails, web site, newsletters, meetings, etc.)

Primarily by e-mails and meetings, including both firm-wide and smaller group meetings.

Who has primary responsibility for leading diversity initiatives at your firm?

Steve Whetstone and Mark Smith, as co-chairs of the firm's Diversity Committee.

Does your law firm currently have a diversity committee?

Yes

Does the committee's representation include one or more members of the firm's management/executive committee (or the equivalent)?

Yes

How many attorneys are on the committee, and in 2003, what was the total number of hours collectively spent by the committee in furtherance of the firm's diversity initiatives?

Total attorneys on committee: 6. *The Diversity Committee is comprised of six partners, three of whom are male and three of whom are female.*

Total hours spent on diversity: Over 400. The current Diversity Committee was formed in 2004 and therefore there is no 2003 hours data to report. That said, Steve and Mark, as well as other attorneys and staff, spent more than 400 hours on diversity issues in 2003 that presaged the formation of the Diversity Committee.

Does the committee and/or diversity leader establish and set goals or objectives consistent with management's priorities?

Yes

Has the firm undertaken a formal or informal diversity program or set of initiatives aimed at increasing the diversity of the firm?

Yes, formal

How often does the firm's management review the firm's diversity progress/results?

Quarterly, through, among other lines of communication, management's direct representation and participation on the Diversity Committee.

How is the firm's diversity committee and/or firm management held accountable for achieving results?

The Diversity Committee has articulated its goals at a recent meeting with all attorneys of color at the firm. Members of the Diversity Committee also have met individually with each attorney of color to discuss the committee's goals with respect to that particular attorney. In the first instance, if the Diversity Committee fails to achieve its stated goals, the attorneys of colors likely will say so. In addition, Steve and Mark meet regularly

with firm management to discuss their goals as co-chairs of the Diversity Committee. Firm management will measure their performance against those agreed-upon goals.

LAW FIRM DIVERSITY INITIATIVES	ALREADY COMPLETED	CURRENTLY ADDRESSING	NOT A CURRENT PRIORITY
Undertake communication from firm management that diversity is a top priority of the firm.		✓	
Formalize diversity plan and committee with action steps and accountability to management.	✓		
Conduct firm-wide diversity training for all attorneys and staff.	✓	✓	
Increase the number of minority attorneys at the associate level.		✓	
Increase the number of minority attorneys at the partnership level.		✓	
Develop/expand relationships with minority bar associations to offer firm's support of these networks.		✓	
Focus on strengthening firm's mentoring program, including for benefit of minority attorneys.		✓	
Conduct internal diversity needs assessment and/or retain diversity consultant to examine how firm culture might be more welcoming of minorities.	✓	✓	
Support law firm's internal affinity networks (e.g., women, minority attorney networks).	✓	✓	
Manage/monitor allocation of work assignments and/or hours billed to ensure women and minority attorneys have equal access/inclusion on top client matters.		✓	
We continue to work hard to make sure that minority attorneys are represented on various firm committees (e.g., the Associates Committee, the Recruiting Committee and the Technology Committee) and firm initiatives (e.g., the China Initiative and client marketing pitches).	✓	✓	

Recruitment – New Associates

Does your firm annually recruit at any of the following types of institutions? (Check all that apply and list the schools).

Ivy League schools: Columbia University, Cornell University, Harvard University, University of Pennsylvania, Yale University*

Public state schools: University of California-Berkeley/Boalt Hall, University of Connecticut: Boston Program, University of Michigan, University of North Carolina at Chapel Hill, University of Texas on Tour: Boston Job Fair, University of Toronto, University of Virginia, George Mason University, New York/Northeast Off Campus Recruitment Program (Tulane, Univ. of Iowa, UCLA, Univ. of Minnesota, USC, Univ. of Wisconsin)*

Private schools: American University/Catholic University Boston Interview Program, Boston College, Boston University, Duke University, Franklin Pierce, George Washington University, Georgetown University, McGill

University, New York University, Northeastern University, Northwestern University, University of Notre Dame, Stanford University, Suffolk University, University of Chicago, Vanderbilt University*

Historically Black Colleges and Universities (HBCUs): Howard University*

* Law schools at which TH&T recruited on-campus in 2003.

Of the law schools that you listed above, do you have any special outreach efforts directed to encourage minority law students to consider your firm?

• *TH&T is a founding member and sponsor of The Boston Lawyers Group (BLG), whose principal purpose is to assist Boston law firms and government agencies in identifying, recruiting, retaining and promoting law students and lawyers of color. Among other BLG programs, TH&T participates in the BLG summer college intern program (we currently have two students of color working with us this summer) and the BLG law school mentoring program.*

• Hold a reception for minority law students

• Participate in/host minority law student job fair(s)

• Sponsor minority law student association events

• Firm's lawyers participate on career panels at school

• Outreach to leadership of minority student organizations

• Scholarships or intern/fellowships for minority students

SUMMER ASSOCIATE STATISTICS: SUMMER 2003	MINORITY MEN	MINORITY WOMEN	WHITE WOMEN	TOTAL
Summer associates	2	1	14	33
Summer associates who received an offer of full-time employment	1	1	14	31
Summer associates who accepted an offer of full-time employment	1	1	9	23

Recruitment – Lateral Associates and Partners

What activities does the firm undertake to attract minority and women attorneys?

• *In addition, TH&T relies on its Boston Lawyers Group contacts to attract minority attorneys.*

• Partner programs with women and minority bar associations

• Participate at minority job fairs

• Seek referrals from other attorneys (and make referrals, as well)

Do you use executive recruiting/search firms to seek to identify new diversity hires (partners or associates)?

No. Not in the past, but we have decided to do so going forward.

LATERAL ASSOCIATES AND PARTNERS: 1/1/03 – 12/31/03	MINORITY MEN	MINORITY WOMEN	WHITE WOMEN	TOTAL
Number of lateral associate hires	0	1	1	6
Number of lateral partner hires (equity and non-equity)	0	0	0	0
Number of new partners (equity and non-equity) promoted from associate rank	0	0	1	4
Number of new equity partners	0	0	1	4

Retention & Professional Development

ATTORNEYS WHO LEFT THE FIRM: 2003	MINORITY MEN	MINORITY WOMEN	WHITE WOMEN	TOTAL
Number of attorneys who voluntarily or involuntarily left your firm's employ in 2003	9	11	44	125

How do 2003 attrition rates generally compare to those experienced in the prior year period?

Higher than in prior years (principally due to a one-time layoff in January 2003)

Please identify the specific steps you are taking to reduce the attrition rate of minority and women attorneys.

• *As mentioned above, members of our Diversity Committee have met with each attorney of color at the firm to discuss and address any specific issues of concern. In addition, the Diversity Committee has met, and plans to meet, with associates of color as a group on a quarterly basis in formal and informal settings to continue the dialogue and bridge-building. Finally, the firm recently created the position, director of human relations, which is held by a former female associate, who, among her other responsibilities, will work with the co-chairs of the Diversity Committee to make certain that the needs and concerns of minority and women attorneys are heard and met.*

• Develop and/or support internal employee affinity groups (e.g., minority or women networks within the firm)

• Increase/review compensation relative to competition

• Increase/improve current work/life programs

• Work with minority and women attorneys to develop career advancement plans

• Introduce minority and women attorneys to key clients, including to lead engagements

• Review work assignments and hours billed to key client matters to make sure minority and women attorneys are not being excluded (though the hours/client matter review is not done solely through the diversity lens)

• Strengthen mentoring program for all attorneys, including minorities and women

• Professional skills development program, including minority and women attorneys (through the Boston Lawyers Group and other non-minority specific internal and external development programs)

Does your firm have part-time/flex-time policies that permit attorneys (male or female) to work alternative schedules?

Yes

What impact, if any, will the decision to work part-time have on an attorney's ability to make partner or, if already a partner, to remain a partner at your firm?

None, except that the partnership track may be extended for part-time attorneys depending on the amount of part-time work they undertake. We currently have several associates and partners who work are working part-time and/or flex-time.

Have any attorneys who chose to work a part-time schedule made partner at your firm?

Yes, several attorneys.

Management Demographic Profile (as of 12/31/03)

	MINORITY MEN	MINORITY WOMEN	WHITE WOMEN	TOTAL
Number of attorneys on the Executive/Management Committee or equivalent	0	0	1	3
Number of attorneys on the Hiring Committee or equivalent	2	1	5	16
Number of attorneys on the Partner/Associate Review Committee or equivalent	0	0	1	9

Please provide information regarding all minority and women attorneys who head offices or practice groups of your law firm:

Minorities or women heading offices: None. TH&T currently has just one office, located in Boston. It is currently headed by Bill Asher.

The Firm Says

We at TH&T are particularly encouraged that, as a result of our re-focused and re-energized diversity recruiting efforts in the fall of 2003, our 2004 summer associate class is one of the most diverse classes we have had: of our 39 summer associates, 12 (or 30 percent) are of color (seven minority male and five minority female), and 13 of the 39 summer associates are white women. Even with these encouraging recent gains, we recognize that we have much more work to do, especially in the areas of retention and promotion of lawyers of color.

Commitment to diversity

We are committed to fostering diversity at every level of the firm. This commitment is directly related to the emphasis we place on professional excellence, teamwork and creative thinking.

Our diversity efforts consist of two main categories of activity. First, we strive continuously to assure that our hiring, professional development and promotion practices are free of unfair bias and focused entirely on professional merit. Second, we cultivate an inclusive work environment in which every person is treated with respect, and the differences among us — whether in regard to race, color, gender, religion, age, sexual orientation, national origin, disability, veteran status or national origin — are welcomed and valued.

These efforts support our emphasis on professional excellence and teamwork by keeping us focused on true measures of quality and removing wasteful distractions and impediments to individual and group success. We

are sure that people contribute to their fullest potential and communicate most effectively with their colleagues when they feel valued and supported and are comfortable being themselves at the office.

We also believe that diversity creates a more stimulating work environment for everyone at our firm, which in turn promotes the kind of creative thinking that has been a hallmark of our success. Diversity helps to expand the spectrum of life experiences and perspectives that each of us can draw upon, and respect for the differences among us helps foster a climate of open-mindedness and flexible thinking.

We strive, on an ongoing basis, to understand what we do well, and improve upon the things we can do better, to cultivate diversity at every level of the firm. To assure that these efforts are conducted in a coordinated fashion, we appoint two partners to serve as co-chairs of our Diversity Committee. We also retain nationally recognized consultants to conduct in-house seminars designed to raise consciousness and promote effective communication in regard to diversity issues. Our firm was one of the founders of and is an active participant in the Boston Lawyers Group — a nationally-acclaimed consortium of Boston law firms and public sector legal offices dedicated to making Boston's legal community reflective of the diversity of our city.

Pro bono services

TH&T also is well-known for its commitment to various pro bono matters and programs focused on counseling and assisting persons of color. Among other pro bono programs and matters, TH&T is:

- a sponsor and holds a board seat on the Lawyers' Committee for Civil Rights Under Law of the Boston Bar Association;
- a sponsor and holds a board seat on Discovering Justice: The James D. St. Clair Court Education Project;
- a sponsor and lead participant in the Political Asylum/Immigration Representation Project;
- coordinator of the New England Innocence Project;
- lead sponsor and provides full-time counselors in residence to the Center for Women and Enterprise;
- a sponsor and lead participant in Citizens Schools' 8th Grade Writing Academy;
- a sponsor and board and advisory committee member of The Commonwealth Institute; and
- lead counsel in the ongoing state class action litigation brought by Massachusetts public school students challenging, on constitutional and statutory grounds, the nature of the Massachusetts Comprehensive Assessment System (MCAS) exam and its use in isolation as a high school graduation requirement.

Policy on Freedom from Discrimination and Harassment

Testa, Hurwitz & Thibeault has a fundamental commitment to treating all employees with dignity and respect. The firm's support of equal employment opportunity includes the firm's commitment that employment discrimination or harassment of employees on account of race, sex, national origin, religion, physical or mental disability, marital status, sexual orientation, any veteran status, any military service or application for military service, or membership in any other category protected under the law will not be tolerated. All employees have the right to be free from verbal or physical conduct which constitutes unlawful discrimination and/or harassment.

Any employee who believes that he or she has been the subject of discrimination and/or harassment should report the alleged act to any one of the following individuals as soon as possible: the Director of Human Resources, the Director of Human Relations, the Director of Administration, or their department manager or chair. The employee also should feel free to speak with their immediate supervisor or any partner, if the employee prefers. An investigation of any such complaint will be undertaken immediately, and steps taken when appropriate to resolve or correct the situation. The firm will make every effort to protect the confidentiality of

all parties, and the firm will make every effort to protect the complainant and any witnesses against retaliation for expressing their views or concerns.

Any firm employee who has been found to have engaged in discrimination or harassment or any retaliation against another person for having expressed their views or concerns regarding acts of discrimination or harassment will be subject to appropriate sanctions, including discharge.

We trust that all managers, supervisory personnel and employees will continue to act responsibly to maintain a professional working environment free of discrimination or harassment.

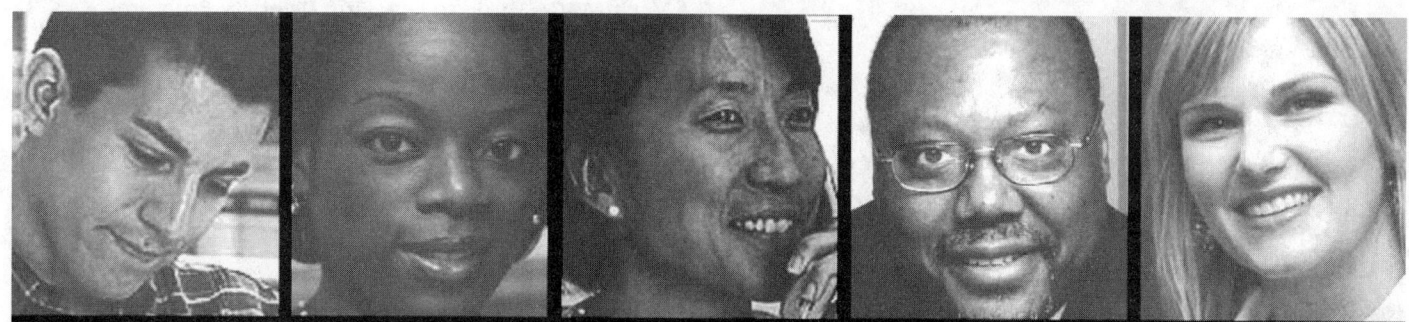

vision |diversity |commitment

Thelen Reid is proudly furthering its commitment to a diverse work force and partnering with clients who share our vision.

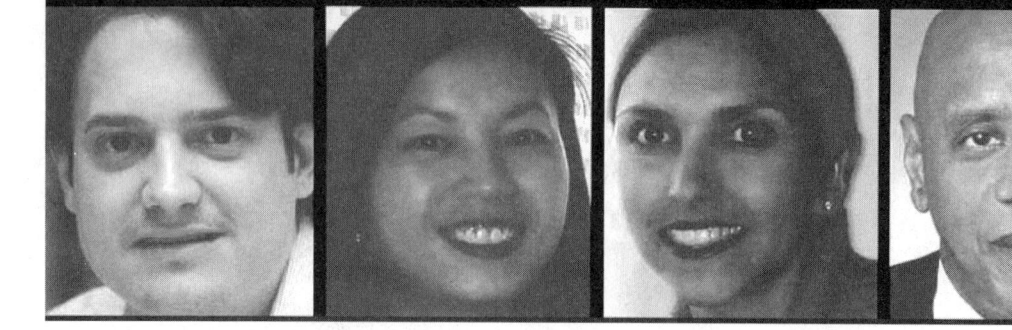

Thelen Reid & Priest LLP

Attorneys At Law

www.thelenreid.com

NEW YORK   SAN FRANCISCO   WASHINGTON, DC   LOS ANGELES   SILICON VALLEY   FLORHAM PARK, NJ

Thelen Reid & Priest LLP

101 Second Street, Suite 1800
San Francisco, CA 94105
Phone: (415) 371-1200
Fax: (415) 371-1211

FIRM LEADERSHIP

Managing Partner: Thomas Igoe Jr., Chairman
Diversity Team Leader: Deborah Broyles,
Partner and Chair of Diversity Committee

LOCATIONS

San Francisco, CA (HQ)
Florham Park, NJ
Los Angeles, CA
New York, NY
San Jose, CA
Washington, DC

LAW FIRM DEMOGRAPHIC PROFILES

FULL-TIME ASSOCIATES	2003	2002
Minority men	18	16
Minority women	31	29
White women	63	54
Total	216	202

SUMMER ASSOCIATES	2003	2002
Minority men	2	4
Minority women	5	10
White women	11	8
Total	26	29

EQUITY PARTNERS	2003	2002
Minority men	8	6
Minority women	5	4
White women	29	27
Total	195	182

NON-EQUITY PARTNERS	2003	2002
Minority men	1	0
Minority women	0	0
White women	2	3
Total	11	10

NEW HIRES	2003	2002
Minority men	5	3
Minority women	7	10
White women	18	13
Total	55	58

Strategic Plan and Diversity Leadership

How does the firm's leadership communicate the importance of diversity to everyone at the firm? (e.g., e-mails, web site, newsletters, meetings, etc.)

The chairman of the firm regularly emphasizes the firm's commitment to diversity in e-mails and at meetings and annual retreats. The chair of the Diversity Committee routinely communicates with the firm through e-mail regarding the committee's diversity initiatives. The firm's ongoing diversity initiatives are also highlighted in firm publications, such as the newsletter and the annual report, as well as the firm web site.

Who has primary responsibility for leading diversity initiatives at your firm?

Deborah Broyles, partner and chair of the Diversity Committee

Does your law firm currently have a diversity committee?

Yes

Does the committee's representation include one or more members of the firm's management/executive committee (or the equivalent)?

Yes

How many attorneys are on the committee, and in 2003, what was the total number of hours collectively spent by the committee in furtherance of the firm's diversity initiatives?

Total attorneys on committee: 47

Total hours spent on diversity: In excess of 700 hours

Does the committee and/or diversity leader establish and set goals or objectives consistent with management's priorities?

Yes

Has the firm undertaken a formal or informal diversity program or set of initiatives aimed at increasing the diversity of the firm?

Yes, formal

How often does the firm's management review the firm's diversity progress/results?

Quarterly

How is the firm's diversity committee and/or firm management held accountable for achieving results?

The Diversity Committee establishes an annual agenda with objectives for the year, and the activities are budgeted accordingly. The chair of the Diversity Committee updates the chairman of the firm quarterly regarding the progress and results of the committee's activities. The firm's evaluation and compensation structure recognizes contributions to firm administration, including furtherance of the firm's diversity initiatives.

LAW FIRM DIVERSITY INITIATIVES	ALREADY COMPLETED	CURRENTLY ADDRESSING	NOT A CURRENT PRIORITY
Undertake communication from firm management that diversity is a top priority of the firm.	✔		
Formalize diversity plan and committee with action steps and accountability to management.	✔		
Conduct firm-wide diversity training for all attorneys and staff.		✔	
Increase the number of minority attorneys at the associate level.		✔	
Increase the number of minority attorneys at the partnership level.		✔	
Develop/expand relationships with minority bar associations to offer firm's support of these networks.		✔	
Focus on strengthening firm's mentoring program, including for benefit of minority attorneys.		✔	
Conduct internal diversity needs assessment and/or retain diversity consultant to examine how firm culture might be more welcoming of minorities.		✔	
Support law firm's internal affinity networks (e.g., women, minority attorney networks).		✔	
Manage/monitor allocation of work assignments and/or hours billed to ensure women and minority attorneys have equal access/inclusion on top client matters.		✔	

Recruitment – New Associates

Does your firm annually recruit at any of the following types of institutions? (Check all that apply and list the schools).

Ivy League schools: Columbia University, Cornell University, Harvard University, University of Pennsylvania, Yale University

Public state schools: University of California-Boalt Hall, UC-Davis, UC-Hastings, UCLA, University of Michigan, University of Virginia, College of William & Mary

Private schools: Brooklyn Law School, Duke University, Fordham University, Georgetown University, George Washington University, Loyola Law School, University of Notre Dame, New York University, Pepperdine University, Santa Clara University, University of Southern California, University of San Francisco, Washington and Lee University

Historically Black Colleges and Universities (HBCUs): Howard University (commencing 2004)

Do you have any special outreach efforts directed to encourage minority law students to consider your firm?

• *The firm commissioned a Study of Minority Student Attitudes (see details below).*

• Hold a reception for minority law students

• Advertise in minority law student association publication(s)

- Participate in/host minority law student job fair(s)
- Sponsor minority law student association events
- Firm's lawyers participate on career panels at school
- Outreach to leadership of minority student organizations

SUMMER ASSOCIATE STATISTICS: SUMMER 2003	MINORITY MEN	MINORITY WOMEN	WHITE WOMEN	TOTAL
Summer associates	2	4	10	24
Summer associates who received an offer of full-time employment	2	3	9	22
Summer associates who accepted an offer of full-time employment	2	3	8	21

Lateral Associates and Partners

What activities does the firm undertake to attract minority and women attorneys?

- *Networking with organizations such as the MCCA and the California Minority Counsel Program*
- Partner programs with women and minority bar associations
- Participate at minority job fairs
- Seek referrals from other attorneys

Do you use executive recruiting/search firms to seek to identify new diversity hires (partners or associates)?

Yes

List all women- and/or minority-owned executive search/recruiting firms to which the firm paid a fee for placement services in the past 12 months:

Mestel & Co.

LATERAL ASSOCIATES AND PARTNERS: 1/1/03 – 12/31/03	MINORITY MEN	MINORITY WOMEN	WHITE WOMEN	TOTAL
Number of lateral associate hires	4	5	17	41
Number of lateral partner hires (equity and non-equity)	2	0	2	9
Number of new partners (equity and non-equity) promoted from associate rank	0	0	2	7
Number of new equity partners	2	0	4	16

Retention & Professional Development

ATTORNEYS WHO LEFT THE FIRM: 2003	MINORITY MEN	MINORITY WOMEN	WHITE WOMEN	TOTAL
Number of attorneys who voluntarily or involuntarily left your firm's employ in 2003	1	4	12	58

How do 2003 attrition rates generally compare to those experienced in the prior year period?

About the same as in prior years

Please identify the specific steps you are taking to reduce the attrition rate of minority and women attorneys.

• *Members of the Diversity Committee sit on the Associate Evaluation Committees for the East and West Coasts, and the chair of the Diversity Committee reviews all associate evaluations firm-wide. Additionally, the chair of the Diversity Committee meets periodically with select committee members to discuss and track the status and professional development of the firm's minority associates.*

• Develop and/or support internal employee affinity groups (e.g., minority or women networks within the firm)

• Increase/review compensation relative to competition

• Increase/improve current work/life programs

• Succession plan includes emphasis on diversity

• Work with minority and women attorneys to develop career advancement plans

• Introduce minority and women attorneys to key clients, including to lead engagements

• Strengthen mentoring program for all attorneys, including minorities and women

• Professional skills development program, including minority and women attorneys

Does your firm have part-time/flex-time policies that permit attorneys (male or female) to work alternative schedules?

Yes

What impact, if any, will the decision to work part-time have on an attorney's ability to make partner or, if already a partner, to remain a partner at your firm?

None, except that an extensive part-time commitment (several years or more) by an associate may result in a deferral of partnership consideration.

Have any attorneys who chose to work a part-time schedule made partner at your firm?

Yes, 10 attorneys. This number includes individuals who worked part-time prior to or at the time of their promotion to partnership, as well as individuals who joined the firm laterally as part-time partners.

Management Demographic Profile (as of 12/31/03)

	MINORITY MEN	MINORITY WOMEN	WHITE WOMEN	TOTAL
Number of attorneys on the Executive/Management Committee or equivalent	0	0	3	13
Number of attorneys on the Hiring Committee or equivalent	1	0	4	15
Number of attorneys on the Partner/Associate Review Committee or equivalent	0	1	3	25

Please provide information regarding all minority and women attorneys who head offices or practice groups of your law firm:

Minorities heading practice groups: Willie E. Dennis, Co-Chair, Private Equity and Venture Capital Group; William A. Kirk Jr., Chair, Government Affairs Department

Women heading practice groups: Linda S. Husar, Chair, Labor and Employment Department

The Firm Says

Thelen Reid & Priest LLP (TRP) is committed to recruiting, retaining and promoting attorneys who reflect the diversity of our society. We believe that a diverse work force enhances our workplace and improves the quality of the services we provide to our clients. Therefore, we strive to create an inclusive environment in which all of our attorneys are able to develop professionally and succeed in the practice of law.

Recruitment and promotion

TRP strives to generate a diverse applicant pool of first-year associates. To achieve this goal, we actively seek women and minority law students during the recruitment process. We also participate in minority student job fairs and have sponsored minority law student scholarships in conjunction with the Bar Association of San Francisco.

TRP continues to improve its diversity at the partner level by attracting a diverse number of lateral partners and counsel to the firm. We are also committed to developing and promoting minority and women associates within the firm's ranks.

In 2002, 62 percent of the associates promoted into our partnership were women, and 37 percent were minority. This trend continued in 2003 and 2004, with the promotion of five more women, which constituted 45 percent of the promotions. In addition, two minority and four woman partners were recently laterally recruited. Two minorities also recently joined as of counsel. A woman was appointed to serve on the firm's Executive Committee and Partnership Council (PC) and two other women were elected to serve on the firm's PC. In addition, a woman was recently appointed to chair our national labor and employment department, and a female minority was appointed to chair our national Diversity Committee.

Diversity initiatives

TRP recognizes that the attrition rate at law firms is higher among women and minority attorneys and therefore has undertaken efforts to combat this disparity and continue our accomplishment in retaining women and minority associates. We have created a national Diversity Committee (DC) consisting of partners, associates and professional staff from all offices. The DC is responsible for reviewing and making recommendations on diversity issues as they affect recruitment, professional training and development, retention and business development. Among the DC's projects is the landmark Study of Minority Student Attitudes (SMSA), conducted by an opinion research and public policy firm retained by TRP to study the perspectives of minority law school students. The study is an enduring project, and TRP views the SMSA as an important step toward strengthening our minority recruitment efforts. The DC also hosted a retreat for the firm's minority and GLBT associates (with management, partner and client participation) to discuss recruitment, retention and professional development issues unique to these attorneys.

TRP has also established the Women's Forum, which addresses the specific and unique concerns of women attorneys at the firm. Women's Forum-sponsored events have included professional development events,

accredited continuing legal education programs and panel discussions focusing on the issues facing women in the legal profession.

TRP also sponsors several career development initiatives that provide networking and professional development opportunities for its minority attorneys. TRP commonly sponsors the Minority Corporate Counsel Association's Annual Conference and the California Minority Counsel Program's Annual Business Development Conference.

The firm has developed longstanding relationships with several minority bar associations. In that regard, TRP regularly sponsors events for local minority bar associations, as well as the Asian American Bar Association, the National Bar Association and the American Bar Association Commission on Racial and Ethnic Diversity in the Profession.

TRP routinely seeks opportunities in which we can collaborate with our colleagues on diversity issues. For example, TRP's Annual National Partner Retreat in October 2003 focused extensively on diversity, including the business case for diversity, with presentations from diversity consultants and in-house counsel. Additionally, TRP has partnered with clients and corporate colleagues on a variety of diversity projects, such as e-mentoring high school students, hosting and participating in diversity presentations, and assisting with the development of a networking resource for in-house counsel women of color.

TRP recognizes and appreciates the importance of diversity to our clients. In 2003, TRP became one of Shell Oil Company's legal "strategic partners" when Shell adopted a strategy to identify a number of firms with which to work based on the legal expertise of those firms as well as their commitment to client service and other important shared values, such as diversity. Shell requires its strategic partners to report on their firm-wide attorney and staff demographics and on the hours worked for Shell by women and minorities. Shell also conducts annual diversity seminars to discuss strategies for retaining and advancing minority lawyers. We are proud to work with Shell and other clients in furtherance of our diversity objectives.

Diversity awards and affirmations

TRP has ranked in the top 15 percent for the past two years in the Minority Law Journal's Diversity Scorecard, which tracks the percentage of minority attorneys at the 250 largest law firms in the United States. Additionally, we recently received the 2003 "Breaking the Glass Ceiling" Award from the Bar Association of San Francisco for our continued efforts and commitment to advancing women to partnership and management ranks. TRP has also received recognition awards from the Charles Houston Bar Association and the California Association of Black Lawyers for ongoing organizational support and sponsorship.

To affirm our commitment to diversity, we became a signatory to the Association of the Bar of the City of New York's Statement of Diversity Principles and to the Bar Association of San Francisco's Diversity Programs and Model Policies. Both of these initiatives call upon law firms to hire diverse incoming classes and to strive to maintain this diversity as the associates rise in seniority and are ultimately considered for partnership.

Thompson & Knight. Making a difference.

TOP FROM LEFT: PARTNERS Victor Alcorta III - Austin, Kennedy Barnes - Dallas, Timothy R. Brown - Houston, Roxella T. Cavazos - Houston, E.F. Mano DeAyala - Houston, Cheryl E. Diaz - Dallas, Marcie Y. Flores - Dallas Boris A. Hidalgo - Houston, Ricky A. Raven - Houston ROW TWO: David M. Abner - Dallas, Isabel Amadeo - Dallas, Melanie S. Bruce - Dallas, Adrienne E. Dominguez - Dallas, Nichole Dotson-Olajuwon - Houston, Pablo C. Ferrante - Houston, Kristen Roberts Gibson - Houston, Tracy L. Hamilton - Dallas, David W. Henderson - Houston, Lily Nguyen Hoang-Dao - Houston ROW THREE: Isaac Johnson, IV - Houston, Jai-Prakash Phillip Kumar - Houston Michelle M. Kwon - Dallas, Jennine R. Lunceford-Ebron - Dallas, Kim McCrea - Dallas, Sarah E. McLean - Houston, Monica M. Smith - Dallas, Luke A. Walker - Dallas, Cara Clophus Wright - Houston, Thomas Yoo - Dallas

Thompson & Knight's impact on our clients' success is energized by the diversity of our lawyers.

Thompson & Knight  through diversity

CORPORATE AND SECURITIES   CORPORATE REORGANIZATION AND CREDITORS' RIGHTS   ENERGY   ENVIRONMENTAL   FINANCE   GOVERNMENT RELATIONS AND PUBLIC POLICY   INTELLECTUAL PROPERTY   INTERNATIONAL   LABOR AND EMPLOYMENT   OIL AND GAS   REAL ESTATE AND BANKING   TAX, BENEFITS, AND ESTATE PLANNING   TECHNOLOGY   TRIAL AND APPELLATE

ALGIERS   AUSTIN   DALLAS   FORT WORTH   HOUSTON   MONTERREY   PARIS   RIO DE JANEIRO   WWW.TKLAW.COM

Thompson & Knight LLP *

1700 Pacific, Suite 3300
Dallas, TX 75201
Phone: (214) 969-1700
Fax: (214) 969-1751

FIRM LEADERSHIP

Managing Partner: Peter Riley, Managing
Partner
Diversity Team Leader: Tim Brown, Partner
and Diversity Committee Chair

LOCATIONS

Dallas, TX (HQ)
Austin, TX
Fort Worth, TX
Houston, TX
Algiers, Algeria
Macaé, Brazil
Monterrey, Mexico
Paris, France
Rio de Janeiro, Brazil
Vitória, Brazil

LAW FIRM DEMOGRAPHIC PROFILES

FULL-TIME ASSOCIATES	2003	2002
Minority men	5	6
Minority women	13	11
White women	53	56
Total	136	141

SUMMER ASSOCIATES	2003	2002
Minority men	5	3
Minority women	5	9
White women	17	26
Total	53	71

EQUITY PARTNERS	2003	2002
Minority men	6	4
Minority women	3	2
White women	31	30
Total	165	164

NON-EQUITY PARTNERS	2003	2002
Minority men	2	4
Minority women	2	0
White women	4	3
Total	11	9

NEW HIRES*	2003	2002
Minority men	0	4
Minority women	7	1
White women	16	18
Total	41	47

*The number of new hires reflects hires made through the
2003 and 2002 calendar years.*

Strategic Plan and Diversity Leadership

How does the firm's leadership communicate the importance of diversity to everyone at the firm? (e.g., e-mails, web site, newsletters, meetings, etc.)

E-mails, web site, newsletters, meetings, retreats, advertising, and evaluations.

Who has primary responsibility for leading diversity initiatives at your firm?

Tim Brown, partner and Diversity Committee chair

Does your law firm currently have a diversity committee?

Yes

Does the committee's representation include one or more members of the firm's management/executive committee (or the equivalent)?

Yes

How many attorneys are on the committee, and in 2003, what was the total number of hours collectively spent by the committee in furtherance of the firm's diversity initiatives?

Total attorneys on committee: 15

Total hours spent on diversity: 2,016

Does the committee and/or diversity leader establish and set goals or objectives consistent with management's priorities?

Yes

Has the firm undertaken a formal or informal diversity program or set of initiatives aimed at increasing the diversity of the firm?

Yes, formal

How often does the firm's management review the firm's diversity progress/results?

Monthly

LAW FIRM DIVERSITY INITIATIVES	ALREADY COMPLETED	CURRENTLY ADDRESSING	NOT A CURRENT PRIORITY
Undertake communication from firm management that diversity is a top priority of the firm.	✓ *		
Formalize diversity plan and committee with action steps and accountability to management.		✓	
Conduct firm-wide diversity training for all attorneys and staff.		✓	
Increase the number of minority attorneys at the associate level.		✓	
Increase the number of minority attorneys at the partnership level.		✓	
Develop/expand relationships with minority bar associations to offer firm's support of these networks.	✓		
Focus on strengthening firm's mentoring program, including for benefit of minority attorneys.		✓	
Conduct internal diversity needs assessment and/or retain diversity consultant to examine how firm culture might be more welcoming of minorities.		✓	
Support law firm's internal affinity networks (e.g., women, minority attorney networks).		✓	
Manage/monitor allocation of work assignments and/or hours billed to ensure women and minority attorneys have equal access/inclusion on top client matters.	✓		
We support women and minority organizations	✓ *		

* We continue to focus on these areas

Recruitment – New Associates

Does your firm annually recruit at any of the following types of institutions? (Check all that apply and list the schools).

Ivy League schools: Harvard University, Yale University, Columbia University, Cornell University, University of Pennsylvania

Public state schools: University of Michigan, University of Texas, University of California at Berkeley (Boalt Hall), University of Kansas, Texas Tech University, Louisiana State University, University of Virginia, University of Oklahoma, University of Houston

Private schools: New York University, University of Notre Dame, Northwestern University, Georgetown University, George Washington University, University of Chicago, Vanderbilt University, Duke University, SMU Dedman School of Law, Tulane University, South Texas College of Law, Baylor University, Stanford University

Historically Black Colleges and Universities (HBCUs): Howard University, Texas Southern University (Thurgood Marshall School of Law)

Of the law schools that you listed above, do you have any special outreach efforts directed to encourage minority law students to consider your firm?

Participate in/host minority law student job fair(s)

SUMMER ASSOCIATE STATISTICS: SUMMER 2003	MINORITY MEN	MINORITY WOMEN	WHITE WOMEN	TOTAL
Summer associates	4	3	13	46
Summer associates who received an offer of full-time employment	3	2	9	33
Summer associates who accepted an offer of full-time employment	3	1	6	17

Recruitment – Lateral Associates and Partners

What activities does the firm undertake to attract minority and women attorneys?

• *Utilize recruiting companies and participate in minority legal conferences.*

• Partner programs with women and minority bar associations

• Participate at minority job fairs

• Seek referrals from other attorneys

Do you use executive recruiting/search firms to seek to identify new diversity hires (partners or associates)?

Yes

LATERAL ASSOCIATES AND PARTNERS: 1/1/03 – 12/31/03	MINORITY MEN	MINORITY WOMEN	WHITE WOMEN	TOTAL
Number of lateral associate hires	0	0	4	4
Number of lateral partner hires (equity and non-equity)	0	0	1	6
Number of new partners (equity and non-equity) promoted from associate rank	0	1	2	7
Number of new equity partners	0	1	0	6

Retention & Professional Development

ATTORNEYS WHO LEFT THE FIRM: 2003	MINORITY MEN	MINORITY WOMEN	WHITE WOMEN	TOTAL
Number of attorneys who voluntarily or involuntarily left your firm's employ in 2003	3	3	17	49

How do 2003 attrition rates generally compare to those experienced in the prior year period?

Higher than in prior years

Please identify the specific steps you are taking to reduce the attrition rate of minority and women attorneys.

- *One-on-one coaching sessions are provided for attorneys seeking image consultation or enhancement in a variety of areas such as client interaction and personal appearance.*
- Develop and/or support internal employee affinity groups (e.g., minority or women networks within the firm)
- Increase/review compensation relative to competition
- Increase/improve current work/life programs
- Work with minority and women attorneys to develop career advancement plans
- Introduce minority and women attorneys to key clients, including to lead engagements
- Review work assignments and hours billed to key client matters to make sure minority and women attorneys are not being excluded
- Strengthen mentoring program for all attorneys, including minorities and women
- Professional skills development program, including minority and women attorneys

Does your firm have part-time/flex-time policies that permit attorneys (male or female) to work alternative schedules?

Yes

What impact, if any, will the decision to work part-time have on an attorney's ability to make partner or, if already a partner, to remain a partner at your firm?

Participation in part-time or flex-time schedules have no impact on an attorney's ability to make or remain partner. Participation in this program is limited to a three-year maximum.

Have any attorneys who chose to work a part-time schedule made partner at your firm?

Yes, three attorneys. This program is available to all attorneys and many have participated in taking the reduced-hours option. It is the attorney's personal option to choose to return to a full-time schedule. Doing so within three years will not impact the attorney's partnership track. However, the majority of the attorneys who have opted for a reduced-hour schedule make a lifestyle choice not to return to a full-time schedule.

Management Demographic Profile (as of 12/31/03)

	MINORITY MEN	MINORITY WOMEN	WHITE WOMEN	TOTAL
Number of attorneys on the Executive/Management Committee or equivalent	0	0	1	10
Number of attorneys on the Hiring Committee or equivalent	2	3	9	33
Number of attorneys on the Partner/Associate Review Committee or equivalent	1	0	4	12

Women heading practice groups: Dororthy H. Bjork, Finance; Elizabeth A. Schartz, Labor and Employment; Martha Harris, Dallas Real Estate and Banking Section

The Firm Says

Thompson & Knight is fully committed to diversity. The firm's managing partner regularly communicates this commitment to partners and others throughout the firm. The managing partner chairs the firm's Management Committee which, in conjunction with the firm's Diversity Committee, is the guiding force behind the development and implementation of a wide variety of diversity initiatives.

The mission statement of the Diversity Committee is to cultivate and maintain diversity, including that of gender, race, thought and action, which we promote internally through employment, mentoring and retention, and externally through community involvement. The firm has a number of programs — e.g., in recruiting, mentoring and part-time lawyer programs, equal employment opportunity and harassment prevention policies, and so on — which assist the firm in meeting its diversity goals. We have also retained consultants to improve our awareness of diversity issues and to identify opportunities for greater diversity in our choice of vendors.

Following are highlights of some of the recent initiatives and long-term programs which the firm uses to support its commitment to diversity.

Thompson & Knight actively seeks and hires qualified minority candidates by participating in the Sunbelt Minority Job Fair, by using recruiting firms and by soliciting recommendations from current attorneys within the firm. In addition to being committed to recruiting qualified minority candidates and women, the firm recognizes the importance of, and is committed to, retaining such attorneys, and has developed programs to foster the development and success of minority and women attorneys in the firm.

The firm recognizes that one of the challenges for minorities and women working in large firms is finding opportunities to work on significant matters. Thompson & Knight has full-time managers in its trial and transactional practices whose responsibilities include coordinating with partners on work assignments. The firm's work assignment system helps to ensure that women and minorities receive the same opportunities as other attorneys and results in more equal distribution of work among all attorneys.

The firm has designed a database to track and report to clients the diversity of lawyers and hours worked on matters for the firm's Top 200 clients. We regularly report this information to clients who request it and periodically review the information to ensure we are meeting our clients' goals as well as our own.

As an adjunct to the Diversity Committee, the firm has formed a Diversity Initiative Group and a Women's Initiative Group. These two groups, comprised of partners and associates, meet monthly and focus on specific issues relating to their groups. Both groups focus on the assimilation of new minorities and women into the firm, marketing opportunities for group members, and ongoing client and professional development. Both groups also serve as mentoring forums for minorities and women, which supplement our firm-wide mentoring program.

The firm is planning a diversity scholarship program for selected minority students. The scholarships would be granted at the end of a law student's first year and will include the opportunity for a summer clerkship after the student has completed his or her second year of law school. We are currently gathering information from approximately 20 law schools to determine the specific details of the scholarship program, including the selection process.

The firm actively supports community projects for women and minorities. One such project, The Juneteenth Film Festival held in Dallas this year, was conceived and successfully implemented by Kennedy Barnes, one of our partners. Kennedy designed the festival to remember and honor the Emancipation Proclamation. This year,

more than 1,500 people attended the six-day event. Twenty-five films directed by, produced by or starring an African-American, or about issues relating to race, emancipation, apartheid, or diversity, were shown during the festival.

The firm sponsors or supports other minority and women's organizations and programs including the MCCA's annual dinner, the ABA's National Conference for Minority Lawyers, the Sandra Day O'Conner Luncheon, and the NAACP Brown v. Board of Education Commemoration.

We have an extensive pro bono program, much of which helps minorities and women. Two notable programs that we support, both of which are open to the entire community but are largely attended by minorities, are The Housing Crisis Center (HCC) in Dallas and the South Dallas Legal Clinic. The HCC is dedicated to preventing homelessness and stabilizing families, the elderly, and the disabled in decent, affordable, permanent housing. Clients who attend these workshops require legal assistance to avoid wrongful evictions or to have their utilities restored. Our attorneys and other personnel staff this clinic once a month. The Volunteer Center of Dallas County has acknowledged the firm for its work with the HCC.

The Dallas Volunteer Attorney Program has awarded the firm two pro bono awards for the significant hours we spend in support of the South Dallas Legal Clinic (SDLC). The SDLC is a clinic for people who fall below the poverty guidelines. Thompson & Knight secretaries and legal assistants perform interviews and check paperwork to ensure that the persons requesting assistance fall within the SDLC's guidelines. Once eligibility is established, our attorneys visit with the individuals and lend our legal expertise to resolving their problems.

Thompson & Knight promotes diversity in thought and action through the organizations we support, through the companies we do business with, through the clinics we serve, and through the employment, development and advancement of a diverse body of highly-valued personnel. We actively seek to recognize all of our employees' efforts to provide our clients with high-quality, cost-effective, and responsive service, and to do so in a way that embodies professionalism, teamwork, and our commitment to ongoing diversity initiatives.

Townsend and Townsend and Crew LLP

Two Embarcadero Center, 8th Floor
San Francisco, CA 94111
Phone: (415) 576-0200
Fax: (415) 576-0300

FIRM LEADERSHIP

Managing Partner: James G. Gilliland,
Chairman
Diversity Team Leader: Byron W. Cooper,
Chair, Diversity Strategy Committee

LOCATIONS

San Francisco, CA (HQ)
Denver CO
Palo Alto, CA
San Diego, CA
Seattle, WA
Walnut Creek, CA

LAW FIRM DEMOGRAPHIC PROFILES

FULL-TIME ASSOCIATES	2003	2002
Minority men	13	15
Minority women	5	6
White women	14	17
Total	77	79

SUMMER ASSOCIATES	2003	2002
Minority men	1	1
Minority women	4	1
White women	4	4
Total	13	11

EQUITY PARTNERS	2003	2002
Minority men	2	2
Minority women	0	0
White women	5	4
Total	42	44

NON-EQUITY PARTNERS	2003	2002
Minority men	6	3
Minority women	0	0
White women	1	0
Total	19	14

NEW HIRES	2003	2002
Minority men	5	1
Minority women	1	2
White women	1	3
Total	21	16

Strategic Plan and Diversity Leadership

How does the firm's leadership communicate the importance of diversity to everyone at the firm? (e.g., e-mails, web site, newsletters, meetings, etc.)

The firm's leadership communicates the importance of diversity through emails, meetings, training sessions and workshops. The importance of diversity is also communicated through the firm's strategic goals.

Who has primary responsibility for leading diversity initiatives at your firm?

Byron Cooper, chair of Diversity Strategy Committee

Does your law firm currently have a diversity committee?

Yes

Does the committee's representation include one or more members of the firm's management/executive committee (or the equivalent)?

No

How many attorneys are on the committee, and in 2003, what was the total number of hours collectively spent by the committee in furtherance of the firm's diversity initiatives?

Total attorneys on committee: 6

Total hours spent on diversity: 87.2

Does the committee and/or diversity leader establish and set goals or objectives consistent with management's priorities?

Yes

Has the firm undertaken a formal or informal diversity program or set of initiatives aimed at increasing the diversity of the firm?

Yes, formal

How often does the firm's management review the firm's diversity progress/results?

Management reviews the progress through regular meetings and through regular reporting to management from the Diversity Strategy Committee.

How is the firm's diversity committee and/or firm management held accountable for achieving results?

Accountability is maintained by making diversity achievements/results an annually reviewed topic of every partner.

LAW FIRM DIVERSITY INITIATIVES	ALREADY COMPLETED	CURRENTLY ADDRESSING	NOT A CURRENT PRIORITY
Undertake communication from firm management that diversity is a top priority of the firm.	✓		
Formalize diversity plan and committee with action steps and accountability to management.	✓		
Conduct firm-wide diversity training for all attorneys and staff.	✓		
Increase the number of minority attorneys at the associate level.		✓	
Increase the number of minority attorneys at the partnership level.		✓	
Develop/expand relationships with minority bar associations to offer firm's support of these networks.		✓	
Focus on strengthening firm's mentoring program, including for benefit of minority attorneys.		✓	
Conduct internal diversity needs assessment and/or retain diversity consultant to examine how firm culture might be more welcoming of minorities.	✓		
Support law firm's internal affinity networks (e.g., women, minority attorney networks).		✓	
Manage/monitor allocation of work assignments and/or hours billed to ensure women and minority attorneys have equal access/inclusion on top client matters.		✓	

Recruitment - New Associates

Does your firm annually recruit at any of the following types of institutions? (Check all that apply and list the schools).

Ivy League schools: Cornell University

Public state schools: University of California-Boalt Hall, University of California-Hastings, University of California-Davis, UCLA, University of Texas, University of Colorado, University of Washington

Private schools: Stanford University, USC, Georgetown University, George Washington University, Santa Clara University, University of Denver, University of San Francisco, Seattle University, Boston College, Northwestern University

Historically Black Colleges and Universities (HBCUs): Howard University(resume collection)

Do you have any special outreach efforts directed to encourage minority law students to consider your firm?

• Sponsor minority law student association events

• Firm's lawyers participate on career panels at school

• Scholarships or intern/fellowships for minority students (Will be offered this year)

SUMMER ASSOCIATE STATISTICS: SUMMER 2003	MINORITY MEN	MINORITY WOMEN	WHITE WOMEN	TOTAL
Summer associates	1	3	3	10
Summer associates who received an offer of full-time employment	1	2	2	8
Summer associates who accepted an offer of full-time employment	1	2	2	7

Recruitment – Lateral Associates and Partners

What activities does the firm undertake to attract minority and women attorneys?

Seek referrals from other attorneys

Do you use executive recruiting/search firms to seek to identify new diversity hires (partners or associates)?

No

LATERAL ASSOCIATES AND PARTNERS: 1/1/03 – 12/31/03	MINORITY MEN	MINORITY WOMEN	WHITE WOMEN	TOTAL
Number of lateral associate hires	4	0	0	13
Number of lateral partner hires (equity and non-equity)	1	0	1	3
Number of new partners (equity and non-equity) promoted from associate rank	2	0	1	8
Number of new equity partners	1	0	0	3

Retention & Professional Development

ATTORNEYS WHO LEFT THE FIRM: 2003	MINORITY MEN	MINORITY WOMEN	WHITE WOMEN	TOTAL
Number of attorneys who voluntarily or involuntarily left your firm's employ in 2003	5	2	4	22

How do 2003 attrition rates generally compare to those experienced in the prior year period?

About the same as in prior years

Please identify the specific steps you are taking to reduce the attrition rate of minority and women attorneys.

• Develop and/or support internal employee affinity groups (e.g., minority or women networks within the firm)

• Increase/improve current work/life programs

• Introduce minority and women attorneys to key clients, including to lead engagements

- Review work assignments and hours billed to key client matters to make sure minority and women attorneys are not being excluded
- Strengthen mentoring program for all attorneys, including minorities and women

Does your firm have part-time/flex-time policies that permit attorneys (male or female) to work alternative schedules?

Yes. The firm is developing a new, more comprehensive policy for implementation later in 2004.

What impact, if any, will the decision to work part-time have on an attorney's ability to make partner or, if already a partner, to remain a partner at your firm?

A part-time schedule may increase the time before an associate is considered for partnership.

Have any attorneys who chose to work a part-time schedule made partner at your firm?

No

Management Demographic Profile (as of 12/31/03)

	MINORITY MEN	MINORITY WOMEN	WHITE WOMEN	TOTAL
Number of attorneys on the Executive/Management Committee or equivalent	0	0	2	6
Number of attorneys on the Hiring Committee or equivalent	1	0	1	6
Number of attorneys on the Partner/Associate Review Committee or equivalent	2	0	1	9

Please provide information regarding all minority and women attorneys who head offices or practice groups of your law firm:

Women heading offices: Karen Dow, Partner in Charge, San Diego, CA; Gwen Peterson, Partner in Charge, Walnut Creek, CA

Minorities heading practice groups: Byron Cooper, Litigation; Richard Hsu, Technology Licensing

The Firm Says

With respect to diversity, Townsend's goals are to:

- Create a working environment where everyone has equal opportunity for achievement and advancement;
- Promote and improve Townsend's leadership position in diversity at all levels by retaining and promoting diverse legal talent;
- Recruit outstanding talent in a manner designed to improve Townsend's diversity;
- Collaborate with existing and potential clients to improve diversity in the legal profession;
- Work diligently with bar associations and other community organizations to foster diversity in the legal profession.

Diversity is one of Townsend's core values. We celebrate differences and honor every team member — male or female, gay or straight, first- or fifth-generation American. Diversity, we believe, contributes to our compassion, our unity and especially our strength as the leading intellectual property law firm. To that end, enhancing diversity is a primary consideration in our hiring practices. We sponsor events for minority and women's groups at law schools, including La Raza Law Students Association, the Black Law Students Association and the Asian Pacific Islander Law Student Association.

Women are represented on every major committee at Townsend, including the policy committee, the compensation committee, the partner nominating committee and the associate review committee. Our female attorneys, technical advisors and patent agents meet quarterly by teleconference and annually in person to discuss issues particular to women professionals, including part-time schedules and networking.

Townsend's nine-member Diversity Committee, comprised of partners, associates and staff from all of Townsend's offices, meets at least once a month. We are so committed to enhancing the firm's diversity that we hired an outside diversity consulting firm to assist us. To remain accountable to our goals, we also periodically report the firm's diversity statistics to our clients.

At Townsend, a commitment to diversity also compels us to act. We provide legal services to low-income individuals, mentor disadvantaged children and donate time and money to human rights organizations. We are also actively involved in the California Minority Counsel Program.

Troutman Sanders LLP

600 Peachtree Street, NE
Suite 5200
Atlanta, GA 30308
Phone: (404) 885-3000
Fax: (404) 885-3900

FIRM LEADERSHIP

Managing Partner: Robert W. Webb, Firm-wide
Managing Partner
Diversity Team Leader: Gordon R. Alphonso,
Diversity Committee Chair

LOCATIONS

Atlanta, GA (HQ)
Norfolk, VA
Raleigh, NC
Richmond, VA
Tysons Corner, VA
Virginia Beach, VA
Washington, DC
Hong Kong
London

LAW FIRM DEMOGRAPHIC PROFILES

FULL-TIME ASSOCIATES	2003	2002
Minority men	12	9
Minority women	17	15
White women	85	69
Total	246	204

SUMMER ASSOCIATES	2003	2002
Minority men	4	3
Minority women	6	6
White women	23	28
Total	55	59

PARTNERS*	2003	2002
Minority men	8	8
Minority women	1	1
White women	28	27
Total	210	205

The firm does not divulge numbers separately for equity and non-equity partners.

NEW HIRES	2003	2002
Minority men	4	3
Minority women	3	3
White women	18	30
Total	51	66

Strategic Plan and Diversity Leadership

How does the firm's leadership communicate the importance of diversity to everyone at the firm? (e.g., e-mails, web site, newsletters, meetings, etc.)

E-mails, web site, newsletters and meetings.

Who has primary responsibility for leading diversity initiatives at your firm?

Gordon R. Alphonso, Diversity Committee chair

Does your law firm currently have a diversity committee?

Yes

Does the committee's representation include one or more members of the firm's management/executive committee (or the equivalent)?

No

How many attorneys are on the committee, and in 2003, what was the total number of hours collectively spent by the committee in furtherance of the firm's diversity initiatives?

Total attorneys on committee: 13

Total hours spent on diversity: Not tracked

Does the committee and/or diversity leader establish and set goals or objectives consistent with management's priorities?

Yes

Has the firm undertaken a formal or informal diversity program or set of initiatives aimed at increasing the diversity of the firm?

Yes, formal

How often does the firm's management review the firm's diversity progress/results?

Quarterly

LAW FIRM DIVERSITY INITIATIVES	ALREADY COMPLETED	CURRENTLY ADDRESSING	NOT A CURRENT PRIORITY
Undertake communication from firm management that diversity is a top priority of the firm.	✓		
Formalize diversity plan and committee with action steps and accountability to management.	✓	✓	
Conduct firm-wide diversity training for all attorneys and staff.		✓	
Increase the number of minority attorneys at the associate level.	✓	✓	
Increase the number of minority attorneys at the partnership level.	✓	✓	
Develop/expand relationships with minority bar associations to offer firm's support of these networks.	✓	✓	
Focus on strengthening firm's mentoring program, including for benefit of minority attorneys.	✓	✓	
Conduct internal diversity needs assessment and/or retain diversity consultant to examine how firm culture might be more welcoming of minorities.		✓	
Support law firm's internal affinity networks (e.g., women, minority attorney networks).	✓	✓	
Manage/monitor allocation of work assignments and/or hours billed to ensure women and minority attorneys have equal access/inclusion on top client matters.		✓	

Recruitment – New Associates

Does your firm annually recruit at any of the following types of institutions? (Check all that apply and list the schools).

Public state schools: University of Georgia, Georgia State University, University of Florida, University of North Carolina, George Mason Univ., Univ. of Michigan, Univ. of Alabama, William & Mary, Univ. of Virginia, Florida State University

Private schools: Emory, Duke, Georgetown, Vanderbilt, Mercer, Univ. of Richmond, Washington & Lee, Wake Forest Univ., George Washington Univ.

Historically Black Colleges and Universities (HBCUs): Howard Unv.

Do you have any special outreach efforts directed to encourage minority law students to consider your firm?

• Participate in/host minority law student job fair(s)

• Sponsor minority law student association events

• Firm's lawyers participate on career panels at school

SUMMER ASSOCIATE STATISTICS: SUMMER 2003	MINORITY MEN	MINORITY WOMEN	WHITE WOMEN	TOTAL
Summer associates	4	6	23	55*
Summer associates who received an offer of full-time employment	2	4	18	41
Summer associates who accepted an offer of full-time employment	1	4	11	30

* Two summer associates withdrew from consideration, so we considered a total of 53 summer associate for permanent offers.

Recruitment – Lateral Associates and Partners

What activities does the firm undertake to attract minority and women attorneys?

• Partner programs with women and minority bar associations

• Participate at minority job fairs

• Seek referrals from other attorneys

Do you use executive recruiting/search firms to seek to identify new diversity hires (partners or associates)?

Yes

If yes, list all women- and/or minority-owned executive search/recruiting firms to which the firm paid a fee for placement services in the past 12 months:

BG Search Associates, The Roux Corporation. We have also entered into a semi-exclusive agreement with Diversity Legal Recruiting, Inc., a minority-owned search firm for lateral associate hiring.

LATERAL ASSOCIATES AND PARTNERS: 1/1/03 – 12/31/03	MINORITY MEN	MINORITY WOMEN	WHITE WOMEN	TOTAL
Number of lateral associate hires	1	0	4	14
Number of lateral partner hires (equity and non-equity)	0	0	1	6
Number of new partners (equity and non-equity) promoted from associate rank	1	0	3	10
Number of new equity partners*	N/A	N/A	N/A	N/A

* The firm does not disclose these numbers.

Retention & Professional Development

ATTORNEYS WHO LEFT THE FIRM: 2003	MINORITY MEN	MINORITY WOMEN	WHITE WOMEN	TOTAL
Number of attorneys who voluntarily or involuntarily left your firm's employ in 2003	7	4	25	76

How do 2003 attrition rates generally compare to those experienced in the prior year period?

Higher than in prior years

Please identify the specific steps you are taking to reduce the attrition rate of minority and women attorneys.

• Develop and/or support internal employee affinity groups (e.g., minority or women networks within the firm)

• Work with minority and women attorneys to develop career advancement plans

• Introduce minority and women attorneys to key clients, including to lead engagements

• Review work assignments and hours billed to key client matters to make sure minority and women attorneys are not being excluded

• Strengthen mentoring program for all attorneys, including minorities and women

• Professional skills development program, including minority and women attorneys

Does your firm have part-time/flex-time policies that permit attorneys (male or female) to work alternative schedules?

Yes. The firm supports part-time work arrangements, which allow its attorneys to pursue family, community and other professional endeavors. All reduced-hours arrangements are determined on a case-by-case basis with practice group approval.

What impact, if any, will the decision to work part-time have on an attorney's ability to make partner or, if already a partner, to remain a partner at your firm?

Decisions with respect to partnership are made on an individual basis. The firm does have partners who have entered into reduced-hour arrangements.

Have any attorneys who chose to work a part-time schedule made partner at your firm?

Yes. The firm has both partners who worked part-time before they made partner and partners who have worked part-time after they made partner.

Management Demographic Profile (as of 12/31/03)

	MINORITY MEN	MINORITY WOMEN	WHITE WOMEN	TOTAL
Number of attorneys on the Executive/Management Committee or equivalent	0	0	0	13
Number of attorneys on the Hiring Committee or equivalent	1	0	3	7
Number of attorneys on the Partner/Associate Review Committee or equivalent	1	0	3	11

Women heading practice groups: Ann Brown (Real Estate Finance), Kay Deming (Products Liability), Ashley Hager and Evelyn Traub (Compensation & Employee Benefits), Roseleen Rick (Multifamily Housing), Jane Schwarzschild (Trusts & Estates)

The Firm Says

Troutman Sanders' commitment to diversity extends beyond the walls of our firm. In addition to recruiting from minority job fairs, we sponsor several programs for women attorneys and take a proactive role in pro bono programs for minorities within our communities. Our dedication to this effort shows the multicultural atmosphere at Troutman Sanders.

The firm's long-term and ongoing commitment to diversity is reflected in its Mission Statement, which provides:

> Troutman Sanders LLP embraces diversity as a cornerstone of our future. It means, in part, a commitment by all of our attorneys to a shared vision and the establishment of a workplace environment that is fully inclusive. Troutman Sanders LLP values diversity in that it enables the Firm both to take full advantage of the knowledge and talents of a multicultural team in order to meet and exceed individual and business goals and client expectations, and to meet the Firm's obligation to provide the broadest possible range of opportunities to the members of the communities served by the Firm.

In keeping with its philosophy, Troutman Sanders LLP defines diversity as an environment of inclusion, in which gender, race, disabilities, sexual orientation, age, religion, national origin, background and social and ethnic group differences are accepted and valued, and all members of the firm can contribute to their fullest potential to achieve the firm's business goals.

Through the dedicated and focused efforts of the members of the Diversity Committee, the firm ensures that its philosophy on diversity is effectively implemented so that its work environment remains welcoming for all of its members and the community continues to benefit from the firm's outreach initiatives.

The firm sponsors and participates in many events which help us with our outreach efforts to minority organizations. Please see the list below as an example of our efforts.

• Sponsored Emory Black Law Students Association Annual Scholarship Banquet

• Participated in the Georgian Association of Black Women Attorney Summer Associate Brunch

• Sponsored Emory Legal Association of Women Students Event for Rape Crisis Line

• Participated in Minorities in the Profession Picnic

• Sponsored University of Georgia Black Law Students Association Reception for 1Ls

• Participated in the Atlanta Legal Diversity Consortium Panel for Summer Associates

• Participated in the Washington Area Legal Recruitment Administrators Association's Summer Associate Diversity Reception

• Sponsored Emory Legal Association of Women Students Race Judicata

• Attended "Attrition of Women from the Legal Profession" conference, hosted by the *Journal of Women and the Law*

• Participated in an event hosted by the Northern Virginia Asian American Association, the Northern Virginia Black Attorneys Association and the Northern Virginia Women's Attorney Association

Vedder, Price, Kaufman & Kammholz, P.C.

222 North LaSalle Street
Chicago, IL 60601
Phone: (312) 609-7500
Fax: (312) 609-5005

FIRM LEADERSHIP

Managing Partner: Charles Wolf and Douglas Hambleton, Executive Committee
Diversity Team Leader: Lawrence Casazza, Chair, Diversity Committee

LOCATIONS

Chicago, IL (HQ)
New York, NY
Roseland, NJ

LAW FIRM DEMOGRAPHIC PROFILES

FULL-TIME ASSOCIATES	2003	2002
Minority men	5	2
Minority women	2	2
White women	34	30
Total	86	78

SUMMER ASSOCIATES	2003	2002
Minority men	2	0
Minority women	0	0
White women	5	4
Total	10	9

EQUITY PARTNERS	2003	2002
Minority men	0	1
Minority women	1	1
White women	16	15
Total	100	98

NON-EQUITY PARTNERS	2003	2002
Minority men	0	0
Minority women	0	0
White women	2	3
Total	18	17

NEW HIRES	2003	2002
Minority men	3	0
Minority women	0	1
White women	10	9
Total	27	27

Strategic Plan and Diversity Leadership

How does the firm's leadership communicate the importance of diversity to everyone at the firm? (e.g., e-mails, web site, newsletters, meetings, etc.)

The firm communicates the importance of diversity through meetings and e-mails.

Who has primary responsibility for leading diversity initiatives at your firm?

The firm's Executive Committee

Does your law firm currently have a diversity committee?

Yes

Does the committee's representation include one or more members of the firm's management/executive committee (or the equivalent)?

Yes

How many attorneys are on the committee, and in 2003, what was the total number of hours collectively spent by the committee in furtherance of the firm's diversity initiatives?

Total attorneys on committee: 8

Does the committee and/or diversity leader establish and set goals or objectives consistent with management's priorities?

Yes

Has the firm undertaken a formal or informal diversity program or set of initiatives aimed at increasing the diversity of the firm?

Yes, formal

How often does the firm's management review the firm's diversity progress/results?

Vedder Price currently reviews the firm's diversity progress and results on an ongoing basis.

LAW FIRM DIVERSITY INITIATIVES	ALREADY COMPLETED	CURRENTLY ADDRESSING	NOT A CURRENT PRIORITY
Undertake communication from firm management that diversity is a top priority of the firm.		✓	
Formalize diversity plan and committee with action steps and accountability to management.		✓	
Conduct firm-wide diversity training for all attorneys and staff.		✓	
Increase the number of minority attorneys at the associate level.		✓	
Increase the number of minority attorneys at the partnership level.		✓	
Develop/expand relationships with minority bar associations to offer firm's support of these networks.		✓	
Focus on strengthening firm's mentoring program, including for benefit of minority attorneys.		✓	
Conduct internal diversity needs assessment and/or retain diversity consultant to examine how firm culture might be more welcoming of minorities.		✓	
Support law firm's internal affinity networks (e.g., women, minority attorney networks).		✓	
Manage/monitor allocation of work assignments and/or hours billed to ensure women and minority attorneys have equal access/inclusion on top client matters.		✓	

Recruitment – New Associates

Does your firm annually recruit at any of the following types of institutions? (Check all that apply and list the schools).

Ivy League schools: Columbia University

Public state schools: University of Illinois, Indiana University, University of Minnesota, University of Michigan, University of Iowa, University of Texas

Private schools: University of Notre Dame, University of Chicago, Northwestern University, Fordham University, Boston University, New York University, DePaul University, Loyola University Chicago, George Washington University, Georgetown University, Chicago Kent College of Law

Do you have any special outreach efforts directed to encourage minority law students to consider your firm?

• Participate in/host minority law student job fair(s)

• Firm's lawyers participate on career panels at school

SUMMER ASSOCIATE STATISTICS: SUMMER 2003	MINORITY MEN	MINORITY WOMEN	WHITE WOMEN	TOTAL
Summer associates	2	0	5	10
Summer associates who received an offer of full-time employment	2	0	5	9
Summer associates who accepted an offer of full-time employment	2	0	4	8

Recruitment – Lateral Associates and Partners

What activities does the firm undertake to attract minority and women attorneys?
- Participate at minority job fairs
- Seek referrals from other attorneys

Do you use executive recruiting/search firms to seek to identify new diversity hires (partners or associates)?
Yes

LATERAL ASSOCIATES AND PARTNERS: 1/1/03 – 12/31/03	MINORITY MEN	MINORITY WOMEN	WHITE WOMEN	TOTAL
Number of lateral associate hires	2	0	8	20
Number of lateral partner hires (equity and non-equity)	0	0	0	4
Number of new partners (equity and non-equity) promoted from associate rank	0	0	1	4
Number of new equity partners	0	0	1	4

Retention & Professional Development

ATTORNEYS WHO LEFT THE FIRM: 2003	MINORITY MEN	MINORITY WOMEN	WHITE WOMEN	TOTAL
Number of attorneys who voluntarily or involuntarily left your firm's employ in 2003	0	0	6	15

How do 2003 attrition rates generally compare to those experienced in the prior year period?
About the same as in prior years

Please identify the specific steps you are taking to reduce the attrition rate of minority and women attorneys.
- Increase/review compensation relative to competition

- Increase/improve current work/life programs
- Work with minority and women attorneys to develop career advancement plans
- Introduce minority and women attorneys to key clients, including to lead engagements
- Review work assignments and hours billed to key client matters to make sure minority and women attorneys are not being excluded
- Strengthen mentoring program for all attorneys, including minorities and women
- Professional skills development program, including minority and women attorneys

Does your firm have part-time/flex-time policies that permit attorneys (male or female) to work alternative schedules?

Yes. Alternative work arrangements are tailored to meet the needs of the individual attorney and the firm. Male and female attorneys may request an alternative work arrangement.

What impact, if any, will the decision to work part-time have on an attorney's ability to make partner or, if already a partner, to remain a partner at your firm?

The decision to work a part-time schedule does not exclude an attorney from partnership consideration, but consideration for partnership may be deferred.

Have any attorneys who chose to work a part-time schedule made partner at your firm?

No

Management Demographic Profile (as of 12/31/03)

	MINORITY MEN	MINORITY WOMEN	WHITE WOMEN	TOTAL
Number of attorneys on the Executive/Management Committee or equivalent	0	0	1	13
Number of attorneys on the Hiring Committee or equivalent	0	0	4	13
Number of attorneys on the Partner/Associate Review Committee or equivalent	0	0	4	14

Please provide information regarding all minority and women attorneys who head offices or practice groups of your law firm:

Women heading practice groups: Denise Blau, Corporate, New York; Garbielle Buckley, Business Immigration; Diane Kehl, Financial Institutions Litigation; Karen Layng, Construction Law; Cathy O'Kelly, Mutual Funds; Donna Pugh, Land Use; Nina Stillman, Employment Class Actions; Pearl Zager, Real Estate

The Firm Says

Vedder, Price, Kaufman & Kammholz, P.C. is strongly committed to equal employment opportunities for all applicants and seeks applications from qualified law students and attorneys who want a challenging practice in an open and flexible firm. The firm is committed to the hiring, training and retention, and promotion of women

and minority attorneys. To that end, the firm strives to be competitive in terms of compensation and benefits in order to attract the best and the brightest attorneys. In addition, the firm offers flexible, part-time work arrangements to its male and female attorneys tailored to the individual needs of the attorney and the firm. Attorneys have taken advantage of these alternative work arrangements in order to achieve a variety of personal goals and interests.

Vedder Price takes the career advancement of its attorneys, including its women and minority attorneys, seriously. The firm's efforts start with recruitment. In 2003, of the nine summer associates who received offers of full-time employment, five were women and two were minority men. Locally, Vedder Price participates in the Cook County Minority Job Fair. The firm, through its Director of Associate Development and marketing department, works with its minority and women associates on an individual basis to develop career advancement and business development plans and offers ongoing professional development counseling. In addition, the firm offers minority and women associates the opportunity to participate in monthly meetings to discuss business development issues and to learn client development strategies from some of the most successful and experienced attorneys in the firm. Many partners routinely introduce minority and women attorneys to key clients and strive to give associates increasing client contact and responsibility as they progress in their careers. Practice group leaders meet regularly to review hours billed and attorney work assignments and strive to ensure that minority and women attorneys are being fully utilized and included in significant deals and cases.

Vedder Price invests substantial time and money in its commitment to mentoring, training and the professional development of its attorneys. The firm's minority and women attorneys are offered, and substantially participate in, a wide array of practice area-specific training through the firm's in-house programs and through outside professional development courses and seminars. Each associate who joins the firm is assigned a mentor to help him or her integrate into the practice and to establish relationships with other attorneys and staff.

Finally, Vedder Price and its attorneys have a strong commitment to participate in and financially support activities that benefit minorities and women. To encourage these efforts, the firm counts a portion of an attorney's pro bono time in these activities as chargeable hour credit. The firm is also a charter member and supporter of the Chicago Committee on Minorities in Large Law Firms, an organization devoted to increasing diversity and diversity awareness in law firms. Among their many contributions, Vedder Price attorneys have been active in adoption and immigration programs to assist minority populations and have represented abused immigrant women seeking legal immigrant status under the Violence Against Women Act. Attorneys have represented minority children in juvenile court and school board administrative hearings and have been active on judicial evaluation committees in conjunction with minority bar associations to ensure that minority candidates are promoted to the bench. Vedder Price attorneys have assisted minorities and women in securing low-cost loans and helped establish tax-exempt status for a program for at-risk children.

Many Vedder Price attorneys contribute to, participate in and support minority and women scholarship and other funds, serve as tutors and career mentors, and support hunger and other community-based programs. Many have been recognized for their efforts. A member of the firm's Board of Directors is co-chair of the ABA Labor and Employment Law Section's Task Force on Sponsorships, Donors and Grants. The Task Force obtained approval from the ABA Board of Governors to establish a Diversity Program Support Fund to serve as a vehicle to help finance the participation of minorities, women and young lawyers in the Section's activities and educational programs. The firm is also a partner in the National Association of Women Business Owners, and several female partners have been honored by the organization for their outstanding contributions to the advancement of women in business.

Venable LLP

575 7th Street, N.W.
Washington, DC 20004
Phone: (202) 344-4000
Fax: (202) 344-8300

FIRM LEADERSHIP

Managing Partner: James L. Shea

LOCATIONS

Washington, DC (HQ)
Baltimore, MD
Rockville, MD
Towson, MD
Vienna, VA

LAW FIRM DEMOGRAPHIC PROFILES

FULL-TIME ASSOCIATES	2003	2002
Minority men	11	13
Minority women	16	12
White women	64	72
Total	173	180

SUMMER ASSOCIATES	2003	2002
Minority men	0	4
Minority women	4	5
White women	4	8
Total	14	27

EQUITY PARTNERS	2003	2002
Minority men	4	1
Minority women	2	0
White women	14	13
Total	141	136

NON-EQUITY PARTNERS	2003	2002
Minority men	5	4
Minority women	1	1
White women	19	20
Total	83	85

NEW HIRES	2003	2002
Minority men	5	4
Minority women	8	2
White women	18	21
Total	58	65

Strategic Plan and Diversity Leadership

How does the firm's leadership communicate the importance of diversity to everyone at the firm?

Website, the firm intranet, meetings of Board, Executive Committee, Hiring Committee, practice groups, staff meetings andpro bono newsletter

Who has primary responsibility for leading diversity initiatives at your firm?

James L. Shea, Managing Partner

Does your law firm currently have a diversity committee?

Yes

Does the committee's representation include one or more members of the firm's management/executive committee (or the equivalent)?

Yes

How many attorneys are on the committee, and in 2003, what was the total number of hours collectively spent by the committee in furtherance of the firm's diversity initiatives?

Total attorneys on committee: 14

Total Hours spent on diversity: Not counted per se

Does the committee and/or diversity leader establish and set goals or objectives consistent with management's priorities?

Yes

Has the firm undertaken a formal or informal diversity program or set of initiatives aimed at increasing the diversity of the firm?

Yes, formal.

How often does the firm's management review the firm's diversity progress/results?

Frequently, depending on which initiative

LAW FIRM DIVERSITY INITIATIVES	ALREADY COMPLETED	CURRENTLY ADDRESSING	NOT A CURRENT PRIORITY
Undertake communication from firm management that diversity is a top priority of the firm.	✔		
Formalize diversity plan and committee with action steps and accountability to management.	✔		
Conduct firm-wide diversity training for all attorneys and staff.		✔	
Increase the number of minority attorneys at the associate level.		✔	
Increase the number of minority attorneys at the partnership level.		✔	
Develop/expand relationships with minority bar associations to offer firm's support of these networks.		✔	
Focus on strengthening firm's mentoring program, including for benefit of minority attorneys.	✔		
Conduct internal diversity needs assessment and/or retain diversity consultant to examine how firm culture might be more welcoming of minorities.	✔		
Support law firm's internal affinity networks (e.g., women, minority attorney networks).	✔		
Manage/monitor allocation of work assignments and/or hours billed to ensure women and minority attorneys have equal access/inclusion on top client matters.	✔		

Recruitment – New Associates

Does your firm annually recruit at any of the following types of institutions? (Check all that apply and list the schools).

Ivy League schools: University of Pennsylvania; Harvard University

Public state schools: University of Michigan, College of William & Mary, University of Virginia, George Mason University, Univeristy of Baltimore; University of Texas

Private schools: Emory University; University of Notre Dame; Georgetown University; Duke University; George Washington University, Catholic University of America, American University

Historically Black Colleges and Universities (HBCUs): Howard University

Do you have any special outreach efforts directed to encourage minority law students to consider your firm?

• Advertise in minority law student association publication(s)

• Participate in/host minority law student job fair(s)

• Sponsor minority law student association events

• Firm's lawyers participate on career panels at school

• Outreach to leadership of minority student organizations

SUMMER ASSOCIATE STATISTICS: SUMMER 2003	MINORITY MEN	MINORITY WOMEN	WHITE WOMEN	TOTAL
Summer associates	0	4	4	14
Summer associates who received an offer of full-time employment	0	3	3	12
Summer associates who accepted an offer of full-time employment	0	2	1	7

Recruitment – Lateral Associates and Partners

What activities does the firm undertake to attract minority and women attorneys?

• Partner programs with women and minority bar associations

• Participate at minority job fairs

• Seek referrals from other attorneys

Do you use executive recruiting/search firms to seek to identify new diversity hires (partners or associates)?

Yes

LATERAL ASSOCIATES AND PARTNERS: 1/1/03 – 12/31/03	MINORITY MEN	MINORITY WOMEN	WHITE WOMEN	TOTAL
Number of lateral associate hires	0	2	7	20
Number of lateral partner hires (equity and non-equity)	4	1	2	16
Number of new partners (equity and non-equity) promoted from associate rank	0	1	0	4
Number of new equity partners	3	1	0	11

Retention & Professional Development

Does your firm have part-time/flex-time policies that permit attorneys (male or female) to work alternative schedules?

Yes

Please identify the specific steps you are taking to reduce the attrition rate of minority and women attorneys.

Develop and/or support internal employee affinity groups (e.g., minority or women networks within the firm)

Does your firm have part-time/flex-time policies that permit attorneys (male or female) to work alternative schedules?

Yes

What impact, if any, will the decision to work part-time have on an attorney's ability to make partner or, if already a partner, to remain a partner at your firm?

Associates who have worked a reduced schedule have made partner while on the reduced schedule and continued as partner in that status.

Have any attorneys who chose to work a part-time schedule made partner at your firm?

Yes, four attorneys.

Management Demographic Profile (as of 12/31/03)

	MINORITY MEN	MINORITY WOMEN	WHITE WOMEN	TOTAL
Number of attorneys on the Executive/Management Committee or equivalent	0	0	1	10
Number of attorneys on the Hiring Committee or equivalent	5	2	2	18
Number of attorneys on the Partner/Associate Review Committee or equivalent	1	0	6	13

Please provide information regarding all minority and women attorneys who head offices or practice groups of your law firm:

Women heading offices: Lindsay B. Meyer, Administrative Partner, Washington, DC

Women heading practice groups: Julie Petruzzelli, IP Litigation; Elizabeth R. Hughes, Business Transactions – South; Barbara E. Schlaff, Employee Benefits; Marcia A. Auberger, Trademark

The Firm Says

Venable is committed to maintaining and building a diverse group of attorneys and staff who reflect not only the diversity of the communities in which we practice but also the clients we serve. We are proud of our record in recruiting, retaining and promoting minority and women lawyers within the firm. Fully 135 of our 435 attorneys (31 percent) are women, including 40 partners, 14 of counsel. 77 associates and four staff attorneys. Our minority attorneys and paralegals represent more than 10 percent of our total partner, of counsel, associate and paralegal staff. Nine of our partners are minorities. We are especially proud of the fact that our minority associates comprise more than 16 percent of all associates, and we continue to nurture and develop this talented group of attorneys. In addition, our minority paralegals comprise more than 20 percent of total paralegals in the firm. Among our non-legal staff, 40 percent are minority. While these percentages represent a strong commitment to diversity, we continue our work to expand the size and scope of our women and minority professional and non-legal staff groups.

Minority recruiting

Venable's Hiring Committee makes a concerted effort to interview minority candidates who have demonstrated factors of success, including academic achievement and other credentials. For the past two decades, all of our entering classes of associates and summer associates have had significant minority representation. In 2003, minorities represented 40 percent of our entering associate class. The percentage of minority summer associates in our summer program has increased from 24 percent in 2001 to 29 percent in 2003. In addition, 31 percent of our lateral partner hires in 2003 were minorities, increasing from 17 percent in 2002.

In our effort to identify and attract minority candidates, we place a strong emphasis on efforts such as on-campus recruiting at law schools and job fairs with significant minority populations as well as outreach efforts to minority student organizations. In addition, Venable has been an active participant and contributor to the Minority Corporate Counsel Association. Venable attorneys are also well represented in the National Bar Association, as well as the American Bar Association's Commission on Racial and Ethnic Diversity in the Profession.

Minority retention, mentoring and professional development programs

Venable has two active retention, mentoring and development programs in place, both of which assist our minority retention, mentoring and professional development efforts. The first is our Preceptor Program, in which all first-and second-year associates are assigned to a preceptor, typically a partner or senior associate, who is responsible for the new lawyer's training and integration into the firm. Each new minority lawyer, like his or her majority colleagues, is matched with a lawyer who has accepted responsibility for the new attorneys' initial success at Venable. In addition, the Venable Success Network is focused specifically on giving our minority attorneys a strong network of colleagues within the firm. Developed several years ago, the Venable Success Network hosts social gatherings of minority lawyers and their spouses several times a year. Through dinners and other events, the attorneys develop relationships and come to support each other, contributing to each other's profile within the firm as well as with clients and community leaders.

Management's commitment to diversity

The management team at Venable realizes that it must lead by example and demonstrate the firm's commitment to diversity. To that end, Venable has invited its leading minority partners and attorneys to play key roles ion the firm's management committees, including Legal Personnel, Associates Evaluation, Hiring, Compensation, Partnership Selection and Diversity. We continue to recruit, develop and promote highly skilled lawyers, paraprofessionals and support staff with varied perspectives and wide range of racial, ethnic, cultural and social backgrounds. The firm's executive management team and board continually review and approve a wide range of programs to enhance further Venable's effectiveness in recruiting, retaining and developing minority attorneys and professionals.

Management's commitment to the minority community

Venable values the opportunities it has to work with the minority community, and our attorneys devote their personal time to special projects within the community. As one of many examples, Venable worked to establish a museum-quality exhibit in our Washington, D.C., office honoring Mary Church Terrell, a prominent civil rights activist and leader in desegregating Washington's dining establishments in the 1950s and the namesake of our Washington, D.C., office. The exhibit is housed in the gallery space of Venable's Washington, D.C., lobby and is located in the neighborhood where Mrs. Terrell fought to end segregation.

Venable partner Robert Wilkins was instrumental not only in the establishment of the Mary Church Terrell exhibit but also has dedicated a significant amount of his time over the past five years to the development of the proposed National Museum of African American History and Culture. Congress passed legalization authorizing the museum and has authorized initial appropriations of $30 million for the museum. Mr. Wilkins and others involved in this historic project are working with the Smithsonian Board of Regents to select an appropriate site for the museum.

Venable's dedication to the minority community extends to our pro bono work as well. For example, our attorneys successfully represented Dr. DeWayne Whittington, the first African-American superintendent of schools in Somerset County, Md., in his civil rights suit against the school system.

Vinson & Elkins L.L.P.

2300 First City Tower
1001 Fannin St., Suite 2300
Houston, TX 77002-6760
Phone: (713) 758-2222
Fax: (713) 758-2346

FIRM LEADERSHIP

Managing Partner: Joseph C. Dilg, Managing
Partner
Diversity Team Leader: Barron F. Wallace,
Partner

LOCATIONS

Houston, TX (HQ)
Austin, TX
Dallas, TX
New York, NY
Washington, DC
Beijing
Dubai
London
Moscow
Tokyo

LAW FIRM DEMOGRAPHIC PROFILES

FULL-TIME ASSOCIATES	2003	2002
Minority men	24	26
Minority women	28	32
White women	156	176
Total	405	459

SUMMER ASSOCIATES	2003	2002
Minority men	18	25
Minority women	23	15
White women	37	50
Total	121	181

EQUITY PARTNERS	2003	2002
Minority men	8	7
Minority women	3	2
White women	49	50
Total	306	308

NEW HIRES	2003	2002
Minority men	7	8
Minority women	3	6
White women	16	40
Total	62	92

Strategic Plan and Diversity Leadership

How does the firm's leadership communicate the importance of diversity to everyone at the firm? (e.g., e-mails, web site, newsletters, meetings, etc.)

Diversity is a key discussion topic at our all attorney meetings, partner retreats, section head meetings, recruiting strategy meetings and attorney orientation sessions, among other firm communication and planning sessions. Our Women's Initiative also publishes a regular newsletter, along with other supplemental e-mail communications. Lastly, a section of our web site is dedicated to our diversity and women's initiatives.

Who has primary responsibility for leading diversity initiatives at your firm?

Barron F. Wallace, partner

Does your law firm currently have a diversity committee?

Yes

Does the committee's representation include one or more members of the firm's management/executive committee (or the equivalent)?

Yes

How many attorneys are on the committee, and in 2003, what was the total number of hours collectively spent by the committee in furtherance of the firm's diversity initiatives?

Total attorneys on Committee: 34 (statistics are for Diversity and Women's Initiative Committees combined)

Total hours spent on diversity: 3,000*

Does the committee and/or diversity leader establish and set goals or objectives consistent with management's priorities?

Yes

Has the firm undertaken a formal or informal diversity program or set of initiatives aimed at increasing the diversity of the firm?

Yes, formal

How often does the firm's management review the firm's diversity progress/results?

The chairs of the Diversity Task Force and Women's Initiative meet with the managing partner on a quarterly basis, or more often, as needed, to review the progress of the two initiatives.

How is the firm's diversity committee and/or firm management held accountable for achieving results?

Our Management Committee evaluates individual partner contributions relating to diversity as a criteria in its biannual review of partner compensation. Additionally, our partnership admission evaluation process requires candidates to describe their efforts to mentor and help develop our more junior lawyers. Finally, it is expected that each section of the firm will formally evaluate how to integrate the diversity strategic plan within their section strategic plans. Section heads and practice group leaders shall report to management on their efforts to

promote diversity within their sections and are asked to consider the following best practice areas that have been adopted by the firm:

- Establishing accountability among partners
- A strategy for communication
- Active participation in firm diversity initiatives
- Diversity-related training and other initiatives
- A plan for associate development, including formalized mentoring activities specific to attorneys of color

LAW FIRM DIVERSITY INITIATIVES	ALREADY COMPLETED	CURRENTLY ADDRESSING	NOT A CURRENT PRIORITY
Undertake communication from firm management that diversity is a top priority of the firm.	✓		
Formalize diversity plan and committee with action steps and accountability to management.		✓	
Conduct firm-wide diversity training for all attorneys and staff.		✓	
Increase the number of minority attorneys at the associate level.		✓	
Increase the number of minority attorneys at the partnership level.		✓	
Develop/expand relationships with minority bar associations to offer firm's support of these networks.		✓	
Focus on strengthening firm's mentoring program, including for benefit of minority attorneys.		✓	
Conduct internal diversity needs assessment and/or retain diversity consultant to examine how firm culture might be more welcoming of minorities.	✓		
Support law firm's internal affinity networks (e.g., women, minority attorney networks).	✓		
Manage/monitor allocation of work assignments and/or hours billed to ensure women and minority attorneys have equal access/inclusion on top client matters.		✓	

Recruitment – New Associates

Does your firm annually recruit at any of the following types of institutions? (Check all that apply and list the schools).

Ivy League schools: Columbia University, Cornell University, Harvard University, University of Pennsylvania, Yale University

Public state schools: Louisiana State University, University of Michigan, University of Georgia, University of Houston, University of Texas, University of Virginia

Private schools: Brigham Young University, Duke University, George Washington University, Georgetown University, New York University, Northwestern University, South Texas College of Law, Southern Methodist University, Stanford University, Tulane University, University of Chicago

Historically Black Colleges and Universities (HBCUs): Texas Southern University, Howard University

Do you have any special outreach efforts directed to encourage minority law students to consider your firm?

• Hold a reception for minority law students

• Advertise in minority law student association publication(s)

• Participate in/host minority law student job fair(s)

• Sponsor minority law student association events

• Firm's lawyers participate on career panels at school

• Outreach to leadership of minority student organizations

• Scholarships or intern/fellowships for minority students

SUMMER ASSOCIATE STATISTICS: SUMMER 2003	MINORITY MEN	MINORITY WOMEN	WHITE WOMEN	TOTAL
Summer associates	14	11	25	82
Summer associates who received an offer of full-time employment	14	9	21	71
Summer associates who accepted an offer of full-time employment	9	8	12	44

Recruitment – Lateral Associates and Partners

What activities does the firm undertake to attract minority and women attorneys?

• Partner programs with women and minority bar associations

• Participate at minority job fairs

• Seek referrals from other attorneys

Do you use executive recruiting/search firms to seek to identify new diversity hires (partners or associates)?

Yes

List all women- and/or minority-owned executive search/recruiting firms to which the firm paid a fee for placement services in the past 12 months:

None

LATERAL ASSOCIATES AND PARTNERS: 1/1/03 – 12/31/03	MINORITY MEN	MINORITY WOMEN	WHITE WOMEN	TOTAL
Number of lateral associate hires	2	0	1	7
Number of lateral partner hires (equity and non-equity)	1	0	0	5
Number of new partners (equity and non-equity) promoted from associate rank	1	0	2	10
Number of new equity partners	2	0	2	15

Retention & Professional Development

ATTORNEYS WHO LEFT THE FIRM: 2003	MINORITY MEN	MINORITY WOMEN	WHITE WOMEN	TOTAL
Number of attorneys who voluntarily or involuntarily left your firm's employ in 2003	7	6	28	99

How do 2003 attrition rates generally compare to those experienced in the prior year period?

Higher than in prior years

Please identify the specific steps you are taking to reduce the attrition rate of minority and women attorneys.

• Develop and/or support internal employee affinity groups (e.g., minority or women networks within the firm)

• Increase/review compensation relative to competition

• Increase/improve current work/life programs

• Work with minority and women attorneys to develop career advancement plans

• Introduce minority and women attorneys to key clients, including to lead engagements

• Review work assignments and hours billed to key client matters to make sure minority and women attorneys are not being excluded

• Strengthen mentoring program for all attorneys, including minorities and women

• Professional skills development program, including minority and women attorneys

Does your firm have part-time/flex-time policies that permit attorneys (male or female) to work alternative schedules?

Yes

What impact, if any, will the decision to work part-time have on an attorney's ability to make partner or, if already a partner, to remain a partner at your firm?

An associate who works part-time will require a longer period to gain the experience necessary for partnership consideration. As a result, consideration for partnership will be delayed in comparison to associates who work full-time. Currently, we have four part-time partners at Vinson & Elkins, whose partnership status is unaffected by their chosen work arrangements.

Have any attorneys who chose to work a part-time schedule made partner at your firm?

None have been eligible for consideration. However, we have four partners who currently work part-time.

Management Demographic Profile (as of 12/31/03)

	MINORITY MEN	MINORITY WOMEN	WHITE WOMEN	TOTAL
Number of attorneys on the Executive/Management Committee or equivalent	0	0	2	15
Number of attorneys on the Hiring Committee or equivalent	1	0	2	11
Number of attorneys on the Partner/Associate Review Committee or equivalent	1	1	7	28

Please provide information regarding all minority and women attorneys who head offices or practice groups of your law firm:

Minorities heading practice groups (list names and departments): Barron Wallace, Public Finance (Houston)

Women heading practice groups (list names and departments): Molly Cagle, Administrative/Environmental Law (Austin); Robbi Hull, Appellate (Austin); Dusty Burke, Employee Benefits & Executive Compensation (Austin); Elizabeth Rogers, Health (Austin); Felicia Finston, Employee Benefits & Executive Compensation (Dallas); Karen Hirschman, Litigation (Dallas); Carol Dinkins, Administrative/Environmental Law (Houston); Sharon Mattox, Administrative/Environmental Law (Houston); Marie Yeates, Appellate (Houston) ; Karen Smith, Business & International (New York)

The Firm Says

Our success depends on our attorneys' collective commitment and ability to anticipate our clients' legal needs and challenges, and on working as a team with our clients to develop solutions for such needs and challenges. We cannot effectively accomplish this goal without diverse people and a culture supportive of such diversity.

~ Joseph C. Dilg, managing partner

At Vinson & Elkins, our approach to diversity is driven by our core values, which emphasize our commitment to attracting and retaining the finest lawyers and staff available, including people of different races, ethnicities, backgrounds and perspectives. We strive to be:

• the "law firm of choice" among clients who place emphasis on firms with diverse talent;
• the "employer of choice" among law firms, offering an inclusive workplace with the most innovative and effective programming; and
• a leader in the communities where we work and live.

We believe our success at achieving these goals is driven through the commitment and accountability of every partner within our firm. Accordingly, diversity is a focal issue in our strategic planning processes and a key discussion topic at each partner retreat, section head meeting, recruiting strategy meeting and attorney

orientation, among other firm communication and planning sessions. At the core of our success, however, lies individual action, which we believe revolves around the following key principles:

- **Inclusion:** Valuing the talents of every attorney within the firm and supporting each attorney's ability to maximize his or her potential as a lawyer.

- **Opportunity:** Proactively ensuring that every attorney at V&E is given opportunities to develop and succeed consistent with all other attorneys.

- **Relationships:** Increasing the ability for every attorney at V&E to form the relationships he or she needs for best performance as a lawyer.

- **Individuality:** Valuing each attorney for his or her unique set of skills and characteristics, maximizing the diversity of perspectives and, ultimately, enhancing client service.

To facilitate our progress, the leadership of the firm has established a Diversity Task Force, which reviews the firm's current efforts with regard to the recruitment, retention and advancement of minority attorneys and recommends strategic initiatives to enhance the firm's efforts in these areas. We have established a Women's Career Development Council for similar purposes. Both committees, working in conjunction with other firm leaders, have established strategic plans from which we have begun to implement specific programs and initiatives.

One of the outgrowths of this process is our New Lawyer Mentoring Program, which is designed to ensure that our new associates become integrated into their sections, the firm and the practice of law. The firm has also adopted core competencies that encompass the requisite skills and abilities our lawyers should focus on developing. These core competencies provide a framework for evaluating associates, for developing and planning training programs, and for facilitating each attorneys' ability to seek out the experiences necessary to develop the expected competencies.

> *Diversity is more than a word, a concept, a goal or a statistic. You must live it, practice it and be an active change agent to make diversity a reality. At Vinson & Elkins, we believe that diversity is achieved through a holistic approach that becomes integrated into every aspect of the firm, its administration and community outreach. This will make us stronger, better lawyers and, more importantly, allow us to provide our clients with continued excellence in legal representation.*
>
> ~ Barron Wallace, chair, Diversity Task Force

For more experienced lawyers, V&E provides the training, community exposure and other opportunities to ensure sucess throughout every step of their careers. As an example, our marketing organization is working to implement a portion of our diversity strategic plan, which calls for each African American, Asian and Latino senior associate to create a business development plan, with the assistance of the marketing organization. The firm is also sponsoring a series of programs in each office on business development for women, featuring a program developed by the ABA Commission on Women in the Profession.

To ensure that these endeavors are perceived as effective and valuable by our associates, we take steps to facilitate communication about these issues. We have created the Associates Subcommittee of the Attorney Development Committee, in order that associates may provide direct input on matters of interest to the ADC. As another example, members of the firm's Partnership Admission Committee meet with each associate to discuss the partner selection process and criteria.

Within our community, the firm makes scholarship awards and contributions to several law schools, as well as to numerous law school organizations serving minority students. We are also planting the seeds, as early as high school, for minority students to become lawyers. Our V&E Scholars Program annually provides five to six $10,000 scholarships to minority high school students who have a financial need, strong academic performance and interest in law. We also provide the scholarship recipients with summer job opportunities and attorney mentors.

Like the recruiting and retention of women at V&E, the recruiting and retention of minorities is critical to our future success. We have always adopted a leadership role in providing client service, in hiring the best lawyers and in leading the causes that impact our communities. It's good and right for us to place this same expectation on creating a workplace that fosters and develops all lawyers.

~ Marie Yeates, co-section head, appellate
Chair, Women's Career Development Council

Wachtell, Lipton, Rosen & Katz

51 West 52nd Street
New York, NY 10019
Phone: (212) 403-1000
Fax: (212) 403-2000

FIRM LEADERSHIP

Managing Partner: Daniel A. Neff, Managing Partner
Diversity Team Leader: Andrew R. Brownstein, Diversity Committee Chairman

LOCATIONS

New York, NY

LAW FIRM DEMOGRAPHIC PROFILES

FULL-TIME ASSOCIATES	2003	2002
Minority men	10	9
Minority women	6	6
White women	16	17
Total	93	99

NON-TRACK ASSOCIATES	2003	2002
Minority men	0	0
Minority women	1	1
White women	8	9
Total	11	9

COUNSEL	2003	2002
Minority men	0	0
Minority women	0	0
White women	2	1
Total	4	0

SUMMER ASSOCIATES	2003	2002
Minority men	6	4
Minority women	2	2
White women	5	7
Total	23	20

EQUITY PARTNERS	2003	2002
Minority men	2	2
Minority women	0	0
White women	10	9
Total	78	77

OF COUNSEL	2003	2002
Minority men	0	0
Minority women	0	0
White women	1	1
Total	7	6

NEW HIRES	2003	2002
Minority men	3	2
Minority women	2	2
White women	2	9
Total	18	30

Strategic Plan and Diversity Leadership

How does the firm's leadership communicate the importance of diversity to everyone at the firm? (e.g., e-mails, web site, newsletters, meetings, etc.)

The firm has a culture of informal communications on all matters, including diversity. All incoming associates and summer associates receive written copies of our policies and attend orientation presentations in which the firm's policies on diversity are clearly communicated. These policies are also posted on the firm's intranet where they are accessible to all employees.

Who has primary responsibility for leading diversity initiatives at your firm?

Andrew R. Brownstein, Diversity Committee chairman

Does your law firm currently have a diversity committee?

Yes

Does the committee's representation include one or more members of the firm's management/executive committee (or the equivalent)?

Yes

How many attorneys are on the committee, and in 2003, what was the total number of hours collectively spent by the committee in furtherance of the firm's diversity initiatives?

Total attorneys on committee: 12

Total hours spent on diversity: N/A. Committee formed in 2004

Does the committee and/or diversity leader establish and set goals or objectives consistent with management's priorities?

Yes. The firm is committed to recruiting and retaining a diverse and talented body of lawyers.

Has the firm undertaken a formal or informal diversity program or set of initiatives aimed at increasing the diversity of the firm?

Yes, informal

How often does the firm's management review the firm's diversity progress/results?

The firm's Recruiting Committee reviews and discusses these issues and communicates with the Management Committee on a routine basis.

How is the firm's diversity committee and/or firm management held accountable for achieving results?

The Recruiting Committee and the Management Committee are accountable to the partnership as a whole.

LAW FIRM DIVERSITY INITIATIVES	ALREADY COMPLETED	CURRENTLY ADDRESSING	NOT A CURRENT PRIORITY
Undertake communication from firm management that diversity is a top priority of the firm.		✓	
Formalize diversity plan and committee with action steps and accountability to management.		✓	
Conduct firm-wide diversity training for all attorneys and staff.		✓	
Increase the number of minority attorneys at the associate level.		✓	
Increase the number of minority attorneys at the partnership level.		✓	
Develop/expand relationships with minority bar associations to offer firm's support of these networks.		✓	
Focus on strengthening firm's mentoring program, including for benefit of minority attorneys.		✓	
Conduct internal diversity needs assessment and/or retain diversity consultant to examine how firm culture might be more welcoming of minorities.		✓	
Support law firm's internal affinity networks (e.g., women, minority attorney networks).		✓	
Manage/monitor allocation of work assignments and/or hours billed to ensure women and minority attorneys have equal access/inclusion on top client matters.		✓	

Recruitment - New Associates

Does your firm annually recruit at any of the following types of institutions? (Check all that apply and list the schools).

Ivy League schools: Columbia University, Harvard University, University of Pennsylvania, Yale University

Private schools: University of Chicago, New York University, Stanford University

Historically Black Colleges and Universities (HBCUs): Howard University

Do you have any special outreach efforts directed to encourage minority law students to consider your firm?

• *1L summer associate program*

• Hold a reception for minority law students

• Participate in/host minority law student job fair(s)

• Sponsor minority law student association events

• Firm's lawyers participate on career panels at school

SUMMER ASSOCIATE STATISTICS: SUMMER 2003	MINORITY MEN	MINORITY WOMEN	WHITE WOMEN	TOTAL
Summer associates	4	1	5	20
Summer associates who received an offer of full-time employment	4	1	5	20
Summer associates who accepted an offer of full-time employment	1	1	2	12*

* Six offers are still outstanding (including three to white women and two to minority men).

Recruitment – Lateral Associates and Partners

What activities does the firm undertake to attract minority and women attorneys?

• *Networking through the firm's partners, associates and summer associates.*

• Participate at minority job fairs

• Seek referrals from other attorneys

Do you use executive recruiting/search firms to seek to identify new diversity hires (partners or associates)?

Yes

If yes, list all women- and/or minority-owned executive search/recruiting firms to which the firm paid a fee for placement services in the past 12 months:

None

LATERAL ASSOCIATES AND PARTNERS: 1/1/03 – 12/31/03	MINORITY MEN	MINORITY WOMEN	WHITE WOMEN	TOTAL
Number of lateral associate hires	0	0	1	2
Number of lateral partner hires (equity and non-equity)	0	0	0	0
Number of new partners (equity and non-equity) promoted from associate rank	0	0	1	1
Number of new equity partners	0	0	1	1

Retention & Professional Development

ATTORNEYS WHO LEFT THE FIRM: 2003	MINORITY MEN	MINORITY WOMEN	WHITE WOMEN	TOTAL
Number of attorneys who voluntarily or involuntarily left your firm's employ in 2003	2	0	8	18

How do 2003 attrition rates generally compare to those experienced in the prior year period?

About the same as in prior years

Please identify the specific steps you are taking to reduce the attrition rate of minority and women attorneys.

• Develop and/or support internal employee affinity groups (e.g., minority or women networks within the firm)

• Increase/review compensation relative to competition*

• Introduce minority and women attorneys to key clients, including to lead engagements**

• Review work assignments and hours billed to key client matters to make sure minority and women attorneys are not being excluded

• Strengthen mentoring program for all attorneys, including minorities and women

• Professional skills development program, including minority and women attorneys

Traditionally our levels of compensation are significantly in excess of those at competitive firms. We believe our compensation not only fairly rewards our associates for their contributions to the success of our firm but also helps attract and retain qualified lawyers.

**Due to the size and unique nature of our practice, all associates, including women and minorities, are introduced to and have significant exposure to key clients.*

Does your firm have part-time/flex-time policies that permit attorneys (male or female) to work alternative schedules?

Due to our size, we do not have a formal policy. However, we have made specific part-time arrangements for a number of attorneys, including women and minorities. In 2003, five attorneys worked on a part-time or flex-time basis.

What impact, if any, will the decision to work part-time have on an attorney's ability to make partner or, if already a partner, to remain a partner at your firm?

All of our partners and partnership-track associates are full-time. Part-time attorneys may resume full-time work and rejoin the partnership track.

Have any attorneys who chose to work a part-time schedule made partner at your firm?

No

Management Demographic Profile (as of 12/31/03)

	MINORITY MEN	MINORITY WOMEN	WHITE WOMEN	TOTAL
Number of attorneys on the Executive/Management Committee or equivalent	0	0	1	9
Number of attorneys on the Hiring Committee or equivalent	1	0	2	14
Number of attorneys on the Partner/Associate Review Committee or equivalent	N/A	N/A	N/A	N/A

Please provide information regarding all minority and women attorneys who head offices or practice groups of your law firm:

Minorities heading offices: N/A (the firm has only one office)

Women heading offices: N/A (the firm has only one office)

Minorities heading practice groups: N/A (the firm does not have practice group leaders).

Women heading practice groups: N/A (the firm does not have practice leaders).

The Firm Says

We are an original signatory to the Association of the Bar of the City of New York's Statement of Goals for Increasing Minority Representation and Retention. The Firm is committed to recruiting a diverse and talented body of lawyers considering diversity in its broadest form. We were one of the first New York City law firms to offer health benefits to Domestic Partners. In the last three years, over twenty-five percent of our new associates are people of color.

We have also signed the Association of the Bar of the City of New York's Statement of Diversity Principles which commits us to a broad set of diversity goals. Along with the other firms that have signed the Statement, we have established a Diversity Committee and we will seek, in summary:

• To hire entry-level classes that reflect the diversity of graduating law students within three years;
• To achieve a level of diversity throughout a class's progression that is at least as great as when the class was first hired;
• To achieve representative diversity in promotions, including counsel and partner; and
• To achieve leadership positions throughout the firm that reflect the diversity among senior legal professionals.

Commitment to Diversity is always

WorthWeil

At Weil, Gotshal & Manges, we are proud of our long tradition of public commitment to diversity and equal opportunity. We work actively to foster an inclusive work environment, support minority-owned vendors and enrich our firm's culture through our diversity and inclusion initiatives for our lawyers and staff.

Our goal is clear – to create a workplace that enables everyone to succeed.
To learn more about Weil Gotshal, please visit us at *www.weil.com*

WEIL, GOTSHAL & MANGES LLP

AUSTIN   BOSTON   BRUSSELS   BUDAPEST   DALLAS   FRANKFURT   HOUSTON   LONDON   MIAMI

MUNICH   NEW YORK   PARIS   PRAGUE   SILICON VALLEY   SINGAPORE   WARSAW   WASHINGTON, D.C.

Weil, Gotshal & Manges LLP

767 Fifth Avenue
New York, NY 10153
Phone: (212) 310-8000
Fax: (212) 310-8007

FIRM LEADERSHIP

Managing Partner: Stephen J. Dannhauser,
Chairman
Diversity Team Leader: Lisa I. Cuevas, Director
of Global Diversity

LOCATIONS

New York, NY (HQ)
Austin, TX
Boston, MA
Dallas, TX
Houston, TX
Miami, FL
Redwood Shores, CA
Washington, DC
Brussels
Budapest
Frankfurt
London
Munich
Paris
Prague
Shanghai
Singapore
Warsaw

LAW FIRM DEMOGRAPHIC PROFILES

FULL-TIME ASSOCIATES	2003	2002
Minority men	56	46
Minority women	64	62
White women	203	186
Total	629	579

SUMMER ASSOCIATES	2003	2002
Minority men	5	18
Minority women	13	7
White women	45	46
Total	115	134

PARTNERS	2003	2002
Minority men	9	8
Minority women	5	4
White women	36	33
Total	233	221

NEW HIRES	2003	2002
Minority men	20	12
Minority women	18	17
White women	54	45
Total	173	160

Strategic Plan and Diversity Leadership

How does the firm's leadership communicate the importance of diversity to everyone at the firm? (e.g., e-mails, web site, newsletters, meetings, etc.)

Web site; formal training program; discussions at partner meetings; memoranda to firm; chairman's "State of the Firm" address; practice group meetings; business planning.

Who has primary responsibility for leading diversity initiatives at your firm?

Professional Relations Committee and Professional Conduct Committee, along with the firm's diversity director.

Does your law firm currently have a diversity committee?

Yes

Does the committee's representation include one or more members of the firm's management/executive committee (or the equivalent)?

No

How many attorneys are on the committee, and in 2003, what was the total number of hours collectively spent by the committee in furtherance of the firm's diversity initiatives?

Total attorneys on committee: 15

Total hours spent on diversity: 1,000+ hours

Does the committee and/or diversity leader establish and set goals or objectives consistent with management's priorities?

Yes

Has the firm undertaken a formal or informal diversity program or set of initiatives aimed at increasing the diversity of the firm?

Yes, formal

How often does the firm's management review the firm's diversity progress/results?

Quarterly

How is the firm's diversity committee and/or firm management held accountable for achieving results?

Partner members of the Professional Conduct Committee are reviewed by the committee chair on an annual basis as part of annual partner reviews; practice groups provide quarterly and annual reports to the Management Committee on diversity; chairs of associate-related committees report to the Management Committee periodically; all annual business plan development includes a diversity component; Professional Relations Committee and Professional Compensation Committee focus on reviewing minority and women associates.

LAW FIRM DIVERSITY INITIATIVES	ALREADY COMPLETED	CURRENTLY ADDRESSING	NOT A CURRENT PRIORITY
Undertake communication from firm management that diversity is a top priority of the firm.	✓		
Formalize diversity plan and committee with action steps and accountability to management.		✓	
Conduct firm-wide diversity training for all attorneys and staff.	✓		
Increase the number of minority attorneys at the associate level.		✓	
Increase the number of minority attorneys at the partnership level.		✓	
Develop/expand relationships with minority bar associations to offer firm's support of these networks.		✓	
Focus on strengthening firm's mentoring program, including for benefit of minority attorneys.		✓	
Conduct internal diversity needs assessment and/or retain diversity consultant to examine how firm culture might be more welcoming of minorities.	✓		
Support law firm's internal affinity networks (e.g., women, minority attorney networks).		✓	
Manage/monitor allocation of work assignments and/or hours billed to ensure women and minority attorneys have equal access/inclusion on top client matters.		✓	

Recruitment – New Associates

Does your firm annually recruit at any of the following types of institutions? (Check all that apply and list the schools).

Ivy League schools: Columbia University, Cornell University, Harvard University, University of Pennsylvania, Yale University

Public state schools: University of California (Boalt Hall), University of California (Hastings), UCLA, Rutgers University (Newark), University of Florida, University of Houston, University of Michigan, University of Texas, University of Virginia,

Private schools: Boston College, Boston University, Brooklyn Law School, Cardozo School of Law, University of Chicago, Fordham University, Duke University, Emory, George Washington University, Georgetown University, New York Law School, NYU, Northwestern University, Santa Clara University, Stanford University, St John's University, Tulane, University of Miami, University of San Francisco, USC, William & Mary

Historically Black Colleges and Universities (HBCUs): Howard University

Other predominantly minority and/or women's colleges: Northeast BLSA Job Fair

Do you have any special outreach efforts directed to encourage minority law students to consider your firm?

• *SEO Program participant;*

• *ABCNY Fellowship Program participant*

• Hold a reception for minority law students

• Advertise in minority law student association publication(s)

• Participate in/host minority law student job fair(s)

• Sponsor minority law student association events

• Firm's lawyers participate on career panels at school

• Outreach to leadership of minority student organizations

• Scholarships or intern/fellowships for minority students

SUMMER ASSOCIATE STATISTICS: SUMMER 2003	MINORITY MEN	MINORITY WOMEN	WHITE WOMEN	TOTAL
Summer associates	2	11	40	98
Summer associates who received an offer of full-time employment	2	11	39	98
Summer associates who accepted an offer of full-time employment	2	9	32	79

Recruitment – Lateral Associates and Partners

What activities does the firm undertake to attract minority and women attorneys?

• *Review minority resumes compiled by law schools; create affinity groups for law school recruiting.*

• Partner programs with women and minority bar associations

• Participate at minority job fairs

• Seek referrals from other attorneys

Do you use executive recruiting/search firms to seek to identify new diversity hires (partners or associates)?

Yes

LATERAL ASSOCIATES AND PARTNERS: 1/1/03 – 12/31/03	MINORITY MEN	MINORITY WOMEN	WHITE WOMEN	TOTAL
Number of lateral associate hires	3	5	19	55
Number of lateral partner hires (equity and non-equity)	1	1	2	9
Number of new partners (equity and non-equity) promoted from associate rank	0	0	1	6
Number of new equity partners	1	1	3	15

Retention & Professional Development

ATTORNEYS WHO LEFT THE FIRM: 2003	MINORITY MEN	MINORITY WOMEN	WHITE WOMEN	TOTAL
Number of attorneys who voluntarily or involuntarily left your firm's employ in 2003	10	17	36	119

How do 2003 attrition rates generally compare to those experienced in the prior year period?

About the same as in prior years

Please identify the specific steps you are taking to reduce the attrition rate of minority and women attorneys.

• Develop and/or support internal employee affinity groups (e.g., minority or women networks within the firm)

• Increase/improve current work/life programs

• Adopt dispute resolution process

• Work with minority and women attorneys to develop career advancement plans

• Introduce minority and women attorneys to key clients, including to lead engagements

• Review work assignments and hours billed to key client matters to make sure minority and women attorneys are not being excluded

• Strengthen mentoring program for all attorneys, including minorities and women

Does your firm have part-time/flex-time policies that permit attorneys (male or female) to work alternative schedules?

Yes

What impact, if any, will the decision to work part-time have on an attorney's ability to make partner or, if already a partner, to remain a partner at your firm?

Time spent working part-time does not have an impact on one's ability to make partner, although it may affect the length of the partnership track. Partners who are working part-time remain partners of the firm.

Have any attorneys who chose to work a part-time schedule made partner at your firm?

Yes. We do not keep formal records, but anecdotally, at least two.

Management Demographic Profile (as of 12/31/03)

	MINORITY MEN	MINORITY WOMEN	WHITE WOMEN	TOTAL
Number of attorneys on the Executive/Management Committee or equivalent	0	0	1	13
Number of attorneys on the Hiring Committee or equivalent	1	1	1	5
Number of attorneys on the Partner/Associate Review Committee or equivalent	0	1	3	12

Please provide information regarding all minority and women attorneys who head offices or practice groups of your law firm:

Minorities heading practice groups: Edward Soto, Miami Litigation; Oscar Cantu, Miami BFR

Women heading practice groups: Marcia Goldstein, BFR; Helene Jaffe, Anti-Trust and Competition; Mindy Spector, Complex Commercial Litigation; Diane Harvey, Bankruptcy Litigation; Melanie Gray, Bankruptcy Litigation; Jane McDonald, Financial Services Practice; Carlyn McCaffrey, Trusts & Estates

The Firm Says

Over the years Weil, Gotshal & Manges has endeavored to create a climate of inclusion, one in which people value individual and group differences, respect the perspectives of others, and communicate openly.

We have made considerable progress in the last 10 years in advancing opportunities for women and minorities. We are committed to finding ways to create career pathways for people from diverse backgrounds who have the personal attributes and the desire to grow in a supportive and collaborative business environment. The firm's diverse work force gives us tremendous strength.

Our diversity efforts span the globe. One of our goals is to seek out and hire from among the best and brightest law school candidates worldwide. By hiring people from diverse cultures and with diverse backgrounds and experiences, we gain essential perspective necessary for achieving our business objectives. We employ focused diversity recruiting strategies to compete effectively for qualified, highly sought-after women and minority graduates.

We were the first major law firm in New York to institute a firm-wide diversity training program and a formal diversity policy, which served as the initial model for the Association of the Bar of the City of New York. In 2002 we implemented another firm-wide diversity assessment and initiated a formal diversity and inclusion training program in the fall of 2003. By the spring of 2004 we conducted nearly 160 training classes in our U.S. and London offices, with close to 100 percent participation among partners, associates and staff. All our firm diversity and inclusion policies have been updated based on feedback from our needs assessment and in line with all equal employment guidelines and laws. We are currently exploring ways to expand the diversity and inclusion initiative to our other offices. As stated by Stephen J. Dannhauser in his address at the annual partner meeting on December 9, 2003: "We have an obligation to future generations of partners to leave behind a strong platform, just as the prior generation left for us. And when I say 'a strong platform,' I mean not just a solid financial position, but ideas, principles, positive values, strong character relationships and networks — held together by an inclusive culture."

The firm places very strong emphasis on the importance of networking and mentoring for success, and we have a very strong formal mentoring program. We believe a formal mentoring system is the first step to developing the informal relationships that may come naturally for some. To help make this process work smoothly, we routinely provide formal mentoring and coaching training to our associates and partners. First-year associates are assigned a peer mentor and a partner mentor. Additionally, we provide training to new associates in our New Associate Orientation Program.

Weil Gotshal has a Supplier Diversity Program that provides opportunities to establish business partnerships with minority- and women-owned businesses. We implemented a diversity-based vendor-purchasing program a decade ago and have received significant coverage in the media and awards from the National Minority Business

Council. The firm continues to significantly increase its use of minority- and woman-owned vendors and has implemented the Supplier Diversity Program in all of its U.S. regional offices.

1,800 Lawyers
38 Offices
25 Countries
52 Languages
50 Nationalities
1 Firm

Worldwide. For Our Clients.

We Understand The
Power Of Diversity

WHITE & CASE LLP

White & Case LLP

1155 Avenue of the Americas
New York, NY 10036
Phone: (212) 819-8200
Fax: (212) 354-8113

FIRM LEADERSHIP

Managing Partner: Duane D. Wall, Managing
Partner
Diversity Team Leader: Alison Dreizen,
Executive Partner in Charge of Diversity

LOCATIONS

New York, NY (HQ)
Los Angeles, CA • Miami, FL • Palo Alto, CA •
San Francisco, CA • Washington, DC • Almaty
Ankara • Bangkok • Beijing • Berlin •
Bratislava • Brussels • Budapest • Dresden •
Dusseldorf • Frankfurt • Hamburg • Helsinki •
Ho Chi Minh City • Hong Kong • Istanbul •
Johannesburg • London • Mexico City • Milan
• Moscow • Mumbai • Paris • Prague • Riyadh
• Rome • Sao Paulo • Shanghai • Singapore •
Stockholm • Tokyo • Warsaw

LAW FIRM DEMOGRAPHIC PROFILES

FULL-TIME ASSOCIATES	2003	2002
Minority men	57	66
Minority women	54	45
White women	137	126
Total	516	486

SUMMER ASSOCIATES	2003	2002
Minority men	9	8
Minority women	5	9
White women	13	21
Total	59	65

EQUITY PARTNERS	2003	2002
Minority men	4	4
Minority women	2	2
White women	14	10
Total	132	124

NON-EQUITY PARTNERS	2003	2002
Minority men	2	1
Minority women	0	0
White women	1	2
Total	22	24

NEW HIRES	2003	2002
Minority men	10	8
Minority women	16	19
White women	37	27
Total	130	114

Strategic Plan and Diversity Leadership

How does the firm's leadership communicate the importance of diversity to everyone at the firm? (e.g., e-mails, web site, newsletters, meetings, etc.)

Policies are posted on the firm intranet. We have launched a mandatory training program in all of our U.S. offices for all attorneys on preventing discrimination and harassment.

Who has primary responsibility for leading diversity initiatives at your firm?

Alison Dreizen, executive partner in charge of diversity

Does your law firm currently have a diversity committee?

Yes

Does the committee's representation include one or more members of the firm's management/executive committee (or the equivalent)?

Yes

How many attorneys are on the committee, and in 2003, what was the total number of hours collectively spent by the committee in furtherance of the firm's diversity initiatives?

Total attorneys on committee: Eight, in 2004

Total hours spent on diversity: 300

Does the committee and/or diversity leader establish and set goals or objectives consistent with management's priorities?

Yes

Has the firm undertaken a formal or informal diversity program or set of initiatives aimed at increasing the diversity of the firm?

Yes, informal

How often does the firm's management review the firm's diversity progress/results?

Annually

How is the firm's diversity committee and/or firm management held accountable for achieving results?

The partners responsible for running diversity initiatives are required to report progress which is taken into account, along with other criteria, in determining partner compensation.

LAW FIRM DIVERSITY INITIATIVES	ALREADY COMPLETED	CURRENTLY ADDRESSING	NOT A CURRENT PRIORITY
Undertake communication from firm management that diversity is a top priority of the firm.	✓		
Formalize diversity plan and committee with action steps and accountability to management.		✓	
Conduct firm-wide diversity training for all attorneys and staff.		✓	
Increase the number of minority attorneys at the associate level.		✓	
Increase the number of minority attorneys at the partnership level.		✓	
Develop/expand relationships with minority bar associations to offer firm's support of these networks.		✓	
Focus on strengthening firm's mentoring program, including for benefit of minority attorneys.		✓	
Conduct internal diversity needs assessment and/or retain diversity consultant to examine how firm culture might be more welcoming of minorities.	✓		
Support law firm's internal affinity networks (e.g., women, minority attorney networks).		✓	
Manage/monitor allocation of work assignments and/or hours billed to ensure women and minority attorneys have equal access/inclusion on top client matters.		✓	
The firm leaders participated in a diversity workshop.	✓		

Recruitment – New Associates

Does your firm annually recruit at any of the following types of institutions?

Ivy League schools: Columbia University, Cornell University, Harvard University, University of Pennsylvania

Public state schools: University of California-Boalt Hall, UC Hastings, UCLA, Rutgers University, University of Florida, University of Illinois, University of Michigan, University of Virginia

Private schools: American University, Boston College, Boston University, Brooklyn Law School, Cardozo School of Law, University of Chicago, Duke University, Emory University, Fordham University, Georgetown University, George Washington University, Hofstra University, Loyola University, McGill University, University of Miami, Northwestern University, University of Notre Dame, New York University, St. Johns University, Santa Clara University, Syracuse University, University of Toronto, Tulane University, USC, Washington University

Historically Black Colleges and Universities (HBCUs): Howard University

Do you have any special outreach efforts directed to encourage minority law students to consider your firm?

• Hold a reception for minority law students

• Participate in/host minority law student job fair(s)

• Firm's lawyers participate on career panels at school

• Scholarships or intern/fellowships for minority students

SUMMER ASSOCIATE STATISTICS: SUMMER 2003*	MINORITY MEN	MINORITY WOMEN	WHITE WOMEN	TOTAL
Summer associates	5	9	12	59
Summer associates who received an offer of full-time employment	8	5	11	56
Summer associates who accepted an offer of full-time employment	5	4	9	48

* Includes New York, Miami, Palo Alto, Los Angeles, Washington, D.C. and San Francisco

Recruitment – Lateral Associates and Partners

What activities does the firm undertake to attract minority and women attorneys?

• Participate at minority job fairs

• Seek referrals from other attorneys

Do you use executive recruiting/search firms to seek to identify new diversity hires (partners or associates)?

No

LATERAL ASSOCIATES AND PARTNERS: 1/1/03 – 12/31/03	MINORITY MEN	MINORITY WOMEN	WHITE WOMEN	TOTAL
Number of lateral associate hires	4	7	18	63
Number of lateral partner hires (equity and non-equity)	0	0	1	7
Number of new partners (equity and non-equity) promoted from associate rank	0	0	2	7
Number of new equity partners	3	0	0	10

Retention & Professional Development

ATTORNEYS WHO LEFT THE FIRM: 2003	MINORITY MEN	MINORITY WOMEN	WHITE WOMEN	TOTAL
Number of attorneys who voluntarily or involuntarily left your firm's employ in 2003	16	8	22	93

How do 2003 attrition rates generally compare to those experienced in the prior year period?

Higher than in prior years

Please identify the specific steps you are taking to reduce the attrition rate of minority and women attorneys.

• Develop and/or support internal employee affinity groups (e.g., minority or women networks within the firm)

• Increase/improve current work/life programs

• Adopt dispute resolution process

• Work with minority and women attorneys to develop career advancement plans

• Strengthen mentoring program for all attorneys, including minorities and women

• Professional skills development program, including minority and women attorneys

Does your firm have part-time/flex-time policies that permit attorneys (male or female) to work alternative schedules?

Yes

What impact, if any, will the decision to work part-time have on an attorney's ability to make partner or, if already a partner, to remain a partner at your firm?

Partnership decisions are based on a number of factors. In the case of a part-time attorney, these factors, in addition to the ones otherwise considered, would include the length of time with the firm and the length of time the attorney has been working part-time. A partner who decides to work part-time would be able to remain a partner, although there may be an adjustment to such person's compensation.

Have any attorneys who chose to work a part-time schedule made partner at your firm?

Yes, one attorney. in the D.C. office worked part-time from 9/6/1994 to 1/1/1997.

Management Demographic Profile (as of 12/31/03)

	MINORITY MEN	MINORITY WOMEN	WHITE WOMEN	TOTAL
Number of attorneys on the Executive/Management Committee or equivalent	0	0	0	8
Number of attorneys on the Hiring Committee or equivalent	1	0	6	15
Number of attorneys on the Partner/Associate Review Committee or equivalent*	0	2	3	10

Lawyers Committee

Please provide information regarding all minority and women attorneys who head offices or practice groups of your law firm:

Women heading practice groups: Maureen Brundage, Securities

Minorities heading practice groups: Victor M. Alvarez, Executive Partner – Miami

The Firm Says

White & Case actively fosters diversity in our workplace. As a global law firm, cultural and ethnic diversity is an essential element of White & Case. The firm has placed an emphasis on creating an environment in our domestic offices that is multicultural and reflective of the international arena in which we operate. We are committed to making White & Case a welcoming and open environment for all who work at the firm.

White & Case's lawyers represent 50 different nationalities, speak more than 52 languages, come from an array of schools and have a variety of backgrounds, work experiences, personalities and personal goals. We are extremely attuned to the potential of smart, motivated people whose backgrounds are diverse and whose resumes may not present a typical, linear path. We are proud to note that of the 11 associates elevated to partnership in the United States as of January 1, 2004, two are minority women and two are minority men. In addition to our lawyers, the firm's managerial staff is ethnically diverse as well.

Alison M. Dreizen, executive partner in charge of diversity, leads the firm's Diversity Committee in the ongoing development and implementation of diversity initiatives throughout the firm, including leadership training sessions, workshops on preventing sexual harassment and discrimination, development of a mentoring program and coordination with the Employment Committee and the Lawyers Committee to ensure that we continually work to implement the diversity principles we support.

Over the years White & Case has maintained a rigorous minority recruitment effort in its offices in New York, Los Angeles, Miami, Palo Alto, San Francisco and Washington, D.C. As a result, nearly a quarter of all domestic associates are minorities. All of the offices in the United States actively recruit minority applicants at the schools where they interview on campus. The New York and Washington offices also recruit at Washington, D.C.-based Howard University Law School, where most of the student body is minority. The firm participates in regional recruiting conferences and job fairs sponsored by minority law student associations.

White & Case was one of the first signatories to the Association of the Bar of the City of New York's Statement of Goals of New York Law Firms and Corporate Legal Departments for Increasing Minority Representation and Retention. The firm is also one of the authors of, and original signatories to, the Statement of Diversity Principles of the Association of the Bar of the City of New York, pursuant to which we have adopted diversity-related goals in hiring, retention, promotion and leadership. For a number of years, we have participated in the Tulane Law School Diversity Clerkship Program. The program is specifically designed to increase the number of minority lawyers in prominent legal positions and places first-year minority students in summer clerkship positions. We also participate in the Northeast and Mid-Atlantic Black Law Students Association (BLSA) job fairs in New York City and Washington, D.C., respectively.

Additionally, White & Case works closely with the Asian American Bar Association, hosting and supporting many events for the organization. White & Case's strong ties to the Association are due in large part to Sylvia Chin, a partner based in the New York office, who has served as president and director of the Association.

White & Case has also recently formed a steering committee led by partner and management board member Tim Goodell, to develop and implement a women's advancement initiative — a program designed to identify opportunities for improving the firm's ability to attract and retain women lawyers. We believe this is important to achieving our goal that White & Case be a place where everyone's talent and contribution is recognized and utilized to the fullest. The business case for doing this is clear. More than half of today's law students are women and we must successfully compete for and retain the best of this segment of the talent pool. Further, more and more of our clients expect to work with women partners on their client relationship teams and in senior leadership positions. We believe that the women's advancement initiative will continue to help us strengthen our efforts in this important area.

The firm's domestic offices also have prominent international legal intern programs, bringing a number of lawyers and professionals from other countries to spend time learning the U.S. legal system.

White & Case lawyers have committed themselves to pro bono work as a way to give back to the community and deepen their experience. This commitment includes providing pro bono services to public interest organizations such as The Appleseed Foundation, where the firm first became involved on one of their projects aimed at getting more immigrants into the banking system. The firm continues to work with the Foundation on the issue of financial literacy and education for recent immigrants, conducting research for, or reviewing drafts of, different consumer brochures to educate Spanish-speaking immigrants about the U.S. banking system and how it can benefit them. As pro bono counsel to the New York Immigration Coalition, White & Case played a central role in convincing the Federal Emergency Management Agency (FEMA) to discontinue their application of an unduly burdensome standard of review of applications to the federal government's mortgage and rental assistance program and continues to work with the organization to ensure that FEMA follows through on its promise to support vulnerable New Yorkers who are still suffering from the effects of September 11.

Diversity is, and will continue to be, a priority for White & Case as the firm builds on the excellent platform it has developed to serve its clients and maintain a productive, challenging and comfortable work environment for all.

Wildman, Harrold, Allen & Dixon LLP

225 West Wacker Drive
Suite 3000
Chicago, IL 60606-1229
Phone: (312) 201-2000
Fax: (312) 201-2555

FIRM LEADERSHIP

Managing Partner: Robert L. Shuftan,
Managing Partner
Diversity Team Leader: Jerald P. Esrick, Chair,
Diversity Committee

LOCATIONS

Chicago, IL (HQ)
Lisle, IL
London

LAW FIRM DEMOGRAPHIC PROFILES

FULL-TIME ASSOCIATES	2003	2002
Minority men	5	7
Minority women	4	4
White women	32	33
Total	92	85

SUMMER ASSOCIATES	2003	2002
Minority men	5	2
Minority women	1	1
White women	8	4
Total	20	20

EQUITY PARTNERS	2003	2002
Minority men	1	1
Minority women	0	0
White women	4	5
Total	51	56

NON-EQUITY PARTNERS	2003	2002
Minority men	3	3
Minority women	0	0
White women	12	19
Total	51	47

NEW HIRES	2003	2002
Minority men	1	0
Minority women	2	2
White women	12	9
Total	33	27

OF COUNSEL	2003	2002
White women	4	4
Total	17	17

MINORITY CORPORATE COUNSEL ASSOCIATION

Strategic Plan and Diversity Leadership

How does the firm's leadership communicate the importance of diversity to everyone at the firm? (e.g., e-mails, web site, newsletters, meetings, etc.)

The firm's Diversity Initiative is part of our Strategic Plan. We have held diversity training sessions with our diversity consultant for the Executive Committee, staff department heads, practice group leaders, partners, associates, staff and summer associates. We reinforce the importance of diversity through our new employee orientation program. We communicate through our internal newsletter, the Wildman Herald, e-mails and our firm web site.

Who has primary responsibility for leading diversity initiatives at your firm?

Robert Shuftan, managing partner, and Jerald Esrick, chair of the Diversity Committee

Does your law firm currently have a diversity committee?

Yes

Does the committee's representation include one or more members of the firm's management/executive committee (or the equivalent)?

Yes

How many attorneys are on the committee, and in 2003, what was the total number of hours collectively spent by the committee in furtherance of the firm's diversity initiatives?

Total attorneys on committee: 12

Total hours spent on diversity: 500 (estimate, does not include recruiting)

Does the committee and/or diversity leader establish and set goals or objectives consistent with management's priorities?

Yes, through the Diversity Initiative

Has the firm undertaken a formal or informal diversity program or set of initiatives aimed at increasing the diversity of the firm?

Yes, formal

How often does the firm's management review the firm's diversity progress/results?

Frequently, but on an ad hoc basis

How is the firm's diversity committee and/or firm management held accountable for achieving results?

Diversity efforts of all partners and associates are reviewed as part of the partner compensation and associate review process and each attorney must provide a self-assessment of her/his efforts toward diversity. Firm management continually reviews both statistical information on the composition of the firm's attorneys and staff and monitors the firm's internal and external activities in support of our Diversity Initiative. The membership

of the Diversity Committee is rotated to obtain fresh ideas and perspectives. Our recruiting of minority attorneys has been targeted and is increasingly successful. Our staff has a high percentage of minority employees.

LAW FIRM DIVERSITY INITIATIVES	ALREADY COMPLETED	CURRENTLY ADDRESSING	NOT A CURRENT PRIORITY
Undertake communication from firm management that diversity is a top priority of the firm.	✓		
Formalize diversity plan and committee with action steps and accountability to management.	✓		
Conduct firm-wide diversity training for all attorneys and staff.	✓		
Increase the number of minority attorneys at the associate level.	✓ *		
Increase the number of minority attorneys at the partnership level.	✓ *		
Develop/expand relationships with minority bar associations to offer firm's support of these networks.	✓		
Focus on strengthening firm's mentoring program, including for benefit of minority attorneys.	✓		
Conduct internal diversity needs assessment and/or retain diversity consultant to examine how firm culture might be more welcoming of minorities.	✓ **		
Support law firm's internal affinity networks (e.g., women, minority attorney networks).	✓		
Manage/monitor allocation of work assignments and/or hours billed to ensure women and minority attorneys have equal access/inclusion on top client matters.	✓ ***		
We retain a diversity consultant; we have adopted a formal mentoring program and affinity networks directly from ideas generated in the Diversity Committee	✓		

* More work to be done.   *** We have done both.*   **** We monitor work allocation.*

Recruitment – New Associates

Does your firm annually recruit at any of the following types of institutions? (Check all that apply and list the schools).

Ivy League schools: Harvard University, Cornell University, University of Pennsylvania

Public state schools: University of Michigan, University of Illinois, University of Iowa, University of Minnesota

Private schools: Northwestern University, University of Chicago, Duke University, Georgetown University, University of Notre Dame, NYU

Historically Black Colleges and Universities (HBCUs): Howard University, CCBA Job Fair

Do you have any special outreach efforts directed to encourage minority law students to consider your firm?

• *We have established a diversity scholarship at Northwestern.*

• Hold a reception for minority law students

• Advertise in minority law student association publication(s)

• Participate in/host minority law student job fair(s)

• Sponsor minority law student association events

• Firm's lawyers participate on career panels at school

• Outreach to leadership of minority student organizations

• Scholarships or intern/fellowships for minority students

SUMMER ASSOCIATE STATISTICS: SUMMER 2003	MINORITY MEN	MINORITY WOMEN	WHITE WOMEN	TOTAL
Summer associates	5	1	6	19
Summer associates who received an offer of full-time employment	5	1	6	19
Summer associates who accepted an offer of full-time employment	3	1	6	15

Recruitment – Lateral Associates and Partners

What activities does the firm undertake to attract minority and women attorneys?

• *Use attorney search firms to hire minority attorneys*

• Partner programs with women and minority bar associations

• Participate at minority job fairs

• Seek referrals from other attorneys

• Utilize online job services (e.g., MCCA/DuPont Primary Law Firm Job Bank)

Do you use executive recruiting/search firms to seek to identify new diversity hires (partners or associates)?

Yes

List all women- and/or minority-owned executive search/recruiting firms to which the firm paid a fee for placement services in the past 12 months:

McCormack-Schreiber

LATERAL ASSOCIATES AND PARTNERS: 1/1/03 – 12/31/03	MINORITY MEN	MINORITY WOMEN	WHITE WOMEN	TOTAL
Number of lateral associate hires	0	1	5	12
Number of lateral partner hires (equity and non-equity)	1	0	3	8
Number of new partners (equity and non-equity) promoted from associate rank	1	0	1	5
Number of new equity partners*	0	0	1	3

* Income partners promoted to equity in 2003.

Retention & Professional Development

ATTORNEYS WHO LEFT THE FIRM: 2003	MINORITY MEN	MINORITY WOMEN	WHITE WOMEN	TOTAL
Number of attorneys who voluntarily or involuntarily left your firm's employ in 2003	1	2	8	27

How do 2003 attrition rates generally compare to those experienced in the prior year period?

Lower than in prior years

Please identify the specific steps you are taking to reduce the attrition rate of minority and women attorneys.

• Develop and/or support internal employee affinity groups (e.g., minority or women networks within the firm)

• Increase/review compensation relative to competition

• Increase/improve current work/life programs

• Adopt dispute resolution process

• Succession plan includes emphasis on diversity

• Work with minority and women attorneys to develop career advancement plans

• Introduce minority and women attorneys to key clients, including to lead engagements

• Review work assignments and hours billed to key client matters to make sure minority and women attorneys are not being excluded

• Strengthen mentoring program for all attorneys, including minorities and women

• Professional skills development program, including minority and women attorneys

Does your firm have part-time/flex-time policies that permit attorneys (male or female) to work alternative schedules?

Yes, we have an alternative Work Arrangement Policy which is part of our Diversity Action Plan.

What impact, if any, will the decision to work part-time have on an attorney's ability to make partner or, if already a partner, to remain a partner at your firm?

It may lengthen the period of time necessary to be considered, depending upon the individual, but everyone is considered on their own merit, without regard to their work arrangement. No impact at all on existing partners (other than possible compensation effect).

Have any attorneys who chose to work a part-time schedule made partner at your firm?

Yes, one attorney (in past five years — no prior records exist).

Management Demographic Profile (as of 12/31/03)

	MINORITY MEN	MINORITY WOMEN	WHITE WOMEN	TOTAL
Number of attorneys on the Executive/Management Committee or equivalent	0	0	0	5
Number of attorneys on the Hiring Committee or equivalent	2	0	2	8
Number of attorneys on the Partner/Associate Review Committee or equivalent	0	0	1	7

Please provide information regarding all minority and women attorneys who head offices or practice groups of your law firm:

Minorities heading practice groups: Demetrius Carney, Governmental Practice Group

Women heading practice groups: Sally Olson, Marketplace Liability Practice Group

The Firm Says

The firm adopted a formal Diversity Initiative and Action Plan in 1999. At the same time the firm established a Diversity Committee. The committee, consisting of 14 partners, associates and staff members, has worked tirelessly to accomplish the action steps called for under the plan. The firm has engaged an outside diversity consultant to work with the firm in implementing these steps. We have created a series of programs designed to increase the diversity of the attorneys we recruit across the board, including attorneys of color and female attorneys. While our non-attorney staff is more diversified than our attorney population, our efforts have fully included staff members. We have conducted diversity training for our Executive Committee, staff department heads, practice group leaders and recruiting committee and a diversity training component for all lawyers within the last year. Recruitment of female and minority lateral associates and partners is a high priority and has resulted in the lateral recruitment of a significant number of female partners in the last year. This year 22 percent of our summer associates are minorities, one of the highest percentages in our history, and 52 percent are women.

We have established a relationship with women's law student associations at local law schools, acting as mentors. We have developed a very successful Women in the Practice of Law affinity program with monthly meetings and ongoing work. (We also have a successful Asian-American affinity group.) We hire as summer interns college students of color, who are often women, as part of a program to encourage greater female and minority enrollment in law school. One of our female partners is the head of the State of Illinois Commission of Women. We have adopted a formal Alternative Work Arrangement Policy designed to mentor and promote

attorneys into the partnership who work on flex-time or alternative work schedules. This year we promoted our first woman partner working on a flex-time basis into the partnership.

The firm periodically presents programs to the entire partnership regarding the importance of our Diversity Initiative. We have brought in clients to discuss the importance of diversity to their businesses and the importance of diversifying our population for our firm's business success.

The firm has been a central player in the Chicago Bar Association Minority Student Job Fair for a number of years. We have volunteered in moot court and other training activities initiated by minority law student associations, provided teaching support for bar examination preparation courses for law students of color and worked with the Chicago Committee for Minorities in Large Law Firms, including hosting its receptions for minority law students. We have formal liaison relationships with the minority bar associations at many local law schools, including Northwestern, University of Chicago, Loyola and University of Michigan. We are committed to expanding this formal liaison program to all of the law schools where the firm recruits.

As a direct outgrowth of work done by the Diversity Committee, the firm has developed programs intended to support the retention, development, training and promotion of a broad and diverse range of attorneys. Some of these programs have been implemented on the theory that any initiative that "raises the tide, raises all boats." Others are designed to improve the firm's retention of specific categories of lawyers and staff. We have developed a mentoring/coaching program in which each new associate is provided a team of three coaches, including a partner, an associate and a member of the team that recruited him or her. These teams have specific assignments to ensure that new associates are introduced to their peers and that work flows and evaluations are properly and timely received.

The firm's efforts in the diversity area have resulted in several awards from minority bar associations, including the University of Illinois Silver Sponsorship Award. The firm regularly supports, both financially and with pro bono activities, minority public interest organizations, including the Public Interest Law Initiative (PILI), the Chicago Committee on Minorities in Law Firms and the Chicago Lawyers Committee for Civil Rights Under Law. Our support of and work with the Welfare to Work program has been recognized by President Bush. We have an ongoing partnership with a Chicago high school with a large Latino population and provide internships for students to earn money for their college educations. We also have handled a large number of pro bono cases for MIHRC (Midwest Immigrant and Human Rights Center). Recently, the firm established a diversity scholarship program at Northwestern Law School.

The firm provides billing credit to its associates for work related to diversity initiatives. Our bonus program for associates specifically includes a category in which associates can improve their bonuses for productive work supporting the firm's Diversity Initiative. As to partners, the firm's Compensation Committee considers partners' efforts in support of the Diversity Initiative as a factor in connection with their compensation, and partners are required to report annually to the Compensation Committee their efforts in this regard.

The firm has a strong hiring and retention policy for attorneys and staff which recognizes opportunities without discrimination of any kind. The Diversity Committee has refined the firm's anti-harassment policy and provided a formalized method by which attorneys and staff can confidentially take advantage of that policy in instances where they believe it has been violated.

In summary, the firm has worked hard, particularly in the last five years since the Diversity Initiative was formalized, to continue to improve its success in hiring and retaining minority and women attorneys. Those efforts have clearly borne fruit. We are not myopic enough to think that we have achieved the success we desire. The Diversity Initiative recognizes that this is an ongoing process. Diversity is an important part of the firm's Strategic Plan for the future.

Willkie Farr & Gallagher LLP

787 Seventh Avenue
New York, NY 10019
Phone: (212) 728-8000
Fax: (212) 728-8111

FIRM LEADERSHIP

Managing Partner: Steven Gartner, Partner
Diversity Team Leader: Kim Walker, Director of
Diversity Initiatives, Special Counsel

LOCATIONS

New York, NY (HQ)
Washington, DC
Brussels
Frankfurt
London
Paris
Rome/Milan

LAW FIRM DEMOGRAPHIC PROFILES

FULL-TIME ASSOCIATES	2003	2002
Minority men	16	20
Minority women	27	22
White women	85	95
Total	304	275

SUMMER ASSOCIATES	2003	2002
Minority men	0	4
Minority women	5	5
White women	23	23
Total	60	57

EQUITY PARTNERS	2003	2002
Minority men	5	5
Minority women	1	1
White women	11	10
Total	113	106

NON-EQUITY PARTNERS	2003	2002
Minority men	0	0
Minority women	1	1
White women	5	4
Total	13	12

NEW HIRES	2003	2002
Minority men	3	2
Minority women	8	6
White women	24	22
Total	66	63

Strategic Plan and Diversity Leadership

How does the firm's leadership communicate the importance of diversity to everyone at the firm? (e.g., e-mails, web site, newsletters, meetings, etc.)

Diversity Committee meetings, monthly Minority Lunches, firm-sponsored diversity events

Who has primary responsibility for leading diversity initiatives at your firm?

Kim Walker, director of diversity initiatives and special counsel

Does your law firm currently have a diversity committee?

Yes

Does the committee's representation include one or more members of the firm's management/executive committee (or the equivalent)?

Yes

How many attorneys are on the committee, and in 2003, what was the total number of hours collectively spent by the committee in furtherance of the firm's diversity initiatives?

Total attorneys on committee: 16

Total hours spent on diversity: 700

Does the committee and/or diversity leader establish and set goals or objectives consistent with management's priorities?

Yes

Has the firm undertaken a formal or informal diversity program or set of initiatives aimed at increasing the diversity of the firm?

Yes, formal

How often does the firm's management review the firm's diversity progress/results?

Quarterly

LAW FIRM DIVERSITY INITIATIVES	ALREADY COMPLETED	CURRENTLY ADDRESSING	NOT A CURRENT PRIORITY
Undertake communication from firm management that diversity is a top priority of the firm.		✓	
Formalize diversity plan and committee with action steps and accountability to management.		✓	
Conduct firm-wide diversity training for all attorneys and staff.		✓	
Increase the number of minority attorneys at the associate level.		✓	
Increase the number of minority attorneys at the partnership level.		✓	
Develop/expand relationships with minority bar associations to offer firm's support of these networks.		✓	
Focus on strengthening firm's mentoring program, including for benefit of minority attorneys.		✓	
Conduct internal diversity needs assessment and/or retain diversity consultant to examine how firm culture might be more welcoming of minorities.	✓		
Support law firm's internal affinity networks (e.g., women, minority attorney networks).		✓	
Manage/monitor allocation of work assignments and/or hours billed to ensure women and minority attorneys have equal access/inclusion on top client matters.		✓	

Recruitment – New Associates

Does your firm annually recruit at any of the following types of institutions? (Check all that apply and list the schools).

Ivy League schools: Harvard University, Yale University, Cornell University, Columbia University, University of Pennsylvania

Public state schools: University of California-Berkeley (Boalt Hall), University of California-Hastings, UCLA, University of Virginia, University of Michigan, Rutgers University

Private schools: NYU, Fordham University, Brooklyn Law School, St. John's University, Georgetown University, Duke University, Stanford University, University of Chicago, Northwestern University, USC

Historically Black Colleges and Universities (HBCUs): Howard University

Do you have any special outreach efforts directed to encourage minority law students to consider your firm?

- *Solicit resumes from members of minority student organizations*
- Hold a reception for minority law students
- Participate in/host minority law student job fair(s)
- Sponsor minority law student association events
- Firm's lawyers participate on career panels at school
- Outreach to leadership of minority student organizations

SUMMER ASSOCIATE STATISTICS: SUMMER 2003	MINORITY MEN	MINORITY WOMEN	WHITE WOMEN	TOTAL
Summer associates	0	5	23	56
Summer associates who received an offer of full-time employment	0	5	23	56
Summer associates who accepted an offer of full-time employment	0	5	19	51

Recruitment – Lateral Associates and Partners

What activities does the firm undertake to attract minority and women attorneys?

- Participate at minority job fairs
- Seek referrals from other attorneys

Do you use executive recruiting/search firms to seek to identify new diversity hires (partners or associates)?

Yes

LATERAL ASSOCIATES AND PARTNERS: 1/1/03 – 12/31/03	MINORITY MEN	MINORITY WOMEN	WHITE WOMEN	TOTAL
Number of lateral associate hires	2	2	7	22
Number of lateral partner hires (equity and non-equity)	0	0	0	2
Number of new partners (equity and non-equity) promoted from associate rank	0	0	4	8
Number of new equity partners	0	0	2	8

Retention & Professional Development

ATTORNEYS WHO LEFT THE FIRM: 2003	MINORITY MEN	MINORITY WOMEN	WHITE WOMEN	TOTAL
Number of attorneys who voluntarily or involuntarily left your firm's employ in 2003	6	2	21	49

How do 2003 attrition rates generally compare to those experienced in the prior year period?

About the same as in prior years

Please identify the specific steps you are taking to reduce the attrition rate of minority and women attorneys.

• Develop and/or support internal employee affinity groups (e.g., minority or women networks within the firm)

• Increase/review compensation relative to competition

• Increase/improve current work/life programs

• Work with minority and women attorneys to develop career advancement plans

• Introduce minority and women attorneys to key clients, including to lead engagements

• Strengthen mentoring program for all attorneys, including minorities and women

• Professional skills development program, including minority and women attorneys

Does your firm have part-time/flex-time policies that permit attorneys (male or female) to work alternative schedules?

Yes

Have any attorneys who chose to work a part-time schedule made partner at your firm?

Yes, two attorneys.

Management Demographic Profile (as of 12/31/03)

	MINORITY MEN	MINORITY WOMEN	WHITE WOMEN	TOTAL
Number of attorneys on the Executive/Management Committee or equivalent	0	0	0	10
Number of attorneys on the Hiring Committee or equivalent	0	2	9	25
Number of attorneys on the Partner/Associate Review Committee or equivalent	0	2	9	25

The Firm Says

In keeping with the belief that everyone benefits from a diverse workplace, Willkie is committed to creating and maintaining a diverse environment by recruiting and retaining people of all backgrounds and cultural experiences. To that end, Willkie has appointed a director of diversity initiatives, Kim A. Walker, who is dedicated not only to the recruitment of minority attorneys but also to their retention, professional development and advancement.

Our commitment and efforts have included participation in various diversity conferences and job fairs, including the American Bar Association National Conference for the Minority Lawyer, MCCA Creating Pathways to Diversity Conference, as well as countless law school conferences sponsored by minority student organizations. We also lend our support to various minority associations, including most recently the Lesbian and Gay Law Association Foundation and the Puerto Rican Legal Defense Fund. Finally, in recognition of the benefits of exposing young persons to the practice of law, we support organizations such as Prep for Prep and provide annual scholarships to minority students at Adlai Stevenson High School.

Much of our efforts in the area of diversity are coordinated through our Diversity Committee. This committee has been in existence for over a decade and meets monthly to address issues of concern or interest to minority associates. The committee's mission is to improve associate retention, promotion and career development and increase the number and tenure of minority and openly gay associates. Recent efforts of the committee have been directed towards improving the partner-mentor program and assigning system, and we have engaged a diversity consultant to assist us in that regard. The consultant has conducted diversity forums and will oversee diversity training early next year. The committee also sponsors monthly lunches and other events to encourage formal and informal discussions among minority associates.

In the area of recruitment, we have made a concerted effort to reach out to minority student organizations and have co-sponsored events, including interview workshops, with several of such organizations. We have also "widened the net" in our recruiting efforts by expanding the number of schools at which we conduct on-campus interviews. In addition, we have engaged diversity headhunters to help us ensure that our lateral hiring is indicative of our commitment to diversity.

Willkie is dedicated to hiring and retaining the best talent available and has long recognized that such talent resides in individuals of all backgrounds and experiences. Our clients, many of whom conduct business on a global scale, expect a superior level of service that is multidimensional and sensitive to the diverse composition of today's marketplace. By building and maintaining a truly diverse team of attorneys, Willkie is able to deliver such service.

**FROM
DIVERSE
PARTS—**

**BUILDING
A GREATER
WHOLE**

Wilmer Cutler Pickering LLP*

2445 M Street, N.W.
Washington, DC 20037
Phone: (202) 663-6000
Fax: (202) 663-6363

FIRM LEADERSHIP

Managing Partner: William Perlstein, Managing Partner
Diversity Team Leader: John Payton and Willam T. Lake, Co-Chairs of the Diversity Committee

LOCATIONS

Washington, DC (HQ)
Baltimore, MD
McLean, VA
New York, NY
Berlin
Brussels
London

* On June 1, 2004, Wilmer Cutler Pickering LLP merged with Hale and Dorr to form Wilmer Cutler Pickering Hale and Dorr LLP. The information below reflects Wilmer Cutler Pickering's diversity programs in 2002 and 2003. The combined firm will report its 2004 diversity initiatives in next year's edition of the Vault/MCCA Law Firm Diversity Guide (2006).

LAW FIRM DEMOGRAPHIC PROFILES

FULL-TIME ASSOCIATES*	2003	2002
Minority men	15	16
Minority women	21	22
White women	117	121
Total	302	308

* Includes counsel

SUMMER ASSOCIATES	2003	2002
Minority men	5	4
Minority women	6	5
White women	23	23
Total	66	60

EQUITY PARTNERS	2003	2002
Minority men	5	5
Minority women	5	4
White women	22	16
Total	121	117

NEW HIRES	2003	2002
Minority men	2	5
Minority women	3	12
White women	32	34
Total	86	99

Strategic Plan and Diversity Leadership

How does the firm's leadership communicate the importance of diversity to everyone at the firm? (e.g., e-mails, web site, newsletters, meetings, etc.)

The Management Committee has discussed the importance of diversity at its own meetings, at several meetings of the partnership and at the meetings of the various leaders of the firm, and it has communicated via e-mail to the entire firm.

Who has primary responsibility for leading diversity initiatives at your firm?

William Perlstein, the managing partner, and the Management Committee; but they have relied on a Diversity Committee chaired by John Payton and Bill Lake (a member of the Management Committee), other partners and associates of the firm. In addition, the New York office has a separate Diversity Committee, chaired by Peggy Kuo, counsel.

Does your law firm currently have a diversity committee?

Yes

Does the committee's representation include one or more members of the firm's management/executive committee (or the equivalent)?

Yes

How many attorneys are on the committee, and in 2003, what was the total number of hours collectively spent by the committee in furtherance of the firm's diversity initiatives?

Total attorneys on committee: 15

Total hours spent on diversity: Not known

Does the committee and/or diversity leader establish and set goals or objectives consistent with management's priorities?

Yes

Has the firm undertaken a formal or informal diversity program or set of initiatives aimed at increasing the diversity of the firm?

Yes, formal

How often does the firm's management review the firm's diversity progress/results?

Unknown

How is the firm's diversity committee and/or firm management held accountable for achieving results?

The success of the firm's diversity initiative is one of the factors considered by the firm's compensation committee in setting partner compensation.

LAW FIRM DIVERSITY INITIATIVES	ALREADY COMPLETED	CURRENTLY ADDRESSING	NOT A CURRENT PRIORITY
Undertake communication from firm management that diversity is a top priority of the firm.	✓		
Formalize diversity plan and committee with action steps and accountability to management.		✓	
Conduct firm-wide diversity training for all attorneys and staff.			✓
Increase the number of minority attorneys at the associate level.		✓	
Increase the number of minority attorneys at the partnership level.		✓	
Develop/expand relationships with minority bar associations to offer firm's support of these networks.		✓	
Focus on strengthening firm's mentoring program, including for benefit of minority attorneys.		✓	
Conduct internal diversity needs assessment and/or retain diversity consultant to examine how firm culture might be more welcoming of minorities.		✓	
Support law firm's internal affinity networks (e.g., women, minority attorney networks).		✓	
Manage/monitor allocation of work assignments and/or hours billed to ensure women and minority attorneys have equal access/inclusion on top client matters.		✓	

Recruitment – New Associates

Does your firm annually recruit at any of the following types of institutions? (Check all that apply and list the schools).

Ivy League schools: Columbia University, Cornell University, Harvard University, University of Pennsylvania, Yale University

Public state schools: University of California-Boalt, George Mason University, University of Maryland, University of Michigan, University of Texas at Austin and University of Virginia

Private schools: American University, Brigham Young University, Catholic University of America, University of Chicago, Duke University, Georgetown University, George Washington University, Northwestern University, New York University, Stanford University and Vanderbilt University

Historically Black Colleges and Universities (HBCUs): Howard University

Do you have any special outreach efforts directed to encourage minority law students to consider your firm?

• Hold a reception for minority law students

• Participate in/host minority law student job fair(s)

• Sponsor minority law student association events

- Firm's lawyers participate on career panels at school
- Outreach to leadership of minority student organizations

SUMMER ASSOCIATE STATISTICS: SUMMER 2003	MINORITY MEN	MINORITY WOMEN	WHITE WOMEN	TOTAL
Summer associates	1	1	4	14
Summer associates who received an offer of full-time employment	1	1	4	14
Summer associates who accepted an offer of full-time employment	0	0	3	5

Reruitment – Lateral Associates and Partners

What activities does the firm undertake to attract minority and women attorneys?

- Partner programs with women and minority bar associations
- Participate at minority job fairs
- Seek referrals from other attorneys

Do you use executive recruiting/search firms to seek to identify new diversity hires (partners or associates)?

No

LATERAL ASSOCIATES AND PARTNERS: 1/1/03 – 12/31/03	MINORITY MEN	MINORITY WOMEN	WHITE WOMEN	TOTAL
Number of lateral associate hires	0	0	6	12
Number of lateral partner hires (equity and non-equity)	1	0	2	5
Number of new partners (equity and non-equity) promoted from associate rank	0	0	0	0
Number of new equity partners	0	1	1	6

Retention & Professional Development

How do 2003 attrition rates generally compare to those experienced in the prior year period?

About the same as in prior years

Please identify the specific steps you are taking to reduce the attrition rate of minority and women attorneys.

• *Support the current affinity groups.*

• Develop and/or support internal employee affinity groups (e.g., minority or women networks within the firm)

• Increase/review compensation relative to competition (partners only)

• Introduce minority and women attorneys to key clients, including to lead engagements

• Review work assignments and hours billed to key client matters to make sure minority and women attorneys are not being excluded

• Strengthen mentoring program for all attorneys, including minorities and women

• Professional skills development program, including minority and women attorneys

Does your firm have part-time/flex-time policies that permit attorneys (male or female) to work alternative schedules?

Yes

What impact, if any, will the decision to work part-time have on an attorney's ability to make partner or, if already a partner, to remain a partner at your firm?

None.

Have any attorneys who chose to work a part-time schedule made partner at your firm?

No, although that may happen this year.

Management Demographic Profile (as of 12/31/03)

	MINORITY MEN	MINORITY WOMEN	WHITE WOMEN	TOTAL
Number of attorneys on the Executive/Management Committee or equivalent	0	0	1	7
Number of attorneys on the Hiring Committee or equivalent*	1	1	2	11
Number of attorneys on the Partner/Associate Review Committee or equivalent	0	1	1	6

* Includes both New York and the Washington offices.

Please provide information regarding all minority and women attorneys who head offices or practice groups of your law firm:

Women heading practice groups: Juanita Crowley, Litigation; Meredith Cross, Corporate

Winston & Strawn LLP

35 W. Wacker Drive
Chicago, IL 60601
Phone: (312) 558-5600
Fax: (312) 558-5700

FIRM LEADERSHIP

Managing Partner: James M. Neis, Managing Partner
Diversity Team Leader: Thomas C. Poindexter, Chair, Diversity Committee

LOCATIONS

Chicago, IL (HQ)
Los Angeles, CA
New York, NY
San Francisco, CA
Washington, DC
Geneva
London
Paris

LAW FIRM DEMOGRAPHIC PROFILES

FULL-TIME ASSOCIATES*	2003	2002
Minority men	28	27
Minority women	41	39
White women	139	140
Total	391	402

Includes staff attorneys and senior attorneys

SUMMER ASSOCIATES	2003	2002
Minority men	3	3
Minority women	5	9
White women	29	27
Total	60	66

EQUITY PARTNERS	2003	2002
Minority men	5	5
Minority women	1	1
White women	19	16
Total	180	171

NON-EQUITY PARTNERS*	2003	2002
Minority men	9	8
Minority women	7	6
White women	45	44
Total	231	211

Includes of counsel and senior counsel

NEW HIRES*	2003	2002
Minority men	6	6
Minority women	9	9
White women	30	30
Total	115	93

Includes attorneys added through acquisition of Murphy Sheneman firm, effective 2/15/03

Strategic Plan and Diversity Leadership

How does the firm's leadership communicate the importance of diversity to everyone at the firm? (e.g., e-mails, web site, newsletters, meetings, etc.)

The firm publishes a regular diversity newsletter ("Diversity@Winston & Strawn") that includes information about diversity and inclusion activities, policies, individual office efforts, sponsorships and interviews with leaders in diversity. Our firm's diversity commitment, official firm diversity charter and diversity achievements also are listed on the firm's web site and intranet site. Recently, the firm also launched a diversity training program, led by an outside diversity consultant. Both the Diversity Committee and Executive Committee have participated in the training, and it will soon be rolled out to all partners and associates.

Who has primary responsibility for leading diversity initiatives at your firm?

Thomas C. Poindexter, partner and chair of the Diversity Committee

Does your law firm currently have a diversity committee?

Yes

Does the committee's representation include one or more members of the firm's management/executive committee (or the equivalent)?

Yes

How many attorneys are on the committee, and in 2003, what was the total number of hours collectively spent by the committee in furtherance of the firm's diversity initiatives?

Total attorneys on committee: 30

Total hours spent on diversity: More than 100

Does the committee and/or diversity leader establish and set goals or objectives consistent with management's priorities?

Yes

Has the firm undertaken a formal or informal diversity program or set of initiatives aimed at increasing the diversity of the firm?

Yes, formal

How often does the firm's management review the firm's diversity progress/results?

Quarterly

How is the firm's diversity committee and/or firm management held accountable for achieving results?

The Diversity Committee is accountable to the Executive Committee for ensuring that adequate programs are in place and that the attorney workforce is adequately informed on how to establish and maintain a diverse work force. All partners are requested to discuss in performance evaluation statements their contribution to diversity.

LAW FIRM DIVERSITY INITIATIVES	ALREADY COMPLETED	CURRENTLY ADDRESSING	NOT A CURRENT PRIORITY
Undertake communication from firm management that diversity is a top priority of the firm.	✔ *		
Formalize diversity plan and committee with action steps and accountability to management.	✔ **	✔	
Conduct firm-wide diversity training for all attorneys and staff.	✔ ***	✔	
Increase the number of minority attorneys at the associate level.		✔	
Increase the number of minority attorneys at the partnership level.		✔	
Develop/expand relationships with minority bar associations to offer firm's support of these networks.		✔	
Focus on strengthening firm's mentoring program, including for benefit of minority attorneys.		✔	
Conduct internal diversity needs assessment and/or retain diversity consultant to examine how firm culture might be more welcoming of minorities.		✔ ****	
Support law firm's internal affinity networks (e.g., women, minority attorney networks).	✔		
Manage/monitor allocation of work assignments and/or hours billed to ensure women and minority attorneys have equal access/inclusion on top client matters.		✔	

* Communication is also sent out on an ongoing basis.

** Formal plan is completed; we are currently addressing action steps and accountability.

*** Our Diversity and Executive Committees have completed training; training to be rolled out for partners and associates.

**** To be initiated in the future.

Recruitment – New Associates

Does your firm annually recruit at any of the following types of institutions? (Check all that apply and list the schools).

Ivy League schools: Columbia University, Cornell University, Harvard University, University of Pennsylvania

Public state schools: Indiana University, Ohio State University, University of California-Berkeley, University of California-Hastings, University of California-Los Angeles, University of Illinois, University of Iowa, University of Michigan, University of Minnesota, University of Virginia, University of Wisconsin

Private schools: Boston College, Boston University, DePaul University, Duke University, Fordham University, George Washington University, Georgetown University, Hofstra University, IIT- Chicago-Kent College of Law, Loyola Law School-Los Angeles, Loyola University Chicago, New York University, Northwestern University, St. John's University, Stanford University, University of Chicago, University of Notre Dame, University of Southern California, Vanderbilt University, Washington University in St. Louis

Historically Black Colleges and Universities (HBCUs): Howard University

Do you have any special outreach efforts directed to encourage minority law students to consider your firm?

- *See narrative section below*
- Hold a reception for minority law students
- Advertise in minority law student association publication(s)
- Participate in/host minority law student job fair(s)
- Sponsor minority law student association events
- Firm's lawyers participate on career panels at school
- Outreach to leadership of minority student organizations
- Scholarships or intern/fellowships for minority students

SUMMER ASSOCIATE STATISTICS: SUMMER 2003	MINORITY MEN	MINORITY WOMEN	WHITE WOMEN	TOTAL
Summer associates	N/A	N/A	N/A	60*
Summer associates who received an offer of full-time employment	N/A	N/A	N/A	N/A
Summer associates who accepted an offer of full-time employment	N/A	N/A	N/A	N/A

* Includes 34 women and 26 men.

Recruitment – Lateral Associates and Partners

What activities does the firm undertake to attract minority and women attorneys?
- Partner programs with women and minority bar associations
- Participate at minority job fairs
- Seek referrals from other attorneys

Do you use executive recruiting/search firms to seek to identify new diversity hires (partners or associates)?

Yes

LATERAL ASSOCIATES AND PARTNERS: 1/1/03 – 12/31/03	MINORITY MEN	MINORITY WOMEN	WHITE WOMEN	TOTAL
Number of lateral associate hires	N/A	N/A	N/A	N/A
Number of lateral partner hires (equity and non-equity)	N/A	N/A	N/A	N/A
Number of new partners (equity and non-equity) promoted from associate rank	1	2	7	37
Number of new equity partners	N/A	N/A	N/A	N/A

Retention & Professional Development

Please identify the specific steps you are taking to reduce the attrition rate of minority and women attorneys. (It is suggested that you elaborate on this issue in the final question of this survey.)

See narrative section below.

- Develop and/or support internal employee affinity groups (e.g., minority or women networks within the firm)
- Increase/review compensation relative to competition
- Work with minority and women attorneys to develop career advancement plans
- Introduce minority and women attorneys to key clients, including to lead engagements
- Review work assignments and hours billed to key client matters to make sure minority and women attorneys are not being excluded
- Strengthen mentoring program for all attorneys, including minorities and women
- Professional skills development program, including minority and women attorneys

Does your firm have part-time/flex-time policies that permit attorneys (male or female) to work alternative schedules?

Yes

What impact, if any, will the decision to work part-time have on an attorney's ability to make partner or, if already a partner, to remain a partner at your firm?

Per the firm's Family Responsibilities Guidelines, associates who have worked or are working part-time may be promoted to partnership. Generally, part-time associates should not expect to advance toward partnership at the same rate as full-time associates.

Have any attorneys who chose to work a part-time schedule made partner at your firm?

Yes, one in 2003 (associate to income partner).

Management Demographic Profile (as of 12/31/03)

	MINORITY MEN	MINORITY WOMEN	WHITE WOMEN	TOTAL
Number of attorneys on the Executive/Management Committee or equivalent	1	0	2	26
Number of attorneys on the Hiring Committee or equivalent	2	0	8	21
Number of attorneys on the Partner/Associate Review Committee or equivalent	1	0	9	25

Please provide information regarding all minority and women attorneys who head offices or practice groups of your law firm:

Women heading offices: Laura Petroff, head of Los Angeles office

Women heading practice groups (list names and departments): Christine Albright, Trusts & Estates; Jennifer Nijman, Environmental

The Firm Says

As part of the Winston & Strawn Diversity Committee Charter, formally adopted in 2003, the firm has both a commitment and a focused effort aimed at, among other things, the recruitment, retention, mentoring and promotion of women and minority attorneys. Highlights of our work follow.

Recruitment of women and minorities

Recruiting women is an integral part of the Diversity Committee Charter and, in recent years, the firm has been successful in this effort. The percentage of women in the summer program and entering classes has generally been consistent with the percentage of women in the law school population.

To interest more minority candidates in our firm, our Hiring Committee has taken extra steps to connect with prospects and provide forums for networking. For example, in Chicago, we participate in the Cook County Minority Job Fair, and in the past few years, we have met a number of future summer associates for the first time at this fair. One of our associates serves as chairperson of this job fair.

We also have reached out to minority law student groups by hosting receptions, open houses and meetings with minority law students from the University of Illinois, Northwestern University and DePaul University. During one visit last year, Latino, Asian American and African American law students were welcomed by our managing partner and learned about our summer program, various practice areas and our associate programs from key partners and associates. Our director of professional development also spoke about our training efforts. The students then mingled with firm attorneys, including members of the Hiring and Summer Committees.

Retention and mentoring efforts

Our Women to Women Initiative (W2W), a subcommittee of the firm's Diversity Committee, was specifically designed last year to create opportunities for women associates to develop meaningful relationships with women partners. To guide their work, the W2W established several goals:

• To promote career satisfaction and firm loyalty
• To provide positive role models
• To supply opportunities for substantive learning in a supportive atmosphere
• To enhance career development

To meet those goals the W2W Initiative launched a formal program series in 2003 and a series of informal mentoring lunches among female attorneys. The program series has included panel discussions led by senior female partners regarding business development strategies; dialogues on practice tips and pragmatic advice on obtaining leadership positions in the firm; and a profile of a new female lateral partner who joined from a major financial institution. The informal mentoring lunches provide a less structured opportunity for small groups of

female associates to meet with female partners to discuss work-related issues and to become more familiar with the firm's leaders.

Diversity scholarships

As part of the firm's 150th anniversary celebration last year, Winston & Strawn established a Diversity Scholarship program. It is our hope the program will help mentor and expand the law school minority population and interest diverse candidates in working at Winston & Strawn after graduation. We will award a scholarship to an entering law student at Columbia, Georgetown, Northwestern and UCLA in the fall of 2004. At Columbia, Georgetown and Northwestern, the scholarship will be awarded to a minority student. At UCLA, it will be awarded to a socio-economically disadvantaged law student. Members of the Hiring and Diversity Committees are now in the process of selecting the scholarship recipients.

Diversity training

The firm has launched a series of innovative diversity training workshops, facilitated by a gender and diversity consulting firm, for all partners and associates in our domestic offices. The sessions discussed such topics as the business reasons for diversity; awareness training on diversity issues related to associate/partner evaluations and promotion; and hands-on skills training in communication, client development, conflict resolution and strategic planning. The sessions also focus on mentoring as a key ingredient in diversity training. The Diversity Committee completed the first phase of the training in 2003, the Executive Committee completed training in January 2004, and we are rolling out sessions for partners and associates in our domestic offices starting in July 2004.

Promotion, leadership and collaboration

We maintain strong ties with numerous organizations that support diversity efforts. For example, we've been a long-time supporter of the Minority Corporate Counsel Association, the Chicago Committee on Minorities in Large Law Firms, the ABA's Commission on Racial and Ethnic Diversity in the Profession, and the ABA's Commission on Women. Many of our attorneys serve in leadership capacities for other organizations including the Black Women Lawyers Association, the Hispanic Lawyers Scholarship Fund of Illinois, the National Conference of Women's Bar Associations and the Chicago Bar Association's Alliance for Women, where they have helped develop programs, sponsor activities, develop policy or host events.

Results of the firm's diversity efforts

While statistics alone cannot measure the success of a diversity program, we are proud of our recent rankings, which recognize our efforts to recruit, retain and promote minorities and women. In the diversity category, the firm was ranked No. 5 in overall diversity, No. 3 for diversity for minorities and No. 6 for diversity for women in the Vault Guide to the Top 100 Law Firms, 2005 edition. The firm also ranked No. 7 for "Dedication to Diversity" in The American Lawyer's Associates Survey. The Chicago Lawyer's 2004 diversity survey also reported that, of firms with more than 100 lawyers, Winston & Strawn was among the top four that had the highest percentage of minority partners. The Minority Corporate Counsel Association also has recognized our diversity efforts by presenting its Sager Award to us three times in the last five years.

Womble Carlyle Sandridge & Rice, PLLC

One West Fourth Street
Winston-Salem, NC 27101
Phone: (336) 721-3600
Fax: (336) 721-3660

FIRM LEADERSHIP

Managing Partner: Keith W. Vaughan, Firm Managing Member
Diversity Team Leader: William A. Davis II, Diversity Committee Chair

LOCATIONS

Winston-Salem, NC (HQ)
Atlanta, GA
Charlotte, NC
Greensboro, NC
Raleigh, NC
Research Triangle Park, NC
Greenville, SC
Tysons Corner, VA
Washington, DC

LAW FIRM DEMOGRAPHIC PROFILES

FULL-TIME ASSOCIATES	2003	2002
Minority men	6	4
Minority women	9	13
White women	62	62
Total	173	161

SUMMER ASSOCIATES	2003	2002
Minority men	2	3
Minority women	3	6
White women	15	19
Total	41	44

EQUITY PARTNERS	2003	2002
Minority men	2	2
Minority women	1	1
White women	22	23
Total	157	149

NON-EQUITY PARTNERS	2003	2002
Minority men	1	0
Minority women	0	0
White women	7	9
Total	47	47

NEW HIRES	2003	2002
Minority men	3	1
Minority women	1	4
White women	22	18
Total	67	51

MINORITY CORPORATE COUNSEL ASSOCIATION

Strategic Plan and Diversity Leadership

How does the firm's leadership communicate the importance of diversity to everyone at the firm? (e.g., e-mails, web site, newsletters, meetings, etc.)

Womble Carlyle is strongly committed to hiring and advancing minorities and women and to maintaining a diverse workplace. Our commitment to diversity is communicated to our attorneys and staff in a variety of ways. First and foremost, it is a priority to our Firm Management Committee (FMC) and is a topic regularly included on FMC meeting agendas. It was announced and discussed at our most recent member retreat and is a part of our long-range strategic plan. The chair of our FMC has made it one of his personal priorities and so he has made it a topic of discussion at his regular monthly meetings with attorneys and management staff in each of our offices. Our commitment is not one of word only, but also one in deed. The firm has taken numerous affirmative steps over the past few years to evidence our commitment to diversity, including creating a diversity committee; adding a director of diversity to our management staff; creating and funding a minority scholarship program; sponsoring minority law school groups; creating a minority student intern program in law firm management in cooperation with a local, historically black college; enrolling in a corporate membership to Diversity, Inc.; partnering with local bar association minority clerkship programs; publishing our firm diversity statement on the web site; supporting attorney involvement in minority and women-focused bar, community and civic organizations; and dedicating pro bono hours and financial support to programs like the Thurgood Marshall Scholarship Fund.

Who has primary responsibility for leading diversity initiatives at your firm?

William A. Davis II, Diversity Committee chair

Does your law firm currently have a diversity committee?

Yes

Does the committee's representation include one or more members of the firm's management/executive committee (or the equivalent)?

Yes

How many attorneys are on the committee, and in 2003, what was the total number of hours collectively spent by the committee in furtherance of the firm's diversity initiatives?

Total attorneys on committee: 12 + one ex-officio FMC member

Total hours spent on diversity: 290 hours

Does the committee and/or diversity leader establish and set goals or objectives consistent with management's priorities?

Yes

Has the firm undertaken a formal or informal diversity program or set of initiatives aimed at increasing the diversity of the firm?

Yes, formal

How often does the firm's management review the firm's diversity progress/results?

Monthly. The firm's diversity program is an FMC agenda item every month to receive a current status report from the Diversity Committee.

How is the firm's diversity committee and/or firm management held accountable for achieving results?

As with all management-level staff, the director of diversity will be responsible for developing a measurable progress plan annually and will be personally evaluated upon the results.

LAW FIRM DIVERSITY INITIATIVES	ALREADY COMPLETED	CURRENTLY ADDRESSING	NOT A CURRENT PRIORITY
Undertake communication from firm management that diversity is a top priority of the firm.	✓		
Formalize diversity plan and committee with action steps and accountability to management.		✓	
Conduct firm-wide diversity training for all attorneys and staff.		✓	
Increase the number of minority attorneys at the associate level.		✓	
Increase the number of minority attorneys at the partnership level.		✓	
Develop/expand relationships with minority bar associations to offer firm's support of these networks.		✓	
Focus on strengthening firm's mentoring program, including for benefit of minority attorneys.		✓	
Conduct internal diversity needs assessment and/or retain diversity consultant to examine how firm culture might be more welcoming of minorities.		✓	
Support law firm's internal affinity networks (e.g., women, minority attorney networks).	✓		
Manage/monitor allocation of work assignments and/or hours billed to ensure women and minority attorneys have equal access/inclusion on top client matters.		✓	
Participation in local bar association minority clerkship programs and creation of a minority scholarship program.	✓		

Recruitment – New Associates

Does your firm annually recruit at any of the following types of institutions? (Check all that apply and list the schools).

Public state schools: University of North Carolina–Chapel Hill, University of Georgia, University of Virginia, College of William & Mary, University of South Carolina

Private schools: Campbell University, Duke University, Emory University, Georgetown University, George Washington University, Wake Forest University, Vanderbilt University, Washington & Lee University

Historically Black Colleges and Universities (HBCUs): Howard University, North Carolina Central University

Other predominantly minority and/or women's colleges: Southeastern Minority Job Fair, Chicago Minority Job Fair, Sunbelt Minority Job Fair, Southeastern Law Placement Consortium

Of the law schools that you listed above, do you have any special outreach efforts directed to encourage minority law students to consider your firm?

• Hold a reception for minority law students

• Advertise in minority law student association publication(s)

• Participate in/host minority law student job fair(s)

• Sponsor minority law student association events

• Firm's lawyers participate on career panels at school

• Outreach to leadership of minority student organizations

• Scholarships or intern/fellowships for minority students

SUMMER ASSOCIATE STATISTICS: SUMMER 2003	MINORITY MEN	MINORITY WOMEN	WHITE WOMEN	TOTAL
Summer associates	1	3	8	18
Summer associates who received an offer of full-time employment	1	3	7	17
Summer associates who accepted an offer of full-time employment	0	1	3	8

Recruitment – Lateral Associates and Partners

What activities does the firm undertake to attract minority and women attorneys?

• Partner programs with women and minority bar associations

• Participate at minority job fairs

• Seek referrals from other attorneys

Do you use executive recruiting/search firms to seek to identify new diversity hires (partners or associates)?

Yes

LATERAL ASSOCIATES AND PARTNERS: 1/1/03 – 12/31/03	MINORITY MEN	MINORITY WOMEN	WHITE WOMEN	TOTAL
Number of lateral associate hires	1	1	14	26
Number of lateral partner hires (equity and non-equity)	1	0	4	32
Number of new partners (equity and non-equity) promoted from associate rank	1	0	6	12
Number of new equity partners	0	0	0	3

Retention & Professional Development

ATTORNEYS WHO LEFT THE FIRM: 2003	MINORITY MEN	MINORITY WOMEN	WHITE WOMEN	TOTAL
Number of attorneys who voluntarily or involuntarily left your firm's employ in 2003	0	6	14	33

How do 2003 attrition rates generally compare to those experienced in the prior year period?

About the same as in prior years

Please identify the specific steps you are taking to reduce the attrition rate of minority and women attorneys.

- Develop and/or support internal employee affinity groups (e.g., minority or women networks within the firm)
- Increase/review compensation relative to competition
- Increase/improve current work/life programs
- Succession plan includes emphasis on diversity
- Introduce minority and women attorneys to key clients, including to lead engagements
- Strengthen mentoring program for all attorneys, including minorities and women
- Professional skills development program, including minority and women attorneys

Does your firm have part-time/flex-time policies that permit attorneys (male or female) to work alternative schedules?

Yes

What impact, if any, will the decision to work part-time have on an attorney's ability to make partner or, if already a partner, to remain a partner at your firm?

If the individual is already a partner, the decision to work part-time will have no impact other than an appropriate pro rata compensation adjustment. If the individual is not yet a partner, the decision may or may not impact the time within which the individual makes partner.

Have any attorneys who chose to work a part-time schedule made partner at your firm?

Yes, two attorneys.

Management Demographic Profile (as of 12/31/03)

	MINORITY MEN	MINORITY WOMEN	WHITE WOMEN	TOTAL
Number of attorneys on the Executive/Management Committee or equivalent	0	0	1	13
Number of attorneys on the Hiring Committee or equivalent	1	0	10	28
Number of attorneys on the Partner/Associate Review Committee or equivalent	0	1	5	18

Please provide information regarding all minority and women attorneys who head offices or practice groups of your law firm:

Women heading practice groups: Karen Carey, Construction Sub-Practice Group; Ellen Gregg, Case Management Facility

The Firm Says

In recognition of Womble Carlyle's strong support of diversity initiatives, our firm was the 2003 recipient of the Thurgood Marshall Scholarship Fund Corporate Leadership Award. We are the first law firm in the nation to receive this honor. Past recipients of this award include Aetna Retirement Services, AOL/Time Warner, Inc., MBNA Corporation, Philip Morris Companies, Reebok International Ltd., Sony Music Entertainment, Inc., UBS Paine Webber, Inc. and Wal-Mart Stores.

Womble Carlyle was chosen as the 2003 recipient of this award because of our dedication to the nation's historically black public colleges and universities through pro bono work, financial support and participation in Fund-sponsored activities. More than 20 Womble Carlyle attorneys have provided pro bono legal support to the Fund during the past three and a half years. Womble Carlyle partner Brent Clinkscale serves as general counsel to the Fund and sits on its board of directors. We are very proud of this award and all of our attorneys who have worked hard to support the Fund.

APPENDIX

Alphabetical List of Firms